WITHDRAWN

Presented to

Kingwood Branch Library
By

Donated by the National Charity
Harris County **League – Kingwood Chapter**
Public Library

your pathway to knowledge

Gale Contextual Encyclopedia of American Literature

Gale Contextual Encyclopedia of American Literature

VOLUME 3

L–Q

GALE
CENGAGE Learning

Detroit • New York • San Francisco • New Haven, Conn • Waterville, Maine • London

GALE
CENGAGE Learning™

**Gale Contextual Encyclopedia
of American Literature**

Project Editors: Anne Marie Hacht and Dwayne
D. Hayes

Editorial: Ira Mark Milne

Rights Acquisition and Management: Kelly Quin,
Robyn Young, and Tracie Richardson

Composition: Evi Abou-El-Seoud

Manufacturing: Wendy Blurton

Imaging: John Watkins

Product Design: Jennifer Wahi and Pam Galbreath

For product information and technology assistance, contact us at
Gale Customer Support, 1-800-877-4253.
For permission to use material from this text or product,
submit all requests online at **www.cengage.com/permissions.**
Further permissions questions can be emailed to
permissionrequest@cengage.com

Cover photographs reproduced by permission. Steinbeck, John, photograph. The
Library of Congress; Angelou, Maya, photograph. AP Images; Fitzgerald, F. Scott,
photograph. The Library of Congress; Twain, Mark, photograph. The Library of Congress;
Poe, Edgar Allan, public domain; London, Jack, photograph. The Library of Congress;
Hughes, Langston, 1943, photo by Gordon Parks. The Library of Congress; Dickinson, Emily.
The Library of Congress; Hemingway, Ernest, photograph. AP Images; Hemingway, Ernest,
photograph. AP Images; Lee, Harper, photograph. AP Images; Tan, Amy, 1993, photograph.
AP Images; Walker, Alice, photograph. AP Images.

While every effort has been made to ensure the reliability of the information presented
in this publication, Gale, a part of Cengage Learning, does not guarantee the accuracy of the
data contained herein. Gale accepts no payment for listing; and inclusion in the publication
of any organization, agency, institution, publication, service, or individual does not imply
endorsement of the editors or publisher. Errors brought to the attention of the publisher
and verified to the satisfaction of the publisher will be corrected in future editions.

Editorial Data Privacy Policy. Does this publication contain information about you as
an individual? If so, for more information about our editorial data privacy policies,
please see our Privacy Statement at www.gale.com.

Library of Congress Cataloging-in-Publication Data

Gale contextual encyclopedia of American literature / editorial, Anne Marie
Hacht, Dwayne D. Hayes.
    p. cm.
    Includes bibliographical references and index.
    ISBN 978-1-4144-3130-7 (set) -- ISBN 978-1-4144-3131-4 (v. 1) --
ISBN 978-1-4144-3132-1 (v. 2) -- ISBN 978-1-4144-3133-8 (v. 3) --
ISBN 978-1-4144-3134-5 (v. 4) -- ISBN 978-1-4144-3139-0 (e-book)
    1. American literature--Encyclopedias. 2. American literature--Bio-bibliography.
3. Authors, American--Biography--Dictionaries. 4. American literature--History and
criticism--Encyclopedias. I. Hacht, Anne Marie. II. Hayes, Dwayne D.

PS21.G36 2009
810'.9--dc22   2008051753

978-1-4144-3130-7 (set)   1-4144-3130-9 (set)
978-1-4144-3131-4 (vol. 1)   1-4144-3131-7 (vol. 1)
978-1-4144-3132-1 (vol. 2)   1-4144-3132-5 (vol. 2)
978-1-4144-3133-8 (vol. 3)   1-4144-3133-3 (vol. 3)
978-1-4144-3134-5 (vol. 4)   1-4144-3134-1 (vol. 4)

This title is also available as an e-book.
ISBN-13: 978-1-4144-3139-0 ISBN-10: 1-4144-3139-2
Contact your Gale, a part of Cengage Learning sales representative for ordering information.

Printed in the United States of America
1 2 3 4 5 6 7 13 12 11 10 09

Contents

VOLUME 2

F-G

H

VOLUME 3

L

VOLUME 4

R

S

Introduction

How to Use This Book

The *Gale Contextual Encyclopedia of American Literature* is a resource for students who seek information beyond the simple biographical details of an author's life or a brief overview of the author's major works. This book is designed to offer a comprehensive view of how an author's work fits within the context of the author's life, historical events, and the literary world. This allows for a greater understanding of both the author's work and the cultural and historical environment in which it was created.

The *Gale Contextual Encyclopedia of American Literature* is divided into entries, each focused on a particular writer who has made significant contributions to literature. In some cases, these individuals may be known primarily for actions and contributions outside the realm of literature. John F. Kennedy and Martin Luther King Jr., for example, are two figures famous for their political activism; Rachel Carson is known primarily as a biologist and ecologist; Cotton Mather is remembered for his connection to the infamous Salem Witch Trials. However, all of these figures have, aside from their other accomplishments and activities, created significant works of literature that have stood the test of time and affected readers beyond the borders of their own cultures.

This book is best used not just to locate the facts of a writer's life and work, but as a way to understand the social, literary, and historical environment in which the writer lived and created. By understanding the context of the writer's work, you are more likely to recognize key themes and stylistic traits as elements of larger trends in the literary world, as well as understand the impact of historical events from a new and unique perspective.

Sections Found within Each Entry in This Book

Each entry in this book is divided into three main parts: Works in Biographical and Historical Context; Works in Literary Context; and Works in Critical Context. These sections are discussed below.

In addition, each entry includes: a Key Facts section, containing birth/death date information as well as a list of major works; a Responses to Literature section, containing discussion and writing activities related to the author in question; a

Further Reading section that includes bibliographic citations as well as reputable sources of additional material about the author in the form of books, periodicals, or Web sites; a Literary and Historical Contemporaries sidebar, listing several famous contemporaries of the author; and a Common Human Experience sidebar, offering examples of other literary or artistic works that share themes or techniques with those of the subject of the entry.

Works in Biographical and Historical Context In this section, you will find information about how events and concerns in the author's life helped to shape the author's work. For example, Kurt Vonnegut's experiences in a German prison camp in Dresden during the Allied bombing of that city in 1945 led him to write *Slaughterhouse-Five* (1969), while events surrounding Watergate (the political scandal that brought about the resignation of President Richard Nixon) led him to write *Jailbird* (1979). This section also includes information on historical events or trends that had an effect on the author. For example, the scientific and technological advancements of the late twentieth century greatly influenced the subject matter of the popular fiction of Michael Crichton, which often centered on the theme of modern technology run amok.

Works in Literary Context In this section, you will find information about how the author's work fits within the context of literature in general. This may include a description of a stylistic trait exhibited in the author's writing; for example, Mark Twain is known for his brilliant use of colloquial speech, and information on this technique—as well as examples of how the author used it—can be found in his entry. This section may also include a discussion of the writer's work as it exists within a specific genre, such as Southern Gothic fiction or modernist poetry. Finally, the Works in Literary Context section may contain discussion of specific themes commonly found in the author's work. The writings of James Baldwin, for example, frequently address the theme of race relations.

Works in Critical Context In this section, you will find a survey of critical and popular opinion related to the author and the author's most important works. The emphasis is on contemporary opinions, or those formed by readers and critics at the time the author's work was first published. In some cases, critical or popular opinion from the time of publication may not be available; this may be due simply to the passage of time, or due to the writer's lack of fame during his or her own lifetime. This section also includes information on how critical or popular opinion of an author has changed over time. Herman Melville's masterwork *Moby-Dick* (1851) met with a tepid reception upon publication, but is now considered one of the finest achievements in American literature. Kate Chopin's novella *The Awakening* (1899) earned her critical scorn and ruined her career, but the work is now considered a breakthrough in women's literature. Conversely, some works that enjoyed widespread acclaim initially are less well regarded or even forgotten today. Joel Chandler Harris's *Uncle Remus* books (published between 1880 and 1905) based on African American folk tales were popular with white and black readers in the North and South at the time; today, many critics accuse Harris (a white journalist) of misappropriating elements of African American culture, and his work has fallen out of favor. Likewise, James Branch Cabell was one of the most celebrated writers of the 1920s, made internationally famous because of the scandal stirred up by the obscenity charges attached to his 1919 novel *Jurgen*; today, his work is rarely read.

Other Information Contained in This Book

In addition to the entries for individual authors, this book also contains a chronology that indicates some major historical events related to the development of American literature. At the end of the book, you will find a glossary of terms—primarily literary and historical in nature—that are used in various entries throughout the book, along with a brief explanation of each term, a general index, and a nationality/ethnicity index.

Advisory Board

Alicia Baker Elley

taught undergraduate and high school literature, composition, and technical writing classes for over ten years. She is currently district librarian for the Harmony Independent School District in Texas.

Maureen Reed

has taught literature, history, and American Studies courses at Minnesota State University Moorhead, Lewis and Clark College, and Portland State University. She earned a Ph.D. in American Studies from the University of Texas at Austin and held a Fulbright Lectureship in American Studies at the University of Regensburg in Germany.

Roger K. Smith

has been a teacher of English, writing, and other humanities courses at such institutions as Ithaca College, Rutgers University, and Edward R. Murrow High School (Brooklyn). He holds a BA from Swarthmore College and an MA from New York University.

Patrick Walsh

holds a Ph.D. in history from the University of Texas at Austin. He has taught English and Multidisciplinary Studies at Concordia College and Minnesota State University, in Moorhead, Minnesota. A Fulbright Lecturer in American Studies at the University of Passau in Germany, he now teaches at the Catlin Gabel School in Portland, Oregon.

Chronology

This chronology contains a brief overview of some of the major events in the history of American literature. This includes the development of technologies and tools that advanced the writing and publishing process, as well as some significant historical events that had an impact on the development of literature.

1500–1700

1576 English explorers begin searching for the Northwest Passage, a hoped-for water route around North America to Asia.

1607 Jamestown settlement established in Virginia.

1620 The Pilgrims traveling from England aboard *The Mayflower* reach Cape Cod and form a settlement at Plymouth, Massachusetts.

1624 The Dutch establish a city called New Amsterdam on the island of Manhattan. The city later became known as New York City, a major center of American commerce and publishing.

1630 Massachusetts Bay Colony Governor John Winthrop begins keeping his journal of life in New England. William Bradford, governor of Plymouth, begins his own book, later titled *History of Plymouth Plantation*.

1650 Anne Bradstreet publishes her first volume of poetry.

1689 Enlightenment thinker John Locke anonymously publishes *Two Treatises of Government*, a work that attacks the idea of the "divine right" of kings and argues for a government that operates with the consent of the governed. The work exerts a strong influence over eighteenth-century French philosophers and America's founding fathers.

1692–1693 The Salem Witch Trials are conducted. One hundred fifty people are arrested and accused of witchcraft, twenty-nine are convicted, and eighteen are executed.

1700–1800

1702 Cotton Mather publishes *Magnalia Christi Americana*, described as an ecclesiastical history of New England. It is one of the first works that attempts to define the American experience.

1718 The city of New Orleans, Louisiana, is founded by French and Canadian settlers.

1732 Benjamin Franklin begins writing *Poor Richard's Almanac*.

1740 Religious leader Jonathan Edwards begins writing his *Personal Narrative*.

1754–1763 The French and Indian War is fought between France and Great Britain and their respective Native American allies. The conflict is part of a broader power struggle between France and Great Britain that is waged in Europe (the Seven Years War).

1762 Jean-Jacques Rousseau publishes *The Social Contract*, a landmark work of political philosophy.

1767   Daniel Boone explores territory west of the Appalachian Mountains.

1770   British soldiers fire into a crowd of rowdy, protesting colonists in Boston, killing five. The event, which helps spark the American Revolution, becomes known as the Boston Massacre.

1773   The British Parliament enacts the Tea Act; in protest, a group of men dressed as Native Americans dump a shipment of tea from Great Britain into Boston Harbor, an event called the Boston Tea Party.

1774   The British Parliament passes measures collectively known as the Intolerable Acts in an effort to punish Massachusetts for the Boston Tea Party.

1775   Patrick Henry gives his famous "Give me liberty, or give me death" speech; Paul Revere goes on his "midnight ride" to warn colonists to take arms against approaching British soldiers; Minutemen fight the British in Lexington and Concord, the first battles of the American Revolution.

1776   Thomas Paine publishes *Common Sense*; Thomas Jefferson writes, and Congress adopts, the Declaration of Independence.

1781   British general Charles Cornwallis surrenders to American General George Washington at Yorktown, ending the American Revolution.

1789   A mob storms the Bastille prison in Paris, France, setting off the French Revolution.

1794   Thomas Paine publishes *The Age of Reason*.

1800–1900

1800   John Chapman, also known as "Johnny Appleseed," travels through the Ohio Valley region giving settlers apple seeds.

1803   President Thomas Jefferson negotiates with France to purchase the Louisiana Territory for $15 million; Jefferson sets Meriwether Lewis and William Clark off on an expedition of the newly acquired territory and the lands west of it for the purpose of determining whether a water route existed between the Missouri River and the Pacific Ocean.

1812–1815

Great Britain and the United States fight the War of 1812.

1819   Washington Irving publishes *The Sketch Book* containing such well-known short stories as "The Legend of Sleepy Hollow" and "Rip Van Winkle."

1820   Congress passes the Missouri Compromise, by which slavery is prohibited in the northern Louisiana territory, Maine is admitted to the Union as a free state, and Missouri is admitted as a slave state. The delicate balance between the interests of slave and free states is preserved for the next three decades.

1821   Sequoyah develops a Native American alphabet and uses it to help Cherokees read and write their own language.

1831   Nat Turner leads a slave rebellion in Virginia in which fifty-five white people are killed; Turner is captured and executed; several eastern Native American tribes are removed from their homelands and forced to march to Oklahoma Territory, a harsh, deadly journey dubbed "the trail of tears."

1832   Samuel Morse invents the telegraph.

1836   Texas declares its independence after revolting against Mexico; Ralph Waldo Emerson publishes *Nature*.

1841   Brook Farm, a utopian cooperative, is established in West Roxbury, Massachusetts, by Unitarian minister George Ripley.

1845   The United States annexes Texas.

1846–1847

Mexican-American War waged; the United States wins the short war, and gains much of what is now the western United States, including present-day California, Arizona, Nevada, Utah, New Mexico, Colorado, and Wyoming.

1848   Women's Rights Convention held in Seneca Falls, New York.

1849   After gold is discovered in California in 1848, a rush of prospectors—known as forty-niners—flood into California in hopes of striking it rich.

1850   Nathaniel Hawthorne publishes *The Scarlet Letter*; after much bitter debate, Congress passes the Compromise of 1850, which includes multiple provisions designed to maintain a balance between the relative power of slave and free states in Congress.

1851   Herman Melville publishes *Moby-Dick*.

1852   Harriet Beecher Stowe publishes *Uncle Tom's Cabin*.

1854   Henry David Thoreau publishes *Walden*.

1855   Walt Whitman publishes his first version of the poetry collection *Leaves of Grass*.

1859   Abolitionist John Brown attacks the U.S. arsenal at Harper's Ferry, West Virginia, in an attempt to gain weapons to start a slave insurrection; he is captured, tried, and hanged.

1861–1865

United States Civil War fought between the Union and the pro-slavery Confederate States of America. The war is effectively ended with the surrender of Confederate general Robert E. Lee to Union general Ulysses S. Grant, in Appomattox, Virginia, in 1865; President Abraham Lincoln is assassinated in 1865.

1869   The Fifteenth Amendment to the Constitution grants African Americans the right to vote.

1876   Alexander Graham Bell invents the telephone.

1879   Thomas Edison invents the electric light bulb.

1884   Mark Twain publishes *Adventures of Huckleberry Finn*.

1890   *The Poems of Emily Dickinson* is published posthumously, by the poet's sister.

1895   Stephen Crane publishes *The Red Badge of Courage*.

1898   The United States and Spain fight the Spanish-American War. The United States quickly wins the war, and gains Puerto Rico, Guam, and the Philippines. The war establishes the United States as a major world power.

1900–Now

1901   A major oil strike is made at Spindletop, Texas.

1903   Orville and Wilbur Wright launch the first successful manned airplane flight in Kitty Hawk, North Carolina; Henry Ford founds the Ford Motor Company.

1909   The National Association for the Advancement of Colored People (NAACP) is formed.

1914   World War I begins in Europe.

1917   The United States enters World War I on the side of the Entente Powers.

1918   Germany and its allies are defeated, and World War I ends.

1920   The Nineteenth Amendment to the Constitution grants women the right to vote.

1925   F. Scott Fitzgerald publishes *The Great Gatsby*.

1926   Ernest Hemingway publishes *The Sun Also Rises*; the Radio Corporation of America (RCA) organizes the National Broadcasting Company (NBC): the first radio network set up for public entertainment and information.

1927   American pilot Charles Lindbergh flies solo across the Atlantic Ocean from New York to France.

1929   The U.S. stock market crashes, causing financial panic; William Faulkner publishes *The Sound and the Fury*.

1929–1939

The Great Depression, a global economic downturn, causes widespread unemployment and deflation.

1932   Amelia Earhart becomes first woman to fly solo across the Atlantic Ocean.

1936   Eugene O'Neill wins Nobel Prize in Literature.

1938   Thorton Wilder publishes the play *Our Town*; Pearl S. Buck wins Nobel Prize in Literature.

1939   World War II begins in Europe with the German invasion of Poland.

1940   Richard Wright publishes *Native Son*; Carson McCullers publishes *The Heart Is a Lonely Hunter*.

1941   Japanese fighter pilots attack the United States naval base at Pearl Harbor, Hawaii. The United States declares war on Japan and, subsequently, on Japanese ally Germany, effecting U.S. entry into World War II; the U.S. begins the Manhattan Project, a secret program to develop an atomic bomb.

1942   President Franklin Roosevelt signs an executive order authorizing the forced relocation of Japanese Americans to internment camps for the duration of the war.

1945   The United States drops atomic bombs on the Japanese cities of Hiroshima and Nagasaki, killing more than 100,000 people. Japan surrenders. Germany surrenders.

1947   Jackie Robinson becomes the first African American major-league baseball player; Tennessee Williams publishes the play *A Streetcar Named Desire*.

1948   Congress approves the Marshall Plan for the reconstruction and assistance of Europe; Jewish state of Israel proclaimed; first television broadcast of *Texaco Star Theater*, hosted by Milton Berle—the first major television program in America.

1949   William Faulkner wins Nobel Prize in Literature.

1950   Senator Joseph McCarthy claims that the United States State Department has been infiltrated by communists; President Harry Truman sends U.S. troops to Korea after communist North Korea invades pro-Western South Korea; Isaac Asimov publishes *I, Robot*.

1951   J. D. Salinger publishes *The Catcher in the Rye*.

1953   Senator Joseph McCarthy becomes chairman of the Senate Committee on Government Operations and launches his notorious investigations into purported communist activity in the United States.

1954   The Supreme Court case *Brown v. the Board of Education of Topeka* declares segregation in public schools unconstitutional; Ernest Hemingway wins Nobel Prize in Literature.

1955   Dr. Martin Luther King Jr. leads the Montgomery Bus Boycott.

1957   Jack Kerouac publishes *On the Road*; Theodore Seuss Geisel (Dr. Seuss) publishes *The Cat in the Hat*; the Soviet Union launches *Sputnik 1*, sparking the U.S./Soviet space race.

1959   Lorraine Hansberry publishes the play *A Raisin in the Sun*.

1960   Harper Lee publishes *To Kill a Mockingbird*; birth control pills are made available to the public.

1962   Cuban Missile Crisis occurs: a tense standoff between nuclear superpowers the United States and the Soviet Union; John Steinbeck wins Nobel Prize in Literature.

1963   President John F. Kennedy assassinated in Dallas, Texas.

1964   Congress passes the Civil Rights Act, prohibiting racial discrimination in public places.

1965   President Lyndon Johnson escalates hostilities against North Vietnam, ordering bombing raids; Dr. Martin Luther King Jr. leads a civil rights march from Selma to Montgomery, Alabama; African American rights activist Malcolm X assassinated; Voting Rights Act passed by Congress.

1968   Martin Luther King Jr. assassinated; presidential candidate Robert Kennedy assassinated.

1969   Kurt Vonnegut publishes *Slaughterhouse-Five*; astronaut Neil Armstrong becomes first human to set foot on the moon.

1974   President Richard Nixon resigns in the wake of the Watergate scandal.

1975   Vietnam War ends.

1976   Saul Bellow wins Nobel Prize in Literature.

1978   Isaac Bashevis Singer wins Nobel Prize in Literature.

1979   Radical Islamists storm the American embassy in Iran and take fifty-two hostages, most of whom are held for 444 days.

1981   The IBM personal computer first becomes available.

1984   Sandra Cisneros publishes *The House on Mango Street*.

1986   Cormac McCarthy publishes *Blood Meridian*.

1989   The Berlin Wall is torn down.

1990   First commercial dial-up access to the Internet becomes available; the Soviet Union collapses, and independent nations are formed of its former territory.

1993   Toni Morrison wins Nobel Prize in Literature.

1998   President Bill Clinton impeached by the U.S. House of Representatives.

2001   In a coordinated suicide mission, radical Islamists associated with terrorist organization al-Qaeda hijack commercial airliners and crash them into the World Trade Center in New York City and the Pentagon building in Virginia, killing nearly 3,000 people; Jonathan Franzen publishes *The Corrections*.

2003   The United States invades Iraq and topples the regime of Saddam Hussein.

2009   Barack Obama sworn in as president of the United States, the first African American ever elected to that office.

L

✸ Jhumpa Lahiri

BORN: *1967, London, England*

NATIONALITY: *Indian-American*

GENRE: *Fiction*

MAJOR WORKS:
Interpreter of Maladies (1999)
The Namesake (2003)

Overview

At thirty-two years old, Jhumpa Lahiri became the youngest writer to ever win the Pulitzer Prize for Fiction for her 1999 book *Interpreter of Maladies*. Marked as an up-and-coming writer from that point on, Lahiri's small output has focused on addressing the experience of minority Americans of immigrant heritage and their attempts to reconcile their forebears' cultural heritage with the American culture they grew up in.

Works in Biographical and Historical Context

Indian Heritage Lahiri was born Nilanjana Sudeshna in London, England, to Bengali parents. When Lahiri was three, her parents, a librarian and a teacher, relocated to South Kingstown, Rhode Island, where she grew up. Her family retained close ties to their cultural homeland, and Lahiri made frequent visits to family members in the city of Calcutta throughout her childhood. Lahiri's mother made a conscious effort to maintain a connection to her family's heritage while raising Jhumpa and her younger sister in America. "It was important to my mother to raise her children as Indian, thinking and doing things in an Indian way, whatever that means," Lahiri recalled to Mervyn Rothstein in the *New York Times*. This duality led to conflicting feelings for Jhumpa while she was growing up. She turned to writing at an early age, penning ten-page "novels" to read to her classmates. "Writing allowed me to observe and make sense of things

without having to participate," she remarked in a *Newsweek International* interview. "I didn't belong. I looked different and felt like an outsider."

After high school graduation, Lahiri attended Barnard College, where she earned a bachelor's degree in English literature, then went on to earn three master's degrees—in creative writing, comparative studies, and literature and the arts—from Boston University. While working on a doctoral dissertation in the field of Renaissance studies, Lahiri turned to writing as an escape from the pressures of academia. After receiving some positive feedback, she began to submit her short stories to magazines. She was awarded the Henfield Prize from *Transatlantic Review* in 1993 and the *Louisville Review* fiction prize in 1997. Eventually, the *New Yorker* reprinted three of her stories in their pages and had named Lahiri as one of the twenty best young writers in America.

Writer of Short Stories Lahiri was inspired with the phrase "interpreter of maladies" after visiting a friend who served as a Russian translator for a Boston doctor. As she recalled to Gillian Flynn in *Entertainment Weekly*, "Over the years it was fading, and every so often I'd come across it and think, 'Am I ever going to do something with it?' Then one day I did." The resulting story catapulted Lahiri into further literary fame when it was selected for inclusion in the *Best American Short Stories 1999* collection. That same year, Lahiri started collecting her stories for publication in a book. Along with "Interpreter of Maladies," which would become the title story of the collection, she assembled eight other stories, some previously published, and some others unpublished.

Interpreter of Maladies was released to immediate critical attention and acclaim. The stories all revolved around Indian and immigrant Indian characters—although Lahiri took pains to specify that none of the characters were biographical, the situations all completely invented. Nevertheless, she could not help but draw upon her own life and family for some of her stories, such as "The Third and Final Continent," which features an Indian librarian very much

Jhumpa Lahiri   *Lahiri, Jhumpa, photograph. AP Images.*

flicted relationships. Lahiri continues to write, "I have all these ideas that are percolating," she told an interviewer. "The more I write, the more I'm learning about how very strange the experience is. It's so difficult, so exasperating, so mysterious."

Works in Literary Context

Lahiri took the writing world by storm with her first book, becoming the youngest author to win the Pulitzer Prize for Fiction. Her work is often praised for its careful balance of precise, dense detail and flowing narrative. According to Lahiri, one motivation for her stories is the "necessary combination of distance and intimacy with a place."

The Search for Identity   In her stories Lahiri tackles the question of identity, an issue familiar to many immigrants in a culturally diverse country like America. "I think that for immigrants, the challenges of exile, the loneliness, the constant sense of alienation, the knowledge of and longing for a lost world, are more explicit and distressing than for their children," she says. "On the other hand, the problem for the children of immigrants—those with strong ties to their country of origin—is that they feel neither one thing nor the other."

"I've often felt," Lahiri told Barbara Kantrowitz in *Newsweek*, "that I am somehow illegitimate in both cultures. A true Indian doesn't accept me as an Indian and a true American doesn't accept me as an American." This feeling of displacement has informed the majority of Lahiri's work. In this, Lahiri is merely the latest in a long and respected tradition of American literature, that of authors exploring what it means to be a "new" American, a recent arrival or the child of immigrants who is attempting to reconcile the culture of the old world with that of the new.

Works in Critical Context

Reviewers of Lahiri's works regard them as "fresh and gripping," combining multiple characters and themes with a conventional search for love. *Newsweek* reviewer Laura Shapiro comments that Lahiri "writes such direct, translucent prose you almost forget you're reading." Caleb Crain writes in the *New York Times Book Review* that "In Lahiri's sympathetic tales, the pang of disappointment turns into a sudden hunger to know more."

Interpreter of Maladies   Although Lahiri is of Indian heritage, her lack of experience with her family's country of origin has led to some of her stories being criticized by some reviewers as inauthentic and stereotypical. *Time International* reviewer Nisid Hajari writes that two of the stories set in Calcutta "survive on little more than smoothness. . . . Lahiri hits her stride closer to home—on the uncertain ground of the immigrant." Other reviewers echo this last sentiment. A *Publishers Weekly* reviewer writes, "Lahiri's touch in these nine tales is delicate, but her observations remain damningly accurate, and her bittersweet stories are unhampered by nostalgia." Hajari, too, offers praise, stating, "The whole is assured and powerful."

in the same vein as her father. "I was filled with anxiety about it," Lahiri commented. "He's not a very [expressive] person, but he said, 'My whole life is in that story.' That's all I could ask for." The publication of *Interpreter of Maladies* immediately established Lahiri's literary reputation, earning her the Pulitzer Prize for Fiction in 2000.

Lahiri's interest in the Indian immigrant experience found more room for exploration in her first novel, *The Namesake* (2003). Described as a "coming of age story" for an entire family, the book follows the progress of an Indian immigrant couple and their gradually growing family's various adjustments to their new surroundings. In particular, Lahiri contrasted the experiences of her native-born parents to their children, born in a new country. Speaking of the son, "Gogol spends most of his life convinced his name is an accident or a random and meaningless misrepresentation of who he is," Lahiri told Edward Nawotka in *Publishers Weekly*. "One of the things I want to have happen for him in the book is for his name to make sense."

In 2008, Lahiri published her second short story collection, *Unaccustomed Earth*, which continues to explore the themes of the Indian immigrant experience and con-

Prema Srinivasan, writing for *Hindu*, calls *Interpreter of Maladies* "eminently readable," and notes that its author "talks about universal maladies in detail, with a touch of humour and sometimes with irony which is never misplaced." In a *New York Times Book Review* article, Michiko Kakutani calls the book an "accomplished collection. . . . She is a writer of uncommon elegance and poise, and with *Interpreter of Maladies* she has made a precocious debut."

Responses to Literature

1. Lahiri often examines the challenges of reconciling Indian heritage with American culture. What other ethnic groups have had to make similar concessions? How have past immigrant cultures been integrated into wider American culture?

2. What is the history of Indian immigration in America? Is it on the rise? How does it compare to the history of Indian immigration in the United Kingdom? How has Indian culture impacted British and American culture?

3. Lahiri sets several of her short stories, such as "A Temporary Matter," in Calcutta. Research the living conditions in Calcutta. Do you think Lahiri's depiction of the city is accurate based on what you've read? Why or why not?

4. What would it be like to attempt to integrate into a new and unfamiliar culture? Pretend that you and your family have moved to a foreign country of your choice; write a story about your experiences attempting to integrate into the new culture, and how you would go about preserving your own American culture.

BIBLIOGRAPHY

Books

"A Temporary Matter." *Short Stories for Students*. Vol. 19. Detroit: Gale, 2004.

Bala, Suman, ed. *Jhumpa Lahiri, the Master Storyteller: A Critical Response to Interpreter of Maladies*. New Delhi: Khosla, 2002.

"Jhumpa Lahiri (1967–)." *Short Story Criticism*. Edited by Jelena Krstovic. Vol. 96. Detroit: Thomson Gale, 2007.

"Lahiri, Jhumpa." *Authors and Artists for Young Adults*. Edited by Dwayne D. Hayes. Vol. 56. Detroit: Gale, 2004.

Periodicals

Patel, Vibhuti. "The Maladies of Belonging." *Newsweek*, Pacific edition (September 20, 1999): 60.

Rothstein, Mervyn. "India's Post-Rushdie Generation." *New York Times* (July 3, 2000): E1.

LITERARY AND HISTORICAL CONTEMPORARIES

Lahiri's famous contemporaries include:

Hugo Chávez (1954–): The current president of Venezuela, Chávez came to power in 1999 riding the wave of a popular movement in his country. His socialist, liberal, anti-American policies have made him a controversial figure.

Michel Houellebecq (1958–): A controversial French author whose fiction has been called "nihilistic" and "repugnant," Houllebecq has also been brought to trial on charges of religious bigotry.

Tiger Woods (1975–): Consistently ranked the number one golfer in the world, Tiger Woods is one of the most successful golfers of all time, a child prodigy who went professional in 1996 and has dominated the sport ever since.

Chuck Palahniuk (1962–): American author Palahniuk is best known as the author of the novel *Fight Club* (1996), which was also adapted into a 1999 movie by director David Fincher.

John F. Kennedy, Jr. (1960–1999): The son of a United States president, young "John-John," as he was called, made an indelible impression at his father's funeral, saluting the passing casket. He died tragically when the plane he was piloting crashed.

COMMON HUMAN EXPERIENCE

Lahiri's focus on the immigrant experience is echoed in many other books from a variety of different cultures originating across the globe who all share a common destination: America.

'Tis: A Memoir (1999), a memoir by Frank McCourt. The sequel to McCourt's memoir of his Irish childhood, *Angela's Ashes* (1996), this autobiography follows McCourt's experiences as a young immigrant in New York City.

House of Sand and Fog (1999), a novel by Andre Dubus. This harrowing story centers on an Iranian army colonel adjusting to his new life in Miami.

In the Year of the Boar and Jackie Robinson (1984), a book by Bette Bao Lord. This is a tale for young adults about a Chinese immigrant girl embracing American life in Brooklyn during the year that Jackie Robinson broke the race barrier in professional baseball.

✸ Louis L'Amour

BORN: *1908, Jamestown, North Dakota*

DIED: *1988, Los Angeles, California*

NATIONALITY: *American*

GENRE: *Fiction*

MAJOR WORKS:

Hondo (1953)

Overview

Louis L'Amour is undoubtedly the most widely read and best-selling author of Western fiction. His domination of the popular Western for over forty years has helped to develop the genre. He has sold more books than nearly every other contemporary novelist. He wrote more million-copy best sellers than any other American fiction writer. By the time he died in 1988, nearly two hundred million copies of his books had been printed.

Works in Biographical and Historical Context

Self-Education, Restless Living L'Amour was born Louis Dearborn LaMoore on March 22, 1908, in Jamestown, North Dakota, the seventh and youngest child in his family. His father, Louis Charles LaMoore, held several jobs. Emily Dearborn LaMoore, a skilled storyteller, was trained as a teacher before her marriage. Her father was a Civil War veteran and had fought in campaigns against the Native Americans. Both parents schooled L'Amour in family and Western lore, laying the foundation for his literary career. Even as a child, L'Amour was a storyteller, beginning his career even before he went to school. He would draw pictures of cowboys and Indians, cut them out, and act out stories with them. As he grew older, he thought that he could write professionally, but it was a long time before he tried to sell his work or found any success in the literary marketplace.

In 1923, at age fifteen, L'Amour's parents moved to Oklahoma. L'Amour decided to end his formal education and begin an extensive self-education consisting of travel and work. He held a variety of jobs, including positions as a longshoreman, lumberjack, miner, and elephant handler. On another job, he helped an old trapper skin 925 dead cattle for a Texas rancher. The old man told L'Amour of his being kidnapped by Indians as a child, riding with the great war chiefs, and fighting the white man. From the trapper's tales L'Amour got the ideas for many later stories and novels. L'Amour also boxed professionally in preliminary events, another skill taught to him by his father. His travels took him up and down the West Coast before he embarked on a sailing trip to Asia. According to one story, L'Amour used the proceeds from sunken treasure he discovered in Macao to visit Paris and other European cities.

Louis L'Amour   *L'Amour, Louis, photograph. AP Images.*

Although L'Amour's early life sounds romantic, almost idyllic, such was not the case. Money and jobs were not always easy to come by, and there were times when he missed meals and slept in lumber piles with newspapers wrapped under his coat for warmth. L'Amour was also often involved in fights, both in and out of the ring.

Settling Down and Writing These early years of wandering freely greatly influenced L'Amour's writing, not only in the knowledge of lore he gained in his journeys but also in his male heroes' conflicting feelings toward settling down. In the late 1930s, L'Amour returned to his parents' home in Oklahoma to begin writing, a career he had always intended to pursue. He did not meet with instant success; he received more than two hundred rejection slips before he learned what he believes to be the secret of telling stories: beginning in the middle of the action to get the reader involved.

After publishing a book of poetry in 1939, L'Amour's career was interrupted by World War II. He entered the army in 1942 and served as an officer in tank destroyer and in transportation units in France and Germany. L'Amour would pass the time by telling other soldiers some of the tales he had picked up on his travels. Their response encouraged him, and in the late 1940s he began submitting his work to the numerous pulp magazines, publishing stories of all varieties, including sports, detective, and adventure magazines. Soon, his work appeared in the magazines

Detective Tales, *Popular Sports*, and *Giant Western*. By the early 1950s, L'Amour was selling to the better-paying slick magazines of *Collier's* and the *Saturday Evening Post*.

Mastery of the Popular Western L'Amour did not intend to concentrate on Westerns, but as he sold work to more Western pulp magazines than any other type, L'Amour began to write mainly in that genre. By the early 1950s many pulp magazines had ceased publication; some never recovered from the paper restrictions of World War II, and the new popularity of original novels in the paperback format drew readers and authors from the pulps. It was in the field of paperback originals that L'Amour was to find his huge success, beginning with the publication in 1953 of *Hondo*.

As a novel, *Hondo* shows all L'Amour's strengths. It is a swiftly told story with touches of sharp, effective violence. It demonstrates L'Amour's understanding of frontier life, the Indians, and nature. As in all L'Amour's books, the Indians are treated with respect. The theme of *Hondo*, and of most of his novels, is best expressed by L'Amour himself in the title of his 1980 short-story collection, *The Strong Shall Live*. The frontier demanded strength of body and strength of character. Those who have both are the survivors in L'Amour's novels. Those who lack either are not likely to last long.

From *Hondo* onward, L'Amour produced three novels a year until his death, gaining steadily in popularity throughout his career and eventually becoming one of the best-selling fiction writers of all time. In 1979 alone, Bantam Books, one of his paperback publishers, shipped over 7.8 million copies of L'Amour titles; and in June 1980, *Yondering*, a collection of the author's early short stories, was published simultaneously in paperback and hardcover editions by Bantam to celebrate one hundred million copies of L'Amour books in print around the world. Although the majority of his novels were Westerns, L'Amour departed occasionally from the Old West in time and place, as in *The Walking Drum* (1984), set in medieval Europe. L'Amour never lost his passion for traveling and researching his novels firsthand, commenting, "I go to an area I'm interested in and I try to find a guy who knows it better than anyone else. Usually it's some broken-down cowboy." President Ronald Reagan was one of L'Amour's fans and awarded L'Amour both the Congressional Gold Medal and the Presidential Medal of Freedom; he was the only novelist in American history to be accorded either honor. L'Amour, who did not smoke, died in Los Angeles, California, on June 10, 1988, of lung cancer.

Even with his prolific output, by the late 1980s, L'Amour had come nowhere near to exhausting the store of research he had gathered as a connoisseur of historical details. At the time of his death in 1988, he had developed outlines for fifty more novels. A year before he died, L'Amour told *CA*, "There's no difference in the Western novel and any other novel.... It's a story about people, and that's the important thing to always remember. Every story is about people—people against the canvas of their times."

LITERARY AND HISTORICAL CONTEMPORARIES

L'Amour's famous contemporaries include:

Klaus Fuchs (1911–1988): Fuchs, a German physicist who had worked for the British, caused a sensation when, in 1950, he confessed to being a spy for the Soviet Union and to passing nuclear secrets from the earliest stages of research during World War II and continuing on for seven years.

Dalton Trumbo (1905–1976): Novelist and screenwriter Trumbo is best known for his antiwar novel *Johnny Got His Gun* and his period of "blacklisting"—professional exile—after he refused to testify before the House Un-American Activities Committee, which was looking for Trumbo to "name names" of communists in Hollywood.

Charles M. Schulz (1922–2000): Shulz is the creator of *Peanuts*, one of the most successful and influential comic strips of all time. Running for fifty straight years, *Peanuts* also spawned a successful series of television specials, with each episode usually focused on a specific holiday.

L. Sprague de Camp (1907–2000): Noted science fiction and fantasy author, publisher, and biographer, de Camp was instrumental in preserving and republishing the pulp fantasy tales of such authors as Robert E. Howard, creator of Conan the Barbarian.

Krystyna Skarbek (1908–1952): Also known by her cover identity of Christine Granville, Skarbek became a legend as one of the most successful British espionage agents who served during World War II. After the war, she had a year-long affair with *James Bond* series author Ian Fleming, who would model at least two of his fictional female agents on Skarbek.

Works in Literary Context

L'Amour wrote of strong heroes, respect for the environment, and straightforward notions of right and wrong. His exhaustive detailing of historical settings was the result of years of research and firsthand observation. L'Amour's heroes, many of them recurring characters from the families Sackett, Talon, and Chantry, create a social order out of a strong loyalty to family and a belief in white Americans' destiny to spread their culture throughout the West. Unlike other pulp Western writers, however, L'Amour examined the often brutal effect of white culture on native culture and endowed his heroes with conflicting feelings about the struggle of Native Americans.

The Values of Oral Tradition L'Amour's subject matter and narrative style are strongly influenced by the oral tradition of storytelling taught him in his youth. L'Amour once said, "I write my books to be read aloud and I think

COMMON HUMAN EXPERIENCE

L'Amour was merely one of several giants of the Western genre. Here are other works that contributed to developing the conventions and elements that would come to define one of America's most beloved genres:

The Virginian (1902), a novel by Owen Wister. Considered to be the first true Western literary novel, this book was a popular sensation upon its publication, showcasing many of the narrative elements that would come to dominate the genre over the coming century.

Lonesome Dove (1985), a novel by Larry McMurtry. One of the most popular of the more recent Western novels by one of the genre's more progressive and literary authors, this story of Texas cattle ranchers was made into a successful television miniseries.

Riders of the Purple Sage (1912), a novel by Zane Grey. One of the key works that catapulted the genre into mass-market success, this novel solidified the narrative themes first outlined in *The Virginian*.

Destry Rides Again (1930), a novel by Max Brand. One of the highest-paid writers of his time, Brand's most popular character is featured in this, his most well-known book, which was made into a classic Western movie in 1932.

of myself in [the] oral tradition." This influence is most predominant in L'Amour's attention to historical detail and a careful portrayal of time and place, typically the nineteenth-century American West. Like the epic plots typical of oral literature, L'Amour's stories are full of adventure, color, and struggle between good and evil.

The Importance of Family and Home A typical L'Amour hero, who often narrates the story in the first person, is a strong, brave white man who struggles with his conscience and sense of independence in his quest to settle the West and make a permanent home for himself. L'Amour's main characters do not stand alone, however, but are typically members of extended families. These families, particularly the Sackett family to which he devoted seventeen novels, provide a framework for L'Amour's philosophy of civilization. Family loyalty and the complex extended family structures L'Amour created comprise the social, moral, and value systems by which his characters behave. Lawlessness is defined by those acting contrary to the values defined by the family. The family is civilization, the protection against the wilderness, and the consistent source of strength in the struggle to settle the West. Unique among other Western genre writers, L'Amour does not confine this definition of civilization to white Americans but endows his Native American characters with the same strong sense of family

as they fight to keep their culture. His white heroes recognize the Native Americans' plight and feel a conflicting admiration for their brand of civilization.

Works in Critical Context

Critical reception of L'Amour's work was often indifferent. Before gaining popularity, his novels often were not reviewed at all. Many critics categorized them as genre fiction and therefore not deserving of critical analysis. Such reviews that L'Amour did garner faulted his wooden, repetitious characters, his confusing tendency to switch between first- and third-person narration in the same passage, and in some cases an overabundance of historical details that detracted from the plot's action. Some critics felt his work would have benefited from some attention to revision. Even Irwyn Applebaum, Western editor at Bantam Books, admits that L'Amour's work may be lacking in literary quality. He emphasizes, however, that a better storyteller is nowhere to be found.

L'Amour's determination to persevere led to increased critical interest in his work; eventually the literary establishment could no longer continue to disregard such a popular writer. *Newsweek* contributor Charles Leerhsen noted that as L'Amour entered his fourth decade as a novelist "the critics back East [were] finally reviewing his work—and praising his unpretentious, lean-as-a-grass-fed-steer style." Some critics maintained that L'Amour's style was the key to his appeal. They applauded his ability to write quick-paced action novels filled with accurate descriptions of the Old West—or whatever other locale his protagonists found themselves in. "Probably the biggest reason for L'Amour's success," wrote Ben Yagoda in *Esquire*, was "his attention to authenticity and detail. ... His books are full of geographical and historical information." Other critics, too, have praised L'Amour's storytelling abilities, memorable characters, ambitious family structures, and evocative, humorous narrative technique. Although L'Amour never achieved a solid critical standing, his legacy is a valuable, entertaining chronicle of an American past, a vital preservation of the "broken-down cowboys" from whom L'Amour gained his inspiration.

Responses to Literature

1. Contrast the themes and styles of L'Amour's Westerns with the content of another popular writer of the genre, such as Larry McMurtry's *Lonesome Dove* or Zane Grey's *Riders of the Purple Sage*. How does L'Amour compare in terms of action, theme, and character development?

2. Read the life stories of some historical outlaws, Native Americans, cowboys, and other notable figures of the Old West. How do they compare to L'Amour's characters? What romantic liberties did L'Amour take with the historical setting of the American West and its people?

3. What, in your opinion, was L'Amour's key to success in such novels as *Hondo*? What was the situation in post–World War II that made L'Amour's tales of the Old West so accessible and popular?

4. Describe the code that L'Amour's heroes live by. How does this compare to the heroic codes of other authors such as Ernest Hemingway or Ken Follett?

BIBLIOGRAPHY

Books

Bold, Christine. *Selling the Wild West: Popular Western Fiction, 1860 to 1960.* Bloomington: Indiana University Press, 1987.

Gale, Robert L. *Louis L'Amour.* Rev. ed. New York: Twayne, 1992.

Hall, Halbert W., with Boden Clarke. *The Work of Louis L'Amour: An Annotated Bibliography & Guide.* San Bernardino, Calif.: Borgo Press, 1995.

Periodicals

Gale, Robert L. "Sack Time: Problems of Chronology in Louis L'Amour's Sackett Novels." *Southwestern American Literature* 10 (Spring 1985): 25–34.

Hinds, Harold E., Jr. "Mexican and Mexican-American Images in the Western Novels of Louis L'Amour." *Latin American Literary Review* 5 (Spring–Summer 1977): 129–141.

Marsden, Michael T. "The Concept of Family in the Fiction of Louis L'Amour." *North Dakota Quarterly* 46 (Summer 1978): 12–21.

———. "The Popular Western Novel as a Cultural Artifact." *Arizona and the West* 20 (Autumn 1978): 203–214.

———. "Remarks Upon an Honorary Doctor of Literature Awarded Posthumously to Louis L'Amour by Bowling Green State University on November 4, 1988." *Journal of Popular Culture* 23 (Winter 1989): 179–190.

Nesbitt, John D. "Change of Purpose in the Novels of Louis L'Amour." *Western American Literature* 13 (Spring 1978): 65–81.

———. "Louis L'Amour—Paper Mache Homer?" *South Dakota Review* 19 (Autumn 1981): 37–48.

Sullivan, Tom. "Westward to Stasis with Louis L'Amour." *Southwest Review* 69 (Winter 1984): 78–87.

❀ Ring Lardner

BORN: *1885, Niles, Michigan*

DIED: *1933, East Hampton, New York*

NATIONALITY: *American*

GENRE: *Fiction*

MAJOR WORKS:

You Know Me Al (1916)

How to Write Short Stories (With Samples) (1924)

Ring Lardner   *Lardner, Ring, photograph. The Library of Congress.*

Overview

Ring Lardner is considered one of the most accomplished humorists and satirists in American literature. Best known for such frequently anthologized short stories as "The Golden Honeymoon," "Champion," "Some Like Them Cold," and "Haircut," he drew upon his background as a small-town Midwesterner and experience as a sportswriter to render his amusing, biting fiction in the idiom of the semi-educated, middle-class American.

Works in Biographical and Historical Context

A Privileged Victorian Upbringing Ring W. Lardner, like so many of the pioneers of modern American literature, grew up in a comfortable family that was a model of late Victorian, middle-class values. Son of a successful businessman and the cultured daughter of an Episcopal minister, Lardner was born in 1885 in the small town of Niles, Michigan. In *Ring: A Biography of Ring Lardner* (1977), Jonathan Yardley gives a vivid picture of the world in which Lardner spent his childhood—a world of teas, musicales, and literary societies; of energetic local theatrical companies; and of riverside picnics. For the affluent Lardners, it also was a world of private tutors and Irish nursemaids.

This idyllic childhood was hard to leave behind, and in the first years after his graduation from high school at sixteen, Lardner drifted between the worlds of childhood and adulthood. He worked a series of odd jobs, flunked out of the Armour Institute in Chicago, and took several extended "rest" periods at the family home. In 1905 he landed a job almost by accident as a reporter for the *South Bend Times*. He took to the work and became a successful and hardworking journalist for most of the rest of his life. One of his principal assignments was sports writing, at which he quickly established himself as an original, often approaching his stories from the perspective of the participants rather than just summarizing events.

A Career as a Sportswriter

In 1907 Lardner took a position on the *Chicago Inter-Ocean* newspaper, and for the next twelve years he worked as a reporter and columnist for such papers as the *Chicago Examiner* and the *Chicago Tribune* and, briefly, for the *Boston American*. During these years he covered many sports, especially baseball, and he traveled with the White Sox and the Cubs. Not quite respectable in the early years of the century, baseball was rough and sometimes violent. Many of the players were illiterate or semiliterate farm-boys, and other figures who hovered around the game were often unsavory.

Lardner was taken with this strange new world, so different from that of his childhood, and he observed it with an amused detachment. He tuned his ear to the awkward but colorful language of the players; he soaked up their tall tales and boasts; he noted with fascination the effects of the big-city spotlight on these boys from the provinces. From 1913 to 1919 he wrote a column called "In the Wake of the News" that appeared on the sports pages of the *Chicago Tribune* and that allowed him free rein to exploit his years of observations. In 1914 he published ten stories in the *Saturday Evening Post*, six of them about a baseball rookie named Jack Keefe. In 1916 these six stories were published in book form as *You Know Me Al*. Ring Lardner's literary career had begun.

Jack Keefe

While domestic affairs run through the book, *You Know Me Al* primarily concerns the day-to-day life of a baseball team, and the book ends with Keefe about to depart on a world tour with the White Sox and the New York Giants. Lardner wrote twenty-six stories about Jack, a busher, or minor-league player. In addition to the six stories appearing in *You Know Me Al*, ten others were each collected in *Treat 'Em Rough* (1918) and *The Real Dope* (1919). Because the quality of the stories in the latter two volumes is uneven, it would seem that these works were motivated by his audience's rather than Lardner's own continuing enthusiasm for the character.

Lardner drew his portrait of Keefe and the other players from his extensive firsthand knowledge of the actual players of the era. In fact, many of them, such as Ty Cobb and Walter Johnson, as well as White Sox owner Charles A. Comiskey, are portrayed as characters in the book. As Otto Friedrich argues in his study *Ring Lardner*, a major result of the busher stories was to undermine forever the all-American image of the professional athlete that had dominated sports fiction. The typical baseball player as Lardner presented him is often petty, can pull cruel practical jokes, and is undisciplined and self-centered. Keefe himself is talented but must always blame his teammates for his failures. In addition, he is too pigheaded to take the usually sound advice of his coaches, and he can be fanatically stingy and supremely egotistical.

How to Write Short Stories

In Gullible, another character that he created during this period, Lardner struck a new rich vein of humor. Gullible is a twentieth-century American Gulliver whose travels are mostly attempts to climb the social ladder. This new character gave Lardner a free hand to explore comically the issue of social class in a supposedly classless society. Keefe and another, less successful character, Fred Gross, are near the bottom of society, but Gullible and his wife are lower middle class, and thus are aware of social strata both below and above.

Lardner's best work during these early years is marked by fairly gentle satire—the shared realization of author and reader that all human beings can be petty fools at times but that no great harm will come of it. Lardner continued to write such stories throughout his career, but as the 1920s began, the vision grew darker and the satire more damning in many of his best works. Some of those stories were collected in *How to Write Short Stories (With Samples)*, published in 1924.

F. Scott Fitzgerald, a noted short-story writer as well as one of the leading novelists of his time, had urged Lardner to publish a collection of his best stories and even suggested the title and the gag preface. He also persuaded his own publisher, the prestigious Charles Scribner's Sons, to publish it. Walton R. Patrick calls the book "the turning point" of Lardner's career because it marked the first time that he received thoughtful scrutiny as an important literary artist. Of the ten stories, six dealt with sport, and nine were written in the familiar first-person narrative voice; but the collection displayed enough range to suggest both where Lardner had been and where he was going as a writer.

How to Write Short Stories (With Samples) was a prelude to what Patrick calls the "peak years" between 1924 and 1929, during which Lardner wrote less than he sometimes had in the past but produced consistently better stories. Many of those stories were collected in *The Love Nest, and Other Stories by Ring W. Lardner* (1926), and the volume clearly indicates a second phase in Lardner's career. Only one of the nine stories concerns athletics; most use third person narration; and the stories are less broadly humorous and more darkly satiric than the earlier works. Lardner, now financially secure and socially prominent, aimed his barbs at a higher social class. Most of his stories from the mid-1920s focus on urbanites of the middle to upper-middle classes.

By the mid-1920s, Lardner had abandoned sports as his principal subject, but his stories of unhappy marriages, such as "The Love Nest," portray the relations between husbands and wives as bitter contests fought with as much ferocity and as little mercy as any competition on the ball field or in the boxing ring. In 1929 Lardner published his last important collection, *Round-Up*. The book rounds up not only Lardner's best writing but also stories that reflect the range of his career. All of his character types are there, from simple baseball players to slick wheeler-dealers, from small-town bumpkins to sophisticated and would-be sophisticated urbanites. In addition, the collection emphasizes the variety of his first- and third-person narrative voices. Finally, the book generously samples the range of Lardner's wit, from stories of rib-poking fun to the dark, acerbic satire of many of the later works.

Throughout much of his career Lardner had struggled unsuccessfully with alcoholism, depression, and insomnia, and during the mid-1920s he had discovered that he suffered from tuberculosis as well. He was frequently hospitalized for these maladies in the early 1930s, although he still managed to write a large number of stories and articles. The most intriguing of these was a series of magazine essays on the state of public radio programming that, to the puzzlement of his readers and critics, was heatedly attacked on what he considered the pornographic lyrics of certain popular songs as well as the prurient humor of radio comedians. Lardner published what Ernest Hemingway—an admirer of Lardner's earlier work—called "those pitiful dying radio censorship pieces" monthly in *The New Yorker* from June 1932 until August 1933. A month after the final installment appeared, Lardner died of a heart attack.

Works in Literary Context

Lardner's writings reflect both the humorous nostalgia as well as the deep bitterness of his personal life. He wrote in the tradition of a long line of American popular journalists and humorists who exploited slang and vernacular speech for comic ends. In doing so, he transmuted what was initially a stock comic device into something much more, an instrument of satire. At the same time, he was, however unwittingly, one of those writers, of whom Mark Twain is the great exemplar, whose sensitivity to the value of the spoken word helped to liberate American prose from the artificial diction that marked so much nineteenth-century writing.

Dialect Narrative Despite his flaws, Lardner's hero Jack Keefe is not a totally unlikable character, thanks to Lardner's choice of a narrative voice—that of Jack Keefe himself, as he relays his exploits in a series of letters to his friend Al Blanchard back in their hometown of Bedford, Indiana. Otto Friedrich considers the busher stories "perhaps the most effective dialect narrative since [Mark Twain's] *Huckleberry Finn*," and readers hear in the opening words of the first story, "A Busher's Letters Home," the voice of another American innocent: "Well, Al old pal I suppose you seen in the paper where I been sold to the White Sox." This sentence establishes the colloquial

voice that includes the decidedly nontraditional grammar, usage, and spelling for which Lardner is probably most famous. Maxwell Geismar claims in *Ring Lardner and the Portrait of Folly* (1972) that "Lardner's new language ... made most of the previous attempts at an American style sound rather like the diction of an Oxford don."

Lardner helped to liberate the language of fiction, doing for his generation what Twain had done for his own fifty years earlier. No writer of his time had a better ear for what H. L. Mencken called "common American." Lardner's linguistic inventiveness paved the way for a generation of otherwise unrelated writers, from Ernest Hemingway to Dashiell Hammett, who felt free to abandon the constraints of formal literary English in order to explore the variety of American speech in their writing.

American Satire Lardner's satiric stories illustrate two things. The first is that Lardner, as Edmund Wilson pointed out in his *Dial* review, had "an unexcelled, a perhaps unrivalled, mastery" of the American language, that he knew equally well the language of the popular-song writer and the "whole vocabulary of adolescent clichés of the middle-aged man from New Jersey," and that he understood the difference between the spoken language of these types and the language they used for writing.

Lardner was essentially a satirist, and increasingly since his death he has been seen as one of the major American practitioners in that genre. As in Mark Twain's *Huckleberry Finn* (1884), the basis for both humor and social criticism is grounded in the dramatic irony that results from the narrator's insufficient understanding of his world and his relation to it. Like Huck, Jack's sense of self is at odds with reality; but whereas Huck has a sense of himself that underestimates his worth, Jack consistently overestimates his abilities both on and off the playing field. Yet Lardner also makes Jack—the ballplayer always on the road—an archetype of rootless modern humanity, longing for stability and connectedness but never quite striving hard enough to achieve them.

As Lardner's writing career progressed, his satire became darker. "Haircut," published in *The Love Nest*, is a first-person narration by a small-town barber who tells a stranger about a local prankster named Jim Kendall while he cuts the stranger's hair. The barber tells his story to praise the local cut-up, but his account quickly reveals the malice that lies behind Kendall's pranks. The barber's story ends with a description of Jim Kendall's being shot and killed by the town "half-wit." The barber assumes that the shooting was accidental, but readers clearly see that it was a case of murder as revenge for the prankster's cruelty. The story is a splendid example of Lardner's finely tuned ear for common speech. It also is a revelation of the dark currents beneath the placid surface of small-town life in the manner of Lardner's contemporaries, Sherwood Anderson and

Sinclair Lewis. Finally, it is a shrewd examination of how malice often is masked in humor, a mask which is, after all, the basis of Lardner's own satiric art.

Works in Critical Context

Many of Lardner's contemporaries expected more of him and felt that he never made full use of his talent. In *The Shores of Light* (1952) Edmund Wilson complained of Lardner's apparent lack of "artistic seriousness." For instance, Wilson lamented that, in *How to Write Short Stories*, Lardner compiled "a book of the best things he has written and then, with his title and comic preface, tries to pretend that he has never attempted to write anything good at all." Fitzgerald, who had suggested that title and preface and who was Lardner's friend and neighbor on Long Island during the 1920s, also thought that Lardner never matured as a writer and blamed it on his years as a baseball reporter. As Fitzgerald declared in "Ring," an essay collected in *The Crack-Up* (1945):

> During those years when most men of promise achieved an adult education, if only in the school of war, Ring moved in the company of a few dozen illiterates playing a boy's game. . . . [Thus, Lardner] fell short of the achievement he was capable of. . . . Ring got less of himself on paper than any other American author of the first flight.

On the other hand, Virginia Woolf felt, as she revealed in *The Moment and Other Essays*, that Lardner, thanks to his mastery of dialect, wrote "the best prose that has come our way. Hence we feel at last freely admitted to the society of our fellows [through their language]."

A generation later, John Berryman offered his opinion in *Commentary* that Lardner was a "squandered talent" because he never recognized his "special gift for . . . nonsense" that could have placed him in the company of "the great fantasists [Edward] Lear and [Lewis] Carroll." Still others, following the lead of Clifton Fadiman's influential *Nation* essay "Ring Lardner and the Triangle of Hate," have argued that Lardner was a misanthrope whose loathing of people, especially himself, blocked his potential to be a fruitful creative artist.

Although most of Lardner's many short stories are unknown by today's readers, and though his work has never attracted a particularly large body of criticism, his most famous stories have been widely praised and his technique widely imitated. Elizabeth Evans has summarized the current critical view of Lardner, calling him "a spokesman of the twenties" who "showed how many people lived, bearing and displaying their foibles, pettiness, misguided ambition, misplaced values. He was a superb humorist, an effective satirist, and a gifted short story writer."

Responses to Literature

1. Write a short story or dialog featuring the vernacular—or common speech—of your hometown or region.

What sayings or phrases are distinct to the area you grew up in? How would you express the vernacular in the written form?

2. What is the significance of Lardner's choice to address his Jack Keefe stories to an imaginary reader? How would the stories have been different if they had been told in standard third person narration?

3. Satire generally pokes fun at a certain group of people or a treasured ideal. Do you think it is necessary to have a low opinion of people in order to be a satirist? Can satire accomplish a positive end, or is it wholly negative?

4. F. Scott Fitzgerald felt that Lardner's career as a sportswriter held him back from developing his true artistic voice, yet without his exposure to the world of pro baseball Lardner would never have had the material to compose his early short stories. Do you agree with Fitzgerald's assessment? Why or why not?

BIBLIOGRAPHY

Books

Bruccoli, Matthew J. and Richard Layman. *Ring Lardner: A Descriptive Bibliography.* Pittsburgh, Pa.: University of Pittsburgh Press, 1976.

DeMuth, James. *Small Town Chicago: The Comic Perspective of Finley Peter Dunne, George Ade, and Ring Lardner.* Port Washington, N.Y.: Kennikat Press, 1980.

Elder, Donald. *Ring Lardner: A Biography.* Garden City, N.J.: Doubleday, 1956.

Evans, Elizabeth. *Ring Lardner.* New York: Ungar, 1979.

Friedrich, Otto. *Ring Lardner.* Minneapolis, Minn.: University of Minnesota Press, 1965.

Geismar, Maxwell. *Ring Lardner and the Portrait of Folly.* New York: Crowell, 1972.

Robinson, Douglas and Ellen Gardiner. *Ring Lardner and the Other.* Oxford: Oxford University Press, 1992.

Yardley, Jonathan. *Ring: A Biography of Ring Lardner.* New York: Random House, 1977.

Periodicals

Fadiman, Clifton. "Ring Lardner and the Triangle of Hate." *Nation* 136 (March 22, 1933): 315–317.

✳ Nella Larsen

BORN: *1891, Chicago, Illinois*

DIED: *1964, New York City*

NATIONALITY: *American*

GENRE: *Fiction*

MAJOR WORKS:

Quicksand (1928)

Passing (1929)

Overview

Nella Larsen is closely associated with the Harlem Renaissance, an era of unprecedented achievement in African American art and literature during the 1920s and early 1930s. Although she is less well known than other black writers of this period, she has been highly praised for her two novels *Quicksand* (1928) and *Passing* (1929). In these works Larsen depicted urban middle-class mixed-race women, and critics praised her for creating complex female characters constrained by society.

Works in Biographical and Historical Context

A Mixed Background Although Larsen disclosed very few details about her childhood, scholars have determined that she was the child of a Caribbean man and a Danish woman and was born in Chicago. Larsen wrote in a short autobiography for her publisher that her father died when she was two years old and that "shortly afterward her mother married a man of her own race and nationality." Larsen grew up among white family members and apparently felt alienated in this environment. She attended Fisk University in Tennessee for a short time, audited classes at the University of Copenhagen in Denmark, and studied nursing in New York City. While she practiced nursing and worked as a librarian in New York, she and her husband, physicist Dr. Elmer S. Imes, befriended writers and artists in Harlem. Thadious Davis—Larsen's foremost biographer—wrote that Harlem's activity seemed like a "whirlwind" to her. Larsen described in a 1925 letter to Carl Van Vechten: "It has seemed always to be tea time, as the immortal Alice remarked, with never time to wash the dishes between while." According to Davis, however, Larsen's affiliation with the creativity of Harlem was "controlled by her conscious desire to achieve recognition and [was] perhaps controlled too by her unconscious hope to belong." He adds: "While for some the stirrings in Harlem may have been racial and aesthetic, for Larsen they were primarily practical. Her objective was to use art to protract her identity onto a larger social landscape as emphatically as possible."

Larsen loved books as much as she did glamour and excitement. Although she was not college educated, she impressed her associates with her knowledge of books. Walter White was so impressed that he recommended her for a position with the Book League of America, while Charles S. Johnson, editor of *Opportunity* magazine, would write that hers was "a most extraordinarily wide acquaintance with past and current literature." An avid reader and collector, Larsen displayed the effects of her reading in her fiction.

She identified Van Vechten and John Galsworthy as her favorite authors; Van Vechten's attention to the details of an "amusing" contemporary scene, and Galsworthy's to social settings, make their way into both of her novels. James Joyce's *Ulysses* (1922), which she requested in 1927

LITERARY AND HISTORICAL CONTEMPORARIES

Nella Larsen's famous contemporaries include:

Eugene O'Neill (1886–1953): One of the first and leading American realist playwrights, O'Neill's plays were generally tragic in tone, often featuring downtrodden characters from the fringes and underbelly of society.

Herbert Hoover (1874–1964): Elected the thirty-first president of the United States during a time of record prosperity, Hoover quickly saw his country slide into the Great Depression. His attempts to solve the worsening economic problems failed, and in 1932 he was defeated in a landslide by Franklin D. Roosevelt.

Clara Bow (1905–1965): The first major Hollywood sex symbol, Bow was nicknamed "the 'It' Girl" during the height of her popularity in the 1920s. Like many silent-era actors, she failed to make the transition to talking motion pictures and died in relative obscurity.

Simone de Beauvoir (1908–1986): French philosopher and author, Beauvoir, among her many important works, published what is largely considered the first work of modern feminism, *The Second Sex*, in 1949.

Louis Armstrong (1901–1971): With his unique baritone voice and masterful trumpet playing, Armstrong did more to popularize jazz music in mainstream America during the 1920s than perhaps any other musician.

from a friend traveling in Europe, inspired her experiments with interior monologues in *Passing*. Carlo Goldoni, an eighteenth-century playwright who reformed the Italian theater and wrote for the French, gave impetus to her treatment of social conventions and injustices. Larsen also admired the works of such modern writers as Marmaduke Pickthall, Taylor Gordon, and Rudolph Fisher.

Career as a Writer Larsen's apprenticeship as a writer was relatively short and included experimentation with the short story. Two of her tales were published in 1926 under a pseudonym, or pen name. Although her short stories do not feature black characters, they present versions of the affluent characters and themes of discontent and concealment that were developed in her novels. Importantly, too, the stories reflect Larsen's penchant for the surprise ending that characterized, and possibly weakened, her longer fiction. In 1926 Larsen began writing her first novel and from that time on considered herself a novelist.

Larsen's novels provide an insight into her own life and the times in which she lived. In 1928 Larsen published her first and best-known novel, *Quicksand*. This semiautobiographical work involves a woman, Helga

Crane, who searches in vain for sexual and racial identity. At the beginning of the novel, Helga, the daughter of a Caribbean man and a Danish woman, is about to leave her teaching position at a Southern black college. She feels stifled by the environment there, so she journeys to Chicago, New York City, and then to Copenhagen, where she is regarded as an exotic novelty and entertained in elite social circles. Helga returns to New York City—specifically Harlem—to reaffirm ties with blacks. There she undergoes a religious experience and marries the minister responsible for her awakening, the "jackleg preacher" Reverend Pleasant Green. Helga and the minister move to his home in the Deep South. While the marriage initially fulfills Helga's longing for an uncomplicated existence and for sexual gratification, she realizes her unhappiness as she is bearing her fourth child. *Quicksand* ends with Helga mired in rural poverty and pregnant with her fifth child.

Larsen followed *Quicksand* with *Passing*, the story of a light-skinned mulatto, or mixed-race, woman, Clare Kendry, who "passes" for white. Clare is attracted to Harlem for its excitement and she daringly risks revealing her racial heritage to her bigoted white husband and to the society in which she lives. In Harlem Clare renews ties with a childhood friend, Irene Redfield, who also passes for white. Like Larsen's first novel, many of the details and situations found in *Passing* bear a similarity to Larsen's own experiences as a mixed-race woman raised in a white environment. Passing was a controversial subject in the African American community, and Larsen herself would be suspected by her former friends of doing the very thing when she disappeared from the Harlem literary scene.

Plagiarism and Disappearance At the height of her popularity in 1930, Larsen prepared for a year in Spain, working on her Guggenheim project and enjoying her first trip to Europe. Before her departure, however, she was accused of plagiarism when a reader of *Forum* magazine noticed that "Sanctuary," the only short story she published under her own name, closely resembled "Mrs. Adis," a story by Sheila Kaye-Smith from a 1922 issue of *Century* magazine. Although Larsen wrote an open letter in *Forum* clearing herself of any wrongdoing and had the support of the editors who had seen the story in draft versions, she suffered a loss of her confidence as a creative writer. Thereafter, she not only wrote more painstakingly but also depended upon outside readings of her works in progress. The incident combined with the deterioration of her marriage to make her fellowship year less than productive, though she tried to complete a novel begun before the publication of *Passing*, and she started two new novels during her stay in Spain and France.

Continued success as a published novelist eluded Larsen. Following her return from Europe, she experienced further marital problems, which she attempted to resolve by moving to Nashville, where her husband was teaching at

Fisk University. She remained committed to her writing during 1932 and 1933 when she began a fourth novel as well as a fifth in collaboration with Edward Donahoe, a young white writer. None of these projects was published. After her divorce in 1933, Larsen moved to the lower east side of New York, where she associated with writers, artists, and literary people who knew her as a novelist. Greenwich Village rather than Harlem became the center of her social life until the late 1930s when she began to withdraw from her friends and acquaintances there. For undisclosed reasons, she chose to change her life and to disappear by moving from one apartment building on Second Avenue to another that was just across the street in a smaller building.

Larsen returned to nursing after her former husband's death in 1941, when she lost the alimony that had freed her from holding a job during the 1930s. She spent the last twenty years of her life working as a night nurse and supervising nurse at hospitals on the lower east side of Manhattan and living quietly in the same Second Avenue studio apartment. There are no extant records suggesting that she continued to write. When Larsen was found dead at the age of seventy-two, she was no longer remembered as a major New Negro writer. Ironically her death in 1964 occurred just as a second rebirth in black letters was under way.

Works in Literary Context

The fragmentation and duality in Nella Larsen's fiction suggest that it may be more bound by her marginality and her milieu than her "modern" explorations of race, the color line, class, and gender might indicate. Her narratives stop abruptly, present no viable solutions, and remain dominated by dissatisfaction; they reflect an accurate and honest perception of the subject matter, but, despite an adept framing of character and incident, Larsen's narratives do not finally penetrate the meaning of that subject. Yet in the very act of displaying tensions that cannot be resolved or concluded, she reveals an extraordinary grasp of the formal, structural, thematic, and symbolic elements of fiction.

Symbolism of the Journey   Throughout *Quicksand*, Nella Larsen is most effective in her use of symbolism to enhance characterization and to underscore theme. Images of entrapment, suffocation, and asphyxiation become more prominent and integral toward the end of the novel, where they skillfully evoke the heroine's mental and physical condition, but from the outset of the novel, they complement the journey, Larsen's major structural device. The literal journey functions symbolically as well, because *Quicksand* is essentially a bildungsroman, or coming-of-age novel, interrelating psychological and social forces in Helga Crane's search for definition and development. Each phase of the spatial journey—Naxos, Chicago, Harlem, Denmark, and Alabama—marks a symbolic stage in her developing con-

sciousness. The narrative structure depends upon the variety of scene changes, yet simultaneously it brings into convergence action and meaning to emphasize Helga's spiritual quest for growth and identity.

Women and Racism   Larsen's fiction is concerned with the lives of middle-class women who, though cast in traditional roles, assume responsibility for their own lives. Her heroines are blacks who resemble whites in their skin coloring, as well as in their mannerisms and lifestyles. They are modern, urban characters who are far removed from the world of Southern blacks and agrarian settings; however, one of Larsen's persistent themes is the relationship of these black characters to their heritage and the legacy of the past. Hers is a sophisticated group enjoying the best that New York has to offer; they attend shows and parties, dress in clothes purchased from smart Fifth Avenue shops, and dine at the best restaurants, but they are not free of the restrictions of racism, a point Larsen is careful to make. Her characters are not free of self-doubt, either, as they search for meaning in their lives; they are vaguely dissatisfied with who and what they are, but they seem basically unable to find a course of action that would allow them to develop fully their potential.

Nella Larsen's work is today generally considered not only a viable reflection of a black world now past but also a precise outlining of a particular female perspective that has endured. Feminist critics especially have praised her portraits of black women and have seen a prototype of the woman artist in her promising but shortened career. Her intricate explorations of the consciousness and the psychology of female character form a legacy of the voice of a woman writer struggling to be heard, to convey her special messages, and thereby to free herself from the restrictions imposed upon the female by society.

Works in Critical Context

Although critics have expressed regret that Larsen's literary career was so brief, they have acknowledged her significance as a portrayer of certain segments of African American society often neglected by other writers, including urban blacks, mulattos, and middle-class society. Of Larsen's importance in the development of black writing, Hazel V. Carby concluded that "she stands as a precursor not only to Richard Wright and Ralph Ellison but to a neglected strand of Afro-American women's fiction." Writes Thadious M. Davis:

> [Larsen's] intricate explorations of the consciousness and the psychology of female character form a legacy of the voice of a woman writer struggling to be heard, to convey her special messages, and thereby to free herself from the restrictions imposed upon the female by society.

Passing   Critics were divided in their reaction to *Passing*, but most found it inferior to *Quicksand*. Several

COMMON HUMAN EXPERIENCE

Nella Larsen was one of several authors active during the Harlem Renaissance, a period of unprecedented artistic expression and freedom in the African American community. Here are some other works by important figures of the Harlem Renaissance:

Not Without Laughter (1930), a novel by Langston Hughes. Although perhaps better known for his poetry on the African American experience, Hughes was also an accomplished playwright and novelist, as evinced here in this character study of African Americans attempting to fulfill their destinies.

Their Eyes Were Watching God (1936), a novel by Zora Neale Hurston. Unlike Larsen and many other Harlem Renaissance writers, Hurston was primarily interested in the rural Southern black culture, as in this novel, which follows the life of an African American woman living in rural Florida.

The Blacker the Berry (1929), a novel by Wallace Thurman. While other black writers of the day were focusing on the experience of racism directed at the African American community from white America, Thurman used this novel to examine the phenomenon of discrimination within the black community based on relative lightness of skin color.

commentators praised the novel for its depiction of the passing phenomenon; the novel is written from an individual psychological perspective instead of in the more usual broad sociological terms. Robert Bone considered *Passing* "the best treatment of the subject in Negro fiction."

Among recent critics *Passing* has received new evaluations that separate it from both the fiction of the tragic mulatto and the literature of passing. Addison Gayle holds the singular view that it is "superior" to *Quicksand* "in terms of character development, organization, and fidelity to language," and that the three-part structure—"Encounter," "Re-encounter," and "Finale"—makes for a more well-knit novel. Gayle, however, believes that Larsen "loses both focus and emotional intensity in her attempt to balance Irene Redfield and Clare Kendry against one another." His assessment of the novel's weakness is similar to the objections voiced by Amritjit Singh and earlier critics who observed the fractured focus of the work. Neither critic Sister Mary Ellen Doyle nor Mabel Youman argues with the opinion that *Passing* is flawed, but both point out that its merits may have been obscured by a mistaken critical emphasis on Clare Kendry and the theme of passing, and they insist that the protagonist is actually Irene Redfield, who must be seen as central for an accurate reading of the novel. Their readings have had an impact on other critics;

for example, Claudia Tate builds upon Youman and Doyle in attempting to rescue *Passing* from charges of being anachronistic and melodramatic.

Responses to Literature

1. Research the history of the Harlem Renaissance. What influence did this period have on Larsen's writing?

2. Some critics have argued that the protagonist of *Passing* is actually Irene Redfield. Make an argument for or against this interpretation, using specific examples from the novel to support your position.

3. Using the library or the Internet, research the phenomenon of blacks or those of mixed race "passing" as white in American society. What were the issues surrounding the topic in Larsen's time? What consequences might be faced by someone trying to pass if they were discovered? What were Larsen's views on the subject?

4. Discuss the process that leads to the entrapment of Helga, the heroine of *Quicksand*.

BIBLIOGRAPHY

Books

Bone, Robert. *The Negro Novel in America*. Rev. ed. New Haven, Conn.: Yale University Press, 1965.

Brown, Sterling. *The Negro in American Fiction*. New York: Atheneum, 1965.

Davis, Arthur P. *From the Dark Tower: Afro-American Writers, 1900–1960*. Washington, D.C.: Howard University Press, 1974.

Davis, Thadious M. *Nella Larson, Novelist of the Harlem Renaissance: A Woman's Life Unveiled*, Baton Rouge: Louisiana State University Press, 1994.

Fulinwider, S. P. *The Mind and Mood of Black America: 20th Century Thought*. Homewood, Ill.: Dorsey Press, 1969.

Gayle, Addison, Jr. *The Way of the New World: The Black Novel in America*. Garden City, N.J.: Anchor/Doubleday, 1975.

Huggins, Nathan. *Harlem Renaissance*. New York: Oxford University Press, 1971.

Kent, George. *Blackness and the Adventure of Western Culture*. Chicago: Third World Press, 1972.

Larson, Charles R. *Invisible Darkness: Jean Toomer and Nella Larsen*. Iowa City: University of Iowa Press, 1993.

Lewis, David Levering. *When Harlem Was in Vogue*. New York: Knopf, 1981.

McLendon, Jacquelyn Y. *The Politics of Color in the Fiction of Jessie Fauset and Nella Larsen*. Charlottesville: University Press of Virginia, 1995.

Perry, Margaret. *Silence to the Drums: A Survey of the Literature of the Harlem Renaissance*. Westport, Conn.: Greenwood Press, 1976.

❁ Jerome Lawrence

BORN: *1915, Cleveland, Ohio*

DIED: *2004, Malibu, California*

NATIONALITY: *American*

GENRE: *Drama*

MAJOR WORKS:

Inherit the Wind (1955)

Auntie Mame (1956)

The Night Thoreau Spent in Jail (1971)

Overview

Along with his writing partner Robert E. Lee, Jerome Lawrence wrote some of the most successful stage plays of all time, including *Inherit the Wind* (1955) and *Auntie Mame* (1956). Despite his great critical and popular success, Lawrence only received one Tony Award nomination for his work.

Works in Biographical and Historical Context

A Productive Partnership Lawrence was born Jerome Schwartz in Cleveland, Ohio. The son of a printer and a teacher, Lawrence was raised in a literary family and earned top honors when he graduated from Ohio State University in 1937. It was during his high school and college years that Lawrence first became involved in theater, acting in and directing school productions.

The works of Jerome Lawrence cannot be fully evaluated without considering his partnership with fellow playwright Robert E. Lee—not to be confused with the famous Civil War general of the same name—a partnership of fifty-two years that produced thirty-nine works for the stage, both in the form of plays as well as musical adaptations.

Lawrence and Lee were both Ohio natives. Born in the same general region of the state, they both attended Ohio universities and worked in the same local industry, commercial radio. Nonetheless, it took a relocation to New York City before the two met in 1942, after which they quickly began their creative partnership, writing a radio play together. Soon after, both men enlisted with the Army; the United States had entered World War II in December of 1941, after the Japanese attack on Pearl Harbor. The two men continued to collaborate, forming the Armed Services Radio Service and producing a series of radio programs for the troops.

From Radio to Stage After World War II ended in 1945, Lawrence returned to civilian life, where he continued writing and producing radio programs in partnership with Lee. With the advent and quickly rising popularity of television in the 1950s, the writing team found their services in increasingly less demand. They decided to shift their efforts towards writing stage plays. With their writing prowess honed over a decade of producing radio scripts for dramas, comedies, musicals, and

LITERARY AND HISTORICAL CONTEMPORARIES

Lawrence's famous contemporaries include:

Elizabeth Taylor (1932–): Notable for her long and distinguished acting career, as well as for her many marriages, Taylor is the prototypical Hollywood celebrity.

Francis Gary Powers (1929–1977): The pilot of a top secret American spy plane, Powers was shot down while flying over the Soviet Union, prompting greater tensions in the Cold War between the two nations.

Harper Lee (1926–): American novelist Lee's considerable reputation rests on her sole novel, *To Kill A Mockingbird* (1960), which remains one of the most widely-read works of American literature.

Andy Warhol (1928–1987): One of the most enigmatic media figures of the latter half of the twentieth century, Warhol revolutionized the art world with his production of so-called "pop" art—art derived from advertisements and other pieces of disposable culture.

variety shows, Lawrence and Lee scored an immediate success with their first dramatic effort for the stage, *Inherit the Wind*.

The play was directly inspired by the so-called "Scopes Monkey Trial," a famous case from the 1920s that put a high school biology teacher on trial for teaching evolution. The trial pitted controversial trial lawyer Clarence Darrow, who defended the teacher, John Scopes, against respected orator and former Presidential candidate William Jennings Bryan. The trial quickly became a national sensation, as it was painted in the press as a showdown between science and religion. The play introduced a theme that Lawrence and Lee would return to many times over the course of their career: using a fictionalized account of a historical incident to comment on current events. In the case of *Inherit the Wind*, Lawrence and Lee were looking back to a time in American history when there was a vigorous debate over intellectual freedom and relating that event to their own time. The America of the 1950s was beset by tensions over suspected Communist infiltration of the government and media. Politicians like Senator Joseph McCarthy, in their zeal to find scapegoats, created a climate of fear and recrimination in which people felt reluctant to speak up or take an unpopular position. The Scopes trial had particular resonance in the wake of a series of hearings that McCarthy called on Capitol Hill to investigate "un-American activities."

Expanding Dramatic Horizons Lawrence and Lee would use their plays to address ongoing cultural concerns again, most notably with *The Night Thoreau Spent in Jail* (1971), which contrasted the civil disobedience of the nineteenth century philosopher Henry David Thoreau,

COMMON HUMAN EXPERIENCE

Lawrence and Lee employed a common theme of using historical events to reflect on current concerns and situations. Other plays have used this approach as well.

Mother Courage and Her Children (1949), a play by Bertolt Brecht. Written by a German playwright in the devastated aftermath of World War II, this antiwar play is set in the seventeenth century, during the Thirty Years' War, which was another multi-national conflict that left Germany in ruins.

The Crucible (1954), a play by Arthur Miller. Set during the Salem Witch Trials of 1692, Miller's play cagily compares the fanatical persecution of innocent Massachusetts colonists in the name of blind ambition with the then-current anti-Communist "witch hunts" of the 1950s.

Saint Joan (1923), a play by George Bernard Shaw. A noted pacifist, Shaw wrote this play about the fifteenth century trial of French national war hero Joan of Arc as a reflection on post–World War I Europe. His suggestion, through the play, that all sides in a war are equally responsible for the destruction and death brought by conflict, proved highly unpopular at the time.

who refused to pay his taxes to support a war he felt unjust, with the then-current Vietnam War, a conflict that many Americas opposed.

Not confining themselves strictly to historical dramas, Lawrence and Lee also penned several highly successful musicals and comedies, including an adaptation of the novel and movie *Lost Horizon* entitled *Shangri-La* (1956) and an adaptation of the 1955 novel *Auntie Mame*, which they also later adapted into a musical entitled *Mame* (1966), with Angela Lansbury in the title role. Both the play and the musical were tremendous hits; the former was adapted into a film starring Rosalind Russell in 1957, the latter, starring Lucille Ball, in 1974.

The American Playwrights Theatre Lawrence and Lee were also instrumental in founding the first true regional theater organization, the American Playwrights Theatre in 1965. The APT was founded in response to the increasingly commercial nature of Broadway productions, in which producers put considerations of potential profitability above artistic merit and controversy. The late 1960s were a time of a burgeoning regional theater movement in America; regional theaters are professional organizations that produce plays according to their own seasons. The success of the APT and its Lawrence-Lee productions—particularly *Thoreau*, which was performed over two thousand times in APT-associated theaters in the two years after its premiere—were instrumental in increasing the popularity and viability of regional theater,

thereby accomplishing the goal Lawrence and Lee had in mind when they founded the APT: bypassing and undermining the power and influence of Broadway.

The writing duo were honored for their work in the dramatic community with a variety of regional and national awards. Lee died in 1994, ending the long-standing and productive partnership with Lawrence. Shortly afterwards, their last publication, *The Selected Plays of Jerome Lawrence and Robert E. Lee* (1994), hit the shelves. That same year, the last Lawrence-Lee play, *Whisper in the Mind* (1994), was produced.

Although most of his efforts were written in collaboration with Lee, Lawrence did produce a biography of the actor Paul Muni by himself. Lawrence died from complications due to stroke in his Malibu home in 2004. Although he had led a long and successful career, he had only been nominated for a single Tony Award, for Best Book of a Musical for *Mame*.

Works in Literary Context

Lawrence told interviewer Nina Couch that "almost if not all of our plays share the theme of the dignity of every individual mind." Again and again, Lawrence and Lee displayed an interest in freedom: of movement, of belief, of individual expression. Both in serious formats, such as *Inherit the Wind*, and in more lighthearted entertainments, such as *Mame*, they held up the independent thinker, often the outsider or outcast who dared to question the status quo, as the hero.

Artistic License A risky proposition for any artist, artistic license is a term that describes the creative process in which facts or accepted dramatic or poetic form are somehow twisted, modified, omitted, or otherwise changed in order to make for a better story. When done well, artistic license (also called dramatic or poetic license) will go either unnoticed, or otherwise be dismissed or ignored by the audience—a phenomenon known as "suspension of disbelief."

However, artistic license can just as easily draw criticism, sometimes extremely harsh and pointed, from those who disagree with the licenses taken by the artist. Lawrence and Lee have come under fire for their artistic license taken with *Inherit the Wind*. The playwrights adapted a historical event, fictionalizing it to fit their dramatic aims. Facts were simplified, characters were mere "sketches" of real-life people, and the actual historical events were subordinated to the dramatic requirements of the play and the intended message. Despite Lawrence and Lee's statements that they never intended for the play to be an accurate depiction of the actual Scopes Monkey Trial, the play continues to draw criticism for the liberties it takes with the historical event.

Works in Critical Context

Successful and well-reviewed, Lawrence's Broadway-produced plays have been the focus of critical attention from the very beginning. Although few fault their plays on pure substance, many critics have called into question the issue of historical accuracy, especially in the case of *Inherit the Wind.*

Despite the success of the APT, critics have been slow to recognize the success of Lawrence-penned regional productions. Although the rise of regional theater has taken much of the attention off of the Broadway stage, critics are still reluctant to give their attention to plays, such as *Thoreau,* that have not premiered or been produced in New York.

Inherit the Wind   From the beginning, Lawrence and Lee stressed that *Inherit the Wind* was not a strict historical adaptation. In their Playwrights' Note, the playwrights state that their play is not history and that the work is meant to stand on its own. While recognizing the historical significance of the Scopes Trial, the authors raise the idea that the issues of the conflict between Clarence Darrow and William Jennings Bryan "have acquired new meaning in the . . . years since they clashed at the Rhea County Courthouse."

Whitney Bolton, in a *Morning Telegraph* review, states: "What is of importance is that from that musty little town . . . came a note of hope; that . . . the accused made it easier . . . for the next accused thinker to take his stand for it." In a review published in the *Christian Science Monitor,* John Beaufort writes that "Drummond's [defense of Brady] is an indictment of all dogma—whether springing from blind ignorance or blind intellectualism."

Responses to Literature

1. In *The Night Thoreau Spent in Jail*, Lawrence and Lee use an extremely expressionistic approach, keeping the time period and stage directions vague, for example. Choose a visual medium, and find an example of an expressionistic work in that medium. Discuss the history behind the work, including how it was received at the time and its current legacy, as well as how you feel the work ties in to at least one of the main themes of the play.

2. Lawrence and Lee saw a similarity between the transcendentalist philosophy of Henry David Thoreau and the counterculture hippie movement of the 1960s and 70s. Research the transcendentalists and the 1960s counterculture. How were they similar? How did the counterculture feel about the transcendentalists? How do you think Thoreau and his like-minded fellows might have viewed the hippie movement?

3. Read further about the lives and careers of the historical personages upon whom the characters in *Inherit the Wind* were based—Clarence Darrow, William Jennings Bryan, and H. L. Mencken. Compare and contrast the historical personalities and their dramatic adaptations.

4. Compare the dramatic and musical adaptations of *Auntie Mame* and *Mame.* What changes were made? How do the two stories differ, and how are they

similar? Outside of the need to insert songs, why were certain changes required to take the play from a stage play to a musical?

BIBLIOGRAPHY

Books

"Inherit the Wind." *Drama for Students.* Edited by David Galens and Lynn Spampinato. Vol. 2. Detroit: Thomson Gale, 1998.

"The Night Thoreau Spent in Jail." *Drama for Students.* Edited by David Galens. Vol. 16. Detroit: Gale, 2003.

Periodicals

Winchester, Mark. "Jerome Lawrence and Robert E. Lee: A Classified Bibliography." *Studies in American Drama, 1945–Present 7* (1992): 88-160.

✻ Emma Lazarus

BORN: *1849, New York City*

DIED: *1887, New York City*

NATIONALITY: *American*

GENRE: *Poetry*

MAJOR WORKS:

"The New Colossus" (1883)

Emma Lazarus   *The Library of Congress.*

LITERARY AND HISTORICAL CONTEMPORARIES

Lazarus's famous contemporaries include:

Robert Louis Stevenson (1850–1894): Scottish-born novelist and poet Stevenson wrote stories for both adults and children, many of which have entered our cultural lexicon and remain as popular today as when they were first published: *Treasure Island* (1883), *Strange Case of Dr. Jekyll and Mr. Hyde* (1886), and *A Child's Garden of Verses* (1885).

Pierre-Auguste Renoir (1841–1919): One of the definitive artists of the French Impressionist school, Renoir's paintings reflected that tradition's interests in the qualities of light, mundane subject-matter, and movement expressed through painting.

Jules Verne (1828–1905): A French novelist, Verne is arguably the first science-fiction writer, and certainly one of the most popular. Many of his predictions— helicopters, rockets to the moon, automobiles, even the Internet—would come to fruition in the hundred years following his death.

Charles "Chinese" Gordon (1833–1885): A living legend in his own time, General Charles Gordon was one of the British Empire's most famous and respected military leaders. He earned his nickname leading an army of Chinese soldiers, and met his death defending the British colonial holding of Khartoum, Sudan.

Henrik Ibsen (1828–1906): A Norwegian playwright who was a lightning rod of controversy in his own time, Ibsen's plays are still produced today thanks to their emotionally gripping, harshly realistic, and thoroughly modern themes and plots.

Overview

Although she was a noted essayist and tireless defender of Jewish rights, Emma Lazarus is chiefly remembered today for her 1883 poem, "The New Colossus," an expression of America as a haven for the oppressed peoples of the world. This poem, with its memorable call to other countries to "give us your tired, your poor," was engraved on a plaque and mounted on the base of the Statue of Liberty, which had itself become a welcoming beacon for newly-arriving immigrants in 1903.

Works in Biographical and Historical Context

Early Life and Writing Emma Lazarus was born to a prosperous Jewish family in New York City. Her heritage was Sephardic, a branch of Judaism that had made its home in Spain and Portugal for centuries before being expelled by the government in 1492, the same year Christopher Columbus reached America. Eventually, some Sephardic Jews began migrating to the New World, with a sizable community existing in America by the time of the American Revolution in 1776.

Like many Sephardic Jews in America, Lazarus's family was interested in social integration with the larger gentile, or non-Jewish, community around them. The Lazarus family took matters a bit further, in fact, all but turning their backs on their cultural and religious heritage. Lazarus's father, Moses, was a member of influential social clubs and counted many of New York City's most prominent businessmen as friends. Lazarus herself was not sent to school, but rather benefited from the best private tutors her father could afford.

Lazarus's home-schooled education was steeped in literature and the arts. She developed an interest in foreign languages and learned to speak Italian, French, and German. She also began writing poetry at the age of eleven, as well as translating poetry from French and German sources. In 1866, at the age of seventeen, Lazarus's poems were privately published with financial help from her father. *Poems and Translations: Written Between the Ages of Fourteen and Sixteen*, containing forty original poems, was reprinted a year later for general distribution. Through her father, Lazarus was able to send a copy of her book to Ralph Waldo Emerson at his home in Massachusetts. Emerson, sixty years old at the time and considered one of America's greatest living poets, wrote back to Lazarus with praise and constructive criticism, thus beginning a long and fruitful correspondence between the two poets.

Lazarus continued to write poetry under Emerson's influence, and gradually she began to develop a name for herself. Her poetry began to appear in *Lippincott's*, the leading literary magazine of the day, and she published her second poetry collection, *Admetus and Other Poems*, in 1871. The collection was well-received both in America and particularly in England, where Lazarus drew comparison to another living legend of poetry, Robert Browning. Lazarus also tried her hand at novel writing, publishing *Alide* in 1874. The book was based on the life of Johann Wolfgang von Goethe, a German philosopher whose work she had translated.

In 1876, the Lazarus family unit was broken up by the death of Lazarus's mother. Shortly thereafter, Lazarus had a chance to finally meet her mentor, Emerson, at his cottage in Concord. After returning to New York, Lazarus branched out into essay writing, critical interpretations, biographical profiles, and book reviews, steadily earning a name for herself in the city's literary world. She also began to question the importance and validity of her work.

"Give Us Your Tired, Your Poor ..." It was during this period of introspection that Lazarus was asked to translate a series of medieval Jewish hymns from German and Hebrew. Although her family had never been particularly religious, Lazarus began to develop an active interest in Jewish culture and history and in the injustices that were being visited upon Russian Jews in her own time.

In a series of *pogroms*, or state-sponsored raids and massacres, Jewish villages in Russia had been attacked and burned, forcing hundreds of thousands of Jews to seek asylum in foreign lands. Many had headed for America, most arriving in New York City. It was during this wave of Jewish immigration, in 1886, that the Statue of Liberty, a gift from France to the United States on the occasion of its centennial, was erected on New York's Ellis Island. The statue quickly became an iconic symbol of freedom to the millions of immigrants who came to America seeking a better way of life.

Lazarus, meanwhile, had begun devoting herself to advocacy on behalf of the newly-arriving Jewish immigrants. She led programs to teach the new arrivals valuable technical skills so that they would be able to quickly become productive members of society. She wrote in defense of the plight of the Russian Jews, and her poetry began to deal almost exclusively with Jewish themes. Her new poetry, along with a verse-drama about Jews being burned at the stake during the Black Death of 1349, was published in *Songs of the Semite* (1882). She also wrote "An Epistle to the Hebrews," an impassioned argument for American Jews to embrace their culture. The essay was controversial, largely due to its open advocacy for the establishment of a Jewish state in Palestine, which at the time was a province of the Ottoman Empire. Lazarus was one of the first Americans to take up this position and was well ahead of her time—many of her fellow members of the Jewish community criticized her for her position on Palestine.

The poem for which Lazarus is chiefly remembered, "The New Colossus," was written during these heady days. Written in 1883 after a successful literary tour of England, the poem was an ode to the Statue of Liberty, which had not yet been erected. In fact, the poem was written to help raise money for the construction of a pedestal which would support the massive statue.

Death and Immortality Lazarus was only thirty-eight when she died of lymphoma, a form of cancer, four years after writing "The New Colossus." As a result, she did not live to see her words immortalized and become almost synonymous with "Lady Liberty." It was through the efforts of one of Lazarus's friends, Georgiana Schuyler, that the poem was inscribed on a plaque and affixed to the base of the statue in 1903, quickly becoming an iconic piece of American verse and securing Lazarus's place in American cultural mythology.

Works in Literary Context

As both a woman and a Jew, Lazarus had to fight against a multitude of cultural prejudices. Despite this, her work earned widespread praise, and inspired her to turn her artistic efforts towards making a difference in the world.

Social Activism Although she did not regard it as one of her greatest poems, "The New Colossus" was a perfect example of Lazarus's social activism, a trait she shared in

---

COMMON HUMAN EXPERIENCE

Lazarus was one of many authors who turned their gift towards trying to make a difference, laying out an agenda of social change or an ideal for their society to aspire to, around the turn of the century. Here are some works by other authors with the same goal:

The Jungle (1906), a novel by Upton Sinclair. Although fictionalized, this novel is an account of the real-life abuses and corruption in the American meatpacking industry. Sinclair, an activist journalist, inspired massive reforms in the industry with his novel.

How the Other Half Lives (1890), a photo essay by Jacob Riis. Like Sinclair, Riis was an activist journalist. This book, a combination of photos and drawings based on photos, revealed the conditions of grinding poverty that existed in New York City's tenement slums.

Strive and Succeed (1872), a novel by Horatio Alger. With his tales of poor young boys working their way up to success with nothing but determination and a bit of luck, Alger's name became synonymous with "rags-to-riches" stories, and reflected the author's Progressive sympathies.

---

common with many writers and journalists of her day. As the nineteenth century drew to a close, many Americans began to feel bothered about the injustices and abuses they witnessed in their society. The so-called Progressive Movement began as a local, grass-roots effort that eventually spread to state and national government levels. Authors and journalists like Upton Sinclair and Jacob Riis attempted to expose the inhumane conditions many of the country's poor and working-class were forced to live in, and writers like Lazarus campaigned for recognition of those elements that society at large deemed "outsiders."

"The New Colossus" is a call to the other nations of the world to send their "wretched refuse," the elements the Old World countries of Europe deemed undesirable, but who were in fact "huddled masses yearning to breathe free." The title is a reference to the Colossus of Rhodes, one of the Seven Wonders of the World that was raised in the third century BCE. But in Lazarus's poem, the "new" colossus is not a symbol of conquering might, but rather a beacon of hope to the rest of the world. It was this sort of optimism that informed many of the Progressive, social activist writers of Lazarus's day.

The fact that "The New Colossus" was placed upon the Statue of Liberty was no coincidence. As fifteen million immigrants streamed into America between 1900 and 1915, a strong "nativist" movement sprang up among Americans who, despite also being descendants of immigrants, considered themselves true American natives. Laws began to be passed limiting the number of immigrants allowed into the country, both in the east and the west, where Chinese immigration was virtually banned outright. Although the content and spirit of Lazarus's poem was quickly eclipsed by a more exclusionary reality, her words continue to provide an ideal towards which the nation can strive.

Works in Critical Context

Upon the publication of her second collection of poetry, *Admetus*, the *Illustrated London News* said Lazarus was "a poet of rare original power." The year of that collection's publication, 1871, was the high watermark for Lazarus critically. Many critics predicted her imminent emergence as a major force in poetry. She was generally well-regarded by other writers and intellectuals of her day in spite of her relatively sparse creative output. When she turned her attention to writing on matters of anti-Semitism, she quickly came to be regarded as one of the leading experts on the subject. Unfortunately, Emerson's refusal to include any of Lazarus's poems in his 1874 compilation *Parnassus* effectively spelled the end of her critical popularity, and Lazarus has been little regarded ever since, despite the widespread anthologizing of "The New Colossus."

Responses to Literature

1. How does Lazarus's view of American idealism contrast with the poetic visions of Walt Whitman, Hart Crane, or John Dos Passos?

2. Study the history of anti-Semitism in Lazarus's time. What were its underlying causes? How prevalent was anti-Semitism in America at the time? How did American anti-Semitism compare to other parts of the world, such as France, Germany, or Russia?

3. Lazarus held a vision of America as a haven for immigrants. Study the history of immigration at the turn of the twentieth century. How closely did Lazarus's vision match reality? Support your conclusions with historical evidence. In your opinion, how well has Lazarus's vision of immigration held up in our current age?

4. Alone or in a group, make a list of American ideals, then choose one to write about in the form of a poem.

BIBLIOGRAPHY

Books

Vogel, Dan. *Emma Lazarus*. Woodbridge, Conn.: Twayne, 1980.

"Lazarus, Emma." *U*X*L Encyclopedia of World Biography*. Edited by Laura B. Tyle. Vol. 6. Detroit: U*X*L, 2003.

"Emma Lazarus." *Encyclopedia of World Biography*. Vol. 9, second ed. Detroit: Gale, 2004.

"Lazarus, Emma." *Gilded Age and Progressive Era Reference Library*. Edited by Rebecca Valentine. Vol. 3. Detroit: UXL, 2007.

Kessner, Carole. "Lazarus, Emma." *Encyclopaedia Judaica*. Edited by Michael Berenbaum and Fred Skolnik. Vol. 12, second ed. Detroit: Macmillan Reference USA, 2007.

"Emma Lazarus (1849–1887)." *Nineteenth-Century Literature Criticism*. Edited by Edna Hedblad and Russel Whitaker. Vol. 109. Detroit: Gale Group, 2002.

❁ Andrea Lee

BORN: *1953, Philadelphia, Pennsylvania*

NATIONALITY: *American*

GENRE: *Fiction, nonfiction*

MAJOR WORKS:

Russian Journal (1981)

Sarah Phillips (1984)

Interesting Women: Stories (2002)

Lost Hearts in Italy (2006)

Andrea Lee   *Lee, Andrea, photograph. © Jerry Bauer. Reproduced by permission.*

Overview

Lee has distinguished herself as a noteworthy journalist and novelist. In her nonfiction work *Russian Journal* (1981), she provides an insightful perspective on contemporary Soviet life, and in her novels, she recounts the lives of various women, many of them expatriates living in Europe.

Works in Biographical and Historical Context

Writing about Soviet Russia The youngest of a Baptist minister's three children, Lee was born in Philadelphia in 1953. She received an MA in English literature from Harvard University and has worked as a staff writer for the *New Yorker* magazine.

Her first book, *Russian Journal*, derives from a diary she kept in 1978 while in the Soviet Union, where her husband was studying for ten months on a fellowship. During a less intense phase of the cold war, the Soviet Union of the 1970s was a totalitarian communist country that wielded strict control over its citizens' lives, from censored speech to government-controlled services. The United States maintained an antagonistic relationship to the Soviet Union as they both amassed military arms for a potential conflict, but relations relaxed somewhat during the 1970s and 1980s as the economic and social failures of the communist country eventually led to its fall in 1991.

Lee's experience in the Soviet Union provided a rare look into a closed country. In her journal Lee wrote that, due to their circumstances, she and her husband "got a view of life in Moscow and Leningrad that was very different from that of the diplomats and journalists we knew."

Turning to Fiction Abroad As if responding to critics' charges that she avoided discussing race in her first book, Lee followed *Russian Journal* with *Sarah Phillips*, an episodic novel explicitly concerned with a contemporary black woman. With *Russian Journal* and *Sarah Phillips* Lee gained recognition as a talented writer of immense promise, but she did not publish other extended works of fiction for nearly twenty years. In 2002 she published *Interesting Women: Stories*, which follows twelve American women living abroad, and in 2006 she produced *Lost Hearts in Italy*, a story detailing a complicated romance taking place in several Italian cities. Lee lives in Turin, Italy.

Works in Literary Context

Travel Narrative Lee's *Russian Journal* fits into the genre of travel narratives, in which the traveler writes about experiences in an unfamiliar place. Travel writing generally focuses both on the differences in the foreign culture as much as it concentrates on the writer's status as outsider in a new location. As is evidenced in Lee's work, this kind of writing recognizes the tension inherent in the visiting experience as the writer navigates seeing new things while at the same time experiencing the phenomenon of being seen as

different by locals. In her book, Lee describes meeting bureaucrats, dissidents, and even contraband sellers. She encounters many cynics and youthful materialists, observes a disturbing number of public drunks, and becomes acquainted with some of Russia's more unsettling aspects, notably government surveillance.

Coming-of-Age Novel In a coming-of-age story, the protagonist grows and changes over the course of the narrative in relationship to at least one conflict. Often, the central action of the book involves family or personal relationships, or, by contrast, an encounter with evil in the world. Lee's work in *Sarah Phillips* embodies these coming-of-age features. The title character is introduced as a woman who has grown disgusted with her boorish, racist acquaintances in Paris, where she has been living in self-exile. At the end of the first chapter, Sarah decides to leave Paris, and in the ensuing sections she recalls events—principally from childhood and adolescence—that have contributed to her present circumstances. Bored with America, Sarah leaves the country after her father's death and her graduation from college. She settles in Paris, but by

COMMON HUMAN EXPERIENCE

Lee writes extensively about Americans living abroad. Other stories that describe Americans traveling in other countries include:

> *Daisy Miller* (1879), a novel by Henry James. This book follows a young American girl as she travels in Europe and reinforces perceptions of unrefined Americans by her seemingly immodest behavior.
>
> *The Sun Also Rises* (1926), by Ernest Hemingway. This modern classic focuses on the Lost Generation in Europe and shows the personal alienation that resulted from World War I.
>
> *Quicksand* (1928), by Harlem Renaissance writer Nella Larsen. This novel follows a young African American woman's search for a place to fit in, including a stay in Denmark where she is treated as an exotic fascination.
>
> *Lost in Translation* (2003), starring Bill Murray and Scarlett Johansson. Directed by Sofia Coppola, this film explores the strange experiences of two Americans who meet in a Tokyo hotel.
>
> *The Quiet American* (1955), by British author Graham Greene. This novel focuses on the dangerous decisions of a young American during the Vietnam War.

novel's end, Sarah realizes the emptiness of her assimilation into white society—both European and American—and reaches a greater understanding of herself and her heritage.

Works in Critical Context

Lee's writing has earned her praise as a keen observer and a consummate technician, one whose probing insights are inevitably rendered with concision and grace. As Susan Richards Shreve notes in the *New York Times Book Review*, "Andrea Lee's authority as a writer comes of an unstinting honesty and a style at once simple and yet luminous."

Russian Journal Following the publication of *Russian Journal*, critics cited the book as a refreshing, if narrow, perspective on Soviet life. Susan Jacoby called Lee's book "a subtly crafted reflection of both the bleak and golden shadings of Russian life" and added: "The subject matter of this journal is highly idiosyncratic. ... What Miss Lee offers are the people, places and experiences that touched her most deeply." Like Jacoby, Peter Osnos cited the book's achievement at "conveying a feeling of place and atmosphere" and declared, "Lee writes very well. There is a warmth and freshness about her style that makes reading [*Russian Journal*] effortless." Osnos was especially impressed with Lee's depiction of the Soviet people, particularly its younger citizens. "What is best

about the book—what distinguishes it from other books about the Soviet Union published in recent years—is her accounts of friendships with young people," he said. Michael Irwin also found Lee an engaging reporter. He praised her "astuteness" and called *Russian Journal* "a considerable exercise in observation, empathy and personal and literary tact."

Responses to Literature

1. After reading *Russian Journal*, research life in the Soviet Union during the 1970s. In your opinion, how does Lee's writing confirm or challenge the American perspective on Soviet Russia?

2. Lee's female characters often come from wealthy, privileged families and have the freedom to travel at will. Choose one character and discuss how her search for personal fulfillment might be different if money were less available to her.

3. Lee's writing introduces the theme of outsider versus insider. Discuss three instances in her work where characters must manage being either part of a group or excluded from it. What conclusions can you draw about identity and belonging?

BIBLIOGRAPHY

Periodicals

Goskowski, Francis. A Review of *Sarah Phillips. Best Sellers* 44, no. 11. (February 1985): 408.

Irwin, Michael. "Hidden Privilege." *London Review of Books* (September 16–October 6, 1982): 20.

Jacoby, Susan. "One Year in Moscow." *New York Times Book Review* (October 25, 1981): 11, 22.

Osnos, Peter. "Blue Jeans in Red Square: An American in Moscow." *Book World: Washington Post* (October 25, 1981): 10.

Shreve, Susan Richards. "Unsentimental Journey." *New York Times Book Review* (November 18, 1984): 13.

Vigderman, Patricia. A Review of *Sarah Phillips. Boston Review* 10, no. 1 (February 1985): 23–24.

Wyngarden, Bruce Van. "Pieces of the Past." *Saturday Review* 11, no. 1 (February 1985): 74.

⊛ Harper Lee

BORN: *1926, Monroeville, Alabama*

NATIONALITY: *American*

GENRE: *Fiction*

MAJOR WORKS:

To Kill A Mockingbird (1960)

Overview

In her first and only novel to date, *To Kill a Mockingbird* (1960), Harper Lee achieved immediate popular acclaim,

Harper Lee   *Lee, Harper, photograph. AP Images.*

University. She left the University of Alabama in 1950, six months short of a law degree, to pursue a writing career in New York City.

Growing up in the pre-Civil Rights South, Lee saw a segregated and harsh cultural attitude toward African Americans. The Jim Crow laws that governed the South in the 1940s and 50s separated most aspects of society by race, from restaurants and stores to schools and hotels. Black Americans were prohibited from entering any establishment dubbed "Whites Only," and the culture was generally aggressive towards them, exhibiting vigilante methods such as Ku Klux Klan tactics and many lynchings. The Civil Rights movement of the 1960s finally led the federal government to intervene to eliminate institutional segregation.

Success of Only Novel Stands Alone   Harper Lee became interested in writing at the age of seven. While she was a student at the University of Alabama, her satires, editorial columns, and reviews appeared in campus publications.

Living in New York in the early 1950s, and supporting herself by working as an airline reservations clerk, she approached a literary agent with the manuscripts of two essays and three short stories. The agent encouraged her to expand one of the stories into a novel that later became *To Kill a Mockingbird*.

With the financial help of friends, she gave up her job and moved into a cold-water flat where she devoted herself to her writing. Although her father became ill and she was forced to divide her time between New York and Monroeville, she continued to work on her novel. She submitted a manuscript to Lippincott in 1957. While editors criticized the book's structure, suggesting it seemed to be a series of short stories strung together, they recognized the novel's promise and encouraged Lee to rewrite it. With the help of her editor, Tay Hohoff, Lee reworked the material, and *To Kill a Mockingbird* was finally published in July 1960, to great success. The novel has been made into a film and continues to be taught in classrooms as an American classic.

The reading public and the critics have been eagerly awaiting more of Lee's writing. In the early 1960s, several short pieces about personal experiences and an article discussing different types of love, "Love—In Other Words" (1961), appeared in popular magazines; none of her work has been published since. Lee still continues to write, however. Although she travels extensively, Monroeville, where her sister Alice Lee practices law, remains home. Whether or not Lee adds to her body of published work, her contribution to American literature is an important one. *To Kill a Mockingbird*, a regional novel with a universal message, combines popular appeal with literary excellence, assuring Lee's place in American letters.

winning the 1961 Pulitzer Prize for literature. Although occasionally faulted as melodramatic, *To Kill a Mockingbird* is widely regarded as one of the most sensitive and revealing portraits of the American South in contemporary literature.

Works in Biographical and Historical Context

Southern Childhood Influences Novel   Although Lee stresses that *To Kill a Mockingbird* is not autobiographical, she allows that a writer "should write about what he knows and write truthfully." The time period and setting of the novel obviously originate in the author's experience as the youngest of three children born to lawyer Amasa Coleman Lee (related to Robert E. Lee) and Frances Finch Lee. The family lived in the sleepy little town of Monroeville, Alabama. After graduating from Monroeville's public schools, Lee spent a year (1944–1945) at Huntingdon College in Montgomery, Alabama, and then attended the University of Alabama for four years (1945–1949), including a year as an exchange student at Oxford

LITERARY AND HISTORICAL CONTEMPORARIES

Lee's famous contemporaries include:

Martin Luther King, Jr. (1929–1968): The most famous civil rights leader, Dr. King led grassroots groups in the Southern U.S. to nonviolently protest racial segregation. He won the Nobel Peace Prize in 1964 and was assassinated in 1968.

Medgar Evers (1925–1963): A prominent civil rights leader, Evers worked for the NAACP in Mississippi. He actively sought to change racist practices such as segregated schooling, and was assassinated by a white supremacist.

J. D. Salinger (1919–): Author of the famous coming-of-age novel *The Catcher in the Rye* (1951), Salinger is also famous for his reclusiveness.

Johnny Cash (1932–2003): Country music legend, Cash grew up in rural Arkansas and became a successful musician during the 1950s.

Truman Capote (1924–1984): Author of well-regarded novels such as *Breakfast at Tiffany's* (1958), Capote was a close friend and childhood neighbor of Lee.

John Steinbeck (1902–1968): Classic American author, Steinbeck is known for his portrayals of struggling workers in books such as *The Grapes of Wrath* (1939). He won the Nobel Prize for Literature in 1962.

Works in Literary Context

Regional Novel A regional novel portrays the distinct characteristics of a specific place, often a small town full of odd and interesting characters. *To Kill a Mockingbird* is about a young girl's coming of age in an era of social and political change. Jean Louise Finch (also known as Scout)—*To Kill a Mockingbird*'s narrator—lives with her bother, Jem, and widowed father, Atticus, in the small fictional town of Maycomb, Alabama, during the 1930s. During the course of the book, readers come to know the residents of Maycomb—good and bad—as well as the misunderstandings and long-held beliefs that lead to the book's tragic climax. The novel's colorful characters include the independent Scout, as well as Scout's brother Jem and mischievous Dill Harris, whose antics and wild plans often get the trio into "worlds of trouble." Calpurnia, the Finch's black housekeeper, helps keep the children in line; she also exposes them to the black community via a trip to her church for Sunday services. Arthur "Boo" Radley, perhaps the most tragic figure in the tale, is the town recluse. As the novel progresses, Scout, Jem, and Dill come to see Boo as less of a scary, shadowy figure, and more of a feeling human being. Through all the book's turmoil, Atticus Finch remains the voice of reason and restraint. While obviously disturbed and dismayed by the nature of Tom Robinson's trial, the lawyer nevertheless takes great pains to explain to his children why his participation, as well as their understanding, is necessary.

Novel of Racial Prejudice Racism appears as a constant theme in American fiction, but especially in Southern literary tradition. With the South's history of slavery, the relationship between the black and white communities has been one writers have focused on regularly. *To Kill a Mockingbird* shows how Scout and her elder brother, Jem, learn about fighting prejudice and upholding human dignity through the example of their father Atticus, who takes on the legal defense of a black man who has been falsely charged with raping a white woman. Lee's story of the events surrounding the trial has been admired for its portrayal of Southern life during the 1930s, not only for its piercing examination of the causes and effects of racism, but because it created a model of tolerance and courage in the character of Atticus Finch. Edgar H. Shuster asserts:

> The achievement of Harper Lee is not that she has written another novel about race prejudice, but rather that she has placed race prejudice in a perspective which allows us to see it as an aspect of a larger thing; as something that arises from phantom contacts, from fear and lack of knowledge; and finally as something that disappears with the kind of knowledge or "education" that one gains through learning what people are really like when you "finally see them."

Works in Critical Context

When *To Kill a Mockingbird* was published in 1960, it brought its young first-time author a startling amount of attention and notoriety. The work was an instant sensation, becoming a best-seller and winning the Pulitzer Prize for Fiction.

To Kill a Mockingbird Initial critical response to Lee's story was mixed. Following the publication of *To Kill a Mockingbird*, some reviewers dismissed the narrative voice of Scout as unconvincing for a girl not yet ten years of age. Harding LeMay, writing in the *New York Herald Tribune Book Review*, praises the author's "grace of writing and honorable decency of intent." "Miss Lee's problem has been to tell the story she wants to tell and yet stay within the consciousness of a child, and she hasn't consistently solved it," observes Granville Hicks in *Saturday Review*. However, subsequent critics have recognized Lee's rendering of a child's perspective through an adult's evaluation as among the most technically expert in contemporary literature. R. A. Dave claims that in the novel "there is a complete cohesion of art and morality. And therein lies [*To Kill a Mockingbird*'s] success. [Lee] is a remarkable storyteller. The reader just glides through the novel abounding in humor and pathos, hopes and fears, love and hatred, humanity and brutality ..." According to commentators, Lee adroitly exposes the turbulence underlying Southern society and psychology while presenting the possibility of its elimination through the understanding of individuals.

Responses to Literature

1. Scout Finch learns tolerance from her father, despite the racial tensions in her culture. Discuss how other characters are influenced by those around them, either towards tolerance or towards racism.

2. Research the American Civil Rights movement. How did leaders like Martin Luther King, Jr. help change the accepted practices of the Jim Crow South?

3. Explore the theme of good and evil in Lee's novel. What symbolism does Lee use to create positive and negative characters? Which characters are all good or all bad, and which characters are more complex in nature?

4. Lee creates many characters whose true identities are different than their external appearance. Choose three characters who turn out to be different than you expected. How does Lee create your initial impression, and then how does she challenge it?

BIBLIOGRAPHY

Books

Bloom, Harold, ed. *Harper Lee's* To Kill a Mockingbird. New York: Chelsea House, 1998.

Dave, R. A. "*To Kill a Mockingbird*: Harper Lee's Tragic Vision." In Naik, M.K., ed. *Indian Studies in American Fiction*. New York: Macmillan, 1974.

Johnson, Claudia Durst. *To Kill a Mockingbird: Threatening Boundaries*. New York: Twayne, 1994.

Periodicals

Harding, LeMay. "Children Play: Adults Betray." *New York Herald Tribune Book Review* (July 10, 1960): 5.

Hicks, Granville. "Three at the Outset." *Saturday Review* (July 23, 1960): 15–16.

Lubet, Steven. "Reconstructing Atticus Finch." *Michigan Law Review* 97 (1999): 1339–1362.

Shackelford, Dean. "The Female Voice in *To Kill a Mockingbird*: Narrative Strategies in Film and Novel." *Mississippi Quarterly* 50 (Winter 1996–97): 101–113.

Schuster, Edgar H. "Discovering Theme and Structure in the Novel." *The English Journal* 52 (1963): 506–511.

COMMON HUMAN EXPERIENCE

Lee describes a close relationship between a father and daughter in her novel. Other famous stories of fathers and daughters include:

King Lear (1608), a play by William Shakespeare. Personal and political conflict ensue when the aging King Lear decides to divide his kingdom between his three scheming daughters.

Pride and Prejudice (1813), a novel by Jane Austen. Elizabeth Bennet is the wittiest of five daughters and shares a close bond with her father. The story follows as she negotiates love and marriage within a society filled with rules.

Empire Falls (2001), a novel by Richard Russo. A divorced father shares an especially close relationship with his daughter as they both navigate life in a small town in Maine. Tragedy strikes when the daughter befriends the high school loner.

Little House on the Prairie (1935), a children's book by Laura Ingalls Wilder, and a television show. This tale of pioneer life follows a family facing challenges in its new home on the Kansas prairie. Daughter Laura maintains a special relationship with her Pa.

"Proof" (2000), a play by David Auburn. The daughter and caretaker of a brilliant mathematician must cope with her father's failing mental health as she also questions both her mathematical abilities and her own sanity.

⊛ Li-Young Lee

BORN: *1951, Jakarta, Indonesia*

NATIONALITY: *American*

GENRE: *Poetry, nonfiction*

MAJOR WORKS:

Rose: Poems (1986)

The City in Which I Love You: Poems (1990)

The Winged Seed: A Remembrance (1995)

Book of My Nights (2001)

Behind My Eyes (2008)

Overview

Considered one of America's most important contemporary poets, Li-Young Lee grapples with questions about family, love, and exile via evocative lyrical experimentation.

Works in Biographical and Historical Context

An International Childhood Li-Young Lee was born on August 19, 1957, in Jakarta, Indonesia, to Chinese

Li-Young Lee   *Writer Pictures 2007*

the State University of New York at Brockport from 1980 to 1981.

Immigrant Work by an Immigrant Writer Lee's international childhood is well featured in his writing. In 1986 Lee published his first book of poetry, *Rose*, which won the Delmore Schwartz Memorial Poetry Award. The poems center on Lee's painful memories of his family's emigration from Indonesia and question his relationship to the past and with his family, particularly with his father. "The Gift," for example, recalls the time when Lee's father cut a metal splinter from Lee's hand as a child. During the painful procedure, his father tells him a story to keep his mind off the knife and the pain. Later in the poem, as an adult Lee removes a splinter from his wife's hand, he remembers his father's earlier care and tenderness. In another poem, "Rain Diary," Lee recounts his father's struggling and bravery in the face of political upheaval in Indonesia. The success of *Rose* led Lee to be featured on Bill Moyers's Public Broadcast System (PBS) series *The Power of the Word* in 1989 and to receive a fellowship from the prestigious Guggenheim Foundation.

Lee continued to build his reputation and impress critics and readers alike throughout the 1990s. *The City in Which I Love You*, Lee's second poetry collection, appeared in 1990 and was selected by the Academy of American Poets for its Lamont Poetry prize. In 1995 Lee published the autobiographical *The Winged Seed*. Since then, Lee has written a third collection of poems titled *Book of My Nights* (2001). Lee has taught at several universities, including Northwestern University and the University of Iowa, and he currently lives in Chicago with his wife and their two sons.

Works in Literary Context

Lee's work draws upon a range of lyrical conventions, from classical Chinese poetry and biblical palmistry to nineteenth-century Romanticism. The recurrent themes of his poetry generally include his perceptions of the Chinese Diaspora, his understanding and acceptance of his own father, and his identity as it has been formed in relation to his native and adopted languages.

Poetry of the Chinese Diaspora Lee's poetry exhibits his sense of being part of a vast global Chinese community. His writing explores the impact his heritage has on his identity's dimensions and textures. He has been praised for expertly representing the aspirations and concerns of post-1965 Asian Americans. The Asian immigrants arriving on United States shores as a result of the 1965 immigration reforms came from a multitude of distinct cultures, so that today the term *Asian American* includes Laotians, Indonesians, Vietnamese, Thai, Hmong, Indians, Sri Lankans, and Chinese from Hong Kong or Taiwan, as well as those from traditional immigrant countries such as Korea and China. The "philosophy" that Lee ponders in his writing explores the question of individual identity in a

parents. Lee's maternal great-grandfather, Yuan Shikai, had been China's first Republican president (serving from 1912 to 1916), and his father, Lee Kuo Yuan (known as Richard), had been a personal physician to Communist leader Mao Zedong. But Lee's parents had escaped to Indonesia after the establishment of the People's Republic of China in 1949, where his father helped found Gamaliel University. The family did not stay in Indonesia long after Li-Young's birth, however. That nation was rife with anti-Chinese sentiment, and Lee Kuo Yuan, who spent a year in jail as a political prisoner, fled Indonesia with his family in 1959.

The Lee family lived in Hong Kong, Macao, and Japan before settling in the United States in 1964. They lived for a time in Pennsylvania, where Lee's father studied at the Pittsburgh Theological Seminary and then became a Presbyterian minister in East Vandergrift, a small mill town. Lee went to high school in Pennsylvania and earned his degree in biochemistry from the University of Pittsburgh in 1979. His meeting with the poet Gerald Stern led him to begin seriously writing poetry, and he went on to study creative writing at the University of Arizona from 1979 to 1980 and again at

world where vast numbers of people have been uprooted from ancestral cultures but are not totally accepted in their adopted lands. In a sense, Lee's poetry is about the desire to establish boundaries in a world where some boundaries—such as those of a nation—no longer exist.

This diaspora theme often merges with others, like his relationship with his father. Lee frequently writes about figuring out where his father's identity ends and his own begins, and about discovering his cultural and artistic lineage. The poems in *Rose*, for instance, center on Lee's memories of his family's escape from Indonesia and introduce many of the themes that have become constants in his body of work: love, family, exile, loss, and mortality. His father's presence is important in *Rose* and also becomes a constant in his writing, not only as a personal and mythical father figure, but as the source of the evocative biblical imagery and powerful language that permeate the poems. Lee's father taught him Chinese poems from the Tang dynasty as well as readings from the biblical book Psalms, and the blending of these lyric forms is evident in his writing.

Symbolic Poetry   One of the most striking technical characteristics of Lee's poetry is the use of a single image that serves to thematically and structurally organize and unify the poem. Indeed, Lee's poems challenge the traditional linear narrative structure: central images link discrete scenes, allowing the poet greater freedom to shift from the concrete to the abstract. This method makes it difficult to separate Lee's poems into thematic categories, since each poem is often a synthesis of multiple themes that draws vitality from their links to diverse life experiences. The narrative structure, though discontinuous and subject to many digressions, allows for a coherence that is supported by the central connective image. The result, as Xiaojing Zhou explains in *The Heath Anthology of American Literature* (1998), is "a capacity for multiple aspects of experience and plural perspectives within one poem."

Works in Critical Context

Lee's highly autobiographical poems have been praised by critics for their tenderness, elegance, and passion, as well as for their insightful perspectives on memory and family within the Chinese Diaspora experience.

The City in Which I Love You   Critical reaction to Lee's collections has been favorable. Writing about *The City in Which I Love You* in *Christianity and Literature*, Walter A. Hesford argues that "motifs, images, and verses from the Song of Songs serve to unify the collection" and that Lee has composed a "distinctly Chinese-American rendition of the biblical Song." Lee's engagement with biblical text, according to Hesford, "does not constitute a critique but a resinging of it, one that restores its erotic, soulful, tribal qualities often lost or ignored in orthodox appropriations."

LITERARY AND HISTORICAL CONTEMPORARIES

Li-Young Lee's famous contemporaries include:

Mao Zedong (1893–1976): Chinese military and political leader of Communist China from its establishment in 1949 until his death. Mao is regarded as one of the most important figures in modern world history and one of the one hundred most influential people of the twentieth century.

Maxine Hong Kingston (1940–): academic and autobiographical writer and professor at the University of California, Berkeley. Known for her often-studied *The Woman Warrior: Memoirs of a Girlhood Among Ghosts* (1975), Kingston writes about her experiences as a Chinese American woman and her struggle to find identity within cultural clashes as well as strict family traditions.

Kazuo Ishiguro (1954–): British writer of Japanese descent, Ishiguro has published short stories, novels, and screenplays that often focus on the destruction of war. He is most famous for his 1989 novel, *The Remains of the Day*.

Zhao Ziyang (1919–2005): leader of China from 1980 to 1987. Zhao ruled during the 1989 Tiananmen Square riots in which thousands of protesting students were gunned down by government military.

Isabel Allende (1942–): Chilean author of numerous novels. Allende's works feature characters who have adventures all over the world. *Daughter of Fortune* (1999), for instance, follows the protagonist in nineteenth-century gold-rush-era California, where she encounters the large Chinese immigrant population.

Universal Appeal   Many reviewers have labeled Lee as a "Chinese-American" poet, maintaining that his experiences as an Asian immigrant to the United States inform much of his work. Other scholars, however, have resisted the conventional urge to confine readings of his poetry to an ethnocentric context, asserting that Lee's thematic concerns are universal. In "Inheritance and Invention," for example, Zhou Xiaojing argues that largely ethnocentric readings of Lee's poems are "not only misleading, but also reductive of the rich cross-cultural sources of influence on Lee's work and of the creative experiment in his poetry." She points out that Lee's cultural influences include classical Chinese poetry, the King James Bible—especially Psalms—and his firsthand experience of life in Asia and America. She concludes that his "position of straddling different cultures and histories leads to an expansion of his conceptual and perceptual horizon," which in turn leads to renewed creativity. Zhou claims that Lee's art transcends "the boundaries of any single

COMMON HUMAN EXPERIENCE

Lee's poems often focus on his difficult relationship with his father. Other stories that examine father-son relationships include:

"Hamlet" (c. 1602), a play by William Shakespeare. Danish Prince Hamlet must decide if he will avenge his father's death after he learns his uncle murdered him. Indecision and self-doubt overcome the character in this classic tragedy.

The Brothers Karamazov (1880), a novel by Fyodor Dostoevsky. A family tragedy of epic proportions, this story is viewed as one of the great novels of world literature. The novel recounts the murder of a corrupt father by one of his four sons, but it is unclear which one committed the crime.

A River Runs Through It (1992), a film directed by Robert Redford starring Brad Pitt. Based on the 1989 autobiographical story by Norman Maclean, this film tells the story of two brothers as they grow up under a domineering minister father.

The Kite Runner (2003), a novel by Khaled Hosseini. The story focuses on an Afghani American immigrant who returns to Afghanistan to rescue the son of a childhood friend whom he betrayed. Once in war-torn Kabul, the narrator learns not only about the fate of his friend's family but also much about his own father.

Field of Dreams (1989), a film directed by Phil Alden Robinson. This movie invokes magical realism to portray a struggling farmer who builds a baseball field on his land in order to understand his father's difficult journey.

cultural heritage of ethnic identity." Even as Lee is regarded as an author with universal appeal, most commentators have situated his works within the cultural context of other Asian American poets, such as Marilyn Chin, Garrett Hongo, and David Mura, detecting similar thematic and stylistic concerns.

Responses to Literature

1. Lee writes about his relationship to his father throughout his poetry. What elements define that relationship? What are his main struggles? Write a short essay in which you consider the elements of Lee's relationship with his father that moved him to write poetry.

2. Lee uses strong images in his poems. Choose one such poem and, with a partner, draw a picture of the image invoked. Compare your picture with your partner's. What elements did each of you focus on? How are the pictures similar? How are they different? How do the pictures reflect the poem you read?

3. Read several poems of Lee's that focus on his Chinese heritage. List specific ways he describes his background. What symbols does he use? What sensory details does he employ? What emotions can you attach to his sense of history and personal identity? Are his feelings and perspectives consistent in his poetry, or do they change?

BIBLIOGRAPHY

Periodicals

Hesford, Walter A. "*The City in Which I Love You*: Li-Young Lee's Excellent Song." *Christianity and Literature* 46 (Autumn 1996): 37–60.

Marshall, Tod. "To Witness the Invisible: A Talk with Li-Young Lee." *Kenyon Review* 22 (Winter 2000): 12–47.

Neff, David. "Remembering the Man Who Forgot Nothing." *Christianity Today* 32 (September 2, 1988): 63.

Pinsker, Sanford. "Review of *Rose*." *Literary Review* 32 (Winter 1989): 256–262.

Yao, Steven G. "The Precision of Persimmons: Hybridity, Grafting and the Case of Li-Young Lee." *Lit: Literature Interpretation Theory* 12 (April 2001): 1–23.

Xiaojing, Zhou. "Inheritance and Invention in Li-Young Lee's Poetry." *MELUS* 21.1 (Spring 1996): 113–132.

Web sites

Li-Young Lee. *Poets.org from the American Academy of Poets.* Retrieved October 10, 2008, from http://www.poets.org/poet.php/prmPID/291.

❀ Robert E. Lee

BORN: *1918, Elyria, Ohio*

DIED: *1994, Los Angeles, California*

NATIONALITY: *American*

GENRE: *Drama*

MAJOR WORKS:
Inherit the Wind (1955)
Auntie Mame (1956)
The Night Thoreau Spent in Jail (1970)

Overview

Playwright Robert E. Lee (who shares his name with a very famous Confederate general of the American Civil War) is best known for popular Broadway works he wrote with his longtime collaborator, Jerome Lawrence. Over the span of five decades, beginning with their first joint venture in 1942, the duo wrote thirty-nine plays, including the well-known Broadway productions *Inherit the Wind, Auntie Mame,* and *The Night Thoreau Spent in Jail.* Lee and Lawrence were successful at using their stage plays, which were often historical, to satirize modern society or comment upon the political conditions of the time periods during which they were written.

Works in Biographical and Historical Context

Depression-era Childhood Lee was born October 15, 1918, in Elyria, a Cleveland suburb. His father, Melvin, was an engineer, and his mother was a teacher. During his childhood in Ohio, Lee witnessed the hardships faced by his community during the Great Depression. Following the catastrophic stock market crash of 1929, economic hardship would affect almost all levels of society; Lee would later use his experiences and observations made during the Great Depression to create works such as *Auntie Mame,* which satirized elite, decadent society.

Collaboration with Lawrence Lee attended Ohio Wesleyan University, and then launched a professional career as a writer and director in commercial radio. In 1942, at the instigation of friends, Lee, who was then overseeing radio ads for a New York City advertising agency, met Jerome Lawrence, a writer for CBS radio. The two ambitious young men immediately formed a writing partnership. Their first collaboration was "Inside a Kid's Head," produced for the radio program *Columbia Workshop* (and later widely anthologized). By the spring of 1942 the two writers were successful enough that they established an office in Los Angeles.

Lee and Lawrence's climb to commercial success was interrupted, however, by America's entry into World War II. Both men went into the armed forces in the summer of 1942 and spent most of the war years creating and producing programs for the Armed Forces Radio Service. These programs, though meant to entertain and educate U.S. Army soldiers, also encouraged Lee and Lawrence to use patriotic rhetoric that spoke out against the tyranny represented by Hitler in Nazi Germany and Mussolini in Fascist Italy. Lee and Lawrence would adopt similar rhetorical strategies when criticizing McCarthyism in *Inherit the Wind* and supporters of the Vietnam War in *The Night Thoreau spent in Jail.*

When the war was over, both Lee and Lawrence returned to civilian life and continued their partnership as radio writers and directors, creating scripts for such programs as *Favorite Story* (starring Ronald Colman), *The*

Frank Sinatra Show, and *Hallmark Playhouse.* In 1948, Lee married Janet Waldo, a radio actress then best known for playing the title role in the popular comedy series *Meet Corliss Archer.* They had two children, Jonathan and Lucy Lee. Lawrence and Lee also landed a contract for their first Broadway show, writing *Look, Ma, I'm Dancin'!* (1948), a vehicle for comedienne Nancy Walker, choreographed by Jerome Robbins and directed by George S. Abbott. Despite the involvement of three theatrical legends—Walker and Robbins at the beginnings of their careers, Abbott already famous—the musical had only a modest success, with 188 performances.

From Radio to Stage From 1948 through 1954 Lawrence and Lee maintained their focus on radio. As producers, directors, and writers, they were responsible for 299 broadcasts of the weekly series *The Railroad Hour,* while continuing work on many other radio and television programs. Lawrence and Lee turned to the stage in the early 1950s, however, as the advent of commercial network television caused the comedy and serial programming of commercial radio to disappear; radio was beginning its transformation to music and news formats. Their first produced play, which proved to be their greatest success (806 performances), was *Inherit the Wind.* With it they established several patterns that recurred in much of their later work.

Inherit the Wind is based on a historical event: the Scopes trial of 1925, which led to the prosecution of a Tennessee high-school biology teacher for teaching the theory of evolution. Lawrence and Lee's play fictionalizes the events, however, and is also seen as a veiled commentary on both the atmosphere of conformity that permeated America in the post-war 1950s, and also the spread of McCarthyism. Joseph McCarthy, a conservative United States senator, spurred the creation of the House Un-American Activities Committee, which aimed to rid America of a perceived Communist threat. In the post–World War II period known as the Cold War, during which America reached a stand-off with Soviet Russia and its allies, many politicians feared that America's post-war enemies (namely Russia) would infiltrate the country with spies and informants. The investigations by McCarthy and his colleagues began a "Red Scare" in which high-profile politicians, artists, and public figures were often unjustly accused of Communist sympathies. Though Lawrence and Lee could not make a blatant attack upon McCarthy and his allies (for fear of being blacklisted or arrested), they satirized the narrow-minded thinking of the members of the House Un-American Activities Committee by comparing them to the creationists of the Scopes trial. Lee and Lawrence would later use the same strategy of historical allegory with their immensely popular *The Night Thoreau Spent in Jail.*

LITERARY AND HISTORICAL CONTEMPORARIES

Robert E. Lee's literary and historical contemporaries include:

Jerome Robbins (1918–1998): From the 1930s to the 1980s, choreographer and director Jerome Robbins was one of America's most influential theater forces both in ballet and on Broadway.

Neil Simon (1927–): One of Broadway's most successful playwrights, Simon is known for capturing the Jewish American experience in such plays as *Brighton Beach Memoirs* (1983) and *The Odd Couple* (1965).

Arthur Miller (1915–2005): Twentieth-century playwright Arthur Miller is the author of the play *The Crucible* (1953), which was an allegorical attack on McCarthyism set in the Puritan era.

Tennessee Williams (1911–1983): Pulitzer Prize–winning Southern playwright Tennessee Williams was best known for his dramas *The Glass Menagerie* (1945), *A Streetcar Named Desire* (1948), and *Cat on a Hot Tin Roof* (1955).

Barry Goldwater (1909–1998): Goldwater was a conservative politician who served nearly forty years in Congress and lost the presidential election to Democrat Lyndon B. Johnson in 1964.

Joe DiMaggio (1914–1999): DiMaggio, one of the most celebrated home-run hitters in major league baseball history, was the longtime star of the New York Yankees, and made even more headlines by marrying movie star Marilyn Monroe in 1954.

John Updike (1932–2009): Prolific, Pulitzer Prize–winning author John Updike is best known for his Rabbit series, which focuses on life in small-town America.

Written in 1970, fifteen years after *Inherit the Wind*, *The Night Thoreau Spent in Jail* similarly uses a specific historical event that Lee and Lawrence present as a way of commenting on a contemporary political situation at the time it was written. In the case of *The Night Thoreau Spent in Jail*, Lee and Lawrence used writer Henry David Thoreau's famed act of civil disobedience—refusing to pay taxes to an America fighting in the Mexican-American War—as an analogy for the Vietnam War of the 1970s. Lee and Lawrence adopted Thoreau's rhetoric of conscientious political objection to reflect their view that the unpopular and lengthy war in Vietnam should be ended.

Aside from writing and producing plays with Lawrence, Lee became an adjunct professor at the University of California, Los Angeles, in 1967, where he taught aspiring actors, playwrights, and screenwriters. Throughout his academic and professional career he adhered to his conviction that the role of a theater artist is to explore political, psychological, and philosophical issues through drama; the ensuing product should then enlighten audiences while also entertaining them. Lee died of cancer in 1994 in Los Angeles.

Works in Literary Context

Throughout his works, Robert E. Lee features eccentrics and idealists (such as Auntie Mame, Henry David Thoreau, and John Scopes) who championed free thinking and free speech. Lee is also remembered for his ability to use settings from past historical time periods to reflect on his own.

Nonconformity and Self-Reliance Lawrence and Lee intended *Inherit the Wind* as a comment on Senator Joseph McCarthy's 1950s campaign against communism, which the playwrights regarded as a thinly veiled attack on the freedoms of speech and thought. Accordingly, the play pits John Scopes, the high school teacher that dared to teach Darwinism and the theory of natural selection, against narrow-minded officials determined to preserve the status quo. For Lawrence and Lee, it was clear that evolution and Darwinism represented progress and the growth of the human spirit, in opposition to the repressive censorship of Brady and Reverend Brown and their efforts to block rational development. The conflict of the play is not between evolution and creationism (a term not in common usage when it was written), therefore, but between freedom of thought and repression of free inquiry. By giving the play that focus, and also by avoiding close reproduction of the historic events in Tennessee, the playwrights were able to emphasize the more universal aspects of the conflict.

Similarly, *The Night Thoreau Spent in Jail* dramatizes an actual historical incident: the night in which writer Henry David Thoreau, protesting the Mexican-American War of 1846–1848, went to jail for refusing to pay his taxes. While the play's structure reflects the kind of theatrical experimentation particularly prominent in the latter half of the 1960s, the content of *The Night Thoreau Spent in Jail* comments as clearly on contemporary social and political events as did *Inherit the Wind*. Thoreau's rejection of his government's involvement in the Mexican-American War mirrors in direct ways the public's growing rejection of the U.S. military involvement in South Vietnam; indeed, the first production of the play in 1970 was abruptly closed when campuses across the country erupted after shootings at Kent State University in Ohio during war protests.

Aside from his political convictions, Thoreau also rejects conventional education and the rigid rules of Deacon Ball. Thoreau's resignation as a teacher after flogging students at Ball's insistence is paralleled with philosopher Ralph Waldo Emerson's resignation as a pastor because of ethical doubts. Later scenes demonstrate further facets of Thoreau's beliefs and unwillingness to conform to the social order of Concord, Massachusetts. As was the case in *Inherit the Wind*, Lawrence and Lee utilize conventional theatrical devices—potential romance, personal tragedy—to connect with the central idea driving the action of the play, yet throughout the protagonist remains an idealistic individual with a fierce dedication to the discovery of the truth.

Satire of Fashionable Society A challenge to conventional authority is the mainspring of Lawrence and Lee's *Auntie Mame*. Patrick Dennis's original novel of the adventures of a madcap free spirit and the nephew she inherits became, in Lawrence and Lee's hands, an episodic comedy with serious undertones. The Great Depression of the 1930s figures largely in the comedy, as do satiric thrusts at ethnic prejudices, trendy education, hidebound conformism, pretentious intellectualism, and social snobbery. The constant redecoration of Mame's Beekman Place apartment in New York provides its own running satire of fashion, and the guests present at the cocktail party in the first scene of the play are a cynical portrait of fashionable society.

Auntie Mame also celebrates freedom of thought (and speech), particularly in Mame's defiance of the anti-Semitism of the Upsons in the second act, and also emphasizes individualism. That it does so comically rather than in a serious dramatic context may have obscured the degree to which *Auntie Mame* shares concerns with *Inherit the Wind* and *The Night Thoreau Spent in Jail*. Unlike the other two well known plays, *Auntie Mame* is not based on a historical event, nor does it comment on specific contemporaneous controversies. Its presentation of the dangers of conformity, however, does reflect a concern of the mid-1950s that is also exhibited in the anti-McCarthyism of *Inherit the Wind*.

Works in Critical Context

Inherit the Wind Lawrence and Lee's *Inherit the Wind* ran for 805 performances on Broadway. Drawing from actual persons, including prosecutor William Jennings Bryan and defense attorney Clarence Darrow, Lee and Lawrence brought to the stage what a *Newsweek* critic called "one of the best serious dramas to hit Broadway and one of the best rounded. Its dialogue moves easily, sometimes brilliantly." A *Life* article noted: "Splashed together in bold colors like a circus poster. . . . [it depicts] a vivid provocative piece of U.S. history."

Auntie Mame *Auntie Mame* and its musical adaptation, *Mame*, are quite different in tone from *Inherit the Wind*. Lighter and less intent on social comment, *Auntie Mame* and *Mame* were among the longest-running productions in Broadway history, lasting 639 and 1508 per-

COMMON HUMAN EXPERIENCE

Lee and Jerome Lawrence's *Inherit the Wind* is considered one of the landmark stage productions of the genre of the courtroom drama. Other works that dramatize legal proceedings in the courtroom include:

To Kill A Mockingbird (1960), a novel by Harper Lee. This Pulitzer Prize-winning novel features the protagonist Atticus Finch, a lawyer who fights for racial equality in the Deep South.

Twelve Angry Men (1954), a play by Reginald Rose. This play focuses on the deliberations of a jury who must decide whether or not to give the death penalty to a man accused of killing his father.

The Crucible (1953), a play by Arthur Miller. This 1950s stage drama, like *Inherit the Wind*, was written in response to the Red Scare introduced by Joseph McCarthy and the House Un-American Activities Committee. Miller likens the 1950s atmosphere of fear to the seventeenth-century Salem witch trials.

"Witness for the Prosecution" (1925), a short story by Agatha Christie. Crime and mystery writer Christie created a tale in which a wife testifies against her husband, who is on trial for murder. While she intends to help her husband, a plot twist at the end of the story reveals that he is actually guilty.

Anatomy of a Murder (1959), a film directed by Otto Preminger and starring Jimmy Stewart. Based on a best-selling novel written by a defense attorney, *Anatomy of a Murder* tells the story of a small-town lawyer in Michigan who must face a powerful prosecutor in order to save the life of his client.

formances respectively. When *Auntie Mame* opened in New York, Wolcott Gibbs described it as "rich in situations whose comic effect I have no reason to suppose has been diminished by age; and the chances are that it will run forever."

The Night Thoreau Spent in Jail In its serious examination of individual freedom, *The Night Thoreau Spent in Jail* is akin to *Inherit the Wind*. Although popular (it was performed more than two thousand times under the auspices of American Playwright's Theatre), the play met with some critical disapproval. A reviewer for *Variety* explained: "Thoreau without warts . . . might still provide dramatic sparks if he had someone to clash with, but the invisible Establishment remains offstage, the reactionary Deacon Ball is mostly comic relief, and Emerson never disagrees." Raymond Crinkley called the play "an idealization of comfortable dissent. . . . It is indicative of the poverty of our creative minds that Thoreau is well thought of." On the other hand, Richard Coe contended that *The Night Thoreau Spent in Jail* attempts "to see in the past striking parallels with the present." He found it "a stirring and a touching play…[that] will prove hauntingly provocative." Critic Gerald Colgan believed it to be "finely and vigorously written, with…a true quality of revelation, a real insight into a mind that has left its stamp on the world's thought."

Responses to Literature

1. Research the reviews that were published after the first productions of Lee's *Inherit the Wind* and Arthur Miller's *The Crucible*, both of which were written in reaction to the climate of fear surrounding the McCarthyism of the 1950s. What do these reviews reveal to you about the social and political conditions of the time period? Do you find that the authors of the reviews themselves were hesitant to address the political natures of the plays, due to fear of being blacklisted?

2. All three of Lee and Lawrence's major works feature protagonists who are eccentrics or idealists, or both. How does Auntie Mame differ from the protagonists John Scopes and Henry David Thoreau? Be sure to address issues of gender, class, comedy, and Lee and Lawrence's choice of historical settings.

3. Both *Auntie Mame* and *Inherit the Wind* have been adapted for film. Locate an adaptation of one of these works, watch it, and compare it to Lee and Lawrence's original text. How true is the adaptation to the original script? While watching, be aware of the time period during which the film was made. Are there any historical analogies you can make between the time period depicted and the time period in which the movie was made?

BIBLIOGRAPHY

Periodicals

Review of *Inherit the Wind*. *Life* (May 9, 1955).
Review of *Inherit the Wind*. *Newsweek* (May 2, 1955).
Review of *The Night Thoreau Spent in Jail*. *Variety* (November 4, 1970).
Coe, Richard. "Auntie Mame is a Whammy!" *Washington Post and Times Herald* (October 17, 1956): C6.
———. "Ms. Justice Loomis, Successor to *Mame*." *Washington Post* (December 18, 1977): L1, 6.
———. "Thoreau: Stirring, Touching." *Washington Post* (October 29, 1970): CI, 14.
Couch, Nena. "An Interview with Jerome Lawrence and Robert E. Lee." *Studies in American Drama*, 1945–Present 7 (1992): 3–18.
Crinkley, Richmond. "Wet TNT." *National Review* (January 12, 1971): 45–46.
Gibbs, Wolcott. "The Theatre: Miss Russell Gets Around." *The New Yorker* (November 10, 1956): 110–122.
Winchester, Mark. "Jerome Lawrence and Robert E. Lee: A Classified Bibliography." *Studies in American Drama* 1945–Present 7 (1992): 88–160.

✸ Ursula K. Le Guin

BORN: *1929, Berkeley, California*

NATIONALITY: *American*

GENRE: *Fiction*

MAJOR WORKS:
A Wizard of Earthsea (1968)
The Left Hand of Darkness (1969)
The Lathe of Heaven (1971)
The Dispossessed: An Ambiguous Utopia (1974)

Overview

An award-winning author of science fiction and fantasy, Ursula K. Le Guin has infused her writing with deep, meaningful explorations of the meaning and importance of culture, language, belief, and gender roles. Her stories, written both for adults and young adults, reflect her interest in Eastern philosophy and anthropology, and have proven consistently popular and successful across age ranges.

Works in Biographical and Historical Context

A Cosmopolitan Upbringing Le Guin is the daughter of a writer, Theodora Kroeber, and a pioneering anthropologist, Alfred Louis Kroeber. She seems to have acquired from her family background a double orientation, both scholarly and humanistic, that shows in all of her writings. The Kroeber household was a stimulating environment to grow up in: Theodora Kroeber describes their summer home in the Napa Valley as a gathering place for scientists, students, writers, and California Indians. In addition to exposing her to history and anthropology, Le Guin's formative environment gave her a perspective on religion different from that of many Americans. She told Jean W. Ross in an interview for *CA*, "I was brought up in an unreligious household; there was no religious practice of any kind. There was also no feeling that any religion was better than another, or worse; they just weren't part of our life."

This was the milieu in which Le Guin began to write, and it may help explain the number of scientists in her stories, who are nearly always humane men deeply

Ursula K. Le Guin   *Dan Tuffs / Getty Images*

concerned about the effect and value of their research. Though she makes no claims to being a scientist herself, she understands what it is to pursue a scientific goal, and the philosophy that underlies anthropological thought, in particular, informs all of her work.

Launching a Writing Career on Her Own Terms   Le Guin started writing, according to an introductory note in her short-story collection, *The Wind's Twelve Quarters* (1975), at about age five. She wrote poetry, some of which was published, and stories, which were not. In the note she mentions a science-fiction story written in 1942, when she was twelve. Le Guin began her professional writing career with short fiction. Her first short story, "An die Musik," appeared in the *Western Humanities Review* in 1961. A later story, "The Dowry of Angyar," appeared originally in *Amazing Science Fiction* in 1964 and provided the impetus for Le Guin's first novel, *Rocannon's World* (1966). "I always wanted to write, and I always knew it would be hard to make a living at it," she explained to *Boston Globe* contributor Maureen Dezell. "I was very arrogant and wanted to be free to write what I wanted to write and see if I could get it published on my own terms. I did, eventually. But it took a long time." Le Guin has been rewarded for her persistence and her vision

on numerous occasions, winning the prestigious Nebula and Hugo awards for her short works, including *The Word for World Is Forest* (1976) and "The Ones Who Walk Away from Omelas" (1974).

Cycles and Earthseas   *Rocannon's World* began a series of works commonly referred to as the Hainish Cycle. These novels and short stories depict the descendants of the first race of humanity, which arose on the fictitious planet Hain and colonized other planets until war isolated the various settlements. *The Left Hand of Darkness* (1969), for which Le Guin received Hugo and Nebula Awards, is generally regarded as one of her best novels. In this work, which continues the Hainish Cycle, an envoy attempts to persuade members of an alien world to join a federation of allied planets known as the Ekuman of Known Worlds. Interwoven with the protagonist's narrative are ethnological reports, accounts of native legends and myths, descriptions of religious ceremonies, and entries from the diaries of the envoy's closest ally. *The Left Hand of Darkness* is particularly noted for its creation of an androgynous alien culture, through which Le Guin explores the ramifications of a society in which individual identities and social status are divorced from stereotypes of gender. Through this approach, Le Guin emphasizes a

LITERARY AND HISTORICAL CONTEMPORARIES

Le Guin's famous contemporaries include:

Yuri Gagarin (1934–1968): A Soviet cosmonaut (astronaut), Gagarin scored an international propaganda coup for his country during the early stages of the Space Race by becoming the first man to be launched into outer space and the first man to orbit the Earth.

Dean Koontz (1945–): An American fiction author, Koontz is considered one of the masters of the suspense genre. His books were among the first to cross genres, often blending elements of suspense, supernatural horror, and techno-thrillers.

Tom Wolfe (1931–): One of the "New Journalists" of the 1960s, Wolfe became a chronicler of underground and counterculture America. In the 1980s he switched gears, becoming a best-selling fiction author.

Bill Graham (1931–1991): One of the most influential behind-the-scenes names in rock history, Graham was instrumental in popularizing and promoting some of the world's biggest musical acts, particularly San Francisco bands like the Grateful Dead, during the 1960s and 70s.

Sergio Leone (1929–1989): Italian film director famous for his series of "Spaghetti Westerns," so called due to the fact that they were filmed in Italy with a largely Italian cast and crew. In particular, his films such as *A Fistful of Dollars* (1967) were notable for launching the stardom of Clint Eastwood, as well as their immediately memorable scores by Ennio Morricone.

favorite theme: the idea that unity is achieved through the interaction and tension of such opposites as likeness and unlikeness, native and alien, male and female. *The Dispossessed* (1974), another winner of Hugo and Nebula awards, garnered praise for its complex characterizations and well-integrated social and political ideas.

Le Guin's *Earthsea* tetralogy is a series based on magic that appeals both to adult and young adult readers in the manner of Tolkien's *Lord of the Rings*. Depicting a world that is both like and unlike our own, Le Guin's Earthsea is a land of forests, islands, and bodies of water that incorporates a variety of nations and customs; although Earthsea is governed by secular rulers, its real laws are made by a hierarchy of wizards, men whose inborn affinity for magic is augmented by disciplined study that teaches them to know, and to be able to name, the essence of each person or thing in the world. The mages of Earthsea are also responsible for keeping the balance or equilibrium of the world: since order is not imposed by a deity, the wizards and other powerful humans act or refrain from acting based on their insights

into both the world and themselves. Thus, individual responsibility and the acceptance of oneself as both good and evil are pivotal qualities in maintaining the balance of Earthsea. Le Guin depicts her wizards as artists, poets, and shamans who devote themselves to retaining an integrated universe, a world in which light and darkness, life and death are equally acknowledged and revered. Throughout her quartet, Le Guin stresses the importance of self-knowledge through each stage of life, especially as it relates to the world. In the first three novels, *A Wizard of Earthsea* (1968), *The Tombs of Atuan* (1971), and *The Farthest Shore* (1972), the main character, Ged, overcomes pride and fear and learns to accept himself and his own mortality as well as to love and trust others; as Archmage of Earthsea, he succeeds in laying the groundwork for a just and peaceful society through his selfless and profoundly dangerous acts of will. In the fourth novel, *Tehanu: The Last Book of Earthsea* (1990), Le Guin suggests that the responsibility for maintaining world equilibrium has shifted from male wizards such as Ged, whose final act as Archmage causes his loss of power, to women, reflecting a growing interest in Le Guin's fiction in feminist themes.

Other Works In addition to her novels, Le Guin has written stories throughout her career that have appeared in numerous science fiction and literary publications. Many of these stories are collected in *The Wind's Twelve Quarters* (1975), *Orsinian Tales* (1976), and *The Compass Rose* (1982). *Orsinian Tales* has been acclaimed for the manner in which it weaves elements of European history, specifically references to events in Central Europe prior to the outbreak of World War II, into a fantastical narrative. Significantly, critics have remarked that Le Guin's Orsinian stories, written in the 1950s and 1960s, constitute the chrysalis out of which her later, and more remote, extraterrestrial fantasies evolved.

Le Guin also offered up a translated version of Chinese poet Lao Tzu's *Tao Te Ching*, the central text of the Taoist belief system. Her interest was first inspired by her father, an avid reader of the text. She reported that she had been working on the project for forty years. Larry Smith, in a review in *Parabola*, says that Le Guin's version "may trouble Taoist purists," but that it is "undeniably refreshing, capturing a language that is casual and clear, reflective and pointed, full of the wise humor of the Way." In her introduction she describes the *Tao Te Ching* as "the most lovable of all the great religious texts, funny, keen, kind, modest, indestructibly outrageous, and inexhaustibly refreshing."

Works in Literary Context

Le Guin has been praised for expanding the scope of the fantasy and science-fiction genres by combining conventional elements of science fiction with more traditional literary techniques, while offering speculations on alternative societies and philosophies. Her works employ psychic phenomena, including telepathy, clairvoyance, and precognition, and commonly incorporate the philosophies of Taoism and Zen, resulting in themes of reciprocity and unity. Le Guin stresses the need for individuals and societies to balance such dualities as order with chaos and harmony with rebellion to achieve wholeness. In her *Earthsea* tetralogy, Le Guin addresses themes common to many of her novels and short fictions: alienation, liberation, and ecological, social, and self awareness.

Critics have often found it difficult to classify Ursula K. Le Guin: while some consider her writing science fiction or fantasy, Le Guin herself discounts any narrow genre categorizations. She told *CA* that "some of my fiction is 'science fiction,' some of it is 'fantasy,' some of it is 'realist,' and some of it is 'magical realism.'"

Using Science Fiction to Explore Metaphysics Le Guin's stories involve reciprocal relationships. There is a sort of golden rule in her fictional world, which states that whatever you touch touches you. This golden rule has a scientific backing in ecology; it also has philosophical underpinnings in Taoism and in Zen. Le Guin is uncomfortable when critics claim her as a great and original thinker, for she works best with what she calls "fortune cookie ideas," ideas proposed by someone else and capable of expression in very simple terms. Beginning with such an idea—ecological balance, for example—she can show through her stories how simple terms hide a mass of complexity and contradiction that surfaces only when the idea interacts with human lives.

The theme of equilibrium between opposing forces works on several levels within the Earthsea books, for example. On the most immediate and recognizable level is the integration of man with himself. In *A Wizard of Earthsea* it is the young mage, or wizard, Ged who undertakes the journey to maturity and self-knowledge; in *The Tombs of Atuan*, it is the girl-priestess, Tenar; and in *The Farthest Shore*, it is the young prince Arran, accompanying Ged on a search for the source of an evil spreading through Earthsea.

Social Criticism Le Guin has incorporated wholesale the question of defining humanity as a dominant theme in her work. In her several major novels, she brings into conflict beings that by appearances and behavior could be human, though there is some factor present that creates doubt or, on the other hand, misguided certainty. Le Guin defines "other" as "the being who is different from yourself." When she uses the term regarding her own work, however, Le Guin means something apart from the usual robot-alien-telepath-superhuman. Her others tend to be less different from us than those of most writers and deliberately suggest conventional humanity. Generally, in Le Guin's work important other-human differences give way to important similarities.

"Two Le Guin novels of unquestionably high standing, even among readers who generally do not care for science fiction, are *The Left Hand of Darkness* and *The*

COMMON HUMAN EXPERIENCE

The Earthsea tetralogy—a series of four books—are sometimes credited as the first series of young-adult fantasy novels, a genre that has proven particularly successful since.

Abarat (2002), a novel by Clive Barker. A young adult novel by an author known more for his grotesque, adult horror stories, this book follows the adventures of a young woman who suddenly finds herself on the brink of a strange, fantastical world.

The Rose and the Beast (2000), a book by Francesca Lia Block. A prolific fantasist, Block turns her attention here to a collection of nine classic fairy tales, retold with a modern perspective and surprising twists.

Artemis Fowl (2001), a novel by Eoin Colfer. A darkly comic cross-genre romp between an evil genius and the realm of the fairies.

First Test (1999), a novel by Tamora Pierce. The first in Pierce's feminist "Protector of the Small" series, the saga of an aspiring female knight in a fantastic, pseudo-medieval world.

Dispossessed," writes *Modern Fiction Studies* contributor Keith N. Hull. "In these novels Le Guin . . . describes herself as writing science fiction based on 'social science, psychology, anthropology [and] history,' . . . . [The result] is an emphasis on culture." *The Left Hand of Darkness* explores the themes of sexual identity, incest, xenophobia, fidelity, and betrayal in a tale of an Earth ambassador, Genly Ai, who is sent to the planet of Gethen, whose inhabitants are androgynous, or both male and female. Through his relationship with a native, Estraven, Ai gains understanding both of the consequences of his fixed sexual orientation and of Gethenian life. As in many of her works, Le Guin incorporates a social message in her science fiction tale. In *The Dispossessed: An Ambiguous Utopia*, another character is an alien in a strange culture; the physicist Shevek, however, is also at odds with his home planet's values. He is devoted to the spread of knowledge, but the development of his theories will inevitably bring his isolated colonial planet and its mother-planet into contact, although the two cultures bitterly oppose one another.

Works in Critical Context

"A significant amount of science fiction has been profoundly thoughtful about the situation of contemporary humanity in the light of its possible futures and its imaginable alternatives," writes Derek de Solla Price in the *New Republic*. "In recent years, no [writer] inside the field of science fiction or outside of it [has] done more to create a modern conscience than . . . Ursula K. Le Guin."

Le Guin, however, "is not competing with [George] Orwell or [Ernest] Hemingway," according to George Edgar Slusser in his book *The Farthest Shores of Ursula Le Guin*. "Her social analysis is acute, but its purpose is not indignation or reform. She has no social program, offers no panaceas." And a *Cambridge Review: Fantasy in Literature* contributor finds Le Guin "an elegant, but not a light writer: not to be trifled with. Superficially, her work charms because it has all the glitter of high intelligence and efficiency."

The Earthsea Trilogy Ursula K. Le Guin's immense reputation as a fantasy writer for children is founded essentially on the Earthsea series. Considered by Le Guin to be among her best work, it displays a holistic conception of the universe. As Robert Scholes suggests in a *Hollins Critic* article, "Where C. S. Lewis worked out of a specifically Christian set of values, Ursula Le Guin works not with a theology but with an ecology, a cosmology, a reverence for the universe as a self-regulating structure." Writing in Joseph D. Olander and Martin Henry Greenberg's *Ursula K. Le Guin*, Margaret P. Esmonde suggests that "all of [the characters'] journeys symbolize the journey every human being must make, one through pain and fear, aided only by trust in the goodness of man, hand holding hand, to the acceptance of mortality." The third book in the series, *The Farthest Shore*, earned Le Guin a National Book Award, and the fourth, *Tehanu: The Last Book of Earthsea*, won the Nebula Award for Best Novel.

Responses to Literature

1. Research the tenets of Taoism, then evaluate how Le Guin incorporates them into stories such as *The Lathe of Heaven*.

2. Le Guin's Earthsea books are set in a fully-imagined world in which magic is real. Why do you think fantasy authors often set their stories in imaginary worlds? Is this more effective than setting magic in the real world, as in the *Harry Potter* novels? Why or why not?

3. Why do you think novels such as the Earthsea tetralogy, supposedly written for younger readers, often prove equally popular with adults? What essential elements of such fantasy stories speak to readers of all ages, and why?

4. Le Guin explores questions of gender roles in *The Left Hand of Darkness*. Do you feel that gender roles are absolute? What would our society be like if there was only one gender?

BIBLIOGRAPHY

Books

Bittner, James. *Approaches to the Fiction of Ursula K. Le Guin*. Ann Arbor, Mich.: UMI Research Press, 1984.

Cogell, Elizabeth Cummins. *Ursula K. Le Guin: A Primary and Secondary Bibliography*. Boston: G. K. Hall, 1983.

———. *Understanding Ursula K. Le Guin*, Columbia, S.C.: University of South Carolina Press, 1990.

Slusser, George Edgar. *Between Two Worlds: The Literary Dilemma of Ursula K. Le Guin*. Second edition. San Bernardino, Calif.: Borgo Press, 1995.

Wayne, Kathryn Ross. *Redefining Moral Education: Life, Le Guin, and Language*. San Francisco: Austin & Winfield, 1994.

✺ Madeleine L'Engle

BORN: *1918, New York City, New York*

DIED: *2007, Litchfield, Connecticut*

NATIONALITY: *American*

GENRE: *Fiction*

MAJOR WORKS:
A Wrinkle in Time (1962)
A Swiftly Tilting Planet (1978)

Madeleine L'Engle   *L'Engle, Madeleine, photograph. © Jerry Bauer. Reproduced by permission.*

Overview

Best known for *A Wrinkle in Time* (1962), a fantasy hailed as the first work of science fiction for children to be regarded as genuine literature, and for a series of naturalistic, autobiographical stories about the Austin family, Madeleine L'Engle has won a devoted following among young readers.

Works in Biographical and Historical Context

Unpopular in Boarding School, Writing Becomes a Haven L'Engle was born in New York City in 1918, the year that World War I ended. Her father, Charles Wadsworth Camp, was a foreign correspondent. Her mother, Madeleine Barnett Camp, was a southern gentlewoman who had studied music extensively and was talented enough to have been a concert pianist, had she so desired. The southern background and love of classical music exerted a strong influence on L'Engle's writing. Several of her works portray the staunch tradition of southern gentility and characters imbued with its ideals. Throughout her works, L'Engle's characters also exhibit a great fondness for classical music—for example, Mrs. Austin vacuuming to it, Katherine Forrester studying it, and Adam Eddington whistling it as a code. In her science fiction works, L'Engle's extraterrestrial beings often speak in voices compared to musical instruments, such as the English horn and the harp.

L'Engle was an only child (her only brother died as an infant) brought up in the formal English tradition her father wished, with a nanny and governess. Because of the rather solitary childhood, she developed a great love of reading, writing stories, and drawing. Her father had been a victim of mustard gas in World War I, a war that produced over forty million casualties during trench warfare mostly occurring in Europe, and resulted in large-scale disillusionment with technology and the idea of progress. As L'Engle's father's physical health deteriorated, his professional work also suffered. His lungs became so afflicted that he could no longer live in New York or any of the other cosmopolitan cities he loved. The family moved to Switzerland, and L'Engle went to the first of a series of boarding schools both in Europe and in the United States. L'Engle graduated from Smith College with honors in 1941 and pursued a career in the theater for the next five years, because she thought it would be good schooling for a writer. Both the boarding schools and theatrical experience provide the dramatic backdrop for L'Engle's first book, *The Small Rain* (1945).

L'Engle again looks to the past for the settings of her next three books: *Ilsa* (1946) takes place in the South and provides a memorable portrait of southern family life; *And Both Were Young* (1949), L'Engle's first "junior" novel, takes place in a Swiss boarding school; and *Camilla Dickinson* (1951) is the story of a sheltered young girl growing up in New York.

Rejections, But Not Defeat While she was writing these three novels, changes were taking place in L'Engle's

life. While acting in a play, she met a young actor named Hugh Franklin; in 1946 they were married. When Franklin decided to leave the theater "forever" (a time span which lasted nine years), the family moved from New York to Connecticut. During these years L'Engle was busy coping with the disadvantages and delights of a 200-year-old house, helping her husband in the general store they purchased, and mothering their three children, Josephine, Maria, and Bion.

As always, L'Engle devoted as much time as she could to reading and writing. This decade was a time of professional discouragement to her; she could not seem to get anything published. Publishers rejected *A Winter's Love* (1957), an adult novel, for being "too moral"; they rejected *Meet the Austins* (1960), a children's book, because it opened with a death; they rejected *A Wrinkle in Time* because it was a "difficult" book—it failed to fit into either their adult or juvenile marketing slots.

All these rejections are chronicled in L'Engle's first nonfiction book, *A Circle of Quiet* (1972). An inveterate journal keeper, L'Engle has written this and three other nonfiction works, largely from journal entries. These books not only give insight into the larger works of L'Engle, but also into the discipline involved in being a writer. *Walking on Water* (1980) discusses at length the interplay between her writing and her Christianity. L'Engle's journals also trace the close parallel of her actual experiences and her writing.

COMMON HUMAN EXPERIENCE

L'Engle writes children's stories that have challenging and seemingly adult content. Other children's stories that offer challenging ideas include:

His Dark Materials Trilogy (1995–2000), three novels by Philip Pullman. This trilogy follows a young girl who not only stumbles on alternate worlds, but learns of both evil and deep truth as she sets out on an epic adventure. The series has been interpreted as presenting anti-Christian sentiment.

The *Harry Potter* Series (1998–2007), seven books by J. K. Rowling. This fantasy series follows a young boy wizard whose parents are murdered by an evil wizard. Harry must avenge his parents' death and save the wizarding community by either sacrificing himself or killing the evil wizard.

The Chronicles of Narnia (1950), a seven-part fantasy series by C. S. Lewis. Lewis's series explores weighty issues such as the nature of evil and individual responsibility through stories of four children who become kings and queens in an alternate universe.

Bridge to Terabithia (1978), a novel by Katherine Paterson. Inspired to write this fantasy story after her son's young friend was killed by lightning, Paterson tells the story of two children who find a magical world together in the woods.

Tuck Everlasting (1975), a novel by Natalie Babbitt. Exploring serious ideas such as death and eternity, the characters in this fantasy novel must grapple with their own mortality when faced with the possibility of everlasting life.

Continuous Publishing in Later Career Of her over sixty books, *A Wrinkle in Time* (which became one in a trilogy) continues to be her most popular book. In it, L'Engle incorporates Albert Einstein's 1919 theory of relativity, a scientific discovery that explains how space and time are influenced by gravity. Einstein's theory made worldwide headlines in the early twentieth century as it was the first since Isaac Newton to significantly explain the science of gravity. L'Engle's inclusion of such weighty scientific content in her novels challenged what was expected of children's literature.

L'Engle passed away in 2007, at the age of eighty-eight. Her ability to entertain both young people and adults throughout her long career as a writer is evidenced by her continued popularity with readers of both her fiction and nonfiction works. That popularity has not waned in the years since: several of L'Engle's books are now considered classics of young adult literature. Her revealing spiritual musings and her sensitive fictional por-

trayals of caring families and individuals attempting to transcend the difficulties of modern life have proved timeless affirmations of the importance of optimism, forgiveness, and love to the human spirit.

Works in Literary Context

A Focus on Children Children's stories generally focus on a young protagonist who must face some kind of challenge. Often the child's parents are either absent or dead; indeed, L'Engle's characters range from orphans to boarding school students, and they always have a moral challenge to overcome. In *A Wrinkle in Time*, the child characters have both normal childhood concerns as well as supernatural challenges. Meg, for instance, worries about school and her "awful" looks, and Calvin longs for honest affection rather than mere popularity. L'Engle has explained that she writes her most difficult works for children since she believes that children's minds are open to the excitement of new ideas, and that they are able to understand what their parents have rejected or forgotten. Yet no matter how difficult the theme L'Engle writes of, or what personal or universal crisis her characters face, there is an underlying joy in her books, a feeling that her characters will eventually make the best choices.

Spiritual Narrative The body of L'Engle's writing is influenced by her deep Christian faith, inspiring both a complicated theology and an underlying hope in her narratives. Although L'Engle uses some broad Christian symbolism in the Time trilogy, such as the unicorn in *A Swiftly Tilting Planet* (1978) or the cherubim in *A Wind in the Door* (1973), her most extensive use of Christian symbolism occurs in the suspense novel *The Arm of the Starfish* (1965). There are several Christian and cosmic ironies in the book: Canon Tallis, a devoted, honorable ecclesiastic, is pointed out to the main character, Adam, as being evil; corrupt Dr. Ball (a name similar to the degenerate deity Baal) is introduced as a caring, benevolent clergyman. Joshua, a Christ-like figure, is really a nonbeliever. Although she is a Christian, some of L'Engle's most theological works have been written as a reaction against what is thought of, in some circles, as Christian piety. Her constant grappling with the idea of God and her all-encompassing theology might well offend readers with a very traditional view of Christianity, while her obviously Christian philosophy might antagonize those who tend toward atheism or agnosticism.

Works in Critical Context

Although occasionally criticized for being pedantic, L'Engle's books have generally been favorably reviewed. Perhaps John Rowe Townsend sums up the critiques best in *A Sense of Story* as he calls her "a curiously-gifted, curiously-learned, curiously-imperfect writer." In 1984 L'Engle received the Catholic Library Association's Regina Award, given for consistent, sustained quality of work.

A Wrinkle in Time Writing in *A Critical History of Children's Literature*, Ruth Hill Viguers calls *A Wrinkle in Time* a "book that combines devices of fairy tales, overtones of fantasy, the philosophy of great lives, the visions of science, and the warmth of a good family story." She proclaims, "It is an exuberant book, original, vital, exciting. Funny ideas, fearful images, amazing characters, and beautiful concepts sweep through it. And it is full of truth." John Rowe Townsend examines the themes in L'Engle's work, explaining that "L'Engle's main themes are the clash of good and evil," and in *A Wrinkle in Time*, "evil is obviously the reduction of people to a mindless mass, while good is individuality, art and love." Susanne Elizabeth Read further comments that L'Engle's work has become one of the foundational works of juvenile science fiction, stating, "Many readers of children's literature meet science fiction for the first time through this novel."

Responses to Literature

1. L'Engle has been criticized for presenting overly mature themes to young children. Read one of her children's books and write an essay discussing any themes in the work that might be considered controversial. How might children respond negatively to this content? How might L'Engle's work help children?

2. L'Engle describes her life as a writer in many of her nonfiction works. Compare her writing process to your own. How do you generate ideas? Under what circumstances do you write (what time of day, for instance, and in what room of the house)? Write a short journal entry describing your writing process.

3. Spirituality is an important concern for L'Engle. Choose one novel and list any spiritual or religious references or themes you can find. What might L'Engle mean by such inclusions? Also write a list of ways spirituality is considered positive in the book, and ways in which it is considered negative. When can religion be dangerous, according to L'Engle?

4. L'Engle's stories are both imaginative and realistic because her fantasies are experienced by realistically-developed characters. Do a character study from one of L'Engle's novels. Describe the character's strengths and weaknesses, and consider what traits L'Engle seems to value most.

BIBLIOGRAPHY

Books

Chase, Carole F. *Madeleine L'Engle, Suncatcher: Spiritual Vision of a Storyteller*. San Diego, Calif.: LuraMedia, 1995.

Gonzales, Doreen. *Madeleine L'Engle*. New York: Dillon Press, 1991.

Hettinga, Donald R. *Presenting Madeleine L'Engle*. New York: Twayne, 1993.

Meigs, Cornelia, ed. *A Critical History of Children's Literature*. New York: Macmillan, 1969.

Reid, Susanne Elizabeth. "New Themes and Trends." *Presenting Young Adult Science Fiction*. New York: Twayne Publishers, 1998, 199–206.

Townsend, John Rowe. *A Sense of Story: Essays on Contemporary Writing for Children*. Philadelphia, Pa.: Lippincott, 1971.

Wytenbroek, J. R. with Roger C. Schlobin. *Nothing is Ordinary: The Extraordinary Vision of Madeleine L'Engle*. San Bernadino, Calif.: Borgo Press, 1995.

✸ Elmore Leonard

BORN: *1925, New Orleans, Louisiana*

NATIONALITY: *American*

GENRE: *Fiction, drama*

MAJOR WORKS:

Stick (1983)

The Big Bounce (1969)

Get Shorty (1990)

Rum Punch (1992)

Elmore Leonard   *Vince Bucci / Getty Images*

Overview

The author of such best-selling novels as *Stick* (1983) and *Glitz* (1985), Leonard has been lauded as one of the finest contemporary crime writers in the United States. His gritty accounts of urban life feature the exploits of lower-class characters trying to make fast money and are often set in the locales of southern Florida and Detroit.

Works in Biographical and Historical Context

Military Service and Marriage Elmore John Leonard Jr. was born on October 11, 1925, in New Orleans, Louisiana. After moving around the Southwest, the family settled in Detroit, Michigan. In the fifth grade Leonard was already writing plays, including a war setting in which the coward redeems himself by rescuing the hero. Called "Dutch" by his classmates (after American League pitcher Dutch Leonard), Leonard still goes by that nickname, and Arbor House has made use of it in titling collections of his novels: *Dutch Treat* (1985) and *Double Dutch Treat* (1986).

After graduating from high school in 1943, Leonard failed a physical for the U.S. Marine Corps and was then drafted into the U.S. Navy. He served in the South Pacific as a Seabee during World War II. Lasting from 1940–1945, World War II united much of the developed world into either Allied or Axis alliances, with the Allies comprising Great Britain, France, the Soviet Union, the United States, and other nations. The Allies ultimately defeated the Axis powers, including Adolf Hitler and his German forces, whose extermination of six million Jews during wartime is referred to as the Holocaust. Leonard later used this background in drawing the character of Walter Majestyk in *The Big Bounce* (1969). On his discharge from the navy, Leonard entered the University of Detroit in 1946 as an English and philosophy major. While at the university, he twice entered short-story contests, and on one occasion earned a second prize. On July 30, 1949, he married Beverly Cline, with whom he subsequently had five children, and in 1950 he graduated. He took a job as a copywriter for the Campbell-Ewald Advertising Agency in Detroit. Though he soon discovered that writing ads was not the least bit satisfying, he remained with the company until 1961. In the early 1950s he developed the habit of rising at 5:00 A.M. so he could write fiction for two hours before going to work to "write zingy copy for Chevrolet trucks." Sometimes he also managed to work on his fiction at the office.

Advertising Leads to Writing In 1953 Leonard published the first of seven western novels. In 1961 Leonard left Campbell-Ewald to write industrial films and educational films for Encyclopaedia Britannica Films. Two years later he started the Elmore Leonard Advertising Agency, which he ran until 1966. During that same decade he began writing contemporary crime fiction.

Publishers shied away from Leonard's first crime novel, *The Big Bounce*, because it did not fit easily into an established genre and featured what were considered immoral protagonists. It was rejected eighty-four times in New York and Hollywood before the film rights were sold for $50,000. Subsequently, the book was sold to Fawcett for publication as a Gold Medal paperback original. The sale of the movie rights allowed Leonard to become a full-time crime fiction and screenplay writer.

In 1973, at the suggestion of his agent, Leonard read the dialogue-driven crime novel *The Friends of Eddie Coyle* (1972), by George V. Higgins, whose technique seems clearly to have influenced Leonard's subsequent works. Yet while many of Higgins's characters deliver rambling monologues, the speech of Leonard's characters tends to be terse, elliptical, and understated.

During the 1970s and early 1980s Leonard built a modest but solid core readership for his crime novels, which were often set in Detroit. He also wrote such screenplays as *Joe Kidd* (1972) for Clint Eastwood and *Mr. Majestyk* (1974) for Charles Bronson. Although he had been writing critically acclaimed crime novels for a decade, and his work was being adapted for the screen, Leonard had only a small cadre of fans until the early 1980s, when his novels began to attract the attention of a larger audience. With the novel *Stick* in 1982, Leonard suddenly became a best-selling writer. One sign of this sudden success can be seen in the agreeable change in Leonard's finances that year. The paperback rights for *Split Images* (1981) earned him $7,000; the rights for *Stick* a year later earned $50,000. Then, in 1983, *LaBrava* won an Edgar Award from the Mystery Writers of America as the best novel of the year. The book sold over 400,000 copies. Leonard's next novel, *Glitz*, hit the best-seller lists in 1985 and was a Book-of-the-Month Club selection. Leonard's popularity continued to increase throughout the 1990s. In *Get Shorty* (1990), for instance, he used his years of experience as a screenwriter to create an intricate story full of inside jokes about the seamy underbelly of Hollywood. Books like *Rum Punch* (1992) continue to be bestsellers, and his newer works include *The Hot Kid* (2006) and *Up in Honey's Room* (2007). Leonard still lives in the Detroit suburb of Bloomfield Village, within one mile of his five children and ten grandchildren, explaining that if he lived in Los Angeles he would spend all his time talking to producers.

Works in Literary Context

Use of Dialect No aspect of Leonard's talent has been more often singled out for critical praise than his ear for dialogue. To get his dialogue right, Leonard listens to the way people really talk and copies it down as faithfully as possible. When writing the novel *City Primeval: High Noon in Detroit* (1980), Leonard even sat in at the Detroit police department's homicide squad room for several months, listening to the way that police officers, lawyers, and suspects spoke. His writing is full of slang terms and peculiarities of speech that mark each of his characters as a true individual. More important, he captures the speech rhythms of his characters. Leonard reproduces speech patterns so well, Alan Cheuse writes in the *Los Angeles Times Book Review*, that "it's difficult to say...who among this novelist's contemporaries has a better ear." Herbert Mitgang of the *New York Times* agrees. The conversations in Leonard's books, Mitgang writes, "sound absolutely authentic." Avoiding narration and description, Leonard moves his novels along with dialogue, letting his characters' conversations tell the story. Speaking of the novel *Freaky Deaky* (1988), Jonathan Kirsch writes in the *Los Angeles Times* that the book "is all dialogue—cool banter, jive talk, interior monologue. Virtually everything we learn about the plot and the characters is imparted through conversation, and so the book reads like a radio script." This emphasis on dialogue also reflects Leonard's experience as a screenwriter.

Crime Novels   Leonard writes realistically about the underworld in the tradition of James M. Cain and W. R. Burnett. His characters on the margins of society are often career criminals looking to get rich quick, hustling for a scam, or primed for the big heist. They may be con artists and they may be psychopathic killers. For most of his characters, survival is difficult enough, and success is impossibly elusive. In one of several unpublished interviews Leonard gave in the spring and summer of 1997, he asserted that his characters are "the kind of people who think they're hip, who are looking for a big score." He attempts to portray "the way they talk, the street parlance. People in crime and on the fringes of crime and people on the other side—they interest me."

Works in Critical Context

Many critics consider Elmore Leonard to be the best living writer of crime fiction in the United States. Since the mid-1980s he has enjoyed enormous commercial success, and his style has influenced a generation of writers.

Glitz   The success of this book brought him national media attention, and Leonard was featured as a *Newsweek* cover story on April 22, 1985. There, Robert S. Prescott wrote that Elmore Leonard "is the best American writer of crime fiction alive, possibly the best we've ever had." Of *Glitz*, Prescott wrote, "If it's not his best story, it's his most carefully textured novel; besides, the margin of difference between Leonard's better and lesser works would admit, with difficulty, a butterfly's wing." Stephen King wrote in his review for *The New York Times* that

> Mr. Leonard moves from low comedy to high action to a couple of surprisingly tender love scenes with a pro's unobtrusive ease and the impeccable rhythms of a born entertainer. He isn't out front, orating at the top of his lungs.... He's behind the scenes where he belongs, moving the props around and keeping the story on a constant roll.

LITERARY AND HISTORICAL CONTEMPORARIES

Leonard's famous contemporaries include:

John Gotti (1940–2002): Once the Mafia boss of the Gambino family in New York, Gotti was a colorful figure in organized crime until his arrest in 1992. He died of cancer while serving a lifetime term in prison.

Clint Eastwood (1930–): The successful actor, director, and producer, Eastwood is well-known for his early roles in westerns such as *The Good, the Bad and the Ugly* (1966). He is also the Oscar-winning director of films such as *Million Dollar Baby* (2005).

Lee Atwater (1951–1991): A controversial Republican Party strategist who was key to the elections of both Ronald Reagan and George H. W. Bush.

Dwight D. Eisenhower (1890–1969): The victorious commander of Allied forces in Europe during World War II and, subsequently, the thirty-fourth president of the United States.

Richard Nixon (1913–1994): The thirty-seventh president of the United States, Nixon, despite making inroads in foreign policy, became known for resigning the presidency in disgrace after the Watergate scandal.

Get Shorty   The protagonist in *Get Shorty* is Chili Palmer, a Miami loan shark who travels to California in pursuit of a man. He is also being pursued, and in the course of the action, he becomes entangled with a third-rate producer, a washed-up actress, and some cocaine dealers. Writing in the *Los Angeles Times Book Review*, Charles Champlin applauds the accuracy of Leonard's portrait of the movie business, calling it "less angry than 'Day of the Locust' but not less devastating in its tour of the industry's soiled follies and the gaminess beneath the grandeurs." Even more sweeping praise comes from Whitney Balliett of *The New Yorker*, who declares that

> book by book (he publishes almost one a year), the tireless and ingenious genre novelist Elmore Leonard is painting an intimate, precise, funny, frightening, and irresistible mural of the American underworld.... Leonard treats [his characters] with the understanding and the detailed attention that Jane Austen gives her Darcys and Emma Woodhouses.

Responses to Literature

1. Leonard's novels are often set in such specific locations as Detroit that affect the storyline. Choose one story and list ways in which the location adds to the narrative. Then consider how the story might change if located in a different city.

COMMON HUMAN EXPERIENCE

Leonard's characterization of criminals is notable because he does not judge the choices they make. Other works that remain morally neutral about questionable lifestyles and behavior include:

"A Good Man is Hard To Find" (1955), a short story by Flannery O'Connor. Focusing on a vacationing family's chance meeting with a serial killer, this story examines who should be considered good, and why.

The Godfather (1969), a novel by Mario Puzo. Chronicling the lives of one mafia family, *The Godfather* was an extremely influential book that launched both a literary and film franchise.

O Brother, Where Art Thou? (2000), a film by the Coen Brothers. A retelling of Homer's epic poem *The Odyssey* this film follows three criminals in the American South of the 1930s, after they escape from a chain gang.

Ocean's Eleven (2001), a film directed by Steven Soderbergh. A remake of the 1960s film, this caper movie starring George Clooney and Brad Pitt shows how eleven thieves pull a heist to ruin a dishonorable businessman.

Matchstick Men (2003), a film directed by Ridley Scott. Based on a novel by Eric Garcia, this film stars Nicolas Cage as an obsessive-compulsive con artist whose life is upended when he meets the teenaged daughter he never knew.

2. Dialect is part of Leonard's style. Choose one character who speaks in a dialect. Rewrite one passage of dialogue that features this character in standard, non-dialect English. Read the original passage out loud; then read the standardized passage out loud. What differences do you notice? How does the language effect the meaning and the characterization in the passage?

3. Criminals and other figures of questionable employ often assume the roles of relatively sympathetic protagonists in Elmore's fiction. What techniques does he use to make criminals sympathetic—or even heroic—to the reader?

4. Some of Leonard's books have been made into movies. Read *The Big Bounce* or *Get Shorty* and then watch the film version. What elements of the narrative were cut or changed for the movie? Why? Which is the better medium for the story?

BIBLIOGRAPHY

Books

Geherin, David. *Elmore Leonard*. New York: Continuum, 1989.

Periodicals

Balliet, Whitney. "Elmore Leonard in Hollywood." *The New Yorker* (September 3, 1990): 106–107.

Champlin, Charley. "Leonard Cocks a Snook at Hollywood." *Los Angeles Times Book Review* (July 29, 1990): 9.

Cheuse, Alan. "A Pleasure for the Hard-Boiled Fans." *Los Angeles Times Book Review* (December 4, 1983): 3.

Hynes, Joseph. "'High Noon in Detroit': Elmore Leonard's Career." *Journal of Popular Culture* 25 (1991): 183–184, 186.

King, Stephen. "What Went Down When Magyk Went Up." *New York Times Book Review* (February 10, 1985): 7.

Kirsch, Jonathan. Review of *Freaky Deaky*. *Los Angeles Times* (May 4, 1988).

McGrath, Charles. "'The Hot Kid': The Old Master." *New York Times Book Review* (May 8, 2005).

Mitgang, Herbert. "Novelist Discovered after 23 Books." *New York Times* (October 23, 1983).

Prescott, Robert S. "Making a Killing: With 'Glitz,' Leonard Finally Brings in the Gold." *Newsweek* 105 (April 22, 1985): 62–67.

Sutter, Gregg. "Getting It Right: Researching Elmore Leonard's Novels, Part I." *Armchair Detective* 19 (1986): 4–19.

———. "Getting It Right: Researching Elmore Leonard's Novels, Part II." *Armchair Detective* 19 (1987): 160–172.

Web sites

The Elmore Leonard Website. Retrieved October 23, 2008, from http://elmoreleonard.com.

✸ Julius Lester

BORN: *1939, St. Louis, Missouri*

NATIONALITY: *American*

GENRE: *Fiction, nonfiction*

MAJOR WORKS:

To Be a Slave (1969)

The Long Journey Home: Stories from Black History (1972)

Uncle Remus: The Complete Tales (1987)

John Henry (1994)

Overview

An African American writer best known for his children's stories focusing on positive presentations of African American folklore and heritage, Lester has published numerous stories, novels, and nonfiction books. His works have received both the Caldecott Honor and the Newbery Honor, among many other awards for children's literature.

Julius Lester   *Julius Lester / Writer Pictures*

Works in Biographical and Historical Context

Racism Clouds Childhood   Lester's early years were spent in the segregated South of the 1940s and 1950s. He was born in 1939 in St. Louis, Missouri, the son of a Methodist minister. At the age of two he moved with his family to Kansas City, Kansas, and as a teenager lived in Nashville, Tennessee, spending summers at his grandmother's farm in rural Arkansas. While Lester's memories of the South were not entirely bad, he was profoundly influenced by the segregated South.

The South, prior to the 1960s, was a segregated and harsh culture for African Americans. Thanks to policies known as Jim Crow laws, the structure of the South during the first half of the twentieth century separated most aspects of society by race, from restaurants and stores to schools and hotels. Black Americans were prohibited from entering any establishment dubbed "Whites Only," and the culture was generally aggressive towards them, with groups such as the Ku Klux Klan responsible for many hate crimes or acts of violence against blacks. The Civil Rights movement of the 1960s finally initiated federal government intervention to eliminate institutional segregation.

Lester's early artistic interests were with music, yet he also had aspirations to become a writer. In books he found an escape from the daily realities of racism, and at a young age became an avid reader. Lester became especially fond of Westerns and mysteries, which he would read into the early hours of the morning.

Political Involvement Inspires Writing   Lester graduated in 1960 from Nashville's Fisk University with a degree in English and became politically active in the struggle to desegregate the South and bring about social change. He became part of political movements in the 1960s in which young people protested traditional cultural attitudes about issues ranging from racial and gender politics to the U.S. involvement, and mandatory

drafting of soldiers, for the Vietnam War. In the mid-1960s Lester joined the Student Non-Violent Coordinating Committee (SNCC), at a time when the group advocated that blacks assume a more militant stance to fight racism. He became head of the SNCC's photo department and traveled to North Vietnam during the Vietnam War to document the effects of U.S. bombing missions. During the same period, he pursued his music interests and played the guitar and banjo at civil rights rallies. Lester went on to record two albums and performed with folksingers Pete Seeger, Phil Ochs, and Judy Collins. His interests in black folk music led to the writing of his first book, *The 12-String Guitar as Played by Leadbelly: An Instructional Manual*, which he coauthored with Seeger in 1965. He then wrote a number of adult books on political themes, including *The Angry Children of Malcolm X* (1966), *Look Out Whitey, Black Power's Gon' Get Your Mama!* (1968), and a book of photographs and poems entitled *The Mud of Vietnam* (1967).

In the late 1960s Lester moved to New York City, where he was the only African American announcer at WBAI-Radio, a noncommercial station featuring alternative programming. He hosted an evening show that featured diverse music styles, including jazz, rock, classical, and experimental, and a morning show entitled "Uncle Tom's Cabin" (a reference to Harriet Beecher Stowe's 1852 bestseller popularizing anti-slavery sentiment prior to the Civil War).

Continuing his varied involvement in black politics, Lester followed the advice of an editor at Dial Press who suggested he branch out into writing children's books. In 1969, he published two books that came to mark his future success as a writer for young people, *To Be a Slave* and *Black Folktales*.

During the 1970s and 1980s, Lester followed with a number of similarly acclaimed books that showed his overlapping interests in African American history, folklore, and political themes, including *The Knee-High Man and Other Tales* (1972) and *The Long Journey Home: Stories from Black History* (1972).

Reclaiming and Retelling African American Stories
A number of Lester's retellings of traditional tales have been collaborations with the illustrator Jerry Pinckney. Both Lester and Pinckney have sought out projects that allow them to reclaim traditional stories, redrawing rich, memorable characters while eliminating taints of racism that may have been part of the original tellings. In 1987, the two produced the first of four volumes of retellings of the "Uncle Remus" tales of nineteenth-century humor writer Joel Chandler Harris. Critics praised the way that Lester reinvented the narrative voice of Uncle Remus to make the storyteller a stronger, livelier presence. Pinckney was the impetus behind the 1994 book *John Henry*, based on a folk legend of an ex-slave whose strength was so great that he beat a steam drill in a contest to dig through a mountain, only to collapse and die afterward.

LITERARY AND HISTORICAL CONTEMPORARIES

Lester's famous contemporaries include:

Martin Luther King, Jr. (1929–1968): An influential African American leader and winner of the Nobel Peace Prize, Dr. King was instrumental in the battle for civil rights during the 1950s and 1960s.

Allen Ginsberg (1926–1997): One of the founders of the American Beat poetry movement of the 1950s, Allen Ginsberg is best known for his poem "Howl" (1956).

Bill Cosby (1937–) Cosby gained prominence as a comedian and actor, but found most recognition in creating the first successful mainstream African American sitcom, *The Cosby Show* (1984–1992).

Harper Lee (1926–): Lee's one novel, *To Kill A Mockingbird* (1960), has become a classic work of American literature. Her story shows a young white girl's encounter with the segregated South.

Spike Lee (1957–): African American screenwriter and director Lee is best known for his controversial films about race and class in America, such as *Do the Right Thing* (1992) and *Malcolm X* (1992).

In 1996, the author-illustrator team also published *Sam and the Tigers*, a new version of the turn-of-the-century tale *The Story of Little Black Sambo*.

Lester is also the author of a 1995 novelization of the William Shakespeare play *Othello*. Reviewers generally found Lester's interpretation to be an accessible story that could serve as an introduction to the play for young readers.

In addition to writing for young readers, Lester has also continued with books for adults, including his novel *Do Lord Remember Me* (1985) and his two-volume compilation *The Seventh Son* (1971), which brings together the writings of the early black political activist W. E. B. Du Bois. He has also authored two autobiographies, *All Is Well* (1976) and *Lovesong* (1988), the latter of which recounts his conversion in the 1980s to Judaism. In addition to his writing career, Lester has served as professor since the early 1970s at the University of Massachusetts in Amherst, first as a professor of Afro-American studies, and then as a professor Near Eastern and Judaic studies.

Works in Literary Context

Modernized Classics Refashioning traditional stories into contemporary forms allows a story to have a longer life within a community. Updates often change or eliminate outdated content and rework themes to be relevant to modern audiences. Lester retells the "Uncle Remus" stories as a way to place the focus on the storyteller in the tales rather than on unpalatable racial stereotypes. Kay McPherson found Lester's Uncle Remus to be "a forceful, witty, and cunning storyteller rather than the subservient character of Harris's creation." *Little Black Sambo* is another example of Lester reclaiming stories with a positive focus on African American heritage. Lester changed the names of all the human characters in the story to Sam, eliminating the original names of Sambo, Mumbo, and Jumbo that many modern readers find offensive. Pinckney, the illustrator, further replaced the original minstrel-like images of the characters in the book with colorful, animated pictures. Lester's work allows traditional stories to retain a place in the culture but with a modern sensibility.

Children's Literature Much of Lester's writing is aimed at children. Generally, children's literature focuses on child characters who must overcome some challenge in their life, often learning important lessons along the way. Lester's work often takes a different angle by presenting historical information and stories to children in a form that entertains them. For Lester, writing for children has been a particularly rewarding area to explore aspects of his African American heritage. Lester explains:

> Children's literature is the one place where you can tell a story. Just, straight, tell a story, and have it received as a narrative without any literary garbage. I've done a fair amount of historically based fiction that would be derided as adult literature because it's not "sophisticated." I'm just telling a story about people's lives. In children's literature, I can do that.

Works in Critical Context

Like most juvenile fiction, Lester's work has not received a great deal of critical attention beyond reviews in a few periodicals. However, his work has received many awards, including the Caldecott Honor, the Newbery Honor, the Coretta Scott King Award, and the Lewis Carroll Shelf Award. *The Long Journey Home* was also a finalist for the National Book Award.

To Be a Slave and Black Folktales *To Be a Slave*, a collection of six stories based on historical fact, evolved from an oral history of slaves Lester was compiling. Runner-up for the Newbery Medal, *To Be a Slave* was acclaimed for its contributions to African American history. "Aside from the fact that these are tremendously moving documents in themselves," writes *Black Like Me* author John Howard Griffin in the *New York Times Book Review*, "they help to destroy the delusion that black men did not suffer as another man would in similar circumstances, a delusion that lies at the base of much racism today." Also in 1969, Lester published his widely praised *Black Folktales*, recasting various human and animal characters from African legends and slave narratives. "Although these tales have been told before, in most of them Lester brings a fresh street-talk language ... and thus breathes new life into them," writes John A. Williams in the *New York Times Book Review*. "It is a tribute to the universality of these tales—and Lester's ability to see it—that we are thus presented with old truths dressed for today."

Responses to Literature

1. Find a copy of one original Joel Chandler Harris "Uncle Remus" story using your computer or your library. Compare it to Lester's version. What changes does Lester make? Why? Can you see any obvious elements of racism in Harris's version?

2. Research the civil rights movement of the 1960s, being careful to verify your sources of information. If you were to write a story about one leader from this era, who would it be and why? Outline the basic details of the person's life.

3. As a child, Lester read as a way to escape his difficult circumstances. At the same time, Lester uses books to convey stories from real history for young readers. Do you think these works would qualify as escapist entertainment? Why or why not?

4. Read at least two of Lester's illustrated children's stories. How do the images add to the story itself? Describe the style of the pictures. Are the colors bold or subtle? Are the characters exaggerated or realistic? How do these choices add meaning to the story?

BIBLIOGRAPHY

Books

MacCann, Donnarae. "Julius Lester." *Twentieth-Century Children's Writers, 3rd edition*. Edited by Tracy Chevalier. Farmington Hills, Mich.: St. James Press, 1989, 575–76.

Periodicals

Foner, Eric and Naomi Lewis. Review of *Long Journey Home: Stories from Black History*. *New York Times Review of Books* (April 20, 1972): 41–42.

Griffin, John Howard. Review of *To Be a Slave*. *New York Times Book Review* (November 3, 1968): 7.

List, Barry. "Julius Lester." *Publisher's Weekly* (February 12, 1988): 67–68.

McPherson, Kay. Review of *The Last Tales of Uncle Remus*. *School Library Journal* (January 1994): 124.

Pingel, Carol Jean. Review of *Othello: A Novel*. *Book Report* (Mar–Apr 1995): 38–39.

Williams, John A. Review of *Black Folktales*. *New York Times Book Review* (November 9, 1969): 10, 12.

Web sites

Julius Lester on Author's Guild. Retrieved October 20, 2008, from http://members.authorsguild.net/juliuslester.

COMMON HUMAN EXPERIENCE

Lester often writes about historical figures in his stories for children. Other children's literature with a historical basis includes:

The Royal Diaries (1999–2005), a series of young adult historical fiction by Kathryn Lasky, Carolyn Meyer, and others. This series of Canadian books tells the stories of young famous world leaders throughout history, but imagines the leaders as young girls.

George Washington's Socks (1991), a novel by Elvira Woodruff. Three young friends are transported back to the Revolutionary War in this story, where they encounter battle as well as George Washington himself as he leads his troops.

Thomas Jefferson: Letters from a Philadelphia Bookworm (2000), a novel by Jennifer Armstrong. A young girl becomes Thomas Jefferson's penpal, writing to him about important issues of the time.

The Night Journey (1981), a novel by Kathryn Lasky. A child convinces her grandmother to tell her story about escaping from her oppressive life in czarist Russia.

The Amazing Thinking Machine (2002), a novel by Dennis Haseley. Two children invent a machine to help their parents survive the Great Depression.

❀ Denise Levertov

BORN: *1923, Ilford, Essex, England*

DIED: *1997, Seattle, Washington*

NATIONALITY: *British, American*

GENRE: *Poetry*

MAJOR WORKS:
The Double Image (1946)
Here and Now (1956)
The Sorrow Dance (1967)

Overview

A leading post–World War II American poet, Denise Levertov infuses descriptions of everyday objects with her personal, political, and religious sensibility. She is best known as part of the Black Mountain school of poetry.

Works in Biographical and Historical Context

Home Schooling and Early Poetry Levertov's father, a Russian Jew who immigrated to Great Britain and became an Anglican minister devoted to combining Christian and Jewish faiths, and her mother, who was well-versed in Welsh and English folklore and literature,

Denise Levertov   *Levertov, Denise, photograph. AP Images.*

the United States—fought to keep German and other Axis forces from seizing control of surrounding regions. Levertov entered the Civil Nursing Reserve and continued to write while working as a civilian nurse in the early 1940s. Levertov's lyrical pieces are set in traditional metrical and stanzaic forms, evidencing Levertov's interest in English Romantic poetry.

Becoming Part of the Black Mountain School

Following the war, Levertov married American novelist Mitchell Goodman. For two years the couple lived in southern France near Goodman's friend Robert Creeley, whose poetic theories greatly influenced the Black Mountain school of poetry. When Goodman and Levertov moved to the United States in the early 1950s, Levertov studied the American modernist poets—Wallace Stevens, Ezra Pound, and, particularly, William Carlos Williams, whose objectivist edict "no ideas but in things" profoundly influenced her verse. During this period, Levertov befriended American poet Robert Duncan, who is also associated with the Black Mountain school and who also wrote extensively about mythology, mysticism, and the occult. Levertov published verse in *Black Mountain Review* and *Origin*, prominent magazines that presented Black Mountain theories and literature. Levertov's collections from this period, including *Here and Now* (1956), firmly established her as an important contemporary poet and contain many frequently anthologized pieces. Her thematic concerns are reflected in the lines "I like to find / what's not found / at once, but lies / within something of a different nature, / in repose, distinct."

Teaching and Political Activism

While holding teaching positions at several United States colleges during the 1960s and 1970s, Levertov participated in demonstrations against American military involvement in the Vietnam conflict as well as other causes. Many writers were part of the radical movements in the 1960s that questioned traditional social, racial, and gender roles. Levertov encouraged draft resisters and helped found the Writers and Artists Protest against the War in Vietnam movement. Her volumes of this period, including *The Sorrow Dance* (1967), *Re-learning the Alphabet* (1970), and *To Stay Alive* (1971), document Levertov's attempt to expand the realm of poetry to encompass social and political themes. In many of these poems, Levertov adopts a more immediate style to convey the urgency of her message. "From a Notebook: October '68–May '69," for example, combines letters, prose passages, and quotations to depict her experiences within the antiwar movement. Many critics faulted this new approach as too harsh and haphazard. Other critics agree, however, that Levertov's political themes are better presented in "The Olga Poems." This sequence concerns Levertov's relationship with her older sister, a political

both exerted strong influences on her poetry. Her father was descended from an eighteenth-century rabbi reputed to know the language of birds and was a founding member of Habid Hasidism, a Jewish mystical movement that opposes rationalism and celebrates the mystery of everyday events. Likewise, Levertov's mother claimed the Welsh tailor and mystic Angell Jones of Mold among her forebears. In her poem "Illustrious Ancestors," Levertov declares an affinity with her heritage.

Levertov's parents assumed all the responsibility for their two daughters' education, relying on the family library and programs aired on the British Broadcasting System. Levertov's only formal instruction occurred at ballet school. She began writing poetry at an early age and mailed several verses to prominent modernist poet T. S. Eliot—who responded with a lengthy and encouraging letter—when she was twelve years old. Her first volume of poems, *The Double Image* (1946), was written during World War II, a conflict that pitted European nations against one another in an attempt to control the political fate of the region. England was a key member of the Allied forces, who—along with Russia, France, and

activist whose death in 1964 had a tremendous impact on Levertov's public and personal life. Levertov's later collections contain many pieces of a political nature and are also noted for poems that explore such personal topics as her growing spirituality and Christian faith.

Levertov continued publishing through the end of her life, writing poetry and prose as well as teaching. She continued to receive many awards, culminating in her election to the American Academy of Arts and Letters in 1980. She died in 1997, in Seattle, after battling lymphoma.

Works in Literary Context

The Black Mountain School of Poetry   Because her poetry was published in the *Black Mountain Review* and because she formed friendships with Robert Duncan, Robert Creeley, and Charles Olson, all associated with Black Mountain College, Levertov came to be considered part of the so-called Black Mountain poetry movement. This loosely defined school had certain theories about poetic composition, most notably Olson's concept of "projective verse," which involves "composition by field." In short, the shape of the poem is determined by its content and by the intuitive judgment of the poet. Levertov embraced the idea that poetic form should not be determined by traditional stanza patterns or preconceived assumptions about the shape of the poem. In the essay "Some Notes on Organic Form" (in *New and Selected Essays*, 1965), Levertov articulates her sense of a poetic form that "is based on an intuition of an order, a form beyond forms" that determines the rhythmic characteristics and the physical appearance of the poem.

Poetry of Nature   Levertov's literary treatment of the natural world developed from neo-Romantic lyrics early in her career to caustic attacks on environmental degradation in the 1980s and 1990s, as she attempted to reveal how the intersection of militarism and technology harms both people and nature. Scholars have long acknowledged Levertov's interest in the natural world, but her nature-oriented poetry has received less attention than her poems of political protest and spiritual exploration. Levertov does, however, make significant contributions to discussions of the relationship between people and nature. Perhaps more than any other poet of her era, she stresses that militarism and an undue obsession with technology lead to various abuses of power that are inseparable from one another. According to Levertov, warfare and other forms of violence threaten not only people but also the nonhuman world. Levertov repeatedly addressed the question of the autonomy of nature and the extent to which the human imagination can comprehend and commune with nonhuman entities. Levertov's sense of the interplay between people and nature is sometimes examined through the lens of Christian spirituality. Levertov is unusual in that she emphasizes that the human relationship with God sets the human species apart from other animals, even as she

LITERARY AND HISTORICAL CONTEMPORARIES

Levertov's famous contemporaries include:

Robert Creeley (1926–2005): Prolific American poet and fellow member of the Black Mountain school of poetry, Creeley was known for his numerous books of poetry and his friendship with Charles Olson.

Adrienne Rich (1929–): Rich is known for her confrontational poetry about the American political landscape. She writes about racism, sexism, and involvement in the Vietnam War.

Betty Freidan (1921–2006): Author of the groundbreaking feminist work *The Feminine Mystique* (1963), Friedan was an activist for women's rights. She was also a founder of the National Organization for Women.

Stokely Carmichael (1941–1958): Political activist and author of the book *Black Power: The Politics of Liberation in America* (1967), Carmichael espoused aggressive methods to achieve equal rights for African Americans. He was a member of the controversial Black Panthers.

Marianne Moore (1887–1972): One of the few female poets associated with the modernist movement, Moore wrote poems focusing on particular objects often found in the natural world.

rejects the notion that this belief implies a hierarchy in which the natural world and its creatures are considered less valuable than people. Her work thus combines elements of traditional theology with a late-twentieth-century ecological sensibility.

Works in Critical Context

Some critics have argued that Levertov's political poetry is overly preachy and not poetic, that she unwisely abandoned her earlier aesthetic principles and experiments with form. Even friends such as Duncan questioned her politically oriented poetics. Others, however, supported her work, and Levertov, in essays and interviews, defended the importance of "engaged poetry," the term she used to describe poetry in touch with political and social issues. A great deal of Levertov's work—not only her antiwar poems but also her meditations on landscapes, animals, and plants—represents her attempt to enter into the experience of people or objects outside herself.

Relearning the Alphabet and To Stay Alive   The poems Levertov wrote about the Vietnam War received a mixed reception. Dorothy M. Nielson praised their discovery of forms and their use of language as being fully appropriate to the political issues they explored, and Hayden Carruth hailed Levertov's political and antiwar

COMMON HUMAN EXPERIENCE

Levertov spent a large part of her career focusing on politics, including protesting the American involvement in Vietnam. Other works that criticize war include:

*M*A*S*H* (1972–1983), a television comedy/drama. Starring Alan Alda, this long-running show mixed drama and comedy and used the thinly veiled backdrop of the Korean War to highlight the contemporary struggles of the Vietnam War.

Goodbye to All That (1929), an autobiography by Robert Graves. Illustrating the brutal trench warfare techniques of World War I, Graves's book reveals the devastation and despair that followed the mass destruction of the war.

"Dulce et Decorum Est" (1920), a poem by Wilfred Owen. A young poet who enlisted in World War I, Owen's most famous poem details the horrors of war and questions those who glamorize it. Owen died in battle in 1918.

poems as work that approached the status of an epic. He writes that her poems are some of "the best products of the recent period of politically oriented vision among American poets." Other poets and critics, however, attacked these works as crude and clunky. In the judgment of Duncan, Levertov accepted too readily the problematic language of public debate and thus denied the poet's responsibility to stretch language and the imagination to their full potential; she did this by employing disclaimers such as that concerning her use of revolution as "[t]he wrong word / . . . / But it's the only / word we have." Other critics faulted the documentary emphasis in the poetry. Charles Altieri criticized Levertov's "aesthetics of presence," with its focus on the concrete image, as being inadequate to represent the complex political and ethical issues and their contexts.

Responses to Literature

1. Levertov used her art to protest things that she believed were harmful, from war to the destruction of nature. What would you protest today? Write an essay describing an issue you find questionable, and then write a brief poem explaining your views on the topic.

2. Research the Vietnam War using your library and the Internet, being careful to consult reliable sources. What were the main issues that caused American protest? Why did the United States remain in the war? What did supporters of the war believe?

3. Conservation of the environment has become a much more popular issue since Levertov's death. Choose one of her poems about nature that would be considered "green" by twenty-first century standards. Describe the elements of Levertov's writing that reflect the environmental movement.

4. Levertov's later work focuses more on her spirituality than her earlier writing. Choose one political poem and one spiritual poem. Compare the subject matter, tone, and style of these poems. How are they similar? How are they different?

BIBLIOGRAPHY

Books

Altieri, Charles. "Denise Levertov and the Limits of the Aesthetics of Presence." In *Denise Levertov: Selected Criticism.* Edited by Albert Gelpi. Ann Arbor: University of Michigan Press, 1993, pp. 126–147.

Carruth, Hayden. "Levertov." In *Critical Essays on Denise Levertov.* Edited by Linda Wagner-Martin. Boston: G. K. Hall, 1991, pp. 30–35.

Gelpi, Albert, ed. *Denise Levertov: Selected Criticism.* Ann Arbor: University of Michigan Press, 1993.

Kinnahan, Linda A. *Poetics of the Feminine: Authority and Literary Tradition in William Carlos Williams, Mina Loy, Denise Levertov, and Kathleen Fraser.* Cambridge: Cambridge University Press, 1994.

Marten, Harry. *Understanding Denise Levertov.* Columbia: University of South Carolina Press, 1988.

Middleton, Peter. *Revelation and Revolution in the Poetry of Denise Levertov.* London: Binnacle Press, 1981.

Rodgers, Audrey. *Denise Levertov: The Poetry of Engagement.* Rutherford, N.J.: Fairleigh Dickinson University Press, 1993.

Wagner, Linda Welshimer. *Denise Levertov.* New York: Twayne Publishers, 1967.

Periodicals

Freidman, Susan Stanford. "Creativity and the Childbirth Metaphor: Gender Difference in Literary Discourse." *Feminist Studies* 13.1 (1975): 328–341.

Nielson, Dorothy M. "Prosopopoeia and the Ethics of Ecological Advocacy in the Poetry of Denise Levertov and Gary Snyder." *Contemporary Literature* 34 (1993): 691–713.

Smith, Lorrie. "An Interview with Denise Levertov." *Michigan Quarterly Review* 24 (1985): 596–604.

Web sites

Robinson, Harriet Hanson. *Dostoevsky and Existentialism.* Retrieved October 31, 2008, from http://fyodordostoevsky.com. Last updated on May 17, 2007.

✸ Philip Levine

BORN: *1928, Detroit, Michigan*

NATIONALITY: *American*

GENRE: *Poetry*

MAJOR WORKS:

They Feed They Lion (1972)

What Work Is (1991)

The Simple Truth (1994)

Overview

Philip Levine is known for poetry grounded in the harsh reality of contemporary urban life. Deeply committed to the plight of the lower-class, blue-collar worker, Levine describes his poetry as an attempt to create "a voice for the voiceless."

Works in Biographical and Historical Context

Raised with Radical Politics Levine was born in Detroit, Michigan, to Russian Jewish immigrants. A. Harry Levine was a businessman, and Esther Priscoll Levine was a bookseller. Both his parents were deeply interested in the radicalism of the Great Depression. With

Philip Levine   *Christopher Felver / Philip Levine*

the economic downturn that resulted from the stock-market crash in 1929—and the high unemployment that followed, leaving one in every four workers out of a job—several radical political movements gained popularity, including anarchism, communism, and socialism. These philosophies sought to redress the inadequacies of capitalism that, because of the suffering caused by the Great Depression, seemed to only hurt working Americans. Popular radical movements included societies that shared resources equally rather than encouraging competition (as in a capitalistic system). Levine grew up in a political household, where he listened to debates about communism and anarchism. He also became fascinated by the Spanish Civil War (1936–1939), a conflict that pitted long-suffering workers against their own military establishment, and even involved support provided by fascist dictators Benito Mussolini and Adolf Hitler.

Levine received his BA from Wayne University (now Wayne State University) in 1950 and then worked at a series of assembly-line jobs in automobile factories before accepting a teaching position at the University of Iowa in 1955. He was awarded an MFA there in 1957, and he has since earned his living teaching poetry, primarily at California State and Tufts Universities.

Poetry of the Working Poor Levine's poetry has changed little since his first collection, *On the Edge* (1961). Although his lines have evolved from traditional meters to freer, more open cadences, and his poems have become increasingly lyrical and less narrative, his themes have largely remained the same—a blend of the personal and the political, the spiritual and the concrete. His rage at the political and economic powers that constrain people's lives features prominently in *They Feed They Lion* (1972), *1933* (1974), and *The Names of the Lost* (1976). Another major theme is the Spanish Civil War, which, as Herbert Leibowitz comments in the *New York Times Book Review*, "embodies for him ... a people's uprising that succeeded, quixotically, for a few rare days in hinting at what a genuinely egalitarian society might be." His best-known descriptions of the war include "For the Fallen" and "Francisco, I'll Bring You Red Carnations." He also evokes his experiences with family members and friends in poems such as "Father," "To Fran," and "My Son and I."

Throughout his career, Levine has rejected the use of self-consciously poetic language, dismissing rhetoric as distracting his readers from what he considers the proper business of his poetry, addressing the truth about life. Critics have often praised Levine for the honesty of his poetry. Other critics, though they admire his personal integrity and the force of his emotion, question whether what he writes can really be distinguished from prose.

Levine received the American Book Award for *Ashes* (1979) and the National Book Critics Circle Award for *Ashes* and *7 Years from Somewhere* (1979). He continues to teach and splits his time between New York and California.

LITERARY AND HISTORICAL CONTEMPORARIES

Levine's famous contemporaries include:

Woody Guthrie (1912–1967): A folksinger and political activist, Guthrie is known for songs like "This Land is Your Land" and "Dust Bowl Refugees."

César Chávez (1927–1993): Arizona-born Chávez was known for protesting unfair working conditions for migrant laborers and eventually succeeded in gaining reforms.

Bruce Springsteen (1949–): American rock and folk singer, Springsteen's music often presents political positions from a worker's perspective, such as protesting the Vietnam War with *Born in the U.S.A.* (1984), or memorializing September 11 with *The Rising* (2002).

Fidel Castro (1926–): Communist leader of Cuba for nearly fifty years, Castro ruled Cuba through a strong dictatorship. His communist policies, while encouraging censorship and control, also brought positive outcomes such as nearly universal literacy. He stepped down in 2008 due to failing health.

Robert Lowell (1917–1977): Lowell was a Pulitzer Prize-winning American poet known for the confessional style and subject matter of his works, as well as his outspoken political and civil rights activism.

Works in Literary Context

Working Class Poetry For more than three decades, Levine has spoken for the working men and women of America's industrial cities. Levine himself explains, "I saw that the people that I was working with ... were voiceless in a way," he stated in *Detroit Magazine*, continuing,

> In terms of the literature of the United States they weren't being heard. Nobody was speaking for them. And as young people will, you know, I took this foolish vow that I would speak for them and that's what my life would be. And sure enough I've gone and done it. Or I've tried anyway.... I just hope I have the strength to carry it all the way through.

In the *Hudson Review*, Vernon Young finds that Levine "has never acknowledged the claim of any society save that of the bluecollar dispossessed, the marginal and crunched for whom he has elected to be the evangelist and spokesman." Critic Herbert Leibowitz comments: "Levine has returned again and again in his poems to the lives of factory workers trapped by poverty and the drudgery of the assembly line, which breaks the body and scars the spirit." However, the speaker in Levine's poems "is never a blue-collar caricature," argues Richard Tillinghast in his *New York Times Book Review*, "but someone with brains,

feelings and a free-wheeling imagination that constantly fights to free him from his prosaic environment."

Poetry of the Human Condition His first book of poems, *On the Edge* (1961), demonstrates Levine's early and abiding preoccupation with narratives and portrait poems that celebrate the heroism of the ordinary individual living out his stubborn joys and hopes in the face of the fear, pain, and loneliness of the human condition. The German officer losing his sense of identity in "The Distant Winter," the deserters from the French-Algerian army in "The Negatives," and the poet himself in the doctor's waiting room in "Passing Out" are all such characters. His portraits, as in "The Drunkard" and "On the Edge," frequently show the subject losing in the struggle, although the portrait is painted with respect. In this and succeeding books, Levine is especially, although not exclusively, concerned with the plight of urban and suburban humans whose pain derives from or is exacerbated by the exploitations of a complex of corporate, industrial, military, and political interests.

Works in Critical Context

Levine's concentration on the negative aspects of working class life has led many critics to describe his work as dark, brooding, and without solace. This sense of defeat is particularly strong when the poet recalls scenes from his Detroit childhood, where unemployment and violence colored his life.

They Feed They Lion Despite its often painful quality, Levine's verse also displays a certain joyfulness, a sense of victory-in-defeat, suggests Marie Borroff. Writing in the *Yale Review*, she describes the title poem of *They Feed They Lion* as "a litany celebrating, in rhythms and images of unflagging, piston-like force, the majestic strength of the oppressed, rising equally out of the substances of the poisoned industrial landscape and the intangibles of humiliation." Edward Hirsch in *Michigan Quarterly Review* finds that while anger and indignation lie at the core of Levine's poetry, his later poems "have developed a softer edge while maintaining their brooding intensity." Robert Mazzocco asserts in *The New York Review of Books* that Levine is "affectionate in his hate, hard in his compassion," and fully aware of "the twilit other world where the negative and the positive seem to be twins of the same coin, where the poet is both victor and victim, and at times blessed because he is both." And Richard Hugo comments in the *American Poetry Review*: "Levine's poems are important because in them we hear and we care." Though Levine's poems tell of despair, pain, and inadequacy, Hugo feels that they still hold out the hope that people can triumph over sadness through language and song. Because Levine has kept alive in himself "the impulse to sing," Hugo concludes that Levine "is destined to become one of the most celebrated poets of the time."

Responses to Literature

1. Research the plight of workers in the United States by reading a book like Howard Zinn's *A People's History of the United States.* How have workers played a role in the creation of America? Do you think that role is adequately reflected in history books? Use specific examples to support your position.

2. Levine writes poetry about his own experiences growing up in a working-class environment. What is an element of your childhood that greatly influenced who you are today? Write an essay describing one aspect of your family or cultural life made you into the person you are now.

3. Levine wants to give a voice to those he thinks have no voice: workers. Whom would you consider voiceless in American society today? Write an essay giving voice to a person or group that you believe is voiceless.

4. Critics often claim that Levine's poetry is more like prose, or nonpoetic writing. Choose three poems. Write a list describing what elements of Levine's style are like nonpoetic writing. Write another list describing what elements of the poem are strictly poetic (rhyme, incomplete sentences, images, and meter, for instance). In your opinion, are Levine's works more like poems or prose? Why?

BIBLIOGRAPHY

Books

Buckley, Christopher, ed. *On the Poetry of Philip Levine: Stranger to Nothing.* Ann Arbor, Mich.: University of Michigan Press, 1991.

Periodicals

Boroff, Marie. Review of *They Feed They Lion. Yale Review* (Autumn 1980).

Hirsch, Edward. "Naming the Lost: The Poetry of Philip Levine." *Michigan Quarterly Review* 28.2 (1989): 258–266.

Hugo, Richard. "Philip Levine: Naming the Lost." *American Poetry Review* 6 (1977): 27–28.

Leibowitz, Herbert. "Lost Souls, Lost Cause." *The New York Times Book Review* (October 7, 1979): 15, 30–31.

Mazzocco, Robert. "Matters of Life and Death." *New York Review of Books* 22 (April 3, 1975): 20–23.

Tillinghast, Richard. "Working the Night Shift." *New York Times Book Review* (September 12, 1982): Sec. 7, 42.

Young, Vernon. *Hudson Review* (Winter 1979).

Web sites

Philip Levine on Poets.org. Retrieved October 26, 2008, from http://www.poets.org/poet.php/ prmPID/19.

COMMON HUMAN EXPERIENCE

Levine consistently highlights the lives and struggles of working people in his poetry. Other works that present sensitive portraits of workers include:

A People's History of the United States (1980), a history book by Howard Zinn. Instead of focusing on traditional movements and leaders, Zinn tells America's history by focusing on the underrepresented voices from colonial times to the present, including Native Americans, slaves, women, and workers.

Nickel and Dimed: On (Not) Getting By in America (2001), a nonfiction book by Barbara Ehrenreich. Writer Ehrenreich chose to work in low wage jobs across America in order to determine how the working poor make ends meet. Her book concludes that one low-wage job, despite its often physically-demanding nature, cannot provide food and shelter, ultimately questioning the minimum wage structure in the U.S.

Life in the Iron Mills (1861), a novella by Rebecca Harding Davis. Focusing on working characters, Davis shows how poverty and desperation take away opportunities for a fulfilled life.

Let Us Now Praise Famous Men (1941), a book written by James Agee with photographs by Walker Evans. Vividly revealing the desperate poverty suffered by Southern sharecroppers, this book combines narrative with numerous stark photographs of farmers and their families.

Norma Rae (1979), a film directed by Martin Ritt. Based on a true story and starring Sally Field, this movie describes one woman's attempts to unionize her Alabama mill and improve the terrible working conditions. The movie won two Academy Awards.

⚙ Meriwether Lewis

BORN: *1774, Albemarle, Virginia*

DIED: *1809, Hohenwald, Tennessee*

NATIONALITY: *American*

GENRE: *Nonfiction*

MAJOR WORKS:

History of the Expedition under the Command of Captains Lewis and Clark (1814)

The Original Journals of the Lewis and Clark Expedition, 1804–1806 (1904–1905)

The Journals of Captain Meriwether Lewis and Sergeant John Ordway, Kept on the Expedition of Western Exploration, 1803–1806 (1916)

Meriwether Lewis   *Lewis, Meriwether, photograph. The Library of Congress.*

Overview

Meriwether Lewis and William Clark led the first American scientific expedition that the United States government sponsored, which was also the first to cross the North American continent within the present United States. Much of the territory they traversed had never been seen by anyone other than native North Americans, and the expedition of the two explorers provided a thoroughly detailed map of the land.

Works in Biographical and Historical Context

Friends with Jefferson   Lewis was born on August 18, 1774, in the prominent Albemarle district of Virginia, near Charlottesville. Among his neighbors was Thomas Jefferson's family. Lewis's father died of pneumonia in 1779 after serving in the Revolutionary War. His mother remarried Capt. John Marks, a wealthy Georgia landowner, in 1780. Lewis was educated by tutors and spent much of his time hunting in the rough terrain where he lived. When his stepfather died in 1792, Lewis brought his mother and the rest of his family home from Georgia and truly took over as head of the family.

While the life of a farmer was more interesting to Lewis than the life of a scholar, he jumped at the chance for adventure in 1794, joining the militia to suppress the Whiskey Rebellion, a farmer's uprising in Western Pennsylvania against a federal tariff imposed on whiskey sales. The action was over before he reached the field, but Lewis loved the military, and fought with the army against Native Americans in the Northwest Territory. Lewis then became part of President Jefferson's White House when the new president asked his old friend to become his personal secretary, a role that Lewis performed for two years.

President Jefferson made an enormous land acquisition in 1804, known as the Louisiana Purchase, in which he doubled the size of United States territory, extending it west to the Rocky Mountains, south to the Gulf of Mexico, and north to the Canadian border. Jefferson purchased the nearly one million square miles from Napoleon Bonaparte, the leader of France, for $15 million. Exploration was already a priority but the Louisiana Purchase increased the urgency; Lewis gained leadership of the project, enlisting his childhood friend William Clark as his partner.

Preparing for the Expedition   Jefferson sent Lewis to Pennsylvania to study extensively scientific topics that would aid the exploration, including botany and astronomy. Jefferson's instructions were lengthy, explicit, and demanding. His first priority was discovering a water route to the Pacific, and the expedition was to note the latitude and longitude of "durable" landmarks for later navigators. In addition to mapping the water route, Lewis was to learn as much as possible about the people he met for the sake of future commerce. These exhaustive ethnographies would eventually aid commerce with the Indians and "those who may endeavor to civilize and instruct them." Lewis and his men were to act as ambassadors, foster peace between the tribes, and to invite their chiefs to visit Washington at the government's expense. Jefferson also suggested that Lewis take some kinepox and teach the Indians how to use it against smallpox.

On top of all this, Jefferson wanted other information regarding the soil, vegetation, animals, mineral deposits, "volcanic appearances," climate, and the seasonal appearances of plants, animals, and insects. In addition to mapping his own route, Lewis was to gather information about other branches of the Missouri and the Columbia and any other rivers that might prove navigable. In particular, Jefferson wanted to learn about the northern source of the Mississippi, as well as the disposition of any Canadian traders.

A Historic Journey Begins   For the expedition, Lewis and Clark chose fourteen soldiers, and included Clark's black servant (actually a slave), York. The party eventually grew to more than forty-five, including Toussaint Chaboneau, whose best claim to fame was his Shoshone wife, Sacajawea, the only woman on the expedition, who proved invaluable as a liaison with other Indians. The Corps of Discovery left Saint Louis in May 1804, proceeding up the lower Missouri River.

By the end of October they were looking for a good spot to spend the winter among the Mandans in what is now North Dakota. By mid-November Fort Mandan was completed, and the company spent the winter of 1804–1805 in councils with the Indians. In April the company left Fort Mandan. By mid-April they were entering territory never before seen by white people.

The Missouri, which at first glance would seem the easiest part of their voyage, became an ever more challenging river of shifting sandbars and collapsing banks. Aboard the boats, deft handling by the men was crucial in order to avoid disaster. The near capsize of a canoe on the Missouri near the Yellowstone (not far from the present-day border between North Dakota and Montana) in May 1805 almost finished the expedition before it ever reached the mountains, as it contained all of the instruments, medicines, and papers that had been generated on the trip. Their first real crisis came in early June 1805 when they had to decide which of two large channels represented the true Missouri. Lewis and Clark made a decision, challenged by their men but on Sacagawea's advice, to follow the southern route, and for five anxious days the two hoped they were not leading their men up a pointless creek they would have to retrace. Finding a great waterfall proved their choice was the correct one.

In August, Lewis crossed the Continental Divide and found the source of the Missouri River. He also located a Shoshoni village, and after pacifying their initial aggression, convinced the chief to guide them. Sacagawea recognized the tribe as her people, and she was able to aid in translation.

From the Missouri to the Pacific, and Back Even with Shoshoni help, the overland journey was arduous for the next few months until the group reached northwest Idaho in September and were cared for by the Nez Percé Indians. October brought them to the Oregon border, and they finally reached the Pacific Ocean in November 1805. There they built a winter shelter in modern-day Oregon, which now is the site of a national monument.

In March, Lewis and Clark began their return trip, scavenging for food at some points, and recovering stashed supplies at others. Lewis and Clark split up in June, with Lewis finding a short path to Montana. He was then accidentally shot in the leg by a hunter, injuring him for a month. Lewis met up with Clark and the rest of the party in August at the Missouri River. The group went on to St. Louis and then back to Washington, D.C.

Celebrated upon their return, Jefferson appointed Lewis governor of the Louisiana Territory, and Clark became superintendent of Indian affairs for the same territory. Lewis was also charged with formally writing the history of the expedition. He seems never to have started on this literary task, and his administrative appointment proved

LITERARY AND HISTORICAL CONTEMPORARIES

Lewis's famous contemporaries include:

James Fenimore Cooper (1789–1851): A popular American writer in the nineteenth century, Cooper wrote stories about the frontier. His most famous novel is *The Last of the Mohicans* (1826).

James Madison (1809–1817): Madison was the fourth president of the United States, and was friendly with the Lewis family.

Samuel Taylor Coleridge (1772–1834): A British Romantic writer, Coleridge is best known for his work with fellow poet William Wordsworth, and for his poem "The Rime of the Ancient Mariner" (1798).

Napoleon Bonaparte (1769–1821): The charismatic Emperor of France, Napoleon waged constant military campaigns throughout Europe in order to strengthen France.

Washington Irving (1783–1859): This American humorist and short story writer is best known for works like "Rip Van Winkle" and "The Legend of Sleepy Hollow" (1820).

disastrous. He encountered mounting political opposition in the territory, and after Jefferson left the presidency, the federal government refused to approve some of his expenditures. The evidence is scanty, but it appears that he became depressed and perhaps began drinking heavily. In the fall of 1809, traveling overland from Natchez, Mississippi, to Tennessee on the Natchez Trace, he set out for Washington, D.C., to attempt to get his account approved. On the night of October 11, 1809, he stopped at a lonely cabin in Tennessee, and he died there of apparently self-inflicted gunshot wounds.

Works in Literary Context

The work of Lewis and Clark had a profound effect on the settlement of the western United States and for that reason their writings have endured as historically significant works. They also continue to provide a detailed view of the region prior to the dramatic changes brought about by the advancement of white settlers, a perspective that might otherwise be lost. However, most scholars agree that the best qualities of their writings are more informational than literary.

Exploration Narrative Lewis and Clark's writing combines both literary flourishes as well as detailed scientific data. The text rarely sounds like typical nature writing, for while Lewis and Clark often refer to a scene as "beautiful," their descriptions were often ordinary, if not downright consumerist: "Our camp is in a beautiful plain, with timber thinly scattered for three quarters of a mile, and

COMMON HUMAN EXPERIENCE

Lewis and Clark kept journals of their expedition. Other famous journals include:

A Midwife's Tale: The Life of Martha Ballard Based on Her Diary, 1785–1812 (1991), a book by Laurel Thatcher Ulrich. Describing the harried life of a nineteenth-century midwife and mother, these diary entries also show the history of medical treatment.

A Year in Thoreau's Journal, 1851 (1993), the writings of nineteenth-century writer Henry David Thoreau. Thoreau's many popular writings about nature and politics find their start in his well-kept journals. This American writer is best known for his book *Walden* (1854), in which he describes living in a cabin in the Massachusetts woods.

The Diary of Virginia Woolf, Vol. I: 1915–1919 (1977), the personal writings of British author Virginia Woolf. Woolf published classics like *Mrs. Dalloway* (1925) and *A Room of One's Own* (1929), and later committed suicide.

Windblown World: The Journals of Jack Kerouac, 1947–1954 (2004), the writings of Beat Generation writer Jack Kerouac. Kerouac is recognized for his contributions to the 1960s American counterculture, especially through his novel *On the Road* (1957).

The Journals of Sylvia Plath (1982), the writings of American poet and novelist Sylvia Plath. Plath's experimental writings are part of the confessional poetry genre. She is best known for her personal narrative, *The Bell Jar* (1963).

consisting chiefly of elm, cottonwood, some ash of an indifferent quality, and a considerable amount of a small species of white oak." Their description of the waterfall begins with an elevated sentiment—"sublime spectacle . . . this stupendous object which since creation had been lavishing its magnificence upon the desert, unknown to civilization"—but these few lines are followed by pages of precise dimensions: "gathering strength from its confined channel, which is only two hundred and eighty yards wide, [the water] rushes over the fall to the depth of eighty-seven feet and three quarters of an inch."

The most important descriptions of all for official purposes were of their position: "The latitude of our camp below the entrance of Portage creek, was found to be 47° 7' 10" 3, as deduced from meridian altitude of the sun's lower limb taken with octant by back observation giving 53° 10". Descriptions of the grand views from bluffs or mountaintops become exercises in triangulation, with mountains described by their directions and positions as compass headings measured in degrees from the observer's position. Clearly, Lewis and Clark viewed the mountains with a cartographer's eye and saw the "durable" landmarks that Jefferson had desired.

Journal Writing Lewis and Clark have become so inseparable in the history of the United States that historians have emphasized their differences in order to distinguish the two. Lewis has been characterized as a moody, sensitive intellectual and Clark as the barely literate frontiersman, perfectly adapted to the wilderness. Both men, however, belonged to land-owning, slaveholding families and might have considered themselves gentlemen. Lewis undoubtedly had more education than Clark, and the literary style of his journals—more verbose and literary than that of Clark—reflects this difference.

Thomas Jefferson noted in his sketch of the writers that Lewis suffered from "hypochondriac affections," which apparently refers to periodic depressions. Yet, Lewis was able to write detailed, technical descriptions of new plant and animal species, while Clark proved to be a skilled cartographer whose detailed maps of the route of the expedition make it possible to locate the position of the party on any given day with some precision. Lewis kept a journal for brief periods of the expedition from Pittsburgh to Saint Louis, and Clark kept one intermittently during their winter camp on the Mississippi and then throughout the rest of the trip. Lewis's journals include substantial gaps in time (prompting some question about whether some of his entries have been lost), but Clark's cover all but about ten days, although he may have copied Lewis's entries for some months in early 1806. Their notebooks and loose sheets also contain undated materials, such as weather diaries, zoological and botanical notes, and digests of information about various tribes.

Works in Critical Context

Not counting the journals of four of the enlisted men, the two captains wrote more than a million words during their preliminary travels to St. Louis and the twenty-eight months of the expedition. The Lewis and Clark journals constitute one of the major travel and exploration accounts of American history, and for this achievement, the two are inseparably linked in history. Their journals, never published in their own lifetimes, constitute their principal literary accomplishment.

The Original Journals of the Lewis and Clark Expedition The journals are not intimate personal records but instead are public documents, and their first purpose was to record valuable information. They were also scientific records of discoveries made in the pursuit of knowledge and records of events that occurred during that pursuit. Neither of the captains regarded them as opportunities to record or analyze their emotions or their philosophies of life. Although it would be difficult to write a psychological profile of Lewis or Clark from the journals alone, this does not deter some writers from trying. Many have found the journals to be works of lasting fascination. They are probably most interesting to readers with an abiding curiosity about Western history and with some knowledge of the country through which the expedition passed. Noted historian Stephen Ambrose, for instance, says the journals are "part guidebook, part travelogue, part booster-like promotion, part text to accompany the master map." Because the full scientific results were not published for a century, they have never received proper credit for their many discoveries about animal and plant life. Nonetheless, the published history of their expedition was, for many years, a primary source of knowledge about the land west of the Mississippi River and was not superseded until the series of expeditions sponsored by the government in the mid-nineteenth century.

Responses to Literature

1. Lewis and Clark took extensive notes on the natural environment. Write your own nature diary, tracking one area near you. Record as much detail as you can, including descriptions at different times of day and in different weather conditions. What did you discover about your surroundings that you had not before noticed?

2. Write an essay in which you describe a recent trip. Discuss both the physical elements of the journey, as well as personal interactions and unexpected challenges. What are the difficulties of recording a physical trip?

3. Lewis and Clark shared the burden of recording their expedition. Choose a partner with whom you share a regular activity, such as a sport or a hobby. Each write a journal entry about that shared interest. Compare essays, and try to compile your perspectives into one coherent narrative. What are the difficulties of writing with a partner? What are the benefits?

4. Research the Louisiana Purchase using your library and the Internet, being careful to focus on reliable sources. How did Jefferson make such a shrewd business deal? Why did Napoleon sell the land at that time in history? How did the land acquisition change America, both physically and in other significant ways?

BIBLIOGRAPHY

Books

Ambrose, Stephen E. *Undaunted Courage: Meriwether Lewis, Thomas Jefferson, and the Opening of the American West.* New York: Simon & Schuster, 1996.

Bakeless, John. *Lewis and Clark: Parnters in Discovery.* William Morrow, 1947; reprinted. New York: Dover Publications, 1996.

Botkin, Daniel B. *Our Natural History: The Lessons of Lewis and Clark.* New York: Putnam, 1995.

Cavan, Seamus. *Lewis and Clark and the Route to the Pacific.* New York: Chelsea House, 1991.

Cutright, Paul Russell. *A History of the Lewis and Clark Journals.* Norman, Okla.: University of Oklahoma Press, 1976.

———. *Lewis and Clark: Pioneering Naturalists.* Chicago, Ill.: University of Illinois Press, 1969.

Hall, Eleanor J. *The Lewis and Clark Expedition.* San Diego, Calif.: Lucent Books, 1996.

Nobles, Gregory H. *American Frontiers: Cultural Encounters and Continental Conquest.* New York: Hill & Wang, 1997.

Ronda, James. *Lewis and Clark among the Indians.* Lincoln, Nebr.: University of Nebraska Press, 1984.

✹ Sinclair Lewis

BORN: *1885, Sauk Centre, Minnesota*

DIED: *1951, Rome, Italy*

NATIONALITY: *American*

GENRE: *Fiction*

MAJOR WORKS:
Main Street (1920)
Babbitt (1922)
Elmer Gantry (1927)
Arrowsmith (1929)

Sinclair Lewis *Lewis, Sinclair, photograph. The Library of Congress.*

Overview

One of the leading American novelists of the 1920s and the first American winner of the Nobel Prize in Literature, Sinclair Lewis created some of the most effective satires in American literature. Along with the noted critic and essayist H. L. Mencken, he vengefully attacked the dullness, the smug provincialism, and the socially enforced conformity of the American middle class.

Works in Biographical and Historical Context

Shedding the Small Town for the East Coast   Lewis was born in the small town of Sauk Centre, Minnesota, and was raised to follow the traditions of his middle-class, Protestant hometown. As scholars have observed, throughout his early life Lewis was torn between two conflicting desires. The first was to conform to the standards of sameness, of respectability, and of financial advancement as dictated by his family and by the town. Opposing this desire was Lewis's need to acknowledge his own nonconformist nature and ambitions: his agnosticism, his literary inclinations, and his general rebellion against the village's preference for unquestioning adherence to established standards of thought, faith, and aesthetics. After writing news stories and working at various odd jobs in the offices of Sauk Centre's two newspapers during his teens, Lewis—to the townsfolks' disapproval—left the Midwest to attend a university in the East. During his years at Yale, which included periods of travel and temporary employment, he read voraciously and published a number of light stories and poems. For a time, Lewis worked as the furnace man at Upton Sinclair's Helicon Hall, a socialist communal experiment in Englewood, New Jersey, and then went on to graduate from Yale in 1908. He married writer Grace Hegger and drifted about America for the next few years, writing and selling short stories to popular journals. A prolific writer with an abundant imagination, Lewis even sold ideas for stories to American novelist Jack London during London's final years.

Gaining Popularity and Refusing the Pulitzer Prize
For the most part, Lewis's early short stories and novels reflect what the author termed the "Sauk-Centricities" of his own nature; they are conventional, optimistic, lightly humorous, and were written for a middle-class audience. In 1920 Lewis published *Main Street*, the novel he had long intended to write in revolt against the sentimental myth of the American small town.

Main Street set the stage for the cultural awakening of the 1920s, a fertile decade of experimentation in the arts. To many intellectuals and a rebellious younger generation, Lewis's novel demolished the myth of small-town America as the locus of "true" American values and showed it for what it really was—the epitome of the provincial, art-hating America they were rebelling against, where standardization reigned, dullness was God, and the

Ford car was the acme of civilization. The success of the novel also reflected the postwar reaction against wartime curbs on free speech and the political repression known as the Red Scare, with its anti-union strike-breaking and wholesale deportation of aliens and radicals. Lewis, a self-styled "parlor socialist," blamed the crackdown on the conservative political and business establishments working in league with radical social groups like the Ku Klux Klan, the Fundamentalists, and the local censors to impose "100% Americanism." *Main Street* was a leading voice in the literary protest against what critic H. L. Mencken called Puritanism, denoting the desire to impose a narrow religious morality on the arts.

Readers, part of the new generation fresh from witnessing the mechanized mass-slaughter of World War I, were ready for literature that would reflect its rejection of genteel optimism, blind nationalism, and traditional religion, and it welcomed Lewis's next two novels as it had earlier embraced *Main Street*. Of Lewis's five major satires, *Babbitt* (1922) and *Arrowsmith* (1929) are widely considered his most accomplished works. Widely acclaimed as one of America's most significant voices of the postwar era, Lewis won the 1926 Pulitzer Prize for Fiction for *Arrowsmith*, but he refused to accept the award, claiming that it was intended only for champions of American wholesomeness. Evidence from Lewis's letters suggests that another, less idealistic reason for his refusal was his anger that Edith Wharton's *The Age of Innocence* had been chosen over *Main Street* as winner of the 1921 Pulitzer Prize.

The Preacher and the Prize   He had been planning what he called "the preacher novel" for nearly a decade, but the spark was the 1925 prosecution of John Scopes by the state of Tennessee for teaching his high-school students about the theory of evolution. Much of the nation followed the trial in the press and on the new medium of radio. The exchanges between the two lawyers representing Scopes and the state, Clarence Darrow and William Jennings Bryan, the aging Populist Party hero, encapsulated the theological battle in Protestantism between the Modernists and the Fundamentalists. The former accepted scientific truth and believed that the theory of evolution should be taught in the schools; the latter believed in the literal biblical account of the creation of the world and supported the state ban on teaching the theory. The resulting novel was *Elmer Gantry* (1927), prompting both protest and praise.

A year after the publication of this, generally considered the weakest but most controversial of his five major novels, Lewis, who had divorced his first wife, married the distinguished journalist Dorothy Thompson. Thompson was a major influence on Lewis's work and thought for the rest of his life. In 1930 the couple traveled to Stockholm, where Lewis received the Nobel Prize for his literary achievement. In his now-famous acceptance speech, Lewis blasted the entire American literary tradition up until roughly his own era and then hailed the rising new generation of the nation's writers, praising Ernest Hemingway, John Dos Passos, Thomas Wolfe, and several others. Lewis's own artistic stature had reached its zenith with the appearance in 1929 of *Dodsworth*, a novel in which a harried, disillusioned American business-man seeks peace of mind through travel in Europe. Con-sidered one of the best of Lewis's satires, *Dodsworth* nonetheless marked the end of his preeminence as a major novelist; he never again wrote with the skill and power exhibited in his landmark satires of the 1920s.

Career Decline Critics continue to speculate about the reasons for Lewis's literary decline during the last two decades of his life. Of all the theories offered, from his failure to complete a proposed novel on American labor to the possibility of his having strained to compete pro-fessionally with his wife, it is fairly certain that the Great Depression, the social and economic downturn as a result of the 1929 stock market crash, had the most damaging effect on his talent; for with much of the American mid-dle class jobless and impoverished, Lewis lost both his reading audience and the target of his satiric jibes. During the rest of his career, Lewis periodically lectured, taught university writing courses, contributed book reviews to various magazines, and turned out a succession of rela-tively undistinguished novels. Lewis was living in Italy, where he had just completed *World So Wide* (1951)—a novel that resurrects businessman Sam Dodsworth of the author's earlier work—when he died of heart disease.

Although Lewis's work is not today the subject of extensive critical discussion, in the author's time, he per-formed the role of American gadfly with a power unequalled except by Thomas Paine, Mark Twain, and H. L. Mencken, according to critic Sheldon Norman Greb-stein. His five major satires not only introduced such defin-itive terms as "Main Street" and "Babbittry" into common usage, but they also paved the way for much of the self-critical realistic fiction of mid-century American literature.

Works in Literary Context

Revolt from the Village Historically, Lewis's novel was in the literary current that Carl Van Doren, books editor for *The Nation*, called in 1920 "the revolt from the village." Other writers, such as Edith Wharton and Willa Cather, had scored the provincialism and dying soul of the American small towns. Lewis joined the so-called revolt from the village by denying the myth of the happy, traditional but progressive small town, and later he would reject the notion of the industrialized but enlightened city. Lewis popularized the revolt in the best-seller *Main Street*, where the partly autobiographical novel portrays the frustrations of Carol Kennicott's idealistic crusades to bring elements of liveliness and culture to her new hus-band's home town of Gopher Prairie, Minnesota, an ugly

little settlement populated by an appalling collection of blustering, inarticulate oafs and prying, vicious shrews. Lewis further satirized a tired business culture in *Babbitt*, explored the thwarted idealism of a scientist in *Arrow-smith*, exposed the hypocrisy and commercialism of evan-gelical religion in *Elmer Gantry*, and depicted the confused values of an American businessman in Europe in *Dodsworth*. With the possible exception of *It Can't Happen Here* (1935), none of his later novels and very few of his short stories equal these confrontations with American culture.

Realistic Satire Lewis recreated recognizable ele-ments of American society by mimicking their lifestyles and speech patterns, and did so in order to reveal their shortcomings. He evoked the American social structure, particularly the role of class distinctions, better than most novelists in his time. He brought the American scene to life in readers' imaginations through his storytelling, his gallery of characters and social types, and his vivid record-ing of their talk and their habitats. *Babbitt*, for example, skewers the loud, hypocritical American businessman as well as members of America's public service organizations and booster clubs, with their endless, vapid speeches and inane rituals. *Arrowsmith* tells of the battles of a human-itarian scientist to conduct medical research against the beckoning forces of fame, commercialism, and material comforts. The power of Lewis's satire was in its realistic style; readers could easily identify the social circles to which Lewis refers, and therefore, fully appreciate his larger social commentary.

COMMON HUMAN EXPERIENCE

Lewis is best known for writing contemporary satires that skewered the people and places he knew best. Other famous cultural satires include:

"A Modest Proposal" (1729), an essay by Jonathan Swift. Swift criticizes the Irish government's handling of poverty by suggesting that hungry families eat their own children.

Adventures of Huckleberry Finn (1885), a novel by Mark Twain. Twain satirizes the racism of the deep South through a young boy's supposedly inappropriate friendship with a black slave.

1984 (1949), a novel by George Orwell. Orwell sets his novel thirty years in the future to illustrate the dangers of socialism and anti-individualism.

Mumbo Jumbo (1972), a novel by Ishmael Reed. Reed targets not only white culture but African American culture as well in this sweeping satire of Western concepts of identity, especially in relation to race.

"The Daily Show" (1996–), a Comedy Central television show. Hosted by comedian Jon Stewart, this show takes the format of a news program but satirizes current political headlines.

Works in Critical Context

Lewis was one of the most astute novelistic social observers of his time. He created larger-than-life types and places that entered the language—Babbitt, Elmer Gantry, Main Street. Although a dedicated realist, Lewis used the tools of caricature, irony, and parody to accentuate his criticisms of American society.

Main Street   *Main Street* sold more than 414,000 copies in the original hardcover edition and more than two million in cheaper editions. Widely reviewed and discussed, it was the literary sensation of 1920–1921—one of those books, like Harriet Beecher Stowe's *Uncle Tom's Cabin* (1852), that becomes a social and cultural event. Lewis had touched a sensitive nerve, the moral and cultural divide between urban and rural America. The heroine, Carol Kennicott, reflected the questioning post–World War I mood. People argued either that the book was a libel upon the village or that it was a revelation of the truths about American pettiness and hypocrisy. One way or the other, it gave America "a new image of itself," as Mark Schorer says. Perhaps the largest block of readers consisted of married women who identified with Carol's struggle against the bonds of domestic servitude. The novel sounded a radical feminist note—a call for liberation from the "gray darkness" of domesticity, which stifled women's desire to lead a "more conscious" life.

Babbitt   Reviewers heaped praise on *Babbitt* when it was published in 1922. Virginia Woolf, writing in the London *Saturday Review*, calls the novel "the equal of any novel written in English in the present century." H. L. Mencken, who had encouraged Lewis since *Main Street*, announced that the title character "simply drips with human juices." Mencken writes in the October 1922 *Smart Set* that "There is more than mere humor" in the novel—it "is a social document of a high order." A few commentators complained that Lewis lacked artistic detachment from Babbitt: that he held the same materialistic values and could envision nothing better for his hero or his country. There was some truth to that; Lewis always insisted that he loved Babbitt, that he was a fine fellow. As John O'Hara, one of many younger novelists who admired and emulated Lewis, told biographer Mark Schorer, many writers were aware of Babbitt and Babbittry, but Lewis was the only one to make him live in a novel. Babbitt is a true creation, a composite of American men seen and overheard in hotel lobbies and Rotary Club luncheons.

Responses to Literature

1. Lewis parodied the weaknesses and excesses he saw in his current society. What weaknesses and foibles could be subject of satire today? List a current topic and list ways in which it could be parodied.

2. Lewis's work contrasts the small town and the big city, a dynamic that remains powerful in twenty-first century society. Compare and contrast the stereotypical country person with the stereotypical city person. Research television shows, movies and books that examine or satire this contrast.

3. Lewis uses realistic dialect in his works in order to create recognizable characters and social settings. Choose a passage of Lewis's dialect and rewrite it in standard English; consider the difference between the two versions. How can dialect influence characterization and meaning in literature?

4. Research the Great Depression by reading a book such as *The Great Crash of 1929* (1954, 1997) by John Kenneth Galbraith. Lewis's writings were based on the more prosperous times prior to the Depression. Write a short essay considering how the shift in cultural perspective may have changed the reception of Lewis's work.

BIBLIOGRAPHY

Books

Bloom, Harold, ed. *Sinclair Lewis.* New York: Chelsea House, 1987.

Bucco, Martin, ed. *Critical Essays on Sinclair Lewis.* Boston: G. K. Hall, 1986.

Hilfer, Anthony C. *The Revolt from the Village*. Chapel Hill, N.C.: University of North Carolina Press, 1969.

Lingeman, Richard. *Sinclair Lewis: Rebel from Main Street*. New York: Random House, 2002.

Kazin, Alfred. "The New Realism: Sherwood Anderson and Sinclair Lewis." *On Native Grounds*. New York: Reynal & Hitchcock, 1942, pp. 217–226.

Lundquist, James. *Sinclair Lewis*. New York: Ungar, 1973.

Mencken, H. L. *H. L. Mencken's "Smart Set" Criticism*. Edited by William H. Nolte. Ithaca, N.Y.: Cornell University Press, 1968.

Schorer, Mark. *Sinclair Lewis: An American Life*. New York, Toronto, and London: McGraw-Hill, 1961.

Woolf, Virginia. *The Moment and Other Essays*. New York: Harcourt, 1948.

Periodicals

Manfred, Frederick. "Sinclair Lewis: A Portrait." *American Scholar* 23 (1954): 162–184.

Thompson, Dorothy. "The Boy and Man from Sauk Centre." *Atlantic Monthly* 206 (1960): 39–48.

✸ Alan Lightman

BORN: *1948, Memphis, Tennessee*

NATIONALITY: *American*

GENRE: *Nonfiction, fiction*

MAJOR WORKS:

A Modern-Day Yankee in a Connecticut Court, and Other Essays on Science (1986)

Einstein's Dreams (1993)

The Diagnosis (2000)

Overview

Alan Lightman is a highly respected astrophysicist who writes both science essays and novels. He has successfully published in both fields, with his work in both areas emphasizing the lives of those behind the work of science.

Works in Biographical and Historical Context

Science and Literature Star from the Start   Born to a movie theater owner and a dance instructor, Lightman grew up in Memphis, Tennessee, in the post–World War II economic boom. After the Allies declared victory over the Axis forces in 1945, the U.S. experienced an unprecedented period of relative peace and economic prosperity. During this time, Lightman was in school, excelling in both science and literature. During high school, for instance, he received awards at science fairs and literary

Alan Lightman   *Lightman, Alan, 2000, photograph. AP Images.*

competitions, both on the state level. He went on to study physics at Princeton, and, in 1974, completed his doctorate in theoretical physics at the California Institute of Technology.

Writer of Science, Lay Science, and Fiction   After completing a postdoctoral fellowship at Cornell and serving as a Harvard professor, Lightman began to write in earnest. While maintaining his research in physics and continuing to write poetry, in the 1980s, Lightman also began to publish essays about science for non-science audiences. He was participating in a recently popular discussion about the origins of the universe, made more mainstream after the 1965 discovery of cosmic microwave background radiation. Arno Penzias and Robert Wilson, two Bell lab employees, accidentally discovered the radiation, which presented itself as large background static on a research telescope; the discovery added a key missing piece in the theory of the earth's origins and provided specific evidence for the Big Bang. Audiences were readily interested in Lightman's writings, which made such complex theories concrete for readers with no background in science. The 1990s also saw the development of string theory, a field of theoretical physics that attempts to explain matter formation in the immediate moments after the Big Bang. Lightman's work incorporates these kinds of highly complex scientific ideas in a manner that regular

LITERARY AND HISTORICAL CONTEMPORARIES

Lightman's famous contemporaries include:

Carl Sagan (1934–1996): A popular astronomer, Sagan is best known for his television show *Cosmos*, as well as for his 1980 book by the same name. His PBS show brought scientific subjects to an enormous viewing audience.

Michael Crichton (1942–2008): Best known for groundbreaking techno-thrillers like *Jurassic Park* and the television medical show *ER*, Crichton wrote adventure novels with detailed scientific content. His background was in medicine, earning his medical degree from Harvard.

Bill Gates (1955–): Founder and Chairman of Microsoft Corporation, as well as the originator of much of the technology that made personal computers widely accessible, Gates became one of the richest individuals in the world by the beginning of the twenty-first century. He also established himself as a successful global philanthropist with the founding of the Bill & Melinda Gates Foundation.

Steven Jay Gould (1941–2002): One of the most popular science writers for mainstream readers, Gould was known for works such as *The Panda's Thumb* (1980) as well as for his scientific work in the field of evolutionary biology.

Al Gore (1948–): Vice president during the Clinton administration and presidential candidate in 2000, Gore has also distinguished himself by winning the 2007 Nobel Peace Prize for his efforts to curb global climate change.

readers can access. His work appeared in publications like *The Atlantic Monthly, Smithsonian,* and *The New Yorker.*

In 1993, Lightman ventured into the world of fiction by publishing *Einstein's Dreams,* a story imagining what worlds Albert Einstein, renowned theorist of relativity, might create in his dreams. Critics embraced his work, which Lightman says is influenced by writers Gabriel García Márquez and Jorge Luis Borges. His next novels continued to receive critical attention, establishing Lightman as a significant voice in both literature and science.

Lightman continues to write, and has taught both physics and writing at MIT. He became the first teacher to serve a joint professorship in science and the humanities. He explains, "Ever since I was a young boy, my passions have been divided between science and art. I was fortunate to make a life in both."

Works in Literary Context

Science for Lay Readers   Lightman has established himself as a legitimate scientist, authoring physics textbooks and originating his own scientific discoveries. But, he has dedicated much of his career to connecting theoretical physics to regular human life. In *Time Travel and Papa Joe's Pipe: Essays on the Human Side of Science* (1984), for instance, Lightman discusses astronomy and particle physics. *A Modern-Day Yankee in a Connecticut Court, and Other Essays on Science* (1986) explores both the life of the scientist and the elements of space travel in an enjoyable way. Some of Lightman's science books attempt to convey technical topics, such as astrophysics, while others review science more generally. *Discoveries: Great Breakthroughs in Twentieth-Century Science* (2005), for example, explains major scientific principles from the theory of relativity to the importance to DNA gene sequencing.

Bending Reality   In the tradition of Argentinean writer Jorge Luis Borges, Lightman's fiction imagines new worlds for his characters that do not abide by regular rules for time and space. His novels present days that do not last for twenty-four hours, hours that do not last for sixty minutes, and minutes that last for much longer than sixty seconds. While establishing new rules for temporal and spatial boundaries, Lightman's work could be classified as science fiction. His characters and themes are not overwhelmed or overshadowed by technological advancements; instead, regular lives are altered by Lightman's bending of physical rules in order for epiphanies to occur.

Works in Critical Context

Critics praise Lightman's work, both nonfiction and fiction, for its ability to convey complex theoretical and philosophical ideas in forms that are easily accessible. Lightman's fiction often toys with concepts such as time and memory, with the ultimate goal of illustrating underlying assumptions of human motivation and identity.

Einstein's Dreams   *Einstein's Dreams* became a bestseller and was translated into thirty different languages. Critics enjoyed the fantastic elements of the novel, in which thirty chapters envision different time/space contingencies that lead to various human lifestyles. The science in the stories is only effective, say reviewers, because of the serious statements about humanity that underlie the fantasy. Michiko Kakutani of the *New York Times* explains, "The dreams...have little to do, for the lay reader anyway, with the technicalities of quantum theory and everything to do with the human condition and its time-ridden existence." He continues, "By turns whimsical and meditative, playful and provocative, *Einstein's Dreams* pulls the reader into a dream world like a powerful magnet." Richard Eder of the *Los Angeles Book Review* concurs, citing Lightman's statements about human nature as more profound than his use of science. He writes, "Lightman has done much more than make relativity visible by seeding it with human stories. He makes his human stories more deeply visible by seeding them with relativity."

Responses to Literature

1. Read one of Lightman's science books, like *Discoveries: Great Breakthroughs in Twentieth-Century Science*. What techniques does Lightman use in order to make complex scientific ideas easy to understand? Provide examples from his work to illustrate the different techniques.

2. Compare a set of Lightman's essays with one of his pieces of fiction. How is his nonfiction style similar to and different than his fiction style? Which do you prefer?

3. Choose a topic of your own expertise. Write a short essay in which you explain one aspect of that topic to someone who knows very little about it. Be sure to avoid or explain any jargon associated with the subject, and try to make the topic enjoyable to read.

4. Much of Lightman's work focuses on the scientists who make important discoveries as much as on the discoveries themselves. Choose one scientist who interests you, and research the scientist's life using the library or the Internet. Can you find details in the scientist's life that relate to his or her later work?

BIBLIOGRAPHY

Periodicals

Eder, Richard. "Time and Time Again." *Los Angeles Book Review* (January 10, 1993): 3, 9.

Harville, Jack. "Dark Humor Helps Leaven Stark Horror in *Diagnosis*." *Charlotte Observer* (November 26, 2000): F6.

Interview with Alan Lightman. *Physics Today* (February 1997).

Interview with Alan Lightman. *Washington Post Book World* (April 23, 2000).

Kakutani, Michiko. "Imagining How Time Might Behave Differently." *New York Times* (January 5, 1993): 16.

Seaman, Donna. Review of *Living with the Genie: Essays on Technology and the Quest for Human Mastery*. *Booklist* (December 2003): 638.

Shires, Nancy P. Review of *The Best American Essays 2000*. *Library Journal* (October 1, 2000): 94.

Web sites

The Massachusetts Institute of Technology Online. *MIT Professor: Alan Lightman*. Retrieved November 9, 2008, from http://www.mit.edu/~humanistic/faculty/lightman.html.

COMMON HUMAN EXPERIENCE

Lightman's first novel imagines what a famous scientist might dream. Other works that fictionalize recognizable characters include:

"Mark Twain Tonight!" (1959), a dramatic performance by Hal Holbrook. Comprised of dramatic recitations of Mark Twain's own writings, this performance includes a detailed impression of the American writer by Holbrook, a well-respected actor.

"The Night Thoreau Spent in Jail," (1971) a play by Jerome Lawrence and Robert E. Lee. This play dramatizes the time in which nineteenth-century American writer Henry David Thoreau served in prison for refusing to pay his taxes. Thoreau was protesting the U.S. involvement in a war with Mexico; Lawrence and Lee used this premise as a parallel of American involvement in the Vietnam War.

The Red Tent (1997), a novel by Anita Diamant. The biblical story of Dinah is reimagined as Diamant presents the world of women that surrounded Jacob and the founding of Israel.

Primary Colors (1998), a novel by Joe Klein. A fictionalized account of Bill Clinton's 1992 primary campaign, this book was initially published anonymously because of its scandalous portrayal of Clinton.

The Hours (1998), a novel by Michael Cunningham. Winning the Pulitzer Prize, this novel presents the day that author Virginia Woolf committed suicide, as illuminated by the lives of two other women in two different time periods. The novel was made into a popular film in 2002 starring Nicole Kidman as Woolf.

✸ Abraham Lincoln

BORN: *1809, Hardin County, Kentucky*

DIED: *1865, Washington, D.C.*

NATIONALITY: *American*

GENRE: *Nonfiction*

MAJOR WORKS:

The Emancipation Proclamation (1863)
The Gettysburg Address (1863)
Second Inaugural Address (1865)

Overview

Abraham Lincoln, the sixteenth President of the United States, is best known for leading the Union forces during the American Civil War, and for composing such works as The Gettysburg Address, The Emancipation Proclamation, and the Second Inaugural Address. As a self-educated

Abraham Lincoln   *Lincoln, Abraham, photograph. The Library of Congress.*

ery advocate and would struggle for the rest of his life with the issue of ending slavery in the United States.

Shortly after his trip down the Mississippi, Lincoln enlisted in the Illinois militia, and served in the Blackhawk War of 1832, a conflict between American settlers and the Sauk, Fox, and Kickapoo Indian tribes, led by Chief Black Hawk. The conflict resulted in hundreds of deaths, and ultimately resulted in the collapse of the last organized Native American resistance to white settlement in Illinois.

After returning from the Blackhawk War, Lincoln himself settled into the growing town of New Salem, where he studied law while working as a postmaster. He made an unsuccessful bid for a seat in the Illinois state legislature, but in 1834 he was elected to the state senate, and in 1836 he received his law license. The next year he moved to the state capital, Springfield, hoping to advance both his professional and political careers. His experience as a successful case attorney sharpened his speaking skills and helped him forge useful political connections in the process. Lincoln married Mary Todd in 1842, and raised a family while continuing his prosperous law practice. In 1846 he was elected to the United States House of Representatives, but his opposition to the Mexican War made him unpopular and he was not reelected. The Mexican War, a dispute fought over the territories of Texas, New Mexico, and southern California, allowed the United States to expand its frontiers and gain more resources—a prospect that was very popular to residents of a frontier state like Illinois. After serving his one term in office, Lincoln returned to his law practice.

Lincoln established his practice by trying cases for the emerging railroad industry. In the first half of the nineteenth century, railroads were being constructed throughout the nation, and provided a crucial infrastructure for commerce and travel unprecedented in the young country's history. Lincoln promoted railroad expansion, and argued that the state and federal governments should be lenient to railroad companies in order to encourage their business. He won many of his cases.

Lincoln decided to return to politics when the Kansas-Nebraska Act threatened to continue the expansion of slavery in the newly acquired western territories. The Act nullified the 1820 Missouri Compromise, which had established that new western states would be free states. In response to this development, Lincoln ran for Senate, associating himself with the Republican Party and, although he lost, he retained his position that slavery should be restricted.

Presidency Over a Nation Divided   Lincoln ran a second time for senate in 1858. During the campaign, Lincoln distinguished himself in a series of seven debates, in which he delineated his views on slavery and other important issues of the time. His moderate views made him a popular spokesperson for the Republican Party. He believed slavery should not be extended to new territories

lawyer from Illinois, Lincoln wrote and spoke in a simple, accessible style that emphasized order and balance.

Works in Biographical and Historical Context

From the Frontier to Washington   Abraham Lincoln was born in 1809 in Kentucky and soon afterward moved with his family to Indiana, which in the early nineteenth century was a frontier area with limited settlement and few conveniences. Both of Lincoln's parents were illiterate, and Lincoln himself received less than one year of formal schooling. As a boy, however, Lincoln learned to read and dedicated himself to his own education. Despite his intellectual pursuits, Lincoln spent much of his youth working as a hand on the family farm. In 1830 Lincoln moved with his family to Illinois, where he continued to farm and also worked as a ferryman and store clerk.

At the age of twenty-two, Lincoln left Indiana and ventured down the Mississippi River on a flatboat expedition. This trip broadened his perspective on American life. In particular, it introduced Lincoln to the institution of slavery then present in the Southern states. After this experience, Lincoln would identify himself as an antislav-

but should be allowed to remain where already established. He did not believe that black Americans were equal to whites, but anticipated the end of bondage as a U.S. institution.

Lincoln continued to promote his antislavery views in an America that was increasingly divided between North and South. The Southern states opposed a strong federal government, and desired more state's rights. By 1860, Lincoln's reputation in the Republican Party led to his presidential nomination. He won the election against several candidates, but a number of Southern states had already seceded from the Union by the time Lincoln entered office in March 1861. In his first inaugural address, Lincoln assured the Southern states that their constitutional right to hold slaves would be upheld, but he insisted that the government must retain a large and concentrated federal power. Lincoln's appeals for unity were overruled, however, and soon after taking office Lincoln found himself presiding over the bloodiest conflict in U.S. history, the American Civil War (1861–1865). Lincoln was unwavering in his conviction that Southern states did not have the right to leave the Union.

During the Civil War Lincoln produced the two works for which he is best known: The Gettysburg Address and The Emancipation Proclamation. Lincoln delivered the Gettysburg Address at a memorial service for the soldiers who fought in the Battle of Gettysburg, the largest and bloodiest conflict of the war. This battle, won by Union troops, was the turning point in which the North gained advantage over its Confederate enemies. In Lincoln's famous, three-paragraph eulogy for the fallen, he urged the nation to finish the war it had started and restore the democratic union. During 1863 Lincoln also drafted The Emancipation Proclamation, which freed slaves in the Southern states. Lincoln's views were hotly debated, but thanks in part to additional military victories, his re-election in 1864 was a landslide victory.

In January 1865, Lincoln guided the passage of the Thirteenth Amendment, which outlawed slavery throughout the United States. His Second Inaugural Address encouraged the healing of a wounded country. The war ended shortly thereafter, with Confederate General Robert E. Lee's surrender at Appomattox Court House in April. Less than one week later, Southern sympathizer John Wilkes Booth assassinated Lincoln while he attended a play at Ford's Theater in Washington, D.C. Lincoln's conflicted public image seems to have been saved by his martyrdom, as his presidency is now seen as one of the most significant in the country's history.

Works in Literary Context

Egalitarian Ideology   President Lincoln delivered his most famous speech, the Gettysburg Address, on November 19, 1863, while dedicating a national cemetery on the Gettysburg battlefield. In his speech of only three paragraphs, Lincoln harkened back to the founding principles

---

LITERARY AND HISTORICAL CONTEMPORARIES

Abraham Lincoln's famous contemporaries include:

Ralph Waldo Emerson (1803–1882): The American Romantic writer most famous for his contribution to Transcendentalist philosophy. Emerson is best known for essays such as "Self-Reliance." Throughout his writing career he supported the abolition of slavery and humanitarian rights for Native Americans.

Ulysses S. Grant (1822–1885): The field commander of the United States Army in the later stages of the Civil War. Grant presided over the Union victory at Vicksburg and received the Confederate surrender at Appamatox Court House in 1865. After the war Grant became the eighteenth President of the United States.

Harriet Beecher Stowe (1811–1896): The author of the bestselling antislavery novel *Uncle Tom's Cabin* (1852). Stowe became an international celebrity in the years leading up to the Civil War. According to legend, when Lincoln met Stowe in 1862, he said to her, "So this is the little lady who started this big war!"

Robert Browning (1812–1889): A British poet and playwright. Browning was as well-known for his literary accomplishments as for his famous marriage to fellow poet Elizabeth Barrett.

William Lloyd Garrison (1805–1879): A radical American abolitionist. Garrison led the American antislavery movement with his newspaper, *The Liberator*, and also supported well-known escaped slave and orator Frederick Douglass.

---

of equality that established the United States, and he invoked those same ideals to restore the grieving nation during the Civil War. The site of a significant Union victory that cost both sides dearly, Lincoln called the Gettysburg battlefield "hallowed ground" because of the "brave men, living and dead, who struggled here." Planned only as a set of cursory remarks, Lincoln's short address stood in stark contrast to the primary speaker's talk, which lasted two hours. But Lincoln's address, at once concise and powerfully eloquent, called for the democratic government to have "a new birth of freedom," and he prophesied that the "government of the people, by the people, for the people shall not perish from the earth."

Antislavery Writing   Throughout his life, Lincoln struggled with the issue of slavery. His perspective grew out of a time when Southern states believed it was their sovereign right to use slaves to support their agricultural economy. Abolitionists in the North, however, argued that slavery was immoral. Lincoln believed in a middle ground, but felt that slavery would eventually divide the

COMMON HUMAN EXPERIENCE

Lincoln's Gettysburg Address, which called for the country's reunification at the height of the Civil War, is considered one of the most influential patriotic speeches ever delivered. Other influential political speeches include:

"We Shall Fight Them On the Beaches" (1940), a speech by British Prime Minister Winston Churchill. In this speech, made after the Battle of Dunkirk in World War II, Churchill states, "We shall fight in France . . . we shall fight on the beaches, we shall fight on the landing grounds, we shall fight in the fields and in the streets, we shall fight in the hills; we shall never surrender."

"I Have A Dream"(1963), a speech by Dr. Martin Luther King, Jr. Delivered at the March on Washington during the American civil-rights movement of the 1960s, King called for a new era in American culture where skin color is irrelevant to opportunity and education.

John F. Kennedy's "Inaugural Address" (1961), a speech at Kennedy's inauguration in Washington, D.C. In it, Kennedy called for a new generation of Americans to embrace the democratic legacy of the American Revolution. In his most famous utterance he said, "my fellow Americans, ask not what your country can do for you—ask what you can do for your country."

"Remarks at the Brandenburg Gate" (1987), a speech by Ronald Reagan in West Berlin, Germany. President Reagan made his famous remarks during the end of the Cold War, calling for the Soviet Union to free East Germany. "Mr. Gorbachev," he said, "tear down this wall."

"Out of Many, One" (2004), Barack Obama's keynote address at the Democratic National Convention. The then-senatorial candidate delivered a powerful speech that launched his national political career and set him up to win the presidency in 2008. Obama speaks of hope and change in his address, stating, "there is not a liberal America and a conservative America—there is the United States of America."

nation and thus should be restricted. In particular, Lincoln was a supporter of the Missouri Compromise, a congressional agreement made in 1820 that prohibited the spread of slavery to new western states. When the Missouri Compromise was repealed in the 1850s Lincoln became a spokesperson for the antislavery Republican Party.

However, Lincoln's view that black Americans were not inherently equal to white Americans distinguished him from the most radical of abolitionists. Lincoln announced the Emancipation Proclamation in 1863—which called for the freeing of slaves in rebel states—as both a moral and strategic decision. Not only did it eradicate a practice he believed was wrong, but it created

a domestic crisis for Southerners in that it interfered with the stability of their society and allowed Southern Blacks to enlist in the Union army. Lincoln is often criticized for his reluctance to free slaves in all states, and detractors have argued that the proclamation was made more on military rather than moral grounds. Many historians agree that Lincoln kept his personal struggles with slavery and equality largely secondary to his primary goal of reuniting a divided country.

Works in Critical Context

Though Lincoln's speeches and writings were often criticized by his political opponents, most literary critics praise Lincoln' simple style, which often fused common sense with balanced sentences and paragraphs. Harriet Beecher Stowe, author of the 1852 bestselling antislavery novel *Uncle Tom's Cabin*, reflected that Lincoln's words "have had that relish and smack of the soil, that appeal to the simple human heart and head, which is a greater power in writing than the most artful device or rhetoric."

The Gettysburg Address Upon its delivery in 1863, Lincoln's *Gettysburg Address* was praised for its simple, direct style, and its artful use of repetition and parallel structure. Reviewing the speech, critic James Burrill Angell commented, "It is often said that the hardest thing in the world is to make a five minute speech, but could the most elaborate and splendid oration be more beautiful, more touching, more inspiring than those few words of the President?" Josiah G. Holland found the speech to be "a perfect gem, deep in feeling, compact in thought and expression, and tasteful and elegant in every word and comma."

However, Lincoln's speech also met with criticism. Many Southern newspapers accused Lincoln of delivering the speech in a sanctimonious attitude unbecoming for a memorial service. And even in the North there were detractors. The *Chicago Daily Times* castigated Lincoln for expressing political partisanship in a eulogy and for misrepresenting the cause for which Union soldiers died at Gettysburg. The review of the speech summarized it as "an offensive exhibition of boorishness and vulgarity."

In general, however, the *Gettysburg Address* is accepted as a model of the ideal short speech. Writer Ralph Waldo Emerson, in his eulogy of Lincoln, said that the *Gettysburg Address* "will not easily be surpassed by words on any recorded occasion." In 1980 literary critic James Hurt claimed that "Lincoln's greatest speeches have the kind of resonance that we associate with poetry."

The Emancipation Proclamation The controversial 1863 *Emancipation Proclamation* freed slaves in the states then in rebellion and heightened the stakes and tension of the Civil War. Many critics, particularly in the North, praised Lincoln for taking the opportunity to make an important ethical decision. Ralph Waldo Emerson, for example, believed that the *Emancipation Proclamation* relieved the country of an immense moral burden, and validated the loss of life that the war wrought. Emerson wrote that with the freeing of slaves, "we shall cease to be hypocrites and pretenders, but what we have styled our free institutions shall be such."

Some critics, however, questioned whether the *Emancipation Proclamation* was an outgrowth of military strategy rather than a compassionate moral decision. The London *Times*, for example, wrote that "the North, as a weapon of war, and not as a concession to principle, has finally decided on emancipation. That this measure is no homage to principle or conviction, but merely a means of raising up a domestic enemy against the Southerners in the midst of their Southern states, is abundantly proved from the fact that slavery, so odious in Alabama, is tolerated in Kentucky." The newspaper argued that if Lincoln were truly dedicated to the ethics of abolishing slavery, the *Emancipation Proclamation* would have applied to all states instead of just the rebellious Southern states.

Second Inaugural Address   Critical reception of Lincoln's 1865 Second Inaugural Address varied widely. The Petersburg, Virginia, *Daily Express* found the speech to be "a compound of philanthropy, fanaticism, and scriptural morality." This newspaper, as well as many other Southern papers, took issue with Lincoln's account of the outbreak of the war. These papers argued that Lincoln presented himself as having no alternative but to start the war. Also, they criticized Lincoln for overemphasizing the issue of slavery, and argued that slavery was not the primary concern at the beginning of the war. Other papers, such as *The New York World*, found the speech to be merely "vague and vacillating." The paper criticized Lincoln for the "vacuity in his speech" and postulated that Lincoln had said very little of substance out of fear he would alienate Southerners. The paper argued that the speech communicated the weakness of Lincoln's political position. The London *Spectator*, however, felt differently. They found the articulateness of Lincoln's speech to be evidence of his growing maturity as a statesman, citing that in his Second Inaugural Address "we can detect no longer the rude or illiterate mould of a village lawyer's thought, but find it replaced by a grasp of principle, a dignity of manner, and a solemnity of purpose."

Responses to Literature

1. The Gettysburg Address is considered to be one of the most important short speeches ever delivered. Choose a subject, person, or object that you would like to commemorate, and write a three paragraph speech in the style of The Gettysburg Address. What difficulties did you encounter in composing your speech? Deliver the speech to your class and survey your classmates' reactions.

2. The 1863 Emancipation Proclamation is one of the most controversial documents in American history. Research the debates for and against the document at the time of its composition. Adopting the personas of statesmen of the period, stage a debate in which you reenact the arguments over the document.

3. One of Lincoln's staunchest supporters was Harriet Beecher Stowe, whose influential best-seller *Uncle Tom's Cabin* raised awareness about the practice of slavery and catapulted the abolitionist movement to widespread public notice. Read Stowe's novel and then research its reception during the years leading up to Lincoln's *Emancipation Proclamation*. In what ways did this novel affect the country, in particular the antislavery movement supported by Lincoln?

BIBLIOGRAPHY

Books

Donald, David Herbert. *Lincoln*. New York: Simon & Schuster, 1995.

Emerson, Ralph Waldo. "Abraham Lincoln." *The Complete Essays and Other Writings of Ralph Waldo Emerson*. The Modern Library, 1940, pp. 917–921.

Fehrenbacker, Don E., ed. *Abraham Lincoln: Speeches and Writings 1859—1865. Vol. I and II*. New York: Library of America-Viking Press, 1989.

Mencken, H. L. "Statesmen: Abraham Lincoln." *A Mencken Chrestomathy*. New York: Alfred A. Knopf, 1949, pp. 221–223.

Oates, Stephen B. *With Malice Toward None: The Life of Abraham Lincoln*. New York: Harper, 1977.

Periodicals

Hurt, James. "All the Living and the Dead: Lincoln's Imagery." *American Literature* 52.3 (1980): 351–380.

Web sites

Biography of Abraham Lincoln. The White House Online. Retrieved November 17, 2008, from http://www.whitehouse.gov/history/presidents/al16.html.

✹ Anne Morrow Lindbergh

BORN: *1906, Englewood, New Jersey*

DIED: *2001, Passumpsic, Vermont*

NATIONALITY: *American*

GENRE: *Nonfiction, poetry*

MAJOR WORKS:

North to the Orient (1935)

Gift from the Sea (1955)

Bring Me a Unicorn: Diaries and Letters of Anne Morrow Lindbergh (1972)

Anne Morrow Lindbergh   *Lindbergh, Anne Morrow, photograph. The Library of Congress.*

Overview

Anne Morrow Lindbergh was best known for her essay collection *Gift from the Sea* (1955), for the publication of five volumes of her diaries, and for her role as the wife of the pioneering aviator Charles Lindbergh. Her perceptive records of the dramatic events of her life and of a woman's role in society garnered public attention and critical acclaim.

Works in Biographical and Historical Context

Wealth Produces Comfortable Childhood   Lindbergh was born into a loving family. Her father, Dwight Morrow, was at various times a partner to banker J. P. Morgan, an ambassador, and a U.S. senator. Her mother, Elizabeth Cutter Morrow, was a poet, a trustee of Smith College, and a crusader for equal education for women. The Morrows' wealth and status ensured that their children were well educated and well traveled at an early age. Lindbergh attended Mrs. Chapin's School in New York and then followed in her mother's footsteps by going to Smith College. After a composition professor encouraged her talent for writing, Lindbergh contributed to college publications and published a poem in *Scribner's Magazine*. She met famous pilot Charles Lindbergh in 1928 at

a family Christmas party in Mexico and married him in 1929. Anne learned the skills necessary to serve as Charles's copilot, navigator, and radio operator, and the couple spent most of the early days of their marriage exploring the world through air travel, including a 1931 survey flight to the Orient via the Arctic Circle.

Writing through Tragedy   The hysterical hero-worship that Charles had inspired since his solo New York–Paris flight in 1927 was only intensified by his marriage to Anne and their subsequent adventures together. "To millions around the world...looking at photographs of the 'perfect'-looking couple...the Lindberghs seemed to enjoy the greatest possible good fortune that a young couple could have," writes Alfred Kazin in the *New York Times Book Review*. The image of perfection was completed in 1930 by the birth of their first child, a son named Charles A. Lindbergh III. But on March 1, 1932, the illusion was shattered. That evening, when Anne went upstairs to check the child before retiring, she found his crib empty; the baby had been kidnapped. While Lindbergh had been in the public eye as an ambassador's daughter and as the wife of a well-known aviator, the 1932 kidnapping of her and Charles's first child generated even greater media coverage. The Lindberghs were besieged by reporters, photographers, and state troopers, and over twelve thousand people, including famous mobster Al Capone, offered their assistance. The baby's body was found on May 12, 1932, in a ditch not far from their home.

Following the death of their child, Charles encouraged Lindbergh to write her first book, *North to the Orient* (1935), an account of their 1931 survey flight. To regain some measure of privacy after the 1935 trial of the alleged kidnapper, Bruno Hauptmann, the couple and their second child moved to England and resided in Europe until the outbreak of World War II. Lindbergh detailed her opposition to the war in *The Wave of the Future* (1940), a controversial book that contributed to the Lindberghs' erroneous reputation as Nazi sympathizers. Lindbergh explains how her individualistic husband Charles was an isolationist, believing that the United States should not get involved in stopping the rise of Adolf Hitler. With war fever mounting, isolationism was popularly considered tantamount to treason, and Charles's status quickly earned him the titles of anti-Semite and pro-Nazi. Although Anne only partly agreed with his position, she felt obliged to support it. She published sporadically from 1944 to 1966, during which time she wrote her most significant work, *Gift from the Sea* (1955), and a volume of poetry, *The Unicorn and Other Poems* (1956). Although John Ciardi's scathing review of *The Unicorn and Other Poems* in the *Saturday Review* generated an extensive debate, the book was commercially successful, as were the diaries. Widowed in 1974, Lindbergh had residences in Connecticut and Hawaii as well as Vermont, where she died on February 7, 2001.

Works in Literary Context

Personal Narrative: Diaries and Letters Lindbergh's audience was considerably widened when publication of her diaries began in 1972. The public was eager to read the inside story on the celebrated couple, and the diaries sold briskly. Lindbergh had at first been reluctant to expose her personal papers. An autobiography was considered as a means of preserving Lindbergh's sense of privacy, but it was finally decided that the original journals would be published. She explains her decision in the introduction to *Locked Rooms and Opened Doors: Diaries and Letters, 1932–1935* (1974):

> When one has processed and packaged part of one's life in books, as I have, it is fair to ask, Why not leave it in that form? Why go back to the imperfect raw material of the diaries? Why publish the grimy minutiae of preparing for a trip; the tedium of long hours of work, the reluctant early risings; the exasperations of cold feet and dusty clothes; the irrational night terrors, lost tempers, and depressions? Because, after sixty, I think, one knows the ups and downs that life holds for everyone, and would like—a last chance—to see and present, truthfully and not glamorized, what happened.

Her decision to print the original journals and letters won the approval of readers and reviewers alike. According to Glendy Culligan of the *Saturday Review*, the "letters and diaries [achieve] both spontaneity and art, thanks in part to her style, in part to a built-in plot and a soul-searching heroine worthy of a Brontë novel."

Feminist Writing *Gift from the Sea* is considered an important feminist document from an era during which little if any dissent was voiced regarding the proper role for women in American life. Lindbergh's struggle with maintaining a sense of self while dedicating the majority of her waking hours in service to children, husband, social obligations, and career is a precursor to the public ruminations of women decades later on the trials and tribulations of "having it all." In fact, her husband Charles "pressed her, almost fiercely, to write and was angry when household chores or children intervened," remarks *Washington Post Book World* contributor Katherine Winton Evans. "Almost all our quarrels," wrote Anne in 1941, "arise from this passionate desire to see me freed to fulfill what there is in me."

Works in Critical Context

Despite the fact that Lindbergh was noted for her explorations of the self in relation to society, for her treatment of the diary as a serious literary form, for her historical documentation, and for her feminist themes, her works received relatively little critical attention.

Gift from the Sea *Gift from the Sea* was to become one of Lindbergh's most enduring works, a book that remained in print thirty years after its first edition. It is a

collection of essays with the central theme of "the tremendous and ever-encroaching problem of how to maintain an inner serenity in the midst of the distractions of life, how to remain balanced, no matter what forces tend to pull one off center," as Sara Henderson Hay writes in *Saturday Review*. Each essay takes the form of a meditation on a seashell, and Elizabeth Gray Vining writes in the *New York Times Book Review* that *Gift from the Sea* "is like a shell itself, in its small and perfect form, the delicate spiraling of its thought, the poetry of its color, and its rhythm from the sea, which tells of light and life and love." She also argues against the notion that it should be seen primarily as a book for women: "A sensitive, tensile, original mind probes delicately into questions of balance and relationship in the world today, and the result is a book for human beings who are mature or in search of maturity, whether men or women."

The Unicorn and Other Poems "There are many beautiful lyrics here," praises Robert Hillyer in the *New York Times Book Review* for *The Unicorn and Other Poems*. "The reader will be well rewarded who joins the poet in this garden by the mortal sea whence, from time to time, rifts in the clouds show flashes from immortality." But *Saturday Review* poetry editor John Ciardi's review is in strong disagreement. "As a reviewer not of Mrs. Lindbergh but of her poems I have, in duty, nothing but contempt to offer," Ciardi writes. He goes on to call it "an offensively bad book—inept, jingling, slovenly,

COMMON HUMAN EXPERIENCE

Lindbergh often wrote about the pain of losing her son. Other works that consider the loss of a child include:

Beloved (1987), a novel by Toni Morrison. Memories and magic follow after an ex-slave chooses to kill her own child rather than allow her to live as a slave.

My Girl (1991), a film starring Macaulay Culkin. Two children become friends under difficult circumstances, and one must cope when the other unexpectedly dies.

The Lovely Bones (2002), a novel by Alice Sebold. After a teenage girl is raped and murdered, she watches from the afterlife as her family grieves her loss.

The Memory Keeper's Daughter (2005), a novel by Kim Edwards. When a doctor delivers his own twin children, he secretly sends one child away because she has Down syndrome. The plan unravels as the truth eventually reveals itself.

The Shack (2007), a novel by William P. Young. A father has an unconventional encounter with God after his daughter is murdered by a serial killer.

illiterate even, and puffed up with the foolish afflatus of a stereotyped high-seriousness, that species of esthetic and human failure that will accept any shriek as a true high-C." A month after Ciardi's review appeared, *Saturday Review* editor Norman Cousins reported:

> John Ciardi's review of Anne Morrow Lindbergh's *The Unicorn and Other Poems* has produced the biggest storm of reader protest in the thirty-three-year history of *The Saturday Review*. Hundreds of readers have hastened to tell us of their pointed disapproval of Mr. Ciardi's review; four have written in his support.... There are few living authors who are using the English language more sensitively or with more genuine appeal [than Lindbergh]. There is in her books a respect for human responses to beauty and for the great connections between humankind and nature that gives her work rare distinction and that earns her the gratitude and loyalty of her readers, as the present episode makes clear.

Responses to Literature

1. Research Charles Lindbergh by reading a book like *Charles A. Lindbergh: Lone Eagle* (2006). Write a short biographical essay on the famous aviator.

2. Should diaries be considered literature? Why or why not? Use examples from Lindbergh's diaries to support your argument.

3. Lindbergh's life was largely defined by her son's kidnapping and death. Can you think of other famous figures who have been defined, more or less, by a singular event—heroic, tragic, or otherwise? Do you think the person chooses to be so defined, or does society define them? Can a person "escape" the effects of the big event in their lives?

4. Identify passages from *A Gift from the Sea* that described women's roles in society during Lindbergh's life. Do you think women's lives have changed since then or remained much the same? In what ways?

BIBLIOGRAPHY

Books

Hertog, Susan. *Anne Morrow Lindbergh: Her Life*. New York: Doubleday, 1999.

Periodicals

Ciardi, John. "A Close Look at the Unicorn." *Saturday Review* (January 12, 1957): 54–57.

Cousins, Norman. "John Ciardi and the Readers." *Saturday Review* (February 16, 1957): 22–23.

Culligan, Glendy. Review of *Bring Me a Unicorn: Diaries and Letters of Anne Morrow Lindbergh, 1922–1926*. *Saturday Review* (March 4, 1972): 72–75.

Evans, Katherine Winton. Review of *Gift from the Sea*. *Washington Post Book World* (March 10, 1974).

Hay, Sara Henderson. Review of *Gift from the Sea*. *Saturday Review* (February 2, 1955).

Hillyer, Robert. Review of *The Unicorn and Other Poems, 1935–1955*. *New York Times Book Review* (March 20, 1955).

Kazin, Alfred. "Hour of Gold, Hour of Lead." *New York Times Book Review* (March 4, 1973): 1, 10.

Vining, Elizabeth Gray. "Islands All—In a Common Sea." *New York Times Book Review* (March 20, 1955): 1.

❋ Vachel Lindsay

BORN: *1879, Springfield, Illinois*

DIED: *1931, Springfield, Illinois*

NATIONALITY: *American*

GENRE: *Poetry*

MAJOR WORKS:

General William Booth Enters into Heaven and Other Poems (1913)

The Congo and Other Poems (1914)

Overview

Lindsay was a popular American poet of the early twentieth century who celebrated small-town Midwestern populism in strongly rhythmic poetry designed to be chanted aloud. Lindsay, in fact, gained recognition for his spirited public readings, and his frequently anthologized poems

Vachel Lindsay   *Lindsay, Vachel, photograph. The Library of Congress.*

"General William Booth Enters into Heaven" (1913) and "The Congo" (1914) are notable for their vividness and vigor.

Works in Biographical and Historical Context

Medical Studies Take Second to Drawing, Poetry

Lindsay was born in Springfield, Illinois, in a house designed by the architect of Abraham Lincoln's home, and in a room said to have been one in which Lincoln himself had slept. In this milieu, Lindsay developed a deep-rooted and abiding respect for Lincoln's love of the common people, which later directed the course of his artistic career. The politics of post–Civil War America, however, also shaped his youth. Lindsay later claimed that the Mason-Dixon Line, the boundary dividing the North and the South and representing conflicting sympathies for the Union and Confederate causes, ran through the middle of his heart, through the middle of his home, and through the middle of Springfield, Illinois, his beloved native city.

Lindsay's father, a physician who fully expected his son to assume the duties of his practice, was a humorless and strict disciplinarian. Lindsay's mother, regarded by her neighbors variously as a social climber and an eccen-

tric, was active in the local Campbellite church and in Springfield literary circles. She undertook her children's education until they were old enough to attend public school, and introduced Lindsay and his two sisters to the fine arts, to classic English and Latin authors, and to a wealth of Greek, Roman, and Nordic legends. It was his mother who encouraged Lindsay in his early artistic pursuits, and to whom he turned for approval and support throughout much of his career. While Lindsay wrote poetry as early as childhood, art was his primary passion.

Skill in Poetry Surpasses Skill in Painting

In 1897 Lindsay attended Hiram College, a small liberal-arts school in Ohio, where he showed little aptitude for medical studies, and largely neglected them for personal reading and writing. Despite his parents' advice that he persevere, he abandoned his medical education and, in 1901, enrolled at the Art Institute in Chicago, where the regimen of technical and anatomical studies made him equally unhappy. Lindsay discovered that while drawing gave him pleasure, a structured learning environment did not; he found, furthermore, that his actual artistic abilities, at least within such an environment, were minimal. Convinced that he would progress more rapidly at the New York School of Art, Lindsay enrolled there in 1903 to study painting with William Merritt Chase and his associate, Robert Henri.

When approached by Lindsay to appraise one of his illustrated manuscripts, Henri, who both respected Lindsay and applauded his determination to succeed at painting as much as he doubted the likelihood of its occurring, candidly advised Lindsay to concentrate instead on writing poems, which he found more impressive than Lindsay's pictorial art. After following Henri's advice, Lindsay took his poetry to the New York streets in 1905, and distributed copies of his verse among merchants and passersby for a nominal sum. A year later, Lindsay left the city for what was to be one of several tramping expeditions across the country. On these journeys, he offered a sheet of his verses extolling beauty and democratic ideals in exchange for bed and board.

While Lindsay spent the summer of 1912 on the road, Harriet Monroe, a Chicago poet who was in the process of launching the periodical *Poetry*, published "General William Booth Enters into Heaven." The poem received wide attention and much praise from readers and critics alike, some of whom had previously rejected Lindsay's work summarily. A collection of Lindsay's poetry, headed by "Booth," was published in 1913. Another collection that included "The Congo," a poem inspired both by the poet's fascination with Africa's spiritualism and Joseph Conrad's *Heart of Darkness* (1899), was published the following year. In *General William Booth Enters into Heaven and Other Poems* (1913) and *The Congo and Other Poems* (1914), Lindsay

LITERARY AND HISTORICAL CONTEMPORARIES

Vachel Lindsay's famous contemporaries include:

Theodore Roosevelt (1858–1919): The twenty-sixth president of the United States, Roosevelt was known for his masculine image, his love of the outdoors, and his previous service in the Spanish-American War, when he led a cavalry unit known as the "Rough Riders."

H. L. Mencken (1880–1956): A prominent journalist and critic, Mencken's strong opinions held sway among intellectuals throughout his lifetime.

Sinclair Lewis (1885–1951): A popular American novelist, Lewis was famed for his scathing portrayals of small-town and business life.

W. E. B. Du Bois (1868–1963): An influential African American leader throughout his lifetime, DuBois believed in equal rights, the value of the arts, and the education of the African American community. He helped found the NAACP.

William Butler Yeats (1865–1935): Yeats was an Irish poet known for such works as *The Tower* (1928); he received the 1923 Nobel Prize in Literature.

attempted to reach a more working-class audience than that addressed by other contemporary poets.

Performance Poetry   With the onset of World War I in 1914, which brought new technologies that resulted in trench warfare and massive casualties on many European battlegrounds, the Modernist period of literature was born. This period encouraged an elitist perspective on art, which looked toward poetry and literature for beauty in life rather than toward traditional institutions like the church. Lindsay's work ran counter to Modernism, his view insisting that poetry is most effective when recited, and many of his poems were accompanied by marginal notations governing the specific volume and tone of voice to be used, among other directives. It had also occurred to Lindsay, in observing the overwhelming popularity of vaudeville, that despite his own reservations about this form of entertainment, he might use certain of its elements to better capture his audience's attention.

Lindsay devised pieces, referred to as "poem games," as ritualistic enactments involving dancing and chanting that required audience participation as well as specific players. These performances of "higher vaudeville" formed part of Lindsay's exhausting schedule of popular (and lucrative) public readings. Although at first encouraged by the enthusiastic response of his audiences and by their eager participation in these "poem games," Lindsay soon wearied of incessant public demand to hear "Booth" and "The Congo" to the exclusion of his other work. It also exas-

perated Lindsay that those dramatic elements employed to entice an audience succeeded, as well, in overshadowing the idealistic visions of beauty and democratic virtue underlying his art.

After the appearance of his first three volumes, Lindsay was both acclaimed as the people's poet and caricatured as a vagabond American minstrel. Conscious of the dangers of actually becoming this caricature, Lindsay nevertheless found it impossible to give up the lucrative entertainer's circuit. Although he constantly had ideas for new works, his exacting schedule did not permit him to pursue most of these. While inwardly distressed over the shape his career was assuming, and while he was not a wealthy man, Lindsay did enjoy moderate success for several years.

By the early 1920s, however, his popularity began to wane as widespread, optimistic faith in America's future was supplanted by pessimism bred of World War I, and as traditional small-town values were viewed ever more critically by urban Americans. Disparagement of Lindsay's work became widespread, and shook the poet's faith in himself. The eminent critic H. L. Mencken mockingly wrote of Lindsay that "what was new in him, at the start, was an echo of the barbaric rhythms of the Jubilee songs. But very soon the thing ceased to be a marvel, and of late . . . ceased to be amusing."

In the last years of his life, Lindsay, who had married at forty-five and now had two children, experienced crushing debts, deteriorating health, and periods of unreasoning rage and paranoia that were directed, by turns, at his family, supporters, and a world he perceived as too urbane to embrace his unfashionable philosophies. In 1931, bitter and disappointed, Lindsay poisoned himself. He announced to those attendant on his deathbed: "They tried to get me; I got them first."

Although Lindsay's work is no longer widely read, most commentators find his contribution to American poetry valuable because of his colorful depiction of American ideals and idealists, and his attempt to address certain sectors of society ignored by other artists. Lindsay's poetic legacy is valued for its vivid presentation of distinctly American characters and ideals.

Works in Literary Context

Narrative of the People   Lindsay's benevolent spirit toward people and nature led some critics to call him a modern-day Saint Francis of Assisi. A *New York Times* reviewer states of the 1914 travel journal *Adventures while Preaching the Gospel of Beauty*, "Here is a genuine, rooted love for fields and simple folk . . . all informed by a prophet's realization of beauty. Here is sweetness and serenity and a nice awareness to the unending comedy of life." Reviewers also noted that the book's presentation of nature could restore inspiration to those who were discouraged by the urban experience. V. D. Scudder writes in *Survey*, "This is a book to commend to all social workers who are saddened . . . by city problems." Lindsay's focus on common people led him to write about historical Americans from modest backgrounds, such as Abraham Lincoln and Johnny Appleseed (John Chapman), who went on to achieve greatness.

Performance Poetry Throughout his career Lindsay was known for reciting his poetry with great theatricality. Referring to his performances as "the higher vaudeville," he supplemented his recitations with sound effects such as tambourines and whistles and sometimes appeared in blackface to recite "The Congo." Dennis Camp related that Harriet Monroe, founder and editor of *Poetry* magazine, once warned Lindsay not to "frighten the ladies" with his loud delivery at one poetry reading, to which he replied, "still I must roar." Traditional verse structures made his poems easy to remember, and often his audiences chanted along with him as he performed. Lindsay was credited with helping keep the oral tradition of poetry alive.

Works in Critical Context

Lindsay's considerable loss of reputation in American letters is a continuing theme in critical evaluations published from the 1970s onward. Publications from Lindsay's own era consistently demonstrate that, from the time of his first trade volume, *General William Booth Enters into Heaven and Other Poems* (1913), to the publication of his *Collected Poems* (1923), few if any other American poets could have presented a serious challenge to Lindsay's stature and popularity. That reputation was not based solely on the published poetry: Lindsay performed his poetry in lecture halls across the United States and Canada, and, for a few weeks in 1920, in England as well.

General William Booth Enters into Heaven and Other Poems and The Congo and Other Poems In 1913 *Poetry* magazine featured Lindsay's poem "General William Booth Enters into Heaven," which helped establish his reputation as a serious literary artist. The poem was included in many anthologies and resulted in the first trade publication of Lindsay's poetry, the book *"General William Booth Enters into Heaven," and Other Poems*. The year after this book appeared came another trade volume, *"The Congo" and Other Poems*. One of Lindsay's most famous poems, the title piece has a rhythmic structure based on African American speech rhythms and jazz. Though Lindsay believed jazz was a decadent art form, he used it in his poems to faithfully relate the regional lore of the South. He recited the poem in a variety of voices ranging from a loud, deep bass to a whisper. A *Springfield Republican* reviewer saw the publication of *The Congo* as the single most interesting event in the American literary scene. "All in all there is an intense and vivid Americanism in these poems—a racy, pungent, authentic note, which, if he fulfills the last measure of his [artistic] promise, will make Mr. Lindsay a prophet of American life," the reviewer explained.

COMMON HUMAN EXPERIENCE

Much of Lindsay's poetry was intended for performance. Other works with strong oral-performance potential include:

"The Bells" (1849), a poem by Edgar Allan Poe. Poe's verse often incorporates strong rhyme and repetition. This poem uses a succession of hard consonants to replicate the actual ringing sound of bells.

Leaves of Grass (1855), a collection of poetry by Walt Whitman. The preeminent nineteenth-century American poet Whitman used stream-of-consciousness techniques in his poetry to suggest a spoken-out-loud quality.

"Howl" (1956), a poem by Allen Ginsberg. One of the Beat Poets who valued stream-of-consciousness and performance poetry above standard poetic forms, Ginsberg is remembered for this famous poem that begins, "I saw the best minds of my generation destroyed by madness."

Red Beans (1991), a collection of poetry by Victor Hernandez Cruz. An American poet of Puerto Rican descent, Cruz's poems combine Spanish and English, popularly called Spanglish, to capture speech patterns of his native Harlem. His work also incorporate musical rhythms and beats.

Uncle Remus: The Complete Tales (1999), a collection of stories by Julius Lester. Updating Joel Chandler Harris's classic versions of African American folktales, Lester retells the famous stories about Uncle Remus and Brer Rabbit, incorporating dialect and natural speech patterns.

Responses to Literature

1. Lindsay was extremely popular during his lifetime, but he has fallen out of favor since his death. Why do you think his work does not appeal to modern audiences? Describe specific elements of style and topic that may not connect with today's readers. Why do you think he was so popular during his time?

2. Lindsay wrote regionally based poetry, including specific accents and elements of local culture. How would you describe an important place in your life? In that place, how do people speak, what do they eat, what rituals or celebrations do they have? How are they different than people in other places? Write an essay or poem that illustrates these specific qualities.

3. Read one of Lindsay's poems silently to yourself, then read it out loud. Imagine how Lindsay would have performed his poems, with accents and specific emphases. What differences do you notice between reading the poem and hearing it? How does Lindsay create meaning through performance of his poems?

4. Lindsay created pictures to accompany many of his pieces of writing. Examine several of these images, and the writing they illustrate. Describe how the images speak to the writings. Do the pictures match the images you have in your head from the writing, or are they different? Why do you think Lindsay chose to illustrate his writings the way he did?

BIBLIOGRAPHY

Books

Flanagan, John T., ed. *Profile of Vachel Lindsay.* Columbus, Ohio: Merill, 1970.

Harris, Mark. *City of Discontent: An Interpretive Biography of Vachel Lindsay.* New York: Bobbs-Merrill, 1952.

Massa, Ann. *Vachel Lindsay: Fieldworker for the American Dream.* Bloomington, Ind.: Indiana University Press, 1970.

Masters, Edgar Lee. *Vachel Lindsay: A Poet in America.* New York: Scribners, 1935.

Mencken, H. L. *Vachel Lindsay: The True Voice of Middle America.* Washington, D.C., 1947.

Wolfe, Glenn Joseph. *Vachel Lindsay: The Poet as Film Theorist.* New York: Arno, 1973.

Periodicals

Review of "The Congo." *Springfield Republican* (October 15, 1914): 5.

Ward, John Chapman. "Vachel Lindsay I 'Lying Low.'" *College Literature* 12 (1985): 233–244.

✦ Robert Lipsyte

BORN: *1938, New York City*

NATIONALITY: *American*

GENRE: *Fiction, nonfiction*

MAJOR WORKS:

The Contender (1967)

SportsWorld: An American Dreamland (1975)

One Fat Summer (1977)

In the Country of Illness: Comfort and Advice for the Journey (1998)

Overview

Robert Lipsyte was for many years a sportswriter for the *New York Times*. He has also written several well-regarded novels for young adult readers, often utilizing sports as subject or background. Lipsyte is recognized as an insightful author who combines enthusiasm for sports with a perceptive awareness of social issues, including the problematic role of sports in American culture. He has also published nonfiction works including biographies, social criticism, history, and memoir.

Robert Lipsyte. *Courtesy of the author*

Works in Biographical and Historical Context

From Copy Boy to Sportswriter Robert Lipsyte was born January 16, 1938, in New York City, and grew up in Rego Park, Queens. His father was a school principal, his mother a teacher and guidance counselor; in the intellectual environment of his home, he read a lot and was not athletically inclined. He was overweight in his pre-teen years, and as he puts it in an autobiographical sketch, "[I] started writing so I could make up stories in which thin kids died horribly." The effort he undertook to lose weight became, later, the source of his novel *One Fat Summer* (1977).

In 1957 Lipsyte received an undergraduate degree in English from Columbia University in New York and planned to attend graduate school. A summer job as night-time copy boy for the *New York Times* sports department led him into a journalistic career. Lipsyte opted to stay and eventually rose from gofer to cub reporter. He earned his first major assignment in 1962, covering the New York Mets' first year in the National League. The expansion team's woeful performance gave him an opportunity to put a colorful stamp on his reporting. In his story on the team's very first spring training game, he talked of an older fan who left in disgust when the Mets fell behind, saying, "Same old Mets!"

Lipsyte's refreshing style and sharp insights made him a standout at the *Times*, and because of the paper's influential status, he soon gained national attention. He later wrote that the 1960s was an especially fruitful period for breaking into sports journalism. The spread of televised sports meant that print reporters had to go beyond summarizing games and provide more detailed information as well as opinion. In addition, the social conflicts of the 1960s, from the civil rights movement to the Vietnam War, profoundly influenced athletics as well as the wider culture. Lipsyte courted controversy by infusing social issues into his sportswriting, reporting about athletes' off-field troubles.

The Champ and The Contender   On the boxing beat, he took interest in a rising heavyweight named Cassius Clay, who converted to the Nation of Islam and changed his name to Muhammad Ali after winning the world title in 1964. Lipsyte defended the fighter, although much of the press corps refused to call him by his new name. In 1967, when Ali refused to serve in Vietnam, Lipsyte was again sympathetic. He later wrote a biography of the charismatic champion, called *Free to Be Muhammad Ali* (1978).

Lipsyte drew upon his experiences as a boxing writer to produce his first novel for young readers, *The Contender* (1967). The book chronicles the metamorphosis of seventeen-year-old Alfred Brooks from an aimless orphan in Harlem to a disciplined young man. He achieves this change by applying principles he learns in training to be a boxer. His trainer, Donatelli, insists, "Everybody wants to be a champion. That's not enough. You have to start by wanting to be a contender.... It's the climbing that makes the man." Alfred does not realize his boxing goals, but his inner resolve helps him form long-term plans to serve his community. As a white author writing about the black experience at a time when such topics rarely appeared in juvenile literature, Lipsyte is credited with vividly describing ghetto life and the boxing world.

Jock Culture   Soon after *The Contender* was published, Lipsyte became a sports columnist for the *Times*. His columns became a vehicle for pointed observations about the intersection of sports and society, with particular skepticism about the role of journalism and the media. For his 1970 book *Assignment: Sports*, he selected and edited his *Times* columns for a younger audience. In a companion volume, *SportsWorld: An American Dreamland* (1975), Lipsyte explores his disillusionment with the impact of sports on young people—for example, the sense of inadequacy normal kids feel when they cannot compete with star athletes and the unhealthy emphasis on winning among coaches and parents. Lipsyte has continued to critique what he calls "jock culture" in fiction as well as essays.

Lipsyte wrote his second young adult novel, *One Fat Summer* (1977), to contend with the pain of his youth and with the summer when he lost forty pounds. He

LITERARY AND HISTORICAL CONTEMPORARIES

Lipsyte's famous contemporaries include:

Robert Kimmel Smith (1930–): Smith is an American novelist for children and adults; he is the author of *Chocolate Fever* (1972) and *Bobby Baseball* (1991).

Joan Didion (1934–): An American journalist, essayist, novelist, and screenwriter, Didion recently wrote a memoir, *The Year of Magical Thinking* (2005), about losing her husband and daughter.

David Halberstam (1934–2007): Halberstam was an American journalist who rose to fame with his reportage of the Vietnam War, and later wrote several books about sports.

Judy Blume (1938–): Blume is an American novelist whose frank depictions of teenage life revitalized the genre of young adult literature; she is the author of *Are You There God? It's Me, Margaret.* (1970) and *Forever* (1975).

Muhammad Ali (1942–): Ali is an American heavyweight boxing champion; many agree with his boast that he was "the greatest of all time."

S. E. Hinton (1948–): An American novelist for young adults, Hinton is the author of several famous works in the genre such as *The Outsiders* (1967).

followed it up with two sequels, *Summer Rules* (1981) and *The Summerboy* (1982), also set in the 1950s and narrated by Bobby Marks, an overweight youngster with a wise mouth, a vivid imagination, and a confidence problem. The novels take Bobby from the ages of fourteen to eighteen and demonstrate how Bobby becomes a thin, independent young man who is unafraid to stand up for what he believes.

Lipsyte was forced to battle his own problems beginning in 1978, when he was diagnosed with testicular cancer. After surgery and chemotherapy, he recovered and returned to an active life. His next book for young adults, *Jock and Jill* (1982), tackles tough topics such as the use of drugs in athletics, gangs, inner-city housing advocacy, and conflicting ethical responsibilities. Following its publication, Lipsyte began another career—in television news. He worked as a correspondent for the program "CBS Sunday Morning," then for NBC. He won an Emmy award in 1990 for hosting the nightly public affairs show "The Eleventh Hour" on New York's public broadcasting station, WNET. In 1991 he returned to the *New York Times* after a twenty-year absence to write two columns, one for the sports section and one for the city section.

Later Career   After two decades fielding young people's questions about Alfred Brooks from *The Contender*,

COMMON HUMAN EXPERIENCE

Lipsyte specializes in telling sports stories that also explore social issues off the field. His writing is in the big leagues of American sports literature, along with these works:

The Natural (1952), a novel by Bernard Malamud. A baseball star returns to the limelight fifteen years after being shot in this dark meditation on heroism.

Bang the Drum Slowly (1956), a novel by Mark Harris. Henry Wiggen, a star pitcher for the New York Mammoths, helps his teammate Bruce Pearson conceal that he is dying of Hodgkin's disease in this touching novel.

Ball Four (1970), a memoir by Jim Bouton. New York Yankee pitcher Bouton blew the cover off baseball myths with this memoir of a major-league season, and the baseball world never forgave him for it.

Shoeless Joe (1982), a novel by W. P. Kinsella. A man hears a voice telling him to turn his cornfield into a baseball diamond. This novel was made into the well-known film *Field of Dreams* (1989).

Eight Men Out (1988), a film written and directed by John Sayles, based on the 1963 book by Eliot Asinof. This period film dramatizes the famous Black Sox baseball scandal of 1919, in which eight Chicago White Sox players intentionally threw the World Series.

Lipsyte decided to pick up the character's story. In *The Brave* (1991), Sonny Bear, a seventeen-year-old half-Indian runaway, meets Brooks, now a forty-year-old New York City police sergeant. Sonny Bear becomes a boxing contender in *The Chief* (1993). *Warrior Angel* (2003) completes the *Contender* quartet.

Robert Lipsyte has continued to distinguish himself in numerous genres of prose. His memoir *In the Country of Illness: Comfort and Advice for the Journey* (1998) sensitively chronicles both his own and his wife's battles with cancer. He has written a series of sports biographies and delved into the history of the American national pastime with *Heroes of Baseball* (2006). The young adult novel *Raiders Night* (2006) looks unflinchingly at the dark side of high school football, including the brutality of hazing rituals and the complicity of adults in covering up their damaging consequences. At age sixty-nine, Lipsyte still connects to teenage readers, and his depictions of jock culture remain penetrating and enlightening.

Works in Literary Context

Young Adult Fiction Lipsyte is widely admired for his novels for adolescent, or young adult, readers. The young adult (or, in literary lingo, "YA") genre is of relatively recent vintage, although such outstanding novels as *Great Expectations* (1860) by Charles Dickens and *The Adventures of Huckleberry Finn* (1884) by Mark Twain feature adolescent protagonists and appeal to that age group. J. D. Salinger's *The Catcher in the Rye* (1951) helped to shape modern young-adult fiction with its troubled hero and edgy subject matter. Contemporary YA authors, such as Robert Cormier, Judy Blume, and Walter Dean Myers, unflinchingly confront serious issues in their novels, issues that teenagers must grapple with in their lives, such as sex, drugs, dangerous behavior, and death. Like his peers, Lipsyte writes about teenage characters facing challenging ethical quandaries, and in so doing, they take steps toward maturity, self-knowledge, and self-esteem.

The Literature of Sport In *The Contender*, Lipsyte presents sports involvement as a form of discipline that will help his protagonist survive and be productive in his environment. This orientation—and the gritty realism that invariably characterizes his portrayal of athletics—makes Lipsyte an exception to the norm of sports storytelling. He is not content merely to tell the story of the game. Nor is he willing to accept the traditional myths of sports, such as that hard-nosed discipline leads inevitably to triumph. His perspective treats the athletic world skeptically and studies it as a source of more complex issues, such as the cultural implications of steroid use and hazing rituals in high school football.

Works in Critical Context

Critics have commended Lipsyte's efforts to portray real and fictional personalities with reverence for their depth and complexity. Lipsyte twice received Columbia University's Meyer Berger Award for Distinguished Reporting, in 1966 (for his sportswriting) and 1996 (for his columns in the *New York Times* city section). In 2001 the American Library Association gave Lipsyte its Margaret A. Edwards Award for lifetime achievement in young adult literature. Teenagers who are attracted to Lipsyte's books often enjoy his descriptions of athletic life as well as his strong characterizations and insights into human nature.

SportsWorld: An American Dreamland and Raiders Night Lipsyte has been criticized, however, for being overly moralistic when reflecting on the evils of society. This tendency is most evident in his commentaries and in the book *SportsWorld: An American Dreamland* (1975), a work of social criticism. This book prompted some reviewers to categorize Lipsyte as a disenchanted writer harboring an intense dislike of sports. Baseball writer Roger Kahn, writing in the *New York Times Book Review*, finds that "*SportsWorld* lacks a sense of joy." On the other hand, in *Newsweek*, Paul D. Zimmerman deems the book "a persuasive volume of dissent." Readers sensitive to Lipsyte's political orientation may be more inclined to accept his sometimes grim conclusions. On the Web site Political Affairs, Dave Zirin calls *Raiders Night* "a book that manages to capture both the seductive adrenaline of sports and the rot beneath the surface." Zirin concludes: "This is the best fictional critique of the athletic industrial complex I've ever read."

Responses to Literature

1. Summarize the picture Lipsyte paints of "jock culture" in *SportsWorld* or in his recent essays. Do you agree with his points? Why or why not?

2. Lipsyte has said that sports biographies for young readers "are really the junk food of publishing"—largely phony stories that perpetuate simplistic myths of success. Yet he himself has written biographies of Muhammad Ali, Jim Thorpe, Michael Jordan, and other athletes. What characteristics, if any, do you think set his works apart from the typical sports biographies?

3. Citing one or more of his novels, evaluate Robert Lipsyte's approach to the young-adult genre. What techniques does he use to relate to young readers? Are these techniques successful?

BIBLIOGRAPHY

Books

Cart, Michael. *Presenting Robert Lipsyte*. New York: Twayne, 1995.

Donelson, Kenneth L., and Alleen Pace Nilsen, eds. *Literature for Today's Young Adults*. Glenview, Ill.: Scott Foresman, 1980.

Scales, Pat. *A Teacher's Resource to Robert Lipsyte*. New York: HarperCollins Children's Books, 1992.

Periodicals

Forman, Jack. Review of *The Chief*. School Library Journal (August 1993): 186.

Miles, Betty. "Robert Lipsyte on Kids/Sports/Books." *Children's Literature in Education* (Spring 1980).

Simmons, John S. "Lipsyte's *Contender*: Another Look at the Junior Novel." *Elementary English* (January 1972): 117.

Watkins, Mel. Review of *Free to Be Muhammad Ali*. *New York Times Book Review* (March 4, 1979): 32.

Web sites

"Robert Lipsyte." Personal home page. Retrieved November 6, 2008, from http://www.robertlipsyte.com.

Zirin, Dave. "*Raider's Night*: Reclaiming Sports as True Fiction." Originally published July 17, 2007. Retrieved November 8, 2008, from http://www.politicalaffairs.net/article/articleview/5585.

■ Malcolm Little

SEE   *Malcolm X*

✱ Jack London

BORN: *1876, San Francisco, California*

DIED: *1916, Glen Ellen, California*

NATIONALITY: *American*

GENRE: *Fiction, nonfiction*

MAJOR WORKS:
The Call of the Wild (1903)
The Sea-Wolf (1904)
White Fang (1906)

Overview

Jack London is recognized as one of the most dynamic figures in American literature. London captured the popular imagination worldwide through his personal exploits as well as through his literary efforts, and his life as a sailor, social crusader, war correspondent, global traveler, and adventurer are legendary. Yet, it is his work of adventure fiction and pioneering literature of social protest that have won him a permanent place in American literature

Jack London   *London, Jack, photograph. The Library of Congress.*

and distinguished him as one of the most widely translated American authors.

Works in Biographical and Historical Context

Unstable Beginnings John Griffith Chaney was born on January 12, 1876, in San Francisco, California. He was the illegitimate child of Flora Wellman, a spiritualist, and her companion William Henry Chaney, a professional astrologer who abandoned Flora when he learned she was pregnant. Flora married John London in September of 1876, and renamed her child John "Jack" London. The couple moved to Oakland, where John London struggled to make a living at various occupations, including farming and managing a grocery store.

London's childhood was financially and emotionally unstable. The family moved frequently from one rented house to another, and London compensated for his loneliness by finding companionship in books. In 1885, London discovered that he could check out books from the Oakland Public Library, an important discovery for a young man longing for escape. London later observed, "It was this world of books, now accessible, that practically gave me the basis of my education." Starting in grade school, London was called upon to help provide for the family. At first the work was part-time: delivering newspapers, setting pins in a bowling alley, sweeping saloon floors, and doing whatever odd jobs would bring a few extra pennies into the family budget. When he finished grade school in 1889, London went to work full-time in a cannery, spending as many as eighteen hours a day at ten cents an hour stuffing pickles into jars. It was a traumatic ordeal, and it impressed upon him a lifelong loathing of manual labor.

An Unquenchable Thirst for Escape The pattern of London's life, reflected in much of his fiction, is a series of escapes—first from the drudgery of poverty, later from the monotony of work. At the age of fifteen, he borrowed money to buy a sloop, a small sailing ship, and achieved notoriety on the Oakland waterfront as "Prince of the Oyster Pirates" by raiding commercial oyster beds. After a year of this dangerous occupation, London switched sides to become a member of the California Fish Patrol. His maritime adventures continued into the next year when, a few days after his seventeenth birthday, he shipped out as a seaman aboard a sealing schooner bound for the northwest Pacific. This seven-month voyage provided the raw materials not only for his novel *The Sea-Wolf* but also for his first successful literary effort: "Story of a Typhoon off the Coast of Japan," a prize-winning sketch published in the *San Francisco Morning Call* in 1893.

Subsequent experiences that winter working in a jute mill—which processed the material used to make burlap—and at the power plant of the Oakland Electric Railway intensified London's wanderlust. At first, London rode with the West Coast contingent of Coxey's Industrial Army, a group of unemployed men who went to Washington to petition Congress for relief following the Panic of 1893, a period of economic crisis marked by massive bank failures. After deserting this army in Missouri, London hoboed northeast on his own. Arrested for vagrancy in New York in June of 1894, he served thirty days in jail, then headed back home to Oakland, determined to educate himself. London's tramping experiences, later recounted in *The Road* (1907), were profoundly influential in shaping his career.

London's series of low-wage jobs quickly taught him the vices of American capitalism, which he viewed as a demeaning caste system. When London was twenty, he joined the Socialist Labor Party and became a political activist, achieving a certain notoriety as the "Boy Socialist" of Oakland. London's essay "How I Became a Socialist" in *War of the Classes: Socialist Essays*, published in 1905, describes his conversion to socialism as the result of intense reading and reflecting on his own personal experiences. London's life experiences helped fuel his desire to be a writer. When he returned to Oakland, he studied intensely to prepare himself for college, and published six stories, three descriptive sketches, and one essay in his school's student literary magazine. After three semesters in high school, London successfully passed the entrance examinations for the University of California, Berkeley, where he studied for one semester. Because of a lack of funds, however, he had to leave. London tried unsuccessfully to earn money by writing but was forced to get a job as a common laborer once again. His next escape came in July of 1897, when London sailed for Alaska with his brother-in-law to take part in the Klondike Gold Rush.

Finding His Voice, Beginning His Career London's experience in the Klondike was the turning point in his career. "It was in the Klondike that I found myself," London later confessed. Forced by an attack of scurvy to return home the next summer, he took back no gold, but a wealth of experiences that his artistic genius then translated into fiction. The year 1898 was for London a time of furiously intense work and a remarkable outpouring of creative energy, subsequently documented in his autobiographical novel *Martin Eden* (1909). By January 1899, he had broken into print in the *Overland Monthly*; within a year his work was appearing in the most prestigious magazines in the country; and in the spring of 1900 his first book, *The Son of the Wolf: Tales of the Far North* was published by a highly respected Boston publishing house. The same year, London also married Bessie Maddern. London and Bessie became the parents of two daughters: Joan, born in 1901, and Bess "Becky," in 1902.

The Son of the Wolf was an immediate success, and became the first volume of London's Northland Saga, a sprawling literary achievement. The Saga included seventy-eight short stories, four novels—including *The Call of the Wild* and *White Fang*, a half-dozen nonfiction essays, and one play. Written during the winter of 1902–1903, *The Call of the Wild* has become one of the great books in world literature, published in hundreds of editions in more than fifty languages. The novel is the heroic journey of Buck, who is transformed from a ranch pet into the Ghost Dog of the Wilderness. An adventure novel, *The Call of the Wild* is also a sophisticated allegory of human nature.

While London had found the key to literary success in his Northland Saga, he was still searching for the key to domestic happiness during the years between the publication of *The Son of the Wolf* and *The Call of the Wild*. During this time, London went to England, presumably en route to South Africa to report on the aftermath of the Boer War for the American Press Association. That assignment was canceled, however, and he reported, instead, on the aftermath of the Industrial Revolution that he found in the London slums. The result was *The People of the Abyss* (1903), a pioneering work of creative nonfiction that championed social-justice issues. London returned home from Europe in November 1902, shortly after the birth of his second daughter, hoping to make his marriage work. But despite his efforts it was increasingly obvious that he and Bessie could not live happily together. In May 1903 he took his family to Glen Ellen, California, and that summer he fell in love with Clara Charmian Kittredge. He left Bessie shortly afterward, and moved into an Oakland apartment, where he completed his novel *The Sea-Wolf*, which became one of his most successful books.

A Life of Adventure and Writing   In the spring of 1905, after his unsuccessful campaign for mayor of Oakland on the Socialist ticket, he took up permanent residence with Charmian Kittredge and purchased Hill Ranch, near Glen Ellen. Now happily engaged, they would be married in 1905 as soon as London's divorce became final. During those months he produced some of his best fiction, including what many critics consider the most artistically successful of his longer novels, *White Fang*, a gripping tale of survival and the power of the environment.

London then embarked on the most publicized of all of his adventures: an attempt to circumnavigate the globe on his own boat, the *Snark*. London carefully planned the construction of the boat, but due in part to the San Francisco earthquake of 1906, it was so poorly built it required extensive repair when it reached Hawaii in 1907. London, suffering from several ailments, ultimately called off the voyage in Australia. The journey became the inspiration for London's nonfiction book, *The Cruise of the Snark* (1911). After this disastrous journey, London focused on building up his ranch in Sonoma Valley, publishing several works that reflected his agrarian interests, including *Burning Daylight* (1911). His interest in socialism also began to wane, and he envisioned less violent solutions to modern man's woes than social revolution.

In the last few years of his life, London suffered from severe health problems and sailed to Hawaii twice in

1915, in the hope of regaining his strength. That same year he published *The Star Rover*, his last great work. It is a science-fiction novel concerning the out-of-body experiences of an intelligent man and convicted murderer, Professor Darrell Standing, who is straitjacketed in San Quentin prison. London died at the age of forty on November 22, 1916, probably from kidney failure. He had achieved an astounding career in just fifteen years as a writer and public figure, becoming the first American author to earn one million dollars from his writing. More importantly, he had become a true literary craftsman, and the best-selling American writer in the world.

Works in Literary Context

Naturalism   London's works are an example of American literary naturalism. The naturalist movement began in the late nineteenth century as an extension of realism, which was concerned with depicting contemporary life and behavior in an authentic, realistic way. By contrast, naturalism was concerned with exploring the social and environmental forces that determined individuals' lives and their behavior. Many naturalistic works focused on exposing the social and environmental inequities that contributed to the harshness of people's lives. In much of London's work, an individual leaves behind the problems of urban life to determine his worth in a natural or primitive environment. Although its hero is a dog, *The Call of the Wild* epitomizes much of the subject matter and style of naturalistic fiction due to its storyline about a domestic dog who must adapt to conditions of the wild.

COMMON HUMAN EXPERIENCE

While his animal stories are powerful on a more literal level, London is widely recognized for employing animals allegorically in *The Call of the Wild* and *White Fang* to explore unconscious human instincts. Here are some other works that utilize animal allegories to explore abstract concepts or issues:

Aesop's Fables (c. sixth century BCE), a collection of stories attributed to Greek storyteller Aesop. *Aesop's Fables* are a commonly recognized set of simplistic moral allegories featuring animals. These tales include the well-known *The Tortoise and the Hare* and *The Fox and the Grapes*.

The Wind in the Willows (1908), a children's novel by Kenneth Grahame. This is a British allegorical tale for children about a group of animals in the Wild Wood.

Flush: A Biography (1933), a novel by Virginia Woolf. An allegory told from the point of view of Elizabeth Barrett Browning's dog, this novel is a comical exploration of Victorian class and gender issues.

Animal Farm (1945), a novel by George Orwell. One of the most critically acclaimed novels of all time, *Animal Farm* employs a cast of farm animals to critique Stalinism.

Firmin: Adventures of a Metropolitan Lowlife (2006), a novel by Sam Savage. The story of Firmin, a rat living in a secondhand bookstore in Boston, this novel is an allegory about the changing urban environment.

Adventure Writing London's work was enormously influential on the expansion of the American tradition of adventure writing, a literary genre that crosses over both fiction and nonfiction. London's contribution to the genre took the form of both short stories, many of which were published in magazines and journals, as well as novels. The subject of adventure writing generally involves richly drawn characters who embark on travel or journeys and are often pitted against nature. London's short story of survival in the wilderness, "To Build a Fire" (1908), is often considered one of the greatest adventure stories ever written.

Works in Critical Context

Although London was an enormously popular and commercially successful writer, his reputation as an author was negligible among critics and members of the literary establishment for many years. As a result, many of his works, including *The Call of the Wild*, *The Sea-Wolf*, and *White Fang* were considered merely works of adventure fiction and relegated to young-adult fiction shelves until the latter half of the twentieth century. Since then, London's work has steadily gained critical recognition for its literary artistry and philosophical depth. Critic Earle Labor concludes that London's greatest achievement is his "artistic modulation of universal dreams."

The Call of the Wild Widely considered a lively, engaging story about the relationship and struggle between civilization and barbarism, *The Call of the Wild* is widely recognized as one of London's best works. Although critics have disagreed about how consciously London applied allegory to his very literal story of Buck, most agree that *The Call of the Wild* is both fascinating as a type of autobiography and as a compelling articulation of London's exploration of human instincts. Critic and novelist Abraham Rothberg writes, "A study of atavism, or reversion to type, it was also an allegory of man's conditions in the society of London's time as well as a revelation of the deepest emotions London felt about himself and that society." Critic Jonathan H. Spinner further appraises the social and symbolic importance of violence in the novel, concluding, "What is presented by London is a syllabus for the twentieth century, a syllabus that states that the way to solve the dilemma of existence in a harsh world is to accept the glory in the cleansing fire of violence."

The Sea-Wolf *The Sea-Wolf* is a novel that charts the transformation of an educated, literary man named Humphrey van Weydon into a rugged individualist who is capable of self-sufficiency aboard a sailing schooner captained by a the colorful character of Wolf Larsen. Critics agree that the novel is a lively engagement with many of the social issues that preoccupied London. James Dickey writes that London "created his most memorable human character, Wolf Larsen, in *The Sea-Wolf*. Larsen exemplifies all of the characteristics London admired most: courage, resourcefulness, ruthlessness, and above all, a strength of will."

Responses to Literature

1. Compare Buck's relationship with Thornton to his relationship with his old master, Judge Miller, in *The Call of the Wild*. How are they different? What is the significance of the difference?

2. In the short story "To Build a Fire," what does the man's inability to build a fire symbolize?

3. How does White Fang perceive humans in the novel *White Fang*? What is the significance of how he perceives people?

4. Choose and read a work of fiction by London. How does the author apply the philosophies of naturalism to the main character in the work? Provide specific details from the work to support your statements.

BIBLIOGRAPHY

Books

Cassuto, Leonard and Reesman, Jeanne Campbell. *Rereading Jack London*. Stanford, Calif.: Stanford University Press, 1996.

Dickey, James. *Introduction to The Call of the Wild, White Fang, and Other Stories by Jack London.* New York: Penguin Books, 1981, pp. 7–16.

Hedrick, Joan D. *Solitary Comrade: Jack London and His Work.* Chapel Hill, N.C.: University of North Carolina Press, 1982.

Johnston, Carolyn. *Jack London: An American Radical?* Westport, Conn.: Greenwood Press, 1984.

Labor, Earle. *Jack London.* New York: Twayne, 1974.

Nuernberg, Susan M., ed. *The Critical Response to Jack London.* Westport, Conn.: Greenwood Press, 1995.

Rothberg, Abraham. *Introduction to The Call of the Wild and White Fang by Jack London.* New York: Bantam Books, 1963, pp. 1–17.

Sinclair, Andrew. *Jack: A Biography of Jack London.* New York: Harper & Row, 1977.

Walker, Dale L. *The Alien Worlds of Jack London.* Grand Rapids, Mich.: Wolf House, 1973.

Periodicals

Spinner, Jonathan H. "A Syllabus for the 20th Century: Jack London's *The Call of the Wild.*" *Jack London Newsletter* vol. 7, no. 2 (May–August 1974): 73–78.

Henry Wadsworth Longfellow   *Longfellow, Henry Wadsworth, photogravure. The Library of Congress.*

✷ Henry Wadsworth Longfellow

BORN: *1807, Portland, Maine*

DIED: *1882, Cambridge, Massachusetts*

NATIONALITY: *American*

GENRE: *Poetry*

MAJOR WORKS:

Voices of the Night (1839)

Evangeline: A Tale of Acadie (1847)

The Song of Hiawatha (1855)

"Paul Revere's Ride" (1863)

Overview

By far the most widely known and best-loved American poet of his time, Henry Wadsworth Longfellow achieved a rare degree of national and international prominence. Poems such as "A Psalm of Life" (1838), *Evangeline, A Tale of Acadie* (1847), and "Paul Revere's Ride" (1863) became mainstays of national culture, long remembered by generations of readers who studied them in school. Longfellow linked American poetry to European traditions beyond England and made pioneering contributions to the nation's literary life. However, his reputation suffered a serious decline in the twentieth century, and he became associated with an outmoded, genteel tradition.

Works in Biographical and Historical Context

A Well-Born American   Longfellow was born on February 27, 1807, in Portland, Maine (though at the time Maine was still a part of Massachusetts). His father, Stephen Longfellow, was an attorney and Harvard graduate active in public affairs; his mother, Zilpah Wadsworth Longfellow, was the daughter of General Peleg Wadsworth, who had served in the American Revolution. The family occupied the first brick house in Portland, built by the general. Henry began his schooling at age three and was educated in private schools, where he became fluent in Latin. His first publication, a four-quatrain elegy to fallen soldiers, appeared in the *Portland Gazette* in 1820. Also that year, he passed the entrance examinations for Bowdoin College in nearby Brunswick, where he attended the following year.

Contrary to his father's wish that he study law, Longfellow preferred a literary career and joined the literary societies on campus. He began publishing poems, sketches, and reviews in numerous periodicals while attending Bowdoin. He hoped to support himself by writing, and fate provided such an opportunity. In 1825, the college trustees offered the young graduate a professorship in modern languages, provided that he prepare for the post by studying Romance (Latin-derived) languages in Europe. He sailed from New York in May 1826, and he spent three years rambling through cities and countryside, absorbing impressions of European cultures. His subsequent work revealed a unique blend of American and European influences.

Professor of Languages   Returning to Maine in 1829, Longfellow as a young professor soon found himself immersed in the unpoetic routines of pedagogy. He married a Portland neighbor, Mary Potter, in 1831, and published his first book, a travelogue called *Outre-Mer: A Pilgrimage Beyond the Sea* (1833–1834). He also wrote essays on French, Spanish, and Italian literature, and material for language textbooks.

Overburdened with instructional tasks, Longfellow leapt at an offer to join the faculty at Harvard. He traveled to Europe again, accompanied by his wife, to ready himself for the new position. In London, he met the British writer Thomas Carlyle, who stimulated Longfellow's interest in German Romanticism, which greatly influenced his later writing. While abroad, Mary Longfellow's health collapsed following a miscarriage; she died in November 1835, leaving her widower stricken and disbelieving. He carried on, immersing himself in German literature in Heidelberg. He subsequently became infatuated with a young American girl visiting Switzerland, Frances "Fanny" Appleton.

Settling down at Harvard, Longfellow wrote poetry along with academic essays. His first poetry collection, *Voices of the Night* (1839), achieved immediate popularity. The poem "A Psalm of Life," from that collection, evokes the theme of *carpe diem*, gently imploring the reader to leave "footprints on the sands of time." His verses, filled with a wistful wisdom born of sad experiences, met an appreciative public response. He also published a romantic novel drawing on his European travels, *Hyperion* (1839).

Evangeline and Fame   Longfellow followed up his poetic success with another collection, *Ballads and Other Poems* (1842). Now that he had discovered his voice and his audience, he achieved personal happiness as well: after a seven-year courtship, Frances Appleton agreed to marry him in 1843. As a wedding gift, her father bought the Craigie House in Cambridge, Massachusetts, and Longfellow spent the rest of his life there, raising six children. Many distinguished friends, such as Nathaniel Hawthorne, were frequent guests.

The professor's academic efforts brought forth a huge anthology of *The Poets and Poetry of Europe* (1845), which he translated and edited. He also began writing the longer narrative poems for which he is primarily remembered. His greatest popular success came with *Evangeline, a Tale of Acadie* (1847). The heroine of this verse romance is separated from her husband during the eviction of the French-speaking Acadians from Nova Scotia. She journeys all over French and British America searching for him. Longfellow's tale of marital fidelity was immediately acclaimed for

its lyrical grace and poignant storyline and became one of the most beloved American poems of the nineteenth century.

Longfellow resigned from Harvard in 1854; he was now the leading American poet and happily withdrew from campus life to devote himself fully to writing. Each new book extended his fame. *The Song of Hiawatha* (1855) was another major success. It was drawn from the tribal folklore of the Ojibway Indians, but it was also inspired by Nordic epics. In the title poem of *The Courtship of Miles Standish and Other Poems* (1858), Longfellow concocted a humorous romance out of familiar historical material from the Plymouth Puritans.

The Christus Trilogy   Fanny Longfellow died tragically on July 9, 1861, when her dress caught fire at home. Trying to smother the flames, her husband burned his face so severely that he couldn't shave again, instead growing the long white beard familiar from portraits. While coping with private tragedy, he suffered the additional trauma of the Civil War, which touched his family directly when his eldest son was wounded while fighting for the Union army. He coped with his sorrow by plunging himself into literary work. The next book he completed, *Tales of a Wayside Inn* (1863), a series of narrative poems reminiscent of Chaucer's *Canterbury Tales* (ca. 1400), reveals Longfellow's versatility and mastery of narrative form. It also contains one of his, and America's, most famous patriotic poems, "Paul Revere's Ride."

Longfellow also took on the ambitious task of translating Dante's *Divine Comedy* (c. 1321) in blank verse. For advice, he gathered weekly sessions of his "Dante Club" of writer-scholars, who included James Russell Lowell and William Dean Howells. Longfellow's translation, still respected for its literary merit, appeared in three volumes from 1865 to 1867.

He then concentrated on what he considered his masterpiece: a trilogy of dramatic poems chronicling the history of Christianity. He had begun the series a decade earlier with *The Golden Legend* (1851), set in medieval Italy; he explored Puritanism and the Salem witch trials in *The New England Tragedies* (1868) and dramatized the passion of Christ in *The Divine Tragedy* (1871). The three works appeared together under the title *Christus: A Mystery* (1872), but sales and critical response were unencouraging.

Despite flagging creative zeal, Longfellow remained productive in his final decade. In 1874, *The New York Ledger* paid him the staggering sum of three thousand dollars for a single poem, "The Hanging of the Crane." At his death in 1882, he was still selling a thousand books a week, and he left his children a sizable estate.

Works in Literary Context

Longfellow displayed an affection for language, literature, and narrative early in life. His early verses imitated British romantic poets and the American William Cullen Bryant. On his first trip to Europe, Longfellow met Washington

Irving, who encouraged him to write and provided a model of an American writer who absorbed European influences. Longfellow's first book, *Outre-Mer: A Pilgrimage Beyond the Sea*, owed an obvious debt to Irving. Longfellow's later immersion in German literature, including works by such writers as Johann Wolfgang von Goethe and Friedrich Schiller, awakened a new sense of poetry as emotional expression. He incorporated much of the artistic philosophy of Goethe, Schiller, and other German poets into his writing and virtually introduced this tradition to American readers, enhancing the worldliness of the young nation's literature.

American Epic Poetry Several of Longfellow's most successful poems—for example, *Evangeline, a Tale of Acadie*, *The Song of Hiawatha*, and *Tales of a Wayside Inn* were epics. Epic poetry is one of the world's oldest literary forms; it extends back at least as far as Homer's *Iliad* and *Odyssey*. Its narrative form is suited to grand themes of history and mythology. By fashioning epics out of Acadian, Native American, and Puritan source material, Longfellow was deliberately offering America a set of founding myths that established a richness and depth of culture like those found in Europe.

Music and Meter Longfellow's poetry combined technical virtuosity with depth of sentiment. He experimented with many forms and meters, from the classical rhythm of *Evangeline, a Tale of Acadie* to sonnets, ballads, and free verse. Musicality was a key attribute of his poetry, and he thought carefully to select formal elements that matched the theme and mood of his subject. The most famous example is *The Song of Hiawatha*, written in an unrhymed meter borrowed from the *Kalevala*, a Finnish folk epic. The poem's steady trochaic meter, stressing the first of each pair of syllables, summons up the beat of a tom-tom: "By the shores of Gitche Gumee, / By the shining Big-Sea-Water." It was so strikingly original that innumerable poets produced parodies of *Hiawatha*. Many of Longfellow's works, however, are remembered less for their formal qualities than for their tender sentimentality; they are lyrics, shorter poems that aim to produce an emotional effect. Examples include his early "psalms," his melancholy lyrics reminiscent of the German Romantics, and his verses extolling moral virtues and paternal affection.

Works in Critical Context

The publication of *Evangeline, a Tale of Acadie* made Longfellow a remarkably popular poet; the book sold out five printings within three months, and hundreds of editions and translations followed. *The Song of Hiawatha* proved even more marketable, earning seven thousand dollars in royalties in its first decade. Although sales of later volumes never matched the popularity of these offerings, and the commercial failure of the *Christus* trilogy was a disappointment, Longfellow lived to experience recognition and rewards seldom enjoyed by other writers at the time. Prominent literary and political figures visited

LITERARY AND HISTORICAL CONTEMPORARIES

Longfellow's famous contemporaries include:

Nathaniel Hawthorne (1804–1864): Hawthorne was an American novelist and short-story writer who wrote about his native New England. One of his most well-known works is the the novel *The Scarlet Letter* (1850).

Ralph Waldo Emerson (1804–1882): Emerson was a preeminent American poet, essayist, and Transcendentalist philosopher.

John Greenleaf Whittier (1807–1892): Whittier was an American poet, Quaker, and advocate for the abolition of slavery.

Charles Dickens (1812–1870): Dickens, the most widely read British novelist of his day, was the author of such immensely popular works as *Great Expectations* (1861) and *David Copperfield* (1850).

Edgar Allan Poe (1809–1849): A master of mystery and the macabre, Poe was an American poet and short-story writer,.

Franklin Pierce (1804–1869): Pierce was the fourteenth president of the United States (1853–1857) and Longfellow's classmate at Bowdoin.

him in Cambridge, and on his final visit to Europe, Queen Victoria received him at Windsor Castle. Longfellow was the only American writer honored with a bust in the Poets' Corner of Westminster Abbey, which was installed there two years after his death.

Posthumous Reputation Plummets Even during his lifetime, Longfellow had his detractors. Edgar Allan Poe famously accused him of imitating the work of other writers; Walt Whitman concurred in this assessment. Numerous critics have found Longfellow's work lacking the originality of Whitman or Emerson, while they have acknowledged his rare popularity. In the twentieth century, however, Longfellow suffered an eclipse of reputation nearly as unparalleled as his original success. In the atmosphere of disillusioned modernity that followed World War I, the gentle simplicity and moralism of his poetry seemed antiquated and even ridiculous. In Herbert Gorman's disparaging 1926 biography, Longfellow became an easy scapegoat for ills attributed to Victorianism and Puritanism. The New Critics of the next generation scorned his didacticism and lack of irony; they looked in vain for complexities and ambiguities his poems do not contain. Because of Longfellow's stature in the canon and the classroom, New Historicist critics leveled the charge that he represented a "high culture" used to indoctrinate immigrants and American children in Puritan norms.

COMMON HUMAN EXPERIENCE

"Listen, my children, and you shall hear / Of the midnight ride of Paul Revere." These famous lines reflect a tradition of war poetry going back centuries. The following works also embody—or parody—that patriotic genre.

"The Star Spangled Banner" (1814), a poem by Francis Scott Key. Key penned this poem while detained on a British warship, after he watched the American Fort McHenry survive a bombardment during the War of 1812.

"The Charge of the Light Brigade" (1854), a poem by Alfred, Lord Tennyson. This poem commemorating a Crimean War battle epitomizes the poetic glorification of warfare.

"Gunga Din" (1892), a poem by Rudyard Kipling. Kipling reveals the folly of racial prejudice in this famous ballad about a soldier "in Injia's sunny clime" and the water-carrier who saves him.

"In Flanders Fields" (1915), a poem by John McCrae. This World War I poem is recited annually in Canada on Remembrance Day.

"With God on Our Side" (1964), a song by Bob Dylan. This sardonic anthem is a short history lesson and a tribute to the hubris that leads civilization to war again and again.

Ironically, it is entirely possible to read Longfellow as a friend of American multiculturalism. In the eyes of sympathetic critics, he was instrumental in introducing European culture to the emerging American mainstream of the antebellum period. Even *The Song of Hiawatha*, as outdated as it may read today, represents an attempt to honor the endangered Native American cultures. In a recent book, *Longfellow Redux* (2008), Christoph Irmscher attempts to overcome the contemporary prejudice against the poet and explore the remarkable connection he maintained with his audience. In Irmscher's argument, Longfellow advanced democratic culture by delivering the international cultural conversation to American readers, bridging social and linguistic divides.

Responses to Literature

1. Identify the German Romantic influence in the poetry of Henry Wadsworth Longfellow, citing specific parts of individual poems.

2. From today's standpoint, how would you evaluate the portrayal of Native American culture in *The Song of Hiawatha*?

3. Explore and evaluate the formal choices, including meter and rhyme scheme, in two or more of Longfellow's poems.

4. Why do you think Longfellow was such a popular poet in his day, and why do you think his reputation has fallen so far in the present?

BIBLIOGRAPHY

Books

Austin, George Lowell. *Henry Wadsworth Longfellow: His Life, His Works, His Friendships*. Boston: Lee and Shepard, 1883.

Brooks, Van Wyck. *The Flowering of New England, 1815–1865*. New York: Dutton, 1936.

Calhoun, Charles C. *Longfellow: A Rediscovered Life*. Boston: Beacon Press, 2004.

Gorman, Herbert S. *A Victorian American: Henry Wadsworth Longfellow*. New York: Doran, 1926.

Hatfield, James Taft. *New Light on Longfellow, with Special Reference to His Relations with Germany*. Boston: Houghton Mifflin, 1933.

Irmscher, Christoph. *Longfellow Redux*. Champaign, Ill.: University of Illinois, 2008.

Kennedy, William Sloane. *Henry W. Longfellow: Biography, Anecdote, Letters, Criticism*. Cambridge, Mass.: Moses King, 1882.

Mathews, Joseph Chesley, ed. *Henry W. Longfellow Reconsidered: A Symposium*. Hartford, Conn.: Transcendental Books, 1970.

Norton, Charles Eliot. *Henry Wadsworth Longfellow: A Sketch of His Life*. Boston: Houghton, Mifflin, 1906.

Schaick, John Van Jr. *The Characters in "Tales of a Wayside Inn."* Boston: Universalist Publishing House, 1939.

Wagenknecht, Edward. *Henry Wadsworth Longfellow: His Poetry and Prose*. New York: Ungar, 1986.

Waggoner, Hyatt H. *American Poets from the Puritans to the Present*. Boston: Houghton Mifflin, 1968.

Williams, Cecil B. *Henry Wadsworth Longfellow*. New York: Twayne Publishers, Inc., 1964.

Periodicals

Ward, Nathan. "The Fire Last Time." *American Heritage* (December 2001).

❀ Barry Lopez

BORN: *1945, Port Chester, New York*

NATIONALITY: *American*

GENRE: *Fiction, nonfiction*

MAJOR WORKS:

Of Wolves and Men (1978)

Arctic Dreams: Imagination and Desire in a Northern Landscape (1986)

Many of Lopez's earliest memories are of adventures that he and his brother had exploring the orchards, fields, and farms of the area. On weekends, his mother would often take the boys to the Mojave Desert, to the nearby beaches, or to the San Bernardino Mountains. These experiences were all instrumental in fostering a love of nature and outdoor life that later infused his writings. In 1955, Lopez's mother married Adrian Bernard Lopez, and the following year the family moved to an apartment in the Murray Hill section of Manhattan, where Barry lived until he entered college. The transition from California to New York City was a jarring one. During his first summer in New York, Lopez and his brother went to a summer camp on the North Fork of Long Island, where they bunked with John Steinbeck's two sons. Feeling a kinship with Steinbeck, another displaced Californian, Lopez read all of Steinbeck's books in the next few years, which had a profound influence on many of Lopez's works. The summer following his graduation from high school, Lopez traveled to Europe, and visited Spain, France, Italy, Switzerland, Austria, West Germany, Portugal, Luxembourg, Liechtenstein, England, and Ireland.

In the fall of 1962, Lopez entered the University of Notre Dame in Indiana, intending to major in aeronautical engineering. During his studies at Notre Dame his love of literature grew, and he later credited such authors as Herman Melville, William Faulkner, Thomas Hardy, Willa Cather, and Ernest Hemingway as being particularly important influences. During this period, Lopez began to write stories of his own, developing an interest in language and narrative that, among other things, helped convince him to change his major to communication arts. During his undergraduate years Lopez also traveled widely throughout the United States and worked on a ranch in Wyoming for two summers. In 1966, he graduated from Notre Dame and briefly considered monastic life. In 1967, he married artist Sandra Landers. The following year, with the vague goal to teach prep school, he enrolled in the master's program in teaching at Notre Dame, and received his teaching degree in 1968.

Lopez developed his love for the land as a child, and his interest in the environment was reflected on a larger scale as the modern environmental movement took shape in America in the 1960s and throughout the 1970s. In 1962, Rachel Carson published her influential work, *Silent Spring*, a book that described the dangers of pesticides to humans and the environment. She also explored the attitudes people have to the land and environment, and her conclusions were a wake-up call to many Americans. The modern environmental movement was concerned with issues of pollution, population, conservation, and the development of a more harmonious relationship with the natural world.

Barry Lopez   *Ulf Andersen / Getty Images*

Overview

Pushcart Prize winner Barry Lopez is an influential American writer on natural history, who focuses on the relationship of human beings to the land and its inhabitants. Lopez's works often defy easy classification—he describes himself simply as "a writer who travels"—but in his works of fiction and nonfiction, Lopez has clearly established a reputation as a masterful and important writer about place and humanity. His writing reveals that our ideas are deeply rooted in humanity's relationship to the environment and that where people live, work, and travel has everything to do with how they treat others.

Works in Biographical and Historical Context

The Landscape of Youth   Barry Holstun Lopez was born on January 6, 1945, in Port Chester, New York, a town located just east of the Connecticut border. They had a second son, Dennis, in 1948, and a short time later the family moved to southern California. Lopez's parents divorced in 1950, and his mother and the two boys moved to a small house in the California town of Reseda.

Native American Influences   After he realized that his primary interest was writing, not teaching, Lopez entered the University of Oregon's MFA program in

LITERARY AND HISTORICAL CONTEMPORARIES

Lopez's famous contemporaries include:

Rachel Carson (1907–1964): Carson, the noted American biologist, environmental activist, and nonfiction writer, is widely recognized for raising the level of American consciousness about environmental issues with her 1962 work *Silent Spring*.

Peter Matthiessen (1927–): An American novelist, nonfiction writer, and environmental activist. Matthiessen is a notable writer in many genres, and his work often focuses on the history and contemporary life of Native Americans.

Leslie Marmon Silko (1948–): A member of the Laguna Pueblo tribe, Silko is the author of the celebrated 1977 novel *Ceremony*, an exploration of the changing cultural identity of a Native American man.

Al Gore (1948–): Vice president of the United States from 1993 to 2001, Gore is also a nonfiction writer and environmental activist. He won the 2007 Nobel Peace Prize for his work on the book and documentary *An Inconvenient Truth* (2006).

Barbara Kingsolver (1955–): An American novelist Kingsolver investigates cultural and social change in books such as *The Poisonwood Bible* (1998).

creative writing in 1968. Although he soon withdrew from the program, he met Barre Toelken, a professor in the English department of the University of Oregon, who introduced Lopez to the narratives of Native American peoples. Lopez found the beliefs and narratives of these cultures, particularly their link between the sacred and the landscape, to have a great deal in common with his own developing beliefs. During this period, he began an intense study of Native American narrative and folklore. In 1970, Lopez and his wife moved to a house in the Cascade Mountains east of Eugene, Oregon, and he launched a career as an independent journalist, contributing articles and photographs to various newspapers and periodicals.

In 1976, Lopez published a collection of short fiction titled *Desert Notes: Reflections in the Eye of a Raven*. The sense of landscape, and of the place of humans within that landscape, is central to the twelve stories in the collection, which are written in an unconventional style that breaks free from traditional ideas of characterization and plot. In contrast to most works of short fiction, these stories focus on their setting—the desert, in this case—over plot or characterization.

In his second published work, *Giving Birth to Thunder, Sleeping with His Daughter: Coyote Builds North America* (1978), Lopez drew on his studies of Native American narratives to retell a series of stories about Coyote, the trickster-hero who appears in many guises in Native American folklore. The book includes more than sixty tales, most of which are no more than two or three pages in length, that are drawn from more than forty different tribes. Coyote, as portrayed in these stories, is a hero, villain, thief, magician, creator, and fool, often playing more than one of these roles in any given story. In contrast to earlier, sanitized versions of Coyote stories intended for mainstream audiences, Lopez's Coyote tales include references to taboo topics, often told for comic effect.

The Call of Nature During the late 1970s, Lopez went on a series of extended trips to Alaska to study wolves, a project that resulted in his breakthrough work, *Of Wolves and Men* (1978). Lopez's first extended work of nonfiction, *Of Wolves and Men* combines the work of scientists, direct observation, interviews, and literary and cultural analysis to create a fascinating portrait of the wolf and its place in the human imagination. Although it is often considered a work of natural history, Lopez's approach to the genre is an inspired one that succeeds not only in describing the subject, but in also calling into question the cultural assumptions behind the attitudes of Western civilization toward the wolf and the natural environment. The book was both a bestseller and a critical success, and it won the prestigious John Burroughs Medal for the best work of natural history published in 1978.

Lopez returned to fiction with his next publications, including a collection of short stories, *River Notes: The Dance of Herons* (1979), the second in a trilogy of short fiction. As in *Desert Notes*, landscape is central to the stories and is a place of spiritual power, but in *River Notes* the presence of humans and their connection to the land is more pronounced. The acute sense of loss that also pervades many of the stories in this collection stemmed from Lopez's mother's death in 1976. Lopez also explored the potential for a spiritual link between humans and the landscape in the nine stories included in *Winter Count* (1981). As in Lopez's earlier collections, these stories often reflect a strong Native American influence, particularly in the spiritual power of the earth and animals and the importance of storytelling. After the publication of *Winter Count*, Lopez was increasingly recognized as a gifted writer not simply of natural history but also of short fiction, and he was awarded the Distinguished Recognition Award from the Friends of American Writers in 1982.

During much of the early 1980s, Lopez traveled extensively throughout the Arctic, studying the land, the wildlife, and the people of the region. The resulting book, *Arctic Dreams: Imagination and Desire in a Northern Landscape* (1986), was an enormous critical and popular success. The book won several prizes, including a National Book Award, and cemented Lopez's reputation as one of the most original and significant contemporary nature writers. In *Arctic Dreams*, Lopez takes his readers on an engaging odyssey through the far North, with chapters on the megafauna of the region, such as the polar bear, narwhal, and musk ox; the rhythms of life in the Arctic landscape; the lifestyles of the native peoples of the region; and the history, often misguided and tragic, of European exploration in the Arctic. At the heart of *Arctic Dreams* is Lopez's conviction that members of Western civilization must learn to approach relations with the land with compassion and dignity rather than a conqueror's mentality.

A Distinguished, Diverse Writer In addition to his full-length works, Lopez has been a longtime contributor to many magazines, including *Harper's, Audubon,* and *Sierra*. Fourteen of his natural history essays were collected and published in *Crossing Open Ground* in 1988. Many of the essays in this work reflect Lopez's deep and abiding interest in non-Western cultures, the importance of narrative, and the need for creating and maintaining an ethical relationship with the land and its inhabitants.

Lopez published *Crow and Weasel,* a Parents's Choice Award-winning fable for young adults, in 1990. The novel follows two young men from a northern plains tribe as they leave their village on a quest to travel farther north than anyone in their village has ever traveled before. Lopez followed *Crow and Weasel* with *Field Notes: The Grace Note of the Canyon Wren* in 1994. This collection completes the trilogy of "Notes" stories he had begun nearly twenty years earlier. In 1998, he published a collection of essays, *About This Life: Journeys on the Threshold of Memory,* documenting his extensive travels and his inner journeys. The autobiographical stories that Lopez tells in *About This Life* reveal the formative influences on his life and career; his family and upbringing; and his beliefs about the importance of rediscovering one's connection to the land. Lopez followed this autobiographical work with *Light Action in the Caribbean* (2000) and *Resistance* (2004). He co-edited *Home Ground: Language for an American Landscape* (2006), a dictionary that compiles and explains regional terms for geographic features. Lopez continues to live and work in western Oregon.

Works in Literary Context

The Literature of Place Although Lopez discourages using the term "nature writing" to describe his work, his output doubtlessly belongs to the American literary prose genre that focuses on the relationship between the natural landscape and culture. Nature writing became popular among writers in many genres during the nineteenth-century American Renaissance, including Herman Melville, Henry David Thoreau, and Ralph Waldo Emerson, and continued throughout the twentieth century with writers such as Wendell Berry, Peter Matthiessen, and Gary Snyder. In Lopez's works, the fate of nature and humanity are inseparable, and among his central concerns is the desire to cultivate an ethical, responsible relationship to the natural environment.

COMMON HUMAN EXPERIENCE

Lopez's fiction and nonfiction is influenced by a central belief that the human imagination is shaped by the natural and man-made landscape it encounters. Here are some other works that explore the way that landscape influences the imagination:

"Hamatreya" (1847), a poem by Ralph Waldo Emerson. In this work, Emerson considers the ways that land ownership influences people and the landscape, while contrasting the spiritual with the real.

Walden (1854), a nonfiction work by Henry David Thoreau. In his famous essay, Thoreau relates his attempt to achieve transcendence through his experiences with nature.

The Grapes of Wrath (1939), a novel by John Steinbeck. Steinbeck's classic novel about the Joad family's journey through the American landscape of the Great Depression won both the Pulitzer Prize and the Nobel Prize in Literature.

Desert Solitaire (1968), a nonfiction work by Edward Abbey. This book by Abbey, a noted essayist and environmental activist, recounts his three years as a park ranger in Utah.

A Pilgrim at Tinker Creek (1974), an essay collection by Annie Dillard. Winner of a Pulitzer Prize, this book is a meditation on the changing seasons of Tinker Creek in the Blue Ridge Mountains of Virginia.

Native American Cultural Influences Lopez's interest in Native American experience and culture influenced many of his works. *Giving Birth to Thunder, Sleeping with His Daughter: Coyote Builds North America* (1978) includes sixty-eight tales of Coyote's adventures drawn from many different Native American tribes. His 1981 collection *Winter Count* is a set of nine stories organized around the Native American practice of marking the passage of one year to the next. Two stories in that collection, "Buffalo" and "The Location of the River," portray the rupture between myth time and storytelling of northern plains tribes with the rational view of natural history and Western scholarship. Many of Lopez's other works include elements drawn from Native American spiritual and cultural traditions as well.

Works in Critical Context

Lopez is widely regarded as an accomplished writer in genres as diverse as natural history, personal essay, and fiction. He is often praised for his thoughtful, meditative approach to subjects and his technique of blending several sources of information. However, some critics have taken issue with his use and appropriation of Native American characters and cultural tradition in his works.

Giving Birth to Thunder, Sleeping with His Daughter: Coyote Builds North America In this ambitious collection of stories, Lopez re-imagines Native American folk tales about the character of Coyote. While critics generally praised Lopez's use of voice and imaginative scenarios, the book received mixed reviews based on Lopez's interpretation of Coyote. There was a disparity between critics those who found these retellings uplifting and others who perceived them as insulting to Native Americans. Lopez's mentor, Barre Toelken, reflected on the potential for misunderstanding Lopez's intentions with the work and concluded in the foreword to the collection that the

> stories are retold in a way that is both faithful to native concepts of Coyote and how his stories should go, and phrased for an audience which reads without listening, for whom literature is studied and reflected upon, for whom Coyote is an imaginary but interesting protagonist.

Arctic Dreams: Imagination and Desire in a Northern Landscape Lopez's longest, most ambitious work, *Arctic Dreams* explores the relationship between the physical details that characterize the Far North and the human perception of it. This book sealed his reputation as one of the most important contemporary natural history writers, and Lopez won the National Book Award for nonfiction the same year the book was published. Lauded as an epic work, critics note the way that Lopez blends natural history with cultural history and personal experience along with scholarship. The book bears both his poetic sensibilities and his scholarly tendencies, including notes, maps, and appendixes, along with a bibliography and index to assist the reader in navigating the geographic and scientific information. Critic John Tallmadge summarizes his assessment of *Arctic Dreams*: "Like all epics it unfolds on a grand scale, moralizing the landscape, detailing feats of heroism, engaging the deepest spiritual, political, and historical questions, and propounding a view of the noblest possibilities for human life."

Responses to Literature

1. *Giving Birth to Thunder, Sleeping with His Daughter: Coyote Builds North America* is composed of short stories about Coyote. Compare the characterization of Coyote in two stories. In what ways are they similar? How are they different? What impact do the different characterizations of Coyote have on your understanding of the role and significance of Coyote?

2. Compare the different perceptions of the wolf in *Of Wolves and Men*. How has the treatment of wolves by different cultures reflect their attitudes and beliefs about the creatures?

3. Lopez is known for writing about the relationship between human beings and the land on which they live. Write a short essay about a specific place you know, emphasizing its relationship to the people who live in the area.

BIBLIOGRAPHY
Books

Paul, Sherman. "Making the Turn: Rereading Barry Lopez." *For Love of the World: Essays on Nature Writers.* Iowa City, Iowa: University of Iowa Press, 1992, pp. 67–107.

Rueckert, William H. "Barry Lopez and the Search for a Dignified and Honorable Relationship with Nature." *Earthly Words: Essays on Contemporary American Nature and Environmental Writers.* Ann Arbor, Mich.: University of Michigan Press, 1994, pp. 137–164.

Slovic, Scott. *Seeking Awareness in American Nature Writing: Henry Thoreau, Annie Dillard, Edward Abbey, Wendell Berry, Barry Lopez.* Salt Lake City, Utah: University of Utah Press, 1992.

Tallmadge, John. "Barry Lopez." *American Nature Writers, Vol. 1.* New York: Scribners, 1996, pp. 549–568.

Wild, Peter. "Barry Lopez." *Western Writers Series, No. 64.* Boise, Idaho: Boise State University, 1984.

Periodicals

Anton, Jim. "An Interview with Barry Lopez." *Western American Literature* 21 (Spring 1986): 3–17.

Bonetti, Kay. "An Interview with Barry Lopez." *Missouri Review* 11 (1988): 59–77.

Evans, Alice. "Leaning Into the Light: An Interview with Barry Lopez." *Poets and Writers* 22 (March/April 1994): 62–79.

Sumner, David. "Nature Writing, American Literature, and the Idea of Community—A Conversation with Barry Lopez." *Weber Studies* 18 (Spring 2001): 2–26.

Todd, Trish. "Barry Lopez Recalls His Arctic Dreams." *Publishers Weekly* 288 (October 11, 1985): 35–36.

✸ Audre Lorde

BORN: *1934, New York, New York*

DIED: *1992, Christiansted, St. Croix (U.S. Virgin Islands)*

NATIONALITY: *American*

GENRE: *Poetry, nonfiction*

MAJOR WORKS:

The Black Unicorn (1978)

The Cancer Journals (1980)

Zami: A New Spelling of My Name (1982)

Audre Lorde   *Lorde, Audre, photograph. The Library of Congress.*

Overview

Audre Lorde described herself as "a black lesbian feminist mother lover poet." She asserted all these identities, and explored their intersections, in powerful works of poetry, autobiography, and social criticism. Her consistently radical, occasionally strident voice helped call attention to the complexities of privilege and oppression in American society, and to the importance of recognizing and celebrating cultural differences.

Works in Biographical and Historical Context

Manhattan Youth   Audrey Geraldine Lorde was born in Harlem, New York City, on February 18, 1934, the third daughter in a Caribbean immigrant family. (She dropped the Y from her first name in her childhood.) As a young child, she was very nearsighted, and did not speak until the age of four or five. She noted that she did not "really" speak until she "started reading and writing poetry." Often she would recite lines of poetry instead of expressing herself in her own words. She began composing poems herself at age twelve or thirteen.

Lorde encountered racism while attending Catholic schools in New York, but found her social niche at Hunter High School, where she became literary editor of the school arts magazine. She published her first poem in *Seventeen* magazine, although her English teachers considered her work "much too romantic." Lorde went on to Hunter College in New York, earning a bachelor's degree in 1959. She spent one year as a student at the National University of Mexico, a period that literally broadened her horizons and helped her affirm her identity.

After college, Lorde completed a master's degree in library science at Columbia University in 1961, and took various odd jobs to support her education. She then accepted a job at the Mount Vernon Public Library, and in 1962 she married attorney Edwin Rollins. They divorced in 1970 after having two children. From 1966 to 1968, Lorde was head librarian at Town School Library in New York City; patrons knew her as the "librarian who wrote." She published poetry in numerous literary magazines and anthologies in the 1960s, and was involved in civil-rights and feminist activism.

Coming Out and Opening to the World   The year 1968 marked a turning point in her career and her life. She received a National Endowment for the Arts Grant, became a poet-in-residence at Tougaloo College, a historically black school in Mississippi, and published her first volume of poetry, *The First Cities*. Amidst the turbulence of the black-power movement and the assassination of Martin Luther King Jr.—an advocate for nonviolence in the struggle for attaining civil rights for African-Americans—Lorde's poems were refreshingly reflective rather than confrontational in tone. While in Mississippi, Lorde met Frances Clayton, a white college professor who became her romantic partner for the next twenty-one years.

Cables to Rage (1970), Lorde's second book, was published outside the United States by Paul Breman, an active supporter of black poetry. This work is less introspective, due to the poet's emerging social concerns and her exploration of guilt and betrayal. Central to this volume is the poem "Martha," in which Lorde reveals her homosexuality for the first time.

With the publication of *From a Land Where Other People Live* (1973), Lorde began to expand the scope of her writing by focusing on racial oppression and worldwide injustice. This publication was nominated for the National Book Award for poetry. Next came *The New York Head Shop and Museum* (1974), often described as Lorde's most radical and political volume of poetry, in which she takes the reader on an odyssey through the decaying city on the verge of bankruptcy, and the hardships of urban poverty.

Beyond White Feminism   Lorde broadened her audience with *Coal* (1976), her first book released by a major publishing house. In the title poem, she celebrates her race: "I am black because I come from the / earth's insides / Take my word for jewel in your / open light." In

The Black Unicorn (1978), her best-known poetry collection, Lorde makes use of African symbols and mythology to integrate the themes of motherhood, black pride, and spiritual renewal.

Now an established poet and professor at the City University of New York, Lorde became a prominent critic and lecturer on the relationship of lesbians and women of color to women's liberation and feminism. She launched an incisive critique of the 1970s women's movement, claiming that it was limited to the concerns of middle-class and affluent white women. In order to truly advance the cause of women's liberation, she argued, white feminists needed to overcome their racism and demonstrate solidarity with all oppressed people. As she put it in the title of a 1979 lecture (reprinted in her essay collection *Sister Outsider* (1984)), "The Master's Tools Will Never Dismantle the Master's House"; that is to say, feminists cannot succeed in bringing about real social change while inwardly accepting hierarchies of power that privilege rich over poor, white over black, straight over gay. In 1980, Lorde cofounded Kitchen Table: Women of Color Press, the nation's first independent press devoted to publishing works by women of color.

The Cancer Journals Lorde's first book in prose was *The Cancer Journals* (1980), an account of her agonizing struggle to overcome breast cancer and mastectomy. She used writing to help her cope with despair and thoughts of death, and to break the silence she perceived around the issue of breast cancer, in the belief that other women could learn from her experience. The book also explains Lorde's decision not to wear a prosthesis after her breast was removed: rather than cover up her wound in shame, she sought to make it visible as another way of accepting and celebrating difference.

Lorde survived for more than a decade after her initial cancer diagnosis. She produced several more volumes of poetry and prose, including *Zami: A New Spelling of My Name* (1982), described by its publishers as a work of "biomythography, combining elements of history, biography and myth." She was named poet laureate of New York State in 1991, a year before cancer took her life.

Works in Literary Context

The first formative influence on Lorde's writing and social outlook was her mother, whose storytelling and use of language reflected the vitality of her Caribbean heritage. Lorde's childhood affection for all kinds of poetry trained her sensibility as well as her self-expression. All through her life, friends and allies said, her way of thinking was that of a poet. Her inner struggle to integrate the many elements of her cultural identity—especially her lesbianism—and define herself on her own terms was probably her major motivation for writing.

Lorde and Black Arts Lorde's early publications coincided with the peak years of the civil rights era in the United States. Poet Amiri Baraka was a leader of the Black Arts Movement, a cultural offshoot of the black power movement, centered in Harlem. Unlike her fellow poets Nikki Giovanni and Maya Angelou, Lorde did not associate herself with Black Arts, although she was active in radical politics. The tone of her early work differed from the militant, confrontational rhetoric of movement-associated literature. Calling *The First Cities* "a quiet, introspective book," poet and publisher Dudley Randall asserted that "[Lorde] does not wave a black flag, but her blackness is there, implicit, in the bone."

Identity Politics The themes of Lorde's poems and political essays primarily relate to emotions and inner development: dealing with pain and loss, and extracting useful life lessons from it; rejecting silence and making one's voice heard; building the capacity to love, and unleashing the liberating energy of sexuality. Above all, Lorde is concerned with accepting the complex and multifaceted nature of personal identity. Asserting herself simultaneously as a woman, an African American, and a lesbian meant that the struggle to embrace herself fully coincided with the struggle against social justice and all kinds of prejudice. Because of this close association between personal and political concerns, her writings had a profound influence on the development of "identity politics" on the political left in the 1980s and 1990s.

Works in Critical Context

Pigeonholed by her radical feminism, Lorde found only a limited audience for her writing at first. Her association with the lesbian poet Adrienne Rich, and her switch to a larger, mainstream publisher, helped bring critical attention and a wider readership to her work. By the 1980s, she had developed a following on the political left and among feminists, although she had antagonized some white feminists with her full-throated criticism of their narrow agenda and implicit racism. Proponents of multiculturalism and women's studies in the academic curriculum championed both her poetry and her social criticism, making her a well-read author on college campuses. Lorde's thematic preoccupation—the complexities of selfhood in a culture where race, class, gender, and sexual orientation largely determine social status—dovetailed with the concerns of both multiculturalists and postmodern critical theorists.

Zami Reviewers and scholars have given attention to Lorde's first prose work, *Zami: A New Spelling of My Name* (1982), for its treatment of the difficult relationship between mother and daughter. In the *New York Times Book Review*, reviewer Rosemary Daniell calls *Zami* "an excellent and evocative autobiography. Indeed, among the elements that make the book so good are its personal honesty and lack of pretentiousness, characteristics that shine through the writing, bespeaking the evolution of a strong and remarkable character." Similarly, Valerie Miner of *The American Book Review* appreciates that Lorde "is explicit about the racism and homophobia she suffered. This social consciousness adds heart and power to an autobiography which moves with the subtle drama of good fiction."

Responses to Literature

1. Write about the imagery Lorde uses in her poetry to express her responses to social injustice. Are there any recurring images or words?

2. How do you interpret Lorde's statement that "the master's tools will never dismantle the master's house"? Do you agree? Why or why not?

3. In what ways does Lorde's poetry reflect her multicultural identity? Analyze one or more poems in which she negotiates several aspects of her social identity.

4. Evaluate Lorde's *Cancer Journals* as a work of literature. What are her objectives in writing the journals, and in publishing them? What literary choices does the author make to achieve these objectives, with what degree of success?

BIBLIOGRAPHY

Books

Addison, Gayle, ed. *Black Expression*. New York: Weybright and Talley, 1969.

Bigsby, C. W. E., ed. *The Black American Writer*. New York: Penguin, 1969.

Christian, Barbara, ed. *Black Feminist Criticism: Perspectives on Black Women Writers*. New York: Pergamon, 1985.

Davies, Carole Boyce. *Black Women, Writing and Identity: Migrations of the Subject*. New Brunswick, N.J.: Rutgers University Press, 1993.

De Veaux, Alexis. *Warrior Poet: A Biography of Audre Lorde*. New York: W.W. Norton, 2004.

Evans, Mari, ed. *Black Women Writers (1950–1980): A Critical Evaluation*. Garden City, N.J.: Doubleday, 1984.

Hall, Joan Wylie. *Conversations with Audre Lorde*. Jackson, Miss.: University Press of Mississippi, 2004.

Keating, AnaLouise. *Women Reading Women Writing: Self-Invention in Paula Gunn Allen, Gloria Anzaldúa, and Audre Lorde*. Philadephia, Pa.: Temple University Press, 1996.

Tate, Claudia, ed. *Black Women Writers at Work*. New York: Continuum, 1983.

Periodicals

Kemp, Yakini B. "Writing Power: Identity Complexities and the Exotic Erotic in Audre Lorde's Writing." *Studies in the Literary Imagination* (Fall 2004).

COMMON HUMAN EXPERIENCE

Lorde explored and honored the life experiences of women of color in America, whose contributions to literature had been somewhat overlooked until the 1980s. Her works, and those listed below, are essential markers in the history of African American and minority women's writing.

Their Eyes Were Watching God (1937), a novel by Zora Neale Hurston. This novel, written in lively Southern dialect, is considered the greatest achievement of the best-known female writer of the Harlem Renaissance.

Annie Allen (1949), a poetry collection by Gwendolyn Brooks. This book of poems about a girl's maturation won the Pulitzer Prize for Poetry, the first time this award was given to an African American.

For Colored Girls Who Have Considered Suicide When the Rainbow is Enuf (1975), a play by Ntozake Shange. This play consists of twenty poems for women of different colors.

This Bridge Called My Back (1981), an anthology edited by Cherrie Moraga and Gloria E. Anzaldúa. This groundbreaking anthology of short writings by women of color became a mainstay of the women's studies curriculum.

The Color Purple (1982), a novel by Alice Walker. This Pulitzer Prize-winning novel, about the struggles and joys of a poor woman in Georgia, is influenced by *Their Eyes Were Watching God*.

Morris, Margaret Kissam. "Audre Lorde: Textual Authority and the Embodied Self." *Frontiers* 23 (2002): 168–188.

Rich, Adrienne. "An Interview with Audre Lorde." *Signs: Journal of Women in Culture and Society* 6 (Summer 1981): 713–736.

✸ H. P. Lovecraft

BORN: *1890, Providence, Rhode Island*

DIED: *1937, Providence, Rhode Island*

NATIONALITY: *American*

GENRE: *Fiction, poetry*

MAJOR WORKS:

"The Colour Out of Space" (1927)

"The Call of Cthulhu" (1928)

"The Dunwich Horror" (1929)

The Shadow over Innsmouth (1936)

At the Mountains of Madness (1936)

Overview

H. P. Lovecraft is considered by many to be the twentieth century's premier writer of supernatural horror. He holds a

H. P. Lovecraft *Writer Pictures*

prominent place in a line of authors that originated with the Gothic novelists of the eighteenth century, was perpetuated by such nineteenth century masters of the macabre as Edgar Allan Poe and Ambrose Bierce, and proliferates today in the work of Stephen King, Clive Barker, and many other writers, artists, and filmmakers. Lovecraft's "weird tales," combining horror, fantasy, and science-fiction elements, were published almost entirely in pulp magazines during his lifetime. Subsequently, however, his work developed a devoted following and made a deep imprint on popular culture.

Works in Biographical and Historical Context

An Isolated Youth Lovecraft was born in Providence, Rhode Island, on August 20, 1890. His father, a traveling salesman, became psychotic in 1893 due to syphilis and was committed to a sanitarium until his death in 1898. Lovecraft grew up in a Victorian home owned by his maternal grandfather, Whipple V. Phillips, a prosperous industrialist who was the dominant intellectual influence on his grandson's early life. A precocious child whose delicate health allowed him only sporadic attendance at school, Lovecraft flourished in a world of cultured adults who fostered his interest in Greco-Roman antiquity, astronomy, eighteenth-century literature, and Gothic tales of horror.

Lovecraft's grandfather died in 1904, and poor management of his estate forced Sarah Phillips Lovecraft and her only child into reduced circumstances. An intensely fearful and overprotective parent, Lovecraft's mother kept him isolated from other children and instilled in him a sense that he was different from other people. He had terrifying nightmares, which would become the source of much of the fiendish material in his writings. Attending high school furthered his interest in science, but in 1908, he suffered a nervous breakdown that prevented him from graduating. Unable to go to Brown University, to his great shame, he instead spent the next five years as a semi-invalid and recluse and continued his self-education.

In this claustrophobic existence, Lovecraft took to writing. He supported himself by ghostwriting, as he would throughout his life, and wrote to newspapers and magazines. In 1914 his isolation was alleviated when he joined the United Amateur Press Association, a group of writers who produced several publications and exchanged letters. The group offered Lovecraft a network of correspondence that provided a major outlet for personal and artistic expression. He also produced his own occasional periodical, *The Conservative*, starting in 1915.

Brooklyn Interlude In his teens, Lovecraft had written some stories modeled after Edgar Allan Poe. Now, encouraged by his fellow writers, he tried short fiction again. His first mature effort, "The Tomb" (1917), was printed in an amateur magazine called *The Vagrant*. Next came "Dagon," which brought Lovecraft a step beyond the amateur world in 1923 when it was printed in *Weird Tales*. This popular pulp magazine became the principal publisher of Lovecraft's fiction during his lifetime. "Dagon" marks the first of the author's many stories concerning ancient gods of his own invention. These gods reflect his own early fascination with classical mythology and other ancient literature.

Beginning around 1919—at about the time his mother was committed to an insane asylum, where she died two years later—Lovecraft began to explore the outside world and traveled in order to socialize with other amateur journalists. In 1921 he met Sonia Greene, a Russian-Jewish businesswoman from New York City. They married in 1924 and Lovecraft went to live with his wife in Brooklyn. However, he was unable to find gainful employment in the city and found metropolitan life disagreeable. When Greene moved to Cleveland for work, the marriage ended cordially and Lovecraft returned to Providence for good.

"The Call of Cthulhu" Back at home, Lovecraft began to pen the works on which his reputation now rests. "The Call of Cthulhu" (1928) introduces the elements of his most sustained and spectacular fantasy: an ancient race of beings banished from the Earth for practicing black magic, but that remains in mysterious and sinister forms, and seeks to return. Lovecraft based many stories around this legend, which later came to be called the "Cthulhu mythos." These stories chart Lovecraft's unique position between the horror and science fiction genres.

Philosophically, Lovecraft was a strict scientific materialist who saw the universe as completely mechanical. In his view, humanity lacked any special dimension of soul or spirit to distinguish it from other forms of matter. At the same time, Lovecraft wrote that his strongest feelings were connected with a sense of unknown realms outside human experience. This tension between scientific sterility and mystic imagination—whose contradictory relationship Lovecraft recognized and relished—accounts for the originality of his work.

Lovecraft published his first longer works, *The Case of Charles Dexter Ward* and *The Dream Quest of Unknown Kadath*, in 1927. Also that year, his story "The Colour Out of Space" appeared in *Amazing Stories*. It was his first and only submission to a strictly science-fiction magazine, for which he received twenty-five dollars. The following year, "The Dunwich Horror" earned him $240 from *Weird Tales*, the largest payment he had received to date.

Later Writing and Posthumous Fame In the 1930s, Lovecraft traveled a bit more widely, up to Quebec and down into the deep American South. As his horizons broadened, his social outlook changed: his conservatism turned into support for Franklin D. Roosevelt. He also softened his racial prejudices; according to biographer L. Sprague de Camp, he was disgusted to hear about anti-Semitic violence in Germany during the Nazi period. His writing also showed a modest increase in nuance and

LITERARY AND HISTORICAL CONTEMPORARIES

Lovecraft's famous contemporaries include:

Aleister Crowley (1875–1947): The British occultist Crowley wrote novels, poetry, and philosophical works in which he created his own brand of philosophy, known as Thelemic mysticism.

Franz Kafka (1883–1924): Kafka was a Hungarian-Jewish author whose famous novels, such as *The Trial* (1925), conjure up nightmarish scenarios.

Aldous Huxley (1894–1963): A British novelist and intellectual, Huxley is most famous as the author of *Brave New World* (1932) and *The Doors of Perception* (1954).

Robert Graves (1895–1985): Graves was a British poet, novelist, historian, critic, and translator of classical mythology.

William Faulkner (1897–1962): An American novelist of high literary stature, some of Faulkner's works have Gothic elements, such as *As I Lay Dying* (1930).

complexity. The novella *At the Mountains of Madness* and the short novel *The Shadow over Innsmouth* were both published in 1936; the latter was his only work published in book form during his lifetime. His last important story was "The Shadow out of Time" (1936), in which a professor gradually realizes that he has been abducted by aliens from the ancient past; on an archaeological dig, he finds a document millions of years old, in his own handwriting.

In addition to his "weird tales," Lovecraft wrote essays (including an influential work on *Supernatural Horror in Literature*, 1945), poetry, and a large body of letters to his many correspondents. He collaborated with and mentored several writers, including August Derleth, Frank Belknap Long, and Robert Bloch, who collectively formed the "Lovecraft Circle." When Lovecraft died painfully of intestinal cancer in 1937, the Lovecraft Circle carried on. Derleth and Donald Wandrei started a publishing company, Arkham House, to collect and preserve the master's scattered writings and many unpublished works. Their efforts are mostly responsible for bringing Lovecraft posthumously to the world's attention. It was Derleth who coined the term "Cthulhu mythos." He also wrote numerous stories based on Lovecraft's imaginative constructions and aroused controversy by listing Lovecraft as his co-author.

Works in Literary Context

Lovecraft was a precocious child and began reading, and absorbing the influence of, literature such as the *Arabian Nights* and Greek and Roman mythology from a very early age. His grandfather also entertained him in his youth with

COMMON HUMAN EXPERIENCE

Lovecraft knew that most critics scorned his "weird tales," but he wrote, "I really have a fairly respectable line of literary predecessors to back me up." His works fit comfortably in a tradition of imaginative horror, along with the following works:

Frankenstein (1818), a novel by Mary Shelley. The classic novel of Victorian horror, this tale is an elegant warning about the limits of scientific endeavor.

The Narrative of Arthur Gordon Pym of Nantucket (1838), a novel by Edgar Allan Poe. In Poe's only finished novel, a young man stows away on a whaler, and his adventures get stranger and stranger.

Invasion of the Body Snatchers (1956), a film directed by Don Siegel, based on the novel *The Body Snatchers* (1955) by Jack Finney. In this science-fiction masterpiece, people are being taken over one at a time by "pods."

The Shining (1977), a novel by Stephen King. In this best-selling novel, a mysterious hotel exerts a powerful force over an alcoholic father and his clairvoyant son.

improvised horror stories on the Gothic model. When he discovered the works of Edgar Allan Poe at the age of eight, he was inspired to write his own macabre tales. Poe remained a formative influence on his literary efforts, as did the Irish fantasist Lord Dunsany, who wrote of mighty beings in enchanted realms, and Arthur Machen, a supernatural-horror writer who imagined the presence of ancient, sinister forces. In addition to identifying these influences on Lovecraft's vision, it is also possible to trace the influences on his unusual writing style—modeled after eighteenth-century stylists Alexander Pope, Joseph Addison and Richard Steele—and his social views, which followed the theories of Oswald Spengler and Friedrich Nietzsche.

Lovecraft's influence on literature and popular culture has been enormous. His first direct impact was on the younger writers he encouraged, who formed the "Lovecraft Circle" and borrowed elements of his fiction in their own writing. August Derleth went furthest of all, concocting a whole cosmology out of the "Cthulhu mythos." Beyond his immediate associates, Lovecraft's impact has made itself felt on the genres of horror, science fiction, and other "weird" fiction. Neil Gaiman, Clive Barker, Harlan Ellison, and Stephen King are among the many who have cited Lovecraft as a key influence. King, the preeminent horror writer of his generation, graced a book jacket of Lovecraft's stories by calling him "the twentieth century's greatest practitioner of the classic horror tale."

Supernatural New England   Lovecraft's stories are commonly divided into three types: those influenced by Dunsany; a group of horror narratives in realistic settings,

reminiscent of Poe; and tales sharing the cosmic legend of Lovecraft's own invention (the Cthulhu mythos). The Dunsanian narratives are related to a tradition of fairy tales and are typified by wholly imaginary settings. The early story "Dagon" (1923) and the novella *The Dream Quest of Unknown Kadath* (1943) are in this vein. Contrasting with these dreamlike romances are tales in which the central element of supernatural horror originates in a realistic New England setting. Lovecraft was captivated by the architecture and landscape of New England, but also depicted a darker side of his native region: one that incorporated degeneracy and superstition in secluded locales, as in "The Picture in the House" (1921) and "The Unnameable" (1925); unearthly rituals practiced in quaint little towns, as in "The Festival" (1925); and ghouls inhabiting modern Boston, in "Pickman's Model" (1927).

Madness and the Insignificance of Humankind
The Cthulhu stories are set in a fictionalized New England dreamscape, in places named Arkham, Dunwich, and Innsmouth, a world possessed by ancient alien entities whose nonhuman nature violates conventional concepts of reality. Again and again in these stories, human beings confront unseen forces that lead ultimately to unspeakable knowledge. Madness or death comes to those who attain full awareness of the mysterious powers lurking in the shadows of ordinary existence. Lovecraft's supernatural beings, alien to the human sphere and blind to the welfare or harm of humankind, reveal the author's belief that human civilization is insignificant in the universal scheme.

Works in Critical Context

Aside from the devoted readers of *Weird Tales*, very few people were aware of the work of Lovecraft during his lifetime. Beginning with the efforts of August Derleth and Donald Wandrei, posthumous publications of Lovecraft's stories have reached an ever-growing audience, attracting considerable critical attention. Critical reception to Lovecraft displays an unusual diversity, from exasperated attacks to reverent celebrations. The uneven quality of his work and his eccentric, old-fashioned prose style have led his severest detractors to regard him as an isolated neurotic. For example, the noted science fiction author Ursula K. Le Guin, in the *Times Literary Supplement*, called Lovecraft "an exceptionally, almost impeccably, bad writer." On the other hand, his many aficionados applaud his ability to make readers' flesh creep by invoking unseen, unearthly powers.

Beyond Victorian Horror   An important controversy in Lovecraft criticism regards how to classify his work in terms of genre. Various labels have been employed, from the broad designations of "horror" and "Gothic" to terms such as "mechanistic supernatural." While his works clearly belong to the tradition of Gothic literature, Lovecraft did not depend on the common mythic concepts associated with the tradition, such as ghosts, vampires, witches, and other figures of folklore. Instead of such hobgoblins, Lovecraft substituted a philosophical viewpoint aligned with modern science, but pulled, as if by gravity, toward the irrational. Donald Burleson writes in *H. P. Lovecraft: A Critical Study*:

> The horror, ultimately, in a Lovecraft tale is not some gelatinous lurker in dark places, but rather the realization, by the characters involved, of their helplessness and their insignificance in the scheme of things . . . their own motelike unimportance in a blind and chaotic universe which neither loves them nor even finds them worthy of notice.

Responses to Literature

1. Read "The Colour Out of Space." Do you think it is accurate to call the story "science fiction"? How is it different from Lovecraft's other tales?

2. Analyze a Lovecraft story of your choosing. How does the author establish an atmosphere of dread, and what techniques does he use to provoke an emotional reaction?

3. Does Lovecraft's idiosyncratic prose style add to the power of his fiction? How?

BIBLIOGRAPHY

Books

Burleson, Donald. *H. P. Lovecraft: A Critical Study*. Westport, Conn.: Greenwood Press, 1983.

Carter, Lin. *Lovecraft: A Look behind the "Cthulhu Mythos."* New York: Ballantine, 1972.

Davis, Sonia H. *The Private Life of H. P. Lovecraft*. West Warwick, R.I.: Necronomicon Press, 1985.

Derleth, August. *H. P. L.: A Memoir*. Chicago: Ben Abramson, 1945.

Joshi, S. T. *H. P. Lovecraft; A Life*. West Warwick, R.I.: Necronomicon Press, 1996.

———, ed. *H. P. Lovecraft: Four Decades of Criticism*. Athens, Ohio: Ohio University Press, 1980.

Levy, Maurice. *Lovecraft: A Study in the Fantastic* (translated by S. T. Joshi). Detroit.: Wayne State University Press, 1988.

Price, Robert M., ed. *H. P. Lovecraft and the Cthulhu Mythos: Essays on America's Classic Writer of Horror Fiction*. San Bernardino, Calif.: Borgo Press, 1995.

Schweitzer, Darrell. *The Dream Quest of H. P. Lovecraft*. San Bernardino, Calif.: Borgo Press, 1978.

Turner, Jim, ed. *Eternal Lovecraft: The Persistence of HPL in Popular Culture*. Collinsville, Ill.: Golden Gryphon Press, 1998.

Wilson, Colin. *The Strength to Dream: Literature and the Imagination*. Boston: Houghton Mifflin, 1962.

✸ Amy Lowell

BORN: *1874, Brookline, Massachusetts*

DIED: *1925, Brookline, Massachusetts*

NATIONALITY: *American*

GENRE: *Poetry, nonfiction*

MAJOR WORKS:
Sword Blades and Poppy Seed (1914)
Some Imagist Poets: An Anthology (editor, 1915)
Can Grande's Castle (1918)
John Keats (1925)
What's O'Clock (1926)

Overview

From 1913 until her death in 1925, Amy Lowell of Boston was a formidable force on the literary scene. She helped bring about the emergence of modern American poetry in the early twentieth century, particularly through the brief but influential phenomenon called imagism. She wrote and published over six hundred and fifty poems herself, but she is remembered more for her contributions as an editor, critic, patron, spokesperson, and popularizer of modern poetry.

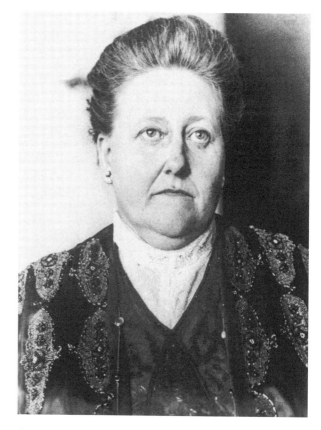

Amy Lowell   © *Bettmann / Corbis*

LITERARY AND HISTORICAL CONTEMPORARIES

Lowell's famous contemporaries include:

Willa Cather (1873–1947): American novelist whose best works, such as *My Antonia* (1918), feature strong heroines.

Robert Frost (1874–1963): American poet of rural New England famous for poems such as "The Road Not Taken" (1916).

Virginia Woolf (1882–1941): British novelist considered a leading modernist; author of the feminist classic *A Room of One's Own* (1929).

D. H. Lawrence (1885–1930): Controversial British poet and novelist who exchanged many letters with Amy Lowell.

Hilda Doolittle (1886–1961): Known simply as H. D., she was an American poet central to imagism and the modernist movement.

Works in Biographical and Historical Context

The Mistress of Sevenels   Amy Lowell was born in Brookline, Massachusetts, on February 9, 1874, the youngest of five children of Augustus and Katherine Bigelow Lawrence Lowell. She descended from a prominent, aristocratic clan with New England roots dating to the seventeenth century; her brother, Abbott Lawrence Lowell, went on to become president of Harvard College. Raised in a stately mansion on the family's ten-acre estate, Sevenels (so named because it housed seven Lowells), she was tutored by governesses and attended private schools in between sojourns to Europe with her family. From an early age, she was encouraged to write. Her first publication was a volume of stories, privately printed, called *Dream Drops or Stories from Fairy Land by a Dreamer* (1887), by Lowell, her sister Elizabeth, and their mother.

She was one of Boston's most popular debutantes in the 1891 season, but no marriage proposal was forthcoming. Her family did not think college education was appropriate for a young woman; instead she diligently educated herself in the huge library at Sevenels, and became, like her father, a fanatical book collector. Lowell continued to live at Sevenels for the rest of her life, purchasing it after her father's death in 1900. For most of that time she lived with her devoted secretary and companion, Ada Dwyer Russell.

One book among the seven thousand in her father's library, a volume of British poetry, struck her deeply, especially the selections by John Keats. She began acquiring books and materials related to the poet until she had amassed a world-famous collection of Keats artifacts and memorabilia. Watching a performance by the famous actress Eleonora Duse in the fall of 1902 inspired to write her first adult poem. Afterwards, she felt that poetry was her calling.

Discovering the Imagists   It was not until 1910, at the age of thirty-six, that Lowell saw the publication of her first poem, "Fixed Idea," in the *Atlantic*. Other poems appeared in various periodicals over the next several years. In 1912, Houghton Mifflin published her first collection, *A Dome of Many-Coloured Glass*; the title was a reference to Percy Bysshe Shelley's elegy to Keats. The book was neither a popular nor a critical success.

The beginning of Lowell's public literary career came at an exciting and complex time for American poetry—the cusp of the high modern era. In 1912, Harriet Monroe founded *Poetry* magazine, which first exposed Lowell to the new departures in contemporary poetry and provided a catalyst for her own writing. Lowell grew interested in several progressive young poets known as imagists, whose strikingly original work honed poetic expression down to its purest, most direct form. Reading some of Hilda Doolittle's poems in the magazine, signed "H. D. Imagiste," Lowell recognized a kinship, and was struck by the realization that she, too, was an imagist.

Spurred by curiosity and a desire to join this new movement, Lowell obtained a letter of introduction to the leader of the imagists, Ezra Pound, from Harriet Monroe, and set out for London early in the summer of 1913. Lowell and Pound became friends, and she also became acquainted with other writers such as John Gould Fletcher and Henry James. Before long, she had met all the major imagists, including Doolittle and Ford Madox Hueffer (who later changed his name to Ford Madox Ford).

"Amygism"   Lowell returned to Boston prepared to campaign for imagism, which she was sure would spark a renaissance in American poetry. She began crisscrossing the country on tour, interpreting the new modern verse in lectures and readings before increasingly large crowds. As a self-appointed propagandist, Lowell was convinced that her mission was not only to advance the poetic enterprise in America but to help refine the taste of the American public. In reviews and critical writing, she praised and encouraged other poets, not only imagists but popular poets like Robert Frost and Carl Sandburg; she also supported several institutions and individuals financially. One of the leading modernists, T. S. Eliot, called her a "demon saleswoman of poetry."

Ezra Pound had included a poem of Lowell's in his 1914 anthology *Des Imagistes*, intended to be the first of an annual series. Later that year, Pound and Lowell had a falling out over the financing of a new periodical and the broader direction of the movement. Pound then abandoned imagism, and Lowell took over editing the annual anthology from 1915 to 1917. Pound subsequently disparaged her as a wealthy dilettante and interloper and derided the movement as "Amygism."

In addition to editing and contributing to the three volumes of *Some Imagist Poets* (1915–1917), Lowell also penned two books of literary criticism, *Six French Poets: Studies in Contemporary Literature* (1915) and *Tendencies in Modern American Poetry* (1917), based on her lectures. She also continued to publish her own poetry in book form. *Sword Blades and Poppy Seed* (1914) was immediately successful, and several more volumes followed.

Biography of Keats Through Pound, Lowell became interested and subsequently influenced by the culture of the Far East. She wrote haikus and other "chinoiseries," poems fashioned after the languages of the Orient. The title of her collection *Pictures of the Floating World* (1919) comes from the Japanese name for a certain style of painting. Some of the short, free-verse lyrics in this collection are highly erotic, with overtones of lesbianism. Lowell also adapted Chinese poems, with translator Florence Ayscough, in the book *Fir-Flower Tablets* (1921).

Lowell's book *A Critical Fable* (1922) was a literary answer to *A Fable for Critics* (1848), a famous satire by her cousin James Russell Lowell. Like the earlier volume, Amy Lowell's *Fable* uses rhymed couplets to poke fun at her fellow poets and the literary profession generally. She also followed her cousin's lead by first publishing her literary joke anonymously.

In the early 1920s, Lowell penned a biography of John Keats, which received enthusiastic reviews at its publication in 1925. Through the wealth of Keats artifacts she had amassed over the years, her biography managed to clarify some issues about the poet's personal life. At thirteen hundred pages, *John Keats* probed the minute details of the poet's life and attempted to depict him as the spiritual antecedent of modern poetry. Lowell's exhaustive scholarship took a toll on her health. She was already plagued by hernia problems. After a severe hernia attack in 1925, she defied doctors' orders and got out of bed. As a result, she was felled by a stroke that took her life. Ada Dwyer Russell edited three posthumous collections of Lowell's poetry, one of which, *What's O'Clock* (1925), won the 1926 Pulitzer Prize for Poetry.

Works in Literary Context

Above all other literary influences on Amy Lowell was that of Keats, with whom she had been fascinated since her youth. Not only does the title of *A Dome of Many-Coloured Glass* obliquely invoke Keats, but the book's elegant design emulates the first edition of Keats's *Lamia* (1820). Lowell's longtime interest in the French novelist Joris Karl Huysmans and her discovery of French *vers libre* (free verse) also influenced various poems in her first collection. Subsequently, the work of her contemporaries, especially the imagists Ezra Pound and H. D., was a decisive influence and a confirmation of the direction her work was taking.

Imagism Imagism was noted as the first modernist movement of English-language writers circulating in the avant-garde before World War I. Its practitioners, in London and the United States, reacted against the sentimental moralism, rigid formats, and ornamental or excessive language of the prevailing Victorian poetry. Imagism aimed to distill poetry to its essence: precise imagery and sharp, clear expression. Its aesthetic was aligned with that of many modern visual artists, notably the cubists. Lowell's own verse headed toward what the French call *vers libre*, but what she termed "unrhymed cadence," a nonmetrical style she felt well-suited for the English language and based on the natural rhythms of speech. With her friend John Gould Fletcher, Lowell is credited with bringing this verse style, also called polyphonic prose, into American poetry—a style closer to the rhythms of prose than of verse. Indeed, many of Lowell's poems lack line breaks and thus appear like paragraphs of prose on the page.

Poetic Mysticism Lowell's approach to life and art was intuitive and mystical. The imagistic mode in which she cast her poems was the one best suited to her gifts and the visionary character of her poetry. In her vision, a transcendent power permeates the world and invests all created things with divinity. Her great sensitivity to sensual impressions, which she used to express this luminous quality of physical objects, gives her poetry a striking visceral impact. Lowell's love poetry similarly depicts the achievement of love as a sacred rite. As a poet her contribution is a rebirth of the human sense of the beauties and mysteries of existence.

Poetic Oracle The imagist movement, although short-lived, was highly influential as an early expression of the modern currents in poetry. Its principles represented a point of embarkation for high modernists such as T. S. Eliot, and even later avant-garde movements such as that of the Beats. Lowell, through her efforts as a promoter, helped to enliven the literary scene and expand the audience for serious poetry in America.

COMMON HUMAN EXPERIENCE

Imagism set out to chisel poetry down to a sleek, hard essence; precise images, no extra words: "no ideas but in things." Some dazzling short poems, such as the following, came out of this movement:

"In a Station of the Metro" (1916), by Ezra Pound. This famous poem by Pound consists of only two lines.
"Fog" (1916), by Carl Sandburg. This poem is famous for its effective imagery, depicting fog as a feline creature.
"Oread" (1919), by H. D. This extended metaphor offers a powerful image of a sea of trees.
"The Red Wheelbarrow" (1923), by William Carlos Williams. This spare, enigmatic poem has been the subject of much scholarly attention.

Works in Critical Context

A Dome of Many-Coloured Glass found few sympathetic reviewers; in the *Chicago Evening Post*, Louis Untermeyer wrote that the collection "can never rouse one's anger. . . . it cannot rouse one at all." *Sword Blades and Poppy Seed* and her later efforts fared better. Some critics tended to admire her poetry for its beauty, and its vivid descriptions of sights, sounds, and smells. D. H. Lawrence, who corresponded with the Bostonian for more than a decade until her death, was impressed with how she captured "the last stages of human apprehension of physico-sensational world." Others scathingly attacked both Lowell's literary work and Lowell herself; her outsized personality, lesbianism, and masculine affectations such as cigar smoking were offensive to conservative sensibilities.

Surface and Depth   Few readers, friendly or critical, have deeply understood the nature of Lowell's verse. Because the language of her most characteristic poetry is chiefly pictorial and descriptive, many dismissed her as a writer who touched only the physical surfaces of the world, failing to comprehend the spiritual vision that lay beneath her richly described imagery. The "New Critics" of the mid-twentieth century perpetuated this misunderstanding. They valued poetry rich in cultural allusions and ironic wit, such as that of Eliot and the later Pound; Lowell's body of work fell outside these aesthetic parameters. Since the rise of feminism and women's studies in the 1970s, scholars have taken another look at Lowell, especially studying her romantic and erotic lesbian love poetry. Recognition of her cultural importance, however, has tended to outshine the lasting literary value of her writing.

Responses to Literature

1. Discuss the significance of flower imagery in the poem "Patterns" (1915), one of Lowell's best-known works.

2. Lowell's free-verse format has been called "polyphonic prose" and "unrhymed cadence." Citing several examples in her work, how would you describe the effect of this loose style?

3. How would you distinguish imagism from other movements in modern poetry? Include examples from one or more poems by Lowell to illustrate your meaning.

BIBLIOGRAPHY

Books

Benvenuto, Richard. *Amy Lowell*. Boston: Twayne, 1985.

Damon, S. Foster. *Amy Lowell: A Chronicle*. Boston and New York: Houghton Mifflin, 1935.

Galvin, Mary E. *Queer Poetics: Five Modernist Women Writers*. Westport, Conn: Greenwood Press, 1998.

Gould, Jean. *Amy: The World of Amy Lowell and The Imagist Movement*. New York: Dodd, Mead, 1975.

Heymann, C. David. *American Aristocracy: The Lives and Times of James Russell, Amy and Robert Lowell*. New York: Dodd, Mead, 1980.

Ruihley, Glenn Richard. *The Thorn of a Rose: Amy Lowell Reconsidered*. Hamden, Conn: Archon Books, 1975.

Periodicals

Faderman, Lillian. "Cigar-Smoking Sappho: Lesbian Laureate Amy Lowell Took her World by Storm." *Advocate* (February 1990).

Francis, Lesley Lee. "A Decade of 'Stirring Times': Robert Frost and Amy Lowell." *New England Quarterly* 59 (December 1986): 508–522.

Healey, Claire. "Amy Lowell Visits London." *New England Quarterly* 46 (September 1973): 439–453.

✸ James Russell Lowell

BORN: *1819, Cambridge, Massachusetts*

DIED: *1891, Cambridge, Massachusetts*

NATIONALITY: *American*

GENRE: *Poetry, nonfiction*

MAJOR WORKS:

The Biglow Papers (1848)

A Fable for Critics (1848)

Among My Books (1870)

Overview

Perhaps the most versatile American intellectual of the nineteenth century, James Russell Lowell was a vital force in American literature and thought. He excelled in an impressive range of pursuits: lyric poet, satirist, literary critic, political essayist, magazine editor, professor of belles lettres, and diplomat. Lowell became in his own time an influential arbiter of literary taste and value and a widely read and internationally respected man of letters.

Works in Biographical and Historical Context

The Magazine Pioneer   James Russell Lowell was born in Cambridge, Massachusetts, on February 22, 1819, the youngest of six children of Rev. Charles Russell Lowell, a Unitarian minister, and Harriet Spence Lowell. Throughout his life, he belonged to the proud, genteel society of the Boston Brahmins, a group descended from the original settlers of New England. Educated according to the best standards of the day, in due time he entered Harvard College. He neglected his class work and got in trouble for high-spirited antics, but he edited the campus literary magazine. His classmates elected him to recite the annual poem on the eve of commencement, but he was suspended before he could deliver the oration. Instead, the *Class Poem* (1838) became his first publication.

Lacking a clear career objective, Lowell earned a degree from Harvard Law School and set up practice in

James Russell Lowell   *Lowell, James Russell, photograph. The Library of Congress.*

Boston. After six months, he abandoned the idea and gambled on finding a literary livelihood. He published a volume of poetry, *A Year's Life*, in 1841, and a second collection in 1844, and contributed verses to a number of magazines. Periodicals had begun wielding a far-reaching influence on American culture in the 1840s. Lowell began a high-minded magazine himself, the *Pioneer*, in 1843, and solicited contributions from an impressive group of writers; Edgar Allan Poe introduced his story "The Tell-Tale Heart" in its pages. Unfortunately, the publication went under after three issues.

Lowell married Maria White, the daughter of a prosperous merchant, in late 1844, just as his first book of literary criticism, *Conversations on Some of the Old Poets* (1845), was being printed. Under his wife's influence, Lowell became increasingly interested and active in political affairs, notably the movement to abolish slavery. He wrote scores of articles and poems, both satirical and polemical, in defense of abolition and other reform causes in the 1840s.

Biglow and A Fable for Critics   Between 1846 and 1848, in the *National Anti-Slavery Standard* and the abolitionist *Boston Courier*, appeared Lowell's most impor-

tant work of this period, the verses of his persona Hosea Biglow. The use of the rustic Yankee as a voice of political reason was not original with Lowell; John Adams had created the character Humphrey Ploughjogger back in the 1760s. Lowell's contribution was in turning the figure into a memorable poet. Using humor and dialect, Lowell launched a forceful satire against the Mexican War, which Congress declared in May 1846 and which the abolitionists, among others, viewed as immoral. In Lowell's view, the aggression against Mexico, and the prior annexation of Texas—which had once been territory belonging to Mexico—were means to extend slavery westward and further cement its pernicious role in American life. The verses of Hosea Biglow were an immediate success, and later compiled in book form as *The Biglow Papers* (1848).

Also in 1848, Lowell published a romantic narrative poem, *The Vision of Sir Launfal*; another poetry collection; and one of his most lasting works, *A Fable for Critics*, a versified commentary on America's contemporary writers. His satirical caricatures of his fellow wordsmiths are bitingly incisive; Edgar Allan Poe, for instance, was incensed by these couplets: "There comes Poe, with his raven, like Barnaby Rudge / Three fifths of him genius and two fifths sheer fudge... / Who has written some things quite the best of their kind / But the heart somehow seems all squeezed out by the mind." The volume quickly sold out three editions and established its author as a wry, audacious observer of the literary scene.

Position at Harvard   In the space of a few years between 1847 and 1852, James and Maria Lowell lost three of their four children; Maria herself died in 1853, leaving Lowell distraught. The joy he found in his sole surviving daughter sustained him, and he made his study a place of refuge and recreation, reading for twelve or more hours a day. He shared the first fruits of this solitary education when he was invited to give a lecture series at the Lowell Institute in Boston in 1855. The overseers at Harvard were so impressed that midway through his twelve lectures, the college offered Lowell the Smith Professorship of Modern Languages, vacated by Henry Wadsworth Longfellow's retirement. Lowell prepared himself for the post with a year of diligent study in Europe, leaving his daughter in the care of a governess, Frances Dunlap. After returning to Cambridge and joining the Harvard faculty, Lowell and Dunlap were married.

Lowell helped to found the *Atlantic Monthly* in the fall of 1857 and became the magazine's first editor, as well as a principal contributor. Under his guidance, the *Atlantic Monthly* set a high mark both for its literary standards and its courageous and outspoken coverage of public affairs, as the nation teetered on the brink of civil war. The dispute between Union and Confederate supporters focused on the rights of states to govern themselves, though the main point of contention was a state's right to practice slavery. Lowell gave up the editorship of

LITERARY AND HISTORICAL CONTEMPORARIES

James Russell Lowell's famous contemporaries include:

Henry David Thoreau (1817–1862): An American author, activist, and naturalist, Thoreau is best known as the author of *Walden* (1854).

Walt Whitman (1819–1892): An American poet whose free-verse declamations celebrated liberty and vitality, Whitman's most enduring work is the collection *Leaves of Grass* (1855).

George Eliot (1819–1880): Eliot was a British novelist who wrote under a male pseudonym; she was known for sophisticated characterizations in novels like *Middlemarch* (1871–1872).

Fyodor Dostoyevsky (1821–1881): Dostoyevsky was Russian novelist whose masterworks include *Crime and Punishment* (1866) and *The Brothers Karamazov* (1880).

Rutherford B. Hayes (1822–1893): Hayes became the nineteenth president of the United States after winning a controversial election in 1876 against Samuel Tilden, in which Tilden won a majority of the popular vote.

Charles Eliot Norton (1827–1908): Norton was a distinguished Harvard professor and coeditor (with Lowell) of the *North American Review*.

the magazine just as the fighting was breaking out, but he continued to submit poetry and prose.

He became coeditor of the *North American Review*, a staid Boston literary journal, in 1863, contributing essays in support of Abraham Lincoln's stewardship of the Union, as well as critical articles on authors such as William Shakespeare, Geoffrey Chaucer, and Dante Alighieri. The war inspired him to write a second, more somber series of *The Biglow Papers* (1862). After the cessation of hostilities and the assassination of Lincoln, Lowell composed and publicly recited an ode commemorating graduates of Harvard who served in the war.

In 1870 the literature professor collected six of his best *North American Review* essays in his first major work of criticism, *Among My Books*. This volume was an enormous success, going through over thirty printings in Lowell's lifetime. Its successor, *My Study Windows* (1871), sold even better and brought its author to the peak of his fame as a critic.

Diplomatic Service   Lowell continued to write essays and satirical poetry in the 1870s. One such effort, "Tempora Mutantur" (1875)—meaning "times have changed"— denounces the corruption that had become synonymous with American politics during the Gilded Age. He entered the political arena in 1876 as a delegate to the Republican convention supporting Rutherford B. Hayes, who won in

that year's disputed presidential election. Hayes appointed Lowell ambassador to Spain in 1877; after three years in Madrid, he moved to London as Minister to England. During his long stay in Europe and after his return home in 1885, he fulfilled his role as America's foremost man of letters by addressing varied audiences on both political and literary subjects. His orations, such as an influential one on "Democracy" (1884), and other writings were collected in several books, including a ten-volume compendium, in his final years. He died on August 12, 1891, in the house in which he was born.

Works in Literary Context

Lowell's wide-ranging intellect absorbed all sorts of influences in cosmopolitan fashion. From his mother he acquired a taste for stories and poetry, and he read widely from an early age. His many critical writings leave a detailed impression of his overall aesthetic. In reviewing literature, he customarily "ranked" poets and judged them against his list of "five indispensable authors": Homer, Dante, Miguel de Cervantes, Johann Wolfgang von Goethe, and Shakespeare.

Lowell as Humorist   One consistent element of Lowell's literary productions is humor. It is never absent from his best poetry, essays, and letters, and its range is as varied as the occasions that elicited it—witty and learned sometimes, boisterous and close to bawdy at others, and always displaying a skeptical, ironic perspective. Of all his writings, the one most often remembered by posterity is his grand literary joke, *A Fable for Critics*, which he wrote for the sheer fun of it. *The Biglow Papers* ranks among the finest political satires in American literature, and its sophisticated use of vernacular dialect inspired later humorists such as Mark Twain and H. L. Mencken.

Public Poetry   Throughout his life Lowell attempted to master a lyrical poetic voice, but his efforts were excessively literary, often didactic, and occasionally awkward and forced. As a public poet, however, both in his satiric verse and his Pindaric odes, Lowell has few equals in American literature. He believed that the poet's role in society is to feel and express the deep meaning of the present. The Biglow poems reflect his intention to employ poetry to contribute to the debate on central social issues. At this aim they succeeded handsomely; in the opinion of Lowell's fellow abolitionist, John Greenleaf Whittier, "the world-wide laugh" caused by the rustic Yankee poet was enough to "have shaken half the walls of Slavery down." Following the Civil War, Lowell lived increasingly in the public eye. In poems like the *Commemoration Ode* (1865) and *The Cathedral* (1870), he spoke nobly and effectively in a manner that can be compared to Walt Whitman's *Democratic Vistas* (1871).

The Critical Habit   Lowell stands alongside Edgar Allan Poe as one of the two most important literary critics

America produced before the Civil War. Much more than Poe, Lowell became an influential judge of taste, a popular and erudite spokesman for the best in American culture. He wrote major essays on dozens of authors, each revealing his vast learning. Yet his criticism was impressionistic, driven by no overriding theoretical viewpoint. One of the clearest statements of his orientation comes from a manuscript fragment called "Criticism and Culture" (unpublished until 1969): "The object of all criticism is not to criticize, but to understand.... Above all, criticism is useful in inducing a judicial habit of mind, and teaching us to keep our intellectual tempers." As one of the century's most distinguished American men of letters, this "judicial habit of mind" was perhaps his most profound legacy.

Works in Critical Context

The early reception to Lowell's poetic offerings was uneven; while he received recognition and wide publication in periodicals, a few people were not impressed. Margaret Fuller and Ralph Waldo Emerson were among those who found his poetry wanting. Although he rose to international fame, Lowell was not in any respect a popular writer. Most readers considered his poetry too difficult; his literary essays appealed to a relatively small class of readers; and his political essays, topical in nature, were not designed to be lasting literary works. It was the combination of his talents that made him eminent—that and a certain quality of character not necessarily reflected on the printed page. Another literary eminence, William Dean Howells, wrote of Lowell: "I knew and felt his greatness somehow apart from the literary proofs of it.... He ruled my fancy and held my allegiance as a character, as a man."

By the early twentieth century, little of the writing Lowell left behind was much read. His reputation had become a matter of received opinion, and that reputation declined significantly in the twentieth century. Modernists and New Critics tended to dismiss him as the embodiment of an outmoded, genteel tradition. In the present era, scholarly interest in Lowell centers on his cultural contributions rather than his literary merits. His works of criticism have received due regard from literary historians, but aside from the satirical *Biglow Papers*, his creative writing has been neglected by contemporary readers and critics.

A Fable for Critics   Given the subject matter of *A Fable for Critics* (1848), it is no surprise the amount of attention the work received from critics and writers when it was published. However, it was not necessarily Lowell himself who received the credit or blame, since the original edition of the book did not carry the author's name—perhaps for fear of repercussion. Despite the original author's anonymity, Poe has no trouble naming the source in his review for the *Southern Literary Messenger*, and its authorship was likely common knowledge soon

COMMON HUMAN EXPERIENCE

Lowell's *Biglow Papers* advanced the abolitionist cause through potent satire. It stands alongside these other American literary works that condemned the institution of slavery:

Walker's Appeal (1829), by David Walker. A radical pamphlet written by a free black man, this work called for immediate and universal emancipation of enslaved African Americans, if necessary through armed insurrection.

Narrative of the Life of Frederick Douglass, an American Slave (1845), a memoir by Frederick Douglass. This escaped slave's memoir was so eloquent that many whites doubted its authenticity, certain that no black man could write so well.

Uncle Tom's Cabin (1852), by Harriet Beecher Stowe. This sentimental novel captured the American imagination like no other work of fiction before or since, and deepened the sectional discord that led to the Civil War.

The Adventures of Huckleberry Finn (1884) by Mark Twain. One of the preeminent works of American literature, Twain's satire confronts the cruelty of slavery and the ethical responsibility of whites.

after publication. The work offered humorous portrayals of many contemporary writers, and the witty gibes made by Lowell sometimes landed on their mark more heavily than he may have expected. Edgar Allan Poe, for example, did not seem to respond well to his portrayal. In his scathing review, he calls the book "ill-conceived and feebly executed, as well in detail as in general." Poe declares, "We laugh not so much at the author's victims as at himself, for letting them put him in such a passion." Poe also takes Lowell to task for his antislavery bias: "Mr. L has not the common honesty to speak well, even in a literary sense, of any man who is not a ranting Abolitionist." He concludes that the book is so "feeble" and "weakly constructed" that Lowell has "lowered himself at least fifty percent in the literary public opinion."

Francis Bowen, writing for *North American Review*, is far more complimentary, calling it "a very pleasant and sparkling poem, abounding in flashes of brilliant satire, edged with wit enough to delight even its victims." Though Bowen does find fault with several elements of the book—including the introduction, the author's choice of subjects, and his too-frequent reliance upon puns, which he calls "wit's bastard offspring"—he nonetheless praises Lowell's audacity to lampoon both authors and critics. It is worth noting that, in *A Fable for Critics*, the anonymous author offers a criticism of himself, noting:

"The top of the hill he will ne'er come nigh reaching / Till he learns the distinction 'twixt singing and preaching."

Responses to Literature

1. Lowell once stated that the point of criticism is "not to criticize, but to understand." Reading some of his own critical works, do you think he followed this guideline? Why or why not? Do you think his approach to studying literature is reflected by critics and scholars today?

2. Try writing your own *Fable for Critics*, with capsule summaries of your favorite (and least favorite) authors. What is it that makes their works unique to them? In what areas could they use improvement?

3. Examine a recent issue of the *Atlantic*. Do you think it holds the same value and importance today as it did in the nineteenth century? Why or why not?

4. In *The Biglow Papers*, how does the elite and well-educated Lowell use "rustic" characters with idiosyncratic diction to convey social commentary?

BIBLIOGRAPHY

Books

Beatty, Richmond Croom. *James Russell Lowell*. Nashville, Tenn.: Vanderbilt University Press, 1952.

Blair, Walter. *Horse Sense in American Humor*. Chicago: University of Chicago Press, 1942.

Duberman, Martin. *James Russell Lowell*. Boston: Houghton Mifflin, 1966.

Foerster, Norman. *American Criticism: A Study in Literary Theory from Poe to the Present*. Boston: Houghton Mifflin, 1928.

Hale, Edward Everett. *James Russell Lowell and His Friends*. Boston: Houghton, Mifflin, 1899.

Heymann, C. David. *American Aristocracy: The Lives and Times of James Russell, Amy, and Robert Lowell*. New York: Dodd, Mead, 1980.

Howard, Leon. *Victorian Knight-Errant: A Study of the Early Literary Career of James Russell Lowell*. Berkeley and Los Angeles: University of California Press, 1952.

Howells, William Dean. *Literary Friends and Acquaintance*. New York: Harper, 1900.

"James Russell Lowell (1819–1891)." *Nineteenth-Century Literature Criticism*. Edited by Laurie Lanzen Harris. Vol. 2. Detroit: Gale Research, 1982, pp. 504–506.

Rourke, Constance. *American Humor: A Study in National Character*. New York: Harcourt, Brace, 1931.

Scudder, Horace Elisha. *James Russell Lowell: A Biography* (two volumes). Boston and New York: Houghton, Mifflin, 1901.

⊛ Robert Lowell

BORN: *1917, Boston, Massachusetts*

DIED: *1977, New York City*

NATIONALITY: *American*

GENRE: *Poetry*

MAJOR WORKS:
Lord Weary's Castle (1946)
Life Studies (1959)
For the Union Dead (1964)
The Dolphin (1973)

Overview

Widely considered the most influential American poet of the mid-twentieth century, Robert Lowell is acclaimed for his mastery of diverse forms, intense expression of personal concerns, and candid commentary on social and moral issues. Lowell's verse reflects his knowledge of European literary traditions as well as the social and literary history of his native New England. His efforts to express his own personal torment, and the contemporary and historical struggles of the nation, fuse in his poetry, resulting in a coherent and distinguished body of work.

Robert Lowell   *Lowell, Robert, photograph. The Library of Congress.*

Works in Biographical and Historical Context

Rebellious Child of Privilege Robert Traill Spence Lowell was born on March 1, 1917, into a prominent Boston family. Among his ancestors were literary figures James Russell Lowell and Amy Lowell. His home was dominated by incessant tension between his parents. Lowell attended St. Mark's School in Massachusetts, where he began writing poetry under the guidance of academic poet Richard Eberhart. In 1935, he went to Harvard, like all Lowells before him, but he left after two years, following a physical fight with his father.

Lowell went south in 1937 to the Tennessee home of Allen Tate, a distinguished poet who proved to be an important influence on the young writer. He pitched a tent in the Tates' front yard and spent the summer there, writing poetry in an almost obsessive way. In the fall, he went to Kenyon College in Ohio, and remained there until 1940, when he graduated summa cum laude with a degree in classics. Also in 1940, he converted to Roman Catholicism and married a young novelist, Jean Stafford.

Lowell and Stafford spent 1942–1943 in Tennessee, sharing a house with the Tates. Here Lowell wrote many of the poems that would appear in his first book. The United States had entered World War II; many adult men were required to report for military service under the draft. Lowell refused induction into the armed forces as protest against the Allied bombing of German civilians and served five months in jail as a conscientious objector.

Against the "Cake of Custom" The poems in Lowell's first collection, *Land of Unlikeness* (1944), reflect the turbulence of the war years as well as the poet's conversion to Catholicism and his reaction to his Protestant heritage. In his introduction to the volume, Allen Tate distinguished between its religious poems, which depict the decline of Christianity in the modern world, and a few more dramatic poems concerning personal experience in the contemporary historical context. Tate had foretold the outline of Lowell's career; his work would ultimately move in the latter direction.

His next publication, *Lord Weary's Castle* (1946), was awarded the Pulitzer Prize for Poetry, and firmly established Lowell's presence in American literature. It was an anguished cry of opposition to war, materialism, and the Puritan ethic. Poet and critic Randall Jarrell, writing in *The Nation*, declared that these poems

> understand the world as a sort of conflict of opposites. In this struggle one opposite is that cake of custom in which all of us lie embedded.... But struggling within this like leaven, falling to it like light, is everything that is free or open, that grows or is willing to change.

Lowell's poetry developed as Tate had predicted, growing more dramatic as it depended less on Christian symbolism. Seven dramatic monologues made up his next

volume, *The Mills of the Kavanaughs* (1951). Most critics considered this an unsuccessful attempt to explore new poetic techniques. By the time of its publication, Lowell had left the Catholic church, divorced Stafford, married the writer Elizabeth Hardwick, and suffered the first serious attack of the manic-depressive illness that would plague him throughout his life, leading repeatedly to hospitalization.

Life Studies and the 1960s A great change came over Lowell's poetry in the late 1950s. He had encountered the revolutionary poetry of Allen Ginsberg and the "Beat" writers; he also revived a friendship with the innovative poet William Carlos Williams, who was a mentor to Ginsberg as well. Lowell began a shift away from conventional form and meter toward free verse and more colloquial language. In 1957 he was writing his autobiography in prose, and this became the source for a group of highly personal poems that resembled prose fragments. In his next publication, *Life Studies* (1959), Lowell found the voice of intense personal concentration that critics would call "confessional" poetry. Winner of the National Book Award in 1960, *Life Studies* was something new on the American literary scene, a breakthrough in both content and style.

Lowell spent the 1960s in New York, commuting to teach at Harvard and writing for the theater. He wrote several loose translations of (or variations on) classic plays,

COMMON HUMAN EXPERIENCE

Lowell's *Life Studies* broadened poetry's reach into the naked psyche. Along with other literary works such as the following, it revealed the power of writing as a tool for exploring the self.

Il Canzoniere (1470), a poetry collection by Petrarch. This collection, a key source of the courtly love tradition, records the Roman poet laureate's unrequited love for a mysterious woman named Laura.

"Howl" (1955), a poem by Allen Ginsberg. Ginsberg's holy rant boldly addresses depravity, homosexuality, and the sterile madness of America in the 1950s.

Heart's Needle (1959), a poetry collection by W. D. Snodgrass. Another inaugural work of confessional verse, the title poem deals with a divorced father's troubled relationship with his young daughter.

Ariel (1965), a poetry collection by Sylvia Plath. Plath cited Lowell as an influence behind this autobiographical work; the published version includes poems written weeks before the poet committed suicide.

including Jean Racine's *Phaedra* (1961) and Aeschylus's *Prometheus Bound* (1969). His most successful theatrical work was a group of short plays called *The Old Glory* (1965), adapted from stories by Nathaniel Hawthorne and Herman Melville. Lowell also published *Imitations* (1961), which consists of reworked translations of poetry by several poets, such as Charles Baudelaire.

Lowell's next book of new poetry, *For the Union Dead* (1964), continued in the confessional vein, but emphasized the interplay of personal and historical narratives. The title poem is suffused with references to period details—advertising slogans, television images, the civil rights struggle. The poet is confident that his private experiences of turmoil parallel his vision of societal decay and alienation. *Near the Ocean* (1967), published during Lowell's most active involvement in national events, extends this concern with politics. In 1965, Lowell declined an invitation to a White House Festival of the Arts, as a protest against the war in Vietnam. Then in October 1967, he participated with several other literary figures in a highly publicized march on the Pentagon. Norman Mailer famously recorded this incident, in which Lowell plays a prominent part, in *The Armies of the Night* (1968).

The Notebook Sonnets For several years starting in 1967, Lowell wrote primarily in unrhymed sonnets. In returning to a time-honored short verse format, Lowell sought a balance between order and spontaneity as a means to describe his moment-to-moment reflections. The first version of this project, published as *Notebook 1967–1968* (1969), comments on contemporary politics while delving into the troubles in the poet's marriage and private life. Lowell published a revised version of the *Notebook* a year later. In 1973, he brought out three volumes of sonnets simultaneously. *History* consists of public poems about literary and political figures past and present; *For Lizzie and Harriet* deals with Elizabeth Hardwick and their daughter; and *The Dolphin* is mostly concerned with Lady Caroline Blackwood, the British author with whom he had another child out of wedlock. *The Dolphin* won the 1974 Pulitzer Prize for Poetry.

In 1970 Lowell moved to England, where he spent most of his next six years. He divorced Hardwick and married Blackwood in 1972. He died of a heart attack on September 12, 1977, in a taxi in New York while on his way to see Hardwick. His last volume of new poetry, *Day by Day* (1977), appeared shortly before he died.

Works in Literary Context

Lowell's elite education gave him a solid grounding in Western literature, and early in life he met and learned from distinguished poets such as Allen Tate and John Crowe Ransom, with whom he studied at Kenyon. He situated himself within the literary tradition of his native New England; he was particularly fond of Herman Melville, to whom he dedicated his acclaimed poem "The Quaker Graveyard in Nantucket," found in *Lord Weary's Castle*. His poetry also reveals the influence of the high modern poets, especially Ezra Pound.

The sense of tension and vigor that distinguishes Lowell's verse derives from his use of highly-charged, concentrated phrasing, sudden bold epigrams, and a profusion of thoughtfully-chosen details ranging from everyday objects to esoteric allusions. He makes skillful use of such poetic devices as assonance, alliteration, symbolism, and conventional verse structures. Throughout his career, Lowell experimented with verse forms and styles. In the 1940s he wrote intricate and tightly patterned poems with traditional meter and rhyme; in the late 1950s he began to write in much looser forms and meters; in the 1960s he wrote increasingly public poetry, and returned to conventional form with his sonnets; and finally, in the 1970s, his poems incorporated and extended elements of all the earlier poetry.

"Confessional" Poetry The poetry of William Carlos Williams, as noted above, influenced Lowell's break in the 1950s from a conventional style to a confessional one—intense poems, open in form, that concentrate on personal conflicts and failings. The first poem Lowell wrote in this style, "Skunk Hour," is the last to appear in *Life Studies* but is one of his best-known verses. The poem begins with a description of a declining seaside town and its inhabitants, recognizable New England character types. The speaker arrives midway, voyeuristically watching the "love-cars" from a hilltop. The poem ends with skunks searching for food in a garbage pail. These final images, arresting and ambiguous, seem to suggest a queasy metaphor for

Lowell's new artistic focus—the poet scavenging for truth in the refuse of psychic life. Hovering in the text is the fact of Lowell's mental illness; the poet bluntly states, "My mind's not right."

Numerous critics have lumped Lowell together with two of his students, Anne Sexton and Sylvia Plath, under the "confessional" label, though their poetry lacks the public dimension of Lowell's. Lowell's influence, however, extends far beyond this specific genre. For several decades in the middle of the twentieth century, he was America's leading poet, setting a standard to which nearly all aspired and by which nearly all were judged. Lowell's bold transformations in style, and the conversational poetics he inaugurated with *Life Studies*, inspired and influenced countless American writers.

Works in Critical Context

For some readers and critics, Lowell stood at the center of his literary generation. He was associated with many of the important American poets of the early twentieth century, and seemed to be their heir. Several of his mentors, including John Crowe Ransom and Robert Penn Warren, were leading figures in the New Criticism, which became the prevailing critical school in mid-century America. Lowell's early poetry, with its erudite intellectual sheen and formal virtuosity, squarely fit the aesthetic of the New Critics. He has remained in high critical regard; his final publication, *Day by Day*, won the National Book Critics Award in 1978. In the decades since his passing, scholarly interest in Lowell has dropped considerably, in favor of some of his colleagues such as Elizabeth Bishop. The introspective nature of his work, and the very public revisions he made to his *Notebook* series, have brought Lowell to the attention of postmodern literary critics.

Lord Weary's Castle   Lowell's friend Randall Jarrell, the noted poet and critic, wrote the most influential commentary on Lowell's early work, a 1947 review of *Lord Weary's Castle* in *The Nation*. Jarrell's description of the work's theme—the "wintry, Calvinist, capitalist world" against which the poet set himself—was the basis for much subsequent analysis.

Life Studies   *Life Studies*, more than a turning point in Lowell's career, is broadly considered a landmark in contemporary American poetry. Its prose-like voice and intensely personal subject matter seemed to represent a bold step toward authenticity and directness and a liberation from the artifice of high modernism. In an essay appearing in *Next-to-Last Things: New Poems and Essays*, Stanley Kunitz calls *Life Studies* "perhaps the most influential book of modern verse since [T. S. Eliot's] 'The Waste Land.'"

Responses to Literature

1. Lowell wrote in many different poetic styles throughout his career—for example, free verse in *Life Studies*, and unrhymed sonnets in *The Dolphin*. Choose a poem by Lowell, describe the style he uses in the poem, and explain why you think he chose that particular style for that poem.

2. Why do you think Lowell's "confessional" poetry in *Life Studies* and subsequent works was considered a breakthrough for American verse?

3. Study some of Lowell's poetry from the 1960s, such as *For the Union Dead*; how does he represent and use artifacts and current events from that colorful era?

4. Explain the significance of the skunks in the poem "Skunk Hour."

BIBLIOGRAPHY

Books

Axelrod, Steven Gould. *Robert Lowell: Life and Art.* Princeton, N.J.: Princeton University Press, 1978.

Bell, Vereen M. *Robert Lowell: Nihilist as Hero.* Cambridge, Mass.: Harvard University Press, 1983.

Cooper, Philip. *The Autobiographical Myth of Robert Lowell.* Chapel Hill, N.C.: University of North Carolina Press, 1970.

Hamilton, Ian. *Robert Lowell: A Biography.* New York: Random House, 1982.

Hart, Henry. *Robert Lowell and the Sublime.* Syracuse, N.Y.: Syracuse University Press, 1995.

Mailer, Norman. *The Armies of the Night.* New York: New American Library, 1968.

Mariani, Paul. *Lost Puritan: A Life of Robert Lowell.* New York: Norton, 1994.

Perloff, Marjorie. *The Poetic Art of Robert Lowell.* Ithaca, N.Y.: Cornell University Press, 1973.

Price, Jonathan, ed. *Critics on Robert Lowell.* Miami, Fla.: University of Miami Press, 1972.

Williamson, Alan. *Pity the Monsters: The Political Vision of Robert Lowell.* New Haven, Conn.: Yale University Press, 1974.

Lois Lowry

BORN: *1937, Honolulu, Hawaii*

NATIONALITY: *American*

GENRE: *Fiction*

MAJOR WORKS:
Anastasia Krupnik (1979)
Number the Stars (1989)
The Giver (1993)
The Willoughbys (2008)

Overview

An author with broad appeal, Lois Lowry has never been one to avoid complexity and controversial topics in her novels for young adults. Her books deal with subjects ranging from the death of a sibling to the Nazi occupation

Lois Lowry   *Lowry, Lois, photograph by Amanda Smith. Reproduced by permission of Lois Lowry.*

of Denmark to the humorous antics of a rebellious teen to futuristic dystopian societies. In her works, Lowry frequently addresses contemporary themes, such as an adopted child's search for her real mother or the loneliness the elderly face. Although Lowry's novels explore a variety of settings and characters, all have a common theme: the importance of the human connection in people's lives.

Works in Biographical and Historical Context

The Military Life   Lowry was born on March 20, 1937, in Honolulu, Hawaii. The daughter of a career military officer—an army dentist—Lowry lived in many different locations. After moving to New York shortly after her birth, Lowry went to live with her mother's family in the Amish country of Pennsylvania, at the beginning of World War II in Europe, in 1939. Although her grandfather adored her and tried to keep her from knowing the horrors of the war, Lowry felt a deep sense of loss because of her father's absence. This emptiness manifested itself in her novels in the form of almost-perfect father figures. At the age of eleven, Lowry briefly lived in Tokyo, Japan, before returning to New York, where she attended high school. By the time she entered Brown University in Rhode Island, her family had moved to Washington, D.C. No matter where she lived, one thing remained constant during her childhood: she tirelessly wrote stories and poems.

In 1956, after finishing her sophomore year in college, Lowry quit school to marry Donald Lowry, an officer in the U.S. Navy. As when she was a child, Lowry frequently moved, wherever the service sent her husband: to California, Connecticut, Florida, South Carolina, and Massachusetts. By the time her husband left the military and enrolled in Harvard Law School, Lowry had four children under the age of five. She was trained as a professional photographer and worked part-time to support her family while her husband finished his law degree. The family then moved to Maine.

Education and Independence   Lowry returned to college and completed her BA degree in writing at the University of Southern Maine in 1972. Later, in graduate school, Lowry wrote two textbooks and had various pieces published in magazines and newspapers. She also produced a book of photographs, *Here in Kennebunkport* (1978), with text by Frederick H. Lewis. Lowry began her career as an author for young adults when an editor at Houghton Mifflin read one of her published short stories about her childhood and asked if she would be interested in writing books for children. Around this time, her marriage ended, and the forty-year-old Lowry moved back to Cambridge, Massachusetts.

Early Books   Lowry's first novel, *A Summer to Die* (1977), inspired by her sister's death from cancer, established a common pattern in her works: she often translates her life into fiction for the purpose of helping others who may have experienced similar circumstances. Following her successful debut, Lowry continued to explore challenging adolescent topics. In her second novel, *Find a Stranger, Say Goodbye* (1978), for example, she documents an adopted child's search for her biological mother. Although neither Lowry nor any of her children are adopted, she felt that the subject was important enough to be dealt with in a sensitive and compassionate way.

Lowry's darkest version of childhood, *Autumn Street* (1979), is autobiographical in content. Like Lowry, the main character's family moves to her grandfather's home in Pennsylvania after America's entrance into World War II takes her father away to war. Elizabeth, again like Lowry, encounters unfamiliar situations, strange people, and cruel realities of the adult world in her new environment.

Anastasia Krupnik   More pleasant memories of her childhood, as well as her experiences as a parent, have led Lowry to her most popular character: Anastasia Krupnik, the spunky, rebellious, and irreverent adolescent who stars in a series of books that began in 1979. In the first book of the series, ten-year-old Anastasia faces numerous comic crises, including the arrival of a sibling and a crush on a boy who is continually dribbling an imaginary basketball. The broad audience appeal and lasting interest in Anastasia have prompted Lowry to write a total of twelve books featuring her young heroine.

Newbery Medals   In 1990, Lowry was awarded the prestigious Newbery Medal for her distinguished contribution to children's literature with *Number the Stars* (1989). Based on a factual account, the story is set during

World War II against the backdrop of Nazi-occupied Denmark, where ten-year-old Annemarie Johansen and her family are drawn into the resistance movement, and shuttle Jews from Denmark into neutral Sweden, where they are safe from the reach of the Nazis. Lowry received the Newbery Medal a second time for her novel *The Giver* (1993), a radical departure from her previous works with its futuristic world where every facet of life—birth, death, work, emotions, even the weather—is strictly controlled in order to maintain a society of "Sameness."

Current Life   Although Lowry lives and does most of her writing in Cambridge, Massachusetts, she also spends time gardening in Maine, where she owns a farmhouse that was built in 1768. She has published young-adult works consistently over the years; her most recent title in that genre being *The Willoughbys* in 2008.

Works in Literary Context

Lowry's primary inspiration has been her personal life, from the perspectives both of a child who grew up without a father and of a mother who observed her children's adolescent struggles. She has said that she draws from her own past, and that she is always mindful of her inner child when writing. Because of her *Anastasia* series, Lowry is frequently compared to Beverly Cleary, for her works offer teen readers the solid, charming writing that Cleary's *Ramona* stories give younger audiences.

Coming-of-Age Stories   While many of Lowry's novels contain lively humor, they also address serious and universal themes; Lowry believes that teenagers must be prepared to live in a complicated world and must not be overprotected from life's realities. Her works are coming-of-age stories, memorable because the main characters endure inner turmoil in their growth and development as human beings. In depicting the difficulties of growing up in a confusing adult world, Lowry helps her readers understand that others have suffered some of the same problems they are facing and have survived.

In the *Anastasia* books, the older Anastasia gets, the more complex her personal problems are. For instance, in 1995's *Anastasia, Absolutely*, Anastasia is troubled by the assignments in her values class at school. She worries that she does not have the right responses to such hypothetical scenarios as what she would do if she saw someone shoplifting or whether she could give one of her own kidneys to save a sibling's life. Each passing crisis gives Anastasia new insight into herself, and by the end of each novel, she is prepared to move on to a new level of maturity. In *The Giver*, childhood is left behind at age twelve, when an individual's adult calling is decided. For Jonas, this passage leads to his knowledge of the darker aspects of human experience—war, death, pain, and euthanasia. For the young child Elizabeth in *Autumn Street*, her father's assurance that bad things will not happen now that he has come home from the war means nothing to her because she has already been initiated into

the terrifying world of experience. Wise beyond her years, Elizabeth no longer has the innocence of a child, nor the capacity to feel safe in a threatening world.

Works in Critical Context

Most critics agree that Lowry's strength as a writer is her ability to create strong central characters whose determination, intelligence, and humor overcome the difficulties they face. However, while some critics praise her lively, diverse characters for reflecting the multiplicity that defines America, others contend that Lowry uses stereotypes of racial and ethnic groups, as well as of the elderly, to create humorous situations. Furthermore, some critics find Lowry's characters too likable and too attractive. For instance, it may seem unrealistic for Natalie in *Find a Stranger, Say Goodbye* (1978) to have it all: beauty and brains, the perfect family life, and even the most attractive, affluent biological mother and father. Nevertheless, the majority of critics agree with Lowry's readers who find her adolescent characters admirable in the way they confront their problems.

The Giver   Some reviewers believe that readers might be disappointed by the ambiguous ending of *The Giver*, which leaves readers to decide if the boys have safely reached "Elsewhere," have been intercepted by their community's security forces, or have died from hunger and exposure. However, in her Newbery Medal acceptance speech, Lowry maintained that the novel has no single "correct" ending. "There's a right one for each

COMMON HUMAN EXPERIENCE

Lowry's *The Giver* is regarded by many to be a dystopian novel. Unlike utopian works, which describe ideal societies, dystopian literature presents a negative view of the future of society and humankind. Other works of dystopian literature include the following:

We (1921), a novel by Yevgeny Zamyatin. Widely considered the first major dystopian novel, *We* features a nightmarish world in which people have designations, not names.

The Handmaid's Tale (1984), a novel by Margaret Atwood. The futuristic dystopia in this work depicts a woman's struggle to survive in a society ruled by misogyny and fascism.

Nineteen Eighty-Four (1949), a novel by George Orwell. Introducing the idea of "Big Brother," Orwell's work is set in a totalitarian state controlled by an all-knowing government that uses constant surveillance to control its citizens.

of us, and it depends on our own beliefs, on our own hopes." She continues, "The truth that we go out and come back, and that what we come back to is changed, and so are we." Reviewer Gary D. Schmidt finds the ending appropriate, explaining that with it "the reader must do what Jonas must now do for the first time: make a choice."

Overall, *The Giver* has been praised by many critics. According to Ann Flowers, "the air of disquiet [in *The Giver*] is delicately insinuated. And the theme of balancing the values of freedom and security is beautifully presented." Reviewer Patty Campbell comments that the novel is so unique, "so rich in levels of meaning, so daring in complexity of symbol and metaphor, so challenging in the ambiguity of its conclusion, that we are left with all our neat little everyday categories and judgments hanging useless." Even when the novel has "occasional logical lapses," says critic Karen Ray, "*The Giver* [is] a powerful and provocative novel."

Responses to Literature

1. How does the society in *The Giver* use euphemisms to distance itself from the reality of "Release"? How does our own society use this device to distance us from aging and death, bodily functions, and political activities? Think of some examples common in modern language. What are the advantages and disadvantages of using euphemisms? Can you think of times when they are actually appropriate?

2. In *Number the Stars*, Annemarie knows that lying is wrong, yet she and her family must lie to protect others. Do you think their lying is justifiable? Or do you think ethics should never be compromised?

3. The ending of *The Giver* is deliberately ambiguous. Write your own ending for the novel that explains what you think might have happened to Jonas and Gabriel.

4. Do such novels as *Number the Stars* and *The Giver* make you feel optimistic or pessimistic about human nature? How does your opinion of human nature shape the way you deal with people? Does it change your approach to life?

BIBLIOGRAPHY

Books

Lowry, Lois. *Looking Back: a Photographic Memoir*. Boston, Mass.: Houghton Mifflin, 1998.

Periodicals

Campbell, Patty. "The Sand in the Oyster." *Horn Book* (November/December 1993): 717–721.

Cart, Michael. "Review of *Anastasia Absolutely*." *New York Times Book Review* (January 14, 1996): 23.

Cooper, Ilene. "Giving and Receiving." *Booklist* (April 15, 1993): 1506.

Flowers, Ann A. "Review of *The Giver*." *Horn Book* (July/August 1993): 458.

Lowry, Lois. "Newbery Medal Acceptance." *Horn Book* (July/August 1994): 414–422.

Ray, Karen. "Review of *The Giver*." *New York Times Book Review* (October 31, 1993): 26.

Schmidt, Gary D. "Review of *The Giver*." *Five Owls* (September–October 1993): 14–15.

Smith, Amanda. "PW Interviews: Lois Lowry." *Publishers Weekly* 229 (February 21, 1986): 152–153.

Web sites

Lois Lowry Biography. Lois Lowry Official Web site. Retrieved November 13, 2008, from http://www.loislowry.com/bio.html. Last updated in 2008.

✹ Robert Ludlum

BORN: *1927, New York*

DIED: *2001, Naples, Florida*

NATIONALITY: *American*

GENRE: *Fiction*

MAJOR WORKS:

The Scarlatti Inheritance (1971)

The Rhinemann Exchange (1974)

The Bourne Identity (1980)

The Prometheus Deception (2000)

Robert Ludlum *AP Wide World Photos*

Overview

Robert Ludlum is a prolific author of best-selling thriller novels that hook readers with intrigue and action from their opening pages. With complicated plots and high-powered suspense, Ludlum's books deal with political scandal and espionage, often involving real historical figures enmeshed in intricate schemes. The premise of almost all of his novels revolves around individuals who find themselves caught up in a web of intrigues, uncertain about whom to trust. Despite criticism that his plots are formulaic and his prose overwritten, Ludlum remains a popular author who has sustained the interest of millions of readers.

Works in Biographical and Historical Context

The Military and the Theater Born in New York in 1927, Ludlum grew up in Short Hills, New Jersey. After leaving home as a teenager to become a stage actor, he enlisted in the United States Marines when he turned seventeen and served as an infantryman from 1945 to 1947. This military experience proved to be a rich source of material for his novels.

Following his military service, Ludlum majored in fine arts at Wesleyan University, where he met Mary Ryducha. When the couple married in 1951, the year Ludlum graduated, they both pursued acting careers. For the next twenty years, Ludlum was an actor, as well as a director and producer. In the 1950s, in addition to having minor roles on Broadway, he appeared in approximately two hundred television dramas and also did voice-overs for commercials. In 1960, he and his wife opened New Jersey's Playhouse-on-the-Mall, the country's first theater in a shopping center. There, Luldlum's most notable production was Bill Manhoff's *The Owl and the Pussycat*, which featured a then-unknown Alan Alda, who later gained fame for his role in the television series *M*A*S*H*.

A Successful Novel at First Attempt After serving as producer at the Playhouse for ten years, Ludlum found himself bored and frustrated with theater work. Eventually, he followed his wife's suggestion that he try his hand at writing. Using an old story idea and outline he had drafted years earlier, Ludlum wrote *The Scarlatti Inheritance* (1971). Based on Ludlum's curiosity about how the early Nazis were financed, the novel follows several financiers, including some Americans, who funded Hitler's Third Reich. Establishing the pattern for Ludlum's career, this story of espionage and corruption became a bestseller.

Encouraged by the success of *The Scarlatti Inheritance*, Ludlum moved his family from New Jersey to Long Island and became a full-time writer. His novels written in the 1970s typically involve international conspiracies and reflect the political climate of the Cold War, a period following World War II and lasting until the mid-1980s that was marked by competition and distrust between the United States and the former Soviet Union. *The Matarese Circle*, for instance, centers on a CIA agent who must work with a KGB equivalent to stop a worldwide revolution. Many readers believed that Ludlum, who traveled widely doing research and gathering material for his works, had worked as a spy himself.

Focus on Terrorism As an end to the Cold War drew near, Ludlum switched his focus to international terrorism. For example, in *The Icarus Agenda* (1988), the world anxiously awaits the fate of two hundred hostages held in Oman, while *The Scorpio Illusion* (1993) tells of Middle Eastern terrorist plans to overthrow the United States government.

By 1984, Ludlum, suffering from osteoarthritis, spent half of each year at his second home in Naples, Florida. Despite heart troubles that led to quadruple bypass surgery in the mid-1990s, Ludlum published six novels in that decade. He died of a heart attack in 2001.

Works in Literary Context

Ludlum himself attributed much of his success as an author to his background in the theater. Besides influencing his methods of character development, Ludlum's

LITERARY AND HISTORICAL CONTEMPORARIES

Ludlum's famous contemporaries include:

Joseph Heller (1927–1999): Based in part on his time in the U. S. Army Air Force, Heller's first and best-known novel, *Catch-22* (1961), is a satiric look at the insanities of war.

William Golding (1911–1993): A master of strange situations, moral allegories, and ironic twists, Golding is noted for the modern classic *Lord of the Flies* (1955).

Orson Welles (1915–1985): Famous for producing the panic-inducing 1938 radio broadcast of H. G. Wells's *War of the Worlds* (1898), Welles, also co-wrote, directed, produced and acted in the masterful film *Citizen Kane*.

John le Carré (1941–): Le Carré, a British novelist, draws from his experiences in the Army Intelligence Corps to explore the moral implications of patriotism and espionage.

Martha Albrand (1915–1981): An established European writer before coming the to United States in 1937, Albrand wrote over forty novels of mystery and suspense.

theatrical training helped him create novels characterized by intricate plots filled with intriguing, complicated conflict. He is often credited with setting the stage for other spy thriller writers, including David Morrell and Gayle Lynds. During the Cold War, Ludlum popularized the idea of American and Soviet covert operations, as well as the conception of illegal operations on American soil by the CIA.

The Spy Thriller Genre   Soon after the first modern government intelligence agencies were formed, the spy thriller emerged as a literary genre. The key elements of Ludlum's spy thrillers—corruption in high places, elaborate secret plans, and unsuspecting civilians drawn into the fray—are what draw readers to Ludlum. The novels' diverse settings and historical periods are enhanced by their main characters, typically ordinary people either accidentally propelled or manipulated into acting as spies. Although they face powerful adversaries who control corrupt global corporations and questionable government and military organizations that threaten international relations, Ludlum's protagonists emerge victorious.

In several of his works, Ludlum unfolds speculative accounts of conspiracy in various aspects of American society. *The Matlock Paper* (1973), for example, is about the criminal activities of a group of New England college professors and the reluctance of the school's dean to assist a government bureau in exposing the teachers. In *The*

Chancellor Manuscript (1977), Ludlum alters history in his story of the assassination of J. Edgar Hoover by a group of government officials who seek control of his private files. International terrorism is also a prominent feature in many of Ludlum's novels, as seen in such works as *The Bourne Identity* (1980), which centers on a Vietnam veteran named David Webb, alias Jason Bourne, who is manipulated by American intelligence officials into becoming a counter-assassin in an effort to eliminate a notorious terrorist.

Works in Critical Context

According to reviewers Susan Baxter and Mark Nichols, Ludlum "has his share of unkind critics who complain of implausible plots, leaden prose, and, as a caustic reviewer once sneered, an absence of 'redeeming literary values to balance the vulgar sensationalism.'" In addition, many reviewers often point to Ludlum's use of mixed metaphors and illogical statements as serious flaws in his books. Despite the abundance of negative evaluations, however, readers have repeatedly voiced their approval of Ludlum in sales, and have made him one of the most widely read writers in the world. As Baxter and Nichols note, "For all his imperfections, Ludlum manages—by pumping suspense into every twist . . . in his tangled plots and by demanding sympathy for well-meaning protagonists afflicted by outrageous adversity—to keep millions of readers frantically turning his pages."

The Icarus Agenda   *The Icarus Agenda* features a plot similar to other Ludlum novels. In this particular work, five wealthy and influential individuals arrange the election of the next United States president. Reviewer Peter L. Robertson acknowledges the power of the novel's storyline: "Ludlum is light-years beyond his literary competition in piling plot twist upon plot twist until the mesmerized reader is held captive, willing to accept any wayward, if occasionally implausible, plotting device." Comments Julie Johnson, "There is a sufficient amount of energy and suspense present in The Icarus Agenda to remind the reader why Mr. Ludlum's novels are best sellers." In his review of *The Icarus Agenda*, journalist Bob Woodward summarizes the media's view of Ludlum: "Ludlum justifiably has a loyal following. Reviews of most of his previous books are critical but conclude, grudgingly, that he has another inevitable bestseller."

The Bourne Trilogy   *The Bourne Identity*, the first in a trilogy of Bourne books, was received more favorably than Ludlum's other novels. The trilogy follows Jason Bourne, a spy who awakens in a doctor's office with amnesia; the story is played out as a remarkable number of killers and organizations attempt to finish Bourne off before he realizes his true identity. "Some of Mr. Ludlum's previous novels were so convoluted they should have been packaged with bags of bread crumbs to help readers keep track of the plot lines," reviewer Peter Andrews writes. "But *The Bourne Identity* is a Ludlum story at its most severely plotted, and for me its most effective." Similarly, critic Don G. Campbell praises the third Bourne book, *The Bourne Ultimatum*, as an example of "how it should be done," concluding that "in the pulse-tingling style that began so many years ago with *The Scarlatti Inheritance*, we are caught up irretrievably." As a result of the their popularity, the Bourne novels were each made into successful movies, and have spawned several literary sequels by Eric van Lustbader.

Responses to Literature

1. In what ways did the end of the Cold War affect Ludlum's fiction? Which approach do you think best describes the focus of his novels: ideological conflicts or conflicts between individuals?

2. How did Ludlum's background in theater enhance his fiction? How do you think this background may have hindered his writing?

3. Many of Ludlum's novels center on high-level conspiracies. Using the library or the Internet, research conspiracy theories of the twentieth century. What conclusions can you make about the theorists themselves? How do the theories relate to their specific time in history?

4. Ludlum wrote novels under the pseudonyms Jonathan Ryder and Michael Shepherd. Investigate some of these works. Why would Ludlum have chosen to write them using a different name? How are the novels credited to Ryder and Shepherd different from those written under his own name?

BIBLIOGRAPHY

Books

Macdonald, Gina. *Robert Ludlum: A Critical Companion.* Westport, Conn.: Greenwood Press, 1997.

Periodicals

Andrews, Peter. "Review of *The Bourne Identity.*" *New York Times Book Review* (March 30, 1980): 7.

Baxter, Susan, and Mark Nichols. "Review of *The Bourne Identity.*" *Maclean's* (April 9, 1984): 50–52.

Campbell, Don G. "Review of *The Bourne Ultimatum.*" *Los Angeles Times Book Review* (March 18, 1990): 8.

Harwood, Richard. "Hooked on the Lure of Ludlum." *Book World* (March 23, 1980): 3.

COMMON HUMAN EXPERIENCE

Although the field of spy thrillers—also called spy fiction or political thrillers—has traditionally merited little critical acclaim, many such works are insightful, informed, and politically astute. Listed below are other spy thrillers praised for their ability to transport the reader into exciting worlds of espionage:

Masquerade (2004), a novel by Gayle Lynds. A secret CIA training camp, a covert world of Washington spies, a shocking underworld in California beach communities, and the treacherous back streets of Paris all drive the action of this novel.

A Spy in the Ointment (1966), a novel by Donald Westlake. Due to a paperwork error by the FBI, the pacifist protagonist in this spy comedy finds himself surrounded by terrorists.

The Great Impersonation (1920), a novel by Edward Phillips Oppenheim. Though one is German and the other British, the two cousins in this novel are almost identical in appearance and, as a result, become entangled in an international web of suspicion.

Johnson, Julie. "Review of *The Icarus Agenda.*" *New York Times Book Review* (March 27, 1988): 16.

Robertson, Peter L. "Review of *The Icarus Agenda.*" *Chicago Tribune Books* (February 28, 1988): 7.

Woodward, Bob. "Review of *The Icarus Agenda.*" *Washington Post Book World* (February 21, 1988): 1.

Web sites

Books and Writers. *Robert Ludlum (1927–2001).* Retrieved October 22, 2008, from http://kirjasto.sci.fi/ludlum.htm

Times Online. *The Times Obituary: Robert Ludlum.* Retrieved October 22, 2008, from http://www.timesonline.co.uk/tol/comment/obituaries/article2262997.ece.

M

⊛ Archibald MacLeish

BORN: *1892, Glencoe, Illinois*

DIED: *1982, Boston, Massachusetts*

NATIONALITY: *American*

GENRE: *Poetry, drama*

MAJOR WORKS:

Streets in the Moon (1928)

Collected Poems 1917–1952 (1952)

J. B. (1958)

Overview

Throughout his career, Archibald MacLeish's verse examined the public and private responsibilities of individual citizens in an increasingly complex world. MacLeish addresses these themes in a wide variety of poetic styles, including sonnets, blank verse, and epics. In addition, he experimented with varied line lengths and speech rhythms in an attempt to create a distinctly modern American voice that would extend beyond the literary world and reach the common people. Indeed, MacLeish is remembered as a writer who promoted poetry and humanism in an age of national cynicism.

Works in Biographical and Historical Context

A Yale Poet MacLeish was born on May 7, 1892, in Glencoe, Illinois, an affluent suburb of Chicago. He attended public schools in Glencoe and a preparatory school in Lakeville, Connecticut. From 1911 to 1915, MacLeish studied at Yale University, where he was a successful football player and swimmer. Also at Yale, he edited and wrote for the *Yale Literary Magazine*, contributed to the *Yale Review*, and composed *Songs for a Summer's Day* (1915), a sonnet sequence that was chosen as the University's Prize Poem. Graduating from Yale that same year, MacLeish entered Harvard Law School.

Before he earned his law degree, he married singer Ada Hitchcock in 1916. The marriage lasted until his death.

From Soldier to Lawyer to Expatriate In 1917, the year America entered World War I, MacLeish enlisted in the U.S. Army as an ambulance driver in France, but he was soon transferred to active duty and rose to the rank of field artillery captain. While MacLeish was in the army, *Tower of Ivory* (1917), his first full-length volume of poetry, was published in the United States. This collection is notable primarily because it first introduces MacLeish's idea of humankind's search to reconcile idealism with reality. When the war was over, MacLeish returned to Harvard Law School, where he was valedictorian of the 1919 graduating class. He remained there for a year to teach constitutional and international law. For the next several years, he was a successful trial lawyer in a Boston firm; however, finding little time to write, he quit his promising career in law to pursue the life of a poet.

In the summer of 1923, MacLeish moved with his wife and two sons to Paris. There, he associated with many of the Lost Generation writers, a group of expatriates who rejected the values of post–World War I America in works that portray humanity's sense of moral aimlessness. Along with MacLeish, such Lost Generation writers as Ezra Pound, Ernest Hemingway, and John Dos Passos revolutionized twentieth-century literature. During this time abroad, MacLeish devoted himself to perfecting his writing and learning to read Dante's epic poem *Inferno* (c. 1321) in the original Italian.

Back in America In 1928, MacLeish returned to the United States the same year *Streets in the Moon* was published. This volume contains MacLeish's most anthologized poem, "Ars Poetica," a modernist manifesto with classical roots that conveys MacLeish's conviction that a poem is a way of knowing and seeing through the senses, the emotions, and the imagination. MacLeish soon began writing the epic poem *Conquistador*, a retelling of Cortez's expeditions in Mexico. Related from the point of view of Bernal Diaz del Castillo, a foot soldier in Cortez's

Archibald Macleish   *Macleish, Archibald, photograph. The Library of Congress.*

army, *Conquistador* objectively chronicles the destruction of native Mexican cultures by Spanish explorers. MacLeish won the Pulitzer Prize for his efforts in 1933.

Political Life   From 1930 to 1938, MacLeish was an editor for *Fortune* magazine. During that period, he wrote two verse plays for radio in an effort to increase patriotism. He also chaired the League of American Writers, an organization that opposed fascism, a political ideology that calls for a dictatorial government and severe economic and social control. Fascism had taken told of the German, Italian, and Spanish governments, with the first two countries forming the European base of the Axis powers during World War II. In 1939, President Franklin D. Roosevelt appointed MacLeish the Librarian of Congress, a position he held for five years. While there, MacLeish both reorganized the Library's administrative offices and instituted a series of poetry readings at the Library. At the same time, MacLeish served as assistant director of the Office of War Information, which specialized in propaganda. In 1944, he was appointed assistant Secretary of State for cultural affairs. After World War II, MacLeish became the first American member of the governing body of the United Nations Educational, Science and Cultural Organization (UNESCO), and chaired the first UNESCO conference in Paris in 1945. MacLeish wrote many essays during these years, and his voice was

powerful and eloquent in its opposition to political indifference and totalitarianism. Not surprisingly, the poetry he published between 1938 and 1948 was also nationalistic and patriotic.

Awards   In 1949, MacLeish become Harvard's Boylston Professor of Rhetoric and Oratory, a position he held until 1962. From 1963 to 1967, he was Simpson Lecturer at Amherst College. MacLeish continued to write poetry, criticism, verse plays, and screenplays to great acclaim. In addition to the National Book Award, MacLeish won a second Pulitzer Prize for his *Collected Poems* (1952). *J. B.* (1958), a verse play based on the book of Job, earned him a third Pulitzer. In 1965, he received an Academy Award for his work on the screenplay of *The Eleanor Roosevelt Story* (1965). MacLeish continued with his writing and public speaking appearances until his death in April 1982 in Boston, Massachusetts.

Works in Literary Context

Much of MacLeish's early work reflects the influence of poets T. S. Eliot and Ezra Pound. MacLeish's *The Pot of Earth* (1925), for instance, has been compared to Eliot's *The Waste Land* for its inclusion of the Adonis myth from Sir James G. Frazer's *The Golden Bough* (1890–1915). Additionally, MacLeish's *Streets in the Moon* (1926) reflects the themes of alienation, despair, and World War I's destruction of cultural traditions that Pound addresses in *Hugh Selwyn Mauberly* (1920). MacLeish's later thematic explorations of the process of aging and the spiritual and physical exile of modern humanity have drawn comparisons to Irish poet William Butler Yeats and French poet St.-John Perse.

The Fall of Man and Woman   In *Tower of Ivory* (1917), his first full-length volume of poetry, MacLeish first introduces the idea of man's searching, fearing nothing, trying to shape his life through his own efforts after his departure from the Garden of Eden. For the title of *Nobodaddy* (1926), a twentieth-century interpretation of the Cain-Abel myth, MacLeish uses one of William Blake's names for God. In the play, MacLeish depicts Adam and Eve emerging from the sleep of Eden, a state in which they had lived in ignorant and unconscious harmony with their surroundings and in obedience to the will of God. Adam chooses to reject God's inexplicable and arbitrary ways and to seek his own knowledge, alone in a desert. Consequently, Adam knows both good and evil. As in *Nobodaddy*, the central character in the poem "Actfive" (1948) endures life without a god; MacLeish's man perseveres because his love of life itself persists.

Eventually, MacLeish turns to the Eve figure and her leaving the Garden of Eden in pursuit of knowledge. In "What Eve Sang," the first poem in the collection *Songs for Eve* (1954), Eve is conscious of her selfhood as she seeks the same knowledge Adam did. In this song, she is aware that human existence surpasses space and time. As the progression of Eve's songs reveals, she is glad to have left the garden and has accepted the wasteland where death is certain. Ironically, however, her knowledge of her mortality permits her to transcend it through the creation of her own world. In the Garden of Eden, "Waking is forbidden," and for this reason Eve says she is thankful for the Fall, despite all the sorrows a life of knowledge brings.

Works in Critical Context

From 1925 to 1960, MacLeish, according to some critics, was among the finest of modern American poets, a distinction he shared with Robert Frost, Wallace Stevens, and William Carlos Williams. However, other commentators argued that his works were too dependent on those of T. S. Eliot and Ezra Pound and that MacLeish had a tendency to change his viewpoint to suit the times instead of sticking to his convictions. In regard to his verse dramas, most academics agree that MacLeish would have earned no enduring reputation as a dramatist at all were it not for *J. B.* This judgment is severe but apt, considering the fact that all other MacLeish plays combined held the stage for fewer than thirty performances.

J. B. The verse play *J. B.* remains one of MacLeish's most critically compelling works and has sparked debate in terms of its humanistic thematic concerns. Addressing the tragic aspects of life—points out critic Joseph Wood Krutch, a contemporary of MacLeish—the play puts the universe rather than sociology at center. With this approach, contends Krutch, MacLeish avoids both superficial optimism and bleak pessimism. Scholar Eleanor Sickles argues that *J. B.* reflects MacLeish's "lasting interest in the fall of man from the Garden of Eden." Sickles views J. B. as a tragic hero whose flaw is a "smug, arrogant assumption that 'the God of Galaxies' is a special friend and patron of his." The strength of the play, she explains, is that the character J. B. grows to recognize the "cosmic power and mystery beyond reach of man's thought," which leads to his acceptance of his separation from paradise. As a result of its main character's spiritual realization, *J. B.* has been remembered for its rarity as a religious verse drama in an age of secular prose.

Detractors such as John Gassner find the resolution of *J. B.* lacking in dramatic impact, revealing MacLeish to be more poet than playwright. Other negative criticism focuses on MacLeish's conception of the character of J. B., thinking of him, in John Ciardi's words, as a "shallow, self-righteous fathead." Such characterization generated controversy when the play was produced, especially among those who accused MacLeish of advocating mere sex as a cure for the devastation depicted in the play. Furthermore, in regard to the play's stylistic elements, critic Kenneth Tynan says *J. B.* is written in

---

LITERARY AND HISTORICAL CONTEMPORARIES

MacLeish's famous contemporaries include:

Ezra Pound (1885–1972): A poet, literary critic, and translator, Pound was instrumental in promoting Imagism, a poetic movement emphasizing the direct treatment of an object without unnecessary rhetoric.

T. S. Eliot (1888–1965): The works of this poet, critic, and dramatist depict the emotional and spiritual emptiness of mankind in an increasingly urban, industrialized age.

E. E. Cummings (1894–1962): Best known for his unconventional use of typography and punctuation, Cummings wrote lyrical love poems, as well as cynical satires about the institutions of his times.

St.-John Perse (1887–1975): Exploring the transitory nature of human existence, the works of this French poet were translated into English by MacLeish and Eliot.

Franklin Delano Roosevelt (1882–1945): The thirty-second president of the United States, Roosevelt dedicated his first term to the New Deal, a program designed to alleviate the economic troubles caused by the Great Depression.

COMMON HUMAN EXPERIENCE

The Lost Generation consisted of expatriate writers—most of whom lived in Paris after World War I—who criticized American culture in works reflecting self-exile and spiritual alienation. Other works that explore the alienation and disillusion of the Lost Generation include the following:

Exiles Return (1934), a nonfiction book by Malcolm Cowley. A chronicle of his experience as a Lost Generation writer, Cowley's memoir explores the development of early twentieth-century literature.

Tender is the Night (1934), a novel by F. Scott Fitzgerald. Set in Europe after World War I, this novel offers a striking portrait of the spiritually barren atmosphere of the time.

The Sun Also Rises (1926), a novel by Ernest Hemingway. Hemingway established his literary reputation with this novel about the disenchantment and dislocation experienced after World War I.

Manhattan Transfer (1925), a novel by John Dos Passos. Consisting of a series of interlocking stories written in experimental style, this work criticizes the superficial exuberance and consumerism that erupted in urban America in the years between World War I and the Great Depression.

"bumpy alliterative verse" and deems it medieval in "narrative technique."

Responses to Literature

1. The verse play *J. B.* is based on the biblical story of Job. The play reflects MacLeish's responses to the horrors he saw during two world wars, including the Holocaust and the bombings of Hiroshima and Nagasaki. How do the men Job and J. B. compare, both in their predicaments and in their responses to them? Do you think MacLeish offers a satisfying answer to the question of human tragedy and suffering?

2. How can a poem be, as MacLeish says in "Ars Poetica," "wordless"? How can it be "motionless in time"?

3. Compare MacLeish's "You, Andrew Marvell" to Marvell's poem "To His Coy Mistress." What is the literal message of both poems? What are the symbolic levels of interpretation? What is the importance of location in the poems?

4. Read MacLeish's poem "Ars Poetica" and then research *Ars Poetica* (ca. 20–23 B.C.E.) by Horace and Aristotle's *Poetics* (ca. 335 B.C.E.. What do these classical scholars consider poetry to be? What are the "rules" each one of them establishes for poetry? What is MacLeish's philosophy of poetry?

BIBLIOGRAPHY

Books

Falk, Signi Lenea. *Archibald MacLeish*. New York: Twayne, 1965.

Gassner, John. *Theatre at the Crossroads*. New York: Holt, 1960.

Mullaly, Edward J. *Archibald MacLeish: A Checklist*. Kent, Ohio: Kent State University Press, 1973.

Smith, Grover. *Archibald MacLeish*. Minneapolis, Minn.: University of Minnesota Press, 1971.

Periodicals

Ciardi, John. "J. B. Revisited." *Saturday Review* 43 (January 30, 1960): 39, 55.

Krutch, Joseph Wood. "Literature and Utopia." *Nation* (October 18, 1933): 442.

Monroe, Harriet. "Archibald MacLeish." *Poetry* 38 (June 1931): 150–155.

Sickles, Eleanor. "Archibald MacLeish and American Democracy." *American Literature* 15 (November 1943): 223–237.

———. "MacLeish and the Fortunate Fall." *American Literature* 35 (May 1963): 205–217.

Tynan, Kenneth. "The Theatre." *The New Yorker* 34 (December 20, 1958): 70–71.

⊛ Naomi Long Madgett

BORN: *1923, Norfolk, Virginia*

NATIONALITY: *American*

GENRE: *Poetry*

MAJOR WORKS:

Exits and Entrances (1978)
Octavia and Other Poems (1988)

Overview

One of the first African American women to publish poetry in the United States, Naomi Long Madgett wrote her first collection of poems, *Songs to a Phantom Nightingale* (1941), while in high school. Though Madgett did not set out to write "African American" poetry, she was influenced by the Harlem Renaissance and the civil rights movement to address racial issues from an African American perspective. In addition to her work as a poet, Madgett has also made her mark as an educator and, since 1974, editor of Lotus Press, a company dedicated to publishing African American authors.

Naomi Long Madgett   *Courtesy of the author*

Works in Biographical and Historical Context

A Minister's Daughter   Born in Norfolk, Virginia, on July 5, 1923, Madgett spent her childhood in East Orange, New Jersey, where her father served as a Baptist minister. Encouraged by her parents, she was an avid reader from a very young age and often sat on the floor of her father's study when she was no more than seven or eight, eagerly reading Aesop's fables and Robert T. Kerlin's anthology *Negro Poets and Their Poems* (1923). In addition to perusing poetry by Alfred, Lord Tennyson and Langston Hughes, Madgett studied a speech book that her mother had used as a student at Virginia State College, and she memorized some of its poems for the impromptu recitations that she, as a minister's daughter, was often called upon to give.

New School, New Worlds   When Madgett was fourteen, her father moved the family from East Orange to St. Louis, Missouri, where she was exposed to a new world. In East Orange, she had studied at an integrated school but was the only black child in her class. At the all-African American Sumner High School in St. Louis, however, she discovered that the achievements of African Americans were respected and honored publicly. At her new school, Madgett, who had been composing poems since she was a young child, was encouraged to continue her writing. Many of her poems from this time reflect the influence of her education at Sumner—her use of Latin phrases and mythological and classical references, for example—while others are inspired by informal educational experiences, such as an overheard street-corner conversation between two homeless men that lent itself to Madgett's earliest uses of colloquial diction and rhythms. In 1941, Madgett published her first collection, *Songs to a Phantom Nightingale*, a few days after graduating from high school.

Family Obligations   In the early 1940s, Madgett attended Virginia State College, earning a BA in 1945. She then began graduate study at New York University, but she withdrew after one semester to marry Julian F. Witherspoon. She moved with him to Detroit in 1946. There Madgett worked as a reporter and copyreader for the *Michigan Chronicle*, an African American weekly, until the birth of her only child in 1947. Because of her obligations as a wife and mother, Madgett did little creative writing. In 1948, her marriage ended, and she worked as a service representative for the Michigan Bell Telephone Company, a position she held until she married William H. Madgett in 1954. Though this marriage also ended in divorce six years later, she has retained Madgett's name.

An African American Poet?   Madgett completed the requirements for a master's degree at Wayne University and began teaching in Detroit public high schools in 1955. The following year, her second book of poetry,

One and the Many (1956), was published. More innovative than her first book, the collection is a record of Madgett's life up to the mid-1950s and reveals her determination to pursue a career as a poet. *One and the Many* also includes several poems with African American themes, including "Refugee," which had been written more than ten years earlier and was chosen by Langston Hughes and Arna Bontemps for their anthology *The Poetry of the Negro: 1746–1949* (1949). However, the selection and ordering of poems in *One and the Many* reflects Madgett's concern with being stereotyped as an African American poet, as opposed to being considered simply a poet.

Madgett's next book, *Star by Star* (1965), contains "Midway," originally written in 1957. This is probably Madgett's best-known poem; its speaker represents all African Americans, relating the many injustices they have faced and the spirit with which they have survived: "You've lashed me and you've treed me / And you've everything but freed me / But in time you'll know you need me and it won't be long." This passage was much quoted at the height of the civil rights movement, for it forcefully expresses the emotions of many African Americans during the 1950s and 1960s.

Impact in Public Schools   While teaching in Detroit, Madgett was appalled to discover that most African American children knew little about such African American poets as Countee Cullen and Langston Hughes, so in the summer of 1965, she taught an experimental course in African American literature—the first course on the subject ever offered in Detroit public schools. After spending 1965–1966 at Oakland University as a Mott Fellow, she returned to the classroom and began teaching the course as a regular part of the curriculum. Madgett's energy and creativity were acknowledged in 1967 when she was honored by the Metropolitan Detroit English Club as the Distinguished English Teacher of the Year.

Poet and Publisher   In 1968, Madgett resigned from the Detroit public school system to accept a position as an associate professor of English at Eastern Michigan University. In 1973 she was promoted to full professor. After marrying Leonard Andrews and visiting Africa in 1972, she published another book of poetry, *Pink Ladies in the Afternoon* (1972). In 1974, Madgett and her husband took over the newly-founded Lotus Press, which has published numerous African American authors, including Madgett herself. Madgett retired from formal teaching at Eastern Michigan in 1984, thereby becoming a professor emeritus.

In 1988, Madgett published her seventh volume of poetry, *Octavia and Other Poems*, indicating a new direction in her work. The long title poem is based on Madgett's family history, as is an appendix containing family pictures, biographies, and family tree. In 1993, Madgett was recognized by the Before Columbus Foundation with an American Book Award for her contributions as publisher and editor of Lotus Press. At the same time, she

LITERARY AND HISTORICAL CONTEMPORARIES

Madgett's famous contemporaries include:

Martin Luther King, Jr. (1929–1968): A powerful speaker who advocated social change through non-violent means, King helped shape the civil rights movement in America.

Robert Hayden (1913–1980): Often using his childhood home in a Detroit slum as a backdrop for his work, Hayden wrote poetry that explores African American social and political struggles.

James Baldwin (1924–1987): Baldwin was an American writer noted for his intelligent essays about civil rights in the United States.

Dudley Randall (1914–2000): An African American poet and publisher from Detroit, Michigan, Randall founded the Broadside Press (1965), which published works by many prominent African American writers.

Gwendolyn Brooks (1917–2000): Brooks, a poet whose work reflects a political consciousness, was the first African American to win a Pulitzer Prize.

COMMON HUMAN EXPERIENCE

Many of Madgett's poems reflect her passion to be a writer, while still meeting her obligations as a wife and mother. Poems such as "The Lost" (1956) and "The Rut" (1956) reveal a fear that life is slipping away, that she is a desperate, trapped homemaker. Other works that depict a woman's struggle to reconcile the responsibilities of family with her art include the following:

The Watermelon Dress: Portrait of a Woman (1984), a narrative poem by Paulette White. Despite the demands of motherhood and a difficult first marriage, the speaker in this poem finds self-awareness as a writer.

The Story of Avis (1877), a novel by Elizabeth Stuart Phelps. Relevant today, this novel offers a painful portrait of a woman's efforts to balance life as a wife, mother, and painter.

Silences (1978), nonfiction by Tillie Olsen. In between work and mothering, Olsen took fifteen years to write *Silences*, which explores the obstacles and frustrations of female writers.

committed to a five-year assignment as poetry editor of the Michigan State University Press. The recipient of numerous awards through the years, Madgett continues to write; her autobiography, *Pilgrim Journey*, was published in 2006.

Works in Literary Context

Madgett's poems are generally divided into two categories: the lyric poems of her youth and the later political works concerned with the civil rights movement. Many of Madgett's early works are sentimental love poems that often use nature to reveal emotion. The primary influence upon the poet at this stage in her life was the Romantic tradition, either directly from John Keats and William Wordsworth or indirectly through Paul Laurence Dunbar and Countee Cullen. Later collections of poetry reveal Madgett's deepening awareness of her power as a writer in the midst of civil disorder and the Vietnam War. Possibly her biggest influence in the writing community—certainly in regard to African American authors—has been her involvement with Lotus Press.

Poetics As Madgett matured, she left behind the youthful imitation of Romantic poetry that so characterizes *Songs to a Phantom Nightingale* and began experimenting with language and the crafting of poetry. As evidenced by the poems in *Star by Star* (1965), Madgett demonstrates a marked improvement in technique, with stronger images, tighter phrasing, and controlled, limited sentimentality. "Beginning and End," for example, opens with images reminiscent of Thoreau's description of spring in *Walden* (1854) and then describes a metaphysical linking of life and death symbolized by worms.

In other poems, Madgett uses the short, clipped lines, the rhyme, and even the imagery of Emily Dickinson. The *Star by Star* collection also contains "Trinity: A Dream Sequence," a series of nineteen short poems. Spoken by a woman, these poems present the intense longing, secrecy, apparent consummation, adoration, guilt, and ending of an illicit romance. The paradoxical but effective use of religious imagery distinguishes "Trinity" from Madgett's simple, straightforward early love poems.

Works in Critical Context

Throughout her career, Madgett has published hundreds of poems that have been collected in seven volumes, reprinted in more than seventy anthologies, and translated into several languages. Nevertheless, her work has never been the subject of extended scholarly study. In part, this neglect is the result of her writing lyric poetry at a time when such poetry has been lightly regarded. Additionally, Madgett has tended to downplay her African American verse—placing her African American poems at the ends of several collections, for instance—despite the fact that much of the favorable attention she has received has come from African American critics, journals, and organizations. However, in *Exits and Entrances* (1978) and, most effectively, in *Octavia and Other Poems* (1988), Madgett has emphasized her African American heritage, which should result in wider recognition of her poems.

Exits and Entrances A combination of autobiography, African American themes, and traditional lyric poetry,

Exits and Entrances satisfied critics in much the same way as her previous collections. According to reviewer Melba Boyd, *Exits and Entrances* displays Madgett's "gentle and distinguished...creative genius." Critic Ray Fleming observes "some fine individual poems in the collection, poems with a wholeness of vision that uncovers the humor and complexity in human relationships." He continues: "The best of Madgett's lyrics resonate with the vibrant, warm humanity of the poet and invite us, with an almost philosophic calm, to look honestly into ourselves."

Although he finds much to praise about *Exits and Entrances*, Fleming also notes some troublesome elements in the collection, including "a disconcerting vagueness about many of these poems that makes it difficult, if not impossible, to locate with precision the dominant idea or emotion that motivates them." For instance, despite their "beautiful haunting quality and tone," "Mufflejaw" and "Fantasia," Fleming says, lack the unifying focus necessary for effective poetry.

Responses to Literature

1. The Naomi Long Madgett Poetry Award competition sponsored by Lotus Press is open only to African American poets. Why do you think the competition is limited to African Americans? In your opinion, is it fair to limit entrants by race? Why or why not?

2. Using the library or the Internet, research Lotus Press, the publishing imprint run by Madgett. What impact has the press had on black poetry? Investigate works that have been published by Lotus Press. What do these works have in common?

3. Madgett recalls that a white teacher once told her, "If you've read one black poem, you've read them all." Is this true? Could the same be said of "white poetry?" Try to identify several general characteristics of African American poetry; how are these traits reflective of African American culture?

4. Many other African American poets of the 1950s and 1960s are much more well-known than Madgett. Why do you think this is? Compare several of Madgett's poems to those of Nikki Giovanni. Do you believe each poet is sending the same message? Why or why not?

BIBLIOGRAPHY

Books

Arata, Esther Spring, and others. *Black Writers Past and Present*. New York: Morrow, 1975.

Hine, Darlene Clark, ed. *Black Women in America: An Historical Encyclopedia*. Brooklyn, N.Y.: Carlson, 1993.

Madgett, Naomi Long. *Star by Star*. Detroit.: Lotus Press, 1965.

Reardon, Joan. *Poetry by American Women, 1900–1975: A Bibliography*. Metuchen, N.J.: Scarecrow Press, 1979.

Redmond, Eugene B. *Drumvoices: The Mission of Afro-American Poetry*. Garden City, N.Y.: Anchor Press, 1976.

Shelton, Pamela L., ed. *Contemporary Women Poets*. Detroit: St. James Press, 1997.

Smith, Jessie Carney, ed. *Notable Black American Women*. Detroit: Gale, 1992.

Periodicals

Boyd, Melba. "Review of *Exits and Entrances*." *Black Scholar* (March–April 1980): 7.

Fleming, Ray. "Review of *Exits and Entrances*." *Black American Literature Forum* (Summer 1980): 91.

Randall, Dudley. "Review of *Pink Ladies in the Afternoon*." *Black World* (September 1974): 32.

Redding, Saunders. "Books Noted." *Negro Digest* (September 1996): 51–52.

⊛ Norman Mailer

BORN: *1923, Long Branch, New Jersey*

DIED: *2007, New York, New York*

NATIONALITY: *American*

GENRE: *Fiction, nonfiction*

MAJOR WORKS:
The Naked and the Dead (1948)
The Armies of the Night (1968)
The Executioner's Song (1979)
Harlot's Ghost (1991)
The Gospel According to the Son (1997)

Overview

An outspoken, independent thinker, Norman Mailer was a significant and controversial figure in twentieth-century American literature. Mailer was famous for conventional novels in which he examined the conflict between social restrictions and the human search for self-actualization, as well as for nonfiction narratives written in the style of New Journalism, a fusion of fiction and reporting. For his penetrating studies of American society, superior prose style, and influential experiments with various literary forms, Mailer was highly regarded as a novelist and a social critic.

Works in Biographical and Historical Context

From Engineering to Literature   Born on January 31, 1923, in Long Branch, New Jersey, Mailer moved with his family to Brooklyn, New York, when he was four. A precocious child, Mailer was an intelligent student

Norman Mailer   *Mailer, Norman, photograph.* © *Jerry Bauer. Reproduced by permission.*

who enjoyed building models. At the age of sixteen, he enrolled in Harvard University to study aeronautical engineering, but he soon became interested in the works of John Dos Passos, Ernest Hemingway, John Steinbeck, and William Faulkner. Inspired to become a great novelist himself, Mailer wrote several short stories and won first prize in *Story* magazine's annual college contest.

Disappointment Follows Early Success Graduating from Harvard with honors in 1943, Mailer was drafted by the United States Army and married his first wife—whom he would divorce in 1952—shortly before leaving to serve in Japan and the Philippines during World War II. Upon his discharge in 1946, he attended graduate school at the Sorbonne in Paris. Mailer recorded his military experiences in his debut novel, *The Naked and the Dead* (1948), which received much critical acclaim and remained number one on the *New York Times* best-seller list for eleven consecutive weeks. *The Naked and the Dead* is frequently cited among the greatest twentieth-century American novels. After publishing his second book, *Barbary Shore* (1951) to generally unenthusiastic reviews, Mailer conceived an ambitious cycle of eight novels centering on a universal mythical hero named Sergius O'Shaughnessy. Three years in the making, *The Deer Park* (1955), the first installment, proved to be the cycle's only volume.

Notorious Celebrity In 1955 Mailer cofounded the *Village Voice*, an alternative weekly newspaper in New York's Greenwich Village covering politics and the arts, and he began to write the contentious political and socially conscious articles that established his reputation in American literary circles as a maverick. The title of his collection of essays from the 1950s, *Advertisements for Myself* (1959), reveals his strategy for cultivating his literary persona. To many, Mailer appeared to play the devil's advocate for no other reason than to elicit a reaction. In 1957 he published "The White Negro," a defiant essay about jazz and the emerging lifestyle of the "hipster" that became a staple of Beat literature and has since been much anthologized. Mailer's unabashed drug and alcohol abuse also became a feature of his writing and personal life around this time. His erratic behavior came to a head in 1960, when he stabbed his second wife with a pocketknife during a night of heavy drinking. When she refused to press charges, Mailer received a suspended sentence. Though the couple quickly reconciled, they divorced in 1962.

During the 1960s, Mailer became known for public acts of defiance and exhibitionism. In Provincetown, Massachusetts, he was arrested for fighting with police. He was jailed for arguing with a bartender over his liquor tab at a New York nightclub. In 1969 he campaigned for the Democratic nomination for mayor of New York, advocating that the city secede from the state. While Mailer's tendency to attract publicity prompted many critics to consider him opportunistic or self-aggrandizing, others asserted that such public demonstrations served as inspiration for his work.

Redemption through New Journalism Mailer's involvement in the turbulent politics of the 1960s became material for much of his writing, including *The Armies of the Night* (1968), a literary triumph that redeemed him in the eyes of those critics who were convinced that he had wasted his talents by playing the part of a national celebrity. Mailer's role as both participant and observer in a massive demonstration against the Vietnam War staged in front of the Pentagon on October 21, 1967, resulted in a night in jail—and a book that won both the Pulitzer Prize and the National Book Award. Furthermore, *The Armies of the Night* marked Mailer's first major contribution to New Journalism, a journalistic style that had emerged in the late 1960s and early 1970s, in which factual events are related from a subjective observer's perspective and incorporate such novelistic prose devices as narrative, dialogue, and multiple points of view.

Arguably Mailer's most damaging controversy concerned his literary association with convicted murderer Jack Henry Abbott. Mailer helped find a publisher for Abbott's book *In the Belly of the Beast* (1981), which became a great success. Mailer successfully petitioned the Utah State Prison parole board to release Abbott; however, one month after leaving prison, Abbott killed another man, causing widespread condemnation of Mailer's role in setting him free. Mailer had met Abbott while conducting research for *The Executioner's Song* (1979), a true-life novel about serial murderer Gary Gilmore, who, on January 17, 1977, became the first convict to be executed in the United States in more than a decade. *The Executioner's Song* was an extraordinary success and Mailer's second work to win a Pulitzer Prize.

Diverse Works   While retreating somewhat from the public eye in the 1980s and 1990s, Mailer continued to produce a diverse body of work, including essays, screenplays, literary criticism, biographies, and several novels. His longest work, coming in at over thirteen hundred pages, was *Harlot's Ghost* (1991), a meticulously researched novel concerning the origins and early history of the U.S. Central Intelligence Agency (CIA), including the covert schemes the agency used to topple foreign governments. In 2003 Mailer published the highly praised *The Spooky Art: Thoughts on Writing* in which he reflects on the craft of writing, using interviews, essay, lectures, and other pieces he had written throughout his tumultuous career. The same year, Mailer published a book scrutinizing the foreign policies of President George W. Bush, titled *Why Are We at War?* and made several television appearances speaking out against the war in Iraq.

The Last Year   Mailer's health declined rapidly in 2007, the same year *The Castle in the Forest*, a retelling of Adolf Hitler's early life, was published. Mailer was hospitalized in Boston for breathing problems; he was transferred to New York, where he recovered from surgery that removed scar tissue from around his lungs. On November 10, 2007, Mailer died of acute renal failure at the age of eighty-four. At the time of his death, he was working on a sequel to *The Castle in the Forest*.

Works in Literary Context

The inspiration for most of Mailer's writing came from his personal exploits and lifestyle as one of America's leading celebrity writers, a distinction he aggressively encouraged. Many of his protagonists are modeled after Mailer himself, and his strongest writing includes explicitly autobiographical elements. Certainly, Mailer's provocative self-portrait as philosophical existentialist and political leftist ensured that his own personality would be a continuing stage for dramatic conflict.

New Journalism   Mailer has influenced other writers with his extensive experimentation with narrative forms and styles as well as his distinctive synthesis of fiction, autobiography, and journalism. Although Mailer considered himself primarily a novelist, he left a more enduring mark as a journalist and essayist. Beginning with his articles for the *Village Voice*, Mailer helped establish New Journalism as a literary style. New Journalism takes creative liberties with the conventions of journalism, seeking to bring events to life and involve readers in major

---

LITERARY AND HISTORICAL CONTEMPORARIES

Mailer's famous contemporaries include:

William S. Burroughs (1914–1997): A leading writer of the Beat movement, Burroughs influenced popular culture as well as literature through his outrageous works such as *Naked Lunch* (1959).

Alex Haley (1921–1992): After retiring from the U.S. Coast Guard in 1959, Haley began a career in writing, publishing the slavery epic *Roots* in 1976.

Menachem Begin (1913–1992): Prime minister of Israel from 1977 to 1983, Begin wrote *White Nights: The Story of a Prisoner in Russia*, which describes his wartime experience in Europe.

John Updike (1932–2009): Best known for his fiction, Updike portrays characters who confront various—and often painful—aspects of love and responsibility.

Gore Vidal (1925–): A prominent American novelist, essayist, and radical social critic, Vidal shocked readers and angered critics with his novel *The City and the Pillar* (1948), which featured undisguised homosexuality.

Hunter S. Thompson (1937–2005): Thompson created "Gonzo journalism," a style of writing in which reporters become part of the action.

---

crises of the modern world so that people have greater understanding of self and society. Several prominent American writers, such as Mailer, Truman Capote, Tom Wolfe, and Joan Didion, are associated with the New Journalism movement, which peaked in the 1970s.

The Theme of Self-Actualization   Miller's preoccupation with the struggle for individuality and free will in the face of natural forces and institutional authority makes it a central theme in his work. In *The Naked and the Dead*, Mailer examines the complex tensions that evolve as the main characters attempt to impose their will upon an essentially uncaring universe. Describing the combat experiences and interaction of fourteen American soldiers as they attempt to seize control of a Japanese-held island in the Philippines during World War II, Mailer presents the diverse members of the platoon as a microcosm of the American people, each with their own geographic, economic, and social backgrounds. Writing in an unsentimental narrative voice, Mailer discourages reader sympathy for a liberal commander who is violently betrayed by an immoral and ambitious sergeant. The conflict between individual willfulness and established power is not only natural, but necessary.

Mailer's theme of the individual's struggle against collective forces that threaten to rob him of his selfhood is perhaps best explained in "The White Negro." In this

COMMON HUMAN EXPERIENCE

In 1973 writer Tom Wolfe coined the phrase "New Journalism" to describe a literary style characterized by the combination of reported truth and personal observation that reads like fiction. With such works as *The Armies of the Night*, Mailer was a forerunner in the New Journalism movement. Other works that illustrate the elements of New Journalism include the following:

Slouching Towards Bethlehem (1968), a collection of essays by Joan Didion. Didion's work describes her often grim experiences amid the California counterculture of the 1960s.

The Electric Kool-Aid Acid Test (1968), a nonfiction work by Tom Wolfe. Delving into the hippie counterculture and the drug experience, Wolfe recounts the travels of Ken Kesey and his Merry Pranksters as they drive across the country in a brightly painted school bus.

In Cold Blood (1966), a fact-based novel by Truman Capote. Capote called this psychological account of a series of murders committed by two men in Kansas a nonfiction novel.

The Gang That Wouldn't Write Straight: Wolfe, Thompson, Didion, and the New Journalism Revolution (2005), a nonfiction work by Marc Weingarten. In this study, Weingarten explains that writers of New Journalism believed that new styles of reporting were necessary to deal with such momentous events as the Vietnam War.

essay, Mailer argues that the American "hipster," a "philosophical psychopath" immune to traditional institutions of social control, is a desirable adaptation of the uninhibited urban African American, whom Mailer praises for placing the needs of the self over those of society. The narrator of *An American Dream* (1965) explicitly illustrates Mailer's comments in "The White Negro" when he violently transgresses social and moral restrictions by murdering his estranged wife in an attempt to shed his conventional social self as a professor and thereby emerge with a new identity.

Works in Critical Context

While most critics acknowledge Mailer as possessing enormous talent and originality, critical evaluation of his writing is problematic due to his multiplicity as an author, political dissident, social critic, and notorious celebrity. Throughout his career, Mailer has both fascinated and angered critics who contend that his fame has been as much the result of his own self-aggrandizement as his writing talent. Though finding that much of his work has become dated due to its focus on current events, scholar Harold Bloom characterizes Mailer as "a historian of the moral consciousness of his era, and as the representative writer of his generation." According to writer Andrew O'Hagan, Mailer has been "as compulsive a literary character as we've had, but he has also been among the most compelling on the page...[because he] risked and emboldened his talent by imagining himself at the core of things."

The Gospel According to the Son With *The Gospel According to the Son*, a first-person account of the life of Jesus, Mailer undertook a project that he told interviewer Bruce Weber was the "largest dare of all" for a writer. Critic Michiko Kakutani assessed the novel as simply another installment in Mailer's self-centered exploration of fame and infamy. Comparing Mailer's Jesus to both a guest on Oprah Winfrey's talk show and Luke Skywalker of the *Star Wars* series, Kakutani asserts that Mailer has turned both Jesus and God "into familiar contemporary types: he has knocked them off their celestial thrones and turned them into what he knows best, celebrities."

As always, opinions of Mailer and assessments of his work vary greatly. While some critics argue that *The Gospel According to the Son* lacks style and is slow, others, such as Brad Hooper, applaud the novel for successfully "[escaping] Mailer's own image." Because of this, Hooper says, Mailer has produced "a provocatively imagined historical novel." As in many of his other works, critics have praised selected passages of narrative brilliance. In addition, critics have noted Mailer's knowledge of canonical texts, as well as his surprising—and to some, disappointing—adherence to tradition.

Responses to Literature

1. Why do you believe New Journalism emerged as a literary form during the late 1960s and early 1970s? What characteristics of nonfiction narrative appeal to readers? Is the style still used today? If so, provide examples from the past five years. If not, then explain why you think New Journalism is no longer a popular style.

2. In the 1970s, Mailer engaged in a sensational public feud with writer Gore Vidal. Investigate this disagreement. What/who was the cause? What did each writer say and do? How was the matter resolved? With which writer would you side?

3. Mailer was fascinated by the sport of boxing. He was close friends with boxer Joe Torres and often used metaphors related to boxing and fighting in his works. Why do you think a sport of violence was so appealing to Mailer? Why would Mailer have wanted to be friends with Torres?

4. Would you label Mailer as egocentric, or megalomaniac? Support your choice with examples not only from Mailer's life but also from his writings. How did his outsized personality contribute to his creativity?

BIBLIOGRAPHY

Books

Bloom, Harold, ed. *Norman Mailer: Modern Critical Views.* New York: Chelsea House, 1986.

Braudy, Leo Beal, ed. *Norman Mailer: A Collection of Critical Essays.* Englewood Cliffs, N.J.: Prentice Hall, 1972.

Ehrlich, Robert. *Norman Mailer: The Radical as Hipster.* Metuchen, N.J.: Scarecrow Press, 1978.

Glenday, Michael K. *Norman Mailer.* New York: St. Martin's Press, 1995.

Jackson, Richard. *Norman Mailer.* Rochester: University of Minnesota Press, 1968.

Periodicals

Hooper, Brad. "Review of *The Gospel According to the Son.*" *Booklist* (April 15, 1997): 34.

Kakutani, Michiko. "Norman Mailer's Perception of Jesus." *New York Times*, April 14, 1997.

O'Hagan, Andrew. "Interview with Norman Mailer." *Paris Review* 181 (Summer 2007): 88–92.

Weber, Bruce. "Yes, His New Book Is Biblical, but Don't Call Him God." *New York Times Book Review* (April 27, 1997): 6–8.

Web sites

Lennon, J. Michael. *A Brief History of Norman Mailer.* Retrieved November 24, 2008, from http://www.pbs.org/wnet/americanmasters/database/mailer_n.html. Last updated in 2008.

⊛ Bernard Malamud

BORN: *1914, Brooklyn, New York*

DIED: *1986, New York, New York*

NATIONALITY: *American*

GENRE: *Fiction*

MAJOR WORKS:
The Natural (1952)
The Magic Barrel (1954)
The Assistant (1957)
The Fixer (1966)

Overview

Bernard Malamud was an internationally acclaimed author of Jewish-American literature, a genre renowned for its tragicomic elements. His novels and short stories, which often depict a Jewish and urban setting, contemplate the individual's struggle for survival in the harsh, modern world. Malamud's fiction draws from both Yiddish folk culture and classic literary traditions, including Greek mythology and Arthurian legend. Although he is best known for such novels as *The Natural* (1952) and *The Fixer* (1966), he is also recognized as a master of the short

Bernard Malamud   *Malamud, Bernard, photograph. The Library of Congress.*

story form with his sympathetic yet ironic treatment of his tragic characters.

Works in Biographical and Historical Context

From New York to Washington D.C. Malamud was born in Brooklyn, New York, on April 26, 1914. His parents, Russian-Jewish immigrants, ran a grocery store where Malamud worked during much of his youth. Even as a young man, Malamud enjoyed a good story— apparently he enjoyed going to the movies (particularly Charlie Chaplin comedies) and relaying their plots to his friends. As a student at Brooklyn's Erasmus Hall High School, Malamud saw his earliest stories published in the school's literary magazine.

Malamud's parents were not highly educated and knew very little about literature or the arts. In fact, Malamud does not have memories of books on the shelves of his home. Yet, he pursued an academic career, and in 1936 received his BA from the City College of New York. In 1942 he earned his master's from Columbia University, where he wrote his thesis about author Thomas Hardy. Interestingly, critics have noted the similarities between Malamud's brooding protagonists and those of Hardy. After graduation, Malamud planned to teach English in

LITERARY AND HISTORICAL CONTEMPORARIES

Malamud's famous contemporaries include:

Dwight D. Eisenhower (1890–1969): An American general who directed the final overthrow of the Nazis in World War II, Eisenhower was President of the United States and served from 1953 to 1961.

Thomas Hardy (1840–1928): An English poet and novelist. Hardy's stories, which tend to focus on life's events and their effects, influenced Malamud and other writers including Robert Frost, Dylan Thomas, and Philip Larkin.

Saul Bellow (1915–2005): The Jewish-American author of Russian descent whose best-known works include *The Adventures of Augie March* (1953), *Herzog* (1964), and *Humboldt's Gift* (1975). Like Malamud, Bellow is considered one of the great Jewish-American authors of the twentieth century.

Philip Roth (1933–): Pulitzer Prize-winning author who, like Malamud, writes about Jewish-American experiences in and around New York City. Famous works include *American Pastoral* (1997) and *The Plot Against America* (2004).

Francis Bacon (1909–1992): One of the first works exhibited by this British painter depicts the sadism of World War II through violent and contorted images.

the New York City public schools. Jobs at the time were scarce, so he took a job in Washington, D.C., with the Census Bureau instead.

Teaching and Writing in Oregon Malamud soon returned to New York, where he wrote during the day and taught English at Erasmus Hall High School at night. In 1945 he married Ann De Chiara, an Italian-American. As both Malamud and De Chiara came from strong ethic backgrounds, neither of their parents approved of the marriage. During the early years of his marriage, Malamud continued to teach and write, and he published several short stories in a variety of magazines. Many of these reflect his experiences with and interest in New York's immigrant populations, including Italians, African Americans, Jews, and others.

In 1949, Malamud accepted a position teaching English at Oregon State University at Corvallis. With the exception of a year he spent in Rome, Italy with his family, he continued teaching there until 1961 and was eventually promoted to the position of associate professor. During his twelve years at Oregon State, Malamud completed and published the first four books that constitute his initial literary phase. Malamud followed his first novel, a mythological baseball story entitled *The Natural*, with *The Assistant*, a novel about a Jewish shopkeeper

based on Malamud's experiences working in his family's store as a youth. The following year, he published a collection of short stories entitled *The Magic Barrel*, which won the National Book Award in 1959. His third novel, *A New Life*, a satire inspired by his experience in the world of academia, was published in 1961.

An International Traveler That same year, Malamud began teaching creative writing at Bennington College in Vermont, where he remained on the faculty until 1986. Periodically, Malamud interrupted his semesters at Bennington College to travel and lecture, experiences he credited with making him a universal writer. In 1963, he visited England and Italy, followed by travels throughout the Soviet Union, France, and Spain during 1965. From 1966 to 1968, he was a visiting lecturer at Harvard University and won the National Book Award and Pulitzer Prize for *The Fixer* before touring Israel in 1968. During the 1970s and 1980s, Malamud continued to publish both novels and collections of short stories. In 1983 he returned to Italy to stay at the Bellagio Study and Conference Center, a retreat for writers and scholars endowed by the Rockefeller Foundation.

During the last few years of his life, Malamud divided his time between a home in rural Bennington and an apartment in New York City. He died of natural causes on March 18, 1986, in New York. At the time of his death, he had written sixteen chapters of a new novel, tentatively titled *The People*. The incomplete novel and several uncollected short stories were published posthumously in 1989.

Works in Literary Context

Although aspects of Jewish tradition are present in Malamud's works, his fiction transcends cultural issues and reflects a universal concern for humanity. Despite unhappy or uncertain endings, his writing assures readers of the presence of goodness in a corrupt world. Malamud has credited American authors Nathaniel Hawthorne and Henry James with influencing his concerns with moral and spiritual struggles. Malamud has also said he was inspired by Russian writers Fyodor Dostoyevsky and Anton Chekhov for their depictions of the self against society.

The Schlemiel In *The Assistant*, Malamud introduces the "schlemiel," a figure that would recur in his later works. The schlemiel is a bungling, ineffectual person who is easily victimized or who continually fails. Such a character commonly appears in Eastern European Yiddish and Jewish literature. Whether the schlemiel epitomizes the born loser, the hard-luck guy, the poignant misfit, or the Jewish world collectively, he has a long and honorable history. He can be traced back to nineteenth-century Yiddish writers such as Shalom Aleichem, whose "Tevye the Milkman" stories (1894) were adapted for the Broadway musical *Fiddler on the Roof* (1964). The schlemiel is a composite of history, legend, myth, and folklore, and underlying all is the tragicomic element. More often than not, the comic figure of the schlemiel seems to be a victim, but because he often manages to redefine his world, in the end he achieves a moral victory frequently denied to others.

The Malamud schlemiel is used to realize a variety of themes and motifs in many of his novels. He is seen in character Roy Hobbs, a downtrodden baseball player, in *The Natural*, and in Frank Alpine, the cynical, homeless, anti-Semitic youth hired by grocery store owner Morris Bober in *The Assistant*. The schlemiel is similarly evident in the unlucky handyman Yakov Bok of *The Fixer* and especially in failed painter Arthur Fidelman, the main character in *Pictures of Fidelman* (1966). In addition to appearing repeatedly in Malamud's novels, the schlemiel also appears in the stories collected in *Rembrandt's Hat* (1973). In "The Silver Crown," for example, a young biology teacher purchases a silver crown from a rabbi for $986, ostensibly to cure his father of cancer—but the father dies anyway. In "Man in the Drawer," writer Howard Harvitz leaves America to forget his troubles, and, in all the great expanse of Russia, happens to encounter a Jewish taxi driver and author who pushes a forbidden manuscript on him. The catch is that if Harvitz agrees to smuggle the manuscript out of the country, he could find himself in a situation much more serious than the one he had originally tried to escape. Unfortunately, as is evidenced by Harvitz and other of Malamud's characters, schlemiels have a tendency to worsen their problems by making the wrong decisions.

Works in Critical Context

Critics have lauded Malamud's imaginative power and narrative skills since the beginning of his career. With the publication of his first works, he won praise for his adept fusion of folk, symbolic, and realistic narratives, as well as for the moral visions and ethical concerns demonstrated in his writings. Scholars have also commended Malamud's presentation of the transcending power of human suffering as well as his proficient use of irony, comedy, and humor in otherwise tragic stories of life. While most early critics recognized Malamud's successful blending of Jewish experience with modern narrative techniques, some argued that Malamud limited himself creatively by relying too heavily on allegory and myth. Others have also been critical of Malamud's tendency to undercut his tragic vision with comic, even grotesque, characterization.

Malamud's stature as an artist has increased steadily since his death in 1986. While the importance of myth and archetype and the redemptive power of human suffering have remained central concerns in critical assessments of his work, a new generation of critics has focused on other issues, such as the nature of free will, human spirituality, Judaic law, the Holocaust, anti-Semitism and the role of women in his narratives. What has ultimately emerged is a view of Malamud as a complex, often con-

---

COMMON HUMAN EXPERIENCE

Malamud writes about the heartaches of simply being human, but he is also firmly grounded in a generation of specifically Jewish-American writers whose work explores the conflicts between gentile society and Jewish tradition. Here are some other works that explore Jewish-American themes and experiences.

> *The Adventures of Augie March* (1953), a novel by Saul Bellow. The protagonist in this work repeatedly finds himself in alternately humorous and tragic events because he will not accept a defining role in life.
> *Portnoy's Complaint* (1969), fiction by Philip Roth. This irreverently funny work describes a man torn between the traditional values of his Jewish mother and his desire to discover for himself what being human means.
> *Call It Sleep* (1934), a novel by Henry Roth. The life of a Jewish immigrant boy living in a New York ghetto becomes a nightmare when his father keeps losing his job.
> *The Pawnbroker* (1961), fiction by Edward Lewis Wallant. A grim novel about a Holocaust survivor working in a Harlem pawn shop, *The Pawnbroker* makes a controversial comparison between Jewish suffering and that of African-Americans.

---

tradictory writer and an artist deeply concerned with the meaning of human existence.

The Magic Barrel The title story of Malamud's prize-winning first short story collection, "The Magic Barrel," is one of his most frequently discussed works of short fiction. Described by author and editor Sanford Pinsker as "quintessential Malamud—in form, content, and perhaps most of all, in moral vision," the story focuses on the interaction of two main characters: a young, unmarried rabbinical student named Leo Finkle, and Pinye Salzman, a vulgar, yet colorful, marriage broker who smells distinctly of fish. The tale of their relationship combines elements of realism and fantasy in an urban, Jewish setting and centers on the protagonist's struggle to break through the barriers of personal isolation. While Malamud's handling of such themes as love, community, redemption, and Jewish identity has been widely praised, he is also noted for his creative use of ambiguity.

Scholars and critics have remarked favorably on Malamud's mixture of folk and realistic treatments of his subject matter, and have proposed links between "The Magic Barrel" and the paintings of Marc Chagall. Commenting on the story's infamously ambiguous conclusion, reviewer Mark Goldman has remarked that the "last scene, like many of Malamud's sudden, summary endings, is a consciously ironic parable and not an escape from tragedy. All the complex meaning is fixed, flashed back upon the story itself in a kind of [James] Joycean epiphany that runs counter to the neatly packaged endings of the naturalistic tale."

The Assistant Critical reaction to *The Assistant* has focused on Malamud's use of symbolism, the theme of duality, and Jewishness as a literary archetype. In regard to protagonist Morris's altruism in dealing with the neighborhood's poor, along with the criminal Frank's decision to repay the money he stole from Morris, critics have discussed Morris and Frank as symbolic representatives of the decency of human nature. Scholar Max F. Schulz has argued that the actions of the two men support the characterization of Morris as a "mythic hero renewing life for the community" and Frank as a "proletarian hero winning justice for society." According to some critics, Malamud uses religious imagery in *The Assistant* to introduce the theme of the double. Citing Frank's identification with St. Francis of Assisi, his namesake and acknowledged hero, and Morris's Christlike selflessness, academics have claimed that Frank's relationship to Morris mirrors St. Francis's celebrated emulation of Christ. Scholars have also identified doubling in Frank's conversion to Morris's faith, the adoption of his humane moral outlook, and the assumption of his duties. Summarizing Malamud's fusion of character and symbolism in *The Assistant*, critic Meyer Levin observed: "Malamud has succeeded . . . in individualizing his people to a point where one feels able to continue conversation with them outside the book and yet he has kept for each of them a symbolic role, so that the tale has moral echoes, almost a runic quality; it is essentially a parable."

Responses to Literature

1. Research the "Black Sox" scandal that involved eight Chicago White Sox players charged with bribery in the 1919 World Series. In *The Natural*, how do the events in Roy Hobbs's career compare with those surrounding the Black Sox scandal?

2. Research the mythological quest for the Holy Grail. What symbolic elements of this quest appear in *The Natural*?

3. According to many critics, the Holocaust lurks below the surface of many of Malamud's works. In *The Assistant*, for example, Morris is almost asphyxiated by gas in his upstairs flat. In your opinion, does the fact that Malamud was not in the Holocaust make his comments about the tragedy less significant than accounts by such Holocaust survivors as author Elie Wiesel? Why or why not?

4. Research the Yiddish term "schlemiel." How has this figure appeared in the history of Jewish literature? Evaluate Malamud's use of the schlemiel in at least two of his works.

BIBLIOGRAPHY

Books

Abramson, Edward A. *Bernard Malamud Revisited.* New York: Twayne, 1993.

Field, Leslie A., and Joyce W. Fields, eds. *Bernard Malamud and the Critics.* New York: New York University Press, 1970.

Helterman, Jeffrey. *Understanding Bernard Malamud.* Columbia, S.C.: University of South Carolina Press, 1985.

Salzberg, Joel. *Critical Essays on Bernard Malamud.* Boston: G. K. Hall, 1987.

Schulz, Max F. *Radical Sophistication: Studies in Contemporary Jewish-American Novelists.* Athens, Ohio: Ohio University Press, 1969.

Wisse, Ruth. *The Schlemiel as Modern Hero.* Chicago: University of Chicago Press, 1971.

Periodicals

Levin, Meyer. "Growth in Brooklyn." *Saturday Review* (June 15, 1957): 28–29.

Mandel, Ruth. "Bernard Malamud's *The Assistant* and *A New Life*: Ironic Affirmation." *Critique* 7 (Winter 1964–1965): 110–121.

Standley, Fred. "Bernard Malamud: The Novel of Redemption." *Southern Humanities Review* 5 (1971): 903–318.

Web sites

My Jewish Learning, Inc. *Bernard Malamud.* Retrieved November 25, 2008, from http://www.myjewishlearning.com/culture/literature/Overview_Jewish_American_Literature/Into_The_Literary_Mainstream/Literature_Malamud_Norton.htm.

⊛ Malcolm X

BORN: *1925, Omaha, Nebraska*

DIED: *1965, New York, New York*

NATIONALITY: *American*

GENRE: *Nonfiction*

MAJOR WORKS:
The Autobiography of Malcolm X (1965)
Malcolm X: Selected Speeches and Statements (1965)

Overview

Malcolm X was a dynamic African-American revolutionary who rose to prominence and notoriety in the mid-1950s. As the outspoken national minister of the Nation of Islam, Malcolm opposed the mainstream civil rights movement, publicly called for black separatism, and rejected nonviolence and integration as effective ways to

Malcolm X   *Malcolm X, 1964, photograph. AP Images.*

combat racism. In Malcolm X's opinion, the African Americans' sole response to racism should be total withdrawal from the culture and society of white America. Malcolm X documented his life experiences in *The Autobiography of Malcolm X* (1965), a work that is often regarded as the most influential book of his generation.

Works in Biographical and Historical Context

Racial Conflict and Violence   Malcolm X was born Malcolm Little in Omaha, Nebraska, on May 19, 1925. He was exposed to violent racism, white supremacists, and the black separatist movement at an early age. His father was Earl Little, a Baptist minister. Little was an avid supporter of Marcus Garvey's "Back to Africa" movement, which condemned the integration of African Americans and whites, and proposed instead that blacks return to Africa and establish their own free state. Because he was often threatened by the Ku Klux Klan, Malcolm's father moved the family to Lansing, Michigan, in 1929.

The racial climate in Michigan proved to be no better for the Littles. The family was attacked by another white-supremacist group, the Black Legion, which burned down their home. The group later murdered Malcolm's father by throwing him under a trolley car. His death was declared a suicide, however, and Malcolm's mother, Louise, was left to care for their children. After his father's death, the family fell into abject poverty. Terribly stricken by her husband's murder and buckling under the demands of raising eight children during the Depression, Malcolm's mother became psychologically unstable and was institutionalized until 1963. As a result, Malcolm and his siblings were made wards of the state and sent to separate foster homes in 1937.

A Life of Crime   Despite the traumas of his early youth, Malcolm was one of the best students in his class at school. He was also popular—his white classmates elected him president of their seventh-grade class. Yet, when he told an English teacher that he wanted to become a lawyer, the teacher suggested carpentry instead and urged Malcolm "to be realistic about being a nigger." Shattered by his teacher's suggestion, Malcolm dropped out of school at the end of eighth grade and went to live with his half sister in Boston, Massachusetts. It was here he discovered the city's African-American underworld. He began to associate with gamblers and thieves and soon acquired a formidable reputation as a hustler, pimp, and drug dealer. A chronic abuser of cocaine and marijuana, he carried out a series of robberies with his longtime white lover until he was arrested in 1946 and given a ten-year prison sentence. The exceptionally long term is thought to reflect the judge's revulsion at Malcolm's liaisons with white women.

Prison Turnabout   Prison marked a turning point in Malcolm's life. Initially, he continued his reckless ways, paying for drugs smuggled in by guards, and his vicious demeanor earned him the nickname "Satan" from other inmates. Eventually, another convict introduced him to the prison's library, and Malcolm began reading as many books as possible. He also began studying the teachings of the Nation of Islam (or Black Muslims), an American sect of Islam that extols the superiority of the African-American race. The Nation of Islam's founder, Elijah Muhammad, counseled his followers—as had Marcus Garvey—to reject white America in favor of an autonomous African-American society.

Muhammad's doctrine of black pride appealed considerably to Malcolm, who seemed to be the perfect candidate for the Nation of Islam. Muhammad taught that drinking, cursing, fighting, dancing, and using drugs—the mainstays of Malcolm's young life—kept the black man under the heel of the white devil. Furthermore, Malcolm was bright, and the Black Muslim doctrine of self-improvement and advancement encouraged and challenged him as public school never had.

The Nation of Islam   Upon his release from prison in 1952, Malcolm took the name "Malcolm X" to signify the loss of the African name that slave owners had replaced when Malcolm's ancestors were brought as slaves to America. He became a close follower of Elijah Muhammad, with whom he studied briefly at the Black Muslim headquarters in Chicago. After serving as an assistant minister at a Detroit mosque, Malcolm X became a minister in New York, where he was recognized as an articulate, energetic spokesperson for the Nation of Islam. He used this position to attack racism, champion separatism, and preach faith in Allah as the salvation of African

Americans. In addition to declaring Christianity an ideology of enslavement, Malcolm X claimed that civil rights, equal opportunity, and integration were all futile within a society that was determinedly racist. As Malcolm X advised blacks to reject white society and unite under Muhammad, the Nation of Islam's membership increased significantly. Acknowledging Malcolm X's effectiveness, Muhammad named him the organization's first national minister.

In the late 1950s, national news media began to focus on the growing numbers of Black Muslims. A CBS documentary entitled *The Hate That Hate Produced* (1959) offered a selective display of incendiary clips of Muhammad, Malcolm X, and other leading Nation of Islam spokesmen preaching what would become the mass media's usual depiction of the Nation of Islam's main message: hate and violence. In response, Malcolm X explained that he merely encouraged African Americans to defend themselves against racial violence, not cause it.

Growing Discord Although Malcolm X always referred to himself as Elijah Muhammad's representative, his fiery speeches against white oppression made him the Black Muslims' leading spokesman. Malcolm rose swiftly in the ranks of the Black Muslims, and in 1954 he was made the head of a major mosque in Harlem. There he achieved a reputation as an articulate, mercurial spokesperson for the radical black community. He denounced integration, nonviolence, and most of the teachings of the more popular civil-rights leader, Dr. Martin Luther King Jr., who used peaceful tactics like sit-ins and marches to demand equal rights for black Americans. Malcolm instead used aggressive language and made radical statements. For example, he famously termed the assassination of President John F. Kennedy in 1963 as a case of "chickens coming home to roost"—implying the president had somehow gotten what he deserved. Malcolm later explained he meant only that "the hate in white men . . . finally had struck down the President," but he was immediately censured by Muhammad. "That was a very bad statement," Muhammad told Malcolm. "The country loved this man." Muhammad ordered him to refrain from public comment for ninety days, and Malcolm complied.

It was around this time that Malcolm X's growing popularity disturbed some leaders in the Nation of Islam, who worried that he was becoming too powerful. Malcolm's remark about the Kennedy assassination gave Muhammad an opportunity to expel his national minister from the organization's hierarchy—indeed, Malcolm had been in conflict with Muhammad for some time. Malcolm had condemned Muhammad's materialism—his expensive cars and business suits and lavishly furnished estate—and was shocked by allegations that Muhammad had seduced several of his secretaries and sired their children. Feeling estranged from Muhammad, Malcolm canceled the original dedication to his autobiography-in-progress (which he had begun in 1963). It was only at the urging of co-author Alex Haley that Malcolm agreed to not turn his autobiography into a polemic against his former mentor.

An Awakening Soon after he was censured, Malcolm proceeded to break officially with the Nation of Islam. It was around this time he learned that disgruntled members of the Nation of Islam were planning his assassination. In April 1964, Malcolm traveled to Mecca, Saudi Arabia, the birthplace of the Muslim prophet Muhammad. Once there, he observed people of all races united in their beliefs, which caused him to undergo a spiritual and political transformation. "Since I learned the *truth* in Mecca," he explained in his autobiography, "my dearest friends have come to include *all* kinds—some Christians, Jews, Buddhists, Hindus, agnostics, and even atheists! I have friends who are called capitalists, Socialists, and Communists! Some of my friends are moderates, conservatives, extremists—some are even Uncle Toms! My friends today are black, brown, red, yellow, and *white*!" In short, the experience was a significant awakening that helped Malcolm gain a greater compassion for people of all races and nationalities. Though he retained his belief that African Americans had to gain control of their own communities and organizations before they could gain their freedom, he dedicated himself to working towards unity and freedom for all peoples. He renamed himself El-Hajj Malik El-Shabazz and, once back in the United States, founded the Organization of Afro-American Unity.

Death Threats Malcolm X's emergence as an independent, revolutionary leader in the fight for African-American rights made him the object of death threats from many groups. Ironically, the threats were overwhelmingly from two diametrically opposed camps—the Nation of Islam and white supremacists. On February 14, 1965, for example, his home was firebombed. Though he and his family escaped unharmed, the house was destroyed. Then, just one week later, on February 21, 1965, he was assassinated while addressing an audience of four hundred in the Audubon Ballroom in Harlem. In front of an audience that included his pregnant wife and four daughters, three men rose and fired sixteen shots, killing Malcolm. Talmadge Thayer, Norman 3X Butler, and Thomas 15X Johnson were apprehended and eventually convicted of the crime. Two of the three were members of the Black Muslims. Although theories about other groups being involved in the murder plot have been discussed, no evidence has ever been produced.

Works in Literary Context

Although Malcolm X's political and religious organizations were on unsteady ground at the time of his death, the posthumous publication of his autobiography insured that his ideas would never be forgotten. Malcolm showed African Americans that they had the right to be angry, to challenge white domination, and to demand change. Decades after his assassination, the teachings of Malcolm X have remained pertinent in race relations. In addition to the plays and movies focusing on him, new scholarly works about Malcolm X continue to be written. Indeed, the words and thoughts of Malcolm X still encourage Americans to fight racism in all forms.

Black Power Despite Malcolm's conversation late in his life to more traditional Islamic thought, he remained strident in his conviction that African Americans deserved their legal equality and should fight against racism whenever they encountered it. As part of a legacy of non-integrationists, Malcolm can be viewed as inheritor of Marcus Garvey's views, and as the forebear of the 1960s and 70s radical Black Power movement. Made popular by the Black Panther group, Black Power sought to aggressively promote black individuality rather than assimilate into white culture. Malcolm's most famous slogan—"By Any Means Necessary"—illustrates this philosophy. He did not agree with Martin Luther King Jr., whose ideas encouraged African-Americans to resist racism nonviolently and passively. Instead, Malcolm always encouraged active resistance. He believed black Americans were regularly discriminated against by both white institutions and white individuals, and black people should resist on both levels. These convictions are evident in his speeches and writings.

African-American Autobiography In part, Malcolm X's legacy can largely be attributed to the fact that his life is preserved in autobiographical form. Besides imparting a sense of immediacy, this firsthand account provides an unflinchingly honest look at the life of a controversial man, from his experiences with violent racism as a youth to his days as a criminal to his role in the Black Muslim movement in America. While the media subjectively portrayed Malcolm X as an enraged activist who demanded violence against whites, *The Autobiography of Malcolm X* presents a more complete view of him as a human being—a chance to defend himself, some say. As a result, such incidents as the incessant threats against his family that resulted in his father's death have a much greater emotional impact because they are recounted in his own words.

Furthermore, Malcolm's book participates in an entire genre of autobiography, particularly of African-American men, which attempts to articulate a kind of double consciousness (so-called by African-American intellectual W. E. B. Du Bois). From this perspective, it is said that a white American male's autobiography needs only to express himself in the world—a black man's autobiography, however, arguably along with women and other minority groups, must articulate the self in relation to a dominant and oppressive society. His autobiography, then, has a double goal: to envision his true self on the page as well as to erase the negative stereotype placed upon him by American culture. Along with other writers such as Richard Wright, W. E. B. Du Bois, and even Frederick Douglass, Malcolm X both narrates the development of his unique self in his autobiography along with the larger journey of the black man in America.

LITERARY AND HISTORICAL CONTEMPORARIES

Malcolm X's famous contemporaries include:

John F. Kennedy (1917–1963): The thirty-fifth President of the United States, Kennedy was assassinated in 1963 in Dallas, Texas.

Martin Luther King Jr. (1929–1968): A civil rights activist who encouraged nonviolence and passive resistance, King gave his famous "I Have a Dream" speech in 1963, a year before he won the Nobel Peace Prize in 1964 and five years before he was assassinated.

Medgar Evers (1925–1963): A prominent civil-rights leader, Evers worked for the NAACP in Mississippi. He actively sought to change such racist practices as segregated schooling. He was assassinated by a white supremacist.

Harper Lee (1926–): An Alabama-born writer of a now-classic piece of Southern literature: *To Kill a Mockingbird* (1960). The story involves conflicted race relations in the South, and is told from the perspective of a young girl.

Betty Shabazz (1936–1997): Wife of Malcolm X. Betty Shabazz took Malcolm's Muslim surname after he returned from his trip to Mecca. After Malcolm's assassination she earned her doctorate in education and became a speaker for civil rights and racial tolerance.

Ishmael Reed (1938–): Reed is best known for his literary theory called the "Neo-HooDoo Aesthetic," which attempts to separate the distinct qualities of African-American culture from white American culture.

Works in Critical Context

The Autobiography of Malcolm X is highly regarded by scholars in many disciplines for its moving account of his own experiences with racism, his criminal past, and his years as an activist. During the late 1960s, Malcolm X's speeches and comments were published in several volumes. Academics agree that, together with the autobiography, these collections offer numerous insights into America's social climate from the mid-1950s to the mid-1960s and articulate the concerns of a significant portion of the black community in those years. As reviewer I. F. Stone notes, "There are few places on earth where whites have not grown rich robbing [African-Americans]. It was Malcolm's great contribution to help make us aware of this."

The Autobiography of Malcolm X *The Autobiography of Malcolm X* was published after Malcolm's death to much critical acclaim. Assessing the work's importance, Charles H. Nichols declared that *The Autobiography of Malcolm X* is arguably the "most influential book read by this generation of Afro-Americans. For not only is the account of Malcolm Little an absorbing and heart-shattering encounter

COMMON HUMAN EXPERIENCE

As a genre, autobiography—the story of a person's life written by that person—is an effective means of expressing the values and history of an era, in addition to one's own philosophical views and personal history. *The Autobiography of Malcolm X*, for example, depicts not only the events in Malcolm X's life and how he responded to them, but also the events of the civil rights movement and how they affected America. Here are some other famous autobiographies:

The Autobiography of Benjamin Franklin (1790), by Benjamin Franklin. Franklin's work reflects his active pursuit of philosophy, politics, religion, and literature during the years before the American Revolution (1775–1783).

Narrative of the Life of Frederick Douglass (1845), by Frederick Douglass. With grace and dignity, Douglass shares his experiences as a slave who overcomes cruelty and oppression.

The Story of My Life, (1903) by Helen Keller. Both blind and deaf, Keller overcame incredible obstacles to become a leading advocate for people with disabilities and an active member of the Socialist party.

The Education of Henry Adams (1907), by Henry Adams. Winner of a Pulitzer Prize in 1919, this autobiography concludes that the nineteenth-century education Adams received was inadequate in preparing him for the conflicts of the twentieth century.

with the realities of poverty, crime and racism. It is a fantastic success story." He continues, "Paradoxically, the book, designed to be an indictment of American and European bigotry and exploitation, is a triumphant affirmation of the possibilities of the human spirit."

As Malcolm X has increasingly been recognized as a leading figure in the African-American struggle for recognition and equality, *The Autobiography of Malcolm X* has grown in importance. Truman Nelson comments:

Viewed in its complete historical context, this is indeed a great book. Its dead-level honesty, its passion, its exalted purpose, even its manifold unsolved ambiguities will make it stand as a monument to the most painful of truths: that this country, this people, this Western world has practiced unspeakable cruelty against a race, an individual, who might have made its fraudulent humanism a reality.

Responses to Literature

1. After reading Malcolm X's autobiography, list four of Malcolm's main goals in eliminating racism. Have any of them been accomplished? In your opinion how much of the racism that existed in Malcolm's lifetime still exists today? Give specific examples of both existing racism and cultural progress in your answer

2. Write a speech that Malcolm X might give today. What issues do you think he would address? How would the themes he addressed during his lifetime apply to modern-day America?

3. Malcolm X is often contrasted with Martin Luther King Jr. Research the two figures by reading a book such as James Cone's *Malcolm & Martin & America* (1991). What did the leaders each believe was the path toward racial equality in America? What areas did they share and where did they disagree?

4. Though they espoused different ideas, both Malcolm X and Martin Luther King Jr. were assassinated because of the ideas they held. In your opinion, how might America be different today if neither man had been assassinated? Why do you think so many people who have tried to reform society have been murdered?

BIBLIOGRAPHY

Books

Bloom, Harold. *The Autobiography of Malcolm X.* New York: Chelsea House, 1995.

Brown, Kevin. *Malcolm X: His Life and Legacy.* Brookfield, Conn.: Milbrook Press, 1995.

Cone, James H. *Malcolm & Martin & America: A Dream or a Nightmare.* New York: Orbis Books, 1991.

Diamond, Arthur. *Malcolm X: A Voice for Black America.* Berkeley Heights, N.J.: Enslow, 1994.

Dyson, Michael Eric. *Making Malcolm: The Myth and Meaning of Malcolm X.* New York: Oxford University Press, 1995.

Lomax, Louise E. *To Kill a Black Man.* Los Angeles: Holloway House, 1968.

Malcolm X, with Alex Haley. *The Autobiography of Malcolm X.* New York: Ballantine, 1965.

McKinley, James. *Assassination in America.* New York: Harper, 1977.

Stone, I. F. *In a Time of Torment.* New York: Random House, 1967.

Wood, Joe. *Malcolm X: In Our Own Image.* New York: Anchor Books, 1994.

Periodicals

Nelson, Truman. "Deliquent's Progress." *The Nation* (Nov 8, 1965): 336–38.

Web sites

The Official Web Site of Malcolm X. *Home.* Retrieved November 15, 2008, from http://www.cmgww.com/historic/malcolm/home.php.

The Malcolm X Project at Columbia University Retrieved
November 24, 2008, from http://www.columbia.
edu/cu/ccbh/mxp.

⚙ David Mamet

BORN: *1947, Chicago, Illinois*

NATIONALITY: *American*

GENRE: *Drama, fiction*

MAJOR WORKS:
American Buffalo (1975)
Glengarry Glen Ross (1984)
The Untouchables (1987)
The Unit (2001)

Overview

David Mamet is a prominent playwright and screenplay
writer who is highly praised for his careful attention to
language and its relationship to behavior. In much of his
work, which reflects the rhythms of fellow dramatist Harold Pinter, he concentrates on creating characters and

David Mamet   *Vera Anderson / WireImage / Getty Images*

atmosphere with sparse, cadenced dialogue—sometimes,
say some critics, at the expense of plot and action. Nevertheless, whether working for the theater or the screen,
Mamet has the reputation of being an extraordinary
craftsman.

Works in Biographical and Historical Context

Linguistic Background David Alan Mamet was born
in Chicago, Illinois, on November 30, 1947, the only son
of Bernard and Leonore Mamet. As a lawyer, Bernard
valued semantics, the branch of linguistics concerned with
the nature, structure, and contextual meaning of words.
Accordingly, he taught Mamet and his younger sister how
to listen, question, and express themselves as precisely as
possible. In fact, Bernard would often stop conversation at
the dinner table until his children found more precise
words for what they were trying to say. Even as a child,
Mamet spent many afternoons in his father's office, composing dialogue at a typewriter. After his parents' divorce
in the late 1950s, Mamet lived with his mother and
attended a private school in Chicago. At the age of fifteen,
he began working backstage at the Hull House Theatre,
where he discovered his life's direction. In high school, he
worked as a busboy at an improvisational-comedy cabaret,
an experience he says helped him understand the rhythms
of action and speech.

An Ear for Language Mamet studied literature and
drama at Goddard College in Plainfield, Vermont. He
received a BA in 1969 after writing his first play, a revue
called *Camel*, to fulfill his thesis requirement in English
literature. Though he studied acting at the Neighborhood Playhouse School of the Theatre in New York City,
he quickly decided he was better suited to writing and
directing for the theater. In 1970, he taught drama at
Marlboro College in Vermont, and then returned to
Chicago, where he worked a variety of odd jobs, including cabdriver, short-order cook, factory worker, and telephone salesman. Many critics attribute Mamet's astute
ear for American idiom and cadence to this apprenticeship among the working class.

In 1971, Mamet returned to Goddard College as a
drama instructor and artist-in-residence. In the process of
teaching his classes, Mamet discovered that writing his
own material for student performances was better than
searching for appropriate material by other dramatists. In
1972, Mamet again went back to Chicago, where he saw
several of his plays staged at experimental theaters. His
play *Sexual Perversity in Chicago* (1974) garnered him
the Joseph Jefferson Award, a prize given annually to the
best new Chicago play. In 1975, a double bill featuring
Duck Variations (1972) and *Sexual Perversity in Chicago*
was produced in an Off-Broadway theater in New York.

Award-Winning Uniqueness The Broadway production of *American Buffalo* (1975) solidified Mamet's

LITERARY AND HISTORICAL CONTEMPORARIES

Mamet's famous contemporaries include:

Sam Shepard (1943–): Shepard is an award-winning playwright, writer, and actor. Before the age of thirty, Shepard had written over thirty plays that were produced in New York.

August Wilson (1945–2005): Wilson was a Pulitzer Prize–winning author of the drama *Fences* (1987). In this and much of his other work, Wilson explores African-American history through kinship and personal connections.

Lanford Wilson (1937–): Wilson is an American dramatist. Wilson's drama often addresses audiences directly and blends conversations with soliloquy. He won the Pulitzer Prize for *Talley's Folly* (1979).

Rob Reiner (1947–): Before his successful career as a director, producer, and writer, Reiner was an Emmy-winning actor on the 1970s sitcom *All in the Family*.

Gregory Maguire (1954–): Maguire is an author and literacy advocate. Maguire's novels for adults often retell classic children's stories from the perspective of another character, as in *Wicked* (1995), based on L. Frank Baum's *The Wonderful Wizard of Oz* (1900).

place in contemporary drama. The play ran for 135 performances and was voted the best American play of 1976–1977 by the New York Drama Critics Circle. More important, however, Mamet's first Broadway production showed he was capable of creating a unique American language for the theater. Indeed, clipped, rapid-fire dialogue is known throughout the world of theater as "Mametspeak." In 1976, Mamet received an Obie award for distinguished playwriting. A prolific dramatist, he followed *American Buffalo* with numerous plays, the most successful of which was *Glengarry Glen Ross* (1984), which earned both the New York Drama Critics' Circle Award for best American play and the Pulitzer Prize in drama in 1984.

Screenplay Writing and Other Genres In 1979, Mamet turned to writing screenplays and made an impressive debut with his work for the 1981 film version of the 1934 novel, *The Postman Always Rings Twice* by James Cain. For Mamet, whose dramas for the stage do not rely on external plot or movement, screenplay writing was a learning experience because he had to focus on plot as well as dialogue. Despite a professed disdain of Hollywood, he has followed *The Postman Always Rings Twice* with a number of critically acclaimed screenplays, including *The Verdict* (1982), which was nominated for an Academy Award, and the gangster epic *The Untouchables* (1987).

A man with numerous creative talents, Mamet has written stage adaptations for several fictional works by Anton Chekov. In 1988, he made his first appearance as a director with the film *House of Games.* At the same time, he wrote *Speed-the-Plow* (1988), in which pop star Madonna made her Broadway debut. In 1994, Mamet published his first novel, *The Village*, and he has published several collections of essays filled with his thoughts, opinions, recollections, musings, and reports on a variety of topics, such as friendship, religion, politics, morals, society, and of course, the American theater.

Throughout the 1990s and 2000s, Mamet has continued to write and direct for both the stage and the screen, working on the movie *Hannibal* (2001), the sequel to the Oscar-winning thriller *Silence of the Lambs* (1991). He ventured into television when he directed an episode of *The Shield* (2001), which he followed in 2006 with the creation of *The Unit*, a CBS action-adventure series featuring a special forces team based on Eric Haney's nonfiction work *Inside Delta Force* (2002). Mamet's most recent work includes directing the martial arts movie *Redbelt* (2008).

Works in Literary Context

Mametspeak Mamet's contributions to the worlds of film and stage are numerous and impressive. One of the movie industry's finest writers and directors, his work has remained in demand, and he established his place in the lexicon of theater with Mametspeak.

Sparse and cryptic at times, Mametspeak is precisely crafted dialogue characterized by a clipped, staccato rhythm unlike natural speech patterns. In many works, Mamet attempts to condense speech into a single line or even a single word, much like the compression found in poetry. Such manipulation of language proves pointed and effective. The power of Mamet's characters lies within their dialogue, and Mamet often emphasizes certain words to draw attention to characters who exploit language in deceitful ways. Characters who engage in Mametspeak are lost in an absurdist society, and they are unable to formulate a complete thought to describe their distress. They interrupt each other, leave sentences unfinished, and are often profane in their expression of frustration.

Because Mametspeak itself creates much of the drama in a play, Mamet's minimalist scripts lack detailed stage directions. In lieu of plot development, he uses italics, parentheses, and quotation marks, all of which tend to become obtrusive for the reader. In the script notation to *American Buffalo*, for example, Mamet explains: "Some portions of the dialogue appear in parentheses, which serve to mark a slight change of outlook on the part of the speaker—perhaps a momentary change to a more introspective regard." For readers of the play, these parentheses set apart the lines they enclose and make the reader wonder whether he is missing some hidden meaning. Not surprisingly, Mametspeak makes large demands upon actors and directors.

Mamet's cadences have frequently been compared to those of Harold Pinter—whom Mamet recognizes as an early influence and who also divided his time between stage and screen. Although Mamet often borrows Pinter's style of pauses, they seem to have a different function in Mamet's plays. In Pinter's plays, for instance, the pauses reflect reality, while the dialogue verbalizes the characters' subconscious thoughts. In Mamet's plays, however, the pauses serve to heighten the realism of the language itself.

Works in Critical Context

David Mamet has acquired a great deal of critical recognition for his plays, each of which is a microcosmic view of the American experience. "He's that rarity, a pure writer," noted reviewer Jack Kroll, "and the synthesis he appears to be making, with echoes from voices as diverse as Beckett, Pinter, and Hemingway, is unique and exciting." Negative criticism of Mamet's work has been aimed at his general focus on the rhythm and form of language rather than on its function and content, resulting in a lack of plot and dramatic conflict. Although some critics have faulted Mamet for failing to control seemingly meaningless repetitions in such plays as *The Woods* (1977) and for his excessive use of profanity, they generally agree he possesses a unique ear for American idiom.

Glengarry Glen Ross   The Pulitzer Prize Mamet received for *Glengarry Glen Ross* not only increased his critical standing, but also helped to make the play a commercial success. Observed reviewer Richard Christiansen, "Craftily constructed, so that there is laughter, as well as rage, in its dialogue, the play has a payoff in each scene and a cleverly plotted mystery that kicks in with a surprise hook at its ending." As in Mamet's earlier plays, the characters and their language are very important to *Glengarry Glen Ross*. As critic Stephen Harvey noted, "The pungency of Glengarry's language comes from economy: if these characters have fifty-word vocabularies, Mamet makes sure that every monosyllable counts."

For the real estate agents in Glengarry Glen Ross, the bottom line is sales. According to critic Robert Brustein, the play is "so precise in its realism that it...takes on reverberant ethical meanings. It is biting...showing life stripped of all idealistic pretenses and liberal pieties." He continues: "Without a single tendentious line, without any polemical intention, without a trace of pity or sentiment, Mamet has launched an assault on the American way of making a living." Commenting on Mamet's criticism of capitalism and society, reviewer Benedict Nightingale called the play "as scathing a study of unscrupulous dealing as the American theater has ever produced."

Responses to Literature

1. Read Arthur Miller's *Death of a Salesman* (1949). Compare and contrast the view of sales in Miller's

---

COMMON HUMAN EXPERIENCE

Many of Mamet's plays deal with the decline of morality in an emotionally and spiritually bereft world. In *Speed-the-Plow*, for example, Mamet depicts the dirty corruption of show business, while *Oleanna* (1991), considered by some to be his most controversial play, dramatizes a relationship between a professor and one of his students that results in sexual-harassment charges. Here are some other works that depict moral and spiritual wastelands in the modern world:

> *Network* (1976), a screenplay by Paddy Chayefsky. Centered around a fictional television network, this work satirizes the dehumanization of contemporary America.
> *The Waste Land* (1922), a poem by T. S. Eliot. With condensed language and many literary and historical references, this long poem explores the spiritual emptiness of society after World War I.
> *The Hamlet of A. MacLeish* (1928), a collection of poetry by Archibald MacLeish. This volume reflects the author's attempt to come to terms with the depravation of society and his loss of faith in mankind.

---

play with that in *Glengarry Glen Ross*. Is Willy Loman anything like the salesmen in Mamet's play? Would you do business with any of the men in either play? Why?

2. Rewrite a page from a Shakespearean drama in Mametspeak. After you finish, explain your process for choosing the language you used and whether you think your work expresses the same mood and meaning as Shakespeare's version.

3. Mamet is known for scripts that lack stage directions. Choose one of Mamet's plays and write detailed stage directions for one of the scenes. What do these directions add to the play? What do they clarify or change?

4. Mamet is extremely specific about italicizing single syllables of dialogue or cutting words off in the middle when appropriate for his meaning. Select a passage of dialogue in one of his plays and determine what Mamet accomplishes by being so attentive to language and its rhythms.

BIBLIOGRAPHY

Books

Bigsby, C. W. E. *David Mamet*. London: Methuen, 1985.
Carroll, Dennis. *David Mamet*. New York: St. Martin's, 1987.

Heilpern, John. *How Good Is David Mamet, Anyway?* New York: Routledge, 2000.

King, Kimball. *Ten Modern American Playwrights.* New York: Garland, 1982.

Periodicals

Brustein, Robert. "Review of *Glengarry Glen Ross.*" *New Republic* (July 12, 1982): 23–24.

Christiansen, Richard. "Review of *Glengarry Glen Ross.*" *Chicago Tribune* (January 18, 1987): 7.

Harvey, Stephen. "Review of *Glengarry Glen Ross.*" *Nation* (April 28, 1984): 522–523.

Kroll, Jack. "Review of *Glengarry Glen Ross.*" *Newsweek* (April 9, 1984): 109.

Nightingale, Benedict. "Review of *Glengarry Glen Ross.*" *New York Times* (March 26, 1984): C17.

Web sites

Fancast. *David Mamet.* Retrieved November 22, 2008, from http://www.fancast.com/people/David-Mamet/7158/biography.

✹ Bobbie Ann Mason

BORN: *1940, Mayfield, Kentucky*

NATIONALITY: *American*

GENRE: *Fiction*

MAJOR WORKS:

Shiloh and Other Stories (1982)

In Country (1985)

Spence + Lila (1988)

Feather Crowns (1993)

An Atomic Romance (2006)

Overview

The people and land of her native rural western Kentucky figure prominently in the fiction of Bobbie Ann Mason, one of the first American writers to use popular culture to illustrate the impact of mass culture on today's society. Faced by the introduction of television, shopping malls, popular music, and fast-food restaurants, Mason's characters find their traditional country lifestyles challenged by modern society. Although she is often categorized a regional writer, Mason offers a universal look at Americans throughout the country whose dreams have been affected—both positively and negatively—by "pop culture."

Works in Biographical and Historical Context

Rural Kentucky Life Mason was born on May 1, 1940, in Mayfield, a small town in western Kentucky. Because her family's farm was located outside of town, Mason attended a rural elementary school that, she told interviewer Lila Havens, had "terrible teachers and poor

Bobbie Ann Mason   *Mason, Bobbie Ann, photograph. © Jerry Bauer. Reproduced by permission.*

students." Quiet and somewhat withdrawn, Mason spent much of her time reading and listening to popular music on the radio. Though she attempted to write fiction when she was a child, she was discouraged by her lack of progress. While a student at Mayfield High School, Mason wrote for the town's local newspaper.

Fan Magazines to Feminist Guide After earning a Bachelor of Arts degree from the University of Kentucky in 1962, Mason moved to New York, where she worked as a writer for *Movie Star* and *T.V. Star Parade* magazines. In 1966, she received a Master of Arts degree from the State University of New York at Binghamton and earned a PhD from the University of Connecticut in 1972. Her doctoral thesis, *Nabokov's Garden: A Guide to Ada*, was published in 1974, and was followed by another non-fiction work, *The Girl Sleuth: A Feminist Guide to The Bobbsey Twins, Nancy Drew, and Their Sisters* in 1975.

Nineteen New Yorker Rejections Mason taught journalism at Mansfield State College in Pennsylvania and began writing short stories involving characters modeled after people she had observed in rural Kentucky. Looking back, Mason has expressed amusement at the arrogance that led her to send the second story she wrote to *The New Yorker*, one of the most prestigious magazines for short fiction. Although this story and the eighteen others that followed it were rejected, the second rejection began a correspondence between Mason and fiction editor Roger Angell, who encouraged her to continue writing. Finally, Mason's twentieth submission to *The New Yorker*, the short story "Offerings," was accepted and published in the February 18, 1980, issue of the magazine. After accepting two more of her stories, *The New Yorker* contracted a first-reading agreement with her. This meant that Mason would submit pieces to that magazine before sending them for consideration anywhere else. This arrangement continues today.

Novels and More In 1982, sixteen of Mason's stories were collected in *Shiloh and Other Stories*, which garnered rave reviews, received several nominations for national book awards and won the 1983 Ernest Hemingway Foundation Award. *In Country*, her first novel, was published in 1985 and has been followed by several other novels and short story collections. Throughout her body of work, Mason has addressed the theme of individual identity in a time of social change.

As part of a series published by Penguin, Mason wrote a brief biography about the legendary singer Elvis Presley in 2003. In *Elvis Presley*, Mason shows a special understanding of her subject, having grown up in approximately the same time and place as the singer and having listened to him throughout his career. The biography includes familiar stories, as well as the author's observations on topics including southern foods, the hiring of Colonel Tom Parker as Presley's manager because of his familiar horse-trading style, and the singer's struggle to be both a poor boy from Tupelo, Mississippi, and the king of rock and roll. In 2005, Mason returned to fiction with *An Atomic Romance*, her first novel in more than a decade. Currently, Mason lives in Kentucky, where she continues to gather material for her work.

Works in Literary Context

Mason has said that her childhood was marked by isolation and a desire to escape the resulting loneliness through books. She identifies Nancy Drew and the Bobbsey Twins as her most powerful and lasting literary influences. The predominance of aloof, disdainful protagonists in twentieth-century literature prompted Mason to write fiction about the antithesis. As a result, her characters are ordinary, working-class citizens of rural western Kentucky, often living in Hopewell, her fictional version of her own hometown of Mayfield.

The Changing South Mason most often explores characters facing overwhelmingly personal events that lead to the acceptance of something new or the rejection or loss of something old. Set primarily in rural western Kentucky, Mason's fiction depicts a rapidly changing South in which individuals who once lived and worked on farms and shared deep-rooted family traditions are now employed by national retail stores, live in subdivi-

sions, and experience the modern world largely through television, popular music, shopping malls, and fast-food restaurants. These adjustments in the characters' lives reflect a general uneasiness that pervades the cultural landscape; the forces of change and alienation are no less frightening because they are universal or unavoidable.

Mason's fiction not only describes the commercial, material aspects of her characters' lives, but also examines the threatening changes in social mores that characterize modern life. Unable to reconcile their present lives with the past, Mason's characters, sometimes viewed as grotesques, are caught between permanence and transience, between their own inherent need for individual expression and their obligations to family and home. Not surprisingly, this struggle affects their relationships, which are often emotionally and intellectually distant. Several of Mason's protagonists are alienated from their heritage and have sought refuge in television evangelism, call-in radio programs, or aerobic dancing. If Mason's characters do find kinship, it is often because they bond over the superficialities of popular culture, including music, movies, and television, and commerce, brand-name products and shopping malls, which invade their formerly remote region. Although she depicts the encroaching impact of suburban America on her rural characters, such as when Wal-Mart replaces the country store, she usually does so not as social criticism, but as a means of providing an

COMMON HUMAN EXPERIENCE

Coined by detractors of the minimalist fiction popular in the late 1970s and early 1980s, the term "dirty realism" refers to a literary genre distinguished by its terse style and its depiction of struggling, working-class characters in dreary rural and suburban settings. Listed below are works associated with the dirty realism movement:

Adcult USA (1996), nonfiction by James B. Twitchell. According to Twitchell, advertising, which simply reflects people's inherent materialism, has become the language of American pop culture, providing a common bond that links all Americans.

Moon Deluxe (1983), a collection of stories by Frederick Barthelme. The short stories in this volume provide a cautionary, humorous, and occasionally depressing portrayal of contemporary suburban life.

"How Dirty is Jayne Allen Phillips?" (2001), a scholarly article by Brian Jarvis. This scholarly piece discusses the genre of dirty realism and how it applies to the works of such writers as Mason and Jayne Allen Phillips, among others.

Where I'm Calling From: New and Collected Stories (1988), short stories by Raymond Carver. Using sparse yet dense language, Carver's stories depict the lives of ordinary people without sentimentality.

accurate and realistic depiction of people within their changing environments. Her inclusion of pop-culture elements enhances the sense of meeting real people engaged in their everyday lives.

Works in Critical Context

Mason has earned critical respect for her compelling and unsentimental portrayals of rural, working-class people attempting to adjust to an increasingly modernized South. Most critics attribute Mason's success to her vivid evocation of Southern dialect and the physical and social geography of the region. R. Z. Sheppard, for example, describes Mason's settings as "ruburbs," places that are no longer rural but not yet suburban, places where subdivisions pop up amongst corn fields. Although some reviewers have faulted Mason's fictional works for employing the same unvarying narrative voice and for lacking definite resolutions, most agree that her works reveal contemporary Southern life with accuracy, humor, and poignancy. Summarizing Mason's significance in *Short Story Criticism*, Roz Kaveney asserts that the author "illuminates ordinary lives with a quiet, clear diction, and celebrates not only the almost unchanging human values which her characters embody, but also the passing details of fashion and social evolution which their personalities refract."

Spence + Lila In *Spence + Lila*, Mason's second novel, the title characters are a Kentucky farm couple who have been married for over forty years. Lila's upcoming surgery is forcing them to face the prospect of being separated for the first time since World War II. As in her other work, Mason looks at the changes in the larger environment as well as those in her characters' lives—as critic John D. Kalb says, "the changes of attitudes and values in the modern world that has intruded in [an] isolated haven." Despite the potential for sentimentality in the story, Mason "manages to avoid the gooey and patronizing muck that is usually described as heartwarming," remarks reviewer Paul Gray. He continues: "Her account is funny and deft, with plenty of gristle." This opinion is shared by Kalb, who writes that "*Spence + Lila* is a novel about real love—not saccharine-sweet sentimentality, but the well-aged version of love between two people who have shared a long, sometimes difficult and trying, life together." Although acknowledging that the book "suffers from a melodramatic predictability absent from Ms. Mason's earlier works," critic Michiko Kakutani concedes that the author treats her subject "without ever becoming sentimental or cliched." Kakutani goes on to praise Mason's "lean stripped-down language" and "nearly pitch-perfect ear for the way her characters speak," adding: "Mainly, however, it's her sure-handed ability to evoke Spence and Lila's life together that lends their story such poignancy and authenticity" to the novel.

Critic Peter S. Prescott, however, finds *Spence + Lila* a "gently tedious" book saved only by Mason's skillful writing. Reviewer Frank Conroy likewise commends Mason's dialogue, but remarks that "one wishes she had risked a bit more in this book, taking us under the surface of things instead of lingering there so lovingly and relentlessly." "Awkward silence in the face of ideas and feelings is a common frailty," observes *Los Angeles Times* writer Nancy Mairs, and such lack of personal expression in *Spence + Lila* leads many reviewers to contend that Mason's plain, lean dialogue prevents the development of fully realized characters.

Responses to Literature

1. In the short story "Shiloh," a couple's child has died from Sudden Infant Death Syndrome (SIDS). Why do you think Mason, who is childless, would choose to write about the topic in her story? How do the ideas in this story relate to recurring themes in Mason's work?

2. *An Atomic Romance* begins as if Reed is watching a movie as he rides into a wildlife refuge. How does this point of view influence one's perceptions? What other references to movies and the way people respond to them can you find in the novel?

3. Such contemporary writers as Raymond Carver, Ann Beattie, and Mason are often referred to as "dirty

realists." What do you think this term means? Research what critics say about the genre of dirty realism. Do you feel it is an accurate description of Mason's writing?

4. Two popular female Southern writers are Flannery O'Connor and Eudora Welty. Read a story by each of these authors and determine how their depictions of the South differ from those of Mason.

BIBLIOGRAPHY

Books

Price, Joanna. *Understanding Bobbie Ann Mason*. Columbia, S.C.: University of South Carolina Press, 2000.

"Bobbie Ann Mason (1940–)." *Short Story Criticism*. Edited by Jelena Krstovic. Vol. 101. Detroit: Thomson Gale, 2007, 209–277.

Periodicals

Booth, David. "San's Quest, Emmett's Wound: Grail Motifs in Bobbie Ann Mason's Portrait of America After Vietnam." *Southern Literary Journal* (Spring 1991): 98–109.

Gray, Paul. "Review of *Spence + Lila*." *Time* (July 14, 1988): 71.

Havens, Lila. "Residents and Transients: An Interview with Bobbie Ann Mason." *Crazy Horse* 29 (Fall 1985): 87–104.

Kakutani, Michiko. "Struggle and Hope in the New South." *New York Times* (June 11, 1988): 13.

Mairs, Nancy. "A Well-Seasoned Love." *Los Angeles Times Book Review* (June 19, 1983): 88.

Sheppard, R. Z. "Review of *Shiloh and Other Stories*." *Time* (January 3, 1983).

White, Leslie. "The Function of Popular Culture in Bobbie Ann Mason's *Shiloh and Other Stories* and *In Country*." *Southern Quarterly* 26 (Summer 1988): 69–79.

Wilhelm, Albert E. "Private Rituals: Coping with Change in the Fiction of Bobbie Ann Mason." *Midwest Quarterly* 28 (Winter 1987): 271–282.

✸ Edgar Lee Masters

BORN: *1868, Garnett, Kansas*

DIED: *1950, Melrose, Pennsylvania*

NATIONALITY: *American*

GENRE: *Poetry, fiction, nonfiction, drama*

MAJOR WORKS:

Spoon River Anthology (1915)

The New Spoon River (1924)

Across Spoon River (1936)

Edgar Lee Masters   Masters, Edgar Lee, photograph. The Library of Congress.

Overview

Edgar Lee Masters is best remembered for *Spoon River Anthology* (1915), a collection of over two hundred free-verse epitaphs—brief statements commemorating the lives of the deceased—spoken from the Spoon River town cemetery. Revealing the secret lives of Spoon River's dead citizens, the volume caused a great sensation because of its frank treatment of sex, moral decay, and hypocrisy. Nevertheless, Masters's treatment of small-town American life paved the way for psychological character studies in literature, influencing generations of writers.

Works in Biographical and Historical Context

Spoon River   Born on August 23, 1869, in Garnett, Kansas, Masters was firmly rooted in the Midwestern society he both praises and criticizes in *Spoon River Anthology*. In 1870 his father's law practice failed, and the family moved to his grandfather's Illinois farm, where they lived until his father was appointed a state's attorney in Petersburg, Illinois. When Masters was eleven, his family moved to Lewistown, Illinois, near the Spoon River, the place that would be immortalized in his poetic masterpiece. Growing up, Masters wrote poetry and read the works of poets James

LITERARY AND HISTORICAL CONTEMPORARIES

Masters's famous contemporaries include:

Edwin Arlington Robinson (1869–1935): The creator of Tilbury Town, Robinson, whose *Collected Poems* (1921) won the first Pulitzer Prize to be awarded for poetry, is best known for his psychological portraits of New England characters.

Robert Frost (1874–1963): Frost is recognized as the voice of New England because his poems describe the people and landscape of that area.

William Butler Yeats (1865–1939): An Irish poet and playwright, Yeats helped encourage the revival of interest in Irish literature and culture that took place at the beginning of the twentieth century.

Richard Strauss (1864–1949): The works of this German composer include what are considered symphonic poems.

A. E. Houseman (1859–1936): Houseman is best known for the poetry collection *A Shropshire Lad* (1896), which contains ironic, melancholy lyrics set in the English countryside.

Cullen Bryant, Edgar Allan Poe, Robert Burns, and Percy Bysshe Shelley. After attending Knox College from 1889 to 1890, Masters began studying law while working in his father's law office. During this time, he submitted poems to magazines and newspapers.

Lawyer and Writer Admitted to the Illinois bar in 1891, Masters soon moved to Chicago, where he joined a law partnership with Clarence Darrow, the attorney famous for serving as the counsel for the defense in the 1925 Scopes evolution trial. Using various pseudonyms to avoid possible damage to his law practice, Masters continued to contribute poems to various journals, and his first collection, *A Book of Verses*, appeared in 1898, the year of his marriage to Helen Jenkins. However, that volume, as well as his second one, *The Blood of the Prophets* (1905), attracted little attention. For the next five years, Masters concentrated on writing dramas, none of which were produced.

Small-Town Life Revealed Masters's private life was seldom tranquil: he was involved in an affair with the sculptor Tennessee Mitchell (who later married author Sherwood Anderson), tried to obtain a divorce from his wife, and dissolved his partnership with Darrow in a bitter dispute over the division of legal fees, all about the same time he began writing *Spoon River Anthology*. Masters originally intended to present a history of the Spoon River area by describing the interconnected lives of its inhabitants in a novel. Following the advice of William Marion Reedy, publisher of the journal *Reedy's Mirror*, Masters began to experiment with poetic forms, bringing to life the sort of people he had known in his boyhood. The resulting poems appeared initially under the pseudonym Webster Ford, but within a year Reedy had revealed Masters's identity, and the poems were gathered and published as *Spoon River Anthology*, a collection that exploded romantic myths about the serenity of small-town life. The book was immediately controversial.

Personal Problems After completing *Spoon River Anthology*, Masters nearly died from a severe bout with pneumonia; when he returned to his law office months later, he was so weak that he could work only a few hours a day. Meanwhile, the number of people seeking legal assistance from him had greatly declined, both because of his enforced absence and because of the notoriety caused by *Spoon River Anthology*. From 1916 to 1922, Masters published seven collections of poetry and the first two of his seven novels. Also during this period, he separated from his wife, and the publicity surrounding their bitter divorce ended what remained of his law practice. In 1923 Masters left Chicago for New York, his property and finances lost in the divorce settlement.

Disappointing Production Although Masters continued to write for the rest of his life, the quality of his work never equaled that of *Spoon River Anthology*. Even *The New Spoon River* (1924), a sequel to his masterpiece, was unsuccessful in its attempt to capture urban life. Part of the reason his later efforts failed lay in his tendency to expound his political views in his work. Overwhelmingly, though, Masters harmed his literary reputation with his injudicious approach to his publications, as he seldom revised his new efforts and often added early and inferior writings to his newer works.

Making History Masters remarried in 1926 and published the first of a series of historical verse plays. In the 1930s, he turned to biography and history, writing about Abraham Lincoln, Walt Whitman, Mark Twain, and Vachel Lindsay. His autobiography, *Across Spoon River*, appeared in 1936, followed by eight more works—fiction and nonfiction in addition to poetry. In his later years, Masters was the recipient of several literary prizes, among them an award from the National Institute and American Academy of Arts and Letters (1942). Masters died in his sleep far from Spoon River in a Melrose Park, Pennsylvania, nursing home in March of 1950.

Works in Literary Context

From late adolescence, Masters had dreamed of making his mark as a writer, and much of his success can be attributed to his own drive and desire. Shortly after the publication of *Spoon River Anthology*, Masters publicly acknowledged the importance of editor William Marion Reedy, for it was Reedy who had encouraged him to write epitaphs. With the publication of *Spoon River Anthology*, Masters established himself as a leader of the Chicago Renaissance, a group of American writers, including Theodore Dreiser, Sherwood Anderson, and Carl Sandburg, who disproved the commonly held notion that great literature came from only East Coast writers. Indeed, from 1912 to around 1925, Chicago was on its way to becoming the literary capital of the United States.

Free-Verse Epitaphs Inspired by *Epigrams from the Greek Anthology*, a collection of some forty-five hundred Greek poems written between about 500 BCE and 1000 CE, *Spoon River Anthology* combines classical forms with innovative ones. Many of the poems in the Greek anthology, like those in *Spoon River Anthology*, are expressed as confessional epitaphs in which the dead comment on their lives. Unlike the ancient Greeks, however, Masters makes his dead recite their speeches in free verse, poetry characterized by short lines of irregular length and meter lacking a set rhythm. Although pioneered by Walt Whitman many years before, free verse still had not gained popular acceptance, and readers often debated whether to consider *Spoon River Anthology* prose or poetry because of its form.

Small-Town Secrets and Broken Dreams Late nineteenth-century literary fashion saw the small town as a mainstay of American values, but Masters shatters this illusion with his portrayals of the deceased citizens of Spoon River as fornicators, adulterers, prostitutes, thieves, and victims of botched abortions. In *Spoon River Anthology*, Masters reveals the spiritual impoverishment of the small Midwestern town as its dead speak of their repressed, hypocritical, stoical, and generally unfulfilled lives. Each person reveals the circumstances of his or her death and, usually, a concealed fact about his or her life as well. Accordingly, a crusading prohibitionist reveals that he died of cirrhosis of the liver caused by drinking; the heir to a fortune confesses that he killed to inherit it; husbands and wives admit that they despised their spouses. The citizens themselves are types rather than historical portraits, which contributes to their universality. For example, the soliloquy of "Lucinda Matlock," although based on Masters's pioneering grandmother, provides a picture of the common experience of the frontier wife and mother rather than outlining the life of a particular person. Above all, what connects readers to the residents of Spoon River is the pathos of their loneliness, alienation, and unrealized hopes.

Works in Critical Context

Despite a prolific writing career, Masters never matched the achievement of *Spoon River Anthology*. Because he feared being dismissed as a writer limited in scope and ability, Masters did not want to produce a similar book; however, in his desire to produce something distinct, critics contend that he never again wrote anything as good. Very few contemporary reviewers acknowledged

COMMON HUMAN EXPERIENCE

Criticizing the complacency and narrow-mindedness of small-town life, Masters challenges the nostalgic, romanticized ideal that many Americans held about the goodness and simplicity of life in a small town. Other works that depict small-town American life include the following:

> *Winesburg, Ohio* (1919), fiction by Sherwood Anderson. This work exposes the loneliness and alienation of inhabitants in a small town in the American heartland.
> *Our Town* (1938), a drama by Thornton Wilder. Although this play includes characters who criticize small-town life, its central message is that people should appreciate the interactions of everyday life in a world of both good and bad.
> *Main Street* (1920), a novel by Sinclair Lewis. In this story, a sophisticated young woman who moves to a small town in the American Midwest struggles against the town's superficial, small-minded residents.

Masters's other works, and even those assessments are altogether dismissed by critics today.

Spoon River Anthology Many of Masters's contemporaries welcomed a new voice in their midst. Proclaiming Masters the first American poet since Walt Whitman to remain in his country and to treat themes unique to America in innovative poetry, fellow poet Ezra Pound rejoiced, "At last. At last America has discovered a poet." Later critics also recognized the volume's importance. "It is safe to say," affirms scholar Ernest Earnest, "that no other volume of poetry except *The Waste Land* (1922) [by T. S. Eliot] made such an impact during the first quarter" of the twentieth century. The "value of the *Spoon River* volume lies in its originality of design, its uniqueness, its effect upon its times," declares Frank Lewis Partee, who emphasizes that the volume's success "started a choir of young poets." "Whether we condemn or praise," says Partee, "we must accept it as a major episode in the history of the poetic movement in the second decade of the new century."

Spoon River Anthology appeared at a time when literary traditionalists were questioning the value of the free verse and imagist movements in modern poetry, along with the realistic and naturalistic tendencies in prose fiction. William Dean Howells, who disparaged many of these trends, declared that what Masters had written in *Spoon River Anthology* was not poetry at all, but "shredded prose." A few years after the volume appeared, T. S. Eliot referred to Masters as a distinguished talent, but he expressed regret that Masters had "not perceived the simple truth that some artificial limitation is necessary" to poetry.

Those commentators who did not object to the free-verse form of the *Spoon River Anthology* epitaphs complained instead of the overwhelmingly negative picture that Masters presents of small-town American life. Here, writes Robert Narveson, "came Masters's ghosts, avowing the presence of vice, corruption, greed, and pettiness" in the American small town, and these revelations made the collection a scandal. Although the uproar over the volume's blunt approach to sex contributed to the popular success of *Spoon River Anthology*, many literary figures were offended. Poet Amy Lowell, for instance, proclaimed that "*Spoon River* is one long chronicle of rapes, seductions, liaisons, and perversions" and wonders, "If life in our little Western cities is as bad as this, why everyone does not commit suicide."

Responses to Literature

1. Unlike many traditionally revered poems, Masters's work is somewhat simple in form and straightforward in message. Yet *Spoon River Anthology* has been both enormously popular with the public and extensively studied by critics. Explain this apparent contradiction. What is the difference between high art and popular art? Is there necessarily a difference between the two? Which category best fits the work of Masters?

2. Read "Richard Cory," "Miniver Cheevy," and "Luke Havergal" by Edwin Arlington Robinson. Compare and contrast the residents in Robinson's fictional Tilbury Town to those of Masters's Spoon River. Did these two writers influence each other? What inspired both poets to write in the voices of small-town residents?

3. How can you summarize a person's life on a gravestone? Write a fictional epitaph from the point of view of a literary character you are familiar with or one of your own creation. In the voice of the character, address the following questions: What were your hopes and dreams? What were the most significant events in your life? How did you die? What advice can you offer the living?

4. In your opinion, does small-town life during Masters's time differ from small-town living today? Do you believe that Masters's Spoon River residents are realistic depictions of inhabitants in a small town in today's times?

BIBLIOGRAPHY

Books

Eliot, T. S. *To Criticize the Critic.* New York: Farrar, Straus and Giroux, 1965.

Flanagan, John T. *Edgar Lee Masters: The Spoon River Poet and His Critics.* Metuchen, N.J.: Scarecrow Press, 1974.

Kramer, Dale. *Chicago Renaissance: The Literary Life in the Midwest, 1900–1930.* New York: Appleton-Century, 1966.

Masters, Hardin W. *Edgar Lee Masters: A Biographical Sketchbook about a Famous American Author.* Rutherford, N.J.: Fairleigh Dickinson University Press, 1978.

Pattee, Fred Lewis. *The New American Literature: 1800–1930.* New York: Appleton-Century, 1930.

Wrenn, John H., and Margaret H. Wrenn. *Edgar Lee Masters.* Boston: Twayne, 1983

Periodicals

Earnest, Ernest. "Spoon River Revisited." *Western Humanities Review* (Winter 1967): 63.

Howells, William Dean. "Somebody's Mother." *Harper's* (September 1915): 523–526.

Pound, Ezra. "Webster Ford [the pseudonym of Edgar Lee Masters]." *Egoist* (January 1, 1915): 11–15.

Sandburg, Carl. "Notes for a Review of the *Spoon River Anthology.*" *Little Review* 2 (May 3, 1915): 42.

⊛ Cotton Mather

BORN: *1663, Boston, Massachusetts*

DIED: *1728, Boston, Massachusetts*

NATIONALITY: *American*

GENRE: *Nonfiction*

MAJOR WORKS:

Wonders of the Invisible World (1693)

Magnalia Christi Americana (1702)

The Christian Philosopher (1721)

Overview

Cotton Mather was a Puritan minister and historian who became well-known in his time because of his role in the Salem witch trials. He wrote prodigiously and produced nearly five hundred volumes of sermons, theological treatises, histories, philosophical speculations, biographies, and meditations.

Works in Biographical and Historical Context

A Prominent Puritan Family Mather was born in Boston on February 12, 1663, into a family whose energies and genius were the backbone of New England Puritanism. His grandfathers, Richard Mather and John Cotton, directed the enthusiasm of the first-generation colonists and in many ways forged the Puritan mindset of New England. Mather's early education was in the classical tradition, and he was educated at Boston Latin

Cotton Mather   *MPI / Getty Images*

School and Harvard College. A melancholy child, he suffered from a stammer that plagued him throughout his life as a minister. He was apparently never very popular with his peers at school or with his congregations, and he was thought by many to be pedantic and self-righteous.

In 1685 Mather, following in the footsteps of his father, Increase Mather, became minister of Boston's Old North Church, a position he held for forty-three years, until his death in 1728. All of the Mathers are identified with New England Puritanism and its harsher doctrines, but Increase and Cotton Mather were unusually enlightened colonists and were responsible for the acceptance of the smallpox vaccination in New England when it was introduced in the early eighteenth century. Mather was married three times, and he was the father of a large family of children, most of whom died, the victims of disease or other tragedies, before him. He lived a full and varied life and was hardly, in an intellectual or historical context, either a biblical fundamentalist or a pulpit-thumping revivalist.

An Active Public Life, A Difficult Personal Life
Though not as politically involved as his grandfathers or his father, Mather was constantly active. He was a strong political advocate of Massachusetts governor William Phips. Mather lost power and prestige when Phips died in 1695. His fitful but productive interest in scientific experiment led

to an honorary degree from the University of Aberdeen (1710) and to fellowship in the Royal Society of London (1713); it also prompted his defense of the smallpox inoculation, an opinion that seems enlightened by current standards but that was unpopular at the time among doctors because of their belief that it did more harm than good.

Mather's life was filled with good works—pastoral care of the flock of his Boston church, responsibilities as husband and father, and constant attention to and engagement in the political and social development of New England. But, his ultimate good work, in his own estimation, was his writing. Voluminous and uneven, this "good work" is surprisingly varied. Although a large proportion of Mather's writing is theological in nature, a substantial part of it can be loosely described as historical, and some of it was overtly scientific.

Mather's personal life was strained when he lost his first wife, Abigail, in 1702 and his second, Elizabeth, in 1713. His third wife, Lydia, became mentally unbalanced. Of his fifteen children, nine died while very young and only two survived him. All too often he was the minister presiding at the funerals of his own wives and children. As if these losses were not enough, three sisters who had lost their husbands became financially dependent on him. Despite his tragic personal life, he was a prolific author and possessed a powerful mind, especially as a historian. His public career was often successful when his personal suffering was the greatest.

Salem Witch Trials
Mather is perhaps best known for his involvement in the Salem witch trials, which took place during the 1690s. Mather was initially a believer in witchcraft, and when the trials began, he wrote a letter to one of the judges, a member of his church, urging them to consider "spectral evidence" (reports of dreams and visions) and to consider the confessions of witches as the best evidence of witchcraft. After a number of executions, based largely on confessions, some of the accused witches began recanting their testimony, and Mather himself began to have doubts about the legitimacy of the trials. He changed his position on the use of spectral evidence and in later life turned away from his belief in the supernatural power of witches. Although he had played an important early role in the trials, he was able to distance himself from the proceedings and later was seen as an opponent of the entire affair. After the trials were over, he wrote *The Wonders of the Invisible World* (1693), a study of the trials, their effects, and the implications of evidence introduced in the trial of a witch. While warning the world of the dangers of judging too hastily and condemning witches without sufficient evidence, the book nevertheless reflected Mather's consistent belief that the Massachusetts Bay Colony authorities should be allowed to deal with what he considered the very real presence of witchcraft.

Scientific Writing
During his later life, Mather produced one of his most important published books, *The*

LITERARY AND HISTORICAL CONTEMPORARIES

Mather's famous contemporaries include:

Daniel Defoe (1661–1731): Defoe was an English writer considered one of the first to craft a modern novel; he is best known for *Robinson Crusoe* (1719).

Jonathan Swift (1667–1745): An Irish writer who wrote well-known satirical essays and poems, Swift is best remembered as the author of *Gulliver's Travels* (1726).

Peter the Great (1672–1725): A tsar (emperor) who expanded the Russian Empire and pushed for the westernization of his country's culture and politics.

William Byrd (1674–1744): An American plantation owner and writer who left an entertaining and varied body of factual reportage about Colonial America.

Alexander Pope (1688–1744): Pope was an English poet renowned for his satirical verses as well as his mastery of the heroic couplet.

COMMON HUMAN EXPERIENCE

Among his voluminous writings, Mather produced a diary of his experiences that reveals much about life in colonial America. Here are some other diaries that reveal aspects of life in colonial America:

History of Plymouth Plantation (1856), a diary by William Bradford. This account kept by the long-time governor of the Plymouth Colony, chronicled the history of the first thirty years of the Plymouth colony.

The Secret Diaries of William Byrd of Westover (1941), by William Byrd. This work, published long after the author's death, presents the perspective of a cultured Virginia plantation owner on life in Colonial America.

A Colonial Quaker Girl: The Diary of Sally Wister, 1777–1778 (2000), edited by Megan O'Hara. This book was written by the daughter of a prominent Quaker family that moved to the country to escape British-occupied Philadelphia during the Revolutionary War.

Christian Philosopher (1721), an example of Mather's scientific writing that exhibited the beginnings of American scientific and philosophical liberalism. In this work, Mather attempted to reconcile revelation in scripture—the truth as the Puritans had known it—with the new truths being found in the natural world by scientific investigators. In this book, Mather displayed a knowledge of contemporary astronomy, quoting such sources as Derham's *Astro-Theology* (1715) and papers published as *Philosophical Transactions* in London in 1705–1707. He also used classification systems that appear in Newton's *Principia* (1687), so it is clear that Mather was well versed in contemporary science, and that his interest was more profound than that of a theologian simply attempting to bolster the tenets of his faith with idly gathered scientific facts.

Dark Later Years, Smallpox Vaccination Effort, and Death Mather continued writing throughout his later years, but his personal life was clouded by tragedy and a general fall from prominence. He lost influence in the church, his congregation shrank, several of his children died (including his favorite daughter Katherine), and his third wife went mad. During a smallpox epidemic in 1721, Mather tried in vain to institute a program of widespread public inoculations, but his plan was fiercely attacked. He nevertheless successfully inoculated his own son and wrote and published an account of it.

Mather died and was buried in Boston in 1728.

Works in Literary Context

Mather lived much of his life in the shadow of his illustrious father, with whom he shared the pulpit of the Old North Church. Unlike his father, he was never to be chosen the president of Harvard College, but his reputation today exceeds that of his father, perhaps because he wrote so voluminously, having published more than four hundred works during his lifetime and leaving large volumes of work in manuscript, such as the learned and lengthy "Biblia Americana," a translation of the Bible from Greek and Hebrew with full annotation and commentary that fills several folio volumes. A citizen of the world and man of his time, Mather was always considered a leading intellectual in New England and Europe.

Biblical Metaphor Like other Puritan historians, Mather considered his own time comparable to the period in Old Testament history in which the Israelites broke free of their enslavement by the Egyptians and set off in search of the Promised Land. In Puritan metaphor, the Puritans themselves are likened to the Israelites, England is likened to Egypt, and Puritan leaders William Bradford, John Winthrop, and even the Mathers themselves are likened to Moses. The New England Puritans made a metaphor out of nearly every experience they had. Thus, the suffering of the Israelites on their journey through the wilderness became a paradigm for the Puritans' arduous crossing of the Atlantic, and like the ancient Israelites, the Puritans were moving in a linear fashion from Babylon, the earthly and corrupt city, to the "City on a Hill," Jerusalem, or the City of God. Ultimately, they were destined for the Heavenly City, for which the earthly "City on a Hill" was but a preparation. Both the "Biblia Americana" and the *Magnalia Christi Americana* reflect this pattern of history, and both are saturated with the symbolic analogies drawn between ancient Israel and the New England Puritan migrations of the first and second generations.

History and Christian Theology Mather, like most of his Puritan contemporaries, perceived the history of the world as a divine drama, in which the eternal conflict between good and evil was continuously being worked out. Mather's strengths and weaknesses as a historian, then, emanate from his conviction that he knew how everything would turn out. Most Christian belief systems share the idea of an omnipotent and all-powerful Divine Providence that irresistibly works out its design in the world, but the idea of predestination—that God has already worked out all of human history—was a particular viewpoint of the radical Calvinism that was accepted by such New England Puritans as Mather. The notion of predestination greatly influenced Mather's historical works.

Works in Critical Context

Much modern opinion about Cotton Mather has tended to condemn him and reduce his writings to a narrow Puritan perspective. As a result, biographies of him are often argumentative in nature, with many of the older versions being openly sympathetic, often defensively so. Most criticism of what Mather wrote has been directed exclusively to the limitations of his religious beliefs. Others, however, have noted that such criticism misses what is most important in Mather's work—the incredibly rich record of the events and personalities central to the New England colonial experience and of one participant's pious and often pained reaction to it. Perry Miller's observations in *The New England Mind* (1953) sparked a modern revision that has tended to treat Mather more objectively, and David Levin has argued that in emphasizing the "Puritan limitations" of our early historians we may blind ourselves to what is best in them. As the *Dictionary of Literary Biography* notes, "Cotton Mather is, then, a historian of narrow but significant interest, whose work must be approached with care."

Responses to Literature

1. Commentators note that Mather's histories reflect a Puritan perspective. In what ways do more recent histories reflect a similar perspective, and in what ways has the writing of history abandoned the types of ideas and approaches embodied in Mather's historical works?

2. Mather was a prolific writer and produced hundreds of volumes during his lifetime. In what ways did the speed of his production affect his writing style? What other factors had an impact on his writing style?

3. Mather was a minister who wrote many sermons. Scholars have noted that even his histories were written to serve the same moral purposes and his sermons. Write an essay that discusses the moral and theological messages in one of Mather's historical works.

4. Mather is noted for the role he played in the Salem witch trials, but commentators have produced conflicting reports about whether he ultimately supported or opposed the trials and executions. Write an argumentative essay taking a position on Mather's role in these events, using passages from his own work to support your position.

BIBLIOGRAPHY

Books

Beall, Otho T., Jr. and Richard Shryock. *Cotton Mather: First Significant Figure in American Medicine.* Baltimore, Md.: Johns Hopkins Press, 1954.

Emerson, Everett. *Major Writers of Early American Literature.* Madison, Wis.: University of Wisconsin Press, 1972.

Gay, Peter. *A Loss of Mastery: Puritan Historians in Colonial America.* Berkeley, Calif.: University of California Press, 1966.

Heimert, Alan, ed. *Cotton Mather: the Puritan Priest.* New York: Harcourt, Brace & World, 1963.

Levin, David. *Cotton Mather.* Cambridge, Mass.: Harvard University Press, 1978.

Levy, Babette. *Cotton Mather.* Boston: Twayne, 1979.

Middlekauf, Robert. *The Mathers: Three Generations of Puritan Intellectuals, 1596–1728.* New York: Oxford University Press, 1971.

Miller, Perry. *The New England Mind: From Colony to Province.* Cambridge, Mass.: Harvard University Press, 1953.

Sibley, John. *Biographical Sketches of Graduates of Harvard University,* volume 3. Cambridge, Mass.: Charles William Sever, 1885.

Ziff, Larzer. *Puritanism in America: New Culture in a New World.* New York: Viking, 1973.

✲ Cormac McCarthy

BORN: *1933, Providence, Rhode Island*

NATIONALITY: *American*

GENRE: *Fiction*

MAJOR WORKS:
Blood Meridian (1985)
All the Pretty Horses (1992)
No Country for Old Men (2005)
The Road (2006)

Overview

Cormac McCarthy has been hailed as one of the finest writers of the twentieth century, with his work compared to that of Herman Melville, William Faulkner, Mark Twain, and even William Shakespeare. McCarthy's writing has been universally recognized for his prose style, which often rises to the level of poetry, but his brutal and

Cormac McCarthy   *Photography by Derek Shapton, wwwderekshaptoncom*

exacting depictions of violence and the seamier side of life in the South and in the West, have drawn both praise and revulsion from readers and critics.

Works in Biographical and Historical Context

Military Service, College, and Marriage   McCarthy was born in Providence, Rhode Island, on July 20, 1933, the eldest of three brothers in a family of six children. In 1937, the family moved to Knoxville, Tennessee, where his father, Charles, began a long tenure as a lawyer for the Tennessee Valley Authority (TVA). The McCarthys raised their children in the Roman Catholic tradition. Cormac attended Catholic High School in Knoxville.

McCarthy entered the University of Tennessee in 1951, majoring in liberal arts, but he left a year later. In 1953, towards the end of the Korean War, McCarthy entered the U.S. Air Force for four years of service. He was not sent to Korea but rather served two of his four years in Alaska, where he also hosted a radio show. After leaving the Air Force, McCarthy resumed his studies at the University of Tennessee and published two stories, "Wake For Susan" and "A Drowning Incident," in the student literary magazine, *The Phoenix*. He won the Ingram-Merrill Award for creative writing for two consecutive years, in 1959 and 1960, while still an undergraduate at Tennessee. McCarthy left the university in 1960 without earning a degree, and in 1961, he married Lee Holleman, who had also been a student at the University of Tennessee. They had a son, Cullen, but the marriage was brief, ending in divorce in the early 1960s.

European Travels   Before the publication of McCarthy's first novel, *The Orchard Keeper* (1965), he received a travel fellowship from the American Academy of Arts and Letters. The fellowship enabled McCarthy to visit Ireland, the home of his ancestors. On the trip he met Anne DeLisle, and the two wed in England in 1966. The same year that he married Anne, McCarthy received a two-year grant from The Rockefeller Foundation. He and Anne toured southern England, France, Switzerland, Italy, and Spain, ending up on the island of Ibiza. Home to so many creative people at that time in the 1960s, Ibiza resembled an artists' colony. During McCarthy's travels in Europe, *The Orchard Keeper* had been published to critical acclaim in the United States and won the author the William Faulkner Award for first-novel achievement. While living on Ibiza, McCarthy completed revisions for his second book, *Outer Dark* (1968).

Awards, Grants, and Writing   McCarthy and his wife returned to the United States in 1967, shortly before the publication of *Outer Dark*, which received favorable reviews. In 1969 the John Simon Guggenheim Memorial Foundation awarded McCarthy a fellowship for creative writing. At this time, McCarthy and his wife moved near Louisville, Tennessee, where they lived in a barn that McCarthy had renovated completely on his own. His next book for Random House, *Child of God* (1974), was inspired by actual events in Sevier County. Unlike McCarthy's previous two novels, *Child of God* garnered mixed reviews.

In 1974 McCarthy took a respite from novel writing and spent a year working on a screenplay for a Public Broadcast Service television movie, *The Gardener's Son*, which had its premiere in 1976. Screened at film festivals in Berlin and Edinburgh, *The Gardener's Son* was nominated for two Emmy Awards in the United States. McCarthy's personal life, however, was suffering. In 1976 DeLisle and McCarthy separated before eventually getting divorced. Soon after the separation, McCarthy moved to El Paso, Texas, where he lived until the late 1990s.

In 1979 McCarthy published his fourth novel, *Suttree*, and two years later, he received a MacArthur Fellowship, also known as a "genius grant." McCarthy used his fellowship funds to support himself while writing his fifth novel, an apocalyptic Western set in Texas and Mexico during the 1840s. McCarthy researched thoroughly and extensively for the novel, attaining a feel for the setting of the book by visiting all the locales mentioned in it and even going so far as to learn Spanish. Although *Blood Meridian* drew little critical attention at the time of its appearance, McCarthy's reputation among critics began to improve following the publication of this novel.

Increasing Critical Attention   Attention to McCarthy's works increased markedly in 1992 and 1993, following publication of *All the Pretty Horses* (1992), which won both the National Book Award and the National Book

Critics Circle Award. As critical response to McCarthy's work grew steadily, McCarthy remained committed to his writing, completing the second and third books of the Border trilogy during the mid-1990s. In the spring of 1998, McCarthy was married for the third time to Jennifer Winkley, a graduate of the University of Texas at El Paso, who majored in English and American literature. They moved to Sante Fe, New Mexico, where they now live with their son, who was the inspiration for McCarthy's Pulitzer Prize-winning novel, *The Road* (2006).

Works in Literary Context

Although McCarthy received awards and grants for his writing, and despite the fact that he had developed a cult-like following, McCarthy was practically unknown until his sixth novel, *All the Pretty Horses*, captured the imagination of the world of letters. Since then, McCarthy's work has been moving toward a higher position in American literature, and he is now regarded as one of the greatest American authors of the twentieth and twenty-first centuries. McCarthy is considered a master of tone and language (one reviewer has said that the English language is the real hero of all McCarthy's books), and his novels are symphonic orchestrations of the tragic, grotesque, lyrical, and comic.

Stark Depictions of Nature McCarthy's narratives have been lauded for their stark depiction of nature as well as for their sheer stylistic beauty, which entwines the lushness and fecundity of Faulkner's prose with the trenchant austerity of Ernest Hemingway's. The metaphysical themes of McCarthy's books emerge out of his loving attention to the natural world and the world of human tools, crafts, and action. Thomas D. Young, Jr., observes that "in all Cormac McCarthy 's work, nature is itself the principal presence." Several commentators have noticed that in McCarthy's world, animal forms—and even the landscape itself—seem to watch people, witnesses to their folly and brutality or to their rare heroism.

Spiritual Nomads McCarthy's novels have grown out of his experiences in, and reading about, Tennessee, Texas, and Mexico. His plots center on spiritual nomads—male characters who are, with varying degrees of consciousness, engaged in quests or anti-quests. This nomadic quality of his protagonists is sometimes magnified—as in *Blood Meridian* and *The Road*—by the author's refusal to even name the characters, referring to them simply as "the kid" or "the man." Many of his novels focus on themes of loss, alienation, and the vanishing of cultures, making McCarthy's novels both demanding and difficult, particularly because his prose style, which is wholly original, is as dark and uncompromising as his view of humanity.

Works in Critical Context

McCarthy has generally been praised by critics, particularly since the mid-1980s. Some critics fault McCarthy for

---

LITERARY AND HISTORICAL CONTEMPORARIES

McCarthy's famous contemporaries include:

Ted Hughes (1930–1998): Hughes was an English poet who was the British poet laureate from 1984 until his death in 1998.

Elvis Presley (1935–1977): Presley was an American musician who has become a pop-culture icon often referred to as "The King."

Richard Brautigan (1935–1984): Brautigan is an American author who is considered one of the links between the Beat Generation and the counterculture generation.

Don DeLillo (1936–): DeLillo is an American novelist prominent as one of the pioneers of post-modern fiction; he is best known for his novel *Underworld* (1997).

Václav Havel (1936–): Havel is a Czech writer and politician who served as the last president of Czechoslovakia (1989–1992) and the first president of the Czech Republic (1993–2003).

Peter Jennings (1938–2005): Jennings was a Canadian-born television news journalist best known for anchoring ABC's national nightly news.

---

excessively florid prose and a relentlessly pessimistic worldview, but others contend that his depiction of the fallen condition of humanity has universal implications. As Robert Coles observes: "[McCarthy] is a novelist of religious feeling who appears to subscribe to no creed but who cannot stop wondering in the most passionate and honest way what gives life meaning." Critics generally praise McCarthy for his probing investigations of the darker side of the human condition. As Irving Malin wrote, McCarthy "is primarily interested in the origins of evil; the search for redemption; the meaning of our brutal existence."

Blood Meridian McCarthy has always been noted for the darkness of his narratives and his ability to explore questions of evil and violence. In *Blood Meridian* (1985), McCarthy parodies values espoused in popular Western films by exaggerating the notion of rugged individuality to the point of demented lawlessness. Critical opinion about *Blood Meridian* has been sharply divided. Vereen M. Bell and other critics see it as a postmodernist masterpiece, a celebration of brutality and violence. Edwin T. Arnold, on the other hand, refuses to accept such a bleak and nihilistic reading of the novel. He maintains that the kid's quest in *Blood Meridian* is, in fact, a moral one. Although some critics found this novel unreasonably grotesque, Andrew Hislop remarks that *Blood Meridian* "is much more than a counterblast of bloody imagery against more cosy perceptions of the West. It is an

COMMON HUMAN EXPERIENCE

Many of McCarthy's works depict the process of cultural practices that are vanishing or being transformed by historical changes. Here are some other works that focus on a similar process:

The Grapes of Wrath (1939), a novel by John Steinbeck. This novel chronicles the profound changes in the life of a family that is displaced from the Midwest during the Great Depression.

Shogun (1975), a novel by James Clavell. This historical novel depicts a period of transformation in Japanese culture that witnessed important changes in the role of the traditional samurai warrior class.

Lonesome Dove (1985), a novel by Larry McMurtry. This novel focuses on the dwindling decades of frontier cowboys by chronicling a cattle drive from Texas to Montana.

exploration, at times explicitly philosophical, of the relationship between culture and violence."

All the Pretty Horses Though McCarthy had often been praised by critics in the past, it was not until the publication of *All the Pretty Horses*, the first installment of his Border Trilogy, that he achieved the wider recognition that was long expected for this author. As Gene Lyons wrote, "For years critics have been promising us a masterpiece from novelist Cormac McCarthy. Now with *All the Pretty Horses*, he seems to have produced one." Praise for *All the Pretty Horses* was nearly universal. A reviewer for *Publisher's Weekly* writes, "This is a novel so exuberant in its prose, so offbeat in its setting and so mordant and profound in its deliberations that one searches in vain for comparisons in American literature." The differences between this novel and McCarthy's previous works was particularly noted. Joseph Poindexter points out that this is the first time that "McCarthy gives us, instead of his usual outcasts, a protagonist we can root for."

Responses to Literature

1. McCarthy has been noted for his bleak view of life and his pessimistic world view. In what ways does he deserve this characterization, and in what ways do his works demonstrate a view of life that is optimistic?

2. Critics have often accused McCarthy of creating main characters that the reader cannot identify with or root for. Are there any characters from McCarthy's novels that you can identify with and that you found yourself rooting for? If so, which ones and why? If not, why not?

3. McCarthy's novels often include disturbing imagery and violent episodes. Write an argumentative essay that takes a position on whether or not these passages are necessary for McCarthy's writing. Be sure to discuss the messages that he is trying to convey in order to assess how appropriate to his themes these disturbing and violent passages are.

4. Critics have praised McCarthy for his ability to reveal the darker side of human nature. Write an analytical essay describing McCarthy's view on human nature. Be sure to use concrete examples from his novels to demonstrate your claims.

BIBLIOGRAPHY

Books

Arnold, Edwin T. and Dianne C. Luce, eds. *A Cormac McCarthy Companion: The Border Trilogy.* Jackson, Miss.: University Press of Mississippi, 2001.

———. *Perspectives on Cormac McCarthy*, revised edition. Jackson, Miss.: University Press of Mississippi, 1999.

Bell, Vereen M. *The Achievement of Cormac McCarthy.* Baton Rouge, La.: Louisiana State University Press, 1988.

Hall, Wade and Rick Wallach, eds. *Sacred Violence: A Reader's Companion to Cormac McCarthy.* El Paso, Tex.: Texas Western Press of the University of Texas at El Paso, 1995.

Jarrett, Robert L. *Cormac McCarthy.* New York: Twayne, 1997.

Wallach, Rick. ed. *Myth, Legend, Dust: Critical Responses to Cormac McCarthy.* New York: Manchester University Press, 2000.

Periodicals

Lyons, Gene. "McCarthy, Cormac. *All the Pretty Horses.*" *Entertainment Weekly* (May 1, 1992): 46.

Malin, Irving. "McCarthy, Cormac. *All the Pretty Horses.*" *Commonweal* (September 25, 1992): 29.

"McCarthy, Cormac. All the Pretty Horses." *Publishers Weekly* (March 16, 1992): 64.

Poindexter, Joseph. "McCarthy, Cormac. *All the Pretty Horses.*" *People Weekly* (July 13, 1992): 27.

✸ Mary McCarthy

BORN: *1912, Seattle, Washington*

DIED: *1989, New York City*

NATIONALITY: *American*

GENRE: *Fiction, nonfiction*

MAJOR WORKS:

The Company She Keeps (1942)

Cast a Cold Eye (1950)

The Group (1963)

Mary McCarthy   *McCarthy, Mary, photograph. The Library of Congress.*

Overview

Mary McCarthy was a fiction and nonfiction writer renowned for her outspokenness and her opposition to what she perceived as hypocrisy. Considered one of America's most eminent intellectuals, she favored the presentation of ideas through fiction and used her sometimes merciless character portraits to dig deeply into the philosophical basis underlying behavior and attitudes.

Works in Biographical and Historical Context

A Conflicting and Troubled Childhood   Coloring all of Mary McCarthy's work are the events of her childhood. The eldest of four children, she was born in Seattle, Washington, on June 21, 1912. Her maternal grandmother, Augusta Morganstern Preston, was a beautiful Jewish woman from San Francisco, and her maternal grandfather, Harold Preston, was a Seattle lawyer whose Protestant ancestors came from New England. Her paternal grandparents were wealthy Irish Catholics from Minneapolis, Minnesota, where they operated a grain elevator business. Her mother, Therese Preston, was a Protestant who converted to Catholicism after marrying Roy McCarthy, a man ten years her senior and a victim of progressive heart disease. The conflicts between the reactionary Catholicism of the McCarthys and the more humane Protestantism of the Prestons, as well as the Jewish heritage of her maternal grandmother, emerge as significant motifs in McCarthy's later writings.

Both of Mary's parents died in the great influenza pandemic of 1918, a devastating worldwide event that resulted in more deaths than all the casualties of World War I. Though many people in modern times associate the flu with only moderate illness, some strains of influenza—coupled with a lack of vaccinations among the general population—can prove to be both highly contagious and potentially deadly.

Mary's Minnesota grandparents assumed the guardianship of the children and placed them in the care of a great aunt, Margaret, and her stern, authoritarian husband, Meyers Shriver. Mary and her brothers were forced to live amid barren conditions, and they received harsh treatment at the hands of their guardians. Although Mary and her brother Kevin occasionally ran away to their grandparents' house in Minneapolis, nothing was done to change conditions for the children until 1923 when Mary's grandfather Preston took her back to live with him in Seattle, sent Kevin and her brother Preston to Catholic boarding schools, and left the youngest boy, Sheridan, with the Shrivers. Although life was more pleasant with her Seattle grandparents, she was never able completely to erase the memories of life in Minnesota. The sense of loss, rejection, and abandonment, and the emotional sterility of the life she endured are recurring echoes in much of McCarthy's fiction.

Becoming a Writer   After moving to Seattle, McCarthy attended schools in the Northwest and eventually became an aspiring young writer studying at Vassar College, which she entered in 1929. In 1933 McCarthy graduated and moved to New York City, where she quickly became a professional writer whose essays and sometimes scathing reviews appeared in many respected publications, including the *New Republic*, *Nation*, and *Partisan Review*. Her work at the *Nation* earned McCarthy some recognition. She joined the staff of the *Partisan Review* in 1937, where she worked as editor until the next year, continuing to contribute drama criticism for several years thereafter. It was during this time that McCarthy came to know the noted literary figures Edmund Wilson (who later became her second husband), Philip Rahv, and Lillian Hellman, among others.

McCarthy began writing fiction at the encouragement of Wilson, shortly after their marriage in 1938. McCarthy's marriage to Wilson was tempestuous from the start, and it ended in divorce after seven years. Scenes from their marriage served as inspiration for short stories even while she still lived with Wilson, and later became material used in her novels. McCarthy taught for a short time at Bard College, but resigned so she could devote more time to writing. By 1955, she had published the novella *The Oasis* (1949), the short story collection *Cast a Cold Eye* (1950), and two novels. Throughout the late

LITERARY AND HISTORICAL CONTEMPORARIES

McCarthy's famous contemporaries include:

Richard Wright (1908–1960): Wright was an author noted for his impact on black fiction because of his naturalistic descriptions of the reality of life for African Americans.

Richard Nixon (1913–1994): Nixon was an influential American politician and the thirty-seventh president of the United States (1969–1974).

Dylan Thomas (1914–1953): Thomas was a Welsh poet known as much for his life of excess as for his iconoclastic, critically acclaimed writings.

Carson McCullers (1917–1967): McCullers was an American writer whose works explored themes of isolation and disenchantment in the South.

Gwendolyn Brooks (1917–2000): Brooks was an African American poet and the first African American writer to win a Pulitzer Prize.

COMMON HUMAN EXPERIENCE

McCarthy often drew on her own life and the lives of people around her to provide material, often shocking and controversial, for her fictional works. Here are some other works based on the author's life and experience that created shock or controversy when published:

Valley of the Dolls (1966), a novel by Jacqueline Susann. This novel about the excesses and self-destruction of three women in the entertainment industry presented the lives of famous people thinly disguised by fiction.

The World is Full of Divorced Women (1975), a novel by Jackie Collins. In this novel, the author draws on her knowledge of the lives of the rich and famous to produce an enticing and scandalous story.

Answered Prayers: the Unfinished Novel (1987), a novel by Truman Capote. Capote used real-life experiences from his jet-set lifestyle to write a revealing novel about the excesses of high-society socialites.

1950s and 1960s, she wrote fiction, nonfiction, and memoirs and published her best-known and most critically-acclaimed book, *The Group* (1963).

Vietnam and Watergate With the international acclaim brought on by the publication of *The Group*, McCarthy felt the need to turn away from the voice of fiction and speak again in her own voice. The war in Vietnam stirred her liberal political interests, and she interrupted a novel in progress to take two trips to Vietnam to get a firsthand look at the situation. Her essays based on these trips were later collected in her books *Vietnam* (1967) and *Hanoi* (1968). *Medina* (1972), a third book of essays about the war, addresses the trial of the U.S. Army captain in command of the soldiers who massacred South Vietnamese civilians in the village of My Lai in 1968. McCarthy also wrote about the Watergate scandal in *The Mask of State* (1974). McCarthy remained politically committed throughout the remainder of her life, continuing to publish essays and memoirs even as her health failed in the 1980s. She died of cancer in 1989.

Works in Literary Context

McCarthy rose to prominence in the 1930s as part of a group of New York City intellectuals that became known for its commitment to political issues. McCarthy's writing—both fiction and nonfiction—is characterized by a spare, elegant style but also by a caustic wit that earned her both high praise and notoriety.

Life as Inspiration For literary inspiration, McCarthy often drew from her life and from the lives of friends and acquaintances, and she made little effort to disguise her sources. Some of her stories shocked contemporary audiences with their sexual candor, and the fact that her subject matter was known to be autobiographical made McCarthy herself into something of a legendary figure. An important element of her style is her bleak view of modern life and her sense of the grotesque and the comic.

Telling, Not Showing McCarthy has been noted for the brutal honesty of her confrontations. Not known for her storytelling abilities, McCarthy's writing has its roots in a neoclassical tradition where art instructs while it delights. In a literary world influenced by romantic traditions and whose critical standards ask fiction to "show" and not "tell," her work has been labeled not courageous enough. Many of her fictional works have been criticized for using long philosophical discussions to tell about a problem rather than dramatizing it. Yet, there is wide agreement that she is a master of the English sentence and her prose style is exceptionally fine.

Works in Critical Context

Debating the Appeal of McCarthy's Style Most discussions of McCarthy's fiction have revolved around debate about the appeal of her literary style. In a review of *Cast a Cold Eye*, George Miles attributed both heartlessness and a detached analytical manner to the author when he spoke of her as "the psychologist and the executioner." Similarly, Jeffrey Walker has remarked that "The reader is aware of McCarthy's own cold eye in presenting these stories of social relationships.... All reveal the coldness of their central characters and form a satiric indictment of urban relationships." Ultimately, approval of McCarthy's writing style appears to depend heavily on personal preference, with critics seemingly split on the issue. *The Company She Kept* was subject to the same dispute about artistic merit as *Cast a Cold Eye*.

The Group McCarthy's early works received considerable attention in literary circles and established her as a writer with a keen critical sense and as a social satirist who focused on the intellectual elite, but it was publication of *The Group*, a novel about eight Vassar girls in the 1930s, that became a bestseller in the U.S. and abroad, which earned McCarthy much wider recognition than she had enjoyed previously. For the very reasons it became popular, critics denounced the book. Some called it nothing more than feminine gossip; some objected to the "shocking" sexual scenes; some maintained that while depicting the surfaces of life brilliantly, she failed to plumb the depths of her material for the larger meanings. Norman Mailer felt that the book was "full of promise," but failed to go far enough and penetrate the "central horror" of our society.

Responses to Literature

1. McCarthy was often accused of telling instead of showing in her fictional works. In what ways does she deserve this charge, and in what ways does she, in fact, dramatize rather than simply talk about the problems that are the center of her novels?

2. Critics have debated the appeal of McCarthy's style, with some suggesting that her style suggests a coldly appraising eye. Does McCarthy merit this characterization of her style? In what ways does this style enhance the messages in her books, and in what ways does it detract from them?

3. McCarthy was an openly political writer who wrote both fiction and nonfiction. Write an essay that discusses the political concerns evident in her nonfiction that show up in her fiction as well. Be sure to consider whether or not the political messages of her fiction and nonfiction are in line with each other, and where there might be points of disparity between these two sides of her work.

4. Commentators consider that McCarthy's view of modern life is a bleak one. Write an argumentative essay that either agrees or disagrees with this characterization. Be sure to use concrete examples from various of her works to support your claims about her view.

BIBLIOGRAPHY

Books

Brightman, Carol. *Writing Dangerously: Mary McCarthy and Her World*. New York: Clarkson Potter, 1992.
Gelderman, Carol W. *Mary McCarthy: A Life*. New York: St. Martin's Press, 1988.
Gelderman, Carol W. *Conversations with Mary McCarthy*. Jackson, Miss.: University Press of Mississippi, 1991.
Grumbach, Doris. *The Company She Kept*. New York: Coward-McCann, 1976.
Hardy, Willene Schaefer. *Mary McCarthy*. New York: Ungar, 1981.
McKenzie, Barbara. *Mary McCarthy*. New York: Twayne, 1966.
Moore, Harry T., ed. *Contemporary American Novelists*. Carbondale, Ill.: Southern Illinois University Press, 1964.
Stock, Irvin. *Mary McCarthy*. Minneapolis, Minn.: University of Minnesota Press, 1968.

Periodicals

Brower, Brock. "Mary McCarthyism." *Esquire* (July 1962): 62–67, 113.
Mailer, Norman. "The Mary McCarthy Case." *New York Review of Books* (October 17, 1963): 1–3.
Niebuhr, Elizabeth. "The Art of Fiction XXVII: Mary McCarthy." *Paris Review* (Winter–Spring 1962): 58–94.

✦ Frank McCourt

BORN: *1930, Brooklyn, New York*

NATIONALITY: *American, Irish*

GENRE: *Nonfiction*

MAJOR WORKS:
Angela's Ashes (1996)

Overview

Frank McCourt is a Pulitzer Prize-winning writer whose memoir, *Angela's Ashes* (1996), became an instant classic among immigrants' tales. Writing with wit, humor, and eloquence, McCourt turns a childhood of disease and poverty into an engaging and entertaining tale that avoids self-pity.

Works in Biographical and Historical Context

A Childhood of Poverty and Suffering McCourt was born in 1930 in Brooklyn, New York, at the beginning of the Great Depression. His parents were unable to find work because of the difficult economic times—when about one in four workers could not find a job—so the family returned to Ireland. Unfortunately, once there, they sank deeper into poverty. McCourt's father was an alcoholic who drank away his earnings and who eventually left the family, forcing the children and mother to go hungry and endure the cold. McCourt's mother, Angela, raised her seven children, three of whom died from diseases made worse by malnutrition, on handouts and

Frank McCourt   *McCourt, Frank, photograph. © Jerry Bauer. Reproduced by permission.*

welfare checks. McCourt nearly died at age ten from typhoid fever. He was a gifted student, but he left school at age thirteen and worked a series of odd jobs and engaged in petty crime in order to help the family survive.

From the Army to the Classroom   McCourt returned to the United States at the age of nineteen and again he worked odd jobs, this time until he was drafted into the U.S. Army at the beginning of the Korean War. The Korean War was a conflict between the Soviet Union-backed North Korea and the United States-supported South Korea, each of which sought to be unified with the other, but neither of which was willing to accept the other's form of government. Ultimately, after years of fighting, the two remained split. McCourt never saw combat, spending the entire war stationed in Germany. After leaving the Army, McCourt used the G.I. Bill to begin attending New York University, where he studied English. After working at night throughout college, he graduated and began a twenty-seven year career in the New York City school system teaching English and creative writing.

Memoir Writing   During his years teaching, McCourt spent summers working on a novel he never completed. Several years after retiring from teaching, he began work-

ing on a memoir of his difficult childhood, which became the best-selling *Angela's Ashes* (1996). Among that book's many honors are included the 1997 Pulitzer Prize for Biography and the National Book Critics Circle Award. McCourt then embarked on writing a second memoir, *'Tis* (1999), which picked up where *Angela's Ashes* left off, and then a third volume, *Teacher Man* (2005), chronicling the time he spent teaching. Since then he has continued to mine his family history for material, adapting an experience from his mother's childhood into the children's book *Angela and the Baby Jesus* (2007).

Works in Literary Context

Presenting the Immigrant Experience   With the publication of his memoir, *Angela's Ashes*, McCourt joined a long line of writers who have chronicled the immigrant experience. Telling of both his childhood in Limerick, Ireland, and his experiences in the United States as a young man, McCourt presents compelling tales of the triumphs and tragedies of immigrants struggling to achieve the American Dream. Although McCourt's memoirs fall within this broader tradition, and his work sometimes "looks like an encyclopedia of Irish cliché," as Malcolm Jones, Jr. noted, he is able to take this clichéd material and turn it into compelling and entertaining reading. As Jones points out, because of his style and storytelling abilities, McCourt is able to "induce in his readers a blissful literary amnesia" so that "you hardly notice that some of this material has come your way before."

Good Humor in the Face of Suffering   One of the most noted features of McCourt's memoirs is his ability to present suffering with not only eloquence but good humor that makes use of both wit and a self-deprecating tone, in which the writer is willing to point out his own faults and foibles. One commentator writes that *Angela's Ashes* is so captivating because of McCourt's "ability to entertain an audience by turning horrifying memories into amusing anecdotes." A critic for *Time* magazine writes, "Like an unpredicted glimmer of midwinter sunshine, cheerfulness keeps breaking into this tale of Celtic woe."

Works in Critical Context

McCourt has enjoyed nearly universal praise from critics who note his wit, eloquence, and storytelling abilities as among his greatest strengths. His three memoirs have all received rave reviews, and he has been likened to some of the greatest biographers of all time. Mary Karr even wrote that "Frank McCourt's lyrical Irish voice will draw comparisons to Joyce. It's that seductive, that hilarious."

Angela's Ashes   *Angela's Ashes* was a smash success upon its publication in 1996. In *Publisher's Weekly*, an unnamed reviewer calls it a "magical memoir," and Malcolm Jones, Jr. of *Newsweek* writes that "McCourt proves himself one of the very best." Best-selling author Thomas

Cahill sums up critical opinion when he writes that *Angela's Ashes*

> is such a marriage of pathos and humor that you never know whether to weep or roar—and find yourself doing both at once. Through each fresh horror of the narrative, you will be made happy by some of the most truly marvelous writing you will ever encounter.

Critically-Acclaimed Follow-Ups McCourt continued to receive praise when he came out with *'Tis* (1999), his second memoir, and *Teacher Man* (2005). One reviewer writes, "Frank McCourt's second memoir, *'Tis*, isn't as good as its predecessor, *Angela's Ashes*, but it's still a moving and impressive work." A reviewer for the *Library Journal* writes that *'Tis* is "as rewarding as *Angela's Ashes*." A reviewer for the *Los Angeles Times*, echoing many others, calls *Teacher Man* "An enthralling work of autobiographical storytelling."

Responses to Literature

1. McCourt has been praised for his storytelling ability and his use of wit and humor to lighten his tales of struggle and hardship. In what ways does his lighthearted tone serve to undermine the impact of his stories, and in what ways does it enhance their impact? On balance, is his approach to presenting his life one that succeeds in putting the reader in his place, or does his storytelling style detract from this?

2. Some reviewers noted that *Angela's Ashes* was full of standard clichés about the Irish. What clichés can you identify? If these are true and accurate depictions of his life, should they be considered clichés? Why or why not?

3. McCourt's works are considered excellent examples of a large body of biography and autobiography on the immigrant experience. Using McCourt's books and at least two others, write an essay that examines the way these authors present the immigrant experience.

4. In *Teacher Man*, McCourt not only tells of his experiences as a teacher in the New York City school system, he describes and analyzes that system, often criticizing its workings. Write an essay that outlines McCourt's criticisms of this educational system and discuss what he seems to be recommending to fix the problems he notes.

BIBLIOGRAPHY

Periodicals

Deignan, Thomas. "McCourt, Frank. *Angela's Ashes*." *Commonweal* (November 8, 1996): 26.

Donoghue, Denis. "Some Day I'll Be In Out of the Rain." *The New York Times Book Review* (September 15, 1996): 13.

Elson, John. "McCourt, Frank. *Angela's Ashes*." *Time* (September 23, 1996): 74.

Jones, Malcolm, Jr. "McCourt, Frank. *Angela's Ashes*." *Newsweek* (September 2, 1996): 68.

Kakutani, Michiko. "Generous Memories of a Poor, Painful Childhood." *The New York Times* (September 17, 1996).

LITERARY AND HISTORICAL CONTEMPORARIES

McCourt's famous contemporaries include:

Gabriel García Márquez (1928–): Márquez is a Colombian fiction writer known for his use of magic realism in novels such as *One Hundred Years of Solitude* (1970); he was awarded the Nobel Prize in Literature in 1982.

Edward Albee (1928–): Albee is an American playwright who writes mainly black comedies in the tradition of the Theater of the Absurd.

Anne Frank (1929–1945): Frank was a German-born Jew who was killed during World War II; she is most famous for the publication after her death of her wartime diaries, known as *The Diary of a Young Girl* (1947).

Ted Hughes (1930–1998): Hughes was an English poet who served as the British poet laureate from 1984 until his death in 1998.

John Barth (1930–): Barth is an American writer who is one of the pioneers of postmodernism in American literature, as shown in works like *Giles Goat-Boy* (1966).

COMMON HUMAN EXPERIENCE

Much of McCourt's work chronicles his struggles trying to survive in Ireland and the United States. Here are some other memoirs that offer similar stories of immigrants' struggles in their home countries and in America:

They Called Me Mustafa, second edition (1999), a memoir by Khachadoor and Helene Pilibosian. This memoir tells the story of a survivor of the Armenian genocide in Turkey who, after escaping from a period of slavery, immigrates to America and eventually opens his own business.

Dear Lizzie (2001), a memoir by Leona Tamarkin. This memoir tells the story of a Jewish refugee from Europe who comes to America after World War I.

Brother I'm Dying (2007), a memoir by Edwidge Danticat. This memoir tells about the difficulties of a childhood in Haiti as well as the struggles and sacrifices of Haitian immigrants to the United States.

King, Nina. "With Love and Squalor." *Washington Post Book World* (September 29, 1996): 1, 10.

"McCourt, Frank. *Angela's Ashes.*" *Publishers Weekly* (July 1, 1996): 49.

Tonkin, Boyd. "McCourt, Frank. *Angela's Ashes.*" *New Statesman* (November 1, 1996): 45.

✸ Carson McCullers

BORN: *1917, Columbus, Georgia*

DIED: *1967, Nyack, New York*

NATIONALITY: *American*

GENRE: *Fiction*

MAJOR WORKS:

The Heart Is a Lonely Hunter (1940)

Reflections in a Golden Eye (1941)

The Ballad of the Sad Cafe (1943)

Overview

Carson McCullers was a novelist who produced a small but important body of work noted for its variety of subtle themes, ranging from examinations of gender, identity, and race to psychological sketches. She is considered one of the most enduring authors of the American Southern

Carson McCullers   *McCullers, Carson, photograph. AP Images.*

literary tradition, alongside her contemporaries Tennessee Williams, Eudora Welty, and Flannery O'Connor.

Works in Biographical and Historical Context

Early Musical Promise   McCullers was born Lula Carson Smith on February 19, 1917, in Columbus, Georgia, a mill town of thirty thousand. With its stifling hot summers and snowless winters, as well as its starkly contrasted classes and races, Columbus inspired the literary landscape for McCullers's most memorable fiction. Although she left her hometown for the North in 1934, and never lived permanently in the South after 1940, she is still widely regarded as a Southern writer, even while her best work is recognized for its universal appeal.

McCullers had exhibited musical talent at an early age. The firstborn child in her family, she was lavished with love and praise but also burdened by expectations of genius. As a girl, she trained to be a concert pianist, and in 1935, McCullers traveled to New York City to study at the Juilliard School of Music. As a result of financial difficulties, however, McCullers never attended Juilliard; instead, she was forced to work part-time, and she began attending writing classes at Columbia University and New York University.

A Quick Succession of Successful Novels   In 1937 she married Reeves McCullers, an aspiring novelist, and in 1940 she published her first novel, *The Heart Is a Lonely Hunter*, which quickly gave her a favorable literary reputation. Written in the closing years of the Great Depression, *The Heart Is a Lonely Hunter* reflected the politically conscious fiction of the 1930s in its realistic portrayal of capitalistic excess and racial injustice, even as it anticipated the 1940s' trend toward fiction about psychological estrangement with its treatment of spiritual isolation.

McCuller's marriage was often unstable. Shortly after their marriage, they moved to North Carolina, where they were briefly happy. They had agreed to support one another's artistic aspirations, but Reeves McCullers never wrote anything publishable. Indeed, he never found steady, satisfying work outside the military. As his wife's career accelerated, he grew more reliant on her income and less sure of his own worth. She and Reeves were divorced in 1940 following their involvement in homosexual affairs. McCullers's second novel, *Reflections in a Golden Eye* (1941), is generally viewed as her reaction to the disintegration of her marriage. Set on an army base, the book depicts archetypal characters whose unfulfilled spiritual and physical needs lead to self-destructive, amoral behavior.

McCullers suffered a series of debilitating cerebral strokes beginning in 1941, but she continued to write, and in 1943, published the novella *The Ballad of the Sad Cafe*. Often considered McCullers's most outstanding achievement, *The Ballad of the Sad Cafe* was described by Irving Howe as "one of the finest novels ever written by an American" and by Tennessee Williams as "assuredly among the masterpieces of our language." In this work, McCullers's characters serve to reveal how individuals seek out their opposites, people who embody traits they desire but cannot attain.

McCuller's fourth novel, *The Member of the Wedding*, came out in 1946. Encouraged by Tennessee Williams, McCullers adapted the novel for the stage in 1950. Retaining its original emphasis on theme, character, and mood, she created a stylistically innovative play noted for being among the few successful dramatic adaptations of a novelist's own work. *The Member of the Wedding* enjoyed a lengthy Broadway run of five hundred and one performances, winning the New York Drama Critics Circle Award for best play in 1950.

A Troubled Personal Life McCullers had remarried Reeves in 1945, but their relationship became increasingly hostile. In 1948, depressed over her increasing invalidism, she slashed one of her wrists. After this suicide attempt, she underwent psychiatric evaluation. She recovered her will to write, leaving Reeves for good in 1953 after he proposed a suicide pact. Later that year he killed himself with an overdose of alcohol and drugs. In 1955, she suffered another devastating loss: the death of her mother, with whom she had periodically shared a home in Nyack, New York.

McCullers used both Reeves and her mother's death as the basis for the central characters of *The Square Root of Wonderful* (1958), a play which many critics viewed as her attempt to reconcile feelings of loss, guilt, and hostility. In McCullers's last novel, *Clock without Hands* (1961), a bigot overcomes his racist beliefs after learning that he is dying from leukemia. Critics, though unimpressed with the book, generally agreed that it offered McCullers's most optimistic treatment of existence, showing a significant shift in her overall tone.

During the last phase of her life, McCullers was largely confined to a bed or a wheelchair. She underwent surgery to repair damaged limbs, survived a heart attack, had a cancerous breast removed, and broke a hip and an elbow in a fall. Following another stroke in 1967, McCullers died in Nyack, New York, at the age of fifty.

Works in Literary Context

McCullers was originally categorized as a Southern Gothic writer due to her portrayal of social misfits and other unconventional characters. However, most contemporary scholars agree with Louis Rubin's contention that her protagonists function as "exemplars of the wretchedness of the human condition" rather than being representative of regional types. She is now considered an important voice in the American literary tradition, not merely a writer of regional interest.

Southern Ambiance, Universal Subject With Eudora Welty, Flannery O'Connor, and Katherine Anne Porter,

LITERARY AND HISTORICAL CONTEMPORARIES

McCullers's famous contemporaries include:

Richard Wright (1908–1960): Wright was an African American author noted for his impact on black fiction because of his naturalistic descriptions of the reality of life for African Americans.

Tennessee Williams (1911–1983): Williams was an American playwright who wrote incisive representations of familial strife; he is best known for his two Pulitzer Prize-winning plays, *A Streetcar Named Desire* (1947) and *Cat on a Hot Tin Roof* (1955).

Gwendolyn Brooks (1917–2000): Brooks was an African American poet and the first African American writer to win a Pulitzer Prize.

J. D. Salinger (1919–): Salinger is an American novelist and short-story writer best known for his best-selling and widely-read novel *The Catcher in the Rye* (1951).

Doris Lessing (1919–): Lessing is British novelist who won the Nobel Prize in Literature in 2007.

Carson McCullers is an explorer of the Southern grotesque, for the ambiance of her fiction is always Southern, whatever its geographic locale, and her characters are the solitary, the freakish, and the lonely. Her work is distinguished from her fellow regionalists' work in the grotesque genre, however, by a deep compassion for the dispossessed. Indeed, she has transcended not only regionalism but Americanism as well, and has become a spokesman for all the lonely and alienated people of the world. Her best work is tenderly lyrical rather than philosophical, but it merits a distinguished place in that eccentric, bleakly poetic body of Southern fiction that takes as its subject the dark corners of the mind.

Isolation McCullers's characters are often seen as universal symbols of psychological isolation and the failure of communication. Her androgynous characters particularly reveal the inadequacy of physical love to fulfill basic human emotional needs McCullers herself explained:

> Love, and especially love of a person who is incapable of returning it, or receiving it, is at the heart of my selection of grotesque figures to write about—people whose physical incapacity is a symbol of their spiritual incapacity to love or receive love—their spiritual isolation.

McCuller's vision of human isolation has inspired continued critical attention to her work. In *Critical Occasions*, Julian Symons has noted: "It is her triumph that from her preoccupation with freaks and with human loneliness she makes fictions which touch and illuminate at many points . . . the world of literal reality."

COMMON HUMAN EXPERIENCE

McCullers's works are filled with isolated and lonely characters who would be considered outcasts. Here are some other novels that feature similar characters:

The Catcher in the Rye (1951), a novel by J. D. Salinger. This novel focuses on the psychological journey of a troubled teenager who feels like an outcast in a word of hypocrisy and stupidity.

Rule of the Bone (1995), a novel by Russell Banks. This novel follows the adventures of a fourteen-year-old dropout and runaway who encounters a large number of characters who are, in some way or another, outcasts or dropouts themselves.

The Book Thief (2005), a novel by Markus Zusak. This novel tells the story of a girl orphaned during the time of Adolf Hitler and navigating the treacherous world of Nazi Germany.

Works in Critical Context

McCullers began her writing career with a successful debut novel, *The Heart is a Lonely Hunter*, then followed up with three more critically-acclaimed books, all written during her twenties. However, she was unable to match this output in her later writings. As Louis Rubin has pointed out, McCullers's first four novels were her major works, and "a very impressive body of fiction indeed," though he added, echoing most other commentators, that "[n]othing that she wrote in the remaining two decades of her life adds much to her achievement."

The Heart is a Lonely Hunter *The Heart is a Lonely Hunter*, McCullers's first novel, established her reputation and was highly praised for its maturity of vision and bleak but lyrical prose style. The book ostensibly revolves around deaf-mute John Singer, a reluctant confidante of four alienated characters who believe that he can comprehend their dreams and frustrations. Critics generally agree, however, that the novel's protagonist is Mick Kelley, an adolescent tomboy whose dreams of becoming a composer are thwarted by sexual discrimination and financial problems. While many reviewers initially maintained that Mick's decision to abandon her ambitions in order to help support her family represents a realistic and appropriate choice, most contemporary scholars contend that her acceptance of a mundane adult life symbolizes the death of her dreams and individuality. Lawrence Graver described *The Heart Is a Lonely Hunter* as "a parable of the human condition, of human isolation, of the craving to communicate and of the impossibility of communication; and also, perhaps, of the inescapable delusions attendant on the inescapable human need to love."

Reflections in a Golden Eye McCullers's second novel, *Reflections in a Golden Eye*, received largely negative reviews, partly due to its unsympathetic characterizations and unorthodox subject matter. Others attributed the reviews to an unfair comparison with her first novel. In his introduction to the 1950 edition of *Reflections in a Golden Eye*, Tennessee Williams declared it a victim of the overly zealous critical scrutiny that usually follows high praise for an author's first work. Despite a disappointing initial reception, *Reflections in a Golden Eye* struck him as an advance over *The Heart Is a Lonely Hunter* because McCullers had reined in her "subjective tenderness" and "youthful lyricism," achieving "absolute mastery of design." Whether one agrees with reviewers who believed that she regressed, or with Williams's assertion that she improved, in neither case can she be accused of having written the same book twice. *Reflections in a Golden Eye* bears only superficial resemblance to its predecessor. Even after efforts to rehabilitate its standing within her body of work, it remains her most controversial work.

Responses to Literature

1. Reviewers disagree about whether or not McCullers improved on her debut novel with her second novel, *Reflections in a Golden Eye*. In your opinion, was *Reflections in a Golden Eye* an improvement over *The Heart is a Lonely Hunter* or a regression? Cite specific examples from both books to support your position.

2. McCullers originally displayed musical talent and had planned to study to be a concert pianist. In what ways are her musical inclinations apparent in her writing? Does her writing benefit from the musical talent that she displayed? If so, how?

3. Commentators have noted that McCullers's characters can be seen as symbols of psychological isolation. Choose one or more of her characters who fit this description and write an essay describing the ways that they demonstrate the isolation of human beings from each other.

4. One commentator called *The Heart is a Lonely Hunter* "a parable of the human condition." Others have noted that McCullers displayed a similar vision of the human condition throughout her major works. Write an essay that describes McCullers' picture of the human condition. Be sure to use concrete examples from different major works to demonstrate your claims.

BIBLIOGRAPHY

Books

Carr, Virginia Spencer. *The Lonely Hunter: A Biography of Carson McCullers*. New York: Doubleday, 1975.

———. *Understanding Carson McCullers*. Columbia, S.C.: University of South Carolina Press, 1990.

Cook, Richard M. *Carson McCullers*. New York: Ungar, 1975.

Edmonds, Dale. *Carson McCullers*. Austin, Tex.: Steck-Vaughn, 1969.

Evans, Oliver. *The Ballad of Carson McCullers*. New York: Coward-McCann, 1966.

Fiedler, Leslie. *Love and Death in the American Novel*, revised edition. New York: Stein & Day, 1966.

Gilbert, Sandra and Susan Gubar. *No Man's Land: The Place of the Woman Writer in the Twentieth Century*. New Haven, Conn.: Yale University Press, 1990.

Graver, Lawrence. *Carson McCullers*. St. Paul, Minn.: University of Minnesota Press, 1969.

Huf, Linda. *A Portrait of the Artist as a Young Woman: The Writer as Heroine in American Literature*. New York: Ungar, 1983.

McDowell, Margaret. *Carson McCullers*. Boston: Twayne, 1980.

Rubin, Louis. *A Gallery of Southerners*. Baton Rouge, La.: Louisiana State University Press, 1982.

✸ Alice McDermott

BORN: *1953, Brooklyn, New York*

NATIONALITY: *American*

GENRE: *Fiction*

MAJOR WORKS:

That Night (1987)

At Weddings and Wakes (1991)

Charming Billy (1998)

After This (2006)

Alice McDermott   McDermott, Alice, photograph. © by Jerry Bauer. Reproduced by permission.

Overview

Alice McDermott is the premier chronicler of the ordinary lives of Irish-Catholic New Yorkers in the twentieth century. Her novels generally explore the lives of a large community of family members and neighbors, and her writing evokes the feel and texture of suburban life on Catholic Long Island in the 1950s and 1960s.

Works in Biographical and Historical Context

A Catholic Suburban Childhood Like many of her characters, McDermott grew up in a middle-class Irish Catholic family on suburban Long Island. She was born on June 27, 1953, the third child and only daughter of Mildred Lynch McDermott, a secretary and homemaker, and William J. McDermott, who worked for Con Edison. Because both parents were first-generation Irish Americans who were orphaned in their youth, McDermott grew up never knowing her biological grandparents. She was, however, part of a large Catholic community, which led her parents to send her to elementary school at St. Boniface in Elmont, Long Island, where classes were taught by nuns. She later attended high school at Sacred Heart Academy in nearby Hempstead.

McDermott claims to have been an indifferent student: "I liked to read books," she told an interviewer, "but I wasn't really a good student. I was not engaged, let's say, with what was going on in the classroom in high school." McDermott also remembers filling up notebooks with stories at the age of nine or ten. Writing was a way of expressing herself privately when dinner-table conversation was dominated by her two older brothers, who both became lawyers. "Writing was a way for me to make my own world and work out my thoughts," she recalls.

Becoming a Writer After graduating from Sacred Heart in 1971, McDermott entered the State University of New York at Oswego. During her undergraduate years, her interest in writing crystallized. At Oswego, McDermott took her first writing class with Paul Briand, who became her mentor. Briand and the other instructors in Oswego's well-regarded writing program offered encouragement and helped her think of herself as a writer and to teach her to analyze her own writing carefully and closely at the sentence level.

Despite the support she received, McDermott still contemplated other career options after graduating from Oswego with a BA in 1975. For a time, she considered

LITERARY AND HISTORICAL CONTEMPORARIES

McDermott's famous contemporaries include:

Ana Castillo (1953–): Castillo is a prominent and prolific Chicana poet, novelist, editor, and translator whose work has been widely anthologized in the United States, Mexico, and Europe.

Oprah Winfrey (1954–): Winfrey is an American television personality best known for her talk show.

Jay McInerney (1955–): A writer considered a member of the American "literary brat pack" that came to prominence in the 1980s.

David Sedaris (1956–): Sedaris is a humorist known for his largely autobiographical essays and contributions to the radio program *This American Life*.

Tama Janowitz (1957–): An American writer famous for her short-story collection *Slaves of New York* (1986).

following in the path of her older brothers and attending law school. She settled, instead, on moving to New York City for a brief stint as a clerk-typist at Vantage Press, a vanity publishing house (a publishing house that publishes books at the author's own expense) that supplied much of the inspiration for the fictional Vista Books of her first novel, *A Bigamist's Daughter* (1982). Soon, though, McDermott enrolled in the master's program in fiction writing at the University of New Hampshire (UNH), where she met a second mentor, Mark Smith. Acting on Smith's advice, McDermott began sending stories to publishers. Her first short story, "Simple Truth," appeared in *Ms.* magazine in July 1978. In the next few years, she published two more stories in *Ms.* and placed others in *Seventeen*, *Redbook*, and *Mademoiselle*. Meanwhile, UNH had hired McDermott as a lecturer after she completed her MA degree in 1978. She taught English at UNH in the 1978–1979 academic year. Also during this period, McDermott met her future husband, David Armstrong, at a bar while she was celebrating the publication of her first short story. The couple married on June 16, 1979, and they now have three children.

Literary Success Inspired by her first taste of literary success, McDermott decided to write a novel, which eventually became *A Bigamist's Daughter*. She and her new husband moved to New York City, where Armstrong finished medical school and McDermott met Harriet Wasserman, an established literary agent who agreed to represent her. *A Bigamist's Daughter* was critically well-received, and following the release of this book, McDermott and her husband moved to La Jolla, California, where Armstrong, by then a neuroscientist, conducted research while McDermott taught at the University of California, Davis. During this time, she worked on her second novel, *That Night* (1987). The book was published to glowing reviews and became a finalist for the National Book Award, the Pulitzer Prize, the PEN/Faulkner Award, and the *Los Angeles Times* Book Award.

In the 1990s, McDermott held a variety of academic positions while she raised her children and continued to write. She taught briefly at American University in 1992, was writer-in-residence at the Virginia Center for the Creative Arts in 1995 and 1997, and settled into a long-term position as creative-writing professor at Johns Hopkins University in 1996. There, she was hired to replace the retiring novelist John Barth.

Although each of her first three novels was quite successful and helped secure McDermott a solid reputation among a small circle of literary critics, writers, and academics, her fourth novel, *Charming Billy*, was the one that won her popular acclaim and a much wider readership. After *Charming Billy* (1998) unexpectedly won the National Book Award, McDermott found herself in demand as a speaker, reader, and interview subject. The book spent several weeks on *The New York Times* bestseller list. She has since written two more well-received novels, including *After This* (2006), which was nominated for the Pulitzer Prize. McDermott won a 2008 Corrington Award for Literary Excellence and lives near Washington, D.C.

Works in Literary Context

The Irish Catholic New Yorker Experience Exploring Catholic Spirituality McDermott is sometimes described as a "quiet" writer whose main purpose is to examine the emotional depth in ordinary lives and commonplace events. Although her novels contain the historically accurate details that bring her characters and their world to life, McDermott states that she is "more interested in what's going on in their heads than what's going on on their couches. . . . The spirituality that is tied to Catholicism is much more important to me." In all of her novels, McDermott probes the dimensions of this spirituality and explores the Catholic viewpoint, particularly on questions relating to life and death.

Works in Critical Context

McDermott has enjoyed almost universal critical acclaim. Several of her novels have been nominated for or won major literary awards. Although her first three novels were successful and helped secure McDermott a solid reputation among a small circle of literary critics, writers, and academics, her fourth novel, *Charming Billy*, was the one that won her popular acclaim and a much wider readership. Since then, critics have tended to accept that McDermott is a major literary voice of the twenty-first century, and they even liken her to such literary notables as Jane Austen.

A Bigamist's Daughter McDermott's *A Bigamist's Daughter* was critically well-received, and reviewers often noted that the book was unusually accomplished for a first novel. Anne Tyler argues that McDermott "sounds like anything but a first-time novelist." Rather, she asserts that McDermott "writes with assurance and skill" and creates a "fascinatingly prismatic story." Stephen Harvey of *The Village Voice* compliments McDermott for writing a tale "which sounds, for a change, like truth" though it grows from "commonplaces mined in so much undistinguished fiction." He admires the author's "spare, acidic prose" as well as her refusal to succumb to romantic illusions on the one hand or to maudlin depression on the other. Le Anne Schreiber in *The New York Times* describes the book as a "shrewd, sad first novel" written by "a very tough-minded and talented young writer." The reviewers, however, did not see the book as flawless. Several commented that Tupper and Elizabeth are not always believable, with Tyler going so far as to say that the book "is almost done in, at times, by the fatuousness of its two central characters."

After This Following her National Book Award-winning fourth novel, McDermott was a finalist for the 2007 Pulitzer Prize for Fiction with her sixth novel, *After This*. As with her previous works, critics were generally impressed with the subtlety of her writing. As Jocelyn McClurg noted, "Alice McDermott writes beautiful, understated sentences so subtle and yet so packed with insight that if you blink, you might miss, say, the death of a character." Even with the praise given to this book, reviewers did not consider this among McDermott's best work. Noting that "McDermott's talent never fails to impress," McClurg nonetheless argues that *After This* "falls short of her best books." A reviewer for *Publisher's Weekly*, while noting that "she flawlessly encapsulates an era in the private moments of one family's life," states that "[t]he story of '60s and '70s suburbia has been told before, and McDermott has little to say about the Vietnam War itself."

Responses to Literature

1. Throughout her adult life and her writing and teaching career, McDermott has lived in various locales in the United States. In what ways does her broader experience of American life inform her writings about the Catholic communities of Long Island? Does she draw on insights from her adult life when writing about a time and place familiar from her childhood? If so, how?

2. McDermott writes primarily about suburban life in the 1950s and 1960s. In what ways has suburban life changed over the past fifty years? In what ways, if any, are the insights into suburban life that are presented in McDermott's novels relevant for understanding its present-day equivalent?

COMMON HUMAN EXPERIENCE

Much of McDermott's work is semi-autobiographical, set in the Long Island suburbs where she grew up. Here are some other similar works from artists who grew up in the suburbs during the middle of the twentieth century:

Avalon (1990), a film by Barry Levinson. This film tells the tale of Jewish immigrants who settle in Baltimore in the first half of the twentieth century in an attempt to attain the American Dream.

The Buddha of Suburbia (1990), a novel by Hanif Kureishi. This novel focuses on a teenager living in the London suburbs in the 1970s and tells the story of his desire to leave his confining life for the big city.

The Namesake (2003), a novel by Jhumpa Lahiri. This novel chronicles the life of Indian immigrant family members as they settle in the Boston suburbs during the 1970s and 1980s.

3. McDermott has been compared to Jane Austen. Write an analytical essay that notes points of similarity between the works of these two authors. Be sure to cite specific novels from each to support your claims.

4. McDermott has been praised for her ability to evoke a particular time and mood in her stories. Draw on your own knowledge and experience of some slice of American life to write a story that, while not necessarily autobiographical, evokes the mood and feel of a particular time and place with which you are familiar.

BIBLIOGRAPHY

Books

Hightower, Laura S., ed. *Newsmakers*. Detroit: Gale Group, 1999.

Periodicals

Cryer, Dan. "Will Success Spoil Alice McDermott?" *Newsday* (March 25, 1998): B06.

Dangel, Mary Jo. "Charming Alice McDermott: Award-winning Novelist." *St. Anthony Messenger* (May 2001).

Gwinn, Mary Ann. "A Top Book Award Brings Changes to the 'Ordinary' Life of Alice McDermott." *Seattle Times* (January 31, 1999): M1.

Heron, Kim. "Redeeming Simple Emotions." *New York Times* (April 19, 1987).

McClurg, Jocelyn. "'After This': A Beautifully Uneven Family Story." *USA Today* (September 5, 2006): D6.

"McDermott, Alice. *After This.*" *Publishers Weekly* (June 19, 2006).

Rothstein, Mervyn. "The Storyteller Is Part of the Tale." *New York Times* (May 9, 1987).

Smith, Wendy. "Alice McDermott." *Publishers Weekly* (March 30, 1992): 85.

Steinberg, Sally Levitt. "L.I. Streets Inspire a Novelist." *New York Times* (October 29, 1989).

Weaver, Teresa K. "Books: Multilayered Stories Are Writer's Forte." *Atlanta Journal-Constitution* (April 21, 2002): F4.

❀ Colleen McElroy

BORN: *1935, St. Louis, Missouri*

NATIONALITY: *American*

GENRE: *Poetry, fiction, drama*

MAJOR WORKS:

Queen of the Ebony Isles (1985)

What Madness Brought Me Here (1990)

A Long Way from St. Louie (1997)

Overview

Colleen McElroy is a poet, dramatist, essayist, and short-story writer with an intense sense of place. One of the country's leading African American female poets, she explores questions of identity and belonging, and her writing has been credited with expanding readers' per-

Colleen McElroy   *Ingrid Pape-Sheldon Photography*

spectives on what it means to be a black woman in today's world.

Works in Biographical and Historical Context

A Childhood on the Move   McElroy was born on October 30, 1935, in St. Louis, Missouri. Her parents divorced in 1938, and she and her mother moved in with her grandmother. Her mother remarried an army sergeant in 1943, and this event began McElroy's childhood as an "army brat." The family moved often, and by the time she was an adult, she had lived in St. Louis, Kansas City, Wyoming, and Munich, Germany, where she attended college for a time. She graduated from Kansas State University with a bachelor's degree in 1958. Her travels as a child had a profound effect on her life and writing. As her writings indicate, she has traveled extensively in Europe, South America, Japan, Majorca, Africa, and Southeast Asia, and much of her work both in poetry and essay form focuses on her experiences during these travels.

Education and Teaching   After finishing her undergraduate degree, McElroy moved to Pittsburgh, where she studied in the speech and hearing program at the University of Pittsburgh. She then returned to Kansas City to work with the speech-impaired at the Rehabilitation Institute. Later, she went back to Kansas State University to earn a master's degree in neurological and language learning patterns.

At the same time she was pursuing a career in speech therapy, she was teaching English. She moved to Bellingham, Washington, to become the director of Speech and Hearing Services at Western Washington University, and from 1966 through 1973, she served as an assistant professor of English. During this time, she continued her education and earned a PhD in ethnolinguistic patterns of dialect differences and oral traditions from the University of Washington in 1973. That year, she became an assistant professor of English at the University of Washington at Seattle in 1973, where she still teaches. In 1983, McElroy became the first black woman to be promoted to full professor at the University of Washington.

Writing Seriously   McElroy began writing seriously in her thirties, when she lived in Bellingham. She developed a passion for the landscape of the Pacific Northwest, and this passion led to the writing of her first poems, which would be offered in her 1973 chapbook, *The Mules Done Long Since Gone.* Her first full collection, *Winters without Snow*, was published in 1979, and in 1983, her *Queen of the Ebony Isles* was selected for the Wesleyan University Press Poetry Series. That collection received the American Book Award in 1985. Since 1985 McElroy has published two short-story compendiums and two poetic memoirs, and she has also written several plays and television scripts.

Works in Literary Context

Travel Poetry   Having traveled extensively throughout her life, McElroy often focuses her writing, both poetry and prose, on her travels and what she has taken from them. She is not, however, a travel writer but a writer who is directly inspired by her travels. She says about her poetic memoir, *A Long Way From St. Louie* (1997), that it is about "impressions of journeys, memories held in fragments: like footprints on a sandy beach, the familiar scent of perfume, or the special spice in a dish prepared by a favorite cook." Her 1990 collection of poems, *What Madness Brought Me Here*, contains a number of "shoe" poems about her travels by foot. In these poems, McElroy takes the reader on journeys not only to different places, but to the questions that arise in her mind as she travels there and contemplates the people and objects she encounters.

McElroy's writings demonstrate her energy not only as a traveler but as a writer as well. Often employing a stream-of-consciousness style, she moves playfully but thoughtfully through a variety of observations and questions. In her poem "A Pièd," she spots a single shoe on a highway, leading her to explore a series of questions about how the shoe got there. Using loosely related images and similes, McElroy takes the reader on a journey that transcends the simple object seen on the road, using sensuality and excitement to explore questions of loneliness, uncertainty, and relationships.

Works in Critical Context

McElroy's work has been well-received by reviewers and readers. She has won several awards for her writing and received support from prestigious institutions, including two fellowships from the National Endowment for the Arts.

What Madness Brought Me Here   McElroy's best-known work is probably *What Madness Brought Me Here* (1990), which includes poems from 1968 through 1988. Denise Levertov writes, "McElroy's work has long interested me. Her poems combine the authenticity of the personal with a strong sense of history. They can surprise and delight the reader." McElroy is particularly praised for her style; as a reviewer for the *San Francisco Review of Books* notes, "McElroy is the master of long, finely-crafted poems, each with a particular melodic intensity and tone." Peggy Kaganoff elaborates a bit more on McElroy's strengths, writing in *Publisher's Weekly* that "language, according to the poet, embodies our madness and cannot succeed in communicating. Madness also serves as a convenient metaphor for her style, which often emphasizes stream-of-consciousness and rifts in association."

A Long Way from St. Louie   McElroy has also received praise for her travel memoir, *A Long Way from St. Louie*. Veronica Chambers describes the book as "humorous, engaging and intelligent," going on to argue that "what

is most impressive is how brave she is, how she is willing to try anything once. She is free in the broadest sense: not anchored to any one place or any one identity." Other reviewers note that McElroy's sense of what it means to be a black woman infuses the book with a particular spirit. As a *Publisher's Weekly* reviewer puts it, "Although skin color is not the primary focus of this delightful book, it is never far from her consciousness, nor from the memory of her grandmother's... belief 'that there are black folks everywhere on this earth.'" Chambers points out, "What sets the book apart is that McElroy broadens our definition and perspective of what it means to be a black woman today."

Responses to Literature

1. McElroy's best-known work, *What Madness Brought Me Here*, collects her poems from a twenty-year period, from 1968 through 1988. In what ways do these poems demonstrate a development in her perspective, and in what ways are there consistent themes and messages despite the poems' two-decade spread?

2. McElroy has moved many times and traveled extensively during her life, and her wanderings seem to inform her writing deeply. In what ways do her writings speak to readers who have not traveled as extensively? Does a reader need to have a similar experience of movement to appreciate McElroy's writings fully, or are her writings accessible to a general audience?

3. Commentators have noted that McElroy explores questions of identity and place in her writings. Write an analytical essay discussing the kinds of questions about identity and place that McElroy raises and the sorts of answers she seems to provide. Be sure to use concrete examples from her writings to demonstrate your points.

4. One critic wrote that "McElroy broadens our definition and perspective of what it means to be a black woman today." Write an essay that discusses what McElroy has to say about being a black woman today.

BIBLIOGRAPHY

Books

Duke, Charles R. and Sally A. Jacobsen, eds. *Poets' Perspectives: Reading Writing and Teaching Poetry*. Portsmouth, N.H.: Boynton/Cook Publishers, 1992.

Koolish, Linda. *African American Writers: Portraits and Visions*. Jackson, Miss.: University Press of Mississippi, 2001.

Page, Yolanda Williams. *Encyclopedia of African American Women Writers*. Westport, Conn.: Greenwood Publishing Group, 2007.

Periodicals

Chambers, Veronica. "A Long Way from St. Louie." *The Women's Review of Books* (December 1997): 5.

Kaganoff, Penny. "What Madness Brought Me Here: New and Selected Poems, 1968–1988." *Publishers Weekly* (December 14, 1990): 62.

"A Long Way from St. Louis." *Publishers Weekly* (March 10, 1997): 57.

Parker, Mary Ann. "A Long Way from St. Louie: Travel Memoirs." *Library Journal* (April 15, 1997): 104.

Watson Sherman, Charlotte. "Walking across the Floor: A Conversation with Colleen J. McElroy—Black Writer and Teacher." *American Visions* (April–May 1995).

Web sites

University of Washington Web site. *Biography of Colleen McElroy*. Retrieved October 31, 2008, from http://faculty.washington.edu/dragnldy/pages/Biography.html.

⊛ Claude McKay

BORN: *1889, Sunny Ville, Jamaica*

DIED: *1948, Chicago, Illinois*

NATIONALITY: *American, Jamaican*

GENRE: *Poetry*

MAJOR WORKS:

Songs of Jamaica (1912)
Harlem Shadows (1922)
Home to Harlem (1928)
Banana Bottom (1933)

Claude McKay   *McKay, Claude, photograph. The Library of Congress.*

Overview

Claude McKay was one of the major voices of the Harlem Renaissance. In all of his works, McKay searched among the common folk for a distinctive black identity, hoping to find a way to preserve the African spirit and creativity in an alienating world. Perhaps more than any other black writer of his time, McKay managed to convert anger and social protest into poems of lasting value.

Works in Biographical and Historical Context

Early Sense of Racial Pride   McKay was born in the hills of Jamaica to peasant farmers whose sense of racial pride greatly affected the young McKay. His father was instrumental in reinforcing this pride, telling him folktales about Africa as well as stories about McKay's African grandfather's enslavement. From accounts of his grandfather's experiences with white men, McKay acquired an early distrust for whites. Under the tutelage of his brother, a schoolteacher and avowed agnostic (one who does not proclaim a belief in a god or gods) McKay was imbued with freethinking ideas and philosophies.

In 1907 he left his rural home to apprentice as a woodworker in Brown's Town, where he met Walter Jekyll, an English linguist and specialist in Jamaican folklore. Jekyll helped further McKay's developing interest in English poetry, introducing him to works by John Milton, Alexander Pope, and Percy Bysshe Shelley. He also encouraged McKay to write verse in his native dialect. In 1909 McKay moved to Kingston, Jamaica's capital, where he later served as a constable. His native town, Sunny Ville, was predominantly black, but in substantially white Kingston, the caste society, which placed blacks below whites and mulattoes, revealed to McKay alienating and degrading aspects of city life and racism. His exposure to overt racism in Kingston soon led him to identify strongly with the plight of blacks, who, he saw to his alarm, there lived under the near-total control of whites.

Establishing Literary and Political Ties   In 1912, with Jekyll's assistance, McKay published his first volumes of poetry, *Songs of Jamaica* and *Constab Ballads*. Both works are collections of lyrical verse written in Jamaican vernacular; the former celebrates nature and the peasant's bond to the soil, while the latter decries injustices of city life. In the same year, McKay traveled to the United States to study agriculture. After attending Tuskegee Institute in Alabama and Kansas State College, he decided to quit his studies in 1914 and move to New York City.

By 1917, because of his associations with two prominent men of letters—Frank Harris, editor of *Pearson's Magazine*, in which McKay's militant poem "To The White Fiends" appeared, and Max Eastman, editor of the Communist magazine *The Liberator*, in which the poem "If We Must Die" was first published—McKay established literary and political ties with left-wing thinkers in Greenwich Village. Partly because of the injustices exposed by World War I and the success of the Russian Revolution, socialism was rising in popularity in the United States, particularly among poor members of the working classes. After the publication of "If We Must Die" in 1919, McKay began two years of travel and work abroad. In London he worked on the socialist periodical *Workers' Dreadnought*.

Starting the Harlem Renaissance   McKay returned to the United States in 1921 and took up various social causes. His most highly acclaimed poetry volume, *Harlem Shadows* (1922), appeared the following year. Although his work would give rise to the Harlem Renaissance—a flourishing of the arts throughout the African American community for which it is named—McKay left the U.S. shortly thereafter and spent twelve years abroad, traveling first to Moscow to attend the Fourth Congress of the Communist Party. McKay was extolled in the Soviet Union as a great American poet, but he grew disenchanted with the Communist party when it became apparent he would have to subjugate his art to political propaganda. Joseph Stalin, in particular, who gained control of the Soviet Union in 1924, believed that all art should have a utilitarian purpose, such as glorifying the state or the working class; any art that called into question the tenets of socialism, or depicted unnecessary or distasteful human behaviors—as defined by the whims of government leaders—was condemned.

By 1923 McKay had moved to Paris; later, he journeyed to the south of France, Germany, North Africa, and Spain. For the next decade, he concentrated on writing fiction, completing his three most important novels, *Home to Harlem* (1928), *Banjo: A Story without a Plot* (1929), and *Banana Bottom* (1933), as well as a collection of short stories.

Return to Harlem   McKay returned to the United States in 1934 to find the Great Depression in full swing. This was a period of deep financial difficulty marked by massive unemployment—with one in four able workers out of a job—as well as devastating agricultural losses throughout the Midwest. Facing financial difficulties and a neglected American literary reputation, he wrote his autobiography, *A Long Way from Home* (1937), in an attempt to bolster his financial and literary status. Following the publication of this work, McKay developed an interest in Roman Catholicism and became active in Harlem's Friendship House, a Catholic community center. His work there led to the writing of *Harlem: Negro Metropolis* (1940), a historical essay collection that sold poorly. By the mid-1940s McKay's health had deteriorated and, after enduring several illnesses, he died of heart failure in Chicago in 1948.

Works in Literary Context

Over the course of his thirty-year writing career, McKay was able to establish his reputation as a master of the

LITERARY AND HISTORICAL CONTEMPORARIES

McKay's famous contemporaries include:

Sinclair Lewis (1885–1951): Lewis was an American author who, in 1930, became the first American to win the Nobel Prize in Literature.

Eugene O'Neill (1888–1953): O'Neill was an American playwright who pioneered realism in dramatic theater; he was awarded the Nobel Prize in Literature in 1936.

Pearl Buck (1892–1973): Buck was an American author and winner of the 1938 Nobel Prize in Literature who helped to introduce American readers to Asian culture through works like *The Good Earth* (1931).

William Faulkner (1897–1962): Faulkner was an American author known for his elaborate writing style and his detailed depiction of fictional Yoknapatawpha County in works like *The Sound and the Fury* (1929). He was awarded the Nobel Prize in Literature in 1949.

Langston Hughes (1902–1967): Hughes was an African American writer best known for his literary influence during the Harlem Renaissance; he remains one of the best-loved American poets by modern readers.

dialect poetry of the Jamaican folk; as a sonnet writer of merit, able to treat subjects as diverse as West Indian flora, European cities, and racial conflicts; as a journalist, reviewer, and essayist with strong political beliefs; as a short-story writer of some force; and as a picaresque novelist whose strength was social and emotional realism. McKay was closely associated with the Harlem Renaissance, but his work also inspired such Francophone poets as Aimé Césaire and Leopold Senghor—authors whose verse espoused tenets of negritude, a movement begun in the 1930s that sought to reclaim African cultural heritage—as well as writers of the Black Arts Movement, which flourished during the 1960s through such acclaimed poets as Amiri Baraka and Haki R. Madhubuti.

The Common People and Cultural Synthesis McKay wrote poems, short stories, and novels expressing the energy and spontaneity of the common people. His work includes dialect verse celebrating peasant life in Jamaica, militant poems challenging white authority in the United States, fictional works depicting black life in both Jamaica and America, and philosophically ambitious novels about the efforts of blacks to cope in Western society. His third novel, *Banana Bottom*, is recognized as his greatest achievement in fiction. Here, as in *Home to Harlem, Banjo: A Story without a Plot*, and several short stories, McKay depicted the black individual in white Western culture. Commenting on the resolution of *Banana Bottom*, Michael B. Stoff notes that "of peasant origin and possessing a

cultivated intellect, Bita Plant represents McKay's first successful synthesis of two cultures."

Contradictory Relationship with the Harlem Renaissance What is generally termed the Harlem Renaissance, a decade of black self-awareness and racial pride, is frequently dated from the appearance in print of Claude McKay's great sonnet "If We Must Die," which commemorated the cataclysmic race riots in the United States during the second half of 1919. The publication in 1919 of "If We Must Die" was at once a shout of defiance and a proclamation of the unbreakable spirit and courage of the oppressed black individual. So great was the effect of that poem that McKay has been proposed as the founder of the Harlem Renaissance and as the prototype of the modern black social-realist contributor to American culture. When in 1925 Alain Locke (the Howard University philosopher and recorder of black literary and artistic achievement) wrote about the "New Negro," he was thinking about those who, in effect, followed in McKay's path in taking pride in African culture, in Negro racial self-consciousness, and in black folkways.

Yet McKay's poetry and his life display the presence of conflicting forces: his sense of identity as a black man and his desire to write out of a traditional literary heritage. McKay made few friends in Harlem during the 1920s, and he resisted characterization as a representative of the Harlem literary community. He was troubled that he was so often identified as a black writer rather than as an individual who was struggling to perfect his poetry, which he wanted to be judged by its merit as verse. His absence from Europe and North Africa from 1922 to 1934, his changing political and religious positions, and his often strained relationships with his friends and supporters resulted in a diminished reputation by the time of his death.

However, the development of black studies and Jamaican nationalism in the 1960s redirected attention to McKay, and resulted in a series of analytic studies that have identified his strengths and weaknesses and reestablished his literary reputation in both the United States and the Caribbean. In 1977 he was posthumously awarded the Order of Jamaica and declared the national poet.

Works in Critical Context

McKay's reputation as an author was never greater than during his period of fame in the 1920s. Despite his apparent decline in later years, his literary accomplishments are acclaimed as pioneering efforts by a black artist, and his influence on later writers is unquestioned. McKay's poetic forms were once thought by some to be too conventional and limiting for the density of his themes; however, he has recently been praised for the intensity and ardor of his poetry.

Home to Harlem and Banjo McKay's first novel, *Home to Harlem*, was the first novel by a black writer to reach the commercial bestseller lists; it was reprinted five times in two months. Its depiction of the racy life that

Carl Van Vechten had presented of Harlem in *Nigger Heaven* (1926) and its ties to the general atmosphere of good-timing made it an instant success. Burton Rascoe, writing for *Bookman*, asserts that the novel is "a book to invoke pity and terror, which is the function of tragedy, and to that extent—that very extent—it is beautiful"; he also applauds the "Negro slang and dialect." The reviewer for the *New York Herald Tribune* compliments the "stark realism" and maintains that "sordid truths" are presented with simplicity. Others claimed that the book was more valuable as folklore than as fiction, suggesting that it was, at times, formless.

McKay's second novel, *Banjo: A Story Without a Plot*, was considered a sequel to *Home to Harlem*. One reviewer, focusing on the picture of waterfront life in Marseilles, commented that McKay had achieved an "unforgettable picture" of it. Others complained that the book had "little consciousness of plot or form," but most agreed that the novel was vigorous and engaging, particularly its "racy Negro idiom." Another critic comments:

> If fault is to be found with the author's manner, let it be that he is more loyal to his characters than they are themselves, that his realism is a shade too natural and his naturalism too real. But such considerations need spoil no one's appreciation of a complex task simply and gustily performed.

Banana Bottom Addison Gayle asserted that in his first two novels, McKay had been exploring the problem of identity, of the place of the outsider in Western civilization, but since he did not resolve the conflict in either of the first two novels, he tried to do so in his third, *Banana Bottom*. Most of the reviewers of the book, however, focused more on the scenery and atmosphere than upon theme. Mary Ross, writing for *Books*, strikes the typical view, pointing out the "glamour of the tropics" as a strong element in the work, and noting, "The vividness of the book is due in large part to Mr. McKay's grasp of the special moods, sights and sounds of his country, its festivals, gayety and ideals." Others commented upon the humor, pathos, and melodrama in the book, but the island scenery remained prominent in the minds of most of the reviewers.

Responses to Literature

1. McKay's poem "If We Must Die," although written about race riots in the United States, was said to have universal significance, and was read by Winston Churchill to the British people during World War II. What aspects of this poem make it apply beyond the particular context in which McKay wrote it? Does the poem's message still have meaning in today's world?

2. McKay was noted for his ability to capture the unique speech patterns and dialects of his characters. Read some of his early poems that display such language. From a reader's perspective, what are some of the advantages and disadvantages of this kind of writing?

3. McKay is often considered the founder of the Harlem Renaissance. Choose another literary figure from the Harlem Renaissance and write an essay tracing McKay's influence on that person's writing.

4. McKay became an adherent of socialism early in his literary career. Write an essay that defines socialism and explores the socialist themes found in one of his works of fiction.

COMMON HUMAN EXPERIENCE

McKay's poetry, short stories, and novels attempted to convey the experiences and struggles of ordinary black people. Here are some other works that attempted a similar depiction of black life:

Their Eyes Were Watching God (1937), a novel by Zora Neale Hurston. This novel tells the story of a woman living in a black town in Florida during the beginning of the twentieth century.

Native Son (1940), a novel by Richard Wright. This novel chronicles the life of an African American struggling through Depression-era Chicago.

Beloved (1987), a novel by Toni Morrison. This novel depicts the life of an African American woman and her daughter after escaping from slavery.

BIBLIOGRAPHY

Books

Bontemps, Arna, ed. *The Harlem Renaissance Remembered*. New York: Dodd, Mead, 1972.

Conroy, Mary James. *Claude McKay: Negro Poet and Novelist*. Ann Arbor, Mich.: University Microfilms, 1968.

Cooper, Wayne F. *Claude McKay: Rebel Sojourner in the Harlem Renaissance: A Biography*. Baton Rouge, La.: Louisiana State University Press, 1987.

Cooper, Wayne F., ed. *The Passion of Claude McKay*. New York: Schocken, 1973.

Gayle, Addison, Jr. *Claude McKay: The Black Poet at War*. Detroit, Mich.: Broadside, 1972.

Giles, James R. *Claude McKay*. Boston: Twayne, 1976.

Lang, Phyllis Martin. *Claude McKay: The Later Years, 1934-48*. Ann Arbor, Mich.: University Microfilms, 1973.

Mphahlele, Ezekiel. *Voices in the Whirlwind*. New York: Hill & Wang, 1972.

Samuels, Wilfred D. *Five Afro-Caribbean Voices in American Culture, 1917–1929*. Boulder, Colo.: Belmont, 1977.

Tillery, Tyrone. *Claude McKay: A Black Poet's Struggle for Identity.* Amherst, Mass.: University of Massachusetts Press, 1992.

Wagner, Jean. *Black Poets of the United States: From Paul Laurence Dunbar to Langston Hughes*, translated by Kenneth Douglas. Urbana, Ill.: University of Illinois Press, 1973.

Periodicals

Smith, Robert. "Claude McKay: An Essay in Criticism." *Phylon* (1948): 270–273.

☸ Terry McMillan

BORN: *1951, Port Huron, Michigan*

NATIONALITY: *American, African American*

GENRE: *Fiction*

MAJOR WORKS:
Disappearing Acts (1989)
Waiting to Exhale (1992)
How Stella Got Her Groove Back (1996)

Terry McMillan   *McMillan, Terry, photograph. © Jerry Bauer. Reproduced by permission.*

Overview

Terry McMillan is an African American novelist whose works often depict the lives of successful contemporary African American women. Her emphasis on love and sexual relationships, her urban, successful characters, and her depictions of realistic friendships between women have garnered her a wide audience beyond the African American community.

Works in Biographical and Historical Context

Developing a Sense of Black Pride   McMillan was born and raised in Port Huron, Michigan, a blue-collar community north of Detroit. Her parents divorced when she was thirteen, and McMillan's mother, who worked in an auto factory as well as performing domestic jobs, assumed almost full responsibility for raising the children. When McMillan was sixteen years old, she began a job at the city library in Port Huron, where she discovered books by African American authors; reading these works gave her a sense of black pride and helped her become aware of issues relevant to African American culture.

Becoming a Writer   In 1968 McMillan left her hometown and moved to Los Angeles. She enrolled in Los Angeles City College, where she studied classic texts by black authors. In 1973 she transferred to the University of California at Berkeley, where she studied journalism and writing and met Ishmael Reed, a well-known author and poet. After receiving her bachelor's degree in journalism, McMillan moved to New York City, where she studied film at Columbia University. For several years she lived with her lover, a drug-dealer, and endured a three-year drug and alcohol addiction before joining Alcoholics Anonymous and regaining control of her life. In 1979 she earned her M.F.A. from Columbia and participated in the Harlem Writers Guild workshop, which was crucial to her development as a writer.

McMillan completed a draft of her first novel, *Mama* (1987), at the MacDowell Colony, where she stayed for two weeks in 1983. She helped promote *Mama* herself instead of relying on publishers to organize readings and market the novel. After the publication of *Mama*, McMillan was offered a position as an instructor at the University of Wyoming at Laramie, where she taught from 1987 to 1990.

Becoming a Best-Selling Author   McMillan's next novel, *Disappearing Acts*, was published in 1989 and became a national bestseller, with more than one hundred thousand paperback copies sold. She taught at the University of Arizona at Tucson from 1990 until 1992 while she published her third novel, *Waiting to Exhale*, which also became a bestseller and was adapted into a feature film in 1995.

McMillan's fifty-nine-year-old mother died of an asthma attack in 1994, and the following year McMillan's best friend died of cancer. She was unable to write after the trauma of these two events. Faced with writer's block, she visited Jamaica to try to overcome her grief; there she met Jonathan Plummer, a twenty-two-year-old resort worker. The two married in 1998. McMillan's fourth novel, *How Stella Got Her Groove Back* (1996), is loosely based on her experience in Jamaica and the beginnings of her relationship with Plummer. A feature film based on this novel was produced in 1998.

McMillan continues to write and has published several novels since *How Stella Got Her Groove Back*, though these works have not received the attention or praise of her first four novels.

Works in Literary Context

McMillan's novels explore issues relevant to African Americans in contemporary American society. McMillan is interested especially in African American women, and her female characters struggle with and celebrate motherhood, cope with troubled romantic relationships, look for successful careers, and search for both personal and cultural identity.

The Struggles of African American Women McMillan's novel *Mama*, based largely on her own family background, tells of Mildred Peacock, a woman who divorces her philandering husband to raise their five children on her own. Mildred overcomes alcohol and drug problems, as well as financial difficulties, to succeed. *Disappearing Acts* and *Waiting to Exhale* focus on successful African American women trying to develop satisfying love relationships while maintaining their business success. In *Disappearing Acts*, McMillan relates the difficulties in the relationship between a blue-collar man and a professional woman. *Waiting to Exhale* takes the form of an ongoing discussion between four friends as they discuss the problems they have in finding and keeping lovers.

Happy Endings for Successful People McMillan's novels all have happy endings, and her characters, especially her women characters, triumph over sometimes incredible odds. As McMillan herself said in a 1996 *Newsweek* interview, "I don't write about victims. They just bore me to death. I prefer to write about somebody who can pick themselves back up and get on with their lives. Because all of us are victims to some extent." Because of this emphasis, McMillan's novels are noted for inspiring readers to set and achieve goals and to encourage women to defy roles prescribed for them by patriarchal societies.

Works in Critical Context

Critics of McMillan's novels have praised her realistic depiction of contemporary, urban African American women. They point out that her characters' language and concerns are handled in a frank and complex manner. Although some critics believe McMillan includes too much profanity in her novels, so much that it sometimes detracts from her story, they also believe that she has

pioneered a new area of African American fiction—the urban romance novel.

Mama *Mama* received quite a bit of critical attention, especially for being the author's first novel. Many reviewers praised the book's realistic portrayal of the struggles of an African American family in the 1960s and 1970s. Although some reviewers pointed out flaws, it was, for the most part, received favorably. Janet Boyarin Blundell writes, "The book's main weakness is that the author apparently could not decide what to leave out....Although the story has power, it lacks focus and a clear point of view." Blundell goes on to note that McMillan appears unable to decide who her audience is: "at times she seems to be writing to blacks, at other times to be explaining things to naive white readers."

Waiting to Exhale McMillan's third novel, *Waiting to Exhale*, continued her string of commercially-successful books. Though the book is populated with African American women, reviewers praised the book for having a universal appeal. As Paula C. Barnes writes, "Although specifically it tells the story of four African-American women, *Waiting to Exhale* addresses the dilemma of career women who want it all." Edward M. Jackson attributes the book's success to McMillan's portrayal of "many themes universal to the contemporary America experience. She wrote about the subjects of divorce, single parenting, weight problems among women, health problems of elderly parents, the insensitivity of males, and the tensions of female friendships." The book was also noted

COMMON HUMAN EXPERIENCE

McMillan's novels explore the difficulties faced by successful professional women, particularly in the area of romance and marriage. Here are some other works that explore similar themes:

Valley of the Dolls (1966), a novel by Jacqueline Susann. This novel follows the career and romantic developments of three young women involved in the entertainment industry in the decades following World War II.

Girlfriends (2000–2007), a television series created by Mara Brock Akil. This comedy series focuses on four very different African American women in their search for romance and success.

Baby Mama (2008), a film by Michael McCullers. This comedy, starring Tina Fey and Amy Poehler, focuses on a professional woman with fertility issues who hires a working-class surrogate to carry her baby to term.

for being, as a reviewer for *Publisher's Weekly* put it, a "racy, zesty, irreverent and absorbing book with broad mainstream appeal."

Responses to Literature

1. McMillan is noted for writing mainly about successful people. In what ways does this limit the relevance of her books? In what ways does it provide her with opportunities to speak to people who are not as successful as her characters?

2. McMillan's novels focus on the struggles of African American women. In what ways are these struggles similar to and different from the struggles of other American women?

3. Although McMillan's characters are primarily African American, she has been noted for the universal relevance of her themes. Write an essay that explores how one or more of her themes have relevance outside the African American community.

4. Write an argumentative essay taking a stand on the question of whether or not readers need a certain level of familiarity with African American culture to appreciate McMillan's works. Be sure to cite specifics from her books to support your position.

BIBLIOGRAPHY

Books

Adjaye, Joseph K. and Adrianne R. Andrews, eds. *Language, Rhythm, and Sound: Black Popular Cultures into the Twenty-First Century*. Pittsburgh, Pa.: University of Pittsburgh Press, 1997.

Patrick, Diane. *Terry McMillan: The Unauthorized Biography*. New York: St. Martin's, 1999.

Richards, Paulette. *Terry McMillan: A Critical Companion*. Westport, Conn.: Greenwood, 1999.

Periodicals

Barnes, Paula C. "A review of *Waiting to Exhale*." *Belles Lettres* (Fall 1992): 56–57.

Dandridge, Rita B. "Debunking the Motherhood Myth in Terry McMillan's *Mama*." *CLA Journal* (1998): 405–416.

Ellerby, Janet. "Deposing the Man of the House: Terry McMillan Rewrites the Family." *MELUS* (1997): 105–117.

Harris, Tina M. "Interrogating the Representation of African American Female Identity in the Films *Waiting to Exhale* and *Set It Off*." *Popular Culture Review* (1999): 43–53.

Harris, Tina M. and Patricia S. Hill. "*Waiting to Exhale* or 'Breath(ing) Again': A Search for Identity, Empowerment, and Love in the 1990's." *Women and Language* (1998): 9–20.

Jackson, Edward M. "Images of Black Males in Terry McMillan's *Waiting to Exhale*." *MAWA Review* (1993): 20–26.

"Review of *Waiting to Exhale*." *Publishers Weekly* (March 23, 1992): 58.

Whitaker, Charles. "Exhaling! Terry McMillan Hits Jackpot in Romance and Finance." *Ebony* (April 2001): 154–157.

✹ Larry McMurtry

BORN: *1936, Wichita Falls, Texas*

NATIONALITY: *American*

GENRE: *Fiction, screenplays*

MAJOR WORKS:
The Last Picture Show (1966)
Terms of Endearment (1975)
Lonesome Dove (1985)

Overview

Larry McMurtry's work is marked by his imaginative connections with the American West. Throughout his career McMurtry has focused on the golden days of cowboys and trail driving and on the transitional time between the early rural life and the new urban one, looking for values to replace the old ones that have disappeared.

Works in Biographical and Historical Context

A Bookish Child in a Bookless Place McMurtry was born June 3, 1936, in Wichita Falls, Texas. He grew up in Archer City, Texas, in a family that had ranched in

Larry McMurtry *McMurtry, Larry, photograph. © Jerry Bauer.*
Reproduced by permission.

what became the most important tools in his workshop—the powers of storytelling and humor. He also discovered one of the chief themes of his work, what he calls the tragic theme of the twentieth- and twenty-first-century Southwest—the end of a way of life signaled by the move off the land. Climbing on the barn at night, young McMurtry looked out across the Texas prairie and sent his imagination with the night trains to Los Angeles and the eighteen-wheelers pointed toward Fort Worth.

College and Teaching In 1954, after graduating with honors from Archer City High School, McMurtry enrolled briefly at Rice University in Houston, where encountering the library became a transforming experience for the boy. Still, he did not stay at Rice, saying his "chief nightmare was a freshman math course (the calculi, trig., analytics) which I failed completely." He transferred to North Texas State College (now the University of North Texas), where he studied literature.

McMurtry also published in an unauthorized literary magazine, the *Coexistence Review*, and the student magazine, the *Avesta*. During his last two years at North Texas State College, McMurtry said he wrote and burned fifty-two "very bad" short stories. Next, he turned to his cowboy past and wrote a story about the destruction of a cattle herd and another about a cattleman's funeral. He then decided to connect the two stories and extend them into a novel. McMurtry sent the manuscript to the *Texas Quarterly*, which was publishing book supplements, and Frank Wardlaw read it and sent it on to a friend at Harper Brothers in New York, who decided to publish it. The novel was released as *Horseman, Pass By* (1961) and was the basis for the acclaimed film *Hud* (1963), starring Paul Newman.

McMurtry went back to Rice University for graduate school and received an M.A. in 1960. He then accepted a Wallace Stegner creative-writing scholarship at Stanford University, and in 1961 he returned to Texas and taught at Texas Christian University in Fort Worth. He began teaching at Rice in 1963 and remained there for most of the 1960s, except for 1964–1965, when he was awarded a Guggenheim Fellowship for creative writing. At Rice University, McMurtry taught literature and creative writing.

Transitions in Life and Writing During the 1960s, McMurtry wrote several well-received novels. In 1969 McMurtry left Texas and moved to Waterford, Virginia, forty miles northwest of Washington, and for most of the 1970s he lived there with his son, James. Later, he moved into the District of Columbia and lived above Booked Up, his rare-book store in Georgetown. He taught briefly at George Washington and American Universities. McMurtry's next three novels followed his personal move, making his transition from examining the effect of change on the frontier values of small towns in Texas to considering the difficult adaptation of the new, urban West to the loss of those values.

Texas for three generations. Archer City was a small town ruled by religious fundamentalism and sexual strictures. The time spent with his friends and acquaintances in Archer City was as important for McMurtry as was the time spent with his family. Classmate Ceil Slack Cleveland is usually acknowledged as the model for Jacy Farrow in *The Last Picture Show* (1966) while Bobby Stubbs provided the outline for Sonny in the first novel and later for Duane in *Texasville* (1987). Before Stubbs's death in the early 1990s McMurtry inscribed books to him, always suggesting that Stubbs was the model for one character or another. Ceil Slack lived only two blocks away from Larry, and they competed for various school awards. Ceil's mother, a poet and painter, encouraged Larry's friendship, and he dedicated *Anything for Billy* (1988) to her and his first agent.

McMurtry was admittedly out of place among the hardworking but anti-intellectual west Texans who lived along the area called Idiot Ridge. He was "insufficiently mean" in a world where meanness meant survival, where violence against animals in the form of bronco-busting, calf throwing, cattle dehorning, and castrating were all part of daily life. He was a "bookish boy" in a "bookless" part of the state. However, he did learn about Southwesterners' violence, intolerance, hypocrisy, and puritanical attitudes, as well as their strength of character, endurance, emphasis on hard work, courage, and particularly

LITERARY AND HISTORICAL CONTEMPORARIES

McMurtry's famous contemporaries include:

Cormac McCarthy (1933–): McCarthy is an American novelist known for his brutal and exacting depictions of violence and the seamier side of life in the South and in the West, particularly in the novels that make up his Border Trilogy.

Elmore Leonard (1925–): A fiction writer whose first successes were Westerns, Leonard has enjoyed even greater success as a crime novelist and screenwriter.

Václav Havel (1936–): Havel is a Czech writer and politician who served as the last president of Czechoslovakia (1989–1992) and the first president of the Czech Republic (1993–2003).

Raymond Carver (1938–1988): Carver was an American short-story writer whose fiction was influential in reviving interest in the short story form.

Peter Jennings (1938–2005): Jennings was a Canadian-born television news journalist best known for anchoring ABC's national nightly news.

In the 1980s, McMurtry began traveling around the country and maintained apartments in California for his movie-writing connections, and in Arizona, after developing a close friendship with the Native American writer Leslie Marmon Silko. In 1985, he published *Lonesome Dove*, a novel that he had been tinkering with for years and which had originally started as a screenplay idea.

McMurtry's life changed following the publication of *Lonesome Dove*, when Archer City, his hometown, after years of being unfavorably characterized by McMurtry, embraced him and welcomed him home. After excoriating his home town in *The Last Picture Show* and portraying it as small-minded and "bookless" in his collection of essays, *In a Narrow Grave* (1968), McMurtry and his family began to transform the small county seat into a literary oasis amid dry, mostly flat cattle and oil country. He renovated the Archer City golf course clubhouse for his residence and bought many of the downtown buildings to house a rare-book operation that is one of the largest in the Southwest.

Late-Career Transition After winning the Pulitzer Prize for *Lonesome Dove*, McMurtry wrote numerous novels alternating between frontier tales and contemporary sequels to his previous works. Early in 1999, he published *Duane's Depressed*, a sequel to *The Last Picture Show* and *Texasville* (1987). Soon afterwards, McMurtry came out with *Crazy Horse* (1999), a biography of the famous Sioux warrior, and then *Walter Benjamin at the*

Dairy Queen: Reflections at Sixty and Beyond (1999), a memoir on cowboying, writing, storytelling, reading and book collecting, aging, and fatherhood. Since 2001, when he released *Sin Killer*, he has alternated between writing fiction and nonfiction.

Works in Literary Context

After garnering initial celebrity by writing about the passing of the Southwest known to the cowboy, McMurtry changed his focus to urban novels cut off from the old Southwest—a change that did not help his critical reputation. In the 1980s McMurtry returned to the settings and themes he had rejected, and the critical fame he had enjoyed previously came back as well.

Through all of his work, McMurtry's Texas background looms large. Growing up on a ranch and learning the ranch work ethic, in which every day began early and ended late, McMurtry approaches his work with intensity and tenacity. In the process he has become the best-known Texas writer of the twentieth century. Fictional Thalia and Hardtop County have become as recognizable to many readers as Faulkner's Jefferson and Yoknapatawpha County.

Demythologizing the West McMurtry has been called the best regional writer that the Southwest has produced, yet his novels are significantly different than such classics of the Western genre as Owen Wister's *The Virginian* (1902) and Jack Schaefer's *Shane* (1949). While these earlier cowboy novels idealized their protagonists by endowing them with epic-sized courage and nobility, McMurtry's writing—particularly his use of satire, black humor, and frequently hyper-realistic detail—demythologizes the West. He portrays people who share the basic human experiences of dissatisfaction, frustration, loneliness, and loss. For example, McCrae and Call, the two cattlemen at the heart of *Lonesome Dove*, display acts of both heroism and pigheadedness in equal measure.

Escape and Return Escape and return—looking-to-leave and longing-to-return—characterize much of McMurtry's life and writing. Drawn to place, McMurtry demonstrates in his work the mythic pattern of escape and return to his "blood's country," his homeland. This is shown most eloquently in *Lonesome Dove*: the novel is set in motion by McCrae and Call's decision to drive a herd of cattle north to Montana and ends with one of the men returning to Texas to bury the other in the place most special to him. Throughout much of his life, McMurtry has found his home territory an awkward, uneasy place. Growing up in Texas created productive tension between his love for the land that nourished him and an equally strong aversion to the narrow-minded elements of his heritage. In his work, he approaches these subjects with a "contradiction of attractions" that produces an "ambivalence as deep as the bone."

Works in Critical Context

Throughout his career, McMurtry has been given mostly praise by critics, and he is considered by many to be Texas's premier novelist. During his early career, as critics gave him high praise, McMurtry himself disparaged his works as juvenile, sentimental, over-edited, and poorly realized. Some critics have faulted McMurtry for inflating insignificant plots and for not fully exploring the important questions posed in his work, preferring instead to pursue the entertainment value of a situation. However, he is consistently praised for his skill in using language to evoke memorable people and places in painstaking, realistic detail.

The "Trash Trilogy" Three of McMurtry's mid-career novels—*Somebody's Darling* (1978), *Cadillac Jack* (1982), and *The Desert Rose* (1983), are often referred to as the "Trash Trilogy." Unlike much of McMurtry's work, these novels have no interconnected characteristics, but of all McMurtry's novels, these three have been generally maligned by critics. Calling them trash makes a ready grouping, and, in the long look at McMurtry's fiction, they are usually ranked low on the list of his achievements. However, as Mark Busby notes in his *Dictionary of Literary Biography* entry, "the term also mirrors the subject matter of the three novels—the tawdry, uncentered worlds of Hollywood and Las Vegas, and the trash and garbage through which Cadillac Jack McGriff sifts." While many critics have given these three books poor reviews, there were also some favorable reviews, and Busby asserts that "all three include commendable elements."

Lonesome Dove McMurtry is best known for his Pulitzer Prize-winning novel, *Lonesome Dove*, an epic tale of cowboy life that chronicles the events of a cattle drive from Texas to Montana during the 1870s. *Lonesome Dove* is the novel his critics had clamored for him to write since he first appeared on the literary scene in the 1960s, and the subject of the novel is the kind he had solidly attacked for fifteen years. Despite some critics' belief that McMurtry contradicted himself by denouncing novels about the past and then writing a novel about the past, *Lonesome Dove* was seen as both extending and transforming the genre. Reviewers observed that while McMurtry confined his story to the conventions of the Western genre, including such archetypal characters as the wily Indian villain Blue Duck and the good-hearted prostitute Lorena, at the same time, he imbued these familiar elements with new life, using them to construct a fresh and poignant story that helps deconstruct the familiar myths and legends of the Old West. Christopher Lehmann-Haupt, in his review for *The New York Times*, writes, "Many of the novel's episodes may smack a little of the tall tale. But Mr. McMurtry has a way of diverting the progress of his clichés in odd and interesting ways."

Responses to Literature

1. McMurtry has criticized his own early works as juvenile, sentimental, over-edited, and poorly real-

---

COMMON HUMAN EXPERIENCE

Throughout his career, McMurty has written about life in the West, depicting both the traditional ways as well as the disintegration of these traditions and the transition to contemporary, urban life. Here are some other works that show these traditional ways and some difficult transitions:

Giant (1956), a film by George Stevens. This film follows the changing lives and fortunes of a Texas family as it makes the transition of from ranching to the oil industry.

Centennial (1975), a novel by James Michener. This historical novel is an epic tale of the land, people, and history of Colorado which centers around the diverse inhabitants of a fictional town called Centennial.

All the Pretty Horses (1992), a novel by Cormac McCarthy. This novel tells the story of a young man who grew up on a West Texas ranch coping with the prospect of leaving the ranching life for a life in town.

---

ized. Read his first novel, *Horseman, Pass By*. Do you agree? Can any of his later writings be given these same criticisms?

2. A number of McMurtry's novels have been sequels to earlier works. In what ways do these sequels help develop the characters and stories more fully, and in what ways do they take away from the power of the originals? Have any of these sequels that changed the meanings and messages of the originals, and if so, are the changes for the better or the worse?

3. McMurtry has stated that he brings to his writing an "ambivalence as deep as the bone." Write an essay that identifies and discusses one or more of the ambivalent attitudes that McMurtry displays in his writings. Be sure to use concrete examples from his novels to demonstrate how this ambivalence plays out in his work.

4. Commentators have noted that McMurtry's cowboy novels both idealize their protagonists and demythologize the West. Write an argumentative essay that takes a stand on whether McMurtry's works, when taken as a whole, tend to glamorize or demythologize the Old West. Use specific examples from his work to support your position.

BIBLIOGRAPHY

Books

Busby, Mark. *Larry McMurtry and the West: An Ambivalent Relationship.* Denton, Tex.: University of North Texas Press, 1995.

Clifford, Craig Edward. *In the Deep Heart's Core: Reflections on Life, Letters, and Texas.* College Station, Tex.: Texas A & M University Press, 1985.

Erisman, Fred and Richard Etulain, eds. *Fifty Western Writers: A Bio-Bibliographical Sourcebook.* Westport, Conn.: Greenwood Press, 1982.

Jones, Roger. *Larry McMurtry and the Victorian Novel.* College Station, Tex.: Texas A & M University Press, 1994.

Landess, Thomas. *Larry McMurtry.* Austin, Tex.: Steck-Vaughn, 1969.

Lich, Lera Patrick Tyler. *Larry McMurtry's Texas: Evolution of the Myth.* Austin, Tex.: Eakin, 1987.

Neinstein, Raymond L. *The Ghost Country.* Berkeley, Calif.: Creative Arts, 1976.

Peavy, Charles. *Larry McMurtry.* Boston: Twayne/G. K. Hall, 1978.

Pilkington, William T. *My Blood's Country: Studies in Southwestern Literature.* Fort Worth, Tex.: Texas Christian University Press, 1973.

Taylor, Golden, ed. *A Literary History of the American West.* Fort Worth, Tex.: Texas Christian University Press, 1987.

Reynolds, Clay, ed. *Taking Stock: A Larry McMurtry Casebook.* Dallas, Tex.: Southern Methodist University Press, 1989.

Schmidt, Dorey, ed. *Larry McMurtry: Unredeemed Dreams.* Edinburgh, Tex.: Pan American University Press, 1978.

Periodicals

Lehmann-Haupt, Christopher. Review of *Lonesome Dove. The New York Times* (June 3, 1985): C20.

Terrence McNally   *McNally, Terrence, photograph. Ron Galella / WireImage / Getty Images.*

✺ Terrence McNally

BORN: *1939, St. Petersburg, Florida*

NATIONALITY: *American*

GENRE: *Drama*

MAJOR WORKS:

Bad Habits (1971)

The Ritz (1976)

Frankie and Johnny in the Claire de Lune (1987)

Kiss of the Spider Woman (1990)

Overview

Terrence McNally is a dramatist of diverse talents whose plays, whether classified as satire, farce, or melodrama, generally attack complacency, outmoded norms, institutions, and human folly by means of black humor and witty, acerbic dialogue. McNally's early plays, in which he examines the effects of current events upon individuals, are often angry, violent, and bitingly satirical. His later works, while remaining true to their author's savage wit, are lighter and more lyrical in tone and increasingly rely on references to New York and its theater community.

Works in Biographical and Historical Context

Early Interest in Music and Theater Terrence McNally was born on November 3, 1939, in St. Petersburg, Florida, but early in his life, his family moved to Corpus Christi, Texas, where McNally was educated. McNally's father operated a small beer distributorship, and by local standards the family was well-off. McNally remembers his childhood as a lonely one, in which he escaped into favorite radio programs, including *Let's Pretend*, *The Lone Ranger*, and *The Green Hornet*, as well as live broadcasts of operas from the Metropolitan Opera. He constructed a miniature model of the Metropolitan and re-created scenes on the stage that, he later recalled, "was more real than life."

McNally's parents encouraged his budding interest in music and theater. Both native New Yorkers, they took him on a visit to their hometown when he was six years old. He was treated to a performance of Irving Berlin's popular Broadway musical, *Annie Get Your Gun* (1946), an experience that McNally never forgot. On subsequent trips he saw as much theater as possible. When his parents journeyed to New York without him, they brought home theater programs and original-cast recordings of musicals and operas for his growing collection. McNally's mother was a high-school English teacher, and she arranged to give McNally and a few other interested classmates extra tutoring in the works of William Shakespeare. During his senior year in high school, McNally wrote a play based on the life of composer George Gershwin. McNally's love of music runs through virtually all of his works—operatic arias, especially, are called for in many of his scripts and the love of opera and its performers is central to his major works.

Working in the Theater World   In 1956 McNally entered Columbia University in New York City, where he majored in journalism. McNally graduated Phi Beta Kappa from Columbia in 1960 with a bachelor's degree. His first play, *The Roller Coaster*, was published in the *Columbia Review* in 1960, and he received a Henry Evans Traveling Fellowship from Columbia that same year. The Evans fellowship made it possible for McNally to spend six months writing in Puerto Vallarta, Mexico. In 1961 he sent samples of his writing to Molly Kazan, wife of director Elia Kazan and a playwright herself. She recognized his potential. McNally's comparative inexperience in theatrical matters led Molly Kazan to secure for him a position as a stage manager at the Actors Studio in New York, where her husband was teaching. McNally was entranced by his experience there. He met noted playwrights, including Edward Albee, William Inge, and Arthur Kopit, and such actors as Geraldine Page and Kim Stanley. He learned more about the roles of playwright, actor, director, designer, and particularly about dramatic structure; he began to apply this learning to his own writings. He also became personally involved for some time with Albee, although their relationship did not last. During the 1960s critics frequently noted the influence of Albee's style on McNally's early plays, although within a decade McNally developed his own distinct style as a dramatist.

In 1961 and 1962, McNally then worked as a tutor to the two teenage children of Nobel Prize-winning novelist John Steinbeck, when the Steinbeck family took a world tour. On returning to New York after the trip, McNally garnered some attention with one of his earliest short plays, *This Side of the Door* (1962), which won the Stanley Drama Award from the department of languages and literature at Wagner College in 1962. To make ends meet, McNally worked for nearly two years (1963–1965) as a movie critic for *Seventh Art* magazine in New York.

Recognition   McNally applied for and won a Guggenheim Fellowship in 1966. Throughout the 1960s and early 1970s he wrote several one-act plays. Most were produced either on stage or public television. The critical success of these works brought him increased recognition. He was a runner-up for a Drama Desk Award for most promising playwright in 1969 and received his second Guggenheim Fellowship that same year.

McNally had a major breakthrough as a playwright when he wrote his first full-length farce, *The Ritz* (1975). The play earned McNally several honors, including an Obie Award for Best Play, an American Academy of Arts and Letters Award, and a National Institute of Arts and Letters Award. Throughout the 1970s, McNally made forays into musical theater, with mixed results. Some of his productions were failures; others were hailed as witty and innovative.

McNally became vice president of the Dramatists Guild in 1981. His involvement with the welfare of playwrights and their works was set in somewhat ironic counterpoint with several of his works during the 1980s. These works were often satiric assaults on the New York theater world.

During the 1980s, McNally wrote increasingly for television, and as he did so, he explored some important social issues of the day, including the emergence of AIDS in America, and particularly among the homosexual community in New York. One of McNally's most effective television dramas was an expanded version of his short one-act play *Andre's Mother*, which was presented on the *American Playhouse* series on PBS in 1990. This drama won McNally a 1990 Emmy Award for its sensitive portrayal of the uncomfortable relationship between the mother of a young man, who has succumbed to AIDS, and his lover, whom she meets at her son's funeral.

Controversy   Throughout his writing career, McNally has always tackled compelling and controversial issues of the day, from the Vietnam War to AIDS. In the late 1990s, he stirred up controversy with the production of his play *Corpus Christi*, which featured a cast of gay characters in Corpus Christi, Texas, putting on a passion play about Jesus Christ's life. This drama set off a furor in the form of criticism from various Catholic organizations. The Manhattan Theatre Club, ostensibly concerned with the safety of its audience in the face of bomb threats, canceled the play. This action inspired a fierce response from the artistic community. Playwright Athol Fugard, who also had a play scheduled to appear in the same venue, withdrew his work in protest of the cancellation of *Corpus Christi*. Tony Kushner, author of *Angels in America* (1992), a play that had also faced similar attempts at censorship, criticized the Manhattan Theatre Club, also. In the face of stinging criticism from Fugard, Kushner, and other playwrights such as Craig Lucas, the Club put the play back on its schedule.

McNally continues to write plays, television scripts, and film screenplays, and in the twenty-first century he is considered a bastion of the New York theatrical community.

LITERARY AND HISTORICAL CONTEMPORARIES

McNally's famous contemporaries include:

Neil Simon (1927–): Simon is American playwright and screenwriter best known the comedies *The Odd Couple* (1965) and *Biloxi Blues* (1985).

Susan Sontag (1933–2004): Sontag was an American writer and political activist who created numerous controversies with her literary and political statements.

Raymond Carver (1938–1988): Carver was an American short-story writer identified with the "dirty realism" school of writing, which generally concerns working-class people and their everyday problems.

Anne Rice (1941–): Rice is an American novelist best known for writing popular vampire tales and other Gothic-style novels.

Tony Kushner (1956–): Kushner is a Pulitzer Prize-winning playwright best known for his drama *Angels in America* (1991).

COMMON HUMAN EXPERIENCE

Many of McNally's works have been satirical treatments of the New York theatrical world in which he lived and worked. Here are some other dramas that provide a critical view of the entertainment industry:

The Producers (1968), a film by Mel Brooks. This film satirizes the New York theater scene through the story of two theatrical producers who try to cheat their investors by intentionally producing a flop that unexpectedly becomes a hit.

Victor Victoria (1982), a film by Blake Edwards. This film, which tells the story of a struggling female singer who pretends to be a male female impersonator, satirizes the nightclub entertainment scene.

Entourage (2004), a television series by Doug Ellin. This series satirizes Hollywood through a look at a rising film star and the people who surround him.

Works in Literary Context

McNally established himself as a playwright with a light-comic gift in the mid-1960s and has matured into one of the most versatile and prolific playwrights in the American theater. Some critics have described him as the American Ben Jonson. (Jonson was an Elizabethan dramatist whose dark view of the contemporary human situation is tem-

pered by a strong vein of humor and satire.) One commentator wrote that McNally "is a playwright, not a polemicist. His view of humanity has to be as generous as that of anyone working in the American theater today."

From Biting Satire to Light Lyricism McNally first achieved prominence as a bitingly comic writer in 1968, when six of his plays were produced. His subjects dealt with the major upheavals of the 1960s and 1970s: the Vietnam War, the draft, middle-class morality, political revolution, presidential assassination, youth and rebellion, popular culture, and changes in sexual codes. McNally's characters in his earliest plays find themselves in a splintered and unfriendly world; the subjects of these works range from the disillusionments of the Vietnam era to the self-deluding popular culture of the late twentieth century. McNally has exhibited an increasingly compassionate and lyrical touch in his plays since the mid-1980s and a life-affirming viewpoint, remarkable for a gay dramatist writing in the midst of the AIDS pandemic. His more recent work is exuberant, lyrical, and absurd, sharply contrasting with the tone of outrage and anger noted in the beginning of his career.

Isolation Throughout his career, McNally has examined the isolation of the individual in contemporary life. He sees "people in a video shop checking out three or four films, and that's who we're going home with at night, this who-needs-anybody attitude, and that bothers me." His plays frequently feature characters fighting against loneliness and isolation with a combination of humor and acceptance of life's harsh realities. For example, in *Sweet Eros* (1968), McNally presents a man who was abandoned by a former lover and who drove his second lover to suicide; he now has kidnapped a woman and bound her to a chair. The man and the woman create a strange type of coexistence, in which both find relief from loneliness and isolation.

Works in Critical Context

McNally had a difficult time achieving critical recognition early in his career. Like most long-time playwrights, he has had his share of failures as well as successes. He is recognized, however, as an important voice in the New York theatrical scene and a playwright whose works have revealed much about the human condition. *New York Times* critic David Richards, in his piece "A Working Playwright Edges Into Fame," states that by the standards of contemporary drama McNally is "an anomaly—a playwright who continues to work regularly at his trade, who believes that a career in the theatre is 'its own reward'...and, most significantly, who grows more accomplished with each successive play." Actress Swoosie Kurtz, who has appeared in McNally's plays, has said his "vision celebrates the bravery of lonely souls; his voice resounds with the anguish and joy of life itself. Out of the mundane, he shapes the opera of the human heart."

And Things That Go Bump in the Night Though he would later meet with Broadway success, McNally's first Broadway play, *And Things That Go Bump in the Night* (1964), was reviewed harshly by critics and ran for only two weeks on Broadway. An anonymous critic for *Time* identifies the play as "coming from the Kopit-Albee playmaking kit" with the result "worse than theatrical incest: it is rather like spreading disease in the guise of curing corruption." John Simon, writing in *New York Magazine*, calls the play "the prize horror of the season," and Wilfrid Sheed of *Commonweal* dismisses it as "a bad play." Some critics were savage, calling *And Things That Go Bump in the Night* "arrant balderdash" and "sick, sick, sick," while others were less emphatic. Writing for *Saturday Review*, Henry Hewes points out McNally's "talent for imagery and an ambitiousness of purpose" but finally concludes that he "appears to lack the discipline or skill necessary to achieve his devastatingly large intention." Despite these reviews, the play was revived twenty-one years later, after McNally had achieved greater success, in Washington, D.C., where it met with more appreciative critics who recognized the pointedly exaggerated qualities of the play.

Bad Habits In 1971 McNally's *Bad Habits*, a bill consisting of two one-act plays, *Ravenswood* and *Dunelawn*, was given a small production at the John Drew Theatre in East Hampton, New York. The bill was well-received in East Hampton, and *Bad Habits* moved to an Off-Broadway production, opening at the Astor Place Theatre, and then returned to Broadway, at the Booth Theatre. *Bad Habits* won the Obie Award in 1974, and it earned McNally the Elizabeth Hull-Kate Warriner Award, a prize given annually by the Dramatists Guild Council for writers whose plays tackle controversial subject matter.

Bad Habits also gave McNally one of his first major critical triumphs. In a review for *Cue* critic Marilyn Stasio applauds the "non-stop hilarity" of the two plays and stresses that although "both plays are casually constructed, the character satire is dead-on accurate, and for all its zaniness has a niceness of logical clarity that is akin to classical farce." Harold Clurman describes McNally as "one of the most adept practitioners of the comedy of insult.... His plays are spoofs and at times quite funny." Similar sentiments would be expressed by critics throughout the rest of McNally's career.

Responses to Literature

1. Commentators note that McNally's early tone of anger and outrage changed to a more lyrical and satirical one later in his career. In what ways can the concerns of his early works be seen in his later works? Which of his early influences are still present in his later works?

2. Much of McNally's work was reviewed at the time of its original production, often making immediate issues the critics' central concerns. Choose one of McNally's works from a previous decade and write a review from the present-day perspective, focusing your critical analysis on how well the work stands up to the test of time and illuminates current problems.

3. McNally has been cited as a dramatist who explores difficult issues about contemporary life. Write an essay that describes some of the issues that he has probed with his works and assesses the effectiveness of his commentaries on contemporary life.

BIBLIOGRAPHY

Books

Anderson, Michael and others, eds. *Crowell's Handbook of Contemporary Drama*. New York: Crowell, 1971.

Bersani, Leo. *Homos*. Cambridge, Mass.: Harvard University Press, 1995.

Bigsby, C. W. E. *Modern American Drama. 1945-2000*. New York: Cambridge University Press, 2000.

Clum, John M. *Acting Gay: Male Homosexuality in Modern Drama*. New York: Columbia University Press, 1994.

Doty, Alexander. *Making Things Perfectly Queer: Interpreting Mass Culture*. Minneapolis: University of Minnesota Press, 1993.

Eddleman, Floyd Eugene, ed. *American Drama Criticism: Interpretations 1890–1977*. Hamden, Conn.: Shoe String, 1979.

Kostenbaum, Wayne. *The Queen's Throat: Opera, Homosexuality, and the Mystery of Desire*. New York: Poseidon, 1993.

Lehman, Peter. *Running Scared: Masculinity and the Representation of the Male Body*. Philadelphia.: Temple University Press, 1993.

Salem, James M. *A Guide to Critical Reviews: Part I: American Drama, 1909–1982*. Metuchen, N.J: Scarecrow Press, 1984.

Sedgwick, Eve Kosofsky. *Tendencies*. Durham, N.C.: Duke University Press, 1993.

Sinfield, Alan. *Out on Stage. Lesbian and Gay Theatre in the Twentieth Century*. New Haven, Conn.: Yale University Press, 2000.

Weston, Kath. *Families We Choose: Lesbians, Gays, Kinship*. New York: Columbia University Press, 1991.

Zinman, Toby Silverman, ed. *Terrence McNally: A Casebook*. New York: Garland, 1997.

✸ D'Arcy McNickle

BORN: *1904, St. Ignatius, Montana*

DIED: *1977, Albuquerque, New Mexico*

NATIONALITY: *American, Native American*

GENRE: *Fiction, nonfiction*

MAJOR WORKS:

The Surrounded (1936)

They Came Here First (1949)

The Indian Tribes of the United States (1962)

Overview

D'Arcy McNickle is regarded as one of the founders of Native American literature and ethnohistory. The product of two cultures, part white and part American Indian, but belonging to neither, he was a writer, historian, policymaker, activist, and educator. His life and work symbolized the potential to bridge two societies and allowed for the survival of the modern Indian and the recognition of tribal culture by American society.

Works in Biographical and Historical Context

Conflicting Identities McNickle was born on January 18, 1904, in St. Ignatius, Montana. His mother, Philomene, was half Cree Indian and half French, the daughter of a recognized half-breed family that had fled Canada after the defeat of the Indians in the Louis Riel Rebellion of 1885. In 1905 his mother was adopted, along with D'Arcy and his two sisters, by the Confederated Salish and Kootenai tribes, and they were listed on the tribal rolls at the Flathead Reservation. His father was a rancher-farmer of Scots-Irish descent, and, although he lived on the reservation and took advantage of the tribal gifts of land made to his family under the Dawes Act, William McNickle was intolerant of his wife and children's heritage. Thus, D'Arcy's parents were often at odds, and this conflict served to aggravate the conflict within him between his Cree and white identities.

Assimilation McNickle and his sisters attended the Jesuit mission school on the Flathead reservation, along with the other Salish and Kootenai children, until their parents divorced. In the custody of his mother, McNickle was enrolled in the Salem Indian Trading School in Chemawa, Oregon, where he was indoctrinated in the ways of white society. At the time, the Chemawa School was one of the schools for Indian children dedicated to the eradication of Indian culture. The children were not allowed to speak in their native language or to have any reminders of their Indian heritage. This assimilation of culture was just one way the U.S. government attempted to subsume distinct Indian culture into mainstream American culture. During this time, McNickle's ties with his Native American heritage were severed at the behest of both of his parents; his father wanted him to grow up "civilized," and his mother, despite her own mixed heritage, encouraged him to adopt white ways so that he would fare better in life. When his mother, who had divorced his father in 1914, married a white man, Gus Dahlberg, three years later, McNickle took his stepfather's surname.

Education and Travels On graduating from the Chemawa school in 1921, McNickle enrolled at the University of Montana, perhaps the first recognized Native American to do so. His interest in writing and historical narrative was stimulated in college. From 1921 to 1925, he studied literature and history. For a poetry class taught by Robert Frost, he wrote an award-winning poem, "Old Isidore," celebrating his maternal grandfather. He also was on the staff of the university's literary journal, *The Frontier*, in which he published some of his poems and two short stories.

Recognizing McNickle's promise and persistence, one of his professors recommended that he go to England to finish his studies. As he had no other way of funding the trip or his tuition, McNickle sold his allotment of tribal lands, a decision he later regretted. He arrived at Oxford in 1925, but the university would not accept enough credits from the University of Montana to allow him to finish his degree. For several months he traveled through England and France. Returning to the United States, McNickle did not go back to Montana to complete his studies; instead, he went to New York City, where he lived for nine years, writing for encyclopedias and newsletters and performing various editorial duties. He also took classes at Columbia University, where he became interested in American history, Native American studies, and Indian-white relations. In 1931 he took advantage of an opportunity to study literature and culture in Grenoble, France.

Writing a Memoir In 1931, as the Great Depression was deepening, McNickle started work on a largely autobiographical novel in which he examined the conflict between his Native American heritage and white society. He struggled for more than five years through revisions and title changes to produce his most highly regarded work, *The Surrounded* (1936). Harcourt, Brace and Company declined the manuscript but said that "perhaps it was the beginning of a new Indian literature," foretelling the impact McNickle's works have on American Western literature and on the public perception of Native Americans. The imminent birth of his daughter in 1933 led him to change his name from Dahlberg back to McNickle; his daughter was christened Antoinette Parenteau McNickle. Finally, in 1936, after having been rejected by more than a dozen publishers, *The Surrounded* was accepted for publication.

Government Work In 1935 McNickle was hired to compose pamphlets about American landmarks for the Federal Writers Project. This government program was part of the New Deal, a series of initiatives spearheaded by President Franklin Roosevelt in an attempt to provide jobs and revitalize the economy. At the same time, the Bureau of Indian Affairs (BIA) was making an effort to hire Native Americans to communicate the policies of the bureau to interned tribes, and in 1936, after applying twice, McNickle was offered a job as an administrative assistant and field representative at the bureau under Commissioner John Collier. At the BIA, McNickle applied his experience and expertise in a variety of capacities, from publishing articles and reviews in the agency's publication, *Indians at Work*, to meeting with tribal leaders to explain new policies. The response to McNickle's articles was positive, and he was often asked to contribute pieces on Native American affairs to psychological, educational, anthropological, religious, and social-welfare journals and poetry reviews. A supporter of Collier's Indian New Deal programs, which he thought would ensure the survival of Indian culture while encouraging tribes to take advantage of modern opportunities, McNickle worked to educate Indian leaders on what the policy would mean to them.

In 1944, McNickle cofounded the National Congress of American Indians, and five years later, he published his second book, *They Came Here First: The Epic of the American Indian* (1949), the first historical survey of Indian-white relations written from a Native American perspective. During this time, McNickle continued to work for the BIA. However, with the Great Depression now well ended and many New Deal programs being phased out by a more conservative federal government, Collier was replaced at the BIA by a director who initiated a "termination policy" to do away with most of the bureau's programs and end all government obligations to the recognized tribes. McNickle left the BIA at that point to become executive director of American Indian Development, Inc., and to head a health education and community development project on a Navajo reservation near Crownpoint, New Mexico.

Working and Writing for Indian Causes McNickle continued to write, publishing forty-six articles while working on the Crownpoint Project, mentoring promising youngsters who later became distinguished anthropologists, and visiting remote reservations in an advisory capacity. In 1959 McNickle and Harold E. Fey published *Indians and Other Americans: Two Ways of Life Meet.* In 1961 McNickle wrote the Declaration of Indian Purpose for an all-Indian conference in Chicago, and he worked with the Indian Claims Commission. In addition to such journals as *American Anthropologist* and *The Nation*, his work frequently appeared in the international publication *American Indigena*. His 1962 book, *The Indian Tribes of the United States*, addressed the theme of enduring ethnicity during an era when the movement to assimilate Indian culture was prevalent and the government was continuing the termination policy that would break up reservations, eradicate tribal government, cease federal aid and ultimately subsume the culture.

McNickle was awarded an honorary doctorate of science by the University of Colorado in 1966 for his work in applied anthropology. Later that year he accepted the invitation of the University of Saskatchewan to establish and head its anthropology department. McNickle was named a fellow of the American Anthropologist Association, and, after retiring from the University of Saskatchewan and moving to Albuquerque, New Mexico, in 1971, he became the founding director of the Native American Research Center at the Newberry Library in Chicago. In October of 1977, when McNickle failed to arrive in Chicago for a Newberry Library board meeting, board members called the Albuquerque police, who discovered that McNickle had died of a heart attack at his home several days previously.

LITERARY AND HISTORICAL CONTEMPORARIES

McNickle's famous contemporaries include:

John Dos Passos (1896–1970): Dos Passos was an American novelist whose nonlinear and stream-of-consciousness style had a major influence on twentieth century fiction.

William Faulkner (1897–1962): Faulkner was an American author known for his elaborate writing style and his detailed depiction of fictional Yoknapatawpha County in works like *The Sound and the Fury* (1929); he won the Nobel Prize in Literature in 1949.

Langston Hughes (1902–1967): Hughes was an African-American writer best known for his literary influence during the Harlem Renaissance.

John Steinbeck (1902–1968): Steinbeck was an American writer widely credited with being one of the best-known and widely-read writers of the twentieth century; he was granted the Nobel Prize in Literature in 1962.

Mourning Dove (1888–1936): Mourning Dove was a Native American author who wrote one of the first novels by and about a Native American female, *Cogewea the Half-Blood* (1927).

Works in Literary Context

Commentators credit McNickle, along with Mourning Dove and John Joseph Matthews, with being one of the first important Native American writers, paving the way for such authors as M. Scott Momaday and Louise Erdrich. McNickle's interests in Native American culture and cross-cultural communication colored his life's work. His career with the government was oriented toward giving Indians more opportunities and educating the public regarding Indian culture. He crafted novels and papers that both argued his political and philosophical points and satisfied his muse.

Conflicting Self-Identity Being part white and part Native American, McNickle experienced a conflict of self-identity. This impacted each different role McNickle took on, from writer and historian to policymaker and activist, as if the quest for his cultural identity needed more than one venue for its expression. Even though his imaginative writing was often put off in favor of his work with Indian affairs, his fiction was a reflection of his work with the government to improve the life of reservation Indians. In many of his works, including *The Surrounded*, he portrayed

COMMON HUMAN EXPERIENCE

Many of McNickle's works traced the effects of white culture on Native American culture. Here are some other works that explored similar issues:

Bury My Heart at Wounded Knee: An Indian History of the American West (1970), a nonfiction work by Dee Brown. This book, which chronicles the settling of the West based on eyewitness reports from the Native Americans who lived there, brought a new perspective to the historical perception of the American frontier and changed the attitude of scholars toward the history of the West by focusing on the racism, deception, and carelessness of the white settlers and United States government.

Trail of Tears: The Rise and Fall of the Cherokee Nation (1989), a nonfiction book by John Ehle. This book about the removal of the Cherokee tribe to the West also provides a portrayal of the Cherokee nation itself, including Native American legend, lore, and religion.

Native American Testimony: A Chronicle of Indian-White Relations from Prophecy to the Present, 1942–2000 (1999), a nonfiction book by Peter Nabokov. This book presents a history of relations between Native Americans and European Americans through Native American eyes and with Native American voices.

the very same identity issues arising from mixed race that he himself experienced.

Harshness and Hope McNickle's historical works present a Native American history to complement and protest against mainstream American history. His tone is realistic, almost pessimistic; as he explained: "I am writing of the West, not of Indians primarily, and certainly not of the romantic West which the best-selling authors have exploited to the detriment of a rational understanding." His works depict the harshness of rural life in the West and the tragedy of reservation life, but he also wrote optimistically about moving Native Americans into the modern world and finding them a place in an urban society.

In this way, McNickle's fiction mixes a sense of impending doom in the face of cultural extinction with a glimmer of hope for adaptation and survival of a modern Indian culture. His themes are amazingly similar throughout his works, from the genesis of his writing career to the end of his life. Seeing the decay of Native American culture around him and observing the wretched existence of his friends, McNickle sought to flee Native American life and achieve the American dream. Eventually, armed with knowledge and experience, he returned, albeit metaphorically, to his Native American heritage. When two roads

were offered, McNickle made a third: he neither held to the "old ways" nor converted to the "white ways." Instead, he learned from both and created himself as a modern Native American. Struggling to temper his romantic sensitivity with the often tragic reality of the Indians' situation that he knew so well, he finally achieved a balance between the two in his fiction.

Works in Critical Context

McNickle was widely praised for his insight into the relations between whites and Native Americans, particularly for exploring the struggles of Native peoples to retain their traditions and identity in the face of white cultural influences. He he has been given acclaim for both his fiction and nonfiction, with critics praising the use he made of genuine Native American materials. Reviewers generally found his novels to be compelling and not overly sentimental, and they have noted his delicate handling of the differences between Native and non-Native perspectives.

The Surrounded The reviews of McNickle's first book, *The Surrounded*, were generally favorable, especially mentioning McNickle's fine descriptions of western life and landscape, though some of the reviewers thought that the novel's plot could have been stronger and more convincing. Pulitzer Prize winner Oliver La Farge wrote of *The Surrounded*, "Perhaps the most interesting aspect of McNickle's book is his success in capturing the whole in small compass by the exercise of a thoroughly artistic selection." None of the other reviewers, however, did more than give passing mention to the Indian themes of the novel.

Responses to Literature

1. Commentators noted that McNickle's historical works presented a different perspective than mainstream American history written up to that point. In what ways has mainstream history changed to reflect the perspectives introduced by writers like McNickle, and in what ways do his historical works still represent an outsider's view even today?

2. McNickle came from a mixture of ethnic and cultural heritages, yet he chose to focus his life's work on his Native American identity. In what ways, if any, were his efforts on behalf of Native American culture a reflection of his mixed heritage?

3. McNickle was involved in government efforts during the 1930s and 1940s to ensure the survival of Native American culture, but he left the Bureau of Indian Affairs in the 1952 when that agency's policies changed. Write an essay that traces the changes in federal policy on Native Americans from 1952 through the end of the twentieth century.

4. McNickle was noted for discussing the struggles of Native peoples to retain their traditions and identity in the face of white cultural influences. Using your

library or the Internet for research, write an essay discussing whether or not Native Americans since McNickle's time have been successful at retaining their traditions and identity.

BIBLIOGRAPHY

Books

Owens, Louis. *Other Destinies: Understanding the American Indian Novel.* Norman, Okla.: University of Oklahoma Press, 1992.

Parker, Dorothy. *Singing an Indian Song: A Biography of D'Arcy McNickle.* Lincoln, Nebr.: University of Nebraska Press, 1992.

Purdy, John Lloyd. *The Legacy of D'Arcy McNickle: Writer, Historian, Activist.* Norman, Okla.: University of Oklahoma Press, 1996.

———. *WordWays: The Novels of D'Arcy McNickle.* Tucson, Ariz.: University of Arizona Press, 1990.

Ruppert, James. *D'Arcy McNickle.* Boise, Idaho: Boise State University, 1988.

Periodicals

Ortiz, Alfonso Ortiz. "D'Arcy McNickle (1907–1977): Across the River and Up the Hill." *American Indian Journal* (April 1978): 12–16.

Owens, Louis. "The Road to Nowhere: D'Arcy McNickle's *The Surrounded* and 'The Hungry Generations.'" *American Indian Quarterly* (Summer 1989): 239–248.

Vest, Jay Hansford C. "Feather Boy's Promise: Sacred Geography and Environmental Ethics in D'Arcy McNickle's *Wind from an Enemy Sky.*" *American Indian Quarterly* (Winter 1993): 45–67.

⊛ John McPhee

BORN: *1931, Princeton, New Jersey*

NATIONALITY: *American*

GENRE: *Nonfiction*

MAJOR WORKS:

Encounters with the Archdruid (1971)
The Curve of Binding Energy (1974)
Coming into the Country (1977)
Annals of the Former World (1998)

Overview

John McPhee is a literary journalist and acclaimed essayist best known for his tetrology *Annals of the Former World* (1998), a study of American geology for which he won the Pulitzer Prize in 1999. As a member of the "New Journalism" movement of the 1960s and 70s, McPhee developed a subjective, accessible style with which he writes about diverse topics—from birch-bark canoes to basketball players to the orange industry—with a special

John McPhee   *AP Images*

emphasis on modern environmental issues. Aside from publishing more than twenty book-length works of nonfiction, McPhee is known for his contributions to *The New Yorker* magazine, where he has been a staff writer since 1965.

Works in Biographical and Historical Context

Immersed in Sports and Nature   John McPhee was born March 8, 1931 in Princeton, New Jersey. McPhee's father, Harry, was a doctor with a specialty in sports medicine who treated Princeton athletes and was a member of the university faculty. As a boy, McPhee spent much of his time biking around campus, hiking in the woods near his home, and attending football and basketball practices with his father. He would later reflect that these aspects of his New England childhood had a profound affect on his writing and in particular his eclectic choices of journalistic subject matter. In an unpublished 1986 interview with Norman Sims, McPhee observed, "If you make a list of all the work I've ever done, and put a little mark beside things that relate to activities and interests I had before I was twenty, you'd have a little mark beside well over ninety percent of the pieces of writing." McPhee's immersion in sports, for example, led him to his first profiles of basketball star and Rhodes Scholar Bill Bradley, and, later, the world-class tennis players Arthur Ashe and Clark Graebner. Also, McPhee's outdoor activities at Keewaydin—a boys' camp where his father worked during the summers as a physician developed McPhee's appreciation for nature and sharpened his skills in the outdoors. He would later use this wilderness knowledge to write such works as *Encounters with the Archdruid* and "Swimming with Canoes" (1998).

McPhee attended Princeton High School, where he developed a love of reading and writing and was also active in sports. In high school, McPhee applied to only one college—Princeton University—and was accepted. Because he was barely seventeen, however, his parents sent him to Deerfield Academy in Massachusetts for an additional year of study before he entered college. There he was taught by Helen Boyden in chemistry and Frank Conklin in geology, who would have a profound influence on his later landmark tetrology *Annals of the Former World*, a geologic survey of the United States. At Deerfield he would also find the subject matter of one of his earliest books: *The Headmaster: Frank L. Boyden of Deerfield* (1966).

Early Writing and The New Yorker

McPhee entered Princeton with the class of 1953, and spent his sophomore and junior years in the creative-writing program, then headed by noted editor Richard Blackmur. At Princeton McPhee joined the staffs of various publications and eventually became editor of the *Princeton Tiger*, for which he wrote a column in imitation of *The New Yorker*'s "Talk of the Town" column. After graduating from Princeton, McPhee went to Cambridge University for a year of postgraduate study in English, and while there he played basketball and worked as a stringer for *Time* magazine. Returning to New York, he worked as a freelancer and wrote short stories.

As a young writer in New York, McPhee steadily submitted articles to *The New Yorker* and eventually took a job at *Time* magazine, where for seven years he wrote articles about people, art, show business, religion, education, and books. During this time he also wrote short stories that were published in *Playboy*, *Reporter*, and the *Transatlantic Review*.

In 1965, McPhee's acclaimed article about Bill Bradley, "A Sense of Where You Are," appeared in *The New Yorker* and proved to be a turning point in McPhee's career. In the same year that the article appeared, Bradley was named an All-American, led his Ivy League team into the Final Four of the NCAA tournament, was designated the most valuable player in the tournament, and was the number-one draft choice of the New York Knicks; Bradley turned down their lucrative offer in favor of a Rhodes Scholarship. McPhee's article continued to resonate in the public imagination, and he quickly expanded his original article into a book-length study of Bradley. Because of

his newfound success, McPhee was offered a coveted staff position at *The New Yorker*, a post that he has held consistently since 1965.

New Journalism and Environmentalism

McPhee's position at *The New Yorker* allowed him to explore many of his early interests, including sports, canoe camp in Vermont, and aviation, along with the subjects, such as geology, that he studied at Deerfield Academy and Princeton University. During the 1960s and 1970s McPhee came to be grouped with "New Journalists," who often wrote about offbeat subjects in a straightforward, accessible style. Over the years, McPhee's journalistic topics have ranged in subject matter from nuclear physics to oranges, from Russian art to Alaskan history, and from birch-bark canoes to parachutes. McPhee also began to distinguish himself as a writer who was particularly attentive to the environmental concerns raised by the scientific community. Though McPhee has stated in interviews that he does not consider himself an ecological activist per se, much of his work focuses on conservation and preservation, the affects of pollution, and man's relationship to nature.

These concerns also influence the more than twenty book-length works of nonfiction that McPhee has published since 1965. McPhee has published acclaimed regional travelogues, including *The Pine Barrens* and *Coming Into the Country* (1977), as well as biographical profiles, including *A Sense of Where You Are* (1965) and *Encounters with an Archdruid* (1977), and the Pulitzer Prize–winning tetrology *Annals of the Former World*. He currently continues to write and teach classes at Princeton University.

Works in Literary Context

Throughout his long career as an author and staff writer for *The New Yorker*, McPhee was closely associated with the style of "New Journalism," through which nonfiction writers sought to fuse a subjective writing style with often offbeat subject matter. Unlike his contemporaries Tom Wolfe and Hunter S. Thompson, who have focused their nonfiction works on the counterculture of the 1960s, John McPhee wedded the genres of adventure and nature writing to the style of New Journalism, creating accessible pieces that both entertain readers and inform them about environmental issues.

Biographical Profiles of Eccentrics and Idealists

Throughout McPhee's career, critics have noted that the writer possesses a laudable talent for biographical writing, and that his choice of living subjects are diverse and engaging. In 1965, McPhee launched his publishing career with *A Sense of Where You Are: A Profile of William Warren Bradley* an early profile of the basketball player who would later lead the New York Knicks to win two NBA championships, be elected to the Basketball Hall of Fame in 1982, become a United States senator from New Jersey, and run for the Democratic nomination for president in 2000. Critic James N. Null has noted that this early work by McPhee established the holistic style that he would develop for his biographical sketches: "The title of McPhee's book, *A Sense of Where You Are*, applies to both Bradley's play on the court and his life off the court," he wrote. "In other words, Bradley has a sense of self, purpose, and direction in life, and this is true of almost all of McPhee's admirable subjects." McPhee continued to present acclaimed, well-researched biographical portraits of individuals for *The New Yorker*. In 1971 he published perhaps his most famous book-length biographical work, *Encounters with the Archdruid*, a portrait of environmentalist and conservationist David Brower, for which McPhee was nominated for a National Book Award.

In his essay on McPhee in *Literary Selves: Autobiography and Contemporary American Nonfiction* (1993), Stull notes that, in his writing, "McPhee may assume . . . the roles of limited participant, foil to more knowledgeable informants, and translator of arcane material to an intelligent but uninformed audience, but his most critical role is that of witness to his subjects' performances, which centers almost exclusively around their commitment to a job or calling."

Regional Writing Several of John McPhee's most acclaimed works are dedicated to capturing the spirit, landscape, and culture of a particular geographical region: *The Pine Barrens* (1968), for example, focuses on the interplay between the ecology and human culture of southern New Jersey, while *The Crofter and the Laird* (1970) describes McPhee's ancestral homeland of Colonsay, a small island in the Hebrides of Scotland. Similarly, *Coming into the Country* profiles the wilderness and industries of Alaska. In all of these works, McPhee fuses descriptions of the region's landscape with its past and present cultural history, as well as vivid descriptions of the modern mode of life of its current residents. McPhee combines interviews with residents with his own firsthand experiences of the region to extensive research of the area's history and politics. As with most of his writing, these pieces pay particular attention to man's relationship with nature.

Works in Critical Context

Using his talent for narrative and vivid characterizations, John McPhee is often regarded as the journalistic liaison between the research specialist and the lay reader. As Michiko Kakutani of the *New York Times* has written, McPhee uses his "pleasantly flexible technique" to both entertain and enlighten readers. In the January 1978 issue of the *Atlantic Monthly* critic Benjamin DeMott commented that "John McPhee . . . has become the name of a standard by which ambitious magazine journalism is now judged."

Encounters with the Archdruid In 1971 McPhee published *Encounters with the Archdruid*, a biographical profile of environmentalist David Brower that would earn McPhee a nomination for the National Book Award. The book was praised primarily for its innovative narrative struc-

ture, which portrayed Brower through his encounters with three other people. McPhee arranged three wilderness journeys with Brower and his "natural enemies"—in Glacier Peak Wilderness of Washington State he traveled with Charles Park, a geologist and mineral engineer, "who believes that if copper were found under the White House,

LITERARY AND HISTORICAL CONTEMPORARIES

McPhee's famous contemporaries include:

Rachel Carson (1907–1964): Carson was a biologist and environmental activist. She is best known for her 1962 treatise *Silent Spring*. She is recognized as one of the first individuals to use nature writing to raise public awareness about such issues as dangerous pesticides and pollution.

Wendell Berry (1934–): Berry is an American poet, novelist, essayist, farmer, and environmentalist who writes frequently about the complex relationship between humanity and the natural world.

Bill Bryson (1951–): Bryson is an American humorist and travel writer. Bryson is the author of the 1998 *A Walk in the Woods: Rediscovering America on the Appalachian Trail*, which documents his hike from Maine to Georgia.

Timothy Egan (1954–): Egan is an American novelist, journalist, and editorial writer best known for creating nonfiction works centered on environmental and moral issues. He won the 2006 National Book Award for his nonfiction book *The Worst Hard Time: The Untold Story of Those Who Survived the Great American Dust Bowl*.

Tom Wolfe (1931–): Wolfe is a noted American writer of novels and nonfiction. Wolfe was a pioneer of the New Journalism movement in the 1960s and 1970s. His well-known book *The Electric Kool-Aid Acid Test* (1968) depicts the experiences of a countercultural group led by writer Ken Kesey in the 1960s.

Hunter S. Thompson (1937–2005): Thompson was an American journalist and author, best known for his novel *Fear and Loathing in Las Vegas* (1972). He is credited with inventing gonzo journalism, a subjective form of writing in which the author injects himself into the subject matter.

Rick Bass (1958–): Bass is a novelist, essayist, and polemicist often regarded as one of America's most prominent environmental writers. Bass is best known for his novels *Where The Water Used to Be* and *The Watch*. A petroleum geologist and ecological activist, Bass is recognized and revered for fusing art and activism to advance wilderness preservation and management.

Cormac McCarthy (1933–): McCarthy is an American novelist known for depictions of the South and the West, particularly in the novels that make up his Border Trilogy (published between 1992 and 1998).

COMMON HUMAN EXPERIENCE

McPhee often writes nonfiction about his experiences in wilderness areas. Here are some other works that feature journeys to distant or remote places:

Into Thin Air (1996), a nonfiction book by John Krakauer. This account describes the author's catastrophic climb to the summit of Mount Everest in 1996.

A Walk in the Woods: Rediscovering America on the Appalachian Trail (1998), a nonfiction book by Bill Bryson. With his trademark wit and eye for detail, nature writer Bill Bryson relates his experiences hiking the Appalachian Trail between Maine and Georgia.

The Reader's Companion to Alaska (1997), a collection of essays edited by Alan Ryan. The essays in this collection are autobiographical accounts of travelers' experiences in the Alaskan frontier.

The Lost Explorer: Finding Mallory on Mount Everest (1999), a nonfiction book by Conrad Anker and David Roberts. This book recreates the 1999 expedition to find the body of famed British climber George Mallory, who perished on Everest in 1924. Though the body was well-preserved due to the cold climate of the mountain, it remains unclear whether or not Mallory became the first man to reach the summit of Everest.

South: A Memoir of the Endurance *Voyage*, autobiography by Ernest Shackleton. This memoir chronicles the extraordinary experiences of the 1914 British Imperial Trans-Antarctic Expedition. Shackleton's ship became embedded in ice, and he and his crew were stranded off Antarctica until 1917.

Road Fever (1991), a nonfiction book by Tim Cahill. This book chronicles the author's record-breaking drive from the southern tip of Argentina to Prudhoe Bay, Alaska.

the White House should be moved"; on Cumberland Island, off the coast of Georgia, with Charles Fraser, a land developer who despite his own interest in the land regards preservationists like Brower as druids, "religious figures who sacrifice people and worship trees"; and in Grand Canyon National Park, with Floyd Elgin Dominy, United States Commissioner of Reclamation, who openly admitted that he cannot stand the sound of open water. Throughout the book McPhee balances the principles presented by both Brower and his detractors, causing critic Mark C. Long to remark that "McPhee is less interested in the truth of Brower's position than in situating him in the ongoing cultural debates over the use of natural resources, development, and the damming of rivers."

Coming into the Country McPhee's book about his Alaskan experience, *Coming into the Country*, is among his most popular works. Ronald Weber, an American Studies professor who specializes in literary journalism, wrote that "the book's roots lie not so much in the effort to emulate the novel as in the attempt to extend the range of journalism while remaining within journalistic forms." *Coming into the Country* sealed McPhee's reputation as one of the best nature and cultural writers in America. Writing in the *New York Times* in November 1977, John Leonard said the book left him enchanted, dreaming of seal oil, caribou, the Yukon River, and grizzly bears. Edward Hoagland in the *New York Times Book Review* called *Coming into the Country* a masterpiece. He said McPhee must have been looking for a "big, long, permanent book, written while he was still in the midst of life and could go after it, because in peripatetic journalism such as McPhee's there is an adventurous, fortuitous element: where the writer *gets himself* and what he *stumbles on*."

Annals of the Former World During the 1980s and the 1990s McPhee worked on a series of books that in 1998 were collected together under the title *Annals of the Former World*. *Annals of the Former World* compiled four previously published books: *Basin and Range* (1981), *In Suspect Terrain* (1983), *Rising from the Plains* (1986), and *Assembling California* (1993) with a fifth and final section, *Crossing the Craton*. The omnibus comprises a geological cross section of North America at about the Fortieth Parallel. Each book, built around an account of travels in the field with a geologist, sketches an overall picture of the science of geology. These collected works are often considered McPhee's masterpiece. He was awarded the Pulitzer Prize for *Annals of the Former World* in 1999.

The collection has been praised both for its factual richness and its accessible style. *Annals of the Former World* begins with McPhee taking a "deceptively simple" road trip across the United States, observed *Los Angeles Times* critic Carolyn See. The author is accompanied by an accomplished geologist who points out the vast history of various western rock formations, and the "ideas do tumble out," according to Rachel Lehmann-Haupt in a *New York Times* article. Among the theories discussed in the collection is one that suggests that moving plates of the Earth will eventually cause one section of the west coast of America to shear off into the Pacific, making part of California an island, as Evan Connell explained in a *Washington Post Book World* review. McPhee covers these theories with ease. "His tone is affable, his meandering appropriate," noted Connell. According to T. H. Watkins of the *Washington Post Book World*, McPhee's *Annals of the Former World* forms a "four-volume literary pilgrimage" through both the remote and urban roots of America. McPhee's writing about the field of geology led writer Wallace Stegner to describe McPhee in a *Los Angeles Times Book Review* article as "our best and liveliest writer about the earth and the earth sciences."

Responses to Literature

1. John McPhee is considered one of the pioneers of literary journalism. Pick up the most recent copy of *The New Yorker* or *The Atlantic Monthly.* Compare the articles in these magazines to those written by McPhee in the 1960s and 70s. Can you trace McPhee's influence? What differences or innovations do you see in modern journalistic writing styles, and how do you account for them?

2. Critics often praise McPhee for his ability to create an authentic sense of the regions about which he writes, such as New Jersey, Alaska, and Scotland. Choose a region you know well and write a piece of literary journalism about it in imitation of McPhee's style. Be sure to include the region's history, a description of it's people, and remarks about the residents's relationship with nature. What difficulties do you encounter while composing the piece?

3. In his innovative biographical profile *Encounters with an Archdruid*, John McPhee studied David Brower through the viewpoints of three outsiders. Following this model, divide your class into groups of four and conduct interviews amongst yourselves, then construct a biography of a classmate based on these interviews. Do you find that you get a fair assessment of the individual about whom you are writing? How does this exercise make you reevaluate McPhee's narrative strategy?

BIBLIOGRAPHY

Books

Colley, John, ed. *Earthly Words: Essays on Contemporary American Nature and Environmental Writers.* Ann Arbor, Mich.: University of Michigan Press, 1994.

Elder, John, ed. *American Nature Writers*, vol. 1. New York: Scribners, 1996.

Kowalewski, Michael, ed. *Temperamental Journeys: Essays on the Modern Literature of Travel.* Athens, Ga.: University of Georgia Press, 1992.

Lounsberry, Barbara. *The Art of Fact: Contemporary Artists of Nonfiction.* Westport, Conn.: Greenwood Press, 1990.

Pearson, Michael. *John McPhee.* New York: Twayne, 1997.

Periodicals

Beem, Edgar Allen. "John McPhee on Maine: Conversation with the Archjournalist." *Maine Times* (November 1, 1985): 14–16.

Connell, Evan. Review of *Basin and Range.Washington Post Book World* (April 19, 1981): p. 4.

Hamilton, Joan. "An Encounter with John McPhee." *Sierra* (May/June 1990): 50–55, 92, 96.

Haynes, Jared. "The Size and Shape of the Canvas: An Interview with John McPhee." *Writing on the Edge* (Spring 1994): 109–25.

———. "The Size and Shape of the Canvas: An Interview with John McPhee (Part 2)." *Writing on the Edge* (Fall 1994): 108–25.

Pearson, Michael. "Twenty Questions: A Conversation with John McPhee." *Creative Nonfiction* (Fall 1993): 76–87.

See, Carolyn. Review of *Basin and Range. Los Angeles Times* (April 27, 1981): p. 8.

Stegner, Wallace. Review of *In Suspect Terrain. Los Angeles Times Book Review* (February 27, 1983): p. 1.

Watkins, T.H. Review of *Assembling California. Washington Post Book World* (March 12, 1995) p. 5.

✸ Herman Melville

BORN: *1819, New York, New York*

DIED: *1891, New York, New York*

NATIONALITY: *American*

GENRE: *Fiction, poetry*

MAJOR WORKS:
Moby-Dick (1851)
Billy Budd (1924)

Herman Melville   Melville, Herman, photograph. The Library of Congress.

Overview

Herman Melville died almost forgotten, although he had once been a popular author and had left behind ten notable books of prose fiction and four of verse. His reputation languished for nearly thirty years after his death, but since the revival of interest in him that began with his centennial in 1919, he has gathered increasing fame, especially for his metaphysical whaling novel, *Moby-Dick*. Much of his writing originates in his experiences as a common sailor and in the complex reactions of his lively mind to ageless spiritual questions.

Works in Biographical and Historical Context

Young Adventurer Born on August 1, 1819, in New York City, Herman Melville had a relatively comfortable childhood until his father's business failure and early death. Melville ended his formal education at age twelve to help support his family. He worked in the family fur business and as a bank clerk and also taught at various schools until, in 1839, he sailed as a cabin boy aboard a merchant ship bound for Liverpool, England. This experience, shocking in its revelation of squalor and human cruelty, inspired his fourth novel, *Redburn: His First Voyage* (1849). Melville's later journey to the South Seas, begun aboard the whaling ship *Acushnet*, provided the background for his greatest works. Finding conditions unbearable aboard the *Acushnet*, Melville deserted the ship in the Marquesas Islands and spent several months in captivity with a tribe of cannibalistic Polynesians. He finally escaped to a passing whaling vessel. Again appalled by the conditions at sea, Melville joined in a mutiny and was briefly imprisoned in Tahiti. He then moved on to Hawaii and later returned to New York aboard a U.S. Navy vessel.

The Writer Emerges Up to this point in his life, Melville had never contemplated a literary career; however, with no prospects on his return to the United States, he was encouraged by family and friends to write about his remarkable journeys. His first novels, *Typee: A Peep at Polynesian Life* (1846) and its sequel, *Omoo: A Narrative of Adventures in the South Seas* (1847), are fictionalized versions of his experiences in the Pacific. These novels were immediately successful and made Melville famous as the "man who lived among the cannibals"—a reputation he was never able to overcome and that interfered with the appreciation of his later works. Although they were generally praised for their excitement, romance, and splendid descriptions of the South Seas, *Typee* and *Omoo* infuriated members of the Christian missionary community, who resented Melville's negative portrayal of their motives and labors.

Melville married Elizabeth Shaw in 1847, and the couple settled in Pittsfield, Massachusetts, where they raised four children. It was there Melville made the acquaintance of author Nathaniel Hawthorne (who lived nearby in Lenox), and the two became friends. Melville drew much support from Hawthorne as he struggled with the creation of his most famous work, *Moby-Dick*, a complicated, ambitious novel about a mentally unbalanced whaling captain and his quest for revenge against a mythic white whale. Like his early novels of the sea, *Moby-Dick* was based on Melville's own experiences as a sailor. Unlike his earlier novels, *Moby-Dick* was a commercial flop—as was Melville's 1852 novel *Pierre*, which was pointedly attacked by critics. Though publishers became wary of his novels following these failrures, Melville published many short stories in periodicals and collected six of his best in *The Piazza Tales* (1856). *The Confidence-Man: His Masquerade* (1857) an allegorical satire of mid-nineteenth-century American life, was the last of Melville's novels to appear during his lifetime. To make money, Melville went on lecture tours from 1857 to 1860, mostly telling audiences about his experiences in the South Seas.

Career as a Poet Whereas Melville's career as a fiction-writer consumed a mere eleven years, his career as a poet unfolded over the final thirty-four years of his life. In 1860 he tried and failed to publish his first volume of poems. Melville's most topical and politically timely work did not reach a large reading public, though it was reviewed or noticed in many American and British publications. Having ceased to court a readership, Melville continued to shape his vision within the rigors of metrical verse. Written in the evenings while Melville was employed as a customs inspector in New York City, the eighteen-thousand-line *Clarel: A Poem and Pilgrimage in the Holy Land* (1876) grew out of Melville's own travels twenty years before. After retiring from government service in 1885, Melville turned his attention to an assortment of verse projects, publishing *John Marr and Other Sailors, with Some Sea-Pieces* (1888) and *Timoleon and Other Ventures in Minor Verse* (1891). At his death in September 1891 of heart failure, Melville left numerous manuscripts of poetry as well as the unpublished *Billy Budd*.

Works in Literary Context

A master of both realistic and allegorical narrative, Melville was also an incisive social critic and philosopher who strove to understand the ambiguities of life and to define the individual's relation to society and the universe.

Allegory and Symbolism The story of Moby-Dick is usually considered allegorical. An allegory is a kind of literary work in which people, objects, places, and actions in a narrative are symbolic of something outside the narrative of the story itself. Some famous allegories in English include John Bunyan's *The Pilgrim's Progress* (1678) and Nathaniel Hawthorne's "Young Goodman Brown" (1835). While the meaning of many allegories is readily apparent, the symbols in *Moby-Dick* are not so easily interpreted. The meaning of the white whale, and the importance of Captain Ahab's quest to kill him, have been, and continue to be, debated.

Sea Stories Melville's *Typee* and *Omoo* fall into the broad literary category of sea stories. Sea stories often feature plenty of action and adventure in the way of pirate attacks, shipwrecks, mutinies, and military battles. They also provide an excellent narrative framework for the consideration of philosophical and political questions, as a ship and its inhabitants can be seen as representative of humankind as a whole. Sea stories have been popular for hundreds of years, but enjoyed a particular surge in readership around the time of the Napoleonic Wars at the turn of the nineteenth century, since so many exciting naval battles occurred during that time and advances in ship building made worldwide sea travel more feasible. James Fenimore Cooper paved the way for the sea story in American literature with his 1824 novel *The Pilot* (the first of several sea novels by Cooper), a best-seller, like the sea stories written later by Melville. Popular twentieth-century sea stories include the eleven-book Horatio Hornblower series by C. S. Forester (published between 1937 and 1967) and the Aubrey-Maturin series by Patrick O'Brian (published between 1970 and 2004).

Works in Critical Context

When Melville died in 1891, he was almost unknown as a writer, and his accomplishments were not fully recognized for over a generation. A tremendous revival of interest in his work began in the 1920s, following the publication of Raymond Weaver's biography, *Herman Melville: Mariner and Mystic* (1921), and constitutes a dramatic reversal nearly unprecedented in American literary history. Melville's works, particularly *Moby-Dick*, have been the subject of innumerable interpretations, and the body of Melville criticism, already immense, continues to grow. Melville is now recognized as one of America's greatest writers, and *Moby-Dick* is widely acclaimed as a work of genius.

Moby-Dick *Moby-Dick* was initially conceived as a realistic narrative about sea life, but it took on a unique literary form as Melville progressed in its composition. As one reviewer said, "It is hardly a novel at all, but a strange combination of prose poem, history and encyclopaedia of the whale wisdom of the mid-nineteenth century." Many contemporary critics appreciated the novel's ambitious scope and inventive structure, while still feeling somewhat befuddled by it. As a reviewer for *London Britannia* wrote: "There is so much eccentricity in its style and in its construction, in the original conception and in the gradual development of its strange and improbable story, that we are at a loss to determine in what category of works of amusement to place it." Today's critics agree that the "eccentricity" of *Moby-Dick* is what marks it as a masterpiece. As critic Clark Davis notes, "Despite its difficult passages, complex philosophical content, and unusual and sometimes awkward form, the book has sustained contin-

---

LITERARY AND HISTORICAL CONTEMPORARIES

Melville's famous contemporaries include:

Edgar Allan Poe (1809–1849): Poe was an American writer best known for his macabre poems and short stories.

Charles Dickens (1812–1870): Dickens was a well-known British writer whose novels explored the social and economic conditions of Victorian Era England.

Henry David Thoreau (1817–1862): Thoreau was an American writer best known for his books *Walden* (1854), an exploration of natural living, and *Civil Disobedience* (1849).

Karl Marx (1818–1883): Marx was a German philosopher and social critic who was one of the founders of the modern communist movement.

Fyodor Dostoevsky (1821–1881): Dostoevsky was a Russian writer whose novels explored human psychology and universal philosophical questions.

Ulysses S. Grant (1822–1885): Grant was an American military leader and statesman who rose to the command of the Union Army during the Civil War, and who later became President of the United States.

---

uous and often extreme attention from readers for the last eighty years."

Billy Budd *Billy Budd*, left in manuscript at Melville's death and considered one of his finest works of fiction, was not published until 1924. It is the story of the execution of a young, popular sailor aboard an English warship. Its ambiguous ending and intriguing symbolism have made it the subject of intense debate among literary scholars interested in Melville's final views on such issues as justice, morality, and religion. As critic Logan Esdale notes, "Herman Melville's *Billy Budd* has produced an astonishing diversity of equally plausible interpretations. Most critics consider finally whether they approve or condemn Captain Vere's decision to try and execute the sailor Billy Budd for the murder of the officer John Claggart." While the rightness or wrongness of Captain Vere's decision is indeed the focus of most of the criticism on *Billy Budd*, the novella is also consistently praised for its philosophical insight, multifaceted narrative technique, and complex use of allegory.

In a review of Melville's body work, Nobel Prize–winning author Albert Camus said

These anguished books in which man is overwhelmed, but in which life is exalted on each page, are inexhaustible sources of strength and pity. We find in them revolt and acceptance, unconquerable and endless love, the passion for beauty, language of the highest order—in short, genius.

COMMON HUMAN EXPERIENCE

Melville frequently drew upon his own sea travels for the subject matter of his books. Here are some other works that draw on the seagoing experiences of their authors:

The Pilot (1824), a novel by James Fenimore Cooper. This book is a sea-novel that follows the adventures of a naval pilot during the American Revolution.

Two Years Before the Mast (1840), a book by Richard Henry Dana Jr. This book details the life of a common sailor by reporting on the two-year voyage of the author on a merchant ship that sailed from Boston to California around the southern tip of South America.

The Log from the Sea of Cortez (1951), a book by John Steinbeck. This book chronicles a six-week voyage made by the author and a friend as they collected specimens in the Gulf of California.

The Secret Sharer (1912), by British writer Joseph Conrad, tells the story of a young sea captain on his first command in the Gulf of Siam. The story is also an exploration of the mind of the captain and the way he comes to acknowledge something vital about his own identity.

Responses to Literature

1. Many critics and scholars agree that *Moby-Dick* is more than just a novel. In what ways did Melville depart from the traditions of the novel in writing this great work? Do these departures enhance the reading experience or detract from it?

2. In what ways are the thematic concerns of Melville's novels evident in his poetry as well, and in what ways do these two sets of work demonstrate different concerns? Is his prose or his poetry more effective at communicating the messages that Melville wants to impart?

3. Much of Melville's fiction was based on his personal experiences as a common sailor. Write an essay that compares and contrasts the experiences of the common sailors in two or more of Melville's novels.

4. Melville's most famous novel, *Moby-Dick*, has been made into a feature-length film three times, in 1930, 1956, and 1978. Write an essay that explores the reasons for this novel's popularity as the basis of films. Discuss whether or not the story is more appropriately set in novelistic or cinematic form.

BIBLIOGRAPHY

Books

Arvin, Newton. *Herman Melville.* New York: William Sloan Associates, 1950.

Anderson, Charles R. *Melville in the South Seas.* New York: Columbia University Press, 1939.

Freeman, John. *Herman Melville.* New York: Macmillan, 1926.

Garner, Stanton. *The Civil War World of Herman Melville.* Lawrence, Kans.: University Press of Kansas, 1993.

Howard, Leon. *Herman Melville: A Biography.* Berkeley, Calif.: University of California Press, 1951.

Leyda, Jay, ed. *The Melville Log: A Documentary Life of Herman Melville, 1819–1891.* New York: Harcourt Brace, 1951.

Metcalf, Eleanor Melville. *Herman Melville: Cycle and Epicycle.* Cambridge, Mass.: Harvard University Press, 1953.

Miller, Edwin Haviland. *Herman Melville: A Biography.* New York: Braziller, 1975.

Mumford, Lewis. *Herman Melville.* New York: Harcourt Brace, 1929.

Parker, Hershel. *Herman Melville: A Biography, Volume I, 1819–1851.* Baltimore: Johns Hopkins University Press, 1996.

Robertson-Lorant, Laurie. *Melville, A Biography.* New York: Clarkson N. Potter, 1996.

Sealts, Merton M., Jr. *The Early Lives of Melville: Nineteenth-Century Biographical Sketches and Their Authors.* Madison, Wisc.: University of Wisconsin Press, 1974.

Weaver, Raymond M. *Herman Melville, Mariner and Mystic.* New York: George H. Doran, 1921.

✸ H. L. Mencken

BORN: *1880, Baltimore, Maryland*

DIED: *1956, Baltimore, Maryland*

NATIONALITY: *American*

GENRE: *Nonfiction*

MAJOR WORKS:
Prejudices, six volumes (1919–1927)
The American Language (1919)
A Mencken Chrestomathy (1949)

Overview

During his lifetime H. L. Mencken was called the "Great Iconoclast" and the "Sage of Baltimore" because of his newspaper and magazine journalism. However, his contributions to American literature were more extensive than those ordinarily found in one who gained fame as a reporter, editor, and columnist. Mencken was the author of at least thirty books and collections of essays and criticism, including a highly acclaimed six-volume study of language, a popular autobiographical trilogy, and volumes on politics, religion, and ethics.

H. L. Mencken   *Mencken, Henry Louis, photograph. The Library of Congress.*

Works in Biographical and Historical Context

A Happy Baltimore Life   Henry Louis Mencken was born on September 12, 1880, in Baltimore, Maryland, the city in which he lived all his life—most of it in the same house. In 1883, his father moved with his growing family into the spacious, three-story row house on Hollins Street, where he and Mencken's mother would live out their lives. Mencken resided in the house until the end of his life, except for the five years of his marriage.

Mencken's prosperous, conservative family was in the tobacco trade—his father and uncle jointly owned a cigar factory—and he took pride in the fact that he came from a long line of European professors and lawyers. Education was stressed in the Mencken household. By the age of nine he was playing the piano and reading voraciously—one of his favorite books as a child was Mark Twain's *Adventures of Huckleberry Finn* (1884), a book he would later claim as a significant personal influence. During his ten years of formal schooling, he became an enthusiastic, systematic reader in all subjects.

Mencken's strong self-assurance derived at least in part from the close family ties he formed from the beginning of his life. In the first volume of his autobiography, *Happy Days* (1940), Mencken recalled his childhood as being "placid, secure, uneventful and happy." There was never an instant, he wrote, when he doubted his father's capacity

> to resolve any difficulty that menaced me, or to beat off any danger. He was always the center of his small world, and in my eyes a man of illimitable puissance and resourcefulness. If we needed anything he got it forthwith, and usually he threw in something that we didn't really need, but only wanted.

His parents were devoted to each other and to their children. As Mencken put it, "We were encapsulated in affection, and kept fat, saucy and contented." He makes it known that he was raised as a member of the comfortable and complacent bourgeoisie, a class that at the time of his writing was under heavy fire from working-class agitators who were intent on saving the nation and the world from all that the middle class represented.

Revolting against Victorian Standards   In 1899, Mencken began his career in journalism at the *Baltimore Herald* as morning editor. By 1903, when he was twenty-three, he was serving as the paper's city editor. In 1906 the *Herald* closed, and Mencken become editor of the *Baltimore Sun*. He retained a lifelong connection with the *Sun* newspaper company, serving as both a reporter and a member of the board of directors.

In 1908 Mencken made a stir in American letters as literary critic of the *Smart Set* magazine, of which he became coeditor with George Jean Nathan from 1914–1923. Nathan's relationship with the magazine ended in August 1925, but Mencken continued as editor until December 1933. As literary critic, he defended writers such as Theodore Dreiser, whose writing represented natural appearances and natural patterns of speech, as well as such satirists as Sinclair Lewis, who wrote with biting humor. He sarcastically opposed the genteel tradition offered by such authors as William Dean Howells and Henry James. He also chided reformers for their high-minded intentions and objected to the banning of "immoral" literature from the mail and libraries.

During these years, he won a following of students, artists, and journalists eager for a revolt against Victorian standards in art, thought, and morality. In 1924 he continued to lead the intellectual rebellion as coeditor with Nathan of the *American Mercury*.

Out of Newspaper Work during the World Wars   During World Wars I and II Mencken saw fit to abstain from newspaper work. His anti-British sentiment made him seem pro-German in the first conflict; and that stance, coupled with his perceived anti-Semitism, had the same effect in the second. He devoted much time to *The American Language* during World War I and

LITERARY AND HISTORICAL CONTEMPORARIES

Mencken's famous contemporaries include:

Theodore Dreiser (1871–1945): Dreiser was an American author noted for his pioneering works in the naturalist school of writing.

Willa Cather (1873–1947): Cather was best known for novels that presented realistic portrayals of pioneer life. Her work often celebrated the courageous endurance of the early Midwestern settlers and the natural beauty of the prairie landscape.

Sherwood Anderson (1876–1941): Anderson was an American short-story writer best known for his influential collection, *Winesburg, Ohio* (1919).

Hermann Hesse (1877–1962): Hesse was a German-Swiss writer whose works explore the individual search for spirituality. Hesse won the 1946 Nobel Prize in Literature.

James Branch Cabell (1879–1958): Cabell was an American author recognized as a pioneering novelist and short-story writer of the Southern literary renaissance. He is best known for his 1919 novel *Jurgen*, which became the focus of a long obscenity case.

Sinclair Lewis (1885–1951): Lewis, noted for his realism, penned stories that were critical of capitalism and American society; in 1930, he became the first American author to win the Nobel Prize in Literature.

Pearl S. Buck (1892–1973): Buck received the 1938 Nobel Prize in Literature for her works that helped introduce American readers to Asian culture.

concentrated on its supplements, partly for the same reason, during World War II.

In 1930 he married author and English professor Sara Haardt. Sadly, Haardt suffered from tuberculosis throughout their marriage, succumbing to the illness in 1935. Afterward, he lived quietly with his brother August in their Baltimore home on Hollins Street. His reputation, somewhat tarnished already because his opinions were rapidly becoming outdated, suffered further during the 1930s because of his scorn for President Franklin Delano Roosevelt and the New Deal programs he initiated, which were an attempt to end the Great Depression and alleviate the suffering of the poor. Mencken called the New Deal "a . . . cow with 125,000 teats." With his views at odds with those of the public and circulation dropping as a result, Mencken left the *Mercury* at the end of 1933 to continue newspaper work and book writing.

In the early 1940s Mencken completed *Happy Days, 1880–1892* (1940), *Newspaper Days, 1899–1906* (1941), and *Heathen Days, 1890–1936* (1943), the autobiographical trilogy that occupied his temporary retirement from newspaper work during World War II. Composed with wit, charm, and pleasant humor, the trilogy records his past from the perspective of a man grown older. In 1948 Mencken suffered a stroke that left him unable to read or write. He was almost completely incapacitated for the rest of his life and was largely forgotten by a once-adoring public. He died in his sleep on January 29, 1956.

Works in Literary Context

Mencken was a prolific writer. He published some twenty-five books—not to mention literally thousands of articles, essays, stories, editorials, and book reviews—during the course of his career, beginning with the now-forgotten *Ventures into Verse* in 1903 and moving in 1905 and 1908 respectively to the more representative *George Bernard Shaw: His Plays* and *The Philosophy of Friedrich Nietzsche.* Throughout his writing career, his style and his messages were very similar to those found in his six-volume collection of opinion *Prejudices*, published between 1919 and 1927.

Writing in the *New York Review of Books*, Murray Kempton likened Mencken to a whale: immense and powerful and difficult to capture. In today's literary world, writers tend to specialize in one medium—but Mencken had careers in three: a book author, a newspaperman, and magazine editor and contributor. Those careers ran concurrently and were often intertwined. The time demanded by one clearly affected his work with the other two. Moreover, as he acknowledged candidly, he would share material among them: what was written for a newspaper column was often revised for a magazine article and then reworked once again for inclusion in a book.

Acidic and Iconoclastic Cultural Commentary
H. L. Mencken's literary reputation was etched by the acidic wit that characterized his commentary on the American culture of his day. Trained as a newspaperman, Mencken reached the height of his powers in the 1920s when, as an associate of the *Sun* in Baltimore and an editor first of the *Smart Set* and then of the *American Mercury*, he became one of the nation's most influential critics.

His messages were intensely iconoclastic—he seemed to enjoy attacking the cherished views and ideals of contemporary American culture. He believed that American culture had become stultified by its rigid adherence to a particularly strange "Puritan" form of Christian morality. He also held that the quality of American politics—and, indeed, of American life—was being compromised by a foolishly persistent belief in egalitarianism. These messages—and the many corollaries he drew from them about literature, art, and society—he published again and again, employing a style that became his signature, a style whose ingredients were the acerbic allusion, the caustic joke, the unusual word, the irreverent comparison.

A Love and Respect for Freedom Mencken was above all else a libertarian. He saw freedom of speech as the most valuable attribute of any society, and insisted, throughout some long and bloody battles, upon the need for civil liberty for all people regardless of color, gender, origin, or social class. One of the most articulate members of America's adversary culture, he reveled in his iconoclasm. "The liberation of the human mind has never been furthered by . . . learned dunderheads," he thundered in *Prejudices: Fourth Series* (1924), "it has been furthered by gay fellows who heaved dead cats into sanctuaries and then went roistering down the highways of the world, proving to all men that doubt, after all, was safe—that the god in his sanctuary was finite in his power and hence a fraud." As both writer and editor, he knocked many false icons from their shaky pedestals. If little proved sacred to Mencken, then it was for the simple reason that, as he saw things, little deserved to be.

Works in Critical Context

Mencken's career generated huge disagreement and controversy during his lifetime, and the uproar has continued into the present day. In the cities, some worshiped Mencken as a demigod; in small-town America, on the other hand, he was reviled as the devil incarnate. For the distinguished critic Joseph Wood Krutch, "Mencken's was the best prose written in America during the Twentieth Century." He reigns as America's most frequently quoted author, and some readers rank him as the country's finest humorist after Mark Twain. Others, however, have judged Mencken as a defectively educated bully who reveled in desecrating the American language.

In 1926 writer Walter Lippmann called Mencken "the most powerful personal influence upon this whole generation of American people." His criticism has been celebrated as beneficial, and he has been extolled for his efforts to make America a saner, more civilized country. On the other hand, he has been scorned as an anti-Semite and racist, a view that has gained strength since the publication of *The Diary of H. L. Mencken* in 1989, which revealed a host of unsavory opinions. Even decades after his death, Mencken is able to stir up the literary scene.

The American Language   In 1919, at the height of his popularity, he had published *The American Language*, a book that he revised and supplemented at various times until 1948. In *The American Language* Mencken sought, as he said in his subtitle, to inquire "into the development of English in the United States." The volume was quickly accepted by linguists, and continues today as a standard reference work in the field. Indeed, it may well account for Mencken's fame long after his other work has become dated and been forgotten. Both reviewers at the time and present-day writers acknowledge Mencken's important contribution with *The American Language*. As one reviewer put it in 2006, Mencken "wrote one of the first influential books on idiomatic American English."

COMMON HUMAN EXPERIENCE

Much of Mencken's work was critical of the state of American culture and language. Here are some other critical inquiries into the American culture and language:

Cultural Literacy: What Every American Needs to Know (1987), a nonfiction book by E. D. Hirsch. This treatise explores the failure of the American educational system to provide students with the basic knowledge to function in contemporary society.

The Closing of the American Mind (1987), a nonfiction book by Allan Bloom. This book critiques the modern university system in the United States and traces how its failings affect American students and society.

The Right Word in the Right Place at the Right Time (2004), a collection of essays by William Safire. These essays originally appeared in the author's *New York Times* language column. Together they explore the ways in which the English language is used and abused in America.

Responses to Literature

1. Throughout his long career, Mencken was consistently critical of the state of American culture. What were the main terms of his critique of American culture? Do his critiques still apply today? In what ways have things improved since Mencken's time, and in what ways have they worsened?

2. Mencken wrote and edited several books about or by German philosopher Friedrich Nietzsche. Consider Nietzsche's writings in *Beyond Good and Evil* (1886). In what ways was Nietzsche's philosophy and literary style an influence on Mencken's writings? Which of Mencken's ideas were borrowed from Nietzsche and applied to American life?

3. Many of Mencken's writings discussed the works of prominent literary figures in the United States and Europe who were living and writing during his lifetime. Choose a prominent literary figure from today, and use Mencken's style of writing to write an essay that analyzes and critiques that figure's works.

4. Mencken commonly wrote about American usage of the English language, which he both described and criticized. Using Mencken's language writings as a model, choose a particular American usage of the English language and write an essay describing its origins and criticizing its effect on American culture and American life.

BIBLIOGRAPHY

Books

Angoff, Charles. *H. L. Mencken: A Portrait from Memory.* New York: Thomas Yoseloff, 1956.

Bode, Carl. *Mencken.* Carbondale, Ill.: Southern Illinois University Press, 1969.

Dolmetsch, Carl R. *The Smart Set, a History and Anthology.* New York: Dial, 1966.

Dorsey, John, ed. *On Mencken.* New York: Knopf, 1980.

Fecher, Charles A. *Mencken: A Study of His Thought.* New York: Knopf, 1978.

Goldberg, Isaac. *The Man Mencken: A Biographical and Critical Survey.* New York: Simon & Schuster, 1925.

Hobson, Fred C., Jr. *Serpent in Eden: H. L. Mencken and the South.* Chapel Hill, N.C.: University of North Carolina Press, 1974.

Kemler, Edgar. *The Irreverent Mr. Mencken.* Boston: Little, Brown, 1950.

Krutch, Joseph Wood. *If You Don't Mind My Saying So ... Essays on Man and Nature.* New York: Sloane, 1964.

Manchester, William. *Disturber of the Peace: The Life of H. L. Mencken.* New York: Harper, 1950.

Mayfield, Sara. *The Constant Circle: H. L. Mencken and His Friends.* New York: Delacorte, 1968.

Nolte, William H. *H. L. Mencken, Literary Critic.* Middletown, Conn.: Wesleyan University Press, 1966.

Scruggs, Charles. *The Sage in Harlem: H. L. Mencken and the Black Writers of the 1920s.* Baltimore: Johns Hopkins Press, 1984.

Stenerson, Douglas C. *H. L. Mencken: Iconoclast from Baltimore.* Chicago: University of Chicago Press, 1971.

Williams, W. H. A. *H. L. Mencken.* Boston: Twayne, 1977.

✹ Eve Merriam

BORN: *1916, Philadelphia, Pennsylvania*

DIED: *1992, New York, New York*

NATIONALITY: *American*

GENRE: *Poetry, fiction, nonfiction, drama*

MAJOR WORKS:
Family Circle (1946)
There's No Rhyme for Silver (1962)
It Doesn't Always Have to Rhyme (1964)
Finding a Poem (1970)

Overview

Eve Merriam's works include fiction, nonfiction, plays, and poetry. She wrote extensively for both children and adults, but has received the most recognition for producing excellent children's poetry. Her contributions to many poetry anthologies and many respected magazines have made her an influential voice in children's literature.

Works in Biographical and Historical Context

A Childhood Filled with Poetry Merriam was born on July 19, 1916 in Philadelphia, the youngest of three girls and one boy. Her parents, who owned a chain of women's dress shops, both emigrated from Russia as young children and grew up in small Pennsylvania towns. According to Merriam, the family joke about her parents' shared occupation was that the women's wear business was the only way they could afford clothing for all three girls. Her lifelong interest in fashion would eventually inspire a book-length study of fashion in America, *Figleaf: The Business of Being in Fashion* (1960), but Merriam's greatest passion was always poetry.

As a child, Merriam loved to read narrative and dramatic poems, and light verse in particular. She was enthralled by the sound of words and their musicality. She loved family trips to see Gilbert and Sullivan musicals, and enjoyed chanting the tongue-twisting verses. She was equally entranced by the poetic quality of language in her favorite childhood books, the classics *Alice's Adventures in Wonderland* (1865), *Swiss Family Robinson* (1812), as well as fairy tales by Hans Christian Andersen and the Brothers Grimm, English and Irish folk tales, and Greek, Roman, and Norse mythology. Her childhood love of poetry was also nourished by reading aloud poems printed in the *Philadelphia Bulletin.*

As an adolescent, Merriam wrote serious poems for her high-school magazine and contributed light verse and political poems to the school's weekly newspaper. Merriam attributes her love for "the richness and the ambiguity of words" to "one very irascible, difficult, tendentious old Latin teacher." She also remembers an English teacher who encouraged her efforts as a writer. However, as a teenager, Merriam never planned to be a writer—she just wrote poems because she felt the need to write them, as if she could not live her life without writing them.

A Love of Fashion and Writing Combine Merriam received her undergraduate education at Cornell University and the University of Pennsylvania. After graduating in 1937, she did graduate work at the University of Wisconsin and Columbia University. In 1939 her writing career began as a copywriter for Columbia Broadcasting System, where she worked on radio documentaries and verse scripts. During World War II, she conducted a weekly program on modern poetry for station WQXR in New York and wrote a daily verse column for *PM.*

After World War II, Merriam began working for fashion magazines. In 1946, she became feature editor for *Deb,* then fashion copy editor for *Glamour* from 1947 to 1948. During these years she also published her first book of poetry, *Family Circle*, in the prestigious Yale Series of Younger Poets.

Becoming a Children's Poet   Merriam continued to write well-received poetry throughout the 1940s and 1950s. She received the William Newman Poetry Award in 1957 and a CBS grant to write poetic drama in 1959. It wasn't until she was in her mid-forties, however, that Merriam turned to the genre that would make her most famous. Her first book of children's poetry, *There Is No Rhyme for Silver*, was named a Junior Literary Guild selection, an encouraging beginning for a neophyte in that field. With impressive regularity, she published book after book of children's verse for the next three decades.

Like other poets at the time, Merriam began to focus on more serious topics in the late 1960s and 1970s. She shifted her concerns to those facing modern children: anxieties, alienation, racial and social injustice, war, inhumane technology, and struggles of urban life. She also published sixteen juvenile books as well as several volumes of poetry and nonfiction for adults. Merriam continued to publish children's poetry throughout the 1980s, and died of cancer in New York City, in April 1992.

Works in Literary Context

Merriam's poetry has given her readers a better appreciation for the varieties of a child's experiences. Her philosophy concerning how children should approach poetry has greatly enhanced the ability of parents and teachers to help them enjoy it. By inviting two generations of readers into her world of words, Merriam has greatly enriched the genre as a whole.

A Delight in Sounds   Merriam's poems are meant to be spoken aloud rather than to remain mute on the printed page. Because of this, her imagery is alive, her diction is colloquial, and every word is significant. Breaking the established rules of children's poetry—which typically demand rigid meter and regular exact rhyme—Merriam delights in playing with the visual, aural, and intellectual effects of words.

Poetry's repetition and musicality are unequaled by any other genre, she believes. Consequently, these rhyming verses prove the special magic of poetry. She has discussed rhyme in critical essays on poetry, calling it "the chime that rings in time . . . like the little bell at the end of a typewriter line." This "bouncy-bouncing quality" of rhyme, however, is not essential, for even without rhyme, other poetic elements such as rhythm, assonance, alliteration, and onomatopoeia (a word that imitates the sound it is describing, such as "woof" or "bang") provide the reader with the special musical effects of poetry. *There Is No Rhyme for Silver*, a collection of fifty-one poems, demonstrates Merriam's special delight in the sound of words, even words that have no rhyme. She invites children to leap right into the rhymes for "all seasons and all times." In fact, her title poem, "There is No Rhyme for

Silver," concludes with this invitation to participate in the medley of rhymes: "Rhymes to whisper, rhymes to yell, / Rhymes to chime like a swinging bell. / Rhymes like a jump rope, now let's begin: / Take a turn and jump right in."

Socially Aware Poetry   In the late 1960s and 1970s, Merriam began to develop into a more socially aware poet. Poems about nature, animals, family, and the everyday experiences children encounter never disappeared from her children's books, but she stretched beyond these traditional sensibilities of childhood to explore the inner emotional conflicts and stark realities of the world facing children. Hence, there is a noticeable transcendence of the safe, socially acceptable poems of *Catch a Little Rhyme* (1966) to bolder statements of social and political realities in *Finding a Poem* (1970). The social awareness in her poetry did not change her basic beliefs about writing verse, however. While her style often changed to reflect her subjects, her poetry always exhibited a continual improvisation and experimentation with language.

Works in Critical Context

Throughout her career, Merriam has been praised by critics and given various poetry awards and grants. The most significant of these was the 1981 NCTE Award for Excellence in Poetry for Children (1981). This award

COMMON HUMAN EXPERIENCE

Much of Merriam's poetry for children explored the realities facing children in the modern world. Here are some other collections of poetry that do the same thing:

Beachy Head (1807), a collection of poems by Charlotte Smith. This expresses the societal concerns of the time in verses that were intended to be enjoyed by both adults and children.

Arthur's Father (1977), a collection of poems by Kit Wright. This work explores the dark undercurrents beneath the everyday world.

Quick Let's Get Out of Here (1983), a collection of poems by Michael Rosen. This illustrated compendium provides a humorous treatment of issues related to friends, family, and daily life.

verified the high regard the teaching profession had for Merriam's contributions to children's poetry, and the recognition gave her added credibility as both a poet and a critic. Following the award, she was often quoted in scholarly journal articles about children's poetry and in textbooks used in courses on children's literature in colleges and universities.

Beginning in the late 1960s, critics noted Merriam's turn towards more socially relevant topics in her poetry, along with the use of social satire. According to critic Judith Saltman, for example, Merriam's work in *Finding a Poem* and *Rainbow Writing* (1976) demonstrates a "dexterous handling of metered verse, free verse, and verbal nonsense . . . allied with social satire and a fierce conscience." According to Saltman, Merriam is considered one of the best writers of popular "sophisticated urban poetry" children enjoy. Her exuberant rhymes and her use of dialogue are not only perfect examples of the oral tradition of children's literature but also excellent illustrations of the contemporary tastes of young readers.

It Doesn't Always Have to Rhyme Barbara Baskin and Karen Harris praise Merriam's use of imagery in *It Doesn't Always Have to Rhyme*, describing it as "sometimes startling." They note the way Merriam works carefully with language in order to evoke a particular response from her readers. The entire collection is designed to teach children with its "remarkable sensitivity to the playful possibilities in language."

Responses to Literature

1. Merriam has been praised for writing poetry that appeals to both children and adults. In what ways does the appeal for these two groups derive from the same sources, and in what ways are there different sources of appeal for children and for adults? In your answer, offer an example from Merriam's work that you think appeals to both children and adults.

2. In the second half of her career, Merriam used poetry to explore social issues she felt were important. In what ways did Merriam's social concerns evolve during the 1970s and into the 1980s? In what areas did she remain consistent in her themes, and in what areas did she have new concerns as the times changed?

3. Commentators have noted that Merriam's poems are meant to be read aloud rather silently. Write an essay that explores how her style is particularly tailored to reading out loud, both by adults to children and by children themselves.

4. Merriam wrote children's poetry that explored the problems children faced in the world in the 1960s and 1970s. Write a poem that explores the kinds of problems you think children face today.

BIBLIOGRAPHY

Books

Baskin, Barbara H., and Karen H. Harris. *Books for the Gifted Child*. New York: Bowker, 1980.

Periodicals

"Eve Merriam Is Named Winner of NCTE's Award for Excellence in Poetry for Children." *Language Arts* (May 1981): 590.

Bosworth, Patricia. "She Ain't Finished Yet." *Working Woman* (March 1982): 136–137.

Hopkins, Lee Bennett. "NCTE Poetry Award Winners on Nonprint Media." *Language Arts* (September 1982): 615–616.

Saltman, Judith, ed. *The Riverside Anthology of Children's Literature*, 6th edition. Boston: Houghton Mifflin, 1985.

Sloan, Gina. "Profile: Eve Merriam." *Language Arts* (November–December, 1981): 957–64.

✸ James Merrill

BORN: *1926, New York, New York*

DIED: *1995, Tucson, Arizona*

NATIONALITY: *American*

GENRE: *Poetry*

MAJOR WORKS:

Nights and Days (1966)

Divine Comedies (1976)

Mirabell: Books of Numbers (1978)

The Changing Light at Sandover (1982)

James Merrill *AP Wide World Photos*

Overview

James Merrill was a lyrical and mystical poet often compared to W. H. Auden and William Butler Yeats. He is best known for his series of poems inspired by the messages of spirit guides he ostensibly received through the medium of a Ouija board. Merrill used formal poetic structures to blend autobiography with archetype and fable, creating a sense of inner tension and authenticity.

Works in Biographical and Historical Context

Wealth and Privilege James Ingram Merrill was born in New York City on March 3, 1926. He was the son of Charles Merrill, the founder of Merrill & Lynch, the stock brokerage company. Merrill's childhood was one of wealth and privilege. He was educated at private schools where the written word and poetry were emphasized and also had a multi-lingual governess who taught him respect for languages. An appreciation for music, especially opera, came early to Merrill, and that dramatic form had a lasting influence on his poetry. Versification was encouraged in the Merrill household, so much so

that in Merrill's senior year at Lawrenceville School, his father privately published his son's first book of poems.

Wealth also meant that Merrill did not have to earn his living from poetry and could live where he wanted as he wanted. Throughout his life, he traveled extensively through Europe and made homes in Stonington, Connecticut; Athens, Greece; and New York City. When his father died, Merrill established the Ingram Merrill Foundation to provide grants to writers and painters.

A Successful Poetry Career Merrill attended Amherst College, where he continued to write poetry, though his studies were interrupted by a year in the infantry during World War II. Returning to Amherst, he published poetry in *Poetry* and the *Kenyon Review* and completed his thesis on Marcel Proust. Proust was fascinated with the everyday and with one's own history, and his work had a lasting influence on Merrill's later poetry.

At the beginning of his career Merrill's poetry was recognized for its elegance and elaborately ornate presentation of artful objects and fanciful scenes. His later work, however, explored themes that were more personal and more historically based, and as a result, critics and readers began to take his writing more seriously. Merrill received the first of his two National Book Awards in 1967 for *Nights and Days*, which added to four early prizes from *Poetry* magazine (in 1947, 1949, 1951, and 1965).

Ephraim and the Ouija Board Merrill and his long-time companion, David Jackson, began experimenting with a home-made Ouija board in 1955. Merrill claims to have made contact with a spirit guide, Ephraim, through these experiments. Although readers and scholars later questioned Merrill's connection to Ephraim—did Merrill believe he was literally a spirit, or was Ephraim merely part of his literary style?—Ephraim was a central presence in and driving force behind Merrill's poetry during the 1970s and 1980s. It was these experiences that lead Merrill to write his most successful and important works, *Divine Comedies*, for which he won the Pulitzer Prize in 1977, and *Mirabell: Books of Numbers*, which won him his second National Book Award in 1979. The National Book Critics Circle Award in 1983 for *The Changing Light at Sandover*, a collection of Ephraim poems, and the Bobbit National Prize for Poetry from the Library of Congress in 1989 for *The Inner Room* (1988) rounded out the poet's many other honors.

Until his death from a heart attack in Tucson, Arizona, in 1995, Merrill continued to produce poetry of note, as well as a memoir, *A Different Person* (1993), which reflected not only on his family, but on his homosexuality in relation to his writing.

Works in Literary Context

Time and Eros With the publication of *Fire Screen* (1969) and *Braving the Elements* (1972), Merrill established in his poetry the themes of time and eros and the

LITERARY AND HISTORICAL CONTEMPORARIES

Merrill's famous contemporaries include:

William Buckley (1925–2008): Buckley was an American writer, editor, and television host who was a leading spokesperson for conservatism in the United States during the second half of the twentieth century.

William De Witt Snodgrass (1926–2009): Snodgrass is an American poet, whose pen name is S. S. Gardons. He won the Pulitzer Prize for Poetry in 1960.

W. S. Merwin (1927–): Merwin is an American poet noted for his stylistically diverse poems that display a moral concern for the state of contemporary society and the natural world.

Edward Albee (1928–): Albee is an American playwright who writes tragicomedies in the tradition of the Theatre of the Absurd.

Ted Hughes (1930–1998): Hughes was a famous English poet and one-time husband of the American writer Sylvia Plath. Hughes served as the British poet laureate from 1984 until his death in 1998.

Frank McCourt (1930–): McCourt is an American writer who won the Pulitzer Prize for his memoir *Angela's Ashes* (1996).

COMMON HUMAN EXPERIENCE

Merrill's poems in *The Changing Light at Sandover* involve a spiritual journey that feature dialogue with a spirit guide. Here are some other poems that feature a spiritual journey:

Inferno (1308–1321), a poem by Dante Aligheri. This epic poem recounts Dante's journey through Hell as guided by the ancient Roman poet Virgil.

The Wanderings of Oisin (1889), a poem by William Butler Yeats. The poem features a conversation between St. Patrick and Oisin, an Irish hero.

Marrow of Flame (2000), poems by Dorothy Walters. The poems in this collection explore the author's mystical experiences during her first attempts at meditation.

The Lovely Bones (2002), a novel by Alice Sebold. This novel presents a girl looking down from heaven after her death to see how her family and friends are coping with their lives.

relationships between them. In this collection and others, Merrill presents love, with its erotic energies of masking and unmasking, as the arena where illusion and reality perform their ritual matings and combats.

Fusing Autobiography and Archetype Merrill's experimentation with a Ouija board alledgedly put him in touch with a spirit guide, Ephraim, who led the poet to a mystical and sacred dialogue reminiscent of a blend of Yeats, Dante, Proust, Byron, and Auden. With these poems, collected in *The Changing Light at Sandover*, Merrill became more than a lyric poet. He fused autobiography and archetype and created an epic and mythological approach to his regular life. As Andrew V. Ettin wrote in *Perspective*, "The transformation of the natural, autobiographical, narrative events and tone into the magical, universal, sonorous, eternal is one of the principal characteristics of Merrill's poetry, perhaps the main source of its splendid and moving qualities." Unlike other autobiographical poets who use the poetry about their lives as a sort of confessional booth, Merrill turns his life into a larger-than-life myth. Helen Vendler wrote in the *New York Times Book Review* that Merrill's poems "are autobiographical without being 'confessional': they show none of that urgency to reveal the untellable or unspeakable that we associate with the poetry we call 'confessional'. . . . It is as though a curtain had been drawn aside, and we are permitted a glimpse of . . . a life that goes on unconscious of us, with the narrator so perfectly an actor in his own drama that his presence as narrator is rendered transparent, invisible."

Works in Critical Context

Merrill was sometimes known in popular circles as "the Ouija poet," a dismissive title based on the skepticism of his Ephraim poems. He was always more interesting to scholarly readers, who considered him one of the twentieth century's finest American poets. Brigitte Weeks wrote in the *New York Times Book Review* that Merrill's "artistic distinction is for the most part acknowledged, particularly in the academy, where he has already become part of the permanent canon. With his technical virtuosity and his metaphysical broodings, he is, like Wallace Stevens, an ideal seminar poet whose complex work lends itself to exhaustive explication."

One of Merrill's most noted accomplishments was his steady growth from gentility to vision, from formal elegance to prophecy and epic poetry. Once he left mere gentility behind and dealt with themes more dramatic and personal, his poetry took on a weight and importance that brought critical acclaim from all quarters.

Divine Comedies Prior to the publication of *Divine Comedies*, Merrill was a well-received, if minor, poet. Critic Paul Christensen wrote that the early poetry "would have assured Merrill a place in poetry as one of our better minor lyricists, one of our perfectionists." But with the publication of *Divine Comedies*, according to Christensen, "Suddenly Merrill has become our grand inquisitor, a poet of metaphysical humor and daring who blithely invents spirits of the Ouija board to confess to us the history of space, the chemical future of man, the heavenly wars at the dawn of being, the whereabouts of old geniuses now reincarnated as scientists and technicians. The whole madcap experiment wobbles and shuffles forward into a sort of greatness."

Indeed, the publication of *Divine Comedies* led many critics to reevaluate Merrill's stature as a poet. As literary critic Harold Bloom wrote in the *New Republic*, Merrill "has convinced many discerning readers of a greatness, or something like it, in his first six volumes of verse, but until this year I remained a stubborn holdout. The publication of *Divine Comedies*...converts me, absolutely if belatedly." Professor William Spiegelman described *Divine Comedies* as "Merrill's supreme fiction, a self-mythologizing within an epic program." Spiegelman went on to praise Merrill for his masterful blending of classic styles into a truly original work: "At last Merrill's masters combine with graceful fluency in a confection entirely his own: the reader finds Proust's social world, his analysis of the human heart and the artist's growth; Dante's encyclopedia of a vast universal organization; and Yeats's spiritualism, for which the hints in the earlier volumes gave only small promise. Added to these are the offhand humor of Lord Byron and W. H. Auden, a Neoplatonic theory of reincarnation, a self-reflexiveness about the process of composition, and a virtual handbook of poetic technique."

The Changing Light at Sandover The sacred books collected in *The Changing Light at Sandover*, which won the National Book Critics Circle Award in 1982, are widely regarded as a major poetic statement, and helped formally cast Merrill as a unique sort of poet—a metaphysical writer who also employed both wit and charm. As Willard Spiegelman noted in the *Dictionary of Literary Biography*, the completion of *The Changing Light at Sandover* "earned [Merrill] his place as one of the most original and major poets of the twentieth century."

Responses to Literature

1. Merrill was often dismissed by the popular press because of his experimentation with a Ouija board, yet he was taken very seriously by scholars. What about Merrill's "Ouija board" poetry do you think interested scholarly commentators so much? Why do you think these elements were missed by readers? In your opinion, did scholars take him more seriously than he deserved, or did others take him less seriously than he deserved?

2. Commentators have noted that Merrill changed his poetic approach and stature during the 1970s when he wrote the poems of *Divine Comedies* and *Mirabell*. In what ways do these works represent a major departure from Merrill's earlier works, and in what ways is there continuity between the earlier and later works?

3. Scholars consider the works collected in *The Changing Light at Sandover* to be a major poetic statement. Write an essay that describes the statement you think Merrill is making in this work, and evaluate its importance for contemporary life.

BIBLIOGRAPHY

Books

Bloom, Harold, ed. *James Merrill*. New York: Chelsea House, 1985.

Howard, Richard. *Alone With America: Essays on the Art of Poetry in the United States Since 1950*. New York: Atheneum, 1971.

Kalstone, David. *Five Temperaments*. New York: Oxford University Press, 1977.

Kamp, Jim, ed. *Reference Guide to American Literature*, 3rd edition. Chicago: St. James Press, 1994.

Labrie, Ross. *James Merrill*. Boston: Twayne, 1982.

Lehman, David and Charles Berger, eds. *James Merrill: Essays in Criticism*. Ithaca, N.Y.: Cornell University Press, 1983.

Moffett, Judith. *James Merrill: An Introduction to the Poetry*, revised edition. New York: Columbia University Press, 1984.

Polito, Robert. *A Reader's Guide to James Merrill's The Changing Light at Sandover*. Ann Arbor: University of Michigan Press, 1994.

Spiegelman, Willard. *The Didactic Muse: Scenes of Instruction in Contemporary American Poetry*. Princeton: Princeton University Press, 1989.

Yenser, Stephen. *The Consuming Myth: The Work of James Merrill*. Cambridge, Mass.: Harvard University Press, 1987.

Periodicals

Brown, Ashley. "An Interview with James Merrill." *Shenandoah* (Summer 1968): 3–15.

Buckley, Christopher. "Exploring *The Changing Light at Sandover*: An Interview with James Merrill." *Twentieth Century Literature* (1992): 415–435.

Kalstone, David. "The Poet: Private." *Saturday Review* (December 2, 1972): 43–45.

McClatchy, J. D. McClatchy. "Lost Paradises." *Parnassus* (Fall/Winter 1976): 305–320.

Sheehan, Donald. "An Interview with James Merrill." *Contemporary Literature* (Winter 1968): 1–14.

❀ Thomas Merton

BORN: *1915, Prades, France*

DIED: *1968, Bangkok, Thailand*

NATIONALITY: *American*

GENRE: *Nonfiction*

MAJOR WORKS:

Thirty Poems (1944)

The Seven Storey Mountain (1948)

Figures for an Apocalypse (1948

The Ascent to the Truth (1951)

The Sign of Jonas (1953)

Thomas Merton   *Merton, Thomas, photograph. The Library of Congress.*

Overview

Thomas Merton was a Trappist monk who became a prolific writer and influential social activist despite his vows of silence. His works are informed by the interplay between his contemplative life, his compassion for humanity, and his desire to work toward nonviolent solutions to world problems. A popular and critically acclaimed autobiographer, poet, and essayist, he was respected for his insight into twentieth-century social problems, his interpretations of the role of religion in modern society, and for helping to introduce Asian religions to the West.

Works in Biographical and Historical Context

Nomadic Youth   Thomas Merton was born in Prades, France, on January 31, 1915. He was the son of two artists, Owen Heathcote Merton, a New Zealander, and Ruth Jenkins Merton, an American. His mother died when he was six years old, and he spent his youth as something of a nomad, living alternately with his father in various Transatlantic settings and with his mother's

family on Long Island, New York. His father died in England when Thomas was fifteen.

His Transatlantic childhood meant that Merton was educated in some of the finest schools in the whole world. He attended the Lycée de Montauban in France and the Oakham School in England, and then spent a year at Clare College, Cambridge. He next went to Columbia University in New York, where he studied English literature, earning a B.A. in 1938 and an M.A. in 1939. At Columbia he was strongly influenced by what became a lifelong friendship with the noted literary critic, Mark Van Doren.

Vow of Silence   Outwardly, Merton seemed destined for a successful career as a university teacher and scholar. Van Doren, for one, thought highly of his prospects, noting in retrospect that he had "never known a mind more brilliant, more beautiful, more serious, more playful." However, in 1941, several years after converting to Catholicism, Merton entered the Trappist monastery Our Lady of Gethsemani in Kentucky. The Trappists require their members to take a vow of silence, which includes strict limitations, though not a complete ban, on writing.

Merton's vocation involved complete isolation from the world. It required silence, austerity, and obedience to his superiors. Monastic life was a mixed experience for Merton—on the one hand, his contemplative side appreciated the deep and lasting silence it offered. But on the other, the artist in him felt the need to celebrate his solidarity with mankind, with the very people whom he had left behind upon entering the monastery. This ambivalence was to remain with him all of his life, and, while it was a source of some anxiety to Merton himself, it is one of the most identifiable features of his writing.

The conditions under which Merton wrote were remarkable. In the 1940s, life at Gethsemani was physically demanding. The monks slept on straw and boards in long dormitories and ate a poor diet. The monastery was marginally heated in the bitter Kentucky winters, and there was no relief in the torrid summers when the monks worked in the fields in mid-July wearing heavy robes (though they were eventually given permission to wear lighter clothes in the heat). Merton spent five years in the monastery living under these conditions.

Expanding Literary Output   Merton's literary output was initially severely restricted by his monastic duties, but at the age of thirty-three he published his autobiography, *The Seven Storey Mountain*, which became a best-seller and made him a reluctant celebrity. He continued to receive expanded responsibilities in the monastery, and in 1955 he achieved the esteemed position of Master of Novices. Though he was frequently frustrated by Trappist censorship, by the 1950s the Trappist leadership was allowing him to publish nearly anything he wished.

Various journals sought contributions from Merton throughout his later years. He often generously complied, sending work frequently to these and other more obscure publications. The pressure he felt to produce writing always brought about the same reaction in him—a desire for solitude, which in turn was followed by a flurry of writing activity and renewed contacts with the world around him.

The majority of his more than fifty books and 300 articles involve expository writing, even though Merton felt most comfortable writing poetry and journal entries. He seems to have had few people to talk to about literary matters, even when his monastic silence was somewhat relaxed in the 1950s and 1960s. He made up for this lack in being an energetic, if somewhat eclectic, reader and notetaker, and by the 1960s, he had developed relationships with a number of writers and artists outside the monastery.

Concerned for the Outside World During the 1950s and 1960s, Merton became increasingly concerned with political events and began advocating awareness and activism rather than isolation as the proper response to the world's problems. Along with political events, Merton became increasingly interested in the study of other religions, particularly Zen Buddhism. Tragically, his activism and writings were cut short when Merton died as a result of accidental electrocution in 1968 in Bangkok, Thailand, where he was attending an ecumenical conference.

Works in Literary Context

James Thomas Baker, one of Merton's biographers, believed that the dichotomy of monk/writer in Merton's personality was an essential ingredient in his writing. As Baker stated in *Thomas Merton: Social Critic*, "There was . . . an oriental paradox about his life and thought, the paradox of a monk speaking to the world, which gave it the quality that was uniquely Merton, and any other career would have robbed his work of that quality."

A Life of Contemplation Nearly all of Merton's major works were directly influenced by his monastic life. The restrictions placed upon the author, along with the lessons he learned leading a life of work and contemplation, informed the content of his writing. Among his best-known publications is his autobiography, *The Seven Storey Mountain*, which relates the events leading to his conversion to Catholicism and advocates a life of contemplation. *The Seven Storey Mountain* offers many examples of the way in which the monastic life seemed ideal for the sort of writing that Merton did. The interval between night and dawn, for example, a very active time for monks, was especially fruitful for writing, as Merton noted: "After two or three hours of prayer your mind is saturated in peace and the richness of the liturgy. The dawn is breaking outside the cold windows. If it is warm, the birds are already beginning to sing. Whole blocks of imagery seem to crystallize out as if it were naturally in the silence and the peace, and the lines almost write themselves." Another work that is a natural outgrowth of Merton's monastic life is *The Sign of Jonas* (1953). This personal journal vividly depicts one five-year period in Merton's life in the monastery, focusing on his evolving understanding of the meaning of his role as a monk

---

LITERARY AND HISTORICAL CONTEMPORARIES

Thomas Merton's famous contemporaries include:

Dylan Thomas (1914–1953): Welsh poet who was one of the most renowned authors of the twentieth century. Thomas was known as much for his life of excess as well as for his iconoclastic, critically acclaimed writings.

Saul Bellow (1915–2005): American novelist of Russian-Jewish origin who won the Nobel Prize in Literature in 1976. He is best known for *The Adventures of Augie March* (1953), and *Herzog* (1964).

Herman Wouk (1915–): American author known for his bestselling novels *The Caine Mutiny* (1951), *The Winds of War* (1971), and *War and Remembrance* (1978).

Anthony Burgess (1917–1993): British author and composer who had a long and prolific writing career that included his best-known novel, *A Clockwork Orange* (1962).

Gwendolyn Brooks (1917–2000): African-American poet and the first African-American writer to win a Pulitzer Prize. Brooks was known for her portrayals of the racism and poverty in the daily lives of urban African Americans.

---

and his attempt to reconcile the conflict between his religious and literary aspirations.

Coming to Terms with Developments in Poetry While Merton's early works focus largely on the development of a spiritual life, many of his later writings address secular questions and focus his thinking on questions of poetic construction. In these later writings, he employs a diverse range of formal and free verse techniques to tackle both religious and secular subjects. Early in his career, he had avoided the forms used by contemporary poets because he associated these with sterile experimentation. By the 1960s, however, he had convinced himself that the use of open forms, with their idiosyncratic variations in line, image, and rhythm, could be harnessed to carry the weight of his spiritual and secular themes. *Cables to the Ace* (1968) represented his first attempt to bring all of these elements together in a lyric/epic format that was to reach consummate expression in *The Geography of Lograire* (1969). *The Geography of Lograire*, Merton's way of coming to terms with developments in American poetry, is widely considered a major poem in recent American writing.

Works in Critical Context

Merton's early works were embraced by both readers and reviewers, in part, according to some critics, because his advocation of a radically different way of life appealed to many people in the years following the chaos of World

COMMON HUMAN EXPERIENCE

Many of Merton's works explore the nature and benefits of a contemplative life. Here are some other works that explore a similar theme:

Walden (1854), a book by Henry David Thoreau. This piece of work describes Thoreau's simple, contemplative, and self-reliant life while living alone in a cabin near Walden Pond.

Zen and the Art of Motorcycle Maintenance (1974), a book by Robert Pirsig. In this autobiographical work, the author wrestles with important philosophical questions of the present, as well as enduring questions of meaning and value in human life.

A Seven Day Journey With Thomas Merton (1993), a book by Esther De Waal. In it, the author describes her own seven-day retreat using the writings and photographs of Thomas Merton as a guide.

The Life of the Mind (2006), a book by James V. Schall. The author explores the delights and pleasures humans take in simply knowing.

War II. Although the shift in his writings from a focus on individual spirituality to social criticism generated mixed responses, some critics feel his later, more political works have yet to be realized as his most important contributions. Assessments of Merton's poetry are varied—some critics find the majority of his verse flawed while others consider him among the most important poets of his generation. Several critics have also observed that much scholarship on Merton's works has yet to be conducted.

The Seven Storey Mountain   Merton's autobiography, *The Seven Storey Mountain*, was an instant success. It sold 6,000 copies within the first month and nearly 300,000 copies the first year, and continues to attract readers year after year. If one accepts T.S. Eliot's rather pragmatic definition of a "classic" as "a work that stays in print," then *The Seven Storey Mountain* has met the test for more than forty years. All the signs point to its continued popularity, as it has been consistently in print since its initial publication.

Critical acclaim for *The Seven Storey Mountain* was immediate upon its publication. In *Catholic World*, Catholic critic F. X. Connolly noted, "The book is bracing in its realism, sincere, direct and challenging.... *The Seven Storey Mountain* is a prolonged prayer as well as a great book." Editor George Shuster had similar praise for the book, as he wrote in the *New York Herald Tribune Weekly Book Review*, "The fervor of [Merton's] progress to the monastery of Gethsemani is deeply moving. It is a difficult matter to write about, but I think there will be

many who, however alien the experience may remain to them personally, will put the narrative down with wonder and respect." The autobiography similarly impressed critic George Miles, who noted in a *Commonweal* review that "the book is written simply; the sensory images of boyhood are wonderful, and the incisive quality of his criticism, that tartness of his humor have not been sentimentalized by Merton's entry into a monastery. ... *The Seven Storey Mountain* is a book that deeply impresses the mind and the heart for days. It fills one with love and hope."

Thirty Poems   Although well known as a poet during his early years as a Trappist monk, Merton did not publish his first book of poetry, *Thirty Poems*, until 1944. The poems in this collection were written both before and after Merton's monastery experience. According to James Thomas Baker, author of *Thomas Merton: Social Critic*, Merton felt "that the poetry which he wrote at that time was the best of his career." The book received favorable reviews, including one written by poet Robert Lowell for *Commonweal*, in which the critic called Merton "easily the most promising of our American Catholic poets."

Merton's next book of poems, *A Man in the Divided Sea* (1946), included all of the poems from *Thirty Poems* plus fifty-six more written during the same period. It was equally praised by critics. John Nerber, reviewing the book in *Poetry*, called it "brilliant" and "provocative," adding, "It is, without doubt, one of the important books of the year." Poet Louise Bogan noted in the *New Yorker* that although Merton "has not yet developed a real synthesis between his poetic gifts and his religious ones ... the possibility of his becoming a religious poet of stature is evident."

Despite the recognition that Merton has received for his religious writings and essays, the literary value of his poetry is still questioned. As artist and critic Richard Kostelanetz admitted in the *New York Times*: "Merton's poems are scarcely anthologized, and his name rarely appears in histories of American literature." William Henry Shannon has been more critical of Merton's literary skills, stating in *Commonweal* that Merton's poetry consists of "over a thousand pages," that contain "a fair amount of ... mediocre or just plain bad" writing.

Responses to Literature

1. Despite the rigors of monastic life, Merton was able to produce a large and varied body of work. In what ways do you think his life in the monastery contributed to his prodigious output, and in what ways might it have hampered even greater productivity?

2. Merton's early works focused on the spiritual life, while many of his later writings were overtly political. Write an essay that compares and contrasts both the style and content of these two stages in his writing career. Be sure to note common themes and to describe continuities and discontinuities in the philosophy underlying his works.

3. Merton's writings often explore spiritual questions and express positions on philosophical matters. Write an essay in which you describe his philosophy on life based upon what you can glean from his writings. In your opinion, how relevant are his ideas for someone who does not live a monastic life?

4. Merton was a poet, an essayist, and a memoirist. Choose two of Merton's writings from different genres that focus on similar themes and write an essay in which you identify how Merton explores the same theme through the different lenses of poetry, essay, or memoir.

BIBLIOGRAPHY

Books

Baker, James. *Thomas Merton—Social Critic.* Lexington: University of Kentucky, 1971.

Finley, James. *Merton's Palace of Nowhere.* Notre Dame, Ind.: Ave Maria, 1978.

Furlong, Monica. *Merton: A Biography.* New York: Harper & Row, 1980.

Hart, Patrick, ed. *The Message of Thomas Merton.* Kalamazoo, Mich.: Cistercian Studies, 1981.

Kelly, Frederic J. *Man Before God: Thomas Merton on Social Responsibility.* Garden City, N.Y.: Doubleday, 1974.

Kramer, Victor. *Thomas Merton.* Boston: Twayne, 1984.

Labrie, Ross. *The Art of Thomas Merton.* Fort Worth: Texas Christian University Press, 1979.

Malits, Elena. *The Solitary Explorer: Thomas Merton's Transforming Journey.* New York: Harper & Row, 1980.

McInery, Dennis Q. *Thomas Merton, The Man and His Work.* Kalamazoo, Mich.: Cistercian Studies, 1974.

Rice, Edward. *The Man in the Sycamore Tree: The Good Times and Hard Life of Thomas Merton, An Entertainment.* Garden City: Doubleday, 1970.

Shannon, William H. *Thomas Merton's Dark Path: The Inner Experience of a Contemplative.* New York: Farrar, Straus & Giroux, 1981.

Twomey, Gerald, ed. *Thomas Merton: Prophet in the Belly of a Paradox.* New York: Paulist, 1978.

Wilkes, Paul, ed. *Merton By Those Who Knew Him Best.* New York: Harper & Row, 1984.

Woodcock, George, *Thomas Merton: Monk and Poet.* New York: Farrar, Straus & Giroux, 1978.

❀ W. S. Merwin

BORN: *1927, New York, New York*

NATIONALITY: *American*

GENRE: *Poetry*

MAJOR WORKS:

A Mask for Janus (1952)

The Lice (1969)

The Carrier of Ladders (1970)

Travels (1993)

Migration: New and Selected Poems (2005)

Overview

W. S. Merwin is one of the most prolific contemporary American poets. He writes stylistically diverse poems that frequently display a moral concern for the state of contemporary society and the natural world. In much of his writing, he presents a despairing view of civilization that is only occasionally tempered by expressions of hope.

Works in Biographical and Historical Context

An Unsatisfying Family Life W. S. Merwin was born September 30, 1927, in New York City. During the early years of his childhood, the Merwin family lived in a "manse," a Presbyterian parsonage, in Union City, New Jersey, on the Palisades, above Hoboken Harbor and the Hudson River. There, when he was perhaps only five years old, Merwin first began to write creatively—hymns for his father's church services. During the late 1930s and

W. S. Merwin   *Merwin, W. S., 1994, photograph. AP Images.*

early 1940s, Merwin attended public school in Scranton, a city set in a landscape dominated by coal mines and factories. He writes that his family life, which had never been especially comforting or satisfying for him, deteriorated even further while he was in high school. His mother and father grew apart, and both held themselves remote from Merwin. During World War II, Merwin's father took a leave of absence from his church and family to serve as a chaplain with American troops in Europe. At about the same time, after graduating from high school in 1943, Merwin left home to attend Princeton University. Thereafter, Merwin only on rare occasions returned to see his parents.

Early Influences   While an undergraduate at Princeton, Merwin did find important mentors who shaped his life. He took classes with and came to know and admire scholar and literary critic R. P. Blackmur. He met and studied with John Berryman, also an instructor at Princeton, who was an established poet. Merwin began to develop a strong interest in both studying and writing poetry. In 1946, at Easter, Merwin visited Ezra Pound in St. Elisabeth's Hospital in Washington, D.C. The meeting had enormous implications for Merwin's future as translator, poet, expatriate, and, perhaps, as social activist.

In 1947 Merwin obtained a Bachelor of Arts degree from Princeton, where he had spent most of his time in the university's libraries reading unassigned texts by Joseph Conrad and Leo Tolstoy, or at the university's stables exercising the neglected polo ponies and Reserve Officer Training Corps horses. Probably largely because of the influence of Pound, Merwin returned to Princeton for another year, to pursue a course of graduate study in modern languages. He also spent a summer at McGill University in Montreal studying Old French. At this point, Merwin began actively to make himself into a writer.

Meeting Poets in Europe   In 1949, influenced by Blackmur and Pound, Merwin left the United States and sailed to Europe without the backing of any program or sponsor. He had left graduate school after a year without obtaining a higher degree because he felt certain that he could learn more living abroad among people for whom the Romance languages were living tongues than he could in the classroom. He found employment as a tutor in France and Portugal, in the household of the Princess of Braganza. In 1950 and 1951 Merwin worked as a tutor to the poet Robert Graves's children while living in the village of Deja on the island of Majorca, Spain. In Deja, receiving some encouragement about his literary aspirations from Graves, Merwin worked at writing the poems that filled his first book. He also began to work on several major translation projects.

In 1951 Merwin moved to London to live and write. That same year he had his first original poem, "The Ballad of John Cable and Three Gentlemen," accepted for publication in *The Kenyon Review*. The next year

Merwin's first book of poems, *A Mask for Janus*, was selected for publication by the Yale Younger Poets Series.

In 1954, when he was twenty-six, Merwin bought a ruined farmhouse in southwest France, an area associated with medieval troubadours and Provençal poetry. Though he only stayed in his farmhouse in France for brief periods of time over the next few years, Merwin's intimate connection with the region and with the people, language, literary history, and natural history of rural France became vital for his intellectual and literary development. Merwin was immediately compelled and haunted by the stony landscape and the stonework of the local architecture. He returned to the region in person and in his writing, again and again, for the next quarter of a century.

From 1951 until 1956 Merwin lived most of each year in London and supported himself by translating Spanish and French classics into radio scripts for the BBC. There, he met and cultivated relationships with several literary persons during these years, most importantly with fellow poets Ted Hughes and Sylvia Plath. The writing in Merwin's first three books, all published when Merwin was in his thirties, is noticeably influenced by the works of other poets.

Return to the United States   In August 1956, with three well-reviewed volumes of poetry to his credit, Merwin flew back to the United States after seven years of residence in Europe. Upon his arrival in the United States, he immediately began actively establishing connections with the American literary organizations that would fund his creative writing for many years to follow. In May 1971 Merwin was awarded the Pulitzer Prize for his poetry in *The Carrier of Ladders* (1970). He used the occasion to publicize his pacifist political beliefs. In his brief statement "On Being Awarded the Pulitzer Prize," Merwin refused to accept the accompanying stipend, suggesting that the money should go to support resistance to the draft (the war in Vietnam was still continuing, and there were large antiwar demonstrations) and to aid a bystander blinded in a police shooting.

Despite his success in the United States, during most of the 1970s Merwin considered his place of residence to be his old farmhouse in Lot, France, though by the end of the 1970s, he decided not to live any longer in Europe. Still, he was unwilling to endure what he deemed to be the uncomfortable cultural climate of the United States. He lived in Mexico for an extended time during the late 1970s. He also began to make visits to Hawaii, and by 1983 he was residing there. After having lived much of his adult life in England and on the European continent, Merwin's relocation to Hawaii compelled him to make a place for himself all over again. Merwin was drawn to Hawaii by personal relationships, as well. In 1983 he married Paula Schwartz and settled where his wife and stepchildren lived. Perhaps most important for his poetry, Merwin was confronted in Hawaii by new landscapes and seascapes, new varieties of birds and insects, new sounds and rhythms, and palm trees. All these brought about an evolutionary step forward in Merwin's literary development.

Continuing a Wide-Ranging Career   If any period of Merwin's poetic career can be said to have had mixed success, it was the 1980s. Critics who had lauded his poetry earlier in his career were unable to find in Merwin's nature writing about rural France and remote, exotic Hawaii the challenging innovations and intellectual complexities of his earlier, Pulitzer Prize-winning work. As for popular regard, much of the American public may have been unprepared as yet to embrace the uncompromising ecological messages that Merwin was already sending in his poetry. As he had earlier in his career with his antinuclear and antiwar views, Merwin resorted to journalistic forums to make more explicit his conservationist and environmentalist views.

W. S. Merwin's published works comprehend an extraordinarily wide-ranging selection of languages and human cultural sources. His investigations of "experience" have also been diverse. While Merwin may seem decidedly a denizen of the wide world, he continues to reside on the island of Maui and considers himself a citizen of the United States. Merwin's literary career has embraced the search for, and apparently the eventual finding of, a purpose, an ethical stance, an imaginative focus that he can believe to be authentic. His writings over the past several decades show that Merwin understands himself to be a lover of nature and an ardent environmentalist.

Works in Literary Context

As a poet and translator, Merwin continues to negotiate, to both popular and critical acclaim, the course of a long, influential, and highly productive literary career. For his literary contributions in poetry, translation, and prose, Merwin has claimed for himself a place among the most widely read and discussed and most frequently imitated writers of his generation. He has also become one of the most honored poets of his generation. Awarded the Pulitzer Prize for Poetry in 1971, over the past half century he has amassed an impressive array of grants, awards, and prestigious literary distinctions. Always a prolific writer, Merwin continually publishes new work in a wide variety of venues and displays his skill in a range of literary genres.

Taking on Large Themes   Merwin's poetry, while displaying some consistency of thematic concern, has evolved throughout his career, with nearly each new book displaying a shift in style. This shift seems to answer the need for a voice that is responsive to the human situation and also to the physical world. The poems from Merwin's early collections are characterized by traditional forms, symbolic imagery, mythical and legendary motifs, and anachronistic language. Many of his themes in these early collections are echoed in his successive works, including explorations of the universal cycle of birth, death, and rebirth; the loss of order and the search for

---

LITERARY AND HISTORICAL CONTEMPORARIES

Merwin's famous contemporaries include:

William Buckley (1925–2008): Buckley was an American writer, editor, and television host who was a leading spokesperson for conservatism in the United States during the second half of the twentieth century.

James Merrill (1926–1995): Merrill was an American poet who won the Pulitzer Prize for Poetry in 1977.

Al Gore (1948–): Gore is a former U.S. senator and vice president of the United States. He is known as an environmentalist; his documentary film about global warming, *An Inconvenient Truth* (2006), won an Academy Award. Gore was awarded the Nobel Peace Prize in 2007.

William De Witt Snodgrass (1926–2009): Snodgrass, whose pen name is S. S. Gardons, is an American poet who won the Pulitzer Prize for Poetry in 1960.

Gabriel García Márquez (1928–): Márquez is a Colombian fiction writer widely considered one of the most important authors of the twentieth century; he was awarded the Nobel Prize for Literature in 1982.

Ted Hughes (1930–1998): An English poet who was the British poet laureate from 1984 until his death.

---

identity in contemporary society; and the tensions between spiritual and temporal existence as well as those between art and experience. Merwin's poetry has consistently addressed the large themes of love, mutability, and mortality, and the relations between language, soul, and nature have always been subjects of his speculations.

Ecopoetry   Since the late 1990s, Merwin has come to be identified as a "conservationist," or "environmentalist" or "environmental activist," and Merwin's latest poetry is frequently identified as "ecopoetry." While Merwin's commentators have only relatively recently begun to recognize his often self-proclaimed environmentalist emphasis, the poet's fascination with nature and his concern for what he insists is a threatened natural world have been parts of his work since almost the beginning of his career. However, in the later stages of Merwin's career, he has produced the most characteristic environmental and ecopoetry of the last quarter of the twentieth century. In this latest and current phase, in poetry of organic form and in attitudes that are literally rooted in the natural landscapes they reflect, Merwin reveals something approaching reverence for nature, and he displays patent environmentalist and ecological sympathies. In much of his later writing, he tempers a profound sense of loss of the natural world with a passionate appreciation of natural beauty and variety, and he exhibits a rhetorical

COMMON HUMAN EXPERIENCE

Merwin's later works have been identified by many as part of the movement of "ecopoetry," poetry that has a strong eco-logical message that entails both personal responsibility towards the environment as well as calls for social change. Here are some works by other poets who are considered "ecopoets":

The White Poem (1988), by Jay Ramsay and Carole Bruce. This book is a collaboration between a poet and a photographer who explore the coastal landscape of Pembrokeshire, a county in southwest Wales.

Heavy Water: a Poem for Chernobyl (2004), a poem by Mario Petrucci. This book-length poem explores the suffering caused by the accident at the Chernobyl nuclear power plant in April 1986 by paying tribute to the courage and humor displayed by the people who were there.

The Thunder Mutters: 101 Poems for the Planet (2005), a collection of poems edited by Alice Oswald. The poems in this collection explore the border between the personal and natural worlds and include works by a geographically and historically diverse group of poets.

devotion to educating all who will listen about the need for the conservation of natural diversity.

Works in Critical Context

Merwin has been consistently praised as a technically accomplished writer and has won several prestigious awards for his works, including the 1971 Pulitzer Prize for Poetry for *The Carrier of Ladders* (1970). While he is consistently praised for rejuvenating traditional forms and for continually challenging and developing his technique and themes, critics have lamented the obscure nature of his work.

Early Collections Reviewers of Merwin's first three collections—*A Mask for Janus*, *The Dancing Bears* (1954), and *Green with Beasts* (1956)—faulted him for intellectual self-indulgence. Although a wealth of detailed critical attention has been lavished on the poetry of Merwin's early years, these poems are seen by some as inferior to his later works. As Clifford Toliver notes in the *Dictionary of Literary Biography*, "the poetry of Merwin's initial three books may be the least innovative and is certainly the least characteristic of his oeuvre." In a similar vein, some critics in the 1960s regarded his evolving style as obscure, but others viewed his new approaches as subtle and rewarding. Scholars have now noted that when Merwin's works are viewed in their entirety, each successive collection shows distinct developments in style and theme from the previous ones.

The Lice Merwin's despair over the desecration of nature is strongly expressed in his collection *The Lice*. "If there is any book today that has perfectly captured the peculiar spiritual agony of our time, the agony of a generation which knows itself to be the last, and has transformed that agony into great art, it is W. S. Merwin's *The Lice*," writes Laurence Lieberman in a *Yale Review* article. He continues:

To read these poems is an act of self-purification. Every poem in the book pronounces a judgement against modern men—the gravest sentence the poetic imagination can conceive for man's withered and wasted conscience: our sweep of history adds up to one thing only, a moral vacuity that is absolute and irrevocable. This book is a testament of betrayals; we have betrayed all beings that had power to save us: the forest, the animals, the gods, the dead, the spirit in us, the words. Now, in our last moments alive, they return to haunt us.

Published in 1969, *The Lice* remains one of Merwin's best-known volumes of poetry. His obsession with the meaning of America and its values makes Merwin like the great nineteenth-century poet Walt Whitman, writes L. Edwin Folsom in *Shenandoah*. "His poetry...often implicitly and sometimes explicitly responds to Whitman; his twentieth century sparsity and soberness—his doubts about the value of America—answer, temper, Whitman's nineteenth century expansiveness and exuberance—his enthusiasm over the American creation." Folsom elaborates:

Merwin's answer to Whitman is begun in *The Lice*, an anti-song of the self. Here, instead of the Whitmanian self expanding and absorbing everything, naming it in an ecstacy of union, we find a self stripped of meaning, unable to expand, in a landscape that refuses to unite with the self, refuses to be assimilated, in a place alien and unnameable.

Travels Many reviewers consider *Travels* one of Merwin's most accomplished collections. In her review of this award-winning volume, Judith Kitchen remarked: "This collection fascinates me. Throughout, Merwin holds onto an established habit of line but finds in certain more traditional forms and techniques a renewed sense of what the line is capable of accomplishing." Gerald Stern asserted that "among the many lovely collections that Merwin has given us over the many years of his writing, this is the finest."

Responses to Literature

1. Merwin has been very active as both a poet and a translator of poetry. Do the works he has translated express themes similar to his own creative works? In what ways are his translations an extension of his creative writing, and in what ways do they appear to demonstrate different concerns?

2. Critics have pointed out that Merwin's concerns about nature, and how nature is threatened, have

been present in his work since his earliest writings. These concerns became central to his poetry during more recent phases of his writing. In what ways have his concerns about nature remained the same throughout his writing career, and in what ways has he developed new concerns through the decades?

3. Merwin has been praised for producing a wide-ranging body of writing. Choose one particular area of his work that you feel is the strongest and most compelling and write an essay explaining your position.

4. Merwin's more recent poetry has been characterized as "ecopoetry." Write an essay comparing and contrasting Merwin's ecopoetic writings with those of other authors who have been similarly categorized. Be sure to pay attention to the types of messages as well as the styles of writing in these different works.

BIBLIOGRAPHY

Books

Brunner, Edward J. *Poetry as Labor and Privilege: The Writings of W. S. Merwin*. Urbana, Ill.: University of Chicago Press, 1991.

Bryson, Scott J., ed. *Ecopoetry: A Critical Introduction*. Salt Lake City, Utah: University of Utah Press, 2002.

Byers, Thomas B. *What I Cannot Say: Self, Word, and World in Whitman, Stevens, and Merwin*. Urbana, Ill.: University of Chicago Press, 1990.

Christhilf, Mark. *W. S. Merwin, the Mythmaker*. Columbia, Mo.: University of Missouri Press, 1986.

Frazier, Jane. *From Origin to Ecology: Nature and the Poetry of W. S. Merwin*. Cranbury, N.J.: Associated University Press, 1999.

Hix, H. L. *Understanding W. S. Merwin*. Columbia, S.C.: University of South Carolina Press, 1997.

Hoeppner, Edward Haworth. *Echoes and Moving Fields: Structure and Subjectivity in the Poetry of W. S. Merwin and John Ashbery*. Lewisburg, Pa.: Bucknell University Press, 1994.

Nelson, Cary, and Ed Folsom, eds. *W. S. Merwin: Essays on the Poetry*. Urbana, Ill.: University of Chicago Press, 1987.

Periodicals

Burt, John. "W. S. Merwin's *The Folding Cliffs*." *Raritan* (Winter 2000): 115–135.

Lieberman, Laurence. "W. S. Merwin: The Church of Ash." *Yale Review* (1973): 602–13.

St. John, David. "The Last Troubadour." *Kenyon Review* (1997): 197–203.

Stern, Gerald. "The Lenore Marshall Poetry Prize—1994." *Nation* (December 12, 1994): 733–36.

✹ James A. Michener

BORN: *1907, New York, New York*

DIED: *1997, Austin, Texas*

NATIONALITY: *American*

GENRE: *Fiction, nonfiction*

MAJOR WORKS:
Tales of the South Pacific (1947)
Hawaii (1959)
The Source (1965)
The Covenant (1980)
Space (1982)

Overview

James A. Michener was among the most popular and prolific of American novelists. He was known primarily for historical epics that chronicle events of various regions and their people from prehistoric times to the present. His novels are often family sagas in which men and women of many heritages intermingle in far-off places.

Works in Biographical and Historical Context

Unknown Origins The exact date or place of Michener's birth is not known. Although many reference books state that it was probably in New York City in 1907, all that is known for certain about his infancy is that Michener's mother, Mabel, picked up the young child whom she would name James from the streets of Doylestown, Pennsylvania, and reared him as her foster child. In 1931, when the young man received a scholarship to study abroad, he obtained a passport only after Mabel Michener and a notary prepared a statement giving him citizenship status. The fact that Michener has never known when or where he was born, or his family

James Michener *Michener, James, 1989, photograph. AP Images.*

background, has impelled him to invent his roots and has enabled him to put himself in the place of characters of exotic heritages.

Michener grew up in the Bucks County countryside in Pennsylvania and attended Doylestown Grammar School. At the age of fourteen he hitchhiked for some months through forty-five American states. On his return home he delivered newspapers, wrote a sports column for the local paper, and was saved from delinquency by his prowess in sports, especially basketball.

Scholarships and Travels   A sports scholarship took Michener to Swarthmore College, and his second novel evokes feelings of an undergraduate of the time in this Quaker institution. During one summer vacation Michener traveled with a Chautauqua tent show and became imbued with a love of the drama, reflected in his fiction, which has often been adapted for the stage and screen.

Michener graduated with honors in 1929 with a degree in English and history as well as a Phi Beta Kappa key. He began teaching at the nearby Hill School. A traveling scholarship enabled him to make his first trip abroad, and he enrolled at St. Andrew's University in Scotland, but he also studied art in London and Siena, Italy, worked on a Mediterranean cargo vessel, and collected folk tales in the Hebrides islands.

The Depression and World War II   Michener returned to the United States during the Depression years. He taught from 1933 to 1936 at George School near Doylestown and in 1937 earned a master's degree at the Colorado State College of Education in Greeley, where he was an associate professor from 1936 through 1939. Michener was inspired through his friendship with an erudite newspaper editor to write a voluminous novel based on the history of that state. The result, many years later, was *Centennial* (1974), which dramatized the lore of Colorado from the creation of the earth up to 1974.

Michener served his writing apprenticeship as the author of some fifteen scholarly articles on the teaching of social studies, published between 1936 and 1942. During 1940–1941 he was a visiting professor at Harvard University, and in 1941 he accepted a post on the editorial staff of the Macmillan Company in New York. Despite his Quaker upbringing (Quakers traditionally emphasize pacifism), he volunteered for service in the U.S. Navy in 1942, after the United States entered World War II, and his first assignment as a lieutenant (junior grade) was a wartime post as "a supersecretary for aviation maintenance" in the South Pacific—a region with which his name is still associated. From 1944 through 1946 Michener served as a naval historian in the South Pacific.

Michener was able to visit some fifty islands during World War II, and as the war wound down, he retreated to a jungle shack and began writing the stories that were to appear as his first novel, *Tales of the South Pacific* (1947), which won a Pulitzer Prize in 1948.

Michener had been discharged from the navy in 1946 as a lieutenant commander and had returned to Macmillan as a textbook editor when in 1949 *Tales of the South Pacific* was made into a successful musical by Richard Rodgers and Oscar Hammerstein II. When *South Pacific* ran for a total of 1,925 performances on Broadway, a share of royalties from the play (which became in 1958 a popular Hollywood film) enabled Michener to devote himself entirely to his career of professional author.

Michener's second book was the semiautobiographical *The Fires of Spring* (1949). With *The Fires of Spring* came an important change in the life of the author. When the book was rejected by Macmillan, Michener traveled by bus up Fifth Avenue and submitted the manuscript to Random House. Thereafter, almost all his books were published by Random House, and Bennett Cerf and Albert Erskine became his meticulous publisher and editor.

Magazine Assignments and More Travels   The Pacific still beckoned, and an assignment from *Holiday* magazine to revisit his wartime haunts sent Michener to write feature articles about the Pacific, its atolls, and places like Fiji, Guadalcanal, and Rabaul. Other assignments allowed Michener to range through Asia, the continent of his early dreams. From these travels, he produced not only several novels but nonfiction works as well, including *The Floating World* (1954), a scholarly study of the art of the Japanese print, the first of four volumes that revealed Michener's serious concern with art, especially that of the Orient.

Into Politics   An avid student of politics, Michener was turning toward involvement in the national political scene. His active campaigning for John F. Kennedy is described in *Report of the County Chairman* (1961). In 1962 Michener himself campaigned vigorously but unsuccessfully as a candidate for the House of Representatives from the Pennsylvania Eighth District. A later study by Michener of the democratic process resulted in *Presidential Lottery* (1969), a plea for reform in the method of choosing an American president.

A Productive Pattern   Michener returned to fiction in 1963, living in the state of Israel and gathering material for a mammoth novel, *The Source* (1965), which became another best seller. The pattern laid down in this novel was repeated throughout the rest of Michener's life: travel, extensive research, and a voluminous treatment of a regional subject matter. His later works include *The Drifters* (1971) in which he focused on a group of disenchanted, contemporary young people, and another saga, *Chesapeake* (1978), set in the great bay of Maryland and its shores; the characters go back to the American Indians, and the story incorporates much fictionalized American history. Still active in his seventies, Michener wrote *The Covenant* (1980), an exploration of the history of South Africa; *Space* (1982), which describes the U.S. space program; *Poland* (1983) and *Caribbean* (1989), which are both fictionalized histories of a country or region.

During his final years, Michener lived in Austin, Texas, where he founded the Michener Center for Writers at the University of Texas. He died of kidney failure in 1997 at the age of ninety.

Works in Literary Context

Epic Treatments   Michener's body of work is largely made up of historical fiction, and many of his novels, some over a thousand pages long, cover large swaths of historical ground. These wide-ranging novels include, among others, *The Covenant*, a saga of the development of South Africa; *Space*, the story of the United States space program; *Poland*, which follows that country's progress from early centuries to the present; *Texas* (1985), a novel commissioned to celebrate the state's sesquicentennial, recounts factual events from 450 years of the region's recorded past; and *Alaska* (1988), which begins with the formation of North America's land mass and follows the state's progress from its early settlement by Russia up to the oil boom that began during the 1970s.

History that Entertains   Michener not only employs an abundance of well-researched information on the social, cultural, and historical background of his subjects that allows him to invest his novels with an encyclopedic quality, he combines this historical information with entertaining and engaging narratives that often center around a particular family or community. A. Grove Day once wrote, "As a literary craftsman Michener has labored to entertain." One *Newsweek* reviewer called Michener "the literary world's Cecil B. DeMille" while a *Time* reviewer praised Michener for being "a popular novelist with an awesome audience for his epic narratives" who was also "an unpretentious, solid craftsman." Michener enjoyed widespread popularity during his lifetime, and his novels have sold over seventy-five million copies worldwide. He remains one of America's most commercially successful authors.

Works in Critical Context

Although commercially successful, Michener's fiction has garnered an uneven critical response. Such early works as *The Bridges at Toko-Ri* (1953) and *Sayonara* (1954) were commended for their steady pace and unified structure. Michener's later, longer novels, however, have been faulted for lacking these same qualities. The frequent time shifts, large casts, and vast scope of events in these works are regarded by some as impediments to serious reader involvement. While some reviewers consider Michener's characters often flat and unrealistic, others laud his entertaining and informative narration of regional histories. Webster Schott, in the *New York Times Book Review*, is in the latter category. Reviewing the breadth of Michener's work, he wrote that Michener

---

LITERARY AND HISTORICAL CONTEMPORARIES

Michener's famous contemporaries include:

John Steinbeck (1902–1968): Steinbeck was an American writer who was one of the best-known and widely read writers of the twentieth century; he was awarded the Nobel Prize in Literature in 1962.

Dee Brown (1908–2002): Brown was an American historian and novelist whose works presented the hardships and challenges involved in the history of the Western frontier.

Leon Uris (1924–2003): Like Michener, Uris was a writer of well-researched historical fiction. His best-known novel was *Exodus* (1958), which told the story of Jewish history from the late nineteenth century to the founding of Israel in 1948. The book topped the best-seller lists in 1959, alongside Michener's *Hawaii*, and was made into a movie in 1960.

Richard Wright (1908–1960): Wright was an African American author noted for his impact on black fiction because of his naturalistic descriptions of the reality of life for African Americans.

Richard Nixon (1913–1994): Nixon was a tenacious American politician and thirty-seventh president of the United States (1969–1974)

---

has found a formula. It delivers everywhere—Hawaii, Africa, Afghanistan, America, Israel, even outer space. The formula calls for experts, vast research, travel to faraway places and fraternizing with locals. And it calls for good guys and bad guys (both real and imagined) to hold the whole work together. It's a formula millions love. Mr. Michener gratifies their curiosity and is a pleasure to read.

Tales of the South Pacific   Although *Tales of the South Pacific* is considered a collection of short stories, Michener considered it a novel due to the book's overall theme of America's fight in the South Pacific theater during World War II. *New York Herald Tribune Weekly Book Review* writer P. J. Searles agreed, stating, "Romantic, nostalgic, tragic—call it what you will—this book seems to me the finest piece of fiction to come out of the South Pacific war." Michener "is a born story teller," *New York Times* writer David Dempsey added, "but, paradoxically, this ability results in the book's only real weakness—the interminable length of some of the tales. Mr. Michener saw so much, and his material is so rich, that he simply could not leave anything out." When the book was published in 1947, Orville Prescott in the *Yale Review* described Michener as

COMMON HUMAN EXPERIENCE

Michener was known for writing historical novels that followed a family or community through multiple generations. Here are some other multigenerational works of historical fiction:

North and South (1982), a novel by John Jakes. This novel, which focuses on two families on opposite sides of the Civil War, traces the family histories from their arrival in the American colonies through the beginning of the Civil War.

The Thorn Birds (1977), a novel by Colleen McCullough. This novel chronicles the trials and tribulations of a family that runs a sheep range in the Australian Outback during the years 1915 to 1969.

The Family Orchard (2000) by Nomi Eve. Eve's highly acclaimed first novel spans two hundred years in the lives of a family of immigrants in Jerusalem.

"Narratives of Empire" (1967–2000), a series of novels by Gore Vidal. This series of seven historical novels follows two fictional American families through the years from 1776 to 1950.

"certainly one of the ablest and one of the most original writers to appear on the American literary scene in a long time."

Hawaii In *James A. Michener*, A. Grove Day described *Hawaii* as "the best novel ever written about Hawaii." It was published a few months after Hawaii was granted statehood in August 1959. According to Day, the book "is founded on truth but not on fact." Michener drew from his own experiences in the Pacific region to develop *Hawaii* and also consulted a variety of other sources, including missionary accounts. As the author stated in his book *Report of the County Chairman*, his goal was to portray "the enviable manner in which Hawaii had been able to assimilate men and women from many different races."

Writing in the *New York Times Book Review*, Maxwell Geismar praised the book as

a brilliant panoramic novel about Hawaii from its volcanic origins to its recent statehood. It is a complex and fascinating subject, and it is rendered here with a wealth of scholarship, of literary imagination and of narrative skill, so that the large and diverse story is continually interesting.

Day reported,

This is not a historical novel in the usual sense, for not one actual name or event is given; rather, it is a pageant of the coming of settlers from many regions; and the main theme might well be: Paradise is not a goal to attain, but a stage to which

people of many colors and creeds may bring their traditional cultures to mingle with those of the others and create what may truly be an Eden at the crossroads of a hitherto empty ocean.

Nevertheless, some of the praise was qualified. A *Times Literary Supplement* writer indicated that "Mr. Michener's zestful, knowledgeable progress through the millennia is absorbing. He cannot, of course, with such enormous slabs of raw material to handle and shape, go anywhere deeply below the surface, but there are some splendid sustained passages in his book." William Hogan wrote in the *San Francisco Chronicle* that "as he has adjusted details in Hawaii's history to suit his fiction, the author is forced to adapt characters to fit into the big historical picture. And that is the book's main weakness." Although *Saturday Review* critic Horace Sutton was of a similar opinion, he maintained that Hawaii "is still a masterful job of research, an absorbing performance of storytelling, and a monumental account of the islands from geologic birth to sociological emergence as the newest, and perhaps the most interesting of the United States."

The Covenant Michener applied this same pattern to explore the history of South Africa in *The Covenant*. In this book, said William McWhirter in *Time*, the author "manages to cover 15,000 years of African history, from the ritual-haunted tribes of Bushmen to present-day Afrikaners obstinately jeering at appeals for 'human rights.'" Michener's method of combining fiction with nonfiction drew some criticism from reviewers. As Andre Brink noted in the *Washington Post Book World*,

in his portrayal of history the author adapts a curious method also characteristic of his earlier novel, *The Source*: even though well-known historical figures appear in it—the Trek leader Piet Retief, the Boer general De Wet, Prime Minister Daniel Malan and a host of others—many of their major exploits are attributed to fictitious characters appearing alongside of them. Imagine a novel prominently featuring Abraham Lincoln but attributing the Gettysburg Address to a fictitious minor character.

However, according to John F. Bums in the *New York Times Book Review*,

the book's accomplishment may be to offer a public inured to stereotypes a sense of the flesh and blood of the Afrikaners, the settlers who grew from harsh beginnings to a white tribe now nearing three million, commanding the most powerful economy and armed forces in Africa.

Space Writing in the *New York Times*, Stephen Farber described Michener's *Space* as a "fictional rendering of the development of the space program from World War II to the present." Michael L. Smith reported in the *Nation* that "real participants make occasional appearances, but Michener relies primarily on fictional approximations." In fact, said Smith, *Space* "is less a historical novel than a tract. In part, it is a celebration of space exploration as a glorious blend of science, American frontiersmanship and human curiosity. But more than that, it's an impassioned denunciation of what Michener considers one of the gravest dangers facing post-Vietnam America: the proliferation of an 'anti-science movement.'"

Ben Bova in the *Washington Post Book World* added that the book "contrasts several varieties of faith, from the simplistic faith of the German rocket engineer who believes that technology can solve any problem, to the faith of the astronauts who believe that flying farther and faster is the greatest good in the world."

Poland Michener's sprawling novel *Poland* (1983), was begun in 1977. Ursula Hegi, writing in the *Los Angeles Times Book Review*, explained that Michener "visited Poland eight times and traveled throughout the country. He talked to people of different backgrounds and enjoyed the assistance of fifteen Polish scholars." Despite the time and effort Michener put into the book, *Poland* received mixed reviews. Bill Kurtis wrote in the *Chicago Tribune Book World* that "Michener's form is familiar. History is seen through the lives of three fictional families.... Around them, Michener wraps a detailed historical panorama." Hegi wrote that "though Michener captures Poland's struggle and development, he presents the reader with too many names and personal histories, making it difficult to keep track of more than a few characters." Other reviewers criticized Michener for oversimplifying history, making notable omissions, and committing historical inaccuracies. Peter Osnos of the *Washington Post*, however, asserted that *Poland* was "Michener at his best," that the book was "prodigiously researched, topically relevant and shamelessly intended for readers with neither will nor patience for more scholarly treatments."

Caribbean *Caribbean* (1989), another of Michener's best-selling novels, is a fictionalized history of the scattered islands between North and South America. Some critics deemed Michener's plot improbable and his characters stereotypical. John Hearne of the *New York Times Book Review* found the characters in the novel "stiff and wooden" and the dialogue unrealistic. Some reviewers, on the other hand, defended the work as informative and entertaining. Hearne commented:

> Given the scope of the task which Michener has set himself, he has done his chosen region proud. *Caribbean* is a work which anybody strange to the islands and wanting to know something about them could read with confidence. All the essentials are there; and a skilled and studious novelist has embedded these essentials in a deeply felt, highly responsible tale.

Karen Stabiner, writing in the *Los Angeles Times Book Review*, claimed that Michener "has perfect best-seller pitch: enough intrigue to make life exciting; enough chronological and geographical distance to make the thrills thrilling, not threatening."

Responses to Literature

1. Michener has been criticized for employing flat and unrealistic characters. Does he deserve his charge, and if so, in what way does this interfere with the reader's enjoyment of his novels? In what ways do his novels not need multidimensional or realistic characters to accomplish what Michener wants them to accomplish?

2. Michener was a best-selling author for much of his career. Did the wide popularity of his novels interfere with his literary development? How was he able to produce high-quality literature while still maintaining his large audience?

3. Although many of Michener's novels are epic sagas, he has also produced novels that are less grand in scope. Choose one of Michener's novels that does not treat a wide-ranging historical topic and write an essay comparing his treatment of the subject in that book to the way he wrote his longer historical epics.

4. Commentators have noted that Michener's novels, despite their diverse topics, share a theme: the defeat of common prejudices and the promotion of harmonious human relations. Write an essay that discusses how he handles this theme in two or more of his novels.

BIBLIOGRAPHY

Books

Becker, George Joseph. *James A. Michener*. New York: Ungar, 1983.

Day, A. Grove. *James A. Michener*. Boston: G. K. Hall, 1977.

Dybwad, G. L., and Joy V. Bliss. *James A. Michener: The Beginning Teacher and His Textbooks*. Albuquerque, N.Mex.: The Book Stops Here, 1995.

Hayes, John Phillip. *James A. Michener*. Indianapolis: Bobbs-Merrill, 1984.

Kings, J. *In Search of Centennial*. New York: Random House, 1978.

Newquist, Roy. *Conversations*. Chicago: Rand McNally, 1967.

Prescott, Orville. *In My Opinion: An Inquiry into the Contemporary Novel*. Indianapolis: Bobbs-Merrill, 1952.

Severson, Marilyn S. *James A. Michener: A Critical Companion*. Westport, Conn.: Greenwood Press, 1996.

Stuckey, W. J. *The Pulitzer Prize Novels*. Norman: University of Oklahoma Press, 1966.

Warfel, Harry Redcay. *American Novelists of Today*. New York: American Book, 1951.

✸ Edna St. Vincent Millay

BORN: *1892, Rockland, Maine*

DIED: *1950, Austerlitz, New York*

NATIONALITY: *American*

GENRE: *Poetry*

MAJOR WORKS:

Renascence, and Other Poems
  (1917)
The Ballad of the Harp-Weaver
  (1922)

Overview

Edna St. Vincent Millay was a popular poet whose verse captured the rebellious mood of post–World War I youth. She is primarily remembered for her early volumes of poetry, which boldly asserted an independent, nonconformist perspective toward contemporary life rarely expressed by women authors of her time.

Edna St. Vincent Millay   *Millay, Edna St. Vincent, photograph. The Library of Congress.*

Works in Biographical and Historical Context

Poetry and Music at an Early Age   Millay, the first of the three daughters of Cora Buzzelle Millay and Henry Tolman Millay, was born in Rockland, Maine, on February 22, 1892. In 1900 Cora Millay divorced her husband, an educator with a fondness for poker, and settled with her girls in Camden, Maine. Millay retained a lifelong devotion and admiration for her mother, who provided for the family by nursing, and who encouraged all her daughters to be self-reliant and to appreciate books and music. In fact, the musical talent of Vincent (as Millay was called by her family) was so obvious that a local teacher gave her piano lessons, hoping to prepare her for a musical career. After a few years the plan was abandoned, but music remained a source of pleasure, a subject for poetry, and the basis for her sense of poetic rhythm.

Published as a Teen   It was Millay's interest in literature that led her to write original poetic compositions while she was still a teenager. At the age of fourteen she had a poem, "Forest Trees," published in *St. Nicholas* magazine, a popular children's periodical that ultimately printed a number of her juvenile works. At Camden High School she wrote for and eventually became editor of the school magazine. At her graduation in 1909 she recited an original poem, and thereby demonstrated a third side of her early interest in the arts: dramatic performance.

In 1912, at her mother's urging, Millay submitted a long poem, which she entitled "Renaissance," in a contest designed to select pieces for an anthology called *The Lyric Year*. Ferdinand Earle, one of the judges, was delighted with the entry from E. Vincent Millay (as she then called herself). He persuaded her to change the title to "Renascence," and fully expected the poem to win first prize. Other judges were not as taken with the poem as Earle, however, and the poem ranked only fourth in the final tally. Nevertheless, when *The Lyric Year* was published in November 1912, "Renascence" received immediate critical acclaim.

The Vassar Years   Millay was already in her twenties when she entered Vassar College in 1914, after a semester of additional preparation at Barnard College. At Vassar, she was very active in campus life. She published poems and plays in the student newspaper, *The Miscellany News*, and acted regularly in school dramas, playing the lead in her own drama, *The Princess Marries the Page* (1932). She also composed lyrics for a marching song for Vassar's Founder's Day—a campus holiday that celebrates the founding of the college—in 1915.

Even with all her extracurricular activities, Millay remained devoted to her coursework. Her studies were concentrated on literature, drama, and both classical and modern languages. Critical biographer Norman Brittin notes, "Her education reinforced the influence of the classics upon her and insured that she would be a learned poet, one more like a Milton, Shelley, or Tennyson than a Whitman or Vachel Lindsay." Indeed, though her poetry would always be termed "American" in flavor, her images and allusions were often based on the classics, while her rhythms and sentiments were forever inviting comparison to established poets from John Donne to A. E. Housman.

Millay's years at Vassar, with their feminine collegiality, also had an effect on the poet's outlook by stimulating and solidifying a healthy regard for the friendship of women and the active feminist principles that were evident in her later poetry. A spirited female independence displayed itself also, particularly in Millay's bridling at rigid dormitory rules.

Greenwich Village Life   In 1917, not long after her graduation, Millay's first volume of poetry, *Renascence and Other Poems*, was published. The appearance of this first volume made Millay a presence in the literary world, but brought her no financial reward. Millay returned to New York City, hoping to make a living through acting. She and her sister Norma moved to Greenwich Village, home of the Provincetown Players, a popular acting troupe of the time.

In the Village, spirits were high and free. It was a new kind of intellectual awakening for Millay, quite different from the formalized education she received at Vassar. Women's rights and free love were an accepted part of the living code, and the determination to experience life to its fullest was heightened by the reality of World War I, with its daily reports of young lives lost. Millay's independent spirit—and the fact that she was an attractive, slender redhead—made her admirably suited for Village life. The young poet who was so recently surrounded by loving female friendships soon had a line of male suitors vying for her attention.

In 1918 Millay met Arthur Davison Ficke, with whom she had corresponded since his first congratulations on her publication of "Renascence." Ficke, an accomplished sonneteer, had influenced Millay's experimentation with the form. Through their correspondence, she had come to think of this married man as her spiritual mentor. While he was in New York on his way to a military posting in France, however, they had an intense three-day affair. The emotional experience found direct expression in love letters and sonnets written to Ficke and indirectly in much of her other work. Though they were to remain lifelong friends, the ardor between them soon cooled.

The whirlwind romances and all-night parties made for an exciting life, but the Village years were also ones of poverty for Millay. She made no money from her acting and had to work hard to sell a few poems. One of her chief sources of revenue at this time was *Ainslee's*, a magazine with no literary pretensions. Since she was paid by the line, poetry did not bring a very great return, so she began turning out prose, along with some light poetry, under the pseudonym "Nancy Boyd."

In 1920 Millay met Edmund Wilson, who would later, unsuccessfully, propose marriage to her. With his

influence, Millay began to have most of her work published in *Vanity Fair*, where Wilson was an editor. This brought much-needed income to the young woman, who was still involved in the exciting but nonpaying world of theater. The *Vanity Fair* exposure helped launch the poet into the national consciousness and earn popularity she would maintain for many years.

The Peak of Popularity   Millay's popularity peaked when she received the Pulitzer Prize in 1923 for *The Ballad of the Harp-Weaver*. In addition to an acclaimed piece of work, the prize was also notable because Millay was the first woman to win the Pulitzer for poetry. Her poems of this period were primarily focused on her own emotional life. At the center of the bohemian milieu in Greenwich Village during the 1920s, Millay had become as famous for her hedonistic lifestyle as for her poetry. Her many failed relationships led her to believe that love could not endure, and she became distrustful of human passion. Accordingly, Millay maintained a dichotomy between soul and body that is evident in many of her works. In 1923, despite her antagonistic relationship with love, she married Eugen Jan Boissevain, though it is reported that the two had an open relationship in which they each took various lovers.

New Priorities   Beginning in the late 1920s, Millay started to reexamine her poetic priorities and became more interested in social and international political problems.

COMMON HUMAN EXPERIENCE

Millay's exploration of mental states anticipated some of the styles of the confessional school of poetry that would become popular in later years. Here are some early works of confessional poetry:

The Waking (1952), a poem by Theodore Roethke. This poem, which describes waking from sleep, is a highly contemplative and self-reflective work that compares waking life to sleep.

Ariel (1965), poems by Sylvia Plath. The poems in this collection are intensely personal, addressing motherhood, sexuality, marriage, and the author's experiences with depression.

The Dream Songs (1969), poems by John Berryman. This collection of poetry consists of lyrical works that explore the associations among emotions provoked by everyday events.

By the time *Wine from These Grapes* appeared in 1934, Millay had suffered the death of her mother and was experiencing increasing anxiety over the fate of mankind itself, as global tensions escalated toward World War II. These two events—one personal and one universal—dominated the contents of the volume. In 1936, more trouble befell Millay when she suffered a back injury in an automobile accident. Added to her already frail health, it was to hamper her work for years. Her next collection of poetry, *Huntsman, What Quarry?*, did not appear until 1939.

Her popularity was already waning as the 1930s wore on, and her series of wartime propaganda poems, published in such volumes as *Conversation at Midnight* (1937) and *Make Bright the Arrows* (1940), further eroded her popularity and put a great strain on her, which resulted in a nervous breakdown in 1944. Her recovery was slow. Several friends died in the 1940s, most notably Arthur Davison Ficke in 1945. Eugen Boissevain, her husband, died in August 1949. Though Millay never recovered emotionally or physically, she continued to write, and was planning another collection when she died of a heart attack on October 19, 1950.

Works in Literary Context

An advocate of individualism and romanticism in her verse, Millay commonly employed rhyme and traditional metrical patterns to convey her nontraditional ideas about the role of women in relationships and society. Millay was one of the most skillful writers of sonnets in the twentieth century and her candid investigations of mental states are credited with helping to herald the confessional school of poetry.

The Voice of Feminism   Millay's earliest works were often a sassy celebration of feminism and free love that caught the mood of Greenwich Village life in the racy postwar period of the 1920s. Millay favored themes of love, death, and nature during this period. Commentators noted that the arch tone of her second volume of poetry, *A Few Figs from Thistles* (1920), reflected the impression that fast life and fleeting loves had made on a young woman always receptive to emotional experiences. The voice of feminism was important in this and other early collections as well, with Millay indicating that women as well as men could be casual in their treatment of sexual love, go on with life when it was over, and look forward to the next affair.

A Political Poet   Beginning in the late 1920s, Millay's poetry began reflecting her political views, with some of her works directly railing against the political conditions in the world at the time. For example, *The Murder of Lidice*, a propaganda piece written for the Writers' War Board in 1942, was a sentimental ballad recounting the German destruction of the Czech village through the story of two village lovers planning to marry on that very day. She brought her intense personal voice to bear on her political poems, but this was considered by critics and readers to harm rather than help these works. As Babette Deutsch wrote, "when she turns to political themes, the gay impudence of her girlhood, the sensitive curiosity of her more mature work, are lost in the shriek of a helplessly angry woman."

Works in Critical Context

After an initial period of resounding praise, critical opinion of Millay's poetry diverged. Later critics most often categorize her as a minor lyric poet who failed to develop beyond her early successes. Detractors termed her writing verbose, pretentious, and artificial, citing Millay's use of archaic words, traditional structures, and a coy tone that weakened her feminist statements. However, some commentators, such as Edmund Wilson, consider Millay one of the few twentieth-century poets whose stature equals that of great literary figures from the past. Millay's champions support this contention by pointing to her pervasive wit, lyric skill, and distinguished contribution to the sonnet form.

Renascence, and Other Poems   Millay's first volume of poetry, *Renascence, and Other Poems*, was a critical and popular success. A collection of lyrics and sonnets celebrating spiritual rebirth, nature, and beauty, *Renascence* was praised by Louis Untermeyer for its "lyrical mastery." The critic added that Millay "has made ecstasy articulate and almost tangible." Harriet Monroe wrote that Millay "has been lavish with details of experience, of emotion, and her agile and penetrating mind has leapt through spaces of thought rarely traversed by women, or by men either for that matter."

The Ballad of the Harp-Weaver *The Ballad of the Harp-Weaver*, which won Millay the Pulitzer Prize for poetry, contains some of her best-known sonnets. Critics were generally impressed with this collection, noting that many female readers saw this work as an important expression of the new woman. As Harriet Monroe wrote in *Poetry* magazine, "How neatly she upsets the carefully built walls of convention which men have set up around their Ideal Woman." Harold Lewis Cook wrote that the sonnets in *Harp-Weaver* "mark a milestone in the conquest of prejudice and evasion." Some critics, however, were disappointed that she did not show a marked maturity or any fresh insights. John Gould Fletcher summarily dismissed the title poem as "the unforgettable rhythm of Mother Goose, the verbal utterance of a primer—all used to deal out an idea which is wishy-washy to the point of intellectual feebleness."

Responses to Literature

1. Critics have faulted Millay for using a coy tone that undermined the feminism of her poetic voice. In what ways does Millay deserve this criticism, and in what ways did she employ a poetic voice that seems appropriate to her feminist themes? Use examples from her poetry in your answer.

2. Millay turned towards political subject matter beginning in the 1930s. In what way was this a significant departure for her, and in what way was this an extension of the kinds of concerns she had displayed in her writing up to that point? In your opinion, did her stylistic approaches change along with her subject matter, or did she use similar styles in her political and personal works?

3. Millay was praised during her lifetime, and particularly during the 1920s, for presenting a new vision of the ideal woman. Write an essay that discusses how well this vision of the ideal woman has stood up to the test of time by comparing contemporary ideals about women with the kinds of ideals Millay put forward.

4. Millay's investigations of her mental and emotional states are said to have prefigured the confessional school of poetry. Write an analytical essay comparing her poetry to the works of at least one of the confessional poets. Be sure to discuss similarities and differences in both style and subject matter.

BIBLIOGRAPHY

Books

Atkins, Elizabeth. *Edna St. Vincent Millay and Her Times.* Chicago: University of Chicago Press, 1936.

Brittin, Norman A. *Edna St. Vincent Millay.* New York: Twayne, 1967; revised, 1982.

Cheney, Anne. *Millay in Greenwich Village.* Tuscaloosa, Ala.: University of Alabama Press, 1975.

Daffron, Carolyn. *Edna St. Vincent Millay.* New York: Chelsea House, 1989.

Dash, Joan. *A Life of One's Own: Three Gifted Women and the Men They Married.* New York: Harper & Row, 1973.

Epstein, Daniel Mark. *What My Lips Have Kissed: The Loves and Love Poems of Edna St. Vincent Millay.* New York: Holt, 2001.

Gould, Jean. *The Poet and Her Book: A Biography of Edna St. Vincent Millay.* New York: Dodd, Mead, 1969.

Gurko, Miriam. *Restless Spirit: The Life of Edna St. Vincent Millay.* New York: Crowell, 1962.

Margaretta, Winifred and Frances Kirkland. *Girls Who Became Writers.* New York: Harper, 1933.

Milford, Nancy. *Savage Beauty: The Life of Edna St. Vincent Millay.* New York: Random House, 2001.

Shafter, Toby. *Edna St. Vincent Millay: America's Best-Loved Poet.* New York: J. Messner, 1957.

Sheean, Vincent. *The Indigo Bunting: A Memoir of Edna St. Vincent Millay.* New York: Harper, 1951.

White, Hilda. *Truth Is My Country: Portraits of Eight New England Authors.* New York: Doubleday, 1971.

◉ Arthur Miller

BORN: *1915, New York, New York*

DIED: *2005, Roxbury, Connecticut*

NATIONALITY: *American*

GENRE: *Drama*

MAJOR WORKS:
All My Sons (1947)
Death of a Salesman (1949)
The Crucible (1953)

Overview

Arthur Miller was one of the major dramatists of the twentieth century. He is frequently ranked with other great figures of American drama as Eugene O'Neill, Tennessee Williams, and Edward Albee. Although Miller's eminence as a dramatist is based primarily on four plays he wrote early in his career, he remained active during a more than sixty-year career, earning awards and premiering new plays until his death at age 89.

Works in Biographical and Historical Context

From Mediocrity to Award-Winning Dramatist
Miller was born and raised in New York City, the son of a prosperous businessman who lost his wealth during the Great Depression. A mediocre high school student with little interest in academic pursuits, Miller's initial application to the University of Michigan was rejected. He was eventually accepted at the University, however, and there

Arthur Miller   *Miller, Arthur, photograph. AP Images.*

began writing for the stage, showing distinct promise as a dramatist and winning several student awards. For a short time after college, he was employed as a scriptwriter for radio plays. Although he found the demands of broadcast writing restrictive, this period, together with his college years, served as a valuable apprenticeship for Miller.

Miller's first Broadway play, *The Man Who Had All the Luck*, was produced in 1944. Although it lasted only four performances, the play nevertheless won a Theatre Guild award and established Miller as an important young playwright. With the production of *Death of a Salesman* in 1949, Miller firmly established his reputation as an outstanding American dramatist. This famous play focuses on the emotional deterioration of Willy Loman, an aging and unsuccessful salesman, who can hardly distinguish between his memories of a brighter past and his setbacks in the dismal present. In the course of the play Willy grapples with the loss of his job and the failure of his two grown sons to achieve wealth, and with it, presumably, happiness. The play was understood to be a scathing indictment of the American system and received overwhelming critical and public acclaim from its initial production.

A Suspected Communist   Miller followed *Death of a Salesman* with an adaptation of Henrik Ibsen's *An Enemy of the People* (1950) and, in 1953, *The Crucible*. Perhaps Miller's most controversial drama, this work is based upon the witch trials held in 1692 in Salem, Massachusetts. Featuring historical characters drawn from this period, *The Crucible* addresses the complex moral dilemmas of John Proctor, a man wrongly accused of practicing

witchcraft. Through his depiction of the mass frenzy of the witch hunt, Miller examines the social and psychological aspects of group pressure and its effect on individual ethics, dignity, and beliefs.

It was through the themes in *The Crucible* that Miller explored and criticized the climate of the early 1950s, in which fear of communism led many national leaders to suspect their fellow Americans of conspiring to overthrow the government. Miller and several of his theater associates became targets for persecution, and in 1957 Miller was himself called to testify before the House Committee on Un-American Activities, which was charged with investigating suspected threats of subversion and communist propaganda in the United States. Although Miller admitted to the committee that he had attended a meeting of communist writers, he refused to identify anyone he had met there and denied ever having been a member of the Communist Party. As a result, he was found guilty of contempt of Congress. This conviction was later overturned.

Miller's next offering, produced in 1955, consisted of two one-act plays: *A Memory of Two Mondays*—a semiautobiographical piece reflecting Miller's own experiences as a young man working in an auto parts warehouse—and *A View from the Bridge*, for which the playwright won his third New York Drama Critics Circle Award. He later expanded this play to two acts. Given Miller's attempts to establish a new, modern form of tragedy, *A View from the Bridge* is significant in that it exhibits many similarities to classical Greek tragedy.

A Break from Playwriting and a Decline in Popularity   A nine-year break from playwriting followed *A View from the Bridge*, during which period Miller embarked on his highly publicized marriage to, and subsequent divorce from, the famous movie actress Marilyn Monroe. Before they separated, however, Miller adapted one of his short stories into the screenplay *The Misfits* (1961) as a vehicle for his wife to demonstrate her acting abilities.

Miller returned to the theater in 1964 with two new works, *After the Fall* and *Incident at Vichy*. These plays explored a theme new to Miller's work: man's hopeless alienation from himself and others. Critics attribute the shift in his work to Miller's emotional response to the horrors of World War II as well as to his personal problems, both of which may have led the dramatist to reject his earlier vision of possible social harmony among humankind. In 1968, Miller returned to realistic family drama with *The Price*, which was his last major Broadway success. His next work, *The Creation of the World and other Business* (1972), a series of comic sketches based on the Biblical Book of Genesis, met with severe critical disapproval when it was first produced on Broadway, closing after only twenty performances. All of Miller's subsequent works premiered outside of New York. In the 1980s, Miller produced a number of short pieces, which reviewers have generally regarded as minor works, inferior to his early masterpieces.

Despite the absence of any notable theatrical success since the mid-1960s, Miller remained an important voice in contemporary American drama throughout the remainder of his life. *Death of a Salesman* and *The Crucible* are still frequently performed, thereby reaching successive generations of playgoers. And though less compelling, his later works continue to probe and explore the nature of the individual as an innately social, interactive creature. Miller died at the age of 89 of congestive heart failure on the evening of February 10, 2005—the 56th anniversary of the Broadway debut of *Death of a Salesman*.

Works in Literary Context

Much of Miller's work displays his deep and abiding concern with conscience and morality, with one's dual—and often conflicting—responsibilities to oneself and to one's fellow human beings. It is only through relationships with others, Miller's plays suggest, that our humanity truly emerges.

Tragedy and the Common Man Throughout his career, Miller continually addressed several distinct but related issues in both his dramatic and expository writings. In his early plays and in a series of essays published in the 1940s and 50s, Miller first outlined a form of tragedy applicable to modern times and contemporary characters, one that challenged traditional notions that suggested only kings, queens, princes, and other members of the nobility can be suitable subjects for tragedy. In "Tragedy and the Common Man," for example, Miller asserts that the "underlying struggle" of all such dramas "is that of the individual attempting to gain his 'rightful' position in society." Consequently, as Miller said in a 1949 essay, "the tragic feeling is invoked in us when we are in the presence of a character who is ready to lay down his life, if need be, to secure one thing—his sense of personal dignity." According to this view, even ordinary people—like Willy Loman, the protagonist of *Death of a Salesman*—can achieve truly tragic stature.

The Individual's Relationship with Himself and Others Another of Miller's abiding concerns is the issue of the individual's relationship with himself and society. Several of his works suggest that people are doomed to frustration when they become cognizant of their own identity, particularly when they search for their identity in a society that frowns upon such an endeavor. In work after work, from *All My Sons* and *The Crucible* to *Incident at Vichy*, Miller has presented dilemmas in which a character's sense of personal integrity or self-interest conflicts with his or her responsibility to society or its representatives. Finally, Miller has repeatedly explored the theme of family relations, particularly interactions between fathers and sons. The families depicted in Miller's plays often serve as vehicles for the author's analyses of the broader relations between individuals and society.

LITERARY AND HISTORICAL CONTEMPORARIES

Miller's famous contemporaries include:

Tennessee Williams (1911–1983): The American dramatist best known for his Pulitzer Prize-winning plays, *A Streetcar Named Desire* (1947) and *Cat on a Hot Tin Roof* (1955).

Angus Wilson (1913–1991): Wilson was an English writer best known as a chronicler of the postwar social revolution in England.

Richard Nixon (1913–1994): An influential American politician and thirty-seventh President of the United States (1969–1974).

Vivian Leigh (1913–1967): Leigh was an English-born actress best known for her on-screen performances in *Gone with the Wind* (1939) and *A Streetcar Named Desire* (1951).

Dylan Thomas (1914–1953): The Welsh poet who was as well known for his life of excess as for his iconoclastic, critically acclaimed writings.

John Berryman (1914–1972): Berryman was an American poet who was one of the founders of the Confessional school of poetry.

Doris Lessing (1919–): A British novelist who won the Nobel Prize for Literature in 2007. Among the many works she has produced are the novels *The Grass is Singing* (1950) and *The Golden Notebook* (1962).

Works in Critical Context

Although Miller's later works are generally considered inferior to his early masterpieces, he remained among the most important and influential dramatists to emerge in the United States following World War II. Critics praise his effective use of vernacular, his moral insight, and his strong sense of social responsibility. As author June Schlueter once commented: "When the twentieth century is history and American drama viewed in perspective, the plays of Arthur Miller will undoubtedly be preserved in the annals of dramatic literature."

Death of a Salesman Critics have generally agreed that *Death of a Salesman* is an important dramatic work. Some commentators, however, have taken issue with Miller's insistence that *Death of a Salesman* is a modern tragedy and that Willy is a tragic hero. For example, the noted dramatic critic Eric Bentley argued that the elements of social drama in this play keep "the 'tragedy' from having genuinely tragic stature." Describing Willy as a "little man," Bentley insisted that such a person is "too little and too passive to play the tragic hero." Bentley and others charged that, according to Miller's own definition, Willy's death is merely "pathetic" rather than tragic. On

COMMON HUMAN EXPERIENCE

Many of Miller's plays dramatize the struggles of common people living ordinary lives. Here are some other works that explore similar struggles:

Of Mice and Men (1937), a novella by John Steinbeck. This work tells of two men trying to survive during the Great Depression.

The Man in the Gray Flannel Suit (1956), a film by Nunnally Johnson. This film, based on a novel of the same name, tells the story of a couple struggling to find happiness and meaning in the materialistic culture of the mid-twentieth century.

Something Happened (1974), a novel by Joseph Heller. This first-person novel expresses the narrator's feelings of alienation and despair as he tells of his futile career, stagnant marriage, and difficulties acting as a parent and friend.

the other hand, several different critics have argued that the salesman does attain tragic dimensions by virtue of what Miller terms the tragic hero's "total compulsion" to preserve his humanity and dignity. Literary critic John Mason Brown, for example, once characterized *Death of a Salesman* as "a tragedy modern and personal, not classic and heroic." Willy Loman is, he observed, "a little man sentenced to discover his smallness rather than a big man undone by his greatness."

Whether or not *Death of a Salesman* can be classified as a true tragedy, it has been generally praised for its innovative structure, which merges elements of both realism and expressionism. Reviewers admired the drama's interweaving of the past with the present and of events inside Willy's mind with those outside. This technique produces a penetrating psychological examination characteristic of dramatic realism. It is appropriate, several critics have noted, that Miller's working title for the play was *Inside of His Head*.

The Crucible *The Crucible* won the 1953 Tony Award for best play, but it received generally lukewarm responses from critics. The piece had a production run that, while respectable, was only one-third the length of *Death of a Salesman*'s premier production. When *The Crucible* was first staged, a number of critics maintained that Miller failed in his characteristic attempt to merge the personal and the social. They complained that many of the figures in the play are poorly developed and merely serve as mouthpieces for Miller's social commentary. As a result, the play was commonly interpreted as a thinly disguised critique of Joseph McCarthy's Senate investigations of communism in the United States, and it was judged as

preachy and overly political. Some commentators also questioned the validity of the parallels Miller established between the Salem witch trials and the congressional investigations of the House Committee on Un-American Activities. The relationship between the historical events depicted in the play and the events of the 1950s has continued to be the subject of much debate among subsequent critics who study *The Crucible*.

However, later generations of critics have been more generous than their historical counterparts with their appreciation of the work. After much of the furor over communist activity in the United States had died down, *The Crucible* was revived off-Broadway. This time, freed from much of its association with "current events," the play was warmly received by critics and enjoyed a run of over six hundred performances. It was now seen to have a more lasting and universal significance than had earlier been apparent. As Robert Martin later maintained, *The Crucible* "has endured beyond the immediate events of its own time. If it was originally seen as a political allegory, it is presently seen by contemporary audiences almost entirely as a distinguished American play by an equally distinguished American playwright."

Responses to Literature

1. Both *Death of a Salesman* and *The Crucible*, though written over fifty years ago, are still frequently performed today. In what ways are the struggles depicted in these two plays relevant to present-day life? Has the meaning of these plays changed over time? If so, in what way?

2. Miller is noted for depicting in dramatic form the struggles of everyday people to cope with life in society. Write an essay that discusses and analyzes the kinds of lessons that Miller's plays can teach to regular people about coping with their lives. Be sure to discuss whether or not these lessons remain as relevant today as they were when the plays were written.

3. While Miller claims that *Death of a Salesman*'s Willy Loman is a tragic hero, a number of critics and commentators disagree. Write a well-argued essay that takes a stand on whether or not Willy is tragic or merely pathetic.

BIBLIOGRAPHY

Books

Abbotson, Susan C. W. *Student Companion to Arthur Miller*. Westport, Conn.: Greenwood Press, 2000.

Bhatia, Santosh K. *Arthur Miller: Social Drama as Tragedy*. New York: Humanities Press, 1985.

Bigsby, C. W. E. *A Critical Introduction to Twentieth-Century American Drama*, volume 2: *Tennessee Williams, Arthur Miller, Edward Albee*. Cambridge, Mass.: Cambridge University Press, 1984.

Bigsby, C.W.E. ed. *The Cambridge Companion to Arthur Miller*. New York: Cambridge University Press, 1997.

Bloom, Harold, ed. *Arthur Miller*. New York: Chelsea House, 1987.

Carson, Neil. *Arthur Miller*. New York: St. Martin's Press, 1982.

Centola, Steven R., ed. *The Achievement of Arthur Miller: New Essays*. Dallas, Tex.: Contemporary Research, 1995.

Corrigan, Robert, ed. *Arthur Miller: A Collection of Critical Essays*. Englewood Cliffs, N.J.: Prentice-Hall, 1969.

Griffin, Alice. *Understanding Arthur Miller*. Columbia, S.C.: University of South Carolina Press, 1996.

Koon, Helen Wickam, ed. *Twentieth Century Interpretations of Death of a Salesman: A Collection of Critical Essays*. Englewood Cliffs, N.J.: Prentice-Hall, 1983.

Moss, Leonard. *Arthur Miller*, second edition. New York: Twayne, 1980.

Otten, Terry. *The Temptation of Innocence in the Dramas of Arthur Miller*. Columbia, Mo.: University of Missouri Press, 2002.

Panikkar, N. Bhaskara. *Individual Morality and Social Happiness in Arthur Miller*. Atlantic Highlands, N.J.: Humanities Press, 1982.

Savran, David. *Communists, Cowboys, and Queers: The Politics of Masculinity in the Work of Arthur Miller and Tennessee Williams*. Minneapolis: University of Minnesota Press, 1992.

Schlueter, June and James K. Flanagan, eds. *Arthur Miller*. New York: Ungar, 1987.

Welland, Dennis. *Miller: The Playwright*, second edition. New York: Methuen, 1983.

❂ Vassar Miller

BORN: *1924, Houston, Texas*

DIED: *1998, Houston, Texas*

NATIONALITY: *American*

GENRE: *Poetry*

MAJOR WORKS:
Wage War on Silence (1960)
If I Had Wheels or Love (1991)

Overview

Vassar Miller has been considered an accomplished poet since her first volume appeared in 1956. Praised by such colleagues as Denise Levertov, Howard Nemerov, James Wright, and Larry McMurtry, her poems have appeared in nine published collections, hundreds of periodicals, and more than fifty anthologies. The defining characteristics of Miller's poetry are clarity, precision, intelligence, honesty, and tenacity.

LITERARY AND HISTORICAL CONTEMPORARIES

Vassar Miller's famous contemporaries include:

Norman Mailer (1923–2007): An American writer who pioneered the New Journalism movement. He received both the Pulitzer Prize and the National Book Award.

Truman Capote (1924–1984): Capote was an American author known for his flamboyant lifestyle as well as for his influential true-crime classic, *In Cold Blood* (1966).

William De Witt Snodgrass (1926–2009): This American poet wrote under the pen name of S. S. Gardons and won the Pulitzer Prize in Poetry in 1960.

James Merrill (1926–1995): An American poet who won the Pulitzer Prize in Poetry in 1977.

Harper Lee (1926–): The American writer best known for her novel *To Kill a Mockingbird* (1960).

Robert Bly (1926–): Bly is a noted American poet who writes visionary and imagistic verse that is pervaded by the landscape and atmosphere of rural Minnesota.

Works in Biographical and Historical Context

Overcoming a Disability Vassar Miller was born on July 19, 1924, in Houston, Texas, to Jesse Gustavus Miller, an important Houston real-estate developer, and Vassar Morrison Miller. The young Miller was born with cerebral palsy. Because her mother died when Miller was only a year old, her stepmother became the dominant female influence in her life. Miller began writing at the age of eight when her father brought home a typewriter, a mechanical aid of profound importance for one afflicted with her disorder.

From her early youth, when a maid took her to evangelistic meetings in a tent, Miller was deeply religious. Despite her formidable physical handicap, she persevered academically and secured a good education in Houston schools. With the assistance and encouragement of her stepmother, she learned to read, attended junior and senior high school, and earned a BS (1947) and an MA (1952) from the University of Houston. For the master's degree she wrote, significantly for her later creative work, a thesis on mysticism in the poetry of Edwin Arlington Robinson. She later became an instructor in creative writing (1975–1976) at St. John's School in Houston.

A Long and Productive Literary Career Because of the appreciation for Miller's work in Houston, the Wings Press was founded as a vehicle for the publication and distribution of her work. During her forty-year literary

COMMON HUMAN EXPERIENCE

Miller's poetic concerns are largely metaphysical in nature. Here are some other works of poetry that center around metaphysical concerns:

God's Determinations Touching his Elect (c. 1680), a collection of poems by Edward Taylor. These works view the grace and majesty of God as a drama of sin and redemption.

Metaphysical Lyrics & Poems of the Seventeenth Century (1921), a poetry collection edited by Herbert J. C. Grierson. This volume collects some of the most representative poems by the early metaphysical poets who influenced later writers.

Divine Poems, Sermons, Devotions and Prayers (1990), by John Donne. The works collected in this volume demonstrate this poet's metaphysical concerns as well as his emotional depth as he explored questions of the divine nature.

career, Miller published ten volumes of poetry, all of which were collected in 1991 under the title *If I Had Wheels or Love*. In addition to numerous poems, she has published several short stories, many book reviews, and an anthology of poems and stories about disabled persons, *Despite This Flesh* (1984).

Notwithstanding her physical handicap, Miller traveled to Europe and elsewhere. Nor did a speech impediment associated with her disability prevent her from teaching and making public appearances. Miller died on October 31, 1998.

Works in Literary Context

Miller's poetry was influenced by Emily Dickinson—whose stylistic and thematic concerns most closely resemble Miller's—Edwin Arlington Robinson, the English metaphysical poets (John Donne, George Herbert, and Richard Crashaw), and Flannery O'Connor. Readers are also occasionally reminded of the American Puritan poet Edward Taylor, though Miller's poetry is not so heavily theological. In the 1960s her work had affinities with the confessionalists Sylvia Plath and Robert Lowell. Indeed, the confessional style has, over the years, become more predominant in Miller's work.

Emotionally Charged Writing Miller's themes center on personal concerns: God (sometimes referred to as "Nada," signifying the ineffable, the unknowable); religious faith (involving both belief and doubt—the need to believe and the necessity of doubt); suffering (physical and spiritual); loneliness (brought about by a life isolated from others); acceptance (the need to be accepted by others,

to be accepted by God, and—perhaps most important—her own need to accept God); silence (the inexpressible, or that which cannot be absolutely or ultimately articulated); sleep (as the seducer, as death (as "the dark nurse" that puts one "to bed," and in terms of suicide, nothingness, and eternity); loss (of innocence, of the joys of childhood, and of friends); the erotic (coupled with conventional yearnings for mystical union with God); the role of the religious poet (whose exuberance is associated with youth and childhood); and the barren inadequacy of modern technology. Readers will observe that humor, most often self-deprecating, is almost always present in Miller's poems, whatever the thematic concerns.

Miller's imagery is emotionally charged, sometimes violent, often erotic, but always appropriate in context. Her father is described as a "ghost, child's god," while her tears of suffering are "orgasmic shivers / along the spine of Midnight Mass." To Miller, Christ is a "pioneer in pain" and her own diseased body is "this house of gutted portals" and "this ravaged stack." Persons intolerant of her physical disability "would sleep upon the margin of my moans." Sexual frustration is "the jig and jerk / of titillated nerves." Finally, the poet's persona is "the dog-self" and time is "an angry little beast / clawing inside us, tearing us to shreds." Each of these are examples of how Miller incorporates vivid, emotional writing into her work.

Poetic Meter Miller's prosody (poetic meter) is now better understood, thanks to Bruce Kellner's 1988 essay "Blood in the Bone: Vassar Miller's Prosody." In Miller's work one finds variations on the Japanese katuata and haiku, blank verse, open verse, dramatic monologues, villanelles, and more. Miller has said, in a 1983 interview with Karla Hammond, that Gerard Manley Hopkins's "sprung rhythm" has influenced her work, but that it is something that "I sense rather than understand." (Incidentally, Miller's first poem was published in the *Hopkins Review*.)

Works in Critical Context

Problems with Critical Evaluation of Miller's Work Three problems typically arise in the critical evaluation of Miller's poetic work. First, she has been approached too often as a Texas poet, implying for some that her work is of regional importance only, an inaccurate view considering her record of national publication. Second, Miller is an unusual phenomenon in contemporary literature: a religious poet. As a result, some readers are quick to reject her work on purely subjective grounds, an antipathy to orthodox religious belief. A careful reading of her poetry will demonstrate, however, that she is a poet, first, and a religious mystic, second. Religious belief provides her work with substance and texture, much as can be said of the work of poet T. S. Eliot. Third, her physical disability has entered into discussions of her literary production. No one will deny that cerebral palsy affected Miller's poetry. Whether her disease has influenced critical evaluation of her work, or whether it ought to do so, is a matter of judgment. The reader and critic must, therefore, be on guard against prejudging Miller's work on provincial, theological, or sympathetic grounds. The poetry speaks for itself, and many critics attest to its power.

Wage War on Silence   Miller's early poetry was praised by reviewers. Her second collection, *Wage War on Silence*, received high compliments from fellow poet James Wright, who wrote in *Poetry* that Miller "has no peer among the younger contemporary writers that I have read." Wright went on to say that "her formal sense is almost always adequate to the meaning, which in turn is to be found in the intensity of her feeling. Her lyrics, invariably brief, are religious and sometimes erotic."

Struggling to Swim on Concrete   With her ninth volume of poetry, *Struggling to Swim on Concrete* (1983), Miller continued to earn the admiration of critics. Critic Paul Christensen wrote in the *Texas Observer*, "Through craftsmanship, she is beautiful, lithe, eager; one misses her spirit in overlooking this telling surface of her work. Her technique is not merely historical, though it connects with a deep past of religious introspection and quest poetry, but rather archetypal, an economy of the soul, as she longs to perfect the ruined part of herself. These poems harrow hell and also glitter like stained glass windows in their rigor and distillations." Christensen went on to praise her vision for being "singularly this hidden self of beasts and fictions, gods and monsters," which connects her to the Southern literary tradition of the twentieth century. According to James Tanner, the sonnet sequence, "Love's Bitten Tongue," which closes the volume, "demonstrates Miller's technical brilliance."

Responses to Literature

1. Miller has often been seen as a regional poet only. In what ways do you think she qualifies as a Texas poet, and in what ways do you think her poetry can be read as more national or even universal?

2. Commentators have noted that Miller's poetry is infused with humor, most often self-deprecating. What role do you think self-deprecating humor plays in Miller's poetry? What messages is she trying to convey by being funny? How does her use of humor affect the reader's reaction to her writings? Support your answer with evidence from the texts you have read.

3. Miller's poetry has focused on religious and personal concerns, particularly about the unknowable God and the various aspects religious faith. Write an essay that describes the nature of Miller's religious views and outlines the religious questions that inform her writing.

4. Miller's cerebral palsy has been a topic of discussion among critics and commentators on her poetry. Write an essay that analyzes the ways in which you can tell cerebral palsy has affected Miller's poetry.

BIBLIOGRAPHY
Books
Brown, Steven Ford, ed. *Heart's Invention: On the Poetry of Vassar Miller*. Houston, Tex.: Ford–Brown, 1988.
Friends of the University of Houston Libraries. *A Tribute to Vassar Miller* [videotape]. Houston, Tex.: University of Houston, 1983.
Poets Laureate of Texas: 1932–1966. San Antonio, Tex.: Naylor, 1966.

Periodicals
Christensen, Paul. "A Dark Texas of the Soul." *Pawn Review* (1984): 1–10.
Hammond, Karla. "An Interview with Vassar Miller." *Pawn Review* (1983): 1–18.
McMurtry, Larry. "Ever a Bridegroom: Reflections on the Failure of Texas Literature." *Texas Observer* (October 23, 1981): 1–19.

Margaret Mitchell

BORN: *1900, Atlanta, Georgia*
DIED: *1949, Atlanta, Georgia*
NATIONALITY: *American*
GENRE: *Fiction*
MAJOR WORKS:
Gone With the Wind (1936)

Overview

Margaret Mitchell is known exclusively for her authorship of *Gone with the Wind*, the best-selling novel in American history. The novel has created the dominant image of the antebellum South for millions of readers.

Works in Biographical and Historical Context

Journalist Turned Novelist   Mitchell was born on November 8, 1900, in Atlanta, Georgia, into an upper-middle-class family. Her father was an attorney and her mother was an activist for women's suffrage. Throughout her childhood, Mitchell was captivated by her parents' and grandmother's stories of Atlanta and their tales of heroic efforts during the Civil War. These stories eventually served as material for her famous literary work. Mitchell attended Smith College, with the goal of becoming a psychiatrist. However, she left school after one year to manage her father's household after her mother's death in 1919.

Margaret Mitchell   *Mitchell, Margaret, photograph. The Library of Congress.*

In 1922, following a brief marriage that ended in divorce, she became a journalist for the *Atlanta Journal* and rose in status from a fledging reporter to one of the newspaper's best feature writers. However, Mitchell's journalism career lasted only four years, and ended when an ankle injury confined her to her home. During her convalescence, and at the suggestion of her second husband, John R. Marsh, Mitchell began to write, with her husband's editorial assistance, a novel with the working title *Tomorrow Is Another Day.* For her story, she drew upon her knowledge of Atlanta and the South, and created fictional characters that were composites of people she knew. Although Mitchell finished most of the work by 1929, she researched historical facts and rewrote sections of the novel for nearly seven more years.

Breaking Publishing Records   In 1935, the manuscript was brought to the attention of Harold S. Latham, editor for Macmillan, who was in Atlanta on a trip to find publishable manuscripts. Never expecting her work to be published, Mitchell reluctantly allowed Latham to read the imposing manuscript, which was over one thousand pages long. He immediately accepted the novel, and after one year of exhaustive revisions, Mitchell's book was published as *Gone with the Wind*—retitled from a line in Ernest Downson's poem "Non sum qualis eram bonae sub regno Cynarae." Upon its entry into the literary market, *Gone with the Wind* broke all publishing records,

selling more than a million copies in its first six months. The book's success also dramatically altered the life of its author. Mitchell spent the remaining years of her life trying to maintain a modicum of privacy for herself and her husband, who became an invalid after suffering a stroke in 1945.

On August 11, 1949, Mitchell and her husband decided to view a film at a local theater. As Mitchell helped her husband across the street, a speeding taxicab came at them from around a corner. The drunken driver hit Mitchell, who died of brain injuries five days later. So many people wished to attend Mitchell's funeral that tickets had to be distributed for the event.

Works in Literary Context

Historical Novel   *Gone with the Wind* was written in the tradition of the historical novel. In her work, Mitchell employed a simple narrative style to combine a sentimental account of the "Old South" with the historical facts of an era that experienced immense social and economic change. From the threat of war between the states to General Sherman's fiery march on Atlanta, and through the Reconstruction period, *Gone with the Wind* depicts the tribulations of Scarlett O'Hara, Rhett Butler, Ashley Wilkes, and Melanie Hamilton—four of the best-known fictional characters in American literature—as they attempt to adapt to the changing circumstances of their homeland. However, only the willful heroine Scarlett and the roguish Rhett emerge as survivors in the "New South," while the ineffectual dreamer Ashley is defeated in spirit and the docile "Southern woman," Melanie, dies. Both Melanie and Ashley are viewed by critics as representatives of the antebellum South—a way of life that was destroyed by Civil War.

While Mitchell may have begun her novel with the retelling of her ancestor's stories of life in the South, what she ended up with was something that spoke to American readers in a way that even Mitchell may never have fully understood. As Anne Edwards, Mitchell's biographer, has put it, "Who can now think of the South before, during, and after the Civil War without images drawn from the pages of *Gone with the Wind*?"

Survival   Mitchell defined the theme of *Gone with the Wind* as simply "survival." The Civil War devastated the economy of Georgia, and Scarlett's determination never to be hungry again, whatever the cost, and her final decision to return to Tara, from which she and her family draw strength, exemplify Mitchell's aim. Melanie may die, Ashley may be a lost soul, Rhett may leave, but Scarlett and Tara endure. In presenting this theme Mitchell offers her readers a plethora of other attractive elements. The novel is nostalgic, regionally patriotic, romantic, filled with stirring events, and crammed with information about the characteristics, customs, beliefs, and manners of antebellum, wartime, and postbellum Georgia. All of these elements, along with the vivid characterization of Scarlett and Rhett, combine to provide an epic account of the fall of a traditional society and the way its inhabitants survived that fall.

Most commentators feel that Scarlett O'Hara is Mitchell's most interesting character, and she is frequently compared to Becky Sharp in William Thackeray's *Vanity Fair*. Similar to Becky's determination, Scarlett's will to survive dictates her actions throughout the novel. In this way, she appears coquettish, clever, selfish, amoral, and even loving in order to suit her needs.

Works in Critical Context

Gone with the Wind   *Gone with the Wind*, Mitchell's only published work during her lifetime, is the most popular novel in American fiction. From the time of its publication in 1936 to the present day, this historical romance has outsold any other hardcover book with the exception of the Bible. By 1976 the work had been translated into twenty-seven languages in thirty-seven countries. Praised as the first Civil War novel to be told from a Southern woman's point of view, *Gone with the Wind* won the 1937 Pulitzer Prize in fiction. Three years after its first publication, Mitchell's novel was adapted into a lavish film that has also become a popular classic.

Although Mitchell is praised for the clarity, vitality, and sheer readability of her story, most critics agree that *Gone with the Wind* suffers in comparison to other works of American Civil War literature. W. J. Stuckey offers a somewhat harsh but representative opinion of the novel, when he states, "While one can hear distant echoes of Fielding, Thackeray (especially), and Emily Bronte in *Gone with the Wind*, Miss Mitchell's art most noisily proclaims its indebtedness to the literature of wish fulfillment—the bosomy and sub-pornographic historical romance, the sentimental novel, and the Hollywood extravaganza." Similarly, Floyd C. Watkins lambasts the novel for being "narrowly patriotic, prudish, melodramatic, and sentimental."

Yet *Gone with the Wind* is always extolled for its detailed telling of this period of American history. In his review for the *New Republic*, Malcolm Cowley described *Gone with the Wind* as "an encyclopedia of the plantation legend." This sentiment was echoed by others, and has remained the prevailing view of the novel.

Responses to Literature

1. *Gone with the Wind* is one of the most famous works of historical fiction in existence. In your opinion, does the historical side or the fictional side dominate this work, and in what ways are the two connected? Would the fictional story have been as compelling without the specific historical setting Mitchell used? Support your answer using specific scenes from the text.

2. Much of the commentary on *Gone with the Wind* focuses on the two main characters, Scarlett O'Hara and Rhett Butler, even though the novel is populated

---

LITERARY AND HISTORICAL CONTEMPORARIES

Margaret Mitchell's famous contemporaries include:

William Faulkner (1897–1962): The American author who is widely considered one of the most important writers of the twentieth century. He was awarded the Nobel Prize in Literature in 1949.

Ernest Hemingway (1899–1961): Hemingway was one of the most prominent writers of the "Lost Generation." During his lifetime, Hemingway received both the Pulitzer Prize and the Nobel Prize.

Langston Hughes (1902–1967): The African-American poet best known for his literary influence during the Harlem Renaissance.

John Steinbeck (1902–1968): Steinbeck is widely credited with being one of the best-known and widely read writers of the twentieth century. He was granted the Nobel Prize in Literature in 1962.

Dee Brown (1908–2002): An American historian and novelist whose works presented the hardships and challenges involved in the history of the Western frontier.

Richard Wright (1908–1960): Wright was a prominent African-American author noted for his naturalistic descriptions of the reality of black American life.

COMMON HUMAN EXPERIENCE

Mitchell's epic novel, *Gone with the Wind*, sets a romantic story amid the backdrop of the Civil War. Here are some other novels that use the Civil War as a setting to tell a story about people and their relationships:

North and South (1982), a novel by John Jakes. This work, which focuses on two families on either side of the Civil War, traces the family histories from their arrival in the American colonies through the beginning of the Civil War.

Lincoln (1984), a novel by Gore Vidal. This account, which forms a part of Vidal's "Narratives of Empire" series of historical novels, describes the personal and political struggles of Abraham Lincoln during his presidency during the Civil War.

Cold Mountain (1997), a novel by Charles Frazier. This tale, set during the final months of the Civil War, tells the parallel stories of a Confederate deserter and the love of his life, a young Southern belle.

---

with many other characters who are struggling through the same circumstances as Scarlett and Rhett. Choose one of the other characters, major or minor, and write an essay comparing that character's personality, circumstances, and reactions to those of either Scarlett, or Rhett, or both.

3. Mitchell's characterization of the antebellum South has been accepted by millions of readers as the way life was in the pre–Civil War South. Write an essay based on historical research that compares and contrasts Mitchell's version of the this period with the version presented by present-day historians.

BIBLIOGRAPHY

Books

Asbury, Darden. *Southern Daughter: The Life of Margaret Mitchell*. New York: Oxford University Press, 1991.

Bridges, Herb. *Gone with the Wind: The Definitive Illustrated History of the Book, the Movie, and the Legend*. New York: Simon & Schuster, 1989.

Edwards, Anne. *Road to Tara: The Life of Margaret Mitchell*. New Haven, Conn.: Ticknor & Fields, 1983.

Farr, Finis. *Margaret Mitchell of Atlanta: The Author of "Gone with the Wind"*. New York: Morrow, 1965.

Pratt, William. *Scarlett Fever*. New York; Macmillan, 1977.

Taylor, Helen. *Scarlett's Women: Gone with the Wind and its Female Fans*. New Brunswick, N.J.: Rutgers University Press, 1989.

Walker, Marianne. *Margaret Mitchell and John Marsh: The Love Story behind Gone with the Wind*. Atlanta, Ga.: Peachtree, 1993.

Watkins, Floyd C. *In Time and Place*. Athens, Ga.: University of Georgia Press, 1977.

Periodicals

Atlanta Historical Bulletin: Margaret Mitchell Memorial Issue (May 1950).

Atlanta Journal Magazine: Margaret Mitchell Memorial Issue (December 18, 1949).

Clark, George R. "G. W. T. W." *Harper's* (February 1949): 97–98.

Drake, Robert Y., Jr. "Tara Twenty Years After." *Georgia Review* (1958): 142–150.

Gaillard, Dawson. "*Gone with the Wind* as Bildungsroman or Why Did Rhett Butler Really Leave Scarlett O'Hara." *Georgia Review*. (1974): 9–18.

✺ N. Scott Momaday

BORN: *1934, Lawton, Oklahoma*

NATIONALITY: *American*

GENRE: *Fiction, nonfiction, poetry, drama*

MAJOR WORKS:
House Made of Dawn (1968)
The Way to Rainy Mountain (1969)

The Gourd Dancer (1976)
In the Bear's House (1999)

Overview

In 1969, the same year that N. Scott Momaday began his tenure as associate professor of English and Comparative Literature at the University of California at Berkeley, he won the Pulitzer Prize in fiction for *House Made of Dawn*, published his autobiographical work, *The Way to Rainy Mountain*, and was initiated into the Kiowa Gourd Dance Society. The critical recognition of Momaday's novel stimulated public interest in Native American literary history as well as in contemporary Native American writers in general. However, the success of Momaday's work results not only from his prowess as a writer but also from his capacity as an engaging mythmaker.

Works in Biographical and Historical Context

Navarro Scott Momaday was born on February 27, 1934, in the Kiowa and Comanche Indian Hospital in Lawton, Oklahoma. He is the only child of Alfred Momaday (of

N. Scott Momaday   *Momaday, Scott, photograph. Ulf Andersen / Getty Images.*

Kiowa heritage) and Natachee Scott (of European and Cherokee ancestry). Six months after his birth, at Devil's Tower, Wyoming, the storyteller Pohd-lohk—who was Momaday's step-grandfather—gave him the Kiowa name Tsoai-talee, which refers to a Kiowa myth about a "rock tree boy" who turns into a bear. This myth of the bear child is so much a part of Momaday's identity that it recurs throughout his works. Momaday's second Indian name is Tsotohah, meaning "Red Bluff." Momaday's many names reflect the fact that he comes from the intermarriage of several Old and New World bloodlines.

An Inherited Love of Learning Momaday's understanding of complex cultural contexts comes naturally out of his own experience. Both of his parents were educators, and Momaday traveled with them as they pursued various teaching opportunities. The Momadays taught among the Navajo for ten years, first at Shiprock, New Mexico, and then in Tuba City and Chinle, Arizona. In 1946 the family moved to the Jemez Pueblo in New Mexico, where Momaday's parents were the only two teachers at the day school there. Both parents taught in Jemez for twenty-five years. Momaday acquired his love of literature and writing from his mother and his love of teaching and painting from his father.

During his youth, Momaday was educated in New Mexico at the Franciscan Mission School in Jemez, the Indian School in Santa Fe, and in Bernalillo County, New Mexico. He also attended the Augustus Military Academy in Fort Defiance, Virginia. He received his undergraduate education at the University of New Mexico (UNM) in Albuquerque, where he studied political science, English, and speech. Momaday interrupted his stint at UNM in 1956–1957 to study law at the University of Virginia. While there, Momaday met and fell under the influence of William Faulkner. In 1958, upon graduating from UNM, Momaday accepted a teaching position on the Jicarilla Apache reservation in Dulce, New Mexico. He married Gaye Mangold on September 5, 1959, with whom he had three daughters—Cael, Jill, and Brit. (His marriage to Mangold did not last, however, and on July 21, 1978 Momaday married a second time, to Regina Heitzer, whom he had met when he was a visiting professor at the University of Regensburg in Germany. Together they have one daughter, Lore.)

In 1959, poet, critic, and scholar Ivor Winters selected Momaday for a Wallace Stegner Creative Writing Fellowship at Stanford University. Under Winters's guidance, Momaday pursued both a career in writing and a PhD in American literature. Winters clearly saw Momaday's talents, and even predicted his future acclaim. Under Winters's influence Momaday wrote and published his dissertation, an edition of the works of nineteenth-century American poet Frederick Goddard Tuckerman (1965). Winters also critiqued several drafts of *House Made of Dawn*, but he died in 1968, a year before Momaday received the Pulitzer Prize for it.

LITERARY AND HISTORICAL CONTEMPORARIES

N. Scott Momaday's famous contemporaries include:

Dennis Banks (1932–): A Native American activist who helped found the American Indian Movement (AIM) in 1968.

Thomas King (1943–): Part Cherokee, King is a writer and champion of Native American causes.

Linda Hogan (1947–): A writer and poet of Chickasaw descent. Hogan's work often focuses on environmental issues.

Leslie Marmon Silko (1948–): The novelist and poet whose book *Ceremony* (1977) helped bring notoriety and respect to Native American writers.

Sherman Alexie (1966–): The American author and comedian. Alexie's short story collection, *The Lone Ranger and Tonto Fistfight in Heaven* (1993) features characters who live on an Indian reservation in Washington state.

Telling Stories, Winning Awards The same year he won the Pulitzer, Momaday published *The Way to Rainy Mountain*, which is generally respected as his greatest contribution to world literature. It is the story of the journey of the Kiowa people from their mythological emergence into the world to Rainy Mountain in Oklahoma and their decline as a people. To write the book, Momaday retraced this journey both intellectually and physically. As he focused his attention on retrieving the remnants of Kiowa oral tradition, he realized how much American Indian oral poetry and mythology had already been lost. He realized that speedy research was needed to salvage what information was still able to be preserved. Deprived of his grandparents as living sources of Kiowa tradition, Momaday collected stories from tribal elders instead.

During the ten years that followed his Pulitzer Prize, Momaday was honored by the National Institute of Arts and Letters, received a Gold Plate Award from the American Academy of Achievement, and in 1979 was also awarded the highest literary award Italy bestows, the Premio Letteraio Internationale Mondelio. In 1992, thirty years after his literary career began, Momaday was given the Returning the Gift Lifetime Achievement Award, an award that acknowledges contributions beyond literary productivity. In 2007, he received a National Medal of Arts from President George W. Bush.

Works in Literary Context

Many of Momaday's works are founded on Kiowa and Navajo mythology. His play *Children of the Sun* (1997), for example, is a dramatic re-creation of the stories of the

COMMON HUMAN EXPERIENCE

Momaday's writing style relies heavily on the Native American tradition of oral storytelling. Many cultures use oral storytelling to pass on their histories and customs to younger generations. Here are some other works that use the structure and style of the oral tradition as a way to tell a tale:

Song of Solomon (1977), a novel by Toni Morrison. The novel's main character, Milkman, focuses on stories of his ancestry to determine his future and to learn to fly.

"The Company of Wolves" (1979), a short story by Angela Carter. Based on the folktale of Little Red Riding Hood, Carter's story warns of wolves and then ignores its own warning.

"Girl" (1978), a short story by Jamaica Kincaid. The story takes place in an island culture, and focuses on a mother who barks orders at her daughter in the hopes she will remember her place in her society.

Green Grass, Running Water (1993), a novel by Thomas King. The plot in this book about contemporary Native American culture revolves around the escape from a mental hospital of four very old Indians.

half-boys of Kiowa mythology also written about in *The Way to Rainy Mountain*. Many of Momaday's themes are clearly established in his collection *The Man Made of Words*, also published in 1997. In this work Momaday explores his conceptions of language, land, and storytelling. Momaday says, "Our stories explain us, justify us, sustain us, humble us, and forgive us. And sometimes they injure and destroy us."

Navajo Tradition Momaday's blending of ancient and traditional material with contemporary and modernist techniques in *House Made of Dawn* has reminded many critics of James Joyce, who combined Catholic religious and Irish political contexts with parallels to classical Greek mythology in such works as *A Portrait of the Artist as a Young Man* (1916) and *Ulysses* (1922). The title of *House Made of Dawn* is taken from the Navajo "Night Chant," one of sixty-two healing rituals held sacred by the Navajo. The house referred to in the title has been identified as one of the prehistoric cliff dwellings along the upper Rio Grande, and the chant alludes to it as the home of the semi-divine personification of the dawn. Throughout the novel, important events and insights occur at dawn or sunrise. Also, throughout the novel Momaday incorporates ceremonial, mythical, and anthropological material from three different American Indian nations—Jemez Pueblo, Kiowa, and Navajo—into the texture of the contemporary story of psychological disintegration and renewal. *House Made of Dawn* is nar-

ratively complex, constructed on a principle of fragmentation and reconstitution somewhat like the modernist poems of Ezra Pound and T. S. Eliot, authors whom Momaday studied while in college and graduate school.

Religious Variety Momaday's work reflects religion and spirituality as it exists in postcolonial Native America, where individuals often live in and learn from multiple sources. Momaday himself is living proof of this blend—he is at once a university professor, a mixed-blood Indian living outside the boundaries of his primary tribe's native lands and customs, and a nomad—one who finds his home in various settings. His mythic vision, therefore, includes Judeo-Christian and Western myths as well as Native American ones. Indeed, many Pueblo ceremonies are Christian and Native conglomerates. Two versions of Indian Christianity exist in *House Made of Dawn*, for example—the Catholicism of the Jemez Pueblo and the peyote cult of the Native American church. Layers of Christianity contribute to the mosaic of values prevalent in the Pueblo. Father Olguin, the primary Christian representative in the novel, is constantly rereading the journal of his predecessor, Fray Nicolas, which exposes changes in attitudes toward Indian ceremonialism. In fact, Father Olguin eventually tries to be a bridge for understanding between Indian and white conceptions of death/murder. When Francisco dies, the protagonist, Abel, prepares Francisco's body in the Pueblo manner and then informs Father Olguin. Amidst so many different belief systems, Abel—and Father Olguin—must figure out his own unique spirituality.

Works in Critical Context

During the First Convocation of American Indian Scholars in 1970, Rupurt Costo asked Momaday's advice on how to preserve a Native worldview in the face of many negative alternatives offered by Western culture. Momaday answered:

> For a long time…the traditional values in the Indian world have not been valued in the terms of the modern dominant society. We've always, I think, thought of acculturation as a kind of one-way process in which the Indian ceases to be an Indian and becomes a white man….But I think more and more we ought to educate the white man. We ought to reconstruct the institutions within the dominant society, so that the Indian values are available to the dominant society.

Perhaps this is the reason Momaday has become such a quintessential Native American writer and figure: Indian values have been made available to the dominant society through Momaday's artistic and myth-making talent.

House Made of Dawn In *House Made of Dawn*, the story of Abel's life is told from multiple perspectives and memories that are, at first read, difficult to navigate. Such difficulties prompted critic Roger Dickinson-Brown in a 1978 article for the *Southern Review* to call the novel a "batch of often dazzling fragments" and "a memorable failure" because of the "incoherence of large parts" of the text. Indeed, psychological, historical, and cultural fragmentation are amply represented in a mosaic of images and memories with few familiar chronological standards.

Susan Scarberry-Garcia in *Landmarks of Healing: A Study of House Made of Dawn* (1990) discusses the strong commonalities between Navajo concepts and *House Made of Dawn*. Of particular importance is her insistence that Abel's final gestures not only help his dying grandfather gain passage into another world but also give his own suffering meaning. *House Made of Dawn* is still an exploration of a particularly male journey, and, as Paul Zolbrod insists, the Navajo creation story "relates how [cosmic] order is to be established and maintained, especially in male-female relationships." In fact, says Zolbrod, "the basic theme of the Navajo creation story is that solidarity must be maintained between male and female if there is to be harmony in the world."

The Way to Rainy Mountain *The Way to Rainy Mountain*, which most critics consider Momaday's best work, is the story of the Kiowas' journey three hundred years ago from Yellowstone onto the Great Plains, where they acquired horses and became a society of sun priests, fighters, and hunters until they were defeated by the U.S. Cavalry in the mid-nineteenth century. Critics note that by the last part the passages begin to blend with one another. The mythic passages are no longer mythic in the traditional sense, because Momaday creates myth out of the memories of his ancestors rather than passing on already established and socially sanctioned tales. According to critic Kenneth Fields, his form forces Momaday "to relate the subjective to the more objective historical sensibility. The writing of the book itself, one feels, enables him to gain both freedom and possession. It is therefore a work of discovery as well as renunciation, of finding but also of letting go."

Responses to Literature

1. Look up the definition of "hero." In your opinion, is Abel, in *House Made of Dawn*, a traditional hero? Why or why not?

2. Compare Abel's spiritual journey in *House Made of Dawn* to Tayo's in Leslie Marmon Silkos's *Ceremony*. What similarities do the journeys have? What differences?

3. Momaday's work is often considered "eco-friendly." Identify at least three passages in *The Gourd Dancer* that champion taking care of the earth and the environment, and write a short essay on what significance these have on the plot.

BIBLIOGRAPHY

Books

Allen, Paula Gunn. "Bringing Home the Fact: Tradition and Continuity in the Imagination," *Recovering the Word: Essays on Native American Literature*. Edited by Brian Swann and Arnold Krupat. Berkeley, Calif.: University of California Press, 1987, pp. 563–569.

Bruner, Edward M. "Experience and Its Expressions." *The Anthropology of Experience*. Edited by Victor W. Turner and Bruner. Chicago: University of Illinois Press, 1986, pp. 3–33.

Costo, Rupert. "Discussion: The Man Made of Words." *Conversations with N. Scott Momaday*. Edited by Matthias Schubnell. Jackson, Miss.: University Press of Mississippi, 1997, pp. 3–19.

Donovan, Kathleen M. *Feminist Readings of Native American Literature: Coming to Voice*. Tucson, Ariz.: University of Arizona Press, 1998.

Dumoulie, Camille. "Eternal Recurrence: Nietzsche's 'Great Thought'," *Companion to Literary Myths, Heroes and Archetypes*. Edited by Pierre Brunel. London: Routledge, 1996, pp. 420–424.

Scarberry-Garcia, Susan. *Landmarks of Healing: A Study of House Made of Dawn*. Albuquerque, N.M.: University of New Mexico Press, 1990.

Schubnell, Matthias, ed. *Conversations with N. Scott Momaday*. Jackson, Miss.: University of Mississippi Press, 1997.

——— *N. Scott Momaday: The Cultural and Literary Background*. Norman, Okla.: University of Oklahoma Press, 1985.

Woodward, Charles L. *Ancestral Voice: Conversations with N. Scott Momaday*. Lincoln, Neb.: University of Nebraska Press, 1989.

Winters, Ivor. *Forms of Discovery*. Chicago: Alan Swallow, 1967.

Witherspoon, Gary. *Language and Art in the Navajo Universe*. Ann Arbor, Mich.: University of Michigan Press, 1977).

Zolbrod, Paul. "When Artifacts Speak, What Can They Tell Us?" *Recovering the Word: Essays on Native American Literature*. Edited by Brian Swann and Krupat. Berkeley, Calif.: University of California Press, 1987, pp. 13–41.

Periodicals

Dickinson-Brown, Roger. "The Art and Importance of N. Scott Momaday," *Southern Review*, 14 (1978): 30–45.

Fields, Kenneth, "More than Language Means," in *Southern Review*, winter, 1970.

Hirsch, Bernard A. "Self-Hatred and Spiritual Corruption in *House Made of Dawn*," *Western American Literature*, 17 (Winter 1983): 307–320.

Kerr, Baine. "The Novel as Sacred Text: N. Scott Momaday's Myth-Making Ethic," *Southwest Review*, 63 (1978): 172–179.

❁ Lorrie Moore

BORN: *1957, New York*

NATIONALITY: *American*

GENRE: *Fiction*

MAJOR WORKS:
Self-Help (1985)
Like Life (1990)
Birds of America (1998)

Overview

Lorrie Moore's short stories are poignant reflections of the human spirit on trial. Alternately hilarious and distressing, Moore's short fiction generally presents a sharp and cynical view of modern existence that often seems like autobiographical reflections on the world of a middle-class woman. Throughout her work a dark humor pervades, lightening the painful plots and charming the reader with wit and irony. Moore's painful yet believable reflections of contemporary existence have gained her a

Lorrie Moore   *Nancy Crampton / Writer Pictures*

rightful place among writers of the late twentieth and early twenty-first centuries.

Works in Biographical and Historical Context

Moore was born on January 13, 1957, in Glens Falls, New York. Both her father, Henry T. Moore Jr., an insurance company executive who came from a family of academics, and her mother, Jeanne (Day) Moore, a former nurse, were avid readers of nonfiction. Moore was the second of four children and, as Don Lee notes in *Ploughshares*, she "remembers her parents as rather strict Protestants, politically minded and culturally alert." She was first published in 1976 at the age of nineteen, as the first-prize winner in a *Seventeen Magazine* writing contest, which she won with her story "Raspberries." After high school Moore went on to complete her undergraduate work, studying writing at St. Lawrence University in northern New York State. At St. Lawrence, Moore studied creative writing with critic and fiction writer Joe David Bellamy, was inducted into Phi Beta Kappa, and graduated summa cum laude in 1978. After graduating Moore moved to Manhattan, where she worked as a paralegal until 1980.

Graduate School and Success   In 1980 she was accepted into the MFA program at Cornell University. At Cornell she studied with Alison Lurie, who was instrumental in getting Moore's first collection published. In 1982 she received her MFA and became a member of the Associated Writing Programs and the Authors Guild. Moore worked as a lecturer at Cornell from 1982 to 1984 and taught there again in 1990 as a visiting associate professor. In 1983 Moore sold to Knopf her first collection, *Self-Help* (1985), made up almost completely of stories from her master's thesis. In 1984 Moore became an assistant professor at the University of Wisconsin, where she subsequently became an associate professor in 1987 and finally a full professor of English in 1991.

Throughout her career Moore has alternated genres, with novels generally following her collections of short stories. She tends to take long periods of time between books due to the time-consuming activities of her "real" life. Often these real-life events become fodder for her fiction. "People Like That Are the Only People Here," from her acclaimed story collection *Birds of America* (1998) revolves around her fictionalized struggles with her son's illness. The story won the O. Henry Award in 1998 for best short story. Moore continues to teach at the University of Wisconsin, Madison, and has a new novel coming out in 2009.

Works in Literary Context

Moore's reflections of life, seemingly confessional, appear as intimate views of real people. This quality, perhaps, is what often leads critics to assume that Moore's stories are autobiographical, an assumption Moore herself has strenuously denied. The major themes of Moore's work center around the trials of contemporary existence—love, loss, loneliness—and often reveal profound psychological implications. As Vince Passaro points out in *Mirabella*: "Certain themes and situations recur: Moore tends toward heroines in their child bearing years, often enduring an erosion of physical health, loneliness, and an exasperation at men and men's stupid vanities."

Moore's fiction has much in common with other writers of her generation, such as Amy Hempel and Deborah Eisenberg. As her work in short fiction evolves, it has moved away from the gimmicky, yet highly amusing, stylistic devices of *Self-Help* and toward a more profound exploration of the psychology of the characters she creates. Certain themes, however, have remained constant: failing relationships and communication breakdowns, the pain of loss compounded by the physical pain of disease, the frustration and guilt of feeling trapped in a relationship, loneliness and the human need for—yet resistance to—real intimacy.

Body Images Physical breakdowns that parallel inner turmoil frequently occur in Moore's work, physicalizing the emotional pain and compounding the trauma. In "What Is Seized" bodily and emotional loss are viciously combined in the mother's life as she loses her husband to divorce and her breasts to cancer. Daughter Lynnie emphasizes this combination in her narration: "Both things happened suddenly, quietly, without announcement. As if some strange wind rushed in and swept things up into it, then quickly rushed out again; it simply left what it left."

Disease and the pain and potential role reversals they bring are common themes in these early stories. The physical breakdown often becomes an embodiment of emotional trauma. After the father's departure the divisions between the interspersed photos and letters and the time line become less clearly defined, and the reader is instead presented with "a series of pictures here of mothers and daughters switching places—women switching places to take care of one another." The title "What Is Seized" reflects both the things that Lynnie observes her mother losing but also the loss of her mother, whose funeral is depicted in the final moments of the story. In this story, abandonment becomes a theme of Lynnie's mother's life, but such loneliness and neediness are not reserved only for women in Moore's fiction.

Isolation Often Moore's characters operate in settings that isolate them, whether in an urban center or tucked away in a monotonous suburb. The vast majority of her protagonists are female, and thus her stories wrestle with issues that are particularly poignant for contemporary women: divorce, love affairs, motherhood, and illness. Throughout her work sadness exists in a tense duality with humor, each offsetting and intensifying the other.

LITERARY AND HISTORICAL CONTEMPORARIES

Moore's famous contemporaries include:

Ronald Reagan (1911–2004): President of the United States during the 1980s, Reagan had previously served as governor of California and was a film star in the 1940s and 1950s.

Alison Lurie (1926–): Moore's former writing professor, Lurie won a Pulitzer for her novel *Foreign Affairs* (1984).

Deborah Eisenberg (1945–): Eisenberg is known for her story collections, such as *Transactions in a Foreign Currency* (1986) and *All Around Atlantis* (1997).

Jay McInerney (1955–): New York writer known for his quintessential novel of the 1980s, *Bright Lights, Big City* (1984).

Pam Houston (1962–): Houston is a nature writer known for her debut story collection, *Cowboys Are My Weakness* (1993), which frankly depicts romances gone wrong.

Works in Critical Context

Lorrie Moore's artful short fiction depicts the pitfalls of modern existence. Throughout, a darkly witty sense of humor pervades the often desperate lives of her characters. Much of the criticism of Moore's work has focused on this humor, described variously as "wry" and "apt." However, as Ralph Sassone points out in his article "This Side of Parody: Lorrie Moore Gets Serious," her use of humor produces dramatic effects:

> Although a cursory reading of her work might make it seem coolly satirical, its aftereffect is the memory of palpable pain. . . . Funniness is simultaneously a leavening agent for her wrenching narratives . . . and a distancing device that perpetuates [her characters'] alienation.

It is also sometimes suggested that because Moore's works are funny, they do not merit serious examination. In an interview with Dwight Garner for the online magazine *Salon*, Moore defends her use of humor by pointing out that the world is funny and that individuals spend much of their time attempting to be humorous: "If you're going to ignore that, what are you doing? You're just saying that part of the world . . . doesn't exist. And of course it exists."

Like Life Several critics have praised *Like Life* for its continued use of dark humor. In this collection, Sassone claims, "she proves that although her natural gift is for kinetic prose about the bright and wired, she can also write understated stories in which the mood is closer to a hush." Other critics found in the collection a broader thematic range and deeper emotional engagement than

COMMON HUMAN EXPERIENCE

In her collection *Self-Help*, Moore uses the second-person point of view. The constant use of the word *you* makes her stories sound authoritative, like a real self-help book. Here are a few other works that utilize this perspective:

Bright Lights, Big City (1984), a novel by Jay McInerney. In this novel, the main character is a cocaine addict who is lamenting the loss of his mother while working a low-level publishing job in New York City.

"How to Talk to a Hunter" (1993), a short story by Pam Houston. In this story, the narrator tells "you" how to seduce a masculine, reserved male.

If on a Winter's Night a Traveler (1979), a novel by Italo Calvino. Every other chapter in this novel is told in second person, preparing the reader for the next chapter.

Half Asleep in Frog Pajamas (1994), a novel by Tom Robbins. The second-person point of view in this novel results in the reader having a very wild ride through Robbins's imagination.

in *Self-Help*. John Casey's review in the *Chicago Tribune* describes Moore's writing as a mix of "comedy and sadness, wisecracks and poignancy." Like many critics, Michiko Kakutani of the *New York Times* compares *Like Life* with *Self-Help*: "Although the stories in *Like Life* are as funny and archly observant as those in Ms. Moore's earlier collection (*Self-Help*), they are also softer, wiser, more minor-key." Kakutani goes on to say that *Like Life* is superior largely due to the addition of "lyrical meditation" and the ability of these characters "to examine—however gingerly—their hurts and missed connections." Again, Moore was praised for her ability to delineate fictional characters that seem somehow familiar, as if they were autobiographical. The reviews also praise Moore's ability to depict varying types of human pain in her exploration of contemporary existence.

Birds of America   Criticism of *Birds of America* has centered on the increasing intensity of Moore's fiction in both plot and language, the greater depth and complexity of her characters, and her use of searing, dark humor. James McManus, in his review for the *New York Times*, called Moore's writing "fluid, cracked, mordant, colloquial." Her sentences can "hold, even startle, us as they glide beneath the radar of ideological theories of behavior to evoke the messy, god-awful behavior itself." McManus observed that in a few instances—in "Charades," for example—the dialogue seems to degenerate into wisecracking but overall praised the collection for articulating the pain and humor of contemporary existence: "it will

stand by itself as one of our funniest, most telling anatomies of human love and vulnerability." In her review for the *Washington Post*, Carolyn See criticizes the fact that so much of Moore's work reflects the unhinged perceptions of upper-middle-class, well-educated women. She praises *Birds of America*, however, for taking on deeper issues such as cancer and death rather than limiting her scope to that of failed relationships.

Responses to Literature

1. *Self-Help* is written mostly in second-person point of view. Why do you think this point of view is so difficult to maintain? In what ways does her choice of this point of view make sense for this work?

2. In her stories "You're Ugly Too" and "People Like That Are the Only People Here," how do Moore's characters use humor to survive illness?

3. Compare Moore's "How to Be an Other Woman" to Pam Houston's "How to Talk to a Hunter." Which story gives more practical advice? What does each story seem to say about relationships between men and women?

4. The title story in *Like Life* is set in the future. How does Moore play with science fiction traditions in this story?

BIBLIOGRAPHY

Books

Schumacher, Michael. *Reasons to Believe*. New York: St. Martin's Press, 1988.

Periodicals

Casey, John. Review of *Like Life*. *Chicago Tribune*, May 20, 1990.

Kakutani, Michiko. Review of *Birds of America*. *New York Times*, June 8, 1990.

Lee, Don. "About Lorrie Moore." *Ploughshares* 24 (Fall 1998): 224–229.

McManus, James. "The Unbearable Lightness of Being." *New York Times*, September 20, 1998.

Passaro, Vince. "Books." *Mirabella* (February 1992): 46, 48, 51.

Sassone, Ralph. "This Side of Parody: Lorrie Moore Gets Serious." *Village Voice Literary Supplement* (June 1990): 15.

See, Carolyn. Review of *Birds of America*. *Washington Post*, September 25, 1998.

Web sites

Garner, Dwight. "Moore's Better Blues: Lorrie Moore Finds the Lighter Side of Ordinary Madness in 'Birds of America.'" *Salon*, originally published October 27, 1998. Retrieved on November 16, 2008, from http://www.salon.com/books/int/1998/10/cov_27int.html.

❂ Marianne Moore

BORN: *1887, Kirkwood, Missouri*

DIED: *1972, New York, New York*

NATIONALITY: *American*

GENRE: *Poetry, nonfiction*

MAJOR WORKS:
Poems (1921)
Selected Poems (1935)
Collected Poems (1951)

Overview

Marianne Moore created a new type of verse, yet she denied that she was a poet. What she wrote was called poetry, she said, because there was no other category in which to put it. There are, in fact, no commonly accepted terms for describing the whole of her work and few accurate tags for designating the most radical forms she perfected. The verse received attention from the avant-garde poets and critics who were her contemporaries and

Marianne Moore   *Moore, Marianne, photograph. The Library of Congress.*

from the generation of poets that followed them. She also became well-known, in the later years of her life, as an American eccentric, but her accomplished work baffled many readers. She continues to be more highly regarded than widely read.

Works in Biographical and Historical Context

A Literary Disposition   As a child, Moore's family experienced frequent changes of fortune and loss. Her mother, Mary Warner, had married John Milton Moore, an engineer and inventor, in 1885, but left him shortly afterwards. Marianne Craig Moore, who was born in 1887 in the house of her maternal grandfather after her parents were separated, never knew her father. After her grandfather died when she was seven, her mother took Marianne and her brother to live in Carlisle, Pennsylvania. Living on a small inheritance, the family was often in strained circumstances, and Mary Moore took a job as a teacher of English at Metzger Institute for Girls, at which her daughter had begun preparatory work in 1896. Marianne never married, and, except for the four years that she was a student at Bryn Mawr College, she lived with her mother until her death in 1947.

Moore's family influenced her literary disposition. Her paternal grandfather, William Moore, was a "bookish man" who owned a large library. During the last years of life he read the *Encyclopedia Britannica* from A through Z. He was also the brother of "Captain Bixby," the steamboat pilot for whom Samuel Clemens—better known as the author Mark Twain—was an apprentice on the Mississippi River. Moore, who majored in biology and histology at Bryn Mawr, told Donald Hall in a 1961 interview that she was sure laboratory studies affected her poetry: "Precision, economy of statement, logic employed to ends that are disinterested, drawing and identifying, liberate—at least have some bearing on—the imagination." She thought seriously of studying medicine.

Fame at Home and Abroad   Upon graduating from Bryn Mawr, Moore took a business course at Carlisle Commercial College in 1909–1910, and went with her mother for the first time to England and Paris in the summer of 1911. Thereafter she taught typing, stenography, bookkeeping, commercial law, and commercial English—and also fixed the typewriters and coached the boys in field sports—at the United States Industrial Indian School in Carlisle. Continuing to write, she contributed ten poems to the Bryn Mawr alumnae magazine during the years 1910–1915.

The following year Moore and her mother joined her brother Warner in Chatham, New Jersey, where he had begun his own Presbyterian ministry. Meanwhile Moore's poems appeared in a variety of "little magazines." They were usually short lyrics or appreciations of admired writers and biblical characters. In 1918 Moore

LITERARY AND HISTORICAL CONTEMPORARIES

Marianne Moore's famous contemporaries include:

Emily Dickinson (1830–1886): Dickinson was an American poet known for her reclusive lifestyle as well as her seemingly simple, fiercely delicate poetry.

William Carlos Williams (1883–1963): Williams was a medical doctor as well as a poet, and was known for his frank, natural imagery.

Georgia O'Keeffe (1887–1986): O'Keeffe is known for her paintings of natural landscapes, particularly of the New Mexican desert and of flowers.

T. S Eliot (1888–1965): Eliot, author of *The Waste Land* (1922), was a friend of Moore's and one of the most important modern poets.

Elizabeth Bishop (1911–1979): Another friend of Moore's, Bishop was selected to be the Poet Laureate of the United States in 1949.

and her mother moved to Greenwich Village in New York City, where Moore worked at the New York Public Library. She began to acquire literary friends, including William Carlos Williams, Alfred Kreymborg, and Wallace Stevens. She also became a contributor to the *Dial*, then the most discriminating literary magazine in America.

In 1921 Winifred Ellerman (known as Bryher), an aspiring English novelist, and Hilda Doolittle, an expatriate American poet who wrote under the initials "H. D.," printed Moore's *Poems* in London. The title of the poem "The Fish" interestingly runs into the first sentence of the poem. In "Poetry," she states her dislike for "all this fiddle" about poetry, referring to poets as "literalists of the imagination."

Publishing Career In 1917, just as the United States entered World War I, Moore's brother joined the U.S. Navy and went immediately on convoy duty. Moore moved with her mother in 1918 to a basement apartment at St. Luke's Place in Greenwich Village, where they lived until 1929.

The year 1925 was pivotal for Moore, who moved from the job of checking out books at the library to that of editor of the *Dial* magazine, where she worked until it ceased publication in July 1929. She remembered later that "those were days when . . . things were opening out, not closing in." The *Dial* concentrated on the arts and sought to connect high culture with all aspects of national life. The work was, Moore said, "a revel," even though she had to contend with the grudges and grievances of contributors. To her discredit, she rejected a section of James Joyce's "Work in Progress"—ultimately published as *Finnegans Wake* (1939)—but she was generally clear-

sighted and prescient. The editing helped her to win her first international recognition, and, after the magazine was discontinued, she was able to support herself and her mother by writing verse and independent reviews or occasional essays.

Later Years Moore's zeal for learning, her resoluteness, her continuing lively responses to what pleased or troubled her became a matter of public interest. She knew how to grow old without ceasing to grow. For instance, in 1955 and 1956, when she was approaching seventy, she attended poetry workshops given by W. H. Auden and Louise Bogan. Having won the triple crown of the National Book Award, the Pulitzer Prize, and Bollingen Prize in Poetry for her *Collected Poems* (1951), Moore could well have conducted the classes herself. Instead, the doyenne of American poets, as Elizabeth Bishop recounts, "took notes constantly, asked many questions, and entered into the discussions with enthusiasm." The other students were timid and nonplussed in the presence of Moore, who said she "was learning a great deal, things she had never known before."

At age seventy, in additions to taking poetry classes and tango lessons, she learned to drive a car, although she never owned one. Famous for liking baseball, she was asked to throw out the first ball for the opening day at Yankee Stadium in 1968 and showed up in midseason of 1967 to practice. She enjoyed being a writer, but, asked when she was seventy-two at what point poetry "had become world-shaking" to her, she replied, "Never!" Marianne Moore died on February 5, 1972, in New York. Despite "the obvious credentials of Moore's chief competitors," including William Carlos Williams and Wallace Stevens, John Ashbery has said, "I am tempted to call her our greatest modern poet."

Works in Literary Context

A variety of sources and modes serves many purposes in Moore's work. Expressing both religious and aesthetic concepts, her poetry is not without political implications and social criticism. Its moral fervor, furthermore, is inseparable from her close attention to language. Having come of age during the period of modernism when writers, following the example of European artists, were highly experimental, Moore, as she wrote later of Elizabeth Bishop, was "archaically new."

Birds as Metaphor From *What Are Years*, Moore's "He 'Digesteth Harde Yron'" showcases Moore's regard for natural history. She writes about extinct birds—the roe known only from its remains and legend, the flightless moa, the great auk—and the flightless ostrich, exploited, threatened, and nearly extinct. The ostrich—a "camel-sparrow"—"was and is / a symbol of justice." The poem fuses observation with interpretations. The sorrow over the plight of an endangered species joins with themes that are essentially religious and political.

Oceanic Imagery Of her four poems published in 1918, the only one Moore chose to include in her later definitive text is "The Fish." It seems to signal a turning point in the poet's development as, in Elizabeth Bishop's words, "the world's greatest living observer" of natural phenomena. Here the ocean is both beautiful and treacherous, a source of life as well as a place of conflict, danger, and destruction. The curious paradox of dying life within the sea, and of the sea dying within what thrives on it, is emphasized in the third and fourth lines of the poem, where a mussel "keeps / adjusting the ash-heaps." The sense of life dying (and growing) within the sea, and of the sea aging (and perhaps renewing), hovers over the poem.

Works in Critical Context

James Dickey has written that, if he had to choose a poet to construct heaven "out of the things we already have," he would choose Moore. Her heaven, he said, would be "Much, most probably, like the earth as it is, but refined by responsiveness and intellect into a state very far from the present one; a state of utter consequentiality." He explained that she "spent her life in remaking—or making—our world from particulars that we have never adequately understood on our own," but that the creative person open to experience can "endow...with joyous conjunctions" and reach "conclusions unforeseeable until they were made."

Moore's work, as Bonnie Costello has pointed out, "does not conform to a strict chronological development." Each book she brought out not only published or republished earlier poems, sometimes reworked, sometimes resurrected in a revised form from her very early output (as with "I May, I Must, I Might"), but also included a variety of poems in very different styles and on very different themes. In her books she assembled her verse in groups that represent a variety of modes from different periods regardless of chronology of composition.

Collected Poems The ambitious modesty of these poems, beginning with "The Fish" and culminating with "The Monkey Puzzle," may be lost, as John Ashbery has pointed out, "in the welter of minutiae" that inhabit some of them. Ashbery also notes an "unassuming but also rather unglamorous wisdom that flashes out between descriptions of bizarre fauna and rare artifacts" that is also evident in the work that would follow. The small detail and the monumental are held together conditionally and depend on each other. Among the first critics to recognize Moore's objectives in 1925 was Yvor Winters, who wrote that their basis is "the transference of the metaphysical into physical terms." "I am," he said, "sure of her genius."

Responses to Literature

1. Read Moore's poem "The Fish." Based on your reading of the poem, how do you think Moore felt about animals and nature in general?

COMMON HUMAN EXPERIENCE

Much of Moore's poetry centers around nature and natural imagery. Because of her educational background, she knew a great deal about science and was apparently fascinated by it. Here are some other works that feature natural imagery and emphasize the thrills of scientific discovery.

Walden (1854), a nonfiction book by Henry David Thoreau. Thoreau documents his time spent near Walden Pond in Massachusetts, on his friend Ralph Waldo Emerson's unspoiled land.

Pelvis with the Distance (1943), a painting by Georgia O'Keeffe. In this painting, a stark white bone frames a vast expanse of blue sky.

Pine Forest in Snow, a photograph by Ansel Adams. One of the most famous landscape photographers, Adams's image is one of beautiful white trees against a black background.

Pilgrim at Tinker Creek (1974), an essay collection by Annie Dillard. Dillard's book of essays about her time reflecting on nature in the Blue Ridge Mountains was awarded the Pulitzer Prize in 1975.

Turtle Island (1974), a book of poetry by Gary Snyder. This book of poems, named after what some natives called America, won the Pulitzer Prize in 1975.

---

2. In "The Fish," how does Moore use rhythm to convey mood and meaning?

3. Do you think Moore really felt that poetry was unimportant—or as she put it, "all this fiddle"? Find evidence in her work that proves otherwise.

4. How might Moore's work as an editor have influenced her poetry writing? Comparing her early work to her later work, can you find evidence of these effects?

5. Compare Moore's "The Fish" to Elizabeth Bishop's poem of the same name. How can you tell Bishop was influenced by Moore?

BIBLIOGRAPHY

Books

Abbott, Craig S. *Marianne Moore: A Reference Guide.* Boston: G. K. Hall, 1978.

Borroff, Marie. *Language and the Poet: Verbal Artistry in Frost, Stevens, and Moore.* Chicago: University of Chicago Press, 1979.

Dickey, James. *Babel to Byzantium.* New York: Farrar, Straus & Giroux, 1968, pp. 156–164.

Hall, Donald. *Marianne Moore: The Cage and the Animal.* New York: Pegasus, 1970.

Phillips, Elizabeth. *Marianne Moore*. New York: Ungar, 1982.

Tomlinson, Charles, ed. *Marianne Moore: A Collection of Critical Essays*. Englewood Cliffs, N.J.: Prentice-Hall, 1969.

Williams, William Carlos. *Selected Essays of William Carlos Williams*. New York: Random House, 1954, pp. 121–131.

Periodicals

Ashbery, John. "Straight Lines Over Rough Terrain." *New York Times Book Review* (November 26, 1967): 1, 42.

Elizabeth Bishop. "Efforts of Affection." *Vanity Fair* 4 (June 1983): 44–61.

Hall, Donald. "The Art of Poetry IV: Marianne Moore." *Paris Review* 7 (Summer/Fall 1961): 41–66.

———. "An Interview with Marianne Moore." *McCall's* 93 (December 1965): 74, 182–190.

Vendler, Helen. "On Marianne Moore." *The New Yorker* 54 (October 16, 1978): 168–193.

Winters, Yvor. "Holiday and Day of Wrath." *Poetry* 26 (April 1925): 39–44.

✹ Pat Mora

BORN: *1942, El Paso, Texas*

NATIONALITY: *American*

GENRE: *Poetry, nonfiction*

MAJOR WORKS:

Chants (1984)

Borders (1986)

Communion (1991)

Overview

Pat Mora has developed one of the broadest audiences of any Hispanic poet in the United States. Her crisp narrative style and the healing messages in her verse appeal to both adult and young readers. As a result, her poems have been reprinted in many elementary, middle, and high school textbooks. While Mora has often been considered a soft-spoken feminist and a regional poet who celebrates life in the desert, her poetic vision has an all-embracing quality. She has written verse that explores the condition of women not only in the Southwest but also in such Third World countries as Pakistan. She has also written deeply humanistic essays and richly diverse children's literature that both encompasses Mexican folk traditions and addresses such modern topics as adoption.

Works in Biographical and Historical Context

Patricia Estella Mora was born on January 19, 1942, in El Paso, Texas, to an optician, Raúl Antonio Mora, and Estella Delgado Mora. She attended Catholic schools in El Paso and received her higher education at institutions in the city, graduating with a BA from Texas Western College in 1963. After finishing college in 1963 she worked as an English teacher in the El Paso Independent School District and El Paso Community College, and then received her MA in English from the University of Texas at El Paso in 1967. Eventually she returned to the University of Texas at El Paso as an instructor, and from 1981 to 1989 served as a university administrator and museum director.

Early Publications Mora began publishing poetry in the late 1970s in minor magazines including the *Americas Review*. Her publications of this period were part of the first wave of the Chicano literary movement. Her first books of poetry clearly indicate her interest in shamanism and biculturalism. *Chants* and *Borders* each received the Southwest Book Award, critical acclaim, and a place in college and high-school curricula. Her third book of poetry, *Communion*, solidified her reputation with scholars and general readers.

Activism and Honors In 1986 Mora received a Kellogg Fellowship to study national and international cultural-conservation issues. Subsequently, she became a consultant for the W. K. Kellogg Foundation and specialized in U.S.-Mexico youth exchanges. In addition to the Kellogg honor, in 1994 Mora received a National Endowment for the Arts fellowship to further the writing of her poetry, which resulted in the publication of *Agua Santa: Holy Water* (1995). With her background in education and interest in exploring issues of cultural development and conflict, Mora has become a popular speaker and guest presenter at gatherings of teachers and education professionals around the country.

Family and Relocation Mora is the mother of three children, William, Elizabeth, and Cecilia, all from her first marriage, to William Burnside. In 1984 she married an archaeologist, Vernon Lee Scarborough, with whom she has traveled extensively. When Scarborough relocated from the University of Texas at El Paso to the University of Cincinnati, Mora made the transition from the West Texas desert to the colder Midwest. Since moving to Ohio, Mora has published several books for children, including *A Birthday Basket for Tía* (1992), *Listen to the Desert* (1994), *Pablo's Tree* (1994), *The Desert Is My Mother* (1994), and *The Gift of the Poinsettia* (1995). She has also produced a collection of autobiographical essays, *Nepantla: Essays from the Land of the Middle* (1993); a family memoir, *House of Houses* (1997); and a volume of religious poems, *Aunt Carmen's Book of Practical Saints* (1997).

Mora now lives in Santa Fe, New Mexico and continues to write. In 2006 she won the National Hispanic Cultural Center Literary Award and in 2008 won the Luis Leal Award for Distinction in Chicano/Latino Letters.

Works in Literary Context

Mora writes much about the people and landscapes of the American Southwest. She personifies the desert in strong, enduring women such as her grandmother who nurtured her when she was growing up. She seems to find strength in Mexican women to bridge gaps in society, whether by commanding respect in an industry or university boardroom, speaking before an audience of educators, or pursuing relationships with men. Her identification with the desert provides a great deal of the power that Mora brings to her poetry readings, in which she often evokes the image of a shaman or curandera (faith healer), another of her alter egos in *Chants*.

The Southwestern Landscape The image of the Desert Mother is the central motif in "Mi Madre" and became the basis for one of Mora's books for children, *The Desert Is My Mother* (1994), which won the Stepping Stones Award in 1995. Of particular significance in *Chants*, however, is the magical relationship between the poet and the Desert Mother. The poet demonstrates shamanistic abilities, tapping into the mysterious power of the desert, its rhythms, its ability to heal with the herbs that grow there, its warmth, and its toughness and strength.

Borders In "Legal Alien" Mora uses the metaphor of the border to represent the outsider status of Mexican Americans. She also sees the border in terms of social class and racism—the skin color of Mexicans is a border to Anglos in "Mexican Maid," for example, and class differences separate Mexicans from Mexican Americans in "Illegal Alien." However, other poems in *Chants*, such as "Legal Alien," and "Curandera," depict the borderland as a center of power in itself. No matter how she is using them, Mora is clearly intrigued by borders and interprets them not only in physical but broad philosophical terms.

Having dwelled on the border between Mexico and the United States for much of her life, Mora came to believe that Mexican Americans, no matter where they resided, lived a type of border existence. While the border can provide a vantage point from which to observe and understand two societies, such a perspective tends to make one feel like an outsider. The result, in Mora's opinion, is that alienation becomes a central condition of the border dweller. Mora has stressed the border as a position of power, a place in which to bridge divisions, heal wounds, and facilitate mutual understanding. This process begins in *Chants*, in which the inhospitable and uninhabitable borderland is envisioned as a mother who nurtures her children: "she: the desert / She: strong mother" ("Mi Madre").

Strong Women In *Chants*, *Borders*, and *Communion*, Mora also attempts to negotiate the border between the past and the present, so as to draw upon the strong women who preceded her: her aunt, Ygmacia Delgado (whom she and her siblings called Tía Lobo, or Aunt Wolf), her grandmother, and mother, as well as healers

---

LITERARY AND HISTORICAL CONTEMPORARIES

Pat Mora's famous contemporaries include:

Frida Kahlo (1907–1954): This famous Mexican painter influenced many fellow artists with her surreal self-portraits.

Maurice Sendak (1928–): Sendak is best known for his classic, *Where the Wild Things Are* (1963).

Dagoberto Gilb (1950–): An American writer of German-Mexican descent who has published *The Magic of Blood* (1994), a story collection about hardworking men in Los Angeles.

Laura Esquivel (1950–): The Mexican author whose novel *Like Water for Chocolate* (1989), set in Mexico, quickly climbed onto American booklists.

Oscar Hijuelos (1951–): A Cuban-American novelist whose book *The Mambo Kings Play Songs of Love* (1989) won a Pulitzer Prize in 1990, making him the first Hispanic to do so.

---

and rebels. Mora envisions herself as a link in the tradition of passing on wisdom to her own daughters and to society at large, choosing the best from the past and making what changes are necessary. As she has explained:

> To transform our traditions wisely, we need to know them, be inspired and saddened by them, choose for ourselves what to retain. But we can prize the past together, valuing the positive female and Mexican traditions. We can prize the elements of the past as we persist in demanding, and creating, change.

Mora rejects the limited roles society has forced on women in the past, especially those that control their sexuality. Such rituals and practices as burying a female child's umbilical cord in the house or placing orange blossoms in the hair of a bride are censured in the poems "Dream" and "Aztec Princess," for example.

Works in Critical Context

Mora's poetry has attracted the attention of Chicano and feminist scholars, along with reviewers from smaller journals who generally appreciate her shamanistic imagery and her idealistic desire to unite and heal.

Chants A reviewer of *Chants* in *Dusty Dog Reviews* asserted: "This is richly feminine poetry, in which a healthy womanly sensuality is being continuously awakened like the living dawn that spreads its westward lights across the world, continuously unveiling a physical magic." The collection has also garnered the praise from fellow poets, such as Anya Achtenberg who wrote in *Contact II* (1995), "Healers, those who restore harmony

COMMON HUMAN EXPERIENCE

Mora has helped people recognize the validity and complexity of literature written by Mexican Americans and other Chicanos. By focusing her writing on her cultural past and her country's future, she has helped make her own customs and traditions interesting to those who know little about them. Here are some other works that have helped spread the Chicano word and vision:

The House on Mango Street (1984), a novel by Sandra Cisneros. This coming-of-age novel centers on Esperanza, a young, impoverished girl.

Like Water for Chocolate (1989), a novel by Laura Esquivel. Cooking intricate recipes helps young Tita solve her romantic problems in this best-seller.

How the García Girls Lost Their Accents (1991), a novel by Julia Alvarez. This novel by the Dominican-American author centers around a group of sisters trying to assimilate in New York City.

Real Women Have Curves (1992), a movie directed by Patricia Cardoso and starring America Ferrara. It tells the story of Ana, a first generation Mexican-American teenager on the verge of becoming a woman.

by bringing together what seems to be separate, often suffer but possess great 'magic,' and Mora's is a healing voice." Novelist Jewelle Gómez is another of Mora's admirers— she wrote in *Hurricane Alice* that "Mora has a powerful grasp of the music of everyday language, and she is not afraid of dark, complex feelings. . . . Mora's simplicity and economy create a haunting sense of timelessness." Gómez went on to say that none of the women in *Chants* "have been bowed by the weighty roles chosen for them in this society. To be old, to speak only one language, are not stigmas; they are conditions in a natural transitory order. . . . This collection is rich, spirited, promising."

Communion Bryce Milligan in the *National Catholic Reporter* found the poems in *Communion* to be "powerful, imaginative and well crafted." In his opinion, "it is clear the poet is giving birth to a new voice." In *Texas Books in Review*, however, Betsy Colquitt found some of the poems in this new voice to be "more engaged intellectually than emotionally" and suggested that Mora's best poems were still those that related to the Southwest and her bilingual, bicultural identity.

A Birthday Basket for Tía Mora's books for children have been acclaimed almost universally for her sensitive and deft portrayals of Mexican American and Mexican culture. Mary Sarber's assessment of *A Birthday Basket for Tía* in the *El Paso Herald-Post*, for example,

could be applied equally to all of Mora's picture books: "This is an outstanding addition to the growing body of literature that will help Hispanic children identify with their culture." Mora's writing for children has also been praised for helping to bring Hispanic culture to non-Hispanic children.

Responses to Literature

1. Explore the use of border imagery in Mora's books. What are some of the struggles people who live on or with borders face, from both sides of the border?

2. The desert is generally thought to be a barren place. Why, then, do you think Mora considers it "Mi Madre"? Support your answer using examples from her poetry.

3. Many of Mora's picture books focus on the need for traditions and celebrations. Why do you think such events so important to children? What traditions and celebrations have been important in your own life?

BIBLIOGRAPHY

Books

Saldívar-Hull, Sonia. "Feminism on the Border: From Gender Politics to Geopolitics." *Criticism in the Borderlands: Studies in Chicano Literature, Culture, and Ideology.* Edited by Héctor Calderón and José David Saldívar. Durham, N.C.: Duke University Press, pp. 203–220.

Periodicals

Achtenberg, Anya. "Healing with Age," *Contact II* (1985): 31–32.

Colquitt, Betsy. Review of *Communion* in *Texas Books in Review* (Winter 1991).

Fox, Linda C. "From *Chants* to *Borders* to *Communion*: Pat Mora's Poetic Journey to *Nepantla*," *Bilingual Review/Revista Bilingue* (1996).

Gómez, Jewelle. Review of *Chants* in *Hurricane Alice* (Spring/Summer 1984).

Milligan, Bryce. Review of *Communion, National Catholic Reporter* (10 May 1991).

Murphy, Patrick. "Grandmother Borderland: Placing Identity and Ethnicity," *Interdisciplinary Studies in Literature and Environment* (1993): 35–41.

Passman, Kristina. "Demeter, Kore, and the Birth of the Self: The Quest for Identity in the Poetry of Alma Villanueva, Pat Mora, and Cherríe Moraga," *Monographic Review*, 6 (1990): 35–41.

Sarber, Mary, review of *A Birthday Basket for Tía* in the *El Paso Herald-Post*.

Web sites

Pat Mora Homepage. Accessed December 14, 2008, from http://PatMora.com.

✸ Toshio Mori

BORN: *1910, San Francisco, California*

DIED: *1980, San Leandro, California*

NATIONALITY: *American*

GENRE: *Fiction*

MAJOR WORKS:

Yokohama, California (1949)

Woman from Hiroshima (1978)

The Chauvinist and Other Stories (1979)

Unfinished Message: Selected Works of Toshio Mori (2000)

Overview

Toshio Mori ranks among the most important early Asian-American writers. His signature work is *Yokohama, California*, a short-story collection that spans the 1920s to the 1940s and features innovative portraits of the Japanese-American community and the internment of the *Issei, Nisei,* and *Young Sansei* (various generations of Japanese immigrants) during World War II. The stories offer vivid, artful, and intimate portraits of Japanese-American life, and often display a wry and ironic sense of humor.

Works in Biographical and Historical Context

Mori's parents, Hidekichi and Yoshi (Takaki) Mori, emigrated from Otake, Japan, in the late 1890s. On his way to the United States, Mori's father briefly stopped and worked in Hawaii before buying a San Francisco bathhouse. His wife then made her way from coastal Miyajima to San Francisco, where Toshio Mori was born on March 3, 1910. Mori's two elder brothers, Masao and Tadashi, subsequently left Japan to join the family, and by 1914 the entire family was reunited. A younger brother, Kazuo, was born in California. From 1913 to 1915 the family co-owned a flower nursery in Oakland, California. In 1915, however, the family acquired their own flower and greenhouse business in San Leandro, California.

California Dreaming As a teenager, Mori dreamed of life as either a professional baseball player or Buddhist missionary. At home, he spoke Japanese to his parents, but spoke English in school and with his brothers. He also read voraciously, and had a particular interest in dime novels, works of fiction that were popular during that time period. When his interest in short-story authorship deepened, he turned to the famous writers and works he mentioned in a 1980 interview with editor Russell Leong: "O. Henry, Stephen Crane, de Maupassant, Balzac, Katherine Mansfield, Chekhov, Gorki, Gogol and *Winesburg, Ohio* [a book of short stories by Sherwood Anderson]."

In the 1930s Mori established a rigorous schedule that included full days working at the nursery and four hours writing stories at night. He sent his stories out for publication but frequently received rejection letters, often on the grounds that his subject matter—Japanese America—was odd fare and would not appeal to a mainstream readership. The acceptance of one of his stories, "The Brothers," by *Coast* magazine in 1938 finally launched his career. His works then made regular appearances in various smaller magazines and journals. Encouraged by the novelist William Saroyan, who had read and admired his stories and became a friend, Mori's work was adopted by a small Idaho publishing house, Caxton Printers, which decided to put his short-story collection, *Yokohama, California*, on its 1942 list.

Mori and the Japanese Internment As was the case with lives of the entire Japanese-American community, Mori's emerging literary career was interrupted on December 7, 1941, when Japan bombed Pearl Harbor, a U.S. naval base in Hawaii. This historic event led President Franklin Delano Roosevelt to declare war on Japan and issue Executive Order 9066, which called for the internment of 120,000 Japanese Americans in camps across the American West. It was believed that Japanese Americans posed such a threat to national security they could not be trusted to live freely in society. Mori and most of his family were sent first to an assembly center at Tanforan Racetrack, California, and then to a Topaz Relocation Camp in central Utah, where Mori spent the whole of World War II as an internee. While interned, Mori and other Japanese Americans lost all the property they left behind. Inside the camps, education was limited, there were few employment opportunities, and detainees had to adhere to a strict schedule.

In the face of widespread anti-Japanese sentiment that resulted from the bombing of Pearl Harbor and the onset of World War II, Caxton made the decision to postpone the publication of *Yokohama, California*. Meanwhile, Mori became camp historian at Topaz, helped found the camp journal *Trek*, had some of his work featured in the *Best Short Stories of 1943* anthology, and witnessed the return from the Italian front of his seriously wounded brother Kazuo, an enlistee in the all-Nisei 442nd Regimental Combat Team.

Mori was not able to return to San Leandro until the war ended in 1945. In June 1947 he married Hisayo Yoshiwara, and in July 1951 they had a son, Steven Mori. In 1949, *Yokohama, California* was finally published, and featured an introduction by Saroyan. Few stories in the collection better represent Mori's strengths than "Lil' Yokohama," a meticulously crafted mosaic of a Japanese-American township in California in the years leading up to World War II. The story emphasizes the everyday life of "our community," reminding readers of how the town's ordinary twenty-four-hour cycles parallel those of cities from Boston, Massachusetts, to Emeryville, California. In his writing, Mori attempted to capture Japanese-American life while facing widespread hostility against the Japanese and anything "Oriental."

LITERARY AND HISTORICAL CONTEMPORARIES

Toshio Mori's famous contemporaries include:

Raymond Chandler (1888–1959): A novelist whose detective Phillip Marlowe was well-rooted in California life.

William Saroyan (1908–1981): This author based his works on the lives of people in Fresno, California, and was a friend of Mori.

Gary Snyder (1930–): A noted San Francisco Bay Area Beat poet who studied Zen Buddhism and became the hero of Jack Kerouac's novel, *The Dharma Bums* (1958).

Armistead Maupin (1944–): A novelist whose series of books, *Tales of the City* (begun in 1978), is set in San Francisco and center on the colorful culture there.

Jessica Hagedorn (1949–): Born in the Philippines, this writer later moved to San Francisco and currently specializes in Asian-American fiction.

Long-Awaited Success *Yokohama, California* sold few copies, and there were few reviews. More than a decade passed before Mori began to make a serious impact on the literary scene. With the close of the family nursery in the 1960s, Mori became an independent flower wholesaler and salesman. However, by the end of that decade America's multicultural literary renaissance opened the way to Mori's recognition as a writer. In the 1970s Mori became a widely celebrated figure. Anthologies featured his stories, lecture and conference invitations were frequent, and he became a mentor to a new generation of Asian-American writers.

Mori published three texts in his waning years. In 1978 a small San Francisco publisher, Isthmus Press, operating with a grant from the National Endowment for the Arts, published Mori's novel *Woman From Hiroshima*. Mori drew upon his family history to present the fictional autobiography of Mrs. Toda, or Toda-san as she is called by her community, as she describes her life for her grandchildren, Johnny and Annabelle. *Woman From Hiroshima* offers Toda-san's life story both for what it says about the individual character and as a tale representative of the larger Japanese-American experience. In 1979 Mori's second story collection, *The Chauvinist and Other Stories*, was published by the Asian-American Studies Center at the University of California, Los Angeles. Featuring twenty-two stories set out in six sections, the book again features Mori's trademark irony and attention to detail.

On April 12, 1980, Mori died in his hometown of San Leandro after suffering several strokes. He was survived by his wife and sons. Mori was mourned in Asian-American circles as well as the larger literary community. In the interview earlier that year with Russell Leong, Mori spoke warmly of his life and writing, of his remembered history of family and community, and of his unyielding commitment to the craft of storytelling. He looked back at the early rejection slips he received from magazines and publishers, explained how he came to focus on "Japanese life-relations" as his main subject matter, and described the delayed publication history of *Yokohama, California*. Mori also spoke of his literary influences and reading and discussed without bitterness his internment at Topaz.

Works in Literary Context

Mori's subtle command of voice and the influence of Zen—quiet self-contemplation and the admiration of the virtues of harmony and balance—are apparent in many of his stories. Mori's writing usually features typical scenes, such as housewives on the porch, old men reading newspapers, and shifts in the weather. Such intimate attention to detail marks all of Mori's work.

Everyday People Mori particularly enjoyed focusing on the simple, common experiences of everyday people, and much of his writing features a "day-in-the-life" quality. In "Lil' Yokohama," for example, small occurrences and commonalities are what draw the community together. Baseball loyalties are divided between the Alameda Taiiku and the San Jose Asahis. The school day parallels the workday. The death of Komai-san, a longtime gardener, occurs at the same time as the Sansei birth of Franklin Susumu Amano. From his window, Yukio Takaki, a painter living on Seventh Street, looks at the scene outside. Sam Suda expands his fruit market, and Satoru Ugaki gets married. The sight of a new Oldsmobile Eight in the neighborhood inspires gossip. Ray Tatemoto leaves to study journalism in New York. The daily *Mainichi News* appears. Radios blast Benny Goodman's jazz, and the school day comes to a close. Mori's portrait closes with, "The day is here, and is Lil' Yokohama's day," a subtle reminder that Japanese America is an unthreatening township at peace both with itself and its fellow citizenry despite the international war. Unmentioned, but implied throughout, is the threat of internment.

Crossing Cultures Cross-cultural themes also abound in Mori's work. In *Yokohama, California*, the story "Tomorrow Is Coming, Children," is a good example of how he employs cross-culturalism to explore the Japanese-American experience and the atmosphere of World War II America. Told by an interned grandmother to her grandchildren, Annabelle and Johnny, it describes the grandmother's emigration from Japan and her adaptation to life in America. She recalls leaving her Japanese village, sailing from the port of Kobe, her seasickness, the sight of the Golden Gate Bridge, and her husband's misgivings about the fact that she wears a kimono instead of Western clothes in their new home in the United States. Over the course of her narrative, the grandmother recalls the kindness of a neighbor, a white American woman who is married to a Japanese acrobat. She and her American neighbor have no common language with which to communicate, but they are able to share compassionate silence, tea, and a love of children. To the narrator, San Francisco represents a larger, more generous America, the life beyond the camps indicated by the "coming tomorrow" of the story's title.

More cross-culturalism is found in the story "The Sweet Potato" (1941) published in *Unfinished Message: Selected Works of Toshio Mori*. The encounter at San Francisco's Treasure Island fairground between the Nisei narrator, his friend Hiro, and an old Japanese-speaking white lady demonstrates a commonality across cultures and generations.

Works in Critical Context

In her introduction to Mori's *The Chauvinist and Other Stories*, Hisaye Yamamoto, a fellow Californian Nisei author, writes admiringly of Mori's "panorama of Japanese America," as well as his "persistence in continuing to write despite the odds." With this statement, Yamamoto summarizes Mori's appeal for Japanese-American readers and mainstream America alike.

Yokohama, California   Many of Mori's numerous short stories in this collection draw on events in his own life, including the decades he spent working in his family's horticultural nursery business. In "Through Anger and Love," the protagonist is a nine-year-old boy, the son of a flower-seller, who, angry at his father, sets off to sell flowers by himself. Another story, "The Chessmen," "is a prize, a heart-rending tale of an old nurseryman-gardener who is about to be put out to pasture," Akira Tofina wrote in *Review of Arts, Literature, Philosophy, and the Humanities* online.

Unfinished Message: Selected Works of Toshio Mori   In 2000, *Unfinished Message: Selected Works of Toshio Mori*, a major retrospective edited by the Sansei poet Lawson Fusao Inada, was published. Inada's introduction to *Unfinished Message* calls attention to Mori's "hard-won mastery of English, his self-taught, masterful technique and style" and his deserved stature as an Asian-American literary "founder." Inada bases his estimation on Mori's treatment of Japanese-American life, including family, school, work, baseball, the Nisei-Sansei triumphs and tensions, the flower-nursery business of his own West Coast family, and World War II and internment. Mori's literary reputation took time to emerge, but his storytelling's gentle ease of manner and his profound observations about human behavior are now widely recognized and celebrated.

Lonny Kaneko, who reviewed the volume in the *International Examiner*, noted that "there are three or four traditional conflict-based stories in the collection,

COMMON HUMAN EXPERIENCE

Mori's work celebrated the everyday minutiae of ordinary people's lives, from daily chores to small hobbies and interpersonal relationships. He specialized in writing about California and portrayed the variety of people who lived in fictionalized neighborhoods there. Here are some other works that depict small—and often surprising—slices of life of a neighborhood or town:

Cannery Row (1945), a novel by John Steinbeck. The characters in this novel all live in a down-and-out neighborhood near Monterey, California, during the Great Depression.

Our Town (1938), a play by Thornton Wilder. This play takes place in the fictionalized Grover's Corners, and details the lives of the people who live there in a rather gossipy fashion.

Winesburg, Ohio (1919), short stories by Sherwood Anderson. George Willard, the book's protagonist, tells stories about his fellow townspeople in this inspirational book.

Shortcuts (1993), a film by Robert Altman. This movie, which features small clips of the lives of people in Los Angeles, was based on the works of the short story author, Raymond Carver.

Tales of the City (1978), a novel by Armistead Maupin. The characters in this book—who all live together in a boarding house in San Francisco—were so interesting that Maupin developed this novel into a series which later became a television miniseries.

but many others demonstrate a touch that is unique and off-the-beaten path." Kaneko called *Unfinished Message* "a delightful read."

Responses to Literature

1. Compare Mori's discussion of internment camps and racism in his story "Slant-Eyed Americans" to Viktor Frankl's discussion of concentration camps in *Man's Search for Meaning* (1946). What similarities exist between the Japanese-American experience in the United States and the Jewish experience in Nazi Germany? What differences?

2. Compare Mori's stories about San Francisco in *Yokohama, California* to Armistead Maupin's version of the same city in his book, *Tales of the City*.

3. Research Zen koans, the poetic sayings of Zen Buddhists. In your opinion, what does the writing style have in common with Mori's style?

BIBLIOGRAPHY

Books

Banhart, Sarah Catlin. "Toshio Mori," in *Asian American Short Story Writer: An A-to-Z Guide*, edited by Guiyou Huang. Westport, Conn.: Greenwood Press, 2003, pp. 195–202.

Davis, Rocío G. *Transcultural Reinventions: Asian American and Asian Canadian Short-Story Cycles*. Toronto: Toronto South Asian Review Publications, 2001.

Horokoshi, Peter. "An Interview with Toshio Mori," in *Counterpoint: Perspectives on Asian America*, edited by Emma Gee. Los Angeles: Asian American Studies Center, University of California, Los Angeles, 1976.

Kim, Elaine. *Asian American Literature: An Introduction to the Writings and their Social Context*. Philadelphia: Temple University Press, 1982.

Lee, A. Robert. *Multicultural American Literature: Comparative Black, Native, Latino/a and Asian American Fictions*. Edinburgh: Edinburgh University Press, 2003.

Mayer, David R. "Toshio Mori: Chronicler of Japanese-American Oakland," in his *Door Stoops and Window Sills: Perspectives on the American Neighborhood Novel*, Nanzan University Academic Publication Series. Kyoto: Yamaguchi, 1992, pp. 55–77.

Trudeau, Lawrence J., ed. "Toshio Mori," in *Asian American Literature: Reviews and Criticism by American Writers of Asian Descent*. Detroit: Gale, 1999.

Periodicals

Bedrosian, Margaret. "Toshio Mori's California Koans," *MELUS*, 15, no. 2 (1988): 47–58.

Keneko, Lonny, review of *Unfinished Message: Selected Works of Toshio Mori* in *International Examiner* (Seattle, WA), April 30, 2001, p. 12.

Leong, Russell. "Toshio Mori: An Interview," *Amerasia Journal*, 7, no. 1 (1980): 89–108.

Mayer, David R. "Akegarasu and Emerson: Kindred Spirits in Toshio Mori's 'The Seventh Street Philosopher,'" *Amerasia Journal*, 16, no. 2 (1990): 1–10.

———"The Philosopher in Search of a Voice: Toshio Mori's Japanese-Influenced Narrator," *Asian American Literature Association Journal*, 2 (1995): 12–24.

———"The Short Stories of Toshio Mori," *Fu Jen Studies: Literature and Linguistics*, 12 (1988): 73–87.

———"Toshio Mori and Loneliness," *Nanzan Review of American Studies*, 15 (1993): 20–31.

———"Toshio Mori's Neighborhood Settings: Inner and Outer Oakland," *Fu Jen Studies: Literature and Linguistics*, 23 (1993): 100–115.

Palumbo-Liu, David. "Toshio Mori and the Attachments of Spirit: A Response to David R. Mayer," *Amerasia Journal*, 17, no. 3 (1991): 41–47.

Sato, Gayle K. "(Self) Indulgent Listening: Reading Cultural Difference in *Yokohama, California*," *Japanese Journal of American Studies*, 11 (2000): 129–146.

Web Sites

Review of Arts, Literature, Philosophy, and the Humanities Online, http://www.ralphmag.org/ (August 16, 2005), Akira Tofina, review of *Unfinished Message*.

Contemporary Authors Online, Gale, 2008. Reproduced in *Biography Resource Center*. Farmington Hills, Mich.: Gale, 2008. http://galenet.galegroup.com/servlet/BioRC

✺ Toni Morrison

BORN: *1931, Lorain, Ohio*

NATIONALITY: *American*

GENRE: *Fiction*

MAJOR WORKS:

Song of Solomon (1977)

Beloved (1987)

Overview

Toni Morrison has established herself as a significant American novelist. She has produced nine extraordinary novels since 1970 and won the Nobel Prize in Literature in 1993. Each of her novels has been critically acclaimed, and despite Morrison's creation of idiosyncratic characters and bizarre circumstances in her novels, the messages she provides have universal appeal.

Works in Biographical and Historical Context

Surviving the Great Depression Morrison was born Chloe Ardelia Wofford in Lorain, Ohio, the second of four children raised in a family that had endured economic and social adversity. Morrison's maternal grandparents, Ardelia and John Solomon Willis, were sharecroppers in Greenville, Alabama, having lost their land at the turn of the century. In 1912 her grandparents decided to head north to escape the hopeless debt of sharecropping and the fear of racism, and eventually settled in Lorain.

While growing up during the Great Depression, Morrison witnessed the struggles of her father, George Wofford, who had migrated from Georgia, and her mother, Ramah Willis Wofford, to support their family. George Wofford often worked many jobs at a time—a shipyard welder, car washer, steel-mill welder, and construction

Toni Morrison   *Morrison, Toni, photograph. AP Images.*

worker. Her parents' willingness to take on hard and sometimes demeaning work was coupled with a distinct unwillingness to relinquish their own sense of value and humanity. Morrison's father was meticulous in his work, writing his name in the side of the ship whenever he welded a perfect seam. Her mother at one point wrote a letter of protest to President Franklin D. Roosevelt when her family received unfit government-sponsored flour.

Though deprived of monetary resources in a hostile world, Morrison's family and community held a remarkable wealth of music, storytelling, love of the supernatural, and black language, which all became major influences on Morrison and her writings. Morrison's mother often sang at home and for the church choir. Though her family could not read music, they could reproduce the music they heard. Other forms of support included storytelling that involved every member of the family. After adults told stories, they invited the children to do the same. Morrison considered this part as important, if not more important, than listening to the stories. Though there were few books in her house, Morrison learned early the importance of reading. Her grandfather was a figure of awe and respect to her because, with the help of his sister, he had taught himself to read. In first grade, Morrison found that she

was not just the only black student in her class, but she was also the only student who already knew how to read. Morrison was encouraged to read at home and did so voraciously, including a wide range of world literature.

Education   After high school Morrison attended Howard University in Washington, D.C., majoring in English and minoring in the classics; her dream was to be a teacher. While at Howard she acquired the nickname Toni. She joined the Howard University Players, thus getting an opportunity to travel in the South, to experience its history and geography, and to relive her grandparents' harrowing flight from poverty and racism. Morrison graduated from Howard in 1953 and then enrolled in graduate school at Cornell University.

Morrison received her master's degree from Cornell in 1955. She wrote her thesis on the theme of suicide in the works of Virginia Woolf and William Faulkner. She then taught English at Texas Southern University in Houston for two years, beginning a teaching career that she proudly continues to this day. In 1957 Morrison, then an English instructor at Howard, began to meet and influence young men who became prominent in the 1960s, among them Amiri Baraka, Andrew Young, and Claude Brown. She even taught the activist Stokely Carmichael in one of her classes.

Marriage and Divorce   Two major events marked her period of teaching at Howard. She began to write, and she married Harold Morrison, a Jamaican architect. During her marriage Morrison joined a writer's group at Howard, where she composed a story that grew into her first novel, *The Bluest Eye* (1970), about a little black girl who longs for blue eyes. With her writing career only in its infancy, her marriage ended around 1964, leaving Morrison with two sons, Harold Ford and Slade Kevin. After her divorce Morrison lived with her parents in Lorain for a year and a half and then accepted an editorial position with a textbook subsidiary at Random House in Syracuse, New York. Her mother expressed dismay that Morrison was a single parent without other family there—a difficult, isolated condition for anyone. For Morrison, writing helped fill the void of family, husband, and, to a great extent, self.

In the late 1960s and early 1970s Morrison's career as a writer paralleled her increasing prominence in the publishing world and as one of the cultural elite of the black community. She left Syracuse to become a senior editor at Random House in New York City. There, she established herself as a mentor to such aspiring African American women writers as Toni Cade Bambara, Gayl Jones, and Angela Davis. The idea for Morrison's second novel, *Sula* (1973), came months after she finished *The Bluest Eye*.

Hitting Her Stride   Morrison's third novel, *Song of Solomon* (1977), expands beyond the time and place of her first two books, moving from North to South and

LITERARY AND HISTORICAL CONTEMPORARIES

Morrison's famous contemporaries include:

William Faulkner (1897–1962): Faulkner is a Nobel Prize–winning American author famous for his tales set in the fictional Yoknapatawpha County in Mississippi.

Martin Luther King Jr. (1929–1968): King's famous and inspiring nonviolent protests and speeches made him a leader of the civil rights movement and the recipient of the Nobel Peace Prize.

Bobby Seale (1936–): Seale cofounded the Black Panthers in 1966 and became one of the more widely known civil rights activists.

Toni Cade Bambara (1939–1995): Stories from Bambara's collection *Gorilla, My Love* (1972) are often anthologized, and Bambara did much to secure rights for women and African Americans.

Alice Walker (1944–): Walker is a Pulitzer Prize–winning American novelist most famous for *The Color Purple* (1982).

from present to past in an endeavor to uncover and rediscover the personal history of an African American family. In *Song of Solomon*, Morrison for the first time uses a male protagonist, Milkman, to undergo a rite of passage—not from innocence to experience but from one history to another, one culture to another, and one value system to another. He undergoes a ritual immersion into the South and his own history in an attempt to understand himself and his culture.

Perhaps Morrison's most acclaimed novel is the much-lauded *Beloved* (1987). Morrison delayed the writing of this novel because she anticipated the pain of recovery and confrontation that writing the book would bring. While her novels since have been strong and praised, *Beloved* continues to haunt American literature. In his Nobel Prize speech, William Faulkner noted that a writer's only true subject is "the human heart in conflict with itself." Morrison, who wrote a master's thesis on Faulkner and Virginia Woolf, seems to agree, for at the core of all her novels is a penetrating view of the unyielding, heartbreaking dilemmas that torment people of all races.

Works in Literary Context

Morrison's rich history of family and community filters directly into her novels, a progression of works that begins by addressing the black family and then broadens to the black community, regions of the United States, foreign lands and alien cultures, history, and reality. In her novels Morrison celebrates the rich heritage and language of the black community and the values it struggles to maintain in a predominantly white society whose own value system, she finds, has lost its collective way. Morrison's thematic consistency is refigured in each novel; each novel is an original revoicing of her previous concerns with the black community and family. She experiments almost relentlessly with language, with narrative forms, and with fictive reality in an endeavor to redefine the African American experience not as marginal or peripheral, but as American.

The Supernatural Although her works are firmly grounded in the often-grim realities of the black experience, Morrison often includes elements of the supernatural to reflect and amplify the mythic qualities of her characters. In *Song of Solomon*, Morrison indulges in myth, fantasy, and the supernatural as a form of transcendence for her African American characters. While she dabbles in the supernatural in both *The Bluest Eye* and *Sula*, in *Song of Solomon* she further blurs the lines between reality and fantasy. Her character Pilate can talk to her dead father, Ruth's watermark does grow each day, and Solomon and Milkman can fly. By casually mingling the real and the bizarre, Morrison negotiates the chasm between reality and fantasy so that the impossible becomes the inevitable.

In *Tar Baby* (1981) Morrison again relies on myth, ghosts, and evil, intensifying their mystical qualities by placing them in the isolated setting of a Caribbean island. Morrison invokes the supernatural as a way to fend off a reality in which whites are set against blacks, women against men, culture against primitivism, and civilization against nature. Morrison challenges these dualities by creating an atmosphere in which the island itself is sentient, competing myths on the island proliferate, and several characters experience psychic occurrences.

Transcending Race Despite the presence of a ghost, supernatural events are not the dominant theme in *Beloved*. Here, Morrison explores the importance of mother-child relationships, the power of memory, the importance of community, and the way in which slavery deprived black parents of child-rearing responsibilities and privileges. Through Beloved's memories, Morrison suggests that the girl is not a supernatural being at all, but rather a young person who has suffered the pains of being brought from Africa to America on a slave ship. Slavery itself, though, has not been the most painful part of Beloved's life. The girl is haunted by the image of her African mother jumping into the ocean, a suicidal act committed, no doubt, to escape the living hell of the slave ship.

When asked by an interviewer for *Newsweek* whether whites could adequately respond to *Beloved*, Morrison replied that she had been misunderstood if people think that she writes only for black readers. Continuing, she explained, "When I write, I don't try to translate for white readers . . . Dostoyevsky wrote for a Russian audience, but we're able to read him. If I'm specific, and I don't over-explain, then anybody can overhear me."

Works in Critical Context

After *Beloved* was published, many African American writers participated in a tribute to Morrison in the *New York Times Book Review* that states in part: "We find your life work ever building to a monument of vision and discovery and trust." The writers argue that Morrison "has yet to receive the national recognition that her five major works of fiction entirely deserve: she has yet to receive the keystone honors of the National Book Award or the Pulitzer Prize." Morrison did indeed go on to win the Pulitzer Prize for *Beloved*.

Song of Solomon *Song of Solomon* was both a popular and critical success, establishing Morrison as one of America's most important novelists. The novel became a paperback best seller, with 570,000 copies in print in 1979. Morrison's success and recognition led to her 1980 appointment by President Jimmy Carter to the National Council on the Arts.

Reviews of *Song of Solomon* were generally enthusiastic. Linda Kuehl in the *Saturday Review* calls Morrison a "romantic revolutionary" whose new novel is "the vision of an original, eccentric, inventive imagination." Several reviewers remarked on Morrison's growth as a writer. In his front-page review for the *New York Times Book Review*, Reynolds Price states that in *Song of Solomon* "the depths of the younger work are still evident, but now they thrust outward, into wider fields." Angela Wigan in *Time* observes that *Song of Solomon* is "an artistic vision that encompasses both a private and a national heritage."

Beloved Reviewers, sensing that they were witnessing a literary phenomenon, lavished *Beloved* with praise. A reviewer for *Publishers Weekly* calls it a milestone in the chronicling of the black experience in America, while Merle Rubin in the *Christian Science Monitor* calls it "a stunning book and lasting achievement [that] transforms the sorrows of history into the luminous truth of art." Walter Clemons in *Newsweek* declares, "I think we have a masterpiece on our hands here." Michiko Kakutani in the *New York Times* writes, "There is a contemporaneous quality to time past and time present as well as a sense that the lines between reality and fiction, truth and memory, have become inextricably blurred."

Responses to Literature

1. In *Beloved*, what indications does the author give that the mysterious girl is a ghost? What evidence is there that the girl is actually a real person? Which do you think is the better explanation, and why?

2. Compare the supernatural elements in *Song of Solomon* to Gabriel García Márquez's *One Hundred Years of Solitude*. Do the authors both use fantastical

---

COMMON HUMAN EXPERIENCE

While Morrison's works transcend race in order to tell honest stories anyone can relate to and empathize with, she grounds her characters in primarily African American struggles and issues. Here are some other works that use African American concerns to convey a universal message about humanity:

Native Son (1940), a novel by Richard Wright. In this novel, a murderer in Chicago explains his crimes.

Another Country (1962), a novel by James Baldwin. This novel, set in Greenwich Village, revolves around the death by suicide of one of its main characters, a troubled jazz musician named Rufus.

Invisible Man (1952), a novel by Ralph Ellison. This novel is narrated by a black man who secretly lives in a New York apartment building basement and perceives himself as being "invisible" to society at large.

The Sound and the Fury (1929), a novel by William Faulkner. In this novel, the demise of the Compton family is told via several different narrative voices.

---

occurrences for the same purpose? In what ways are the two works different?

3. In *The Bluest Eye*, how is beauty viewed as a racial issue by the various characters?

4. Morrison has stated that she was inspired to write *Beloved* by the life of the slave woman Margaret Garner. Using your library or the Internet, research Garner's life and draw comparisons between the novel and historical fact. How closely does Morrison's book match the actual historical details?

BIBLIOGRAPHY

Books

Bloom, Harold, ed. *Toni Morrison*. New York: Chelsea House, 1990.

Furman, Jan. *Toni Morrison's Fiction*. Columbia: University of South Carolina, 1996.

McKay, Nellie Y., ed. *Critical Essays on Toni Morrison*. Boston: G. K. Hall, 1988.

Taylor-Guthrie, Danille. *Conversations with Toni Morrison*. Jackson: University Press of Mississippi, 1994.

Periodicals

"Black Writers in Praise of Toni Morrison." *New York Times Book Review* (January 24, 1988).

Blake, Susan L. "Folklore and Community in *Song of Solomon*." *MELUS* 7 (Fall 1980): 77–82.

Clemons, Walter. Review of *Beloved*. *Newsweek* (September 28, 1987).

Kakutani, Michiko. Review of *Beloved. New York Times* (September 2, 1987).

Kuehl, Linda. Review of *Song of Solomon. Saturday Review* (September 17, 1977).

Price, Reynolds. Review of *Song of Solomon. New York Times Book Review* (September 11, 1977).

Reed, Harry. "Toni Morrison, *Song of Solomon* and Black Cultural Nationalism." *Centennial Review* 32 (Winter 1988): 50–64.

Rubin, Merle. Review of *Beloved. Christian Science Monitor* (October 5, 1987).

Strouse, Jean. "Toni Morrison's Black Magic." *Newsweek* 97, March 30, 1981, pp. 52–57.

Wigan, Angela. Review of *Song of Solomon. Time*, September 12, 1977.

✹ Walter Mosley

BORN: *1952, Los Angeles, California*

NATIONALITY: *American*

GENRE: *Fiction, nonfiction*

MAJOR WORKS:

Devil in a Blue Dress (1990)

RL's Dream (1995)

Always Outnumbered, Always Outgunned (1997)

Overview

In 1992, when President Bill Clinton was asked who his favorite mystery writer was, he replied, "Walter Mosley." Although Mosley had already won critical acclaim, the president's endorsement brought him to the attention of a larger public. His next book, *Black Betty* (1994), the third in his Easy Rawlins series, sold one hundred thousand copies in hardback. His Easy Rawlins books, as well as his novels featuring Fearless Jones, are set in the African American community of Los Angeles, from the post–World War II years into the turbulent 1960s. More than just a genre writer, Mosley, in his Easy Rawlins books, presents a social history of the black experience in America at a crucial period in the struggle for civil rights.

Works in Biographical and Historical Context

A Legacy of Oppression Born on January 12, 1952, in Watts, a poor inner-city section of South Central Los Angeles, Mosley was the only son of a custodian, LeRoy Mosley, whom the writer has frequently named as the most important influence in his childhood. His father became the partial model for Mosley's best-known fictional detective, Easy Rawlins, as well as for Socrates Fortlow. Mosley's mother, Ella, who worked for the Los Angeles Department of Education, was Jewish, and growing up, Mosley experienced cross-cultural influences

Walter Mosley   *Lee Celano / WireImage for Roberson PR / Getty Images*

that became the focus of his life and novels. He is acutely conscious of the traditions and the history of the oppressed peoples that were his legacy.

Mosley's family left Watts, the locus of notorious race riots in 1965, for West Los Angeles when he was twelve. His parents were able to buy two duplexes and began renting out three of the four apartments—an important event for Mosley's later novels as Easy Rawlins similarly becomes a property owner. Meanwhile, Mosley enrolled at Louis Pasteur Junior High School and then Hamilton High School, from which he graduated in 1970. In the early 1970s, Mosley grew long hair and traveled to Northern California and then to Europe.

A Technical and Creative Education A determined Mosley worked his way to a higher education, going to school in Vermont, first at Goddard College and then at Johnson State College, where he earned a bachelor of arts degree in political science. Seeing the future importance of computers in American life, he trained as a computer programmer. In 1981 he moved to New York City, where he met the dancer and choreographer Joy Kellman, whom he married in 1987 (they divorced in 2001). His interest in technology forecast the books he has written in the science-fiction genre, *Blue Light* (1998) and *Futureland: Nine Stories of an Imminent World* (2001).

Although his technical training led to a position with Mobil Oil, Mosley found his work as a programmer tedious. He pursued means of self-expression, including painting and pottery. Inspired by having read Alice Walker's *The Color Purple* (1982), he tried writing. In a December 1995 interview for *Ebony*, he recalls being excited by a sentence he wrote one Saturday at work—"On hot sticky days in southern Louisiana the fire ants swarmed." He says he "stumbled onto writing somewhere around 33 or 34 and I went, 'Oh, this is interesting. This is kind of fun.'" At first he studied poetry because he "believed that you really can't write fiction unless you know poetry in some way or another . . . . you have to understand the music of poetry to write good fiction." In 1985 he began to take night classes in the graduate writing program of the City University of New York.

First Publications   For a while, Mosley was unable to find a publisher for his first novel, *Gone Fishin'* (1987), about a young Easy Rawlins coming of age in the borderland between Texas and Louisiana. Mosley credits the success of Terry McMillan's best-selling books *Disappearing Acts* (1990) and *Waiting to Exhale* (1992) with changing the perceptions of publishers. When *Devil in a Blue Dress* was published in 1990, critics compared Mosley's writing to the work of Raymond Chandler, whose cynical portrait of Los Angeles set the tone for hardboiled urban detective fiction, and to the hardened voice and style of Chester Himes, the African American detective writer.

Devil in a Blue Dress introduces Ezekiel "Easy" Rawlins, an unemployed black veteran returned from World War II who finds America just as racist as it was when he left to fight for it. Determined not to be ground down by the social, political, and economic system that crushes so many black men before they have a chance to succeed, Easy has a canny business sense and a willingness to do what he has to do to survive. At first, his only refuge from his brutal world is his house, and he understands the importance of the property to his sense of identity. *Devil in a Blue Dress* is representative of Mosley's writing in that he portrays both white and black worlds, neither in a particularly flattering way.

Mosley went on to write several more Easy Rawlins novels, including *A Little Yellow Dog* (1996). Set in 1963, the novel shows Easy trying to lead a reformed life. At the heart of *A Little Yellow Dog* as well as in most of Mosley's other work, lies Los Angeles—colorful, varied, culturally rich, and full of contradictions and untold stories.

Mosley published his next book, *Gone Fishin'* (1997)—the first Easy Rawlins novel he wrote, which had been rejected by publishers in the late 1980s—with a small black publishing house, Black Classic Press in Baltimore. A stew of sex, voodoo, and death, the novel takes Easy back to

LITERARY AND HISTORICAL CONTEMPORARIES

Mosley's famous contemporaries include:

James Ellroy (1948–): A native of Los Angeles, Ellroy is a mystery writer known for his works set in Los Angeles during the 1950s, such as *L. A. Confidential* (1990).

John Edgar Wideman (1941–): Wideman is one of the country's most prominent African American writers, known for his nonfiction and fiction alike, including his novel *Sent for You Yesterday* (1983).

Alice Walker (1944–): Walker's award-winning novel *The Color Purple* (1982) inspired Mosley and a host of other young writers.

Terry McMillan (1951–): McMillan's publications not only helped Mosley get published, but she also had a hand in starting the "chick lit" genre with *Waiting to Exhale* (1992) and *How Stella Got Her Groove Back* (1998).

Oprah Winfrey (1954–): Winfrey is a wildly successful talk-show host who frequently features discussion of literary works through her televised book club.

his early manhood in Houston in 1939, when he accompanies his best friend, Mouse, on a journey to the Louisiana bayou town of Pariah to get money from his stepfather. Later in 1997, Mosley published *Always Outnumbered, Always Outgunned*, a book set in contemporary Los Angeles featuring Socrates Fortlow, a former convict who spent twenty-seven years in an Indiana penitentiary for rape and murder. Eight years out of prison and living in a shack in Watts, the nearly sixty-year-old Socrates strives to overcome the angry legacy of hatred from his prison days. Fortlow is based in part on Mosley's childhood growing up in the often tumultuous neighborhood.

Recent Works   In 2003 Mosley brought out two mystery books—the eighth book in the Easy Rawlins series, *Six Easy Pieces*, and the novel *Fear Itself*—as well as his response to the events of September 11, 2001, and the war on terror, *What Next? A Memoir Toward World Peace*. In 2004 Mosley published two works, the non-genre novel *The Man in My Basement*, and his ninth book about Easy Rawlins, *Little Scarlet*.

At fifty-two, Walter Mosley is respected as a writer beyond genre. He was named the first Artist-in-Residence at the Africana Studies Institute of New York University, where he directs a lecture series titled "Black Genius." He is a director on the board of the National Book Awards, the Poetry Society of America, a member of the executive board of PEN American Center (and founder of its Open Book Committee), and a past president of the Mystery Writers of America.

COMMON HUMAN EXPERIENCE

Mosley writes primarily about Los Angeles, the city where he grew up. Here are some other works that celebrate the complicated city:

Ask the Dust (1939), a novel by John Fante. Set in a depressed, dry Los Angeles, this novel centers around a down-and-out writer and his love for a Mexican waitress.

L.A. Confidential (1990), a novel by James Ellroy. This twisted tale of corrupt policemen was later made into a movie starring Kevin Spacey and Russell Crowe.

The Big Sleep, (1939) a novel by Raymond Chandler. Chandler's Los Angeles is full of hot winds and lying millionaires in this classic detective novel.

Day of the Locust (1939), a novel by Nathaniel West. This tale of a Hollywood scenery painter and his struggling acquaintances reveals the less-than-glamorous side of the film industry.

Works in Literary Context

Use of Color   One notable aspect of Mosley's novels, particularly his Easy Rawlins series, is his treatment of color. Blue, red, white, black, yellow, and brown are used in the titles of the first six novels of the series. In the collection *Six Easy Pieces*, the title of each story includes a color word: "Smoke," "Crimson Stain," "Silver Lining," "Lavender," "Gator Green," "Gray-Eyed Death," and "Amber Gate." Mosley often interweaves various images of color. His characters are not simply "black"; they are "coffee-colored," "pale brown," "ebony," "chocolate," and dozens of other colors. Mosley has said that his purpose is twofold: to counter the white stereotype that blacks all look alike, and also to stress the variety of humanity.

Historical Themes   At the beginning of *Black Betty*, set in 1961, Easy awakes from a disturbing dream and

> tried to think of better things. About our new young Irish president and Martin Luther King; about how the world was changing and a black man in America had the chance to be a man for the first time in hundreds of years.

Mosley often gives readers a recognizable moment in American history viewed through the eyes of a single black man. This perspective, rare in crime fiction, vivifies not only the black experience, but the larger event as well. Thus, the hot winds that would eventually ignite the Watts riots are seen, not as abstract issues in race relations, but as emotions in the hearts of individuals we have come to know and care about. In Easy's bitterness and in the bone-weary fatigue with which he greets each new act of senseless violence, the reader feels the ineffable sadness that has come to envelop this urban landscape.

Money and Property   Many of Mosley's works depict the economic realities of being black during the 1950s and 1960s. In *A Red Death* (1991), Easy has invested the money he ended up with in *Devil in a Blue Dress* in property but is so wary of drawing attention to himself that he pretends to be only the handyman and employs a shady businessman named Mofass to act as the landlord. As in the first novel, Easy's financial situation—in this case his acquisition of the apartments with off-the-books money—makes him vulnerable. He is threatened by two conflicting elements of white oppression: a racist IRS agent looking for money and an even more dangerous FBI agent who wants to use Easy to frame suspected communist sympathizers—whether they are actually communists or not.

Works in Critical Context

Mosley has been praised for his evocative style and for staking out new territory for the hard-boiled detective genre. "Mosley's L.A." writes David L. Ulin in the *Los Angeles Times Book Review*, "is ... a sprawl of black neighborhoods largely hidden from the history books, a shadow community within the larger city, where a unique, street-smart justice prevails."

Devil in a Blue Dress   As critic Marilyn C. Wesley notes in her 2001 essay "Power and Knowledge in Walter Mosley's *Devil in a Blue Dress*," the writer's real objective is not the resolution of the crime narrative or of the problems of society: "In *Devil in a Blue Dress* and the other Easy Rawlins novels, Walter Mosley represents rather than resolves complicated historical issues of the multiracial society Easy uncomfortably inhabits." A reviewer for *The New York Times* notes that *Devil in a Blue Dress* marks "the debut of a talented author with something vital to say about the distance between the black and white worlds, and with a dramatic way to say it."

Always Outnumbered, Always Outgunned   *Always Outnumbered, Always Outgunned* was a great critical success. Writing in the *The New York Times*, Sven Birkerts praises the believability of the character of Socrates:

> Mosley models Socrates from all sides, many unflattering, yet he manages to leave us with the impression of a man whose soul is tuned to the pain of others. Socrates acts decently, not because he hews to a code of right action, but because decency follows from this susceptibility.

"Mosley's style," Birkerts asserts, "suits his subject perfectly. The prose is sandpapery, the sentence rhythms often rough and jabbing. But then—sudden surprise—we come upon moments of undefended lyricism."

Responses to Literature

1. Compare the city of Los Angeles as shown in *Devil in a Blue Dress* and *The Big Sleep*. How is Mosley's portrait of the city different from Raymond Chandler's?

2. How are women portrayed in Mosley's *Devil in a Blue Dress*? Provide examples from the work to illustrate your statements.

3. Easy's friendship with Mouse is complicated. Track it over the course of Mosley's Easy Rawlins series. What do they seem to argue about most?

4. Why is having property so important to Easy Rawlins in particular, and why might the notion of property be significant to African Americans in general? Use your library or the Internet to research the history of African American property ownership in the United States.

BIBLIOGRAPHY

Books

Cawelti, John G. *Adventure, Mystery and Romance: Formula Stories as Art and Popular Culture.* Chicago: University of Chicago Press, 1977.

Periodicals

Berger, Roger A. "'The Black Dick': Race, Sexuality and Discourse in the L.A. Novels of Walter Mosley." *African American Review* 31 (Summer 1997): 281–295.

Birkerts, Sven. Review of *Always Outnumbered, Always Outgunned. The New York Times* (November 9, 1997).

Bunyon, Scott. "No Order from Chaos: The Absence of Chandler's Extra Legal Space in the Detective Fiction of Chester Himes and Walter Mosley." *Studies in the Novel* 35 (2003).

Jaggi, Maya. "Socrates of the Streets." *Guardian* (September 6, 2003): 7, 20.

Lock, Helen. "Invisible Detection: The Case of Walter Mosley," *MELUS* 26 (2001).

"The Mystery of Walter Mosley." *Ebony* (December 1995).

Ulin, David L. *The Los Angeles Times Book Review*, (August 6, 1995).

Wesley, Marilyn C. "Power and Knowledge in Walter Mosley's *Devil in a Blue Dress*." *African American Review* 35 (2001).

✹ Mourning Dove

BORN: *1888, Bonner's Ferry, Idaho*

DIED: *1936, Medical Lake, Washington*

NATIONALITY: *Native American*

GENRE: *Fiction*

MAJOR WORKS:

Cogewea, the Half Blood: A Depiction of the Great Montana Cattle Range (1927)

Coyote Stories (1933)

Overview

Christine Quintasket, also called Mourning Dove, is credited as one of the first Native American women to publish a novel. Her work documents the practice of assimilation, or the adoption of mainstream habits by people from a minority culture.

Works in Biographical and Historical Context

Assimilation Policies of the 1880s The life and works of also called Mourning Dove (Humishuma in her native tongue) point to an extraordinary, although almost unremarked, period in the history of European American settlement, the end of open military conflict with indigenous peoples and the beginning of assimilation policies. The Court of Indian Offenses was established in 1883, making it a crime for Native Americans to speak their own dialects, wear traditional clothing, or practice rituals. The Dawes Act of 1887 began the process of forcing Native Americans to give up portions of their land to white settlers and participate in the practice of monetary exchange for land. It was assumed by supporters of assimilation that no American Indian tribes would survive into the twenty-first century, but would instead adopt a more "civilized" mainstream way of life. It was in this historical context that Christine Quintasket came into the world.

Growing up in the Colville Tribe According to her writings, Christine Quintasket was born in a canoe crossing the Kootenai River near Bonner's Ferry, Idaho, in April of 1888. Her parents were Joseph Quintasket, an Okanogan from British Columbia, Canada, and Lucy Stukin, a Colville (Salishan) from north central Washington State. Her mother died in 1902; although Quintasket had no children of her own, she was responsible for rearing her younger brother and two younger sisters—Julia, born in 1891, Mary Margaret, born in 1892, and Louis, born in 1896. Two other younger siblings, John and Marie, both died before age five.

In June 1891, Quintasket's name appears on a tribal census as an eight year old but this is one of several conflicting records of her age. In 1895, Quintasket entered the Sacred Heart School at the Goodwin Mission in Ward, Washington. She could only speak Salishan and the nuns were hard on her for not speaking English. After several months, she became ill from the constant punishment and was sent home. In 1896, she returned to school and remained there until 1899. At that time, U.S. government funding for Indian schools was cut, and all the Indian students were sent to school at Fort Spokane.

Last Wild Buffalo Roundup Leaves Impression In 1902, Quintasket returned home to care for her brother and sisters after her mother died. When her father remarried in 1904, Quintasket was able to return to school. She enrolled at Fort Shaw Indian School in

LITERARY AND HISTORICAL CONTEMPORARIES

Quintasket's famous contemporaries include:

T. S. Eliot (1888–1995): Eliot was an American-born poet who moved to England, becoming a British subject, in 1927; he was awarded the 1948 Nobel Prize in Literature for his life's work, including the poetic works *The Waste Land* (1922) and *Four Quartets* (1935–1942).

Katherine Mansfield (1888–1923): New Zealand short story author, heavily influenced by the work of Anton Chekhov, who was considered one of the best short story writers of her day.

Eugene O'Neill (1888–1953): An American playwright credited with being one of the first to bring realism to the American stage, O'Neill was awarded the 1936 Nobel Prize in Literature for his work.

Vicki Baum (1888–1960): Austrian author who wrote more than fifty novels—of which many have been adapted to film—including *People at a Hotel* (1929) and *A Tale from Bali* (1937).

John Steinbeck (1902–1968): American author who was awarded the Pulitzer Prize in 1940 and the Nobel Prize for Literature in 1962 for his compassionate portrayals of the poor during the Great Depression and the Dust Bowl years of the 1930s.

Great Falls, Montana. While at school, she saw the last roundup of a wild buffalo herd in 1908. This roundup made a strong impression on Quintasket, and she used this event as the basis for her first novel, *Cogewea, the Half Blood: A Depiction of the Great Montana Cattle Range* (1927). Quintasket also met her first husband, Hector McLeod, a Flathead Indian, while she was at Fort Shaw Indian School. They married in 1909 and divorced several years later. His abusive nature led to his shooting death while playing cards in April 1937.

Quintasket worked as a housekeeper to support herself. She was able to purchase a typewriter with money she had saved. In 1912, Quintasket was living in Portland, Oregon, where she began writing her first novel. When she began to write, she used the name Morning Dove, but changed it to Mourning Dove when she saw the name on a bird exhibit at a museum in Spokane, Washington. The Okanogan tribal name for this bird is Humishuma. From 1913 until 1915 she attended Calgary Business School, where she developed a greater understanding of writing styles and typing skills.

Quintasket Meets Lucullus McWhorter Around 1915, Quintasket went to the Walla Walla Frontier Days Celebration. There she met Lucullus Virgil McWhorter. He was a local businessman and took a serious interest in

the Yakima tribe from the central Washington state area. He was an advocate for Yakima rights and ensured that the tribe received compensation for past due government promises. The Yakima tribe held him in high regard and gave him the Indian name of Hemene Kawan, or Old Wolf. He was also called Big Foot because of his size. He befriended Quintasket and helped her with her writing, using his influence to get her first book published in 1927. Fifteen years passed from when she first began writing the novel until its publication. The delay was due not only to endless editing and rewriting, but also to World War I. Criticism by some influential local people, who insinuated that McWhorter wrote the book and Quintasket just put her name on it, also played a part in the delay.

Writing in Spite of Ill Health In 1919, Quintasket married Fred Galler. He was a Wenatchi Indian from the Colville Indian Reservation in north central Washington State. Their marriage had difficulties, but they stayed together on Colville Reservation.

L.V. McWhorter knew that Quintasket could go to the elders on the Colville Indian Reservation and hear centuries-old traditional stories and legends. He urged her constantly to collect the stories for her book about the tribal heritage. He thought these old stories would soon be lost in the process of assimilation into the white culture. Quintasket found that each family group usually had slightly different versions of the same legend. She heard some of the most influential stories by attending Colville funerals, which would last throughout the night. To help relieve the grief, and to help keep everyone awake during the funerals, the older Indian women would tell the most colorful and humorous of the stories. This was the basis for Quintasket's second book, *Coyote Stories* (1933), and the posthumously published *Tales of the Okanogans* (1976). McWhorter helped her edit and rewrite the legends. In the evenings, despite illness and exhaustion, Quintasket found the energy to type her novels and correspond with McWhorter. She frequently suffered from pneumonia, rheumatism, and general poor health during much of her adult life.

First Publication Yields Tribal Recognition When Quintasket's book *Cogewea* was finally published in 1927, she became a well-known personality in the Washington state area and especially on the Colville Indian Reservation. Quintasket eventually became active in local Indian politics. She joined with other Indian women and started social organizations and handicraft clubs. She began to speak at local gatherings and, on several occasions, went east to lecture. She found these long trips tiring and expensive, since she paid for most of the travel expenses herself.

A Trailblazing Woman From the late 1920s until her death in 1936, Quintasket was an activist for Indian rights. In 1930, she and others organized the Colville

Indian Association. Through their efforts, unresolved land claims, past due payments for lands purchased, and money owed to the tribe on leases for land, timber, and water rights were secured for the tribe. She was the first woman elected to the Colville Tribal Council.

Quintasket continued with her activities and writing while working on her autobiography throughout the late 1920s and early 1930s. The combined efforts of writing, activism, and family were a strain on her fragile health, and she became more despondent. At times she became disoriented; on July 30, 1936, she was taken to the state hospital at Medical Lake for treatment. Quintasket died on August 8, 1936; exhaustion from manic depressive psychosis was listed on her death certificate.

Heister Dean Guie, editor of the local newspaper in Yakima, collaborated with Quintasket and McWhorter for many years. The year before *Coyote Stories* was published, Quintasket had stayed with the Guies. Quintasket wanted Guie to review and edit her autobiography, but the manuscript was stored away. Several years later Quintasket died; Guie's widow found manuscript pages stored away in a trunk in the home attic in 1981. She turned them over to a scholar friend, who was unable to put the manuscript into any order. The papers were then sent to the University of Washington Press, where editor Jay Miller put the autobiography together. Quintasket's autobiography, *Mourning Dove: A Salishan Autobiography* was published in 1990, fifty-four years after she died.

Works in Literary Context

Mourning Dove is considered by some to be the first Native American female novelist. Her work was influenced by her contact with elder members of the Colville (Salishan) tribe, the relationships she built with white settlers who had an interest in the preservation of Native American culture, and her struggles as a woman trying to reconcile the cultural differences that existed between her tribe and other Americans.

Racial Identity and Culture Clash Mourning Dove's novel, *Cogewea, the Half Blood: A Depiction of the Great Montana Cattle Range*, is semi-autobiographical. Mourning Dove creates a heroine struggling with a mixed-blood identity. Cogewea has been given a white education, but she also retains the knowledge of her own Indian traditions and language. She experiences herself at times in the no-man's land of interpreter or mediator. She does move easily between cultures but cannot find a home in either world. She values actions based on community needs (the Indian way) and actions guided by individual wants (the white way). She believes, and does not believe, in Native American rituals. Mourning Dove also does not shy away from exploring the poignant aspect of being a mixed-blood, the sexual exploitation of indigenous peoples that often went hand-in-hand with conquest and colonization.

Were it not for the Women's Movement of the 1970s and the explosion of a stunning series of major

---

COMMON HUMAN EXPERIENCE

Among the themes in Mourning Dove's work is exploitation of Native Americans by foreign settlers. Other works that confront this theme include the following:

Custer Died for Your Sins: An Indian Manifesto (1969), a nonfiction book by Vine Deloria, Jr. This work attempts to replace the stereotypes of American Indians with a commentary about the history of U. S. race relations, bureaucracies, churches, and social scientists.

The Wild Frontier: Atrocities during the American-Indian War from Jamestown Colony to Wounded Knee (2000), a nonfiction work by William M. Osborn. This work attempts to detail the exploitation and massacres of Native Americans that occurred from 1511 until 1890.

Conquest: Sexual Violence and American Indian Genocide (2005), a nonfiction book by Andrea Smith. Winner of the 2005 Gustavus Myers Outstanding Book Award, this work presents the history of violence against indigenous women in a way that speaks to the global implications of imperialism.

American Indian texts, Mourning Dove's life and works may have been forgotten. Instead, the social activism of the 1960s led to a substantive challenge of the American literature canon as it was then conceived, and precursors of contemporary women writers were sought to recover an historical and literary past. Issues of coming to voice as a Native American woman writer at the turn of the last century, of understanding the settlement of the West from an Indian perspective, and of learning how to read collaborative texts, have drawn considerable attention to Mourning Dove works.

Works in Critical Context

In 1927, the first work of Mourning Dove was published, *Cogewea*. However, because the publishers did not promote the novel in any way, Mourning Dove made less than twenty five dollars for the publication, and the final settlement between the authors and the publisher gained her only scores of copies of the unsold novel.

Cogewea Debate Continues Of all who read *Cogewea*, perhaps Mourning Dove herself was its biggest critic. She received a copy in 1928 and immediately wrote to McWhorter on June 4:

I have just got through going over the book *Cogewea*, and am surprised at the changes that you made ... I felt like it was some one else's book and not mine at all. In fact the finishing touches are put there by you, and I have never seen it ...Oh my Big Foot, you surely roasted the Shoapees strong. I think a little too strong to get their sympathy. Her criticism of McWhorter's additions were insightful and are at the core of the ongoing interpretive debate about the novel. Some critics argue that the plurality of voices in *Cogewea* adds compelling complexity to the work. For example, Choctaw-Cherokee novelist and critic Louis Owens writes, "the reader feels throughout *Cogewea* the presence of a political disturbance permeating the text as the voices of Mourning Dove and McWhorter struggle to be heard one over the other—with Mourning Dove's easily winning out."

On the whole, the published works of Mourning Dove have received favorable appraisal for their contribution to Native American women's history and writing. Criticism continues to focus on what some scholars argue is an inaccurate and overtly Eurocentric editorializing of her work on the part of contributors, including ethnohistorian Jay Miller and L. V. McWhorter. For example, while commenting on Miller's editorial contribution to *Coyote Stories*, Alana Brown argues that Miller "evidently felt the need to assert male authority over the text and to discredit Mourning Dove even as he brings her to our attention."

Responses to Literature

1. Using your library or the Internet, research the place of the trickster in Native American myth. What was the character and purpose of the trickster? To what extent does Mourning Dove serve as a "trickster"?

2. Research the difficulties Mourning Dove encountered while writing her books and explain them in their historical context.

3. *Cogewea* brings up issues related to assimilation of a minority culture into the mainstream. What are the benefits and disadvantages of the absorption of one culture into another? In your opinion, is assimilation a reasonable solution? Why or why not?

4. What aspects of identity does Mourning Dove seem to value? How does this accord with your view of identity?

BIBLIOGRAPHY

Books

Allen, Paula Gunn. *The Sacred Hoop: Recovering the Feminine in American Indian Traditions.* Boston: Beacon, 1986, pp. 81–84, 151.

Ammons, Elizabeth and Annette White-Parks. *Tricksterism in Turn-of-the-Century American Literature.* New York and Oxford: Oxford University Press, 1991, pp. 121–122, 136–138, 197–199.

Dearborn, Mary. *Pocahontas's Daughters: Gender and Ethnicity in American Culture.* New York and Oxford: Oxford University Press, 1986, pp. 12–30.

Fisher, Alice Poindexter. "The Transformation of Tradition: A Study of Zitkala Sa and Mourning Dove, Two Transitional American Indian Writers." *Critical Essays on Native American Literature.* Boston: G. K. Hall, 1985, pp. 202–211.

Larson, Charles R. *American Indian Fiction.* Albuquerque, N.Mex.: University of New Mexico Press, 1978.

Miller, Jay. *Being and Becoming Indian: Biographical Studies of North American Frontiers,* edited by James A. Clifton. Chicago: Dorsey Press, 1989.

Owens, Louis. "Origin Mists: John Rollin Ridge's Masquerade and Mourning Dove's Mixedbloods." *Other Destinies: Understanding the American Indian Novel.* Norman, Okla. and London: University of Oklahoma Press, 1992, pp. 32–48.

Viehmann, Martha. "Cogewea, The Half-Blood, A Narrative of Mixed Descent." *Early Native American Writing: New Critical Essays,* edited by Helen Jaskoski. New York and Oxford: Oxford University Press, 1996, pp. 204–222.

Periodicals

Bernardin, Susan. "Mixed Messages: Authority and Authorship in Mourning Dove's Cogewea, the Half-Blood: A Depiction of the Great Montana Cattle Range." *American Literature* 67 (September 1995): 487–509.

Biedler, Peter. "Literary Criticism in Cogewea: Mourning Dove's Protagonist Reads The Brand." *American Indian Culture and Research Journal* 19, no. 2 (1995): 45–65.

Brown, Alana. "A Voice from the Past." *The Women's Review of Books* Vol. VIII, 2 (November 1990): 19–20.

Karell, Linda. "'The Story I Am Telling You Is True': Collaboration and Literary Authority in Mourning Dove's Cogewea." *American Indian Quarterly* 19 (Fall 1995): 451–465.

Bharati Mukherjee

BORN: *1940, Calcutta, India*

NATIONALITY: *Indian, American*

GENRE: *Fiction, nonfiction*

MAJOR WORKS:
The Tiger's Daughter (1972)
Wife (1975)
The Middleman and Other Stories (1988)
Desirable Daughters (2002)

Overview

Finding a voice to express a cross-cultural sensibility is the literary mission of Bharati Mukherjee, one of the major Indian writers in the United States. Dislocation, cultural

Bharati Mukherjee *AP Wide World Photos*

alienation, survival, and adaptability are persistent themes in the fiction of this versatile author, whose own biographical trajectory spans India, Canada, and the United States. Through an array of vibrant, larger-than-life characters and their often extraordinary experiences, Mukherjee charts the lives of immigrants in North America: their trials and tribulations as well as their zest for survival. As a writer who straddles multiple cultures, combining history, myth, and philosophy, Mukherjee has carved a niche for herself in the burgeoning field of Indian writing in English.

Works in Biographical and Historical Context

Mukherjee was born in Calcutta (called Kolkata since 2001), India, on July 27, 1940. She was the second of three daughters. Her father, Sudhir Lal Mukherjee, was of the elite Brahmin class, a respected chemist who had done advanced research in Germany and earned a doctorate from the University of London. His ancestral home was in Faridpur, East Bengal (now Bangladesh). Her mother, Bina (Bannerjee) Mukherjee, was from Dhaka. Both Faridpur and Dhaka became part of Pakistan when the region was partitioned in 1947, at the time of India's independence. During the years preceding the partition, their families moved to Calcutta, where Mukherjee spent her early years.

Childhood Growing up in an "extraordinarily close-knit family" (as she put it in *Days and Nights in Calcutta*, a 1977 memoir she wrote with her husband, Clark Blaise), Mukherjee was accustomed to having aunts, uncles, cousins, and other members of the extended family all around her, but the major influence on her life at this stage was her father. A vibrant, impressive personality, he encouraged his daughters to study and actively promoted Mukherjee's interest in creative writing. Her mother, like many Bengali women of her time, was not highly educated. Though outwardly quiet, Bina Mukherjee nursed a lifelong craving for the education that had been denied her and did not want her daughters to be similarly deprived. She also wanted to protect her daughters from the constraints endured by many middle-class Indian women trapped in conventional arranged marriages.

At the age of three, Mukherjee was sent to a school run by Protestant missionaries. Though the instruction was bilingual, the school laid greater emphasis on fluency in English than did other similar institutions in Calcutta. This early exposure to an Anglicized education bred in Mukherjee a degree of detachment from Calcutta culture. Though orthodox and traditional in their approach to religion, her parents encouraged their daughters to pursue education, independent careers, and self-fulfillment. All three sisters rejected arranged marriages and chose instead to marry for love; all left home in pursuit of work and education. When she left India to settle abroad, Mukherjee carried with her deep ties to her native land and an abiding faith in the Hinduism she had learned from her parents.

Opportunities Abroad After a successful start to his pharmaceuticals company in Calcutta, Sudhir Lal Mukherjee's business floundered when he and his partner developed differences. In 1947, he moved with his wife and daughters to England, where he engaged in chemical research. His business partner pursued him to England to seek reconciliation and persuaded him to represent the company's interests by continuing his research. The scientific work of Mukherjee's father later took the family to Basel, Switzerland. Part of Mukherjee's childhood was thus spent in London, where she attended a small private school and became proficient in English, and Basel, where she went to a German school. She and her sisters were successful, prizewinning students.

When the family returned to Calcutta in 1951, Sudhir Lal Mukherjee's business was flourishing. Instead of returning to the joint family home, he moved his wife and daughters into a luxury mansion within his factory compound. The house had all the comforts that money could buy—a lake, a swimming pool, and many servants—but the girls were now isolated from the world of middle-class

LITERARY AND HISTORICAL CONTEMPORARIES

Mukherjee's famous contemporaries include:

Rajiv Ghandi (1944–1991): Ghandi was an Indian political leader who became Prime Minister of India after his mother, Indira Gandhi, was assassinated in 1984.

V. S. Naipaul (1932–): Naipaul is a novelist from Trinidad and winner of the Nobel Prize in Literature (2001). He is famous for his novel *The House of Mr. Biswas* (1961).

Anita Desai (1937–): Desai is an acclaimed Indian novelist living in the United States. Her daughter, Kiran Desai, is also an award-winning novelist.

Maxine Hong Kingston (1940–): Kingston is an American author known for her autobiographical work *The Woman Warrior* (1976).

Clark Blaise (1940–): Blaise is a well-known Canadian-American author and Mukherjee's husband.

Salman Rushdie (1947–): Rushdie is an award-winning British-Indian author whose novel, *The Satanic Verses* (1988), made him the target of international death threats.

Calcutta and no longer felt a sense of belonging to the city of their childhood.

Education Mukherjee attended the University of Calcutta, graduating with honors in English in 1959. She continued her studies at the University of Baroda in western India, earning an M.A. degree in English and ancient Indian culture in 1961. Her education at Baroda gave her a thorough grounding in Indian tradition and heritage, counterbalancing the influence of her earlier Anglicized education, and also enhanced her understanding of the Hindu religious beliefs she had received from her parents.

Mukherjee had displayed an interest in writing from an early age. While in London, she had begun writing a novel about English children. As a student at Loreto Convent, she published short stories based on European history in the school magazine. In college, she decided to become a writer, a decision her father encouraged. After consulting with a visiting American scholar, he wrote to the poet Paul Engle, who at that time was associated with the Creative Writing Program at the University of Iowa. In September 1961, Mukherjee was admitted to the Writers' Workshop at the university. In 1963 she was awarded an M.F.A. Her thesis, a collection of short fiction, earned her admission to the doctoral program in English. She completed her doctorate in 1969.

Marriage At the Writers' Workshop, Mukherjee met Clark Blaise, a Canadian American and fellow student, and the couple married during a lunch hour one day in September 1963. Mukherjee has described their relationship as "an intensely literary marriage." Not only do both have distinguished independent careers as writers and academics, but also, each has influenced the other's work, and they have collaborated on more than one literary venture. Over the years, though sometimes forced to live separately for professional reasons, they have spent most of their time together, raising their two sons and simultaneously pursuing their literary vocations.

Publication and Success Her first novel, *The Tiger's Daughter*, was published in 1972, and the following year, Mukherjee went on a sabbatical with her husband, spending a year in India, where she began work on *Wife* (1975), her next novel. She received a grant from the Canada Arts Council to support her project. Though best known as a writer of fiction, Mukherjee has also published several works of nonfiction. *Kautilya's Concept of Diplomacy*, the first of three books she has written on politics in India, appeared in 1976. The following year, she was awarded another Canada Arts Council grant and in 1978–1979 a Guggenheim Foundation Award.

In 1980 Mukherjee and Blaise gave up their tenured positions at McGill University, leaving Canada to move to New York. The following year, she published the essay "An Invisible Woman" (*Saturday Night*, March 1981), in which she attacked the Canadian policy of multiculturalism and described the racism encountered by immigrants in Canada. She describes her own experience of racial discrimination—how she became "a housebound, fearful, aggrieved, obsessive, and unforgiving queen of bitterness"—placing it in the context of the overall situation of Asians in Toronto. "An Invisible Woman" received the second prize at the National Magazine Awards.

Awards and Recent Publications *The Middleman and Other Stories* (1988), which won the National Book Critics Circle Award for Fiction in 1988, was recognized as the work of an artist developing her craft and enlarging her vision. Around that time, Mukherjee became an American citizen, and in 1989, the year she took a position as a distinguished professor at the University of California at Berkeley, she published her third novel, *Jasmine*, which was acclaimed by reviewers for its representation of cultural diversity in America. Her novel *Desirable Daughters* earned her further fame in 2002.

Works in Literary Context

The immigrant's experience of the clash of cultures and the question of identity the immigrant must face continue to be Mukherjee's major preoccupations. She draws upon multiple cultural traditions, combining ancient Indian philosophy with the modern mythology of the American Dream and the oral folktales of India with the speech rhythms and cultural iconography of contemporary California. She uses violence, a frequent feature of her fiction, as a metaphor for cultural conflict. Her immigrant protagonists frequently undergo changes of identity and metamorphoses.

Female Voices "Finding the right voice," as she told *Iowa Review* interviewers, remains the prime feature of Mukherjee's aesthetic: "The sense of voice being the way one controls fiction. Voice can be the sum total of every artistic trick in your bag. It's how to use texture, how to use metaphor, how to choose the right point of view, character, and therefore the idioms, the language." Although she deals with the lives of women who resist imposed destinies, Mukherjee does not think of herself as a feminist: "For some non-white, Asian women, our ways of negotiating power are different. There is no reason why we should have to appropriate—wholesale and intact—the white, middle-class women's tools and rhetoric." Mukherjee seeks to give characters voices in the context of social and political realities to create a fuller representation of the immigrant experience.

Melding East and West In Mukherjee's first novel, *The Tiger's Daughter* (1972), the central character, Tara, is a Vassar-educated expatriate who returns to India after several years abroad to find a different world from the one she has preserved in her memory. Instead of being comforted by middle-class Brahmin traditions, she is now struck by overwhelming impressions of poverty, hunger, and political turmoil. Tara's awareness of change, and of sharp cultural difference between East and West, also parallels Mukherjee's own perceptions about contemporary India. Mukherjee's early fiction shows the influence of English literature, and the writer's appreciation of the work of Jane Austen is apparent in her use of irony and the omniscient point of view in *The Tiger's Daughter*. At the same time, the novel reveals a sense of self that is non-Western, especially in Tara's belief in rebirth and reincarnation.

Although Bharati Mukherjee is not the first author to address the issue of immigration and dual identities, her importance as a writer of Indian background in the United States is enduring. Her courage and success have helped to inspire a generation of younger authors of South Asian origin, including Jhumpa Lahiri, Shauna Singh Baldwin, and Anita Rau Badami, who write today with confidence about the immigrant experience.

Works in Critical Context

In *India Today* (March 17, 2003), Geeta Doctor notes the ways that Mukherjee's writing deliberately places an exotic aura around Indian culture:

> It's as if Mukherjee is asked to join an American quilting bee where each woman may contribute a small square in which she is permitted to embroider her own story within the fixed colors of the main design. Their skill is in stitching in pieces of folk wisdom and sequined fragments of exotic scenery that they have kept hidden in the treasure chest of their past life.

COMMON HUMAN EXPERIENCE

Mukherjee praises the American "melting pot" theory. In "A Four-Hundred-Year-Old Woman," an essay published in *The Writer and Her Work* (1991), Mukherjee describes herself as "a four-hundred-year-old woman, born in the captivity of a colonial, pre-industrial oral culture, and living now as a contemporary New Yorker." She finds America interesting because immigrants there, according to her, are initiated into a fluid reality with great liberating potential. Here are some other works that celebrate the unique position of immigrants around the world.

Midnight's Children (1981), a novel by Salman Rushdie. The hero of this humorous novel bounces back and forth between Pakistan and India; his story parallels the post-colonial history of the Indian subcontinent.

My Beautiful Laundrette (1985), a film directed by Stephen Frears. Personal and political conflicts arise for Omar, the gay Pakistani-British protagonist of this film.

When We Were Orphans (2000), a novel by Kazuo Ishiguro. Christopher Banks moves from China to England and back to unravel the mystery of his life.

White Teeth, (2000) a novel by Zadie Smith. This novel studies the friendship of a Bangladeshi immigrant and a British man in London.

In America (2002), a film by Jim Sheridan. An Irish family moves to the New York neighborhood, Hell's Kitchen, in this tragicomedy.

Wife *Wife* received a mixed reception from reviewers and critics, both in the United States and India. In her 1985 essay "Foreignness of Spirit: The World of Bharati Mukherjee's Novels" in *Journal of Indian Writing in English*, Indian critic Jasbir Jain argues that the novel's indictment of patriarchy in the Indian social system is undermined because the character Dimple's mental instability makes her an unreliable point of reference. Others, however, praised Mukherjee's novel for its representation of the plight of Indian expatriates in North America. In his essay on the author for *International Literature in English: Essays on the Modern Writers* (1991), Liew-Geok Leong approved her exploration of "the psychology and geography of displacement." *Wife* was short-listed for the Governor General's Award in Canada.

Desirable Daughters Reviewers found strengths as well as weaknesses in *Desirable Daughters*. Ken Forster of the *San Francisco Chronicle* chided Mukherjee for choosing melodrama when "her prose is strong enough to carry subtler shades of storytelling," but he still found the novel compelling: "Readers are certain to pick up on the seismic, rumbling machinations of the plot, but even the most reluctant of them will find it hard to deny the result is compulsively entertaining." Lee Siegel, in his review in the *Washington Post*, detects a pattern in Mukherjee's cultural observations: "The 'desirable daughters' of this novel represent three ways of relating, as South Asian women, to modernity and the West, three ways of understanding the manifold meanings of culture itself."

Responses to Literature

1. What does Mukherjee determine is the cause of the plane crash in her nonfiction work *The Sorrow and the Terror* (1987)?

2. How does the main character handle the loss of her family in Mukherjee's story "The Management of Grief" (from *The Middleman and Other Stories*)?

3. In *Jasmine*, why do you think Mukherjee has her main character change identities so often? What might she be trying to say about the challenges of immigration?

4. What are the advantages and disadvantages of arranged marriages, according to Mukherjee's novel *Wife*?

BIBLIOGRAPHY

Books

Alam, Fakrul. *Bharati Mukherjee*. New York: Twayne, 1996.

Lal, Malashri. *The Law of the Threshold: Women Writers in Indian English*. Shimla: Indian Institute of Advanced Study, 1995.

Leong, Liew-Geok. "Bharati Mukherjee," in Ross, Robert L., ed., *International Literature in English: Essays on the Modern Writers*. New York: St. James, 1991.

Nelson, Emmanuel S., ed. *Bharati Mukherjee: Critical Perspectives*. New York: Garland, 1993.

Periodicals

Carb, Alison B. "An Interview with Bharati Mukherjee." *Massachusetts Review* 29 (1988): 645–654.

Connell, Michael, Jessie Grierson, and Tom Grimes. "An Interview with Bharati Mukherjee." *Iowa Review* 20 (Spring 1990): 7–32.

Doctor, Geeta. Review of *Desirable Daughters*. *India Today* (March 17, 2003).

Forster, Ken. Review of *Desirable Daughters*. *San Francisco Chronicle* (April 28, 2002).

Jain, Jasbir. "Foreignness of Spirit: The World of Bharati Mukherjee's Novels." *Journal of Indian Writing in English* 13 (July 1985): 12–19.

Siegel, Lee. Review of *Desirable Daughters*. *Washington Post* (April 28, 2002).

✸ Walter Dean Myers

BORN: *1937, Martinsburg, West Virginia*

NATIONALITY: *American*

GENRE: *Fiction, nonfiction, poetry*

MAJOR WORKS:
Where Does the Day Go? (1969)
It Ain't All for Nothin' (1978)
The Young Landlords (1979)
Motown and Didi: A Love Story (1984)

Overview

Walter Dean Myers is one of modern literature's premier authors of fiction for young adults. Two of his novels for teens, *The Young Landlords* (1979) and *Motown and Didi: A Love Story* (1984), have won the prestigious Coretta Scott King Award, and his text for the picture book *Where Does the Day Go?* (1969) received the Council on Interracial Books for Children Award in 1969.

Works in Biographical and Historical Context

Working-Class Child Takes Up the Pen Walter Myers was born into an impoverished family on August 12, 1937 in Martinsburg, West Virginia, and at age three was adopted by Herbert and Florence Dean, who settled

Walter Dean Myers *Myers, Walter Dean, photograph by David Godlis. Reproduced by permission of Walter Dean Myers.*

in New York City's Harlem district. Although he wrote poems and stories from his early teens onward, and won awards for them, his parents did not encourage his literary talents. "I was from a family of laborers," he remembers in an autobiographical essay in *Something about the Author Autobiography Series*, "and the idea of writing stories or essays was far removed from their experience. Writing had no practical value for a Black child." The dawning realization that his possibilities were limited by race and economic status embittered Myers as a teen. "A youngster is not trained to want to be a gasoline station attendant or a clerk in some obscure office," he states. "We are taught to want to be lawyers and doctors and accountants—these professions that are given value. When the compromise comes, as it does early in Harlem to many children, it comes hard."

Young Adulthood Myers admits that he was not ready to accept that compromise. Through high school, and a three-year enlistment in the army, he read avidly and wrote short stories. After his discharge from the service, he worked in a variety of positions, including mail clerk at the post office, interoffice messenger, and interviewer in a factory. None of these tasks pleased him, and when he began to publish poetry, stories, and articles in magazines, he cautiously started to consider a writing profession.

Myers won a contest, sponsored by the Council on Interracial Books for Children, for his text of *Where Does the Day Go?* In that story, a group of children from several ethnic backgrounds discuss their ideas about night and day with a sensitive and wise black father during a long walk. Inspired by the success of his first attempt to write for young people, Myers turned his attention to producing more picture books. During the early 1970s, he published three: *The Dancers* (1972), *The Dragon Takes a Wife* (1972), and *Fly, Jimmy, Fly!* (1974). In more recent years, he has concentrated on longer works for older children and continues to write texts for picture books occasionally. In 1980 he released a fable set in India, *The Golden Serpent*, and in 1984, an animal adventure, *Mr. Monkey and the Gotcha Bird*.

Career A graduate of the City College of New York, Myers accepted a job as a senior trade book editor for the Bobbs-Merrill Publishing Company in New York in 1970, and worked there until 1977. His seven-year tenure taught him "the book business from another viewpoint," as he puts it in his autobiographical essay. Myers benefited from his experiences at Bobbs-Merrill, even though he was laid off during a restructuring program. "After the initial disillusionment about the artistic aspects of the job, I realized how foolish I had been in not learning, as a writer, more about the business aspects of my craft," he concludes. Armed with the pragmatic knowledge of how the publishing industry works, Myers has supported himself by his writing alone since 1977.

LITERARY AND HISTORICAL CONTEMPORARIES

Myers's famous contemporaries include:

Coretta Scott King (1927–2006): King was the wife of Martin Luther King, Jr. and and an activist who lended her name to the prestigious literary prize.

Martin Luther King, Jr. (1929–1968): King, Jr. was an American civil rights leader known for his inspirational speeches and nonviolent protest methods.

Wilt Chamberlain (1936–1999): Chamberlain was a professional basketball player known for his height; "Wilt the Stilt" holds many NBA records, including most points scored in a single game (100).

Bill Cosby (1937–): Cosby is an African-American comedian, actor, and author, known for his comic creations including *The Cosby Show*, one of television's best-loved comedies.

Ishmael Reed (1938–): Reed is a prominent and sometimes controversial African-American novelist, poet, and critic.

Judy Blume (1938–): Blume is an author of books for children and teenagers that help them deal with troubling issues, such as sexuality and racism.

By the time he left Bobbs-Merrill, Myers had already established a reputation as an able author of fiction for black children, based largely upon his highly successful novels for teens, such as *Fast Sam, Cool Clyde, and Stuff* (1975) and *Mojo and the Russians* (1977). Central to the stories is the concept of close friendships, portrayed as a positive, nurturing influence. Myers followed these two upbeat novels with a serious one, *It Ain't All for Nothin'* (1978), the account of a boy caught in a web of parental abuse and conflicting values.

A Publishing Frenzy One year after the publication of *It Ain't All for Nothin'*, Myers published *The Young Landlords* (1979), a novel that focuses once again on the intensity of ghetto living. One summer, a group of young people form an Action Group designed to improve the community. *Hoops* (1981), Myers's next novel, focuses on Lonnie Jackson, a recent high school graduate, whose life lacks direction until he gets an opportunity to play in a basketball tournament. In 1981, Myers also published his only young adult novel set in Africa. *The Legend of Tarik* tells of a young African boy who witnesses the cruel slaughter of his entire family by the dreaded El Muerte.

In addition to his novels, Myers has written two nonfiction works for young people, *The World of Work: A Guide to Choosing a Career* (1975) and *Social Welfare* (1976), which examines the welfare system and suggests alternatives to it.

COMMON HUMAN EXPERIENCE

Myers writes about many facets of urban life, particularly those that take place in the colorful New York City neighborhood of Harlem. One thing that he often writes about is the sport of basketball, which draws people of all classes and colors onto the court. His *Hoops* (1983) and *Slam* (1998), are two novels that revolve around the sport. Here are some other works that center on sports and the pressures of athletic competition.

The Natural (1952), a novel by Bernard Malamud. This book follows Roy Hobbs's baseball career after he is shot.

The Basketball Diaries (1978), a novel by Jim Carroll. The narrator here moves rather quickly from basketball success to hopeless drug addiction in this autobiographical novel set in New York City.

Shoeless Joe (1982), a novel by W.P. Kinsella. This novel about baseball dreams in a small town was made into a movie, *Field of Dreams* (1989).

Hoop Dreams (1994), a documentary by Steve James. This documentary shadows two boys from inner-city Chicago as they try to reach professional basketball stardom.

Friday Night Lights (2004), a movie directed by Peter Berg and Josh Pate. In this film, the west Texas town of Odessa is obsessed with its high school football teams, which puts a lot of stress on the players.

In 1980 Myers received the Coretta Scott King Award for *The Young Landlords*. During the course of his career, Myers's focus has shifted from children's picture books to novels for young adults. This shift is an important one, for by appealing to the consciousness of young adults, Myers is touching, perhaps, the most important element of society. As Myers states, "If you choose to deal with my children then you must deal with them as whole people, and that means dealing with their blackness as well as their intellect." The Coretta Scott King award for outstanding children's literature was again awarded to Myers for the novel *Fallen Angels* (1988). His 2006 novel, *Jazz*, which his son Christopher illustrated, won the American Library Association Children's Notable Book Award.

Works in Literary Context

Whether he is writing about the ghettos of New York, the remote countries of Africa, or social institutions, Myers captures the essence of the developing experiences of youth. His tone can be funny or serious, but his concern for young people is clearly demonstrated in the basic themes of each work. He is concerned with the development of youths, and his message is always the same:

young people must face the reality of growing up and must persevere, knowing that they can succeed despite any odds they face. Furthermore, this positive message enables youths to discover what is important in life and to reject influences that could destroy them.

Responsibility and Choice Myers strives to present characters for whom urban life is an uplifting experience, despite the potentially dangerous influences. In his first Coretta Scott King Award-winner, *The Young Landlords*, several teens learn responsibility when they are given a ghetto apartment building to manage. Lonnie Jackson, the protagonist of *Hoops* (1981), profits from the example of an older friend who has become involved with gamblers. Tippy, the protagonist of *It Ain't All for Nothin'*, is a boy whose life reaches the crossroads from which he can travel in one of two directions. He can choose the values of his father, which would not improve his situation, or he can uphold the values of his God-fearing grandmother with whom he had lived before her illness. After experiencing life with his father and becoming a participant in petty crimes, Tippy decides to reject his father's world and to live with Mr. Roland, a man who befriended him in his moment of need. A poignant, sad book, *It Ain't All for Nothin'* reflects much of the pain and anguish of ghetto life. At the end of the novel, Tippy turns his father in to the police.

Equality Concerned with stereotyping of a sexual as well as a racial sort, Myers creates plausible female characters and features platonic friendships between the sexes in his works. "The love in *Fast Sam, Cool Clyde, and Stuff* is not between any one couple," writes Alleen Pace Nilsen. "Instead it is a sort of general feeling of good will and concern that exists among a group of inner city kids." Nilsen, among others, also notes that Myers's fiction can appeal to readers of any race. She concludes that he "makes the reader feel so close to the characters that ethnic group identification is secondary."

Works in Critical Context

Myers has received consistent praise for the realism of his depiction of disadvantaged youth, his knack for capturing the language and dialogue of teenagers, and for his engaging prose. Critics have identified the skill with which his narratives reveal the inner resources that enable young adults to navigate difficult situations and relationships.

Fast Sam, Cool Clyde, and Stuff In 1975, Myers published the first in a series of novels for young adults. *Fast Sam, Cool Clyde, and Stuff*, set in the neighborhood of 116th Street in New York City, tells of a group of preteen youths growing up in an adverse environment, yet making the most of their situation. This novel proved to be Myers's springboard into young adult literature. In his *School Library Journal* review, John F. Caviston commented that the novel is "alternately funny, sad, and sentimental, but it is always very natural and appealing." *Booklist* described the narrative as "engrossing and infused with dramatic impact," and *Horn Book* asserted that the novel has not only "the flavor of a Harlem Tom Sawyer or Penrod" but also "the merit of being swift in narrative and natural and vivid in dialogue."

It Ain't All for Nothin' Myers's third novel has more serious implications. Jane Pennington praised the novel in *Interracial Books for Children Bulletin* as a "devastating book...one which needs to be written.... Not only does it delineate the sufferings of [the main character], it also details the caring and support offered to him by members of the community." *It Ain't All for Nothin'* "pretties up nothing; not the language, not the circumstances, not the despair," according to Pennington.

Responses to Literature

1. In *It Ain't All for Nothin'*, list ways in which the main character learns to make his hard decisions.

2. What are the benefits of basketball in Myers's novels? What other community activities does he write about?

3. How is Myers's New York City in *Fast Sam, Cool Clyde, and Stuff* different from Judy Blume's in her novel *Tales of a Fourth Grade Nothing* (1972)? How are they similar?

4. Explore the theme of responsibility in several of Myers's novels.

BIBLIOGRAPHY

Books

Bishop, Rudine Sims. *Presenting Walter Dean Myers.* Boston: Twayne Publishers, 1990.

Patrick-Wexler, Diane. *Walter Dean Myers.* Austin: Raintree Steck-Vaughn, 1995.

Rush, Theresa G., ed. *Black American Writers: Past and Present.* Metuchen, N.J.: Scarecrow Press, 1975.

Periodicals

Brown, Jennifer M. "Walter Dean Myers Unites Two Passions." *Publishers Weekly* (March 22, 1999): 45.

Caviston, John, review of *Fast Sam, Cool Clyde, and Stuff. School Library Journal* 21 (March 1975): 108.

Corbett, Sue. "Walter Dean Myers Has Been Writing Poignant, Tough Stories For and About At-Risk Kids." *Knight Ridder/Tribune News Service* (January 26, 2000): K6508.

Higgins, Jim. "Former 'Bad Boy' Taps into Youths' Minds, Struggles." *Milwaukee Journal Sentinel* (May 26, 2002): 1.

McElmeel, Sharron L. "A Profile: Walter Dean Myers." *Book Report* (September-October 2001): 42.

Nilsen, Alleen Pace, "Love and the Teeenage Reader." *English Journal* (March 1976): 90–92.

Pennington, Jane, review of *It Ain't All for Nothin'. Interracial Books for Children Bulletin* 10 (1979): 18.

Smith, Amanda. "Walter Dean Myers: This Award-Winning Author for Young People Tells It Like It Is." *Publishers Weekly* (July 20, 1992): 217.

Something about the Author Autobiography Series, Volume 2, Gale, 1986.

N-Q

Azar Nafisi

BORN: *1950, Tehran, Iran*

NATIONALITY: *Iranian; American resident*

GENRE: *Nonfiction*

MAJOR WORKS:

Anti-Terra: A Critical Study of Vladimir Nabokov's Novels (1994)

Reading Lolita in Tehran: A Memoir in Books (2003)

Overview

Azar Nafisi is most famous for her memoir, *Reading Lolita in Tehran: A Memoir in Books*, which became an international best-seller and piqued the world's interest in the silent world in which many Iranian women live. A depiction of the Islamic revolution of 1979, the book shows what life was like in Iran under the Ayatollah Khomeini and how the new regime changed the lives of Nafisi and her literature students.

Works in Biographical and Historical Context

When Azar Nafisi was thirteen years old her parents sent her from her home in Tehran, Iran, to Lancaster, England, so that she could finish her schooling. When Nafisi returned to her birthplace things had changed. She returned in 1979 after the revolution of Ayatollah Ruhollah Khomeini. Khomeini had enforced a strict moral code, and his ideological revolution kept many people—particularly women—from expressing themselves. Women were forced to wear veils and morality police patrolled the streets. According to Michael Harris of the *Los Angeles Times*, Nafisi has said that "in the course of nearly two decades the streets have been turned into a war zone, where young women who disobey the rules are hurled into patrol cars, taken to jail, flogged, fined ... and sometimes raped or executed."

The Islamic revolution affected many parts of the world, including America, when the Iran hostage crisis took place in 1979. A group of Islamic students held fifty-two staff members of the American embassy hostage for over a year, until the Algiers Accords were signed in 1981 and the hostages were released.

Finding Solace in Literature In 1981 Nafisi was fired from the University of Tehran, where she had taught literature, because she refused to wear a veil. She did not teach again until 1987. From 1995 to 1997 she set up weekly secret meetings with seven female students to discuss literature. *Reading Lolita in Tehran: A Memoir in Books* is the story of Nafisi, her students, and the books that they discussed during those meetings. The book has been translated into more than ten languages and is in its fifteenth printing. It has won a number of awards, including the 2004 Nonfiction Book of the Year Award from Book Sense, the Frederic W. Ness Book Award, the 2004 Latifeh Yarsheter Book Award, and it was a finalist for the 2004 PEN/Martha Albrand Award for the Art of the Memoir. Nafisi says that "my passion has always been books and literature, and teaching. In the U.S. I teach—and I also write. The main difference is of course that the book that I recently wrote could not have been written had I lived in my homeland."

In an interview for *Newsweek*, Nafisi claimed that she is grateful to the Islamic Republic of Iran. "The Islamic Republic took away everything I'd taken for granted. It made me appreciate the feel of the wind on my skin. How lovely the sun feels on your hair. How free you feel when you can lick ice cream in the streets." Nafisi now resides in the United States and teaches literature at Johns Hopkins University in Baltimore, Maryland, where she is a professor of aesthetics, culture, and literature.

Azar Nafisi   *Getty Images*

Works in Literary Context

Influences on Nafisi's work are not primarily Iranian. Instead, they include a broad array of Western authors and works: F. Scott Fitzgerald's *The Great Gatsby* (1925), Gustave Flaubert's *Madame Bovary* (1857), and, of course, Vladimir Nabokov's *Lolita* (1955). All of these works deal, in some way, with a character who desires to be liberated and to break free from the confines of society; perhaps that is what draws Nafisi, as an Iranian-born woman in a male-dominated culture, to them.

Diversity As depicted in Nafisi's *Reading Lolita in Tehran*, the seven students who meet weekly at the author's home are all very different from each other. Some are married, some are divorced, some are rich, some are poor. Their personalities and passions vary, they have different beliefs, but they are uniquely bonded by the shared experience of reading these novels together and discussing what they mean in their lives. Nafisi divides the book into four sections. Each section discusses a piece of literature. As readers are taken through the sections they come to know daily life in

Iran, the author, and her students and how these great works of literature fit into their lives; as well as how the pieces are relevant and meaningful in and of themselves.

Works in Critical Context

While Nafisi continues to write, she is most known for *Reading Lolita in Tehran*, her groundbreaking memoir. Readers and critics became instantly interested in the book, which impresses mainly because of its devotion to literature in a time when many books were banned or discouraged.

Reading Lolita in Tehran In the *New York Times*, Michiko Kakutani gave *Reading Lolita in Tehran* a decidedly positive review. Kakutani described it as "a visceral and often harrowing portrait of the Islamic revolution in that country and its fallout on the day-to-day lives of Ms. Nafisi and her students." Further describing the book as "a thoughtful account of the novels they studied together," Kakutani concludes, "And it is, finally, an eloquent brief on the transformative powers of fiction—on the refuge from ideology that art can offer to those living under tyranny, and art's affirmative and subversive faith in the voice of the individual." In an article for the *Guardian Unlimited* Paul Allen was equally enthusiastic. He wrote, "The charismatic passion in the book is not simply for literature itself but for the kind of inspirational teaching of it which helps students to teach themselves by applying their own intelligence and emotions to what they are reading." "*Reading Lolita in Tehran* is more than a collection of keen perceptions of the nature of literature—though it is certainly and formidably and beautifully that. It is also a portrait of daily life under despotism," noted Charles Matthews in the *Manila Times*.

In a review for *Library Journal*, Ron Ratliff commented on the lives of Nafisi's students: "Their stories reflect the oppression of the Iranian regime but also the determination not to be crushed by it." He went on to say, "Nafisi's lucid style keeps the reader glued to the page from start to finish." In an article for the *Star Tribune*, Andrea Hoag commented that Nafisi's memoir "is a reminder that a safe, illusory world exists within the imaginary constraints of our great novels, a place where all of us can still take comfort."

Responses to Literature

1. Why does Nafisi choose *Lolita* as her title, rather than one of the other books her group discusses?

2. How is the study of literature an act of defiance for Nafisi's reading group?

3. Does *Reading Lolita in Tehran* help you to appreciate your own relative freedom? Explain.

4. If you were living under an oppressive regime and you decided to make a list of works of literature or films that you would try to read or watch, what titles would be on your list, and why?

BIBLIOGRAPHY

Periodicals

Harris, Michael. Review of *Reading Lolita in Tehran: A Memoir in Books. Los Angeles Times* (May 14, 2003) (E13).

Hoag, Andrea. Review of *Reading Lolita in Tehran: A Memoir in Books. Star Tribune* (April 6, 2003).

Huntley, Kristine. Review of *Reading Lolita in Tehran: A Memoir in Books. Booklist* (April 15, 2003): 1443.

Jackson, Marni. Review of *Reading Lolita in Tehran: A Memoir in Books. Globe & Mail* (April 19, 2003).

Kakutani, Michoko. "Book Study as Insubordination Under the Mullahs." *New York Times* (April 15, 2003).

Matthews, Charles. Review of *Reading Lolita in Tehran: A Memoir in Books. Manila Times* (May 14, 2003).

Power, Carla. Review of *Reading Lolita in Tehran: A Memoir in Books. Newsweek* (May 5, 2003): 58.

Review of *Reading Lolita in Tehran: A Memoir in Books. Kirkus Reviews* (February 15, 2003): 289.

Review of *Reading Lolita in Tehran: A Memoir in Books, Publisher's Weekly* (March 17, 2003): 62.

Ratliff, Ron. Review of *Reading Lolita in Tehran: A Memoir in Books. Library Journal* (April 1, 2003): 98.

Sandip, Roy. "To Be an Iranian Girl—Here and There." *San Francisco Chronicle* (June 15, 2003): M1.

Simpson, Mona. Review of *Reading Lolita in Tehran: A Memoir in Books. Atlantic Monthly* (May 27, 2003).

Web sites

Allen, Paul. Review of *Reading Lolita in Tehran: A Memoir in Books. Guardian Unlimited* (November 3, 2003). Accessed December 10, 2008, from http://books.guardian.co.uk/.

Birnbaum, Robert. "Interview with Azar Nafisi." *Identity Theory* (March 15, 2004). Accessed December 10, 2008, from http://identity theory.com/interviews/.

"Azar Nafisi." Accessed December 10, 2008, from http://azarnafisi.com/home/.

Wasserman, Elizabeth. "The Fiction of Life." *Atlantic Unbound* (March 15, 2004). Accessed December 10, 2008, from http://www.theatlantic. com/.

LITERARY AND HISTORICAL CONTEMPORARIES

Azar Nafisi's famous contemporaries include:

Ruhollah Khomeini (1902–1989): Also known as the Ayatollah Khomeini, he overthrew the pro-American Shah (monarch) of Iran and began an Islamic revolution in 1979.

Ronald Reagan (1911–2004): Fortieth President of the United States, Reagan gave his inaugural speech on the day the Iranian hostages were freed in 1981.

Mohammed Reza Pahlavi (1919–1980): The monarch of Iran until Khomeini's revolution in 1979, Mohammed Reza Pahlavi was the last Shah of Iran.

Salman Rushdie (1947–): Rushdie is an Indian-born British novelist, the author of *The Satanic Verses* (1988), which offended some Muslims because of its portrayal of the prophet Mohammed. The Ayatollah Khomeini declared the novel blasphemous and issued a *fatwa* (religious edict) calling for Rushdie's execution.

Zahra Eshraghi (1964–): The granddaughter of the Ayatollah Khomeini and a figure of feminist reform in Iran; she is against mandatory veils for women.

COMMON HUMAN EXPERIENCE

Despite the struggles she has endured in order to be heard and read, Nafisi is part of a long-standing tradition. Beginning with the legendary Persian queen Scheherazade, there have been many Iranian or Persian women who have enthralled audiences with their tales. Here are some other works by or centered upon Iranian women.

One Thousand and One Nights (c. ninth century; first English translation, 1838), a collection of stories by many authors. The clever heroine Scheherazade must tell her new husband a story a night in order to avoid execution, in this collection of ancient stories about Aladdin's lamp, Sinbad's voyages, and other classic tales.

Funny in Farsi (2003), a memoir by Firoozeh Dumas. This humorous memoir begins with the author's move from Iran to California during the 1970s, when she was only seven years old.

Persepolis: The Story of a Childhood (2004), a graphic novel by Marjane Satrapi. The author uses a comic-strip format to unveil the horrors of the Iranian revolution.

The Circle (2000), a film by Jafar Panahi. The short, interconnected stories in this film help the viewer appreciate the difficulties that all kinds of Iranian women must face.

⦿ Ogden Nash

BORN: *1902, Rye, New York*

DIED: *1971, Baltimore, Maryland*

NATIONALITY: *American*

GENRE: *Poetry*

MAJOR WORKS:

Hard Lines (1931)

Free Wheeling (1931)

Happy Days (1933)

I'm a Stranger Here Myself (1938)

Overview

During his lifetime, Ogden Nash was the most widely known, appreciated, and imitated American creator of light verse. Many Nash admirers, both scholars and the general public, maintain that the poet's reputation has grown still further in the years since his death. Certainly, few writers of light or serious verse can claim the same extensive dissemination of their poems that Nash's works enjoy. Certain Nash lines have become bits of popular American folklore. Nash's peculiar variety of poetic buffoonery combines wit and imagination with eminently memorable rhymes.

Ogden Nash   *Nash, Ogden, photograph. AP Images.*

Works in Biographical and Historical Context

Frederick Ogden Nash was born in Rye, New York, to Edmund Strudwick and Mattie Chenault Nash. Nash's great-great-grandfather was governor of North Carolina during the American Revolution, and that ancestor's brother was General Francis Nash, for whom Nashville, Tennessee, was named. Nash was raised in Savannah, Georgia, and several other East Coast cities, as his father's import-export business necessitated that the Nashes make frequent moves. Nash described his unique accent as "Clam chowder of the East Coast—New England with a little Savannah at odd moments."

Schooling and Early Career   Following his secondary education from 1917 to 1920 at St. George's School in Newport, Rhode Island, Nash attended Harvard for the 1920–1921 academic year, and then, as he put it, he "had to drop out to earn a living." He first tried teaching at his alma mater, but left after a year.

After St. George's Nash tried working as a bond salesman on Wall Street. The results left something to be desired; following his failure at high finance, Nash took a job writing streetcar advertising for Barron Collier. He moved on in 1925 to the advertising department at the Doubleday, Page publishing house, which was to become Doubleday, Doran in 1927. Nash had considerable aptitude for advertising, according to George Stevens, a colleague at Doubleday, Doran, who felt that Nash could have made quite a success at the business. Stevens later recalled Nash's ad copy for Booth Tarkington's *The Plutocrat* (1927), one of the house's titles which was then high on the bestseller lists. Nash's slogan, "First in New York, First in Chicago, and First in the Hearts of his Countrymen," was effective and catchy but, much to Stevens's delight, Nash's paraphrase of the epithet commonly applied to George Washington scandalized an elderly vice-president at the company.

Nash's humorous advertising sallies were by no means his sole writings during this period. In off hours, he tried to write serious poetry. "I wrote sonnets about beauty and truth, eternity, poignant pain," he remembered. "That was what the people I read wrote about, too—Keats, Shelley, Byron, the classical English poets." Yet, Nash's final judgment on his serious literary efforts was that he had better "laugh at myself before anyone laughed at me," and he restricted himself increasingly to writing the whimsical verse that was to make him famous.

Writing "Seriously"   Early in his stay at Doubleday, Doran, Nash made his first attempt at writing a children's book, collaborating with his friend Joseph Alger on *The Cricket of Carador* (1925). This slight but imaginative fantasy forecast his lifelong fascination with animals. While working at Doubleday, Doran, Nash collaborated with Christopher Morley and another colleague to create his first published piece of comic writing, an effusion of youthful good spirits that parodies various forms of serious literature: *Born in a Beer Garden or, She Troupes to Conquer: Sundry Ejaculations* by "Christopher Morley, Cleon Throckmorton, and Ogden Nash, and Certain of the Hoboken Ads, with a Commentary by Earnest Elmo Calkins" (1930). It was at Doubleday, Doran, as he faced Stevens across their desks, that Nash began scrawling brief verses on pieces of yellow paper and pitching them over to his friend. Nash's first published humorous poem occurred to him one summer afternoon in 1930 as he gazed out his office window at an urban prominence, a mound covered by high-rise buildings. He titled the verse "Spring Comes to Murray Hill" and mailed the poem to *The New Yorker*, which accepted it. The poem shows the characteristic mental process of the Nash character's voice: a moment's boredom spiraling into an absurd festival of fractured rhyme.

Nash soon had a second poem taken by *The New Yorker*, quickly gained additional acceptances from other periodicals, and in 1931 saw his first collection of verses, *Hard Lines*, with Otto Soglow's illustrations, published by Simon and Schuster. The book's success was immediate and substantial as seven printings of *Hard Lines* were sold out in 1931 alone. In a very short time Nash noticed that he was making more money from selling poetry— about forty dollars a week—than he was receiving from his advertising job. Quitting the advertising business, he took a position on the staff of *The New Yorker* in 1932, but kept the job for only three months and thereafter wrote on a freelance basis.

Family Life   Nash married Frances Rider Leonard in 1931 and shortly afterwards began a family. *The Bad Parents' Garden of Verse* (1936) expresses a variety of new concerns. His wife had borne him two baby girls by this time, and Nash, in his role as protective father, had developed new views on boys, which he mocked in verse. As he settled, supposedly with much comic catastrophe, into parenthood, Nash continued to feature his thoughts on children along with his original themes in *I'm a Stranger Here Myself* (1938), *The Face is Familiar* (1940), *Good Intentions* (1942), and *Many Long Years Ago* (1945).

Multimedia Efforts   From 1936 to 1942 he had a well-remunerated but frustrating sojourn in Hollywood. He wrote three screenplays for MGM, though none of these met with success. During this screenwriting interlude, however, Nash met S. J. Perelman, who was in Hollywood on similar business. The two quickly became friends and decided to collaborate on a musical, for which Kurt Weill was recruited to provide the score. The resulting effort, a book by Perelman, lyrics by Nash, and music by Weill, was *One Touch of Venus*, a smash hit of the 1943 Broadway season. Although Nash was to try two more musicals, he did not repeat the success he achieved with his first attempt.

Nash had more consistent, if less spectacular, luck with radio and television than he did with the stage. In the 1940s he was heard on radio's "Information, Please!" and on the Bing Crosby and Rudy Vallee shows. He was

LITERARY AND HISTORICAL CONTEMPORARIES

Nash's famous contemporaries include:

Julia Moore (1847–1920): Known for her notoriously sentimental and bad poetry, Moore's style was often mocked by Nash.

Dorothy Parker (1893–1967): Parker was an American writer during the Jazz Age known for her wit and her publications in *The New Yorker*.

James Thurber (1894–1961): Thurber was one of the original cartoonists for *The New Yorker*, as well as a successful humor writer.

E. E. Cummings (1894–1962): Cummings was an American poet known for his often whimsical and always nontraditional use of punctuation and language.

Kurt Weill (1900–1950): Nash worked with this German-American composer, famous for *The Threepenny Opera* (1928), on the Broadway musical *One Touch of Venus* (1943).

a regular panelist on the guess-the-celebrity show "Masquerade Party" in the 1950s and was in frequent demand as a panelist for other such shows. He wrote lyrics for the television show *Art Carney Meets Peter and the Wolf*, based on Sergei Prokofiev's *Peter and the Wolf*, and for two other television specials for children.

Later Output   In the 1950s and 1960s Nash gave increasing attention to writing children's poems, while he continued his steady output of adult-oriented whimsy. Works such as *Parents Keep Out: Elderly Poems for Youngerly Readers* (1951), *The Christmas That Almost Wasn't* (1957), and *Girls are Silly* (1962) give a sense of Nash's increasing emphasis on poetry for children and poetry addressed to adults that focuses on children. In Nash's adult-oriented later works, considerable emphasis is given to mild complaints about aging and sickness, yet the comedy that always introduces and accompanies the complaint, the implied criticism that introduces the complainer, gives a very limited sense of morbidity. Nash always saw his role as that of cheerful light entertainer and maintained it to the last in his writing.

Nash's much less comic consideration of death in "Old Men" suggests his awareness of death and the ominous possibility of one's passing meaning very little to others However, Nash's own death was not unmourned. Throughout his life he enjoyed not only the popularity accorded him by his sizable readership, but also the much rarer tribute of respect from his competitors in the creation of light verse. At the time of his death in 1971, his admirers, both amateur and professional, accorded Nash the sincerest form of flattery as, with varying degrees of

COMMON HUMAN EXPERIENCE

Nash is known for his nonsense rhymes which, upon closer inspection, are quite accurate depictions of society and more complicated than they first seem. Here are some other works that make sense out of nonsense, thereby helping us to see the humor and irony in everyday situations.

"The Scroobius Pip" (1888/1968), a poem by Edward Lear. Nash finished this posthumous nonsense poem by Lear, who is generally considered the father of nonsense verse.

"Jabberwocky" (1871), a poem by Lewis Carroll. The nonsense word "chortle" comes from this famous poem first featured in *Through the Looking Glass, and What Alice Found There*.

The Gashlycrumb Tinies (1963), a book by Edward Gorey. Gorey's rhyming couplets detail the gory deaths of twenty-six children, in alphabetical order.

success, they attempted to couch their farewell tributes in Nash-like mangled meter.

Works in Literary Context

Satirizing Suburbia The events Nash most often satirizes are the social gatherings in upper-middle-class suburban homes and country clubs. For instance, in "Out is Out," from *I'm a Stranger Here Myself*, Nash scowls poetically upon suburban hosts and hostesses who find it novel to eat dinner outside.

Nash was also intrigued with the friction between his friends and neighbors during their recreation at the country club. In one verse, his speaker plays a somewhat Machiavellian role when he introduces two fellow country clubbers, who, considering their personal temperamental peculiarities, ought to destroy each other once they get tennis rackets in their hands. Watching the two decimate one another with violent outbreaks of temper, Nash's speaker is satisfied at the outcome of his harsh experiment in human relations: "To both of you more power, and may your meeting flower / In the slaughter of a vixen and a bully." Nash's other themes always keep to the comic treatment of the everyday—dining, buses and taxis, cocktails, the common cold, fashion, love, language, the theater, travel, conscience, money, birthdays, card games, the weather, football, matrimony, child rearing, family arguments, and even death.

Inverted Language In Nash's verse, the unusual usages are wild; the standard clichés, literary borrowings, and moralistic saws of banal poetry become altered and refocused with hilarious effects and considerable loss of

the expected conventional moral relevance in such lines as "A good way to forget today's sorrows / is by thinking hard about tomorrow's." The reader's expectations are constantly overturned. *Hard Lines* shows the variety of ways in which Nash first demonstrated his cheerful sabotage of conventional spelling, which was to be his trademark, with such lines as "Philo Vance / needs a kick in the pance" and "Like an art lover looking at the Mona Lisa in the Louvre / is the *New York Herald Tribune* looking at Mr. Herbert Houvre."

Works in Critical Context

Any attempt to place Nash's work in the context of other American humorous writing, or the humor of any other country, for that matter, tends to highlight his singularity. George Stevens notes this particularity:

Nash was not the only writer who could make frivolity immortal. But, he was unique—not at all like Gilbert or Lear or Lewis Carroll, still less like his immediate predecessors in America: Dorothy Parker, Margaret Fishback, Franklin P. Adams. By the same token, he was and remains inimitable—easy to imitate badly, impossible to imitate well.

In his most characteristic pose, Nash is a good-natured observer of the passing scene, hopeful that it is going to yield him adequate curiosities to turn into comic capital. One critic has called Nash "a philosopher, albeit a laughing one," who writes most typically of the "vicissitudes and eccentricitudes of domestic life as they affected an apparently gentle, somewhat bewildered man."

I'm a Stranger Here Myself *I'm a Stranger Here Myself* was published at a time when Nash's style was already well-established, and even well-parodied by lesser writers. Still, the collection was highly regarded by critics. Thomas Sugrue, in his review for *New York Herald Tribune Books*, states, "Mr. Nash is alone in his field these days, for the other spirits who were born into our century with the souls of eighteenth century essayists seem to have lost their sense of humor and become psychologists and psychoanalysts." Peter Monro Jack of *The New York Times Book Review* concludes, "He covers almost everything, and we may as well lie down and die laughing at almost everything." Louis Untermeyer writes in *Saturday Review*, "Nonsense and criticism elbow each other in Nash; he is a crazy story-teller one moment, a satirist the next, a wit who takes to clowning to correct pretense and expose hypocrisy." Untermeyer also predicts that Nash's humorous verse will one day win him a Pulitzer Prize—an event that unfortunately never transpired.

Responses to Literature

1. Nash loved animals. Find a few lines from his earlier poems which demonstrate this fascination. Compare these to his "city" poems and determine what the allure of nature was for him.

2. Nash often wrote of animals. For example: "The cow is of the bovine ilk; / One end is moo, the other, milk." Pick any animal and try to write a Nash-like poem about it. Is it harder than you thought?

3. How do you think Lewis Carroll's poem "Jabberwocky" influenced Nash's verse?

4. What would you say to someone who thinks Nash is not serious enough? Prepare a defense of the poet's work against such a charge.

BIBLIOGRAPHY

Books

Axford, Lavonne B. *An Index to the Poems of Ogden Nash.* Metuchen, N.J.: Scarecrow, 1972.

Benet, Laura. *Famous American Humorists.* New York: Dodd, 1959.

Blair, Walter. *Horse Sense in Literature, from Benjamin Franklin to Ogden Nash.* New York: Russell and Russell, 1942.

Parker, Douglas M. *Ogden Nash: The Life and Work of America's Laureate of Light Verse.* Chicago: Ivan R. Dee, 2005.

Newquist, Roy. *Conversations.* Chicago: Rand McNally, 1967.

Stuart, David. *The Life and Rhymes of Ogden Nash.* Boulder, Colo.: Madison Books, 2000.

Periodicals

Hasley, Louis. "The Golden Treasury of Ogden Nashery." *Arizona Quarterly* 27 (Spring 1971): 241–250.

Jack, Peter Monro. "Odgen Nash, Whose Verses Are Highly Contagious." *The New York Times Book Review* (June 19, 1938): 2.

Sugrue, Thomas. "Ogden Nash as Essayist-Poet." *New York Herald Tribune Books* (June 5, 1938): 2.

Untermeyer, Louis. "Inventory of Nash: 1938." *Saturday Review* (June 4, 1938): 6–7.

✺ Gloria Naylor

BORN: *1950, Queens, New York*

NATIONALITY: *American*

GENRE: *Fiction*

MAJOR WORKS:

The Women of Brewster Place (1982)

Mama Day (1988)

The Men of Brewster Place (1998)

Overview

Since the publication of her American Book Award-winning first novel, *The Women of Brewster Place* (1982), Gloria Naylor has become one of the most critically acclaimed and popular black authors at work in America today. Along with

Gloria Naylor *Naylor, Gloria, 1986, photograph. AP Images.*

Alice Walker and Toni Morrison, she is one of the key forces in the black feminist literary movement. Her novels characteristically explore the experiences of women struggling against poverty and racism in urban America.

Works in Biographical and Historical Context

Segregation in the South and the City   Naylor was born in New York City in 1950, the daughter of Roosevelt Naylor, a transit worker, and Alberta Naylor, a telephone operator. Prior to the birth of their daughter, Naylor's parents had lived in Mississippi, where they worked as sharecroppers. Sharecroppers farmed parcels of land owned by someone else in exchange for a share of the final crop; this system took the place of slavery in many parts of the South after the Civil War, and many sharecroppers existed much like slaves, due to the terms of their agreements with landowners. The Naylors left Mississippi to avoid the widespread racism of the still-segregated Deep South and to seek new opportunities for both themselves and their children in the emerging industries of the north. Naylor was raised in low-income African American neighborhoods in New York City, and her experiences there would inform the later writing of her celebrated novel *The Women of Brewster Place.*

LITERARY AND HISTORICAL CONTEMPORARIES

Naylor's famous contemporaries include:

Toni Morrison (1931–): Morrison, author of *Beloved* (1988) and *Song of Solomon* (1977), was the first African American woman to win the Nobel Prize.

Oprah Winfrey (1954–): A talk-show host, actress, and philanthropist, Oprah Winfrey has promoted the popularity of women's African American writing through her "Oprah's Book Club."

Bill Clinton (1946–): Clinton, the forty-second president of the United States, is known for advocating policies aimed toward racial equality. Upon his induction to office he selected African American poet Maya Angelou to compose an inaugural poem.

Alice Walker (1944–): Walker is a writer and feminist who won the Pulitzer Prize and the National Book Award for her novel *The Color Purple* (1982).

Amy Tan (1952–): Tan is an Asian American novelist best known for her book *The Joy Luck Club* (1989), which describes the relationships between a group of Chinese women that meet every week to play the card game mahjong and exchange the stories of their lives.

Henry Louis Gates, Jr. (1950–): Gates is an African American academic, writer, literary critic, and activist. He currently teaches at Harvard University, where he directs the W. E. B. DuBois Institute for African and African-American Research.

Reading became a passion for Naylor at a young age mostly due to her mother's influence. Alberta Naylor struggled to obtain books because, in rural Mississippi, she was barred from taking them out of public libraries. After moving with her family to New York in 1949, she made sure her children got an early introduction to the wonders of reading, and Gloria was given her first library card at about age four. A quiet, precocious child, Naylor began writing prodigiously even before her teen years, filling many notebooks with observations, poems, and short stories.

The Civil Rights Movement and Missionary Work

An excellent student, Naylor was placed into advanced classes in high school. Her first exposure to English classics helped shape the foundation of her later writing efforts. "The passion of the Brontës, the irony of Jane Austen, and the social indignation of Dickens fed my imagination as I read voraciously," she said in the *New York Times Book Review*. However, her evolution as a writer was stalled during her senior year in high school as a result of Civil Rights Movement leader Martin Luther King, Jr.'s assassination. King's death had a major impact on Naylor, leaving her bewildered about the black community and her own future. Her search for meaning led her to serve as a missionary for the Jehovah's Witnesses in New York, North Carolina, and Florida for the next seven years. The Christian society of Jehovah's Witnesses is a religious organization that emphasizes missionary work; while working as a missionary in New York City and in the South, Naylor became well-acquainted with the issues of poverty and racism affecting African Americans across the nation.

Return to Reading and Writing

Naylor left the mission at age twenty-five and went back to school. As she wrote in the *New York Times*, "I had used that religion as a straitjacket—for my budding sexuality, for my inability to accept the various shadings of life—while doing it and myself an injustice." After taking nursing courses at Medgar Evers College, she transferred to Brooklyn College to pursue her interest in English literature. She helped pay for her schooling by working the night shift as a switchboard operator at various New York City hotels.

College was a pivotal time for Naylor. While there her black consciousness, especially as a black woman, began taking form and compelled her to explore her creative powers. Her eyes were opened greatly by reading the works of black female authors such as Zora Neale Hurston, Toni Morrison, and Alice Walker. During this time she read Toni Morrison's novel *The Bluest Eye* (1970), which was a pivotal experience for her. She began to avidly read the work of other black women novelists as well, none of which she had been exposed to previously. She went on to earn an M.A. in African American studies at Yale University; her thesis eventually became her second published novel, *Linden Hills* (1985).

Critical Success

Drawing on these authors as role models, Naylor found her stride as a writer and was recognized for her talent soon after she began writing fiction. One of the first short stories she penned appeared in a 1980 issue of the magazine *Essence* and helped her secure a contract with Viking publishers. In 1982 Naylor published her first novel, *The Women of Brewster Place*, to almost immediate success. *The Women of Brewster Place* is made up of seven interconnected stories, involving seven black women who live in a dreary apartment complex that is isolated from the rest of the city. Though they are from widely varying age groups and social backgrounds and have very different outlooks and approaches to life, the women become a strong support group for each other as they struggle with the pain and frustration of finding their dreams constantly thwarted by the forces of racism and sexism. Naylor's work won the prestigious American Book Award for best first novel in 1983. After the success of her first novel, Naylor continued to publish fiction that explores the African American experience in America; her novels *Linden Hills*, *Mama Day* (1988), *Bailey's Café* (1992), and *The Men of Brewster Place* (1998) have received widespread critical attention.

Naylor's other writings have included one work of nonfiction, as well as essays and screenplays. She is also the founder of One Way Productions, an independent film company that she formed to bring *Mama Day* and other projects to the screen. After a brief marriage during her years as a missionary, Naylor has decided not to remarry or have children because she feels that her solitude is vital for her work. Her commitment to her craft resulted in her becoming one of the few black women to win the coveted Guggenheim Fellowship for creative writing and has made her one of the most important voices in black feminist literature.

Works in Literary Context

Gloria Naylor is often categorized as a member of the black feminist literary movement of the 1980s and 1990s. Along with authors such as Alice Walker, Toni Morrison, and Maya Angelou, Naylor sought to make political statements about racial and gender issues by depicting the personal lives of African American women. Unlike many of her contemporaries, however, Naylor focuses most of her works on modern urban settings rather than past historical time periods.

Feminism Shattered Stereotypes Naylor's *The Women of Brewster Place* is a saga of seven women of different ages, backgrounds, and lifestyles and how they confronted poverty, racism, sexism, and domestic strife both alone and together. Chief among Naylor's goals in *The Women of Brewster Place* was to shatter stereotypes about black women and demonstrate that their experience is as varied as that of any other demographic of American society. The novel is set on a symbolically dead-end street that is cut off from "accepted" society by an ugly brick wall, much as blacks are pushed into ghettos by white society. Throughout the novel, the women of the neighborhood must balance concerns regarding money and livelihood with more intimate issues related to marriages and children. Naylor covered the entire gamut of human experience, from Kiswana Browne, who defects from a comfortable middle-class existence to ally with the people of the street, to Cora Lee, whose overriding passion is the care of her beloved babies.

Classical Allusions Many critics have pointed out that Naylor's works take their inspiration from the classics of English literature: *Linden Place* has been compared to Dante's *Divine Comedy*, while *Bailey's Café* has led reviewers to point out similarities with Edith Wharton's *The House of Mirth*. The plot twists and thematic concerns of *Mama Day* have led several reviewers to compare the work to that of Shakespeare, particularly *The Tempest*. By incorporating classic allusions into work that focuses on African American experiences, Naylor makes an argument for the democratic nature of language and its ability to inspire all members of society no matter what their race, gender, or age.

COMMON HUMAN EXPERIENCE

In *The Women of Brewster Place* and *Mama Day*, Naylor portrays the experiences of African American women struggling to formulate their identities despite the challenges presented by poverty, racism, and chauvinism. Other works by African American female authors which develop this theme include:

Their Eyes Were Watching God (1937), a novel by Zora Neale Hurston. This seminal work of African American feminist literature chronicles the life of Janie Crawford, a woman who lives in Eatonville, Florida, America's first all-black community, in the early twentieth century.
I Know Why the Caged Bird Sings (1969), an autobiography by Maya Angelou. Angelou's memoir of her childhood in Depression-era Stamps, Arkansas, explores her development as an African American female artist.
The Color Purple (1982), a novel by Alice Walker. This novel by Alice Walker describes the lives of women living in the rural South in the 1920s and 30s. The protagonist, Celie, is abused by her father and husband, but finds hope in her friendship with another woman, Shug, and in the hope of being reunited with her long-lost sister.
Beloved (1987), a novel by Toni Morrison. Morrison's novel explores slavery and the trauma it causes. The book won the Pulitzer Prize in 1987 and is considered one of the most important novels ever written by an African American author.

Works in Critical Context

Many critics, such as Vashti Crutcher Lewis, have commented on the "brilliance" of Naylor's first novel, and praised her for "her rich prose, her lyrical portrayals of African Americans, and her illumination of the meaning of being a black woman in America." In *The Women of Brewster Place* and her other novels, Lewis states that Naylor focuses on

> themes of deferred dreams of love (familial and sexual), marriage, respectability, and economic stability, while observing the recurring messages that poverty breeds violence, that true friendship and affection are not dependent on gender, and that women in the black ghettos of America bear their burdens with grace and courage.

The Women of Brewster Place *The Women of Brewster Place* was both a critical and popular success. *Publishers Weekly* called it "a remarkable first novel." The book appeared on the *Publishers Weekly* trade paperback bestseller list, and was later made into a television movie starring Oprah Winfrey. Assessing Naylor's appeal, *Washington Post* reviewer Deirdre Donahue observes: "Naylor is not afraid to grapple with life's big subjects: sex, birth, love, death, grief. Her women feel deeply, and she unflinchingly transcribes their emotions." Lewis describes *The Women of Brewster Place* as "a tightly focused novel peopled with well-delineated, realistically portrayed African-American women. Naylor's use of authentic African American vernacular and precise metaphors are hallmarks."

Mama Day   Naylor's third novel is named for its main character—a wise old woman with magical powers whose name is Miranda Day, but whom everyone refers to as Mama Day. *New York Times Book Review* contributor Bharati Mukherjee states that "the portrait of Mama Day is magnificent." Writer Rita Mae Brown states in the *Los Angeles Times Book Review* that the strength of the book is "that the women possess the real power, and are acknowledged as having it." Mukherjee concludes that "Gloria Naylor has written a big, strong, dense, admirable novel … designed to last and intended for many levels of use."

The Men of Brewster Place   Naylor revisited her first success in 2000 with *The Men of Brewster Place*. Male characters were very marginal in her first novel, functioning mainly as people who wreaked havoc upon the lives of the women of Brewster Place. In *The Men of Brewster Place*, the author fills in the background of those characters, giving insight into their actions. *African American Review* writer Maxine Lavon Montgomery calls Naylor "a skillful writer adept at creating a range of uniquely individual characters." The author's look at the plight of the black man is rendered "in such a way as to render a compelling fictional exposé of his dilemma." *Black Issues in Higher Education* reviewer Jackie Thomas praises *The Men of Brewster Place* as "a profound work that explores the other side of the gender issue." He approves of Naylor's depiction of them as rational beings who "are able to think for themselves and who realize that they have problems they must solve."

Responses to Literature

1. Many critics have pointed out that Gloria Naylor makes frequent allusions or references to classic works of literature in her works. Research the characters often pointed out as inspirations for female protagonists in Naylor's novels—for example, Miranda from Shakespeare's *The Tempest* or Lily Bart from Edith Wharton's *The House of Mirth*. Write an essay in which you compare and contrast these characters to the characters in Naylor's works. Why do you think Naylor was influenced or inspired by these specific characters?

2. From the beginning of her career, Gloria Naylor has been considered a spokesperson for the African American feminist movement. Compare her treatment of men and women in *The Women of Brewster Place* to that in *The Men of Brewster Place*. What differences do you see? Can *The Men of Brewster Place* be considered a feminist novel?

3. *The Women of Brewster Place* was adapted into a TV movie starring Oprah Winfrey in 1989. Locate a copy of the miniseries and compare it to your reading of the book. What liberties does the film take with the plot and characters of the novel? Do you think these changes improved or detracted from the overall story? What changes would you have made in terms of script or casting?

BIBLIOGRAPHY

Books

Fowler, Virginia C. *Gloria Naylor: In Search of Sanctuary*. New York: Prentice-Hall, 1996.

Hall, Chekita T. *Gloria Naylor's Feminist Blues Aesthetic*. New York: Garland, 1998.

Periodicals

Brown, Rita Mae. Review of *Mama Day*. *Los Angeles Times Book Review* (February 24, 1985).

Donahue, Deirdre. Review of *The Women of Brewster Place*. *Washington Post* (October 21, 1983).

Montgomery, Maxine Lavon. Review of *The Men of Brewster Place*. *African American Review* (Summer 1994): 173.

Mukherjee, Bharati. "There Are Four Sides to Everything." *New York Times Book Review* (February 21, 1988): C25.

Thomas, Jackie. Review of *The Men of Brewster Place*. *Black Issues in Higher Education* (December 10, 1998): 31.

✺ Howard Nemerov

BORN: *1920, New York City*

DIED: *1991, University City, Missouri*

NATIONALITY: *American*

GENRE: *Poetry*

MAJOR WORKS:

The Salt Garden (1955)

The Collected Poems of Howard Nemerov: 1947–1975 (1977)

Trying Conclusions: New and Selected Poems, 1961–1991 (1991)

Overview

One of the most significant American poets of the late twentieth century, Howard Nemerov wrote verse that is noted for its technical excellence, intelligence, and wit. Written in a variety of forms and styles—including lyrical, narrative, satirical, and meditative—his poems are, according to critic Phoebe Pettingell, "concerned less with the nature of things than with how we perceive them." Nemerov focuses on the individual consciousness and how it is affected by the external, modern world.

Howard Nemerov   *Bettmann / Corbis*

Works in Biographical and Historical Context

Fighter Pilot and Poet   Nemerov was born in New York City in 1920, the son of well-to-do parents heavily involved in the world of art and culture. Both he and his sister, the photographer Diane Arbus, displayed great artistic talent at an early age and were encouraged by their parents to read and create. Nemerov attended the Society for Ethical Culture's Fieldston School, one of the most elite preparatory schools in the country. He was an outstanding student and entered Harvard after graduating in 1937. During his years at the university, his interest in literature deepened and he began to write poems.

After graduating from Harvard in 1941, Nemerov served in World War II as a fighter pilot, first with the Royal Canadian Air Force from 1942 to 1944, and later with the U.S. Army Air Force between 1944 and 1945, where he achieved the rank of first lieutenant. Nemerov's experiences in combat would often inform his later poetry, which emphasized humanity's alienation and disillusionment with the modern world. As a pilot, Nemerov

was keenly sensitive to the role technology played both in warfare and in the experience of the individual; throughout his long literary career he would frequently describe the anxiety that science and new technology create in society. After the war, he taught war veterans at Hamilton College for two years before taking posts at Bennington College, Brandeis University, the University of Minnesota, and Hollins College. Also, from 1946 to 1951 he served as associate editor for *Furioso*, developing his skills as a keen-witted reviewer of contemporary poetry. He served as poetry consultant at the Library of Congress in 1963–1964. Between 1964 and his death in 1991, Nemerov was a distinguished professor on the faculty of Washington University in St. Louis.

Finding a Modern Voice   Nemerov's early poems, such as those found in *The Salt Garden* (1955), were praised, though many critics found them lacking in voice, often academic, and derivative of prominent poets from the earlier half of the century, such as T. S. Eliot and W. H. Auden. Not until the publication of *The Collected Poems of Howard Nemerov: 1947–1975* (1977) did the poet receive widespread acclaim and a place in American letters. The volume won both the National Book Award and the Pulitzer Prize and is generally considered by critics to be one of the most important poetry collections published in the latter half of the twentieth century.

Following the success of *The Collected Poems of Howard Nemerov: 1947–1975*, Nemerov was the recipient of numerous awards and honors, including fellowships from the Academy of American Poets and the Guggenheim Foundation, a National Endowment for the Arts grant, and the National Medal of the Arts. Aside from publishing poems, he continued to teach, lecture, and to contribute literary criticism to journals and periodicals. He also served as poet laureate of the United States from 1988 to 1990. Nemerov died of cancer in 1991 in University City, Missouri. Many of the poems upon which he had been working at the time of his death were published in 1991 in the collection *Trying Conclusions: New and Selected Poems, 1961–1991*, to wide acclaim.

Works in Literary Context

Because of his detached stance and firm grounding in formal verse, Nemerov has frequently been labeled an academic poet. Yet, his poetry is often marked by humor, the occasional use of slang, and everyday objects and events. Critics have noted that Nemerov's humor provides a counterbalance to the urbanity and intellectual weight of his poems, making his work difficult to categorize.

Duality of Vision   Nemerov's work characteristically is based on opposed elements and a duality of vision. As critic F. C. Golffing explains in *Poetry*, "Mr. Nemerov tells us that he dichotomizes the 'poetry of the eye' and the 'poetry of the mind,' and that he attempts to exhibit in his verse the 'ever-present dispute between two ways of looking at the world.'" Nemerov's frequent use of

LITERARY AND HISTORICAL CONTEMPORARIES

Nemerov's famous contemporaries include:

Philip Larkin (1922–1985): British poet Philip Larkin is generally considered one of the most important poets to publish in the era after World War II, as shown in works like *The Less Deceived* (1955).

Randall Jarrell (1914–1965): Poet and critic Randall Jarrell was a leading voice in poetics until his untimely death in a car accident in 1965. He frequently reviewed Nemerov's poems, pointing out the influence of such poets as T. S. Eliot and W. H. Auden on their tone and form.

Diane Arbus (1923–1971): Arbus, the sister of Nemerov, was an American photographer famed for her portraits of members of widely varying countercultures.

John Ashbery (1927–): This Pulitzer Prize–winning American poet is best known for his surrealist meditation *Self-Portrait in a Convex Mirror* (1975).

Jackson Pollock (1912–1956): Pollock was an American abstract expressionist painter famous for his singular method of dripping liquid paint on large canvasses laid on his studio floor.

Frank O'Hara (1926–1966): A leader of the New York School of Poetry, O'Hara is best known for his volume titled *Lunch Poems* (1964).

opposing elements also has led reviewers to criticize his work for being derivative of earlier modern poets, such as T. S. Eliot, W. H. Auden, William Butler Yeats, and Wallace Stevens.

Alienation and the Modern Age Throughout his work, Nemerov describes the anxiety modern man feels in the face of a world increasingly affected by technology, warfare, globalization, and mass production. Critic Peter Meinke contends that it is Nemerov's "modern awareness of contemporary man's alienation and fragmentation combined with a breadth of wit" that "sets Nemerov's writing apart from other modern writers." *Saturday Review* contributor I. L. Salomon has claimed that Nemerov combines a classical, formalist "instinct for perfection" and unity with a modern "carelessness in expression."

The Natural World Beginning with the collection *The Salt Garden*, Nemerov's poetry has shown a growing concern with nature. In 1966 Nemerov wrote in *Poets on Poetry* of the impact of the natural world on his work: "During the war and since, I have lived in the country, chiefly in Vermont, and while my relation to the landscape has been contemplative rather than practical, the landscape nevertheless has in large part taken over my poetry." This interest in the landscape has led many critics to compare Nemerov's work to that of Robert Frost; Nemerov, like Frost, brought philosophical issues into his poetry, while focusing on the natural world.

Paradox and Irony Many of Nemerov's critics have pointed out that his poetry combines a witty, ironic manner and a serious, often pessimistic, philosophy. Writer James Dickey observed the seriousness that underlies Nemerov's wit. Dickey maintains that although Nemerov is witty, "the enveloping emotion that arises from his writing is helplessness: the helplessness we all feel in the face of the events of our time, and of life itself." Julia A. Bartholomay argues that Nemerov's double view is expressed in his poetry through the use of paradox. The paradoxes reflect the "divisiveness, fragmentation, complexity, and absurdity of modern existence."

Works in Critical Context

The Salt Garden Upon its publication in 1955, Nemerov's *The Salt Garden* received recognition and praise but also drew criticism for being derivative. "The accents of Auden and [John Crowe] Ransom," observes Louis Untermeyer, "occasionally twist his utterance into a curious poetic patois." Similarly, the poet Randall Jarrell states that "he isn't, as yet, a very individual poet." Peter Meinke, too, maintains that Nemerov in his early work is "writing Eliot, Yeats, and Stevens out of his system." Yet, at the same time that critics faulted Nemerov for his imitation, they were also impressed by his natural talent as a poet. Jarrell comments that "as you read *The Salt Garden* you are impressed with how much the poet has learned, how well he has developed," while Peter Meinke observes that in this volume "Nemerov has found his most characteristic voice: a quiet intelligent voice brooding lyrically on the strange beauty and tragic loneliness of life."

The Collected Poems of Howard Nemerov The *Collected Poems of Howard Nemerov* presented verse from all of the earlier volumes, and its publication in 1977 met with widespread acclaim, winning both the National Book Award and the Pulitzer Prize in 1978. Phoebe Pettingell notes in the *New Leader* that the book shows "a gradual intensifying of a unified perspective," the poet's obsession with the theme of "man's sometimes tragic, sometimes ludicrous relation to history, death and the universe." Tom Johnson offers this assessment in the *Sewanee Review*: "Nemerov has written more incisively of science and its place in our imaginations than anyone else has yet managed to do. ... The breadth of accomplishment and depth of insight are one's most striking impressions." Robert Shaw recommends *Collected Poems* to readers whose interest in poetry stems more from curiosity than from experience with the genre. "Such readers," Shaw states, "can expect to be charmed by the easy flow of Nemerov's reasoned discourse, and moved by those fine moments in his poems in which reason is overcome by awe."

Trying Conclusions: New and Selected Poems, 1961–1991 Many reviewers found great value in *Trying Conclusions: New and Selected Poems, 1961–1991*, published the year of Nemerov's death. This volume collects many of the poems first published in *The Blue Swallows* (1967) and *The Winter Lightning* (1968) and also includes newer, previously unpublished poems that Nemerov wrote close to the time of his death. Sidney Burris, writing in the *Southern Review*, finds the collection significant because, in addition to containing a dozen new poems, it provides an excellent selection of Nemerov's previous work, thus functioning as a "companion volume" that encapsulates the poet's career. Burris goes on to state that "his poems aim ultimately to dignify the world of our recognizably common experience." Several reviewers also saw in the collection the humor and versatility frequently associated with Nemerov. Phoebe Pettingell, in *Sewanee Review*, notes the poet's "mean, satirical wit," and points out that the title, *Trying Conclusions*, could be interpreted in many ways, in keeping with Nemerov's penchant for plays on words.

Responses to Literature

1. Critics have frequently pointed out that Nemerov was heavily influenced by the modernist poets of the early twentieth century, such as T. S. Eliot, W. H. Auden, and Wallace Stevens. Research the major works of one of these poets and compare them to the works of Nemerov. What similarities do you find in terms of theme and form? Why do you think Nemerov found inspiration in these writers?

2. Nemerov himself has stated that the natural world plays a central role in his poetry. Choose two to three poems in which Nemerov uses images or symbolism from nature to make a philosophical point or to comment upon the human world. What type of language does he use to describe nature? In your opinion, what is Nemerov's larger message about man's relationship with the natural world?

3. Nemerov frequently uses paradox to illustrate the modern condition of humanity. A paradox is something that appears contradictory but expresses a basic truth. Locate some of these paradoxes in his work and identify how they function. Then, write your own poem incorporating a paradox that affects the world in which you currently live. Is the use of paradox more or less powerful than a straightforward approach? Discuss this with classmates.

BIBLIOGRAPHY

Books

Bartholomay, Julia A. *The Shield of Perseus: The Vision and Imagination of Howard Nemerov.* Gainesville: University of Florida Press, 1972.
Dickey, James. *Babel to Byzantium: Poets & Poetry Now.* New York: Farrar, Straus & Giroux, 1968.
Meinke, Peter. *Howard Nemerov.* Minneapolis: University of Minnesota Press, 1968.

COMMON HUMAN EXPERIENCE

The Collected Poems of Howard Nemerov: 1947–1975 captured the alienation and fragmentation felt by modern society in the latter half of the twentieth century. Other works written by Nemerov's contemporaries that capture a similar sense of modern anxiety include:

Life Studies (1959), a poetry collection by Robert Lowell. This immensely influential volume of poetry abandoned traditional form and meter and introduced the concept of "confessional," highly subjective poetry to American verse.
The Whitsun Weddings (1964), a book of poems by Philip Larkin. This collection meditates on the meaning of marriage and tradition in the modern age.
Lunch Poems (1964), a volume of poetry by Frank O'Hara. O'Hara wrote these poems on his lunch breaks while working in an advertising firm. They often meditate upon items of American popular culture, drawing inspiration from pop art and jazz.
The Lost World (1966), a poetry collection by Randall Jarrell. This book, often considered Jarrell's finest, explores the themes of childhood and loss.
Self-Portrait in a Convex Mirror (1975), by John Ashbery. This highly experimental book of poetry, inspired by a Renaissance painting, explores the ability of language to make meaning through volatile human consciousness.

Periodicals

Burris, Sidney. "A Sort of Memoir, A Sort of Review." *Southern Review* 28 (Winter 1992): 184–201.
Johnson, Tom. "Ideas and Order." *Sewanee Review* 86 (Summer 1978): 445–453.
Pettingell, Phoebe. "Knowledge Turning into Dream: Recollections of Howard Nemerov." *Sewanee Review* 100, no. 4 (1992): 706–715.
Shaw, Robert B. "Making Some Mind of What Was Only Sense." *Nation* 226 (February 25, 1968): 213–215.

Frank Norris

BORN: *1870, Chicago, Illinois*
DIED: *1902, San Francisco, California*
NATIONALITY: *American*
GENRE: *Fiction*
MAJOR WORKS:
McTeague (1899)
The Octopus (1901)
The Pit (1903)

Frank Norris   *Norris, Frank, photograph.*

Overview

Writer Frank Norris played a major role in introducing naturalism to late nineteenth- and early twentieth-century American literature. Influenced by the French naturalist writer Émile Zola, he achieved an unprecedented and sometimes shocking realism in his novels *McTeague* (1899), a depiction of San Francisco's lower social depths, and *The Octopus* (1901) and *The Pit* (1903), which dramatized brutal economic forces affecting American labor and big business. While laying the foundations for his career as a serious fiction writer, Norris also established himself as a critic and as an author of light, popular novels, short stories, and newspaper articles.

Works in Biographical and Historical Context

Paris and Zola   Born in Chicago in 1870, Norris was the elder son of a prosperous wholesale jeweler and a onetime actress. When he was fourteen, he moved with his family to San Francisco, where his father entered into real estate development while retaining his successful jewelry business. Norris was educated in private schools, including Belmont Academy and the Boys' High School in San Francisco, and his mother shared with him her love of poetry and art. His parents' marriage, however, became

increasingly unstable, and the young Norris would witness frequent domestic disputes, many of which would become models for his later novels.

In 1886 Norris enrolled at the San Francisco Art Associations school, where he received instruction in drawing and painting under the direction of the French-trained instructor Emil Carlsen. In 1887, entertaining ambitions to become a painter, Norris remained in Paris following a family tour abroad and enrolled in the Atelier Julien art school. Over the next three years, while studying art, Norris also became acquainted with the works of French naturalist writers, such as Émile Zola. These French naturalists attempted to capture life in its most realistic sense and frequently depicted man in constant struggle against a harsh world driven by human greed and market capitalism. Though Norris still harbored a fondness for the adventure novels he read as a youth, he developed an interest in the politics and aesthetics associated with the naturalist movement. While in Paris, he began writing, sending installments of a medieval romance to his younger brother, Charles, at home in California. In 1890 Norris returned to the United States and, at his father's insistence, entered the University of California in preparation for assuming a position in the family jewelry business.

Return to the States   Although Norris entered the university against his will and later considered his education practically useless, the experience he gained during his four years at the University of California is considered pivotal to the maturation of his writing. While in his freshman year he wrote a romantic narrative poem, *Yvernelle: A Legend of Feudal France*, which was published in book form in 1892. During the same period his father divorced his mother, remarried, and moved back to Chicago; Norris never saw him again. By the time *Yvernelle* was published, Norris had lost his youthful interest in purely romantic literature and soon began to use more realistic subject matter in his writing. By the time he left the university—without a degree due to his failure to meet the mathematics requirement—he had begun the novel *McTeague*. In 1894 Norris entered Harvard University as a special student in English and French, and during his year there he worked on both *McTeague* and another novel, *Vandover and the Brute*. These two volumes are considered by critics to be the most naturalistic and the most ambitious of his early work. Under the direction of Professor Lewis Gates, Norris cultivated his affinity for the works of Zola and began to base his own fiction on a more realistic foundation than he had previously considered.

Journalism, Naturalism, and Fiction   In 1895 Norris left the university and served as a foreign correspondent in South Africa for the *San Francisco Chronicle*. During this time South Africa was in between the First (1880–1881) and Second (1899–1902) Boer Wars, and hostilities were still pronounced between British colonials and the Boers (residents descended from Dutch settlers). Witnessing the constant violence between the Boers, the British soldiers, and the native tribes of South Africa deepened Norris's naturalistic views on the condition of man. After a year Norris returned to San Francisco to become an editor, contributor, and journalist for a local periodical titled the *Wave*. While on staff for the magazine, he wrote articles, short fiction, and sketches that often focused on grittier aspects of West Coast life. During this time he also finished *McTeague*, for which he could not find a publisher, and *Moran of the Lady Letty: A Story of Adventure off the California Coast* (1898), a more conventional adventure story that was serialized by the *Wave* and by the S. S. McClure syndicate in New York. The novel caught the attention of S. S. McClure himself, who hired Norris as a journalist for *McClure's* magazine and as a reader for the Doubleday and McClure Company. During this time Norris outlined an epic trilogy about the production, sale, and consumption of wheat. The first two novels, *The Octopus* and *The Pit*, were well received. However, before he could begin the final installment of the series, he died from appendicitis at the age of thirty-two.

Works in Literary Context

Regionalism   Norris centered the majority of his work on California, exploring the lifestyle and social concerns that influenced the formation of the American West in the late nineteenth century. His novels pay close attention to the relationship between class and language, using diction and dialect as markers for specific characters. Norris believed strongly that America was too large to have a "national" literary character and argued that American literature was, by virtue of the size of the country, given to regionalism. In his essay titled "The Great American Novel," Norris insists that a significant American novelist could not, strictly speaking, claim to have written a national work because of the extraordinary sectional diversity in the United States. Every noteworthy American author he cited when arguing the point was known for a regional sensibility and a local-color focus in his fiction, and Norris was, of course, implying the same about himself. Five of his seven novels are situated in California, and his canon of approximately three hundred works repeatedly demonstrates how appropriate it is to view him as a self-conscious and deliberate regional writer.

Naturalism   In such works as *McTeague*, *The Octopus*, and *The Pit*, Norris adopted the methods of the French novelist and literary theorist Émile Zola in representing poverty, degradation, and physical cruelty, which had previously been ignored by writers of the genteel tradition in American literature. Zola's harsh realism and attention to social inequalities came to be known as the naturalist movement and was espoused by Norris and other American writers, including William Dean Howells, Theodore Dreiser, Jack London, and Stephen Crane.

The works of these authors document a remarkable period of intellectual and artistic transition at the end of the nineteenth century and the beginning of the twentieth. This shift was due largely to the works of biologist and evolutionary theorist Charles Darwin, who argued

LITERARY AND HISTORICAL CONTEMPORARIES

Norris's famous contemporaries include:

Jacob Riis (1849–1914): a Danish American journalist, photographer, and social reformer, Riis's monumental photo-essay *How the Other Half Lives* (1890) spurred labor reform and the late nineteenth-century movement to improve living conditions in New York slums.

Buffalo Bill Cody (1846–1917): Cody, a soldier, scout, and buffalo hunter-turned-showman, became an international celebrity while touring with his Wild West show in the latter half of the nineteenth century.

Jack London (1876–1916): London, a California-born writer, was best known for his tales of adventure in the American West and for novels such as *The Call of the Wild* (1903), which described the Klondike Gold Rush.

Thomas Alva Edison (1846–1931): Influential turn-of-the-century inventor Thomas A. Edison patented such important technological innovations as the light bulb, phonograph, and the Kinetoscope, an early forerunner to celluloid films used in movie theaters.

Émile Zola (1840–1902): French writer Émile Zola led the naturalist movement of the late nineteenth century and is best known for his epic work *Les Rougon-Macquart* (1871–1893).

Elizabeth Cady Stanton (1850–1902): An American women's rights activist, abolitionist, and social reformer, Stanton advocated women's parental and custody rights, property rights, employment and income rights, divorce laws, and birth control.

Charles W. Chesnutt (1858–1932): Chesnutt was an influential African American novelist, essayist, and activist who is remembered for his regionalist short stories set in the rural South.

that man and ape were descended from a common ancestor, and that man's behavior depended as much on genetics as on social environment. The need to redefine man's situation in the "new world" revealed by evolutionary scientists, by antitraditional social theorists, and by new schools of philosophical inquiry was a primary motivation for Norris as he shaped his more serious writings. Conventional certainties about man, God, nature, and society had waned. Norris was one of many writers who sought to clarify the troubling questions of the age and to provide new explanations of life in his descriptions of characters and environments.

Works in Critical Context

Although Norris published a great number of short stories and essays throughout his career, he is best known for his naturalistic novels. His career as a novelist was remarkably

COMMON HUMAN EXPERIENCE

Norris's naturalistic novels sought to capture realistically the social conditions caused by the mechanization and alienation of the late nineteenth and early twentieth centuries. Other works of the same era written in a naturalistic style include:

> *Sister Carrie* (1900), a novel by Theodore Dreiser. This story chronicles the move of a young girl who migrates from the countryside to Chicago, where she falls into a desperate economic situation and is mistreated by advantage-seeking men.
>
> "The Open Boat" (1897), a short story by Stephen Crane. Crane's story describes the experiences of four shipwrecked men who must struggle against the harshest forces of nature to survive.
>
> *The House of Mirth* (1905), a novel by Edith Wharton. *The House of Mirth* follows the life of New York socialite Lily Bart, who possesses intelligence and manners but no fortune. Eventually she falls out of favor with the elite, moves to a boarding house, and must work in a low-end millinery shop.
>
> *Les Rougon-Macquart* (1871–1893), a collection of novels by Émile Zola. This twenty-novel collection is considered the cornerstone of French naturalism. In epic scope, it traces a single family through the Franco-Prussian War and the reign of Napoleon III.

short; however, the few works that he wrote have endured among literary scholars.

McTeague *McTeague* is generally considered the most important of Norris's early works and is rated a masterpiece by some observers. Depicting the financial, social, and moral degradation of a dentist and his wife in San Francisco, *McTeague* was inspired by a sensational murder case in 1893 in which a husband murdered his wife in the kindergarten where she worked as a janitor. While admitting that some readers would judge its subject unpleasant and its central characters contemptible, John D. Barry, writing in a review in *Literary World*, asserts that "every figure is perfectly realized; every episode has its significance." Continuing, Barry calls the work a "volume which seems to me worthy to rank among the few great novels produced in this country," and he accords high praise to "its profound insight into character; its shrewd humor; its brilliant massing of significant detail, and … its dramatic force." Writing in 1911, the critic Frederic Taber Cooper asserts:

> *McTeague* does not begin to show the breadth of purpose or the technical skill of *The Octopus* or *The Pit*; yet there are times when one is tempted to award it a higher place for all-around excellence. There is a

better balance between the central theme and the individual characters,—or to state it differently, between the underlying ethics and the so-called human interest. If Norris had never written another book, he would still have lived on in *McTeague*.

The Octopus Set in the San Joaquin Valley in California, *The Octopus* depicts the clash between wheat farmers and railroad operators, a symbol of the broader conflict of agriculture with the monetary interests of capitalism. Both aspects are depicted in the novel as inexorable forces beyond the control of the individuals involved, with wheat representing the supply and the railroad the means of fulfilling the demand. In a review of *The Octopus*, Norris's contemporary, Jack London, writes enthusiastically that "the promise of … McTeague has been realized. Can we ask more?" In a retrospective essay in 1935, Granville Hicks notes inconsistencies in Norris's philosophy and approach to his subject, yet writes of Norris, "He had at least one quality of greatness: he could seize upon the central issues of his time and create people in whose lives those issues were reflected." Charles Child Walcutt, who traced the influence of Zola's theories and technique on Norris's works, calls *The Octopus* "one of the finest American novels written before 1910. It towers immeasurably far above the sickly sentiment of Norris's contemporaries."

The Pit The sequel to *The Octopus*, *The Pit* centers on a wealthy trader, Curtis Jadwin, whose greed leads to his financial ruin after he attempts to corner the market on the wheat harvest, thereby upsetting the balance of a system that serves as the chief source of the world's grain supply. Frederic Taber Cooper notes, "*The Pit*, considered as a human story, has a stronger, more direct appeal" than *The Octopus* because "the interest [is] focused more directly on the central characters. … One feels that somehow and somewhere he had gained a deeper insight into the hearts of the men and women about him."

Responses to Literature

1. In nearly all of his major works, Norris explored corruption in big business, and dramatized how this affected the ordinary American citizen. Research the issue of corruption in big business today. You may want to consider the Enron scandal, recent mortgage firm bailouts, and bank failures. How might Norris and his fellow naturalists react to these events? Choose one item of recent news and outline how a naturalist might depict it in fiction.

2. In his critical writing of the late nineteenth century, Norris argued that all literature written in America would perforce be regional literature, given the size and social diversity of the country. Do you agree with Norris? Taking into consideration today's movement toward globalization, do you think you could now argue for a unilateral, specifically "American" literature? If so, what are its characteristics?

3. The naturalistic philosophies of Zola and his followers were heavily influenced by the works of the scientist Charles Darwin. Research Darwin's evolutionary theories, particularly as set forth in the 1859 work *On the Origin of Species.* How did these scientific theories inform beliefs about human social interactions? Present your findings to the class, being sure to tie them to ideas explored in Norris's novels.

BIBLIOGRAPHY

Books

Cooper, Frederic Taber. *Some American Story Tellers, 1911.* Freeport, N.Y.: Books for Libraries Press, 1968.

Hicks, Granville. *The Great Tradition: An Interpretation of American Literature since the Civil War.* New York: Macmillan Publishing Company, 1935.

Pizer, Donald. *The Novels of Frank Norris.* Bloomington: Indiana University Press, 1966.

Walcutt, Charles Child. *American Literary Naturalism: A Divided Stream.* Minneapolis: University of Minnesota Press, 1956.

Periodicals

Barry, John D. Review of *McTeague. Literary World* (March 18, 1899): 88–89.

✸ Jim Northrup

BORN: *1943, Fond du Lac Indian Reservation, Minnesota*

NATIONALITY: *American*

GENRE: *Fiction, poetry, drama*

MAJOR WORKS:

Walking the Rez Road (1993)

Rez Road Follies: Canoes, Casinos, Computers, and Birch Bark Baskets (1997)

Overview

Jim Northrup is a Native American novelist and newspaper columnist whose work offers political commentary on modern American Indian life in an accessible, folksy style. His syndicated column, *Fond du Lac Follies* chronicles Northrup's life on a reservation in northern Minnesota. Northrup is best known for his books *Walking the Rez Road* (1993) and *Rez Road Follies: Canoes, Casinos, Computers, and Birch Bark Baskets* (1997), which has been adapted to the stage and performed in theaters across America.

Works in Biographical and Historical Context

American Indian Heritage and the Vietnam War Native American (Anishinaabe) writer Jim Northrup was born in a government hospital in northern Minnesota's

Jim Northrup   *Courtesy of the author*

Fond du Lac Indian Reservation in 1943. At the age of six he was separated from his family and sent to a federal boarding school, one which he would later describe in his autobiography, *Walking the Rez Road*, as a harrowing place where he was often physically and mentally abused. Northrup was sent to a Christian boarding school in North Dakota for his secondary education.

After graduating from high school, he joined the United States Marine Corps, in which he served in the Vietnam War. During this highly controversial conflict, Northrup became active in the American civil rights movement. During the 1960s and 70s, civil-rights activists organized rallies and protests aimed at achieving racial equality. Hoping to obtain improved conditions on Indian reservations and such federally funded boarding schools as the one he attended as a boy, Northrup supported political initiatives that espoused equal rights and desegregation. After the end of the Vietnam War, he also actively supported rights for veterans. Northrup's brother, who also fought in Vietnam, suffered a severe case of post traumatic stress disorder, and frequently was an inspiration for Northrup's poetry and politics.

Stories and Poems from Fond du Lac In the 1980s Northrup began expressing his political convictions through poetry and performance. In addition, Northrup started writing the column *Fond du Lac Follies*, which presented humorous anecdotes of reservation life with political undertones and commentary on the relationship of the United States government to Native American tribes. The column achieved widespread success and was awarded the prize for "Best Column" in 1999 by the Native American Press Association. In addition, Northrup published *Three More: Poems* (1992) and *Days of Obsidian, Days of Grace* (1994).

LITERARY AND HISTORICAL CONTEMPORARIES

Northrup's literary and historical contemporaries include:

N. Scott Momaday (1934–): This Native American (Kiowa) writer is credited with having brought mainstream attention to Native American literature with the publication of his Pulitzer Prize-winning work *House Made of Dawn* (1968).

Paula Gunn Allen (1938–2008): The poet, scholar, and feminist Paula Gunn Allen has raised awareness of the experiences of Native American women through her various works.

Louise Erdrich (1954–): A Native American author best known for her story collection *Love Medicine* (1984), which describes the lives of people who live on an Indian reservation.

Gerald Vizenor (1934–): A prolific author, Native American activist, and teacher of Native American literature and history.

Leslie Marmon Silko (1948–): This Pueblo Laguna writer is the author of the acclaimed novel *Ceremony*, published in 1977 to widespread acclaim.

Jimmy Santiago Baca (1952–): A poet of mixed Hispanic and Apache descent. Baca writes primarily about race and the prison system in the American Southwest.

These secured his reputation as a vital voice in American Indian literature. Northrup achieved his greatest success, however, with his two story collections, *Walking the Rez Road* (1993) and *Rez Road Follies: Canoes, Casinos, Computers, and Birch Bark Baskets* (1997). Readers and reviewers appreciated Northrup's candor and humor. Northrup subsequently adapted the stories from his memoirs to public-performance pieces.

Northrup continues to work as a writer, columnist, and activist, and is frequently anthologized in collections of Native American writing. In addition he volunteers as a mentor to students, promotes creative writing in schools, and is often sought as a public speaker. In 1997 Northrup was featured in a film directed by Mike Riven entitled *Jim Northrup: With Reservations*. In this film, Northrup leaves his home in northern Minnesota, travels across the United States, and visits the Vietnam Veterans Memorial in Washington, D.C. Northrup's regular column, the *Fond du Lac Follies*, continues to be syndicated in several Native American papers, including *The Circle*, *The Native American Press*, and *News From Indian Country*.

Works in Literary Context

As critic Roseanne Hoefal has commented, Jim Northrup's work is "about survivors of oppression, trying to outlive the circumstances to which they've been sentenced and attempting to withstand acculturation, or alcoholism, or the struggle to obliterate someone else's oppression yet furthering their own in the process." Northrup tends to depict characters that have suffered through hardships such as war, poverty, and discrimination. Often, these characters persevere through the use of humor. Writer Gerald Vizenor states that "the wild and wondrous characters in [Northrup's] stories are survivors in the best trickster humor, no one is a passive victim."

Life on American Indian Reservations Northrup's stories and poems capture, often humorously, the daily life of American Indians living on reservations. Indeed, reservation culture is a key recurring focus of Northrup's work. In his introduction to *Touchwood*, a 1987 collection of Anishinaabe prose, Vizenor notes that Northrup's "direct and humorous stories are inspired by the rich language that people speak on the reservation" Throughout his works, Northrup focuses on traditional Anishinaabe rites and traditions, the importance of developing a relationship with the natural world, and a recognition of the cyclical nature of life. Also, he often cites the storytelling tradition of Native Americans tribes as one of their most important assets, and one that can be used to heal wounds and reaffirm faith.

The Vietnam War In his poetry and prose, Northrup develops his most important themes—those of survival and rehabilitation—around his experience in the Vietnam War. His writing laments the trauma experienced by Vietnam veterans, and often portrays the horrors of post-traumatic stress disorder, which afflicted a large number of those returning from the conflict. The poem "Wahbegan," for example, is a eulogy to Northrup's brother, who "died in the war / but didn't fall down / for fifteen tortured years." These lines express how Northrup's brother, while not killed in the line of duty, was led by his misery and stress to commit suicide years later. "How about a memorial," the speaker asks, "for those who made it / through the war / but still died / before their time?"

Works in Critical Context

Though he is also recognized for his poetry and journalism, Jim Northrup has received most of his critical attention for his collection *Walking the Rez Road*.

Walking the Rez Road *Walking the Rez Road* is a collection of twenty-one poems and twenty-one stories whose subjects include the Vietnam war, Anishinaabe culture and history, and contemporary reservation life. The book received high praise upon its publication, and continues to be considered one of the most significant works produced by an Anishinaabe writer.

In *Studies in American Indian Literatures*, reviewer Roseanne Hoefal writes that "Northrup employs everyday language and rejects conventional euphemisms in ways that allow the reader to bear witness to crucial moments."

She goes on to comment that "Northrup is generous to walk readers through not only the minefields he and the Anishinaabe have already negotiated and continue to negotiate, but also through the veritable gold mine of riches they inhabit." In particular, reviewers praised Northrup's frank style and abundant humor. A reviewer in the *Denver Post*, for example, remarked that "it's nice to have an authentic, nonfiction voice telling it like it is."

Responses to Literature

1. Watch Mike Riven's documentary film, *Jim Northrup: With Reservations*. What are your impressions of Jim Northrup as a person and as an artist? How does his Native American identity affect his viewpoint of the world? In small groups, discuss his reaction to the Vietnam Veterans Memorial.

2. Jim Northrup writes extensively about his experiences both in the Vietnam War and as a veteran of the war. How does race inform his view of the war and of the historical time period during which it was fought?

3. Jim Northrup was born on an American Indian reservation in 1943, and has dedicated the bulk of his work to depicting the lives of Native Americans who remain on them. Research the history of American Indian reservations. What laws pertain to these Native American communities? How have Native Americans been educated, and what is their typical socioeconomic position? How are these factors reflected in Native American literature?

BIBLIOGRAPHY

Books

Coltelli, Laura, ed. *Winged Words: American Indian Writers Speak*. Lincoln, Neb.: University of Nebraska Press, 1990.

Danziger, Edmund. *The Chippewas of Lake Superior*. Norman, Okla.: University of Oklahoma Press, 1990.

Johnston, Basil. *Ojibway Heritage*. Lincoln, Neb.: University of Nebraska Press, 1990.

Vizenor, Gerald, ed. *Touchwood: A Collection of Ojibway Prose*. Minneapolis: New Rivers, 1987.

———. *Crossbloods: Bone Courts, Bingo, and Other Reports*. Minneapolis: University of Minnesota Press, 1990.

Periodicals

Hoeful, Roseanne. *Walking with Jim Northrup and Sharing His "Rez"ervations*. Studies in American Indian Literatures 9, no. 2 (Summer 1997), pp. 11–21.

LaLonde, Chris. *Stories, Humor, and Survival in Jim Northrup's* Walking the Rez Road. *Studies in American Indian Literatures* 9, no. 2 (Summer 1997), pp. 23–40.

COMMON HUMAN EXPERIENCE

Northrup's works describe the experiences of Native Americans, particularly those living on American Indian reservations. Other works that focus on Native American culture and heritage include:

Jim Northrup: With Reservations (1996), a documentary film directed by Mike Riven. The film follows Northrup as he leaves his home in northern Minnesota and makes a pilgrimage across the United States.

Love Medicine (1984), a story collection by Louise Erdrich. This innovative collection tells stories from an American Indian reservation using a variety of differing viewpoints.

Ceremony (1977), a novel by Leslie Marmon Silko. This highly acclaimed novel tells the story of Tayo, a Pueblo veteran of World War II, who returns from overseas duty to poverty and struggle on an Indian reservation.

House Made of Dawn (1968), a novel by N. Scott Momaday. Momaday's acclaimed novel, for which he won the Pulitzer Prize in 1969, tells the story of a man returning to a Pueblo reservation in New Mexico after serving in World War II.

Darkness in Saint Louis Bearheart (1978), a novel by Gerald Vizenor, and one of the first Native American works of science fiction.

Trailing You (1994), a collection of poems by Kimberly Blaeser in which the author describes her upbringing in the Minnesota Ojibwa tribe.

✸ Naomi Shihab Nye

BORN: *1952, St. Louis, Missouri*

NATIONALITY: *American*

GENRE: *Fiction, poetry*

MAJOR WORKS:
Hugging the Jukebox (1982)
Habibi (1996)
Nineteen Varieties of Gazelle (2002)

Overview

Naomi Shihab Nye is known for award-winning poetry that lends a fresh perspective to ordinary events, people, and objects. A great deal of her work is written for children. In *Contemporary Women Poets*, critic Paul Christensen has stated that Nye "is building a reputation … as the voice of childhood in America, the voice of the girl at the age of daring exploration." Nye's poetry is informed by her Palestinian-American background, yet her dedication to a multicultural viewpoint does not negate a sense of common humanity in her work. As critic Jane Tanner has declared, Nye "is international in scope and internal in focus."

Naomi Shihab Nye   *Nye, Naomi Shihab, photograph. Reproduced by permission.*

Works in Biographical and Historical Context

An International Childhood Nye was born on March 12, 1952, in St. Louis, Missouri. Her father, Aziz Shihab, was Palestinian, and her mother, Miriam Naomi Allwardt Shihab, was an American of German and Swiss descent. As a young girl, Nye read voraciously and listened to her father's stories about his homeland and family. She began writing poems at age six and had them published in a children's magazine at age seven.

After spending much of her childhood in St. Louis, Nye moved with her family to Jerusalem, which was then part of Jordan. Nye attended a year of high school in Ramallah, Jordan before her family moved back to the United States, this time to San Antonio, Texas. The period in which Nye lived in Jordan was plagued with violence between Jewish and Arab citizens in the area, who disagreed over religious matters as well as the boundaries and territories established by the creation of the state of Israel in 1948. Nye's experience of this violent conflict would later be featured prominently in her poems and stories, most of which are dedicated to improving relations between members of differing religious and ethnic groups.

After returning to the United States, Nye began to write about the conflict in the Middle East while studying English and world religions at Trinity University in San Antonio. She graduated from the university in 1974 and married photographer and lawyer Michael Nye on September 2, 1978. She published *Different Ways to Pray* in 1980 and *Hugging the Jukebox* in 1982, both to great success.

An Award-Winning Global Activist In addition to her three major collections and four chapbooks, Nye has published short stories, essays, and more than one hundred individual poems in journals and anthologies. She has also recorded two albums of original songs, *Rutabaga-Roo* (1979) and *Lullaby Raft* (1981), and a reading of her poetry, *The Spoken Page* (1988). Nye has worked as writer-in-residence in Texas, Wyoming, Maine, California, Hawaii and Oregon; as a teacher at the University of California, Berkeley, the University of Texas at San Antonio, and Our Lady of the Lake in San Antonio; and as poetry therapist at Horizon House in San Antonio.

Nye has also traveled to the Middle East and Asia for the United States Information Agency to promote international goodwill through the arts. Throughout her works, Nye addresses issues of mixed heritage and cross-cultural understanding. As Nye herself wrote in a press release for Four Winds Press, "My poems and stories often begin with the voices of our neighbors, mostly Mexican American, always inventive and surprising. . . . I never get tired of mixtures." A contributor to *Contemporary Southern Writers* wrote that Nye's poetry "is playfully and imaginatively instructive, borrows from Eastern and Middle Eastern and Native American religions, and resembles the meditative poetry of William Stafford, Wallace Stevens, and Gary Snyder." Nye's work was selected for the Pushcart Prize in 1982 and 1984. In 1988 she was chosen by poet W. S. Merwin to receive the Academy of American Poets' Lavan Award. In the same year she was also a cowinner, with Galway Kinnell, of the Charity Randall Citation for Spoken Poetry from the International Poetry Forum. Nye and her husband currently live in San Antonio with their son, Madison Cloudfeather, born in 1986.

Works in Literary Context

Cultural Diversity Throughout her career, Nye has promoted, both in her writing and political activism, cross-cultural understanding. In her first full-length collection, *Different Ways to Pray*, Nye explores the differences between, and shared experiences of, cultures from California to Texas, and from South America to Mexico. As critic Jane Tanner observed, "with her acceptance of different 'ways to pray' is also Nye's growing awareness that living in the world can sometimes be difficult." In more recent works, such as *Habibi*, Nye addresses religious and ethnic conflict by depicting its effects on the lives of children and adolescents.

The Arab-American Experience While cultural diversity is a focal point of her work, Nye also draws heavily from her Palestinian background and a childhood partially spent in Jordan. As a result, she addresses the Arab-American experience in nearly all of her primary works. Often, Nye will weave descriptions of Palestinian traditions, stories, and daily life with portrayals of the modern conflict and cultural challenges faced by Palestinians in both America and in the Middle East. In *Hugging the Jukebox*, for example, Nye depicts the experience of living in an urban setting affected by indiscriminate violence, racial hatred, and poverty. More recently, in *Habibi*, Nye offers an extended meditation on war and its effects and calls for peace and cultural understanding.

Feminist Perspective Though critics usually focus on the Arab-American themes in Nye's works, Nye is considered one of the leading figures in the poetry of the American Southwest, especially poetry expressing a woman's point of view. A contributor to *Contemporary Poets* wrote that she "brings attention to the female as a humorous, wry creature with brisk, hard intelligence and a sense of personal freedom unheard of." Indeed, Nye's depictions of women cross cultures, generations, and historical periods. She has written both of modern Arab women and of the pioneer women that helped settle the American West.

Works in Critical Context

Hugging the Jukebox Nye's poetry collection *Hugging the Jukebox* appeared in 1982, winning much acclaim and the Voertman Poetry Prize. Reviewers praised *Hugging the Jukebox*, noting Nye's warmth and celebratory tone. Writing in the *Village Voice*, Mary Logue commented that in Nye's poems about daily life, "sometimes the fabric is thin and the mundaneness of the action shows through. But, in an alchemical process of purification, Nye often pulls gold from the ordinary." According to *Library Journal* contributor David Kirby, the poet "seems to be in good, easy relation with the earth and its peoples." In critic Paul Christensen's view, Nye "does not avoid the horrors of urban life, but she patches together the vision of simple nature struggling up through the cracks of the city."

Habibi In 1997 Nye published *Habibi*, her first young-adult novel. Readers meet Liyana Abboud, an Arab-American teen who moves with her family to her Palestinian father's native country during the 1970s, only to discover that the violence in Jerusalem has not yet abated. Autobiographical in its focus, Habibi was praised by Karen Leggett, who noted in the *New York Times Book Review* that the novel magnifies through the lens of adolescence "the joys and anxieties of growing up" and that Nye is "meticulously sensitive to this rainbow of emotion." Appraising *Habibi* in *Horn Book*, Jennifer M. Brabander agreed, saying, "The leisurely progression of the narrative matches the slow and stately pace of daily life" in Jerusalem "and the text's poetic turns of phrase accurately reflect Liyana's passion for words and language." As Nye explained to a *Children's Literature Review* contributor: "To counteract negative images conveyed by blazing headlines, writers must steadily transmit simple stories closer to heart and more common to everyday life. Then we will be doing our job."

Nineteen Varieties of Gazelle In her 2002 collection of poetry, *Nineteen Varieties of Gazelle*, Nye explores the Middle East through her Palestinian-American poet's

***

LITERARY AND HISTORICAL CONTEMPORARIES

Nye's famous contemporaries include:

Yasser Arafat (1929–2004): Arafat was the longtime leader of the Palestinian Liberation Organization, a group dedicated to the creation of a Palestinian state.

Ariel Sharon (1928–): Sharon, an Israeli politician and military leader, served as Prime Minister of Israel from 2001–2006.

Fadwa Tuqan (1917–2003): Tuqan was aPalestinian poet whose works often chronicled the sufferings of Palestinians living in Israeli occupied areas.

Naguib Mahfouz (1911–2006): Mahfouz is a Nobel Prize–winning author known for novels that capture the history and politics of the author's home in Egypt.

Latifa Baka (1964–): Baka is a Moroccan short-story writer and novelist.

Edward Said (1935–2003): Said was a Palestinian-American literary critic and political activist best known for his book *Orientalism* (1978), in which he argues that Western writings about the East contain an inherent colonial bias.

Galway Kinnell (1927–): Kinnell is an acclaimed American poet known for his dedication to promoting international human rights.

***

eye, recording the sights, sounds, smells, tastes, and people she encounters. She particularly focuses on her experiences in Jerusalem as the city is besieged by terror and struggle. Nye offers readers a view into the lives of the many innocent people who live in the Middle East in a post–September 11 world. A contributor to *Kirkus Reviews* said that reading the poems will "elicit a gasp of surprise, a nod of the head, a pause to reflect." Reviewer Hazel Rochman agrees, as evidenced by her report in *Booklist*, that claimed *Nineteen Variations of Gazelle* "will spark discussion and bring readers up close" to what war and vengeance really mean. Nina Lindsay, writing in *School Library Journal*, observed that Nye's book is "a celebration of her heritage, and a call for peace."

Responses to Literature

1. Nye lived in the Middle East as a teenager, and for that reason the Arab-Israeli conflict heavily influences her work. Research the history of Jordan and Israel, particularly during the times Nye lived in the area. What are the roots of the conflict Nye writes so much about? How can you apply the issues at stake to Nye's poetry?

2. Critics have pointed out that though both *Hugging the Jukebox* and *Habibi* address ethnic conflict, the

COMMON HUMAN EXPERIENCE

Nye has become well-known for promoting awareness of the Arab-Israeli conflict and for presenting a point-of-view informed by her Palestinian background. Other works by Palestinian writers that have addressed the conflict in the Middle East include:

Fadwa, A Tale of Palestinian Poetess (1999). This documentary film, directed by writer Liana Badr, explores the life of Palestinian poet Fadwa Tuqan.

The Night and the Horseman (1969) a collection of poems by Fadwa Tuqan. Considered one of the most avant-garde writers of the Arabic world, Tuqan explores the lives and experiences of female Palestinian refugees in this landmark work.

Covering Islam: How the Media and the Experts Determine How We See the Rest of the World (1981), a book by cultural studies theorist Edward Said. In this work, Said argues there is evidence of anti-Arab prejudice in Western media.

The Secret Life of Saeed, the Ill-Fated Pessoptimist: A Palestinian Who Became a Citizen of Israel (1974), a novel by Emile Habibi. Habibi's work chronicles the difficulties of being an Arab in the state of Israel.

Identity Card (1964), a collection of poems by Mahmoud Darwish. In this collection Darwish expresses his resistance to Israeli occupation of formerly Palestinian lands.

works emphasize not war but daily life. In your opinion, how does this approach affect Nye's overall themes? Explain why you think she chooses to describe daily life and ordinary people in her works.

3. While Nye is most often identified as an Arab-American poet, she also pursues feminist themes throughout her work. By looking at the texts of both her poetry and prose, discuss with your class the symbols and images Nye associates with women. How are women portrayed? What differences between female generations does Nye highlight? Support your answers with evidence from the texts you have read.

BIBLIOGRAPHY

Books

Christenson, Paul. *Contemporary Women Poets*. Detroit: St. James Press, 1997.

Periodicals

Brabander, Jennifer M. Review of *Habibi. Horn Book* November–December, 1997, pp. 683–684.

Kirby, David. Review of *Hugging the Jukebox. Library Journal*, August 1982.

Leggett, Karen. Review of *Habibi. New York Times Book Review*, November 16, 1997, p. 50.

Lindsay, Nina. Review of *Nineteen Varieties of Gazelle, School Library Journal*, May 2002, p. 175.

Logue, Mary. Review of *Hugging the Jukebox. Village Voice*, January 18, 1983, p. 37.

McKee, Louis. "Ranting and Raving about Naomi Shihab Nye," *Swamp Root* Spring 1989: 83–93.

Rochman, Hazel. Review of *Nineteen Varieties of Gazelle. Booklist*, April 1, 2002, p. 1315.

✸ Joyce Carol Oates

BORN: *1938, Lockhart, New York*

NATIONALITY: *American*

GENRE: *Fiction*

MAJOR WORKS:

them (1969)

Bellefleur (1980)

Black Water (1992)

Blonde (2000)

I'll Take You There (2002)

Overview

One of America's most prolific and versatile contemporary writers, Joyce Carol Oates has published more than forty novels, nearly thirty volumes of short stories, nine collections of verse, several plays, and numerous nonfiction works since her first book appeared in 1963. In her fiction, Oates focuses upon the spiritual, sexual, and intellectual decline of modern American society. Employing a dense, elliptical prose style, she depicts such cruel and macabre actions as rape, incest, murder, mutilation, child abuse, and suicide to delineate the forces of evil with which individuals must contend. Oates's protagonists often suffer at the hands of others as a result of emotional deficiencies or socioeconomic conditions. Critic Greg Johnson commented: "[Oates's] particular genius is her ability to convey psychological states with unerring fidelity, and to relate the intense private experiences of her characters to the larger realities of American life."

Works in Biographical and Historical Context

"Dull, Ordinary" Origins Joyce Carol Oates was born on June 16, 1938 into a working-class Catholic family outside Lockport, New York, and she was raised amid a rural setting on her maternal grandparents' farm. She attended a one-room schoolhouse in Erie County, a parallel community to the fictitious Eden County where many of her works are set. She displayed an early interest in storytelling by drawing picture-tales before she could write. Oates has said that her childhood "was dull, ordinary, nothing people would be interested in" but has admitted

Joyce Carol Oates   © Colin McPherson

that "a great deal frightened me." In 1953, at age fifteen, Oates wrote her first novel, though it was rejected by publishers who found its subject matter, which concerned the rehabilitation of a drug dealer, exceedingly depressing for adolescent audiences.

Education in Literature   Oates began her academic career at Syracuse University and graduated from there as class valedictorian in 1960. In 1961, she received a Master of Arts degree in English from the University of Wisconsin, where she met and married Raymond Joseph Smith, an English educator. With the encouragement of Smith and her professors, Oates began to write and publish short stories. The following year, after beginning work on her doctorate in English, Oates inadvertently encountered one of her own stories in Margaret Foley's anthology *Best American Short Stories*. This discovery prompted Oates to focus on writing professionally, and in 1963 she published her first volume of short stories, *By the North Gate* (1963). Oates's first novel, *With Shuddering Fall* (1964), foreshadows her preoccupation with evil and violence in the story of a destructive romance between a teenage girl and a thirty-year-old stock car driver that ends with his

death in an accident. Following the success of this debut novel, Oates published a critically acclaimed trilogy that explores three distinct segments of American society. Critics attribute the naturalistic ambience of these works to the influence of such twentieth-century authors as William Faulkner, Theodore Dreiser, and James T. Farrell. The first volume of the trilogy, *A Garden of Earthly Delights* (1967), is set in rural Eden County and chronicles the life of the daughter of a migrant worker who marries a wealthy farmer in order to provide for her illegitimate son. The woman's idyllic existence is destroyed, however, when the boy murders his stepfather and kills himself. In *Expensive People* (1967), the second work in the series, Oates exposes the superficial world of suburbanites whose preoccupation with material comforts reveals their spiritual poverty.

Detroit and the Civil Rights Movement   Oates taught at the University of Detroit between 1961 and 1967, a time period when the city suffered not only from widespread economic hardship, but racial tensions heightened by the civil rights movement, which advocated racial equality and spurred several political protests in the city. Oates's critically acclaimed novel *them* (1969), the third installment of her trilogy and winner of the National Book Award for fiction, depicts the violence and degradation endured by three generations of an urban Detroit family. Critics acknowledge that Oates's experiences as a teacher in Detroit during the early 1960s contributed to her accurate rendering of the city and its social problems. Betty DeRamus stated: "Her days in Detroit did more for Joyce Carol Oates than bring her together with new people—it gave her a tradition to write from, the so-called American Gothic tradition of exaggerated horror and gloom and mysterious and violent incidents."

Continuing Versatility   In 1967, Oates and her husband moved to Canada to teach at the University of Windsor, where together they founded the influential literary journal *Ontario Review*. Since leaving the University of Windsor in 1977, Oates has been writer-in-residence at Princeton University in New Jersey. A continually versatile and prolific writer, Oates has published and been recognized for such novels as *Bellefleur* (1980), *Black Water* (1992), *Blonde* (2000), and *I'll Take You There* (2002). Oates has also composed several dramas that were produced off-Broadway in New York and has published numerous volumes of poetry. In addition, she is a respected essayist and literary critic whose nonfiction works are praised for the logic and sensibility with which she examines a variety of subjects.

Works in Literary Context

Oates has established a reputation for consistently versatile work, ranging in genre from stories of upper-class domesticity to horror and psychological crime, but throughout her work, she reveals "an uncanny knack for understanding middle America, suburbia, and the temper of the times," to

LITERARY AND HISTORICAL CONTEMPORARIES

Oates's famous contemporaries include:

Toni Morrison (1931–): Morrison, author of *Beloved* (1988) and *Song of Solomon* (1977), was the first African-American woman to win the Nobel Prize.

Philip Roth (1933–): Roth is one of the most popular and celebrated contemporary American novelists, and a two-time winner of the National Book Award.

Martin Luther King, Jr. (1929–1968): American minister and activist, King was the leader of the American civil rights movement, best known for his 1963 "I Have a Dream" speech.

John Updike (1932–2009): Prolific, Pulitzer Prize-winning author John Updike is best known for his Rabbit series, which focuses on life in small-town America.

Richard Nixon (1913–1994): The thirty-seventh President of the United States. Nixon resigned from office after the Watergate scandal, in which he was implicated in the cover-up of a theft from the headquarters of the National Democratic Party.

Joe DiMaggio (1914–1999): DiMaggio, one of the most celebrated home run hitters in major league baseball history, was the longtime star of the New York Yankees and made even more headlines by marrying movie star Marilyn Monroe in 1954.

quote a *Contemporary Novelists* critic. Violence and victimization are often featured in Oates's stories and novels, but existential questions of self-discovery abound as well. She writes about real people in real situations; as one *Publishers Weekly* reviewer put it: "Reading an Oates novel is like becoming a peeping tom, staring without guilt into the bright living rooms and dark hearts of America."

Gothic Americana Oates has been linked with the Gothic tradition in literature because of the prevalence of horror, evil, and the supernatural in her work. Her novels of the 1970s explore characters involved with various American professional and cultural institutions while interweaving elements of human malevolence and tragedy. *Wonderland* (1971), for example, depicts a brilliant surgeon who is unable to build a satisfying home life, resulting in estrangement from his wife, children, and society. *The Assassins: A Book of Hours* (1975) is a psychological tale that dramatizes the effects of the murder of a conservative politician on his wife and two brothers. In these and all her fiction, the frustrations and imbalance of individuals become emblematic of U.S. society as a whole.

Nineteenth Century Parody During the early 1980s, Oates published several novels that parody works by nineteenth-century authors, including Louisa May Alcott,

Charles Dickens, Edgar Allan Poe, and Charlotte and Emily Bronte. *Bellefleur* (1980) follows the prescribed formula for a Gothic multigenerational saga, utilizing supernatural occurrences while tracing the lineage of an exploitative American family. Oates included explicit violence in this work; for example, a man deliberately crashes his plane into the Bellefleur mansion, killing himself and his family. *A Bloodsmoor Romance* (1982) displays such elements of Gothic romance as mysterious kidnappings and psychic phenomena in the story of five maiden sisters living in rural Pennsylvania in the late 1800s. In *Mysteries of Winterthurn* (1984), Oates borrowed heavily from the works of Poe as she explored the conventions of the nineteenth-century mystery novel. The protagonist of this work is a brilliant young detective who models his career after the exploits of Sir Arthur Conan Doyle's fictional sleuth, Sherlock Holmes. While some critics viewed these works as whimsical, others, citing Oates's accomplished depiction of evil, maintained that they are significant literary achievements. Though fanciful in form, the books often examine such sensitive issues as crimes against women, children, and the poor, as well as the role of family history in shaping destiny.

Obsession Some of Oates's novels explore the nature and ramifications of obsession. *Solstice* (1985) revolves around a relationship between a young divorcée and an older woman that evolves into an emotional power struggle. In *Marya: A Life* (1986), a successful writer and academician attempts to locate her alcoholic mother, who had abused and later abandoned her as a child. With *You Must Remember This* (1987), Oates returned to a naturalistic portrait of families under emotional and moral distress. Suicide attempts, violent beatings, disfiguring accidents, and incest figure prominently in this novel, which centers on an intense love affair between a former boxer and his adolescent niece.

Works in Critical Context

Short Fiction Most critics contend that Oates's short fiction, for which she has twice received the O. Henry Special Award for Continuing Achievement, evokes the same urgency and emotional power as her principal novels. Such collections as *By the North Gate*, *Where Are You Going, Where Have You Been?: Stories of Young America* (1974), *The Lamb of Abyssalia* (1980), and *Raven's Wing* (1986) contain pieces that focus upon violent and abusive relationships between the sexes. One widely anthologized story, "Where Are You Going, Where Have You Been?" (1966), a tale of female adolescence and sexual awakening, is considered a classic of modern short fiction and was adapted for film.

them The novel *them* chronicles three decades, beginning in 1937, in the life of the Wendall family. *New York Times* reviewer John Leonard wrote, "*them*, as literature, is a reimagining, a reinventing of the urban American experience of the last thirty years, a complex and powerful novel." Leonard added: "*them* is really about all the private selves, accidents and casualties that add up to a public violence." *Christian Science Monitor* contributor Joanne Leedom also noted the symbolic importance that violence assumes and links it to the characters' search for freedom: "The characters live, love, and almost die in an effort to find freedom and to break out of their patterns. ... The quest in them is for rebirth; the means is violence; the end is merely a realignment of patterns."

Bellefleur *Bellefleur* is a five-part novel that encompasses thousands of years and explores what it means to be an American. It is the saga of the Bellefleurs, a rich and rapacious family with a "curse," that settles in the Adirondack Mountains. Wrote *New York Times* contributor John Leonard: "On one level, *Bellefleur* is Gothic pulp fiction, cleverly consuming itself." Oates herself has acknowledged that the book was partially conceived as a critique of the American dream, and critics generally agreed that this dimension enhances the story, transforming the Gothic parody into serious art. Susan Tekulve in *Book* felt that, like nineteenth-century writer Edgar Allan Poe, "Oates merges Gothic conventions with modern social and political concerns, creating stories that feel at once antique and new. But she also shares Poe's love of dark humor and a good hoax." Greg Johnson believed that "the Gothic elements throughout her fiction, like her use of mystical frameworks, serve the larger function of expanding the thematic scope and suggestiveness of her narratives."

Black Water Oates fictionally reconstructs a familiar historical scenario in her award-winning *Black Water*, a 1992 account of a tragic encounter between a powerful U.S. senator and a young woman he meets at a party. While driving to a motel, the drunken senator steers the car off a bridge into the dark water of an East Coast river, and although he is able to escape, he leaves the young woman to drown. The events parallel those of Senator Edward Kennedy's fatal plunge at Chappaquiddick in 1969 that left a young campaign worker dead, but Oates updates the story and sets it twenty years later. Told from the point of view of the drowning woman, the story "portrays an individual fate, born out of the protagonist's character and driven forward by the force of events," according to Richard Bausch in the *New York Times Book Review*. Bausch called Oates's effort "taut, powerfully imagined and beautifully written ... it continues to haunt us." It is a fusion of "the instincts of political and erotic conquest," wrote Richard Eder in the *Los Angeles Times Book Review*.

Blonde Published in 2000, one of Oates's most successful novels to date is *Blonde*, a fictional re-working of the life of Marilyn Monroe. *Booklist* contributor Donna Seaman commented that the author "liberates the real woman behind the mythological creature called Marilyn Monroe." A *Publishers Weekly* contributor found the novel "dramatic, provocative and unsettlingly suggestive," adding that Oates "creates a striking and poignant portrait of the mythic star and the society that made and failed her."

COMMON HUMAN EXPERIENCE

Throughout her work, Oates combines a sense of the Gothic with the setting of the American suburb. Other works that examine life in American suburbs include:

The Stepford Wives (1972), a novel by Ira Levin. A woman who has just moved to the quiet suburb of Stepford wonders why the married women in her neighborhood seem so very mild-mannered and submissive. This creepy horror story has been filmed twice, once in 1975 and again in 2004.

The Ice Storm (1994), a novel by Rick Moody. This book captures suburban Connecticut life in the 1970s, and in 1997 was adapted into a film directed by Ang Lee and starring Kevin Kline, Elijah Wood, Christina Ricci, and Tobey Maguire.

Far From Heaven (2002), a film written and directed by Todd Haynes, starring Julianne Moore and Dennis Quaid. This film explores domestic and racial tensions in a Connecticut suburb in the 1950s.

The Virgin Suicides (1993), a novel by Jeffrey Eugenides. This debut novel by Eugenides describes the bizarre suicides of five in the rich suburb of Grosse Pointe, Michigan, in the 1970s. The popular book was adapted into a film by director Sofia Coppola in 1999.

subUrbia (1994), a play by Eric Bogosian. This play focuses on the lives of men and women in their twenties living in American suburbs. In 1996 director Richard Linklater adapted Bogosian's play into an independent film starring Parker Posey and Giovanni Ribisi.

American Beauty (1999), a film directed by Sam Mendes, starring Kevin Spacey and Annette Bening. This film, which won the Oscar for Best Picture in 1999, is narrated by a depressed suburban advertising executive (Spacey) who becomes infatuated with one of his teenage daughter's friends.

I'll Take You There Oates moved to the self-discovery of early adulthood in *I'll Take You There*. Cited as her most autobiographical novel to date, the book deals with an unnamed protagonist as she comes of age at Syracuse University in the early 1960s. *Los Angeles Times Book Review* critic Stanley Crouch praised Oates's "masterful strength of the form, the improvisational attitude toward sentence structure and the foreshadowing, as well as the deft use of motifs."

Responses to Literature

1. Throughout the 1980s, Joyce Carol Oates published several novels that parodied the Gothic works of nineteenth-century writers such as Charles Dickens

and Edgar Allan Poe. Research the works and writing styles of these authors, and compare them to Oates's *Bellefleur*. Why did Oates choose the nineteenth century as a point of comparison for the twentieth? How does she adapt a sense of the Gothic to fit the condition of modern America?

2. Critics often disagree in their assessment of Oates's fictionalized treatments of popular culture icons. Make a careful study of Oates's recreation of Marilyn Monroe in *Blonde* and Ted Kennedy in *Black Water*. How does Oates present these characters to her audience? Does she humanize or objectify them? What significance do these celebrities have in terms of American culture?

3. Violence is a constant presence in the works of Joyce Carol Oates. Take one of her books set in a city— such as *them*—and compare it to one of her many books set in the suburbs. How are the treatments of violence different between the urban and suburban settings? What overall argument does Oates put forward about the importance of violence in modern America? What roles do race and gender play in her treatments of violence?

BIBLIOGRAPHY

Books

Bender, Eileen. *Joyce Carol Oates.* Bloomington, In.: Indiana University Press, 1987.

Bloom, Harold, ed. *Modern Critical Views: Joyce Carol Oates.* New York: Chelsea House, 1987.

Daly, Brenda O. *Lavish Self-Divisions: The Novels of Joyce Carol Oates.* Jackson, Miss.: University Press of Mississippi, 1996.

Johnson, Greg. *Understanding Joyce Carol Oates.* Columbia, S.C.: University of South Carolina Press, 1987.

Wagner, Linda W, ed. *Joyce Carol Oates: The Critical Reception.* Boston: G. K. Hall, 1979.

Periodicals

Bausch, Richard. Review of *Black Water. New York Times Book Review* (May 10, 1992): 1.

Crouch, Stanley. Review of *I'll Take you There. Los Angeles Times Book Review* (January 26, 2003): 3.

Eder, Richard. Review of *Black Water. Los Angeles Times Book Review* (May 10, 1992): 2.

Leedom, Joanne. Review of *them. Christian Science Monitor* (October 30, 1969): 12.

Leonard, John. Review of *them. New York Times* (October 1, 1969): 45.

Leonard, John. Review of *Bellefleur. New York Times* (July 20, 1980): 1.

Seaman, Donna. Review of *Blonde. Booklist* (January 1, 2000): 835.

Tekulve, Susan. Review of *Faithless: Tales of Transgression. Book* (March 2001): 70.

✺ Tim O'Brien

BORN: *1946, Austin, Minnesota*

NATIONALITY: *American*

GENRE: *Fiction*

MAJOR WORKS:

Going after Cacciato (1978)
The Things They Carried (1990)
In the Lake of the Woods (1994)

Overview

Award-winning author Tim O'Brien is perhaps best known for his fictional portrayals of the Vietnam conflict, in work that describes the experiences of American soldiers and veterans, as well as Vietnamese civilians. Based on his own combat exposure, O'Brien delves into the American psyche and the human experience as he writes not only of what actually happened, but also the emotional and psychological impact of the war. In highly praised works such as *The Things They Carried* (1990), *Going after Cacciato* (1978), and *In the Lake of the Woods* (1994), he explores the war and its aftershocks from many vantage points, some intimate and some more distant. "But to label O'Brien a Vietnam author seems limiting, even simplistic," *Library*

Tim O'Brien   *O'Brien, Tim, photograph. © Jerry Bauer. Reproduced by permission.*

Journal contributor Mirela Roncevic maintains, "for his work has incessantly challenged his storytelling skills, demonstrating his ability to write both lucidly and succinctly while exploring the arcane relationship between fact and fiction, reality and imagination."

Works in Biographical and Historical Context

From Minnesota to My Lai O'Brien was born in 1946 in Austin, Minnesota, to William T. O'Brien, an insurance salesman, and Ava Schulz O'Brien, a teacher. O'Brien moved with his family to Worthington, Minnesota when he was ten years old. As a youth, he studied and practiced the techniques of magic; he has often indicated that this early fascination with the mystery of illusion influenced his later writings, which often incorporate dream scenarios and experimental meta-fictional forms.

In the years following World War II, the country of Vietnam—which had for a time been ruled as a colony of France—became an independent nation partitioned into a region under Communist rule (North Vietnam) and a republic (South Vietnam). The two sides were to be united by free election, but instead they began battling in a civil war to determine the political and ideological fate of the country. The United States supported the government of South Vietnam, and sent nearly three million Americans to the region over the course of the war. Many Americans, however, felt that the conflict was not one in which the United States should have been directly involved.

In 1968 O'Brien graduated summa cum laude from Macalester College in St. Paul, Minnesota, with a bachelor's degree in political science. Soon after graduating he was drafted into the U.S. Army during the height of the Vietnam War. Though O'Brien, having studied political science and witnessed the controversy over the war, held reservations about conscription, he reported to the army. He completed basic and advanced-infantry training at Fort Lewis, Washington, and arrived in Vietnam in 1969. He served with the 198th Infantry (Alpha Company) in the Quang Ngai region, near the South China Sea, where he earned a Purple Heart for wounds suffered at My Lai a year after the infamous massacre. This massacre, in which American soldiers tortured, shot, and killed hundreds of unarmed civilians in South Vietnam, caused international outrage and escalated the anti-war protests in the United States. O'Brien would later integrate the legacy of My Lai into his fiction; the protagonist of *In the Lake of the Woods*, a politician named John Wade, is revealed to have been a participant in the massacre at My Lai.

Critical Success During his time in Vietnam, O'Brien began writing vignettes about his army experience. Following an honorable discharge as an infantry sergeant in 1970, O'Brien accepted a scholarship to attend Harvard University as a graduate student in government studies. He left Harvard, however, in 1976, without completing

---

LITERARY AND HISTORICAL CONTEMPORARIES

O'Brien's famous contemporaries include:

David Halberstam (1934–2007): Journalist David Halberstam won a Pulitzer Prize for his reporting on the Vietnam War, and was the author of *The Best and the Brightest* (1972), a book that traces the development of America's involvement in Vietnam.

John McCain (1936–): Arizona senator and 2008 Republican presidential candidate John McCain was a pilot during the Vietnam War, and spent six years in a prisoner of war camp after being shot down in combat.

Richard Nixon (1913–1994): The thirty-seventh president of the United States, was in office during much of the Vietnam War. Nixon resigned from office after the Watergate scandal, in which he was accused of aiding in the robbery of the Democratic Party's headquarters.

Oliver Stone (1946–): Stone, an American filmmaker, served as a soldier during the Vietnam War in 1967 and 1968, earning a Purple Heart and a Bronze Star. His wartime experiences inspired his 1986 film *Platoon*, which won the Academy Award for Best Picture.

Maya Lin (1959–): Lin is a Chinese American artist who designed the Vietnam Veterans Memorial in Washington, D.C.

---

the Ph.D. program. Afterwards, he served as an intern at the *Washington Post* and later worked there as a national affairs reporter. O'Brien continued writing fiction, and in 1973 published *If I Die in a Combat Zone, Box Me up and Ship Me Home*, a book of memoirs that also reveals considerable emphasis on fictional technique. The series of vignettes reflects O'Brien's experience as a foot soldier and struck a chord with a wide public for both its autobiographical nature and evocative language, becoming both a popular as well as a critical success. With his publishing career firmly established, O'Brien focused solely on writing, publishing *Northern Lights* in 1975, followed by *Going After Cacciato*, a novel that gave him a permanent foothold in American literature, and for which he received the 1979 National Book Award in Fiction. O'Brien followed the success of *Going after Cacciato* with *The Things They Carried*, a collection of short stories that many critics consider a novel, given the interwoven nature of the individual stories. Depicting the men of Alpha Company and a fictional character named Tim O'Brien, *The Things They Carried* won France's prestigious Prix du Meilleur Livre Étranger, the *Chicago Tribune*'s Heartland Prize, and was nominated for the Pulitzer Prize. *In the Lake of the Woods* (1994), O'Brien's next novel, takes place after the Vietnam War. It received the James Fenimore Cooper Prize from the Society of

COMMON HUMAN EXPERIENCE

O'Brien is best known for his books and short stories that capture the experiences of American soldiers before and after the Vietnam War. Other works that focus on Vietnam War soldiers and veterans include:

Hearts and Minds (1974), a documentary film directed by Peter Davis. This controversial film offers differing viewpoints on the war in Vietnam, many of which suggest that American racism and imperialism prolonged the conflict.

Meditations in Green (1983), a novel by Stephen Wright. This acclaimed war novel focuses on the experiences of James Griffen, a heroin-addicted soldier in Vietnam.

The Best and the Brightest (1972), a nonfiction book by David Halberstam. In this nonfiction work, Vietnam War journalist David Halberstam researches and records the history of U.S. involvement with armed conflict in Vietnam.

Maya Lin: A Strong Clear Vision (1994), a documentary film directed by Frieda Lee Mock. This film explores the life and works of Chinese American artist Maya Lin, who designed the Vietnam Veterans Memorial in 1981 at the age of twenty-one.

Dispatches (1977), a book by Michael Herr. Herr compiled this book based on his notes as a war correspondent in Vietnam.

American Historians and was selected as the Best Work of Fiction of 1994 by *Time* magazine. O'Brien currently holds the Roy F. and Joann Cole Mitte Chair in Creative Writing on alternating years at Texas State University, and he has been a member of the graduate program with the Creative Writing faculty since 1999.

Works in Literary Context

War Literature *Going after Cacciato*, *If I Die in a Combat Zone*, and *The Things They Carried* have all been widely praised as canonical works within the genre of American war literature. Almost all of O'Brien's writings deal with the Vietnam War and his stories commonly blend memories of his own experiences with fictional treatments of such themes as courage, heroism, brutal violence, and emotional upheaval in the face of death and destruction by impersonal, global forces. Commenting on this element of O'Brien's writing, as evidenced in the short story "Spin," Robin Blyn wrote: "[The story] offers the ambiguous, the unfinished, and the wound that will not succumb to the narrative cure. Keeping the wound open, O'Brien's text prevents the neat closure and false redemption of the traditional war story."

Postmodernism Throughout his career, O'Brien has been hailed as a postmodern novelist, a natural outgrowth of what some consider a postmodern war. The American postmodern novel, which emerged with writers such as Joseph Heller and Thomas Pynchon after World War II, generally features a sense of disillusionment and irony, and focuses on the absurdity of the modern, mechanized world. In addition, postmodern works often incorporate wordplay and self-referential allusions—for example, using "Tim O'Brien" as a fictional character in *The Things They Carried*. O'Brien's overt references to his stories as both artifact and truth have caused him to be labeled a postmodern, meta-fictional writer; scholars have noted that truth, artifact, illusion, and fantasy are vehicles through which O'Brien explores the troubling nature of reality, knowledge, and the healing power of literature. Critic Pico Iyer remarked that "O'Brien's clean, incantatory prose always hovers on the edge of dream, and his specialty is that twilight zone of chimeras and fears and fantasies where nobody knows what's true and what is not."

Works in Critical Context

Critics have frequently noted that though O'Brien's work focuses on the Vietnam War, his narratives branch out into broader themes—for example, conflict among family members, betrayal, gender conflict, loss of faith, and social ideology.

Going After Cacciato O'Brien combined experimental narrative with the Vietnam theme in *Going after Cacciato*, winner of the National Book Award in 1979. The chapters read like short stories; several were published separately before the book's compilation, with two tales winning O. Henry awards. *Cacciato* records the dream journey of Paul Berlin, a U.S. infantryman in Vietnam, and alternates this with the "dreamlike" actualities of war. "The fantasy journey is an unworkable idea that nearly sinks the book," claims a reviewer in *Newsweek*. And Mary Hope, writing in *Spectator*, labels *Going after Cacciato* a "strained effort." Other critics issued more positive reviews, praising the writing style and the author's abilities. "O'Brien's writing is crisp, authentic and grimly ironic," declares Richard Freedman in *The New York Times Book Review*. *Washington Post Book World* contributor Robert Wilson also comments on the dream elements, calling them "out of place, hard to reconcile with the evocative realism of the rest of the narrative," but closes by writing that "O'Brien knows the soldier as well as anybody, and is able to make us know him in the unique way that the best fiction can."

The Things They Carried O'Brien returns to the subject of Vietnam and the soldier's viewpoint with *The Things They Carried*, a fictional memoir filled with interconnected stories about the conflict and the people involved. The volume is narrated by a character named "Tim O'Brien," whom the author states is not himself, although there are many similarities. The title, *The Things They Carried*, refers to the things a soldier takes into combat with him: not necessarily all physical items, like weapons, but also intangibles such as fear, exhaustion, and memories. Many reviewers praised O'Brien's work, such as *The New York Times Book Review* contributor Robert R. Harris, who proclaims it "a stunning performance. The overall effect of these original tales is devastating." "O'Brien convinces us that such incredible stories are faithful to the reality of Vietnam," declares Julian Loose in *Times Literary Supplement*. Michiko Kakutani praises O'Brien's prose, describing it as a style "that combines the sharp, unsentimental rhythms of Hemingway with gentler, more lyrical descriptions … [giving] the reader a shockingly visceral sense of what it felt like to tramp through a booby-trapped jungle," and concludes, "With *The Things They Carried*, Mr. O'Brien has written a vital, important book—a book that matters not only to the reader interested in Vietnam, but to anyone interested in the craft of writing as well."

In the Lake of the Woods *In the Lake of the Woods* features a character named John Wade who has just seen his political career destroyed by the public revelation of his presence at the My Lai massacre—a fact he worked hard to hide. O'Brien does not provide definitive answers to certain plot questions, an element that prompted discomfort among some reviewers. Many critics, however, pointed out that the ambiguity of the novel is fitting for the unresolved subject of the war and the My Lai massacre. A critic in the *New York Times Book Review* comments that the book is "a novel about the effects of suppressing a true war story, about the unforgivable uses of history, about what happens when you try to pretend that history no longer exists."

Responses to Literature

1. O'Brien's *In the Lake of the Woods* focuses on the massacre at My Lai, through the viewpoint of an American soldier that participated in it. Research the fiction, history, and documentary films available on the subject of My Lai. How is the massacre represented, and whose viewpoints are favored? Report your findings to the class, and hypothesize what role the My Lai massacre played in the ultimate outcome of the Vietnam War.

2. Scholars have often noted that O'Brien's work has a close kinship with that of postmodern writers such as Thomas Pynchon and Joseph Heller. Research the works of these two authors and compare their depictions of the war experience to that of O'Brien's in *The Things They Carried*. In your opinion, how does the experience of combat lend itself to the development of the postmodern style of writing?

3. Many critics have noted that though O'Brien's works generally feature male protagonists, they often examine gender conflicts faced by soldiers or veterans. Focus on one male/female relationship in

O'Brien's works—for example, that of John Wade and his wife in *In the Lake of the Woods*—and try to form a statement about the roles women play in O'Brien's works.

BIBLIOGRAPHY

Periodicals

Freedman, Richard. Review of *Going After Cacciato*. *New York Times Book Review* (February 12, 1978): 1, 22.

Harris, Robert R. "Too Embarrassed Not to Kill." *The New York Times Book Review* (March 11, 1990): 8.

Hope, Mary. Review of *Going After Cacciato*. *Spectator* (November 25, 1978): 23.

Kakutani, Michiko. Review of *The Things They Carried*. *The New York Times Book Review* (March 11, 1990): 8.

Loose, Julian. Review of *The Things They Carried*. *Times Literary Supplement* (June 29, 1990): 708.

Review of *Going After Cacciato*. *Newsweek* (February 20, 1978).

Wilson, Robert. Review of *Going After Cacciato*. *Washington Post Book World* (February 19, 1978): E4.

⬡ Flannery O'Connor

BORN: *1925, Savannah, Georgia*

DIED: *1964, Milledgeville, Georgia*

NATIONALITY: *American*

GENRE: *Fiction*

MAJOR WORKS:
A Good Man is Hard to Find (1955)
Wise Blood (1952)
Everything That Rises Must Converge (1965)

Overview

Flannery O'Connor is considered one of the foremost short-story writers in American literature. She was an anomaly among post–World War II authors—a Roman Catholic from the Bible-belt South whose stated purpose was to reveal the mystery of God's grace in everyday life. Aware that not all readers shared her faith, O'Connor chose to depict salvation through shocking, often violent actions upon characters who are spiritually or physically grotesque. Moreover, her work shows a penchant for employing ironic detachment and mordant humor within compressed, polished prose. She also infused her fiction with the local color and rich comic detail of her southern milieu, particularly through her skillful presentation of regional dialect. A complex system of symbolism and allegory adds further resonance to O'Connor's writing.

Flannery O'Connor   *O'Connor, Flannery, photograph. AP Images.*

Works in Biographical and Historical Context

Roman Catholic Upbringing   Born in 1925 in Savannah, Georgia, Flannery O'Connor was the only child of devout Roman Catholics from prominent Georgia families. She attended parochial schools in Savannah and public high school in nearby Milledgeville, where the family moved after her father developed disseminated lupus, a degenerative disease that O'Connor later inherited. During this time in the Deep South, Roman Catholics were a small minority in an otherwise Protestant region and were often discriminated against. This may account for O'Connor's fervent identification with the Catholic religion throughout her life and works.

Soon after her father's death, when she was nearly sixteen, O'Connor entered the nearby Georgia State College for Women, where she majored in social sciences.

In her spare time she edited and wrote for school publications to which she also contributed linoleum-block and woodcut cartoons. After graduation, O'Connor enrolled in the graduate writing program at Iowa State University, where she earned her master's degree in 1947 with six stories, including "The Geranium," which had appeared the previous year in the periodical *Accent.*

Return to Georgia   O'Connor began her first novel, *Wise Blood,* while living at Yaddo writers' colony in upstate New York in 1947–48. She continued working on the novel while living in New York City and then in Connecticut, where she boarded with her friends Sally and Robert Fitzgerald, a young married couple who shared O'Connor's Catholic faith and literary interests. However, O'Connor's independent lifestyle ended abruptly at age twenty-five when she suffered her first attack of lupus. From that point onward, O'Connor lived with her mother at Andalusia, a small dairy farm outside Milledgeville, Georgia.

During this period she witnessed the effects of segregation and racial tension in a state heavily influenced by the "Jim Crow" laws that divided Southern society into black and white. She maintained a steady writing pace, publishing *Wise Blood* in 1952, followed by the story collection *A Good Man Is Hard to Find* in 1955, and a second novel, *The Violent Bear It Away,* in 1960. Each volume attracted significant critical attention, and she was awarded three O. Henry prizes for her short stories in addition to several grants and two honorary degrees. Throughout her career, O'Connor's stories were readily published, occasionally by popular magazines, such as *Mademoiselle,* but more often by prestigious literary journals including *Sewanee Review, Shenandoah,* and *Kenyon Review.* As her reputation grew, she traveled when her health permitted to give readings and lectures. O'Connor also enjoyed oil-painting and raising exotic fowl—peacocks, her particular favorites, bear significant symbolic weight in some of her stories. Even during her final illness, which was triggered by abdominal surgery, O'Connor wrote devotedly, and she finished her final story, "Parker's Back," several weeks before she died in 1964.

Works in Literary Context

Influences   O'Connor's artistic style and vision were shaped by a variety of influences. Critics have noted that her stark imagery, caustic satire, and use of the grotesque reflects the black humor tradition exemplified by Nathanael West, whose novel *Miss Lonelyhearts* (1933) was among the twentieth-century works O'Connor most admired. While some commentators were eager to align O'Connor with her Southern contemporaries, including Eudora Welty, Carson McCullers, and Erskine Caldwell, she resisted being confined to regional status, and critics now generally recognize that her aims were wholly different from those of her contemporaries. Nevertheless, many critics note the influence of William Faulkner's fiction on her vision of the southern gothic and her masterful prose rhythms and cadences. Most crucial, however, and underlying all O'Connor's fiction, is her deep grounding in biblical tradition and Catholic theology, which she nurtured all her life with intense reading in not only early Catholic literature, but also works by twentieth-century Catholic apologists. Particularly significant among modern influences were the French Catholic authors Georges Bernanos, François Mauriac, and Pierre Teilhard de Chardin, whose philosophical writings inspired the title of O'Connor's posthumous 1965 short story collection, *Everything That Rises Must Converge*.

Convergence and Redemption   The major theme of *Everything That Rises Must Converge* is derived from Pierre Teilhard de Chardin's *The Phenomenon of Man* (1955). In this work, Teilhard de Chardin asserts that all matter and spirit will eventually converge at what he refers to as the Omega Point. The stories from O'Connor's collection are about man's resistance to this convergence. O'Connor's characters use different methods to avoid convergence or union with mankind, including isolating themselves in intellectualism like Julian and Sheppard, or by clinging to a romanticized version of the past like Julian's mother. It is only through the destruction of pride and false identities that O'Connor's characters have a chance at convergence or redemption, hence the violent climaxes of many of the stories: Julian loses his sense of superiority over and separation from his mother as he watches her die from a stroke; Sheppard realizes the error of his judgment when he finds his son hanging in the attic.

Religion and Spiritual Conflict   In her fiction O'Connor frequently criticizes the materialism and spiritual apathy of contemporary society, faulting modern rationalism and advanced technology for its negation of the need for religious faith and redemption. Employing scenes and characters from her native southern environment, she depicts the violent and often bizarre religiosity of Protestant fundamentalists as a manifestation of spiritual life struggling to exist in a nonspiritual world. Hermione Lee in the *New Statesman* wrote, "Essentially, O'Connor's subject is acceptance: the point at which her sinners become aware of the awful unavoidability of Grace. ... Its masterly realism springs from the life in Georgia, but its intellectual energy, and its penetration of grotesque extremes, derives from the faith." The protagonists of both of her novels—Hazel Motes in *Wise Blood* and Francis Marion Tarwater in *The Violent Bear It Away*—experience intense spiritual conflict. Often considered "Christ-haunted" characters, they are tormented by visions of God and the devil and by the temptation to deny the reality of their revelations. Critics have described O'Connor's protagonists as grotesque in personality, inclined to violence, and isolated and frustrated by their spiritual struggle.

Reflecting the religious themes of her novels, a recurring motif in O'Connor's short stories is that of divine grace descending in an often bizarre or violent manner upon a spiritually deficient main character. She often depicts a rural

LITERARY AND HISTORICAL CONTEMPORARIES

O'Connor's literary and historical contemporaries include:

Eudora Welty (1909–2001): This short story writer and Pulitzer Prize-winning novelist was known for stories that captured the landscapes and people of her native Mississippi.

William Faulkner (1897–1962): One of the most famous American authors of the twentieth century, Mississippi-born Faulkner is best known for his novels *Absalom, Absalom!* (1936) and *Light in August* (1932).

Carson McCullers (1917–1967): McCullers, a native of Georgia, was known to employ the Southern gothic tradition in such works as *The Heart is a Lonely Hunter* (1940).

Tennessee Williams (1911–1983): This Pulitzer Prize-winning Southern playwright was best known for his dramas *The Glass Menagerie* (1945), *A Streetcar Named Desire* (1948), and *Cat on Hot Tin Roof* (1955).

Walker Percy (1916–1990): Like Welty, Percy was a Southern Catholic writer. His most famous novel, *The Moviegoer* (1961) won the National Book Award in 1962.

domestic situation suddenly invaded by a criminal or perverse outsider—a distorted Christ figure who redeems a protagonist afflicted with pride, intellectualism, or materialism. In one of O'Connor's best-known stories, "A Good Man Is Hard to Find," for example, a smugly self-complacent grandmother is shocked into spiritual awareness by a murderer who kills first her family and then her.

The New South   A religious writer who defined her "subject in fiction" as "the action of grace in territory held largely by the devil," O'Connor nevertheless believed good writing begins in a concrete "experience, not an abstraction." Her writing reflects this by being firmly rooted in her native South. Her Catholic family lived in Milledgeville, Georgia, since before the American Civil War, and O'Connor herself witnessed and wrote about the racial tensions of the Deep South during the decades of the twentieth century still affected by segregation and the Jim Crow laws. "Ours is a real Bible Belt," she once said. "We have a sense of the absolute ... a sense of Moses' face as he pulverized the idols ... a sense of time, place and eternity joined." Alice Walker noted that it was for O'Connor's characterizations "that I appreciated her work at first ... these white folks without the magnolia ... and these black folks without melons and superior racial patience, these are like the Southerners that I know." John Idol summed up Flannery O'Connor's fiction as follows: "In the twelve or fifteen of her best stories Miss O'Connor aptly blended satire and reverence, the concrete and the abstract, the comic and the cosmic, earning for herself a secure place among the writers of the Southern Renascence."

COMMON HUMAN EXPERIENCE

O'Connor is known for employing the Southern gothic into her works. Her novels and stories often use bizarre or grotesque characters or situations to present ideas related to religious or spiritual themes. Other works that sustain a sense of the Southern gothic include:

Absalom, Absalom! (1936), a novel by William Faulkner. In this acclaimed novel, often considered a Modernist masterpiece, Faulkner tells the story of the rise and fall of plantation owner Thomas J. Sutpen and his family.

Bastard Out of Carolina (1993), an autobiographical memoir by Dorothy Allison. In this controversial work, Allison tells of her upbringing in a poor family in a small town, and describes the sexual abuse she suffered at the hand of her stepfather.

A Confederacy of Dunces (1980), a novel by John Kennedy Toole. This novel, published eleven years after the author's suicide, chronicles a young man's experiences in the French Quarter of New Orleans in the 1960s.

Raney (1985), a novel by Clyde Edgerton. This novel chronicles the first two years of marriage of the protagonist Raney Bell and her husband, a devout Southern Christian.

The Heart is a Lonely Hunter (1940), a novel by Carson McCullers. This story focuses on misfits and outcasts of a small Southern town.

Works in Critical Context

A. L. Rowse called Flannery O'Connor "probably the greatest short-story writer of our time," and this opinion is not unique among critics. Considering her limited output as a writer, the critical response to her canon has been extraordinary. More than a dozen books, chapters in many more, and hundreds of articles have been devoted to O'Connor's work. As Josephine Hendin noted in *The World of Flannery O'Connor*, the author produced "a body of work of remarkable uniformity and persistent design." Her themes have been identified by Stanley Edgar Hyman as the "profound equation of the mysteries of sex and religion ... change of identity, transformation, death-and-rebirth ... the perverse mother ... [and] the transvaluation of values in which progress in the world is retrogression in the spirit."

A Good Man is Hard to Find Though Flannery O'Connor's stories in *A Good Man is Hard to Find* deal with the violent and grotesque, the collection received almost universal praise. As critic Ted R. Spivey explained, O'Connor dealt with violent and grotesque people because "man has in his soul a powerful destructive element, which often makes him behave in a violent and grotesque manner. ... [Her writing is about] the existen-tial struggle with the principle of destruction traditionally called the Devil." Numerous critics see this preoccupation with the demonic as a central characteristic of O'Connor's work. In opposition to this evil force O'Connor places a God whose "grace hits the characters in [her] stories with the force of a mugging," Josephine Hendin wrote. The climactic moments of grace in her stories and in her characters' lives have been described by Preston M. Browning, Jr., as "those moments when her characters undergo a traumatic collapse of their illusions of righteousness and self-sufficiency." As *Washington Post* critic William McPherson put it, "the question behind Miss O'Connor's stories is not whether God exists—he's there, all right—but whether men can bear it."

Wise Blood Initial reviewers of *Wise Blood* praised O'Connor's rich imagery, powerful symbolism, and skillful rendering of Southern dialect, but found her characterizations two-dimensional and shockingly monstrous. Later critics generally discussed the book's satirical, theological, and ironic elements, the quest motif, and whether the protagonist, Haze, is finally redeemed. Obsessed with Christ and the notion of original sin, Haze has a mechanical rigidity and monomaniacal obsession with beliefs that are absurdly comic. While some commentators found O'Connor's portrayal of Haze cartoonish, others argued that realism was not her intention in *Wise Blood*. Lewis A. Lawson explained that Haze was conceived "as an exemplum, as a vehicle whose attitudes and actions would personify a spiritual view which [O'Connor] wished to reveal." Lawson added that Haze represents an example "of the deadly effect that Southern fundamentalism could have on the soul, warping and terrorizing it so completely with its perversion of Christian doctrine that the soul in rebellion rejects entirely the idea of orthodox Christianity."

Some commentators have considered Haze a madman unable to redeem others or to be redeemed himself. While most believe that he is saved, others concur with Ben Satterfield: "Those who claim Haze is redeemed mistake his acts of penance, if that is what they are, for the goal they are employed to achieve; they mistake the means for the end. But atonement is not redemption and should not be confused with it." Satterfield has accused some critics of guilelessly accepting O'Connor's own comments about her work and of being too eager to find redemption in everything she wrote. Richard Giannone stated: "[In] his own mental way Haze is a martyr in the original sense of the word as giving testimony to the truth, sealed in his own suffering and unwise blood."

Everything That Rises Must Converge Most critics discuss the relationship of *Everything That Rises Must Converge* to the ideas of Catholic theologian Pierre Teilhard de Chardin, who believed that all spiritual and physical matter would eventually converge and that the soul would be redeemed. The title's obvious allusion to Teilhard de Chardin's work is commonly accepted. However, reviewers disagree about O'Connor's intentions. Some argue that she accepts Teilhard de Chardin's ideas, and the stories are her attempt to portray true convergence. Others, including Robert Fitzgerald in the introduction to the work, assert that O'Connor uses the title ironically. As Fitzgerald wrote, "There is quite a gamut of [comedy,] running from something very like cartooning to an irony dry and refined, especially in the treatment of the most serious matters."

Responses to Literature

1. Flannery O'Connor was born in Georgia in 1925, and died there in 1964, just before the height of the American civil rights movement. Research the history of race relations in the Deep South during this period, paying special attention to Jim Crow laws and the landmark court case, *Brown v. The Board of Education*. In your opinion, how do these historic events affect the characters and situations in O'Connor's works? Can you see a shift in perspective in her treatment of race between early and later stories?

2. Critics have often noted that the title for Flannery O'Connor's last collection is taken from the works of French Catholic theologian Pierre Teilhard de Chardin. Research his *The Phenomenon of Man* and try to find thematic links to O'Connor's stories. Do you think that O'Connor is attempting to portray the idea of convergence in a straightforward manner, or do you agree with critic Robert Fitzgerald, who believes that O'Connor treats the concept with a spirit of irony?

3. Since the publication of *Wise Blood* in 1952, critics have argued over Flannery O'Connor's portrayal of the Southern fundamentalist, Haze. Some critics consider Haze a madman, while others believe he is redeemed by the end of the novel. Review the novel and read the critical interpretations of Haze. What is your opinion of this character? Construct an essay in which you argue for or against Haze's redemption.

BIBLIOGRAPHY

Books

Baumgaertner, Jill P. *Flannery O'Connor: A Proper Scaring*. Chicago: Cornerstone Press, 1998.

Bloom, Harold, ed. *Flannery O'Connor*. New York: Chelsea House Publishers, 1998.

Driskell, Leon V., and Joan T. Brittain. *The Eternal Crossroads: The Art of Flannery O'Connor*. Lexington, Ky.: University Press of Kentucky, 1971.

Enjolras, Laurence. *Flannery O'Connor's Characters*. Lanham, Md.:University Press of America, 1998.

Hendin, Josephine. "The Enduring Conflict: Parents & Children in *Everything That Rises Must Converge*." In *The World of Flannery O'Connor*. Bloomington: Indiana University Press, 1970, 97–130.

Lawson, Lewis. "Flannery O'Connor and the Grotesque: *Wise Blood*." In *Flannery O'Connor*, edited by Robert Reiter, 52. St. Louis: B. Herder Books, 1968.

McMullen, Joanne Halleran. *Writing Against God: Language as Message in the Literature of Flannery O'Connor*. Macon, Ga.: Mercer University Press, 1996.

Oates, Joyce Carol. "The Visionary Art of Flannery O'Connor." In *New Heaven, New Earth: The Visionary Experience in Literature*. New York: The Vanguard Press, Inc., 1974, 174–76.

Spivey, Ted Ray. *Flannery O'Connor: The Woman, the Thinker, the Visionary*. Macon, Ga.: Mercer University Press, 1995.

Whitt, Margaret Earley. *Understanding Flannery O'Connor*. Columbia, S.C.: University of South Carolina, 1995.

Periodicals

Satterfield, Ben. "*Wise Blood*, Artistic Anemia, and the Hemorrhaging of O'Connor Criticism," *Studies in American Fiction*, Vol. 17, No. 1, Spring, 1989, pp. 33–50.

Lee, Hermione. Review of Flannery O'Connor. *New Statesman*, December 7, 1979.

Howe, Irving. "Flannery O'Connor's Stories." In *The New York Review of Books*, Vol. V, No. 4, September 30, 1965, pp. 16–7.

Rosenfeld, Isaac. "To Win by Default." In *New Republic*, July 7, 1952, pp. 19–20.

Schott, Webster. "Flannery O'Connor: Faith's Stepchild." In *The Nation*, Vol. 201, No. 7, September 13, 1965, pp. 142–44, 146.

✸ Clifford Odets

BORN: *1906, Philadelphia, Pennsylvania*

DIED: *1963, Los Angeles, California*

NATIONALITY: *American*

GENRE: *Drama, screenplays*

MAJOR WORKS:

Waiting for Lefty (1935)

Awake and Sing! (1935)

Golden Boy (1937)

None But the Lonely Heart (1944)

The Country Girl (1950)

Overview

One of the most prominent American playwrights of the 1930s, Clifford Odets realistically portrayed Depression-era Americans searching for a place in modern society. He never lived up to early critical acclaim which compared him favorably with Anton Chekhov and Eugene O'Neill, however, and eventually settled into a financially successful, yet lackluster, Hollywood career. His best plays retain

Clifford Odets   *Odets, Clifford, photograph. AP Images.*

historical significance for their portrayal of American, especially Jewish American, life during and after the Great Depression. His play *Awake and Sing!* (1935) is regarded as a major turning point in the portrayal of Jews on the American stage.

Works in Biographical and Historical Context

Finding His Own Path   Born on July 18, 1906, in Philadelphia, Pennsylvania, Odets was the son of Louis J. Odets, and his wife Pearl (Geisinger). His father was a printer when he was born, but by the time Odets was six, the family moved to a Jewish neighborhood in the Bronx, New York. There, his father moved from working as a feeder at a printing plant, to becoming the plant's owner. The family was solidly middle-class, and eventually returned to Philadelphia where his father became the vice president of a boiler company and later owned an advertising agency.

A melancholy child, Odets quit Morris High School in 1923 and pursued poetry writing for a time, provoking his father's anger and disappointment, as he expected his son to follow him into the family advertising business. At fifteen, Odets decided to become a stage actor, to which his parents gave their qualified approval. He acted with small theater groups, and also performed in radio plays, vaudeville acts, and summer stock productions. While Odets was

still finding his way in the world, he allegedly attempted suicide three times before the age of twenty-five.

Influenced by the Great Depression   By 1930, Odets was living alone in New York City. While his family's business was still prospering, he grew increasingly aware of the destructive impact of the Great Depression on the city's suffering masses. The stock market crash of 1929 had effectively launched the Great Depression. The stock market crashed because an investment boom, which began in 1924, was fueled by investors buying stocks on margin (in which investors took out loans to buy stocks for as little as a ten percent down payment) and with purely speculative money. The stocks themselves became wildly overvalued, and their value plummeted as the economy took a downturn. The failure of the stock market caused the economy, first in the United States and then the world, to fall into a dramatic and sustained depression which lasted through the 1930s. Nearly every American was affected in some way by this economic crisis, with one out of every four able-bodied workers unable to find a job at the height of the troubles.

In 1930, Odets joined the Group Theatre, founded by Harold Clurman, Cheryl Crawford, and Lee Strasberg. This theatre was intended to be both a training ground for actors and an idealistic collective which would attempt to change society through the onstage presentation of alternative values. Odets gained little recognition in the organization as an actor—he was apparently a poor one—but did gain prominence as a playwright. His plays reflected the leftist values he espoused after briefly joining the Communist Party in 1934. A small number of Americans joined the Communist Party in the 1930s, believing communism—with its philosophy of sharing wealth equally among the working class—was the answer to the United States' economic problems.

Successful Playwright   Odets became an immediate sensation with the Group Theatre's production of his play *Waiting for Lefty* (1935). This play centers around a taxi drivers' union preparing to vote on whether or not they should go on strike. Though it was popular on Broadway, its production was later banned in several cities. Later in 1935, Odets garnered wide popular acclaim for *Awake and Sing!* It focuses on a poverty-stricken Jewish family living in the Bronx and dealing with difficult life circumstances. In later years, this play became seen in retrospect as perhaps Odets' most important work.

Soon after, Odets accepted an offer from Paramount Studios to work as a scriptwriter. He was accused by his peers of selling out, but Odets contended that his earnings could help finance the Group Theatre. Among his early screenplays was an adaptation of *The General Died at Dawn* (1936) from the novel by Charles G. Booth.

Greatest Commercial Success   Having moved away from leftist politics, Odets returned to New York City and the Group Theatre in 1937. He wrote more plays for the company, including *Golden Boy* (1937), which was the first of four to focus on personal relationships rather than direct social criticism. *Golden Boy* became the greatest commercial success of his career. The story of a young man trying to decide between careers as a violinist and a boxer, who ultimately destroys himself, the play reflected Odets's love of music and anticipated his own idealistic turmoil as well.

Following the failure of Odets's play *Clash by Night* (1941), the Group Theatre disbanded and he returned to Hollywood. In 1944, he wrote a screenplay adaptation of *None But the Lonely Heart* (1943), a novel by Richard Llewellyn. It is considered one of his best screenplays, along with *Humoresque* (1946), which he co-adapted with Zachary Gold from the short story by Fannie Hurst.

During this time period, the United States—like much of Europe and Asia—was embroiled in World War II. The war began when Nazi Germany, led by Adolf Hitler, invaded Poland in September 1939 and overran the country. England and France declared war on Germany, but Germany soon controlled much of the European continent. The United States entered the war in 1941, after Japan bombed an American naval base in Hawaii. The war was fought in a number of theaters in Europe, Asia, Africa, and the South Pacific, involving sixty-one countries and leaving fifty-five million people dead.

Old Ghosts and Stalled Plays In the late 1940s, Odets continued to occasionally write dramas, primarily semi-autobiographical dramas with psychological overtones and little social commentary. *The Country Girl* (1950)—about an alcoholic actor who attempts a comeback on Broadway with the help of his wife, upon whom he is totally dependent—was his last major success in the theater. *The Flowering Peach* (1954), his last completed play, was an adaptation of the biblical story of Noah in terms of Jewish life.

In 1952, Odets was forced to testify in front of the House Un-American Activities Committee (HUAC). In the late 1940s and early 1950s, HUAC investigated charges of Americans working in government, Hollywood, and other professions about alleged Communist activities, beliefs, and leanings. Over six million people were checked by a security program implemented by President Harry S. Truman, and several hundred lost their jobs and/or were jailed as a result of the hearings. When Odets appeared, he spoke about his earlier Communist activities—including a brief trip to Cuba in 1935 to investigate conditions there with other Communists—but his statements did little to enhance his personal reputation as he mentioned the names of individuals he believed to have been Communist Party members in the 1930s. Odets was not blacklisted like other prominent entertainment figures, however, and returned to California.

After the death of his second wife, actress Betty Grayson, in the mid-1950s, Odets started several plays but failed to complete them. He was, however, able to write for the screen. Thus, Odets continued to live and work in Holly-

LITERARY AND HISTORICAL CONTEMPORARIES

Clifford Odets's famous contemporaries include:

Lee Strasberg (1901–1982): A co-founder of the Group Theatre, Strasberg was a stage director who became better known as the artistic director and primary force behind the Actors Studio. This highly respected acting school taught the "Method" approach to the craft.

Fritz Lang (1890–1976): This Austrian-born film director helmed the film adaptation of Odets's play *Clash by Night* (1952). Lang also directed such classics as *Metropolis* (1927).

Joseph McCarthy (1908–1957): This American senator conducted a highly controversial campaign against supposed Communist infiltration of the U.S. government during the late 1940s and early 1950s. His actions led to the term "McCarthyism."

Arthur Miller (1915–2005): Considered the preeminent playwright of the twentieth century, Miller's realistic dramas explored the complex psychological and social issues that plagued mankind in the post–World War II period. His best known work is *Death of a Salesman* (1949).

Ring Lardner, Jr. (1915–2000): This American screenwriter won two Academy Awards for his work, but saw his career essentially destroyed by the HUAC hearings conducted by Joseph McCarthy. Among Lardner's best known works was *Woman of the Year* (1941), which he co-wrote with Michael Kanin.

wood, but continued to alternately defend and disparage his film work as he had for the years he worked in Hollywood. He wrote such screenplays as *The Story on Page One* (1960) and *Wild in the Country* (1961). Odets also directed *The Story on Page One*, and Elvis Presley starred in the latter. Working on a dramatic series for television at the time of his death, Odets died in Los Angeles, California, on August 14, 1963.

Works in Literary Context

Very much a product of his time, Odets was spurred to write plays of social impact by the events of the 1930s, primarily the Great Depression. While his early plays have an explicit socialist message, later plays moderated this tone. Although his techniques changed considerably during the course of his career—from the strident call to action of *Waiting for Lefty* to the quiet allegory of *The Flowering Peach*—Odets primarily wrote about the individual trying to preserve a sense of identity in an often hostile world. His plays are filled with brilliant dialogue (including an emphasis on Jewish idioms), an emphasis on the importance of family, and a profound belief in the

COMMON HUMAN EXPERIENCE

Many plays by Odets—including *Golden Boy*, *Clash by Night*, and *Paradise Lost*—examine the spiritual consequences of self-determined inaction. Here are some other dramas with a similar theme:

> *The Glass Menagerie* (1944), a play by Tennessee Williams. In this drama, a young man reminisces about a sad incident in his youth while living in a St. Louis tenement in the 1930s with his domineering mother and handicapped sister.
>
> *Desire Under the Elms* (1924), a play by Eugene O'Neill. In this drama, set in 1850 at the Cabot family farm, the characters in the play vie for its possession and their possessiveness generates isolation and loneliness.
>
> *Winterset* (1935), a play by Maxwell Anderson. This tragedy in verse follows the quest of Mio Romagna to prove his father's innocence in the years after Bartolomeo Romagna was executed for a robbery and murder he did not commit. Complicating his journey is Mio's love relationship with Miriamne Esdras and her family.
>
> *Orpheus Descending* (1958), a play by Tennessee Williams. In this drama, a young charismatic musician descends on a small, repressive Southern town, and forms a relationship with a passionate woman with a tragic past who is trapped in a bad marriage.

dignity of the human race. As a writer, Odets was influenced by the events of the 1930s, the communal life influence of the Group Theatre, and his Jewish background and childhood. Authors such as Victor Hugo also inspired Odets as a writer.

Proletarian Drama   Odets was briefly a member of the Communist Party in 1934, and his first three produced plays—*Waiting for Lefty*, *Awake and Sing!*, and *Paradise Lost*—were all written during his brief association with that group. These plays confirm leftist principles while declaring archaic the values of middle-class America in the 1930s. Odets also employed Jewish street idioms to great effect. With *Waiting for Lefty*, Odets structured the play so that the personal problems of the characters reflected the conflict between the union and the taxi company, mirroring the struggle of the working class, or proletariat, against the wealthy business owners that Communists were rebelling against. *Awake and Sing!* examines the aspirations of a Jewish working-class family that has become disillusioned by an oppressive economic system. In *Paradise Lost*, a middle-class businessman and his family are destroyed by a series of disasters. Each character in the play represents a particular middle-class value, and the catastrophes that befall them symbolize the fall of these values in the 1930s.

Individual Integrity   The basic theme of all Odets's plays is simply the struggle of the individual to maintain his or her integrity. This integrity, as well as sense of self, was challenged by the events of the Great Depression of the 1930s, and impacted family and love relationships as well as corrupt businesses. *Golden Boy*, for example, focuses on Jon Bonaparte, a musician turned prizefighter who becomes successful, but destroys himself by going against his nature. In the play, Odets depicts his loss of integrity as a tragedy, the result of faulty decisions and changes in values which corrupted him. Mid-career plays like *Rocket to the Moon* (1938), *Night Music* (1940), and *Clash by Night* (1941) are love stories which touch on the topic of integrity. *Rocket to the Moon*, in particular, deals with loneliness and the need for love, noting how conditions within and outside humans impede attaining love. In *The Big Knife* (1949), a movie actor is offered a multi-million-dollar contract but wants to escape the corruption of the film industry and return to the New York stage, thereby regaining his integrity.

Works in Critical Context

By the end of 1935, Odets's impressive first year as a playwright, many critics praised him as a genius who spoke for the American people. Later, however, critics, labeled Odets's early works as propaganda, with stereotypical characters and obvious messages. More recently, critics have re-appraised his plays, and his work became appreciated for its dialogue—especially for realistically capturing Jewish American idioms—and the author's belief in the nobility of humanity. Once criticized for a lack of character development in his plays, Odets also impressed such critics for delivering emotional impact to his audiences while skillfully communicating the economic and spiritual insecurity of the American experience. In general, whatever faults have been found in Odets's plays have been transcended by his writing skill, especially regarding his character presentation and language.

Awake and Sing!   Many critics believe that *Awake and Sing!* is among Odets's finest plays. When first performed, most critics found the play enjoyable and indicative of the emergence of a new important playwright. Stark Young writes in the *New Republic*, "*Awake and Sing* shows great promise, especially in the field of melodrama. It begins, moves along and develops with real skill. The attention it exacts is definite and constant." Another contemporary critic, Grenville Vernon of the *Commonweal*, was even more enthusiastic. Vernon lauds Odets and his work by writing, "Mr. Odets's play proves to be one of the truest, most vital productions of the year, a play which deserves a place in the front rank of American drama." Scholars who later wrote about *Awake and Sing!* were impressed about how the play resonated over time. Richard H. Goldstone in *Proceedings of the IVth Congress of the International Comparative Literature Association* writes:

What makes the play both arresting and important is that from unpromising basic materials—the Bergers are, after all, a commonplace group—Odets has created characters who join the line of older American families: the Laphams, the Babbitts, the Compsons, the Gants, and the Joads.

Golden Boy Many critics consider *Golden Boy* Odets's most successful play and the first to gain a wide audience. In *The Nation*, Joseph Wood Krutch gives much praise to the play, noting "the piece exhibits unmistakable power and genuine originality." Krutch also writes, "There are moments when *Golden Boy* seems near to greatness ..." Young, reviewing the play in the *New Republic*, was particularly impressed by the way Odets drew his characters. Young writes, "He has a sense of character drawing that exhibits the courage of outline. An unusual number of the characters in *Golden Boy* are set beside one another with the right bold theatre instinct ..." In *The New York Times*, Brooks Atkinson calls it "one of his best plays" and concludes that "it is a pithy and thoroughly absorbing drama that restores to the theatre a pungent theatrical talent."

Responses to Literature

1. Research HUAC's investigation into Communist influence in Hollywood. In a paper, address how Odets's experience while testifying compares to other Hollywood figures. Do you think such hearings could be held today? Why or why not?

2. In a small group, watch the film *Evan Almighty* (2007) and read Odets's *The Flowering Peach* as well as the biblical story of Noah on which both stories are based. Discuss how the different authors interpret the story. Which version do you think is most effective? Why?

3. Research the Great Depression and its effect on Americans, especially those living in New York City. Create a presentation in which you explore one of Odets's early plays and the effect the Great Depression had on its characters—economically, socially, or otherwise.

4. Research Americans embracing Communism in the 1930s. In an essay, link your findings to one of Odets's first three plays. How do you interpret the leftist influence on the play?

BIBLIOGRAPHY

Books

Brenman-Gibson, Margaret. *Clifford Odets, An American Biography: The Years from 1960 to 1940.* New York: Athenaeum, 1981.

Gladstone, Richard H. "The Making of Americans: Clifford Odets's Implicit Theme." *Proceedings of the IVth Congress of the International Comparative Literature Association*, edited by François Jost. Paris: Mouton & Co., 1966, pp. 654–660.

Weales, Gerald. *Clifford Odets, the Playwright.* New York: Methuen, 1985.

Periodicals

Atkinson, Brooks. "*Golden Boy*: Clifford Odets Rewards the Group Theatre with One of His Best Plays." *The New York Times* (November 21, 1937): sec. 2, p. 1.

Krutch, Joseph Wood. A review of *Golden Boy*. *The Nation* (November 13, 1937): 540.

Vernon, Grenville. A review of *Awake and Sing! The Commonweal* (March 15, 1935): 570.

Young, Stark. A review of *Golden Boy*. *The New Republic* (November 17, 1937): 44–45.

———. "Awake and Whistle at Least." *The New Republic* (March 13, 1935): 134.

❋ Frank O'Hara

BORN: *1926, Baltimore, Maryland*

DIED: *1966, Mastic Beach, New York*

NATIONALITY: *American*

GENRE: *Poetry, art criticism*

MAJOR WORKS:
Lunch Poems (1964)

Overview

A member of the New York School of Poets, Frank O'Hara applied the techniques of Abstract Expressionist painting and French Surrealism to his writing. He constructed poems in which he often employed words as units of form and sound without meaning, and juxtaposed seemingly random images and ideas. His poetry is noted for its rather cluttered style. In his verse, O'Hara eschewed

Frank O'Hara *O'Hara, Frank, photograph. AP Images.*

traditional meter and poetic diction in favor of a random outpouring of objects and imagery. Often compared to Walt Whitman and William Carlos Williams, O'Hara drew on mundane details from urban life to create poetry characterized by immediacy and apparent superficiality.

Works in Biographical and Historical Context

Music and War Born Frances Russell O'Hara on March 27, 1926, in Baltimore, Maryland, he was the son of Russell J. O'Hara and his wife, Katherine (Broderick). O'Hara was raised in Grafton, Massachusetts, a suburb of Worcester. While growing up, he was a serious music student and wanted to be a concert pianist. O'Hara traveled every Saturday to Boston to take piano lessons, while attending St. John's High School in Worcester during the week. When O'Hara completed his high school education, World War II was already underway.

The war began when Nazi Germany, led by Adolf Hitler, invaded Poland in September 1939 and overran the country. England and France declared war on Germany, but Germany soon controlled much of the European continent. The United States entered the war in 1941, after Japan bombed an American naval base in Hawaii. The war was fought in a number of theaters in Europe, Asia, Africa, and the South Pacific, involving sixty-one countries and leaving fifty-five million people dead. O'Hara himself served in the U.S. Navy as a sonarman third class on the destroyer U.S.S. *Nicholas* for two years in the South Pacific during the conflict.

Harvard and a Hopwood After the war's end and his discharge from the military, O'Hara entered Harvard College in 1946. He first studied music, with the goal of becoming a concert pianist. O'Hara later switched to English for his major, and decided he wanted to be a writer. While a student, he wrote his first poems and met John Ashbery and Kenneth Koch, poets with whom he was later associated as a member of a literary circle known as the New York School of Poets. O'Hara was also a founder of the Poet's Theatre in Cambridge, Massachusetts.

After graduating from Harvard in 1950, O'Hara entered a master's program in English and creative writing at the University of Michigan in Ann Arbor. While a student, he won a Hopwood Award for a collection of poems, "A Byzantine Place," and the verse play *Try! Try!* in 1951. O'Hara was granted his master's degree that year and then moved to New York City.

Immersed in the World of Art In 1952, O'Hara published his first poetry collection, *A City Winter, and Other Poems*, followed by *Oranges* (1953). Both were published by the Tibor de Nagy Gallery. He was also employed briefly first as a private secretary to photographer Cecil Beaton, then at the front desk of the Museum of Modern Art as a sales clerk. O'Hara resigned the latter post to become an editorial associate of the publication *Art News* from 1953 to 1955. While working there, he, at times, contributed reviews and occasional articles. O'Hara rejoined the Museum of Modern Art in 1955 as a special assistant in the International Program. By 1960, he had been promoted to associate curator.

During this period, O'Hara organized many seminal exhibitions by Abstract Expressionist painters such as Willem de Kooning and Mark Rothko, as well as the sculptor David Smith and painters of the New York School, including Grace Hartigan and Michael Goldberg. O'Hara was an astute art critic and wrote an influential monograph on painter Jackson Pollock, a close friend. His art criticism was collected posthumously in *Art Chronicles 1954–66* (1975) and *Standing Still and Walking in New York* (1983).

Growing Popularity While working at the Museum of Modern Art, O'Hara published five collections of poetry. Like his earlier works, most were published in limited editions and not widely available. He was an improvisational writer who often dashed off poems on his lunch hour or in the company of other people. *Mediations in An Emergency* (1957) was the first of his poetry collections to be widely circulated. *Odes* (1960) included five serigraphs by Michael Goldberg.

That same year, O'Hara published a long poem, *Second Avenue* (1960), which had been written in 1953. The ambitious poem was composed of eleven parts which featured a catalogue of random juxtapositions. With the publication of *Lunch Poems* (1964), his reputation gained ground. The last collection published while O'Hara was alive was *Love Poems* (1965), which included a number of poems about his male lovers, including a series dedicated to dancer Vincent Warren. O'Hara was gay at a time when homosexuality was not accepted by mainstream America. Certain urban areas like New York City, however, had an active gay community and subculture.

Early Death After being struck by a dune buggy taxi cab on Fire Island, a well-known gay resort near New York City, O'Hara died on July 24, 1966, at the age of forty. After his death, his poetry received more attention than while he was alive. He won a National Book Award in 1972 for one of many posthumous collections of his poetry, *The Collected Poems of Frank O'Hara* (1971). O'Hara also wrote a number of plays gathered retrospectively in *Selected Plays* (1978), while his essays were collected in *Standing Still and Walking in New York* (1975).

Works in Literary Context

A highly innovative postmodern poet, Frank O'Hara's work was unusual in its stylistic diversity. His work ranges from early surrealistic pieces to his exuberant and highly original "I do this I do that" poems, which chart his walks around New York during his lunch hour. Above all an urban poet, O'Hara wrote poems that are notable for the way they map New York in the 1950s and 1960s, but also link it to wider global, historical, and psychological spaces.

The joyful profusion of visual detail in his poetry reflects the poet's exuberant vision of life, especially of the urban scene. O'Hara was also influenced by the gay culture and lifestyle of which he was a part, and included mentions of his male lovers, as well as close male and female friendships in his poetry. As a poet, O'Hara was influenced by a variety of authors and interests including European symbolism and surrealism; the American poetic tradition of Walt Whitman, William Carlos Williams, and Hart Crane; Abstract Expressionist painting; Pop Art; cinema; and classical and contemporary music.

Influence of Gay Culture O'Hara's poetry contains many allusions to gay culture and activities, such as cruising and cross-dressing, and his poems sometimes adopt attitudes that are campy or ethically transgressive. His poetry, nonetheless, is not as unambiguously gay as that of Allen Ginsberg. In some O'Hara poems, it is not apparent that the poet's lover is male. His homosexuality is most obvious in the vocabulary and style of some of his poems: it has a linguistic, as much as a thematic, presence in his work. This more implicit referencing of his sexuality does not, however, stem from political or social evasiveness about his sexual identity. Instead, his poems convey a fluid and open sense of gender and sexual boundaries, creating a "morphing" sexuality that is more reflective of today's discourses and practices than of those most visible in the 1950s and 1960s.

Everyday Details of Urban Life Personal but not confessional, many of O'Hara's poems document daily experiences. It is poetry of observation, not mediation. O'Hara did not distinguish between art and life—for him the two were inexorably linked. Often described as spontaneous and nonreferential, O'Hara's poems create a collage of seemingly insignificant details from urban life. He often treats significant events in a trivial fashion, and often includes fleeting images that lack a frame of reference. "The Day Lady Died," for instance, contrasts the mundane activities of an ordinary day with a few concluding lines concerning Billie Holiday and her death. "Personal Poem" lacks any periods or rests, suggesting that objects and ideas are events that should be immediately consumed and dropped. O'Hara's focus on everyday details reveals the significance inherent in all aspects of experience, and suggests that the value of life is equivalent to the vitality with which it is experienced. O'Hara's focus on the present, as evidenced by his fast-paced style, has also been interpreted as a warning against dwelling on the past, an explicit theme in *The General Returns from One Place to Another* (1962), a play in which a caricature of General Douglas MacArthur attempts to recapture past glory.

Cultural Images and Myths Many of O'Hara's poems reflect his interest in cultural images and myths. In his poem "On Seeing Larry Rivers' Washington Crossing the Delaware at the Museum of Modern Art," for example, O'Hara mocks America's first president, George

---

LITERARY AND HISTORICAL CONTEMPORARIES

Frank O'Hara's famous contemporaries include:

Larry Rivers (1924–2002): This Abstract Expressionist painter was a close friend of O'Hara's. Rivers first made a reputation for himself as a jazz saxophonist, then came to prominence for his figurative paintings which combined the highbrow with low culture.

Edward Gorey (1925–2000): O'Hara's roommate at Harvard, Gorey became a well-known illustrator, writer, and designer. His pen-and-ink drawings and books were noted for their arch humor and gothic sensibility. Among his books is *The Doubtful Guest* (1957), aimed at young readers.

Jack Kerouac (1922–1969): This Beat Generation writer was known as the father of the movement. Among his best-known works is the novel *On the Road* (1957).

Robert Creeley (1926–2005): One of the "Black Mountain Poets," his poetry is noted as much for its concision as its emotional power. Among his best-known poetry collections is *Later* (1979).

Charles Olson (1910–1970): Considered a major influence on American poetry after World War II, Olson was a central figure in the Black Mountain school of poetry. Among his best-known works is *The Maximus Poems 1–10* (1953).

Washington, as well as the heroic myth associated with the general. O'Hara depicts him as anxious, cold, and fearful. At the same time, however, he pays tribute to Washington and re-mythologizes the crossing by approaching an authentic rendering of the historical event, while portraying Washington as a complex person engaged in a dangerous and difficult endeavor.

Works in Critical Context

Although early critical reaction to O'Hara's poetry was mixed, his reputation increased steadily after his death, and critics have noted his immense influence on subsequent poets. Most critics have focused on the importance O'Hara imputes to the present and the trivial. In explaining the apparent superficiality of his poetry, critics have argued that O'Hara's poems lack depth because of the way he treats significant events. Many reviewers believed that the full range and power of O'Hara's work was revealed only posthumously in editions of his work like *The Collected Poems of Frank O'Hara* and *Poems Retrieved* (1977). Currently, his reputation is secure as an important and even popular poet in the great upsurge of American poetry following World War II.

COMMON HUMAN EXPERIENCE

O'Hara was a member of the New York School of Poets. Here are some poetry collections by other poets in the group:

Poems (1953), a poetry collection by Kenneth Koch. In this collection, Koch employs the bizarre humor of surrealism and the techniques of Abstract Expressionism in poems that emphasize form and sound.

Freely Espousing (1969), a poetry collection by James Schuyler. The first major collection by Schuyler demonstrates his range in form, style and subject. Frequently autobiographical in his poetry, he catalogs the sights and sounds of daily life in simple and direct language.

Self-Portrait in a Convex Mirror (1975), a poetry collection by John Ashbery. This award-winning collection features Ashbery engaging in self-analysis and metaphysical exploration, particularly in the long title poem.

Moscow Mansions (1973), a poetry collection by Barbara Guest. This collection reflects Guest's interest in the arts in general, considering the problem of artistic composition and consciousness itself in such poems as "Roses" and "The Poetess."

The Collected Poems of Frank O'Hara Published several years after his death, the award-winning collection, *The Collected Poems of Frank O'Hara*, received generally positive reviews from critics. Writing in *Parnassus*, Helen Vendler judges this inclusive collection as overwhelming. Vendler writes, "His charms are inseparable from his overproduction. ... [T]hey remind us ... of the rapid unfinished sketches done by an artist to keep his hand in, or to remind him of some perishable composition of the earth." She concludes, however, "In O'Hara, modern life is instantly recognizable, and a modern ethos of the anarchically personal receives its best incarnation yet." In *Contemporary Literature*, Marjorie G. Perloff notes, "O'Hara was nothing if not learned. His command of language and verse forms, his knowledge of European literature, rivaled not only Lowell's but Eliot's and Pound's ..." Herbert A. Leibowitz in *The New York Times* concludes, "The pleasures of the *Collected Poems* confirm his place as one of our best minor poets."

Art Chronicles 1954–66 *Art Chronicles 1954–66* is a collection of O'Hara's art criticism published while he worked at the *Art News* and for other publications. Critics generally regarded his art criticism as highly as his poetry. In *The New Republic*, Marjorie Perloff comments that this "set of essays suggest to me that O'Hara will eventually emerge as the Ezra Pound of the postwar period." She adds that "his impressionistic criticism takes on a different cast when one notes that, like Pound, he

had an unerring eye for genius, an amazing sense of the difference between the first-rate and the second best." However, Thomas Byrom was more tempered in his praise. In the *Times Literary Supplement*, he writes, "This art criticism ... is light, fanciful, and untheoretical. When he fashions himself after Apollinaire ... we should not take him as serious as his immortalizers have done. The emulation is a respectful bit of cheek ..."

Responses to Literature

1. Create a presentation about the New York School of Poets, focusing much of your attention on O'Hara. Define the group and what made their poetry distinctive. What was O'Hara's place within the group?

2. Research Abstract Expressionism and read O'Hara's poems which were inspired by this artistic movement. In an essay, analyze one of his poems in terms of your findings. What elements of Abstract Expressionism can you find in his poetry?

3. Many of O'Hara's poems were observations of his everyday life in New York City, including observations he made while walking the streets during his lunch hour. Write several poems of your own, inspired by your daily life and what you observe as you go about your daily activities.

4. Read O'Hara's poem "On Seeing Larry Rivers' *Washington Crossing the Delaware* at the Museum of Modern Art" and view the painting that he is describing. In an essay, offer your interpretation and thoughts on O'Hara's poem and the painting that inspired it. Does O'Hara's poem treat the depiction of the significant event respectfully? How does his poem serve to enhance a viewer's appreciation for the painting?

BIBLIOGRAPHY

Books

Gooch, Brad. *City Poet: The Life and Times of Frank O'Hara*. New York: Knopf, 1993.

Perloff, Marjorie. *Frank O'Hara: Poet Among Painters*, second ed. Chicago: University of Chicago Press, 1998.

Smith, Hazel. *Hyperscapes in the Poetry of Frank O'Hara: Difference, Homosexuality, Topography*. Liverpool, England: Liverpool University Press, 2000.

Periodicals

Byrom, Thomas. "The Poet of the Painters." *Times Literary Supplement* (January 27, 1968): 78–79.

Leibowitz, Herbert. "A Pan Piping on the City Streets." *The New York Times* (November 28, 1971): 7, 28.

Perloff, Marjorie. "Poetry Chronicle: 1970–71." *Contemporary Literature* (Winter 1973): 97–131.

———. "They Were There." *The New Republic* (March 1, 1975): 23–24.

Vendler, Helen. "The Virtues of Alterable." *Parnassus* (Fall/Winter 1972): 5–20.

John O'Hara

BORN: *1905, Pottsville, Pennsylvania*

DIED: *1970, Princeton, New Jersey*

NATIONALITY: *American*

GENRE: *Fiction, nonfiction, screenplays*

MAJOR WORKS:

Appointment in Samarra (1934)

BUtterfield 8 (1935)

Ten North Frederick (1955)

From the Terrace (1958)

Elizabeth Appleton (1963)

Overview

In his novels and short stories, John O'Hara explored America's obsession with power, status, and sex in the early and mid-twentieth century. His chosen milieu was often the small town, and the fictitious community of Gibbsville, the county seat of Lantenengo County, Pennsylvania, which recurs in much of his work. O'Hara's fiction depicts the intense and destructive rivalry between the wealthy establishment and the upwardly mobile ethnic

John O'Hara   *Carl Mydans / Time Life Pictures / Getty Images*

classes. O'Hara never received the critical recognition awarded some of his contemporaries, though his popularity with readers remained consistent throughout his career.

Works in Biographical and Historical Context

Tumultuous Childhood   Born on January 31, 1905, in Pottsville, Pennsylvania, O'Hara was the son of Patrick Henry O'Hara and his wife Katherine Elizabeth. His father was a physician and surgeon, and O'Hara was the eldest of eight children born into this prominent Irish family. His hometown of Pottsville was a small industrial town which would later inspire his fictional creation of Gibbsville. He was raised in the Roman Catholic faith, and was observant of the town's Protestant elite and their disdain of the Irish Catholic community. An unruly but gifted student who enjoyed drinking alcohol from an early age, O'Hara was expelled from Fordham Preparatory School and the Keystone State Normal School. He eventually graduated as valedictorian from the Niagara Preparatory School in New York in 1924.

Because of his father's unexpected death in March 1925, O'Hara was unable to attend Yale as he had planned, and the family was reduced to genteel poverty. For the next ten years, O'Hara worked as a ship steward, railroad freight clerk, gas meter reader, amusement park guard, soda jerk, and press agent. Among his most important positions was that of journalist. O'Hara began his journalism career writing for newspapers in Pottsville. In 1925, he was hired as a reporter for *The Pottsville Journal*, where he worked for two years. After spending a year working as a waiter on an ocean liner bound for Europe, he then moved to Chicago in an unsuccessful attempt to find work as a journalist.

A Journalist and Fiction Writer   O'Hara eventually moved to New York City when he was hired as a reporter for the *New York Herald Tribune* in 1928. That same year, he sold his first short story, "Alumnae Bulletin," to *The New Yorker*. Though he lost his *Herald* job because of his drinking, O'Hara soon had other journalism jobs and became a regular contributor to the magazine. He later wrote for such periodicals as *Newsweek* and *Time*. O'Hara also worked briefly as a literary secretary and as a press agent.

As O'Hara's career was taking off, the United States, was in the midst of the Great Depression. The stock market crashed in 1929, effectively causing this economic crisis. The stock market crashed because an investment boom which began in 1924 was fueled by investors buying stocks on margin (in which investors took out loans to buy stocks for as little as a ten percent down payment) and with purely speculative money. The stocks became wildly overvalued, and their value plummeted as the American economy took a downturn. The failure of the stock market caused the economy first in the United

LITERARY AND HISTORICAL CONTEMPORARIES

O'Hara's famous contemporaries include:

Dorothy Parker (1893–1967): This American writer was the leading light and most scathing wit of the "Algonquin Round Table," a circle of literary notables in New York City in the 1920s and 1930s. Like O'Hara, she published short stories in *The New Yorker*.

Robert Benchley (1889–1945): An American humorist, theater critic, newspaper columnist, radio performer, and movie actor, Benchley contributed to such periodicals as *Life* and *The New Yorker*.

Wolcott Gibbs (1902–1958): Gibbs was an American critic, short story writer, and parodist who was closely associated with *The New Yorker* throughout his career. In addition to serving as an editor, he was a reporter, fiction writer, and drama critic for the magazine.

Lorenz Hart (1895–1943): This American lyricist worked with composer Richard Rogers on many hit Broadway musicals of the 1930s, including *The Boys from Syracuse* (1938). Hart collaborated with Rogers and O'Hara on the hit musical adaptation of *Pal Joey*.

Elizabeth Taylor (1932–): Taylor is a British-born American actress who won an Academy Award for her work in the film adaptation of *BUtterfield 8*.

States and then around the world to fall into a dramatic and sustained depression which lasted through the 1930s.

Published First Novel In this environment, O'Hara published his first successful novel in 1934, *Appointment in Samarra*. Like much of his best work, it is an ironic picture of the members of a country club in a fictional Pennsylvania town, and a study of status in Pennsylvania society. The novel focuses on the tragedy of Julian English, who initiates his own downfall by throwing a drink into the face of a social superior. O'Hara's next novel, *BUtterfield 8* (1935), was also a popular bestseller. In 1935, O'Hara also published one of his first highly respected short story collections, *The Doctor's Son*.

By the time *BUtterfield 8* and *The Doctor's Son* were published, O'Hara had begun working as a screenwriter in Hollywood for Paramount Studios. He spent nearly a decade writing scripts as his primary occupation, though he continued to produce fiction on the side. While his works from the late 1930s—including the Hollywood-based novel *Hope of Heaven* (1938) and short story collection *Files on Parade* (1939)—were not as popular, he found greater success in 1940.

Broadway Success That year, O'Hara published his well-respected short story collection *Pal Joey*, which consisted of loosely connected vignettes about a small-time nightclub entertainer and his attempts to gain professional and social respectability. He later collaborated with Richard Rogers and Lorenz Hart to turn the collection into what became the hit musical comedy of the 1941 theater season. *Pal Joey* was also later made into a movie.

In 1944, O'Hara left Hollywood to work as a war correspondent for *Liberty* magazine. By this time, World War II had been raging for five years. The war had begun in September 1939 when Nazi Germany, led by Adolf Hitler, invaded Poland and overran the country. England and France declared war on Germany, but Germany soon controlled much of the European continent. The United States entered the war in 1941, after Japan bombed an American naval base in Hawaii. The war was fought in a number of theaters in Europe, Asia, Africa, and the South Pacific, involving sixty-one countries and leaving fifty-five million people dead.

Popular Success, Critical Failure After World War II, O'Hara returned to writing novels and short stories. While he remained commercially successful, his works became less appreciated by critics. For example, the novel *A Rage to Live* (1949) had huge sales but mixed reviews. *Ten North Frederick* (1955) and *From the Terrace* (1958) were both best-selling novels that were made into movies. *Ten North Frederick* deals with the contrast between the public and private lives of Joe Chapin, an aspiring politician who becomes an alcoholic, while *From the Terrace* details the life of a wealthy man. While *Frederick* was critically acclaimed, *Terrace* received especially bad reviews.

Despite such negative reviews, O'Hara continued a prodigious output in the last decade of his life. He wrote several novels, including *Elizabeth Appleton* (1963), which focuses on the life of a privileged woman, and *The Lockwood Concern* (1965). O'Hara also put out seven short story and novella collections, including *Sermons and Soda Water* (1960) and *The O'Hara Generation* (1969). The stories collected in *The Cape Cod Lighter* (1962), *The Hat on the Bed* (1963), and *The Horse Knows the Way* (1964), demonstrate his mastery of the short story form and are considered to be his best later works.

After suffering a heart attack at his home in Princeton, New Jersey, O'Hara died there on April 11, 1970. Two multi-generational sagas that he wrote in his last years were published after his death: *The Ewings* (1972) and its sequel *The Second Ewings* (1977).

Works in Literary Context

As a writer, O'Hara favored realism in his prose style, and wrote highly regarded naturalistic dialogue which reveals much about his characters. He often examined the codified class system in the United States in the mid-twentieth century. Many of his works take place in the fictional town of Gibbsville, the counterpoint to O'Hara's hometown of Pottsville, Pennsylvania. In his early novels, especially, he explored the jealousy and hostilities between the Protestant elite and ethnic groups, primarily the Irish, struggling for social ascendancy there and in the United States as a whole. While other works were not as concerned with class struggles, O'Hara chronicles the material trappings of success in every social strata as well as the effects of such pursuits on his characters' lives. Later in his career, his emphasis on the sexual relationships of his characters and its effect on them became an increasing focus of concern. As a writer, O'Hara was greatly influenced by Ernest Hemingway, F. Scott Fitzgerald, John Steinbeck, Sinclair Lewis, Ring Lardner, and Dorothy Parker.

Status-Driven, Destructive Americans As an author, O'Hara said he was picturing, as honestly as he could, how twentieth-century Americans were driven by money, sex, and a struggle for status. In pursuit of these goals, many of his characters lead themselves to their own destruction. For example, *Appointment in Samarra* focuses on the last three days in the life of Julian English, a wealthy but insecure man whose antagonistic behavior towards his family, Gibbsville's social elite, and the town's Irish community drives him to suicide. Similarly, *BUtterfield 8* is based on a real-life scandal in which a young Manhattan socialite with questionable morals dies under mysterious circumstances. Later novels, novellas, and short stories share this theme. For example, in *Ten North Frederick*, Joe Chapin earns great wealth and prestige with the help of his family name, a Yale law degree, and considerable intelligence. But Chapin aspires to be president of the United States, so he attempts to buy the lieutenant governorship, is duped by an Irish politician, and drinks himself to death. Such works show O'Hara's concern with American ambition and desire for social status.

Realism A realist-naturalist writer, O'Hara emphasized complete objectivity in his books, writing frankly about the materialistic aspirations and sexual exploits of his characters. Known for his extraordinary ear for language, O'Hara also was exacting in his depiction of American social customs and the wardrobes of his characters. Such realism was not limited to the upper classes as his characters included workers, shopkeepers, and racketeers whose lives were delineated in authentic detail as well. *A Rage to Live* was among his first long and elaborately documented novels. Set in Fort Penn from 1900 to 1920, the novel includes a detailed, serious social history. Not all of his works were filled with such an overwhelming amount of detail. O'Hara's short stories were also realistic, but early on, many were brief. For example, the stories in *The Doctor's Son and Other Stories* were distinguished by economy of treatment and close observation of human behavior. Stories in *The Doctor's Son* as well as *Files on Parade* (1939) and *Pal Joey* were also highly praised for their convincing, realistic dialogue.

Works in Critical Context

When O'Hara originally published his novels and short stories, critics had a mixed reaction to his works and chosen literary style. Some found him to be skillful but

---

COMMON HUMAN EXPERIENCE

Many critics believe that the musical adaptation of O'Hara's *Pal Joey*, written by Richard Rogers, Lorenz Hart, and John O'Hara, helped define the musical comedy. Here are some other musical comedies which were equally influential:

No, No Nanette (1925), a musical by Vincent Youmans. This work tells the story of a young woman who rescues her uncle from financial ruin and finds romance in the process.

Girl Crazy (1930), a musical by George and Ira Gershwin. In this musical, a wealthy young playboy is sent to an all-boys school in Arizona to get his mind off girls. Once, there he becomes interested in a local girl who is not interested in him.

Anything Goes (1934), a musical by Cole Porter. This production focuses on a case of mistaken identity aboard a ship, and includes a colorful list of characters, including an evangelist turned nightclub signer, a stowaway, a debutante, and a wanted criminal.

Babes in Arms (1937), a musical by Richard Rogers and Lorenz Hart. This musical focuses on young but impoverished stage apprentices who overcome challenging circumstances to put on a revue to help out the nice but financially challenged co-owner of the summer stock theater to which they are attached.

---

cynical, labeling him a post–Jazz Age follower of Hemingway and Fitzgerald. Others recognized him as a gifted social commentator. When his novels, published in the 1950s and 1960s, became bestsellers, some critics objected to the simple precision of his dialogue and detail, to the superficial reality of his American scenes, and to the social climbing and sexual conduct of his characters, who some believed were not worth writing about. Though such critics often dismissed him as a hack, his books were widely read and reviewed. Author John Steinbeck even called O'Hara the most underrated writer in America. A number of critics came to acknowledge O'Hara as the master of the short story, publishing at least a dozen highly admired collections. Indeed, some reviewers have called him America's best short story writer.

Appointment in Samarra Reviewers in the 1930s were shocked by O'Hara's frank treatment of sex and social snobbery in his first novel *Appointment in Samarra*. In the *Saturday Review of Literature*, Henry Seidel Canby complains of a "thoroughgoing vulgarity in this book." Even a literary hero of O'Hara's, Sinclair Lewis, dismissed the book. Lewis writes in another edition of the *Saturday Review of Literature* that "this book, for all the cleverness of its observation, the deftness of its tempo, the courage of its vocabulary, was inherently nothing but infantilism." Today, critics consider *Appointment in Samarra* a stronger work than later O'Hara efforts. As Edmund Wilson writes in *Classics and Commercials: A Literary Chronicle of the 1940s,* "*Appointment in Samarra* is a memorable picture, both of a provincial snob, a disorganized drinking-man of the twenties, and of the complexities of the social organism in which he flourished and perished."

A Rage to Live One of O'Hara's most ambitious books, *A Rage to Live,* is a lengthy novel about a marriage that is destroyed after the wife commits adultery. It addresses almost all of the author's concerns about social stratification, materialism, and the dangers of sexual passion. While extremely popular with readers, many contemporary critics felt the novel was poorly plotted and contained too many unnecessary details. One reviewer, Brendan Gill, writes in *The New Yorker* that the book is "discursive and prolix" and remarks that it resembles "one of those 'panoramic,' three-or-four generation novels that writers of the third and fourth magnitude turn out in such disheartening abundance." Later critics found more to like about the novel. For example, Douglas Robillard in *Essays in Arts and Sciences* comments that "novels like *A Rage to Live* (1949) and *Ten North Frederick* (1955) are fine, strong books, well planned and thoroughly realized."

Responses to Literature

1. Research the death of Jazz Age celebrity Starr Faithfull, whose body washed up on a Long Island beach in 1931. She was allegedly the inspiration for Gloria Wondrous in *BUtterfield 8.* In an essay, describe your interpretation of the link between Faithfull and Wondrous. What do you think O'Hara saw in Faithfull that would make her an inspiration for his fictional character?

2. Many critics believe that in his short stories set in Gibbsville, O'Hara helped invent his own sub-genre, the prototypical *New Yorker* magazine story—full of contemporary dialogue, a focus on everyday events, indeterminate in its resolution, and sometimes maddeningly elliptical. Using these guidelines, write your own short story in a similar style.

3. Research the friendship between O'Hara and F. Scott Fitzgerald. Create a presentation in which you describe their relationship and how you see Fitzgerald's influence on O'Hara's writing.

4. In a small group, examine the moral fabric of American life during the 1930s as presented in *BUtterfield 8* and O'Hara's other major novels published in or set in this time period. Do circumstances appear drastically different from modern times? In what ways are they similar?

BIBLIOGRAPHY

Books

Bruccoli, Matthew Joseph. *The O'Hara Concern: A Biography of John O'Hara.* Pittsburgh, Pa.: University of Pittsburgh Press, 1995.

Long, Robert Emmet. *John O'Hara.* New York: Ungar, 1983.

Wilson, Edmund. *Classics and Commercials: A Literary Chronicle of the Forties.* New York: Farrar, Straus, 1950.

Periodicals

Canby, Henry Seidel. Review of *Appointment in Samarra. Saturday Review of Literature* (August 18, 1934).

Gill, Brendan. Review of *A Rage to Live. The New Yorker* (August 20, 1949).

Lewis, Sinclair. Review of *Appointment in Samarra. Saturday Review of Literature* (October 6, 1934).

Robillard, Douglas. "'A Great Character Study': John O'Hara's Letters and Fiction." *Essays in Arts and Sciences* (May 1979): 73–79.

✸ John Okada

BORN: *1923, Seattle, Washington*

DIED: *1971, Los Angeles, California*

NATIONALITY: *American*

GENRE: *Fiction*

MAJOR WORKS:
No-No Boy (1957)

John Okada *Okada, John, photograph. From a cover of No-No Boy. University of Washington Press, 2001. Reproduced by permission.*

Overview

Japanese American author John Okada published only one novel, *No-No Boy* (1957), which came to be recognized as a significant contribution to American literature. The book was not popular when first published, and many in the Asian American community were upset that Okada was raising issues about cultural division and internment camps that many preferred to forget. Though the author died an unknown, *No-No Boy* began making an impact in the late 1970s when a group called Combined Asian-American Resources Project in Seattle revived the book. The novel has come to inspire other Asian American writers, as well as writers who address the issue of ethnic discrimination in the United States.

Works in Biographical and Historical Context

A War-Torn Childhood   John Okada was born on September 23, 1923, in Seattle, Washington. He was the son of immigrants from Japan. His father, Freddy Okada, owned several hotels in the city. Okada, his two brothers, and his sister were raised in Seattle, where he attended Bailey Gatzert Elementary School and Broadway High School.

World War II broke out while Okada was still a high school student. World War II began in Europe when Nazi Germany, led by Adolf Hitler, invaded Poland in September 1939 and overran the country. England and France declared war on Germany, but Germany soon controlled much of the European continent. The United States entered the war in December 1941, after Japan bombed an American naval base in Hawaii. The war was fought in a number of theaters in Europe, Asia, Africa, and the South Pacific, involving sixty-one countries and leaving fifty-five million people dead.

Internment Camps   Japan and the United States fought each other primarily in the Pacific Theater. Because the countries were enemies, even on American soil, natives of Japan and Japanese Americans were regarded with suspicion. On February 19, 1942, President Franklin D. Roosevelt issued Executive Order 9066, which ordered 110,000 Japanese Americans to be removed from their homes—it was believed these people posed such a threat to U.S. security that they could not be trusted to live freely in society. Most of those affected by the order lived on the West Coast, and they were sent to internment camps in remote areas without being charged or tried of any crime. At the time of the Japanese internment, Okada was a college student at the University of Washington. Because they were of Japanese descent, he and his family were sent to live at a detention center in Minidoka, Idaho.

While living in these camps, many Japanese Americans lost all the property they left behind. Inside the camps, education was limited, there were few employment opportunities, and detainees fragmented into sometimes hostile factions. A few Japanese Americans were sent to prison for alleged or perceived disloyalty. After the war, the interned people were allowed to return to what remained of their homes and lives. While questions about their loyalty lingered for years, many preferred to forget the experience.

A Nisei Fights   When the United States first became involved in World War II, many young Japanese American men who had been born in the United States—known as Nisei—had registered for the draft. However, they were classified as 4-C, aliens who were ineligible for service. As the American military changed, so, too, did the status of the 4-Cs. In early 1943, the secretary of war restored the Nisei's right to volunteer for service and changed their draft status to 1-A. As a result, the War Department soon began recruiting young Nisei men in internment camps to serve in an all-Japanese American army unit, the 442nd Regimental Combat Team. This unit ultimately became the most decorated fighting unit of the whole of World War II.

Okada was a Nisei who chose to join the army. He served in army intelligence in the Pacific, flying over Japanese-held islands broadcasting radio messages asking Japanese soldiers to surrender. Okada reached the rank of sergeant before his discharge in 1946. These experiences—both being forced to live in an internment camp and serving in the American military—would affect him so profoundly that he would be moved to write about them later in life.

After the war, Okada continued his education at the University of Washington, where he earned a BA in English and library science. He later earned a master's degree in English from Columbia University in 1949. Okada then returned to Seattle, where he worked in the business reference department of the Seattle Public Library. He later moved to Detroit to work for the Detroit Public Library. By this time, Okada was working on what would become his only published novel.

A First—and Only—Novel   Because his job at the Detroit Public Library was unrewarding and required long hours, Okada did not have time to work on his novel. Seeking a better position, he became a technical writer for Chrysler Missile Operations. He still could not find enough time to write, and the community in Michigan did not embrace his family. In 1956 Okada moved his family to Los Angeles, where he again found a job as a technical writer and was able to complete his novel.

Okada published his only novel in 1957. *No-No Boy* was deeply inspired by his experiences during World War II. The story is a realistic treatment of the effects of racism and generational tension in the Japanese American community in Seattle after World War II. In the novel, Ichiro, the young American-born protagonist, returns to his parents' home after they have all been interned in relocation camps. Ichiro has just served a prison term for resisting the draft. His mother, still fiercely loyal to her native land, cannot understand how torn her son is between his ancestry and his citizenship. Others in the community also reject him as he struggles with his own rehabilitation into society.

LITERARY AND HISTORICAL CONTEMPORARIES

Okada's famous contemporaries include:

Norman Y. Mineta (1931–): This Japanese American politician spent time in an internment camp during World War II. He later became the mayor of San Jose, California. He also served as a congressman, as secretary of commerce during President Bill Clinton's administration, and as secretary of transportation in President George W. Bush's administration.

Spark M. Matsunaga (1916–1990): This Hawaiian-born Japanese American fought with the 442nd Regimental Combat Team during World War II. He later became a member of the U.S. House of Representatives and then the U.S. Senate, where he devoted himself to the cause of peace and seeking redress for the Japanese Americans interned during World War II.

Minoru Yasui (1917–1987): This Japanese American lawyer fought President Franklin D. Roosevelt's Executive Order 9066 in courts during World War II. He continued to fight the federal government to right the wrongs done to Japanese Americans during the war for the rest of his life.

Daniel K. Inouye (1924–): This Japanese American was a hero during World War II as a member of the 442nd Regimental Combat Team. He was also the first Japanese American to serve in the U.S. Congress, representing Hawaii beginning in 1959.

Franklin D. Roosevelt (1882–1945): This American president was elected to office four times. During his years as president, he led the country out of the Great Depression and through much of World War II.

Unfinished Second Novel *No-No Boy* was a failure. The Japanese American community was still emotionally raw from the events of World War II and so rejected the book. The greater reading public reacted similarly to Okada's work. The fifteen hundred copies of the first edition of the book never sold out. Okada continued to write, however, but published no other novels during his lifetime.

Okada was working on a second novel about Japanese immigrants when he died of a heart attack on February 20, 1971, in Los Angeles. His widow, Dorothy, destroyed the manuscript and his other writings after the University of California, Los Angeles, refused his papers for their manuscript collection.

Works in Literary Context

Okada published only one novel, but *No-No Boy* is considered a classic, pioneering Asian American novel. Set in Seattle after the end of World War II, it tells the story of

Ichiro Yamada, a young Japanese American who refuses to serve in the U.S. armed forces during the war and is consequently imprisoned for two years. Following his release, Ichiro regrets his decision, must deal with the reactions and rejections of his family and community, and fears he has no future in the United States. Over the course of the novel, he gradually learns to put aside his self-hatred and rediscover a sense of hope and belonging.

Because of its subject matter, the novel opens a window on the Japanese American experience in the immediate period after World War II. It particularly illuminates the generational conflict between the Issei (the first generation of Japanese immigrants, who were born in Japan) and the Nisei (the second generation, born in the United States) and the struggles of the Nisei to come to terms with their dual heritage.

Questions of Loyalty In *No-No Boy*, Okada also explores the idea of loyalty, specifically the fragmentation many Japanese Americans felt within themselves and in their community as a result of their experiences during the war. Indeed, much of the novel focuses on questions about loyalty and disloyalty. For example, the main character, Ichiro Yamada, is recruited by the U.S. War Department and required—as were all Japanese American men recruited into the army—to fill out a form that asked questions about willingness to serve in the U.S. armed forces as well as swearing full allegiance to the United States while forswearing allegiance to the Japanese emperor or any other foreign government. Yamada answers no to such questions and is jailed for two years for being disloyal. He is met with taunts and jeers from war veterans and even from his own brother, Taro. Over the course of *No-No Boy*, Ichiro comes to feel shame over his choice, demonstrated by his wish to trade places with a dying veteran Kenji, whose missing leg and mortal injuries are slowly draining him of life. Ichiro still loves the country of his birth, and though he feels he belongs to neither side, he comes to see himself as an American again, albeit one who must construct his identity while confronting such issues as assimilation.

Fragmentation When Ichiro returns to Seattle after serving his term in prison, he finds both the Japanese American community and the people that are part of it fragmented because of the experiences they have suffered. Sons, like Ichiro, have defied parents, while husbands have left wives, and wives have committed adultery. Parents, such as Ichiro's father, have turned to alcohol to cope, while Ichiro's mother, like others, is on the verge of insanity. Ichiro's mother refuses to believe that Japan lost the war, and her pride and resistance becomes a destructive force that furthers the fragmentation she and others experience. Dying veteran Kenji is physically fragmented, having lost a leg and suffering other injuries that will eventually take his life. None of the characters in the novel is whole—each one is fractured in some way by the war. The community shows its fragmentation by its rejection of Ichiro, who had been cut off from them. Yet, Okada concludes that it is the hope of America and its ideals that make Ichiro whole again and give optimism to other members of the greater Japanese American community.

Works in Critical Context

Okada's only novel, *No-No Boy*, received poor reviews or was just ignored by critics when published in 1957. The novel was disregarded not only by the mainstream American literary community but by the Japanese community as well. It was published only twelve years after the end of the war, a time when many Japanese Americans preferred to remain quiet about their painful wartime experiences. The book was essentially forgotten until the late 1970s when it was revived by the Combined Asian-American Resources Project in Seattle. Because of renewed interest in *No-No Boy* in the years after Okada's death, the novel has come to be seen as a significant piece of Asian American literature by critics.

No-No Boy   Though initial critical responses to *No-No Boy* were generally negative, later critics and scholars saw the novel as a powerful statement about the Japanese American community in the post–World War II period. Stan Yogi, writing in *MELUS*, saw the novel as exploring "Ichiro's attempt to claim an identity as an American." He concluded "Through Ichiro's journey to reestablish himself as an American, Okada explores the gray area between the oppositions that develop around polarized definitions of 'Japanese' and 'American,' individuality and community, assimilation and cultural maintenance." In *Three American Literatures: Essays in Chicano, Native American, and Asian-American Literature for Teachers of American Literature*, Lawson Fusao Inada concluded that the book is "a testament to the strength of a people, not a tribute to oppression. ... In spite of the camps and prison, the death and destruction he experiences, Ichiro emerges as a positive person who says yes to life." *Kliatt* reviewer Janet Julian called Okada's *No-No Boy* "a haunting, beautifully written book that stays in the heart."

Responses to Literature

1. Research the history behind President Franklin D. Roosevelt's Executive Order 9066 and its effect on Japanese Americans. In an essay, write about your findings by linking them to *No-No Boy*. Could you imagine such an order being issued today? Why or why not?

2. In a small group, talk about Ichiro's dilemma in *No-No Boy*. Why do you think he says no to the loyalty tests? Why do you think he considers suicide? How would you react in this situation?

3. Create a presentation about life in internment camps for Japanese Americans during World War II. Include information about the treatment of children, daily activities and routines, and how Japanese Americans reacted to their internee status.

COMMON HUMAN EXPERIENCE

In *No-No Boy*, Okada offers a fictionalized account of the Japanese American experience during World War II. Here are some other works that explore this subject:

Farewell to Manzanar: A True Story of Japanese American Experience During and After World War II Internment (1973), a memoir by Jeanne Wakatsuki Houston and James D. Houston. This autobiography chronicles Wakatsuki Houston's memories and reflections about her family's experience living in an internment camp during World War II.

Under the Blood-Red Sun (1995), a novel for young readers by Graham Salisbury. This work of historical fiction takes place in Oahu, Hawaii, in the time just prior to and immediately after the bombing of Pearl Harbor. It is told from the perspective of Tomi, a young boy whose mother is Japanese American and who struggles with issues related to his Japanese heritage.

Nisei Daughter (1953), a memoir by Monica Sone. Sone's autobiography about her experiences as a Japanese American internee during World War II was the first autobiography of its kind published in the postwar period. The book also includes details about her childhood, how her neighbors treated her after the bombing at Pearl Harbor, and her evacuation experience.

Poston Sonata (1992), a musical work by Glenn Horiuchi. This experimental jazz artist is influenced by traditional Japanese instruments and music. This work is intended to evoke the experiences of Japanese American internees at the Poston, Arizona, internment camp during World War II.

BIBLIOGRAPHY

Books

Inada, Lawson Fusao. *Three American Literatures: Essays in Chicano, Native American, and Asian-American Literature for Teachers of American Literature*, edited by Houston A. Baker, Jr. New York: Modern Language Association of America, 1982, pp. 254–266.

Sato, Gayle K. Fujita. "Momoaro's Exile: John Okada's *No-No Boy*." In *Reading the Literature of Asian America*, edited by Shirley Geok-Lim and Amy Ling. Philadelphia: Temple University Press, 1992, pp. 239–258.

Periodicals

Amoko, Apollo O. "Resilient ImagiNations: *No-No Boy, Obasan*, and the Limits of Minority Disclosure." *Mosaic* (September 2000): 35.

Gribben, Bryn. "The Mother That Won't Reflect Back:
Situating Psychoanalysis and the Japanese Mother in
No-No Boy." *MELUS: The Journal of the Society for
the Study of the Multi-Ethnic Literature of the United
States* (Summer 2003): 31–46.

Julian, Janet. A review of *No-No Boy. Kliatt* (Fall
1978): 13.

Ling, Jinqi. "Race, Power and Cultural Politics in John
Okada's *No-No Boy.*" *American Literature* (June
1995): 359–381.

Usui, Masami. "An Issei Woman's Suffering, Silence, and
Suicide in John Okada's *No-No Boy.*" *Chu-Shikoku
Studies in American Literature* (June 1997): 43–61.

Yeh, William. "To Belong or Not to Belong: The
Liminality of John Okada's *No-No Boy.*" *Amerasia
Journal* 19, no. 1 (1993): 121–133.

Yogi, Stan. "'You had to be one or the other'
Oppositions and Reconciliation in John Okada's
No-No Boy." *MELUS: The Journal of the Society for
the Study of the Multi-Ethnic Literature of the United
States* (Summer 1996): 63–77.

✸ Sharon Olds

BORN: *1942, San Francisco, California*

NATIONALITY: *American*

GENRE: *Poetry*

MAJOR WORKS:

Satan Says (1980)

The Dead and the Living (1984)

The Gold Cell (1987)

The Father (1992)

The Unswept Room (2002)

Strike Sparks: Selected Poems, 1980–2002 (2004)

Overview

American poet Sharon Olds is a highly regarded, prize-winning poet who uses an intensely personal voice to explore themes of domestic and political violence, sexuality, and family relationships. Frequently associated with the confessional school of poetry, Olds has attained the status of a major figure in contemporary American poetry. Her poems are considered highly accessible, and they appeal to a wide audience. Olds's work is viewed in the tradition of Walt Whitman as a celebration of the body, in all its pleasures and pains, and is believed to particularly resonate with female readers.

Works in Biographical and Historical Context

A Counter-Culture Childhood Olds was born in San Francisco, California, on November 19, 1942. She was raised in Berkeley, California. Because she does not dis-

Sharon Olds   *Christopher Felver / Corbis*

cuss her family publicly, little is known or has been confirmed about her childhood and family. What is known is that she was an avid reader as a child, wrote poems from an early age, and was raised in a very "hellfire-and-brimstone"-type religious family. When Olds was sixteen years old, a shoe shop opened in Berkeley where custom-made sandals were designed from an outline of a customer's foot. This shop was her first look at a different world, what became the counter-culture movement of the 1960s whose ideals she embraced.

Much of the 1960s counter-culture movement was centered on the West Coast and the emerging generation of baby boomers. On campuses like the University of California at Berkeley, student groups led massive rallies to protest the Vietnam War and military research being conducted on campus in the mid-1960s, and to defend their freedom of speech and the civil rights movement. Also during this time, the Black Panthers, a major group affiliated with the Black Power movement, was organized in San Francisco. They demanded civil rights for African Americans and supported militant action to get them. Also in San Francisco, a new bohemian lifestyle emerged that supported ideals of free love, legalized marijuana, and the use of drugs such as LSD to have groundbreaking visions and experiences. These hippies were the second generation of beatniks and they refused to conform to the values and ways of greater American society. The climax of the hippie movement was the Summer of Love in

1967, when the hippie message began to significantly affect mainstream American society.

A Poet Emerges   Though Olds was greatly influenced by this era, she was initially educated far away from it—at the Dana Hall School in Wellesley, Massachusetts. In the early 1960s, she returned to California to attend Stanford, where she earned her BA with honors in 1964. Olds then moved to New York City to enter a graduate program in English at Columbia University. There she studied Ralph Waldo Emerson and wrote her own poetry. She earned her PhD in 1972.

From 1976 to 1980, Olds was a lecturer-in-residence on poetry at the Theodor Herzl Institute. Olds was thirty-seven years old when she published her first book of poetry in 1980, *Satan Says*, an event that she said was partly due to pure luck. Many of the poems focus on the primal emotions produced by child abuse. In the title poem, for example, Olds juxtaposes sexually charged imagery with feelings of rage toward her parents. However, in purging herself of violent emotions, the narrator moves unexpectedly toward love and reconciliation.

During the early and mid-1980s, Olds worked on her next volume while holding a number of positions as visiting teacher of poetry at reputable institutions. These included the Manhattan Theater Club and the Poetry Center at the YMCA of New York City (where she taught in 1982), New York University (where she taught in 1983 and 1985), and Sarah Lawrence College (where she taught in 1984). Her next collection of poetry, *The Dead and the Living* (1984), won two major awards: the Lamont Poetry Selection of the Academy of American Poets in 1984 and the National Book Critics Circle Award in 1985.

Focus on Trauma   In *The Dead and the Living*, Olds expands her focus on her traumatic childhood to include poems that tenderly depict the activities of her children and her own role as a mother. Her concern with victims and their emotional healing is extended to the public sphere in poems that describe crimes of political persecution and social injustice. She also uses photographs to illustrate these problems. Olds continued to explore similar themes in *The Gold Cell* (1987), which likewise emphasizes sexuality, the primacy of body, and family life. The poems employ autobiographical material to tell stories of birth, sex, and death with an unflinching, unsentimental honesty. She also celebrates the erotic mother-child relationship.

By the publication of *The Dead and the Living*, Olds was working as a visiting teacher of poetry at Goldwater Hospital, an institution for the severely physically disabled. She held this position from 1985 to 1990 but continued to teach there in some capacity for years afterward as well. Olds was also a visiting teacher of poetry at Columbia University from 1985 to 1986 and held the Fanny Hurst Chair at Brandeis University from 1986 to 1987. In 1992 Olds became an associate professor at

New York University and later helmed the school's graduate program in creative writing.

Continued Intensity   Even with these many teaching appointments, Olds continued to create her own original work. In 1991 she published *The Sign of Saturn: Poems 1980–1987* (1991), a selection of poems from previous books titled under the baleful influence of Saturn, the father who ate his children. *The Sign of Saturn* was followed by a new collection, *The Father* (1992). The poems in this volume express the poet's grief and compassion for her father during his death from cancer. She uses scatological and sexually explicit language to describe the deterioration of his body, which becomes a metaphor for his dismal failings as an abusive, alcoholic parent. Similarly, the well-constructed verse poems in *The Wellspring: Poems* (1996) continued to look at her childhood and tense relationship with her parents, her own children and ideas about motherhood, and love in marriage.

After receiving the Walt Whitman Citation of Merit for Poets in 1998 and beginning a four-year tenure of the New York state poet laureateship, Olds published *Blood, Tin, Straw* in 1999. This collection continued the exploration of childhood abuse. Her next volume of poetry, *The Unswept Room* (2002), moves away from father-related imagery to focus on mothers and maternal-related images. It also reflects the happier perspective of a

COMMON HUMAN EXPERIENCE

Olds has identified herself with a number of female poets who specialize in similarly evocative, personal works. Here are some writings by these poets:

The Bell Jar (1963), a novel by Sylvia Plath. This semi-autobiographical novel reveals an intensely personal struggle with self-consciousness, bold metaphors for death and sexuality, and a pioneering examination of societal limitations experienced by women.

The Gates (1978), a poetry collection by Muriel Rukeyser. This collection of poems documents the author's experiences as a single mother in the straitlaced 1950s.

In the Mecca (1968), a poetry collection by Gwendolyn Brooks. This collection focuses on the inhabitants of a slum tenement where Brooks worked when she first graduated from college. The title poem is a grim account of a mother's search for her missing child who has been brutally raped and murdered by another resident of the housing complex.

Ordinary Words (1999), a poetry collection by Ruth Stone. These poems explore the poet's painful life as a young widow left to single-handedly raise three children after her husband's suicide. She also touches on issues related to country life, hysteria, chaos, and madness.

late-middle-aged woman. The title poem, "The Unswept Room," describes a depiction of a feast rendered on the mosaic-tiled floor of Museo Gregoriano Profano.

Another Era of Activism A year after she published another retrospective—*Strike Sparks: Selected Poems, 1980–2002* (2004)—Olds made national headlines when she refused an invitation from First Lady Laura Bush to come to the White House. Olds turned it down in order to protest the ongoing war in Iraq, believing her acceptance of the invitation would be seen as condoning the war and the Bush presidency. In early 2003, a United States-led coalition invaded Iraq, toppling the regime led by Saddam Hussein. The invasion was controversial, as was the long-term occupation that followed. Though Olds declined the White House invitation, she did attend the related National Book Festival on the National Mall in Washington, D.C.

In 2008 Olds published *One Secret Thing*, which included a section of poems titled "War" as well as four sections about family, mother, sex, and emerging womanhood. Olds continues to live in New York City, teach at New York University, and write poetry.

Works in Literary Context

In much of her early verse, Olds examines her roles as daughter and mother. Her painful memories of her parents are rendered in uncompromising, often sexually explicit, language. In other poems, she expresses sorrow and outrage for the victims of war and political violence. Her seamless linkage of domestic and public abuse indicates the universal scope of her compassion and poetic vision. While Olds also focused on her father in early collections, maternal and mother-related images predominate in later volumes. The poet herself regarded her poems as observations inspired by ordinary life that were not simple or abstract but reflective of the way she experienced life. Her poetry falls within the modernist tradition of poets such as Walt Whitman and Gertrude Stein, who sought to use the contemporary idiom of language in poetry. As a writer, Olds was also influenced by her life and family as well as the events and counter-culture of the 1960s.

Specific Language and Imagery As Olds is intimate and candid in her writing, her poetry is precise and concrete in its use of imagery. Her language has an exhilarating, vibrant, and celebratory quality, despite the often morbid and unhappy subjects of her poetry. She daringly presents the familiar details of a woman's life using frank language traditionally taboo to female writers. In short, Olds uses language very explicitly. This blunt use is evident in her very first collection, *Satan Says*. These poems explore the difficulties of finding a language sufficiently broad and expansive with which to define one's relationship with others without compromising the complexities and differences of those relationships. In *The Dead and the Living*, Olds uses complex and sharp images as she attempts to re-create the past as a means of liberating the present and the future. Similarly, the poems in *The Gold Cell* are written with clarity and precision. They feature engrossing metaphors and a carefully crafted tone that runs the risk of sentimentality but does not fall into it—instead, truthfulness and integrity prevail in the poems. Later collections like *One Secret Thing* also feature well-written free verse with raw and vivid poems about similar subjects.

Focus on Self and Family Because much of Olds's inspiration for her work apparently comes from own life and her family, the themes of many of her poems are related to these subjects, including personal relationships and self-perception. For example, *Satan Says* is a passionate volume that is divided into sections titled "Daughter," "Woman," "Mother," and "Journey." The poems explore the central meanings of love and shared experience through an investigation of the "other," which is estranged from the self, such as the alter ego, family, friends, and lovers. In *The Dead and the Living*, many of the poems focus on the family, which, like Olds's first book, tell the story of a traumatic childhood in graphic physical and emotional detail. The cast of characters include a cruel grandfather, drunken and violent father, a bitter and passive mother, and a sadistic sister. The book also contains poems that seem to be about Olds's children and her experience as a mother, so that in this book the child victim becomes the mature survivor. *The Gold Cell* also concentrates on personal relationships with poems about motherhood, love, and lust. In poems like "Boy Out in the World" and "Looking at Them Asleep," Olds writes tenderly about her children. The poems in *The Father* are more concretely about family concerns as they explore the responses of a daughter to her unloving father's slow death from cancer. Olds describes his illness, final days, and death in a series of graphic, narrowly focused poems. Later collections share these concerns, including *The Unswept Room*, which includes more mother-daughter poems as well as the poet's own reflections on reaching middle age.

Works in Critical Context

For many critics, Olds's predilection for sexual description and horrific subject matter is integral to the emotional catharsis of the narrator and necessary to create empathy for both victims and their abusers. Other reviewers, while recognizing the struggle for forgiveness and redemption in her work, contend it exhibits a morbid obsession with violence and profanity. Some critics have also felt her work lacks depth, revels in graphic images, and is narcissistic. In spite of these objections, Olds's poetry has been widely praised for its compelling narration, inventive use of metaphor, and scrupulous honesty in rendering extremely personal emotions and experiences.

The Dead and the Living   Many critics judged Olds's second collection as compelling and moving. In a review for the *Nation*, Richard Tillinghast commented that "While *Satan Says* was possible to ignore because of its raw power, *The Dead and the Living* is a considerable step forward. ... Olds is a keen and accurate observer of people." Writing in *America*, Elizabeth Gaffney also found the collection to be strong. She wrote, "Out of private revelations she makes poems of universal truth, of sex, death, fear, love. Her poems are sometimes jarring, unexpected, bold, but always loving and deeply rewarding." However, Tillinghast felt that Olds's attempts "to establish political analogies to private brutalization ... are not very convincing. ... This becomes a mannerism, representing political thinking only at the superficial level." Nevertheless, Tillinghast conceded that *The Dead and the Living* "has the chastening impact of a powerful documentary."

The Unswept Room   Like *The Dead and the Living*, *The Unswept Room* also received generally positive reviews. Writing in the *Guardian*, Carol Rumens stated that "*The Unswept Room* has a maternal slant." She added, "Often perceived as a faltering, otherwordly voice, a nymph or dryad crying, singing, or softly complaining, mother elicits a more fluttering and uncertain response from her daughter-confessor." Kate Daniels in *Women's Review of Books* found the collection challenging. She wrote that "without abandoning her characteristic intensity, [Olds] continues to disquiet and decenter, but in a newly ruminative voice that bespeaks the journey of mid-life." Daniels also observed that "as carefully as an archeologist, [Olds] combs through the accoutrements of a life in late

middle age," and added that "clearly, the philosophical and spiritual development within so many of the poems in *The Unswept Room* suggests a poet who is preparing herself for the remainder of life rather than mourning her past or bemoaning lost opportunities."

Responses to Literature

1. In interviews, Olds has stated that she believes there should be a poet in every school and hospital as well as similar institutions. Stage a debate over this idea for your class. What benefit do you see to this concept? Do you think it is unnecessary?

2. It is believed that many of Olds's poems are inspired by her difficult relationship with her parents, as well as her childhood, her marriage, and her children. However, she has never spoken publicly about the circumstances of her personal life. What inferences can you make about Olds's life from reading her poems? What elements do you think are fictionalized, and why? Support your answer using evidence from the texts you have read.

3. Research the counter-culture movement in the Bay Area in the 1960s. In an essay, link your findings to some of Olds's poems, especially those concerned with social issues. How do you see the influence of the 1960s in her poetry?

4. Read Olds's poetry collections *Satan Says* and *The Unswept Room*. In a small group, discuss how Olds evolved as poet. How do you think her themes changed over time? Do you prefer the poems in one collection over another?

BIBLIOGRAPHY

Books

Swiontkowski, Gale. *Imagining Incest: Sexton, Plath, Rich and Old on Life with Daddy.* Selinsgrove: Susquehanna University Press, 2003.

Periodicals

Bornstein, Jonah. "Sharon Olds: Painful Insights and Small Beauties." *Literary Cavalcade* (January 1989).

Daniels, Kate. "Gritty and Alive." *Women's Review of Books* (May 2003): 16.

Dillon, Brian. "'Never Having Had You, I Cannot Let You Go': Sharon Olds' Poems of a Father-Daughter Relationship" *Literary Review: An International Journal of Contemporary Writing* (March 1993): 108–118.

Gaffney, Elizabeth. A review of *The Dead and the Living. America* (June 30, 1984).

Rumens, Carol. A review of *The Unswept Rom. Guardian* (April 26, 2003).

Scheponik, Peter C. "Olds's 'My Father Speaks to Me from the Dead.'" *Explicator* (Fall 1998): 59–62.

———. "Olds's 'The Pope's Penis.'" *Explicator* (Fall 2000): 52–54.

Tanner, Laura E. "Death-Watch: Terminal Illness and the Gaze in Sharon Olds' 'The Father.'" *Mosaic: A Journal for the Interdisciplinary Study of Literature* (March 1996): 103–121.

Tillinghast, Richard. A review of *The Dead and the Living*. *America* (October 13, 1984).

✾ Mary Oliver

BORN: *1935, Maple Heights, Ohio*

NATIONALITY: *American*

GENRE: *Poetry, nonfiction*

MAJOR WORKS:

The River Styx, Ohio, and Other Poems (1972)

American Primitive (1983)

House of Life (1990)

New and Selected Poems (1992)

Thirst (2006)

Overview

Mary Oliver's poems celebrate nature and explore the mysteries of life, death, and regeneration. The winner of the 1984 Pulitzer Prize for poetry, Oliver writes naturalist poetry that seems deceptively simple, yet its conventional form masks a unique and original vision.

Mary Oliver   *Malcolm Greenaway*

Works in Biographical and Historical Context

Following in the Footsteps of Millay Mary Jane Oliver was born on September 10, 1935, in Maple Heights, Ohio. She was the daughter of Edward William Oliver, a teacher, and his wife, Helen M. (Vlasak). By the age of thirteen, Oliver knew she wanted to write. When she was fifteen years old, she wrote to Norma Millay Ellis, the sister of recently deceased poet Edna St. Vincent Millay. She requested permission to visit Steepletop, Millay's home in upstate New York. Oliver visited the home several times, including an extensive stay during which Oliver assisted in the task of organizing Millay's papers. Millay's lyrical style and themes influenced Oliver's early work, and, like Millay, she embraced country life and later lived in artist colonies in Provincetown, Massachusetts.

When Oliver was a high school student, school integration was a hot-button issue. For decades, qualified black Americans had been denied admission to whites-only colleges and public schools. In the 1950s, black students began petitioning for equal rights. In 1954 the Supreme Court ruled in the landmark case *Brown v. Board of Education* that the "separate but equal" doctrine denied black students equal protection under the law. Though schools legally had to be integrated, many school districts resisted, and it took several decades for integration to be achieved. It was in this environment that Oliver went to school and developed her interest in writing.

Published First Collection After high school, Oliver first attended Ohio State University from 1955 to 1956, then went east to Vassar College (as Millay had done) from 1956 to 1957. She did not earn a degree from either, however. During this time, Oliver held what she has called "ordinary jobs" and saved her intellectual energy for writing poetry. In 1963 Oliver published her first poetry collection, *No Voyage and Other Poems*, of which she published an enlarged edition in 1965. Oliver's first poetry collection established her reputation for treating nature in a direct and unsentimental, yet lyrical, fashion. Oliver then drew on her Ohio heritage for her next collection, *The River Styx, Ohio, and Other Poems* (1972). In 1978 Oliver published two chapbooks, *Night Traveler* and *Sleeping in the Forest*.

Evolution of Poetry By the early 1980s, Oliver was teaching at Case Western Reserve University in Cleveland, Ohio, as a Mather Visiting Professor. She also served as a poet-in-residence at Bucknell University in 1986. As Oliver held these posts, her poetry continued to evolve. Such collections as *Twelve Moons* (1980) and *American Primitive* (1983) saw the poet delving further into the natural world for subject matter. Thematically, the poems in these collections unflinchingly face nature. They study its continuous—and often vicious—cycle of life and death to embrace the stark beauty of this process. In 1984 Oliver won the Pulitzer Prize for *American Primitive.*

Oliver shifted her perspective in her next project, *Dream Work* (1986), which featured some human-centered themes of personal suffering and the past. For example, this collection includes a poem that deals with the Holocaust (the extermination of millions of Jews, homosexuals, Gypsies, and other groups in Nazi Germany from 1941 to 1945). However, most of the poems focus on her favorite topic: the agony and awe of nature. With *House of Light* (1990)—which won the Christopher Award—Oliver returned to a nature-based focus. The poems feature themes of isolation from human concerns and assimilation into various aspects and beings of nature. In 1992 Oliver won the National Book Award for her collection *New and Selected Poems*, which was published that same year. This volume included poems from her previous eight books as well as previously unpublished newer works.

An Academic Poet By the publication of *New and Selected Poems*, Oliver held a new academic post. In 1991 she was named the Margaret Banister poet-in-residence at Sweet Briar College. Three years later, she published her first work of prose, *A Poetry Handbook: A Prose Guide for Writing and Understanding Poetry* (1994). In this book, Oliver drew on her years of writing experience to explore and explain various elements and processes of poetry writing. She also continued her exploration of natural phenomenon in poetry through such collections in the mid- to late-1990s, including *White Pine: Poems and Prose Poems* (1994), *West Wind: Poems and Prose Poems* (1997), and *Winter Hours* (1999). Oliver also published other prose works, including *Blue Pastures* (1995) and *Rules for the Dance: A Handbook for Writing and Reading Metrical Verse* (1998). The latter broached the same subjects as *A Poetry Handbook.*

The second half of the decade saw Oliver in yet another academic post. Beginning in 1996, she held the Catharine Osgood Foster Chair for Distinguished Teaching at Vermont's Bennington College. There, she continued to challenge herself as a poet and prose writer, publishing prolifically in the early twenty-first century. In 2000 Oliver published the book-length poem *The Leaf and the Cloud.* After *What Do We Know* (2002), Oliver published four books in 2004: *Why I Wake Early, Boston Iris: Poems and Essays, Long Life: Essays and Other Writings*, and *New and Selected Poems, Volume 2.* She followed these books with two more collections about nature and life—*Thirst: Poems* (2006) and *Red Bird: Poems* (2008)—as well as *Our World* (2007), a collection of notes, comments, and poems featuring photographs by the late Molly Malone Cook, Oliver's long-time partner. Oliver continues to live and work in Vermont.

Works in Literary Context

Oliver is considered a New England nature or pastoral poet, a literary descendant of New England pastoralist

---

LITERARY AND HISTORICAL CONTEMPORARIES

Oliver's famous contemporaries include:

Alan Freed (1921–1965): A pioneering radio disc jockey on WJW, Freed helped make Cleveland, Ohio, an early hotbed of rock-n-roll music in the 1950s.

Betty Friedan (1921–2006): This American author launched the modern American women's rights movement with her book *The Feminine Mystique* (1963).

Audre Lorde (1934–1992): This African American poet explored social concerns and the themes of guilt and betrayal in such collections as *Cables to Rage* (1970).

Maria Irene Fornes (1930–): This Cuban American lesbian playwright specializes in very visual works that often address issues related to sexuality. Her plays include *Tango Palace* (1963).

Michael Cunningham (1952–): This American novelist won the Pulitzer Prize for fiction for his book *The Hours* (1998). In his novels, he explores themes of family, friendship, identity, and commitment.

---

writers, including William Thoreau and Robert Frost. As an author, she is greatly influenced by these writers, along with Edna St. Vincent Millay, William Butler Yeats, Walt Whitman, William Blake, and William Wordsworth. Oliver was also inspired by the Midwest and her Midwestern childhood.

Oliver's work in this genre reflects a curiosity of plants, animals, and ecosystems far more than human beings and civilization. Typical themes involve the beauty, power, and wonder of nature, and how humans would benefit from appreciating nature. When Oliver writes about people, it is usually to consider their personal, painful experiences, her perspective as a writer, and elements of the greater human condition, including death. She suggests that individuals need to experience life more carefully if they are to transcend ordinary moments and find meaning in the world.

A Fascination with Nature Much of Oliver's poetry—such as her Pulitzer Prize–winning collection *American Primitive* as well as *White Pine: Poems and Prose Poems*—glorifies humankind's natural relationship to animals, plants, and the nonhuman world. She writes lyrical poetry that observes the natural world with a careful eye, one acutely tuned to the rhythm of nature and its often powerful forces. Her language lends a tactile beauty to her observations as she focuses on the quiet of occurrences of nature, such as industrious hummingbirds, graceful egrets, and motionless ponds. Indeed, Oliver's work forges an individual alliance with nature that finds expression in an often rapturous lyricism. Her vision emphasizes

COMMON HUMAN EXPERIENCE

Oliver is primarily identified as a nature poet. Here are some other collections of poetry by twentieth-century authors who employ nature imagery:

The Signature of All Things: Poems, Songs, Elegies, Translations, and Epigrams (1950), a poetry collection by Kenneth Rexroth. This collection features an intense exploration of spiritual transcendence through communion with nature and humanity.

Flagons and Apples (1912), a poetry collection by Robinson Jeffers. This early collection features traditional structures, rhyme schemes, and diction. It uses the natural world as a backdrop for semiautobiographical lyrics about frustrated love.

Turtle Island (1974), a poetry collection by Gary Snyder. This Pulitzer Prize–winning volume focuses, like many of Snyder's collections, on ecological concerns and the poet's interest in instilling an ecological consciousness in his readers.

The Vixen: Poems (1996), a poetry collection by W. S. Merwin. The poems in this volume explore a rural forest in southwestern France that the poet called home for many years.

beauty and simplicity, achieved through a nonviolent portrait of nature's ecosystems.

Oliver's poems also reveal her extensive and authentic knowledge of plants and animals. She presents this knowledge in beautiful—though often not realistic—images. Her poems give readers the illusion that the natural world is graspable, controllable, and beautiful. She promotes a vision of gentleness and possibility, one that says the natural world is obtainable and belongs to anyone who simply opens his or her eyes to it. Oliver also often relates animals and plants to the human condition. The poems of *Twelve Moons*, for example, explore natural cycles and processes, equating them with what is deepest and most enduring in human experience.

Personal Emotions   Another predominant theme in Oliver's poetry is emotion and emotional situations, especially those that are personal. In *No Voyage*, for example, she explores the theme of emotional distance arising out of an inability to grieve adequately for others and their losses. One poem in particular—"The Murderer's House"—features the shame of those who heartlessly pass by a house that is haunted by sadness and loss. The poems in *The River Styx, Ohio, and Other Poems* and *The Night Traveler* are similarly personal and call on childhood memories to explore themes of loss, unconscious fears, and death. Yet, like nature, Oliver's vision of death

is often gentle, pastoral, and haunting rather than fearful and violent.

Works in Critical Context

Critics have commended Oliver's poetry for its clarity, simplicity, and descriptive precision. Stylistically, reviewers have noted the lyrical beauty of Oliver's lines and turns of phrase, and she has found favor for serving up her rapturous visions of nature without lapsing into sentimentality. While some feminist literary critics have neglected her poetry because of her perceived status as a "woman in nature" poet, other critics have noted that Oliver forges outside of traditional Romantic poetry stereotypes to claim her own individual space in nature poetry. Oliver's prose, such as *A Poetry Handbook*, has been praised for providing an incisive, knowledgeable, and artistic guide to the mechanics of poetry writing.

Dream Work   The book *Dream Work* was highly regarded by critics. Reviewing the collection for the *Nation*, Alicia Ostriker called Oliver as "visionary as [Ralph Waldo] Emerson" and said she considered Oliver "among the few American poets who can describe and transmit ecstasy, while retaining a practical awareness of the world as one of predators and prey." Colin Lowndes of the *Toronto Globe & Mail* similarly considered Oliver "a poet of worked-for reconciliations" whose volume expertly deals with thresholds or the "points at which opposing forces meet." Many critics also appreciate Oliver's gift for lyricism. Holly Prado of the *Los Angeles Times Book Review*, for example, called the poetry of *Dream Work* "the best of the real lyrics we have these days." Ostriker concluded that *Dream Work* is ultimately a volume in which Oliver moves "from the natural world and its desires, the 'heaven of appetite' … into the world of historical and personal suffering. … She confronts as well, steadily what she cannot change."

Thirst   Later collections by Oliver, such as *Thirst*, received similar praise from critics. In *Library Journal*, E. M. Kaufman wrote, "In these self-effacing poems, Oliver continues her work of loving the world, acknowledging that not all love is returned." Fred Dings in *World Literature Today* was impressed by her words and creative choices. Dings noted, "the beautiful lyricism of Oliver's voice in these hymns to the Earth and prayers to her God will make good company, regardless of our own religious persuasions." Reviewing the collection in *America*, Angela O'Donnell was similarly awed, calling *Thirst* "elegiac in genre and in spirit. … To read *Thirst* … is to feel gratitude for the simple fact of being alive. This is not surprising as it is the effect her best work has produced in readers for the past 43 years."

Responses to Literature

1. Oliver draws on nature imagery sometimes inspired by her childhood in Ohio. Write several poems of your own based on your childhood memories of

your natural surroundings. What natural environment did you grow up in? Were there particular plants, animals, or ecosystems that affected you? Describe these settings in detail, along with how they made you feel.

2. Read Oliver's first poetry collection, *No Voyage and Other Poems*, and one of her latest collections, such as *Thirst*. In an essay, discuss how you think she has evolved as a poet. Has her poetic voice changed? What thematic differences do you notice in her work?

3. Create a presentation for your class about *Our World*, focusing on how Oliver uses her words to illustrate Cook's photographs. How does this book relate to her poetry? Does it broaden your understanding of Oliver and her motivation for writing poetry? In what way?

BIBLIOGRAPHY

Periodicals

Alford, Jean B. "The Poetry of Mary Oliver: Modern Renewal through Mortal Acceptance." *Pembroke* 20 (1988).

Bond, Diane S. "The Language of Nature in the Poetry of Mary Oliver." *Women's Studies* 21, no. 1 (1992): 1–15.

Burton-Christie, Douglas. "Nature, Spirit, and Imagination in the Poetry of Mary Oliver." *Cross Current* (Spring 1996): 77–87.

Dings, Fred. Review of *Thirst*. *World Literature Today* (November–December 2007): 72.

Kaufman, E. M. Review of *Thirst*. *Library Journal* (January 1, 2007): 113.

Lowndes, Colin. Review of *Thirst*. *Globe & Mail* (August 23, 1986).

O'Donnell, Angela. Review of *Thirst*. *America* (October 9, 2006): 23.

Ostriker, Alicia. Review of *Dream Work*. *Nation* (August 30, 1986): 148–150.

Prado, Holly. Review of *Dream Work*. *Los Angeles Times Book Review* (February 27, 1987): 8.

Russell, Sue. "Mary Oliver: The Poet and the Persona." *Harvard Gay and Lesbian Review* (Fall 1997).

✸ Tillie Olsen

BORN: *1913, Omaha, Nebraska*

DIED: *2007, Oakland, California*

NATIONALITY: *American*

GENRE: *Fiction, nonfiction, poetry, drama*

MAJOR WORKS:

"I Stand Here Ironing," (1955)

Tell Me a Riddle: A Collection (1961)

Yonnondio: From the Thirties (1974)

Silences (1979)

Tillie Olsen *AP Wide World Photos*

Overview

An author and political activist, Tillie Olsen writes about the struggles of working people, particularly women, with insight that comes from personal experiences. While her output was slender, her work is considered of the highest quality by most critics. Using a strongly emotional style, Olsen is widely considered a chronicler of the poor and powerless, as well as a leading feminist writer. Among her best-known works is the award-winning short story collection *Tell Me a Riddle: A Collection* (1961).

Works in Biographical and Historical Context

Radical Background Born Tillie Lerner on January 14, 1913, in Omaha, Nebraska, Olsen was the daughter of Samuel Lerner and his wife, Ida (Berber). Her parents were Russian Jewish immigrants who had been political activists in Russia. They immigrated to the United States after the failed 1905 Russian Revolution. (This revolution was launched by workers demanding better conditions from Czar Nicholas II. While their revolt led to drastic changes in the Russian government, such as the introduction of Russia's first elected legislative assembly, the imperial regime remained in place.) In the United States,

LITERARY AND HISTORICAL CONTEMPORARIES

Olsen's famous contemporaries include:

Michael Gold (1893–1967): This American communist author and journalist served as the editor of the *Liberator* from 1920 to 1922 and *New Masses* from 1928 to 1932. His books include *The Hollow Man* (1941).

Nathanael West (1904–1940): This American fiction author and screenwriter wrote about the horror and emptiness of modern life in his best-known works, the novels; *Miss Lonely-Hearts* (1933) and *The Day of the Locusts* (1939).

Eleanor Roosevelt (1884–1962): This American philanthropist and author was the wife of President Franklin D. Roosevelt. A champion of liberal causes, she focused on securing equal opportunities for women under the New Deal's work relief programs, among other issues.

Harry F. Ward (1873–1966): This British-born American Methodist minister was a prominent supporter of organizations associated with the Communist Party during the 1930s.

Clifford Odets (1906–1963): This American playwright and screenwriter was a leading dramatist in the 1930s. Briefly a member of the Communist Party in the 1930s, he had three hit plays in 1935: *Waiting for Lefty*, *Awake and Sing*, and *Paradise Lost*.

Samuel Lerner worked as a laborer and later became an official in the Nebraska Socialist Party.

As a young girl, Olsen became passionate about writing. As a teenager, she was especially inspired by reading Rebecca Harding Davis's fictional work *Life in the Iron Mills* (1861). Olsen was so moved by Davis's descriptions of the working class that she vowed to become a writer. After dropping out of Omaha Central High School in 1917, Olsen held a variety of jobs, such as factory worker, to help support her family, but continued to educate herself through books at public libraries. She also joined the Young Communist League and Young People's Socialist League when she was seventeen years old and became a political activist.

Begins Writing First Novel Olsen was jailed in Kansas City, Kansas, for helping packinghouse workers organize unions in 1932. While in prison, she developed pleurisy (an inflammation of the membrane that surrounds and protects the lungs) and incipient tuberculosis (a bacterial lung infection for which the only treatment, in this time period before the development of antibiotics, was bed rest). After her release, Olsen moved to Fairbault, Minnesota, to recover from the first stages of tuberculosis. While living there, she began working on her novel *Yon-*

nondio (1974), about a migrant family. A chapter of it, the short story "The Iron Throat," was published in the *Partisan Review* in 1934.

Work on the book was put aside when she moved to California. By this time, Olsen was a mother, having given birth to her daughter, Karla, in 1932. She also made a move to San Francisco, California—the city that would become her long-time home—in 1933. While living in San Francisco, Olsen was arrested for taking part in the San Francisco Maritime Strike. She also wrote poetry and contributed poems, essays, and reportage to left-wing journals such as *Waterfront Worker* and *Daily Worker*.

Break From Writing Olsen's professional writing career then took a nearly two decade long hiatus because of family, economic, and social concerns. She had three more daughters and married Jack Olsen, a longshoreman and union organizer, in 1936. Olsen also held a succession of low-paying jobs—such as waitress, punch press operator, secretary, and trimmer in a slaughterhouse—to help support her family and participated in community, union, and political activities. She, like many Americans, faced economic challenges in the 1930s because of the Great Depression. The failure of the stock market in 1929 caused the economy, first in the United States, then the world, to fall in a dramatic and sustained economic depression which lasted through the 1930s.

Despite the many demands on her time, Olsen stole moments to write. By the 1950s, she was devoting more time to her writing. She also studied creative writing at San Francisco State College from 1953 to 1954, then won a Stegner Fellowship in creative writing at Stanford University in 1955. That same year, Olsen published "I Stand Here Ironing," a short story that announced the resurrection of her career. She no longer held working-class jobs but obtained numerous grants and fellowships that provided the financial resources needed to devote her time to writing.

Wins O. Henry Award A few years later, Olsen published what many critics consider her most significant work, the short story collection *Tell Me a Riddle: A Collection* (1961). That same year, the title story won the O. Henry Award for the year's best American short story. This short story focuses on the female half of an elderly couple who is forced to reevaluate her past, family life, and marriage in the face of her impending death. The rest of the four stories—among them "I Stand Here Ironing"—in the collection also explore human relationships.

During the rest of the 1960s, Olsen received numerous fellowships, teaching appointments, and several stays at the MacDowell Colony. As a writing teacher, Olsen promoted works by neglected women writers, such as Davis, Charlotte Perkins Gilman, and Agnes Smedley. In 1972, Olsen published an edition of Davis's *Life in the Iron Mills*, which included a biographical and literary commentary on the book, as well as restoring that story to the canon.

Greater Acclaim Olsen gained greater recognition as an author in the 1970s as she published several works. In 1971, she published the novella, *Requa*, which told the story of a young boy raised by his bachelor uncle after his mother dies. In 1973, Olsen rediscovered the *Yonnondio* manuscript and began working on it again. It was published in 1974 as *Yonnondio: From the Thirties* to widespread acclaim. The novel focuses on the struggles of a family living in the Midwest during the Great Depression. In 1979, Olsen published a collection of lectures and essays, *Silences*. The book looks at the issue of unnatural silences and hiatuses in literary production through the prism of her own experiences as well as that of other authors. Her thesis is that the social and economic circumstances surrounding class, color, and gender have adversely affected the potential to create literature.

Olsen's reputation also expanded because she began working internationally as a visiting scholar beginning in the late 1970s, traveling to such countries as Norway, the Soviet Union, and China. She also continued to teach in the United States, holding visiting professor and lecturer positions at the University of Minnesota and the University of California Los Angeles in 1986 and 1987, respectively. Her literary output continued to expand as she wrote her first play in 1981, *I Stand Here Mourning*. It is a monologue of a mother who is mourning the blighting of her nineteen-year-old daughter's life. In 1984, Olsen edited the nonfiction collection, *Mother to Daughter, Daughter to Mother: A Day Book and Reader*. Three years later, she co-authored *Mothers and Daughters: That Special Quality: An Exploration in Pictures*.

After her husband's death in 1989, Olsen's original output decreased, though revised editions of *Silences* and *Yonnondio* were published in 2003 and 2004, respectively. She also suffered through years of declining health, including Alzheimer's. Olsen died of complications from the disease on January 1, 2007, in Oakland, California, at the age of 94.

Works in Literary Context

In both her fiction and nonfiction works, Olsen writes about people who, because of their class, sex, and/or race, have been denied the opportunity to express and develop themselves. Her stories repeatedly embrace and affirm the humanity of underprivileged individuals who suffer the exigencies of subsistence-level work, grueling hours, and lack of free time to devote either to the development of creative talents, or the sensitive rearing of children. Olsen particularly focuses on the lot of working-class women and their frequently heroic ability to persevere. She pays close attention to the pain of being a wife and mother, while also esteeming those who endure and prevail in spite of suffering. Olsen combines in her writing her socialist upbringing, her concern for the poor, and her love of language. As an author, she was also greatly influenced by such authors as Rebecca Harding Davis.

COMMON HUMAN EXPERIENCE

Olsen is often considered one of the leading women writers of the 1930s who focused on poverty, the working class, and the lives of women. Here are some works by other women authors who tackle many of the same themes:

Pity Is Not Enough (1933), a novel by Josephine Herbst. This semi-autobiographical novel is the first of the "Trexler" trilogy and is based on the life of Herbst's uncle who went South after the Civil War as a carpetbagger. The novel covers American history from the period of Reconstruction to the Great Depression.

The Unpossessed (1934), a novel by Tess Slesinger. This modernist novel focuses on a marriage destroyed by the husband's insistence that parenthood would compromise the couple's political ideals.

Daughters of the Earth (1929), a novel by Agnes Smedley. This semi-autobiographical novel covered the challenges of Smedley's early years of poverty and hardship, emphasizing the many obstacles facing a poor young woman.

The Girl (1979), a novel by Meridel Le Sueur. This novel was written in 1939 but not published until 1979. It is the story of a girl who moves from her unhappy rural existence to urban Minnesota, where she faces the ravages of the Great Depression and sexual and emotional abuse by men until she is rescued by a community of homeless women who are associated with the Communist Party.

Working-Class People Many of Olsen's writings focus on working-class families and their search for self-fulfillment. She returns again and again to the tension in characters' lives, between the demands of living in poverty and the need for accomplishment and meaning. Olsen's only novel, *Yonnondio*, follows the lives of a poor working-class family as they struggle during the Great Depression. Centering on two strong women, the novel presents their lives in terms of failures and successes, always locating the source of their strength within themselves. Two other short stories—"Hey Sailor, What Ship?" and "Requa"—feature male characters dealing with the human condition. In the former, for example, a sailor named Whitey enjoys his time ashore with an adopted family in San Francisco. While Whitey goes on drinking bouts, the family enjoys his visits because they bring a sense of romance and adventure. From them, Whitey gets a feeling of security and understanding. The relationship is marred when the eldest daughter, embarrassed by Whitey in front of her friends, turns on him. Many of the essays in *Silences* touch on the obstacles to writing that some people face, including poverty and prejudices against class, color, and gender.

Olsen lamented the literary void created by the silences of these people.

Mothers, Children, and Lost Dreams Another predominant theme in Olsen's works is the relationship between mothers and their children. She argues that the greatest demands are placed upon mothers, often to the detriment of the women's hopes and dreams. The title story of *Tell Me a Riddle* focuses on a grandmother's efforts to make sense of her life as she is dying of cancer, surrounded by the family for whom she has sacrificed all her own ambitions. "I Stand Here Ironing" focuses on a mother's internal conflict as she remembers all the trials and failures she has encountered as she tried to raise her daughter. She mourns that her daughter has not had more advantages and fears that her daughter will be forced to endure a life much like her mother's. Olsen's nonfiction works touch on these ideas as well. In *Silences*, a collection of essays and speeches, she discusses the sacrifices that women writers have had to make for their families and refutes the common claim that women writers have not been as successful as men because they are not as talented. Instead, Olsen points out, such writers have to focus on child rearing while dealing with prejudice.

Works in Critical Context

Critics have been nearly unanimous in their praise of Olsen's fiction. Although she published very little, reviewers agree that her short stories and novel are peerless in their portrayal of the working class, women, and the powerless. Stylistically, scholars praise Olsen's use of dialect, internal conflict, and flashbacks, as well as her ability to evoke a sense or experience with an economy of words. Critics were less impressed by Olsen's nonfiction, often considering such works far less evocative and convincing than her fiction.

Yonnondio: From the Thirties When *Yonnondio* was published in the mid-1970s, it was generally well-received. Some critics, however, found the story too depressing and hopeless. A contributor to the *New Yorker* wrote that the novel "is the story of real people who are visibly shackled by having no money at all and by the daily insults offered by the world to their pride." Similarly, Susannah Clapp of the *Times Literary Supplement* stated that "By the end of the novel ... pain, rather than building the Holbrook characters, has bleached it out." While *Nation* reviewer Catherine R. Simpson noted that the condition of poverty "seeks to destroy" the characters, "Olsen's compelling gift is her ability to render lyrically the rhythms of consciousness of victims." Despite such doubts, critics like Peter Ackroyd of the *Spectator* declared "*Yonnondio* is one of the most powerful statements to have emerged from the American 'thirties'."

Silences Of Olsen's nonfiction works, *Silences* was considered a powerful statement about the difficulties some people face in writing. "Tillie Olsen's remarkable power comes from having almost never written at all," observed *Times Literary Supplement* reviewer Helen McNeil. "First a silent, then a vocal conscience for American women's writing, Olsen writes with an elegance, compassion, and directness rare in any period." Commenting on Olsen's emotional voice, *Antioch Review* contributor Nolan Miller noted that *Silences* "bears the stamp of a passionate and reasonably angry voice. What is said here needed to be said."

Responses to Literature

1. Read "The Death of Ivan Ilyich" (1886), a short story by Leo Tolstoy and "Tell Me a Riddle," a short story by Olsen. Olsen's story is often compared to Tolstoy's. In an essay, compare and contrast the two stories, focusing on the roles of patient and physician.

2. In a small group, discuss Olsen's short story "Hey Sailor, What Ship?" as an example of modernist literature. What are the modernist literary allusions and motifs? How does it compare to such books as Virginia Woolf's *The Waves* (1931), and T.S. Eliot's *The Waste Land* (1922)?

3. Read "Yonnondio" (c. 1891), the poem by Walt Whitman from which Olsen took the name of her novel. In an essay, explain what you believe the link is between the poem and *Yonnondio*.

4. Create a presentation for the class about the communist and socialist parties in the United States in the 1930s. Include examples from Olsen's stories and nonfiction works to illustrate how these groups influenced her writing.

BIBLIOGRAPHY

Books

Cardoni, Agnes Toloczko. *Women's Ethical Coming of Age: Adolescent Female Characters in the Prose Fiction of Tillie Olsen*. Lanham, Md.: University Press of America, 1997.

Faulkner, Mara. *Protest and Possibility in the Writing of Tillie Olsen*. Charlottesville: University Press of Virginia, 1993.

Orr, Elaine Neil. *Tillie Olsen and A Feminist Spiritual Vision*. Jackson: The University of Mississippi, 1987.

Periodicals

Ackroyd, Peter. Review of *Yonnondio: From the Thirties*. *Spectator* (December 14, 1974).

Clapp, Susannah. Review of *Yonnondio: From the Thirties*. *Times Literary Supplement* (January 10, 1975).

McNeil, Helen. Review of *Silences*. *Times Literary Supplement* (November 14, 1980).

Miller, Nolan. Review of *Silences*. *Antioch Review* (Fall 1978): 513.

Review of *Yonnondio: From the Thirties*. *New Yorker* (March 25, 1974).

Simpson, Catherine R. Review of *Yonnondio: From the Thirties*. *Nation* (April 10, 1972).

✿ Charles Olson

BORN: *1910, Worcester, Massachusetts*

DIED: *1970, New York, New York*

NATIONALITY: *American*

GENRE: *Poetry, nonfiction*

MAJOR WORKS:

Call Me Ishmael: A Study of Melville (1947)
The Maximus Poems (1960)
The Maximus Poems, IV, V, VI (1968)
The Maximus Poems, Volume Three (1975)

Overview

A major figure in the Black Mountain school of postmodernist American poetry, Charles Olson has also written influential essays on literary theory. Seeking to break from conventional poetics, he tried to make his work spontaneous, reflecting the rhythms of ordinary conversations. He rejected the traditional European-influenced system of symbols, images, and classical allusions in poetry, prefer-

Charles Olson *Nat Farbman / Time Life Pictures / Getty Images*

ring to express a world view that was multicultural, yet specifically rooted in the America of his time. Among his best known works is *The Maximus Poems* (1960) and its two subsequent volumes, which form a significant epic verse cycle of three hundred poems.

Works in Biographical and Historical Context

Gifted Student   Born Charles John Olson on December 27, 1910, in Worcester, Massachusetts, he was the son of Karl Joseph and Mary (Hines) Olson. His father was a letter carrier, who raised his family in Massachusetts. Young Olson spent his summers in the fishing village of Gloucester, which would later become the focus of what critics consider his most important work, the three-volume epic cycle that began with *The Maximus Poems* (1960). During the school year, Olson proved himself to be a gifted student from an early age and graduated from Classical High School in 1928.

Olson attended Wesleyan University, earning his bachelor's degree in 1932 and master's degree in 1933. He was a Phi Beta Kappa and a candidate for the Rhodes Scholarship while a student at Wesleyan. Olson then entered Harvard University where, by 1939, he completed all the requirements for a doctorate in the school's new American Civilization program, except for his dissertation. Instead of finishing his thesis, Olson chose to accept a Guggenheim fellowship to write about Herman Melville. His book on Melville was eventually published as *Call Me Ishmael* (1947) and established his literary reputation. This book was a study of the influence of William Shakespeare and other authors on Melville's classic novel *Moby Dick*.

Quits Promising Political Career   During World War II, Olson worked in the Office of War Information in Washington, D.C., as the assistant chief of the Foreign Language Division. World War II began in Europe when Nazi Germany, led by Adolf Hitler, invaded Poland in September 1939 and overran the country. England and France declared war on Germany, but Germany soon controlled much of the European continent. The United States entered the war in 1941, after Japan bombed an American naval base in Hawaii. The war was fought in a number of theaters in Europe, Asia, Africa, and the South Pacific, involving sixty-one countries and leaving fifty-five million people dead. Olson eventually resigned in protest against bureaucratic meddling and inefficiency.

After the war's end, Olson remained in Washington and built a promising political career with the Democratic National Committee as an adviser and strategist. He had previously served on several committees for President Franklin D. Roosevelt, who had been elected to the presidency four times before his death in 1945. By the time Olson was in his mid-thirties, he abandoned politics to concentrate on literature, publishing his first poetry

LITERARY AND HISTORICAL CONTEMPORARIES

Olson's famous contemporaries include:

Cid Corman (1924–2004): This American poet and essayist is often compared to Robert Creeley, and was an influential figure among the Beat and Black Mountain poets. Corman's poetry collections include *For Instance* (1962).

Jonathan Williams (1929–2008): This American poet is usually associated with both the Black Mountain poets and Beat poets. Like Olson, he was greatly influenced by William Carlos Williams. Jonathan Williams' poetry collections include *Petite Country Concrete Suite* (1965).

Michael Rumaker (1932–): This American novelist and short story writer was considered the most promising prose writer to come from the Black Mountain school after his short story, "The Pipe," was printed in the journal the *Black Mountain Review* in 1956.

William S. Burroughs (1914–1997): This American experimental novelist and short story writer was the consummate outsider and rebel and had tremendous influence on the Beat generation of writers. His novel, *Confessions of an Unredeemed Drug Addict* (1953), was greatly influenced by his own life as a morphine addict.

Allen Ginsberg (1926–1997): This American poet and essayist enjoyed a prominent place in post-World War II American culture. A leading example of the Beat generation of writers, he first came to public attention with the publication of *Howl and Other Poems* (1956).

collection *To Corrado Cagli* in 1947, as well as his critical nonfiction work *Call me Ishmael*. In 1948, Olson took a temporary teaching post at Black Mountain College in North Carolina. He also published his second collection of poetry, *Y&X* (1948). Two years later, Olson published the influential essay "Projective Verse" in *Poetry New York*, which became a manifesto for the postmodernist poetry movement in America.

Black Mountain Poet Olson returned to Black Mountain in 1951 to serve as a lecturer as well as the school's rector. Olson soon became the charismatic leader of what came to be known as the Black Mountain poets. He also published his second collection of poetry *In Cold Hell, In Thicket* (1953), and a collection of essays, *Mayan Letters* (1953). When Black Mountain College closed in 1956 because of financial difficulties, Olson returned to Gloucester, Massachusetts, where he lived in modest circumstances among fishermen. There, he devoted himself to writing *The Maximus Poems* and other poetry collections. In 1959, Olson published *O'Ryan 2.4.6.8.10*, followed by *The Distances* in 1960.

Olson's most important poetry collection, *The Maximus Poems*, came next. These epic poems were published in two volumes, *The Maximus Poems* in 1960 and *The Maximus Poems, IV, V, VI* in 1968. The subject of the poems is Gloucester—both its historic past and present condition—from the point of view of Maximus, a character representing the poet himself.

Posthumous Accolades While Gloucester remained his home base, Olson took several visiting professorships at the State University of New York from 1963 to 1965, and the University of Connecticut in 1969. He also continued to put out both poetry and prose works. Olson published two more poetry volumes in addition to the two *Maximus* volumes: *O'Ryan 1, 2, 3, 4, 5, 6, 7, 8, 9, 10* (1965) and *West* (1966). His nonfiction works of this time period included the essay collections *Human Universe and Other Essays* (1965) and *Proprioception* (1965).

Olson died on January 10, 1970, in New York City from liver cancer. After his death, several more volumes of his poetry were published, including the comprehensive edition of his short poems *Archaeologist of Morning* (1970) and *The Maximus Poems, Volume Three*, as well as a volume of criticism, *The Special View of History* (1970). Olson also received several posthumous awards, including the American Book Award from the Before Columbus Foundation in 1988 for the *The Collected Poems of Charles Olson* (1987).

Works in Literary Context

In his essays, Olson argues that poetic language must be spontaneous, expressing what is actually seen and felt, rather than obeying conventional rules of logic and order. The poet followed these ideas in his own major poetic works, particularly the rejection of tradition-bound European ways of thinking and a striving towards less artificial, more direct methods of writing and experiencing life. Olson believed that his "projective"—open—verse transmitted energy from the poet's inspiration to the reader. As a poet and theorist, Olson was greatly influenced by Ezra Pound, William Carlos Williams, and Edward Dahlberg, while his theories also reflect the inspiration of Alfred North Whitehead and Carl Jung. He attempted to carry on their innovations while discovering his own radically new means of expression. Olson was also inspired by his childhood summer home of Gloucester, Massachusetts, and the fishermen who lived there, as well as the depth and breadth of his intellectual reading.

Projective Poetry In his influential essay, "Projective Verse," Olson defined poetry in terms of the dynamic world his contemporaries were discovering while he redefined the possibilities of language. The essay became the fundamental theory of the Black Mountain school, as well as a powerful influence on American poetry written in the 1960s. In the essay, he wrote "A poem is energy transferred from where the poet got it ... by way of the poem itself ... to the reader." The poet's own energy as he or she writes is among that which is embodied in the poem. The syllable, Olson argued, reveals the poet's act of exploring the possibilities of sound in order to create an oral beauty. The line reveals the poet's breathing, where it begins and ends as he works. Conventional syntax, meter, and rhyme must be abandoned, Olson argued, if their structural requirements slow the swift currents of the poet's thought. The predictable left-hand margin falsifies the spontaneous nature of experience. Poems such as "The Kingfishers" (1949) and *The Maximus Poems* demonstrate his sustained effort to practice his poetic theories. The latter poems require the reader to experience the world through Maximus's senses as reflected by the spatial arrangement of words on a page.

Gloucester Gloucester, a favorite haunt of Olson while he was growing up in Massachusetts, figures symbolically in his writing, particularly because one of his primary artistic considerations was the effect on an individual of the social evolution of place. The several volumes of *The Maximus Poems* especially employ Gloucester as a major symbol. The books are dense with antiquarian knowledge about Gloucester, beginning with the establishment of the Massachusetts Bay Colony to modern Gloucester as an emblem of contemporary society and its travails. Among the themes treated in the *Maximus* cycle are the values and heroism of the working people of Gloucester, and how what might have been an idyllic community was violated by modern American consumer culture. Olson is also viewed as having restored the use of myth to contemporary poetry; his account of Gloucester as a community in conflict with mass society is regarded as a timeless paradigm of order versus tyranny in a world mythology.

Works in Critical Context

During his lifetime, Olson inspired admiration within his circle of colleagues and students. He also attracted controversy with his radical challenges to traditional and modernist literary conventions. Because his seemingly cryptic, often ungrammatical, manner of writing can be difficult to read, contemporary reviewers expressed frustration with, and skepticism about, his methods. As postmodernism became an established literary movement, critics focused on exploring Olson's characteristic themes and style, often comparing his theoretical writings with his own verse. Still, critical assessment of the importance of Olson's projective verse theory varies depending on a given critic's enthusiasm for Olson as phenomenon in American poetry.

The Maximus Poems Many critics, as well as readers, find *The Maximus Poems*, as well as the *Maximus* poems in the two subsequent volumes, difficult to follow because of Olson's experiments with form and content. Some contemporary reviewers have judged it to be a failure in terms of its epic intentions, though others found the verse quite challenging. Later critics came to regard the work as an important testament of the second half of the century. In a contemporary review of the first ten *Maximus* poems, Robert Creeley—whose review was

published in his *A Quick Graph: Collected Notes and Essays*—noted "They are truth because their form is that issue of what is out there, and what is part of it can come into a man's own body." Critics and scholars discussed and debated many aspects of the poems, with individuals offering their own interpretation. Referring to Olson's vision, for example, Robert von Hallberg in *Contemporary Literature* noted "Olson defines for Gloucester (an always, by extension, for America) its heritage of values and conflicts; he cautions a firm grip on those values and a sharpened understanding of those conflicts in the present time of national slide and decadence." In *Modern Poetry*, Phillip E. Smith II concluded, "The unity of humanism in place as well as person is the great accomplishment of *The Maximus Poems*."

Collected Prose Published in 1997, *Collected Prose* included much of Olson's nonfiction writing, including essays, criticism, and reviews. Critics acknowledged his widespread influence as well as his contrarian nature. In *Publishers Weekly*, the reviewer commented, "While scattershot, Olson's hardheaded declarations are never boring." Other critics found his style challenging. David Kirby, in *Library Journal*, said that "Olson wrote in a muscular style, one as individualistic as it is exasperating." Janet St. John, in *Booklist*, acknowledged that "In a Pound-like manner, Olson brought to literature a modern sensibility." She added, "To readers and thinkers, one of Olson's most obvious gifts is to urge understanding by drawing connections where we might not have thought to draw them." Writing in *America*, Fidel Fajardo-Acosta concluded, "His quest for personal truth and freedom, the product of a humane and generous spirit, is accompanied by a truly Whitmanian acceptance of, and search for, unity with the individual and the collective other."

Responses to Literature

1. In a paper, compare and contrast Olson's epic *Maximus* poem sequence with one of the other major verse epics of the modern period such as Ezra Pound's *Cantos* (1925–69), William Carlos Williams' *Paterson* (1946–58), or Hart Crane's *The Bridge* (1930). Which poem do believe is most valuable?

2. Read "Projective Verse." Based on your understanding of the essay and Olson's ideas, write several poems of your own using these ideas.

3. Create a presentation for the class about the Black Mountain school of poetry. What were its defining ideas? Why did it become so influential? Use poems and ideas of Olson's in your presentation.

4. Read Olson's *In Cold Hell, in Thicket* (1953), a collection of primarily shorter poems. Some of the poems are written in projective mode, while others are free verse. Identify poems of both types, and in an essay, compare and contrast the effectiveness of each type. Which poems speak more to you?

BIBLIOGRAPHY

Books

Butterick, George. *A Guide to the Maximus Poems of Charles Olson*. Berkeley: The University of California Press, 1978.

Christensen, Paul. *Charles Olson: Call Him Ishmael*. Austin: University of Texas Press, 1979.

Clark, Tom. *Charles Olson: The Allegory of a Poet's Life*. New York: Norton, 1991.

Creeley, Robert. "Charles Olson: 'The Maximus Poems, 1–10'." In *A Quick Graph: Collected Notes and Essays*, edited by Donald Allen. San Francisco: Four Seasons, 1970, pp. 157–58.

Maud, Ralph. *What Does Not Change: The Significance of Charles Olson's "The Kingfishers."* Cranbury, N.J.: Farleigh Dickinson University Press, 1998.

Paul, Sherman. *Olson's Push: Origin, Black Mountain, and Recent American Poetry*. Baton Rouge: Louisiana State University Press, 1978.

Merrill, Thomas. *The Poetry of Charles Olson: A Primer*. Newark: University of Delaware Press, 1982.

Periodicals

Fajardo-Acosta, Fidel. Review of *Collected Prose. America* (November 28, 1998): 21.

Kirby, David. Review of *Collected Prose. Library Journal* (January 1998): 100.

Review of *Collected Prose. Publishers Weekly* (November 17, 1997): 50.

Smith, Phillip E. II. "Descent into Polis: Charles Olson's Search for Community." *Modern Poetry Studies* (Spring 1977): 13–22.

St. John, Janet. Review of *Collected Prose. Booklist* (December 15, 1997): 680.

Von Hallberg, Robert. "Olson's Relation to Pound and Williams." *Contemporary Literature* (Winter 1974): 15–48.

✸ Eugene O'Neill

BORN: *1888, New York, New York*

DIED: *1953, Boston, Massachusetts*

NATIONALITY: *American*

GENRE: *Drama*

MAJOR WORKS:
Beyond the Horizon (1920)
Anna Christie (1921)
Strange Interlude (1928)
The Iceman Cometh (1946)
Long Day's Journey Into Night (1956)

Eugene O'Neill   *O'Neill, Eugene, photograph. AP Images.*

Overview

The four-time winner of the Pulitzer Prize and the Nobel laureate for literature in 1936, Eugene O'Neill is considered a ground-breaking figure in American dramatic literature. He enlarged the scope, material, and technique of American drama while setting high aspirations for himself. Many of O'Neill's plays focus on the anguish and pain experienced by sensitive people. His work did not merely enrich American drama: he reinvented it and prepared the way for the playwrights who followed. O'Neill's masterpieces include *Anna Christie* (1921), *Strange Interlude* (1928), *Mourning Becomes Electra* (1931), and *Long Day's Journey into Night* (1956).

Works in Biographical and Historical Context

Difficult Childhood　Born Eugene Gladstone O'Neill in a New York City hotel in 1888, he was the third son of James and Ella Quinlan O'Neill. His father was an outstanding romantic actor, best known for his portrayal of the lead in the stage version of *The Count of Monte Cristo* six thousand times, and O'Neill spent the first seven years of his life on tour with his parents. Although he received much exposure to the theater, he disliked living in hotel rooms, and the constant traveling drove his mother to become addicted to drugs, particularly morphine. Throughout his childhood, his family life was dysfunctional and tormented.

From the age of seven to fourteen, O'Neill was educated at Catholic schools. He then rebelled against any further Catholic education, and his parents sent him to high school at the Betts Academy in Connecticut. O'Neill began spending time with his elder brother James, a heavy drinker, who introduced him to debauchery. O'Neill's formal education ended in 1907 with an unfinished year at Princeton University, which ended with his dismissal from the school. By this time, his only interests were alcohol, books, and women, though he also held a job for a mail-order firm.

Focus on Playwriting　After his 1909 marriage to Kathleen Jenkins, O'Neill left for Honduras to mine for gold. He later worked at sea and held odd jobs in Buenos Aires, Argentina. Over the years, nearly half of his published plays show his interest in the sea. In 1912, O'Neill's marriage broke up, he attempted suicide, and he developed tuberculosis. (Tuberculosis was a bacterial lung infection for which the only current treatment was bed rest. Antibiotics had not yet been developed, limiting treatment options.) By the time he was released from the hospital after a six-month hospital stay in June 1913, he had decided to become a dramatist.

O'Neill began to read every modern play he could find and wrote constantly. With his father's help, five of O'Neill's one-act plays were published in 1914. After spending a term in George Pierce Baker's playwriting class at Harvard University, O'Neill planned on returning in the fall of 1915, but instead lived at a bar and hotel in New York City known as the "Hell Hole." There, he drank heavily and produced nothing.

Success as a Playwright　During this period, World War I was being fought. This conflict began in Europe in 1914 after the assassination of Archduke Franz Ferdinand, the heir to the Austro-Hungarian throne. Because of political tensions and entangling alliances, nearly all of Europe soon became involved in the conflict. In 1917, the United States joined the war on the side of Great Britain and France after Germany's naval fleet began sinking American merchant ships in British waters. Ultimately, ten million soldiers died and twenty million were wounded during the course of the "Great War."

O'Neill resumed his playwriting when he joined the Provincetown Players in Cape Cod, Massachusetts. (He later became the co-manager of the Provincetown Players, beginning in 1923.) There, several of his plays about the sea were produced, including *Bound East for Cardiff* (1916), which made him well known by 1918. Also in 1918, O'Neill married his second wife, Agnes Boulton, with whom he had two children, Shane and Oona.

Popular Full-Length Plays　Until this point, O'Neill concentrated heavily on the one-act form. In 1920, his first one-act play, *Beyond the Horizon*, was produced, for which he won his first Pulitzer Prize. This play was similar to the one-act form in its structure, but by adding a poetic and well-spoken character, O'Neill was able to reach high dramatic moments.

Over the next fifteen years, O'Neill wrote twenty-one plays. Some were brilliant successes, such as *Anna Christie* and *Strange Interlude* (1928), both of which won Pulitzers. Other significant plays include *Desire Under the Elms* (1924) and *Mourning Becomes Electra* (1931). Other plays, such as *Diff'rent* (1920) and *All God's Chillun Got Wings* (1924), received mixed reviews, while his plays *Dynamo* (1929) and *Days Without End* (1934) were outright disasters. Yet, O'Neill's importance as a dramatist was confirmed with his winning the Nobel Prize for literature in 1936.

Late Struggles　O'Neill's personal life was turbulent as well. During the early 1920s, O'Neill's father, mother, and brother all died within a three-year span. His marriage also became troubled, and he divorced Boulton in 1929. O'Neill married actress Carlotta Monterey soon after. She brought a sense of order to his life, managing it in order to facilitate his work. Her care helped him remain productive and also made it possible for him to give up alcohol. Suffering ill health after 1937, O'Neill became a virtual recluse in France, Bermuda, Sea Island, Georgia, and California.

O'Neill continued to write original works until 1943 when he was prevented from writing by a hand tremor resulting from Parkinson's disease. However, few of these late plays were produced during his lifetime. For example, O'Neill wrote about his tormented upbringing in his

LITERARY AND HISTORICAL CONTEMPORARIES

O'Neill's famous contemporaries include:

Charlie Chaplin (1887–1977): This British actor and filmmaker was a silent film comedy star best known for his on-screen persona, the Little Tramp. Chaplin married O'Neill's daughter, Oona, late in life.

Paul Robeson (1898–1976): This African American actor, singer, and political activist performed the title role in the original New York production of O'Neill's *The Emperor Jones* to much acclaim.

John Reed (1887–1920): This American revolutionist, poet, and journalist became a symbol in many American minds of the communist revolution in Russia. A Marxist writer, Reed was friends with O'Neill.

Louise Bryant (1885–1936): This American editor and writer witnessed the Soviet revolution in Russia and became one of its outspoken defenders. Married to John Reed, Bryant was the inspiration for the lead character in O'Neill's *Strange Interlude*.

Elmer Rice (1892–1967): This American playwright and novelist wrote several popular plays produced in New York in the 1920s, 1930s, and 1940s. Among his best-known works is *Street Scene* (1929).

tour-de-force autobiographical play, *Long Day's Journey into Night*. While the play was written in 1940, he ordered it withheld from production for twenty-five years. However, in 1956, a few years after his death, his widow allowed its first staging in New York.

Posthumous Acclaim   One late original play that was produced in New York was *The Iceman Cometh*, which was written earlier but first produced in 1946. This play fascinated audiences despite its length. It concludes that humans require self-lies to sustain them; life without pipe dreams is too terrible for most people. At the time of his death, O'Neill had six unfinished original plays. When he knew that death was near, he tore up the plays rather than have someone else rewrite them.

O'Neill died of pneumonia on November 27, 1953, in Boston. In the years after his death, a number of his late plays were produced to acclaim and great success. For example, O'Neill won his last Pulitzer posthumously for *Long Day's Journey into Night*. The success of this play—which also won the Antoinette Perry Award for best play—solidified O'Neill's reputation with audiences who had not seen his plays in the 1920s or 1930s.

Works in Literary Context

O'Neill's plays focus on themes of family guilt and strife, the destructive power of love, the constrictions of mar-

riage, the necessity for sensitive and gifted characters to escape their environments, the need for "pipe dreams," and—perhaps his main recurring theme—the tragic effects on people who betray their temperaments or violate their natures. His most memorable characters are obsessed by fixed ideas or romantic ideals. Many of O'Neill's plays are extremely long—running typically four or five hours on stage—and tend to feature marathon monologues and profound themes touching on the human condition. His early plays employed realism and naturalism, using realistic speech and detail. However, later plays featured "supernaturalism"—the systemic use of symbolism in a realistic work. As an author, O'Neill was influenced by Friedrich Nietzsche, August Strindberg, and historical dramas. The destructive love and guilt of his family also especially inspired O'Neill's later family dramas.

Expressionistic Techniques   O'Neill introduced expressionistic techniques into American drama in his endeavor to objectify the inner experiences of his characters. Expressionism is an artistic style that departs from the conventions of realism and naturalism and seeks to convey inner experience by distorting, rather than representing, natural images. In expressionistic works, such as O'Neill's plays, distortion, simplification, exaggeration, and symbolic settings are employed. His *The Emperor Jones* (1920) is regarded as the first American expressionist play; it was followed by *The Hairy Ape* (1922). In *The Emperor Jones*, Brutus Jones moves from reality, to conscious memories of the past, to subconscious roots of his ancient heritage, as he flees for his life. The play ends with the reality of his death. O'Neill also employed techniques from the classics and gave them expressionistic treatments. In *The Great God Brown* (1926), masks indicate the characters' efforts to hide their conflicts of mind and soul. *Lazarus Laughed* (1927) employs mask and chorus.

Autobiographical Troubled Families   In the 1930s and 1940s, O'Neill wrote many plays about troubled people and their families, inspired by his own life. He was dealing with his "private demons" by using his own experience to make broad statements about human nature. *All God's Chillun Got Wings*, for example is a symbolic account of his parents' marriage that shows a black man—"Jim"—and a white woman—"Ella"—who struggle to love each other despite their differences. While *Mourning Becomes Electra* is an adaptation of the "Oresteia" trilogy of Aeschylus, the tale of passion, murder, and divine retribution suggested to O'Neill his family's buried relationships. For O'Neill, the psychology of family life, not the ancient gods, determines each character's fate. *Long Day's Journey into Night* portrays even more tragic family dynamics. Set in New London, Connecticut, on one day in 1912 at the home of the Tyrone family, the members of the family try to be kind to each other as the day begins, but ugly memories repeatedly emerge and inspire intensifying rounds of soul-searching, recrimination, and apology. Not all plays with this theme were dark, however. The nostalgic comedy,

Ah, Wilderness! (1933), was inspired by his youth in New London, Connecticut. The main character is Richard Miller, a good-natured seventeen-year-old who prompts a minor scandal by quoting "decadent" poetry to his girl-friend. Chastised by adults, he rebels by visiting a bar and a prostitute with a heart of gold. When he comes home drunk, his alcoholic Uncle Sid gently sees him to bed.

Works in Critical Context

While O'Neill is now generally considered among America's foremost dramatists, his plays were not always well received when originally produced. Despite receiving the Nobel Prize in literature in 1936, O'Neill's reputation as a playwright declined steadily after 1935, reaching an all-time low shortly after his death in 1953. However, a number of his late plays were produced for the first time beginning in the mid- to late 1950s. The O'Neill revival in the late 1950s credited him with making American drama into literature and with bringing the combination of personal and cultural memory to the American stage. Critics downplayed his so-called morbidness by emphasizing the theme of salvation through tragedy. His detractors, however, claimed that O'Neill was over-ambitious, that his plays were too long and obscure, faulting his strange combination of mysticism and melodrama and calling his writing thin. Furthermore, feminist reassessments pointed out O'Neill's vilification of women, questioning the possibilities for women in realism itself. Nonetheless, most critics agree that his influence on American theater history is undeniable.

Desire Under the Elms Regarded as one of O'Neill's best early dramas, *Desire Under the Elms* established his reputation as one of the foremost American dramatists of the twentieth century. Because of its controversial themes of incest and infanticide, the play was unfavorably reviewed on its debut but has subsequently been regarded as what Travis Bogard in *Contour in Time: The Plays of Eugene O'Neill* terms "the first important tragedy to be written in America." Contemporary critics were more divided, with commentators like the *Nation*'s Joseph Wood Krutch praising the play without trying to discover a redeeming social message. He wrote that "The meaning and unity of [O'Neill's] work lies not in any controlling intellectual idea and certainly not in a 'message,' but merely in the fact that each play is an experience of extraordinary intensity." Noting that the play transcended its themes and setting, Krutch concluded, O'Neill's play is "interested less in New England as such than in an aspect of the eternal tragedy of man and his passions."

Long Day's Journey into Night When *Long Day's Journey into Night* made its premiere in 1956, O'Neill's reputation among critics was that of an outdated, over the hill, third-rate thinker. After the play made its debut in Boston, and then in New York City that fall, critics changed their thinking about the playwright and his talent. From its earliest productions, *Journey* was regarded as a master-

---

COMMON HUMAN EXPERIENCE

The destructive effects of drug addiction is a theme in O'Neill's play, *Long Day's Journey Into Night*. Here are some more works that feature this theme:

Confessions of an English Opium-Eater (1821), a memoir by English writer Thomas de Quincey. This book was first published anonymously in two magazine installments. An immediate success with the public, it was reprinted in book form the following year. De Quincey had been addicted to opium since 1804. He had first taken it, following standard medical practice at the time, for pain relief.

Trainspotting (1996), a film directed by Danny Boyle. This film is based on the novel of the same title by Irvine Welsh (1993). The film follows the lives of a group of young heroin addicts in the poverty-stricken areas of otherwise prosperous Edinburgh, Scotland, in the 1990s.

The Man with the Golden Arm (1949), a novel by Nelson Algren. Algren presents a gritty tale about the life of a young man, known as Frankie Machine, who is addicted to morphine following treatment for an injury sustained in World War II. The morphine was used to control his pain. He has just been released after detoxing at a federal prison for drug addicts, but his life is about to spiral downward. The novel won the National Book Award in 1950.

The Naked Lunch (1959), a novel by William Burroughs. This novel is narrated by a drug addict, William Lee, as he flees the United States for Mexico. Burroughs used some of his own experiences as a heroin and morphine addict in this controversial, but widely praised, novel that tells its story in an unconventional, nonlinear fashion.

---

piece. In the *New York Daily News,* John Chapman wrote that the Tyrones "become larger than their own small lives. They become humanity, looking for something but not knowing exactly what it is looking for." Chapman concluded, "This is O'Neill's most beautiful play. . . . And it is one of the great dramas of any time." Similarly, Harold Clurman in the *Nation* wrote, "The play is the testament of the most serious playwright our country has produced." Over the years, critics remained impressed by the play, with Leó Miralas noting in *Eugene O'Neill's Critics: Voices from Abroad,* "It would be difficult to point out a piece written more at the margin of all conventions, more contrary to all the tastes of the public, more bitter, and more painful, which cleanses the soul and at the same time is constructed without the least deference to theatrical canons, classical forms, and patron saints of theatre."

Responses to Literature

1. Research why O'Neill's plays like *The Fountain* (1925), *Marco Millions* (1927), and *Lazarus Laughed* (1927) were considered failed experiments by most critics. In an essay, explain your findings and, focusing on one play in particular, delineate why you think that play was a failure.

2. In a small group, discuss O'Neill's early plays inspired by his time at sea. Why do you think the sea held such an attraction for O'Neill? How do the themes in the early plays compare to those in his later full-length plays?

3. In a paper, discuss O'Neill's pipe-dream plays, such as *The Iceman Cometh*. How do you think the concept of a pipe dream plays out in them? How does the idea of a pipe dream relate to modern society? Could such plays be updated and still retain their meaning?

4. Create a presentation about *Ah, Wilderness!*, the only lighthearted comedy O'Neill produced. How does the play contrast with O'Neill's other works? How do its themes, characters, dialogue, and structure compare with his other plays?

BIBLIOGRAPHY

Books

Alexander, Doris. *Eugene O'Neill's Creative Struggle: The Decisive Decade, 1924–1933*. University Park: Pennsylvania State University Press, 1992.

Bagchee, Shymal, ed. *Perspectives on O'Neill: New Essays*. Victoria, B.C.: University of Victoria, 1988.

Black, Stephen A. *Eugene O'Neill: Beyond Mourning and Tragedy*. New Haven, Conn: Yale University Press, 1999.

Bogard, Travis. *Contour in Time: The Plays of Eugene O'Neill*. New York: Oxford University Press, 1972.

Dubost, Thierry. *Struggle, Defeat, or Rebirth: Eugene O'Neill's Vision of Humanity*. Jefferson, N.C.: McFarland, 1996.

Mirlas, León. "The Scope of O'Neill's Drama." In *Eugene O'Neill's Critics: Voices from Abroad*, edited by Horst Frenz and Susan Tuck. Carbondale: Southern Illinois University Press, 1984, pp. 101–09.

Sheaffer, Louis. *O'Neill, Son and Artist*. Rev. ed. Boston: Little, Brown, 2002.

Periodicals

Chapman, John. Review of *Long Day's Journey into Night. New York Daily News* (November 8, 1956).

Clurman, Harold. Review of *Long Day's Journey into Night. The Nation* (March 3, 1956).

Krutch, Joseph Wood. "The God of the Stumps." *The Nation* (November 26, 1924): 578–80.

✲ Simon J. Ortiz

BORN: *1941, Pueblo of Acoma, New Mexico*

NATIONALITY: *Native American*

GENRE: *Poetry, fiction, nonfiction*

MAJOR WORKS:

Going for the Rain (1976)

A Good Journey (1977)

Fighting Back: For Sake of the People, for the Sake of the Land (1980)

From Sand Creek: Rising in This Heart Which Is Our America (1981)

The Good Rainbow Road (2004)

Overview

An Acoma Pueblo Indian, Simon J. Ortiz is considered an important Native American writer in contemporary American literature. Considered part of the Native American Renaissance, he draws on oral tradition, folk tales, and other elements of his native culture to address themes of Native American heritage and contemporary identity. Writing poetry, short stories, nonfiction, and literature for children, Ortiz won the Pushcart Prize for Poetry for *From Sand Creek: Rising in This Heart Which Is Our America* (1981) and the 1993 Lifetime Achievement Award for Literature from the Native Writers Circle of the Americas.

Works in Biographical and Historical Context

Influenced by Storytelling Simon Joseph Ortiz was born on May 27, 1941, at the Pueblo of Acoma, near Albuquerque, New Mexico, the son of Joe L. and Mamie Toribio Ortiz. His father was a woodcarver, clan leader, and laborer for the Santa Fe railroad, while his mother was a potter. While growing up in a large family, which belonged to the Eagle clan of the tribal people of the

Simon J. Ortiz   *AP Images*

Acoma reservation, Ortiz suffered financial hardships but was particularly inspired by storytellers. He was especially moved by stories people told about their lives and social situations, especially those about Native Americans trying to survive in contemporary life. Speaking the Acoma language of Keres at home, Ortiz learned English as a second language at McCartys Day School, his elementary school. He then briefly attended a boarding school, St. Catherine's Indian School, until homesickness and disillusionment compelled him to transfer to Albuquerque Indian School. By this time, Ortiz was collecting stories and thoughts and was an avid reader.

Though Albuquerque was a trade school, Ortiz liked to read and study, to learn about the world, though being a writer seemed out of the realm of possibility for him. He transferred again to Grants High School in Grants, New Mexico, where he was a successful student who earned awards in both academics and sports and saw his leadership skills emerging. He then briefly worked in the uranium mines and processing plants of the Grants Ambrosia Lake area. His work experience as a mining laborer later provided the material for his writing in *Fighting Back: For Sake of the People, for the Sake of the Land* (1980). From 1961 to 1962, he attended Fort Lewis College, in Durango, Colorado. There, Ortiz studied chemistry but became interested in drama and English studies. Also a leader of the Indian Student Organization, Ortiz became involved in issues of fair treatment for native peoples.

Enlisted in Army Ortiz enlisted in the U.S. Army in 1963, remaining in the service until 1966. At this time, the United States was becoming more involved in what became the Vietnam War. Vietnam had been divided into a communist North and noncommunist South in the mid-1950s, but communist efforts to gain control over all of Vietnam continued. In the early 1960s, the United States began to provide military aid to South Vietnam, hoping to stop the spread of communism. At first the aid came in the form of advisors, but after 1964, an ever-increasing number of American troops entered the conflict. Though unpopular, the war in Vietnam continued until the early 1970s. Approximately 58,000 American soldiers and two million Vietnamese soldiers and civilians lost their lives in the conflict.

After his discharge, Ortiz attended the University of New Mexico at Albuquerque. Completing his bachelor's degree in 1968, he then entered the University of Iowa, where he earned his M.F.A. in creative writing in 1969. From 1970 to 1973, Ortiz served as a newspaper editor for the National Indian Youth Council in Albuquerque. His first book of poetry, *Naked in the Wind*, was published in 1971. Ortiz began receiving national attention as an author when four of his short stories appeared in *The Man to Send Rain Clouds* (1974), an anthology of Native American writing edited by Kenneth Rosen. Two of them were to become his best-known stories: "Kaiser and the War" and "The Killing of a State Cop."

Native American Conflict In this time period, some Native Americans were demanding greater civil rights, inspired by the success of the African American civil rights movement. In the 1960s, Native Americans were among the poorest, most unhealthy, and worst educated minority groups in the United States. To draw attention to their plight, Native American activists took over Alcatraz Island in 1969 and a trading post in Wounded Knee, South Dakota, in 1973. While these tactics won national attention, other activists lobbied the federal government for new laws that would grant them more control over their own lives. By the mid-1970s, these efforts paid off as the federal government returned millions of acres of land and passed the Indian Self-Determination and Educational Assistance Act of 1975.

Ortiz had struggled with alcoholism for many years, and during the mid-1970s, received treatment for the disease at the Veterans Administration hospital in Fort Lyons, Colorado. After his release, *Going for the Rain* (1976) was published. This volume is regarded as Ortiz's first significant poetry collection and emphasizes the importance of returning to traditional culture, languages, and stories as a means of spiritual healing in an alienating modern world. *A Good Journey* (1977) continues this thematic concern. The short story collection, *The How-bah Indians* (1978), describes the everyday struggles of Native Americans living on reservations in America, while his first children's book, *The People Shall Continue* (1978), offers colorful drawings to accompany the story, a panorama of the history of American Indians from before the arrival of the first settlers to the present.

Continued Success Ortiz also began teaching writing and American Indian literature at various colleges and universities, including San Diego State University, the College of Marin, Institute of American Arts, the University of New Mexico, and Lewis and Clark College. While holding these posts, Ortiz became the consulting editor of Pueblo of Acoma Press, beginning in 1982. He also continued to publish significant books, including *Fight Back* (1980), which contained poetry, prose, and essays. It was published on the three-hundredth anniversary of the Pueblos' revolt against their Spanish colonizers in 1680, and was dedicated to the Pueblo Indians. Similarly, *From Sand Creek* contains more than forty lyric poems, each paired on facing pages with a prose piece ranging in length from one sentence to one page. Next, Ortiz published the short story collection *Fightin'* (1983). The nineteen new and previously published works explore the interactions between Native Americans and whites.

In 1989, Ortiz became the first lieutenant governor for the Acoma Pueblo in New Mexico. He continued to write, publishing his first poetry collection in over a decade in 1992. *Woven Stone* contains three out-of-print poetry collections—*Going for Rain, A Good Journey,* and *Fight Back*—in one volume along with an autobiographical introduction describing Ortiz's development as a writer. Two

LITERARY AND HISTORICAL CONTEMPORARIES

Ortiz's famous contemporaries include:

Duane Niatum (1938–): This Native American poet, short story writer, and essayist focuses on the realities of being Indian in contemporary American society. His poetry collections include *Digging Out the Roots* (1977) and *Songs for the Harvester of Dreams* (1981).

Jane Smiley (1949–): This American novelist earned her M.F.A. from the University of Iowa. She won a Pulitzer Prize for her novel *A Thousand Acres* (1991).

Joan Baez (1941–): This American folk singer is widely recognized for her nonviolent, antiestablishment, and anti-war positions. She has used her singing and speaking talents to criticize violations of human rights in a number of countries.

Toni Cade Bambara (1939–95): This African American novelist and short story writer was a consistent advocate for civil rights. Among her works is the short story collection *Gorilla, My Love* (1972).

Gerald Vizenor (1934–): This Native American novelist, short story writer, and poet draws on the strong oral traditions of his Indian ancestors. His novels include *Darkness in Saint Louis Bearheart* (1973).

years later, Ortiz published *After and Before the Lightning* (1994), which consists of journal entries written in verse and prose, dating from November 1985 through March 1986, and set on the Lakota Sioux Rosebud reservation in South Dakota, where Ortiz spent a semester as a visiting professor. These pieces continue to explore themes of Native American community and identity, with particular focus on man's relationship to the land in the harsh conditions of a South Dakota winter.

Returning to short fiction collections, Ortiz put out *Men on the Moon* (1999), which also focuses on tensions and interactions between Native Americans and whites. After another nearly decade-long break from publishing verse, Ortiz published another new volume in 2002, *Out There Somewhere*. These poems contain further examinations of the concepts of identity, culture, and history.

Throughout his career, Ortiz published a number of books for younger readers. The illustrated *The Good Rainbow Road* (2004) relates an original story in the form of a traditional fable or legend about two brothers trying to rescue their village from drought. Ortiz continues to write while teaching at Arizona State University.

Works in Literary Context

Ortiz's writings are emotionally charged and complex. His expressions of anger, passion, love, fear, and threats to human existence make the reader question the backdrop of the society in which he or she exists. Pertinent to both Native and non-Native American readers, Ortiz's subjects are those that affect daily life. Writing in English, Ortiz uses language to confirm, verify, and affirm the essence of the land and people together and their existence based on the concept of "wholeness." His storytelling relates traditions of his culture and blends experience and oral traditions. Language is also important, and he often conveys a message with political overtones. Many of his poems warn that the abuse and exploitation of the land ultimately lead to the destruction of all life, including human life. As an author, Ortiz was greatly influenced by historical events involving Native Americans, the oral storytelling traditions of his people, and works of literature.

Coyote In several volumes of Ortiz's poetry, the poet employs the mythical trickster figure Coyote as a symbol of Native American survival. This recurring figure of the Coyote throughout his oeuvre representative of a fusing of optimistic humor and survival skills. Coyote makes his debut in *Going for the Rain* and plays a number of roles in the collection: Western rascal, wise Acoma grandfather, and Coyote Lady. Coyote plays a prominent role in four poems in *A Good Journey*. One poem in the latter collection, "Two Coyote Ones," features a speaker who recalls and generates his own stories about Coyote as a way of making sense of his experiences. In another, "Telling about Coyote," the Coyote takes on existential meaning.

War and Conflict In many of his works—including poetry, prose, and essays—Ortiz uses wars and other conflicts as a source of inspiration. The poetry and prose collection, *Fight Back*, uses the three hundredth anniversary of the Pueblos' revolt against their Spanish colonizers in 1680 as a point of comparison for modern times. The book is divided into two sections. "Too Many Sacrifices" combines poetic prose and lyric poetry in a series of short pieces set in the "Uranium Belt"—a region in the Southwest where both Native Americans and working-class whites were exploited as mine workers echoing the relationship between Pueblos and their colonizers. Similarly, in *From Sand Creek*, the poems and prose pieces are set in the Colorado veterans hospital where Ortiz was treated for alcohol abuse along with other Native American Vietnam War veterans. The title of the volume refers to the infamous Sand Creek massacre in 1864 in Colorado, in which more than a hundred peaceful Cheyenne and Arapaho Indian women and children were murdered by the U.S. military. Ortiz juxtaposes descriptions of his own experiences in the hospital with historical events of the massacre. Ortiz's short stories also employ war as a means of exploring Indian cultural identity. "Kaiser and the War" features a Pueblo Indian, Kaiser, running to the wilderness to hide from authorities, who have come to draft him into the army during World War II. Although divided in their opinions of Kaiser, the Pueblo community refuses to turn him into the authorities. Kaiser later emerges from hiding and tries to volunteer for the army but is sent to prison. While Kaiser's motivations remain unclear, his story serves as a focal point for encounters between the U.S. government and the Pueblo community.

Works in Critical Context

Critics have praised Ortiz for his explorations of Native American cultural heritage and for his emphasis on incorporating traditional cultural practices into the lives of modern Native Americans. He is lauded for his integration of oral storytelling traditions from his heritage into his work. Closely linked with oral tradition is the implicit connection in Ortiz's writing between language, culture, and worldview. Critics have also noted Ortiz's highlighting of the importance of the land and natural environment in his works and have commended his consistent expressions of hope and optimism in the face of oppression. Also commended is Ortiz's sense of humor, descriptive language, recurring motifs, unity of theme, political messages, and his drawing connections between Native Americans and those of other oppressed and exploited peoples.

From Sand Creek: Rising in This Heart Which Is Our America When *From Sand Creek: Rising in This Heart Which Is Our America* was first published in 1981, it was generally well received by critics. The reviewer in the *Small Press Review* called it "a gracefully designed and carefully crafted book," concluding "The poems are a rare gift." The critic in *Choice* also praised Ortiz and his poems, writing "No one has traveled the paths Ortiz has and returned to tell the tale of his travel. . . . No other Indian poet presently writing can equal Ortiz in evoking such a range of experience and emotion." Reviewing the volume in the *Nation*, Harold Jaffe is similarly positive. He stresses that although Ortiz's poetry refers to the sufferings of Native Americans both past and present, "the cumulative impression, is, admirably, not of gloom and despair, but of a renewed faith in the prospect of relationship with the land and solidarity among the dispossessed."

Out There Somewhere Like many of Ortiz's poetry collections, *Out There Somewhere* received mostly positive reviews by critics when it was published in 2002. The diversity of subject matter led a *Publishers Weekly* contributor to comment that if Ortiz "moves too easily from the sunset . . . to a series of questions about cultural appropriation, this book still asks crucial questions as much as it argues for beauty." More positively, Donna Seaman in *Booklist* praised *Out There Somewhere* for poems that express Ortiz's despair and hope. These are verses, she concludes, that are "permeated by gentleness and in which silence is every bit as eloquent as words."

Responses to Literature

1. Research Native American life on reservations, especially the treatment and education of children. In an essay, link your findings to Ortiz's experiences as a child. How do you believe his young life affected his

---

COMMON HUMAN EXPERIENCE

Ortiz is a member of the generation of writers that formed the Native American Renaissance of the 1960s and 1970s. The themes addressed by these writers are Native American history, culture, and identity, and the challenges faced by contemporary Native Americans. Here are some works by other members of this movement that explore these themes:

House Made of Dawn (1968), a novel by M. Scott Momaday. This Pulitzer Prize-winning novel chronicles the struggles of a young Native American man named Abel, a war veteran, who is having problems finding his place in the world.

Ceremony (1975), a novel by Leslie Marmon Silko. This novel depicts the struggles of its mixed-blood protagonist, Tayo, in his attempts to find healing after World War II. Tayo also must come to terms with conflicts arising from the colonization of his people, the Laguna.

Winter in the Blood (1974), a novel by James Welch. Set on the Fort Belknap Indian Reservation, this novel offers a realistic portrayal of life on a Montana reservation. Using sharp poetic imagery, Welch describes the life of the unnamed narrator, a thirty-two-year-old Blackfoot Indian who seemingly has no purpose in life.

Custer Died for Your Sins: An Indian Manifesto (1969), a nonfiction work by Vine Deloria, Jr. In this book, Deloria argues against federal policy of termination, advocates self-determination, and the upholding of treaties, while exposing the callousness and hypocrisy on the part of white specialists such as anthropologists, government bureaucrats, and the missionaries who ministered to Indian people.

---

writing? Use examples from his work to illustrate your point.

2. Many of Ortiz's poems are about coming to certain places and they underscore his ability to locate himself in human geography. Write several of your own poems inspired by your own sense of place.

3. Create a presentation for the class about the Native American Renaissance in literature. How does Ortiz fit within this tradition? What are some common elements in these writers?

4. In a small group, discuss how Ortiz uses Coyote as a symbol in his poetry. Why is this symbol so effective? Does he use other powerful symbols in his other works?

BIBLIOGRAPHY

Books

Evars, Lawrence J. "The Killing of a New Mexican State Trooper: Ways of Telling an Historical Event."

Critical Essays on Native American Literature, ed. Andrew Wiget. Boston: G. K. Hall, 1985, pp. 246–261.

Wiget, Andrew. *Simon Ortiz.* Boise, ID: Boise State University Press, 1986.

Periodicals

Brewster, E. Fitz. "Undermining Narrative Stereotypes in Simon Ortiz's 'The Killing of a State Cop'." *MELUS* (Summer 2003): 105–21.

Brill de Ramirez, Susan B. "Walking with the Land: Simon J. Ortiz, Robert J. Conley, and Velma Wallis." *South Dakota Review* (Spring 2000): 59–92.

Jaffe, Harold. "Speaking Memory." *Nation* (April 3, 1982): 406–08.

Rader, Dean. "Luci Tapahonso and Simon Ortiz: Allegory, Symbol, Language, Poetry." *Southwestern American Literature* (Spring 1997): 75–92.

Review of *From Sand Creek: Rising in This Heart Which Is Our America. Choice* (January 1982): 628.

Review of *From Sand Creek: Rising in This Heart Which Is Our America. Small Press Review* (November 1981): 8.

Review of *Out There Somewhere. Publishers Weekly* (March 18, 2002): 94.

Seaman, Donna. Review of *Out There Somewhere. Booklist* (March 15, 2002): 120.

Cynthia Ozick   *AP Wide World Photos*

✸ Cynthia Ozick

BORN: *1928, New York, New York*

NATIONALITY: *American*

GENRE: *Fiction, nonfiction, drama*

MAJOR WORKS:

The Pagan Rabbi and Other Stories (1971)

The Shawl (1989)

The Puttermesser Papers (1997)

Heir to the Glimmering World (2004)

Overview

Considered one of the most important twentieth-century Jewish American authors, Cynthia Ozick emerged as the dominant voice for new directions in Jewish American writing. She brings considerable learning to her imaginative work. Her esteemed reputation is primarily based on her short fiction, in which she repeatedly addresses the difficulty of sustaining a Jewish identity and heritage in a predominantly secular society and resisting pressures to assimilate. She also examines the calling and accountability of the artist, especially in the context of the Jewish moral code, in her fiction. Ozick won three O. Henry Prizes in short fiction.

Works in Biographical and Historical Context

Raised in the Bronx Born April 17, 1928 in New York City, Ozick is the daughter of William and Celia (Regelson) Ozick. Her parents were both Yiddish-speaking Russian Jewish immigrants. Her father owned a pharmacy and was a Jewish scholar who raised his family in the Bronx. As a young child, Ozick was subject to much degradation because of her religion, but found solace in reading and writing. She also lived through the Great Depression, which was prompted by the stock-market crash of 1929. The stock market crashed because an investment boom that began in 1924 was fueled by investors buying stocks with borrowed money. The stocks themselves were also wildly overvalued and their value plummeted as the economy took a downturn. The failure of the stock market led to a dramatic and sustained worldwide depression that lasted through the 1930s. The American economy recovered in the early 1940s as the nation entered World War II. Ozick was in her teens, attending the prestigious Hunter College High School in Manhattan, while the devastating conflict raged abroad.

Launched Writing Career Ozick earned her under-graduate degree in English from New York University (NYU) in 1949, and then an MA in literature from Ohio State University in 1950. At Ohio State, she wrote a thesis on the later novels of Henry James, who became an influence on Ozick's own novels. After completing her graduate studies, Ozick worked as an advertising copy-writer for Filene's Department Store. She married lawyer Bernard Hallote in 1952, with whom she had a daughter, Rachel. She also launched a writing career in the early 1950s, and produced two unpublished novels. She taught English at NYU from 1964 to 1965, and published some poems in a Jewish magazine in 1965.

For six years, she worked on the manuscript of *Trust*, which became her first published novel in 1966. The book focuses on a young woman's search for identity amid the confusion of modern American life in the after-math of World War II. The work received only lukewarm critical and commercial reception. Ozick then turned to writing short stories and novellas, which were published in such periodicals as *Commentary*, *Esquire*, and *The New Yorker*.

Success with Short Fiction In 1971, Ozick began pub-lishing collections of short stories and novellas to great success. Her first was *The Pagan Rabbi and Other Stories* (1971), which won the Jewish Council Book Award and B'nai B'rith Jewish Heritage Award. The title story is a fantasy about a young rabbi's struggle between Pan and Moses, nature and Judaism, while "Envy; or, Yiddish in America," explores the conflict of the traditional Jew living in a gentile world. Subsequent short fiction collections include *Bloodshed and Three Novellas* (1976) and *Levitation: Five Fictions* (1982). The former explores issues and moral dilemmas facing the Jewish writer, while the latter tells the story of a World War II orphan who becomes fixated on the idea that he is the son of Bruno Schulz, a famous Polish Jewish writer killed by the Nazis in their effort to exterminate the Jews of Europe during World War II.

Ozick returned to longer fiction in the early 1980s with the novel *The Cannibal Galaxy* (1983), which told the story of a young Orthodox Jew who survives World War II hidden in a priest's library. After the war, he attempts to launch a Jewish school that would bring together the best of Jewish and Western traditions. This novel was followed by *The Messiah of Stockholm* (1987)—which was thematically similar to *Bloodshed*. *The Shawl* (1989), considered her most powerful and controversial work, consists of two novellas about Holocaust survivors.

Intellectual Nonfiction In the early 1980s, Ozick began publishing her literary criticism and intellectually challenging essays in collections. They included *Art and Ardor* (1983), which focuses on the idol-making charac-ter of fiction. Other essay collections include *Metaphor and Memory* (1989). These essays make it clear that at least some imaginative works can be numbered on the side of the angels and that literature can be an abiding,

LITERARY AND HISTORICAL CONTEMPORARIES

Cynthia Ozick's famous contemporaries include:

Chaim Potok (1929–2002): This American rabbi and author was a critical scholar of Judaic texts as well as a novelist who included Jewish theology, history, and scholarship in his works. His novels include *My Name Is Asher Lev* (1972).

Joseph Heller (1923–1999): This Jewish American author's reputation rests principally on his first book, the darkly comic antiwar novel *Catch-22* (1961), inspired by the author's own combat experiences in World War II.

Joseph Baer Soloveitchik (1903–1993): Soloveitchik was among the most widely influential Orthodox Jewish theologians of the twentieth century and one of Ortho-dox Judaism's key American religious leaders.

Allen Ginsberg (1926–1997): The son of a Russian Jew-ish immigrant, Ginsberg was an American poet and leader of the mid-twentieth century Beat movement. He revitalized American poetry in the 1950s with the con-troversial poem "Howl" (1955).

Elie Wiesel (1928–): Born in Romania to Jewish parents, Wiesel wrote of his imprisonment in the Nazi concen-tration camps in *Night* (1958), and went on to win the Nobel Peace Prize in 1986.

even necessary, moral force. Other nonfiction collections include *Fame and Folly* (1996), *Quarrel and Quandary* (2000), and *The Din in the Head* (2006).

In the mid-1990s, Ozick turned to playwriting with *Blue Light*, which was first produced on Long Island in 1994. It was an adaptation of *The Shawl* and had an Off-Broadway run under that name in 1996. After this play, Ozick returned to fiction, albeit with a lighter tone. The comic novel *The Puttermesser Papers* (1997) uses fantasy and an episodic structure to delineate the magical adven-tures of Jewish attorney Ruth Puttermesser. In 2004, she published a realistic novel, *Heir to the Glimmering World*, which focuses on a teenage orphan working for a German immigrant family head by a professor who obsessively studies the Karaites, an obscure Jewish sect.

By the early 2000s, Ozick was living and working in New Rochelle, New York, and contributing to a variety of publications including the *New York Times* as well as her own original books. In 2008, she won two lifetime achievement awards, the PEN/Malamud prize for short fiction and the PEN/Nabokov award.

Works in Literary Context

Ozick's fiction is written with great intelligence, elegant incisiveness, and sharp, often satiric, wit. She focuses

COMMON HUMAN EXPERIENCE

Ozick is part of a tradition of twentieth-century Jewish American writers who focus on Jewish concerns as well as secular culture. Here are some other fiction works by authors who often take a similar point of view:

The Days of Awe (2005), a novel by Hugh Nissenson. In this novel, the author focuses on the events of September 11, 2001, as they intersect in the lives of his protagonist, Artie Rubin, his wife Joanna, and their friends. Artie must deal with death on many fronts, and his experiences push him back into his Jewish faith.

In the Days of Simon Stern (1973), a novel by Arthur A. Cohen. Written from the perspective of a blind, oracular narrator named Nathan, the novel recounts the emergence of the Messiah during the 1940s in New York. Through the narrative, it deals with the question of post-Holocaust faith.

The Bellarosa Connection (1990), a novella by Saul Bellow. This novella tells the story of a Holocaust survivor while at the same time delving into Jewish issues of memory and the ethical and psychological problems faced by American Jews living safe lives while their European brethren suffered and died.

Goodbye, Columbus, and Five Short Stories (1959), short fiction by Philip Roth. The title novella, *Goodbye, Columbus*, depicts the Patimkins, a *nouveau riche* Jewish family, as boorish creatures of leisure while exploring the relationship between Brenda Patimkin and Neil Klugman, a lower-middle-class native of Newark, New Jersey.

primarily on facets of Jewish life and thought. Among her favored topics are: the Holocaust and its legacy; the Jewish presence in contemporary life; and Jewish mysticism and legend. Ozick also addresses a wide range of other literary and political subjects, including gender politics. Sophisticated and erudite prose is a hallmark of her writing style, especially of her short fiction. As a fiction writer, Ozick was greatly influenced by Henry James as well as the literature, history, and philosophy of Judaism.

Jewish Identity In most of Ozick's short fiction, the plot revolves around the dilemma of being Jewish in modern Western society, particularly the United States. In "Levitation," found in *Levitation: Five Fictions*, a couple in a mixed Jewish and Christian marriage fail to understand each other's priorities due to the basic incompatibility of their worldviews. Ozick sees American culture as predominantly pagan, concerned with nature and the physical realm of existence, and therefore inherently in conflict with the worship of the intangible God of Judaism. For example, in "The Pagan Rabbi" from *The Pagan Rabbi and Other*

Stories, the title character is torn between love of religions and scholarship on one hand and attraction to nature and magic on the other. In "Envy; or Yiddish in America" from the same collection, the protagonist Edelshtein is an immigrant Yiddish poet who cannot get translated or published in English, and satirically attacks the successful but secular Yiddish novelist Ostrover, a figure based on Isaac Bashevis Singer. Edelshtein reveals Ozick's belief that for Jewish literature to be valuable, it must remain focused on Jewish themes and must reject assimilation.

Usurping Another recurring theme in Ozick's work is that every writer borrows material from other writers and, more importantly, usurps God's domain by attempting to replicate or transform reality through fiction. This theme is best illustrated in the story "Usurpation (Other People's Stories)," published in *Bloodshed and Three Novellas*. The idea of a person taking on the role of a godlike creator is given a humorous twist in "Puttermesser and Xanthippe," in which Ruth Puttermesser creates a female golem (a creature made in clay and brought to life by magical incantations) to help with her housework. The creature is useful at first, but begins to run amok, forcing her creator to destroy her. A similar religious offense is treated in Ozick's story "The Shawl," and its sequel, "Rosa" (also published in *The Shawl*). The focus of the narratives is a woman who idolatrously worships the memory of her infant daughter, who was murdered in a Nazi death camp. Even the essays in *Art and Ardor* focus on the idol-making characters of fiction. However, the essays in *Metaphor and Memory*, scrutinizing the works of writers from Primo Levi and S. Y. Agnon to Anton Chekhov and Henry James, make it clear that at least some imaginative works can be numbered on the side of the angels.

Works in Critical Context

Ozick's short fiction has always been extremely well-received by critics. Many commentators have said that her stories are free of the opaque language that made the novel *Trust* so difficult to read. Reviewers have generally recognized Ozick's strengths to be her challenging ideas and evocative style, while noting weaknesses in her characterizations and her portrayal of the emotional realm. Some critics question the accessibility of Ozick's fiction to average readers, describing her style as overly pedantic and parochial, with its strong emphasis on Jewish concerns. Critics have compared Ozick to T. S. Eliot, Flannery O'Connor, and Grace Paley.

The Messiah of Stockholm Many critics praised *The Messiah of Stockholm* as the first of her books to reconcile her need to create fiction with her desire to remain a follower of the Jewish tradition. In the *New York Times*, the well-known critic Harold Bloom writes that "The novel is a complex and fascinating meditation on the nature of the writing and the responsibilities of those who choose to create—or judge—tales." Bloom also notes that the novel can "be, at times, very funny indeed about the daily operations of one of the city's newspapers and . . . [the protagonist's] peculiar detachment from everyday work and life." *The Messiah of Stockholm* also garnered praise for its stylistic vitality. Writing in the Chicago *Tribune Books*, Mona Simpson calls the book "a poetic yet often raucously comic epic," and also maintains that "of course, no work of Ozick's can be talked about without first acknowledging the simple brilliance of her prose." John Calvin Batchelor of the *Washington Post Book World* enthuses that *The Messiah of Stockholm* "is a superb read, with prose so deft that were it fisticuffs the author would be forbidden by law to combat mortals."

Heir to the Glimmering World *Heir to the Glimmering World* (published as *The Bear Boy* in England) also received positive reviews. Reviewing the novel in *Women's Review of Books*, Jan Clausen writes that "This uncharacteristically hefty volume revisits prior themes—tensions between faith and heresy; the irreducibly individual impact of the Holocaust on each of its victims; textuality as a way of life; the Jewish intellectual woman as hero—in the startling form of neo-Victorian realist pastiche." John Leonard in the *New York Times Book Review* finds that the novel "is both a chambered nautilus and a haunted house—a fairy tale with locked rooms, mad songs, secret books and stolen babies. And a children's story, an Oedipal grief, about killing fathers and moving on. And a sendup of Victorian novels that solve their problems with fortuitous marriage, sudden death, miraculous inheritance, emigration to Australia or all of the above." *Guardian Online* reviewer Ali Smith concludes that "like all the best fiction, while it knows that books are a necessary refuge, it doesn't once dodge the heresies and complexities of the real and it works, like all Ozick's fine, uncompromising and paradoxical oeuvre, to leave both books and world at once more properly mysterious and better understood."

Responses to Literature

1. Research the concept of a golem. Create a presentation for the class about golems, using Ozick's story "Puttermesser and Xanthippe" to illustrate your findings.

2. A number of Ozick's fictional works focus on women, childbearing, and the struggle between mothers and their children. Select one or more stories, novels, or novellas by the author that focus on this theme. Write a paper in which you discuss how she portrays these ideas.

3. As a group, research the Holocaust and Holocaust survivors. Using your findings, discuss how Ozick uses this monumental event and the people it affected in her fiction. Can you relate the event, the people, and the stories to any contemporary event?

4. Write a paper on the American Jewish renaissance in the twentieth century. How does Ozick fit into the movement? Does her fiction reflect the concerns of the greater movement?

BIBLIOGRAPHY

Books

Bloom, Harold. *Cynthia Ozick: Modern Critical Views.* New York: Chelsea Publishers, 1986.

Cohen, Sarah Blacher. *Cynthia Ozick's Comic Art: From Levity to Liturgy.* Bloomington, Ind.: Indiana University Press, 1994.

Kasuvar, Elaine M. *Cynthia Ozick: Tradition and Invention.* Bloomington, Ind.: Indiana University Press, 1993.

Kielsky, Vera Emuna. *Inevitable Exiles: Cynthia Ozick's Views of the Precariousness of Jewish Existence in a Gentile Society.* New York: Peter Lang, 1989.

Periodicals

Batchelor, John Calvin. Review of *The Messiah of Stockholm. Washington Post Book World* (March 8, 1987).

Bloom, Harold. Review of *The Messiah of Stockholm. New York Times Book Review* (March 22, 1987): 1.

Clausen, Jan. Review of *Heir to the Glimmering World. Women's Review of Books* (November 2004): 3.

Halkin, Hillel. "What Is Cynthia Ozick About?" *Commentary* (January 2005): 49–55.

Parrish, Timothy L. "Creation's Covenant: The Art of Cynthia Ozick." *Texas Studies in Literature and Language* (Winter 2001): 440–464.

Leonard, John. Review of *Heir to the Glimmering World. New York Times Book Review* (September 5, 2004).

Scrafford, Barbara. "Nature's Silent Scream: A Commentary on Cynthia Ozick's 'The Shawl.'" *Critique* (Fall 1989): 11–15.

Simpson, Mona. Review of *The Messiah of Stockholm. Tribune Books* (March 1, 1987): 7.

✸ ZZ Packer

BORN: *1973, Chicago, Illinois*

NATIONALITY: *American*

GENRE: *Fiction*

MAJOR WORKS:

Drinking Coffee Elsewhere (2003)

Overview

African-American author ZZ Packer is best known for works of short fiction, for which she has received much critical acclaim. She has published one highly lauded collection of short stories, *Drinking Coffee Elsewhere*. In her stories, Packer explores issues of racial identity, troubled family relationships, and being an outsider.

Works in Biographical and Historical Context

Emphasis on Education Zuwena Packer was born on January 12, 1973, in Chicago, Illinois. Her father owned

ZZ Packer *Marc Brasz / Corbis*

where she changed her major from science to literature. Shortly before she earned her BA in 1994, she published her first short story in *Seventeen*.

Published in the New Yorker After earning her degree, Packer moved to Baltimore, Maryland, where she taught English in a public high school and began working toward an MA program at Johns Hopkins in 1995. Packer then entered the writing program at the University of Iowa, where her mentor was the African-American short-fiction author James Alan McPherson. She earned her MFA there in 1999. That same year, she earned both the Ms. Giles Whiting Award and Bellingham Review Award.

In 1999, Packer was also named a Wallace Stegner Fellow at Stanford University. The two-year fellowship is designed for emerging fiction and poetry writers, and gave the young author time to work on what became her first short story collection. In 2000, she published a short story, "Drinking Coffee Elsewhere," in the *New Yorker*'s annual "Debut Fiction" issue. The magazine honor sparked interest from publishers, and led to a hefty advance for her first book.

Highly Praised First Collection Before Packer's debut was completed, she married software engineer Michael Boros in 2001. The couple has since had two sons. Like many Americans, she also was forced to deal with the events of September 11, 2001. On that day, Al-Qaeda terrorists hijacked commercial airliners and crashed them into the World Trade Center in New York City and the Pentagon in Washington, D.C. Thousands of people lost their lives in the attacks, and the event had an unsettling effect on American society in the years following.

In 2003, Packer published her first short story collection, *Drinking Coffee Elsewhere*. The anthology of eight stories was highly acclaimed, named by both the American Library Association and the *New York Times* as a notable book. *Drinking Coffee Elsewhere* was also lauded by the *San Francisco Chronicle* as the best book of the year in 2003.

Continued Work on Novel As Packer continued working on her fiction, she also began teaching at various universities. From 2003 to 2004, she was a visiting assistant professor at her alma mater, the University of Iowa's Writers' Workshop. In 2005, she held a Guggenheim Fellowship for fiction. She also has held a Truman Capote fellowship at Stanford University. In 2008, Packer served as the editor of a collection of twenty short stories about Southerners, *New Stories from the South*.

By 2008, Packer was residing in Pacifica, California. She continues her writing career and holds various writer-in-residence and visiting professorships, including a 2008 term at San Jose State University. She also continues to work on her first novel, about the adventures of Buffalo Soldiers set in the aftermath of the American Civil War. The work is tentatively entitled *The Thousands*. (Buffalo Soldiers were part of six all-African-American army

a lounge and bar, while her mother worked for the Social Security Administration. When she was five years old, the family moved to Atlanta, Georgia. After her parents' divorced when she was twelve, she and her mother moved to Louisville, Kentucky. By the time she was in junior high school, Packer became so frustrated by people pronouncing her first name wrong that she adopted her family nickname, ZZ. Throughout her childhood, she was exposed to the Pentecostal Church, to which some in her family belonged. The church is known for the strict personal discipline of its adherents and an emphasis on "speaking in tongues" to demonstrate that one is possessed by the Holy Spirit.

While Packer would later draw upon some elements of Pentecostalism in her short stories, it was not until her high-school years that she discovered her literary gifts. Her focus until this time had been math and science, but one teacher made her write short stories for class and she realized that the goal of writing well was by no means out of her reach. Still, after graduating from high school, Packer entered the Massachusetts Institute of Technology, where she studied electrical engineering for a time. In the early 1990s, Packer transferred to Yale University,

regiments created by an act of Congress in 1866 immediately after the Civil War. They served primarily in the western United States and its territories in struggles against Native American, and in Cuba during the Spanish-American War.) The British magazine *Granta* ran an excerpt of this novel in 2007. The magazine also named Packer one its "Best Young American Novelists."

Works in Literary Context

Much of Packer's fiction focuses on the African-American experience and issues of race, primarily between blacks and whites. She often focuses on uncomfortable topics like racial tensions and the difficulties of being black at a time when race has supposedly become insignificant. Packer handles such dilemmas and problems with empathy, frankness, humanism, and a sense of humor. Some of her explorations of racial identity and related political issues are considered a new kind of comedy of manners. Many of her characters suffer from self-hatred, a sense of not belonging or of being outsiders in their own lives. Packer's influences as a writer included her mentor, McPherson, as well as Toni Morrison, Leo Tolstoy, Mark Twain, Ralph Ellison, Marilynne Robinson, and James Baldwin.

African-American Experiences The short stories included in *Drinking Coffee Elsewhere* and *New Stories from the South* focus on African-American characters dealing with racial discrimination and race-related tensions. In "Drinking Coffee Elsewhere," Dina is a college student at Yale who is confused by both her sexuality and the racism she encounters at the mostly white school. "Brownies," also included in *Drinking Coffee Elsewhere*, takes place at a sleepaway camp for Brownie troops. There, a group of African-American Girl Scouts becomes obsessed with an all-white troop and plans an act of revenge for what they believe is a racial slur. Also found in *Drinking Coffee Elsewhere* is "The Ant of the Self," which focuses on a young man forced to drive his deadbeat father to the Million Man March where he hopes to sell some exotic African birds. The young man and his father get into a fistfight and the boy is abandoned by his father in an unfamiliar city.

Pentecostalism A number of Packer's short stories also touch on the theme of Pentecostalism. The author neither condemns nor praises the religion, but uses its perceived extremes as a catalyst. In "Speaking in Tongues," included in *Drinking Coffee Elsewhere*, fourteen-year-old Tia runs away from her Pentecostal family after resisting the efforts of her sternly religious aunt who wishes her to "get saved." She goes to Atlanta in order to search for the drug-addicted mother who abandoned her, but instead allows a hustler-and-prostitute couple to become her substitute family for a time.

Works in Critical Context

Packer is extolled by critics for her stories that emphasize social context and starkly illuminate the African-American experience. Reviewers also praise her for scene descrip-

---

LITERARY AND HISTORICAL CONTEMPORARIES

ZZ Packer's famous contemporaries include:

Colson Whitehead (1969–): This African-American author graduated from Harvard and received a MacArthur Foundation "genius grant" in 2002. His novels include *The Intuitionist* (1998).

Zadie Smith (1975–): A black novelist considered one of the most talented young authors in Britain. Her novels include *White Teeth* (1999) and *On Beauty* (2005).

Jonathan Safran Foer (1977–): A young American author who made a splash with his first novel, *Everything is Illuminated* (2002).

Barack Obama (1961–): This African-American politician was serving his first term in the U.S. Senate when he was elected President of the United States in 2008. He became the first black to assume that office.

Lisa Bonet (1967–): An African-American actress who starred in such popular 1980s situation comedies as *The Cosby Show* and *A Different World*.

---

tions, word choices, toughness, and realism. While commentators admire how Packer unflinchingly and provocatively takes on uncomfortable issues about race with a sense of humor and humanism, they also acknowledge that her stories have universal appeal.

Drinking Coffee Elsewhere Packer's first short-story collection, *Drinking Coffee Elsewhere*, received many critical accolades upon its publication in 2003. In the *Village Voice*, Joy Press admired the stories, noting that "Packer specializes in goody-goodies—most of her heroines are young, wholesome African American women caught at a formative moment, ducking bitterness as it settles in around them." *New York Times* writer Jean Thompson hailed Packer as a fresh new literary voice, commending her talent for creating "a world already populated by clamoring, sorrowing, eminently knowable people, and with the promise of more to come." *Publishers Weekly* believed that *Drinking Coffee Elsewhere* was particularly noteworthy because the stories' conclusions fail to resolve "neatly or easily. Packer knows how to keep the tone provocative and tense at the close of each tale, doing justice to the complexity and dignity of the characters and their difficult choices." In *Independent on Sunday*, David Isaacson concluded that "each study has a universal, human dimension that subtly transcends the immediate subject."

Responses to Literature

1. Create a presentation for the class about the Pentecostal religion. Use the short story "Speaking in

COMMON HUMAN EXPERIENCE

Packer is an African-American author who sometimes explores uncomfortable issues related to race. Here are some other works by authors who touch on these tensions:

Corregidora (1975), a novel by Gayl Jones. This novel explores the psychological effects of slavery and sexual abuse on a modern black woman.

A Glance Away (1967), a novel by John Edgar Wideman. This novel focuses on a day in the life of a drug addict, reflecting the harsh realities of life in black urban America.

Meridian (1976), a novel by Alice Walker. This novel focuses on a young African-American woman who was born in the South and uses education as a means of escape.

Invisible Man (1952), a novel by Ralph Ellison. This novel is brutally honest and graphic in its depiction of the humiliating treatment its African-American protagonist suffers at the hands of whites in both the South and the North.

Tongues" to illustrate your findings. How does the story depict the religion?

2. Many of Packer's stories seem influenced by such personal experiences as growing up in the South and attending the elite, predominantly white Yale University. Write a short story of your own influenced by your own personal experiences.

3. Research the Million Man March, which provides the backdrop for "The Ant of the Self." In a paper, link your findings about the inspiration for and intention of the march with the actions of and tensions between the characters. How does the march really affect the father and son characters?

4. In a small group, discuss the short story "Brownies." Why does the troop of black girls feel slighted? Should they? How could the situation have been handled differently? Should they have acted differently once they learned the truth?

BIBLIOGRAPHY

Periodicals

Isaacson, David. Review of *Drinking Coffee Elsewhere*. *Independent on Sunday* (March 14, 2004): 35.

Press, Joy. Review of *Drinking Coffee Elsewhere*. *Village Voice* (February 26, 2003): 58.

Review of *Drinking Coffee Elsewhere*. *Publishers Weekly* (December 16, 2002).

Thompson, Jean. Review of *Drinking Coffee Elsewhere*. *New York Times* (March 16, 2003).

Web sites

Birnbaum, Robert. "Interview: ZZ Packer." *IdentityTheory.com*. Retrieved December 7, 2008, from http://www.identitytheory.com/interviews/birnbaum103.html. Last updated on April 29, 2003.

Janssens, Jeff, and S. Zoe Wexler. "Being Part of the World: An Interview with ZZ Packer." *nīdus*. Retrieved December 7, 2008, from http://www.pitt.edu/~nidus/current/packer.html.

"A Writer's Life: ZZ Packer." London *Telegraph*. Retrieved December 7, 2008, from http://www.telegraph.co.uk/arts/main.jhtml?xml=/arts/2004/04/25/bopacker.xml&sSheet=/arts/2004/04/25/bomain.html. Last updated on April 18, 2004.

"ZZ Packer." *WordSmitten*. Retrieved December 7, 2008, from http://www.wordsmitten.com/author_zzpacker.htm.

⊛ Thomas Paine

BORN: *1737, Thetford, England*

DIED: *1809, New York, New York*

NATIONALITY: *American*

GENRE: *Nonfiction*

MAJOR WORKS:

Common Sense (1776)
The American Crisis (1776–1783)
Rights of Man (1791–1792)
The Age of Reason (1794–1795)
Agrarian Justice (1797)

Overview

Thomas Paine was one of the most colorful and successful political pamphleteers during the age of the American and French Revolutions. He was among the first writers to realize the power of the press to bring about political and social reform. In his writings, Paine expressed his beliefs that man is rational and basically good but corrupted by society, that all men are equal, and that justice is dependent on a nation's economic system. Though he was shunned at the end of his life for his later controversial views, Paine is still regarded as an important figure in American history.

Works in Biographical and Historical Context

Unhappy Childhood Paine was born in Thetford, England, on January 29, 1737, the son of John Pain and his wife, Frances (Cocke). His Quaker father was a farmer and a corsetiere (a maker of women's corsets). Paine was raised in poverty and had a miserable childhood. After attending local schools for seven years, Paine began an apprenticeship to his father at the age of thirteen. Unhappy, Paine ran away when he was sixteen years old to sail on a British

Thomas Paine   *Paine, Thomas, photograph of painting by Romney.*
National Archives and Records Administration.

privateer in the Seven Years' War. (Called the French and Indian War in North America, this conflict was fought between the British and French in a number of locations across the globe. The British won, ending the French empire in North America.)

Returning to London, Paine finished his apprenticeship and briefly worked as a corsetiere, then held a minor government post and taught school for a short time. Later the owner of his own general store, he secured a post as an excise officer (a collector of taxes on goods produced and sold in a country). While holding these jobs, Paine was married to his first wife, Mary Lambert, who died in childbirth with their child in 1760, only a year after their marriage. After a second marriage, to Elizabeth Ollive in 1768, he continued his education by reading books, attending lectures, and conducting scientific experiments.

His First Pamphlets   Paine's second marriage ended in separation because his wages as an excise officer were too low to support his family; another shop he owned did not produce enough income, either. At the request of other excise officers, Paine wrote a pamphlet in 1772 urging Parliament to raise their wages. When the idea was formally presented in 1773, Parliament was not persuaded and he was fired by his superiors. Divorced from his wife and

forced to declare bankruptcy, Paine had to sell the family's shop to escape imprisonment for debt.

Seeking a chance to become successful, Paine boldly called on Benjamin Franklin. This American politician was in London serving as the foremost American spokesman in Great Britain in this time period. Franklin was impressed by Paine, and gave him a letter of recommendation. Paine went to America, arriving in November 1774 to start a new life. There, Paine found work with printer Robert Aitken, who published *Pennsylvania Magazine*. Paine began contributing essays to the periodical. Within a few months, Paine's vigorous literary style had attracted more readers and circulation more than doubled. Paine's essays called for an end not only to slave trade but also to slavery. He also attacked British colonial policies both in America and India. Encouraged by Franklin and Benjamin Rush to write a history of the dispute between England and the American colonies, Paine published the influential pamphlet *Common Sense* on January 10, 1776.

Impact of Common Sense   More than 500,000 copies of *Common Sense* circulated in the colonies, and long excerpts appeared in newspapers and magazines. The real importance of *Common Sense* lay not so much in its vigorous call for independence as in its call for leveling the old order and starting anew. Most Americans believed that governments evolved naturally from society, and the English government, for example, reflected the country's social organization. This, Paine said, was wrong. For him, society and government were two different things. Paine called for independence, but he also urged Americans to reject the British model of government, which gave too much power to the king and the aristocrats. *Common Sense* had a profound influence on American opinion, and it helped convince Americans that they were fighting for essential human rights that could only come with independence.

Though independence had not yet been declared, a revolution had begun. General George Washington forced the British to abandon Boston and royal authority was collapsing in all the American colonies. Though independence was indeed declared in the summer of 1776, the situation for the colonists looked dire by the end of the year. The British had captured New York, and Washington's army was driven through New Jersey and into Pennsylvania. In December 1776, the British fleet threatened Philadelphia, and Congress fled to Baltimore. Paine was fighting in the fledgling Continental Army as a member of the Pennsylvania regiment. He accompanied Washington's retreating army in what seemed to be the final moments of the struggle. Sitting by a campfire, Paine wrote a new pamphlet that addressed the problems of the moment, *The American Crisis*. On Christmas Eve, Washington had his troops assemble to listen to the first four essays of the pamphlet before they rowed across the Delaware River to surprise the British at Trenton.

LITERARY AND HISTORICAL CONTEMPORARIES

Thomas Paine's famous contemporaries include:

Benjamin Rush (1745–1813): This American physician was an outspoken abolitionist and supported the revolutionary cause. Rush suggested to Paine that he should write what became *Common Sense*.

Marquis de Lafayette (1757–1834): Lafayette was a French noble of liberal inclination who volunteered his time and money to support the American cause during the Revolutionary War. He also played an important role in two revolutions in France.

Edmund Burke (1729–1797): A British statesman who was also a noted political theorist and philosophical writer. His disdain of the French Revolution led to *Reflections on the Revolution in France* (1790), which compelled Paine to respond with *Rights of Man*.

James Monroe (1758–1831): Monroe served with distinction in the Continental Army during the Revolutionary War. He later served two terms as U.S. President, from 1817 to 1825.

Thomas Jefferson (1743–1826): This preeminent American revolutionary drafted the Declaration of Independence. He held a number of important roles in the federal government, including Minister to France, Secretary of State, Vice President, President for two terms.

Revolutionary War Activities Paine's pamphlet emphasized the importance of freedom, and rallied Washington's troops. Their surprise victories in Trenton and Princeton rallied public opinion. Paine went on to publish fourteen *Crisis* essays over the next seven years. All were designed to strengthen American resolve and to comment on specific issues of a moment. The final number of the series, published on the eighth anniversary of the battle of Lexington, April 19, 1783, urged the American people to adopt a stronger central government that could protect liberty against a hostile world.

Later in the Revolutionary War, Paine served in a number of political positions, including secretary to Congress's Committee on Foreign Affairs and as a clerk of the Pennsylvania Assembly. As clerk, Paine drafted the preamble to Pennsylvania's law abolishing slavery in 1780. He had been advocating this cause since his first months in America. Paine continued to write on political questions, and spoke out against the establishment of a national bank and criticized the citizens of Rhode Island for scuttling the proposed five-percent import duty. Paine was committed to the independence of America, and he had little patience with local political grievances that he felt detracted from American unity and strength.

Influence in France In the early days of the United States, Paine also focused his attention on scientific matters, trying to develop a smokeless candle and inventing an iron bridge that would not require piers to support its span. To perfect the bridge, Paine sailed for Europe in April 1787. He first went to England, then was invited by the Marquis de Lafayette to visit France. There, Paine met with Thomas Jefferson, then the American Minister to France. To Lafayette he offered advice on a new constitution in France, and in fact helped draft France's Declaration of the Rights of Man and of the Citizen. When the Bastille fell on July 14, 1789—marking the beginning of the French Revolution that led to the end of the monarchy in France—Lafayette entrusted its key to Paine, who was to present it to Washington.

Returning to London, Paine was stunned to read Edmund Burke's speech denouncing the French Revolution. Burke had supported the American cause, but believed the French Revolution was a mistake. Paine was outraged at Burke's attack, outlined in *Reflections on the French Revolution* (1790). Paine responded with a vigorous defense, the two-part *Rights of Man*. Paine not only vindicated the French Revolution but also argued for the power of all people to construct whatever government they choose.

Shunned in Last Days Because he criticized the British monarchy in print, Paine was charged with seditious libel in England. He fled to France, where he was elected to the French National Convention. He arrived in September 1792, days before the Convention declared France a republic, a decision Paine supported. However, Paine opposed the mob violence of the French Revolution as well as the execution of French king Louis XVI, and was labeled a traitor. Arrested on December 18, 1793, Paine narrowly escaped execution by the guillotine and nearly died in prison. The American minister to France, James Monroe, secured his release in November 1794.

Paine recovered from his imprisonment at Monroe's home, where he completed two more pamphlets. He had begun writing *The Age of Reason* while in prison in France. This pamphlet was an attack on organized religion. *Agrarian Justice* called for redistribution of wealth by implementing heavy inheritance taxes on the wealthy to support social welfare programs. *The Age of Reason* led to accusations of atheism and alienated Paine from many Americans, including Samuel Adams, who otherwise supported his political views. Paine also criticized Presidents Washington and John Adams for their pro-British and anti-French policies. This led to further estrangement from many Americans. Still, President Thomas Jefferson invited Paine to return to the United States in 1802. Paine spent his last years ignored and in poverty on a farm in New Rochelle, New York, and in New York City, where he died on June 8, 1809.

Works in Literary Context

As a writer, Paine's thoughts were rarely original. He mostly used ideas that already existed. What made him an admirable author was the way he combined those ideas and presented them in a language best understood by the common man. Paine's sentences were simple and direct, and his arguments turned on one or two accessible principles and pursued persuasion through clarity and repetition. He chose references that would be available to common laborers and tradespeople. Sharing these standards, his major works differed from one another primarily in their focuses, which were often determined by the moment in which they were written. His writings were forceful and persuasive, affecting real change in the American colonies, the United States, France, and Great Britain. Paine defended liberty not only for the people in America, but also those in England and in France. Paine's writings also reflected his support for humanitarian causes and social welfare policies as well as his belief in deism as opposed to the organized religions of his day. As a writer, Paine was greatly influenced by the times in which he lived, the ideas of the Enlightenment, his background as a Quaker, and such authors as Jean Jacques Rousseau, Baron de Montesquieu, John Locke, and Thomas Hobbes.

Support of American Revolution   During the period of the American Revolutionary War, Paine published several works that supported the American cause and helped rally Americans when spirits and resources ran low. *Common Sense* is credited with almost single-handedly convincing the American colonies to enter into armed rebellion against Great Britain. In this work, Paine popularized the Enlightenment concept that government is a social contract that exists by the consent of the people for the protection of their natural rights. Attacking the idea of monarchy, Paine catalogued the abuses that the British king had imposed upon his American subjects, and he called for the establishment of a new government, independent of Britain. Equally popular and equally effective was the 13 parts of the essay series, *The American Crisis.* Issued at periods during the war when the patriot cause seemed desperate, these essays lifted the morale of soldiers and civilians alike and helped secure the revenues and determination needed to see the conflict through to a successful conclusion. After the war, with works such as *The Rights of Man* and *The Age of Reason*, Paine set out to accomplish for the world what he had already accomplished for America.

Art of Persuasion   It is generally conceded that what distinguishes Paine from other writers of his time was his tremendous talent for persuasion. While Paine sometimes ignored the niceties of conventional grammar and was capable of subverting logic to suit his ends, in the works of Paine can be seen a truly extraordinary grasp of the principles of effective rhetoric. Speaking with conviction as a common man in the idiom of the common man, Paine at his best could generate a unique sense of identification between himself and his audience. Disavowing the complex neoclassical rhetoric of his day, Paine espoused a style that was forceful, direct, clear, and simple. Easily under-

COMMON HUMAN EXPERIENCE

Paine's *Common Sense* and *The American Crisis* played a significant part in the American Revolution. Here are some other works that affected or reflected on aspects of the conflict:

Letters from a Pennsylvania Farmer (1768), nonfiction by John Dickinson. In this work, Dickinson summed up colonial grievances against their British rulers.

M'Fingal (1772–1782), a poem by John Trumbell. This mock-epic satire was a burlesque of a typical Tory magistrate, and it celebrated the struggle for independence.

"Burgoyne's Proclamation" (1777), a poem by William Livingston. This verse parody ridiculed the titular British general as well as the language of authority itself.

Edict by the King of Prussia (1773), a satirical work by Benjamin Franklin. This piece was an account of a claim to British territory supposedly presented by Prussian King Frederick the Great. The claim is based on the fact that England itself had been settled by colonists from Germany who had never been emancipated.

stood, his prose was carefully structured to move his audience to action. A master at the use of such rhetorical devices as parallelism, repetition, invective, rhetorical questions, and ethical appeals, Paine was able to garner widespread support for the causes he espoused.

Works in Critical Context

Few American writers have generated as much controversy as that surrounding Paine and his works. Revered as a folk hero during the American Revolution, Paine died an object of ridicule in the very country that his writings had done so much to establish. Nonetheless, Paine is considered among the most successful persuasive writers of all time. Even Paine's most strident adversaries have been forced to admit that without him there might not have been an American Revolution. Yet by the time Paine died, he had fallen far from the pinnacle of his celebrity in revolutionary America. He was forgotten at best and despised at worst. Despite some isolated efforts to reassess his image in the nineteenth century, Paine's reputation was not revitalized until the twentieth century, when scholars gradually developed a new view of the significance and complexity of Paine's writings.

Common Sense   Published in early 1776, the pamphlet *Common Sense* reached its popular audience of skeptical artisans and farmers eager to read something that appealed to them in their language. Twenty-five editions of the pamphlet were printed during the year, spreading the argument for revolution to all classes of free people throughout the colonies. In Virginia, Edmund Randolph commented that with the diffusion of *Common Sense*, "the public sentiment which a few weeks before had shuddered at the tremendous obstacles, with which independence was environed, overleaped every barrier." As *Common Sense* enjoyed a circulation unprecedented in the eighteenth century, George Washington was one of many impressed by what he called Paine's "sound doctrine and unanswerable reasoning." Twentieth century writers were equally impressed by the power of Paine's words. In *Main Currents in American Thought: Volume I: 1620–1800, The Colonial Mind*, Vernon Parrington commented, "The amazing influence of *Common Sense* on a public opinion long befogged by legal quibble flowed from its direct and skillful appeal to material interests."

The Rights of Man With the publication of the first part of his pamphlet *The Rights of Man*, Paine secured his standing as a radical defender of human liberty. His pamphlet again appealed to readers of his time with its emotional, familiar style. Because his words came at the right moment, Paine's message found a large and eager audience. According to historian Eric Foner in *Tom Paine and Revolutionary America*, "The response to *The Rights of Man* can only be described as overwhelming." Particularly in Britain, Paine "captured the public imagination" by contrasting France's new democracy—reputedly providing the people a voice in their government in addition to freedom of religion, for example—with the British regime. The publication of the second part of *The Rights of Man* broadened Paine's appeal and furthered the controversy surrounding his opinions. Yet Olivia Smith in *The Politics of Language, 1791–1819* also noted, "Paine was not denounced as a vulgar author until he had written *The Rights of Man*." Still, the pamphlet continued to affect radical thought in the nineteenth century. Twentieth-century authors also praised *The Rights of Man*, with Smith noting, "There is more fulness to Paine's writing than that of *Common Sense* or *The Crisis*. ... A greater use of metaphor, a more vividly present narrator, and a keener awareness of his audience are the characteristics of Paine's prose."

Responses to Literature

1. Read *Common Sense* and write a paper identifying and analyzing the specific persuasive techniques Paine uses in the pamphlet. What are his rhetorical strategies, and why do you think they worked so well at the time?

2. Stage a debate for the class over the pamphlet *The Rights of Man*. Touch on such issues as the validity of Paine's argument, its effect on history, and its place in Paine's canon.

3. Read several numbers of *The Crisis*, then write your own pamphlet to inspire people about an issue central to life in the twenty-first century.

4. Write a paper in which you link Paine's Quaker background to one or more of his published works. How was his philosophy affected by Quaker beliefs?

BIBLIOGRAPHY

Books

Foner, Eric. *Tom Paine and Revolutionary America.* New York: Oxford University Press, 1976.

Fruchtman, Jack, Jr. *Thomas Paine: Apostle of Freedom.* New York: Four Walls Eight Windows, 1994.

Keane, John. *Tom Paine: A Political Life.* New York: Little, Brown, 1995.

Meltzer, Milton. *Tom Paine: Voice of Revolution.* New York: Franklin Watts, 1996.

Parrington, Vernon. *The Politics of Language, 1791–1819.* New York: Clarendon Press, 1984.

Smith, Olivia. *Main Currents in American Thought: Volume I: 1620–1800, The Colonial Mind.* New York: Harcourt, Brace and Company, 1954.

Vail, John J. *Thomas Paine.* New York: Chelsea House, 1990.

Periodicals

Everton, Michael. "'The Would-Be Author and the Real Bookseller': Thomas Paine and Eighteenth-Century Printing Ethics." *Early American Literature* (2005): 79–110.

Rago, Joseph. "Doubting Thomas." *New Criterion* (October 2006): 67–69.

Thompson, Tommy R. "The Resurrection of Thomas Paine in American Popular Magazines." *The Midwest Quarterly* (Autumn 1991): 75–92.

❀ Chuck Palahniuk

BORN: *1962, Pasco, Washington*

NATIONALITY: *American*

GENRE: *Fiction*

MAJOR WORKS:

Fight Club (1996)

Invisible Monsters (1999)

Choke (2001)

Diary (2003)

Snuff (2008)

Overview

Novelist Chuck Palahniuk is best known for his dark comedies that explore themes of commercialism, personal identity, nihilism—a belief that life has no objective meaning—and free will. Beginning with the award-winning *Fight Club* (1996), his unconventional novels feature shocking, if not bizarre, premises, and are sustained by his black humor and cynical viewpoint. Critics often give Palahniuk's novels mixed reviews, admitting to

Chuck Palahniuk   © *Colin McPherson*

be entertained amidst often disturbing material. He also has published at least two collections of nonfiction.

Works in Biographical and Historical Context

Violent Background Born Charles Michael Palahniuk on February 21, 1962, in Pasco, Washington, he was the son of Fred and Carol Palahniuk. His father was a railroad brakeman while his mother was an office manager at a nuclear power plant. Raised in a mobile home in Burbank, Washington, his childhood was unspectacular, but colored by a violent past. His paternal grandfather killed his wife and would have killed his three-year-old son had he been able to find him. Instead, his paternal grandfather killed himself. When his parents separated and divorced when Palahniuk was fourteen, he and his siblings were frequently left in the care of their maternal grandparents, who lived in eastern Washington.

In the early 1980s, Palahniuk entered the University of Oregon, where he studied journalism and discovered that he had a talent for words. While a student, he worked as an intern for KLCC, a National Public Radio member station in Eugene, Oregon. Palahniuk earned his B.A. in 1986. After earning his degree, Palahniuk moved to Portland, Oregon, where he wrote for a newspaper. He also worked as a diesel mechanic for Freightliner for thirteen years and wrote manuals on repairing trucks. Being a mechanic allowed him to observe people, allowing him to be fascinated by what drives people to behave as they do.

Launched Fiction Career Still an avid reader and lover of books, Palahniuk decided to start writing fiction. He began attending writing workshops hosted by Tom Spanbauer, a Pulitzer Prize-nominated author. Spanbauer influenced Palahniuk to write in what became a signature minimalist style. Palahniuk completed two unpublished novels in the early 1990s, then published his disturbing first novel, *Fight Club*, in 1996. The novel features a secret fight club in which men beat each other bloody, and whose members eventually develop into an anarchist army that is funded by selling soap made of liposuctioned human fat. It was inspired by his own fights, and the lack of response his bruised and bloody face got from coworkers. *Fight Club* won the 1997 Pacific Northwest Booksellers Association Award and the 1997 Oregon Book Award.

Fight Club was made into a cult hit film of the same name in 1999, bringing more attention to Palahniuk as an author. Because of the success of the book and film, Palahniuk was able to focus on writing full-time. Also in 1999, he published two more novels, *Survivor* and *Invisible Monsters*. *Survivor* focuses on the survivor of a cult who becomes a celebrity before his death in the Australian desert, while *Invisible Monsters* was a revised version of one of his first unpublished works, a shocking, twisted tale about a former model, out for revenge.

Personal Tragedy Just as Palahniuk was achieving success, he suffered a personal tragedy. In 1999, his father and his father's girlfriend, Donna Fontaine, were murdered by her abusive ex-husband, Dale Shackelford, whom she had put in jail for battery. After his release, Shackelford had followed them home, shot them, and tried to cover up the murder by setting the house on fire. In 2001, Shackelford was caught and found guilty on two counts of first degree murder. Palahniuk attended the trial and found inspiration for a later book.

As Palahniuk was dealing with his own tragedy, many Americans were also facing a wide-scale trauma. On September 11, 2001, al-Qaeda terrorists hijacked a number of commercial airliners and crashed them into the World Trade Center in New York City and into the Pentagon in Washington, D.C. Thousands of people lost their lives in the attacks and unsettled American society in the years following the event.

Continued Success Palahniuk's next novel was *Choke* (2001), which was a *New York Times* bestseller. The novel focuses on Victor Mancini, a medical school dropout who works at a historical village and supplements his

LITERARY AND HISTORICAL CONTEMPORARIES

Chuck Palahniuk's famous contemporaries include:

Alice Sebold (1963–): Best-selling American author, Sebold, is known for her novel *The Lovely Bones* (2002), in which a girl narrates the tale of her murder and its effect on those she leaves behind.

Brad Pitt (1963–): This American film star is as known as much for his looks as his varied film choices. He played the role of Tyler Durden in the film adaptation of *Fight Club* (1999).

Stephen King (1947–): This American author is known for his prolific array of novels, short stories, and screen work. Much of his output focuses on horror, fantasy, and science fiction—often with humorous touches—including such classics as *The Shining* (1977).

Irvine Welsh (1958–): Scottish author, Welsh, writes controversial novels about drug abuse and the question of the identity of the Scottish working class beginning in the 1960s. His works include *Trainspotting* (1993) and *Glue* (2001).

Clark Gregg (1962–): An American actor, screenwriter, and director, Gregg wrote the screenplay for the Robert Zemeckis film, *What Lies Beneath* (2000). He also directed the film adaptation of Palahniuk's 2001 novel, *Choke* (2008).

income by faking choking in restaurants, hoping for a payout from whoever saves him. *Choke* was followed by the novel, *Lullaby* (2002), in which the author attempts to come to terms with the violence in his own family. The story focuses on a poetic verse that can kill someone if sung or even hummed, and was to be the first in a horror trilogy. Palahniuk won both the 2003 Pacific Northwest Booksellers Association Award and the 2003 Bram Stoker Award for *Lullaby*.

In 2003, Palahniuk published two more books, the novel, *Diary*, and nonfiction travelogue, *Fugitives and Refugees: A Walk in Portland, Oregon*. His next book was also nonfiction, a collection of articles and essays on figures in American culture, such as Juliette Lewis and Marilyn Manson, as well as a take on his own life, *Stranger Than Fiction: True Stories* (2004). Continuing to write challenging fiction, *Haunted* (2005) centers on seventeen writers who answer an ad for a writer's retreat. Once they arrive at the retreat, they find themselves trapped in a huge theater working to write their masterpieces. The result is seventeen horror stories by writers who soon learn that they may also be kidnap victims.

Publishing two novels in two years, Palahniuk put out *Rant: An Oral Biography of Buster Casey* in 2007, and

Snuff in 2008. The former tells the story of the life of a folk hero, from his small-town beginnings to his time with the Nighttimers group in the big city, while the latter focuses on three men waiting their turn to have sex with a porn star who wants to break a world record for serial fornication. Continuing to work on novels and nonfiction, Palahniuk lives with his partner on a former church compound outside of Vancouver, Washington.

Works in Literary Context

As an author, Palahniuk favors a limited vocabulary and short sentences, telling a story in what might be called a conversational tone. The narratives of his novels often start at the story's end, with the main character then relating the events that led to the moment where the novel beings. Through his novels, Palahniuk offers his views on societal problems, such as materialism. His characters are usually working-class individuals who struggle to sustain their personal needs. His stories always emphasize the rampant consumerism of American contemporary society. As a writer, Palahniuk was greatly influenced by Amy Hempel, Gordon Lish, Ira Levin, Søren Kierkegaard, Jean-Paul Sartre, Michael Foucault, and Albert Camus.

Personal Transformation Palahniuk's early novels often focus on the concept of identity, how the protagonist can transform, and the consequences of that transformation. *Fight Club, Survivor, Invisible Monsters,* and *Choke* all deal with this subject. *Fight Club*, for example, revolves around an unnamed man who is disillusioned with American society. He has a bland, unhappy life, and has been seeking solace, however undeserved, by faking terminal illness at support group meetings. He also befriends Tyler Durden, an unpredictable young man who suggests they start a fight club, where men participate in fist fights as a way of dealing with personal demons. In *Survivor*, Tender Branson moves from being a member of the Creedish Death Cult who worked as an unpaid servant in exchange for donations to the church. After a raid on the cult and a mass suicide of most of its members, media interest in Branson turned him into a celebrity and book-selling self-help guru. The transformation in *Invisible Monsters* is both physical and personal and concerns several characters. Shannon McFarland is a former model who lost the lower half of her face in a shooting. She is left without a career and filled with anger at her ex-boyfriend, Manus, and ex-girlfriend, Evie, who had an affair after the shooting. Convinced that the pair may be responsible for her wounds, she goes on a cross-country trip with a new friend, the transgendered Brandy Alexander, to confront Evie in Texas. In the process, Shannon and Brandy kidnap Manus and start secretly feeding him female hormone pills.

Violence Palahniuk often uses and incorporates acts of violence into novels. *Fight Club* revolves around a club for men who are required to participate in fist fights. The first fight club inspires countless others. Durden, the force behind the clubs, has larger, destructive plans for his army of thousands of nihilists. His Project Mayhem is a plan to terrorize corporate America by attacking the world's tallest building. Similarly, *Survivor* begins with a focus on Tender Branson moments before his death, as his plane is about to crash into the Australian desert. Throughout the story, it is revealed that his brother, Adam, might be a serial killer and the mass suicide at the Creedish Death Cult may, in fact, be murders. Suicide is also found in *Diary*, in which artist Misty Marie Kleinman writes a diary for her carpenter husband, Peter Wilmot, who lies in a coma following a suicide attempt. The prevention of violence is at the heart of the horror novel, *Lullaby*. A newspaper reporter named Carl Streator discovers a link between an ancient African tribal poem and the death of five babies from SIDS. The poem was originally intended as a way to decrease the tribes' population in desperate times, but has now been carelessly reprinted in a book. Teaming up with a real estate agent, Helen Hoover Boyle, who knows about the verse, Streator seeks to destroy all known copies of the book. *Rant* focuses on a folk hero who may have been a serial killer. Palahniuk's infamous short story, "Guts," which has reportedly caused dozens of people to faint upon hearing it read aloud by the author, contains descriptions of disturbing accidents that result in serious bodily injury.

Works in Critical Context

Though Palahniuk is considered a "cult figure" in the American literary scene, critics have generally reviewed his works unfavorably. He has been labeled a "shock writer" because of the often lurid subjects presented in his novels. Many reviewers claim that his books promote nihilism, sexism, and self-destruction. Despite the negative reviews, Palahniuk has been praised for his logical, philosophical, and futuristic style of storytelling. Other critics have lauded his sense of humor, use of language, and touches of surrealism.

Fight Club   Critics were both disturbed and fascinated by *Fight Club*. A *Publishers Weekly* reviewer warns that almost any reader is likely to find something offensive. The reviewer calls the book "caustic, outrageous, bleakly funny, violent and always unsettling" as well as "utterly original." Stuart Jefferies, in the *Guardian Unlimited*, considers the literary and social relevance of *Fight Club*, calling the novel "the 90s reply to *American Psycho*, Bret Easton Ellis's satire on youthful white-collar greed and banality in Wall Street in the 80s." In *Booklist*, Thomas Gaughan describes *Fight Club* as "gen X's most articulate assault yet on baby-boomer sensibilities" and a work sure to disturb young reader's parents. He concludes that the novel is "powerful, and possibly brilliant."

Lullaby   Like *Fight Club* and other novels by Palahniuk, the horror novel *Lullaby* received mixed reviews. Janet Maslin in the *New York Times* is both fascinated and repelled by Palahniuk's "tireless pursuit of the outrageous" in *Lullaby*. Like Kurt Vonnegut, she writes, Palahniuk "juggles nihilism and idealism with fluid, funny ease, and he repeats and rephrases word patterns until

---

COMMON HUMAN EXPERIENCE

Palahniuk's novels often focus on violence and its relationship to human nature. Here are some other novels which touch on similar ideas:

Crash (1973), a novel by J. G. Ballard. In this novel, Ballard tells the story of crash victim James Ballard and photographer Vaughan, a man obsessed with the idea of dying in an auto crash with Elizabeth Taylor.

The Contortionist's Handbook (2002), a novel by Craig Clevenger. This novel focuses on John Vincent, a young man born with an extra finger on each hand. Encouraged to pursue magic, he develops a talent for sleight-of-hand tricks which leads to a life of petty crime and drug addiction.

American Psycho (1991), a novel by Bret Easton Ellis. This novel centers on Patrick Bateman, a young wealthy investment banker who describes both his materialistic lifestyle and the series of brutal murders he committed in a flat, dispassionate narrative.

The Virgin Suicides (1994), a novel by Jeffrey Eugenides. This novel revolves around the life of the Lisbons, a Catholic family with five daughters. The novel narrates the daughters' lives and how they work their way to committing suicide.

---

they take on an almost mystical aspect." Virginia Heffernan, reviewing the novel for the *New York Times Book Review*, is less impressed, dubbing the novel "a nauseating picaresque" with "less than zero sacred." A *Kirkus Review* contributor saw more to like in the novel, calling it the kind of "outrageous, darkly comic fun ... you'd expect from Palahniuk." *Booklist* reviewer John Green concludes that what separates *Lullaby* from Palahniuk's earlier work "is its emotional depth, its ability to explore the unbearable pain of losing a child just as richly as it laments our consume-or-die worldview."

Responses to Literature

1. Watch the film adaptation of one of Palahniuk's novels. In an essay, compare and contrast the two versions of the story. Which version do you believe is more effective? Why?

2. In a small group, discuss the themes and plot lines of *Lullaby*. What do you believe is the metaphor for the verse at the heart of the story? How do you interpret the story?

3. Taking cues from the novel, *Diary*, write your own short story in diary form. Use the concept of a diary to reveal your character's innermost thoughts and tensions.

4. Stage a debate for the class about the way masculinity is portrayed in *Fight Club*. Do you think Palahniuk is accurate in the way he depicts the inner workings of men? Which elements are realistic and which are based in fantasy?

BIBLIOGRAPHY

Periodicals

Bunn, Alison. "Open Book." *The Advocate* (May 20, 2008): 42.

Gaughan, Thomas. Review of *Fight Club. Booklist* (July 1996): 1804.

Green, John. Review of *Lullaby. Booklist* (August 2002): 1887.

Heffernan, Virginia. Review of *Lullaby. New York Times Book Review* (October 20, 2002): 17.

Maslin, Janet. Review of *Lullaby. New York Times* (September 12, 2002): E9.

Randall, Lee. "Devilishly Funny Chuck Palahniuk's Exhaustively Researched Work is No Joy-Ride, but *Snuff* Will Tickle Every Funny Bone You've Got." *The Scotsman* (August 13, 2008): 40.

Review of *Fight Club. Publishers Weekly* (June 3, 1996): 60.

Review of *Lullaby. Kirkus Reviews* (June 15, 2002): 834.

Tuss, Alex. "Masculine Identity and Success: A Critical Analysis of Patricia Highsmith's *The Talented Mr. Ripley* and Chuck Palahniuk's *Fight Club*." *The Journal of Men's Studies* (Winter 2004): 93.

Web sites

Jeffries, Stuart. "Bruise Control." *Guardian Unlimited*. Retrieved December 8, 2008, from http://www.guardian.co.uk/books/2000/may/12/fiction.chuckpalahniuk. Last updated on May 12, 2000.

✦ Grace Paley

BORN: *1922, New York City*

DIED: *2007, Thetford Hill, Vermont*

NATIONALITY: *American*

GENRE: *Fiction, poetry*

MAJOR WORKS:

The Little Disturbances of Man: Stories of Women and Men at Love (1959)

Enormous Changes at the Last Minute (1974)

Later the Same Day (1985)

Long Walks and Intimate Talks (1991)

Fidelity (2008)

Overview

Considered one of the most innovative contemporary American short fiction writers, Grace Paley combines traditional subject matter with postmodern fictional tech-

Grace Paley   *Paley, Grace, 1986, photograph. AP Images.*

niques to depict modern urban life in the United States. A feminist and political activist, she addresses many social concerns in her stories, often focusing on female and Jewish protagonists who contend with issues of oppression, community, and cultural heritage. Marked by lively, colloquial prose and a combination of humor and poignancy, Paley's stories are also characterized by narrative ambiguities and inconclusive endings. Celebrating precarious human relationships in a society, and a world, of dangerous inequalities, Paley's voice is comically appalled, yet positive.

Works in Biographical and Historical Context

Inspiring Childhood   Born Grace Goodside on December 11, 1922, in New York City, she was the youngest child of Dr. Isaac Goodside, a physician, and his wife, Manya (Ridnyik), a photographer and medical assistant. She lived much of her life in the city, which later provided the setting for many of her short stories. Her parents were Jewish immigrants from Europe who supported leftist and Zionist (the political philosophy that follows the idea of a national homeland for the Jewish people) movements. Growing up on stories of discrimination, racism, and exile, in an environment of radicalism, she was sensitive to everyone's shortcomings. Her parents' activities influenced Paley's own lifelong political activism. She also grew up in a household where three languages were spoken—Yiddish, Russian, and English. As a writer of fiction, she would pick up on the music of all three tongues, celebrating their rhythms and idioms.

Paley began writing poetry at an early age. When she was sixteen years old, she enrolled at Hunter College, but dropped out in 1939 before receiving a degree. She also attended New York University. By the time she left school, World War II had broken out. The war began when Nazi Germany, led by Adolf Hitler, invaded Poland in September 1939, and overran the country. England and France declared war on Germany, but Germany soon controlled much of the European continent. The United States entered the war in 1941, after Japan bombed an American naval base in Hawaii. The war was fought in a number of theaters in Europe, Asia, Africa, and the South Pacific, involving sixty-one countries and leaving fifty-five million people dead. Although Paley was not directly involved in the war effort, the experience of living through wartime helped to shape her opinions about militarism and steeled her resolve in her antiwar activities later in life.

Failed Marriage   In 1942, Paley married Jess Paley, a cinematographer. They had two children—Nora and Danny—but separated three years later, although they were not divorced until the 1970s. Many critics believe that Jess Paley is the model for many absent husbands of many of Paley's characters. Paley also began studying poetry in the early 1940s under acclaimed poet W. H. Auden at the New School for Social Research.

Paley wrote poetry exclusively until the age of thirty-three, when she began writing short stories. She published these early short stories in her first collection, *The Little Disturbances of Man: Stories of Women and Men at Love* (1959). With this acclaimed collection, Paley established a reputation as a masterful stylist, able to vividly capture the idiomatic speech of native New Yorkers of various ethnicities. Her protagonists in this and later collections are characterized by their vivaciousness and indomitability of spirit, which they maintain in spite of economic difficulties and painful personal relationships.

Antiwar Activities   After founding the Greenwich Village Peace Center in 1961, Paley taught at Columbia University and Syracuse University in the 1960s. Also in this time period, Paley became increasingly active in a number of political movements, including opposing the war in Vietnam. She was arrested during antiwar demonstrations. Vietnam had been divided into a Communist North and noncommunist South in the mid-1950s, but Communist efforts to gain control over all of Vietnam continued. In the early 1960s, the United States began to provide military aid to South Vietnam, hoping to stop the spread of communism. At first the aid came in the form of advisors, but after 1964, an ever-increasing number of American troops entered the conflict. Though unpopular, the war in Vietnam continued until the early 1970s. Approximately 58,000 American soldiers and two million Vietnamese soldiers and civilians lost their lives in the conflict. Paley traveled to Vietnam in 1969, representing the anti-war movement.

During this period, Paley also began writing a novel, an attempt to satisfy others' expectations. She called the novel a huge mistake, and never finished it. In addition, beginning in 1966, Paley began teaching creative writing at Sarah Lawrence College, a position she would hold until 1988. Because of her teaching duties, political activism (including being active in the anti-nuclear war movement),

and commitment to raising her children, her literary output remained limited. After finally divorcing Jess Paley in 1972, Paley was married to her second husband, Bob Nichols.

Lauded Short Story Collections   In 1974, Paley published the short story collection, *Enormous Changes at the Last Minute.* Beginning with this collection of short stories, she focused increasingly on political and social themes, and began experimenting with different forms of narrative which helped her enhance her reputation as a major postmodernist writer. After being elected to the American Academy of Letters in 1980, Paley began teaching City College of New York in 1983. Two years later, she published both a significant short story collection—*Later the Same Day* (1985)—and a poetry collection, *Leaning Forward* (1985).

While continuing to teach, Paley's literary output increased in the 1990s. In 1991, Paley published *Long Walks and Intimate Talks*, a collection of poetry and short stories. A year later, she put out more poetry with *New and Collected Poems* (1992). In 1994, Paley gave the same treatment to her short fiction with *Grace Paley: The Collected Stories*, which was a finalist for the Pulitzer Prize. In 1998, she published the memoir *Just As I Thought.*

Death from Cancer   By this time, Paley was spending much of the year in Vermont with her second husband, where she served as the state's poet laureate for a time.

COMMON HUMAN EXPERIENCE

In her short stories, Paley often features female characters strongly dealing with the problems and joys of everyday life. Here are other short story collections by women who focus on deeply human struggles:

Twilight of the Superheroes (2006), a short story collection by Deborah Eisenberg. This volume of short stories focuses on the idea that humanity is basically powerless in the face of fate.

Woman Hollering Creek and Other Stories (1991), a short story collection by Sandra Cisneros. This collection of twenty-two stories focuses on numerous Mexican-American characters living near San Antonio, Texas. They contain the interior monologues of individuals who have been assimilated into American culture despite their sense of loyalty to Mexico.

Days (1979), a short story collection by Mary Robison. Written with humor and extreme detail, these stories focus on characters who are seemingly oblivious to both the bizarre and mundane aspects of their lives.

Dance of the Happy Shades (1968), a short story collection by Alice Munro. This short story collection focuses on the ordinary lives of characters growing up and coming of age in small towns in southwestern Ontario, Canada.

She continued to publish works, including another collection of poetry, *Begin Again: Collected Poems* (2000). Paley succumbed to breast cancer on August 22, 2007, at her home in Thetford Hill, Vermont, at the age of 84. After her death, a last original collection of poems was published, *Fidelity* (2008).

Works in Literary Context

Paley's work celebrates the positive powers of womanhood. Her work reflects her own experience as a child of the Jewish Bronx, a young wife and mother staked out with the kids in Greenwich Village's Washington Square Park, and an activist involved in many of the important political movements of her time. In her stories, Paley employs techniques that are more commonly associated with experimental, nonrepresentational fiction. Sometimes dubbed an "experimental realist," the author draws on the sociology of metafiction, or writing in which the author self-consciously plays with the traditional rules of fiction. As an author, Paley was greatly influenced by her own ethnic background and family, Jewish oral tradition, feminism, postmodernism, political activities, and life in New York City.

The American Female Experience Throughout Paley's short stories, the status of women in American society is a predominant theme. Her female protagonists rebel against authority by protesting government actions or asserting their independence in romantic relationships. Frequently, these women are single mothers—abandoned or "unmarried on principle"—who develop informal, independent communities of support. Several of Paley's stories feature the recurring character Faith Darwin, a writer who shares a number of biographical characteristics with Paley. Faith, like other Paley heroines, maintains an awareness of the relationship between politics and personal life. She also expresses many of Paley's principles on the nature of art and the role of the writer in society. For example, in "A Conversation with My Father," Faith's father, hospitalized with heart disease, reproaches her for not writing simple, tragic stories in the vein of Anton Chekhov. Much of Paley's fiction also compares the value systems of male and female characters. Whereas women in Paley's stories are generally concerned with establishing communal bonds and finding peace, men pursue wealth and individual honor and frequently abandon their families in order to do so. She outlines these differences in beliefs in such stories as "An Interest in Life," in which the female protagonist speculates on the differences between a woman's idea of happiness and a man's, noting that women prefer the comfort of a husband and children, while men are obsessed with their own individual fame.

Jewish Background The majority of Paley's characters are either Jewish immigrants or their descendants who must come to terms with past oppression as well as with contemporary prejudices. The burden of Jewish history is a recurrent theme in Paley's stories. In the story "In Time Which Made a Monkey of Us All," victims of the Holocaust are described with bitter humor as those who "died in the epidemics of Jewishness." Similarly, in "Zargrowsky Tells," a Jewish immigrant charges that an "American-born girl has some nerve to mention history." In such stories, Paley faithfully reproduces the cadences of Yiddish speech. In "Debts," the narrator, a writer, says that her work is like the oral storytelling of the past—an act necessary to the preservation of the culture and dignity of one's people and family.

Works in Critical Context

Paley's combination of traditional oral storytelling aesthetics with a postmodern narrative self-awareness and approach to plot has led critics to hail her as a major renovator of the short story. Critics generally consider the stories featuring Faith Darwin her most successful, and some have speculated that, taken together, these works might comprise a novel. Some reviewers have charged that Paley's political views overwhelm her later stories, but others argue that while she writes about politically engaged characters, she never aims to preach or argue political issues. While critics sometimes fault Paley for incompletely rendering her subject matter, particularly in her shorter stories, the emotional intensity of her narratives and the fullness of her characters have earned her widespread respect.

The Little Disturbances of Man: Stories of Women and Men at Love While initial sales of Paley's first collection of short stories, *The Little Disturbances of Man: Stories of Women and Men at Love*, were modest, the collection drew a loyal following and generally good reviews. A reviewer for *The New Yorker* assesses Paley's writing in it as "fresh and vigorous," noting that "her view on life is her own." Discussing the story "An Interest in Life," Jonathan Baumbach of the *Partisan Review* explains how "the matter-of-fact, ironic voice of the protagonist, Ginny, distances the reader from the conventions of her pathos ... only to bring us ... to an awareness of the character as if someone known to us intimately for a long time." Baumbach concludes, "Paley's comic stories deal in exaggerated understatement, disguise their considerable ambition in the modesty of wit." In the introduction to the Virago edition of the volume, A. S. Byatt states that

> we have had a great many artists, more of them women than not, recording the tragedies of repetition, frequency, weariness, and little disturbances. What distinguishes Grace Paley from the mass of these is the interest, and even more, the inventiveness which she brings to her small world.

Enormous Changes at the Last Minute Paley's next collection, *Enormous Changes at the Last Minute*, was challenging for critics. Writing in the *New Republic*, Michele Murray comments, "Even with the glitter of its style ... *Enormous Changes* is a book of losses and failures. It's not tragedy that weighs down these stories, it's no more than despair and repetition." Yet the *Nation*'s Burton Bendow argues that Paley "is right to avoid looking tragedy in the face; she knows where her talent lies. It is, if not for comedy exactly, for virtuoso mimicry." In the *Village Voice*, Vivian Gornick lauds the collection, writing, "Paley when she is good is so good that she is worth ninety-nine 'even' writers, and when one hears that unmistakable Paley voice one feels what can be felt only in the presence of a true writer: safe." Walter Clemons of *Newsweek* concludes, "*Enormous Changes at the Last Minute* was well worth the wait."

Responses to Literature

1. Paley's short stories were often influenced by her childhood and life as a single mother in New York City. Write a short story of your own reflecting the influences of your surroundings.

2. Research the antiwar movement surrounding the Vietnam War, of which Paley took part. In an essay, link one or more stories or poems by Paley which reflect antiwar concerns to your findings.

3. Create an oral presentation about Paley's use of language and dialogue. Include information about the three languages spoken in her childhood home, the Jewish oral tradition, and related literature.

4. In a small group, discuss how Paley depicts women and their lives in her stories. Can you relate to her depiction? Do you think her concerns still have relevance in today's society? Are her women complex or simple?

BIBLIOGRAPHY

Books

Arcana, Judith. *Grace Paley's Life Stories.* Champagne, Ill.: University of Illinois Press, 1993.

Bach, Gerhard, and Blaine H. Hall. *Conversations with Grace Paley.* Jackson, Miss.: University Press of Mississippi, 1997.

Byatt, A. S. "Introduction." *The Little Disturbances of Man.* London: Virago, 1980.

Taylor, Jacqueline. *Grace Paley: Illuminating the Dark Lives.* Austin, Tex.: University of Texas Press, 1990.

Periodicals

Baba, Minako. "Faith Darwin as Writer-Heroine: A Study of Grace Paley's Short Stories." *Studies in Jewish American Literature* (Spring 1988): 40–54.

Baumbach, Jonathan. Review of *The Little Disturbances of Man: Stories of Women and Men at Love. Partisan Review* (Spring 1975): 303–306.

Bendow, Burton. "Voices in the Metropolis." *Nation* (March 11, 1974): 597–598.

Clemons, Walter. Review of *Enormous Changes at the Last Minute. Newsweek* (March 11, 1974).

Gornick, Vivian. Review of *Enormous Changes at the Last Minute. Village Voice* (March 14, 1974).

Murray, Michele. Review of *Enormous Changes at the Last Minute. New Republic* (March 16, 1974).

Review of *The Little Disturbances of Man: Stories of Women and Men at Love. The New Yorker* (June 27, 1959).

✸ Américo Paredes

BORN: *1915, Brownsville, Texas*

DIED: *1999, Austin, Texas*

NATIONALITY: *American*

GENRE: *Poetry, nonfiction, fiction*

MAJOR WORKS:

Cantos de adolescencia (1937)

"With His Pistol in His Hand": A Border Ballad and Its Hero (1958)

George Washington Gomez: A Mexicotexan Novel (1990)

Between Two Worlds (1991)

The Hammon and the Beans and Other Stories (1994)

Américo Paredes   *Paredes, Americo, photograph by Ralph Barrera. Reproduced by permission of Ralph Barrera.*

Overview

A renowned scholar and folklorist who specialized in the border culture of the American Southwest, Américo Paredes wrote both poetry and academic works on the *corrida*, or Mexican ballad. Through his work, he sought to correct what he regarded as the misrepresentation of his people and culture. Paredes was instrumental in the development of the field of folklore in academia as well as in the field of Mexican American studies. His groundbreaking book, *"With His Pistol in His Hand": A Border Ballad and Its Hero* (1958), is considered highly influential in the founding of folklore studies and Chicano studies.

Works in Biographical and Historical Context

Brought Up on the Rio Grande   Born on September 3, 1915, in Brownsville, Texas, Paredes was the son of Justo Paredes and his wife, Clotilde Manzano-Vidal. His father's family had been ranchers on both sides of the Rio Grande, beginning in the mid-1700s, while his mother's family had

come to the region from Spain in the mid-1800s. One of eight children in his family, Paredes learned to read and write Spanish at home, but received his formal education at the English-language public schools in Brownsville. While a student at Brownsville High School, Paredes began writing poetry and took first prize in a state-wide poetry contest.

After graduating from high school in 1934, Paredes entered Brownsville Junior College, aspiring to be a poet and fiction writer. At the time, the United States, and indeed the whole world, was dealing with a deep economic downturn known as the Great Depression. It began with the stock market crash of 1929. The stock market crashed because an investment boom which began in 1924 was fueled by investors buying stocks on margin (in which investors took out loans to buy stocks for as little as ten percent down), and with purely speculative money. The stocks themselves were also wildly overvalued and their value plummeted as the economy took a downturn. The failure of the stock market caused the economy, first in the United States then the world, to fall in a dramatic and sustained depression which lasted through the 1930s.

Published First Book of Poetry   While a college student, Paredes did not lack for employment, as many Americans did. He worked as a translator and writer for the local newspaper, *The Brownsville Herald*, as well as for Pan American Airways. Paredes also found occasional work as a professional singer and studied piano and guitar during this time. In addition, he continued to write poetry, though it remained unpublished for many years. Some of the poetry Paredes had written in high school began appearing in the paper, as well as "Los lunnes literarios," the literary supplement of San Antonio's Mexican-American newspaper *La Prensa*. Poems from this time period were collected in Paredes' first volume of poetry, *Cantos de adolescencia* (1937). These poems recount an adolescent's struggle to fit into a culture that is neither Mexican or American.

In 1939, Paredes married Consuelo Chelo Silva, a local singer. The marriage was brief, but produced a son, Américo Paredes, Jr. When Paredes married Silva, World War II was beginning in Europe. The war began when Nazi Germany, led by Adolf Hitler, invaded Poland in September 1939 and overran the country. England and France declared war on Germany, but Germany soon controlled much of the European continent. The United States entered the war in 1941, after Japan bombed an American naval base in Hawaii. The war was fought in a number of theaters in Europe, Asia, Africa, and the South Pacific, involving sixty-one countries and leaving fifty-five million people dead.

Served in World War II   During World War II, Paredes served in the U.S. Army from 1941 to 1946. After a stint as an infantryman, he worked as a reporter and editor for the U.S. military newspaper, *Stars and Stripes*, in Japan. Paredes remained there after the war and worked for the

Red Cross for five years doing public relations work. He met his second wife, Amelia Shidzu Nagamine, during his time in Japan. The couple married in 1948 and eventually had three children together.

In the early 1950s, Paredes returned to Texas, entering the University of Texas at Austin. He earned his B.A. in English, summa cum laude in 1951, then remained at the school for graduate work. Paredes was given his M.A. in 1953 and Ph.D. in 1957, both in English (folklore) and Spanish, with a specialty in the folklore of the Texas-Mexican border region. While a graduate student, he published his first collection of short stories, *Border Country* (1952).

Dissertation Turned Book After earning his graduate degrees, Parades held a variety of positions in academia. He first taught at Texas Western University, then organized and worked as an archivist at the University of Texas at Austin's Folklore Archives from 1957 to 1967. In 1958, Paredes published the scholarly work, *"With His Pistol in His Hand": A Border Ballad and Its Hero*. Based on his doctoral dissertation, it was a study of the ballad form, passed down as part of the Texas-Mexican border region's oral tradition and performed by anonymous balladeers.

As an academic, Paredes was the editor of an acclaimed collection of translated folklore, *Folktales of Mexico* (1970). He also published several scholarly studies of folklore, including *A Texas-Mexican Cancionero: Folksongs of the Lower Bridge* (1976), *Uncle Remus con Chile* (1992), and *Folklore and Culture on the Tex-Mex Border* (1993). In addition, Paredes was also the co-founder of the University of Texas's Mexican-American Studies Program. For his work as a humanist, he was given the Charles Frankel Prize by the National Endowment of the Arts in 1989.

Works Old and New In the 1990s, Parades published a number of original works in a variety of genres. In 1990, he published his first novel, *George Washington Gomez: A Mexicotexas Novel*, perhaps his best known work of border literature, and originally written while he was a young journalist in Brownsville. His second novel, *The Shadow*, was published in 1998. Paredes put out his second volume of original poetry, *Between Two Worlds*, in 1991. These poems were written in the 1930s, but were unpublished at the time of their composition. Among the best-known poems was "The Mexico-Texan," which had been used in south Texas political campaigns and entered the local oral tradition. His second collection of short stories came out in 1994, *The Hammon and the Beans and Other Stories*, which featured stories primarily written in the 1930s and 1940s. It was also considered a significant contribution to border literature as it vividly describes the Brownsville of his youth where Mexican Americans struggled against poverty, prejudice, and the loss of cultural identity.

In his last years, Paredes served as a professor emeritus of English and anthropology at the University of Texas. He died of pneumonia on May 5, 1999, in Austin.

LITERARY AND HISTORICAL CONTEMPORARIES

Américo Paredes's famous contemporaries include:

César Chávez (1927–1993): This Hispanic American labor leader was a champion of migrant rights. He organized the first effective union of farm workers in the history of California agriculture.

Douglas MacArthur (1880–1964): This American army general served as the commander of forces in the Pacific during World War II. He also oversaw the rebuilding of Japan and led United Nations forces in the Korean War.

J. Frank Dobie (1888–1964): This American scholar and professor was a leading American folklorist. He was a professor of English at the University of Texas, and his nonfiction books include *Coronado's Children* (1939).

Luis Valdez (1940–): This American playwright and director was the founder of the El Teatro Campesino in California, and is considered to be the father of Mexican American theater. He also wrote and directed the hit film, *La Bamba* (1987).

Rodolfo "Corky" Gonzáles (1928–2005): This Mexican American author and activist started the Crusade for Justice, an organization which worked to help poor Mexican Americans. He was also known for his work, *I Am Joaquin/Yo Soy Joaquin: An Epic Poem* (1967), which expresses his ethnic pride.

Works in Literary Context

Paredes was a pioneer in the academic study of the Mexican-American experience and of the culture of the U.S.-Mexico border. His poetry, fiction, and scholarly work were all informed by his conviction that his people, and his region, had been misrepresented in the literature of the dominant American culture. Paredes's poetry was specifically inspired by the ballads and stories passed down to him by his father when he was a boy, works that also greatly shaped his fiction and nonfiction work. As a writer, Paredes was also influenced by childhood summers spent in northern Mexico, listening to storytellers, as well as the culture in which he was raised. Authors that inspired his work include Gustavo Adolfo Bécquer.

Mexican and Southwestern Folklore Much of Paredes's scholarly work focuses on folklore, specifically Mexican, Mexican American, and southwestern types. His first academic work was *"With His Pistol in His Hand": A Border Ballad and Its Hero*. This pioneering study on Mexican American folklore focuses on the legend of Gregorio Cortez, a Mexican American ranch hand who shot a Texas sheriff and then became a hero as he eluded capture. In his *"With His Pistol in His Hand,"* Paredes discusses all facets of Cortez's story and how the ballad

"El corrido de Gregorio Cortez" developed out of actual events. He also provided the folk background out of which it came. His next major work on folklore was *Folktales of Mexico*, a collection of tales edited and translated by Paredes. In addition to including folktales, his introduction offered a complete history of folklore societies and folklore studies in Mexico. *A Texas-Mexican Cancionero: Folksongs of the Lower Border* is a comprehensive anthology and study of traditional songs in the border area.

Bicultural Heritage and Cultural Conflict In his poetry and fiction, Paredes often explores—and sometimes celebrates—his bicultural heritage as a Mexican-American living on the border between Texas and Mexico. He includes information about what it means to grow up in this society and reflects the era in which the work was written. For example, his first poetry collection, *Cantos de adolescencia*, features a poetic voice of an adolescent, whose existence as an Hispanic in an Anglo American world, compels him to treasure his ancestral roots. Paredes's second collection of poetry, *Between Two Worlds*, also reflects his bicultural heritage with poems which reflect, among other topics, the conflict arising from the poet's Mexican-American identity. His novel, *George Washington Gomez: A Mexicotexan Novel*, was written between 1936 to 1940, reflecting the Great Depression, the beginning of World War II, and conflict of cultures in the Rio Grande Valley. It is a portrayal of an era of hardships that left a deep mark on the Chicanos of south Texas through the character of Guálinto, who lives in this environment riddled with cultural conflict. His father is murdered by the Texas Rangers, who incorrectly assume that he is part of a seditionist movement seeking to establish a Spanish-speaking republic in the southwest. Guálinto himself faces prejudice in school, as was common in the place and time.

Works in Critical Context

Critics have offered high praise for Paredes as a pioneer in the field of border culture, and in what came to be known as "border writing." He was lauded for his attempts to capture more accurately the culture of his people and his region. Much of Paredes's fiction and poetry was highly regarded by critics, though there is limited criticism of his work.

George Washington Gomez: A Mexicotexan Novel Much scholarly attention has been paid to what is generally considered the better of Paredes's two novels, *George Washington Gomez: A Mexicotexan Novel*. Writing in *MELUS*, Hector Perez offers his interpretation of the novel, examining its themes and the history of the region and times in which it was written. He asserts, "*George Washington Gomez* can be read as a radical novel, though its radical quality can best be appreciated in the context of its setting: the U.S.-Mexico border and the era's literary and intellectual environment." Another scholar finds the novel to be an example of a new form of modernism. Christopher Schedler in *Texas Studies in Literature and Language* writes, "... Paredes develops a form of Mexican-American modernism to depict a new period of linguistic and ideological—rather than armed—cultural conflict and to represent the pluralistic identity of an emerging Mexican-American middle-class subject." In a popular publication, *Texas Monthly*, Don Graham concludes,

> Paredes ... focused his whole career on the uphill struggle to assert the claims of border culture against those of the prevailing Anglo history. In *George Washington Gomez* he did just that, leaving behind a powerful critique of another side of race relations in South Texas.

Between Two Worlds Similarly, Paredes's second collection of poetry, *Between Two Worlds*, received little critical attention, though scholars found the work to be both significant and praiseworthy. In *The Ethnic Canon: Histories, Institutions, and Interventions*, Ramón Saldívar points out how far ahead of its time the poetry of *Between Two Worlds* was. He writes, "*Between Two Worlds* might well emblematize the features of ... postmodern border writing were it not for the fact that it predates the notion by more than a half a century." In another essay by Saldívar, included in *The Borderlands of Culture: Américo Paredes and the Transnational Imaginary*, he concludes that all of Paredes's works of fiction and poetry, including *Between Two Worlds*, "imagine the predicaments of contemporary ethnic cultural politics, identity formation, and social transformation in the context of what I am here calling bilingual modernity and transnational modernization."

Responses to Literature

1. Create a presentation for the class about Paredes's studies of folklore, using *Folktales of Mexico* as one potential source. How does Paredes link folktales to greater culture? Can you find parallels with folk stories in today's society?

2. Read the short stories in *The Hammon and the Beans: And Other Stories*, written between 1940 and 1953 and reflect on the time and place in which they were written. Taking a cue from Paredes' stories, write your own short story which reflects your own life and the time, place, and cultural forces in which you live.

3. Research the post-revolutionary Mexico setting which is the backdrop of Paredes's novel, *The Shadow*. In an essay, use your findings to discuss the novel and how it reflects the history and culture of the time.

4. In a small group, read *"With His Pistol in His Hand": A Border Ballad and Its Hero* and watch the PBS television movie adaptation of it, *George Cortez* (1982). In your discussion, compare and contrast the two versions. How does the movie reflect Paredes's scholarly concerns?

BIBLIOGRAPHY

Books

Limon, Jose E. "Américo Paredes, Tradition, and the First Ephebe: A Poetic Mediation on the Epic Corrido." *Mexican Ballads, Chicano Poems, History and Influence in Mexican-American Social Poetry.* Berkeley, Calif.: University of California Press, 1992, pp. 45–80.

———. *The Return of the Mexican Ballad: Américo Paredes and His Anthropologist Text as Persuasive Political Performance.* Stanford, Calif.: Stanford Center for Chicano Research, 1986.

Saldívar, Ramón. "Bilingual Aesthetics and the Law of the Heart." *The Borderlands of Culture: Américo Paredes and the Transnational Imaginary.* Durham, N.C.: Duke University Press, 2006, pp. 264–288.

———. "The Borders of Modernity: Américo Paredes's *Between Two Worlds* and the Chicano National Subject." *The Ethnic Canon: Histories, Institutions, and Interventions*, edited by David Palumbo-Liu. Minneapolis, Minn.: University of Minnesota Press, 1995, pp. 71–87.

———. "The Folk Base of Chicano Narrative: Américo Paredes's *With His Pistol in His Hand* and the Corrido Tradition." *Chicano Narrative: The Dialectics of Difference.* Madison, Wis.: University of Wisconsin Press, 1990, pp. 26–42.

Periodicals

Graham, Don. "Don Graham's Texas Classics: Amémerico Paredes' novel *George Washington Gomez.*" *Texas Monthly* (January 2000): 26.

Leal, Luis. "Américo Paredes and Modern Mexican American Scholarship." *Ethnic Affairs* (1987): 1–11.

Limon, Jose E. "Américo Paredes: Ballad Scholar." *Journal of American Folklore* (Winter 2007): 3.

Perez, Hector. "Voicing Resistance on the Border: A Reading of Américo Paredes's *George Washington Gomez.*" *MELUS* (Spring 1998): 27.

Saldívar, Ramón. "The Borderlands of Culture: Américo Paredes's *George Washington Gomez* and Chicano Literature at the End of the Twentieth Century." *American Literary History* (Summer 1993): 272–293.

Schedler, Christopher. "Inscribing Mexican-American Modernism in Américo Paredes's *George Washington Gomez.*" *Texas Studies in Literature and Language* (Summer 2000): 154.

❂ Dorothy Parker

BORN: *1893, West End, New Jersey*

DIED: *1967, New York City*

NATIONALITY: *American*

GENRE: *Poetry, fiction, nonfiction, drama*

MAJOR WORKS:

Enough Rope (1926)

Sunset Gun (1928)

Laments for the Living (1930)

Death and Taxes (1931)

A Star Is Born (1937)

Overview

During the 1920s and 1930s, Dorothy Parker was a literary celebrity whose often quoted witticisms were as well-known as her poetry and short fiction. Her verse, modeled on such traditional forms as the lyric, ballad, and sonnet, frequently addressed women's issues and the starkness of urban life through irony, parody, and hyperbole. Her short stories examine the social mores of the middle-class, often through bitterly cynical portrayals of stagnant marriages and unhappy love affairs. Despite her flamboyant reputation, Parker regarded herself as a social satirist rather than a humorist and often wrote from a liberal sensibility alternating between outrage and sentimentality.

Dorothy Parker   *Parker, Dorothy, 1933, photograph. AP Images.*

Works in Biographical and Historical Context

Unhappy Childhood   Born Dorothy Rothschild in 1893, in West End, New Jersey, she was the daughter of J. Henry Rothschild, a wealthy Jewish clothier, and his Protestant Scottish wife, Eliza A. (Marston). Her mother died when she was four. Her father later remarried, and Parker was raised by her father and her devoutly Catholic stepmother. Parker had issues with both parents, resenting her father's authoritarian personality and disliking her stepmother, whom she considered a religious fanatic. She also grew up ashamed of her mixed ethnic and religious background, and later stated that if she had written an autobiography, she would have entitled it "Mongrel."

Parker also detested her stepmother for sending her to Blessed Sacrament Convent—a convent school in New York City—in order to save Parker's soul from her "Jewish upbringing." While at the convent, Parker began writing poetry, but her education among the nuns ended early. Already showing signs of a rebellious streak, Parker described the Immaculate Conception as "spontaneous combustion" and was expelled.

Began Literary Criticism Career   In 1907, Parker's father and stepmother sent the young girl to an exclusive finishing school, Miss Dana's School, in Morristown,

New Jersey, where she graduated in 1911. During her time at the finishing school, Parker began developing as a writer. Her persistence paid off in 1915 when one of her poems captured the attention of a *Vogue* editor, who hired her to write captions for the magazine's fashion illustrations. She worked there from 1916 to 1917.

In 1917, an editor hired her at *Vanity Fair* as a drama critic. Parker's acerbic wit again brought trouble, and she was fired from this post in 1920, after writing a blistering review of a play starring the wife of one of the magazine's financial backers. Parker continued writing as a literary critic for *The New Yorker*'s book review column under the pseudonym, "Constant Reader."

Literary Star   As Parker's literary career blossomed, she married Wall Street broker, Edwin Pond Parker II, in 1917. He spent two years in military service at the end of World War I. This conflict began in Europe in 1914 after the assassination of Archduke Franz Ferdinand, the heir to the Austro-Hungarian throne. Because of political tensions and entangling alliances, nearly the whole of Europe soon became involved in the conflict. The United States joined the war on the side of Great Britain and France in 1917 after Germany's naval fleet began sinking American merchant ships in British waters. Ultimately, ten million soldiers died and twenty million were wounded during the course of the "Great War."

During the 1920s, Parker became well-known in New York literary and theatrical circles as a member of the Algonquin Round Table. The group, which included other prominent writers such as Robert Benchley, George S. Kaufman, and Franklin Pierce Adams, met regularly at the Algonquin Hotel and became famous when newspaper columnists reported their activities and quoted their conversations. Many of Parker's derisive Round Table remarks, such as "Men seldom make passes / At girls who wear glasses" were often quoted and achieved catchphrase status.

Published Acclaimed Poetry   As she achieved literary fame, however, Parker's life was punctuated by unhappiness, which was mirrored in her poetry. She published two collections of poetry in the 1920s, the bestseller, *Enough Rope* (1926), and *Sunset Gun* (1928). Both collections achieved widespread acclaim, and featured poems which explored the threat of losing love and unveiling the hypocrisy and mawkishness of romantic jargon. After gaining such laudatory reviews, Parker retired from magazine work to focus on writing verse and short stories, and later expanded into other genres. By the end of the 1920s, however, Parker was also drinking heavily, had a string of affairs, an abortion, and had attempted suicide three times.

As Parker's personal life degenerated, the United States and, indeed the world, was mired in an economic crisis. In 1929, a stock market crash launched the Great Depression. The failure of the stock market caused the economy, first in the United States, then the world, to fall in a dramatic and sustained depression which lasted through the 1930s.

Well-Received Short Stories   In this atmosphere, Parker published a more morose book of poetry, *Death and Taxes* (1931), followed by her collected poems, *Not So Deep as a Well* (1936). By the mid-1930s, she was writing more prose and poetry. Parker put out three collections of short stories—*Laments for the Living* (1930), *After Such Pleasures* (1933), and *Here Lies* (1939). Many of these stories had originally appeared in other publications, including *The New Yorker*, beginning in the 1920s. One story, "Big Blonde," won the O. Henry Award for best short story in 1929.

After the dissolution of her first marriage in 1928, Parker married the actor, Alan Campbell, in 1933. The relationship was also far from happy, and was marked by bickering, divorce in 1947, remarriage in 1950, separation in 1953, and reuniting again in 1956 until Campbell's death in 1963. The couple lived in California for much of their married life and collaborated on twenty-one screenplays in the 1930s and 1940s. Their most notable effort was the script for *A Star is Born* (1937), which was nominated for an Academy Award.

Hollywood Years   Despite the success, Parker disliked what she considered Hollywood superficiality, and became increasingly involved with such organizations as the fledgling Screen Actors Guild (which she helped organize in 1934) and the Anti-Nazi League in 1936. Her association with these left-wing groups impelled the House Un-American Activities Committee (HUAC) to investigate her as a possible Communist subversive in the 1950s. In the late 1940s and early 1950s, HUAC investigated charges of Americans working in government, Hollywood, and other professions about alleged Communist activities, beliefs, and leanings. Approximately 6.6 million people were checked by a security program implemented by President Harry S. Truman, and several hundred lost their jobs and/or were jailed as a result of the hearings. Parker refused to cooperate with the investigation. Though no charges were filed against her, she was blacklisted, or kept from receiving work from the major Hollywood studios.

During this time period, Parker also wrote two plays—*The Coast of Illyria* (1949) and *Ladies of the Corridor* (1954)—though neither were particularly popular successes. Finding it increasingly difficult to write because of ill health, Parker only published an occasional book review during the 1960s, and adapted a few of her short stories for television. She died of a heart attack on June 7, 1967, at the Hotel Volney in New York City.

Works in Literary Context

As a writer, Parker was witty, sardonic, elegant, and often profound. In her poetry and short stories, she used her wit and a highly developed sense of humor to attack hypocrisy and intolerance, and to express sympathy towards victims of sexual and racial oppression. As a poet, Parker favored primarily traditional forms. She packed caustic sarcasm into sonnets, lyrics, ballads, Horation odes, epigrams, and epi-

LITERARY AND HISTORICAL CONTEMPORARIES

Dorothy Parker's famous contemporaries include:

Ernest Hemingway (1898–1961): This American author won the Nobel Prize in Literature, and was one of the most celebrated and influential literary stylists of the twentieth century. His novels include *A Farewell to Arms* (1929).

F. Scott Fitzgerald (1896–1940): This American author and screenwriter defined the 1920s with such novels as *This Side of Paradise* (1920) and *The Great Gatsby* (1925).

Lillian Hellman (1906–1984): This American playwright is considered one of the major American dramatists. Her works include *The Little Foxes* (1939). Hellmann also helped organize the Screen Actors Guild.

Dashiell Hammett (1894–1961): This American writer helped develop the hard-boiled detective story through such novels as *The Maltese Falcon* (1930). He also helped organize the Screen Actors Guild.

Bartolomeo Vanzetti (1888–1927): This Italian-born anarchist became, with Nicola Sacco, the center of a major legal controversy in the 1920s after they were convicted of robbery and murder. Parker, like many others, protested the harshness of the sentence they received, which was death.

taphs. Her early short fiction was marked by precise, economical language and simple plot structures, though later stories were longer, more involved, and demonstrated a deeper understanding of interpersonal relationships. Thematically, Parker favored gender roles, failed love, false promises, communication problems, and emotional isolation, among other topics in both poems and short stories. As an author, Parker was greatly influenced by her personal background and unhappiness; the era in which she lived and its morals; and such authors as James Joyce, Ernest Hemingway, F. Scott Fitzgerald, and Ring Lardner.

Wit, Humor, and Ridicule   In her poetry, short stories, quips from the Algonquin Round Table, and criticism, Parker's sharply witty voice is considered one of the most memorable of the 1920s, 1930s, and 1940s. Her use of scorn, bitterness, and acerbic wit was molded into a profoundly moving art. Beginning her career as a skillful reviewer and critic, Parker developed a scathingly epigrammatic style, best displayed in using wit in demolishing inept or pretentious literary or dramatic productions. Humor-charged ridicule punctuates most of Parker's poetry and prose, allowing her to lance through the hypocrisy of social customs, vows, and the inconsistency of love ("Scratch a lover and find a foe.") Parker's

COMMON HUMAN EXPERIENCE

As an author, Parker is often identified as a member of the Algonquin Round Table. Here are some works by authors who were also part of this group:

> *Of All Things* (1921), a nonfiction collection by Robert Benchley. This collection of humorous essays focuses on familiar topics ranging from social life issues to bridge playing and fuel-saving.
>
> *To the Ladies* (1922), a play by George S. Kaufman. This satiric play focuses on a vapid woman who is wrecking her bright husband's plans.
>
> *So Big* (1924), a novel by Edna Ferber. This Pulitzer Prize-winning novel focuses on a young widow on a farm in Illinois who sacrifices everything for her son's happiness.
>
> *While Rome Burns* (1928), a nonfiction collection by Alexander Woollcott. This collection of essays appeared in leading periodicals of the era and are often humorous sketches of such personalities of that era, including Parker and Charlie Chaplin.

writing is often an attempt to use her wit as a defense—first against pain, then despair. In all her works, she also employs a complex use of irony and satire to explore the contradictory nature of human behavior. Parker's sense of wit is on display in such stories as "The Little Hours," in which an insomniac invokes La Rouchefoucauld (one of Jonathan Swift's masters), and a horde of half-remembered literary citations in lieu of counting sheep. Stories such as "Big Blonde," "Mr. Durant," "The Waltz," and "A Telephone Call" document with both humor and sadness the realities of being a woman in a male-dominated world.

Gender Roles and Failed Love   In her poetry and short stories, Parker often addressed women's issues, soured love relationships, and the vacuous, superficial lives of upper-crust society women who lived in the 1920s and 1930s. In her characteristic burlesque style, Parker lampoons cloying women who depend too much on men for emotional and economic well-being, as well as the types of men who twist these female traits to their advantage. In poems like "One Perfect Rose" from *Enough Rope*, Parker mimics the frilly language of romantic greeting card verse, rambling about a rose from a suitor. But Parker adds an unexpected twist in the last stanza: "Why is it no one ever sent me yet / One perfect limousine, do you suppose / Ah no, it's always just my luck to get / One perfect rose." Parker's short stories addressed similar themes, with a number of them focusing on the emotional idiosyncrasies of anxious, self-involved women in the midst of crises. Such stories dem-

onstrated her belief that self-absorption hampers communication and leads to emotional isolation. For example, many of the female characters in *Laments for the Living* and *After Such Pleasures* are socialites who attempt to hide their insecurities behind fancy language and pompous behavior.

Works in Critical Context

While Parker's literary reputation rests on her ability to see humor in the most bitter human tragedies, as well as her incisive wit, sense of pathos, and her more serious attempts at satire, most critics found her explorations of gender roles and romantic relationships the most significant and lasting facet of her short fiction. Parker's skill in packaging modern issues into classical poetic forms also won the praise of many critics, who noted that her lilting verse is often deceptively airy, which allows her to explore the contradictory nature of human behavior. Other critics have described her work as melodramatic, sentimental, and trivial because of the witticisms that thread throughout her poetry. In recent years, critics have found deeper meanings in Parker's work than many of her contemporaries were able to appreciate—particularly in the poems and short stories that center on women's issues.

Not So Deep As a Well   This collection of poems by Parker—which included verse from her first three volumes as well as a few other works—was well-received by contemporary critics. Writing in the *Saturday Review of Literature*, William Rose Benét comments, "Here is a lively plenty. . . . Here is also an exquisitely distilled bitterness that improves with age. Tenderness, bravado, the arrantly colloquial inimitably made use of, and Dorothy Parker's own version of the Voice of Experience." Monica Redlich of the *Spectator* was similarly impressed, calling her stories "a perennial delight" and noting, "No other writer can so perfectly portray not only sophistication but the obverse of sophistication—the knotted back of the canvas, the tangle of emotion and passion and fear that shall never be seen in public." Louis Kronenberger of *The New York Times* concludes, "After ten years Mrs. Parker strikes me as having achieved . . . a kind of historical signficance." He also notes, "One comes back to Mrs. Parker's light verse with the greatest pleasure: with its sharp wit, its clean bite, its perfectly conscious—and hence delightful—archness, it stands re-reading amply."

After Such Pleasures   Like her poetry, Parker's short story collections, such as *After Such Pleasures*, were also generally well-received. A reviewer for *The New York Times Book Review* found that the source of the stories' power lay in their combination of humor and emotion. The critic notes that "Dorothy Parker at the present moment finds herself at the very front of the movement which for years last, especially in America, has been tending toward the comedy of character and away from the comedy of situation." The reviewer also declares, "She has the inestimable gift of jeering at sentimentality without utterly destroying it . . ." Similarly, a reviewer for *The Nation* comments that "she is an authentic wit and an excellent satirist and she is just enough surprised to find that love descends to boredom to make her description of it passionate as well as pointed."

Responses to Literature

1. Read some of Parker's short stories, which many critics believe are still relevant to modern readers. In a small group, discuss why you believe Parker's fiction is timeless or not. Are there any era-specific details of her work that are confusing or that might be lost on modern readers?

2. In an essay, examine several of Parker's short stories or poems that focus on women and failed love. How does she discuss the subject? How does she depict men in relation to women? Can you relate to her depiction of these situations?

3. Drawing on examples from both her published criticism and her fiction and poetry, create a presentation about how Parker's journalism writing influenced her writing style as a fiction writer and poet.

4. Research the Algonquin Round Table; its members, focusing on Parker; and the era in which it happened. Write an essay in which you link your findings together. How were Parker and the Round Table influenced by the era in which they lived? Could such writers have the same influence today? Is there a modern equivalent of the Round Table?

BIBLIOGRAPHY

Books

Frewin, Leslie. *The Late Mrs. Dorothy Parker.* New York: Macmillan, 1986.

Keats, John. *You Might as Well Live: The Life and Times of Dorothy Parker.* New York: Simon and Schuster, 1970.

Meade, Marion. *Dorothy Parker: What Fresh Hell Is This?* New York: Penguin, 1988.

Melzer, Sondra. *The Rhetoric of Rage: Women in Dorothy Parker.* New York: Peter Lang, 1996.

Periodicals

Barranger, Milly S. "Dorothy Parker and the Politics of McCarthyism." *Theatre History Studies* (2006): 7–30.

Benét, William Rose. "Deep, At That." *Saturday Review of Literature* (December 12, 1936): 5.

"Dorothy Parker's Stories and Other Recent Works of Fiction." *The New York Times Book Review* (October 29, 1933): 6.

Kronenberger, Louis. "The Rueful, Frostbitten Laughter of Dorothy Parker." *The New York Times* (December 13, 1936): 2, 28.

Redlich, Monica. Review of *Not So Deep a Well. The Spectator* (April 16, 1937): 726.

Review of *After Such Pleasures. The Nation* (December 20, 1933): 715.

✸ Gordon Parks

BORN: *1912, Fort Scott, Kansas*

DIED: *2006, New York City*

NATIONALITY: *American*

GENRE: *Fiction, nonfiction, drama*

MAJOR WORKS:

The Learning Tree (1963)

A Choice of Weapons (1966)

A Poet and His Camera (1968)

To Smile in Autumn: A Memoir (1979)

Voices in the Mirror: An Autobiography (1990)

Overview

Considered by some a modern Renaissance man, Gordon Parks was a groundbreaking photojournalist for *Life*, a noteworthy musician, composer, and film director, as well as an acclaimed novelist and screenwriter. He achieved great success by overcoming racial, social, and economic barriers, triumphs he discussed in three autobiographies as

Gordon Parks   *Parks, Gordon, photograph. AP Images.*

well as one autobiographical novel, *The Learning Tree* (1963). The multi-talented Parks is perhaps best known for directing *Shaft* (1971) and *Shaft's Big Score* (1972), the first two entries in the popular film series about a black private detective played by Richard Roundtree.

Works in Biographical and Historical Context

Raised in Poverty   Born Gordon Roger Alexander Buchanan Parks on November 30, 1912, in Fort Scott, Kansas, he was the youngest of fifteen children of Andrew and Sarah (Ross) Jackson Parks. Parks' father was a dirt farmer, and the family lived in extreme poverty. Despite their lack of funds and the oppression caused by the intense racial segregation in the community, the strict Methodists taught Parks and his siblings to value honesty, justice, courage, and perseverance. As a young child, Parks displayed an innate talent for music and was able to play instruments by ear, including piano. When he was fifteen years old, however, his mother died and members of the family dispersed. Parks went to St. Paul, Minnesota, to live with an older sister. There, he attended Central High School and Mechanical Arts High School.

After Parks fought with his brother-in-law, he was told to leave his sister's home while still a high school student. He survived by taking odd jobs like mopping floors and working as a waiter. Parks tried to finish high school for a time, but he soon dropped out and drifted in search of work. Parks found a job as a piano player in a brothel. Later, he joined the Larry Funk Orchestra and went on tour with the group until it dissolved in New York in 1933. By this time, the United States, and indeed the world, was caught up in the Great Depression.

Continued Economic Struggles   The stock market crash of 1929 launched the Great Depression. The stock market crashed because an investment boom which began in 1924 was fueled by investors buying stocks on margin (in which investors took out loans to buy stocks for as little as ten percent down) and with purely speculative money. The stocks themselves were also wildly overvalued, and their value plummeted as the economy took a downturn. The failure of the stock market caused the economy, first in the United States, then the world, to fall in a dramatic and sustained depression, which lasted through the 1930s.

Part of President Franklin D. Roosevelt's plan for creating jobs and helping the economic recovery was such entities as the Civilian Conservation Corps, which Parks joined in 1933. For the corps, he cleared forest land. He used this employment to return to Minnesota, where he married the first of three wives, Sally Avis. In 1935, he went to work on the railroad as a waiter on a dining car. By the late 1930s, Parks was working as a porter on the North Pacific Railroad line when he purchased a 35 millimeter camera from a pawn shop in Seattle. He used the

camera, a Voightlander Brilliant, to take some pictures of seagulls over Puget Sound. The pictures were so impressive, that within weeks they were on display in a developer's shop in Minnesota.

Success as a Photographer   Photography soon became Parks's profession. Moving to Chicago at the behest of boxer Joe Louis's wife, Marva, in 1941, she helped him gain some photography assignments shooting fashion and society photos. By early 1942, Parks was working as an apprentice with Roy Stryker at the Farm Services Administration, then taking photographs of his own. Many early pictures that Parks took, such as "Washington, D.C. Government Charwoman" (1942), became highly regarded classics.

By 1943, Parks was a valued employee of Stryker, transferring with him to the Office of War Information, where he also gained valuable writing experience. By this time, the United States was fighting in World War II. The war had begun when Nazi Germany, led by Adolf Hitler, invaded Poland in September 1939 and overran the country. England and France declared war on Germany, but Germany soon controlled much of the European continent. The United States entered the war in 1941, after Japan bombed an American naval base in Hawaii. The war was fought in a number of theaters in Europe, Asia, Africa, and the South Pacific, involving sixty-one countries and leaving fifty-five million people dead.

Challenging Photographs and First Books   As part of his assignment in the Office of War Information, Parks documented the activities of the Tuskegee Airmen, a group of all-black fighter pilots whose achievements contributed greatly to the desegregation of the armed forces in 1948. In 1945, Stryker and Parks left the federal government's employ to work for Standard Oil's Photography Project in New Jersey, where Parks photographed small towns and urban views through 1948. At that time, Parks embarked on what became a twenty-year-long distinguished career as the first African American member of the photography staff of *Life* magazine. He photographed both famous and everyday people and traveled to Europe to take assignments. In 1948, he began working with color photography, and in 1959, added poetry to his repertoire. *Life* published a series of photographs by Parks which included verses of his own poems.

Published The Learning Tree   In the 1960s, Parks continued to produce memorable photojournalism, though his creative work expanded to include novels, beginning with the bestseller, *The Learning Tree* (1963). The novel was inspired by his own childhood and family in Kansas. Like many of Parks's photographs, it gave a positive view of black people while also exposing the miserable conditions of daily life. He also wrote his first autobiography, *A Choice of Weapons* (1966), then published a volume of poetry, self-illustrated with his own photographs, *A Poet and His Camera* (1968).

After leaving *Life* in 1968, Parks moved to Holly-wood where he worked as a screenwriter and director. His first project was his own adaptation of the *The Learning Tree*. Parks wrote the screenplay, produced and directed the film, and wrote the score. Following the critical success of *The Learning Tree*, Parks created the *Shaft* franchise in the early 1970s, and became instrumental in launching the blaxploitation genre of films that catered to African American audiences. In 1976, Parks filmed *Leadbelly*, about the life of the folksinger and guitarist Huddie Ledbetter.

Continued Work in Multiple Genres While working in film, Parks continued to publish books as well, including a second autobiography, *To Smile in Autumn: A Memoir* (1979). In the 1980s, Parks continued to challenge himself by writing a work of adult fiction, the historical novel *Shannon* (1981). In 1989, he wrote a ballet about civil rights leader Martin Luther King, Jr., entitled *Martin*, as well as its libretto, or accompanying text, and contributed to the choreography. Parks then published his third autobiography, *Voices in the Mirror: An Autobiography* (1990). Living in New York City at the end of his life, the Corcoran Gallery of Art in Washington, D.C., sponsored a major retrospective of Parks' entire career in 1997. Ill in his last years with prostate cancer and high blood pressure, he died of the diseases on March 7, 2006, in New York City.

Works in Literary Context

While known mostly as a photographer, Parks was also a gifted storyteller in words, using his personal experiences to illustrate such themes as overcoming social prejudice and personal hardship in order to succeed. His books celebrate the black family, black strength, and the determination of blacks to survive. As a writer, he was inspired by his varied life experiences from childhood to successful photographer and beyond.

A Social Documentarian in Words and Pictures
A key part of Parks's life and art was his photography. Parks's photography, like his writing, deals with many substantive issues, from politics and entertainment to the lives of ordinary men and women in their struggles to survive. Intertwining real life and art became a distinctive characteristic of Parks's work throughout his career. A number of his pictures and writings reflect his interest in documenting the challenges faced by those who live in poverty and/or with effects of racism, both features of his own life. A significant proportion of his work focuses on the everyday lives of African Americans, including his Farm Security Administration pictures as well as his novel, *The Learning Tree*. Parks also used his photographs to illustrate his own writings. Most of his volumes of poetry, for example, were self-illustrated with photographs to illuminate the poems. Even his only collection of essays, *Born Black*, used photographs to underscore his discus-

sion of race and what it meant to be African American in the United States during the mid-twentieth century.

Works in Critical Context

Critics have warmly embraced Parks as both a photographer and as a writer. Considered a gifted storyteller, each of his books has been generally praised by critics. Many have admired the candor of Parks's autobiographies, which they feel reveal complexities about himself and race in America. However, critics generally disparage his studio films, though they admit that, like some of his best-known photographs, they combine social awareness with a vulgarian's love of glitz and excess.

The Learning Tree Perhaps Parks's best known literary work, the autobiographical novel, *The Learning Tree*, was highly regarded by critics. Nat Hentoff in the *New York Herald* writes that the book "is an honest, craftsman-like sketch of a boyhood obviously similar to his own …" He added, "… Negro boys will be to identify much more strongly and hopefully with Newt Winger's story than they can with many books about alien American experiences, which they are now required to read." A *Time* reviewer notes that Parks's "unabashed nostalgia for what was good there, blended with sharp recollections of staggering violence and fear, makes the novel an immensely

COMMON HUMAN EXPERIENCE

Parks is perhaps better known for his pictures than his writings, though his work in both genres emphasizes his commitment to bringing those living in poverty to greater public attention. Here are some collections of photographs by other photographers who worked for the Farm Security Administration and made a similar commitment:

Ben Shahn's New York: The Photography of Modern Times (2000), a photography collection by Ben Shahn. These Depression-era photographs underscore the artist's concern for social justice as well as his compassion.

Puerto Rico Mio (1990), a photography collection by Jack Delano. This collection of photos of Puerto Rico includes pictures shot while Delano was working there for the Farm Security Administration in 1941 and 1942.

Dorothea Lange: American Photographs (1994), a photography collection by Dorothea Lange. Considered one of the most talented photographers to take photographs during the Great Depression, the book contains some of her best-known images, which opened the eyes of the government and a generation to the effects of the Depression on poor Americans.

Let Us Now Praise Famous Men (1941), a nonfiction work by James Agee with photographs by Walker Evans. This study of three tenant families living in Alabama in the mid-1930s is now considered a classic representation of the time period.

readable, sometimes unsettling book." Another critic, Louise Giles, concludes that the book was written not with resentment "but rather with rueful reminiscence, even humor. It is an unassuming and thoroughly conventional book, but it has freshness, sincerity, and charm."

A Choice of Weapons Parks's first autobiography, *A Choice of Weapons,* was considered by critics to be a powerful first-person narrative. Some reviewers consider it the most insightful of his series of autobiographies, and a number believe that *A Choice of Weapons* has greater impact than *The Learning Tree* because Parks documents his life with few artistic embellishments. Saunders Redding of *The New York Times Book Review* writes of *Choice* that it "is not the overwrought, introspective and gut-wrenched jeremiad of a martyr to racial bigotry and hatred. It is, rather, a perceptive narrative of one man's struggle to realize the values ... he has been taught to respect." Writing in the *Saturday Review,* Edwin M. Yoder Jr. concludes that *A Choice of Weapons* is "an excellent introduction to what it must have been like to be black and ambitious—and poor—in the America of [the 1930s], when nearly every door was sealed to Negros."

Responses to Literature

1. Compare and contrast the novel and film versions of *The Learning Tree* in an essay. How do the versions differ? Which version is more effective? Would you have made any different creative choices?

2. Look at some of Parks's pictures and pictorial essays published during his long tenure at *Life* magazine, then create your own pictorial essay about your life, an event in your area, or your school. Concentrate on trying to use pictures to relate a story.

3. Research the civil rights movement and create a presentation for the class using Parks's words and pictures to illustrate your findings.

4. Write a research paper about *Shaft* and the blaxploitation film genre. What was Parks's role in the development of the genre? How does it fit in with the rest of his work?

BIBLIOGRAPHY

Books

Bush, Martin H. *The Photographs of Gordon Parks.* Wichita, Kans.: Wichita State University, 1983.

Harnan, Terry. *Gordon Parks, Black Photographer.* Champaign, Ill.: Garrard, 1972.

Midge, Turk. *Gordon Parks.* New York: Crowell, 1971.

Periodicals

Briggs, Joe Bob. "Who Dat Man? *Shaft* and the Blaxploitation Genre." *Cineaste* (Spring 2003): 24–29.

Henry, Matthew. "He Is a 'bad mother *$%@!#\': *Shaft* and Contemporary Black Masculinity." *Journal of Popular Film and Television* (Summer 2002): 114.

Hentoff, Nat. Review of *The Learning Tree. New York Herald Tribune* (August 25, 1963): 6.

Kevles, Barbara. "The Marketing of *Leadbelly." Cineaste* (Spring 2003): 34–35.

Redding, Saunders. Review of *A Choice of Weapons. The New York Times Book Review* (February 13, 1966).

Review of *The Learning Tree. Time* (September 6, 1963).

Yoder, Edwin M., Jr. "No Catch for the Hawk." *Saturday Review* (February 12, 1966): 40.

❀ Suzan-Lori Parks

BORN: *1963, Fort Knox, Kentucky*

NATIONALITY: *American*

GENRE: *Drama, screenplays, fiction*

MAJOR WORKS:

Imperceptible Mutabilities in the Third Kingdom (1989)

Venus (1996)

Topdog/Underdog (2001)

Getting Mother's Body (2003)

Suzan-Lori Parks   *Parks, Suzan-Lori, photograph. AP Images.*

Overview

Innovative and sometimes controversial, Suzan-Lori Parks is one of the most highly acclaimed African American playwrights working in contemporary theater. Her use of "rep & rev" (repetition and revision) to re-examine and reconfigure historical episodes is lauded for providing an "Afrocentric" history and identity—elements that are largely missing from the "Eurocentric" historical record. Often depicting and exaggerating black stereotypes, Parks draws attention to their invalidity and the ignorance upon which they are based. In 2002, she became the first African American woman to receive the Pulitzer Prize for drama, for her play *Topdog/Underdog* (2001).

Works in Biographical and Historical Context

German-Based Childhood   Parks was born in Fort Knox, Kentucky in 1964, the daughter of Donald and Francis Parks. At the time of her birth, the United States was becoming more deeply involved in the Vietnam War. Vietnam had been divided into a Communist North and noncommunist South in the mid-1950s, but Communist

efforts to gain control over all of Vietnam continued. In the early 1960s, the United States began to provide military aid to South Vietnam, hoping to stop the spread of communism. Though unpopular, the war in Vietnam continued until the early 1970s. Approximately 58,000 American soldiers and over two million Vietnamese soldiers and civilians were lost in the conflict.

Parks began writing at an early age, but because Parks's father was then an officer in the U.S. Army, the family moved frequently in her childhood. She lived in six different states before moving to Germany. There, she attended a German public high school. Parks credited her European experience with giving her a different, valuable perspective on her identity. For the first time in her life, she was identified as an American, not an African American.

Encouraged to Write Plays   After graduating from high school, Parks entered Mount Holyoke College in Massachusetts, where she studied under the celebrated author, James Baldwin. Baldwin appreciated Parks's talent and encouraged her to begin writing for the stage. Her first play, *The Sinner's Place* (1984), helped her receive honors for her English degree, but was rejected for staging by Mount Holyoke because the play called for the stage to be covered in dirt. The drama department refused to accommodate the request.

Parks earned her B.A. in German and English from Mount Holyoke in 1985, then briefly studied acting at the Drama Studio in London before moving to New York City, where she worked as a legal assistant. She wrote two more plays, *Betting on the Dust Commander* (1987) and *Imperceptible Mutabilities in the Third Kingdom* (1989). The former focuses on family relations, upheaval, and movement, while the latter is a tetralogy of four short plays about African American identity. *Imperceptible Mutabilities* was produced Off-Broadway, winning an Obie Award and recognition of Parks as a significant up-and-coming playwright.

Acclaimed Works   In the late 1980s and early 1990s, Parks continued to receive significant awards and honors. In 1989, she was given a National Endowments for the Arts grant. In 1990, Parks received grants from the New York Foundation for the Arts grantee and the Rockefeller Foundation, and she wrote her first screenplay, the short *Anemone Me* (1990). She also continued to produce original plays, including *The Death of the Last Black Man in the Whole Entire World* (1990) and *The America Play* (1993). Parks's play, *Venus* (1996), based on the life of Saartjie Baartman, won the playwright her second Obie Award. That same year, Spike Lee directed her screenplay *Girl 6*.

As the century turned, Parks was again honored with major fellowships, including a Guggenheim fellowship in 2000 and a MacArthur Foundation "genius grant" in 2001. Her plays were also innovative as she explored Nathaniel Hawthorne's *The Scarlet Letter* (1850) in two plays, *In the Blood* (1999) and *Fucking A* (2000). Parks's play, *Topdog/Underdog* (2001), focuses on two brothers

LITERARY AND HISTORICAL CONTEMPORARIES

Suzan-Lori Parks's famous contemporaries include:

James Baldwin (1924–1987): This African American novelist, essayist, and playwright wrote introspective critiques of race, homosexuality, and cultural issues. His novels include *Go Tell It on the Mountain* (1952).

Richard Foreman (1937–): This avant-garde theater director and writer directed the first production of *Venus* at the New York Shakespeare Festival. His plays include *Hotels for Criminals* (1975).

Wendy Wasserstein (1950–2006): This New York-based playwright won the Pulitzer Prize in 1989 for her play, *The Heidi Chronicles* (1988).

Mos Def (1973–): This African American rap artist and actor appeared in an early production of *Topdog/Underdog*. His albums include *The New Danger* (2005).

Don Cheadle (1964–): This African American actor appeared in an early production of *Topdog/Underdog*. His film appearances include *Ocean's Eleven* (2001) and *Hotel Rwanda* (2004).

Spike Lee (1957–): This acclaimed African American film director often focused on the contemporary African American experience in his early films. He directed *Girl 6* (1996), written by Parks, as well as *Do the Right Thing* (1989) and *Bamboozled* (2000).

Barack Obama (1961–): Obama, a first-term senator from Illinois, won the 2008 election to become the first African American President of the United States.

who struggle to succeed in life. In 2002, the play was honored with the Pulitzer Prize for Drama.

Wrote First Novel   While Parks was reaching the pinnacle of her career, she and other Americans were dealing with a devastating act of terrorism in the United States. On September 11, 2001, al-Qaeda terrorists hijacked a number of commercial airliners, and crashed them into the World Trade Center in New York City and the Pentagon in Washington, D.C. Thousands of people lost their lives in the attacks and unsettled American society in the years following the event.

In 2003, Parks moved to a new genre, publishing her first novel, *Getting Mother's Body*. Well-received by critics, it is set in West Texas, where she spent part of her youth. The novel focuses on a sixteen-year-old girl named Billy Beede. When she finds herself pregnant by an older, married man, she decides she needs to raise enough money to have an abortion. To do so, she enlists the help of an aunt and an uncle, then travels to Arizona to dig up her late mother's body and retrieve the jewelry with which she was reportedly buried.

Diverse Success   Two years later, Parks co-wrote the script for a television movie, the adaptation of Zora Neale Hurston's *Their Eyes Were Watching God*, which aired on ABC. In 2007, she co-wrote the screenplay for the film, *The Great Debaters* and wrote the musical, *Ray Charles Live!*, which debuted at the Pasadena Playhouse in 2007. In 2008, Parks became writer-in-residence at the Public Theater in New York, and began a stint as a visiting professor at New York University. She also continued to write plays, screenplays, and novels.

Works in Literary Context

As a playwright, Parks is known for her wildly experimental plays that featured linguistically creative dialogue and provocative, historically-based subject matter. Her plays are often noted for their originality, non-linear progression of time, poetic dialogue, political and social agendas, and depiction of the search for identity. She employs language reminiscent of African American dialects and vernacular to give multiple meanings to the spoken word and expose the hidden message behind the dialogue of her characters. Parks's lyrical, creative dialogue is often compared to jazz and hip-hop. As a writer, Parks was influenced by her mentor, James Baldwin; other authors, including James Joyce, Virginia Woolf, and William Faulkner; and her experiences as an African American woman, both in the United State and abroad.

African American Identity   Throughout her plays, Parks often touches on issues related to African American identity. She explores such subjects as the loss of identity, the creation of new identities, and what identity really means. *The Third Kingdom*, a short play included in *Imperceptible Mutabilities*, re-enacts the Middle Passage from Africa across the Atlantic Ocean, that many slaves endured at the beginning of their captivity. In lieu of the dearth of known history from these' subjugated people, Parks provides memories and cultural references that create a new, solid history for African Americans to follow. In another short play that makes up *Imperceptible Mutabilities*, *Open House*, a former slave named Blanca is dying, and her memories are being stolen from her—symbolized by continuous tooth extractions—linking her loss with African Americans' loss of culture, identity and voice. Her fourth play, *The Death of the Last Black Man in the Whole Entire World*, centers on the character, Black Man with Watermelon, who is continually beaten, enslaved, and killed, yet always returns to the stage to tell his story. Parks highlights the importance of "telling the story" as a way to fight the negation of African Americans, whose literary silencing during the years of the slave trade, has rendered their story almost forgotten. The characters in *The America Play* are also searching for clues to their identities. The wife and son of the main character, Foundling Father, dig in the sand around "the great hole of history" for clues to the truth about issues like identity. The objects they uncover suggest that many accepted truths are, in fact, lies and distortions based on perception.

Use and Abuse of Women In a number of Parks's plays, she depicts the use, abuse, and degradation of women—primarily African American—and how they subvert and overcome this circumstance. While some of these women are objectified and have their humanity stripped away, a few turn the tables. In *Snails*, one of the short plays in *Imperceptible Mutabilities*, a white naturalist disguises himself as an exterminator so he can "bug" the home where three African American women live, thereby gaining insight into the actions of these women in a non-white-influenced surrounding. Through this "study," the women lose identity and respect and become objects to manipulate and examine. While *Open House* is primarily about African-American identity, Parks uses a female protagonist, Blanca, who undergoes much pain to symbolize this loss. More concretely, the focus of *Venus* is a real-life woman who was used by European society. In reality, Saartjie Baartman was an African brought to Europe during the Victorian era and put on display as Venus Hottentot because of her African physical features. In the play, Parks rewrites history, refusing to let Baartman be a docile pawn in her own life. She makes Baartman an accomplice in her fame and destiny as Venus becomes a willing participant, and receives financial rewards for her work. Baartman uses her African "otherness" to obtain wealth and love. In both *In the Blood* and *Fucking A*, Parks explores ideas about women brought up in Nathaniel Hawthorne's *The Scarlet Letter*, which focuses on the condemned Hester Prynne. In *In the Blood*, Parks's Hester is a woman who lives under an overpass with her five multi-ethnic illegitimate children. Hester is abandoned and ill-treated by society and her lovers, and her story ends tragically.

Works in Critical Context

Critical reception to Parks's plays has been largely favorable. Although some commentators charge that she reinforces racial misconceptions with her use of stereotypical language and gestures, most reviewers contend that Parks's over-the-top depiction of stereotypes lampoons these misconceptions, and makes a farce out of the underlying prejudices that drive stereotyping. Reviewers often applaud Parks for her attempts to fill in the gaps of African American memory and history, and for her refusal to rely on the Eurocentric history that has been dominant for centuries. Her innovative use of language and staging has also been praised. Parks's history-heavy work has been called provocative, demanding, challenging, controversial, experimental, and avant-garde.

Topdog/Underdog Like many of her plays, Parks's *Topdog/Underdog* was well-received in both its Off-Broadway and Broadway runs. Writing in the *Christian Science Monitor*, Iris Fanger called the play "a cross between a hip-hop riff and a Greek tragedy; as entertaining as the former and as gripping as the latter." Ben Brantley of the

---

COMMON HUMAN EXPERIENCE

Parks is considered a leading African American woman playwright of the late twentieth and early twenty-first centuries. Here are some other works by African American women playwrights who touch on issues similar to Parks:

for colored girls who have considered suicide/when the rainbow is enuf (1976), a play by Ntozake Shange. This play focuses on issues of sexism and racism in African American women's lives. Despite many harrowing scenes, the work is essentially optimistic, showing the "infinite beauty" of black women.

A Raisin in the Sun (1959), a play by Lorraine Hansberry. This play centers on the financial and emotional struggles of an African American family in Chicago in the 1950s. Despite obstacles, their dream of owning and living in a new home in a white neighborhood is realized.

Fires in the Mirror (1992), a play by Anna Deavere Smith. This play uses real events surrounding the accidental killing of an African American child by a Hasidic Jew in the Crown Heights section of Brooklyn to explore issues of tension, violence, identity, and the historical conflict between these communities.

Funnyhouse of a Negro (1964), a play by Adrienne Kennedy. This one-act play focuses on a young mixed-race woman's efforts to come to terms with her racial heritage.

New York Times hails *Topdog/Underdog* as a "dizzying spin" on the Cain and Abel story. In the play, Brantley wrote, "Brotherly love and hatred is translated into the terms of men who have known betrayal since their youth ... and who will never be able to entirely trust anyone, including (and especially) each other." In the *San Francisco Chronicle*, Robert Hurwitt concluded, "As an almost naturalistic, two-character one-set drama of wounded sibling rivalry, *Topdog* looks pretty conventional compared with the fractured plots and poetically complex language of Parks's earlier works. But the complex interweaving of social, imagistic and emotional metaphor beneath its surface makes *Topdog* as richly provocative as it is undeniably powerful."

Getting Mother's Body Parks's first novel, *Getting Mother's Body*, was generally as acclaimed as her plays. *Publishers Weekly* praised the novel's "easy grace and infectious rhythms." Karen Valby in *Entertainment Weekly* noted, "A master of pitch and mood, Parks occasionally veers off her novelistic course. Her story struggles a bit to find its stride; for all the brilliant scenes, the connective tissue sometimes lacks thrust." But Beth Kephart in *Book* found that "there's jazz and spunk in the writing here, tremendous humor that ultimately yields to tenderness."

Booklist's Vanessa Bush concluded that "Parks offers a collection of exuberantly loony characters, longing for better lives and a means of realizing their meager dreams."

Responses to Literature

1. Research the life of Saartjie Baartman and both the African and European cultures in which she lived. Create a presentation about her, using Parks's play, *Venus*, to illustrate your findings. Could someone be treated that way today?

2. Read Nathaniel Hawthorne's novel, *The Scarlet Letter* (1850), and Parks's two plays inspired by it, *In the Blood* and *Fucking A*. How do the texts relate? What do the plays add to Hawthorne's original? How does each depict women and their place in society?

3. In an essay, discuss how Parks uses Abraham Lincoln as a symbol in plays such as *The America Play* and *Topdog/Underdog*. What does Lincoln represent in each play? Are the depictions linked?

4. In a small group, discuss how Parks depicts issues related to African American identity in her plays. What images does she use? How does she use them? Is the way that she looks at issues of identity effective? How has her depiction of identity evolved over the course of her plays?

BIBLIOGRAPHY

Periodicals

Geis, Deborah R. *Suzan-Lori Parks*. Ann Arbor: University of Michigan Press, 2008.

Periodicals

Brantley, Ben. "Not to Worry Mr. Lincoln, It's Just a Con Game." *New York Times* (April 19, 2002): B2.

Bush, Vanessa. Review of *Getting Mother's Body. Booklist* (May 1, 2003): 1581.

Fanger, Iris. Review of *Topdog/Underdog. Christian Science Monitor* (April 12, 2002).

Frieze, James. "Imperceptible Mutabilities in the Third Kingdom: Suzan-Lori Parks and the Shared Struggle to Perceive." *Modern Drama* (1998): 523–532.

Hurwitt, Robert. "*Topdog* Is Worthy of Pulitzer." *San Francisco Chronicle* (April 9, 2002): D1.

Kephart, Beth. Review of *Getting Mother's Body. Book* (May-June 2003): 44.

Review of *Getting Mother's Body. Publishers Weekly* (May 19, 2003): 54.

Smith, Wendy. "Words as Crossroad: Suzan-Lori Parks." *Publishers Weekly* (May 12, 2003): 37.

Solomon, Alisa. "To Be Young, Gifted, and African American." *Village Voice* (September 11, 1989): 99–102.

Valby, Karen. "Drawl She Wrote: In Her Debut Novel about a Downtrodden Texas Family, Suzan-Lori Parks Spins Dialogue into Gritty Poetry." *Entertainment Weekly* (May 9, 2003): 80.

✸ Ann Patchett

BORN: *1963, Los Angeles, California*

NATIONALITY: *American*

GENRE: *Fiction*

MAJOR WORKS:

The Patron Saint of Liars (1992)

Taft (1994)

The Magician's Assistant (1997)

Bel Canto (2001)

Run (2007)

Overview

Best known for her fourth novel *Bel Canto* (2001), which was awarded the PEN/Faulkner Award and the Orange Prize for Fiction in 2002, Ann Patchett is a contemporary novelist who has earned a reputation for her compelling exploration of how humans form meaningful connections with each other.

Ann Patchett *AP Wide World Photos*

Works in Biographical and Historical Context

Indifference to Roman Catholic Education   Patchett was born on December 2, 1963, in Los Angeles, California. When she was six years old, Patchett's parents divorced and she moved with her sister and mother to Nashville, Tennessee. Her father remained in California, working as a detective for the Los Angeles Police Department. As a child, Patchett attended private Roman Catholic schools but remained indifferent to her education. While reflecting on her school years, Patchett recalled a two-year period in which she was barred from recess because of a series of disciplinary infractions. As reported by Carol Brennan in *Newsmakers*, Patchett attributes her behavior during those years partly to her home life. "We had peculiar circumstances," she said of her family in a *Publishers Weekly* interview with Elizabeth Bernstein. "She was a very loving mother, but we were scrambling; we had bigger things going on in our lives than whether or not I could read."

Penchant for Storytelling   Despite her poor performance in other areas of school, Patchett impressed her teachers with her ability to tell stories. By the time she reached her teenage years, she had begun submitting poetry to national magazines, with the hope of becoming a poet. With this goal in mind, Patchett enrolled in New York's Sarah Lawrence College. However, partway through her studies, she experienced a case of writer's block. In an attempt to jumpstart her writing, Patchett enrolled in a creative writing class taught by novelist Allan Gurganus and began writing short stories. By 1984, she had graduated and her first short story, "All Little Colored Children Should Learn to Play Harmonica," was published in the prestigious *Paris Review*. The story, about an African American family—the Smileys—in the 1940s, attracted attention within literary circles and was later included in several subsequent anthologies.

Professional Training in Creative Writing   After graduating, Patchett worked for a stint as an editorial assistant before enrolling in the University of Iowa's graduate writing program, a noted professional training ground for upcoming writers. Although she completed her M.F.A. in 1987, Patchett reported that she learned little during her stay at Iowa. She tried to expand her first story into a longer work but failed to develop a satisfying plot. After retreating briefly to Yaddo, a writer's colony in Saratoga Springs, New York, and Millay, a writer's colony in Austerlitz, New York, Patchett got married and taught classes at Allegheny College in Pennsylvania. After her relationship ended abruptly, Patchett moved back to her mother's house in Nashville, wrote, and supported herself by working at T. G. I. Friday's. After selling them one of her short stories, Patchett worked for *Seventeen* magazine as a contributing writer for nine years.

Early Success   From 1990 until 1991, Patchett was a fellow at the Bunting Institute at Radcliff College. There she met the opera singer Karol Bennett, who she later used as a model for the character Roxane Coss in *Bel*

Canto. Not long after, Patchett completed her first novel, *The Patron Saint of Liars* (1992), which was awarded the 1989 James A. Michener Copernicus Award from the University of Iowa for a work in progress and was a New York Times Notable Book for 2002. Set in the 1960s, the novel concerns a young pregnant woman who abandons her marriage and takes refuge at a home for unwed mothers. Patchett published her second novel, *Taft* (1994), two years after her first. Like the plot of her first book, *Taft* concerns a group of strangers who are brought together, in this case at a bar, and end up forming deep emotional relationships with one another. *Taft* was awarded the Janet Heidinger Kafka Prize for best work of fiction in 1994.

While visiting her father in California, Patchett found inspiration for her third novel at a dinner theater magic show, where she was chosen to assist one of the performers. Soon afterward, she won a Guggenheim Fellowship to complete *The Magician's Assistant* (1997), which was shortlisted for England's prestigious Orange Prize. While living in Nashville, Patchett helped her mother publish her own writing, including her first novel, *Julie and Romeo* (2000).

Literary Breakthrough with Bel Canto   After completing *The Magician's Assistant*, Patchett spent the next four years writing her most famous novel, *Bel Canto* (2001), a story inspired by a real-life hostage situation at the Japanese Embassy in Lima, Peru, which occurred during four months in 1996. In her book, Patchett leaves the South American country unnamed but draws many parallels to the real crisis. Upon its publication, *Bel Canto* was nominated for the National Book Critics Circle Award

COMMON HUMAN EXPERIENCE

Patchett's writing often explores the conflicts that exist between an individual's inner nature and society. Other works that explore this theme include the following:

"The Man that Corrupted Hadleyburg" (1879), a short story by Mark Twain. An offended stranger vows to corrupt Hadleyburg, a town known for incorruptibility, and thus exposes the social weakness caused by individual temptation.

The Awakening (1899), a novel by Kate Chopin. While away for a summer, Edna Pontellier realizes that her true nature is at odds with the role she is asked to play in society as the wife of a successful businessman.

Nineteen Eighty-Four (1949), a novel George Orwell. The protagonist of this science-fiction tale, Winston Smith, grows increasingly uncomfortable with the role he is forced to play in a totalitarian regime and, ultimately, rebels.

A Confederacy of Dunces (1980), a novel by John Kennedy Toole. Idealistic to the point of delusion, Ignatius J. Reilly, the protagonist, undergoes a quest for employment in the French Quarter of New Orleans, but feels that he does not belong in his surroundings.

and took several other honors, including the $15,000 P. E. N./Faulkner Award in 2001 and the Orange Prize in 2002. Immensely popular, the novel has sold over one million copies in the United States alone and is now available in more than thirty foreign languages.

Recent Nonfiction After her success with *Bel Canto*, Patchett continued writing and also became the editor of the 2006 edition of *Best American Short Stories*. Since 2001, Patchett has published one novel, *Run* (2007), and two nonfiction books: *Truth & Beauty*, a memoir chronicling her friendship with the writer Lucy Grealy, which won several awards, and *What Now?* (2008), an expanded version of the commencement address she gave at Sarah Lawrence College in 2006.

Patchett continues to live and work in Nashville, Tennessee.

Works in Literary Context

Patchett's fiction frequently focuses on socially charged issues like racism, political divergence, and gender, depicting them through the lens of chance and circumstance. Most of her novels bring strangers together and explore how they form friendships and identities once they are forced to interact with one another. Patchett has stated that Thomas Mann's *The Magic Mountain* (1924) and Saul Bellow's *Humboldt's Gift* (1975) are among the most influential works she has read. She also includes Anton

Chekhov, Eudora Welty, John Updike, Joan Didion, and her close friend, Elizabeth McCracken, among the authors who have influenced her work.

The Universal Potential for Human Connection
In her work, Patchett explores the potential for human connection between unlikely groups of strangers by placing them together in unusual circumstances. Confinement, whether physical or metaphorical, plays a key role in the development of the bonds that develop between people in Patchett's stories. For example, in *Bel Canto*, a group of upper-class partygoers and guerilla terrorists connect with one another during a four-month hostage situation despite the barriers of language, class, and circumstance that exist between them. In *The Patron Saint of Liars*, Patchett confines her characters to an abandoned hotel in Kentucky that has been converted into a home for unwed mothers. In *The Magician's Assistant*, her characters are confined to a tract house in snowy Nebraska. Such confinement shields her characters from the prejudices of society and allows them to connect, forever changing their lives. For example, *Taft* concerns the taboo bond that develops between an old bartender and a teenage girl as she helps him come to terms with being abandoned by his girlfriend and son.

Works in Critical Context

As an author, Patchett has enjoyed considerable success. Her first novel won an award prior to its publication, and her subsequent works have received largely positive reviews. In a review of her work, *Washington Post* writer Joseph McLellan praises the author's realism: "Patchett's psychological observations are usually intriguing and most often convincing." McLellan also praises her accessibility by noting, "Her style is fluent and highly readable." Pulitzer Prize-winning author Robert Olen Butler offers his assessment of Patchett: "She is a genius of the human condition," he states. "I can't think of many other writers, ever, who get anywhere near her ability to comprehend the vastness and diversity of humanity, and to articulate our deepest heart."

Bel Canto *Bel Canto*, Patchett's fourth novel, enjoyed a warm reception from critics. Discussing the book's central theme, James Polk of *The New York Times Book Review* writes, "*Bel Canto* often shows Patchett doing what she does best—offering fine insights into the various ways in which human connections can be forged ... whatever pressures the world may place upon them." Despite widespread praise, not all reviewers responded favorably to the novel. For example, Helen Brown of the *Daily Telegraph* criticized the book's characterization, arguing that

the uptight chief executive, the compassionate diva, the rebel leader who wants only the best for his country, and the quiet translator are all disappointing, two-dimensional stereotypes. They are like opera characters who require soaring art, bel canto, to move their audience.

Run Like *Bel Canto*, Patchett's most recent novel, *Run*, has enjoyed a warm reception from critics. Writing for the *St. Louis Post-Dispatch*, reviewer Holly Silva describes the novel as "moody and thoughtful, gentle in its handling of weighty topics, and quietly suspenseful." In her assessment, what makes the novel "technically astonishing" is "[t]he range of big issues, as they are expertly intertwined and paced." Sarah Weisman of *Library Journal* found the novel "engrossing and enjoyable." Patrick Ness of *The Guardian* praises the thematic content of the book, which is "about good people who try to do their best by each other," as well as Patchett's ability to "accomplish this without sentiment or stupidity." Leah Hager Cohen, writing for *The New York Times*, says that Patchett's "lack of frivolity in her prose" makes her different from other writers. Commenting on Patchett's writing style, Cohen says that Patchett "doesn't dally excessively over a pretty phrase," and that she is "more hammer and nails than glue and lace," thus making her books "solid, weight-bearing constructions." Janet Maslin, another *New York Times* reviewer, agrees by saying that the novel "shimmers with its author's rarefied eloquence, and with the deep resonance of her insights."

Responses to Literature

1. The ending of *Bel Canto* is foreshadowed early on in the novel. Why do you think the author chose do this? How does this impact your reading of the book?

2. What role does Roxane's singing play in *Bel Canto*?

3. *Run* has been criticized for dealing superficially with the issue of race, and with providing characters that are stereotypical. Read the work and decide for yourself if this is a valid criticism. Find specific examples within the work that either support or refute this contention.

4. Patchett is known for combining unlikely characters in a single location and documenting their interactions and connections. Try writing a short story set in a confined space—such as a single room—with four characters that are dramatically different in several ways; think about each character's background, education, temperament, and philosophy of life when determining how the characters will act toward each other.

BIBLIOGRAPHY

Periodicals

Berne, S. "The Magician's Assistant. By Ann Patchett." *The New York Times Book Review* 102, no. 46 (November 16, 1997): 17.

Cohen, L. H. "Run by Ann Patchett." *The New York Times Book Review* 112, no. 39 (September 30, 2007): 7.

Oates, Joyce Carol. "Truth & Beauty: A Friendship. By Ann Patchett." *The New York Times Book Review* 109, Part 20 (May 16, 2004): 10.

Sayers, V. "Run by Ann Patchett." *Commonweal* 135, no. 2 (January 31, 2008): 27–28.

Somerville, Kris. "Truth & Beauty (review)." *Missouri Review* 27, no. 2 (2004): 197–199.

Updike, J. "Ann Patchett's 'Run.'" *New York Magazine* (October 1, 2007): 98–100.

Web sites

Ann Patchett. Accessed November 30, 2008, from http://www.annpatchett.com.

✸ Katherine Paterson

BORN: *1932, Tsing-Tsiang Pu, China*

NATIONALITY: *American*

GENRE: *Fiction, nonfiction*

MAJOR WORKS:
The Master Puppeteer (1975)
Bridge to Terabithia (1977)
The Great Gilly Hopkins (1978)
Jacob Have I Loved (1980)
Bread and Roses, Too (2006)

Katherine Paterson   *Landov*

Overview

Katherine Paterson is a popular author of children's fiction whose work has won international popular and critical acclaim. Collectively, her books have swept every conceivable award for children's literature.

Works in Biographical and Historical Context

A Childhood of Continual Change   Katherine Paterson was born of American missionary parents, George Raymond and Mary Goetchius Womeldorf, in Tsing-Tsiang Pu, China, on October 31, 1932, the third of five children. As a child, Paterson dreamed of becoming a famous movie star or growing up to be a missionary like her parents, never imagining herself as a writer. The Japanese invasion and occupation of China, beginning in 1937, forced the family to return twice to the United States, the second time permanently. Moving about between China and various locations in Virginia, North Carolina, and West Virginia, the young Paterson experienced a variety of cultures and almost continual change. Before she graduated summa cum laude from King College in Bristol, Tennessee, in 1954, she had attended thirteen schools and moved at least eighteen times.

Preparation for Missionary Work   As part of her preparation to become a missionary, Paterson spent one year teaching sixth grade at a school in rural northern Virginia. This experience later inspired the setting for one of her more famous books, *Bridge to Terabithia* (1977), winner of the 1978 Lewis Carroll Shelf Award and the Newberry Medal. Since its publication, Paterson has learned that some of her students know about the book and have read it. She writes, "I hope they can tell by reading it how much they meant to me."

In 1957 Paterson received an M.A. in English Bible from the Presbyterian School of Christian Education in Richmond, Virginia. At this point, she was still pursuing her childhood dream to return to China as a missionary. However, at that time China, which had undergone a communist revolution in 1949, was closed to Americans, forcing Paterson to look elsewhere for missionary work.

Move to Japan   As a child living in China under Japanese assault, Paterson had hated and feared the Japanese. She remembered Japan as the enemy who had dropped bombs and occupied the cities where Paterson lived during childhood. However, as an adult she shifted her perspective; she recalls in a brief autobiographical sketch that a Japanese friend urged her to "put aside those childish feelings and give myself a chance to view the Japanese in a new way." Later in 1957, Paterson enrolled at the Naganuma School of Japanese Language in the Japanese city of Kobe. She then served as a Christian education assistant for eleven pastors in rural areas of Shikoku Island. During the four years she spent in Japan, she came to love the country and its people.

These years in Japan inspired at least three of her books. In *The Sign of the Chrysanthemum* (1973) and *Of Nightingales That Weep* (1974), the twelfth-century civil wars between the rival Heike and Genji clans provide a finely detailed background and create the circumstances which incite the protagonists' quests. Paterson later returned to Japan to conduct research for *The Master Puppeteer* (1975), winner of the National Book Award. A mystery novel, *The Master Puppeteer* is set in eighteenth-century Osaka, when the famine of 1783–1787 had reduced the populace to bestial scavengers who plunder and burn their city. The two young heroes of *The Master Puppeteer*—Jiro, the initiate, and Kinshi, the scapegoat—represent hope. The story suggests that hope for redemption of debased worlds, like eighteenth-century Osaka, may well lie in people like Kinshi, self-possessed and altruistic, who will give of themselves until it hurts.

Return to New York: Starting a Family   Paterson returned to New York City where, on a fellowship to the Union Theological Seminary, she earned a Master's in Religious Education in 1962, and met and married John Barstow Paterson, a Presbyterian minister. Within a few years, Paterson had become the mother of four, two natural sons, John and David, and two adopted daughters, one Chinese, Elizabeth Polin, and one Apache Kiowa, Mary Katherine. Her insecurities as a new foster mother later inspired *The Great Gilly Hopkins* (1978), winner of the Christopher Award, the National Book Award, and the Newberry Honors Book award. In *Gates of Excellence* (1981) Paterson calls the novel "a confession of sin," the sin of not dealing with problems.

Writing Career Begins   According to Paterson, her career as a writer began in 1964 while she was living in Maryland. As a gesture of gratitude to the Presbyterian Church that had given her an academic scholarship, she agreed to write curriculum materials for fifth and sixth grade students. The experience cultivated within her a desire to write and she quickly shifted her focus to fiction, her favorite genre. However, as a busy mother juggling the needs of four small children, Paterson struggled and did not publish any of her work. A friend suggested that she take an adult education course in writing and she agreed. The novel she wrote during the course became her first publication in fiction and launched her career as a writer.

Throughout her career, Paterson has built upon work she originally created for her community. The nine short stories in *Angels & Other Strangers: Family Christmas Stories* (1979) were originally written at the suggestion of John Paterson for reading aloud in lieu of a sermon at Christmas Eve services in his Takoma Park Church. Because of the hearty response of the congregation, she published the collection. More explicitly Christian than her novels, the stories reflect the author's concern for the modern world's lost and lonely.

Paterson won her second Newberry Medal for *Jacob Have I Loved* (1980), a provocative story of an adolescent's submergence by, and victory over, her bitter jealousy of her twin sister, which blinds her to her own worth and to others' appreciation of it. With *Rebels of the Heavenly Kingdom* (1983), Paterson turns again to historical fiction, this time to China in the mid-nineteenth century, during the 1850–1853 revolt of the Taiping Tienkuo (the Heavenly Kingdom of Great Peace) against the corrupt Manchu rulers. This starkly realistic adventure-romance tells the stories of Wang Lee and Mei Lin, two young people caught in the devastation wrought by fanatic warlords whose religious ideals are shot through with political ambitions. Neither her most provocative nor most profound novel, *Come Sing, Jimmy Jo* (1985) is the story of a shy, gifted mountain boy, James Johnson, who, within six months, becomes a country-music star. This novel recapitulates several themes from Paterson's earlier books.

The Healing Power of Writing   Wrestling with literary problems has helped Paterson through wrenching situations in her personal life. For example, when her son David was eight years old, his best friend was killed by a lightning strike. Trying to make sense of the event, Paterson wrote *Bridge to Terabithia*, a story of friendship and loss that became her best-known work. Likewise, Paterson fell back on writing while undergoing surgery for and recovering from cancer, and after the death of her mother.

After thirteen years in Takoma Park, Maryland, the family moved to Norfolk, Virginia, where John Paterson served as pastor of Lafayette Presbyterian Church until August 1986. Paterson and her husband, now retired, live in Vermont where she continues to write. She has received many awards for her work, including numerous lifetime achievement awards and honorary degrees. *Bridge to Terabithia*, first adapted to film in 1985, was filmed again by Disney/Walden Media in 2007. Another movie based on her book *The Great Gilly Hopkins*, is expected to be released in 2009. Since 2007, Paterson has been serving as Vice President of the National Children's Book and Literacy Alliance, a non-profit organization. Paterson published *Bread and Roses, Too*, her fifteenth novel, in 2006.

Works in Literary Context

Paterson's fiction is influenced by the continual change of her childhood, her work as a teacher, and her family life. She credits her husband with providing the most influential support, and as to the question of whether her own children have influenced her writing, Paterson, in *Gates of Excellence* (1981) answers in the affirmative: "the very persons who have taken away my time and space are those who have given me something to say."

Redemption for the Lost and Lonely   Paterson writes of Japanese and American youngsters, who, despite their cultural differences, are in many ways alike. Entangled in chaotic childhoods, her sensitive but tough young protagonists, each a social or a spiritual outsider, set out to achieve self-determined goals. During the course of each story, the child, caught in potentially tragic circumstan-

---

LITERARY AND HISTORICAL CONTEMPORARIES

Katherine Paterson's famous contemporaries include:

Shel Silverstein (1930–1999): American author who combines humorous poetry and reflective prose with simple, skillful line drawings.

John Updike (1932–2009): A major contemporary American author, Updike is particularly noted for the subtle complexity of his fiction.

C. S. Adler (1932–): Since the publication of *The Magic of the Glits* (1979), Adler has written over forty books for children and young adults.

Judy Blume (1938–): American author, perhaps the most popular contemporary author of works for upper elementary to junior high school readers. Blume's frank, often humorous stories focus on the emotional and social concerns of adolescents.

Maurice Sendak (1928–): During his distinguished career in children's books, Sendak has provided pictures for more than 80 works, such as *Where the Wild Things Are* (1963).

---

ces, must come to grips with the limitations with which reality circumscribes one's dreams. In each Paterson story, the protagonist turns tragedy to triumph by bravely choosing an unselfish path. In relinquishing vainglorious dreams and opening themselves to tenacious love, Paterson's protagonists gain dignity and happiness. They embody the theme of redemption through the sacrifice of oneself and one's ambitions.

Paterson's contribution to children's literature has been recognized with numerous awards, for her individual works and for her lifetime achievement, including the 1998 Hans Christian Anderson Medal for Writing, the 2000 Library of Congress Living Legend recognition, and the 2006 Astrid Lindgren Memorial award, along with her two National Book Awards and pair of Newberry Medals.

Works in Critical Context

In addition to the many accolades Katherine Paterson has won for her writing, her works have been translated into over fifteen languages, selling millions of copies worldwide. Critic and translator Anthea Bell approvingly notes the subtlety with which Paterson is able "to make her own Christian convictions evident while not letting them become obtrusive."

Bridge to Terabithia   In his book *Katherine Paterson* (1994), scholar Gary D. Schmidt calls *Bridge to Terabithia* "perhaps the most moving and painful of her books." Writing in a similar vein, critics Linda Bachelder, Patricia Kelly, Donald Kenney, and Robert Small in their article

COMMON HUMAN EXPERIENCE

Redemption is a common theme in Paterson's fiction. Other works that explore this theme include the following:

Paradise Lost (1667), an epic poem by John Milton. In this classic work, the author justifies the actions of God by offering a presentation of the fall of man, which includes the possibility for man's redemption.

"Young Goodman Brown" (1835), a short story by Nathaniel Hawthorne. In this allegory about the nature of good and evil, Goodman Brown journeys with the devil to an unholy ceremony which includes many familiar figures, including his wife.

A Tale of Two Cities (1859), a novel by Charles Dickens. In this historical novel of the French Revolution, a rogue named Sydney Carton redeems himself by sacrificing his life to save the husband of the woman he loves.

Paradise (1997), a novel by Toni Morrison. This work explores the tension between a group of men in Ruby, Oklahoma and a group of women who live in a convent down the road.

"Young Adult Literature: Looking Backward" (1980), note that "Paterson's treatment of the death of Leslie, who died in a freak accident while swinging over a flooded creek to the magical kingdom of Terabithia, is sensitively portrayed." Judging Paterson to be among the best writers of children's fiction, Norma Bagnall admires Paterson's craft in her article "Bait/Rebait: Literature Isn't Supposed to be Realistic" (1981): "The best writers understand how literature works. ... It is why Katherine Paterson, in *Bridge to Terabithia*, uses foreshadowing to set the stage for the death."

Responses to Literature

1. Unlike many children's books, the characters in *Bridge to Terabithia* use swear words. Why do you think Paterson includes this type of dialogue? What impact does it have on your reading of the story?

2. Compare Leslie to the other students at Lark Creek School in *Bridge to Terabithia*. How do her differences impact the way others treat her? Can you relate to these social dynamics?

3. Explain the meaning of the title *Bridge to Terabithia*. What might the bridge symbolize? Explain your interpretation using quotations from the story.

4. Katherine Paterson has a religious background, and has written many Christian stories. Do you detect religious themes or concerns in her children's novels?

BIBLIOGRAPHY

Books

McGinty, Alice B. *Katherine Paterson*. New York: Rosen Publishing Group, 2002.

Schmidt, Gary D. *Katherine Paterson*. New York: Maxwell Macmillan International, 1994.

Smedman, Sarah M. and Joel Chaston.*Bridges for the Young: The Fiction of Katherine Paterson*. Lanham, Md.: Children's Literature Association and the Scarecrow Press, 2003.

Periodicals

Bell, Anthea. "A Case of Commitment." *Signal* 35 (May 1982): 73–81.

Buckley, Virginia. "Katherine Paterson." *Horn Book* 54 (August 1978): 368–371.

Goforth, Caroline. "The Role of the Island in *Jacob Have I Loved*." *Children's Literature Association Quarterly* 9 (Winter 1984–1985): 176–178.

Gough, John. "*Bridge to Terabithia*: The Subtlety of Plain Language." *Idiom* 18 (Summer 1983): 19–22.

Haskell, Ann. "Talk with a Winner." *New York Times Book Review* 26 (April 1981): 52, 67–68.

Huse, Nancy. "Katherine Paterson's Ultimate Realism." *Children's Literature Association Quarterly* 9 (Fall 1984): 99–101.

Jones, Linda T. "Profile Katherine Paterson." *Language Arts* 58 (February 1981): 189–196.

McGavran, Jr., James H. "Bathrobes and Bibles, Waves and Words in Katherine Paterson's *Jacob Have I Loved*." *Children's Literature in Education* 17 (Spring 1986): 3–15.

Powers, Douglas. "Of Time, Place, and Person: *The Great Gilly Hopkins* and Problems of Story for Adopted Children." *Children's Literature in Education* 15 (Winter 1984): 211–219.

Rees, David. "Medals and Awards." *Painted Desert, Green Shade*. (Boston: Horn Book, 1984): 89–101.

Smedman, M. Sarah. "'A Good Oyster': Story and Meaning in *Jacob Have I Loved*." *Children's Literature in Education* 14 (Autumn 1983): 180–187.

Web sites

Paterson, Katherine. *The Official Website of Author Katherine Paterson*. Retrieved November 13, 2008 from http://www.terabithia.com/.

✸ James Patterson

BORN: *1947, Newburgh, New York*

NATIONALITY: *American*

GENRE: *Fiction*

MAJOR WORKS:

The Thomas Berryman Number (1976)

James Patterson   *Supplied by Capital Pictures*

Along Came a Spider (1992)
The Alex Cross series (1992–present)
Women's Murder Club series (2001–present)
Maximum Ride series (2005–present)

Overview

James Patterson is a popular contemporary author, best known for his *Alex Cross* and *Women's Murder Club* mystery-thriller series. As an accomplished writer, he has won a variety of awards including the Edgar, BCA Mystery Guild's Thriller of the Year, and the International Thriller of the Year awards. Once dubbed "the man who can't miss" by *Time* magazine, Patterson's books have sold over 130 million copies worldwide.

Works in Biographical and Historical Context

Academic Excellence in New York   James Patterson was born on March 22, 1947, and grew up in Newburgh, New York. As a child, Patterson envisioned himself as a writer but his interest in literature did not fully emerge until his late teens. In school, Patterson excelled as a student; he graduated from Manhattan College summa cum lade with a BA in English in 1969. In 1971, he again graduated summa cum laude with a master's degree from Vanderbilt University.

Successful Career in Advertising   After graduating from Vanderbilt, Patterson built a highly successful career in the corporate sector, and worked for the J. Walter Thompson advertising agency. He began in 1971 as a copywriter and climbed the company's ladder until he found himself at the top, as the firm's youngest executive. Among his accomplishments at J. Walter Thompson, his most famous is the popular tag line "I'm a Toys R Us Kid," a slogan he is credited with creating. Patterson's corporate experience set him up for success as a best-selling author.

Literary Debut   In 1976, Patterson published his debut novel, *The Thomas Berryman Number*. Before being accepted, the novel was turned down by twenty-six publishers. Despite this initial difficulty, the work proved highly successful and was awarded the 1977 Edgar Award for Best First Novel. In it the protagonist, a professional hit man named Thomas Berryman, is pursued by a southern journalist who is trying to thwart his attempt to kill Nashville's revered African-American mayor.

Introducing Alex Cross   Patterson's next literary efforts were similar to his first, a string of mystery thrillers including *The Jericho Commandment* (1977), *Black Market* (1986), and *The Midnight Club* (1988). However, it was his novel in what would later become the best-selling *Alex Cross* series, *Along Came a Spider*, that brought Patterson popularity and secured for him a place in the line of highly acclaimed mystery fiction writers. The success of *Along Came a Spider* allowed Patterson to leave his job at Thompson agency and write full-time. As of 2008, there are fourteen novels in the *Alex Cross* series, with the fifteenth planned for publication in November 2009. Three novels in the series, *Along Came a Spider*, *Kiss the Girls* (1995), and *Roses Are Red* (2000) have been adapted for film.

The Women's Murder Club Series   Patterson's second popular series, the *Women's Murder Club*, began with the publication of *1st to Die* (2001) and has already produced seven best-selling novels, with an eighth scheduled for release in April 2009. The series is unique in that Patterson collaborated with other authors in writing six out of the seven published works—two of the novels were coauthored by Andrew Gross and four by Maxine Paetro. The *Women's Murder Club* was made into a TV series by ABC in 2007 and a video-game set.

The Maximum Ride Series   Patterson's third and most recent series began with the publication of *Maximum Ride: The Angel Experiment* (2005), a story about a group of teenagers with superpowers, and includes four installments, with a fifth scheduled for release in March 2009. The series was originally intended for teenagers and young adults but after sales indicated that the books were extremely popular with adults, the publisher adjusted its marketing and relabeled the series adult fiction. According to *Publishers Weekly* over six million copies of books in the

LITERARY AND HISTORICAL CONTEMPORARIES

James Patterson's famous contemporaries include:

Stephen King (1947–): A prolific and immensely popular American author of horror fiction, King blends elements of the traditional gothic tale with those of the modern psychological thriller, detective, and science fiction genres.

Tom Clancy (1947–): An American author of popular fiction about adventure and espionage, Clancy is best known for his Jack Ryan novels, which include *The Hunt for Red October* (1984) and *Patriot Games* (1987).

Michael Crichton (1942–2008): Crichton is an American author best known for his science fiction and techno-thriller novels such as *Jurassic Park* (1990).

Dean Koontz (1945–): An American author, Koontz is best known for novels in which he combines the popular literary genres of science fiction, horror, suspense, and romance.

John Grisham (1955–): An immensely popular author of legal thrillers, Grisham is best known for his novel *The Firm* (1991), which centers around a recent Harvard Law School graduate who, after learning that his firm is heavily involved in organized crime, risks his life to help the FBI indict his associates and their mob bosses.

series have been sold to date. A movie adaptation of the first three novels is scheduled for release in 2010.

Popularity and Monetary Success Patterson's popularity is reflected in his current standing as the record-holder for most books on the *New York Times* best-seller list, with thirty-nine titles making the list. To date, he has sold over 150 million book worldwide and according to *Forbes* magazine, he ranked second only to J. K. Rowling as the highest paid author of 2007, earning $50 million that year alone. The *New York Times* reported that he wrote one out of every fifteen books sold in the United States during 2007. Patterson is not showing any signs of slowing his productivity and has at least four new novels scheduled for release in 2009: *Run for Your Life*; *MAX*, the latest book in the *Maximum Ride* series; *8th Confession*, the latest book in the *Women's Murder Club* series; and *Swimsuit*. In addition to his own work, Patterson is known for his collaboration with other authors and artists, including Michael Ledwidge, Ned Rust, Leopoldo Gout, NaRae Lee, Peter DeJonge, Howard Roughan, Andrew Gross, Gabrielle Charbonnet, Hal Friedman, and Maxine Paetro. Patterson, his wife Susan, and his son Jack live in Palm Beach, Florida.

Works in Literary Context

Patterson, one of the top-selling mystery writers of all time, is known for his novels that are regarded by fans as compelling page-turners. While there is little scholarship on Patterson's work, his popularity and high sales place him alongside contemporaries like Stephen King and Tom Clancy. Among the authors admired by Patterson are Frederick Forsyth, William Peter Blatty, and Gabriel Garcia Marquez—he has named *One Hundred Years of Solitude* (1967) as his favorite book.

Crime Fiction Patterson's work belongs in the sub-genre of crime fiction. Alex Cross, Patterson's most famous character, is a retired forensic psychologist of the Washington, D.C. Police Department who works as a private psychologist and a government consultant. In Patterson's first best-selling novel, *Along Came a Spider*, Cross pursues a psychotic killer who abducts two children. Later installments in the series follow Cross as he works to solve murder mysteries. Similarly, the *Women's Murder Club* series follows the activities of four intelligent and hardworking women—Lindsay Boxer, a homicide detective of the San Francisco Police Department, Cindy Thomas, an up-and-coming reporter for the *San Francisco Chronicle*, Claire Washburn, the chief medical examiner for San Francisco, and Yuki Castellano, a district attorney, as they solve crimes in San Francisco.

Works in Critical Context

Patterson's reputation rests on the popular appeal of his fiction, which has made him one of the best-selling mystery writers in history. Many fans of his work report enjoying the suspenseful charity in his thrillers that inspire them to faithfully follow his works. Patterson's appeal is consistent, and he regularly attains best-seller status. Despite his success, however, many critics and members of the literary community remain unimpressed by his style and thematic focus.

Roses Are Red According to *Time*, "In a culture that values high style over storytelling, pretty prose over popularity and pulse-pounding plots, he's [Patterson] at the extreme wrong end of the spectrum, and he knows it. And, yes, it irks him a little." Critics find Patterson's page-turner style to be lacking literary significance. David Lazarus of *San Francisco Chronicle* wrote in his review of *Roses Are Red*: "As usual, Patterson knows how to keep the pages turning, and his short, tight chapters make for a brisk pace. They do not allow for much depth, thought, which prevents *Roses Are Red* from getting too far into the psychological makeup of the story's characters."

Kiss the Girls In her review of *Kiss the Girls*, "Thriller Built on Slice-and-Dice Female victims," published in the *San Francisco Chronicle*, Patricia Holt labeled the work "loathsome" saying that the author's "sloppy descriptions of people betray [his] bent for lazy characterizations." Like some of Patterson's other critics, Holt's main complaint is against what she calls "the Female Dismemberment and Mutilation School of Mystery Writing."

You've Been Warned One of Patterson's most recent novels, *You've Been Warned* (2007) has attracted similar criticism to his other work. The reviewer for *Publishers Weekly* commented that "The Patterson bestseller factory has turned out another high-drama thriller," but added that the narration by the character Kristen is "breathless [and] superficial … [and] doesn't generate a lot of reader sympathy or interest in figuring out the source of her macabre experiences."

Responses to Literature

1. Discuss the literary techniques Patterson uses to make his fiction "page-turning." What does he add or omit to make his stories compelling to readers?

2. Patterson's *Maximum Ride* series was originally intended for teenagers and young adults. However, sale records indicate that most books have been bought by older readers instead. Why do you think these books appeal more to adult than to young audiences?

3. Why does Patterson switch narrators throughout *Along Came a Spider*? Use examples from the novel to support your answer.

4. Discuss the moral lesson of the five balls (work, health, family, friends, and integrity) in *Suzanne's Diary for Nicholas*. Do you think Suzanne was destined to drop one of the glass balls (her health) or was there something more she could have done to change the course of her life?

BIBLIOGRAPHY

Books

Gregoriou, Christiana. *Deviance in Contemporary Crime Fiction*. Basingstoke, England: Palgrave Macmillan, 2007.

Kotker, Joan G. *James Patterson: A Critical Companion*. Westport, Conn.: Greenwood Press, 2004.

Periodicals

Holt, Patricia. "Thriller Built on Slice-and-Dice Female Victims." *San Francisco Chronicle* (January 13, 1995): D10.

Lazarus, David. "Detectives and Sleuths Need Love Too." *San Francisco Chronicle* (December 3, 2000): RV-6.

Review of *You've Been Warned*. *Publishers Weekly*. No. 30 (July 30, 2007).

Zvirin, S. "Story Behind the Story." *Booklist* 102, no. 18 (2006): 54.

"James Patterson Gets Bestsellers but No Respect." *Time* 167, no. 12 (March 20, 2006): 108–116.

Web sites

James Patterson: The Official Website. Retrieved December 5, 2008, from http://www.james patterson.com/index.html.

Rose, Lacey, and Lauren Streib. "The World's Best Paid Authors." *Forbes.com* Retrieved December 6, 2008, from http://www.forbes.com.

Thornton, Matthew. "Patterson Aplenty." *Publisher's Weekly*. Retrieved December 6, 2008, from http://www.publishersweekly.com.

COMMON HUMAN EXPERIENCE

Murder mysteries appears frequently in Patterson's work. Other works that explore this theme include the following:

"The Three Apples," also known as "The Tale of a Murdered Young Woman" (c. ninth century), a story by an unknown author within *One Thousand and One Nights* (first English translation, 1838). In this tale, the Abbasid Caliph orders his vizier to solve a murder crime under the threat of execution, but is then surprised when two men show up, each claiming to be the murderer.

Murder! (1930), a film directed by Alfred Hitchcock. An actress in a traveling theatre group is murdered and a female colleague is found standing over her body when police arrive. However, during her trial a member of the jury becomes convinced of her innocence and sets out to find the real murderer before the innocent women is put to death.

The Day of the Jackal (1971), a novel by Frederick Forsyth. An assassin is hired to murder the president of France, Charles de Gaulle, but his efforts are thwarted by a French intelligence inspector who is hired to track him down.

Homicide: A Year of Killing on the Streets (1991), a nonfiction book by David Simon. In this Edgar Award–winning book, the author describes the year he spent with the Baltimore Police Department homicide squad.

❀ Gary Paulsen

BORN: *1939, Minneapolis, Minnesota*

DIED:NATIONALITY: *American*

GENRE: *Fiction, nonfiction*

MAJOR WORKS:
Dogsong (1985)
Hatchet (1987)
The Winter Room (1989)
The Haymeadow (1994)
Lawn Boy (2007)

Overview

A prolific author of juvenile fiction, Gary Paulsen is known for his coming-of-age stories, including three winners of

Gary Paulsen   *Paulsen, Gary, photograph. Courtesy of Gary Paulsen.*

the Newbery Honor: *Dogsong* (1985), *Hatchet* (1987), and *The Winter Room* (1989).

Works in Biographical and Historical Context

Growing Up as an Army Brat   Gary Paulsen was born on May 17, 1939, in Minneapolis, Minnesota. Since his father was stationed in England during World War II and his mother worked long hours in a factory, Paulsen's primary caregivers during his early years were his grandmother and a few aunts. At the end of World War II, Paulsen and his family moved overseas to the Philippines. The next few years, from 1946 until 1949, were marked by frequent moves and the instability caused by his mother and father's alcoholism.

Discovering Literature   A self-described 'army brat,' Paulsen grew up as a shy boy who remained miserable until he discovered the world of literature. Paulsen told Marguerite Feitlowitz in an interview that, "School was a nightmare because I was unbelievably shy, and terrible at sports. I had no friends, and teachers ridiculed me … One day as I was walking past the public library in twenty below temperatures … I went in to get warm and

to my absolute astonishment the librarian … asked me if I wanted a library card. … When she handed me the card, she handed me the world." Although his library card did little to change his less-than-dedicated attitude toward school, Paulsen did develop a passion for reading and spent countless hours reading alone in the basement of his apartment building.

Eclectic Experiences as an Adolescent   Paulsen ran away from home at the age of fourteen and traveled with a carnival, experiences which piqued his interest in adventure. Paulsen frequently draws from this period in his life for the thematic content of his fiction. Alone in the world, Paulsen worked at a variety of jobs in order to support himself. His experiences during this time included working on a farm and jobs as an engineer, construction worker, ranch hand, truck driver, and sailor.

Move to Minnesota Proves Conducive to Writing   After abruptly leaving his job at an aerospace firm in California, where he worked as a satellite technician, Paulsen made a decision to work as a magazine proofreader in Hollywood while simultaneously working on his own writing at night. After a year, he moved to Minnesota and rented a cabin on a lake, where he completed his first novel, *Special War* (1966).

Racing the Iditarod   While living in rural Minnesota, Paulsen became interested in the sport of dog-sled racing and eventually picked it up himself. After training up to twenty hours a day, Paulsen entered the 1983 Iditarod, a 1,180-mile Alaskan dog-sled race. In 1985, after a second run of the same race, Paulsen suffered an attack of angina, a painful tightness in his chest, which forced him to give up his dogs and direct his concentrated efforts elsewhere. It was at this time that Paulsen began to focus more seriously on writing. "I write because it's all I can do," Paulsen once reflected. "Every time I've tried to do something else, I cannot." The author continues to write—even though the task is often daunting to him—because he wants his "years on this ball of earth to mean something. Writing furnishes a way for that to happen. … It pleases me to write—in a very literal sense of the word."

Coming Full Circle   Since his first publication in 1966, Paulsen has written more than two hundred novels for children and young adults as well as numerous magazine articles, short stories, plays, and nonfiction books. Of these, several have been recognized by the literary community, earning awards for their artistic merit. Perhaps most significantly, three of his novels, *Dogsong*, *Hatchet*, and *The Winter Room* were recognized with the Newbery Honor, the runner-up prize for the Newbery Award. In addition, *The Haymeadow* (1994) was awarded the Western Writers of America Golden Spurs Award. "It's like things have come full circle," Paulsen reflected in an *AAYA* interview. "I felt like nothing the first time I walked into a library, and now library associations are giving me awards. It means a lot to me."

Paulsen's own colorful life was the basis for his auto-biographical book entitled *Eastern Sun, Winter Moon: An Autobiographical Odyssey* (1993). In it, Paulsen chronicles a journey he took by car across the country to meet his long-absent father, his family's unsettling life in the Philippines, and the break-up of his parents's marriage.

Paulsen and his wife, Ruth Wright Paulsen, divide their time between their home in New Mexico and a boat in the Pacific. His novel *Lawn Boy* (2007) was selected for the 2008 New Mexico Book Award.

Works in Literary Context

Paulsen is a prolific author of coming-of-age stories and has published hundreds of novels, many of which include wilderness settings. In addition, he has also written non-fiction works on topics including hunting, trapping, farming, animals, medicine, and outdoor life. His experiences growing up with his grandmother and aunts as strong female role models is reflected in a collection of stories lauding women for their ability to handle so much responsibility and adversity with equanimity.

Coming-of-Age in the Wilderness   Many of Paulsen's books combine an outdoors theme with the story of a boy's coming-of-age. For example, in *Tracker* (1984), the thirteen-year-old protagonist learns to hunt and come to terms with the death of his grandfather, simultaneously. Similarly, *Dogsong* (1985) concerns a fourteen-year-old Eskimo who races a dog team across Alaska. Along the way, he encounters a pregnant girl who suffers from exposure to the cold. Themes of growing up and survival are also present in one of Paulsen's most famous books, *Hatchet*. In it, Brian, who is struggling to deal with his parent's divorce, is the only survivor of a plane crash in the Canadian wilderness and must overcome his worries in order to survive.

Works in Critical Context

While many of his books are no longer in print, Paulsen is well respected within the literary community as one of the most significant writers of young adult fiction. Critics often point to Paulsen's sensitive treatment of adolescent concerns. "There is poetic majesty in the descriptions without a touch of condescension to the young," writes Eugene J. Lineham in *Best Sellers*. Of all of his works, one of his earlier novels, *Hatchet*, has received the most critical praise.

Hatchet   Reviewing *Hatchet* in *Voice of Youth Advocates*, Eve Wilson states, "Paulsen's knowledge of our national wilderness is obvious and beautifully shared. Beyond that Paulsen grips Brian (and the reader) by the throat, shaking him into enlightenment and self-confidence after having endured several life-threatening events." Margery Fisher's assessment, in *Growing Point*, is equally positive: "The theme has been used before, most notably by Ivan Southall, but the book stands well on its own for firm concrete detail and an equally firm pattern of the boy's moods and

reactions to danger." Audrey Laski, in *The School Librarian*, has a similar reaction to the way the protagonist is depicted: "The passionate, repetitive rhythms of the writing, though sometimes a little overdone, powerfully communicate his terrors and triumphs."

The success of the novel involved more than just earning positive reviews. When it was published in 1987, "something extraordinary happened," writes Sarah L. Thomson in her biography, *Gary Paulsen* (2003). "*Hatchet* was more than a critical and popular success. It was a phenomenon." Anita Silvey has judged the book to be "the best modern survival story for young readers." Speaking to the novel's believability, Silvey notes that it "leaves readers feeling as if they have been living alone in the wilderness." Perhaps this explains the flurry of letters Paulsen has received asking him what happened to Brian, the novel's protagonist, after his rescue. Commenting on Paulsen's popularity with young readers, James B. Blasingame asserts that "without a doubt, *Hatchet* ... is one of the most widely read young adult novels in the world today."

Responses to Literature

1. Why does Brian put the rifle he finds in the survival pack aside in *Hatchet*? What does it represent for him? Explain your answer using examples from the novel.

COMMON HUMAN EXPERIENCE

Survival in the wilderness in a central focus of Paulsen's writing. Other works that focus on this theme include the following:

Robinson Crusoe (1719), a novel by Daniel Defoe. In this fictional autobiography, the title character—a cast-away—spends almost three decades on an island near Venezuela and manages to overcome his despair after reading the Bible and becoming religious.

The Swiss Family Robinson (1812), a novel by Johann David Wyss. On their way to Australia, a Swiss family is shipwrecked in the East Indies.

The Jungle Book (1894), a story collection by Rudyard Kipling. In the most well-known stories of the collection, Mowgli, an abandoned man cub, is raised by wolves in the jungles of India.

Stone Fox (1980), a children's novel by John Reynolds Gardiner. This is a short tale about a boy, Little Willy, who enters a dog sled race in the hopes of winning the $500 prize so that he can pay off his grandfather's debt.

Life of Pi (2001), a novel by Yann Martel. In this story, the young protagonist is stranded on a lifeboat in the Pacific Ocean, which he shares with a variety of animals, including a tiger.

2. What role does Brian's past play in *Hatchet*? What techniques does Paulsen use to bring the past into the action of the novel?

3. To what extent does Brian change throughout the course of *Hatchet*? How would you describe these changes?

4. Why do you think Paulsen chose to name his novel *Hatchet*? Explain your opinion using examples from the text.

BIBLIOGRAPHY

Books

Blasingame, James. *Gary Paulsen*. Westport, Conn.: Greenwood Press, 2007.

Feitlowitz, Marguerite. "Interview with Gary Paulsen." *Authors and Artists for Young Adults* Vol. 2, Detroit, Mich: Gale, 1989, pp. 165–73.

Fine, Edith Hope. *Gary Paulsen: Author and Wilderness Adventurer*. New York: Enslow, 2000.

Macken, JoAnn Early. *Gary Paulsen: Voice of Adventure and Survival*. Berkeley Heights, N.J.: Enslow Publishers, 2006.

Salvner, Gary M. *Presenting Gary Paulsen*. New York: Twayne Publishers, 1996.

Thomson, Sarah L. *Gary Paulsen*. New York: Rosen Central, 2003.

Periodicals

Campbell, Patty. Review of *The Cookcamp. New York Times Book Review* (May 5, 1991): 22–23.

Fisher, Margery. Review of *Hatchet. Growing Point* Vol. 28, No. 4 (November 1989): 5234–39.

Laski, Audrey. Review of *Hatchet. The School Librarian* Vol. 37, No. 4 (November 1989): 161, 163.

Linehan, Eugene J. Review of *Dogsong. Best Sellers* (July 1985).

Rausch, Tim. Review of *The Car. School Library Journal* (May 1994): 131–32.

Sapia, Yvonne. "Sisters in Search of America." *Los Angeles Times Book Review* (February 27, 1994): 2, 13.

Wilson, Evie. Review of *Hatchet. Voice of Youth Advocates* Vol. 10, No. 6 (February 1988): 283.

Winton, Tim. "His Own World War." *Los Angeles Times Book Review* (March 21, 1993): 1, 11.

Web sites

Gary Paulsen. Retrieved November 29, 2008, from http://www.randomhouse.com/features/garypaulsen.

⊕ Richard Peck

BORN: *1934, Decatur, Illinois*

NATIONALITY: *American*

GENRE: *Fiction*

MAJOR WORKS:
Dreamland Lake (1973)
Are You in the House Alone? (1976)
A Long Way from Chicago (1998)
A Year Down Yonder (2000)
The River Between Us (2003)

Overview

Richard Peck is a contemporary American novelist best known for his young adult fiction, including *A Year Down Yonder* (2000), which was awarded the 2001 Newbery Medal.

Works in Biographical and Historical Context

Growing Up in Illinois during the Great Depression
Richard Peck was born on April 5, 1934, in Decatur, Illinois, to Wayne Morris, a merchant, and Virginia (Gray) Peck, a dietitian. The Great Depression, which began with the stock market crash on October 29, 1929, was in full swing, and many families across the United States struggled to make ends meet. Although he was still young by the time the war economy of World War II began to relieve the widespread economic hardship, Peck was inspired enough by the climate of the 1930s to use the

Richard Peck   *Peck, Richard, photograph by Don Gallo. Reproduced by permission of Richard Peck.*

Great Depression as the backdrop for one of his most successful novels, *A Year Down Yonder.*

Education in English   Peck attended DePauw University in Indiana and spent his junior year, from 1955 until 1956, at the University of Exeter in England. He graduated from DePauw in 1956. Before going back to school, he served in the U.S. Army in Stuttgart, Germany, for two years. The United States had maintained a military presence in the city ever since the Allied forces took control of Germany in 1945, at the end of World War II. After returning to the United States, he pursued graduate education at Southern Illinois University, earning his MA in 1959, and then enrolled at the University of Washington from 1960 to 1961. While at Southern Illinois University, Peck taught English. After graduating, he taught high school English at Glenbrook North High School in Illinois before taking a job in Chicago as a textbook editor.

After two years, Peck left Chicago and moved to New York where he taught for six years at Hunter College High School. He left his position in 1971 to work first as the assistant director of the Council for Basic Education in Washington, D.C., and then as a fellow at Oxford University in England. It was during these years that Peck submitted his first books for publication.

Leaving Teaching   Peck became familiar with contemporary adolescent problems while teaching high school.

He liked his students but, after several years, became discouraged and quit. He once said that teaching "had begun to turn into something that looked weirdly like psychiatric social work." Peck decided instead to write books for teenagers that featured the problems he had seen. "Ironically, it was my students who taught me to be a writer, though I had been hired to teach *them*," he said in a speech published in *Arkansas Libraries.* "They taught me that a novel must entertain first before it can be anything else."

First Novel Confronts Teen Pregnancy   Peck's first novel, *Don't Look and It Won't Hurt* (1972) is about a teenage pregnancy. In it, he tells the story of alienation and healing from the viewpoint of the young mother's younger sister. The fifteen-year-old manages to keep her troubled family together, "parenting" her parents in a role reversal that appeals to readers of this age group. She is also helpful in the sister's recovery after she decides to give her baby up for adoption. The novel received much critical praise and became a popular success, and it continues to sell in both paperback and hardcover editions.

Success and Recognition   Since his first novel, Peck has published numerous novels for young adults, several poetry anthologies, a short story collection, and several nonfiction books for adults. Of these, his novels for young adults have been most successful, and several have won prestigious awards. For example, his novel *Dreamland Lake* (1973), was nominated for the 1994 Edgar Allan Poe Award. Two years later, Peck's controversial novel about a teenage girl who is raped, *Are You in the House Alone?* (1976), received the Edgar Allan Poe Award for best juvenile fiction in 1976. In 1999, *A Long Way from Chicago* (1999) was recognized with the Newbery Honor. Perhaps most significantly, *A Year Down Yonder* (2000) won the 2001 Newbery Medal. Peck has also won numerous awards for his lifetime accomplishments, including the National Humanities Medal in 2001.

In contrast to many of his peers, Peck refuses to write on a computer, preferring instead to compose his written works on a typewriter. For similar reasons, he does not maintain a personal Web site. Peck's most recent books include several novels for young adults, *The Teacher's Funeral* (2004), *Here Lies the Librarian* (2006), *On the Wings of Heroes* (2007); a short story anthology, *Past Perfect, Present Tense* (2004); and a nonfiction book, *Escape! The Story of The Great Houdini* (2007).

Works in Literary Context

While teaching high school, Peck observed that young adults are most concerned with winning approval from their peers and seeking reassurance from their reading material. Peck believes that American attitudes about public education have resulted in a system that discourages young people instead of equipping them for survival in the real world. With these needs in mind, Peck writes about the passage from childhood to adulthood. He believes that in a young adult novel, typically "the reader

LITERARY AND HISTORICAL CONTEMPORARIES

Richard Peck's famous contemporaries include:

Gary Paulsen (1939–): A prolific author of juvenile fiction, Paulsen is known for his coming-of-age stories, which include three winners of the Newbery Honor: *Dogsong* (1985), *Hatchet* (1987), and *The Winter Room* (1989).

Judy Blume (1938–): Blume is an American children's author of *Are You There God? It's Me Margaret.* (1970) and other novels.

Nancy Garden (1938–): Garden is an American author of children's and adult fiction whose novel *Annie on My Mind* (1982) attracted controversial attention for dealing with the romantic relationship between two seventeen-year-old girls.

Robert Cormier (1925–2000): An American author of award-winning books for young adults, Cormier's books include *The Chocolate War* (1974), *I Am the Cheese* (1977), and *After the First Death* (1979).

Cynthia Voigt (1942–): Voigt, an American author of young adult fiction, was awarded the Newbery Medal for her novel *Dicey's Song* (1982).

Lois Lowry (1937–): Lowry is a highly acclaimed author of children's literature who has won the Newbery Medal twice, for *Number the Stars* (1989) and *The Giver* (1993).

meets a worthy young character who takes one step nearer maturity, and he or she takes that step independently." Peck's writing is heavily influenced by his experience as a high school English teacher.

Realism: Teen Issues   Peck's books that deal with important teenage problems such as suicide, unwanted pregnancy, death of a loved one, and rape have won critical praise for their realism and emotional power. He has written over a dozen very popular books for young adults, books that help young readers to develop self-confidence. Peck does not ignore social issues related to gender. In his books, he realistically portrays women in a period of social change in a variety of social roles.

Overcoming Peer Pressure   Peck's female heroes are known for making their own decisions and exercising their freedom from the demands of peer pressure. He feels that these qualities are especially important for characters in teenage fiction. Writing in *Literature for Today's Young Adults*, Peck explains that young people need to see that the confining codes of behavior they live with as adolescents will not be imposed on them for the rest of their lives. He believes they need to see characters rewarded for making the kinds of free choices that young

readers will soon have to make on their way to adulthood. He concludes that the future of young adult fiction is in "books that invite the young to think for themselves instead of for each other." "After twelve novels," he said in the speech, "I find I have only one theme. ... It is simply that you will never grow up until you begin to think and act independently of your peers."

Works in Critical Context

Peck's first novel, *Don't Look and It Won't Hurt* was well received and brought him praise from critics and young readers alike. Over the course of his writing career, Peck has developed a reputation for his ability to engage young readers and confront difficult aspects of being a teenager with sensitivity.

Are You in the House Alone?   Peck's controversial novel about a teenage girl who is raped received the Edgar Allan Poe Award in 1976. Zena Sutherland, writing in the *Bulletin of the Center for Children's Books*, was impressed by the novel's scope, saying that the author "sees clearly both society's problem and the victim's: the range of attitudes, the awful indignity," the fear and shame that is part of this kind of crime. Peck explained in his speech, "I did not write the novel to tell the young about rape. They already know what that is." He said he wrote it to warn the young that, regrettably, criminals are sometimes treated with more respect than victims, even though victims of crime live in the shadow of that experience for the rest of their lives. Alix Nelson in the *New York Times Book Review* thought that Peck should be commended for reaching his audience and for teaching them about a topic that many other people prefer to avoid.

A Year Down Yonder   This novel, a sequel to the earlier *A Long Way from Chicago* (1998), is about a fifteen-year-old girl who goes to live with her grandmother in a small town in Illinois during the Great Depression. It was awarded the Newbery Medal in 2001 and received appreciative reviews. In *Booklist*, Hazel Rochman commented on the book's "combination of wit, gentleness, and outrageous farce." The reviewer admired the well-developed characterization, as well as the dialogue and storytelling. She concluded that "The heart of the book is Grandma—huge and overbearing, totally outside polite society. Just as powerful is what's hidden: Mary Alice discovers kindness and grace as well as snakes in the attic. Most moving is Mary Alice's own growth." Kitty Flynn in *The Horn Book Magazine* was of the opinion that "while the escapades are diverting," the novel does not possess the "cumulative power" of the first novel. "Grandma, who was an indefatigable source of surprise and bewilderment to her grandchildren in the first book, doesn't come across as such a mythic figure this time around." This mild criticism aside. Flynn praised the humor in the novel and concluded that "Peck presents memorable characters in a satisfying sequel."

Responses to Literature

1. What technique(s) does Peck use to engage your attention in his novels? Provide several examples from his fiction to support your views.

2. Peck has a reputation for confronting serious teenage issues with sensitivity and compassion, while holding the attention of young readers. Do you agree with this assessment of his strengths? Explain your opinion using examples from his fiction.

3. What does Mary Alice learn from her grandmother in *A Year Down Yonder*? How does her experience living with Grandma change her?

4. How would you characterize Grandma's system of values, or way of telling right from wrong, in *A Year Down Yonder*? Give some examples from the story to support your opinion.

BIBLIOGRAPHY

Books

Donelson, Kenneth L., and Alleen Pace Nilsen, eds. "Richard Peck." *Literature for Today's Young Adults*. (New York: Longman, 2001).

Periodicals

Betts, Wendy E. Review of *The Last Safe Place on Earth*. *Five Owls* (March/April 1995): 88.

Crew, Hilary. "Blossom Culp and Her Ilk: The Independent Female in Richard Peck's YA Fiction." *Top of the News* (Spring 1987): 297–301.

Flynn, Kitty. Review of *A Year Down Yonder*. *The Horn Book Magazine* 76, no. 6 (November 2000): 761.

McHenry, Dorinda. Review of *Lost in Cyberspace*. *Children's Book Review Service* (January 1996): 60.

Mercier, Jean F. "Interview with Richard Peck." *Publishers Weekly*, March 14, 1980.

Nelson, Alix. "Ah, Not to Be Sixteen Again." *New York Times Book Review* (November 14, 1976): 29.

Peck, Richard. "People of the Word." *Arkansas Libraries* (December 1981): 13–16.

Phelan, Carolyn. Review of *Lost in Cyberspace*. *Booklist* (October 15, 1995): 402.

Rochman, Hazel. Review of *A Year Down Yonder*. *Booklist* 97, no. 4 (October 15, 2000): 436.

Sutherland, Zena. Review of *Are You in the House Alone?* *Bulletin of the Center for Children's Books* (March 1977): 111–112.

Sutton, Roger. "A Conversation with Richard Peck." *School Library Journal* (June 1990): 36–40.

Voss, Lana. Review of *Bel-Air Bambi and the Mall Rats*. *Voice of Youth Advocates* (December 1993): 298.

Youree, Beverly. Review of *Love and Death at the Mall*. *Voice of Youth Advocates* (April 1994): 58.

COMMON HUMAN EXPERIENCE

Much of Peck's writing focuses on the problems teenagers encounter in modern society. Other works that explore this theme include the following:

Great Expectations (1860), a novel by Charles Dickens. This story follows orphaned Pip through his experiences growing up as a member of the working class who strives to achieve social mobility.

Heidi (1880), a novel by Johanna Spyri. Heidi, an orphan, has many challenging experiences while growing up alongside her grandfather, Peter the goat-herder, and Klara, an invalid.

The Catcher in the Rye (1951), a novel by J. D. Salinger. Holden Caulfield, a teenage boy, is expelled from high school and wanders the streets of New York City before ending up at a mental institution.

Reviving Ophelia (1994), a nonfiction book by Mary Pipher. The author discusses the reasons that teenage girls frequently suffer from depression and eating disorders, and why some commit suicide.

Veronika Decides to Die (1998), a novel by Paulo Coelho. Twelve-year-old Veronika struggles to find a reason to live after she attempts suicide by taking a handful of sleeping pills.

✺ Walker Percy

BORN: *1916, Birmingham, Alabama*

DIED: *1990, Covington, Louisiana*

NATIONALITY: *American*

GENRE: *Fiction, nonfiction*

MAJOR WORKS:
The Moviegoer (1961)

Overview

Walker Percy was a highly respected American author who, through more than thirty years of writing, balanced interesting, accessible fiction with serious ideas. After the publication of his National Book Award-winning novel *The Moviegoer* in 1961, he established himself as a major Southern novelist with a unique place in American fiction.

Works in Biographical and Historical Context

Youth in the Deep South Percy was born on May 28, 1916, in Birmingham, Alabama, where he spent his childhood. His youth in the Deep South was far from ordinary; events from his formative years and young manhood often served as the experiences upon which his

Walker Percy   *Percy, Walker, photograph. © Jerry Bauer. Reproduced by permission.*

New York City. Working as a pathologist in New York, Percy was called upon to perform autopsies on indigent alcoholics, many of whom had died of tuberculosis. Within a year, Percy contracted the dreaded lung disease himself; he spent most of the following three years in a sanatorium, while World War II raged. While convalescing, he explored the humanistic interests that he had been unable to pursue during his medical training—French and Russian literature, philosophy and psychology. He found himself drawn particularly to the works of Albert Camus, Jean-Paul Sartre, and Fyodor Dostoevsky. In addition to his reading, Percy's philosophical outlook was shaped by his uncle, who, according to Percy, instilled in him "the Greek-Roman Stoic view" that informs much of his fiction.

Pursuit of a Modern Conundrum   World War II saw an exponential increase in the technologies available for human warfare. After people witnessed the destructive power of new weaponry—particularly the atomic bomb, which decimated the Japanese cities of Hiroshima and Nagasaki, killing tens of thousands of civilians—many struggled to comprehend the meaning of man's existence in the modern world. In 1944, Percy had recovered sufficiently to return to Columbia to teach pathology, but he suffered a relapse and decided to quit medicine. The illness was somewhat fortuitous, because Percy had become deeply interested in a whole new realm of intellectual endeavor. After studying the beauty of the scientific method, he told *Bookweek,* "An extraordinary paradox became clear: that the more science progressed and even as it benefited man, the less it said about what it is like to be a man living in the world." Percy searched for a solution to this paradox and began to consider a career, however humble, through which he could expose the unique modern conundrum. Writing provided him the means to that end.

Marriage and Conversion to Catholicism   Percy's first published works were philosophical essays that appeared in scholarly journals; these essays dealt with self-estrangement in the twentieth century, its causes and ramifications. In 1946, he married Mary Bernice Townsend and, in 1947, converted to Catholicism. Christianity, and Roman Catholicism in particular, figure prominently in all his work as a source of morality and reform.

Interest in Semiotics   Percy and his wife moved to New Orleans, and then to Covington, Louisiana, living on an inheritance from a relative. When one of his children was born deaf, Percy became fascinated by a branch of philosophy that consumed him from that point forward—semiotics, the study of symbols and how they are used in human communication.

Success as a Novelist   Percy wrote two unpublished novels before beginning *The Moviegoer.* He finally found his fictive niche, however, when he decided to follow Albert Camus's example and write about a character, a stockbroker named Binx Bolling, who serves as "an embodiment of a certain pathology of the twentieth century," to use his

fiction is based. When Percy was thirteen, his father committed suicide, as had his grandfather twelve years earlier. His mother died two years later in an automobile accident. Percy and his two brothers were then adopted by their father's cousin, William Alexander Percy, a wealthy and learned gentleman who lived in Greenville, Mississippi. Uncle Will, as they called him, was himself a writer whose poetic memoir, *Lanterns on the Levee: Recollections of a Planter's Son* (1941) was a popular exploration of postwar gentility in the South. As a teenager, Percy encountered intellectuals of all sorts in his adoptive parent's home—historians, novelists, psychologists, and poets all enjoyed the elder Percy's hospitality. But though Walker Percy dabbled in writing during his school years (he sold sonnets to less-talented English classmates who needed them for assignments), when he left these stimulating surroundings for college in 1934, he turned to science, planning to pursue a career in medicine.

Career in Medicine Halted by Tuberculosis   Percy studied chemistry at the University of North Carolina and, in due course, was admitted to medical school at the Columbia College of Physicians and Surgeons. He received his medical degree from that institution in 1941, and that same year he began his residency at Bellevue Hospital in

own words from the *Southern Review. The Moviegoer* was published in 1961 when Percy was forty-five, and although the publisher, Alfred A. Knopf, did little to promote the book, it was discovered and given the National Book Award.

Despite some surprise and disgruntlement over the awarding of the National Book Award to a new, untested author, most literary critics have, in retrospect, given high praise to *The Moviegoer* for its tightness and control of the material. Percy's subsequent works included *The Last Gentleman* (1966); *Love in the Ruins* (1971), which won the National Catholic Book Award in the year it was published; *Lancelot* (1977); *The Second Coming* (1980); and *The Thanatos Syndrome* (1987).

Exploration of Semiotics and Existentialism in Nonfiction In addition to fiction, Percy published several non-fiction works that explore his interests in semiotics and existentialism. *The Message in the Bottle* (1975) consists of scholarly essays on linguistics, existentialism, and psychology. As in his novels, Percy probes the relationship between alienation and communication. In *Lost in the Cosmos* (1983), Percy parodies "how-to" manuals and various forms of popular culture with the intention of promoting understanding of the human predicament.

Contributions to the Literary Community In addition to his direct contributions to American letters, Percy helped found the Fellowship of Southern Writers. He also helped ensure that John Kennedy Toole's novel *A Confederacy of Dunces* (1980; posthumous) was published after the author committed suicide. Toole's book was later awarded the Pulitzer Prize in Literature.

Percy died of prostate cancer on May 10, 1990, at his home in Covington, Louisiana.

Works in Literary Context

Best known for his first novel, *The Moviegoer*, Percy explores such conditions of modern life as alienation, malaise, and conformity. Percy has named Soren Kierkegaard as the philosopher who probably influenced him most. But he was also drawn to Martin Heidegger; he became absorbed in the existentialist ideas of Jean-Paul Sartre and Albert Camus and the Christian existentialism espoused by Gabriel Marcel. He found that he shared the existentialist view of man as being in a predicament, troubled by uprootedness, estrangement, and anxiety. Like him, these men were interested in what it is like to be a man in a world transformed by science. And it was from these philosophers, rather than from fellow Southern writers, that Percy fashioned his literary credo. Scholars have identified Percy's two major themes, the problem of existence in the modern age and the hope that one can overcome despair, as the most enduring qualities of his work.

Existential Christianity Drawing upon the religious and philosophical ideas of Kierkegaard and Marcel and imbued with his knowledge of semiotics, science,

---

LITERARY AND HISTORICAL CONTEMPORARIES

Walker Percy's famous contemporaries include:

Jean-Paul Sartre (1905–1980): French author regarded as among the most influential contributors to world literature in the twentieth century and a leading proponent of the philosophical concept of existentialism.

Flannery O'Connor (1925–1964): American author considered one of the foremost short story writers in American literature. She was an anomaly among post-World War II authors—a Roman Catholic from the Bible-belt South whose stated purpose was to reveal the mystery of God's grace in everyday life.

Albert Camus (1913–1960): Algerian-born French author who, in his varied career, passionately explored his major theme: the belief that people can attain happiness in an apparently meaningless world; he was awarded the Nobel Prize for Literature in 1957.

George Orwell (1903–1950): English author significant for his unwavering commitment, both as an individual and as an artist, to personal freedom and social justice; while he wrote a variety of works, his novels *Animal Farm* (1945) and *Nineteen Eighty-Four* (1949) are best known and most widely read.

J. D. Salinger (1919–): Best known for his controversial novel *The Catcher in the Rye* (1951), Salinger is recognized by critics and readers alike as one of the most popular and influential authors of American fiction to emerge after World War II.

Iris Murdoch (1919–1999): Irish-born English author and scholar of philosophy, who makes use of intricately developed plots and witty observations to examine emotional, spiritual, and intellectual pursuits of well-educated, upper middle class British characters.

Southern history, and popular culture, Percy's works promote Christian and existentialist values as means for counteracting contemporary psychological and social ills. Percy's heroes are usually contemplative, affluent, middle-aged men who seek spiritual meaning, identity, and love. These protagonists reject scientific humanism in favor of traditional Christian ideals to overcome despair and to confront an increasingly valueless, chaotic, and swiftly changing world. A major concern in Percy's work is the relationship between language, identity, and reality. Although some critics fault Percy for creating one-dimensional characters, many laud his insightful probing of social, moral, and philosophical issues.

Recovery from Despair Percy admits that his main writing motivation is usually a desire to correct wrongs. But he does not think that an author's philosophy should

COMMON HUMAN EXPERIENCE

The problem of existence in the modern age is a central focus of Percy's work. Other works that explore this theme include the following:

Being and Time (1927), a philosophical text by Martin Heidegger. In this classic work, the author explores the essence of, and constraints on, being as such.

Nausea (1938), a novel by Jean-Paul Sartre. One of the author's most famous books, this work tells the story of a researcher named Roquetin who becomes acutely aware of the nauseating quality of his existence in the world.

The Stranger (1942), a novel by Albert Camus. Set in pre-World War II Algeria, this book tells the story of an alienated French man who eventually commits murder and must await his fate in prison.

be imposed on a work; it must be an integral part of the work, as it is of the author's being. Often the enemy is everyday life, a condition of numbness and devitalized existence resulting from routine. A second cause of modern malaise is inauthenticity, the antithesis of meaningful life, involving the surrender of individuality through such habits as conformity. A third cause is abstraction, the absorption of concrete personality into its theoretical shadow through estrangement from the self. Fortunately for troubled mankind, Percy posits solutions to these ills. Man can recover himself through ordeal, such as a shock that disrupts everyday life. Alternatively, he can attempt a rotation, through novel experiences that transcend his expectations; initiate a repetition, a reliving of a past experience; or cultivate intersubjectivity—that is, authentic and compassionate relations with other human beings. All of Percy's protagonists suffer from at least one of these causes of despair and recover, or attempt to recover, by one of these means.

Works in Critical Context

Critics generally agree that *The Moviegoer* is Percy's best novel, with scholars noting, in particular, the tight control he exercised over his material. Also well-received were his next two novels, *The Last Gentleman* and *The Second Coming*. Commentators argue that these novels do more than represent Percy's moral and philosophical ideas; they are also well-told stories with imagination and interesting characters and events. Percy is frequently praised for his poignant satire and his talent for deftly incorporating profound ideas into accessible, well-written stories. *Love in the Ruins* is cited frequently as his most humorous work; Percy used humor and affirmation to overcome despair.

Lancelot, which received mostly negative reviews, has been criticized for lacking the sense of affirmation common to Percy's other works and for its confessional format, which, argued commentators, created severe problems with characterization.

Enthusiastic Reception of The Moviegoer After the publication of his National Book Award-winning novel *The Moviegoer* in 1961, Percy "claimed a position, never relinquished, as not only a major Southern novelist, but as one of the unique voices in American fiction," according to Malcolm Jones in the *New York Times Magazine*. As Charles Poore noted in the *New York Times*, Percy "shows us the modern world through the distorting mirrors that the modern world foolishly calls reality." Gail Godwin offered a concurrent description in the *New York Times Book Review*. "Walker Percy," Godwin wrote, "has the rare gift of being able to dramatize metaphysics." In the *Mississippi Quarterly Review*, John F. Zeugner concluded: "*The Moviegoer* seems to have been composed in joy—a muted celebration of Bolling's departure from despair. Written in the first person, shaped with a tranquil irony, *The Moviegoer* hums with the exhilaration of a man who has argued his way out of darkness."

Responses to Literature

1. Discuss the literary techniques Percy employs in *The Moviegoer*. How does the quality of the protagonist's narration impact your reading of the work and your interpretation of its themes?

2. Percy's fiction has been called philosophical. How does he bring the encounter with ideas to the center of his narratives? Explore the relationship between plot and philosophy, looking closely at one or more of his texts.

3. In *The Moviegoer*, why is Kate depressed? What is at the root of her fear?

4. How do Percy's novels represent the issue of religious faith in modern society?

5. In *The Moviegoer*, what makes John think that everyone else is "dead" despite their outward appearances of living?

BIBLIOGRAPHY

Books

Coles, Robert. *Walker Percy: An American Search.* Boston: Little, Brown, 1978.

Elie, Paul. *The Life You Save May Be Your Own: An American Pilgrimage.* New York: Farrar, Straus, and Giroux, 2003.

Hobson, Linda Whitney. *Understanding Walker Percy.* Columbia: University of South Carolina Press, 1988.

Luschei, Martin. *The Sovereign Wayfarer: Walker Percy's Diagnosis of the Malaise.* Baton Rouge: Louisiana State University Press, 1972.

Montgomery, Marion. *With Walker Percy at a
    Tupperware Party: In the Company of Flannery
    O'Connor, T. S. Eliot, and Others.* South Bend, Ind.:
    St. Augustine's Press, 2008.

Samway, Patrick H. *Walker Percy: A Life.* New York:
    Farrar, Straus, and Giroux, 1997.

Tolson, Jay. *Pilgrim in Ruins: A Life of Walker Percy.*
    New York; Simon & Schuster, 1992.

Tharpe, Jac. *Walker Percy.* Boston: Twayne Publishers,
    1983.

Periodicals

Blouin, Michel T. "The Novels of Walker Percy: An
    Attempt at Synthesis." *Xavier University Studies* 6
    (1968): 29–42.

Byrd, Scott. "Mysteries and Movies: Walker Percy's
    College Articles and *The Movie Goer." Mississippi
    Quarterly* 25 (Spring 1972): 165–181

Gaston, Paul L. "The Revelation of Walker Percy."
    Colorado Quarterly 20 (Spring 1972): 459–470.

Johnson, Mark. "The Search for Place in Walker Percy's
    Novels." *Southern Literary Journal* 8 (Fall 1975):
    55–81.

Kazin, Alfred. "The Pilgrimage of Walker Percy."
    Harper's Magazine 242 (June 1971): 81–86.

Lawson, Lewis A. "Walker Percy's Indirect
    Communications." *Texas Studies in Literature and
    Language* 11 (Spring 1969): 867–900.

Lehan, Richard. "The Way Back: Redemption in the
    Novels of Walker Percy." *Southern Review* 4 (April
    1968): 306–319.

Zeugner, John F. "Walker Percy and Gabriel Marcel: The
    Castaway and the Wayfarer." *Mississippi Quarterly*
    28 (Winter 1974–1975): 21–53.

✸ Ann Petry

BORN: *1908, Old Saybrook, Connecticut*

DIED: *1997, Old Saybrook, Connecticut*

NATIONALITY: *American*

GENRE: *Fiction, nonfiction*

MAJOR WORKS:

The Street (1946)

*Harriet Tubman, Conductor on the Under-
    ground Railroad* (1955)

Miss Muriel and Other Stories (1971)

Overview

Most famous for her stories of hardship and resilience in
Harlem, Ann Petry is among the most respected African
American authors of the twentieth century. Her work
continues to be praised for its ability to transcend racial
boundaries, speaking to the universality of prejudice in
the human experience.

Ann Petry *Petry, Ann, 1946, photograph. AP Images.*

Works in Biographical and Historical Context

Comfortable Childhood in Connecticut Ann
Lane (later Petry) was born in Old Saybrook, Connecticut, to Peter C. Lane and Bertha James Lane on October
12, 1908. She was the youngest of three children, the
oldest child having died at age two. The Lanes lived a
rather comfortable and stable life. The family, early on,
had established a tradition in the sciences, with specific
concentration in chemistry that was to extend for three
generations. Her father, a native of New Germantown,
New Jersey, was a pharmacist who had been apprenticed
to a druggist and licensed in 1890. He owned a drugstore
in Old Saybrook. Her aunt and uncle were also druggists,
owning a drugstore in the neighboring town of Old
Lyme, Connecticut. Equally accomplished, her mother,
a native of Hartford, Connecticut, graduated from the
New York School of Chiropody and was licensed to
practice her profession in 1915. The Lanes were one of
two black families in the small New England town, a fact
that helped to shape Ann's perspective and provided her
with raw materials for later stories and novels.

Career in Pharmacy In 1925 Ann Lane, the only
person of African American descent in her class, graduated from Old Saybrook High School. She found that
her classes at the Connecticut College of Pharmacy (now

the University of Connecticut School of Pharmacy) had a similar racial composition. She graduated from this institution with a PhD degree in 1931. For the next seven years Ann worked as a pharmacist in the family-owned drugstore.

Embracing Change: Marriage and Move to Harlem
In 1938 Ann Lane made some crucial decisions. On February 22, 1938, she married George D. Petry in Old Saybrook, and jointly they decided to sever ties with her native town. She resolved to go to New York, learn to write, and become good at it. In New York the need to earn money and an inclination toward writing led her to newspaper work. A job as a newspaper reporter for the *People's Voice*, a Harlem weekly, plunged her into the streets of Harlem. She spent some years in Harlem learning of its people and transmitting their yearnings, feelings, and fears to the printed page. Her experiences in the inner city educated her to the economic hardships of the poor, deepened her sensitivity to the plight of millions of less fortunate black Americans, and made her painfully aware of the degree to which bigotry can erode the personal lives of its victims.

Acquiring Skills for Creative Writing   Not content with the writing experience provided by her stint with the *People's Voice*, Petry enrolled in creative writing courses at Columbia University in the evenings to learn about fictional technique, effective dialogue, and dramatic structure. A tireless, disciplined, and single-minded worker, Petry spent hours polishing her craft, writing and rewriting her stories. She deliberately set out to understand the anxieties and frustrations that stimulated abnormal behavior in the human species, reading voraciously in the fields of psychology and psychiatry. She taught in a Harlem experimental school, which gave her an opportunity to observe firsthand the degree to which ghetto existence affected the lives of black children. In those years Petry taught salesmanship, became a member of what is now the American Negro Theater, and became affiliated with Negro Women Incorporated, a political group, eventually becoming its executive secretary.

In the midst of a career and an active civic life, Petry was not prepared for the editorial rejections that came her way. In response, she made up her mind to focus exclusively on her writing and eventually her efforts paid off. In 1943 *Crisis* published her short story "On Saturday the Siren Sounds at Noon," which is set in the middle of New York's Harlem. Told in flashbacks through the consciousness of a nameless black father whose memory is triggered by the weekly Saturday noon air raid siren, the story depicts his returning home one day to find that a tragic fire has claimed the lives of all his children. The story is representative of Petry's early work in that it is based in part on true incidents, including a newspaper story she covered while working as a journalist.

Success as a Fiction Writer   In 1945 Petry produced one of her best-known short stories for *Crisis* magazine, "Like a Winding Sheet." Set in Harlem, it chronicles a

day in the life of Johnson, a black factory worker. "Like a Winding Sheet" drew Petry national acclaim, winning her a place in Martha Foley's *Best American Stories of 1946*. Its publication kindled the interest of major book publishers. Within months after it appeared, she had written the first five chapters and a synopsis of her first novel, *The Street* (1946), which had won a Houghton Mifflin Literary Fellowship Award of $2,400 in 1945.

After ten months of writing in near seclusion, Petry's first novel appeared in January of 1946 and drew favorable reviews. *The Street* tells the story of Lutie Johnson, an intelligent, industrious, and attractive young black woman who struggles to survive and maintain her dignity in a brutal environment.

Petry's second novel, *Country Place* (1947), is a story about the inevitability of change and of the tragic disillusionment that those who refuse to adjust to it must suffer. The major characters are white, and many of the minor ones are of varying nationalities and ethnic origins. Like Petry's first novel, *Country Place*, a selection of the British Book Club, enjoyed a warm reception from reviewers.

Country Place was followed by a series of separately published stories. Two of the stronger stories, "The Necessary Knocking at the Door" (in *'47*, 1947) and "The Bones of Louella Brown" (in *Opportunity*, 1947), though radically different in tone, illustrate Petry's technical proficiency at its best. One of Petry's most popular stories is "In Darkness and Confusion," a novella based on the Harlem riots of August 1943.

Return to Old Saybrook   Petry returned to Old Saybrook in 1948. In 1949 for *Holiday* magazine she produced a long nostalgic essay titled "Harlem," which reviewed in pictorial and historical form the world's most famous black community. That was followed by publication of her first children's book, *The Drugstore Cat* (1949). A delightful story for youngsters six to ten years of age, this piece marks the author's first departure from adult writing. Set in an environment Petry knew well, it focuses on Buzzie, the country cat who comes to live with the town druggist and emerges as a hero when he saves the store from robbers.

Defending the Novel as Social Criticism   Another product of this reflective period was Petry's 1950 critical essay, "The Novel as Social Criticism," an eloquent defense of the problem or thesis novel. In her essay Petry eschews the idea that art ought to exist for its own sake and asserts that most of the world's greatest novelists, from Charles Dickens to Leo Tolstoy to William Faulkner, have written social criticism, for each suggests "how society affected the lives of his characters."

In 1953 Petry's novel *The Narrows* was published. It is set in the black section of a small Connecticut community. The plot centers around black Link Williams and his relationship with Camilo Treadway, daughter of the town's most revered white family and heiress to an industrial fortune. Some critics admired its memorable characterization and stylistic experimentation.

Children's Literature Generally unhappy with the lack of black nonfiction for juveniles, Petry wrote *Harriet Tubman, Conductor on the Underground Railroad* (1955). Dedicated to Petry's only child, Elisabeth Ann, *Harriet Tubman* is a moving and sensitive portrayal of the famous former slave and abolitionist who was personally responsible for delivering over three hundred slaves out of bondage in Dorchester County, Maryland. The book has a wealth of historical detail, and its informational value is increased by the clever manner with which Petry juxtaposes Tubman's private history with the public history of the nation during the years before the Civil War.

Petry's next two children's books were *Tituba of Salem Village* (1964) and *Legends of the Saints* (1970). *Tituba of Salem Village* tells the story of a female slave from Barbados who finds herself branded a witch and caught up in the hysteria of the Salem witch trials of the late 1600s. *Legends of the Saints*, illustrated by Ann Rockwell, presents in simple language the miraculous lives of ten holy people of varying nationalities and time periods.

Later Short Stories Reveal a Shift in Thematic Focus Petry produced some excellent short stories after 1953. "Has Anybody Seen Miss Dora Dean," published by *New Yorker* magazine in 1958, is a refreshing blend of humor, folklore, and suspense. One thinly disguised autobiographical story, "The New Mirror," which appeared in the *New Yorker* in 1965, and another, "Miss Muriel," the lengthy piece that became the title story of *Miss Muriel and Other Stories* (1971), show evidence of a new thematic thrust. "The New Mirror" tells the story of a black family in an all-white town and their attempts to maintain privacy in an environment where color keeps them constantly on display. "Miss Muriel," told from the perspective of a young black girl, is a romantic story with racial overtones. It depicts the pursuit of an attractive aunt by two lovers of different ethnic origins. Both stories make a powerful comment about the barriers that prevent meaningful human relationships in modern society.

Petry remained in Old Saybrook to raise her daughter until her death on April 28, 1997.

Works in Literary Context

Petry's dual personal history—living first in a middle-class community in Connecticut and then in Harlem—gave her an unusual literary vantage point from which she was able to isolate and dramatize essential aspects of the human condition that transcend geographical and racial boundaries. She credited the time she spent working as a journalist among the largest influences on her writing.

Naturalism Many scholars consider Petry's work strongly naturalistic. Its focus is on racism as an environmental force adversely affecting human lives so that its victims can neither understand nor control the devastating effects upon them and those they love. Like Theodore Dreiser, Jack London, Stephen Crane, and Frank Norris, she trained in journalism, and characteristic of her work from this period is a detailed documentary style. Her short stories and *The Street* parallel

LITERARY AND HISTORICAL CONTEMPORARIES

Petry's famous contemporaries include:

Richard Wright (1908–1960): Best known for *Native Son* (1940) and *Black Boy: A Record of Childhood and Youth* (1945), Wright was a seminal figure in black literature and one of the first writers to portray the dehumanizing effects of racism on blacks.

Margaret Walker Alexander (1915–1998): Alexander was an African American author, lecturer, and expert on the Harlem Renaissance of the 1920s.

Chester Himes (1909–1984): Himes was an African American author whose earliest novels, including *If He Hollers Let Him Go* (1945), are often identified as works of social protest; later writings are regarded as pleas for social reform.

Sterling Brown (1901–1989): Brown was an important American poet and critic and one of the first writers to infuse his poetry with black folklore.

Nella Larsen (1891–1964): Although she was less well known than other black writers of the Harlem Renaissance, Larsen has been highly praised for her two novels *Quicksand* (1928) and *Passing* (1929).

William Attaway (1911–1986): Attaway was an African American author who is most remembered for two novels: *Let Me Breathe Thunder* (1939) and *Blood on the Forge* (1941).

the work during the 1940s of Richard Wright, Chester Himes, William Attaway, and Willard Motley, African American naturalists.

While Petry's work has declined in popularity, her place in the history of American letters is secure. She continues to be regarded by critics and scholars alike as a powerful writer whose work is highly relevant to the climate of modern society.

Works in Critical Context

When Petry initially submitted her work to publishers, she received many rejections. However, she refined her craft considerably throughout her adult life and eventually achieved success when "On Saturday the Siren Sounds at Noon" was accepted for publication. Afterward, her works enjoyed increasing success and national acclaim, and her first novel was met with enthusiastic reviews. She achieved the height of her popularity during the 1940s and 1950s.

Reviews of The Street When *The Street* first appeared, it won generally favorable reactions and drew commendable reviews. Writing in *Phylon* (March–June 1947), Alain Locke deemed it "the artistic success of the year." Alfred Butterfield, *New York Times Book Review* critic, noted that the novel was "a work of close documentation and

COMMON HUMAN EXPERIENCE

Much of Petry's fiction concerns negative social dynamics in the United States that develop from racial prejudice against African Americans. Other works that explore this theme include the following:

Iola Leroy (1892), a novel by Frances Harper. The protagonist of this story, a mulatto woman, the child of a slave owner and a slave, refuses to conceal her racial identity but instead chooses to fight for racial equality.

The Autobiography of an Ex-colored Man (1912), an autobiography by James Weldon Johnson. In this work, the biracial author struggles in post-Reconstruction American to choose between expressing his racial identity as half African American and hiding in obscurity by pretending to be white.

Not Without Laughter (1930), a novel by Langston Hughes. In this story about the reality of being black in a small Kansas town during the 1920s, the protagonist Sandy struggles to live life in the face of racial prejudice and discrimination.

Black Boy (1945), an autobiography by Richard Wright. This book tells the story of the author's difficult experiences growing up in the racially prejudiced South.

Invisible Man (1952), a novel by Ralph Waldo Ellison. Because of racial prejudice and inequality, the narrator of this story, an African American man, feels socially invisible to mainstream culture.

intimate perception." Praising Petry for her artistry, he wrote, "It deals with its Negro characters without condescension, without special pleading, without distortion of any kind." Arna Bontemps, writing in the *New York Herald Tribune Weekly Book Review*, praised Petry for her "unblushing" realism and noted that it was "part of her achievement, however, that the carnal life of the slums never seems to be hauled in for its own sake." The general consensus seemed to be that *The Street* was, in the words of Henry Tracy (*Common Ground*, Summer 1946), "an outstanding novel from any angle." Even those who had begun to sour on social criticism acknowledged that Petry had breathed new life into the naturalistic novel. Noting the absence of sociological and political propaganda, and commending Petry for control and restraint, David Dempsey of the *Antioch Review* (September 1946) wrote: "Petry underscores her meaning with action rather than editorials and avoids the sentimentalization of character which one finds in such a 'protest' writer as Steinbeck."

While changing directions in literary taste in later decades have undercut the popular acclaim that she enjoyed in the 1940s and 1950s, Petry's works retain vitality for discriminating readers.

Responses to Literature

1. What effect(s) does Lutie's belief in the American Dream have on her life in *The Street*? Explain your view using examples from the novel.

2. In several places throughout *The Street*, Lutie alludes to Benjamin Franklin. What role does this allusion serve in furthering the novel's themes and why does the author choose Franklin?

3. Explain why Lutie abandons her child in *The Street*. Are her actions justified? Support your opinion citing examples from the text.

4. Analyze the ending of *The Street*. What statement, if any, do you think the author is trying to make about life for people in Harlem?

BIBLIOGRAPHY

Books

Christian, Barbara. *Black Women Novelists: The Development of Tradition 1892–1976*. Westport, Conn.: Greenwood Press, 1980.

Evin, Hazel Arnett. *Ann Petry: A Bio-Bibliography*. New York: G. K. Hall, 1993.

Gates, Henry Louis, Jr. "In Her Own Write." Forward. *The Schomburg Library of Nineteenth-Century Black Women Writers*. New York: Oxford University Press, 1988.

Holladay, Hilary. *Ann Petry*. New York: Twayne, 1996.

McKay, Nellie. "Ann Petry's *The Street* and *The Narrows*: A Study of the Influence of Class, Race, and Gender on Afro-American Women's Lives." *Women and War*, edited by Maria Diedrich and Dorothea Fischer-Hornung. New York: Berg, 1990.

Washington, Mary Helen. *Invented Lives: Narratives of Black Women, 1860–1960*. Garden City, N.Y.: Doubleday, 1987.

Periodicals

Greene, Majorie. "Ann Petry Planned to Write." *Opportunity* 24 (April–June 1946): 78–79.

Ivy, James W. "Ann Petry Talks about First Novel." *Crisis* 53 (January 1946): 48–49.

McDowell, Margaret. "The Narrows: A Fuller View of Ann Petry." *Black American Literature Forum*. 14 (1980): 135–141.

Shinn, Themla J. "Women in the Novels of Ann Petry." *Critique: Studies in Modern Fiction*. 16, no. 1 (1974): 110–120.

Weir, Sybil. "The Narrows, a Black New England Novel." *Studies in American Fiction* 15 (Spring 1987): 81–93.

Web sites

O'Donnell, Heather. *Ann Petry*. Retrieved November 21, 2008, from http://voices.cla.umn.edu.

❀ Marge Piercy

BORN: *1936, Detroit, Michigan*

NATIONALITY: *American*

GENRE: *Fiction, nonfiction, poetry*

MAJOR WORKS:

Going Down Fast (1969)
Woman on the Edge of Time (1976)
Gone to Soldiers (1987)
City of Darkness, City of Light (1996)
Sleeping with Cats (2003)

Overview

Marge Piercy's reputation as an important fiction writer began with the appearance of her first published novel, *Going Down Fast* (1969). Since then, she has lectured at over four hundred institutions, won countless awards for her work, and has taken her place in the history of American letters as an important feminist writer.

Works in Biographical and Historical Context

Growing Up in Inner-City Detroit Born on March 31, 1936, Marge Piercy grew up in inner-city Detroit as

Marge Piercy   *Piercy, Marge, photograph. © Jerry Bauer. Reproduced by permission.*

part of a patriarchal working-class family. Her father, Robert Douglas Piercy, who was born into a Presbyterian family but observed no religion, came from Welsh-English stock and grew up in a soft-coal mining town in Pennsylvania. He worked for Westinghouse all his adult life but was laid off for a year and a half during the Great Depression in the 1930s. Piercy's mother, Bert Bernice Bunnin Piercy, grew up in poverty and never finished the tenth grade. She taught her daughter to observe closely, value curiosity, and love books, fostering in her the characteristics that Piercy claims made her a poet and writer of fiction.

Early Career Shadowed by Divorce After attending public schools in Detroit, Piercy enrolled at the University of Michigan, winning Hopwood Awards for poetry and fiction in 1956 and for poetry in 1957. She earned her BA in 1957, having been elected to Phi Beta Kappa and Phi Kappa Phi. After earning an MA from Northwestern University in 1958, Piercy married Michel Schiff, a Jewish particle physicist, and went with him to live in France. Piercy ascribes the breakup of this marriage to Schiff's inability to pay serious attention to her writing. Divorced at twenty-three, Piercy supported herself with various part-time jobs: secretary, switchboard operator, department store clerk, artists's model, and instructor at the Gary extension of Indiana University (1960–1962). During this time she wrote several unpublished novels and also became active in the civil rights movement.

Second Marriage, to Robert Shapiro In 1962 Piercy married Robert Shapiro, a computer scientist. The open marriage that they established meant that other men and women often shared the house with them. Over the next few years the couple lived in Cambridge, San Francisco, and Boston. In spring 1965, Piercy and her husband moved to New York City, where she did research on the Central Intelligence Agency (CIA), helped found the North American Congress on Latin America (NACLA), and continued to be active in Students for a Democratic Society (SDS). As she continued writing and attempting to get her work published, Piercy and her husband became increasingly active in the anti-Vietnam War movement. Her time was consumed by these political and literary activities during 1969, the year in which her first published novel appeared. During this period, Piercy also published the first of seventeen volumes of poetry, *Breaking Camp* (1968).

Feminist Beliefs Find Literary Expression Growing out of her political involvement during the 1960s, *Going Down Fast* demonstrates how power corrupts even when it seems to represent progress. Such progressive developments as urban renewal and the building of a university extension may result in mere demolition, which Piercy likens to legalized rape. In *Going Down Fast* and the novels that followed, Piercy's radical beliefs about the oppression of women found literary expression.

Involvement in Women's Movement In the years following the publishing of *Going Down Fast* the political

LITERARY AND HISTORICAL CONTEMPORARIES

Piercy's famous contemporaries include:

Wendell Berry (1934–): American author acknowledged as a master of many literary genres, but whether he is writing poetry, prose, or essays, his message is always essentially the same: humans must learn to live in harmony with the natural rhythms of the earth or perish.

Sylvia Plath (1932–1963): Considered an important poet of the post–World War II era, Plath became widely known following her suicide and the posthumous publication of *Ariel* (1965), a collection containing her most startling and acclaimed verse.

Audre Lorde (1934–1992): American writer Lorde described herself as "a black lesbian feminist mother lover poet." She often expressed anger toward racial oppression, urban blight, and personal hardship in her poetry, but she has also cultivated a unique blend of hope and spiritual renewal.

Gregory Corso (1930–2001): American author best known as one of the Beat poets, though his place in the Beat movement was often considered secondary to such better-known writers as Allen Ginsberg, Jack Kerouac, and William S. Burroughs. Poems such as "Marriage" (1958) and "Bomb" (1958) secured Corso's place in the history of American poetry.

Linda Pastan (1932–): American author known for poetry in which she relates the battles of everyday life.

Gary Snyder (1930–): American author whose stature as both a counterculture figure and an innovative and important mainstream poet places him in an uncommon position in contemporary literature; he is the recipient of several literary honors and awards, including a Pulitzer Prize for his poetry collection *Turtle Island* (1974).

movement Piercy was part of gradually fragmented, and she became involved in the women's movement—writing articles, organizing consciousness-raising groups, and attending feminist functions. In 1971 Piercy and her husband moved to Cape Cod, where she still lives. Once there, Piercy's creativity and sense of peace blossomed. She discovered that she loved gardening, became active with local women's groups, and made frequent trips to Boston. However, Piercy's marriage began to fail, and she and Shapiro were divorced in 1980.

During these years, Piercy's fiction grew progressively stronger, and her intense interest in history and politics is again evident in *Dance the Eagle to Sleep* (1970). Classified as dystopian science fiction, the novel recalls the author's experiences as a member of SDS and anticipates her later interest in futuristic worlds. In *Small Changes* (1973) Piercy takes these ideas further, register-

ing the meager alterations in the lives of women in spite of the so-called radical movements of the 1960s.

In an autobiographical essay in volume one of *Contemporary Authors Autobiography Series*, Piercy says that her next novel, *Woman on the Edge of Time* (1976), arose from "a tension between the harshness of much of my earlier life and the gratitude I felt toward the land where I was living."

Piercy's works of the late 1970s and early 1980s emphasize the politics of city planning and the poet's sensual pleasure in such activities as gardening, making love, and cooking. For example, in *The Twelve-Spoked Wheel Flashing* (1978), she captures sense of place within a structure based upon the four seasons. Secure in love, Piercy employs a gentle wit while exploring the vicissitudes of political and domestic life. *Stone, Paper, Knife* (1983) contains poems championing nature, women, animals, and the pleasures of gardening, as well as pieces assailing such figures of oppression as the slum landlord, pornographers, and the military.

Third Marriage On June 2, 1982, Piercy married Ira Wood, whom she had known for six years. Early in their relationship they wrote a play, *The Last White Class* (1979), and poems. Later they wrote a novel, *Storm Tide* (1998). Piercy credits Wood with giving her an emotional and artistic security that nourishes her activism and her writing.

Later Fiction From the beginning Piercy's novels expressed a fundamental belief in the possibilities of freedom for all people, regardless of age, sex, race, religion, or sexual preference. She recognizes history as a continuing lesson in how people may exist together as true individuals while creating a stable society based on understanding and respect. Piercy continues to build on her progressive themes in her later fiction.

Piercy's next novel, *The High Cost of Living* (1978), is set in Detroit and focuses on the types of compromises a lesbian graduate student must make in her search for love, acceptance, financial security, and self-respect. *Vida* (1980), like *Dance the Eagle to Sleep*, is based on Piercy's experiences with SDS. In *Braided Lives* (1982), considered Piercy's most autobiographical novel, the conformist atmosphere of the late 1950s is evoked in intensely poetic language. *Fly Away Home* (1984) is perhaps Piercy's most successful attempt to combine political themes with domestic drama.

Gone to Soldiers (1987) takes a bold step forward from her previous work. The book is a war story that examines women's position in what has traditionally been masculine terrain. Piercy uses war to present a religious, gay, feminist-psychological slant on ethnicity. In *He, She, & It* (1991), language—specifically the power of naming—is central, as it often is in Piercy's work, and she speaks of failed relationships, violence, oppression, and humankind's inability to conserve and use well the habitable earth. In 1993 *He, She, & It* won the Arthur C. Clarke Award for Best Science

Fiction Novel published in the United Kingdom during the previous year. *City of Darkness, City of Light* (1996) views the French Revolution from a feminist perspective. The novel also focuses on the roots of modern feminism in the French Revolution, examining how revolutionaries abandon their original ideals as they become corrupted by power.

Throughout the late 1990s and early 2000s, Piercy continued to publish poetry and fiction but turned increasingly toward nonfiction work, including *So You Want to Learn to Write* (2001), her memoir *Sleeping with Cats* (2003), and *Pesach for the Rest of Us* (2007).

Works in Literary Context

Piercy is a prominent feminist writer whose political commitment informs her works, which focus on individuals struggling to escape restrictive social roles to realize personal potential. Frankly polemical, Piercy's colloquial, free verse poetry passionately excoriates such phenomena as sexism, capitalism, and pollution, using exaggerated imagery and unabashed emotionalism in service of her social commentary. Piercy's novels share these characteristics while concentrating on individuals often deemed marginal by mainstream American society, including working-class Jews, lesbians, urban African Americans, and immigrants of various nationalities. Although Piercy's depiction of the evils of poverty are often bleakly realistic, her works display a fundamental optimism in the power of the collective will expressed in political action.

Gender Politics Piercy is one of the best known of that group of American women writers who have created popular fictions about the changing face of radical America and, in particular, about changing perceptions of and about women. Piercy writes about, and on behalf of, radical political causes, but her main interest is in sexual politics. Taken together, her novels offer a feminist's eye-view of American history from World War II (*Gone to Soldiers*), through the 1950s (*Braided Lives*) to the heady days of the 1960s' student activism and anti-Vietnam war campaigns (treated retrospectively in *Vida*), and the raising of consciousness of the women's movement of the late 1960s and 1970s (*The High Cost of Living*, *Small Changes*, and *Fly Away Home*).

There seems to be a general consensus that by far the most interesting and accomplished of Piercy's novels is one of her earliest creations, *Woman on the Edge of Time*. Like much contemporary feminist fantasy fiction *Woman on the Edge of Time* uses the science fiction genre to enact the vision of women overcoming oppressive social and psychological conditions by transcending both the physical and ideological constraints of patriarchal society.

Works in Critical Context

"Almost alone among her American contemporaries, Marge Piercy is radical and writer simultaneously, her literary identity so indivisible that it is difficult to say where

COMMON HUMAN EXPERIENCE

In Piercy's writing and political activities she is particularly concerned with gender inequality and its implications for women. Other works that explore this theme include the following:

A Vindication of the Rights of Women (1792), a philosophical work by Mary Wollstonecraft. In this work the British author argues for educational opportunities for women, stating that they are human beings and not property.

A Room of One's Own (1929), an extended essay by Virginia Woolf. In this work, the author explores the status of women writers in a society where women are not afforded the same opportunities that are available to men.

The Second Sex (1949), a philosophical work by Simone de Beauvoir. In this work the author explores questions of gender construction and the implications of gender inequality for women.

The Feminine Mystique (1963), a nonfiction book by Betty Friedan. In this work, which was a highly influential part of the women's movement, the author argues that women lose their identities while believing that they must find meaning solely through the family identity.

The Handmaid's Tale (1985), a novel by Margaret Atwood. This novel is set in the near future in which a totalitarian theocracy has overthrown the United States government. The theocracy enforces a new social order that increases the existing subjugation of women, including the narrator, Offred, who tries to escape her life as an enslaved Handmaid.

one leaves off and the other begins," writes Elinor Langer in the *New York Times Book Review*. Piercy's moralistic stance, more typical of nineteenth- than twentieth-century writers, has alienated some critics, producing charges that she is more committed to her politics than to her craft. Other critics maintain that Piercy at her angriest is Piercy at her best.

For example, Piercy considers *Braided Lives* one of her best and most original works. In general, critics liked the writing too, but some note that the novel deals too excessively with the problems of women. Brina Caplan in a review for the *Nation* points out that *Braided Lives* seems "to accommodate almost every humiliation to which women are liable." Similarly, Katha Pollitt in the *New York Times* finds that Piercy "makes Jill & Company victims of every possible social cruelty and male treachery, usually more than once." Pollitt hails, however, Piercy's representation of female characters as fighters by noting that even those who did not survive the cultural oppression fought against the attitudes of the day. Pollitt concludes that the book "is a tribute to Piercy's strengths" and "by virtue of her sheer force of conviction, plus a flair for scene writing, she writes thought-provoking, persuasive novels, fiction that is both political and aimed at a popular audience but that is never just a polemic or just a potboiler."

Responses to Literature

1. Read Piercy's poem "Barbie Doll" from the collection *To Be of Use* (1973) and her essay "Through the Cracks: Growing Up in the Fifties" from *Part Colored Blocks for a Quilt* (1982). Can you relate to the social pressures Piercy criticizes? To what extent do you think these pressures on women (and men) have shifted since the 1950s?

2. Discuss the technical innovations that help create a nonsexist world in *Women at the Edge of Time*. Is such a world possible in the future and, if so, is there anything problematic about Piercy's vision of utopia?

3. Compare and contrast one of Piercy's early works with one of her later ones. How has her approach to issues developed or changed? Is the later work more or less powerful and convincing than the earlier one? Has the tone in which she writes changed?

4. Piercy is often described as an angry writer. To what extent does the emotional content of Piercy's work succeed in persuading readers to empathize with her message? Give several examples from her writing to support your answer.

BIBLIOGRAPHY

Books

Bartkowski, Frances. *Feminist Utopias.* Lincoln: University of Nebraska Press, 1989.

Freedman, Diane P. *An Alchemy of Genres: Cross-Genre Writing by American Feminist Poet-Critics.* Charlottesville: University of Virginia Press, 1992.

Hansen, Elaine Tuttle. "The Double Narrative Structure of Small Changes." In *Contemporary American Women Writers: Narrative Strategies*, edited by Catherine Rainwater and William J. Scheick. Lexington: University of Kentucky Press, 1985.

Hoegland, Lisa Maria. *Feminism and Its Fictions.* Philadelphia: University of Pennsylvania Press, 1998.

Jones, Anne Hudson. "Feminist Science Fiction and Medical Ethics." In *The Intersectional of Science Fiction and Philosophy*, edited by Robert E. Myers. Westport, Conn.: Greenwood Press, 1983.

Keulen, Margarete. *Radical Imagination: Feminist Conception of the Future in Ursula Le Guin, Marge Piercy, and Sally Miller.* New York: Peter Lang, 1991.

Kress, Susan. "In and Out of Time." In *Future Females: A Critical Anthology*, edited by Marlene Barr. Bowling Green: Bowling Green State University Popular Press, 1981.

Michael, Magali Cornier. *Feminism and the Postmodern Impulse: Post-World War II Fiction.* Albany: State University of New York Press, 1996.

Musleah, Rachel. *One on One: Portrait of Marge Piercy.* New York: Hadassah, The Women's Zionist Organization of American, Inc., 2000.

Ruddick, Sara. "Thinking Mothers / Conceiving Self." In *Representations of Motherhood*, edited by Donna Bassin, Margaret Honey, and Meryle Mahrer Kaplan. New Haven: Yale University Press, 1994, pp. 29–45.

Shands, Kerstin W. *The Repair of the World: the Novels of Marge Piercy.* Westport: Greenwood Press, 1994.

Thielmann, Pia. *Marge Piercy's Women: Visions Captured and Subdued.* Frankfurt, Germany: R. G. Fischer, 1986.

Walker, Sue, and Eugenie Hamner, eds. *Ways of Knowing: Essays on Marge Piercy.* Mobile, Ala.: Negative Capability Press, 1991.

Periodicals

Orr, Elaine. "Mothering as Good Fiction: Instances from Marge Piercy's *Woman on the Edge of Time.*" *Journal of Narrative Technique* 23 (Spring 1993): 61–79.

Sizemore, Christine W. "Masculine and Feminine Cities: Marge Piercy's *Going Down Fast* and *Fly Away Home.*" *Frontiers: A Journal of Women Studies* 13, no. 1 (1992): 90–110.

Web sites

Marge Piercy. Retrieved November 18, 2008, from http://margepiercy.com.

☸ Sylvia Plath

BORN: *1932, Jamaica Plain, Massachusetts*

DIED: *1963, London, England*

NATIONALITY: *American*

GENRE: *Poetry, fiction, short stories*

MAJOR WORKS:

Colossus (1960)

The Bell Jar (1963)

Ariel (1965)

The Collected Poems (1981)

Overview

Considered an important poet of the post–World War II era, Plath became widely known following her suicide in 1963 and the posthumous publication of *Ariel* (1965), a collection containing her most startling and acclaimed verse.

Sylvia Plath   *AP Wide World Photos*

Works in Biographical and Historical Context

Father's Death Leaves Lasting Damage   Born in Jamaica Plain, Massachusetts, Plath enjoyed what she described as an idyllic early childhood near the sea. Her father, a German immigrant, was a professor of entomology who was especially interested in the study of bees. But his sudden death from diabetes in 1940 devastated the eight-year-old Plath, and many critics note the significance of this traumatic experience in interpreting her poetry, which frequently contains both brutal and reverential images of her father as well as sea imagery and allusions to bees.

Mental Collapse and Partial Recovery   Plath began publishing poetry at an early age, in such periodicals as *Seventeen* and the *Christian Science Monitor*, and in 1950 she earned a scholarship to Smith College. After spending a month during the summer of her junior year in New York City as a guest editor for *Mademoiselle* magazine, Plath suffered a mental collapse, which resulted in her attempted suicide and subsequent institutionalization. Mental health care in the 1950s was vastly superior than at any point in the past, as various advocacy groups had succeeded in pushing through reforms in the late 1940s.

Still, treatment for depression was limited, and mental illness was stigmatized.

Plath later chronicled the circumstances and consequences of this breakdown in her best-selling novel, *The Bell Jar* (1963), a work considered groundbreaking for its open description of mental illness. Following her recovery, Plath returned to Smith and graduated summa cum laude. After winning a Fulbright fellowship to study at Cambridge University, Plath met and married Ted Hughes, an English poet. The eventual failure of their marriage during the early 1960s—and the ensuing struggles with severe depression that led to her suicide—are considered to have played crucial roles in Plath's most critically acclaimed poetry.

Posthumous Winner of the 1982 Pulitzer Prize
Plath's verse is well-represented in several different volumes. *The Colossus* (1960), the only book of her poems published during her lifetime, collects pieces dating from the mid- to late 1950s; *Ariel* contains poems selected by Hughes from among the many works Plath composed during the final months before her death; *Winter Trees* (1971) collects several more of the *Ariel* poems and reflects Hughes's plan to publish Plath's later works in intervals; *Crossing the Water: Transitional Poems* (1971) reprints most of her post-*Colossus* and pre-*Ariel* verse; and *The Collected Poems* (1981), which won a Pulitzer Prize in 1982, features all of her verse, including juvenilia and several previously unpublished pieces in order of composition.

Frustrations Displayed in Later Works   Critics generally believe that some of the later poems in *The Colossus* heralded a new phase in Plath's career. Generally speaking, Plath's later work displays the increasing frustration of her aspirations. Her ambitions of finding happiness through work, marriage, and family were thwarted by such events as hospital stays for a miscarriage and an appendectomy, the breakup of her marriage, and fluctuating moods in which she felt vulnerable to male domination and threatening natural forces, particularly death. After the dissolution of her marriage, Plath moved with her two children from the Devon countryside to a London flat, where Irish poet William Butler Yeats had once resided, and wrote feverishly from the summer of 1962 until her suicide in February of the following year. Plath was writing during a relatively conservative period that lasted from the end of World War II until the civil rights movement of the 1960s. In Western Europe and the United States, suburban development and the nuclear family became symbols of the era that were later sharply contrasted by the social revolution of the 1960s. Plath likely felt stymied by the constraints of a society that valued men's career goals more than women's.

Haunted by Her Past   Plath published *The Bell Jar*, which appeared shortly before her death, under the pseudonym of Victoria Lucas. She was unsure of the quality of

LITERARY AND HISTORICAL CONTEMPORARIES

Among Plath's famous contemporaries were:

Anne Sexton (1928–1974): An American poet and writer who, along with Plath, advanced the genre of confessional poetry.

Robert Lowell (1917–1977): Considered by many to be one of the best American poets of the twentieth century, the work of this American writer frequently concerns questions of history and the self.

Karl Jay Shapiro (1913–2000): A poet who won the Pulitzer Prize in Poetry for his work *V-Letter, and Other Poems* (1945).

Ted Hughes (1930–1998): An English poet and children's writer who served as the British poet laureate from 1984 until his death; over the course of his life, Hughes maintained a significant interest in the work of Plath, his one-time wife.

Simone de Beauvoir (1908–1986): A French author and philosopher who wrote an extended analysis of the oppression of women in her treatise *The Second Sex* (1949).

the work and feared that it might offend those people, particularly her mother, on whom the characters are based. This novel details a college student's disappointing adventures during a summer month in New York City as a guest editor for a fashion magazine, her despair upon returning home, her attempted suicide, and the electroshock treatments and institutionalization she undergoes to "cure" her of depression and lethargy. The narrator of *The Bell Jar* encounters many of the pressures and problems Plath examined in her verse: Her attempts to establish her identity are consistently undermined, she projects an ambivalent attitude toward men, society remains indifferent to her sensitivity, vulnerability, and artistic ambitions, and she is haunted by events from her past, particularly the death of her father.

Ultimately, Plath became overwhelmed by the trials of her personal life. By February 1963 her marriage was over and she was ill, struggling to care for her two small children in a cramped flat in London. Outside, the winter was the coldest the city had seen in decades. On Monday, February 11, she committed suicide.

Works in Literary Context

Plath's early verse reflects various poetic influences, evoking the mythic qualities of the works of William Butler Yeats and Ted Hughes, the diverse experiments with form and language of Gerard Manley Hopkins and W. H. Auden, and the focus on personal concerns that dominates the verse of Robert Lowell and Theodore

Roethke. Her later works are marked by the influences of her failed marriage and haunting past.

Themes of Despair and Mental Illness Through bold metaphors and stark, often violent and unsettling imagery, Plath's works present nature and human experience as mythic, or larger than life. Her vivid, intense poems explore such topics as personal identity, individual suffering and oppression, as well as the inevitability of death. Deeply informed by autobiographical elements, Plath's writings poignantly reflect her struggles with despair and mental illness.

Plath's *Ariel* poems reflect her increasing anger, bitterness, and despair toward life and feature intense, rhythmic language that blends terse statements, sing-song passages, repetitive phrasing, and sudden violent images, metaphors, and declarations. For example, in "Daddy," perhaps her most frequently discussed and anthologized work, Plath denounces her father's dominance over her life and, among other allusions, associates him with Nazism and herself with Jewish victims of the Holocaust: "I have always been scared of *you* / With your Luftwaffe, your gobbledygoo. / And your neat moustache / And your Aryan eye, bright blue. / Panzer-man, panzer-man, O You—." Plath explained in a radio broadcast that the poem's narrator is "a girl with an Electra complex. Her father died while she thought he was God."

Academic Interest in Plath's Unique Voice Plath's efforts to assert a strong female identity and to balance familial, marital, and career aspirations have established her as a representative voice for feminist concerns. While Plath is frequently linked with confessional poets Robert Lowell, Anne Sexton, and John Berryman, all of whom directly express personal torments and anguish in their work, critics have noted that many of Plath's poems are dramatic monologues voiced by a character who is not necessarily autobiographical. Although sometimes faulted as self-indulgent and preoccupied with death and psychological suffering, Plath continues to be read widely, and her work has generated numerous scholarly studies.

Journals, Verse Plays, and Short Stories The posthumous publication of Plath's writings in other genres, many of which were edited by Ted Hughes, reflects the continuing interest in her work. *Three Women: A Monologue for Three Voices* (1968) is a verse play originally presented on British radio in 1962, in which three women discuss pregnancy. *Letters Home: Correspondence, 1950–1963* (1975) reveals Plath's reactions to pivotal events in her adult life through the publication of letters she exchanged with her mother. *Johnny Panic and the Bible of Dreams, and Other Prose Writings* (1977) collects short stories and excerpts from her diaries in which Plath reworked the personal experiences, themes, and topics she frequently explored in her verse. *The Journals of Sylvia Plath* (1982), which includes most of the extensive diary entries Plath compiled during her lifetime, has received substantial critical attention. Katha Pollitt described this latter collection as "a storehouse of ideas for stories, novels, and poems; of stray phrases and incidents that would turn up, sometimes years later, in her finished work. They are the place, too, where she chronicled an almost unbroken parade of depressions, blocks, and visits of the 'Panic Bird,' and where she urged herself, over and over, year after dragging year, to throw herself into writing."

Works in Critical Context

Critics often maintain that during her brief career, Plath's verse evolved from an early style in which she seemed to model her work on that of other, earlier poets to a later display of a unique and accomplished poetic voice. Katha Pollitt commented: "Plath's was one of those rare poetic careers—Keats' was another—that moved consistently and with gathering rapidity and assurance to an ever greater daring and individuality." Although critical reception of her work *The Bell Jar* was mixed, reviewers praised the novel's satiric portrait of American society and its poignant study of the growing disillusionment of a talented young woman.

Building Sanity in the Ariel Poems Response to "Daddy" reflected the general critical opinion toward much of Plath's later work. Some critics contended that Plath's jarring effects are extravagant, and many objected to her equation of personal sufferings with such horrors as those experienced by victims of Nazi genocide. Others praised the passion and formal structure of her later poems, through which she confronts her tensions and conflicts. Some recent readings of her work have emphasized the connection between Plath's struggle to maintain her own unstable mental health and the thematic content of her poetry. Jon Rosenblatt wrote, for example, "What her poems reveal again and again is her tremendously violent struggle to gain control of the psyche. Each of Plath's poems portrays in different but parallel settings a momentary ordering of the symbols of life and death." Likewise, Stanley Plumly stated that "behind the separate masks, all the masks of [Plath's] good poems, there is a unity, an integrity, and an integrating of imagination— that whatever the hammer-splittings of the self, behind the sad mask of the woman is the mind and heart of someone making transcendent poems."

Responses to Literature

1. Analyzing specific passages from the text, discuss the reasons for Esther's madness in *The Bell Jar*.

2. Select a recurring image from *The Bell Jar*—like mirrors, blood, or trees—and trace the evolution of its meaning from its first appearance to its last.

3. Compare and contrast the imagery Plath uses in her poetry with that of her novel, *The Bell Jar*.

4. Discuss aspects of the feminine experience as they appear in Plath's poetry collection *Ariel*. What do these poems suggest about life for women in the 1990s?

COMMON HUMAN EXPERIENCE

Foremost among Plath's themes is mental illness. Other works that explore this theme include:

Madness and Civilization: A History of Insanity in the Age of Reason (1961), a nonfiction book by Michel Foucault. This work traces the shifting meaning of insanity in Western history.

One Flew over the Cuckoo's Nest (1962), a novel by Ken Kesey. Inspired by Kesey's tenure at a mental health facility, this story is narrated by a Native American, the Chief, who has been institutionalized in a mental hospital since World War II.

Girl, Interrupted (1993), a memoir by Susanna Kaysen. In this work, successfully adapted for film in 1999, the author describes her experiences receiving treatment for a borderline personality disorder as a patient in a psychiatric hospital.

"The Yellow Wallpaper" (1892), a short story by Charlotte Perkins Gilman. In this popular and disturbing short story, Gilman chronicles the experience of an apparently sane female writer whose husband and doctor insist on her mental illness—confining her to her room, preventing her from writing, and ultimately driving her mad.

BIBLIOGRAPHY

Books

Aird, Eileen M. *Sylvia Plath*. New York: Barnes & Noble, 1973.

Butscher, Edward. *Sylvia Plath, Method and Madness*. New York: Seabury, 1976.

Hobrook, David. *Sylvia Plath: Poetry and Existence*. London: Athlone, 1976.

Kroll, Judith. *Chapters in a Mythology: The Poetry of Sylvia Plath*. New York: Harper & Row, 1976.

Melander, Ingrid. *The Poetry of Sylvia Plath: A Study of Themes*. Stockholm: Almquist & Wiksell, 1972.

Meyering, Sheryl L. *Sylvia Plath: A Reference Guide, 1973–1988*. Boston: G. K. Hall, 1990.

Newman, Charles H., ed. *The Art of Sylvia Plath*. Bloomington: Indiana University Press, 1970.

Northouse, Cameron, and Thomas Walsh. *Sylvia Plath and Anne Sexton: A Reference Guide*. Boston: G. K. Hall, 1974.

Steiner, Nancy Hunter. *A Closer Look at Ariel: A Memory of Sylvia Plath*. New York: Harper's Magazine Press, 1973.

Wagner, Linda W., ed. *Critical Essays on Sylvia Plath*. Boston: G. K. Hall, 1984.

Wagner-Martin, Linda. *Sylvia Plath: A Biography*. New York: Simon & Schuster, 1987.

✸ George Plimpton

BORN: *1927, New York, New York*

DIED: *2003, New York, New York*

NATIONALITY: *American*

GENRE: *Nonfiction*

MAJOR WORKS:

Paper Lion (1966)

Overview

George Plimpton is best known as the cofounder of the *Paris Review* and as the author of *Paper Lion* (1966), a highly acclaimed account of his experiences in a professional football training camp. Plimpton occupies a unique niche in sports literature, one marked by his own participation in the sports he covers, sound reportage, and elegant prose.

Works in Biographical and Historical Context

Growing Up in New York   A New Yorker most of his life, George Ames Plimpton was born on March 18,

George Plimpton   *Plimpton, George, photograph. AP Images.*

1927, to Pauline (Ames) Plimpton and Francis T. P. Plimpton, a lawyer, who was appointed ambassador to the United Nations in the Kennedy administration (1961–1963). Plimpton attended St. Bernard's School and Phillips Exeter Academy, where he wrote for the student newspaper, the *Exonian*. At Harvard University, which he entered in 1944 and left to serve in the United States Army from 1945 to 1948, he became editor of the *Lampoon* (the college's humor magazine) before graduating with an AB in 1950. He earned an additional BA and MA from King's College, Cambridge University, which he attended from 1952 to 1954.

Co-founding the Paris Review   Along with several other Americans, including Peter Matthiessen and Donald Hall, Plimpton helped to found the *Paris Review* in 1953. The magazine established itself almost immediately as an influential American literary journal, and Plimpton remained its editor thereafter. The literary quarterly is best known for its probing interviews with contemporary novelists, poets, and dramatists, many of which Plimpton conducted in the early days of the journal. Also in those early years, Viking published his first book, *The Rabbit's Umbrella* (1955), which Plimpton wrote in Paris.

Vanderbilt Interview Begins Career in Sports Writing   Plimpton's sports writing career began after a chance meeting with a friend, Whitney Tower, a writer for the fledgling *Sports Illustrated* when Plimpton was in his early twenties and teaching at Barnard College. He was asked to write a piece on Harold S. Vanderbilt, whose J-Boats helped defend the America's Cup titles in the 1930s. Vanderbilt had proved to be an unforthcoming subject for other writers, but Plimpton relied on his Harvard ties to get an interview with the elder alumnus.

Career with Sports Illustrated Begins   An early piece, "Dreams of Glory on the Mound" (*Sports Illustrated*, April 10, 1961), later expanded to book form that same year in *Out of My League* (1961), began Plimpton's long-time relationship with *Sports Illustrated*. "Miami Notebook: Cassius Clay and Malcolm X," published a few years later in the June 1964 issue of *Harper's*, was the first of many pieces Plimpton wrote on the great heavyweight boxing champion, Muhammad Ali, formerly Cassius Clay.

The mid-1960s was a prolific period for Plimpton at *Sports Illustrated*. In "World Champion Is Refused a Meal" (May 17, 1965), he covered Cassius Clay (or more precisely Clay's trainer, Bundini Brown) on a private bus trip to Clay's Chicopee Falls, Massachusetts, training camp. In Yulee, Florida, the heavyweight champion of the world and his mostly Muslim entourage were refused a meal at a segregated restaurant. In "Celestial Hell of the Superfan" (*Sports Illustrated*, September 13, 1965), Plimpton offers a study of professional football's superfans. In contrast to the superfan piece, Plimpton wrote "But Why Me, Coach?" (*Sports Illustrated*, December 13, 1965) about the waiving of New York Giant defensive tackle Mike Bundra. Having bounced around with several clubs before losing his job again, Bundra saw his own woes mirrored by his relatives who called to console him.

In 1966 Plimpton had expanded his *Sports Illustrated* articles (as well as two other sections that appeared in the *New Yorker* and *Harper's*) on his experiences as a quarterback with the Detroit Lions into the best seller (twenty-four weeks) *Paper Lion*, which was later made into a movie. After learning about five plays of the Lions during a three-week training session, Plimpton got to play a series of downs during a preseason intersquad scrimmage.

Plimpton Named Contributing Editor Plimpton's reputation was growing quickly by the late 1960s. In 1967 he earned a distinguished achievement award from the University of Southern California and was also named contributing editor to *Sports Illustrated*. On March 28, 1968, at age forty-one, Plimpton married photography studio assistant Freddy Medora Espy. They had two children: Medora Ames and Taylor Ames.

His next book, *The Bogey Man*, appeared in 1968. With the financial backing of *Sports Illustrated*, Plimpton spent a month touring with the Professional Golfers' Association. The book covers his participation in the Bing Crosby National Pro-Amateur, the San Francisco Lucky, and the Bob Hope Desert Classic. Portions of the book appeared in several issues of *Sports Illustrated*. The book was reviewed favorably in general, but several critics, Dick Schapp among them, felt that it did not measure up to *Paper Lion*.

Eclectic Interests Plimpton published several non-sports-related books, including several collections of *Paris Review* interviews; three volumes of *The American Literary Anthology* (1968, 1969, 1970) with Peter Ardery; and *American Journey: The Times of Robert F. Kennedy* (1970) with Jean Stein. He served as associate editor of *Harper's* and contributing editor at *Food and Wine*.

Sports Coverage during the 1970s Several Plimpton books on sports were published during the 1970s. First came *Pierre's Book: The Game of Court Tennis* (1971) by Pierre Etchebaster, which Plimpton edited and for which he wrote the introduction. *Mad Ducks and Bears* (1973) addresses two seemingly unrelated subjects: the first is NFL linemen, in particular the Lions's offensive guard John Gordy (the "Bear" of the title) and defensive lineman Alex Karras (the "Mad Duck"); the second was Plimpton's diary as he prepared to play quarterback again, this time for the Baltimore Colts against the Detroit Lions, for a 1971 television special, *Plimpton! The Great Quarterback Sneak*. Some critics were critical of the two-pronged approach, arguing that it weakened the book considerably. Henry Aaron's record-breaking 715th home run was the occasion for "Final Twist of the Drama" (*Sports Illustrated*, April 11, 1974), which Plimpton later expanded into book form as *One for the Record: The Inside Story of Hank Aaron's Chase for the Home-Run Record* (1974).

Plimpton continued to contribute sports essays to *Harper's*. "Baseball Stories" (May 1976), which also appeared in *The Game and the Glory: The Commissioner's Official Bicentennial Volume* (1976), ruminated on the bullpen.

One More July: A Football Dialogue with Bill Curry (1977) utilizes Plimpton's great interviewing skills and seems to wrap up his decade-long infatuation with the game of football. The dialogues with Curry, who played professional football from 1965 to 1975, helped put a coda on a football era that was coming to an end just as a new one was beginning. The events in the book are recalled during a long car trip Plimpton took with Curry, whom he met during his brief foray with the Colts, as the two men travel from Lexington, Kentucky, to Green Bay, Wisconsin, where Curry, a former all-pro center, was hoping for one last shot with the Packers.

Shadow Box was also published in 1977; like Plimpton's other sports books, participatory or otherwise, it is an attempt by the author to understand a sport he really "never understood." The admission is not merely to feign ignorance but to acknowledge that one can never really get to know a sport or any subject—Plimpton has also tried his hand at stand-up comedy in Las Vegas, acting with John Wayne in the 1970 movie *Rio Lobo*, and guest conducting with the Cincinnati Symphony—unless one gets inside his material either by taking part in it or by studying it thoroughly.

Thus, in *Shadow Box* Plimpton returns to 1959 and his three-round exhibition bout with light heavyweight champion Archie Moore (in which he was assisted by an Ernest Hemingway-recommended trainer) and moves forward to a detailed account of the Muhammad Ali-George Foreman match in Kinshasa, Zaire, in 1974, in which the aging Ali reclaimed the heavyweight title. Plimpton also recalls the Ali he had profiled in an earlier essay for *Sports Illustrated*, "Return of the Big Bopper" (December 23, 1974), just after the 1974 fight, when the magazine named Ali "Sportsman of the Year."

Professional Recognition By the end of the 1970s and early 1980s, during which Plimpton received the Mark Twain Award from the International Platform Association and a few honorary degrees, he published a coffee-table book, *Sports!* (1978), with photographs by Neil Leifer, and *A Sports Bestiary* (1982), with cartoons by Arnold Roth, in which Plimpton lampooned such sports clichés as "the Cliffhanger."

When Plimpton was in his fifties, he turned one last time to participatory journalism to experience ice hockey. *Open Net* (1985) tells the story of his playing goaltender for the Boston Bruins.

An Elaborate Hoax Plimpton next published his first novel, *The Curious Case of Sidd Finch* (1987). The novel was the outgrowth (urged on by a six-figure advance

LITERARY AND HISTORICAL CONTEMPORARIES

Plimpton's famous contemporaries include:

Roger Kahn (1927–): Known to many as "the dean of sports writing," respected sports journalist Kahn gained nationwide attention with the publication of his memoir *The Boys of Summer* (1972).

Walter "Red" Smith (1905–1982): Smith was an American sportswriter who was awarded the Pulitzer Prize for Commentary in 1976.

Joan Didion (1934–): Didion is an American author respected as a novelist, screenwriter, and a writer of personalized, journalistic essays.

Dick Schaap (1931–2001): Schaap was an American author and broadcaster who wrote more than thirty books and served as a mentor and father figure for Bobby Fischer, world chess champion.

David Allen Chip (1927–2008): Chip was an English writer who served as editor-in-chief of Reuters and the Press Association; his passions included rowing, storytelling, and opera.

James Murray (1919–1998): Murray was an American sportswriter of the *Los Angeles Times* for more than thirty years.

Dave Anderson (1929–): Anderson is an American sportswriter who was awarded the Dick Schaap Award for Outstanding Journalism in 2005.

from Plimpton's publisher) of an April Fool's piece he had written for *Sports Illustrated* in 1985, which claimed that "a converted cricket-bowler from Pakistan" who could throw the ball 168 miles per hour had signed with the New York Mets. The article was part of an elaborate hoax (with the cooperation of the Mets organization and players), but it read like a straightforward work of investigative journalism, with interviews and biographical information on Finch's Harvard days and later life as an aspirant Buddhist monk. The story managed to fool the media for a short time and caused a minor controversy.

Exploring Other Interests in the 1980s Plimpton continued to edit and write non-sports books throughout the 1980s, including *Edie: An American Biography* (1982), about model and actress Edie Sedgwick, with Jean Stein; *D. V.* (1984), the memoir of Diana Vreeland, edited by Plimpton and Christopher Hemphill; and *Fireworks: A History and Celebration* (1984); as well as several additional *Paris Review Interviews* anthologies.

He also published a December 26, 1988, *Sports Illustrated* piece, "A Sportsman Born and Bred," which featured president-elect George H. W. Bush as an all-around American sportsman with perhaps the greatest sporting pedigree of any U.S. president since Theodore Roosevelt. "The Wild Blue Yonder" (*Sports Illustrated*, April 3, 1989) tells the story of "the upper reaches" of Madison Square Garden. The piece contrasts Plimpton's well-mannered sensibilities against the coarse, spontaneous actions of working-class hockey fans.

Searching for the "X-Factor" Plimpton, who was divorced from his first wife after twenty years of marriage, married Sarah Whitehead Dudley in 1991; they have twin daughters, Olivia Hartley and Laura Dudley. He also published more books in the 1990s: *The Best of Plimpton* a collection of various material, including several sports pieces; *The Norton Book of Sports* (1992), for which he selected the pieces and wrote the introduction and which allowed him to reintroduce his literary theories of sports; and *The Official Olympics Triplecast Viewer's Guide* (1992), a commemorative edition of the Barcelona Summer Olympics. In 1990 *The X-Factor* appeared, in which Plimpton attempted to define the qualities and character of the pure champion. His last sports book, for which he served as guest editor and wrote an introduction, was *The Best American Sports Writing, 1997.*

"The Man in the Flying Lawn Chair" Near the end of the century Plimpton continued to write about sportsmen, always searching for the new subject and the new adventure that would stretch his curiosity. In 1998 he profiled Larry Waters, "The Man in the Flying Lawn Chair" (*New Yorker*, June 1, 1998), who in 1982 had soared to 16,000 feet in a "Sears, Roebuck lawn chair to which were attached four clusters of helium-filled weather balloons, forty-two of them in all." Although Plimpton reluctantly agreed not to write about his flight (so that Waters could take advantage of lecturing before aviation clubs), Waters's suicide at a campsite near Mt. Wilson occasioned Plimpton to return to his subject, whose lonely death seemed to parallel his one great flight.

Plimpton died of natural causes in his sleep on September 25, 2003.

Works in Literary Context

Plimpton occupies a unique place in American letters as both the esteemed editor and cofounder of the *Paris Review*, a journal known for its author interviews, and as an award-winning sports journalist who participated in the sports he covered. He has attributed much of his success to his failure at Phillips Exeter Academy.

Participatory Journalism Whether playing tennis against Pancho Gonzales, swimming against Don Schollander, or playing for two minutes in a Boston Celtics game, Plimpton insists on engaging directly with the subjects of his writing. Over the course of his career, Plimpton covered and participated in nearly every professional sport in the United States. He first ventured into participatory sports journalism with *Out of My League*. Like in his other works, Plimpton sees himself as a sort of *espantaneo*, the man who hurls himself impulsively into the bullring to win the crowd's applause. The idea for the piece came from something James Thurber once wrote: "The majority of American males put themselves to sleep by striking out the batting order of the New York Yankees." While *Out of My League* deals with some of the arrangements, details, and technicalities involved in getting Plimpton actually on the mound to face American and National League all-stars in a postseason exhibition game, the book recounts no Walter Mittyesque triumphs but rather Plimpton's total humiliation, failure, and disappointment.

Likewise, the climactic moment of *Paper Lion*, Plimpton's most famous work, occurs when he plays in the game himself. "I *felt* myself a football quarterback, not an interloper," Plimpton notes. Yet, on the first play, despite his brief feelings of contentment and empowerment at the quarterback position, he realizes how out of his depth he is (a seasoned quarterback cannot take "the extra second" it takes Plimpton "to control the ball"). Finding himself in the path of one of his own blockers, Plimpton describes it as "coming around a corner in a high speed car to find a moose ambling across the center line." All of these events lead Plimpton to an epiphany as he hears applause upon leaving the field, which he believes was because he had played so poorly. Had he performed spectacularly, their cheers would have been disingenuous. "Their concept of things would have been upset. The outsider did not belong, and there was comfort in that being proved."

Works in Critical Context

Plimpton enjoyed popularity among both scholars and critics throughout his career as an editor, sportswriter, and small-time actor. Most critics consider *Paper Lion* to be his best work, and criticisms of his later work are often based on comparisons to it.

Critical Acclaim for Paper Lion Reviewers consider *Paper Lion*, Plimpton's book about his football adventures with the Detroit Lions, a classic of sports writing. It "is the best book written about pro football— maybe about any sport—because he captured with absolute fidelity how the average fan might feel given the opportunity to try out for a professional football team," explains Hal Higdon in *Saturday Review*. The book attracted sports fans not only through its innovative concept—a writer actually taking the field with a professional team— but also through the author's command over language. "Practically everybody loves George's stuff because George writes with an affection for his fellow man, has a rare eye for the bizarre, and a nice sense of his own ineptitude," declares Trent Frayne in the *Toronto Globe and Mail*. "[Ernest] Hemingway … [once] said, 'Plimpton is the dark side of the moon of Walter Mitty.'" Many writers echo Hemingway's statement. However, although Plimpton's adventures superficially resemble those of James Thurber's famous character, there are many differ-

<aside>

COMMON HUMAN EXPERIENCE

The world of professional athletics is a central concern in Plimpton's work. Other works that explore this theme include the following:

"Field Sports" (1742), a poem by William Somervile. This poem is about hawking, a sport in which participants use trained hawks to hunt other birds.

I Never Had It Made (1972), an autobiography by Jackie Robinson. The author tells of his journey to become the first African American to play professional baseball.

It's Not about the Bike: My Journey Back to Life (2001), an autobiography by Lance Armstrong with Sally Jenkins. The author tells of his struggle against cancer in the context of his career as a professional cyclist.

Seabiscuit: An American Legend (2001), a nonfiction book by Laura Hillenbrand. This work is about a thoroughbred racehorse named Seabiscuit who overcame a life of misfortune and became a sporting sensation during the Great Depression.

Amazing Pace (2006), a biography by Paul McMullen. In this work the author chronicles the career of U.S. swimmer Michael Phelps on his way to becoming one of the most successful Olympic athletes of all time.

Playing for Pizza (2007), a novel by John Grisham. In this story a quarterback who can no longer get work with the National Football League joins a semiprofessional team in Italy.

</aside>

ences between the two. "In his participatory journalism [Plimpton] has been described wrongly as a Walter Mitty, and he is nothing of the sort. This is no daydreaming nebbish," declares Joe Flaherty in the *New York Times Book Review*. Plimpton's adventures are tangible rather than imaginary. Yet, while Mitty in his dreams is a fantastic success at everything he undertakes, Plimpton's efforts almost invariably result in failure and humiliation. "Plimpton has stock in setting himself up as a naif … many of us are familiar with his gangling, tweedy demeanor and Oxford accent. He plays the 'fancy pants' to our outhouse Americana," Flaherty asserts. "George Plimpton doesn't want to be known as an athlete," explains Cal Reynard in the *Arizona Daily Star*. "He figures his role in sports is that of the spectator, but he wants to get closer to the game than the stands."

Responses to Literature

1. Discuss the type of language Plimpton uses in his most famous work, *Paper Lion*. What makes it accessible? What literary techniques does Plimpton use throughout the book?

2. Discuss the perspective Plimpton brings to professional football in *Paper Lion*. Does his writing shift your view of what it means to "participate" in sports as a spectator?

3. By the end of *Paper Lion*, Plimpton has failed as a quarterback and is pulled from the game. How does this ending impact your reading of the story?

4. Do you agree with Plimpton's belief that in order to really understand a sport (or any subject), you need to actively participate in it?

BIBLIOGRAPHY

Books

Aldrich, Nelson W. *George Being George: George Plimpton's Life as Told, Admired, Deplored, and Envied by 200 Friends, Relatives, Lovers, Acquaintances, Rivals, and a Few Unappreciative Observers.* New York: Random House, 2008.

Moore, Marianne. *A Marianne Moore Reader.* New York: Viking, 1965, p. 244.

Orodenker, Richard. *The Writers' Game: Baseball Writing in America.* New York: Twayne, 1996, pp. 113–199, 132–134, 159–160.

Periodicals

Nadel, Alan. "'My Mind Is Weak but My Body Is Strong': George Plimpton and the Boswellian Tradition." *Midwest Quarterly* 30 (Spring 1989): 372–386.

Severo, Richard. "George Plimpton, Urbane and Witty Writer, Dies at 76." *New York Times*, September 26, 2003.

"A Swinging Walter Mitty." *Time*, April 7, 1967, p. 40.

"Obituary, George Plimpton, American Writer and Madcap."*Economist* 369, no. 8345, (2003): 104.

Welton, Clark. "Paper Plimpton." *Esquire* (January 1976): 115–17, 142, 144, 146.

❂ Edgar Allan Poe

BORN: *1809, Boston, Massachusetts*

DIED: *1849, Baltimore, Maryland*

NATIONALITY: *American*

GENRE: *Fiction, nonfiction, poetry*

MAJOR WORKS:

The Narrative of Arthur Gordon Pym of Nantucket (1838)

Tales of the Grotesque and Arabesque (1840)

The Prose Romances of Edgar Allan Poe (1843)

Tales (1845)

The Raven and Other Poems (1845)

Edgar Allan Poe   *Poe, Edgar Allan, photograph.*

Overview

Edgar Allan Poe is recognized as one of the foremost progenitors of modern literature, both in its popular forms, such as horror and detective fiction, and in its more complex and self-conscious forms, which represent the essential artistic manner of the twentieth century.

Works in Biographical and Historical Context

Orphaned in Early Childhood Edgar Allan Poe was born on January 19, 1809. His mother was a minor actress named Elizabeth Arnold married to a sometime actor and reputed alcoholic, David Poe. By the time Edgar was three years of age, his father had mysteriously disappeared from the scene, and Elizabeth Poe was on her deathbed in Richmond, Virginia. Poe and his older brother, William Henry, and younger sister, Rosalie, were suddenly orphans. Poe was raised in the home of John Allan, a prosperous exporter from Richmond, Virginia, who never legally adopted his foster son. As a boy, Poe attended the best schools available and was admitted to the University of Virginia at Charlottesville in 1825. While there he distinguished himself academically but was forced to leave after less than a year because of bad debts and inadequate financial support from Allan.

Financial Trouble Limits Education   Poe's relationship with Allan disintegrated upon his return to Richmond in 1827, and soon after, Poe left for Boston, where he enlisted in the army and also anonymously published his first poetry collection, *Tamerlane, and Other Poems* (1827). The volume went unnoticed by readers and reviewers, and a second collection, *Al Aaraaf, Tamerlane, and Minor Poems* (1827), received only slightly more attention. That same year Poe was honorably discharged from the army, having attained the rank of regimental sergeant major, and was then admitted to the United States Military Academy at West Point. However, because Allan would neither provide his foster son with sufficient funds to maintain himself as a cadet nor give the consent necessary to resign from the academy, Poe gained a dismissal by ignoring his duties and violating regulations. He subsequently went to New York City, where *Poems* (1831), his third collection of verse was published, and then to Baltimore, where he lived at the home of his aunt, Mrs. Maria Clemm.

Money from Writing Fails to Pay the Bills   Over the next few years Poe's first short stories appeared in the *Philadelphia Saturday Courier*, and his "MS. Found in a Bottle" (1833) won a cash prize for best story in the *Baltimore Saturday Visitor*. Nevertheless, Poe was still not earning enough to live independently, nor did Allan's death in 1834 provide him with a legacy.

Rise to Prominence   In 1835 Poe's financial problems were temporarily alleviated when he accepted an editorship at the *Southern Literary Messenger* in Richmond. He brought with him his aunt and his twelve-year-old cousin Virginia, whom he married in 1836. The *Southern Literary Messenger* was the first of several journals Poe would direct over the next ten years and through which he rose to prominence as a leading man of letters in America.

Poe made himself known not only as a superlative author of poetry and fiction but also as a literary critic whose level of imagination and insight had hitherto been unapproached in American literature. While Poe's writings gained attention in the late 1830s and early 1840s, the profits from his work remained meager, and he supported himself by editing *Burton's Gentleman's Magazine* and *Graham's Magazine* in Philadelphia and the *Broadway Journal* in New York City.

Romantic Affairs and Mysterious Death   After his wife's death from tuberculosis in 1847, Poe became involved in a number of romantic affairs. It was while he was preparing for his second marriage that Poe, for reasons unknown, arrived in Baltimore in late September of 1849. On October 3, he was found in a state of semi-consciousness; he died four days later without regaining

LITERARY AND HISTORICAL CONTEMPORARIES

Poe's famous contemporaries include:

Henry Wadsworth Longfellow (1807–1882): Longfellow was an American author who was instrumental in introducing European culture to the American readers of his day. Moreover, he simultaneously popularized American folk themes abroad, where his works enjoyed an immense readership.

Margaret Fuller (1810–1850): American author, journalist, and feminist theoretician, Fuller is best known for her book *Woman in the Nineteenth Century* (1845); she was also a leading figure in the transcendentalist movement and edited its journal, the *Dial*.

Nathaniel Hawthorne (1804–1864): Hawthorne was an American novelist. His novel *The Scarlet Letter* (1850), with its balanced structure, polished prose style, and skillful use of symbols, is acknowledged as a classic of American literature; along with Poe, Hawthorne is regarded as one of the principal architects of the modern American short story.

Herman Melville (1819–1891): A major American literary figure of the nineteenth century, Melville is best known as the author of *Moby-Dick; or, The Whale* (1851), a complex metaphysical novel involving a quest for a white whale.

Charles Darwin (1809–1882): Darwin was an English naturalist whose book *The Origin of Species by Means of Natural Selection* (1859) is considered one of the most influential scientific works of all time.

Lord Alfred Tennyson (1809–1892): Considered one of the greatest poets of the English language, Tennyson was immensely popular in his lifetime, especially in the years following the publication of his lengthy elegiac poem *In Memoriam* (1850).

Elizabeth Browning (1806–1861): Browning was an English author best remembered for her masterful *Sonnets from the Portuguese* (1850), considered one of the most beautiful love cycles in English literature.

the necessary lucidity to explain what had happened during the last days of his life.

Works in Literary Context

Poe's stature as a major figure in literature is primarily based on his ingenious and profound short stories, poems, and critical theories, which established a highly influential rationale for the short form in both poetry and fiction. In his use of the demonic and the grotesque, Poe evidenced the impact of the stories of E. T. A. Hoffman and the Gothic novels of Ann Radcliffe, while the despair and melancholy in much of his writing reflects an affinity

COMMON HUMAN EXPERIENCE

The death of a loved one is a central focus throughout Poe's fiction. Other works that explore this theme include the following:

> *Othello* (c. 1622), a tragedy by William Shakespeare. Driven by jealousy to murder his wife, Desdemona, Othello is consumed by grief upon realizing she had not betrayed him as he was led to believe.
>
> "A Mother's Lament for the Death of Her Son" (1788), a poem by Robert Burns. As its title implies, a mother mourns the loss of her son, who has been taken from her by fate.
>
> *A Grief Observed* (1961), a poetry collection by C. S. Lewis. After his wife died of bone cancer, the author wrote these poems that reflect his experiences of loss and grief.

with the Romantic movement of the early nineteenth century. His early verse reflects the influence of such English romantics as Lord Byron, John Keats, and Percy Bysshe Shelley, while also foreshadowing his later poetry, which demonstrates a subjective outlook and surreal, mystic vision.

Art for Art's Sake Regarded in literary histories and handbooks as the architect of the modern short story, Poe was also the principal forerunner of the "art for art's sake" movement in nineteenth-century European literature. Whereas earlier critics predominantly concerned themselves with moral or ideological generalities, Poe focused his criticism on the specifics of style and construction that contributed to a work's effectiveness or failure. In his own work, he demonstrated a brilliant command of language and technique as well as an inspired and original imagination.

Psychological Realism Aside from a common theoretical basis, there is a psychological intensity that is characteristic of Poe's writings, especially the tales of horror that comprise his best and best-known works. These stories—which include "The Black Cat" (1843), "The Cask of Amontillado" (1846), and "The Tell-Tale Heart" (1843)—are often told by a first-person narrator, and through this voice Poe probes the workings of a character's psyche. In his Gothic tales, Poe also employed an essentially symbolic, almost allegorical method that gives such works as "The Fall of the House of Usher" (1840), "The Masque of the Red Death" (1842), and "Ligeia" (1838) an enigmatic quality that accounts for their enduring interest, as well as linking them with the symbolic works of Nathaniel Hawthorne and Herman Melville.

Science Fiction and the Detective Story In addition to his achievement as creator of the modern horror tale, Poe is also credited with parenting two other popular genres: science fiction and the detective story. In such works as "The Unparalleled Adventure of Hans Pfaall" (1835) and "Von Kempelen and His Discovery" (1849), Poe took advantage of the fascination for science and technology that emerged in the early nineteenth century to produce speculative and fantastic narratives that anticipate a type of literature that did not become widely practiced until the twentieth century. Similarly, Poe's three tales of ratiocination (or exact reasoning)—"The Murders in the Rue Morgue" (1841), "The Purloined Letter" (1844), and "The Mystery of Marie Roget" (1842)—are recognized as the models that established the major characters and literary conventions of detective fiction, specifically the amateur sleuth who solves a crime that has confounded the authorities and whose feats of deductive reasoning are documented by an admiring associate.

Poetry In some of his most famous poems—"To Helen" (1831), "Lenore" (1843), and "The Raven" (1845) in particular—Poe investigates the loss of ideal beauty and the difficulty in regaining it. These pieces are usually narrated by a young man who laments the untimely death of his beloved. "To Helen" is a three-stanza lyric that has been called one of the most beautiful love poems in the English language. The subject of the work is a woman who becomes, in the eyes of the narrator, a personification of the classical beauty of ancient Greece and Rome. "Lenore" presents ways in which the dead are best remembered, either by mourning or celebrating life beyond earthly boundaries. In "The Raven," Poe successfully unites his philosophical and aesthetic ideals. In this psychological piece, a young scholar is emotionally tormented by a raven's ominous repetition of "Nevermore" in answer to his question about the probability of an afterlife with his deceased lover.

The influence of Poe's tales may be seen in the work of later writers, including Ambrose Bierce and H. P. Lovecraft, who belong to a distinct tradition of horror literature initiated by Poe. Poe's poetry and short stories greatly influenced the French symbolists of the late nineteenth century, who in turn altered the direction of modern literature. It is this philosophical and artistic transaction that accounts for much of Poe's importance in literary history.

Works in Critical Context

While his works were not conspicuously acclaimed during his lifetime, Poe did earn due respect as a gifted fiction writer, poet, and man of letters, and occasionally he achieved a measure of popular success, especially following the appearance of "The Raven." After his death, however, the history of his critical reception becomes one of dramatically uneven judgments and interpretations. This state of affairs was initiated by Poe's one-time friend and literary executor R. W. Griswold, who, in a libelous obituary notice in the *New York Tribune* bearing the byline "Ludwig," attributed the depravity and psychological aberrations of many of the characters in Poe's fiction to Poe himself. In retrospect, Griswold's vilifications seem ultimately to have elicited as much sympathy as censure with respect to Poe and his work, leading subsequent biographers of the late nineteenth century to defend, sometimes too devotedly, Poe's name. It was not until the 1941 biography by A. H. Quinn that a balanced view was provided of Poe, his work, and the relationship between the author's life and his imagination. Nevertheless, the identification of Poe with the murderers and madmen of his works survived and flourished in the twentieth century, most prominently in the form of psychoanalytical studies, such as those of Marie Bonaparte and Joseph Wood Krutch. Added to the controversy over the sanity, or at best the maturity of Poe (Paul Elmer More called him "the poet of unripe boys and unsound men"), was the question of the value of Poe's works as serious literature. At the forefront of Poe's detractors were such eminent figures as Henry James, Aldous Huxley, and T. S. Eliot, who dismissed Poe's works as juvenile, vulgar, and artistically debased; in contrast, these same works have been judged to be of the highest literary merit by writers Bernard Shaw and William Carlos Williams. Complementing Poe's erratic reputation among English and American critics is the more stable, and generally more elevated, opinion of critics elsewhere in the world, particularly in France. Following the extensive translations and commentaries of Charles Baudelaire in the 1850s, Poe's works were received with a peculiar esteem by French writers, most profoundly those associated with the late nineteenth-century movement of symbolism, who admired Poe's transcendent aspirations as a poet; the twentieth-century movement of surrealism, which valued Poe's bizarre and apparently unruled imagination; and such figures as Paul Valery, who found in Poe's theories and thought an ideal of supreme rationalism. In other countries, Poe's works have enjoyed a similar regard, and numerous studies have been written tracing the influence of the American author on the international literary scene, especially in Russia, Japan, Scandinavia, and Latin America.

"The Raven"   Poe scholar Gary Richard Thompson notes in his book *Poe: Essays and Reviews* (1984) that in 1845 "when 'The Raven' first appeared in the January *Evening Mirror* [it was] an enormous popular and critical success, inviting many reprints and parodies." Ian M. Walker in his book *Edgar Allan Poe* (1997) goes so far as to declare that the poem's publication "made an impact unsurpassed by any previous American poem." However, not everyone was so impressed. Scholar Eric Carlson notes that the Nobel laureate William Butler Yeats denounced "The Raven" as "insincere and vulgar." In contrast, Charles Baudelaire noted in his introduction to the French edition of "The Raven," "It is indeed the poem of the sleeplessness of despair; it lacks nothing:

neither the fever of ideas, nor the violence of colors, nor sickly reasoning, nor drivelling terror, nor even the bizarre gaiety of suffering which makes it more terrible."

Contemporary Perspectives on Poe   In contrast to earlier critics who viewed the man and his works as one, criticism of the past twenty-five years has developed a view of Poe as a detached artist who was more concerned with displaying his virtuosity than with expressing his "soul," and who maintained an ironic rather than an autobiographical relationship to his writings. While at one time critics such as Yvor Winters wished to remove Poe from literary history, his works remain integral to any conception of modernism in world literature. Herbert Marshall McLuhan wrote in an essay titled "Edgar Poe's Tradition," "Poe never lost contact with the terrible pathos of his time. Coevally with Baudelaire, and long before Conrad and Eliot, he explored the heart of darkness."

Responses to Literature

1. How does the narrator's attitude toward the raven change throughout the poem "The Raven"? How does this shift relate to the narrator's experience of grief, isolation, and the loss of his love Lenore?

2. To what extent do you trust the speaker's memory of his relationship with Annabel Lee? Explain your answer using examples from the poem "Annabel Lee."

3. How does Poe establish the mood of "The Fall of the House of Usher"? Identify specific parts of the text that establish the tone of the story.

4. Explain Poe's use of the *doppelgänger*, or character double, in "The Fall of the House of Usher." What other literary techniques does he use throughout the story? What purpose do they serve?

BIBLIOGRAPHY

Books

Bittner, William. *Poe: A Biography*. Boston: Little, Brown, 1962.

Bonaparte, Marie. *The Lie and Works of Edgar Allan Poe: A Psycho-analytic Interpretation*, translated by John Rodker. London: Imago, 1949.

Gill, William Fearing. *The Life of Edgar Allan Poe*. New York: Dillingham, 1877.

Hutchisson, James M. *Poe*. Jackson: University Press of Mississippi, 2005.

Ketterer, David. *Edgar Allan Poe: Life, Work, Criticism*. Fredericton, New Brunswick: York, 1989.

Krutch, Joseph Wood. *Edgar Allan Poe: A Study in Genius*. New York: Knopf, 1926.

Mankowitz, Wolf. *The Extraordinary Mr. Poe*. New York: Simon & Schuster, 1978.

Meyers, Jeffrey. *Edgar Allan Poe: His Life and Legacy*. New York: Scribners, 1992.

Moss, Sidney P. *Poe's Literary Battles: The Critic in the Context of His Literary Milieu.* Durham, N.C.: Duke University Press, 1963.

Pope-Hennessy, Una. *Edgar Allan Poe, 1809–1849: A Critical Biography.* London: Macmillan, 1934.

Quinn, Arthur Hobson. *Edgar Allan Poe: A Critical Biography.* New York: Appleton-Century, 1941.

Silverman, Kenneth. *Edgar A. Poe: Mournful and Never-ending Remembrance.* New York: HarperCollins, 1991.

Symons, Julian. *The Tell-Tale Heart: The Life and Works of Edgar Allan Poe.* New York: Harper & Row, 1978.

Wagenknecht, Edward. *Edgar Allan Poe: The Man behind the Legend.* New York: Oxford University Press, 1963.

Whitman, Sarah Helen. *Edgar Poe and His Critics.* New York: Rudd & Carleton, 1860.

Winwar, Frances. *The Haunted Palace: A Life of Edgar Allan Poe.* New York: Harper, 1959.

Periodicals

Hoffman, Daniel. "The Artist of the Beautiful." *American Poetry Review* 24, no. 6 (November/December 1995).

Zimmerman, Brett. "A Catalogue of Selected Rhetorical Devices Used in the Works of Edgar Allan Poe." *Style* (Winter 1999).

Katherine Anne Porter   *Porter, Katherine Anne, 1940, photograph by George Platt Lynes. NYWTS / The Library of Congress.*

Katherine Anne Porter

BORN: *1890, Indian Creek, Texas*

DIED: *1980, Silver Spring, Maryland*

NATIONALITY: *American*

GENRE: *Fiction, nonfiction*

MAJOR WORKS:
Flowering Judas (1930)
Noon Wine (1937)
Pale Horse, Pale Rider (1939)
Ship of Fools (1962)
The Collected Stories of Katherine Anne Porter (1964)

Overview

Although her output was relatively small, Katherine Anne Porter was one of the most recognized and acclaimed American writers of short fiction of the mid-twentieth century. In 1966 she won both the Pulitzer Prize and the National Book Award for *The Collected Stories of Katherine Anne Porter* (1964), a collection comprising stories mainly written between 1922 and 1940.

Works in Biographical and Historical Context

A Roving Spirit Is Born Porter was born in Indian Creek, Texas. When she was two years old, her mother died, and the family moved to a farm in Hays County, near Austin, where Porter and her four siblings were reared by their paternal grandmother. This milieu provided the setting and characters for many of Porter's short stories. For example, Uncle Jimbilly and Nannie—emancipated slaves who appear in several works—are based upon two of the farm's domestic servants, and Porter's grandmother, Catherine Anne, often surfaces as the authoritative, strong-willed matriarch. After her grandmother died in 1901, Porter was sent to several convent schools in Texas and Louisiana, until, at the age of sixteen, she ran away to get married. This marriage, her first of four, ended in divorce, and Porter subsequently moved to Chicago, where she worked as a journalist and as a movie extra for Essanay Studios. Porter referred to herself as "a roving spirit," and her myriad travel experiences typically yielded the ideas for her stories.

Inspired by Mexico and Europe In 1918, while employed as the drama critic for the *Rocky Mountain*

News in Denver, Colorado, Porter fell ill with influenza. The virus was life-threatening and caused her hair to turn white, an ordeal that later formed the basis for *Pale Horse, Pale Rider* (1939). After a brief, unhappy stint as a ghost writer while living in New York City's Greenwich Village, Porter traveled to Mexico, where she studied art and became involved in the Obregon Revolution of 1920, a movement to overthrow the regime of President Venustiano Carranza, who had failed to move Mexico toward social reform. The revolutionary program of educational, agrarian, and labor reorganization intrigued Porter and influenced the nature of social commentary in her works. Porter's first published short story, "Maria Concepcion" (1922), and several other early tales take place in Mexico—the country Porter felt she knew best.

During the 1920s, Porter's stories appeared in the literary journals *Century Magazine*, *Hound and Horn*, and the *Virginia Quarterly Review*, and were later collected in *Flowering Judas* (1930), her first volume of short fiction. The stories won Porter critical acclaim and a Guggenheim fellowship that allowed her to travel extensively in Europe for many years. A cruise to Germany in 1932, where she met, among others, Adolf Hitler and Hermann Goering, inspired her only novel, *Ship of Fools* (1962). Although she generally disliked Germany, Porter stayed there for a year following her cruise, and her experiences later rendered material for "The Leaning Tower" (1941), a short story concerning an American expatriate in Nazi Germany.

After leaving Berlin in 1933, Porter lived in Paris, and the four years she spent there greatly influenced her life and career. In Paris, Porter renewed many literary acquaintances and developed several lifelong friendships, most notably with such authors as Glenway Wescott and Ford Madox Ford. Porter also remarried, and her writing flourished. Such nostalgic works as *Old Mortality* (1937), "The Witness," and "The Grave" were composed or developed in Paris, and the distance and contrast of the city from Porter's native Texas gave her a fresh perspective on her childhood that allowed her to write of it with genuine warmth. Porter's perspective on her strict Southern upbringing was so changed that when she returned to the United States in 1936, she visited her family for the first time in eighteen years.

Commercial Success Brings Financial Independence

Porter continued to travel in America, and the books that evolved in Paris, *Pale Horse, Pale Rider* and *The Leaning Tower, and Other Stories* (1944), were eventually published. Porter's critical acclaim brought her employment offers from many universities, and for years she earned income as both a lecturer and a writer-in-residence. With the publication and commercial success of *Ship of Fools*, Porter became financially independent, drastically reduced her speaking appearances, and moved to College Park, Maryland. Her final work, *The Never-Ending Wrong* (1977), was published when she was eighty-seven and concerns the

LITERARY AND HISTORICAL CONTEMPORARIES

Porter's famous contemporaries include:

Robert Penn Warren (1905–1989): American author who received Pulitzer Prizes for both fiction and poetry, Warren was appointed by the Library of Congress as the first poet laureate of the United States in 1986.

Allen Tate (1899–1979): Tate was an American poet associated with the Fugitives, the small group of southern poets who were led by John Crowe Ransom at Vanderbilt University in Nashville during the early 1920s.

Glenway Wescott (1901–1987): Wescott was an American author whose current reputation as a stylist is based primarily on *The Pilgrim Hawk: A Love Story* (1940). He was a friend of Katherine Anne Porter and wrote long essays about her and other authors.

Ezra Pound (1885–1972): Among the foremost literary figures of the twentieth century, Pound is credited with creating some of modern poetry's most enduring and inventive verse.

James Joyce (1882–1941): An Irish author considered to be one of the most prominent English-speaking literary figures of the first half of the twentieth century, Joyce's virtuoso experiments in prose contributed to a redefinition of the form of the modern novel.

T. S. Eliot (1888–1965): As an eminent poet, critic, and playwright, Eliot has maintained an influence upon literature that some critics claim is unequaled by any other twentieth-century writer. His poetry and prose are frequently cited as having helped inaugurate the modern period in English and American letters.

Sacco and Vanzetti murder trial. Written from fifty-year-old notes that detail conversations Porter had with policemen, journalists, and protesters, *The Never-Ending Wrong* reflects Porter's concern with what she termed the "political injustice" involved in the case. Porter's lifelong pursuit to complete a biography of Cotton Mather remained unrealized when she died after a succession of cerebral hemorrhages in 1980, at the age of ninety.

Works in Literary Context

Porter is widely acknowledged as one of the finest modern authors of short fiction. Writing in an unadorned prose style, Porter endowed her works with vivid, sensitive characterizations and garnered much critical praise for her arresting blend of imagery, detail, and subtle irony. Her stories often revolve around the relationships and emotions of her characters and explore such concerns as the differences between appearance and reality and the consequences of self-deception. Porter's perceptive psychological studies typically draw from personal experience and depend

COMMON HUMAN EXPERIENCE

Betrayal in human relationships plays a central role in Porter's fiction. Other works that explore this theme include the following:

The Gospel of John (c. 90–100 CE), a religious text ascribed to John the Evangelist. This work contains the story of Judas, one of the disciples of Jesus who betrayed him for monetary gain.

The Divine Comedy (c. 1320), an epic poem by Dante Alighieri. In this work the innermost circle of hell is reserved for those who have committed acts of betrayal.

Sense and Sensibility (1811), a novel by Jane Austen. Compromised by the loss of their provider, the Dashwood women move into a cottage in Devonshire, the setting where many characters experience the pain of betrayal in their intimate relationships with lovers and friends.

on moments of illumination to express the essence of an incident. She is perhaps most highly regarded for her lengthier works of short fiction, particularly the novellas *Noon Wine* (1937) and *Pale Horse, Pale Rider*, which emphasize personal consequences within a social context.

Psychological Fiction George Hendrick observed that from the beginning of her career, Porter sought to "explore the human heart and mind and society itself, without lapsing into popular clichés." Porter often realized this ideal through treatment of grim, uncomfortable realities. The stories in *Flowering Judas*, for example, are united by the theme of betrayal. *Pale Horse, Pale Rider* is composed of three novellas that explore the uneasy correlations between life and death. *Old Mortality* is an ironic work that probes the authenticity of a family legend from the point of view of Miranda, a young girl commonly acknowledged as Porter's fictional counterpart. Throughout the story, Miranda becomes increasingly aware of her elders' misconceptions of the past, and *Old Mortality* ends as Miranda, determined not to repeat the mistakes of her family, naively makes a vow to live life free of illusion and deception. Porter continued her portrayal of Miranda in *Pale Horse, Pale Rider*, a treatment of wartime psychology set in Denver during World War I. In *Noon Wine*, which many contemporary critics consider her most outstanding work, Porter shifts the focus of her central theme of betrayal to a complex, cerebral study of murder. In her final short story collection, *The Leaning Tower*, Porter contemplates the constant change and growth of human relationships, often using a character's personal experience to represent the greater failures or triumphs of humanity.

Porter was an important influence on the generation of writers that followed her, including William Humphrey, William Goyen, Tillie Olsen, Carson McCullers, Flannery O'Connor, and Eudora Welty.

Works in Critical Context

During Porter's lifetime, critical response was skewed by her flamboyant personality and by the distortions in her biographical record. She was seen as an aristocratic daughter of the Old South whose depictions of "plain" people were excursions into foreign territory. Critics treated her in a manner befitting an exquisite Southern belle, vying in their praises. She was subjected to little rigorous criticism, but her work was the focus of close readings, which led to minor shifts in emphasis in the interpretations of her stories. Although she received pervasive critical acclaim during her career, she never enjoyed wide readership or financial success until she wrote *Ship of Fools*. Ironically, critics concluded from the novel that Porter's excellence in short fiction could not be sustained in a longer work.

With the revival of interest in women's writing in the wake of the feminist movement, much of Porter's body of work was collected or republished in response to the reconsideration of her work by scholars. Commenting on the reasons for the reexamination of Porter's work only after a long period of neglect, Reynolds Price has this to say in the *New York Times Book Review*: "Porter's stories take an aim as accurate and deadly as Nathaniel Hawthorne's, and her prose is leaner, for dissecting deeper. The results are dazzling."

Collected Stories Porter's reputation rests firmly on the strength of the twenty-seven stories included in her *Collected Stories*, which are marked by an economy of style and a controlled portrayal of character and emotion. Laurie Johnston notes in the *New York Times* that Porter's "storytelling had a quality of translucence—a smoothly polished, surface objectivity that nevertheless moved the reader to share the underlying turmoil of her characters and their often frightening interrelationships." Robert Penn Warren in the *Washington Post* states that Porter was "certainly unsurpassed in our century or country—perhaps any time or country—as a writer [of] fiction in the short forms of story or novella. ... Her work remains a monument to a tremendous talent—even genius."

Responses to Literature

1. Discuss the theme of betrayal in Porter's short story "Flowering Judas." To what extent does Laura commit an act of betrayal? Who or what else is betrayed in the story?

2. How does Porter's novel *Ship of Fools* relate to the traditional allegory of the same name? How does the story and theme differ?

3. Analyze the strengths and weaknesses of Granny in "The Jilting of Granny Weatherall." Identify key points in the story where her character traits are revealed.

4. What literary techniques does Porter use in *Pale Horse, Pale Rider* to portray Miranda's character? To what extent are they effective?

BIBLIOGRAPHY

Books

Brinkmeyer, Robert H. *Katherine Anne Porter's Artistic Development: Primitivism, Traditionalism, and Totalitarianism.* Baton Rouge: Louisiana State University Press, 1993.

DeMouy, Jane. *Katherine Anne Porter's Women: The Eyes of Her Fiction.* Austin: University of Texas Press, 1983.

Emmons, Wilfred S. *Katherine Anne Porter: The Regional Stories.* Austin, Tex.: Steck-Vaughn, 1967.

Givner, Joan. *Katherine Anne Porter: A Life.* New York: Simon & Schuster, 1982.

Hendrick, Willene, and George. *Katherine Anne Porter.* Rev. ed. Boston: Twayne, 1988.

Hilt, Kathryn. *Katherine Anne Porter: An Annotated Bibliography.* New York: Garland, 1990.

Lopez, Enrique Hank. *Conversations with Katherine Anne Porter: Refugee from Indian Creek.* Boston: Little, Brown, 1981.

Unrue, Darlene Harbour. *Truth and Vision in Katherine Anne Porter's Fiction.* Athens: University of Georgia Press, 1985.

Warren, Robert Penn, ed. *Katherine Anne Porter: A Collection of Critical Essays.* Englewood Cliffs, N.J.: Prentice-Hall, 1979.

Periodicals

Allen, Charles A. "Katherine Anne Porter: Psychology as Art." *Southwest Review* 41 (Summer 1956): 223–230.

Core, George. "The Best Residuum of Truth." *Georgia Review* 20 (Fall 1966): 278–291.

Curley, Daniel. "Katherine Anne Porter: The Larger Plan." *Kenyon Review* 25 (Autumn 1963): 671–695.

Givner, Joan. "The Genesis of *Ship of Fools.*" *Southern Literary Journal* 10 (Fall 1977): 14–30.

Hartley, Lodwick. "Katherine Anne Porter." *Sewanee Review* 48 (April 1940): 206–216.

Johnson, James William. "Another Look at Katherine Anne Porter." *Virginia Quarterly Review* 36 (Autumn 1960): 598–613.

Perry, Robert L. "Porter's 'Hacienda' and the Theme of Change." *Midwest Quarterly* 6 (Summer 1965): 403–415.

Schwartz, Edward Greenfield. "The Way of Dissent: Katherine Anne Porter's Critical Position." *Western Humanities Review* 8 (Spring 1954): 119–130.

Stein, William Bysshe. "'Theft': Porter's Politics of Modern Love." *Perspective* 11 (Winter 1960): 223–228.

Walsh, Thomas F. "Deep Similarities in 'Noon Wine.'" *Mosaic* 9 (Fall 1975): 83–91.

———. "Xochitl: Katherine Anne Porter's Changing Goddess." *American Literature* 52 (May 1980): 183–193.

Warren, Robert Penn. "Katherine Anne Porter (Irony with a Center)." *Kenyon Review* 4 (Winter 1942): 29–42.

■ William Sydney Porter

SEE *O. Henry*

◉ Chaim Potok

BORN: *1929, The Bronx, New York*

DIED: *2002, Merion, Pennsylvania*

NATIONALITY: *American*

GENRE: *Fiction*

MAJOR WORKS:
The Chosen (1967)
I Am Asher Lev (1972)
I Am the Clay (1992)

Chaim Potok   *Potok, Chaim, photograph. © Jerry Bauer. Reproduced by permission.*

Overview

Chaim Potok was a novelist, rabbi, and critical scholar of Judaic texts. His work, notably the novel *The Chosen*, strives to show characters in relation to God and to dramatize the importance of religion in a secular age and society.

Works in Biographical and Historical Context

Early Life Chaim Potok was born Herman Harold Potok on February 17, 1929, in New York City, to Polish Jewish immigrants Mollie Friedman and Benjamin Max Potok. His Hebrew name, Chaim (which means "alive" or "life") was the one he used personally and professionally. He spent his formative years in a traditional Jewish home (Mollie was descended from a prominent Hasidic dynasty) and he attended Jewish schools. He was instructed in secular subjects, as mandated by the state, but also well educated in Jewish religious texts. Potok was shielded from the secular world and later called his upbringing "essentially a fundamentalist" one, both "repressive and joyous." A natural aptitude for art—he harbored ambitions to become a painter—was dismissed by his parents as foolishness, a distraction from his Talmudic studies.

He had a transformative experience in early adolescence, when he furtively read Evelyn Waugh's *Brideshead Revisited* (1945), and then *Portrait of the Artist as a Young Man* (1916) by James Joyce. These works greatly influenced his decision to become a writer. Potok recognized in Waugh's writing the capacity of literature to transport readers into cultural environments foreign from their own. He determined that fiction would be his vehicle to present Jewish civilization in American literature. With that end in mind, he undertook a rigorous religious and secular education at Yeshiva University, where he earned a BA summa cum laude in 1950. His determination to write held, even with the knowledge that, at some point, his relationships with family and community would suffer.

His studies at Jewish Theological Seminary of America, a Conservative school (actually more liberal than his Orthodox upbringing), where he received rabbinic ordination in 1954, were very upsetting to his family. Potok was forced to create a new life and community from scratch, but he was able to devote himself to writing. He took up a Judaic professional role in conjunction with that of the creative artist. He served as a U.S. Army chaplain in Korea with a front-line medical battalion and a combat engineer battalion from 1955 to 1957. He married Adena Sarah Mosevitzky upon his return to the United States. He also taught at the university level, and served as editor-in-chief of the Jewish Publication Society, the beginning of a distinguished career in Jewish literary letters. Potok also earned a PhD in philosophy at the University of Pennsylvania in 1965.

Novel as Tool In 1967, Potok's first novel, *The Chosen*, was published. *The Chosen* examines modern Orthodox Jewish identity in America, and religious conflict in the Crown Heights and Williamsburg sections of Brooklyn, an area that was heavily populated by Jews. The antagonists are Hasidim, known for their mystical interpretation of Judaic sources and intense devotion to their spiritual leaders, and Orthodox Jews, who emphasize a rational, intellectual approach to Judaic law and theology. The supportive relationship that later develops between two boys, one Hasidic and the other Orthodox, begins in strife, dramatized in a quintessentially American baseball rivalry. The novel chronicles the boys' experiences and reactions as sons of fathers who strive to sustain religious life and tradition in a predominantly secular age and society.

In addition to using religious and scholarly interests to authenticate the lives of the characters in *The Chosen*, Potok parallels his youths' inner quests for Jewish identity with historic events: the Nazi mission to destroy Jewry and the search for physical and spiritual salvation in a Jewish national homeland. Although the Holocaust remains a muted topic in this first novel, it is presented as a hovering pestilence in the larger context of America at war. Potok links the Holocaust and the creation of the State of Israel, a theme to which he will return in later works. The final third of the novel is narrated in the context of the struggle to create and maintain the state of Israel, and the experiences of the characters are intimately bound with that of Israel. *The Chosen* was notably the first book published in the United States that closely examined Hasidic Jewry in America. It was a best-seller, adapted as both a film and a musical, and was a finalist for the National Book Award.

I Am Asher Lev Potok would write a sequel to *The Chosen*, then embark on his third novel, *I Am Asher Lev*, about the coming-of-age of an artist living in a Hasidic society inherently hostile to his vocation. Asher Lev rejects his designated role of Hasidic emissary for his career as an artist. Potok again uses the first-person narrative of his previous novels and achieves immediacy and vividness through the artist's retrospective portrait of his childhood. The pretext for the narrative is Lev's response to Hasidic detractors, with whom he has become notorious due to a painting of his that particularly upset his community. The mature Lev offers a reexamination of his attitudes and the external forces that shaped his vision and judgment. Although Lev remains an observant Jew, the community judges him guilty of betraying his religious heritage and encroaching upon a tradition sacred to Christianity.

Beyond disappointment in their son's failure to work in behalf of Jewish causes, the Levs despair of his dedication to art, considering it blasphemous at worst and mere indulgence of personal vanity at best. This is a thematic element almost identical to Potok's own past, except that Asher persistently defies his father's demand that he sacrifice art to religion, and a deep rift develops between them. Asher Lev shares with James Joyce's Stephen Dedalus the knowledge that his vocation as an artist demands a period of exile. Potok, like Joyce, treats the artist's isolation and alienation from family, school, and religious community, culminating in exile, as a progressive step that will lead to reconciliation of the artist's spiritual and aesthetic natures.

Life as Scholar, Novelist Chaim Potok, in his post as editor of the Jewish Publication Society of America, spent a great deal of his life in scholarly pursuits, in addition to returning to his love of painting. He published six novels and two works of non-fiction. In 2002 he succumbed to brain cancer and died in Merion, Pennsylvania, at the age of seventy-three.

Works in Literary Context

Jewish Literature Commitment to Judaism and the influence of Evelyn Waugh, James Joyce, and Flannery O'Connor are evident in Potok's efforts to show characters in relation to God and to dramatize the importance of religion in a secular age and society. The genesis and substance of almost every Potok novel is Jewish religious, historic, and cultural experience in a non-Judaic world. Potok's philosophical and ethical views—his affirmative vision, veneration of life, positive assessment of human nature, and pervasive striving for meaning in the midst of chaos and for good in the face of evil—derive from Judaism. He joins other Jewish American novelists in advocating the Jewish view of a sanctified world and enduring and noble humanity, revealing a vital philosophy to counter twentieth-century alienation and despair. His characters are conversant with Jewish theology, liturgy, and rabbinic commentaries, and it is through these intellectual resources and their life experiences that they strive to comprehend the human condition. Michael Chabon, the Pulitzer Prize–winning author of *The Amazing Adventures of Kavalier and Clay* (2000) is an heir to Potok's unique melding of Jewish themes and secular ones, in addition to his focus on father-son relationships.

The Coming-of-Age Novel Potok's novels, while not technically marketed for young adults, are books that can appeal to sensitive young people. *The Chosen* is his most poignant effort at a coming-of-age novel, but in a rare occurance of a Potok book featuring a female protagonist, *Davita's Harp* is also a stirring look into the life of a girl in the Hasidic world. Jonathan Safran Foer's much-lauded *Everything is Illuminated* (2002), with its themes of a young man seeking his Jewish identitiy, and indeed his identity in the larger world, have much in common with Potok's characters.

Works in Critical Context

Critical response to Potok's writing has ranged from denunciation to acclaim, with the bulk of the response falling in the latter category. Potok's detractors frequently

LITERARY AND HISTORICAL CONTEMPORARIES

Chaim Potok's famous contemporaries include:

Saul Bellow (1915–2005): A Jewish American novelist and Nobel Prize winner, Bellow is best known for *The Adventures of Augie March* (1953) and *Humboldt's Gift* (1975).

Flannery O'Connor (1925–1964): O'Connor was an American author whose Southern Gothic novels and short stories, including *Wise Blood* (1952), brought her literary acclaim.

Jack Kerouac (1922–1969): An American author, Kerouac was one of the principal founders of the Beat movement, and he is known for his 1957 novel *On the Road*.

Joan Didion (1923–2007): American novelist and essayist Didion is the author, among other works, of the non-fiction collection *Slouching Towards Bethlehem* (1968), which is about her time in California.

George H. W. Bush (1924–): The forty-first American president (1989–93), a Republican, Bush was defeated in his bid for a second term by Bill Clinton, who was succeeded by Bush's son, George W. Bush, in 2001.

center their criticism on the novelist's style, charging him with composing banal speech and employing a pompous tone. Others have complained about the predictability and lack of complexity in his characters. In the November 1967 *Midstream*, Curt Leviant judges the dialogue between the young men of *The Chosen* "more like a mature man's bookish presumption of what their talk should sound like than authentic speech itself" and objects to Potok's rendition of Hasidim as void of humor and zest for life. Most often, Potok is extolled for examining serious social, philosophical, and theological problems and praised for his concern with ideas and issues. In the *New York Times Book Review*, the critic reviewing *The Chosen* wrote that "Long afterwards, it remains in the mind, and delights. It is like those myths that, as C. S. Lewis reminds us, do not essentially exist in words at all."

The Chosen As is the case with many first novels, *The Chosen* received mixed criticism from reviewers. *New York Times* contributing critic Eliot Fremont-Smith describes the book as "a long, earnest, somewhat affecting and sporadically fascinating tale of religious conflict and generational confrontation in which the characters never come fully alive because they are kept subservient to theme: They don't have ideas so much as they represent ideas." While *New Republic* contributor Philip Toynbee observes that Potok's prose has "too many exhausted phrases and dead words," he maintains that *The Chosen* "is a fascinating

COMMON HUMAN EXPERIENCE

Chaim Potok wrote richly and deeply about his characters' struggle to choose between the sacred and the secular in their own lives. Here are other artistic works where this conflict is explored:

The Confessions (398), an autobiography by St. Augustine of Hippo. This is a classic of Western civilization, and among the many themes are Augustine's post-conversion attempts to reconcile his youthful indiscretions (he even laments over childhood sins he cannot remember) with his deep longing to follow the rule of God.

Portnoy's Complaint (1969), a novel by Philip Roth. The titular character of Roth's book is torn between what he sees as his manic sexual appetite (which is probably not that unusual for his peer group) and his ethical Judaism, which he suspects would not be tolerant of his urges.

Mad Men (2007–), a television series created by Matthew Weiner. The character Peggy Olson, who begins as a secretary and works her way up, gives in to pressure by her family to attend mass. However, she resists her parish priest's attempts to make her feel guilty about her out-of-wedlock child.

Chariots of Fire (1981), A film directed by Hugh Hudson. This Oscar-winning movie tells the story of two champion runners, training for the 1924 summer Olympics in Paris. One of the men, Eric Liddell, was known as the "Flying Scotsman," and he almost missed his chance to win an Olympic gold medal because he, a former missionary, would not run on a Sunday.

Responses to Literature

1. Potok has long credited his fateful encounter with *Brideshead Revisited* (which he plucked, almost at random, from a public library shelf) as the impetus for his own writing career. Read *Brideshead Revisited* and *The Chosen*. Write a paper comparing the relationships of Charles Ryder and Sebastian Flyte in Waugh's novel with those of Reuven Malters and Daniel Saunders. How is the presentation of relationships in the latter book influenced by those of the former?

2. Potok was very moved by his military experience in Korea. Though raised to believe that the Jewish people were integral to God's plan on earth, he encountered a place with virtually no Jewish presence (and consquently, no anti-Semitism) that was profoundly spiritual nonetheless. Read Potok's 1992 novel *I Am the Clay*, and write a paper discussing the meeting of different cultures in the story.

3. Potok's dreams of becoming a professional visual artist were disparaged by his parents, and he eventually gave up the pursuit, even as he continually returned to the theme in his novels—notably in *I Am Asher Lev*. Write a two-page fictional obituary of Chaim Potok, imagining that, instead of becoming a novelist, he had been a successful painter. Research the obituaries of other artists from the recent past to give you an understanding of how they should be written.

4. Potok said that he was shocked by the runaway success of *The Chosen*—he expected only a few hundred people would want to read it. Read *The Chosen* and discuss with other students the qualities that make it so universal. What in your opinion made Potok think it would only be attractive to a limited audience?

BIBLIOGRAPHY

Books

Abramson, Edward A. *Chaim Potok*. Boston: Twayne, 1994.

Sternlicht, Sanford V. *Chaim Potok: A Critical Companion*. Westport, Conn.: Greenwood Press, 2000.

Walden. Daniel, ed. *The World of Chaim Potok*. Albany, N.Y.: State University of New York Press, 1985.

Periodicals

Fox, Margalit. "Chaim Potok, 73, Dies; Novelist Illumined the World of Hasidic Judaism's Corner." *New York Times* (July 24, 2002).

Web Sites

Chaim Potok. Retrieved December 7, 2008, from http://www.jewishvirtuallibrary.org/jsource/biography/Potok.html.

Chaim Potok: Biography. Retrieved December 8, 2008, from http://potok.lasierra.edu/Potok.biographical.html.

book in its own right. Few Jewish writers have emerged from so deep in the heart of orthodoxy: fewer still have been able to write about their emergence with such an unforced sympathy for both sides and every participant." Hugh Nissenson noted in the *New York Times Book Review* that "the structural pattern of the novel, the beautifully wrought contrapuntal relationship of the boys, and their fathers, is complete. We rejoice, and we weep a little, as at those haunting Hasidic melodies which transfigure their words." For Granville Hicks, in *Saturday Review*, the novel "suggests that almost any situation, no matter how unfamiliar to the population in general, may have meaning for the multitude if the author goes deep enough. Who cares about the Hasidim? Not many people, I suppose. But we all know about fanaticism and can recognize that it may have power for good as well as evil. And many of us are either fathers or sons or both. ... It is hard to make good boys credible and interesting; it must have been even harder for Chaim Potok to bring to life a pair of good fathers, good in such different ways. But he succeeded, and the result is a fine, moving, gratifying book."

⊛ Ezra Pound

BORN: *1885, Hailey, Idaho*

DIED: *1972, Venice, Italy*

NATIONALITY: *American*

GENRE: *Poetry, nonfiction*

MAJOR WORKS:

A Lume Spento (1908)

The Spirit of Romance (1910)

Cathay: Translations by Ezra Pound for the Most Part from the Chinese of Rihaku, From the Notes of the Late Ernest Fenollosa, and the Decipherings of the Professors Mori and Ariga (1915)

Jefferson And/Or Mussolini (1935)

The Pisan Cantos (1948)

Overview

Ezra Pound's influence on the development of poetry in the twentieth century has perhaps been greater than that of any other poet. Few writers have devoted as much energy to the advancement of the arts in general. Through his criticism and translations, as well as in his own poetry, particularly in the *Cantos*, Pound explored poetic traditions from different cultures ranging from ancient Greece and China to England and America.

Ezra Pound   *Pound, Ezra, photograph. The Library of Congress.*

Works in Biographical and Historical Context

Early Literary Experiences Born to Homer and Isabel Weston Pound in the frontier town of Hailey, Idaho, in 1885, and raised in the suburbs of Philadelphia from June 1889 on, Pound had a rather ordinary middle-class upbringing but extraordinary personal ambitions. In his fifteenth year he decided that by age thirty he would know more about poetry than any man living.

Pound attended the University of Pennsylvania in 1901, and it was there he met several individuals who would influence him greatly through the years. William Carlos Williams and Pound would begin a friendship which would continue, despite a variety of stand-offs—largely on Williams's part—until Williams's death in 1963. Pound also befriended poet Hilda Doolittle (who wrote under the initials "H. D."), to whom he was briefly engaged.

He transferred to Hamilton College in 1903, receiving his bachelor's degree in 1905. He again attended the University of Pennsylvania, and he received an M. A. in Romance languages in 1907. He abandoned pursuit of a Ph.D. after failing a course on the history of literary criticism. In the fall of 1907, he received an appointment as an instructor in Romance languages at Wabash College in Indiana, but he was fired early in 1908. Though it was probably not clear to Pound at the time, this event initiated a break, not only with American academic life, but with America.

Early Career in London and the Imagists In February 1908, Pound sailed from New York to Gibraltar. He spent three months in Venice, and although he was short of money, the city was an especially rich source of romantic inspiration for his poetry. He collected forty-four of his poems and published them himself in Venice under the title, *A Lume Spento*, in June 1908. Soon after, he departed for London, where *A Quinzaine for this Yule, Exultations and Personae* (1908) was published.

In February 1909, he gave a series of six lectures which became the basis for his first published book of criticism. *The Spirit of Romance* (1910) examined a large body of poetry, stretching from Ovid to Dante Alighieri and William Shakespeare. Pound also contributed scores of reviews and critical articles to various periodicals. He articulated his aesthetic principles and indicated his literary, artistic, and musical preferences, thus offering information helpful for interpreting his poetry. Soon after settling in London, Pound met novelist Olivia Shakespear and her daughter Dorothy, whom he would marry in 1913. From 1908 to 1911, Pound published six volumes of his poetry, most of it a reflection of his love for Romance language and Renaissance works. His abiding goal was to contribute to a general renaissance in humane letters, though his views would shift in troubling directions in the future. His first big step was the creation of the Imagist movement.

Pound founded the Imagists in 1912, marking the end of his early poetic style. Imagism favored economy and precision of language, a focus on common language, and a movement away from overly adorned verse. In this first of the Modernist movements, there was also a determination to draw from classic sources, including ancient Asian poets. So it was also around this time that Pound began to study Chinese and Japanese writings. In 1915, he would publish his translation of *Cathay*, a collection of poems, mostly by the Chinese poet Li Bai. Pound's free-verse translation, working from the notes of Ernest Fenollosa, managed to produce a series of translations whose accuracy to the spirit, if not the letter, of the originals is still admired by scholars of Chinese literature.

Pound was even able to persuade William Butler Yeats, whom he had befriended through Olivia Shakespear, to rethink his own poetic practice, to some extent, in the light of Imagist ideas. In 1913, Yeats invited Pound to stay with him for three months at Stone Cottage in Sussex, and it was there that Pound first heard of James Joyce, and included an early poem of his in the anthology *Des Imagistes*.

Editor and Advocate

The outbreak of World War I, and its long, painful course, had deep and lasting effects on Pound. Begun in 1914, the war, fought primarily in Europe, was a clash between the Allied forces (which included Britain, France, and eventually the United States) and the Central forces (Germany and the Ottoman Empire). Treaty agreements brought the majority of Europe into battle, where trench and chemical warfare led to a degree of casualties that had never been seen before. Like so many others, Pound was shaken by the waste of young life, and an immediate result was that his aggressively militant tone became greatly muted. After years of sniping at America and England, his writings during this time indicate that his only political hope lay in a coalition of England, France, and America. His poem, *Hugh Selwyn Mauberly*, published in 1920, condemns the war and the circumstances—including consumerism and a lack of values—that led to it. Themes of this work would also be found in T. S. Eliot's *The Waste Land*.

Pound was instrumental in the publishing of T. S. Eliot's "The Love Song of J. Alfred Prufrock." In 1921, he edited Eliot's *The Waste Land*, possibly the most important poem of the modernist era. Eliot, in turn, dedicated the poem to Pound. He also continued his support of Irish novelist James Joyce. Other writers Pound praised while they were still relatively unknown included D. H. Lawrence, Robert Frost, H. D., and Ernest Hemingway.

Pound was also committed to battling the poverty of his artistic peers. He matched patrons with writers, and connected buyers with painters and sculptors. His disdain for the banks and capitalism was aided by what he saw as the humiliating requirement of day jobs for the artistic geniuses he so admired. Against this background, Pound would become committed to the cause of economic reform.

Paris and the Cantos

In January 1921, Pound left England for France and became interested in the work of Ernest Hemingway, Jean Cocteau and the Dadaists. His three years in Paris were transitional ones for his career, a time for reorienting his thinking about his future role as a socially committed writer, and also for making some important decisions about the *Cantos*, his most ambitious work, which was scarcely begun.

The composition of the *Cantos* would take up a considerable part of Pound's life. They are considered unfinished, though one hundred and twenty of them were completed. In 1924, Pound left Paris for Italy in favor of an engagement with the strong political and social currents that were flowing through Italy.

A Turn Toward Fascism

In Italy, in the years following World War I, he became a convert to the economic ideas of C. H. Douglas. This system involved removing financial power from the banks and placing it in a neutral institution which would consult only the good of the public as a whole—an assault on the basic assumptions of a capitalist economy. Pound was vehemently opposed to usury, the private appropriation of the power to lend money, and in his writings of the 1920s and 1930s, he returns obsessively to the need to eliminate it from civilized life. In *Jefferson And/Or Mussolini* (1935), Pound defended the Fascist revolution in Italy as the legacy of the American Revolution, and insisted that the similarities between Jefferson and Mussolini were more profound than their differences. Both, he argued, sought to protect the nation as a whole from the particular interests that threatened to dissolve it. Fascism, like Jeffersonian democracy, understood that the best government is the one which most speedily translates the best thought into action. Pound saw in Benito Mussolini, the Italian Fascist leader, an image of the role he himself had sought in the realm of art, the strong-willed leader who can impel a collection of individuals into a common movement and who is able to convert ideas into action.

Incarceration and Illness

When World War II broke out, Italy was part of the Axis Powers, aligned with Nazi Germany and Japan against the Allied Powers of England, France, Russia, and eventually, the United States. Pound stayed in Italy, broadcasting a series of controversial radio commentaries. These commentaries often attacked Roosevelt and the Jewish bankers whom Pound held responsible for the war. By 1943, the U.S. government deemed the broadcasts to be treasonous; at war's end, the poet was arrested by the U.S. Army and kept imprisoned near Pisa, Italy. Eventually judged to be mentally incompetent to stand trial, Pound was incarcerated in St. Elizabeth Hospital in Washington, D.C. During this time, he would compose the *Pisan Cantos* (1948). He stayed in the hospital until 1958, when Robert Frost led a successful effort to free him.

Upon his release from St. Elizabeth Hospital in 1958, Pound returned to Italy, where he lived quietly for the rest of his life, mostly with his mistress, Olga Rudge, an accomplished violinist. By 1962, he was speaking less and less; neither his memory nor his sense of orientation was impaired, and when he did talk his comments were precise and correct. His psychiatrist's findings were that, while he was rational and in touch with reality at almost all points, in one area—the assigning of blame—his thinking appeared psychotic. His psychiatrist noted that he was not depressive except in the one area of self-accusation. Pound died in 1972 at age eighty-seven, and was buried in Italy.

Works in Literary Context

Imagism   Imagism was marked by a clarity of thought and language, in addition to rigorous requirements for writing. An Imagist poem relies heavily upon visual description over abstract ideas or feelings. Imagist poems are generally free verse, and they place no limits or rules on subject matter. The Imagist Manifesto attacked the artifice that had come to dominate poetry and to restore the method of direct presentation and clear speech.

The original Imagist clique—Pound, Richard Aldington, and Hilda Doolittle—would grow to include William Carlos Williams and Amy Lowell, who would become its leader. Having read about imagism in *Poetry*, she had come to London in 1913 with a letter of introduction from Harriet Monroe to Pound. He asked for permission to include "In a Garden" in *Des Imagistes*. Pound's most notable Imagist works include *Cathay* (1915), *Hugh Selwyn Mauberly* (1920), and *Ripostes* (1912).

Chinese Philosophy and Literature   Confucius offered to Pound a perspective radically removed from the age in which he felt he had the misfortune to live. The embrace of Confucian thought—with its attendant emphasis on justice and morality—allowed him to pass beyond the problems of Christianity and capitalism, democracy and liberalism, romanticism, and classicism, even advocating the replacement of Greek with Chinese in academia.

Perhaps the best way to account for Pound's attraction to Confucius is to notice that it allowed him to transfer some of his earliest literary principles into the domain of social thought. He repeatedly quoted the Confucian opinion on the first responsibility of government: "call things by their right names"—a maxim that echoes Imagist principles.

Gary Snyder, part of the San Francisco Renaissance and a peripheral member of the Beats, counts Pound as an influence and as a predecessor in the arena of Asian literature and thought.

LITERARY AND HISTORICAL CONTEMPORARIES

Ezra Pound's famous contemporaries include:

T. S. Eliot (1888–1965): Eliot was an American-born, Nobel Prize-winning poet, playwright, and critic. Discovered and promoted by Ezra Pound, Eliot was well-known for, among other works, the Modernist masterpiece poem, *The Waste Land*.

James Joyce (1882–1841): The visionary Irish author of *Ulysses* (1922), Joyce wrote with searing insight about the inner lives of his characters and about Dublin, his home town and the setting for his books.

Boris Pasternak (1890–1960): A Russian novelist and poet, Nobel Prize-winner Pasternak is best known for his 1958 novel, *Doctor Zhivago*, which was banned in the U.S.S.R.

Franklin D. Roosevelt (1882–1945): Elected thirty-second president of the United States, Roosevelt was the only President to serve more than two terms. Roosevelt shepherded the country through the Great Depression, implementing New Deal programs to cope with American poverty and unemployment, and was notable for his commitment to liberal government.

Willa Cather (1873–1947): American author Cather is best known for her depictions of frontier life and the immigrant experience, as in the novel *My Ántonia* (1918).

Works in Critical Context

More widely recognized than any other writer by his poet-contemporaries for his influence on their work, opinions about Pound as a poet range from uncritical adulation to bitter condemnation.

Cantos   Written for over four decades and in one hundred and twenty parts, encompassing subjects as diverse as John Adams, Economics, Chinese History, and his own life, The *Cantos* are Ezra Pound's most lasting achievement. Reestablishing a poetic tradition traced from Homer's *Odyssey* and Dante's *Divine Comedy*, the *Cantos* are a modern epic, a poem that would contain and elucidate history, and, as critical opinion would come to understand, contain and elucidate the essence of Pound's own mind. Notes Donald E. Herdeck in *Bloomsbury Review*, "the *Cantos* are Ezra L. Pound's letters to all of us—the rant, the stubbornness, the pith and humor of the *Cantos* are here, as first drafts, or widening ripples of the life that became the *Cantos*."

A work unintended for the casual reader, their significance was recognized early. In a 1931 review, the critic Dudley Fitts called the *Cantos* "without any doubt, the most ambitious poetic conception of our day." The long poem, however, presents innumerable difficulties to

COMMON HUMAN EXPERIENCE

The Divine Comedy (early fourteenth century), an epic poem by Dante Alighieri, had a profound influence on both the structure and substance of Pound's *Cantos*. Here are some other works which have followed from Dante's masterpiece:

> *On Translating the Divina Commedia* (1864–1866), a series of four sonnets by Henry Wadsworth Longfellow. Inspired by the process of translating *The Divine Comedy*, these sonnets were first published in the *Atlantic*, where Longfellow was a founding editor.
> *The Gates of Hell* (1917), an unfinished sculpture by Auguste Rodin. These enormous bronze doors feature several notable reliefs inspired by *The Divine Comedy*.
> *The Dante Quartet* (1987), a six-minute silent film by avant-garde filmmaker Stan Brakhage. Brakhage utilizes a technique for combining painting and film to speed the viewer on a journey through Dante's *Inferno*.
> *The Amber Spyglass* (1999), a novel by Philip Pullman. The Whitbread prize-winning third novel in Pullman's *His Dark Materials* trilogy, features the hero, Lyra, and her companion venturing into hell, and eventually being able to emerge from it.

its readers. In 1927, when a draft of *XVI Cantos* appeared, his old friend, William Carlos Williams, lamented, "Pound has sought to communicate his poetry to us and failed. It is a tragedy, since he is our best poet."

Critics have produced a host of explanatory texts designed to help readers understand and evaluate the *Cantos*. George Kearns in his *Guide to Ezra Pound's Selected Cantos* warns that such understanding requires a significant investment, time-wise, since if "one wants to read even a single canto, one must assemble information from a great many sources." Notably, it was during his imprisonment in Italy that Pound completed the *Pisan Cantos* (1948), which Paul L. Montgomery of the *New York Times* called "among the masterpieces of this century." The poems won him the Bollingen Prize in 1949.

Poet Allen Ginsberg reported that Pound had "felt that the *Cantos* were 'stupidity and ignorance all the way through,' and were a failure and a 'mess.'" Ginsberg responded that the *Cantos* "were an accurate representation of his mind ... a model of his consciousness over a fifty-year time span—they were a great human achievement."

Responses to Literature

1. Pound performed one of his most important critical labors in helping T. S. Eliot edit and revise *The Waste Land*. Read *The Waste Land: Facsimile Edition* (1974), which provides the original manuscript, and shows Pound's edits (in addition to those by Eliot and Eliot's wife). Write a paper in which you discuss the progression of the poem from the original to the final edited version. Which do you find more satisfying? Do you consider any of the edits misguided? Which do you think were the most crucial to a coherent final version?

2. Pound would receive some of his greatest laurels for the *Pisan Cantos*, composed while he was incarcerated. Read the *Pisan Cantos* and then read the manuscript resulting from Oscar Wilde's imprisonment, *De Profundis* (1905). Do you sense any similar themes between these two works? In each case, is the context of the writing—the fact that the author was imprisoned—important to understanding the work?

3. Pound's legacy will always be tarnished by his entanglement with Fascism, his anti-Semitic writings, and his perceived mental illness. In 1999, the dean of the Cathedral of St. John the Divine vetoed the election of Pound into its Poets' Corner (honoring American poets, including T. S. Eliot and Emily Dickinson), citing these indiscretions. Have a discussion in which you debate both sides of this issue. Do you think a government-sponsored monument would have a different responsibility to inclusion than a private one?

4. An individual canto is a division within a long poem, and comes from the Latin word meaning "song." These divisions were possibly first designated as lyrics to accompany music. Read one of Pound's *Cantos*. In what ways, if any, does it exhibit musical qualities that would make it suitable to be adapted as a song?

BIBLIOGRAPHY

Books

Bell, Ian F. A. *Critic as Scientist: The Modernist Poetics of Ezra Pound*. London and New York: Methuen, 1981.
Davie, Donald. *Ezra Pound*. New York: Viking, 1976.
de Rachewiltz, Mary. *Discretions*. Boston: Little, Brown, 1971.
Doolittle, Hilda. *End to Torment: A Memoir of Ezra Pound by H. D.* New York: New Directions, 1985.
Eastman, Barbara. *Ezra Pound's Cantos: The Story of the Text*. Orono, Maine: National Poetry Foundation, University of Maine, 1979.
Eliot, T. S. *Ezra Pound: His Metric and Poetry*. New York: Knopf, 1917.
Heyman, C. David. *Ezra Pound: The Last Rower*. New York: Viking, 1976.
Moody, A. David. *Ezra Pound: Poet I: The Young Genius 1885–1920*. New York: Oxford University Press, 2007.
Wilhelm, James H. *The American Roots of Ezra Pound*. New York: Garland, 1985.

Periodicals

Smith, Dinitia. "Cathedral Bars Ezra Pound from its Poets' Corner." *The New York Times* (October 23, 1999).

Web Sites

Imagism. Retrieved December 3, 2008, from http://www.writing.upenn.edu/~afilreis/88/imagism-def.html.

Wilmer, Clive. *Pound's Life and Career.* Retrieved December 3, 2008, from http://www.english.uiuc.edu/maps/poets/m_r/pound/bio.htm.

❀ Helen Prejean

BORN: *1939, Baton Rouge, Louisiana*

NATIONALITY: *American*

GENRE: *Nonfiction*

MAJOR WORKS:

Dead Man Walking: An Eyewitness Account of the Death Penalty in the United States (1993)

The Death of Innocents: An Eyewitness Account of Wrongful Executions (2004)

Sister Helen Prejean   *Frederick M. Brown / Getty Images*

Overview

Sister Helen Prejean is the most prominent anti–death penalty activist in the United States, devoting her life to ending capital punishment. Her 1993 memoir *Dead Man Walking*, brought these issues to the forefront of national debate.

Works in Biographical and Historical Context

Early Life and Devotion   Sister Helen Prejean was born on April 21, 1939, in Baton Rouge, Louisiana, into a tight-knit, happy, middle-class Catholic family in 1939. Her mother was a nurse and her father was a lawyer. She received a loving and religious upbringing.

The Prejean family was keen on road trips, and it was on these protracted excursions that Helen learned to tell a story and, conversely, to meditate in silence. At St. Joseph's Academy for girls in Baton Rouge, using the rhetoric skills she learned from her father, she was a bright and popular student, elected to class office.

In 1957, when she was eighteen, Prejean took her vows, becoming a sister of St. Joseph of Medaille, an order focused on charitable works and education. She received a BA in English and education from St. Mary's Dominican College and later an MA in religious education from St. Paul's University in Ottawa, Canada. For over twenty years, Prejean taught middle- and high-schoolers, in addition to working in parish religious education. In 1981 the sisters of her order and Prejean herself began to rethink their mission, which, until that point, had not been devoted to Joseph of Medaille's dictum to serve those most in need.

A New Dedication   Desiring a position more in keeping with her responsibilities to the poor, Prejean took a post at the St. Thomas Housing Project in New Orleans, and it was during this time that she began her prison ministry. She has referred to the path of the New Orleans poor—specifically African Americans—to prison as a "greased rail," and she reasoned that inmates, undeniably lacking in material goods, fit with her dedication to serve those most in need. In 1982 in Louisiana, an unofficial moratorium had prevented the state from executing anyone for two decades. When Prejean received a request from a representative of the Louisiana Coalition on Jails and Prisons to begin an epistolary communication with Patrick Sonnier, she agreed. Sonnier had murdered two teenagers and had been sentenced to die at Angola State Prison. At the time her letter writing began, Prejean still did not believe the state would execute him. When Sonnier asked her to come and visit him, she agreed to this as well. She would continue to visit him for two and a half years, until the date of his execution.

Diary of a Spiritual Adviser   Sonnier, along with his brother, Eddie, had been convicted in 1977 of rape and two brutal murders. Eddie's sentence was life in prison, while Patrick received the death penalty. Prejean did not

LITERARY AND HISTORICAL CONTEMPORARIES

Sister Helen Prejean's famous contemporaries include:

Susan Sarandon (1946–): American actress Sarandon won an Academy Award for her portrayal of Prejean in the film *Dead Man Walking*. She is also notable for her devotion to liberal causes, notably as an anti-war activist.

Tenzin Gyatso, fourteenth Dalai Lama of Tibet (1935–): The Buddhist spiritual leader of the Tibetan people, the Dalai Lama has been in political exile in India since 1959, while his homeland remains in serious conflict with China over Tibetan sovereignty. He won the Nobel Peace Prize in 1989.

William Sloane Coffin Jr. (1924–2006): American minister and former chaplain of Yale University, Coffin was a civil rights activist and anti-war crusader.

Elie Wiesel (1928–): A Holocaust survivor and winner of the Nobel Peace Prize, Wiesel is best known for his devastating memoir about his imprisonment at the hands of the Nazis, *Night* (1960).

Mitch Albom (1958–): A writer who first achieved success as a sports journalist, Albom became a best-selling author with his memoir about his experiences visiting with his terminally ill former professor, *Tuesdays with Morrie* (1997).

doubt Sonnier's guilt, but she felt a call to compassion that surmounted her innate disgust with him; she became his spiritual adviser. Polite visitations turned into deeper meditations and prayerful encounters with Sonnier, who, by several accounts other than Prejean's, was a remorseful prisoner.

Prejean kept detailed diaries during this time, which she used to write her best-selling account of her time (including the details of execution) with two death-row inmates, *Dead Man Walking*. The other man, Robert Lee Willie, whom Prejean found far less repentant, was also executed, and the family of his victim would continue to publicly disdain Prejean for her perceived unwillingness to sympathize with their pain, prompting her to begin her work counseling the grieving families. *Dead Man Walking* catapulted Prejean and her cause into the spotlight. The book would go on to be nominated for the Pulitzer Prize and was turned into a feature film starring Susan Sarandon.

Over the years, Prejean became increasingly appalled by the capital punishment system. As she gained exposure to capital punishment's intricacies—the secretive nature of the execution, the mental anguish wrought upon the individuals charged with carrying out the gruesome task—she also became more sensitive to the fact that the death pen-

alty is meted out with a clear bias against the poor, uneducated, and nonwhite.

A Shift in Focus Whereas *Dead Man Walking* focused its anti–capital punishment argument on the stance that it is morally and ethically repugnant for the state to put its citizens to death, *The Death of Innocents* (2004) seeks to persuade readers that by virtue of sheer incompetence, capital punishment cannot continue. She tells the stories of two death-row inmates, Louisianan Dobie Gillis Williams, a man with an I.Q. of sixty-five, poor and black, convicted of rape and murder, and Joseph Roger O'Dell, a career criminal from Virginia who was convicted of murder, rape, and sodomy in Virginia.

The misconduct at the two trials was stunning. The attorney for Williams was staggeringly inept, and O'Dell was allowed to represent himself, all with disastrous results. Both men were eventually executed, although in 2002 the Supreme Court decided that the Constitution bars execution of the mentally handicapped.

Prejean continues to council death row inmates and advocate for the abolition of the death penalty. Her numerous accolades have brought increased awareness to the cause, and she founded a support group, SURVIVE, for the families of the victims.

Works in Literary Context

The Fight against Capital Punishment Prejean is part of a long tradition of memoirists who have, out of a sense of duty, placed themselves into difficult or even dangerous situations in order to educate the public. Her striking ability to meld a personal story with a larger social and political one accomplishes these educational goals. Upton Sinclair, the journalist who immersed himself in the revolting Chicago meatpacking industry in order to report on the horrendous conditions for both animals and workers, is her forebear in this work. Prejean's stories have influenced the film adaptation of *Dead Man Walking*, but other creative attempts to discredit capital punishment, among them the 2003 film *The Life of David Gale*, owe a debt to her message.

Works in Critical Context

Prejean's books have been well received, and critics find her prose an engaging vehicle for her extraordinary personal story—worthy of praise in its own right.

Dead Man Walking When *Dead Man Walking* appeared, Laura Shapiro in the *New York Times* wrote, "[Prejean] is an excellent writer, direct and honest and unsentimental; her accounts of crime and punishment are gripping, and her argument is persuasive." Adam Liptak, reviewer for the *New York Times Book Review*, writing about *The Death of Innocents*, noted that Prejean's first effort was a "fine, furious" piece of social activism literature, and much of that was echoed in the second book. He did find, however, that the work suffered from an overload of Catholic theology and tenuous attempts to wrestle with the intricate legal issues involved.

Responses to Literature

1. In many ways, *Dead Man Walking* and *The Death of Innocents* are reconstituted journal entries. Prejean utilized these records of events and her own internal states to write accurately and with a profound immediacy. Keep a detailed journal for one week and then write a one-page paper based on the entries. Wait one week, and write another one-page paper about that week, this time using no journal or diary entries. Compare and contrast the two papers. Which is more interesting? Which is more reflective of your preferred writing style?

2. Read *Dead Man Walking* and then, with parental permission, view the film. Compare and contrast the interpretation with the original source material. Did you feel it was successful as an adaptation? Why or why not?

3. Read famed attorney Clarence Darrow's argument to the court on behalf of Nathan Leopold and Richard Loeb, two teenagers who confessed to murdering a fourteen-year-old neighbor for thrills. Darrow convinced the court to spare the lives of his clients. Write a paper in which you explore Darrow's remarks. Are they contrary or complimentary to those of Prejean? Do you find one or the other more convincing?

4. Capital punishment, in some form or another, is legal in most states in America. Research the history of capital punishment in your state and write a paper, making your best prediction for the future of the issue. Take into consideration recent political events and incorporate what you have noticed in your own community and with your own family and friends.

BIBLIOGRAPHY

Periodicals

Bragg, Rick. "Visiting Death Row with Sister Helen Prejean; Making Executions Personal." *New York Times*, March 21, 1996.

Liptak, Adam. "'*The Death of Innocents*' A Reasonable Doubt." *New York Times Book Review* (January 23, 2005).

Prejean, Sister Helen. "Death in Texas." *New York Review of Books* (January 13, 2005).

Shapiro, Laura. "I Would Not Want My Murderer Executed." *New York Times*, July 4, 1993.

Web Sites

The Nobel Peace Prize 1986. Retrieved December 6, 2008, from http://nobelprize.org/nobel_prizes/peace/laureates/1986/press.html.

PBS: Sister Helen Prejean Interview. Retrieved December 6, 2008, from http://www.pbs.org/wgbh/pages/frontline/angel/interviews/hprejean.html.

Sister Helen Prejean. Retrieved December 6, 2008, from http://prejean.org.

COMMON HUMAN EXPERIENCE

Prejean writes and advocates for an almost universally detested minority (criminals), yet she is compelled by her faith to see every individual as worthy of respect and dignity. Here are other instances in film and literature in which the ostensible hero supports or defends a despicable character, with mixed results:

The Last King of Scotland (1998), a novel by Giles Foden. This fictionalized account of Idi Amin, the Ugandan dictator, is told through the eyes of Nicholas Garrigan, a Scottish doctor. Garrigan becomes Amin's personal physician and also becomes complicit in his reign of terror.

John Adams (2002), a biography by David McCullough. This Pulitzer prize–winning biography tells the story of a prepresidential John Adams as he defends the British soldiers who slew civilians during the Boston Massacre in 1770.

Bel Canto (2000), a novel by Ann Patchett. Inspired by a real-life hostage crisis in Lima, Patchett's story centers around the very real bonds and relationships that form between a group of terrorists and their hostages.

The Penultimate Peril and *The End* (2005), the twelfth and thirteenth novels in the *Series of Unfortunate Events* books by Lemony Snicket (Daniel Handler). The Baudelaire orphans, hitherto the objects of substantial abuse and murderous intent at the hands of Count Olaf, must first help him escape and burn down a hotel in the penultimate novel. In the final book, they bury him honorably after his final act is one of kindness.

✸ Annie Proulx

BORN: *1935, Norwich, Connecticut*

NATIONALITY: *American*

GENRE: *Fiction*

MAJOR WORKS:
Postcards (1992)
The Shipping News (1993)
Close Range: Wyoming Stories (1999)

Overview

Annie Proulx is a successful and highly praised novelist and short-story writer. Her stories, published in four collections, deal with themes of a changing American way of life in areas invaded by civilizing forces adverse to the inhabitants. Proulx's novels, which deal with similar themes, have brought her popularity and success; yet, her short stories, she admits, are the works that give the swift and stunning insights into human behavior she desires most.

E. Annie Proulx   *Proulx, E. Annie, photograph. © Jerry Bauer.
Reproduced by permission.*

Works in Biographical and Historical Context

Early Life of Wandering   Born Edna Annie Proulx to George Napoleon Proulx and Lois "Nellie" (Gill) Proulx in Norwich, Connecticut, on August 22, 1935, Proulx was the first of five daughters. Her mother's family came to New England from England in 1635; her father's family came to Canada from France in 1637 and to New England in the 1860s. Although her family's roots on this continent were set down early, Proulx's father moved his family from state to state in New England and then to North Carolina, no doubt contributing to his eldest daughter's penchant for travel and relocation.

From Freelance Journalist to Novelist   An early chapter in Proulx's life could have led to a very different existence for the author. After receiving her B.A. and M.A. in history, Proulx completed doctoral orals in Renaissance economic history, the Canadian North, and China; but in 1975 she abandoned academia for fear of not finding a teaching job. The end of her academic career coincided with the end of her third marriage; as a result, Proulx raised her three sons as a single parent.

While she was certainly not an overnight sensation, having written stories from the age of ten and published short fiction since her early twenties, Proulx did present her own remarkable success story, one characterized by hard work and a fierce independence. Proulx was transformed into a novelist after nineteen years of work as a freelance journalist. She wrote articles for magazines on a myriad of topics, including weather, mountain lions, African beadwork, cider, and lettuces. Her work appeared in the publications *Country Journal*, *Organic Gardening*, and *Yankee*. In the early 1980s, Proulx produced a shelf full of on-assignment "how-to" books on food, gardening, and carpentry. Another journalistic venture cast Proulx as the founder and editor of a rural newspaper, the *Vershire Behind the Times*, from 1984 to 1986. The financial rewards for such work were meager; devoting time to writing short stories was a luxury—Proulx averaged two a year, nearly all of which were published. The experience of working for a rural newspaper would later inform her novel *The Shipping News* (1993).

In 1983, Proulx's career as a fiction writer was boosted by a notice in *Best American Short Stories*, an honor that was repeated in 1987. Proulx published her first book, *Heart Songs and Other Stories*, in 1988. This collection introduced the reading public to Proulx's gritty themes and deft, if unconventional, use of language. Against the starkly beautiful backdrop of the New England countryside and in the guise of hunting and fishing stories, Proulx depicts the struggles of men trying to cope with their emotionally and morally tangled lives. Proulx illustrates the stories with vivid verbal pictures, such as a man who eats a fish "as he would a slice of watermelon" or a woman who is as "thin as a folded dollar bill, her hand as narrow and cold as a trout."

When Scribner's editor Tom Jenks drew up Proulx's contract for *Heart Songs and Other Stories*, he suggested that they include a novel in the agreement. The resulting work, *Postcards* (1992), proved to be a liberating experience for Proulx, who had never before considered undertaking such a task. In many ways, *Postcards* resembles the stories found in *Heart Songs*, but given a larger scope.

Several Awards for Fiction   *Postcards* was a professional and personal success; it proved Proulx's skill and comfort working in the new form. The most tangible evidence of her achievement was receiving the 1993 PEN/Faulkner Award for fiction and its $15,000 bonus. Proulx also enjoyed the distinction of being the first woman to be so honored.

The very next year, Proulx capped this success by writing *The Shipping News* (1993). This novel is a dark but comic tale set in Newfoundland, the story of a luckless newspaper reporter named Quoyle. It is packed with details of the island's landscape, weather, food, and language, all drawn in a choppy yet vibrant style. The book resulted in a steady stream of awards, all topped by the 1994 Pulitzer Prize for Fiction.

The Shipping News was the result of a canoeing trip to Newfoundland, followed by careful research. After falling in love with the place, the author took at least seven trips to the island, talking to residents and absorbing the atmosphere. She pulled her characters' names from telephone directories and words from the *Dictionary of Newfoundland English*. Here the journalist and historian in Proulx surfaced, both in her interest in seemingly arcane details and in her passion for "getting it right." Proulx also took inspiration from *The Ashley Book of Knots* (1944), an expansive encyclopedia of knot-tying she bought at a yard sale.

With this approach to writing fiction, Proulx breaks with the standard advice to "write what you know." In researching her next novel, Proulx became an expert on accordion music. She studied not how to play the instrument, but how to take one apart and then reconstruct it. *Accordion Crimes*, published in 1996, is the tale of an accordion as it moves from owner to owner over the course of one hundred years. In 1999, she followed up with a collection of short stories entitled *Close Range: Wyoming Stories*. The collection earned her the New Yorker Award for fiction in 2000.

Reluctant Celebrity In the wake of her fame, Proulx was hard-pressed to find the time she needed to research and write. On top of her schedule of book signings and readings, she was inundated with requests for interviews, many of which took place in her remote Vermont home. As a result, Proulx developed a reputation for shunning the media and coveting her private life. She soon bought a second place in Newfoundland, and by the spring of 1995, she had moved to Wyoming, where she resides today. The author's latest collection of short stories, *Fine Just the Way It Is: Wyoming Stories 3*, was released in 2008.

Works in Literary Context

Proulx has made an important contribution to the American short story. Her realistic, carefully researched and detailed stories have been collected and published in four volumes. She is known for her carefully chosen details that pare down the narrative to the essential kernel of meaning, and her artful use of characterization to make her people vital and real. Two important themes that emerge in her writing include the idea of rural life interrupted and accidental love.

Rural Life Interrupted Many of Proulx's stories show rural life in great detail and exposition. She questions the effects of modernization on such an existence. In "On the Antler," the first story in *Heart Songs*, the outdoors become a central image. The story presents the lore that has been kept alive by men throughout the centuries in"how-to" books and hunters and fishermen's true adventures, which preserve a way of life that seems to be disappearing. The Hawkheel character sees the nature he loves and lives for becoming devalued and stolen from him; the skills he has learned for survival are useless in the

cruel competitive environment of the late twentieth century. Proulx uses this type of character when writing about rural New England, Wyoming, and other the locales of her novels.

In her statements about rural life, Proulx often pits outsiders against locals. Her story "Stone City" shows an outsider coming to Chopping County mainly for grouse hunting. Proulx uses humor in satirizing the narrator, a city dweller who infiltrates the backwoods territory, feeling superior to the locals. Interestingly, the story deals with the mean slyness and murderous rage of the Stones, a family with deeply entrenched roots in the area. The tale deals with the complexities of human emotion and both the nobility and squalor of rural life.

Accidental Love "Brokeback Mountain," the last story in the *Close Range: Wyoming Stories*, won prestigious awards and attracted notice from a wide audience. A film adaptation of the story was released in 2005 to critical acclaim. The story describes the relationship between two men, Ennis Del Mar and Jack Twist, who meet in their late teens; fall in love without calling it that; separate and marry women; and have children. However, they meet for short vacations, keeping alive their secret relationship until one dies in early middle age. The story is simply and significantly a love story. The enemy in the story is the hard, narrow, and violent antipathy toward such a relationship in the male-dominated society of the West. Their love for each other surprises and confuses them, and the

COMMON HUMAN EXPERIENCE

The effects of modernization on rural life is an important theme in Proulx's work. Other works that explore the theme of losing a way of life include the following:

The Fountainhead (1943), a novel by Ayn Rand. This work presents a modern society that does not encourage individualism but instead invites a tyranny of bland mediocrity.

All the Pretty Horses (1992), a novel by Cormac McCarthy. This book depicts the great beauty of the natural world, but also examines the origins of evil, the search for redemption, and the meaning of humankind's brutal existence.

Pride and Prejudice (1813), a novel by Jane Austen. This work explores the preference of simple country living over the shallow posturing of city life.

course of their relationship is beset by the same jealousy, tenderness, and disputes as any heterosexual love. Proulx's message seems to be that people find love only accidentally and improbably in this world, and the love lives on only with great sacrifice and suffering.

Works in Critical Context

Proulx first attracted widespread critical and public attention when her novel *Postcards* (1992), won the 1993 PEN/Faulkner Award for fiction. Critics have praised her affirmative portrayal of the human condition through the lives of quirky, often less than heroic characters, and her juxtaposition of lavish language against the stern northern settings of her short stories and novels.

Heart Songs   The publication of *Heart Songs* (1988), a collection of short stories, marked the beginning of Proulx's transformation from journalist to full-time fiction writer. Of these tales, critic Kenneth Rosen of the *New York Times Book Review* concludes: "Their sometimes enigmatic, often lyrical images seem to complement New England's lavish but barren beauty." There were also some more critical of her work. Jane Gardam concedes Proulx's command of language: "She describes the minute, unspoken ritual events in these lives. ... She is very funny." However, Gardam adds that "in spite of her good dialogue and distilled construction ... I find these stories quite unconsciously derivative, and ... rather ordinary."

The Shipping News   Proulx's second novel, *The Shipping News*, won a Pulitzer Prize for fiction in 1994. Howard Norman of the *New York Times Book Review* acknowledges "Proulx's surreal humor and her zest for the strange foibles of humanity." Sandra Scofield, writing

for the *Washington Post Book World*, also praises Proulx's humor, calling the book a "wildly comic, heart-thumping romance ... [Proulx] uses language that is riotous yet clearly under control. ... She is capable of precision, the perfect description, the keenest insight." William Green writes in the *Los Angeles Times Book Review*: "Proulx captures the flavor of Newfoundland as convincingly as if she were born there. ... *The Shipping News* is brimming with eccentric characters and rich subplots."

Still, there were some who thought that the novel lacked emotional depth. Verlyn Klinkenborg writes that there is "a distinction to be made between a successful writer and the gravy that is ladled over that writer by the literary press." She goes on to say that Proulx was "served up hot." More often than not, however, Proulx's works collectively have been received with enthusiasm from popular and scholarly reviews.

Responses to Literature

1. The short story "In the Pit" from *Heart Songs* contrasts city life and country life. In it, Proulx seems go beyond this distinction to say that humans make their own destiny, irrespective of their conditions. How does she convey this message in the story?

2. Read *Heart Songs* and Cormac McCarthy's *All the Pretty Horses*. How do the two works depict violence differently? How are these depictions similar in both works?

3. Describe the connection of Wyoming's harsh, unyielding and treacherous landscape to the events and characters depicted in *Close Range: Wyoming Stories*. In your opinion, does Proulx use place as a character in her stories?

BIBLIOGRAPHY

Books

Rood, Karen L. *Understanding Annie Proulx*. Columbia, S.C.: University of South Carolina Press, 2001.

Periodicals

Bolick, Katie. "Imagination Is Everything." *Atlantic Unbound* (November 1997).

Gardam, Jane. "Rather Ordinary Horror and Hatred." *Spectator* (March 25, 1995): 33–34.

Green, William. "Oh, to Be Less of an Oaf in Newfoundland." *Los Angeles Times Book Review* (July 18, 1993): 9.

Klinkenborg, Verlyn. "The Princess of Tides." *New Republic* (May 30, 1994): 35–37.

Scofield, Sandra. "Harbors of the Heart." *Washington Post Book World* (August 1, 1993): 5.

Steinberg, Sybil. "E. Annie Proulx: An American Odyssey." *Publishers Weekly* (June 1996): 57–58.

Withworth, John. "Was Love Then a Bag of Sweets?" *Spectator* (December 1993).

"An Interview with Annie Proulx." *Missouri Review* 22, no. 2 (1999): 77–79.

Web sites

Rosen, Kenneth. *In Short; Fiction*. Retrieved November 23, 2008, from http://query.nytimes.com/gst/fullpage.html?res=950DE0DF153EF93AA15752C0A96F948260.

Norman, Howard. *In Killick-Claw, Everybody Reads The Gammy Bird*. Accessed November 23, 2008, from http://partners.nytimes.com/books/99/05/23/specials/proulx-shipping.html.

✱ Thomas Pynchon

BORN: *1937, Glen Cove, New York*

NATIONALITY: *American*

GENRE: *Fiction*

MAJOR WORKS:

V. (1963)

The Crying of Lot 49 (1966)

Gravity's Rainbow (1973)

Mason & Dixon (1997)

Against the Day (2006)

Thomas Pynchon   *Writer Pictures*

Overview

Thomas Pynchon is widely regarded as one of contemporary America's eminent literary stylists. Using elements of science fiction, fantasy, satire, myth, and advanced mathematics, his novels illustrate the chaos and randomness of modern life. They are characterized by black humor, a large cast of unusual and allegorical characters, and an encyclopedic use of Western history and popular culture. Critics have praised Pynchon's work for its wide-ranging subject matter, innovative synthesis of narrative perspectives, and profound philosophical insights into the nature of truth and historical reality.

Works in Biographical and Historical Context

Intelligent and Irreverent   Pynchon was born in Glen Cove, New York, on May 8, 1937, to a prominent family. Pynchon's ancestors include a sixteenth-century London high sheriff; a seventeenth-century Massachusetts Bay Colony patentee and treasurer, who was also a founder of both Roxbury and Springfield, Massachusetts; and a nineteenth-century Trinity College president. In 1953, Pynchon graduated from Oyster Bay High School, where he was class salutatorian and the recipient of an award for English at graduation. The pieces Pynchon submitted for his high school newspaper during his senior year revealed, even then, his irreverence for authority and his playfulness in naming characters.

College Years   In 1953, Pynchon entered Cornell University as a scholarship student in the engineering physics program. Although Pynchon remained in this program only one year, his early academic interest and excellence in the sciences were evident later in his fiction, in which scientific theories serve as suggestive and complex metaphors. As a sophomore, Pynchon transferred to Cornell's college of arts and sciences before interrupting his college education for a two-year stint in the U.S. Navy. In a rare biographical statement, Pynchon said that his navy experience provided him with one of his favorite characters: Pig Bodine, the archetypal AWOL sailor in the short story "Low-Lands."

In 1957, Pynchon returned to Cornell to complete his degree in English, graduating in June 1959. During those two years, he became friends with Richard Farina, to whom he would later dedicate *Gravity's Rainbow* (1973). Throughout his junior and senior years, Pynchon wrote short stories that were later published in various literary journals; most of these pieces can be found in the collection, *Slow Learner: Early Stories* (1984). Pynchon has characterized the stories he wrote at Cornell as apprentice fiction; nevertheless, these early pieces provide insight into themes and character types that would become central to his novels.

Establishing a Reputation   After graduating from Cornell, Pynchon turned down a teaching offer there to

LITERARY AND HISTORICAL CONTEMPORARIES

Pynchon's famous contemporaries include:

Don DeLillo (1936–): DeLillo, an American writer, is a masterful satirist with a linguist's appreciation for words.

Stanley Kubrick (1928–1999): This acclaimed director, screenwriter, and producer was known for his meticulous attention to artistry and detail, as well as for his reticence about his personal life.

Frank Chin (1940–): A defiant voice from the margins of American culture, Chin has helped shape contemporary Asian American literature.

William Gibson (1948–): Gibson is a science fiction writer whose novels focus on the effects of computer networks and cybernetics on humans.

John Gardner (1933–1982): Known for his unique writing style, Gardner was a philosophical novelist and a controversial critic.

Pier Paolo Pasolini (1922–1975): In his native Italy, Pasolini was recognized as a complex novelist, poet, and filmmaker.

pursue his writing. In 1960, passed over for a Ford Foundation Fellowship to work with an opera company, Pynchon worked for a time as a technical writer and engineering aide for the Boeing Company in Seattle, Washington. During his years there, he worked on his first novel, *V.* (1963). It was awarded the William Faulkner Foundation Award in 1963 for the best first novel of the year.

Widely regarded as Pynchon's most accessible work, due to its concise development, *The Crying of Lot 49* (1966) won the Rosenthal Foundation Award of the National Institute of Arts and Letters. With 1973's *Gravity's Rainbow*, Pynchon secured his reputation as a writer of major importance. In addition to winning the National Book Award, *Gravity's Rainbow* won the Howells Medal of the National Institute of Arts and Letters, and was chosen the American Academy of Arts and Letters best novel of the decade. The novel was also a unanimous choice by the Pulitzer Prize committee for fiction; however, the nomination was revoked when the advisory board ruled that *Gravity's Rainbow* was obscene, overwritten, incomprehensible, and pretentious.

A Writing Recluse As Pynchon increasingly immersed himself in his writing, the known history of his life became progressively more hazy, until the most significant biographical fact about him is his obscurity. Pynchon is so reclusive and wary of publicity, that even what he looks like is unclear because most published photographs of him have been taken from his high school yearbook.

He surfaced briefly in 1983 with his introduction to the new edition of Richard Farina's *Been Down So Long It Looks Like Up to Me* and in 1984, with the introduction to *Slow Learner*. Afterwards, Pynchon again disappeared from public view. He did not emerge even when, in 1988, he was awarded a five-year fellowship by the John D. and Catherine T. MacArthur Foundation—he did, however, accept the $310,000 grant.

Nearly seventeen years passed between the publication of *Gravity's Rainbow* and Pynchon's next novel, *Vineland* (1990), a work satirizing the conservative political climate of the Reagan administration in the 1980s. In 1992, he provided the introduction to a posthumously published collection of Donald Barthelme's work, paying homage to an admired contemporary and an old friend. In 1997, Pynchon published *Mason & Dixon*, a novel concerned with the national identity of the United States. As biographical information on Pynchon is limited, the literary world was excited when 120 letters the author wrote to a former agent became public in 1998. The *New York Times* published excerpts from the letters, which gave new insight into Pynchon as a young author. Since then, the reclusive Pynchon has been rumored to live in California, Mexico, and New York City. His latest work is *Against the Day* (2006), a novel spanning the period between the Chicago World's Fair of 1893 and the years just after World War I. Characteristically, Pynchon uses obscure languages and a long list of characters living in an era of uncertainty in this work.

Works in Literary Context

In the introduction to *Slow Learner*, his collection of early short stories, Pynchon lists the writers—Jack Kerouac, Allen Ginsberg, Saul Bellow, Herb Gold, and Philip Roth—who helped him develop a perception of voice by showing him how different kinds of English could exist in fiction. He also confirms thematic influences that various critics have noted as consistently important in his work: Niccolo Machiavelli's *The Prince* (1532), Norbert Wiener's expositions of information theory, *The Education of Henry Adams* (1907) by Henry Adams, and the guidebooks of German printer, Karl Baedeker. Even more expansive in its inspiration is *Mason & Dixon*, Pynchon's most consciously literary novel, which contains echoes of Rudyard Kipling, Franz Kafka, D. H. Lawrence, Joseph Conrad, Nathaniel Hawthorne, Herman Melville, and Mark Twain.

Entropy Of all Pynchon's short stories, "Entropy" (1960) has received the most critical attention because its theme, reflected in its title, appears so central to understanding Pynchon's fiction as a whole. The scientific concept of entropy, the tendency for any system to move from a state of order to one of disorder, can be interpreted as characterizing, not only physical forms, but also information and communication. For Pynchon, the theme of entropy, as used in his early story, prepares the reader for the metaphor of entropy representing the breakdown in everyday life that will recur throughout his body of work.

Indeed, "Entropy" provided the testing ground for the contrast between Meatball Mulligan—who attempts to make order out of chaos—and Callisto—who is obsessed by the potential for entropy to reduce his life to its final equilibrium—that would reappear in *V.* by way of the characters Benny Profane and Herbert Stencil. Stencil, in particular, confronts the unavoidable forces of entropy, unfortunately discovering that the past is virtually erased as entropy takes over. Even more explicit than *V.* at demonstrating the unraveling of the universe through an equalization of energy, is *The Crying of Lot 49*, with its use of the concept of entropy as a metaphor for the forces that contribute to social decline.

Works in Critical Context

Since *V.* was published in 1963, Pynchon's works have been the subject of meticulous scholarly interpretation, and critics have commended their ambitious subject matter, dark humor, and innovative narrative constructs. Other reviewers, however, have derided his undeveloped characters, fragmented and convoluted plots, and abundance of inane word play and meaningless allusions. Recent criticism has explored *Mason & Dixon* as a poetic act and a meditation on American national identity. Other recent studies have examined the influence of other authors and works on Pynchon's novels, such as the impact of Bruno Schulz's 1930s short story "The Comet" on *Gravity's Rainbow*. While many critics perceive Pynchon's interest in binary oppositions as a strategy for exposing the hypocrisy of extremes, others view his divisions and ambiguous endings as simplistic and evasive. A highly imaginative and original postmodern novelist, Pynchon continues to be viewed as one of America's most challenging, and thought-provoking authors.

Gravity's Rainbow While Pynchon's detractors have variously faulted this controversial novel as obscene, nihilistic, or incomprehensible, many designate *Gravity's Rainbow* a masterpiece, contending that Pynchon has fashioned a work of profound implications by connecting a wide variety of human activities and ideas with the mass destruction of World War II. Scholar Joseph Slade hails Pynchon as "the first American novelist to accept the duty of which [Aldous] Huxley speaks," the duty "to seek powerful means of expressing the nature of technology and the crises it has generated." On the contrary, reviewer Richard Poirier suggests that scientific data permeate the book, not to provide solutions to conceptual difficulties, but to compound these difficulties by offering yet another tradition to which the language can allude. As a result, the central symbol of the novel, the V-2 rocket, carries more weight than traditional symbols; it is, says Poirier, "Moby Dick and the Pequod all in one, both the Virgin and the Dynamo of Pynchon's magnificent book."

COMMON HUMAN EXPERIENCE

A postmodern literary movement, metafiction, or fiction about fiction, includes such general characteristics as history that becomes fiction, arbitrary language, an author who appears powerless over his narrative, or reality that becomes no longer understandable. Involving hundreds of characters with several perspectives of historical events, *Gravity's Rainbow* is a complex narrative exemplifying metafiction.

Listed below are other examples of metafiction:

Libra (1988), a novel by Don DeLillo. This work weaves two discrete narratives with historical and invented characters in the story of Lee Harvey Oswald and the circumstances leading to his assassination of President Kennedy.

Grendel (1971), fiction by John Gardner. Based on the Anglo-Saxon *Beowulf* (c.1000), *Grendel* narrates the epic from the monster's point of view.

Operation Shylock: A Confession (1993), a novel by Philip Roth. The protagonist of this humorous puzzle of a novel, a novelist named "Philip Roth," travels to Israel to search for a man who has assumed Roth's identity.

The Curious Incident of the Dog in the Night-Time (2003), fiction by Mark Haddon. Chronicling an autistic boy's investigation—inspired by his literary hero, Sherlock Holmes—of the death of his neighbor's dog, this book offers the reader no help in how to interpret and decipher the boy's narrative.

Poirier continues, "More than any living writer, including Norman Mailer, [Pynchon] has caught the inward movements of our time in outward manifestations of art and technology so that in being historical he must also be marvelously exorbitant," and this "exorbitant" quality of *Gravity's Rainbow* may well constitute its greatest threat to traditional ideas of what is literary.

Indeed, as reviewer Khachig Tölölyan observes, *Gravity's Rainbow* surpasses many traditional definitions "of what can be considered literary," upsetting "narrow generic and modal categories" of criticism and refusing "to fulfill a set of expectations nurtured by reading the great novels of the nineteenth century, or the slighter fictions of our time." Reflecting its thematic concerns, the structure of *Gravity's Rainbow* allows characters, situations, and events to proliferate beyond control or limit. Scholar Louis Mackey observes that the tone of narration undermines "every ingredient of form—myth, symbol, archetype, history, allegory, romantic quest, even the ritual sanctities of science." Furthermore, the refusal to be pinned down into comprehensible meanings is part of the novel's achievement. Mackey concludes, "Whatever it says garrulously and disconcertingly fails to make the point. And that of course is the point."

Responses to Literature

1. Though *Gravity's Rainbow* is a work of fiction, many parts are based on historical facts. Investigate a factual aspect of the plot, such as the German rocket program. How does Pynchon blend fact and fiction to contribute to the meaning of the novel? Do you think such an approach obscures the meaning?

2. *The Crying of Lot 49* deals extensively with history and its messages. What can you gain by understanding the history of the Tristero? How does it relate to the novel's themes of chaos and communication?

3. *V.* has an ambiguous ending. Why do you think Pynchon leaves the mystery unsolved? Do you think the entire novel could be Pynchon's joke on the reader?

4. What is your opinion of Pynchon's exploration of various technologies in American culture: television, radio, electronics, the telephone, and the automobile, for instance? What impact do such technologies have on the lives of Pynchon's characters? What point do you think he is making?

BIBLIOGRAPHY

Books

Berressem, Hanjo. *Pynchon's Poetics: Interfacing Theory and Text*. Urbana, Ill.: University of Illinois Press, 1993.

Dugdale, John. *Thomas Pynchon: Allusive Parables of Power*. New York: St. Martin's Press, 1990.

Hume, Kathryn. *Pynchon's Mythography: An Approach to Gravity's Rainbow*. Carbondale, Ill.: Southern Illinois University Press, 1987.

Pearce, Richard, ed. *Critical Essays on Thomas Pynchon*. Boston: G. K. Hall, 1981.

Slade, Joseph W. *Thomas Pynchon*. New York: Warner, 1974.

Periodicals

Mackey, Louis. "Paranoia, Pynchon, and Preterition." *Sub-Stance* 30 (Winter 1981): 16–30.

Poirier, Richard. "Rocket Power." *Saturday Review of the Arts* 13 (March 1973): 59–64.

Tölölyan, Khachig. "Prodigious Pynchon and His Progeny." *Studies in the Novel* 11 (Summer 1979): 224–234.

Weisenburger, Steven. "Thomas Pynchon at Twenty-two: A Recovered Autobiographical Sketch." *American Literature* 62 (December 1990): 692–697.

Web sites

"San Narciso Community College." *Entropy*. Retrieved December 12, 2008, from http://pynchon.pomona.edu/entropy/index.html. Last updated in 1997.

⊛ Anna Quindlen

BORN: *1952, Philadelphia, Pennsylvania*

NATIONALITY: *American*

GENRE: *Fiction, nonfiction*

MAJOR WORKS:
Living Out Loud (1988)
One True Thing (1995)
Black and Blue (1998)

Overview

Anna Quindlen, author of several best-selling novels and the recipient of the 1992 Pulitzer Prize for commentary, emerged as an important novelist and commentator during the last decades of the twentieth century. While Quindlen has sometimes been viewed as a novelist addressing women's issues, her work possesses universal appeal.

Works in Biographical and Historical Context

A Successful Career in Journalism Quindlen was born on July 8, 1952, in Philadelphia, Pennsylvania, the oldest of five siblings. Her father was a management consultant

Anna Quindlen *Quindlen, Anna, photograph. AP Images.*

of Irish heritage, and her mother was a homemaker who came from an Italian family. Even as a youth, Quindlen found herself drawn to writing. Raised in the upper-middle-class neighborhood of Drexel Hill, Quindlen attended private schools and earned her B.A. in English literature from Barnard College in 1974. Because of her parents' backgrounds, Quindlen's upbringing was steeped in the strong traditions of Catholicism, which would be an influential topic for her novels and essays. A young girl, raised during the oppressive 1950s, Quindlen came of age during the turbulent decade of the 1960s, which was marked by culture clashes, disagreement over the Vietnam War, and the civil rights movement. Quindlen was undoubtedly influenced by the various progressive movements of that decade, particularly feminism, on which she would reflect numerous times in her works.

Although fiction was her first love, Quindlen pursued a journalism career as the most viable, stable outlet for her writing activity. When she was just eighteen, Quindlen was hired by the *New York Post* as a part-time reporter, and by the time she completed her degree at Barnard, she had earned a spot as a full-time reporter. While Quindlen was at Barnard, her mother was diagnosed with cancer, and she died when Quindlen was nineteen. In 1977, Quindlen left the *New York Post* for a job with the prestigious *New York Times*. She began work there as a general-assignment reporter and was soon assigned to City Hall, which she covered until 1981. In 1978, Quindlen married Gerald Krovatin, a criminal defense attorney. By 1983, Quindlen had been promoted to deputy metropolitan editor, and was contributing two editorial columns a week, in addition to her other writing duties at the *New York Post*.

Quindlen gave birth to her first son, Quin, in 1983 and another son, Christopher, in 1985. By that time, Quindlen felt drawn to stay home with her children, and she decided to resign from the newspaper. Her editor, however, offered her a chance to write a weekly column, which later turned into "Life in the 30s." Quindlen's columns became enormously popular and soon gained syndication across the United States. Her topics ranged from reminiscences about her childhood to difficulties in raising children, and working outside the home to feminist issues. Her columns were largely drawn from personal experience and addressed subjects that she found important—primarily issues affecting women and children. As a result, Quindlen often received scathing letters of disagreement regarding her views about politics and women's issues. For the most part, however, her writing appealed to many who became loyal readers. In 1988, Quindlen retired her column, and in the same year, she published her first work, *Living Out Loud*, which was a collection of her "Life in the 30s" pieces. Her daughter, Maria, was born that same year, and Quindlen felt that it was time to move toward fiction writing rather than journalism, though she still wrote freelance pieces. In 1992, Quindlen was honored with the Pulitzer Prize in commentary for her work as a columnist.

LITERARY AND HISTORICAL CONTEMPORARIES

Anna Quindlen's famous contemporaries include:

Anne Tyler (1941–): Tyler is a Pulitzer Prize–winning novelist noted for her strong depiction of family-oriented stories.

Hillary Clinton (1947–): One of the most important female politicians in American history—having served as both a United States Senator and the First Lady—Clinton has become an important feminist icon.

Jane Smiley (1949–): American fiction writer Smiley is the award-winning author of the feminist re-imagining of *King Lear, A Thousand Acres* (1991).

Maureen Dowd (1952–): A prominent reporter and columnist for *The New York Times*, Dowd received the Pulitzer Prize for her commentary in 1999.

Jonathan Franzen (1959–): American novelist and winner of the National Book Award for his scathing family portrait, *The Corrections* (2001), Franzen is noted for his sharp social criticism.

Branching Out to Fiction While writing her "Life in the 30s" column, Quindlen had begun work on a novel, *Object Lessons*, which was published in 1991. *Object Lessons* chronicles the lives of three generations of the Scanlans, an Irish-Italian-American family. The novel is related through the perspective of Maggie Scanlan, a thirteen-year-old who observes the activities of adults who perplex her as she watches them. The pivotal summer of Maggie's life in the novel includes her grandfather's death, the revelation of family secrets, and her own coming of age. *Object Lessons* received favorable acclaim from readers, yet critics often panned the book for its inadequacies. Despite the fact it failed to bring strong critical reviews, the book was quite popular among readers.

Quindlen's next project was a children's book. It was followed by *Thinking Out Loud: On the Personal, the Political, the Public, and the Private* (1993), an essay collection in which Quindlen examines a range of social issues. Quindlen's second work of fiction, *One True Thing* (1994), is a loosely autobiographical depiction of the lives of an upper-middle-class family dealing with the mother's diagnosis of cancer. Ellen Gulden gives up a prestigious job to care for her dying mother, for whom she has possessed little respect over the years. While caring for her mother, Ellen learns about herself and the family that she has long taken for granted. Quindlen illustrates the demands placed upon women in familial relationships, and explores the controversial topic of euthanasia. Unlike the response to her first novel, critics hailed *One True Thing* as astounding and triumphant, and that same year, a major feature film version of the novel appeared.

COMMON HUMAN EXPERIENCE

Black and Blue focuses on the issue of domestic violence. Here are some other works that take up the topic of domestic abuse:

The Color Purple (1982), a novel by Alice Walker. Winner of the Pulitzer Prize for Fiction and the National Book Award, Walker's novel examines an African American woman's struggle to survive the abusive men in her life in 1930s Georgia.

Bastard Out of Carolina (1993), a novel by Dorothy Allison. This work is a semi-autobiographical novel about an abusive Southern family that explores issues of class and sexuality.

"Woman Hollering Creek" (1991), a short story by Sandra Cisneros. This work focuses on a Mexican woman living in the Southwest who struggles with her cultural and sexual identity in the face of a constricting, abusive relationship.

"Bedrock" (1995), a short story by Annie Proulx. This short story explores the life of a man who is abused by his wife and examines issues of poverty.

The Woman Who Walked into Doors (1997), a novel by Roddy Doyle. Acclaimed Irish novelist Doyle presents the story of a working-class battered woman.

Commercial Success, Mixed Critical Response Quindlen's exploration of controversial issues and secrets reappeared in her third novel, *Black and Blue* (1998), which followed another children's book and two coffee-table books with photographer Nick Kelsh. *Black and Blue* recounts the story of Fran and Bobby Benedetto's painful and turbulent marriage. Literary critics were more pleased with *Black and Blue* than her previous two novels, and the novel was commercially a bestseller. It became a television movie in 1999.

Quindlen continued her success across writing genres. In 2000, she published *A Short Guide to a Happy Life*, which was an expanded version of a commencement speech. With that work, Quindlen became the first writer ever to have books appear on the fiction, nonfiction, and self-help *New York Times* bestseller lists. Following this book, Quindlen wrote another novel, *Blessings*, which was published in 2002. *Blessings* is the story of a nontraditional family forged after an older woman and her handyman find an abandoned baby. Critical response was split over the merits of the novel and, as a result, it was not as successful as Quindlen's other novels. In the wake of *Blessings*, Quindlen continued to produce prolific commentary in many prestigious publications and magazines and a novel about family life in New York, *Rise and Shine*, in 2006.

An outspoken and influential commentator, Quindlen has secured her place among the important voices in the late twentieth century. Her fiction also maintains a strong social agenda, and throughout all of her novels, she emphasizes the importance of realistic and believable characters. Her novels have drawn legions of loyal readers; and critics, while sometimes not entirely impressed with Quindlen's plots, almost always praise her ability to articulate family life, and to create interesting stories and strong characters.

Works in Literary Context

As a journalist, Quindlen is known for her unique strategy of covering national issues with a focus on domestic and daily events that are interpreted from a feminist perspective. For instance, she based a discussion of the economic recession of the 1980s on the household grocery budgets of families, arguing that the checkout counter was a worthy indicator of the economy. Quindlen's fiction employs the same type of strategy: she explores larger social and cultural issues by focusing on daily or domestic events, which are often semi-autobiographical. Her fiction is also deeply informed by her experience in journalism. Quindlen often transforms the issues and observations she comments on in her columns into the subjects of her fiction.

Domestic Fiction Quindlen's focus on family relationships and her concern with exploring women's lives fits within a twentieth-century extension of the domestic fiction genre. Principally regarded as a nineteenth century genre, domestic fiction (sometimes referred to as "sentimental fiction") is a category of novel that is usually popular among female readers and depicts family life and the relationships of a female heroine. For instance, *Object Lessons* focuses on the twelve-year-old Maggie Scanlan and her struggle to interpret the conflicts in her family that have resulted from her father's rebellion against his own father, as well as come to terms with her newfound interest in boys, her cousin's unwed pregnancy, and her difficult mother. In *One True Thing*, Quindlen focuses on a self-absorbed, ambitious magazine journalist who is manipulated into caring for her dying mother by a father whom the narrator has always idolized. Some of Quindlen's works are semi-autobiographical, and add elements of memoir to give her stories more depth. Her journalistic eye for observation and keen detail also enables her to develop domestic fiction that is strikingly realistic. As a twentieth-century author of domestic fiction, Quindlen is very conscious about utilizing a feminist perspective in her works. Quindlen is also unafraid of focusing on challenging subjects in her domestic fiction, such as abortion and euthanasia, and she also imagines non-traditional family structures.

Works in Critical Context

Quindlen has enjoyed tremendous commercial success, but her fiction has often received mixed critical reviews. It has been criticized for being too pedantic it its examination of social issues, and too simplistic in its examination of characters and relationships. Yet many critics view Quindlen as a keen observer of detail and remark on her ability to translate the observations on life and culture she made famous in her columns to successful literature. Commenting on the realistic way she depicts family triumphs as well as struggles, critic Laura Green writes, "Quindlen balances her readers' longing to experience the protagonist's triumph with the knowledge that to end by simply rewarding virtue would betray the very realism we enjoy."

One True Thing Quindlen's second novel received much more praise than her first. *One True Thing*, the story of a daughter who gives up her prestigious career to care for her dying mother, left critics impressed with Quindlen's ability to capture the nuances of family life and investigate the dimensions of the complex relationships she established. Author and critic Michael Dorris writes, "All along the way to the novel's believable, satisfying conclusion, we are presented with insights and challenges to ponder, ideas that resonate concerning the nature and the method of change." Some critics, however, found the novel lacking in depth and the ability to provide insight on its subjects. In his *New York Times Book Review* review of the novel, Frederick Busch writes, "It will, at times, feel like a good conversation about daughters and parents. But it will not offer a way of saying what had seemed unsayable to and about and for the dead."

Black and Blue Despite some criticisms that Quindlen's novel did not provide enough depth in her treatment of the abusive relationship at the center of *Black and Blue*, the novel was generally received well and sold well commercially. Many critics lauded Quindlen's ability to deal with extremely complex social and emotional issues in the novel. As Faith McLellan observes, "Quindlen, who gave up a highly acclaimed *New York Times* column to become a novelist, shows that her eye for domestic detail focuses just as sharply in fiction as it did in another kind of 'real life.'" Critic Autumn Stephens notes that Quindlen "sweeps aside sound-bite clichés on the subject of spousal abuse," and makes the following appraisal about the novel: "Sensitive, suspenseful and haunting, *Black and Blue* depicts the unique travails—and also the unexpected triumphs—of a 'recovering battered woman.'"

Responses to Literature

1. What are the main "object lessons" that Maggie Scanlan learns in her family observations in *Object Lessons*?

2. In *One True Thing*, a daughter becomes her mother's caretaker. How does she come to terms with this reversal of roles? What is Quindlen saying about the traditional roles of family?

3. Throughout *Blessings*, Quindlen presents many different types of families. Compare two of the families presented in the novel. What do they have in common? What is different about them? What is Quindlen saying about the nature of family in this novel?

4. Quindlen began writing *Object Lessons* while she was still writing her "Life in the 30's" column. Compare the narrative voice and subject matter Quindlen uses in *Object Lessons* with the tone and subjects Quindlen uses in her column collection *Living Out Loud*. What are the similarities? What are the differences?

BIBLIOGRAPHY

Periodicals

Stephens, Autumn. "Quindlen Gets Inside the Head of a Battered Woman." *San Francisco Chronicle* (January 25, 1998): RV-1.

Busch, Frederick. "A Death in the Family." *The New York Times Book Review* (September 11, 1994): 11.

Dorris, Michael. "Finding Truth as Death Looms." *Los Angeles Times* (August 25, 1994): E6.

Fenichel, Marilyn. "Spokeswoman for Our Time." *Psychology Today* no. 4 (April 1989): 71.

McDaniel, Maude. "Anna Quindlen Writes a Wise Coming-Of-Age Novel." *Chicago Tribune Books* (April 21 1991): 6.

McLellan, Faith. "Where the Bruises and the Hurts Live On." *Lancet* (1998): 1970.

Paley, Maggie. "Taking Flight." *The New York Times Book Review* (February 8, 1998): 11.

Quindlen, Anna and Rose A. Adkins. "Reporting the Details of Life." *Writer's Digest* 73, no. 3 (1993): 35–37.

Quindlen, Anna and Marilyn Gardner. "Columnist Anna Quindlen." *Christian Science Monitor* 80, no. 223 (1988): 21–22.

Quindlen, Anna and Alexander M. Santora. "Anna Quindlen: From the '60s to the '90s." *Commonweal* 119, no. 3 (February 14, 1992): 9–13.

Quindlen, Anna and Sybil Steinberg. "Anna Quindlen." *Publishers Weekly* 238, no. 13 (March 15, 1991): 40–41.

Web sites

Green, Laura. "*Black and Blue*, by Anna Quindlen." *Salon*. Retrieved November 23, 2008, from http://www.salon.com/books/sneaks/1998/02/10review.html. Last updated February 10, 1998.

■ Christine Quintasket

SEE *Mourning Dove*

Glossary of Literary Terms

The glossary contains terms found in various entries throughout the *Gale Contextual Encyclopedia of American Literature*. This glossary includes terms for various literary components or techniques relevant to the work of the authors, terms for important artistic movements or groups discussed in relation to the authors, and terms for social, political, or philosophical ideas that profoundly impacted American literature. Definitions for more basic literary terms, such as "figurative language," have not been included.

ALLEGORY: A work in which the entire narrative serves as a symbol for something beyond the surface-level story.

ANACHRONISM: A thing or idea mentioned in a work of art that occurs outside its normal place in time. In William Shakespeare's play *Julius Caesar*, for example, the author mentions the striking of a clock to indicate time passing—even though no such clocks existed in ancient Rome, the time period in which the play is set.

ANTI-HERO: A main character in a literary work whose actions and ideals would not generally be regarded as heroic, though the character may still be portrayed sympathetically by the author. Holden Caulfield, the protagonist of J. D. Salinger's novel *The Catcher in the Rye* (1951), is an example of an anti-hero.

AVANT-GARDE: Meaning "advance guard" in French, a term used to describe artists or artistic works that are considered innovative or nontraditional.

BALLAD: A poetic work written in the form of a traditional song that commonly relates a folk tale, myth, or legend. Ballads are often written in four-line stanzas with alternating lines of eight and six syllables, in which the lines with six syllables contain end-rhyme.

BEAT GENERATION: A collective term for a group of writers who rose to prominence in the late 1940s and 1950s. Their work and their lifestyles were marked by defiance of legal and cultural authority, experimentation with drugs and unconventional sexual relationships, interest in Eastern religions, and an affinity for improvisational jazz music. Famous Beat writers include: Allen Ginsberg, Jack Kerouac, and William S. Burroughs.

BILDUNGSROMAN: Taken from a German term meaning "novel of formation," a novel that documents the maturation of the protagonist. The bildungsroman is also commonly known as a "coming of age" novel.

BLANK VERSE: A type of poetry which follows a set pattern of stressed and unstressed syllables in each line, but does not feature consistent rhyme. Poet Robert Frost wrote many of his poems in blank verse.

CAPTIVITY NARRATIVE: A first-hand, nonfiction account of the captivity of a white American settler by Native Americans.

COMEDY: In classical Greek drama, a play that ends happily for its major characters; many ancient comedies poked fun at political figures or cultural stereotypes, which inspired the laughter modern audiences now associate with the term.

CONFESSIONAL POETRY: Confessional poetry is a kind of poetry popularized in the 1950s and 1960s characterized by revelations of extremely intimate, often unflattering details of the poet's private life. Subjects often include sex and drug use. Major confessional poets include Sylvia Plath and Anne Sexton.

ENJAMBMENT: In poetry, the splitting of a continuous phrase or sentence into two or more lines. The result is that a single line may appear to express an incomplete thought, though the work as a whole is afforded a more complex rhythm and structure. Poet e. e. cummings made frequent use of enjambment.

EPIC: A literary work, originally a work in poetic form, that focuses on large-scale events and themes, and often takes place over a long period of time. *The Odyssey*, an ancient Greek epic by Homer, is one of the earliest examples. The term is now often applied to long works that cover a time span of many years, such as Margaret Mitchell's 1936 novel *Gone With the Wind*.

EPIGRAM: A short, clever statement—often in the form of a couplet—intended to impart humor and insight. Dorothy Parker was famous for her witty epigrams.

EPISTOLARY NOVEL: A novel in which the story is told through letters written by one or more characters. Samuel Richardson was an early practitioner of the epistolary novel, with works such as *Pamela* (1740) and *Clarissa* (1748). Alice Walker produced a more recent version with her 1982 novel *The Color Purple*.

EXISTENTIALISM: A philosophical movement that gained popularity in the first half of the twentieth century, thanks to literary works by Jean-Paul Sartre and Simone de Beauvoir, among others. Existentialism is characterized by the idea that life does not have a greater meaning or purpose beyond that which people choose to create for themselves. Many prominent African American writers have been labeled existentialist, including Ralph Ellison and Richard Wright.

EXPERIMENTAL NOVEL: A work which defies the traditional structure or subject matter of a novel, and emphasizes style or technique over content. Thomas Pynchon's 1973 novel *Gravity's Rainbow*, for example, is considered an experimental novel.

FABLE: A short tale whose purpose is to impart a message or lesson, usually featuring animals as characters. "The Tortoise and the Hare" is a well-known example of a fable. James Thurber and Joel Chandler Harris are known for their fables.

FARCE: A dramatic work characterized by characters being put into comedic situations that are unlikely or improbable, as in Thornton Wilder's *The Matchmaker* (1954).

FLASH FICTION: Short fiction, usually under one thousand words, that despite its length contains all the traditional elements of story such as a protagonist and conflict that is somehow resolved. O. Henry and Ray Bradbury are both authors of flash fiction.

FRAME NARRATIVE: A literary device in which the main story being told to the reader is presented as a story being told by one of the characters within the work, as in "The Celebrated Jumping Frog of Calaveras County," an 1865 short story by Mark Twain.

GONZO JOURNALISM: A subjective style of journalism in which events are described from the reporter's point of view. Gonzo journalism originated with Hunter S. Thompson.

GOTHIC FICTION: A literary sub-genre that emerged in the last half of the eighteenth century and was characterized by eerie atmosphere, melodrama, mystery, and romance.

IMAGISM: A poetic movement of the early twentieth century that emphasized direct expression through concise imagery and non-standard structure. Ezra Pound was instrumental in the development of the Imagist movement, and poet Amy Lowell was a leading practitioner.

IMPRESSIONISM: An artistic movement that emerged during the latter half of the nineteenth century, and focused on artistic impression over realistic representation. In literature, impressionism was characterized by a focus on the depiction of the interior, mental landscapes of characters, and was associated with other literary movements such as Symbolism.

IRONY: A literary device in which a character's perception of reality differs from actual reality, or in which a character's words do not express their true feelings. Sarcasm is a well-known form of irony. Dramatic irony occurs when an audience is given information that is not known by one or more characters in the play.

LIBRETTO: A text for the vocal portion of an opera or other musical work, often written in verse form. Composers frequently employ well-known writers to write libretti for their works, and writers such as Paul Laurence Dunbar, Langston Hughes, and Gertrude Stein sometimes worked as librettists.

LOST GENERATION: A term used to describe a loosely defined group of American writers who spent time in Europe—especially Paris—following World War I. These writers, including Ernest Hemingway, F. Scott Fitzgerald, and Sherwood Anderson, were notable for themes of disillusionment in their works.

MAGICAL REALISM: A literary style developed primarily in South America in which fantastic or supernatural elements are woven into otherwise realistic tales. Writers commonly associated with magic realism include Jorge Luis Borges, Alejo Carpentier, Gabriel García Márquez, and Carlos Fuentes; however, the work of some North American writers has been labeled magical realist, including Toni Morrison's 1987 novel *Beloved* and John Cheever's famous 1947 short story "The Enormous Radio."

MELODRAMA: A literary work which contains heightened or exaggerated emotions from the characters. The term originally applied to theatrical productions in which music (or melody) was used to accentuate the drama occurring on the stage.

MODERNISM: An artistic movement during the early twentieth century influenced by the rapid industrialization, scientific advancements, and devastating warfare of the time. Modernist writers were noted for their radical departure from traditional literary forms, with notable Modernist works including T. S. Eliot's poem "The Waste Land" (1922) and James Joyce's novel *Ulysses* (1922).

MUCKRAKERS: A term applied to journalists and fiction writers of the late nineteenth and early twentieth century whose work uncovered corruption in the government and big business. Authors Frank Norris and Upton Sinclair were both considered muckrakers.

NATURALISM: A literary movement of the late nineteenth century that focused on realistic portrayals of people and situations, and specifically dealt with the effects of heredity and environment on a characters's personality and development. Stephen Crane is widely regarded as a Naturalist.

NEOCLASSICISM: A term describing art that sought inspiration in ancient Greek and Roman forms, with emphasis on rationalism and proportion. Phillis Wheatley is considered a neoclassical poet.

NEW JOURNALISM: A style of journalism popularized in the 1960s and 1970s in which the journalist employed such literary techniques as setting scenes, presenting subjects as fleshed out "characters," and offering details of setting and scene.

NIHILISM: A philosophical movement that first appeared in the nineteenth century and is characterized by the belief that life has no objective purpose, moral code, or value. Writers associated with nihilism include Ivan Turgenev, whose novel *Fathers and Sons* (1862) described the Russian Nihilist movement and popularized the concept. More recent fiction has also been labeled Nihilist, including Bret Easton Ellis's 1985 novel *Less Than Zero*.

PARABLE: A short tale meant to impart a message or lesson to the reader. Parables are similar to fables, but do not include supernatural or fantastic elements such as talking animals.

PARODY: A literary work designed to mock or criticize another, usually well-known literary work or genre. An early example is *Shamela* (1741), Henry Fielding's parody of the successful Samuel Richardson novel *Pamela* (1740). Wendy Wasserstein's *Sloth* (2006) is a recent example of a parody.

PASTORAL: Literature that depicts rural life, nature, and the people of a rural region in a highly idealized way. The *Eclogues* (c. 40 B.C.E.) by the ancient Roman poet Virgil are among the oldest examples of pastoral poetry. Some works by Willa Cather and Wallace Stegner contain pastoral elements.

PICARESQUE: A type of novel first developed in Spain that focuses on the adventures of a rogue, or clever antihero. Among many others, James Branch Cabell's 1919 novel *Jurgen* exhibits the key traits of the picaresque.

POSTMODERNISM: A post-World War II literary movement characterized by nonlinearity, or a nonstandard narrative timeline, as well as metafiction, in which the author shows awareness of the story as a work of fiction and may even appear as a character within it.

PSEUDONYM: An alternate name used by a writer, often to hide the writer's identity. For example, William Sydney Porter used the pen name O. Henry when writing his celebrated short stories.

PSYCHOLOGICAL FICTION: A type of fiction in which a great deal of attention is paid to the thoughts and feelings of the characters, as opposed to external action. Henry James was well known for his psychological fiction.

REALISM: An artistic movement characterized by a desire to portray characters and environments as objectively, or as close to reality, as possible. Realism relies heavily upon physical descriptions, and Gustave Flaubert's novel *Madame Bovary* (1856)—with its almost grotesque precision to detail—is considered a landmark work of realism. Prominent American realists include Mark Twain and Edith Wharton.

ROMAN À CLEF: A literary work containing fictionalized depictions of real people and events. The work may be autobiographical, as in Sylvia Plath's *The Bell Jar* (1963), or it may refer to thinly disguised versions of well-known people, as in Truman Capote's *Answered Prayers* (1987).

ROMANTICISM: An artistic and philosophical movement that developed throughout Europe in the late eighteenth and early nineteenth centuries, and was popular in the United States throughout the nineteenth century (thought it reached its peak near the middle of the century). Romantic literature is notable for its expression of powerful emotions and use of natural settings. The work of Walt Whitman, Ralph Waldo Emerson, and Harriet Beecher Stowe is considered Romantic.

SATIRE: A type of literature intended to attack a person, group, institution, or idea through parody or irony. Very often, the satirist exposes the shortcomings of its subject by ironically expressing a position in support or praise of the subject. Benjamin Franklin, Stephen Crane, and Dorothy Parker are a few of the many American writers known for their satires.

SERIAL PUBLICATION: The printing of consecutive portions of a novel or other lengthy work of literature in successive issues of a periodical. Some of Mark Twains's works were first printed through serial publication.

SOCIAL REALISM: An artistic movement of the nineteenth century defined by sympathetic yet realistic depictions of the working class and the poor conditions in which they lived. Upton Sinclair's 1906 novel *The Jungle* is an example of social realism.

SONNET (ELIZABETHAN): A poetic form typically consisting of fourteen ten-syllable lines and an alternating rhyme scheme. William Shakespeare is perhaps the most famous practitioner of English-language sonnets.

SOUTHERN GOTHIC FICTION: A type of Gothic fiction (see definition) in which grotesque, supernatural, melodramatic, and mysterious elements are deployed for the sake of exploring the culture of the American South. Prominent authors of Southern Gothic literature include Flannery O'Connor, William Faulkner, Carson McCullers, and Tennessee Williams.

STREAM OF CONSCIOUSNESS: A literary technique meant to emulate the flow of thought in a character's mind. This is sometimes expressed through disjointed or run-on sentences, repetitions of words or phrases, or tenuous associations between different subjects. Notable works that use the stream of consciousness technique include *The Sound and the Fury* (1929) by William Faulkner and *On the Road* (1957) by Jack Kerouac.

SURREALISM: An artistic movement of the early twentieth century noted for its embrace of the irrational. Surrealist literary works often contained jarring juxtapositions of unrelated things, seemingly random or nonsensical phrases, and dreamlike situations. William Burroughs is considered a surrealist.

TRAGEDY: In classical Greek drama, a play that focuses on themes such as love, fate and betrayal, and does not end happily for one or more of the main characters. The play *Antigone* (c. 442 B.C.E.) by Sophocles is a typical Greek tragedy. Eugene O'Neill wrote several famous tragedies that drew heavily on ancient Greek models.

TRANSCENDENTALISM: A philosophical movement that originated in New England in the first half of the nineteenth century, Transcendentalism prized individualism and forwarded the idea that each individual has the ability to achieve a transcendent spirituality by communing with nature and remaining true to his or her essential self.

VERNACULAR: The casual and natural speech of a group of people or culture. Mark Twain's 1884 novel *Adventures of Huckleberry Finn* makes masterful use of the American vernacular of the 1830s.

Index

B

B

C

C

D

E

F

G

H

H

I-J

K

M

N

O

P

Q-R

R

S

S

T

U-W

W

Y-Z

Nationality/Ethnicity Index